The Garland Encyclopedia of World Music
Volume 5

South Asia

Garland Reference Library of the Humanities, Volume 1191

Volume 1
AFRICA
edited by Ruth M. Stone

Volume 2
SOUTH AMERICA, MEXICO, CENTRAL AMERICA, AND THE CARIBBEAN
edited by Dale A. Olsen and Daniel E. Sheehy

Volume 3
THE UNITED STATES AND CANADA
edited by Ellen Koskoff

Volume 4
SOUTHEAST ASIA
edited by Terry E. Miller and Sean Williams

Volume 5
SOUTH ASIA: THE INDIAN SUBCONTINENT
edited by Alison Arnold

Volume 6
THE MIDDLE EAST
edited by Virginia Danielson, Scott Marcus, and Dwight Reynolds

Volume 7
EAST ASIA: CHINA, JAPAN, AND KOREA
edited by Robert C. Provine, Yosihiko Tokumaru, and J. Lawrence Witzleben

Volume 8
EUROPE
edited by Timothy Rice, James Porter, and Chris Goertzen

Volume 9
AUSTRALIA AND THE PACIFIC ISLANDS
edited by Adrienne L. Kaeppler and J. Wainwright Love

Volume 10
THE WORLD'S MUSIC: GENERAL PERSPECTIVES AND REFERENCE TOOLS

Advisory Editors
Bruno Nettl and Ruth M. Stone

Founding Editors
James Porter and Timothy Rice

The Garland Encyclopedia of World Music
Volume 5

South Asia

The Indian Subcontinent

Alison Arnold
Editor

GARLAND PUBLISHING, INC.
A member of the Taylor and Francis Group
New York and London
2000

The initial planning of *The Garland Encyclopedia of World Music* was assisted by a grant from the National Endowment for the Humanities.

Published by Garland Publishing, Inc.
A member of the Taylor & Francis Group
19 Union Square West
New York, New York 10003

Library of Congress Cataloging-in-Publication Data

The Garland encyclopedia of world music / [advisory editors, Bruno Nettl and Ruth M. Stone ; founding editors, James Porter and Timothy Rice].
p. cm.
Includes bibliographical references, discographies, and indexes.
Contents: v. 5. South Asia / Alison Arnold, editor
ISBN 0-8240-4946-2 (alk. paper)
1. Music—Encyclopedias. 2. Folk music—Encyclopedias.
3. Popular music—Encyclopedias. I. Nettl, Bruno, 1930– .
II. Stone, Ruth M. III. Porter, James, 1937– . IV. Rice, Timothy, 1945– .
ML100.G16 1998
780′.9—dc21 97-9671
CIP
MN

For Garland Publishing:

President: Colin Jones
Publisher: Ken Wright
Editor, Music: Soo Mee Kwon
Assistant Editor, Music: Gillian Rodger
Production Director: Laura-Ann Robb
Project Editor: Barbara Curialle Gerr
Copy Editor: Samuel Bartos
Proofreaders: Usha Sanyal, Patterson Lamb
Desktop publishing: Betty and Don Probert (Special Projects Group)
Index: Marilyn Bliss
Music typesetting: Hyunjung Choi
Line art: Nigel Orme
Maps: Indiana University Graphic Services
Cover design: Lawrence Wolfson Design, New York

Cover illustration: A Kalbeliā Jogī ensemble plays *tālī* 'brass plate' and *puṅgī* 'gourd with two single-reed pipes for melody and for drone' to accompany a female dancer whose movements imitate the hooded cobra, at the annual camel fair in Pushkar, Rajasthan. CORBIS / © R. Ian Lloyd. Used by permission.

Printed on acid-free, 250-year-life paper
Manufactured in the United States of America

10 9 8 7 6 5 4 3 2 1

Contents

List of Audio Examples

The following list identifies the recorded selections on the compact disc that accompanies this volume and gives page references to text discussions of each selection. Track numbers on these pages allow immediate location of the discussion. Descriptive notes on the audio selections can be found on pages 1029–1034 and on an insert in the CD pocket.

List of Maps

About *The Garland Encyclopedia of World Music*

Scholars have created many kinds of encyclopedias devoted to preserving and transmitting knowledge about the world. The study of music has itself been the subject of numerous encyclopedias in many languages. Yet until now the term *music encyclopedia* has been synonymous with surveys of the history, theory, and performance practice of European-based traditions.

In July 1988, the editors of *The Garland Encyclopedia of World Music* gathered for a meeting to determine the nature and scope of a massive new undertaking. For this, the first encyclopedia devoted to the music of all the world's peoples, the editors decided against the traditional alphabetic approach to compartmentalizing knowledge from A to Z. Instead, they chose a geographic approach, with each volume devoted to a single region and coverage assigned to the world's experts on specific music cultures.

For several decades, ethnomusicologists (following the practice of previous generations of comparative musicologists) have been documenting the music of the world through fieldwork, recording, and analysis. Now, for the first time, they have created an encyclopedia that summarizes in one place the major findings that have resulted from the explosion in such documentation since the 1960s. The volumes in this series comprise contributions from all those specialists who have from the start defined the field of ethnomusicology: anthropologists, linguists, dance ethnologists, cultural historians, folklorists, literary scholars, and—of course—musicologists, composers, and performers. This multidisciplinary approach continues to enrich the field, and future generations of students and scholars will find *The Garland Encyclopedia of World Music* to be an invaluable resource that contributes to knowledge in all its varieties.

Each volume has a similar design and organization: three large sections that cover the major topics of a region from broad general issues to specific music practices. Each section consists of articles written by leading researchers, and extensive glossaries and indexes give the reader easy access to terms, names, and places of interest.

Part 1: an introduction to the region, its culture, and its music as well as a survey of previous music scholarship and research

Part 2: major issues and processes that link the musics of the region

Part 3: detailed accounts of individual music cultures

The editors of each volume have determined how this three-part structure is to be constructed and applied depending on the nature of their regions of interest. The concepts covered in Part 2 will therefore differ from volume to volume; likewise, the articles in Part 3 might be about the music of nations, ethnic groups, islands, or subregions. The picture of music presented in each volume is thus comprehensive yet remains focused on critical ideas and issues.

Complementing the texts of the encyclopedia's articles are numerous illustrations: photographs, drawings, maps, charts, song texts, and music examples. At the end of each volume is a useful set of study and research tools, including a glossary of terms, lists of audio and visual resources, and an extensive bibliography. An audio compact disc will be found inside the back cover of each volume, with sound examples that are linked (with a TRACK icon in the margin) to discussions in the text.

The Garland Encyclopedia of World Music represents the work of hundreds of specialists guided by a team of distinguished editors. With a sense of pride, Garland Publishing offers this new series to readers everywhere.

Preface

This volume, on the music and dance of South Asia, is the first of its kind to cover such a broad range of material—from ancient traditions to modern pop genres, from village folk music to classical art forms, and from the Pashtun music of Afghanistan to the Sinhala music of Sri Lanka. To say that the task has been challenging would be an understatement indeed. And yet, given the limitations on time, energy, and expense that naturally affect any single publication, the South Asia volume represents a wonderfully rich source of information on music making and music theory, musicians and dancers, performers and audiences, musical transmission, mass media, and many other topics.

Over sixty-five authors—representing fourteen countries on four different continents—have contributed to this work. Each has carried out field research and gained firsthand experience of the peoples, cultures, and musics they have written about. Several are also performers and dancers. It is their combined expertise and their shared respect for the music and dance of South Asia that fill the pages of this volume.

HOW THIS VOLUME IS ORGANIZED

Like most of its companion volumes, volume 5 of *The Garland Encyclopedia of World Music* follows a three-part structure. Part 1 introduces the region of South Asia as a whole, first in an overview article profiling its geography, societies, cultures, religions, and history. For places whose names have been changed within the last few decades, readers will generally find the older, more familiar names in use throughout the book: Madras instead of Chennai, Bombay rather than Mumbai, Banaras in place of Varanasi. Following the overview are two complementary articles that examine the history of musical scholarship, from the most ancient treatises, possibly dating from before the Common Era, to works of the late twentieth century. The chronological division into these two chapters, THEORETICAL TREATISES and SCHOLARSHIP SINCE 1300, reflects the approximate time in the history of South Asian music when theoretical concepts and ideas being written about in the northern regions began to show the influence of the conquering Muslim (Persian) culture. However, the duration and extent of this influence is a matter of debate among specialists.

Issues and Processes

Part 2, the largest section of the volume, focuses on issues and processes general to South Asia as a whole and encompasses the great traditions of classical and religious music; the relation of music to art; musical instruments; the social organization of music; learning and transmission; music in theater and dance; mass media; and the music of the South Asian diaspora. Certain topics, such as musical instruments and dance, are divided into separate articles on northern and southern areas, which follow the contrasting histories of these two halves of the Indian subcontinent through recent centuries, as well as the resulting gravitation of scholars toward the one or the other area. In one sense, these general themes reflect the way researchers today view and study performance theory and practice in South Asia; however, they often overlap. To gain an understanding of the complex worlds of North Indian (also known as Hindustani) or South Indian (also called Karnatak) classical music, for example, the interested reader might consult not only the respective articles in THE CLASSICAL TRADITIONS, but also the sections on MUSICAL MATERIAL CULTURE, for instruments used in their performance; MUSIC AND SOCIAL ORGANIZATION, on performers and patrons; MUSIC LEARNING AND TRANSMISSION, on the ways performance traditions are passed on; as well as MASS MEDIA AND CONTEMPORARY MUSICAL EXCHANGE, for an account of the spread of these musical traditions nationally and internationally through both recordings and live performances. Other sections of Part 2 focus on music in relation to religion, ritual, drama, and dance, and on music in the South Asian communities to be found in many other parts of the world. Within these broad topics, fundamental issues are examined regarding how and why music is made, where and when it is performed, by whom and for whom it is created, what role it plays in South Asian society, and how it has changed over time in both conception and practice.

Geographical and musical regions

The sections of Part 3 are organized by geographical region. We begin in the north, grouping Indian states into three regions—the northwest, north, and central—and the far north bordering on China into the Himalayan region; and the countries of Pakistan, Afghanistan, and Bangladesh are each treated as a single region. Due to the strong historical and musical links between the present-day Indian state of West Bengal and the neighboring Republic of Bangladesh, these two lands are grouped as one region. In the south, two regions cover the four states of South India and Sri Lanka. Since peoples and cultures do not necessarily fall neatly within such political boundaries, the grouping of states and countries into regions aims to bring together discussions of peoples and cultures with similar or shared musical practices, and to highlight different musics to be found within geographically close communities—differences that often relate to people's social, cultural, or religious backgrounds. The articles within these "music regions" deal with musics specific to them; in most cases, they focus on "regional traditions," a term that is used in the context of South Asian music to refer to nonclassical music, that is, the traditions usually called "folk" or "tribal."

These "musical regions" are not intended as strict geographical categories; they serve as a useful structure for the volume, though at the price of some apparent contradictions. The Indian state of Orissa, for example, is grouped within central India in Part 3, whereas its musical instruments are discussed in MUSICAL INSTRUMENTS: NORTHERN AREA, and its classical dance tradition is described in MUSIC AND DANCE: SOUTHERN AREA. Such overlapping only serves to underscore the links and connections that make categorization very difficult, as well as the flexibility one must adopt when attempting to fit any dynamic cultural tradition into a coherent structure.

Over the centuries, writers and scholars have tended to study and document theoretical concepts and traditions relating to the great traditions of South Asian music, and culture in general, paying little or no attention to the more local "little tradiitoins." It was in the 1950s that the terms "great" and "little" traditions were first proposed in connection with South Asian culture, by a group of scholars at the University of Chicago led by the anthropologist Milton Singer. The "great" traditions, in particular the classical art forms, were those that enjoyed wide geographical dispersion, a codified theory, and an orally transmitted performance tradition practiced by a professional class of artists. The "little" traditions, roughly analogous to the "folk" category of European scholarship (see the introduction to Volume 8, *The Music of Europe*), were local forms of expression circumscribed by linguistic, ethnic, sectarian, or social-caste identities. In the twentieth century, the performance practices and theories of Hindustani and Karnatak classical traditions have remained the primary focus of music researchers both native and foreign; however, a relatively small but growing number of musicologists and anthropologists have explored regional and local musical traditions maintained by villagers, tribal groups, and ethnic populations. These musics are the subject matter of Part 3, and although no single work can really do justice to the enormous variety of local musics in South Asia, this part of the volume goes well beyond the scope of any previous publication in presenting information on so many "little traditions."

The approach of the authors of Part 3 has generally not been one of individual case studies; rather, an attempt is made to introduce readers to the broad variety of traditions found in any one region. Coverage differs from one author to another, but the articles largely begin with a brief summary of a region's geography, peoples, cultures, and languages, and go on to discuss such topics as indigenous concepts of music and their relation to performance and behavior; music and identity; musical styles, genres, and instruments; aesthetics; learning and transmission; performance contexts; and the impact of mass media. All the authors give colorful descriptions of musical life in the villages and towns of South Asia, and the variety of focus and style among them is one of the strengths of this book.

Much research remains to be done, as evidenced by the omission of articles on geographical areas, such as the states of Haryana and Himachal Pradesh in northwest India, the northeastern states of Arunachal Pradesh, Assam, Bihar, Manipur, Meghalaya, Mizoram, Nagaland, and Tripura, and certain parts of Afghanistan and Pakistan. Recent political unrest—particularly in Kashmir and Afghanistan—is just one of a number of reasons why music research has been hindered or is lacking.

Research Tools

The volume provides a variety of research aids, beginning with a table of contents that guides readers to broad areas of interest and to specific articles. Each article starts with an outline of its major subdivisions and ends with a list of references; this list generally includes only works cited in the article. Some articles include a section identifying further reading and listening materials, and some include musical examples, either in Western notation or in Indian solfège notation (explained in HINDUSTANI RAGA). The top of every fourth page highlights a key excerpt from the article text; cross-references cited in brackets (as, for example, "[see MUSIC AND TRANCE]") provide links to other articles.

Throughout the book readers will find many illustrations, including photographs, drawings, tables, and charts, which enhance the presentation of possibly unfamiliar material, whether it be musical instruments, dance costumes, or intricate musical concepts. A series of maps, listed at the beginning of the volume, help locate the places mentioned in the text; for place names referred to in Part 2, readers should consult either the general maps of South Asia in Part 1 or the more detailed regional maps of Part 3. Although the peoples, cultures, castes, and communities of the region cannot be shown on the maps due to their enormous number, Map 3 does provide information on South Asian populations in other parts of the world, and ethnic groups, musical communities, and musicians discussed in articles will be found in the index and glossary at the end of the volume.

Glossary

The Glossary provides brief definitions and page references for many of the terms mentioned in this volume; in the articles, definitions are generally given following the first occurrence of a term and are often repeated within the text for the benefit of readers who are consulting individual article sections only. In the text, a quick definition or gloss usually follows the term immediately in single quotes. Glossed terms include musical genres, instruments, performance techniques, theoretical concepts, and musical communities. If two or more terms have the same meaning, the variant spellings or words appear in parentheses following the initial term; those with their own glossary entry are in boldface.

Guides to Publications, Recordings, and Films and Videos

Selective lists of published materials are to be found at the end of this volume, representing a compilation of sources in broad areas of the performing arts of South Asia. These lists include references from articles in the volume as well as further sources on particular topics that can supplement knowledge or steer readers in new directions, and they reflect an emphasis on written materials in English. Effort has been expended to keep articles relatively free of academic text references, with the guides at the end of the volume providing more extensive listings of written, aural, and visual sources.

The guiding principle in selecting the recordings listed, as in the selection of publications, films, and videos, has been availability to a wide variety of readers. Commercial recordings of North and South Indian classical music are numerous, and the Guide to Recordings provides a sampling of this rich resource. Relatively fewer recordings of regional, devotional, tribal (*ādivāsī*), and other musical traditions—including South Asian popular music—are readily available in the West; consequently, they form a smaller part of the volume's guide. Finally, a growing number of CD-ROMs relating to South Asian music and dance is now available in the marketplace, and the Guide to Recordings includes a small number of these materials.

Compact disc

The compact disc accompanying this volume contains thirty-four samples of music illustrating topics covered in the articles. The selected examples include field recordings made in various regions of South Asia, by the authors, that in some cases represent music not readily available on commercial recordings. In the interest of providing a broad representation of the musical sounds in South Asia, excerpts from Hindustani and Karnatak classical performances have been included as well. These samples allow those listeners unfamiliar with such traditions to experience the unique soundscape of Indian classical music, and those with limited familiarity to compare similar genres in the Hindustani (tracks #1–3, 7) and Karnatak (tracks #4–6, 8) traditions. Tracks 1 and 4 are both slow vocal improvisations; 2 and 5 are instrumental improvisations with an underlying rhythmic pulse but no strict meter; excerpts 3 and 6 present metered compositions that then serve as the basis for further improvisation; and 7 and 8 are examples of solo drumming. The North Indian tabla performance (track 7) is of particular value due to its age, as it was taken from a 78-rpm recording believed to date from the 1930s or 1940s.

TRANSLITERATION AND ORTHOGRAPHY

In this volume, the romanization of terms follows the Library of Congress system, to be found in *ALA–LC Romanization Tables: Transliteration Schemes for Non-Roman Scripts*, compiled and edited by Randall K. Barry (Washington, D.C.: Library of Congress, 1991). While this system specifies Roman letter equivalents for all characters of the non-Roman scripts of South Asian languages, the sheer quantity of different languages spoken in South Asia and represented in this volume has made consistency a near impossibility. For the languages of the northern regions, the pronunciation guide below encompasses many of the sounds encountered in Hindi, Urdu, and regional languages and dialects. For South Indian languages, the Telugu transliteration scheme, also reflected in the pronunciation guide, has generally been adopted for terms associated with the Karnatak music tradition. Consequently, for Tamil terms certain general principles have been adopted for consistency, such as a preference for *ḍ* or *d* over *ṭ* or *t* in medial position (for example, *naḍai* not *naṭai*), for *b* rather than *p*, and for *g* rather than *k*; also a preference for *t* over *d* in initial position (*tēvāram* not *dēvāram*) and likewise for *p* over *b*, and *k* over *g*.

For ease of pronunciation, personal names and the names of gods and deities are presented in this volume with anglicized spelling and without diacritical marks (Krishna rather than Kṛṣṇa, for example), as they are commonly written in English. Social, religious, and musical groups likewise appear in roman and not italic script, although these, like the names of festivals, seasons, and song titles appear with diacritics for more precise representation. Musical genres, instruments, theoretical terms, and titles of books and treatises are largely in italics. So too are general terms for musician, singer, instrumentalist, and so forth. However, a number of commonly used terms and titles can now be found in English dictionaries, and appear here in roman script. These include: raga, tala, sitar, sarod, tabla, ghazal, bhajan, qawwali, the Vedas, the Mahabharata, and the Ramayana. In the case of raga and tala, the North and South Indian forms of these terms have been retained when they qualify specific raga and tala names, as in the Hindustani *rāg jaunpurī* and *tīntāl*, and the Karnatak *rāga śankarābharaṇa* and *ādi tāḷa*.

The following pronuncation guide gives approximate English equivalents for the sounds of romanized letters in South Asian languages.

Vowels and diphthongs

Romanization	Pronunciation
a	b*u*t
ā	f*a*ther
i	b*i*t
ī	f*ee*t
u	p*u*t
ū	b*oo*t
ṛ	*re*turn
ḷ	*lu*cky (tongue touching the roof of the mouth)
e	l*a*te
ai	*e*ver
o	b*oa*t
au	*cow*

Consonants

All consonants have an inherent *a* (pronounced as in "*a* letter") following their initial sound. Especially at the end of words, the romanization of South Indian terms usually incorporates the final *a*, as in *rāga*, while that of modern-day North Indian terms, following pronunciation, generally drops the final *a*, as in *rāg*. This convention has been followed in the volume.

The consonants *ka*, *qa*, *ga*, *ja*, *ta*, *da*, *pa*, *ba*, and *za* are pronounced as in English; all have aspirated forms that add an *h* sound (as in *h*ug), otherwise described as an expiration of air, to the pronunciation of the consonant: *kha* as in *Kh*mer, *gha* as in *gh*ost, and so on. Consonants *ya*, *ra*, *la*, *va*, and *ma* are unaspirated letters that sound like their equivalents in English. The sounds transliterated as *ca*, *cha*, *na*, *sa*, and *sha* vary as follows: *ca* is pronounced like *ch* in *ch*urch, and *cha* has the added breath of air; varieties of *na* include *ṅa*, *ṇa*, and *ña*, and range in sound from a nasalization (*ṅa* and *ña*) to a retroflex *n* spoken with the tongue curled back and touching the roof of the mouth (*ṇa*); *sa* is pronounced as in English, and the aspirated *sha* and aspirated retroflex *sha* (different from each other in pronunciation but not in English spelling) are romanized as *śa* and *sha*, respectively. The retroflex consonants *ṭa*, *ṭha*, *ḍa*, *ḍha*, *ṛa*, and *ṛha* are all pronounced with the tongue touching the roof of the mouth.

ACKNOWLEDGMENTS

Of all the many people who have helped to create and produce this volume, it is the almost seventy authors to whom I am most indebted. Their hard work, their specialized knowledge, their patience and understanding during the editorial process, and their support of this endeavor have been invaluable to me during my editorship. We have shared times of concentrated work and times of silence, periods of frustration and moments of humor, but in particular we have shared a sense of combined effort. For our essential communication—between the United States and South Asia, Australia, New Zealand, Canada, and Europe—we clearly owe recognition to the speed and reliability of electronic mail, express mail, fax, and other computer-related technologies, without which this project would certainly not have been completed in four years. But more important, for our knowledge and our skills, we as writers and performers owe our deep gratitude to our teachers, our gurus and ustads, and the countless musicians, dancers, actors, and other performing artists of South Asia who have shared with us their creativity and their love of music.

I sincerely thank my three advisors—Matthew Allen, Regula Qureshi, and Bonnie Wade—whose wisdom and experience have guided me from the earliest planning of this volume to its final stages of production. Always willing to share their thoughts and ideas, they assisted in designing the volume's structure, selecting and locating authors, determining a workable volume-wide transliteration and romanization system, and in many other aspects of the process. I am grateful to them, as well as to Charles Capwell, Daniel Neuman, and Lorraine Sakata, for reading and providing critical comments on the seventy-five articles submitted. In particular, I extend my warm gratitude to Lorraine Sakata and John Baily for their advice and assistance in planning the Pakistan and Afghanistan sections, respectively. One notable example of the dedication afforded this production by its advisors and authors occurred at the Society for Ethnomusicology meeting in Los Angeles in 1995. Matthew Allen, Rolf Groesbeck, Gayathri Kassebaum, and Richard Wolf gave of their time and energy to discuss and create guidelines for a consistent spelling and transliteration of all Dravidian languages in the Garland South Asia volume. I appreciate both their willingness to help and their invaluable transliteration supplement, subsequently submitted by Matthew Allen.

I would like to thank the many people who have provided photographs and slides, including Nancy Martin, Carol Babiracki, and George Pallivathucal, as well as the volume authors and others credited in figure captions. Cristina Magaldi at the University of California, Los Angeles, and Beth G. Raps of Tallahassee, Florida, translated articles for the volume. Bob Haddad of Music of the World and Randy Friel of Soundwave Audio Productions and Services, both of Chapel Hill, North Carolina, provided valuable assistance in producing the compact disc, of which I am most appreciative.

I am grateful for the assistance of various individuals connected with the editing and production processes. I enjoyed a brief collaboration with Jacob Love, the first copy editor of the South Asia volume, followed by a longer association with Samuel Bartos; both worked carefully and diligently copy editing article texts. I would like to thank the managing editors of this encyclopedia series during my tenure—Richard Wallis until 1998 and Soo Mee Kwon thereafter, as well as former Garland Vice President Leo Balk—for their strong commitment to the project and their efforts to bring about the timely release of this and other volumes. Two particular individuals have been enormously helpful to me during the past year: project editor Barbara Curialle Gerr and project assistant Gillian Rodger. Their friendship and their tireless work dealing with the seemingly endless details of text and illustration preparation and production have been a great encouragement. And to all other Garland employees and contracted specialists who have worked on this volume, I give my thanks.

Although deeply involved in the preparation of the South Asia volume, I have benefited from sporadic but informative and supportive communication with the other volume editors of *The Garland Encyclopedia of World Music* over the past four years. I am honored to have had such distinguished colleagues, and I am grateful for the sharing of ideas and experiences I have encountered at joint editorial meetings and via e-mail and telephone. To Ruth Stone especially, I extend my warm congratulations on her completion of the first published volume *Africa.* She has been an inspiration and incentive to me as a "sole" volume editor, and I give thanks for the thoughtful and helpful advice she gave me as I undertook this daunting task.

At the time I began work on this project in 1995, I was juggling teaching (both at a university and at a community music school) and raising a family. Four years later, my Garland work has temporarily supplanted teaching and has become a full-time occupation, as my long-suffering family will assuredly attest. I cannot thank them enough for their support and their understanding. My elder son Adam's clerical assistance was especially appreciated, as well as his creation of a computer database for the volume. I am also grateful to my younger son Nathan for his cheerful companionship during numerous trips to copy shops and post offices and the long hours when I sat at the computer. Throughout this period, my husband, Gordon, has been my unwavering partner—emotionally, psychologically, intellectually, and financially. Words cannot express my gratitude; this published volume is without doubt a testament to his faithful and generous support.

—Alison Arnold

List of Contributors

Mohammad Akbar
Manor Park, London, England

Matthew Allen
Wheaton College
Norton, Massachusetts, U.S.A.

Andrew Burton Alter
The University of New England
Armidale, New South Wales, Australia

Alison Arnold
University of North Carolina, Chapel Hill
Chapel Hill, North Carolina, U.S.A.

Gordon K. Arnold
IBM Corporation
Research Triangle Park, North Carolina, U.S.A.

Sabir Badalkhan
Istituto Universitario Orientale
Naples, Italy

John Baily
Goldsmiths College, London University
New Cross, England

Guy Beck
Tulane University
New Orleans, Louisiana, U.S.A.

Jan Van Belle
Arnhem, Netherlands

Gregory D. Booth
University of Auckland
Auckland, New Zealand

Donald Brenneis
University of California at Santa Cruz
Santa Cruz, California, U.S.A.

Charles Capwell
University of Illinois at Urbana-Champaign
Urbana, Illinois, U.S.A.

Amy Catlin
University of California, Los Angeles
Los Angeles, California, U.S.A.

Peter J. Claus
California State University, Hayward
Hayward, California, U.S.A.

Monique Desroches
University of Montreal
Montreal, Quebec, Canada

Brigitte DesRosiers
University of Montreal
Montreal, Quebec, Canada

Veronica Doubleday
School of Historical and Critical Studies,
University of Brighton
Brighton, England

Gerry Farrell
City University
London, England

Reis Flora
Monash University
Victoria, Australia

Karunamaya Goswami
Narayanganj Women's College
Narayanganj, Bangladesh

Paul D. Greene
Penn State University, Delaware County Campus
Media, Pennsylvania, U.S.A.

John Andrew Greig
U.S. Department of State
Washington, D.C., U.S.A.

Rolf Groesbeck
University of Arkansas at Little Rock
Little Rock, Arkansas, U.S.A.

Mireille Helffer
Centre National de Recherche Scientifique,
Musée de l'Homme
Paris, France

Edward O. Henry
San Diego State University
San Diego, California, U.S.A.

Wayne Howard
Winona, Mississippi, U.S.A.

William Jackson
Indiana University–Purdue University at Indianapolis
Indianapolis, Indiana, U.S.A.

Gayathri Rajapur Kassebaum
Bharatiya Vidyabhavan
Bangalore, India

Saskia Kersenboom
University of Amsterdam
Amsterdam, Netherlands

James R. Kippen
University of Toronto
Toronto, Ontario, Canada

Peter Manuel
John Jay College, City University of New York
New York, New York, U.S.A.

Scott L. Marcus
University of California, Santa Barbara
Santa Barbara, California, U.S.A.

Joyce Middlebrook
Brownsville, California, U.S.A.

Allyn Miner
University of Pennsylvania
Philadelphia, Pennsylvania, U.S.A.

Nabi Misdaq
School of African and Asian Studies
University of Sussex, England

Pirkko Moisala
Abo Akademi University
Turku, Finland

Helen Myers
Central Connecticut State University
New Britain, Connecticut, U.S.A.

Mekhala Devi Natavar
Duke University
Durham, North Carolina, U.S.A.

Adam Nayyar
Lok Virsa Research Centre
Islamabad, Pakistan

David Paul Nelson
Amherst College
Amherst, Massachusetts, U.S.A.

Robert Ollikkala
Algoma Conservatory of Music
Sault Ste. Marie, Ontario, Canada

Józef M. Pacholczyk
University of Maryland
College Park, Maryland, U.S.A.

Joseph J. Palackal
City University of New York
New York, New York, U.S.A.

Jayendran Pillay
Hampshire College
Amherst, Massachusetts, U.S.A.

Jennifer C. Post
Middlebury College
Middlebury, Vermont, U.S.A.

Regula Burckhardt Qureshi
University of Alberta
Edmonton, Alberta, Canada

N. Ramanathan
University of Madras
Chennai, India

Ashok D. Ranade
Mumbai, India

David B. Reck
Amherst College
Amherst, Massachusetts, U.S.A.

David Roche
Sonoma State University
Rohnert Park, California, U.S.A.

Gene H. Roghair
Nevada City, California, U.S.A.

Lewis Rowell
Indiana University
Bloomington, Indiana, U.S.A.

George Ruckert
Massachusetts Institute of Technology
Boston, Massachusetts, U.S.A.

Hiromi Lorraine Sakata
University of California, Los Angeles
Los Angeles, California, U.S.A.

T. Sankaran
Chennai, India

Susana Sardo
Universidade de Aveiro, Campus de Santiago
Aveiro, Portugal

Anna Schmid
South Asia Institute
Heidelberg, Germany

Anne Sheeran
Seattle, Washington, U.S.A.

Zöe C. Sherinian
Franklin and Marshall College
Lancaster, Pennsylvania, U.S.A.

Brian Q. Silver
International Music Associates
Washington, D.C., U.S.A.

Robert Simms
University of Toronto, Scarborough College
Toronto, Ontario, Canada

Gora Singh (deceased)
New York, New York, U.S.A.

Karna Singh
New York, New York, U.S.A.

Stephen Slawek
University of Texas, Austin
Austin, Texas, U.S.A.

Gordon R. Thompson
Skidmore College
Saratoga Springs, New York, U.S.A.

Bonnie C. Wade
University of California, Berkeley
Berkeley, California, U.S.A.

Richard Widdess
University of London, School of Oriental and African Studies
London, England

Richard K. Wolf
Harvard University
Cambridge, Massachusetts, U.S.A.

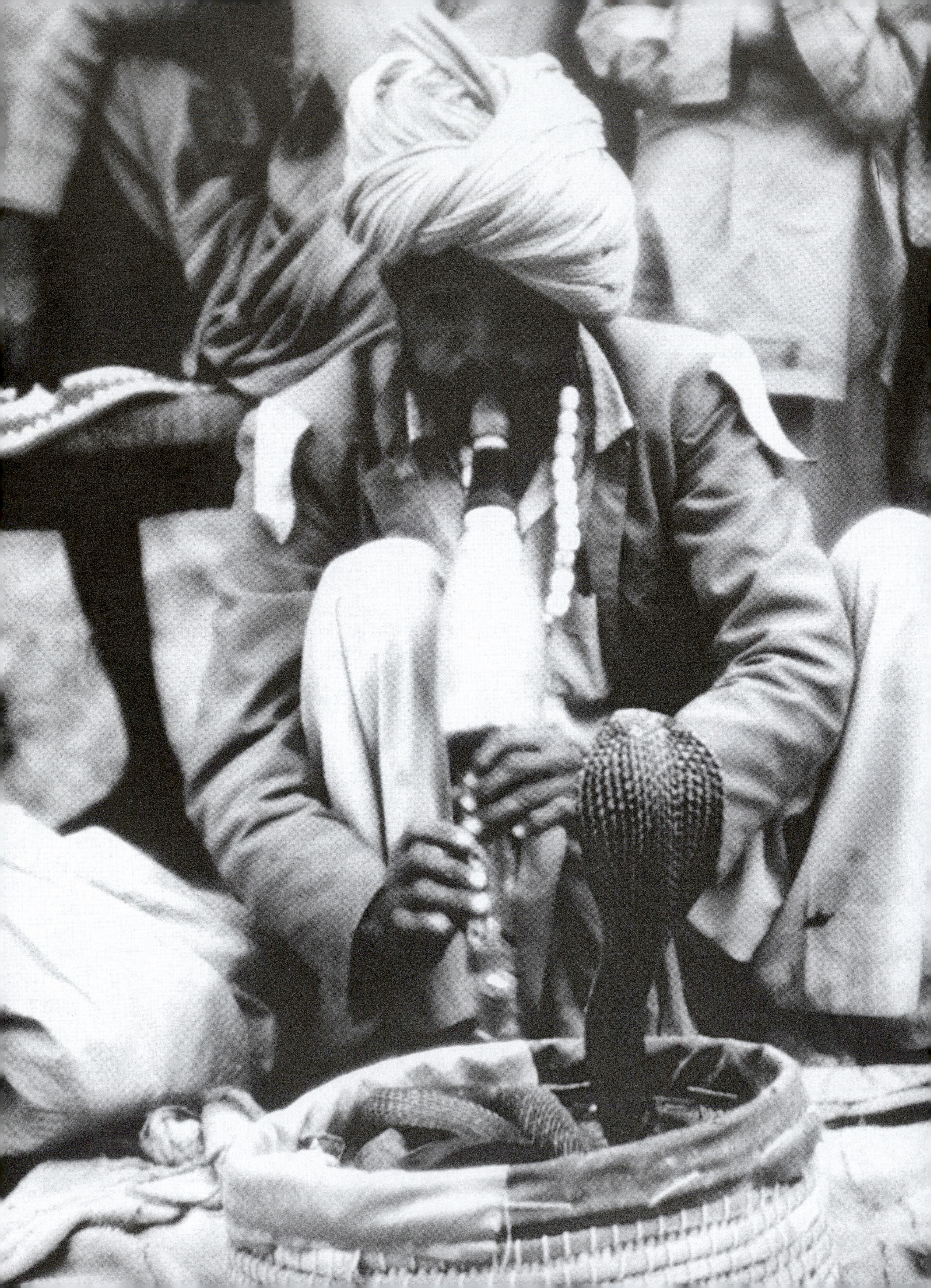

Part 1
Introduction to the Music of South Asia

Music, dance, and drama are all integral parts of South Asian culture and society. These performing arts—classical music traditions, devotional songs, tribal dances, regional dance dramas, life-cycle songs, and many more—are passed on orally within families, social groups, and stylistic schools. In this land, home to roughly one-fifth of the world's people, performing artists and their communities infuse these musical practices of the past with vital meaning and expressivity that reflect the present. South Asian music is thus at once traditional and modern. It is also part of our global marketplace, where popular music and culture are rapidly transmitted from one continent to another. South Asians, at home and in the diaspora, are entertaining new ideas and creating new musical syntheses. These varied and vibrant expressions of culture and identity today remain a testament to the value of music, dance, and drama in the lives of South Asians.

Whether on the streets, in temples, or in concert halls, music is an integral part of life in South Asia. In Karachi, Pakistan, a snake charmer plays a *puṅgī* to entertain onlookers. Photo by Nazir Jairazbhoy, 1983.

Profile of South Asia and Its Music

Alison Arnold

Geography
Peoples, Cultures, and Languages
Social Structure
Religious Practice
Political History

South Asia covers just over 5 million square kilometers, a mere 11 percent of the Asian continent, yet it encompasses the world's second most populous nation (India), it boasts the world's highest elevations (the Himalayas), and its history extends back to one of the world's oldest civilizations (that of the Indus Valley). The region is defined primarily by its physical location, extending from the Himalayas south through the Indian subcontinent and from the eastern border of India to the western borders of Pakistan and Afghanistan. Within these geopolitical boundaries, the peoples of South Asia belong to the seven nation states of Afghanistan, Bangladesh, Bhutan, India, Nepal, Pakistan, and Sri Lanka (map 1). Compared with the population of Europe (excluding Russia and the countries of the former Soviet Union), which comprises over twenty-five nations within an area just under 5 million square kilometers, the population of South Asia might appear less diverse. However, the identities of South Asians reside not so much in their nationalities as in their particular ethnic backgrounds, regional cultures, languages, religions, and social categories, which all cut across national and political lines.

The music and dance of South Asia reflect this diversity of peoples in their variety of regional folk genres, religious and devotional expressions, tribal forms, theater and dance-drama accompaniment, urban popular genres, and cultivated art traditions. But more than this, the many music and dance styles and genres are the products of South Asia's history, society, and culture. Modern-day performance practices therefore not only inform us about life and culture in the present but provide a window into the past. Within the Indian subcontinent two classical music traditions prevail, Karnatak in the south and Hindustani in the north (figure 1). In a manner somewhat analogous to West European classical music, these traditions are rooted in older musical practices and are performed over a wide geographical area by people of different ethnic and social backgrounds. Few other forms of music are similarly panregional in South Asia; devotional singing, linked with the spread of the bhakti devotional movement especially in the fifteenth to seventeenth centuries, is common throughout the area, and popular music in the form of film songs has gained nationwide audiences through modern-day mass media channels. But in the thousands of villages and rural communities throughout India and its neighboring countries, local

opposite: MAP 1 South Asia.

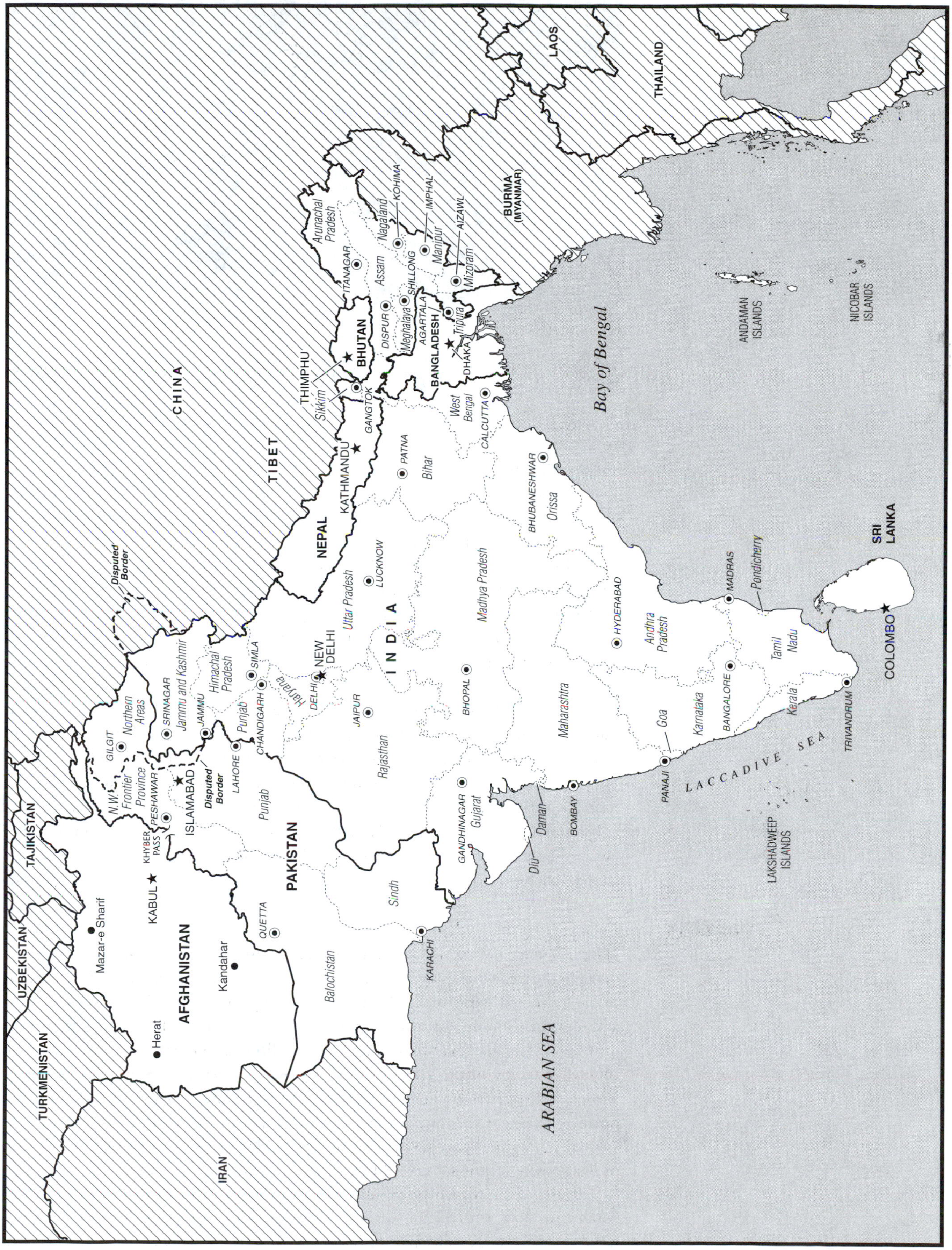
CHINA
TIBET
LAOS
THAILAND
BURMA (MYANMAR)
Arunachal Pradesh
ITANAGAR
Nagaland
KOHIMA
IMPHAL
Manipur
AIZAWL
Mizoram
Assam
SHILLONG
DISPUR
Meghalaya
AGARTALA
Tripura
BANGLADESH
DHAKA
BHUTAN
THIMPHU
Sikkim
GANGTOK
West Bengal
CALCUTTA
Bay of Bengal
ANDAMAN ISLANDS
NICOBAR ISLANDS
KATHMANDU
NEPAL
PATNA
Bihar
BHUBANESHWAR
Orissa
SRI LANKA
COLOMBO
Pondicherry
MADRAS
LUCKNOW
Uttar Pradesh
Madhya Pradesh
HYDERABAD
Andhra Pradesh
Tamil Nadu
BANGALORE
Kerala
TRIVANDRUM
Karnataka
Goa
PANAJI
LACCADIVE SEA
LAKSHADWEEP ISLANDS
Disputed Border
Jammu and Kashmir
Himachal Pradesh
SIMLA
NEW DELHI
DELHI
Haryana
INDIA
BHOPAL
Maharashtra
BOMBAY
Daman
Diu
SRINAGAR
Northern Areas
GILGIT
JAMMU
Punjab
CHANDIGARH
JAIPUR
Rajasthan
N.W. Frontier Province
PESHAWAR
ISLAMABAD
Disputed Border
LAHORE
Punjab
GANDHINAGAR
Gujarat
TAJIKISTAN
KHYBER PASS
KABUL
Mazar-e Sharif
AFGHANISTAN
PAKISTAN
QUETTA
Sindh
KARACHI
UZBEKISTAN
Kandahar
Balochistan
Herat
TURKMENISTAN
ARABIAN SEA
IRAN

FIGURE 1 Hindustani classical music performance by Ustad Ali Akbar Khan (*center*) playing sarod, accompanied by (*from left*) Zakir Hussain on tabla drums, two *tambūrā* players (Rajiv Taranath on the right), and Ali Akbar Khan's son Ashish Khan, also playing sarod. The thirtieth Sawai Gandharva Music Festival in Pune, 1982. Photo by Gordon Arnold.

music and dance traditions abound; although the pan–South Asian forms present a certain degree of musical unity, it is these local forms that manifest the rich diversity of South Asian musical culture. Such diversity results in part from the region's former political organization, particularly the subcontinent's division into 562 princely states before India's independence in 1947. Yet these regional and tribal music and dance traditions remain viable even at the end of the twentieth century. The pervasive force of mass media and technology, spreading pop music to the remotest habitats [see POP MUSIC AND AUDIO-CASSETTE TECHNOLOGY], and the greater mobility of people both migrating and emigrating [see MUSIC AND THE SOUTH ASIAN DIASPORA] are now speeding up musical change. Thus the regional forms documented here, which will doubtless take on new characters and meanings in the new millennium, present a valuable picture of South Asian musical culture c. A.D. 2000, a moment in its musical history that has not been captured elsewhere in such broad and rich detail.

This profile of South Asia introduces the world region and its music through a series of broad "frames": geography, peoples, cultures, languages, social structures, religions, and political history. Through these frames, which also serve to situate the music of South Asia within the context of the volume, the reader can view the material that follows.

GEOGRAPHY

The land mass of South Asia comprises several distinctive physical regions, prominent among them being the high mountain ranges of the Himalaya and Hindu Kush to the north and northwest, which geographically separate the Indian subcontinent and Afghanistan from northern Asia (see map 2). This physical boundary has historically divided peoples, cultures, and musical traditions, and has allowed contact only through a few mountain passes. It has also acted as a meteorological barrier, enabling a tropical climate to extend beyond the tropical zone to northern India. Rising in the northern peaks are the three major rivers, the Ganges, Indus, and Brahmaputra, fed year-round by snow and heavy monsoon rains. The Ganges meets the Brahmaputra in Bangladesh, forming the world's largest and most fertile river delta.

To the south, the Indian peninsula encompasses the Western and Eastern Ghat Mountains bordering the broad central Deccan Plateau. The Vindhya and Satpura ranges distance the southern regions of India from their northern neighbors. Beyond

India's shores, South Asia extends to several groups of islands—Lakshadweep, the Andamans, and the Nicobars—as well as Sri Lanka. Sandwiched between the southern peninsula and northern mountains lie the densely populated Ganges plain and the Indus river valley, separated by the Thar (Great Indian) Desert. These river valleys have allowed life and culture to thrive for millennia, influenced time and again by foreign invasions, by the establishment of foreign rulers, and by the introduction of new ideas, religions, languages, and musical traditions.

PEOPLES, CULTURES, AND LANGUAGES

The current population of South Asia constitutes over one-third of Asia's people. This statistic reflects the vast population of India, estimated in 1998 at over 984 million (Brunner 1999:153–155). Although India's population has more than doubled since independence fifty years ago, the peoples of this world region reflect a multilayering of cultures and languages brought about by millennia of migrations and invasions.

The majority of people in South Asia live outside urban areas, despite the enormous growth of the port cities of Bombay (Mumbai), Calcutta, and Madras (Chennai), which developed as important centers of trade and industry in the eighteenth and nineteenth centuries and as havens of commercial and economic opportunities in the twentieth century. Only 26 percent of India's population is urban (compared with 75 percent in the United States); the only South Asian nation with a higher urban population is Pakistan, with 28 percent (Famighetti 1997). The enormous rural population lives in predominantly agricultural villages and towns, each of which sustains cultural and musical traditions of local, regional, or national identity. Villages have always had connections with larger towns and cities through trade, politics, and religious practices, and such links have strengthened musical practices by connecting audiences and performers (especially itinerant musicians and entertainers, for example).

The peoples and languages of Afghanistan and Pakistan in the northwest, and of Nepal and Bhutan in the north, reflect their proximity and historical connections with the neighboring regions of Iran, central Asia, and Tibet. The population of Afghanistan comprises mostly Pashtun, Tajik, Uzbek, and Hazara peoples, who speak Pashto and Dari (both of the Persian branch of the Indo-European language family), and Turkic languages; in Pakistan, the principal languages are Urdu (the national language), Punjabi, Sindhi, Pashto, Balochi, and English (map 2). The Newars, Guruṅgs, and Tibetans (among others) in Nepal speak Nepali (an Indic language), Newari, and Tibetan and Tibeto-Burman dialects, as do the primarily Bhote and Nepalese peoples in Bhutan, whose official language is Dzongkha.

The Indian constitution recognizes sixteen principal languages, of which two (Hindi and English) are the official national languages; India has a further 1,652 dialects. The principal language spoken in the Gangetic plain is Hindi, of the Indic branch of the Indo-European family, with several North Indian dialects—including Rajasthani, Braj Bhasha, Bhojpuri, Magadhi, and Maithili—all considered closely related. To the south, on the Chotanagpur Plateau, various tribal groups speak languages belonging to three different language families: Indo-European (Sadani, for example), Dravidian (Kurukh, spoken by the Oraon), and Austro-Asiatic (Mundari, Santali, Ho, etc.) (Babiracki 1991). In the southern peninsula, four major Dravidian languages predominate—Kannada, Malayalam, Tamil, and Telugu—with other Dravidian languages such as Gondi, Tulu, and Kota spoken by specific ethnic and tribal groups. The Dravidian (Sanskrit *drāviḍa)* language family is linked to the ancient Australoid race of that name in the Indian subcontinent. Sri Lanka has three principal languages: English, Tamil, and the Indic Sinhala spoken by the majority

TIBETAN
HIMALAYA
Disputed Border
NEPALI
DZONGKHA
ASSAMESE
Brahmaputra R.
BENGALI
Ganges River
ORIYA
EASTERN GHATS
TAMIL
SINHALA
HINDI
(URDU)
Yamuna R.
GANGE
Narmada R.
VINDHYA RANGE
SATPURA RANGE
DECCAN PLATEAU
MARATHI
TELUGU
KANNADA
MALAYALAM
Kaveri R.
Tungabhadra R.
Krishna River
Godavari River
WESTERN GHATS
Chambal R.
KASHMIRI
PUNJABI
THAR DESERT
GUJARATI
PASHTO
HINDU KUSH
KHYBER PASS
Indus River
SINDHI (URDU)
DARI
BALOCHI

FIGURE 2 Gujarati musicians playing *alghoza* double flute and frame drum at a folk music festival in Bhuj, Kutch, organized by India National Theatre, 1982. Photo by Gordon Arnold.

Sinhala population. And to the east, the people of Bangladesh speak two principal languages, Bengali and English.

In 1956, the Indian government reorganized state boundaries on the basis of language, aiming to create a single dominant ethnolinguistic group in each state, in response to intense agitation and separatist demands (Wolpert 1997:368–370). This political restructuring recognized the importance of ethnicity and language in the regional identities of India's peoples, and resulted in the division of Bombay into predominantly Marathi-speaking Maharashtra and Gujarati-speaking Gujarat in 1960, the separation of Nagaland from Assam in 1963, the division of Indian Punjab into Sikh-majority Punjab and Hindu-majority Haryana in 1966, and the creation of tribal states in northeastern India in the 1970s and 1980s (Stern 1993:106–110). Within the new states, local cultural and musical traditions as well as local dialects and mother tongues have lived on, enriching the cultural and linguistic matrix. In Rajasthan, within the northern Hindi-speaking belt, for example, members of the Rajput caste, descended from the ancient ruling Rajput warrior clans, have patronized music and the performing arts for generations; their support of various professional hereditary musician families such as the Manganihārs and Ḍholīs has created a rich heritage of musical traditions [see RAJASTHAN]. In the same western desert region, as in other parts of northern India, men and women of various castes separately and informally perform devotional, seasonal, and life-cycle songs within their own communities, upholding local and regional cultural traditions (figure 2). Professional narrative singers, such as the various Mīrāsī groups who document genealogies and beliefs [see PAKISTAN: PUNJAB] and the *māṇ bhaṭṭ* epic storytellers [see GUJARAT], express their ethnic identity through their cultural performances.

opposite: MAP 2 Principal languages and physical features of South Asia

The new political state and province boundaries encircled large geographical areas, but some ethnic groups nevertheless found their peoples and lands divided. Balochistan, the home of the Baloch people, straddles western and southwestern Pakistan, southeastern Iran, and southwestern Afghanistan [see BALOCHISTAN]. The people of the Punjab are divided between Pakistan and India, with the present Indian state of Punjab, created in 1966, providing a homeland for the large Sikh population there [see INDIA: PUNJAB and PAKISTAN: PUNJAB]. Likewise in the east, the people of Bengal found part of their land apportioned to Pakistan at the time of India's independence, the territory now adjacent to the Indian state of West Bengal and known

FIGURE 3 A *ḍhol* drummer accompanies a troupe of Gujarati male dancers rehearsing for their performance in the Kutch folk festival in Bhuj, 1982. Photo by Gordon Arnold.

as Bangladesh. In such cases where nationality has intersected with cultural, ethnic, and linguistic populations, the issue of identity has become more complex, and musical traditions have developed in new directions.

Within ethnic populations in South Asia, gender defines roles both in life and in musical culture. Women in traditional ethnic communities rarely sing or dance in public, but they often perform in gender-segregated gatherings during wedding and childbirth celebrations [see PAKISTAN: MUSIC AND GENDER]. They tend to use minimal musical accompaniment, such as hand clapping, hand cymbals, and sometimes drumming. Instrumentalists, both amateur and professional, are typically men (figure 3). Professional musical performance is traditionally passed through family lineages, ranging from classical musicians (*gharānā*) to regional caste artists, from temple drummers to epic singers, from dance and theater accompanists to snake charmers. Some tribal populations have similar gender distinctions in social and musical contexts [see TAMIL NADU], while others foster greater intermixing of men and women in musical performance, often with no distinction between performers and audience [see MAHARASHTRA; MADHYA PRADESH].

Beyond locality, region, language, and ethnicity, other factors play a significant role in the ways the people of South Asia distinguish and identify themselves and others and in the cultural and musical traditions they foster. Most important among these factors are social and religious categories, both of which have been shaped by the region's political history.

SOCIAL STRUCTURE

Music and the performing arts in South Asia have been strongly affected throughout history by the evolving social organization in this world area. Both music and dance today reflect the hierarchical social order of India's dominant religion, Hinduism—in the value placed on music by different social groups, in the social status of performers, in the relationships among musicians, patrons, and society at large, and in the range of performance contexts. Unlike in the West, where extraordinary talent and expertise can lead to fame and fortune for artists regardless of their social background, in the Indian subcontinent social class and caste play a major role in defining the limits of an artist's expectations and opportunities, with the possible exception of the popular music industry. Lower-caste musicians who perform for upper-caste

FIGURE 4 A Brahmin priest performs *sarasvatī pūjā*, blessing library books at the newly opened Archive and Research Center for Ethnomusicology at the American Institute of Indian Studies in Pune, 1982. Photo by Alison Arnold.

patrons, for example, may reach an outstanding level of artistry, but their traditional caste affiliation limits their ability to rise above a subordinate rank.

From c. 1500 B.C. to the present, Indian society has recognized a hierarchy of classes and castes, each with its own *dharma*—associated behavior patterns, duties, and obligations toward the larger society. According to ancient laws of the Aryans (seminomadic tribes who entered northwest India during the second millennium B.C.), people belonged to one of four social groups, sometimes described as classes (*varṇa*). The upper three—Brahmins, Kshatriyas, and Vaishyas—held initiation ceremonies for young boys, after which they were considered twice-born (*dvija*). The duties of these three *varṇa* within the traditionally articulated scheme included studying and sacrificing. In addition, the Brahmins' function was to teach, and many became professional priests (figure 4); Kshatriyas served to protect people as rulers and fighters; and the Vaishyas were merchants and traders. A fourth group, the Shudras, comprised a rich variety of professions, including artisans and musicians whose role was to serve the upper classes. According to the developing Hindu belief system, Shudras were further subdivided by profession and social behavior into those "excluded" from Hindu society and treated as outcasts, and those "not excluded." Those lowest in the social hierarchy, whose occupations included sweeping, tanning leather, and cremating corpses, later became known as untouchables (called Harijans by Mahatma Gandhi). After independence, the Indian constitution expressly abolished untouchability, but the government keeps a schedule or register of formerly untouchable castes (hence the euphemism "scheduled castes") and both legislates against discrimination and reserves educational and employment opportunities for this sector of the population. This hierarchical social order has dictated not only duties but degrees of religious purity. Within the belief system, those born into low social levels have been considered "unclean," but have always theoretically had the possibility of escaping their associated ritual pollution through proper conduct in their present life leading to rebirth into a higher level (Stern 1993:74–83).

The relationship between *varṇa* 'social category, class' and the more commonly used term *jāti* 'caste' is fluid and has little historical documentation. The English word *caste*, from the term *casta* 'tribe' or 'clan' first used by Portuguese traders in the sixteenth century to describe the many Hindu groups they encountered, refers in modern South Asia to hereditary social groups distinguished by occupation, race,

At the end of the twentieth century, caste still remains an important aspect of society in the subcontinent, and continues to play a distinctive role in regional music.

region, and religion. Caste affiliation also determines inherited status, wealth, and relationships within the caste system. Caste organization has been a strong characteristic of Hinduism for centuries, and has traditionally imposed rigid rules of social interaction and mobility. The system has allowed some degree of change—-castes have risen and fallen, castes have been formed and have died out—-but for the most part the hierarchical structure is fixed. Most significantly, the caste system has provided social identity, and not only to native-born Hindus: Sikhs, Muslims, and Christians in South Asia have all experienced the influence of the caste structure (Basham 1959:151). At the end of the twentieth century, caste still remains an important aspect of society in the subcontinent, and continues to play a distinctive role in regional music [see REGIONAL CASTE ARTISTS AND THEIR PATRONS], but its hold is being undoubtedly challenged by the increasing spread of foreign technology, communications, ideas, and education.

The social structure outlined above has penetrated all aspects of life, including music; perhaps one of its more unfortunate realities has been the relatively low social status afforded professional male instrumentalists in the past, especially those playing instruments made of animal skin or gut (considered polluting by Hindus) and those accompanying solo musicians, and professional female artists as well [see WOMEN AND MUSIC]. In South India in particular, the distinction between Brahmin and non-Brahmin musicians is an integral part of music history, which documents both separate traditions of, and interaction between, the two sociomusical communities [see THE SOCIAL ORGANIZATION OF MUSIC AND MUSICIANS: SOUTHERN AREA].

Beyond the borders of predominantly Hindu India, the populations of Pakistan and Afghanistan to the northwest are almost entirely Islamic (97 percent and 100 percent of the populations, respectively). Here ethnic groups derive their social cohesion from locality and from the larger Muslim community. Other areas where caste is present but plays a less significant role than in India are Sri Lanka and Bhutan, both of which have large Buddhist populations (see below), as well as Bangladesh, where 83 percent of the people are Muslim.

RELIGIOUS PRACTICE

The two major religions practiced in South Asia today are Hinduism and Islam. With more than 850 million Hindus—65 percent of the South Asian population—living predominantly in India, South Asia is the only region in the world (besides the Indonesian island of Bali) with a dominant Hindu population (figure 5). The 375 million Muslims who reside largely in Afghanistan, Bangladesh, India, and Pakistan, make up 28.5 percent of South Asia's people; they represent only a fraction of the estimated one billion followers of Islam worldwide (Brunner 1999:406).

Hinduism arose in India from the ancient traditions and the divine pantheon recorded in the Vedas, the earliest Hindu sacred writings, comprising four canonical

FIGURE 5 Thirukkalikundran, a South Indian Hindu temple in Tamil Nadu. Photo by Gordon Arnold, 1983.

collections of prayers, liturgical formulas, and hymns. Over time Hinduism acquired many popular divinities, as well as an enormous body of sacred literature ranging from the esoteric Vedas, Brahmanas, and Upanishads to the more widely accessible Puranas (ancient stories) and epic tales, especially the Mahabharata and the Ramayana. These writings have inspired generations of poets and singers to compose devotional songs that are still sung in both northern and southern areas [see RELIGIOUS AND DEVOTIONAL MUSIC]. Modern-day Hinduism owes much to the mendicant poet-singers of devotional hymns who traversed the Tamil region of South India in the sixth to ninth centuries and more northern areas in medieval times (thirteenth to seventeenth centuries), spreading the tradition of bhakti (devotion). The singing of bhajans and other devotional forms is now fundamental to Hindu worship throughout South Asia, and has even led to the composition of pop bhajans that appear in commercial Indian films and are played through loudspeakers at religious festivals and parades. With no single doctrine, Hinduism has always allowed its followers great freedom of belief and religious expression.

The first of several incursions of Islamic peoples into South Asia occurred in the eighth century, when Arabs from Iraq occupied Sindh, in present-day Pakistan (Wolpert 1997:105–106). A more potent Islamic force arrived with the Muslim Turks, who ruled northern India in the twelfth century and even spread into the south, until the Hindu kingdom of Vijayanagar (established c. 1335) pushed them back north of the Krishna River. With the Islamic empire of the Persian-speaking Mughals, from Central Asia, spreading throughout the northern regions and spanning two and a half centuries (early 1500s to mid 1700s), Islam became a pervasive influence in South Asia (figure 6). Islamic doctrine does not sanction the use of music in mosques; however, Muslims cultivated musical traditions on the subconti-

FIGURE 6 Mosque at the Taj Mahal in Agra, Uttar Pradesh. Photo by Gordon Arnold, 1982.

nent in both religious and secular life [see MUSIC, THE STATE, AND ISLAM]. Devotional music in the form of qawwali and *kāfī* is performed, particularly at the shrines of Sufi saints (figure 7; see PAKISTAN: DEVOTIONAL MUSIC).

Other minority religions in present-day South Asia include Buddhism, Jainism, and Sikhism, all native to the subcontinent and currently practiced by approximately 22.5 million, 5 million, and 19.5 million South Asians, respectively (1.75 percent, 0.35 percent, and 1.5 percent of the population). Buddhism began after the enlightenment of Siddhartha Gautama (c. 563–483 B.C.) at Bodh Gaya (in modern-day Uttar Pradesh) in the fifth century B.C. and spread throughout India and elsewhere in Asia through the early centuries after Christ, when Hinduism was becoming established. The major Buddhist populations today are found in China, Korea, Japan, Tibet, Mongolia, and Southeast Asia; in South Asia, Buddhists form a majority in Sri Lanka (69 percent of the population) and Bhutan (75 percent). The conservative Theravada tradition in Sri Lanka, which offers salvation only to a select few, has

FIGURE 7 The tomb of the Sufi saint Nizamuddin in Delhi. Photo by Gordon Arnold, 1982.

employed music to a lesser extent than the more liberal Mahayana tradition of universal salvation followed in the north. Sinhala Buddhist music includes Buddhist chanting and music by a lay instrumental ensemble called *hēvisi* [see SRI LANKA]. In the Himalayan regions, the monastic communities and schools of Tibetan Buddhism continue their practices of singing (*dbyangs-yig*) and playing ritual instruments [see TIBETAN CULTURE IN SOUTH ASIA].

The founder of Jainism (the "religion of the conquerors"), Vardhamana Mahavira (c. 540–468 B.C.), was a contemporary of the Buddha and followed a life of asceticism from the age of thirty, reached enlightenment (becoming a *jina* 'conqueror') in his early forties, and thereafter preached and practiced self-torture and death by starvation. Jainism, like Buddhism, is essentially atheistic, assigning no role to personal deities, but unlike Mahayana Buddhism and Hinduism, it teaches that salvation is possible only to those living a rigorous monastic life. By the first century of the common era, Jainism had split into two sects, the Digambaras, who went naked, and the Svetambaras, who wore white clothes, but their doctrines remained fundamentally the same. Jainism never spread beyond India, save in the diaspora.

Sikhism was founded in 1496 by Guru Nanak (1469–1533), the son of a Hindu living in Punjab. Its rejection of caste and idolatry and its monotheistic doctrine attracted both Hindus and Muslims at a time when Muslims were ruling this area of the subcontinent. Throughout its history, Sikh gurus and musicians have employed North Indian classical ragas and talas as a basis for their musical settings of religious texts and poetry, and in Sikh gurdwaras, or temples, *kīrtan* singing with harmonium and tabla accompaniment is an important part of worship [see NORTH INDIA: PUNJAB].

Also introduced from outside South Asia was Christianity, which reached South India and Sri Lanka (then Ceylon) during the early centuries of the Christian era. At this time, missionaries from Persia set up churches both in Ceylon and along the Malabar Coast (Moraes 1964), and the musical traditions that developed reflected both native music as well as Christian music elsewhere [see KERALA; TAMIL NADU; GOA]. More recently, waves of Hindu conversion to Christianity have occurred during the past few centuries, particularly during British colonial rule, but Christianity has remained a minority religion in South Asia, with approximately 25 million followers today (figure 8).

FIGURE 8 Saint Thomas Cathedral in Madras, Tamil Nadu. Photo by Alison Arnold, 1983.

Many changes occurred for classical musicians in particular during the first half of the twentieth century, in part resulting from the changeover from private and court patronage by the Muslim rulers to public support through concerts, broadcasting, and recording.

POLITICAL HISTORY

The history of South Asia, closely linked with both its social organization and religious traditions, reveals a dynamic political environment. Throughout the region's history, major migrations have moved into South Asia primarily through the high mountains of the northwest, in particular via the Khyber Pass between present-day Afghanistan and Pakistan. In the second millennium B.C., the Vedic Aryans pushed their way southward to find an advanced civilization along the fertile Indus River Valley that had flourished (especially in the great cities of Harappa and Mohenjo Daro) from c. 2600 to c. 2000 B.C. The Aryans introduced the Sanskrit language and the Vedic religion, the forerunner of Hinduism; the four canonical collections of Vedic hymns, prayers, and liturgical formulas served as the basis for religious chant [see VEDIC CHANT]. In the sixth century B.C., India's northwest region of Gandhara (whose capital was Taxila, near present-day Islamabad, Pakistan) fell to the Persian Achaemenid emperor, Darius I, and remained under Persian control until Alexander the Great of Macedonia, with tens of thousands of Macedonian and Greek soldiers, conquered lands down to the mouth of the Indus River in 326 B.C. Alexander's heirs brought Greek culture to the northwestern region. Like the later incursions by Iranian, Turkish, Central Asian, and Arab peoples up to the eighteenth century, the Greco-Macedonian invasion led to varying degrees of assimilation of people, language, culture, and music in South Asia.

FIGURE 9 Dancer carved on a stone pillar in the marriage hall, Sri Varadaraja Temple, Kanchipuram, Tamil Nadu.. Photo by Gordon Arnold, 1983.

As Aryan influence penetrated the entire Indian peninsula and led to a strong cultural synthesis with Dravidian culture in the south, Islamic rulers in the north attempted but failed to subjugate completely the Dravidian people. Hindu temples and courts in the south lavishly patronized music and dance, as did the later Mughal courts in northern cities (figure 9). Little documentary evidence of these performance practices exists, since the performing arts in South Asia have always been transmitted orally [see VISUAL SOURCES]. Theoretical treatises, however, provide us with details about early musical scales, modes, melodies, compositions, improvisation, instruments, and so forth [see THEORETICAL TREATISES]. Treatises written after the thirteenth century reveal a divergence from musical doctrines (*saṅgīta śāstra*) set down before that time, as well as a growing dissimilarity between the musical traditions *(sampradāya)* developing in the south and those in the Muslim-influenced north, comparable to the differing sociocultural settings [see SCHOLARSHIP SINCE 1300]. Musicians traveled back and forth between Hindu and Muslim courts, but by the late sixteenth century, when the center of Karnatak music shifted from Vijayanagar down to Tanjavur (called Tanjore by the British) in the far southeast, the separate canonical traditions now known as Hindustani and Karnatak music were already taking root.

Mughal emperors ruled much of the subcontinent, except for the far south and southwest, between 1526 and 1748 (in decline from 1712 onward), and their ostentatious, aristocratic lifestyles encouraged the gradual adoption of Persian culture and language and the patronage of art and music at the imperial courts. The vocal genres now performed as Hindustani classical music—*dhrupad, khyāl, ṭhumrī*—together with the Hindustani instrumental *ālāp-jor-jhālā-gat* structure owe their early stylistic development largely to the vocalists and musicians patronized by the Mughal courts in Gwalior, Delhi, Agra, and elsewhere [see Hindustani Vocal Music; Hindustani Instrumental Music]. In the south, Karnatak music also developed under royal patronage, but in close connection with Hindu temples and the devotional (bhakti) tradition [see Karnatak Vocal and Instrumental Music]. The earliest musical compositions still performed today in Karnatak concerts were created by three poet-saints of the Tamil bhakti movement who lived in the seventh to ninth centuries. Of the later singer-composers responsible for creating the modern Karnatak repertoire, Purandara Dasa (sixteenth century) gave up a comfortable lifestyle to become a wandering religious singer. The three Trinity composers of the eighteenth and nineteenth centuries—Tyagaraja, Muttusvami Diksitar, and Syama Sastri—spent their lives seeking to combine devotion and musical creativity.

In addition to the Mughals, who arrived by land, the sixteenth century saw yet another influx of peoples and cultures into South Asia, this time by sea. The arrival of the Portuguese navigator Vasco da Gama in Kozhikode (then called Calicut) in 1492 opened the gates to European colonial expansion, which not only brought about the gradual decline of court patronage of the arts but put an end to Muslim rule some two centuries later. The British presence in South Asia dates from the arrival of the first East India Company ship at Surat, Gujarat, in 1608 and the Company's ensuing establishment of trade centers, particularly in Calcutta, Madras, and Bombay (Gardner 1971). As Britain's position became more dominant in the mid-1700s, leading to direct colonial rule from 1858 to 1947, thousands of English people lived and worked in India, introducing the English language and culture to the subcontinent. Their interests lay far from the performing arts of South Asia, but their views had long-lasting effects on music and dance performance. Their disapproval of temple dancing, for example, and of music and dancing connected with the courtesan tradition (a view that was adopted by the new Indian middle class in the early twentieth century) led to the prohibition of the former in Madras in 1947 (Marglin 1985) as well as the decline of the latter [see Women and Music].

Many changes occurred for classical musicians in particular during the first half of the twentieth century, in part resulting from the changeover from private and court patronage by the Muslim rulers to public support through concerts, broadcasting, and recording. The family lineages (*gharānā*) through which musical knowledge had been passed down orally from one generation to the next had to find new adaptive strategies to ensure the continuity of their livelihood in the new social and political environment (Neuman 1980). Music education was broadening to incorporate public and private teaching institutions in both North and South India [see Institutional Music Education]; with the arrival of Western technology and equipment, a new popular music was also created, produced mainly by the growing Indian film industry. The dissemination and popularization of film songs via radio, cinema, and gramophone recordings (later also via cassettes and CDs) resulted not only in the development of the largest film industry in the world but in the largest body of recorded music produced on the subcontinent (figure 10; see Film Music).

FIGURE 10 Film-song lyric booklets for sale on Grant Road, Bombay, 1982. Photo by Gordon Arnold.

Since the final years of colonial rule, India (and indeed South Asia) has undergone major political reorganization. The redrawing of national and regional boundaries, the movements of peoples, and the accompanying social, ethnic, and religious unrest have divided populations and fractured their artistic traditions. The present division of India into twenty-five union states and seven union territories as well as

FIGURE 11 Cassette store in Connaught Place, New Delhi, advertising popular Sikh devotional music. Photo by Gordon Arnold, 1982.

the creation of present-day Pakistan and Bangladesh have all occurred since India's independence in 1947.

In that year, Pakistan came into being as a new homeland created for Muslims, carved out of former Indian territory in the northwest and northeast (the two predominantly Muslim regions of the subcontinent). The massive movement of people flowing both ways across the new India-Pakistan borders led to bitter conflicts, enormous loss of life, and huge refugee populations in the new nation-states. The two Pakistan territories were united by religion but separated both geographically (by some 1,600 kilometers) as well as culturally, linguistically, and politically. Further rupture occurred in 1971, when East Pakistan declared its independence as the People's Republic of Bangladesh, an entity not officially recognized by Pakistan until 1974. Such recent reorganizations have had devastating effects on the peoples and cultures of South Asia. Yet they have also had positive effects, such as new alliances, new art forms, and the further spread of existing musical practices.

Within present-day South Asia some areas, notably Afghanistan, Kashmir, and northern Sri Lanka, continue to be affected by political turmoil and social unrest, while others enjoy relative calm and even prosperity. Modern technology and communications are spreading widely throughout the subcontinent, with computer and cable-TV networks becoming more pervasive. The popular music industry is thriving, as new styles, artists, and recording companies appear with great frequency, adding to the huge amounts of readily available pop music both native and foreign (figure 11). And both beyond and amidst the world of popular culture, local and regional, secular and devotional music genres still continue to find expression, and classical music traditions have strong followings both at home and abroad, served by recordings and world-traveling artists. South Asia today is a world region with a wealth of cultural and musical diversity, and although political, technological, and other forces in some cases threaten to homogenize or even destroy traditional practices, music, dance, and drama at the turn of the millennium remain integral components of South Asian life and culture.

REFERENCES

Babiracki, Carol. 1991. "Music and the History of Tribe-Caste Interaction in Choṭanāgpur." In *Ethnomusicology and Modern Music History*, ed. Stephen Blum, Philip Bohlman, and Daniel Neuman, 206–228. Urbana: University of Illinois Press.

Basham, A. L. 1959. *The Wonder That Was India.* New York: Grove Press.

Brunner, Borgna, ed. 1999. *Time Almanac 1999.* Boston: Information Please LLC.

Famighetti, Robert, ed. 1997. *The World Almanac and Book of Facts, 1997.* Mahwah, N.J.: K-III Reference Corporation.

Gardner, Brian. 1971. *The East India Company: A History.* New York: Dorset Press.

Marglin, Frédérique A. 1985. *Wives of the God-King: The Rituals of the Devadasis of Puri.* Delhi: Oxford University Press.

Moraes, George M. 1964. *A History of Christianity in India: From Early Times to St. Francis Xavier A.D. 52–1542.* Bombay: Manaktalas.

Neuman, Daniel M. 1980. *The Life of Music in North India: The Organization of an Artistic Tradition.* Detroit: Wayne State University Press.

Powers, Harold S. 1980. "India, Subcontinent of, I." *The New Grove Dictionary of Music and Musicians*, ed. Stanley Sadie. London: Macmillan.

Singer, Milton. 1972. *When a Great Tradition Modernizes.* New York: Praeger.

Stern, Robert W. 1993. *Changing India: Bourgeois Revolution on the Subcontinent.* Cambridge: Cambridge University Press.

Wade, Bonnie C. 1979. *Music in India: The Classical Traditions.* Englewood Cliffs, N.J.: Prentice-Hall.

Wolpert, Stanley. 1997. *A New History of India*, 5th ed. Oxford: Oxford University Press.

Theoretical Treatises

Lewis Rowell

We know about the music of ancient and medieval India (up to c. C.E. 1300) only through the documents in which scholars sought to describe and prescribe it. The transition between the so-called ancient and medieval eras of Indian history was gradual, and was the result more of a trend toward feudalism and an evolving state of mind than of the rise and fall of kingdoms and dynasties. Historians have consequently dated the onset of the Middle Ages anywhere from the fall of the Gupta kingdom (c. 540) to the first Muslim invasions (c. 1000). But in terms of intellectual history, the records of early Indian music reveal a tradition of relative cultural continuity. Musical ideas and the remarkable clarity of the Sanskrit language in which these ideas were expressed proved more durable than the societies in which their authors lived.

Unlike Western music, Indian music was and still is primarily an oral tradition. Musical scholars of the ancient Mediterranean employed notation perhaps a millennium before their Indian counterparts, but by doing this Western musicians paid a twofold price. First, musical notation restrained complexity and encouraged grossly simplified melodic traditions. Second, since many ancient Western musics died out, the authority of their surviving musical texts is questionable because they lack the sustaining support of a continuous oral tradition.

In contrast, the recorded details of music in South Asia have never lacked the support of a living performance tradition. Nor have Indian musicians ever regarded notation as anything more than a convenient jog to the memory. We know virtually nothing about the musical consequences of the cultural friction between the indigenous Dravidian peoples and the Indo-Aryans advancing through the northern mountain passes from c. 2000 B.C. However, for the last two thousand years, Indian culture has maintained a central core of musical understanding that can assimilate new musical ideas and yet withstand innovations incompatible with existing tradition.

Such historical explanations risk glossing over cultural upheavals that must have seemed cataclysmic at the time; moreover, the authors of early music-theoretical treatises had a habit of wishful thinking, suggesting a more homogeneous tradition than could ever have existed. Nevertheless ancient and medieval Indian music is alive in contemporary practice, whereas the musics of ancient Greece, Egypt, Sumeria, Israel,

Ancient Indian thinkers held liberation from the endless cycle of birth and rebirth to be the ultimate purpose of music.

and the rest of the Middle Eastern world survive only in a few handfuls of notated fragments and partially documented theoretical systems.

This article is an introduction to the musical documents of early India, which span over a thousand years (from the beginning of the common era to 1300). It focuses on musical concepts and systems, not compositions, because authors were primarily concerned with making new music—not preserving music that already existed. Authors sought above all to provide guidelines within which valid music making could occur—in ways that would give pleasure and take advantage of fresh sources of inspiration, but which would also be in harmony with the existing tradition. These documents record a continuous attempt to provide theoretical authority for every conceivable type of musical expression; it was expected that music makers would select the most pleasing varieties according to personal and regional tastes.

The earliest extant texts date from the first few centuries of the common era, although much of the material they contain is considerably older. The present article provides brief descriptions of eleven major monuments of early Indian musical scholarship, then examines three of these texts in greater detail, for quite different reasons: the *Nāṭyaśāstra* of Bharata, for its documentation of the ritual and incidental music of the Gupta theater; the *Nāradīyaśikṣā*, for its valuable material on Vedic chant traditions and the musical influence of ancient speech science; and the *Saṅgītaratnākara* of Sarngadeva, for its masterly synthesis of previous musical learning. A final section samples representative verses from early treatises.

Readers who are familiar with the present stylistic division between the musical systems of North and South India may be surprised to find here virtually no information on the history of this split. But the latest of the treatises mentioned was written before the full impact of the successive Muslim intrusions was felt. Specialists are still debating the extent to which today's North Indian music reflects Persian influence, and (more controversial) the extent to which today's South Indian music may contain traces of older, indigenous Indian musics. We know little about the origin and provenance of the major music treatises, but enough copies have been discovered in southern locations and in several of the southern scripts (e.g., Malayalam, Kannada, and Tamil) to suggest that music performed in South Indian cities today may be closer to pre-Islamic musical practice than that in North Indian cities. Nevertheless, the literary tradition recorded in the documents here surveyed is, with two exceptions, a Sanskrit one, and it remains the common heritage of modern India's art music.

MUSIC AS A SUBJECT

The anthropologist Alan Merriam has proposed a valuable model for ethnomusicology that divides the subject of music into three compartments: concepts, behaviors, and sounds—what we think, do, and hear (Merriam 1964). In the case of early Indian music, most of our information is in the form of concepts. For the actual

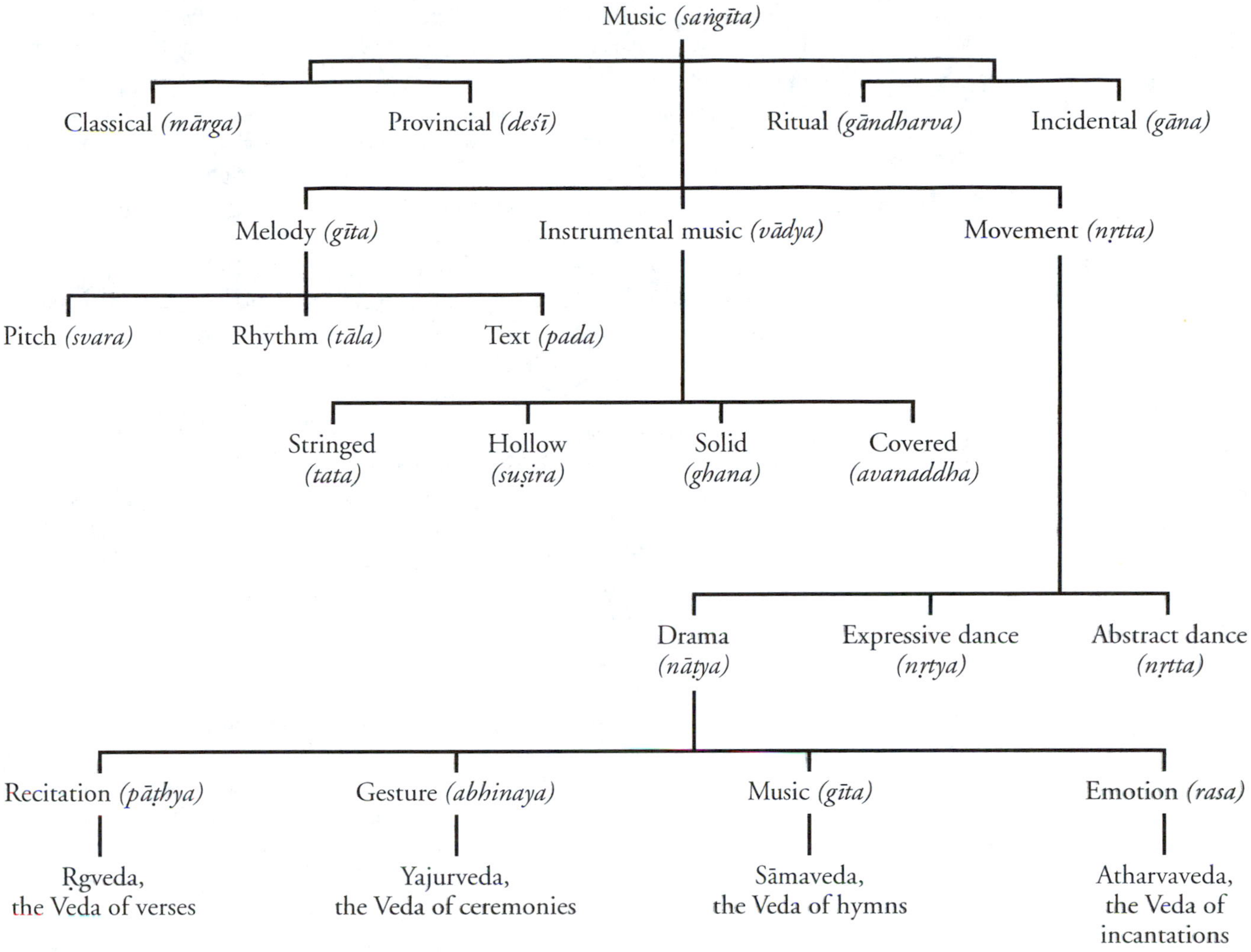

FIGURE 1 The divisions of music, representing a synthesis of categories presented in early Indian treatises on music.

behaviors and sounds of music in ancient and medieval India, we have two sources of evidence: surviving verbal descriptions and our experience of Indian music today.

The English word *music* fails to capture the exact sense of early terms such as the Sanskrit *saṅgīta* and the Greek *mousike.* Students of ancient music, in India as in the West, must make their way through a verbal obstacle course for two main reasons. First, music emerged only gradually as a subject in itself. Second, music covered a somewhat different and wider range of topics than it does today. In ancient Greek civilization, for example, music was lumped together with astronomy, dance, drama, history, and several genres of poetry, and was itself divided into categories that do not match our modern ones (see below).

Indian authors classified music according to behavioral, functional, historical, literary, and technical divisions. The schematic diagram in figure 1 is a display of the major categories, pathways, and connections. This picture of Indian classical music has not altered radically in the intervening centuries.

Music (*saṅgīta*)

The Sanskrit word *saṅgīta,* an exact cognate of the Latin *concentus* 'sung together', conveys the core of the ancient Indian conception of music. It is formed from the prefix *sam* 'together' and the noun *gīta* 'song'. *Gīta* underscores the message that the essence of Indian music is vocal sound. The larger implications of *saṅgīta* include, first, melody, and then organized sound in general. Its three technical divisions are melody (*gīta*), instrumental music (*vādya*), and movement (*nṛtta*), the last of which includes abstract dance, mime, and acting. Each of these divisions opens out into its own array of topics and subtopics, some overlapping.

The distinction between classical (*mārga*) and provincial (*deśī*) musics was an early attempt to sort music into two simultaneous historical layers. *Mārga* meant the original, classical tradition with its emphasis on composition, strict rhythmic and metric structure, and its own set of melodic modes and formulas. Authors used *deśī* to refer to newer styles of music that developed during the second half of the first millennium. These featured song texts in the many provincial languages (in addition to classical Sanskrit), greater rhythmic and structural freedom, a greater role for improvisation, and a new assortment of modes (ragas) and meters (talas). Music was evidently shedding some of its earlier ritual restrictions and moving in the direction of entertainment for the princely courts.

The distinction between ritual (*gāndharva*) and incidental (*gāna*) musics refers to their functions in the musical theater that flourished in courts and temples throughout India during the first millennium. *Gāndharva* was music appropriate for the elaborate ceremony of dedication that preceded a play—strict, formulaic, composed music. By *gāna,* authors meant the more loosely regulated incidental music performed during a play—plot songs, instrumental interludes, entrance music, and background music.

The goals of music

There is "a place for everything" in Indian thought, and authors of music treatises did not neglect to enumerate the goals of music. Their context was the ancient Hindu doctrine of the four goals of life: righteousness (*dharma*), material gain (*artha*), pleasure (*kāma*), and liberation (*mokṣa*) from the endless cycle of birth and rebirth. Ancient Indian thinkers held liberation to be the ultimate purpose of music. Musicians and their listeners achieve this state through the control of the senses (*yoga*) that comes when performing or listening to music with total absorption. The immediate goal of music is sensory pleasure, but its ultimate goal is spiritual release.

THE DIVISIONS OF MUSIC

Melody (*gīta*)

The first technical division of *saṅgīta*, melody (*gīta*), is itself divided into pitch, rhythm, and text. This three-part subdivision recalls the ancient Greek classification of music into harmonics, rhythmics, and metrics. In writing about pitch, authors understood the word *svara* both as the subject of pitch organization in general, and the name for an individual unit of pitch—a note or scale degree. Its domain extended from individual notes, scales, and modes to the various types of ornaments and melodic frameworks on which entire compositions and improvisations were built. Tala similarly covered a wide territory that included virtually every aspect of rhythm and meter, from individual time units, patterns, and hand gestures to musical lines, sections, whole compositions, and general concepts such as tempo. The subdivision of poetic meter (*pada*) was considered to be a musical topic, but its chief contribution was the many durational and accent patterns in the musical text settings.

Instrumental music (*vādya*)

The ancient Indian classification of musical instruments was based on their acoustic principle, as was the 1914 Hornbostel-Sachs classification into strings (chordophones), winds (aerophones), self-vibrating instruments (idiophones), and drums (membranophones) (Baines and Wachsmann 1961). Most Western scholars conceived of music either as human breath (whether sung or blown through an instrument) or sound produced by impact (upon a string, cymbal, or drum). Acoustical scientists of ancient China classified instruments according to the materials from which they were made: metal, stone, clay, skin, silk, wood, gourd, and bamboo.

The vina was the basic stringed instrument in the earliest Indian literature. Authors tended to focus more on its music than its performing techniques. The bamboo flute was the archetypal hollow instrument, but early authors had relatively little to say about wind instruments in general. In contrast, the chapters on "solid" instruments (idiophones) often provided an excuse for a complete exposition of the rhythmic-metric system. Only in the chapters on drums and drumming do we find equal emphasis on making and playing the instrument and on typical rhythmic and metric patterns.

Movement (*nṛtta*)

Authors construed *nṛtta,* the third technical component of *saṅgīta,* not as dance but as movement in general, which encompassed pure dance, expressive dance (pantomime), and acting. This last division, drama (*nāṭya*), was an enormous field including the composition, performance, and production of plays, and was also divided into choice and delivery of text (*pāṭhya*), gesture (*abhinaya*), accompanying music (*gīta*), and underlying emotion (*rasa*) (see figure 1). Motivated by a passion for drawing connections between different sets of categories—a tendency that is evident in all Indian literature—authors related each of the four main components of drama to one of the four Vedas [see VEDIC CHANT]. Note that *gīta* appears twice in figure 1—as one of the major technical topics of music and again as a subtopic of drama.

THE WRITTEN TEXT

The Sanskrit word for treatise is *śāstra*. As the final part of a compound word, it has the same force as "-ology"; the monuments of Indian musical learning were referred to collectively as *saṅgītaśāstra.* The term thus signifies both an individual treatise and an entire field of learning.

An ancient Indian treatise is really an expanding datafile, not a fixed, bound text. If it has a proper beginning, it is in some nucleus of primordial wisdom that was revealed to a sage—one who was worthy to receive this information by virtue of the gifts of insight, prophecy, and spiritual integrity. Such "original" knowledge may be encoded in cryptic form, but it is infallibly true, and the older, the better. The task of later scholars is to interpret and amplify—not to contradict. The sages (treatise authors) received their learning orally, hence their knowledge (as in the Vedas) is referred to as "that which has been heard" (*śruti*). Post-Vedic accumulations of knowledge are referred to as "that which has been remembered" (*smṛti*)—in a word, tradition.

The records of musical knowledge begin with short statements (*sūtra*) and poetic couplets (*śloka*), intellectual index cards that provide a base for subsequent explanation and elaboration. As the original datafile expands and scribes copy and recopy a text, it becomes impossible to distinguish between primary and secondary material. At some point scholars determine that a text is "complete"; subsequent layers of analysis and amplification are added in the form of commentaries. What began as an index card may eventually become an entire library.

In an oral tradition, book learning is never as reliable as learning from a living teacher. A student must therefore know and respect the limitations of written knowledge. No text can ever be presented exhaustively in any single version, spoken or written. The main reason for setting a text down in writing is to provide a convenient index to the information preserved in individual and collective memory.

In Hindu thought, the world of illusion in which we live draws a veil between us and the truth, but a treatise is the "all-seeing eye" that pierces the darkness like a lamp and reveals things as they really are.

From a physical perspective, a book is a pile of palm leaves or strips of bark trimmed to a uniform size, dried, and tied with cord. The perishability of these materials in India's unfavorable climate and the resulting need for scribal recopying have led to predictable results—worms have feasted on such books, semiliterate copyists have made mistakes. Scholars must assume that any manuscript may be riddled with errors and place their faith in the meaning and internal consistency of the text. Grammaticians (pandits) can provide an essential source of expertise, but their expertise quickly becomes strained in technical subjects such as music.

AUTHORSHIP AND DATES

Authorship of treatises is multiple, consisting of a team of sages, teachers, editors, commentators, and copyists—most of whom have never met, and some of whom may be as mythical as the author of the *Iliad.* In the case of ancient writings, no one can say when the process of authorship began. We must assume that the subject matter of a book was transmitted orally through a long line of teachers and students before becoming fixed in written form. In the case of medieval treatises, the team was often a group of contemporary scholars assembled by a ruler to compile a private encyclopedia or library. Their job was to sift through everything they could find on a given subject and produce a synthesis of previous learning. The author in this case can best be described as the chairman of a committee. The group may be working with a living tradition or, as often happened, with neither knowledge of a living tradition nor technical command of the subject.

We can determine the dates of later medieval texts (for example, *Mānasollāsa*, *Saṅgītaratnākara*, and *Saṅgītasamayasāra*) with some precision, but the date by which a text was compiled or reached its final form is by no means an accurate indicator of the age of the material. Books were often written over a long span of time—perhaps as long as five hundred to one thousand years. In the case of earlier texts such as the *Nāṭyaśāstra* and *Bṛhaddeśī*, scholars have attempted to estimate the date by which the text achieved its canonical form, but these estimates may differ by as much as five hundred years. It is often possible to determine the relative order of texts by comparing them and studying the manuscript tradition. But determining the absolute date of any early treatise can only be a matter of conjecture.

THE PURPOSES OF SCHOLARSHIP

The Sanskrit word *śāstra* derives from a root meaning to correct, punish—and hence to teach(!). Music treatises seek to prescribe, not merely describe. Knowledge is always imperfect and incomplete, but false knowledge is to be feared above all else. The theory of music sets forth the details of music as they are presumed to have been, and therefore ought to be. In Hindu thought, the world of illusion (*māya*) in which we live draws a veil between us and the truth, but a treatise is the "all-seeing eye" that pierces the darkness like a lamp and reveals things as they really are.

What does a reader do with a book?

"Read it" is the obvious answer, but there is more to it than that. A reader should also memorize it, or as much of it as possible, and be prepared to recite it on demand—chapter and verse. A text exists to be delivered by the power of the spoken word, or, at times, chanted. Oral testimony is best because sound has an elemental power that can preserve or change the world. The daily rituals of Hinduism depend on the efficacy of the word. So, in the end, the transmission of musical knowledge and acts of worship have much in common. Part of a teacher's authority rests on his ability to select and recite appropriate passages (all teachers at that time were male).

A book is also an index to a larger body of knowledge stored in the reader's memory. It is a form of intellectual insurance against loss. The reader memorizes knowledge in encoded form, and the thought or sound of each keyword should call to mind further details of the subject, stored in a less accessible part of the memory. The text rhythm and metric structure and the predictable stylistic features aid this process. When a text becomes corrupt—as all texts eventually do—because of scribal error or the limitations of memory, scholars familiar with the language, codes, and tradition can often restore it. A book is thus not for everyone—only for those whose study has prepared them to decipher the codes with which the knowledge has been encapsulated. If a reader does not already know a great deal about a subject, a book is of little use.

What should a book contain?

A text on music, like a text on any other artistic or scientific subject, should begin with a benedictory verse (*maṅgalācaraṇa*) and state its authority, supported if possible by appropriate quotations for the sake of credibility. It should then proceed with a list of the topics to be expounded (*uddeśa* 'table of contents'), arranged in proper order, followed by clear expositions of each individual topic. It should conclude with a summary, which often consists of an enumeration of all that has been discussed, and a final moralizing verse.

Name, number, and definition are the goals of a proper exposition of any subject. An author should divide a given topic into a number of subtopics, state their names, and define each term in the fewest possible words. This strategy provides additional insurance against loss or corruption. Special code words and colophons serve as markers in the text. They indicate, among other things, the beginning of a new subject, the end of a quotation, or the omission of material that the reader is expected to know. Two particular strategies are popular in this body of literature: (1) definition by "characteristic marks" (*lakṣaṇa*), a particular cluster of features unique to the item being defined (see "On vocal quality" and "On ornaments," for example, in "Extracts from Early Treatises" below); and (2) sets of merits and demerits (*guṇa* and *doṣa*), practical lists of "do's and don'ts" (as in the extract from the *Nāradīyaśikṣā*, "On singing," cited below). A musical explanation must do more than merely inform; it must be an explicit affirmation of values.

DESCRIPTIONS OF EARLY TREATISES

Nāṭyaśāstra 'Treatise on Drama' is a massive text of about six thousand verses attributed to the legendary sage Bharata. Scholars believe that the *Nāṭyaśāstra* was compiled during the first two centuries of the common era. The work is a comprehensive guide to all aspects of early Indian theater, including the mythical origin of drama, theater design and construction, dedication rituals, play writing, acting, declamation, dancing, music, poetry, casting, costume, makeup, and emotion. Six (or in some editions, seven) chapters on music provide detailed information on the theater orchestra and its various instruments, the system of pitch, rhythm and meter, musical form, songs, singing, and drumming.

Dattilam (named after its author) is a short work of 244 verses by this otherwise unknown author. Written at about the same time as the *Nāṭyaśāstra*, *Dattilam* is limited to two topics: pitch organization (*svara*) and time organization (*tala*). Dattila, like Bharata, focuses on the ritual music for the Gupta theater and, because his approach differs considerably from Bharata's, his treatise provides valuable corroboration for the teachings of the *Nāṭyaśāstra*.

Cilappatikāram 'The Epic of an Anklet' is a long narrative poem by the Tamil author Ilanko Atikal. Written near the beginning of the fifth century, the *Cilappatikāram* contains many references to the theory and practice of music in the ancient Tamil kingdoms at the southern tip of India.

Nāradīyaśikṣā 'The Phonetic Manual of Narada' is a treatise of 239 verses ascribed to another of India's mythical sages. Compiled in the fifth or sixth centuries, the *Nāradīyaśikṣā* is a book of practical instructions for young priests learning to chant the hymns of the Sāmaveda.

The Kudumiyamalai rock inscription (seventh century) is carved into a cave temple wall on a hill near Pudukkottai in Tamil Nadu. The short inscription is a musical notation illustrating an important set of early ragas.

Bṛhaddeśī 'The Great Treatise on *Deśī*' is attributed to the sage Matanga and was written in the ninth century. Provincial music (*deśī*) is the subject of this text of about five hundred verses, indicating that the ancient Indian musical tradition was gradually becoming enriched by the local ragas, talas, styles, and tastes of India's various geographical regions.

Abhinavabhāratī 'Abhinavagupta on the treatise of Bharata' is a long and elaborate commentary on the *Nāṭyaśāstra* by Abhinavagupta. It was written c. 1000.

Sarasvatīhṛdayālaṅkāra 'Ornament of the Heart of Sarasvati' was written by King Nanyadeva of Mithila (now Tirhut, in northern Bihar), c. 1100. Because of its alternative title, *Bhāratabhāṣya* 'Commentary on Bharata', scholars have incorrectly presumed the work to be a commentary on the *Nāṭyaśāstra*.

Mānasollāsa 'Diversions of the Heart' was compiled in 1131 by a team of scholars under orders from King Somesvara III of Kalyani (in modern Karnataka). An enormous treatise on royal sports and entertainments, *Mānasollāsa* includes three substantial sections on music (song, instrumental music, and dance), along with material on politics, elephant taming, architecture, painting, jewelry, perfumes, hunting, and games.

Saṅgītaratnākara 'The Jewel Mine of Music' was written by Sarngadeva in 1240. The author was an Ayurvedic physician and royal accountant at the court of King Singhana at Devagiri (now Daulatabad, in Maharashtra).

Saṅgītasamayasāra 'The Essence of Musical Teachings' was written in 1250 by the Jain author Parsvadeva. It consists of 1,168 verses on raga, tala, sound, songs, dance, and instrumental music.

THREE MUSIC TREATISES

A closer examination of three important texts will provide a more comprehensive picture of the world of early Indian musical scholarship. Each of the texts represents a distinctive point of view and reflects the professional concerns of its author(s). Bharata's *Nāṭyaśāstra*, the major monument of ancient musical learning, approaches the subject of music from the perspective of a theatrical producer and director. The *Nāradīyaśikṣā*, a work of uncertain age but unquestioned authority, is an instruction manual for chanting the hymns of the Sāmaveda and places music within the field of articulatory phonetics. Sarngadeva's *Saṅgītaratnākara*, a massive synthesis of the subject of *saṅgīta* as it was understood near the end of India's medieval era, situates music within the Ayurvedic world of human anatomy and physiology, and summarizes the entire field of musical theory and practice. This unique mixture of dramatic and poetic theory, speech science, religious practice, the healing arts, and princely entertainment is the heritage of Indian music today.

The *Nāṭyaśāstra* and music for the theater

The name Bharata (literally 'he who is to be maintained') has many meanings in India: the fire god Agni, the Vedic priests who upheld the world order by their stewardship of the sacred fire, numerous ancient rulers who took the name as a symbol of their role as protectors of their subjects, the legendary author of this treatise, and the Sanskrit/Hindi name for the modern state of India. No one knows who the sage Bharata was or when he lived, but much of the material in the *Nāṭyaśāstra* must have been set down before the beginning of the common era. The text apparently achieved its final form sometime between A.D. 100 and 500, and copies spread widely throughout the subcontinent in the original Sanskrit and then in all major regional languages. Virtually every Indian musical author knew it and quoted from it extensively; the eleventh-century Kashmiri commentator Abhinavagupta amplified and illustrated its six thousand verses in great detail.

Drama, for Bharata, was a blend of ritual and entertainment, from a play's elaborate ceremonial prelude (*pūrvaraṅga*) to the romance, comedy, and conflict of the play itself. The music described in the *Nāṭyaśāstra* includes both formal (*gāndharva*) and informal (*gāna*) genres of song, instrumental music, and dance. The plays, which were originally performed in temple corridors and open fields, eventually migrated to the royal courts, where they were lavishly presented. A theatrical performance was at once a ritual offering to a deity (usually Shiva), a feast for the senses, and a lesson in appropriate emotion and social behavior. Dramatic critics and theorists held that a successful performance would not only be pleasing to the gods, but would also help to maintain the established world order and lead to "unseen benefit" (as Abhinavagupta put it) in this world and the next.

Ritual and incidental music

The elaborate opening ceremonies are the most remarkable feature of early Sanskrit drama. From descriptions of these prologues in the *Nāṭyaśāstra* we can glean specific information about theater music. The musical ensemble, seated in a niche at the rear center of the stage, consisted of a male singer and several female singers, vina and flute players, a drummer, and another percussionist who played the small cymbals and regulated the metric structure (tala). The ensemble thus employed a minimum of seven to eight performers and (on festive occasions) a maximum of perhaps fifty to sixty. The singers sat closest to the audience and faced each other, while the percussion section faced the audience from behind the singers (see "On the theater ensemble" below). It was essential that the players and singers maintain eye contact with

If the *Nāṭyaśastra* were the only text to focus on rhythmic/metric patterns and not poetic meters, we would still know more about time organization in Indian music than in any of the other musics of the ancient world.

one another in order to synchronize their actions with the tala gestures that controlled the metric structure of the music.

The prologue consisted of as many as nineteen separate items of music, recitation, and dance. Lasting from five minutes to more than a half hour, it began with a suite of nine purely instrumental numbers, each marking a gradual transition from tuning and musical exercises to formally conceived music. The final ten numbers featured the stage director (*sūtradhāra* 'he who holds the strings') and his two assistants—all of whom played roles in the following play—and a small group of female dancers. The purposes of this latter half of the prologue included a blessing of the stage, a salutation to the patron deity, "warming up" the audience, and a gradual introduction of poetic text, physical movement, the play's theme, and the dominant emotion to be evoked (*rasa*). The final item was the director's address to the spectators, after which the play proper began. Because of its ritual function, the prologue's music followed strict rules governing its text, rhythm, and meter. It was composed, not improvised, and therefore meticulously rehearsed.

The other main category of theater music was the incidental music performed during the play. This included songs, dance numbers, instrumental interludes, and music for entrances and exits. We know little about the music in this category apart from the many sample song texts given in chapter 32 of the *Nāṭyaśāstra* and some general material on rhythmic patterns, accompaniment styles, and synchronization of music with stage movement. Some of the song texts were part of the formal text of a play; others were to be inserted in individual productions, often with topical references that would be familiar to the audience. As a performance unfolded, spectators would experience a general progression from strict formality (in the prologue) to greater freedom (in the incidental music).

Musical organization

Our knowledge of ancient Western musics is, for the most part, limited to matters of pitch organization such as scales, intervals, and modes. Indian theoretical treatises are therefore all the more valuable because of the specific information they provide on rhythm, meter, tempo, and form. The *Nāṭyaśāstra* tells us little about the melody and rhythm—the actual notes, durations, and tunes—of Sanskrit theater music but much more about the musical system—rhythmic/metric patterns, underlying scales, and poetic meters. If the *Nāṭyaśāstra* were the only text to focus on these slippery issues, we would still know more about time organization in Indian music than in any of the other musics of the ancient world.

Rhythmic and metric patterns

Chapter 31 of the *Nāṭyaśāstra*, on tala, contains the most valuable information. In that chapter we learn how complete musical compositions were constructed from a variety of short rhythmic patterns, phrases, and larger formal units. Bharata describes these patterns, phrases, and sections with code words indicating the number and order of their events—not the individual drum strokes, melodic durations, and groupings of poetic syllables, but the underlying structural rhythms of the music. Two important principles govern the ancient Indian concept of musical form. First, hand motions symbolize and communicate the metric patterns and structural rhythms. Second, rhythmic structure is inflatable—somewhat like a design on a balloon—in that the same patterns control musical organization over short, intermediate, and long spans of time.

The *Nāṭyaśāstra* and later treatises refer to rhythmic and metric patterns by listing their prescribed sequence of hand gestures: claps, silent waves, and finger counts similar to many of the gestures used in modern Indian music (see figure 2, and the passage "On tala" below). In performance, each such pattern was expandable by prefixing additional gestures or "beats." Generally, each musical component could appear in three different versions or "states": (1) a syllabic state, in which audible gestures accompany various combinations of the three basic durations (short, long, and protracted, in a strict ratio of 1:2:3); (2) a twofold state, in which a silent gesture precedes each sounding beat; and (3) a fourfold version with three silent gestures preceding each sounding beat.

Figure 2 is a diagram of one of the compositions described in the tala chapter. The *uttara* consists of an opening epigram (a typical beginning strategy in this repertoire) followed by a pair of parallel stanzas, each with a brief refrain, and a coda that features a set of permuting variations. The name *uttara* means the "northern" song, or perhaps the "best" or "last" song (because it is the last listed of the seven major types of compositions). The reconstruction in figure 2 is a selection from among the many authorized performance variables. In this interpretation the *uttara* comprises ninety-four beat units, with an estimated performance time of about two minutes, twenty seconds. Each formal section is displayed in numbered beat units and in letters representing the four silent and three audible gestures. In interpreting this diagram, it is important not to assume that the foursquare sequence of identical durations would have limited the melodic lines and drum patterns to repetitive binary rhythms. The text descriptions make it clear that the melodic curves and arabesques of the vocal and instrumental lines were spun out over this solid metric framework in intricate, overlapping patterns.

The spacing in figure 2 (into groups of one, two, or four units) indicates the "state" of each formal section—syllabic, twofold, or fourfold. The sequence of gestures is also a clue to the state, with silent gestures appearing only in the expanded (twofold or fourfold) states. The *uttara* further demonstrates three formal features that are characteristic of ritual theater music. First, beats 1 through 6 of each of the two stanzas are sung with meaningless syllables; meaningful text begins only on the seventh beat. This procedure is an obvious ancestor of the improvised presentation of a raga that begins most performances of modern Indian music. Second, each of the two refrains is a repetition of the text and melody of the previous stanza at twice the speed; Karnatak music today features similarly abrupt changes of speed. Third, the process of systematic permutation of melody and rhythm was (and still is) a typical strategy of closure. Music, like the world, exists in a perpetual state of transformation.

Musical scales

The *Nāṭyaśāstra* also provides the first detailed information on the scales of ancient India. In chapter 28 the author has outlined a set of eighteen modes (*jāti,* sometimes referred to as mode classes). Seven of these form a complete set of rotations of the diatonic scale, that is, equivalent to white-key scales running from C to C, D to D,

FIGURE 2 Reconstruction of the *uttara* form described in Bharata's *Nāṭyaśāstra*, chapter 31 (on tala). Numbers indicate beat units, letters represent hand gestures.

Epigram	1	2	3	4	5	6	7	8	9	10	11	12	13	14	15	16
	A	B	C	Y	A	B	C	X	A	Y	C	X	A	B	C	Z

Stanza 1	1	2	3	4	5	6	7	8	9	10	11	12
	B	D	X	Y	B	X	B	Y	X	D	B	Z
Refrain	1	2	3	4	5	6						
	Z	X	Y	X	Y	X						
(durations)	P	S	L	L	S	P						
Stanza 2	1	2	3	4	5	6	7	8	9	10	11	12
	B	D	X	Y	B	X	B	Y	X	D	B	Z
Refrain	1	2	3	4	5	6						
	Z	X	L	L	S	P						
(durations)	P	S	L	L	S	P						

Permuting Coda:

set 1 ("even" variations)	1	2	3	4	5	6	7	8
	B	Y	B	X	B	D	B	Z
	1	2	3	4	5	6	7	8
	B	Y	Y	X	Y	X	Y	Z
	1	2	3	4	5	6	7	8
	B	Y	B	X	B	D	B	Z
set 2 ("odd" variations)	1	2	3	4	5	6		
	B	Y	X	D	B	Z		
	1	2	3	4	5	6		
	Z	X	Y	X	Y	X		
	1	2	3	4	5	6		
	B	Y	X	D	B	Z		

A = palm with fingers folded (silent)
B = palm down with fingers extended (silent)
C = open hand waves to the right (silent)
U = fingers closed with palm downward (silent)
X = left hand slaps down on right hand or left knee (audible)
Y = right hand slaps down on left hand or right knee (audible)
Z = hands clap together (audible)
S = short duration (M.M. = 60–72)
L = long duration (twice as long as the short)
P = protracted duration (three times as long as the short)
All durations long unless otherwise indicated.

and so forth; the remaining eleven are mixtures. These are clearly ancestors of the later ragas. Combinations of ten characteristic features (*lakṣaṇa*) provide the basis for identifying and classifying each of the modes: the initial note, the most prominent note, the highest note, the lowest note, versions with only five scale degrees, versions with six scale degrees, scarcely used notes, frequently used notes, the final note, and notes appropriate for internal cadences. Other possible variants include chromatic alterations, back-and-forth swings between two notes and—most interesting of all—note sequences that mark an "internal pathway" (*antaramārga*). This intriguing concept of internal pathway strongly suggests that the modes were more than neutral scales, and that they were in fact skeletal melodies with individual contours.

Performance practice

Throughout the chapters on music, we find more attention paid to theoretical topics than to performance topics. The details of the musical system were evidently a matter of greater importance than learning practical techniques. The purpose of a treatise was, after all, to support the oral tradition, not to take its place. The brief chapter on the flute (chapter 30) consists of only thirteen verses and is limited to tuning variations produced by fingering. The material pertaining to the vina in chapter 29 dwells mostly on different finger strokes and ornaments. And the chapter on tala (chapter 31) has nothing to say about making or playing the cymbals and everything to say about the system of rhythm and meter.

Only in the drum chapter (chapter 33) do we find a comprehensive exposition of instrument-making and performance techniques, organized around sixteen major topics—from individual drum syllables, strokes, and their combinations to matters of tempo, accompaniment, style, and the ceremonies for installing and dedicating a drum. The fact that abstract principles of rhythm and meter and practical instructions in drumming appear in two separate chapters illustrates an understanding of their roles in Indian music as valid and important today as it was two thousand years ago. The drummer is not solely responsible for timekeeping; tala is the mutual responsibility of all the performers, freeing the drummer to develop his role as antagonist to the soloist, playing a rich sonic counterpoint to the main melody. The popular stereotype of Indian music as solo melody over a drone and a timekeeping drummer is not and never has been true to the fact. Indian music is more accurately conceived as an interaction between two sets of syllables—one (the melody) distinguished primarily by pitch and the other (the drum accompaniment) by a wide variety of both pitched and nonpitched sounds that are controlled and synchronized by the patterns of tala.

One crucial matter is entirely absent in the *Nāṭyaśāstra* and its successors. There is no evidence whatsoever that the continuous drone of modern Indian music was a part of ancient and medieval practice. Not until the fifteenth and sixteenth centuries do we find evidence for the drone in music treatises, and it is most unlikely that early authors would have ignored such an important musical component. One important reason for the absence of a drone lies in the tonal structure of the earliest modes and ragas. The text descriptions of the *Nāṭyaśāstra* reveal that modes and scales did not share a single tonic note at their lower end. They revolved instead around a prominent note in the middle of their range, a note that was not always the same—something like the way reciting tones of Gregorian chant revolve around the dominant of their mode. If indeed the melodies of ancient India did not feature this impulse to sink to a common final tone, it follows that one set of drone tones would not serve for all.

Emotion

As valuable as the foregoing information on India's ancient musical systems is, another strand of material in the *Nāṭyaśāstra* is still more valuable. The theory of aesthetic emotion (*rasa*) outlined in detail in chapter 6, and never far beneath the surface throughout the rest of the treatise, is India's most significant contribution to the philosophy of art. Although well developed by the time the *Nāṭyaśāstra* had reached its canonical form, the fullest explanation of this idea came in Abhinavagupta's eleventh-century commentary (*Abhinavabhāratī*). The literal meaning of *rasa* is 'juice', as in the sap of a tree. It signifies a continuous current of emotion—emotion that composers imagine, that actors and dancers represent, and that arises spontaneously in the awareness of spectators as a play unfolds. In Abhinavagupta's elegant phrasing, the dramatic spectacle transforms the hearts of the spectators into "spotless mirrors"

The theory of aesthetic emotion (*rasa*) is India's most significant contribution to the philosophy of art. It signifies a continuous current of emotion that composers imagine, that actors and dancers represent, and that arises spontaneously in the awareness of spectators as a play unfolds.

that receive and reflect the main emotion and subsidiary emotions called forth by the play.

It is rare to find in any ancient culture such an explicit catalogue of the range of human feeling. The *Nāṭyaśāstra* identifies and illustrates eight main emotional states: erotic, comic, compassionate, furious, heroic, terrible, disgusting, and wondrous. Later authorities added a ninth *rasa*, a state of beatific peace (see "On emotion in performance" below). The task of each play and production was to develop a single pervading emotional theme.

The idea of *rasa* is still valid today. It is taken for granted in Indian musical thought that each raga has its own distinctive emotional flavor and is therefore assigned to one of the traditional sentiments, in much the same way that each raga signifies a particular time of day. What these conventional associations rest on is not clear. There are too few main emotions and too many distinct melody types to permit any one-to-one correspondence between mood and mode. But the concept is self-fulfilling: if we assume that a given musical construction represents and communicates a particular emotion, awareness of that emotion will automatically inform the intent of the poet and composer, the actions of the performer, and the perceptions and reactions of the empathetic listener. We do not need to search for meaning in Indian music; it is there.

The *Nāradīyaśikṣā* and Vedic chant

It is an abrupt transition from the glittering secular world of Bharata's theater to the mystical asceticism of the Sāmavedic priest's world described in the *Nāradīyaśikṣā*. The title means "the phonetic manual [*śikṣā*] of Narada." There are numerous legends about the sage Narada but no solid information on when or where he lived, if there ever was such a person. The *Nāradīyaśikṣā* is a short treatise of 239 verses, divided roughly half and half between musical and phonetic issues. Its age is uncertain (although estimated as being from the fifth or sixth century C.E.), its text is hopelessly corrupt in many places, and many of its meanings are far from clear. The earliest layers of text duplicate passages in other phonetic treatises compiled before the beginning of the common era, but editors may have added the rest of the material as much as a thousand years later. The text was substantially complete by sometime in the eighth or ninth century. Despite its textual problems, the *Nāradīyaśikṣā* is the best surviving representative of this important school of thought.

The contents are a hodgepodge of material, including a brief history of the evolution of Vedic chant, technical details of the system of musical pitch, mythical associations between musical notes and animal cries, the qualities of good and bad singing, the hand motions and ceremonies of Vedic chant, the three Vedic accents, poetic meters, correct enunciation and word separation, and practical advice for the daily life of a priest in training. The *Nāradīyaśikṣā* offers both general instructions for chanting the four Vedas and specific precepts that apply only to the Sāmaveda. What little coherence there is in this material lies in the conventional belief that the sounds and organizing principles of music arose from the sounds and organizing principles of sacred chant. This may or may not be true. Just as recitation and chanting are heightened forms of speech (the argument continues), so is song a heightened form of recitation and chant. The line between them is impossible to draw.

The standard list of the six topics of phonetic theory applies equally to music, chanting, and reciting: (1) individual sounds and letters, (2) qualitative distinctions of sound (accent, pitch, timbre), (3) quantitative distinctions of sound (duration, syllable, meter), (4) dynamic distinctions of sound (force, resonance, place of articulation), (5) performance and delivery, and (6) the proper separations and transitions between sounds. Authors of the phonetic treatises were obsessed with word separation and continuity between syllables because of the distinctive nature of the Vedic language, the ancestor of classical Sanskrit. Because an oral language does not need the graphics of the printed page, speakers delivered the sacred texts in a continuous flow and depended on conventional phonetic changes at the junctions between words (*sandhi*) to convey the meaning of the text. This concern for melodic continuity with minimal (but clear) interruptions is responsible for two characteristic features of Indian singing today: the precision with which singers enunciate song texts and the preference for ornamental transitions (*gamaka*) between notes.

Musical pitch and duration

The first two verses of book 1, chapter 5, contain one piece of vital information that appears nowhere else in ancient Indian musicological literature. The author of the *Nāradīyaśikṣā* has outlined a set of correspondences between the scale used for chanting the Sāmavedic hymns and the "worldly" musical scale. The passage in question appears below (see "On scales"), and the two scales appear in Western staff notation in figure 3. Their exact tunings are unknown, and modern schools of Sāmavedic chant differ considerably in their choice of intervals between the notes, but it is clear that the secular musical scale described here was equivalent to a diatonic scale widespread in the ancient world. Its pattern, expressed in figure 3 as the series of white notes starting on D, was known both to the ancient Greeks and the composers of Gregorian chant, and is known today as the Dorian mode. The two scales differ in that the Sāmavedic scale runs downward from a nucleus of three of its upper notes (as their names indicate), whereas the secular scale runs upward.

Narada's main objective was to demonstrate the variety of ways in which one tone could differ from another: in pitch, in timbre, in dynamic force, in duration, and in function within a scale. Two terms, *svara* and *śruti*, are particularly important. The general term for a single conceptual unit of pitch is *svara* 'note', meaning either (1) one of the degrees of a musical scale, or (2) one of the accents in Vedic chanting.

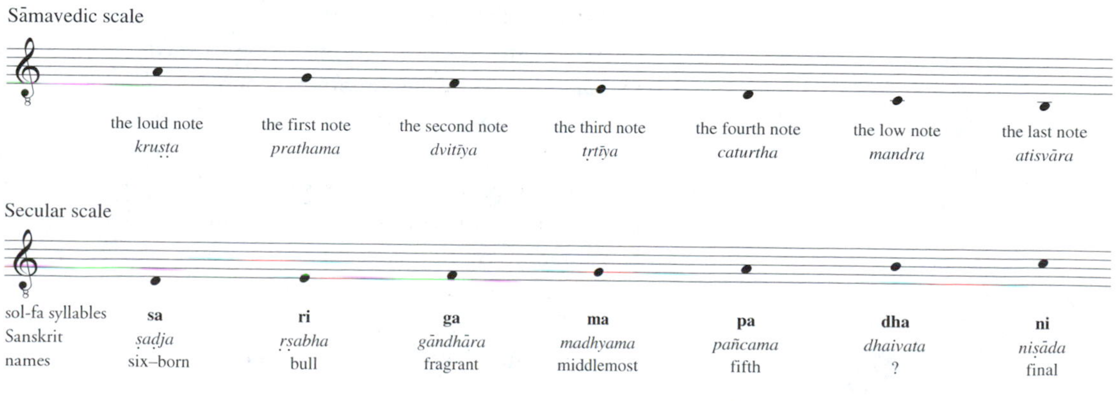

FIGURE 3 The Sāmavedic and secular scales, based upon the *Nāradīyaśikṣā*.

Western equivalents are, for example: (1) the sol-fa syllables (*do, re, mi, fa, sol, la, ti*) and (2) the acute, grave, and circumflex accents of French. *Śruti* is another general term for smaller distinctions of pitch, color, and dynamics. Although the mind can grasp musical tones (*svara*), the ear cannot distinguish potential musical tones arranged in a continuous scale of microintervals (*śruti*).

Distinctions between durations are more obvious; individual syllables are short, long, or protracted, in a ratio of 1:2:3 (as previously indicated in the *Nāṭyaśāstra*). The distinctions between pitches, tonal colors, and accents, which are both complex and interesting, demonstrate how difficult it is to describe musical sound with words. If we hear a sound as "sharped" when compared with another sound or to some neutral standard we have in mind, is it higher, brighter, louder, more impacted, more tense, or a combination of some or all of these? The author of the *Nāradīyaśikṣā* mentions three sets of distinctions: (1) the seven notes of the scale (Sa, Ri, Ga, Ma, Pa, Dha, and Ni), (2) the five qualitative types of tonal color (bright, extended, mournful, soft, and moderate), and (3) the three Vedic accents (high, low, and compound, equivalent to acute, grave, and circumflex).

The Vedic accents are difficult to equate with other musical characteristics, no doubt because they functioned as accents of poetic recitation, not musical tones. In modern practice they appear to be a complex blend of pitch, intensity, and timbral distinctions.

The sol-fa syllables derived from the names of the seven scale degrees remain the standard oral notation of modern Indian music and the basis by which it is learned, remembered, and taught. The Sanskrit names for the notes are

Sa	from *ṣaḍja,* born of the six organs (of speech)
Ri	from *ṛṣabha,* like a bull
Ga	from *gāndhāra,* the fragrant note
Ma	from *madhyama,* the middlemost note (of seven)
Pa	from *pañcama,* the fifth note
Dha	from *dhaivata* (etymology unclear)
Ni	from *niṣāda,* the final note

The *Nāradīyaśikṣā* presents this technical information in a colorful tapestry of mythological and cosmological references, in which each of the seven musical notes refers to a specific color, animal cry, social class, place of resonance within the human body, sage, and deity. Indian musicians thus conceived of musical sounds as an index to all the audible, visible, tangible, and mental components of the chanter's world, a world structure that the priests helped to maintain in proper order by the symbolic resonance of their gestures and by the sounds they uttered during their daily routines of prayer and praise.

Performance and daily life

Physical gesture is an important issue in the *Nāradīyaśikṣā.* Narada gives precise instructions for the hand motions that accompany and must be synchronized with the chant syllables. The right and left hands have specialized functions: chanters use the right hand primarily to mark the various notes and the bodily regions from which the notes derive their special resonance; they use the left hand to signal durations, accents, and text repetitions. In these gestures we see the possible ritual origins of the hand motions used to represent the patterns of tala. We may also compare these practices to the hand diagrams of the European Middle Ages, which assign each note of the scale to one of the finger joints. The function of the hand motions in Vedic chanting is thus both symbolic and mnemonic.

The *Nāradīyaśikṣā* also offers valuable (and often humorous) glimpses of the daily life of a young priest, a grinding routine of study, practice, and the obligations of ritual performance in an all-male environment. Certain salutations, prayers, and hymns were recited daily, and other, more elaborate sacrifices were performed on demand and for special occasions. These included recitation of Vedic hymns, fire offerings, and the ceremonial pressing of juice from the intoxicating soma plant—which has not been conclusively identified. The purpose of the sacrifices was to maintain the cosmic order, and the *Nāradīyaśikṣā* warns chanters of the fearful consequences that would result from a slip of the tongue, mind, or finger.

The *Saṅgītaratnākara*, a medieval synthesis of musical learning

In Sarngadeva's massive *Saṅgītaratnākara* 'The Jewel Mine of Music' we encounter a third perspective. The author, like his father, the royal accountant to King Singhana of Devagiri (now Daulatabad) on the Deccan Plateau, was of Kashmiri ancestry, a devotee of Shiva, and an Ayurvedic physician. The treatise, written in the first half of the thirteenth century, reflects the author's physiological, musical, and arithmetical interests in its focus on the generation of sound within the human body, its masterly synthesis of previous learning, and its attempts to formalize the details of the ancient Indian musical system. It circulated rapidly throughout India and became the subject of at least seven commentaries, of which three are extant. The *Saṅgītaratnākara* is unquestionably the most important and influential of all medieval Indian treatises on music.

Sarngadeva's organization of musical knowledge into seven major topics became a model for later authors. The topics are (1) pitch organization in general (*svara*), including microtones, notes, intervals, consonance and dissonance, scales and their variables, melodic contours, ornaments, mode classes (*jāti*), text setting, and melodic styles; (2) raga, under which the author classifies and illustrates the characteristics of a large number of ancient and contemporary ragas and explains procedures for improvising a raga; (3) miscellaneous topics (*prakīrṇa*), which include sets of standards for singers and instrumentalists, descriptions of performance ornaments (*gamaka*), further material on improvisation, and a description of the theater ensemble; (4) "art" songs (*prabandha*); (5) tala, including outlines of both ancient and medieval talas and the musical forms assembled from the various tala patterns; (6) instruments (*vādya*), including physical descriptions, playing techniques, and appropriate repertoires for the four classes of musical instruments; and (7) dance (*nartana*), including individual movements, poses, expressive styles, and a valuable discussion of the nine emotions (*rasa*).

The organization and emphases of the *Saṅgītaratnākara* signaled important developments in Indian musical scholarship in the closing years of the Middle Ages. First, *saṅgīta* had by now evolved into something approaching what modern Westerners would define as "music." It had become an independent subject, no longer dependent upon its previous dramatic and liturgical contexts; its main context was now the world of princely courts and royal patrons, its main aim entertainment. Second, the musical details of the ancient *mārga* system of pitch, rhythm, and form had become a closed system, and medieval authors had begun to place equal emphasis on the scales, meters, and talas of the various provincial "little traditions" known collectively as *deśī*. Sarngadeva outlined a total of 120 *deśī* talas and 264 ragas, of which some have still further subdivisions.

Third, improvisation now occupied a much larger role in musical practice than before, and treatises on music had begun to offer more detailed instructions for presenting and developing a raga in performance. Fourth, instrumental music had become a single category; authors now began to treat organological information and

The *Saṅgītaratnākara* is unquestionably the most important and influential of all medieval Indian treatises on music.

performance techniques in greater detail and with more respect. Fifth, the aim of musical scholarship was still to enumerate and describe more than to systematize and formalize, but much progress had been made in the latter direction. And finally, treatises had become much more explicit in addressing aesthetic issues.

Students of Indian music are often surprised by Sarngadeva's leisurely introduction to the opening chapter, in which he literally traces the generation and emergence of sound within the body "back to creation" and beyond. ("Back to creation" is a standard learned Indian answer to the question "Why?") He devotes 168 verses to primordial sound (*nāda*) produced in the human body, beginning with ultimate, timeless, unmanifested reality (Brahman) and drawing upon various doctrines of the Sāṅkhya, Yoga, and Vedanta philosophies, as well as on Ayurvedic teachings. The result emphasizes that the principles of musical sound are ultimately grounded in metaphysics, and that the quintessence of musical sound is human, vocal sound.

Raga

The subject of raga had become highly developed by Sarngadeva's time; the number of raga classes and individual ragas had proliferated greatly. The opening chapter explains the principal topics of pitch, including the mode classes (*jāti*), by then a closed category of ancient music and neither subject to change nor relevant to contemporary practice. In chapter 2 Sarngadeva turns from the abstract to the concrete, from melodic material to tune—recalling the distinction ancient Greek authors drew between melodic substance (*melos*) and melody (*melodia*).

The chapter on raga classifies the many types of ancient ragas and those currently in vogue, to show lines of development from one class to another and to illustrate the most important of these with short notated examples and descriptions of their features. In this enormously valuable chapter, the author enumerates a total of 264 ragas and groups them into ten distinct classes representing evolutionary stages. He identifies five general styles of ragas: pure and plain, curving and delicate, ornate, elaborate and athletic, and "mixed"—a typical final category in Indian classification schemes.

Sarngadeva was not the first Indian author to include musical examples in notation, but his corpus of notated raga melodies is by far the most comprehensive and informative collection in any of the early treatises. Because he reproduced many of the examples appearing in earlier works such as Matanga's *Bṛhaddeśī* (eighth or ninth century), and because several later authors reproduced his examples, it is often possible to detect the many errors and omissions and arrive at accurate replicas of the original melodies. The ethnomusicologist Richard Widdess has written a valuable guide to the early history of the raga system (Widdess 1995).

Several types of notated examples appear in the *Saṅgītaratnākara*: short melodies demonstrating ornamental contours, melodies illustrating typical performance options in the mode types, short examples of text setting, instrumental melodies in

ca– lat– ta– raṅ– ga– bhaṅ– gu– ram a–
ne– ka– re– ṇu– piṃ– ju– ram su–
rā– su– raiḥ su– se– vi– tam pu–
nā– tu jāh– na– vī– ja– lam

FIGURE 4 Transcription of a metrical song from Sarngadeva's *Saṅgītaratnākara* 'The Jewel Mine of Music' (2.2.79ff), adapted from Widdess 1995:183. By permission of Oxford University Press.

unmeasured rhythm suitable for establishing the characteristic features of a raga (*ālāpa*), and metrical songs (*ākṣiptikā*) with texts in Sanskrit or regional languages. Figure 4 is a transcription of one of these metrical songs (*Saṅgītaratnākara* 2.2.79ff). The transcription and translation are adapted from Widdess 1995:183.

calattaraṅgabhaṅguram	May the water of the Ganges,
anekareṇupiṃjuram	wrinkled with shifting waves,
surāsuraiḥ susevitam	golden with much sand,
punātu jāhnavījalam	much revered by gods and demons, be purifying.

The basic notation for the musical examples in the *Saṅgītaratnākara* consists of sol-fa syllables, modified by dots and other signs to indicate a lower or upper octave or a lengthened duration. In texted melodies, the texts appear in the Devanagari script of Sanskrit, with syllables of short and long durations distributed under the corresponding melodic syllables. Vertical strokes often divide the melodies into groups of four syllables, giving the misleading impression of a regular, pervading binary rhythm. There is no implication, however, that these examples represent anything other than a skeletal version of the melody; what they demonstrate is that the idea of raga was considerably more specific than a scale with special functions, such as initial, predominant, final, profuse, and scarce notes. Individual ragas were further particularized by their own melodic shape and characteristic patterns.

Performance

The third chapter, on miscellaneous topics, offers the most vivid glimpses of performance practice in the musical life of medieval India. Sarngadeva focuses mainly on singers and singing, but the chapter concludes with a brief but valuable section on the theater ensemble. As elsewhere in the treatise, the author's purpose is more to classify, to name and enumerate, than to give full details. Sarngadeva's perceptive and often amusing remarks begin with job descriptions—what composers, poets, male singers, female singers, and members of the ensemble ought to know and be able to do. These requirements include mental and physical characteristics, knowledge of specific subject areas, sensitivity, various talents, and proficiency in a wide range of performance skills. Nowhere else in the musical literature of the ancient and medieval world do we find such revealing descriptions of what is expected of musicians, although we may rightly wonder how often such demanding specifications were met. "On dancing" below includes one such set of qualifications.

Blatant gender stereotypes pervade this and other early Indian treatises. Sweetness, youth, and beauty are universal requirements for "songstresses," requirements from which male performers were apparently exempt. We learn not only the attributes of ideal singers and composers, but also what characteristics would place performers in the mediocre or deficient categories, often accompanied by blunt and sardonic descriptions of what was to be avoided. Censured singers fall into twenty-five types: those who close their eyes in apparent rapture, those whose voices are harsh like a crow's, those whose limbs shake with fear, those whose facial veins stand out, those with voices of limited range, those who make frequent musical errors or memory slips, and so on.

Sarngadeva next proceeds to vocal sound in the abstract. He divides it into four main categories based on the predominance or mixture of the three humors (phlegm, bile, and wind—not four as in the West), with thirty subcategories based on combinations of fourteen descriptors: creamy, wide-ranging, sweet, hollow, dense, deep, shrill, dry, heavy, tender, delicate, blending, harsh, and soft. The author continues with definitions of fifteen "merits" and eight "demerits" of singing. Many if not most of these performance standards did not arise in the context of music but were borrowed from poetic and dramatic criticism.

Sarngadeva enumerates and describes a large number of other performance accomplishments in the remainder of the third chapter. These fall into two main categories—ornamentation and improvisation. Compositional ornaments (*alaṅkāra*) are included in an earlier chapter. Here the author focuses on two types of performance ornaments: *gamaka* (of which Sarngadeva lists fifteen) and *sthāya* (of which there are ninety-six). Although the term *gamaka* appears in many earlier treatises, this new focus on performance ornaments is characteristic of thirteenth-century music treatises and signals the growing role of improvisation in musical practice. A contemporary description of a set of seven *gamaka* appears in the *Saṅgītasamayasāra* (see "On ornaments" below). Sarngadeva's *gamaka* are all varieties of shakes (*kampita*). Other types of ornament, including slides between notes, ornamental clusters, and other variations in pitch, duration, and/or dynamics fall under the heading of *sthāya*, for which there is no common denominator. We may compare them to the repertoire of "licks" that a jazz musician must have at his command. The chapter continues with some brief but important advice on how to present and explore a raga in performance.

Songs

Songs (*prabandha*) are the subject of the fourth chapter. The term *prabandha* signifies a formal "art song," not a spontaneous improvisation (although some of the song sections could be and probably were at least partially improvised). These were the songs sung in royal courts, usually in praise of the ruler. Sarngadeva tells us nothing about the accompaniments, if there were any, but focuses instead on matters of text, poetic meter, form, and style. Matanga's *Bṛhaddeśī* was the first treatise to discuss song forms; by Sarngadeva's time the number of possible types had grown from Matanga's forty-eight to many thousands. Most of this chapter is an ingenious, mind-boggling exercise in classification, but several vital pieces of information give us a penetrating glimpse into the tradition of secular court song.

Art songs generally began with an extensive introduction followed by a short ornamental interlude, a main section of text, and a final section introducing the names of the royal patron and the singer/composer—in effect a signature. A variant of this pattern exists today in the structure of the *kriti,* one of the main forms of Karnatak vocal music [see KARNATAK VOCAL AND INSTRUMENTAL MUSIC].

Remaining chapters

Chapters on tala, instruments, and dance conclude the *Saṅgītaratnākara*. The most notable feature of Sarngadeva's chapter on tala is the list of 120 *deśī* talas. These consist of cyclical rhythmic patterns gathered from various geographical regions and ranging from one to twenty-two durations, each having one of five relative lengths: three, two, one, half, and quarter. Sarngadeva did not specify the type and sequence of gestures for these newer talas, but describes in another passage a set of gestures similar to those seen today.

With tala as with raga, ancient and contemporary practice remained in separate compartments: a venerated central tradition of ritual music (*mārga*) that was closed to further innovation and inaccessible except through treatises, and a living tradition (*deśī*) blended from a large number of regional preferences—in effect, a classical and a vernacular music. But this division cannot compare to the division between ancient and modern music in the West. Indian musical traditions have not suffered the disruptions and stylistic upheavals that have marked the history of music in Europe and the rest of the Western world. Indian musicians today can thus rightly claim the support of a continuous tradition extending back more than two thousand years. We may know the early stages of this tradition only through the surviving documents, but the past is clearly audible in what we hear today.

EXTRACTS FROM EARLY TREATISES

The following seventeen passages from early Sanskrit theoretical treatises provide a sample of writings on various aspects of Indian music and dance. Translations are by Lewis Rowell unless otherwise indicated.

On sound:

> We worship that divine sound, the life of consciousness in all beings and the supreme bliss, manifested in the form of the universe. By the adoration of sound, the gods Brahma, Vishnu, and Shiva are truly worshiped, for they are the embodiment of sound. The Soul, having a desire to speak, stirs the mind. The mind strikes the fire abiding in the body, and that fire strikes the wind. Then that wind . . . , rising along the upward paths, manifests the sound successively in the navel, the heart, the throat, the head, and the mouth. (*Saṅgītaratnākara* 1.3.1–4)

Commentary: The ancient Indian concept of sound is based not on the five elements (atmosphere, fire, wind, water, and earth) but on their properties: (1) the World Soul (Atman), a vaporous continuum of vital spirit, consciousness, atmosphere, and latent energy; (2) the stimulating warmth and friction produced by fire; (3) human breath; (4) the watery channels of the respiratory system; and (5) the gross form of earth, once sound has emerged from the body and become manifest in the outer world. Sound is a link between the human and the divine worlds. The utterance of sound is at once an act of worship and an affirmation of its role in the creation, maintenance, and ultimate dissolution of the universe.

On vocal quality:

> Sound is fourfold, divided into the following varieties: excess of air, excess of bile, excess of phlegm, and balance of the humors. And thus the sage Tumburu spoke: "Dry, higher sound is acknowledged to be born of air. . . . Sound that is deep, solid, and continuous is known to be born of bile, while sound that is creamy, delicate, and sweet is born of phlegm. The sound that results from a harmonious balance of these three qualities is declared to be born of conjunction. (*Bṛhaddeśī* 1.24)

Commentary: The author's classification of vocal sound is similar to the Western doctrine of the four bodily fluids or "humors," each with its characteristic tempera-

Even legendary sages were unable to perceive the individual microtones because of their subtlety. How can we of limited ability hope to do better?

ment: blood (sanguine), yellow bile (choleric), black bile (melancholic), and phlegm (phlegmatic). Ancient Indian science recognized only three humors. The keywords in the above descriptions still provide a practical catalogue of the desirable qualities of Indian vocal sound.

On singing:

> The ten meritorious qualities of singing are these: color, abundance, ornament, clarity, distinctness, loudness, smoothness, evenness, great delicacy, and sweetness. These are the faults of singing: lack of confidence, timidity, excitement, lack of clarity, nasality, a shrill tone, a tone produced too high in the head or in the wrong register, a discordant sound, tastelessness, interruptions, rough enunciation, confusion, and inability to keep time. (*Nāradīyaśikṣā* 1.3.1, 1–12)

Commentary: Indian authors set down their system of musical and other artistic values in the form of practical lists of "do's and don'ts" (*guṇa* and *doṣa*). The above lists are a mixture of composition and performance values, and it is not clear whether they pertain specifically to singing, to chanting (of the Vedas), or both. In no other ancient musical culture do we find such explicit aesthetic statements.

On instrumental music:

> . . . He took up
> A seven-stringed lute and tuned its scale
> By tightly fastening the leather straps
> On the curved arm. He placed the bridge
> Along the fingerboard, and tuned the strings
> Beginning with the fourth and ending with the third.
> On his ear he then tested the mode
> That had seven notes in its descending scale
> And five in the ascending, and was dear to the goddess
> Of the leaping stag. He played it
> With three variations according to tradition. (*Cilappatikāram* 13.131–41, translated by R. Parthasarathy)

Commentary: In this passage from a great Tamil epic, we find a description of tuning that permits an accurate reconstruction of the musical system (when combined with information from other sections of the poem). It also provides an early glimpse of the raga system, in which a scale often differs in ascent and descent and serves as a melodic framework for improvised variations.

On scales:

> The first note of the Sāman singers corresponds to Ma on the flute. The second corresponds to Ga, the third to Ri. The fourth note corresponds to Sa, and the fifth to Dha. The sixth note corresponds to Ni, the seventh to Pa. (*Nāradīyaśikṣā* 1.5.1–2)

Commentary: Figure 3 displays this equation between the Sāmavedic and secular scales, in Western staff notation. The word *sāman* means hymn, hence the title Sāmaveda, the Veda of hymns. The text contains one glaring contradiction, reversing the positions of Dha and Ni of the secular scale. Despite all the efforts of scholars to explain this contradiction away, it is probably the result of scribal miscopying.

On notes and intervals:

> The scale steps composed of four microtones (*śruti*) correspond to the priestly class; those of three, to the warrior class; those of two, to the merchant class; and those of one, to the menial class. (*Bṛhaddeśī* 1.61)

Commentary: The author here compares the intervals between notes of the scale to the traditional four classes of Hindu society: the priestly (*brāhmaṇa*), warrior (*kṣatriya*), merchant (*vaiśya*), and menial (*śūdra*) classes. Indian musicians divided the octave into twenty-two microtones (*śruti*), and the scale into intervals of four, three, or two such microtones. The interval of one microtone was only a theoretical possibility.

On intonation:

> Just as the path of fishes swimming in the sea cannot be perceived, nor that of the birds in the sky, so is it with the microtones that pass through the steps of the musical scale. Just as one cannot churn butter from curds or strike fire from wood without effort, so is it when one attempts to perceive the microtones. (*Nāradīyaśikṣā* 1.6.16–17)

Commentary: The author continues to say that even legendary sages such as Tumburu and Matanga were unable to perceive the individual microtones because of their subtlety. How can we of limited ability hope to do better? Indian music is hard to hear in all its full detail but then, how can anyone hope to perceive the world in all its reality?

On ornaments:

> The seven ornaments (*gamaka*) are these: bursting forth, quivering, melting, meandering, impacting, oscillating, and manifesting [the three registers]. (*Saṅgītasamayasāra* 1.47)

Commentary: This passage is one of the earliest lists of performance ornaments. The author proceeds to describe them as follows: (1) a rapid ascending scale passage; (2) a rapid shake on a single note; (3) portamento from one note into another; (4) a rapid, aimless succession of notes; (5) one note impacting sharply upon its neighbor; (6) a delicate back-and-forth swing between two notes; and (7) a passage swooping through the low, middle, and high registers without interruption.

On tala:

> The gesture known as *āvāpa* is formed by folding the fingers with the palm upwards. *Niṣkrāma* is formed with palm downwards and the fingers extended. Casting of the hand to the right is defined as *vikṣepa.* And folding it with palm downwards should be known as *praveśa.* The beat made with the right hand is *śamyā,* that with the left, *tāla.* The clap of the hands together is known as *sannipāta.* (*Dattilam* 118b–121a)

Commentary: Dattila here defines the four silent and three audible gestures of the ancient tala system. See figure 2 for an entire composition delineated by these gestures.

On raga:

> The *ālāpa* of a raga is that section in which there is a manifestation of the initial, low, and high notes; likewise of the final and confinal, and also of the scarceness and profusion of certain notes and of the hexatonic and pentatonic versions of the raga. (*Saṅgītaratnākara* 2.23–24)

Commentary: This passage is one of the earliest descriptions of the process of *ālāp*, in which a soloist begins a performance with an improvised display of the characteristic features of the chosen raga. Each raga has its own set of characteristic marks, which will not necessarily include all of those mentioned in the above passage.

On style:

> The three styles are slow, moderate, and colored. In the first, song dominates; in the second, vocal and instrumental music are equal; and in the third, instrumental playing dominates. (*Dattilam* 43)

Commentary: Indian musical concepts tend to come in sets of three, that is, with a moderate version and two extremes. In this passage we have very early evidence of a slow, drawn-out vocal style and a brilliant, fast instrumental style.

On the theater ensemble:

> The members of the group should be seated on the stage facing east. The orchestra is placed between the two entrance doors. The player of a *muraja* should face the stage; to his right should sit the player of a *paṇava,* and to his left the player of a *dardara*. . . . A male singer will face the north, with a vina player to his left and two flute players to his right. A female singer will face the male singer. So much for the seating of the orchestra. (*Nāṭyaśāstra* 33.221)

Commentary: It is not clear whether the three drums mentioned in this passage were played by one or more drummers. For additional information on the theater ensemble, see "The *Nāṭyaśāstra* and music for the theater" above.

On listener preferences:

> Master teachers prefer evenness in performance, whereas learned pandits prefer the distinct separation of words. Women prefer sweetness in music, but men prefer loudness. (*Nāradīyaśikṣā* 1.3.14)

Commentary: Scholars prefer to hear clear delivery of the text, both in singing and in chant, while teachers are more attracted to an even musical line. Gender stereotypes are rampant in Indian musical texts: a similar verse from the *Nāṭyaśāstra* states that women may be forgiven for poor intonation, but not men.

On emotion in performance:

> There are nine accepted emotional states: the erotic, the comic, the pathetic, the furious, the heroic, the fearful, the odious, the wondrous, and the tranquil. . . . The actor does not enjoy any emotion; rather the audience tastes the emotion. The actor is the vessel from which they taste. (*Saṅgītaratnākara* 6.1358–61)

Commentary: For the theory of aesthetic emotion (*rasa*), see "The *Nāṭyaśāstra* and music for the theater" above.

On songs:

> That song which is sung with raga at its beginning, with ornaments, and is then accompanied by tala, well-rendered with sol-fa and recited drum syllables, and also containing passages of meaningful text in various regional languages—this one is named 'parrot-beak,' a favorite of people everywhere. (*Bṛhaddeśī* 402–03)

Commentary: The meaning of raga is 'colored', and the author is drawing a punning comparison between the improvisatory beginning of this song and the colorful beak of a parrot. This description of a particular type of medieval song would probably fit a typical song heard in modern Karnatak music.

On dancing:

> Beauty of limbs, perfection of form, a charming and full face, large eyes, lips red as the Bimba fruit, attractive teeth, a neck beautiful like the spiral conch, arms straight like moving creepers, slender waist, hips that are not too heavy, thighs resembling the trunk of an elephant, not too tall, crippled, or too fat, without prominent veins, conspicuous in charm, beauty, sweetness, courage, and generosity, and being either fair or dark in color—experts declare these to be the merits of a [female] dancer. That dancer who with delicate movements of the body, beautiful rhythms, and correct timing seems to bring out the very letters of the songs and instrumental music, and who seems to make visible through her limbs the sound of the songs and instruments, and dances while carrying her limbs like flowers, fully manifesting the dominant emotion, is declared by experts to be the best dancer. (*Saṅgītaratnākara* 6.1231–36; translation adapted from K. Kunjunni Raja and R. Burnier.)

On drumming:

> I shall next relate the characteristics of an excellent drummer. He must be expert in songs, instrumental playing, rhythm, and timing, and must know how to begin a song and bring it to a proper conclusion. He must have a nimble hand, be able to play all the strokes, know what leads to success in performance, and should be able to sing. He must also be able to concentrate, to produce a pleasing tone by applying paste to the drumheads, and he must be strong in body, regular in his physical and intellectual habits, and an accomplished artist. Such a drummer is declared to be the best. (*Nāṭyaśāstra* 33.293–94)

Published editions of these works are listed in the Guide to Publications at the end of this volume.

REFERENCES

Hornbostel, Erich M. von, and Curt Sachs. 1961 [1914]. "Classification of Musical Instruments: Translated from the Original German by Anthony Baines and Klaus P. Wachsmann." In *The Garland Library of Readings in Ethnomusicology* 6, ed. Kay K. Shelemay, 119–145. New York: Garland.

Merriam, Alan P. 1964. *The Anthropology of Music*. Evanston, Ill.: Northwestern University Press.

Rowell, Lewis. 1992. *Music and Musical Thought in Early India*. Chicago: University of Chicago Press.

Widdess, Richard. 1995. *The Rāgas of Early Indian Music: Modes, Melodies and Musical Notations from the Gupta Period to c. 1250*. Oxford: Clarendon.

Scholarship since 1300

Robert Simms

In broad terms, the history of scholarship on Indian music begins with the insular elaboration of a tradition by Indian writers and proceeds toward increasing Western influence, international authors, and a multitude of approaches. This has been by no means an evolutionary progression, but rather the Indian scene responding to the impact of Western colonialism and the global spread of technology. Scholarly sources during the first half of the period are generally theoretical treatises and court chronicles; later contacts with European scholarship resulted in increasingly diversified forms of monographs.

The most significant difference between scholarship of this period and that of earlier centuries is the emergence of two distinct classical music traditions, which evolved into the present-day Northern (Hindustani) and Southern (Karnatak) traditions. The exact nature and causes of the split are complex matters of some conjecture, and have been discussed by scholars throughout the twentieth century. The most common explanation is that music in the North was increasingly influenced by the conquering Muslim (specifically Persian) culture from the thirteenth century on and gradually drifted away from the "original" Indian tradition, subsequently maintained in the South. This explanation, however, glosses over the fact that common musical features were often merely given Persianized names, and that the political situation was constantly changing, with musicians shifting between Muslim and Hindu courts. There has always been considerable interchange and communication between the two musical cultures. The Hindustani vocal style of *dhrupad*, for example, shares many structural, aesthetic, and stylistic affinities with the Karnatak *kīrtana* genre. In terms of scholarship after the mid-sixteenth century, most texts are clearly aligned with one or the other tradition, and readers view them exclusively from that perspective.

THEORETICAL AND PRACTICAL TOPICS

Scholarship since 1300 has dealt with a broad range of topics, with varying degrees of emphasis throughout this long period. As in earlier scholarship, most topics have reflected one of two basic points of view, the theoretical (*śāstra*), or the practical (*sampradāya*), dealing with music as it was performed at particular points in history.

In many ways this division (like the scholarly enterprise itself) highlights the social, intellectual, and practical boundaries of literary and applied musical activity. To this day, musicians still transmit orally the knowledge and information required to perform Indian music—instrumental and vocal technique, repertoires of ragas, talas, and individual compositions, formal structures, performance practices, and pedagogical technique. The presentation of practical information in the form of instructional and scholarly texts is the work of Indian writers who tend to treat a subject as a theoretical science, and show a proclivity for organizing and categorizing the diverse range of human, natural, and supernatural phenomena.

The theoretical/practical bifurcation of Indian scholarship is useful, but should be viewed with flexibility, since topics overlap and the study of one inevitably leads to another. Theoretical topics include acoustics and tuning systems, instrument structure and categories, aesthetics, the cosmological and spiritual significance of music (in Western terms, speculative music theory), and melodic and rhythmic principles—raga and tala. Writers since 1300 have also been increasingly concerned with contemporary musical performance; they provide insights into the practical conventions of musical form, instrumental technique, melodic ornamentation, improvisation, and concert structure. Beginning in the nineteenth century, these descriptions were often consolidated in the form of more or less comprehensive instruction manuals for various instruments. Establishing criteria for judging good performance (that is, music criticism) could be considered both a practical area of scholarship and a theoretical one, as it relates to the topic of aesthetics. Some of the early writers in this period offered notated repertoire (usually very skeletal), a highly practical enterprise that expanded markedly in the twentieth century.

Another important branch of scholarship has dealt with the social aspect of music history, describing important musicians, collecting anecdotes and lore, and describing the social context of music and musicians. Visual art has provided a key source for studying the development and history of musical instruments as well as for insights into the social context of musical performance. The Western and Western-influenced ethnomusicological approach of the late twentieth century forms a scholarly area of its own, incorporating a variety of approaches and perspectives. Perhaps the most significant twentieth-century development is the study and archival storage of sound recordings.

GENERAL FEATURES OF SCHOLARSHIP

Throughout this historical period—though to a lesser extent in the twentieth century—writers exhibited a concern for the continuity of musical tradition, and tried to reconcile contemporary practice and theory with ancient theory. Music normally undergoes change in any musical culture, and undoubtedly did so quite radically in India between the thirteenth and sixteenth centuries, but Indian theorists seem to have had difficulty letting go of old ideas and generating new ones that would more accurately account for contemporary practices. Sarngadeva's thirteenth-century treatise, the *Saṅgītaratnākara*, itself a consolidation of ancient music theory and tradition, casts a particularly long shadow in this respect, as it became the standard by which most writers worked for several centuries.

This concern for the continuity of musical traditions reflects the respect for tradition that is general in Indian culture. Key treatises such as the *Saṅgītaratnākara* and Bharata's second-century work, the *Nāṭyaśāstra,* appear to have functioned similarly to revealed sacred scriptures (*śruti* in Hinduism), which writers comment on and supplement (*smṛti*). Throughout the period, writers of theoretical treatises frequently followed Sarngadeva's seven-chapter format and quoted portions of his text to establish their authority and to retransmit his original statements. In general, by following Sarngadeva's format, the early writers produced comprehensive works discussing speculative theory, tuning, features of the tonal system, raga classification, performance practice, ornamentation, improvisatory techniques, compositional forms, tala, instruments, and dance. Many treatises served mainly to restate the ideas of previous writers, but they show varying degrees of emphasis and often include important exceptions, details, or supplementary sections that provide new insights into a topic.

Across the broad range of subjects within Indian musical scholarship, perhaps the most common threads in the literature of the entire period were a pervasive focus on tuning theory and the definition and categorization of the existing raga repertoire. On the whole, writers increasingly tended to treat music as a unique activity, distinct from its traditional role as a component of dance (*nṛtya)* and theater (*nāṭya*).

The earliest scholarship on periodization remained consistent until a decisive shift in the mid-sixteenth century, which established theoretical and practical approaches common to the Hindustani and Karnatak traditions today. The late eighteenth and nineteenth centuries saw vast political changes as a result of British colonization and marked another phase of scholarship, showing increasing European involvement while laying a practical foundation for Indian (especially Hindustani) music as it entered the age of recording technology. In the twentieth century, the diverse nature and enormous quantity of research can be seen roughly as forming two halves: early Indian and British studies, and the thoroughly international contributions made and influenced by Western ethnomusicologists after 1960. Sources on Indian music through this time period are in Sanskrit; Farsi; vernacular Indian languages, particularly Hindi and Urdu; English; German; and French.

SCHOLARSHIP FROM 1300 TO 1550

Texts and commentaries on the *Saṅgītaratnākara*

Scholarly writings of this period generally reinforced the ancient canon, deliberately consolidating earlier scholarly views; they particularly reflected and commented upon Sarngadeva's thirteenth-century treatise, the *Saṅgītaratnākara*. At least seven such commentaries emerged during this time, constituting almost a genre of scholarship in themselves (figure 1). These early sources are all in Sanskrit, and are significant for several reasons. Their authors often quote or draw upon sources that are now lost; they clarify obscure passages in treatises that may reflect the oral tradition of the period; and they occasionally provide insights into contemporary practice and theory by a method of comparison with classical models. Modern scholars have tried to piece together this complex jigsaw puzzle of somewhat random source fragments, sources quoted in other sources, and bits of contemporary information likely considered incidental and digressive by the original authors.

A treatise by the Jain author Sudhakalasa, *Saṅgītopaniṣad-sāroddhāra* (c. 1350), together with Parsvadeva's twelfth-century work, *Saṅgītasamayasāra,* made important contributions to early scholarship; the writers describe a tradition that differs in some ways from that of the *Saṅgītaratnākara,* supporting the notion that musical practice and theory were not entirely uniform during this period. Unlike most music treatises of the time, Sudhakalasa's points forward with its discussion of tala, including the kind of definitive drum patterns that later find currency in the prescribed drum syllable patterns (*ṭhekā*) of Hindustani talas, and with its iconographical personifications of ragas (*rāgmālā*)—an approach that would occupy Hindustani scholars from the sixteenth to the eighteenth centuries.

Two other significant treatises are commentaries on the *Saṅgītaratnākara*. Simhabhupala's *Sudhākara* (c. 1330) basically paraphrases and clarifies Sarngadeva;

FIGURE 1 Some important Indian treatises, 1300–1550.

Title	*Author*	*Date*	*Language*
Sudhākara	Simhabhupala	c. 1330	Sanskrit
Saṅgītopaniṣad-sāroddhāra	Sudhakalasa	c. 1350	Sanskrit
Gunyat al-Munyat	Anon.	c. 1375	Persian
Saṅgītaśiromaṇi	under Sultan Malika Shahi	1428	Sanskrit
Kalānidhi	Kallinatha	c. 1450	Sanskrit
Saṅgītarāja	Kumbhakarna	1453	Sanskrit
Lahjat-i Sikandar Shāhi	Umar Sama Yahya	c. 1500	Persian
Mān Kutūhal	Man Singh	c. 1500	Hindi

the writer adds little of his own by way of supplementary material, but draws on other earlier sources. Kallinatha's commentary *Kalānidhi* (c. 1450) is valuable for its additional insights into contemporary practice in his native Vijayanagar (in modern Karnataka), especially with regard to raga. Kallinatha's work is generally more critical and incisive than Simhabhupala's.

Scholarship sponsored by aristocratic patrons

The patronage of royalty and nobility has played a major role in Indian musical scholarship. The Muslim ruler Sultan Malika Shahi organized a conference of musicologists to review and edit his musicological manuscript collection into a single volume, which resulted in the *Saṅgītaśiromaṇi* (1428). The work, in Sanskrit, follows Sarngadeva's seven-chapter archetypal format. It reveals little about contemporary practice, focusing instead on concordant points of the ancient texts: descriptions and classifications of ragas and compositional forms according to the ancient *grāma-jāti* scale system—which was at that time no longer relevant. The text is significant, however, for it includes treatises now obscure or lost, and reflects the cooperative rapport that often existed between Hindu and Muslim musicians and music scholars. The chapter on compositional form provides details not found elsewhere.

The *Saṅgītarāja* (1453), written by or under the direction of King Kumbhakarna of Rajasthan, is a large compilation of musical theory. The work draws heavily upon the *Saṅgītaratnākara* and the *Saṅgītopaniṣad-sāroddhāra*, and also refers to the *Saṅgītaśiromaṇi*. Because of its large size, only two chapters of the *Saṅgītarāja* have been published, but these contain many details that both corroborate other works and provide fresh insights into lost sources. Kumbhakarna is credited with other musicological works, including a commentary on the *Saṅgītaratnākara*, but the *Saṅgītarāja* seems to stand as an untapped resource for future scholarship.

Around 1500, the first translations of Sanskrit sources into vernacular and foreign languages appeared, including the Hindi *Mān Kutūhal*, compiled under the patronage of the Hindu raja Man Singh, and Umar Sama Yahya's *Lahjat-i Sikandar Shāhi* in Persian. This attraction toward translating sources marks a growing interest in musical scholarship beyond a Sanskrit (and Brahmin) readership, with vernacular translations reaching out to an unprecedentedly large audience. Not only was Sanskrit an exclusive, erudite language, but most practicing musicians were illiterate. Even the literate minority probably would not have been able to read Sanskrit.

SCHOLARSHIP FROM 1550 TO 1780

A greater number of treatises appeared during the first half of this period than during the second half: many of them expounded fresh approaches and ideas (figure 2). The Karnatak/Hindustani division is clearly apparent; while there are some interesting cases of overlap, most treatises from this time onward are generally affiliated with one

Around 1550, the rise of scholarship on the Hindustani musical tradition coincided with the establishment of the Mughal empire and its court patronage of music.

FIGURE 2 Some important Indian treatises, 1550–1940.

Title	*Author*	*Date*	*Language*
Svaramelakalānidhi	Ramamatya	c. 1550	Sanskrit
Sadrāgacandrodaya	Vitthala	c. 1590	Sanskrit
'Ain-i Akbarī	Abu Fazl	1597	Persian
Rāgavibodha	Somanatha	1609	Sanskrit
Caturdaṇḍī Prakāśikā	Venkatamakhi	c. 1620	Sanskrit
Saṅgītaśudha	Raghunatha Naik	c. 1620	Sanskrit
Saṅgītadarpaṇa	Damodara	c. 1625 (Hindi trans. 1673)	Persian
Saṅgītapārijāta	Ahobala	c. 1650 (Persian trans. 1724)	Sanskrit
Tuḥfat al-Hind	Mirza Khan	c. 1675	Persian
Saṅgītasāramṛta	under Tukkoj II	c. 1730	Sanskrit
Saṅgītsār	under Maharaja Pratap Singh	c. 1800	Hindi
Naghmāt-i Āsafī	Mohammad Reza	1813	Persian
Saṅgītasārasaṅgraha	S. M. Tagore	1875	Sanskrit
Saṅgīta Sampradāya-Pradaśinī	Subbarama Diksitar	1904	Telugu
Hindustānī Saṅgīt-Paddhati	V. N. Bhatkhande	1910–1932	Marathi
Kramik Pustak-Mālikā	V. N. Bhatkhande	1920–1937	Marathi

or the other tradition. Scholarship of the period describes practices and advances theories that establish direct continuity with the modern tradition. The dominant topics are the definition and classification of the contemporary raga repertoire. Three basic approaches to classification emerge: according to scale type (Karnatak *mela*, Hindustani *ṭhāṭ*), iconographic and poetic personification (*rāgmālā*), or position in a hierarchical structure of raga families. Karnatak scholars were largely concerned with developing a tightly structured system based on scale types, while the Hindustani tradition maintained a looser and more subjective conception of raga characterized by iconographic and familial categorization. Summary discussions in English of treatises from this period may be found in Gangoly (1989) and Bhagyalekshmy (1991).

Scale-type raga classification

Early sixteenth-century musicians and scholars of Vijayanagar developed a raga classification system based on scale type (*mela*), first described by the writer Ramamatya in *Svaramelakalānidhi* (c. 1550). A series of treatises from Tanjore further refined the concept, the most significant being *Caturdaṇḍī Prakāśikā* (c. 1620) by Venkatamakhi, whose system, with slight modifications, prevails to this day in the Karnatak tradition. Venkatamakhi theoretically posits seventy-two scale types (*mela*), each capable of generating many ragas [see KARNATAK RAGA]. Following in the scholarly tradition of speculative theory, the author numbers each and associates them with particular deities and cosmological correspondences (the moon, winds, seasons, Vedas, directions, and so on). His discussion of scale types also includes verse descriptions, showing an affinity with Hindustani practices. The *Saṅgītasārāmṛta,* written under Tukkoj II (c. 1730), further paves the way to modern Karnatak theory by refining theoretical ideas dating back to Sarngadeva and synthesizing them with contemporary practice.

Iconographic and family raga classification

Around 1550, the rise of scholarship on the Hindustani musical tradition coincided with the establishment of the Mughal empire and its court patronage of music (except during the rule of Emperor Aurangzeb, r. 1659–1707). Hindustani scholars adopted and advanced approaches to raga classification based on iconographic and poetic personifications that dated back to Sudhakalasa (fourteenth century) and Matanga (ninth century), and on categorization according to gender as discussed in Narada's *Saṅgītamakaranda* (c. eleventh century). The latter text was possibly a precedent for linking raga performance with specific times of day, a doctrine that many music theorists, particularly Hindustani writers, have been developing ever since [see HINDUSTANI RAGA].

The family system of classification generally posited six main ragas, each with five subordinate ragas (*rāgiṇī*), resulting in a thirty-six-mode system. The essential duality of the *rāg/rāgiṇī* scheme was masculine/feminine (lord and lady, husband and wife). Especially after 1600, iconographic and verse representations usually accompanied descriptions of raga families (figure 3). Writers generally listed the relationship and presented the verse iconography without attempting to explicate the musical structure of the ragas. By the standards of the Karnatak *mela* scheme and Western scientific sensibilities, the *rāg/rāgiṇī* taxonomy is imprecise. But the extramusical associations are deeply rooted in Indian speculative values, where music exists in the continuum of a greater cosmological harmony. This perspective places more value upon (and focuses attention toward) the subtle and ultimately inexplicable inner essence of a raga, and how this corresponds with the essence of other seemingly disparate phenomena. As with many expressions of Hindu and Sufi metaphysics, this approach downplays exterior forms that veil the true inner nature of things.

FIGURE 3 A *rāgmālā* verse iconography for *rāgiṇī megh malhār*, from Rajasthan, c. 1725. (Shirali 1977:50). Courtesy of the Trustees of the Prince of Wales Museum of Western India, Mumbai.

Damodara's *rāg/rāgiṇī* classification, in the *Saṅgītadarpaṇa* (c. 1625), gained wide currency and by 1800 had become the standard system. Damodara's work is essentially a *rāg/rāgiṇī* compilation with verse iconographies; his classification system is based on the legendary school (*mata*) of Hanuman, a system of obscure origin that had not previously been documented. Translated into Hindi in 1673, the *Saṅgītadarpaṇa* became influential among both Indian and early European scholars. In the *Saṅgītapārijāta* (c. 1650, translated into Persian in 1724), Ahobala likewise based a raga classification on the Hanuman *rāg/rāgiṇī* system. He was also perhaps the first to describe intervals in terms of string-length divisions, although a treatise by Hrdaya Narayana Deva from the same period features this as well. The work devotes attention to performance time and sentiments associated with particular ragas.

Interaction of Hindustani and Karnatak scholarship

In the sixteenth and seventeenth centuries, a significant number of Karnatak scholars migrated northward seeking patronage, and the resulting interaction between the two musical traditions produced treatises somewhat ambiguous in their traditional affiliation. The biography and writings of Ahobala (author of the *Saṅgītapārijāta*) suggest that this writer may have been a Karnatak scholar who moved north and wrote about

Hindustani music (Powers 1980). A similar but smaller migration of Northern scholars moving south completed the exchange, and musical practices that shared characteristics of both traditions may well have existed in the sixteenth century. A key scholar of this mold is Pundarika Vitthala, whose *Sadrāgacandrodaya* (c. 1590) lies on the cusp of both traditions, and who was among the first writers to introduce the concept of scale type into the Hindustani tradition. His other works point more decidedly toward the North: *Rāgamālā* (1576) follows the Hindustani system of raga family classification with verse iconographies, but also includes descriptions of their musical structure; his *Rāgamañjarī* (c. 1600) mentions Persian modes and notes their correspondence with particular ragas.

Another important figure straddling Hindustani and Karnatak traditions is the Telugu author Somanatha, whose Sanskrit work *Rāgavibodha* (1609) is significant for openly acknowledging the normality of musical change. Like Vitthala, Somanatha describes ragas in terms of scale type and provides verse iconographies. But unlike authors of other *rāgmālā* sources, Somanatha provides a theoretical basis for the visual raga representation. He also provides detailed notations of the short improvisatory introductions *(ālāp)* to various ragas, as performed on the vina, which shed light on raga structure as well as on other general aspects of raga performance such as ornamentation, variation, development, and instrumental technique. Somanatha's repertoire of ragas has modern equivalents in both Karnatak and Hindustani traditions, highlighting his pivotal historical position—and modern authors variously claim him to be a Karnatak or Hindustani scholar.

After initial contacts in the fourteenth century, or possibly earlier, Muslim rulers and scholars showed considerable interest in Indian music. The *'Ain-i Akbarī* (1597), Abu Fazl's Persian chronicle of the Emperor Akbar's Mughal court, includes a summary of classical Indian music theory, and documents the movements, origins, and social status of court musicians, as well as their repertoire, and various aspects of the social context of musical activities. The work describes a multicultural court, where many of the musicians were from South India and Persia, reflecting both the general historical situation and Akbar's own outlook. Musicians were expected to know the styles, repertoire, and texts of Hindustani, Karnatak, and Persian traditions. There is no contemporary scholarly equivalent on the scale of this chronicle, but effects of the musical interaction quite likely trickled into scholarly perspectives. A portion of Mirza Khan's *Tuḥfat al-Hind* (c. 1675) compiles Indian music theory, chronicles musical patronage and other lore, and lists several *rāg/rāgiṇī* systems and Persian modes.

SCHOLARSHIP FROM 1780 TO 1900

European involvement

Missionaries and travelers were the first to provide Europeans with descriptions of Indian art and music as early as the late seventeenth century. Although their documentation was not always scholarly, their works provide early source material for the study of Indian music history. Indeed, these early descriptions of Indian music are part of a literature that was truly global. Accounts of "Customs and Habits of Local Inhabitants" appeared, covering every region visited by European missionaries, settlers, and traders. European scholarship in Indian music was fostered during the Enlightenment, a philosophical movement of the eighteenth century that emphasized essential human equality and the value of rational and systematic research.

Along with the more practical enterprise of colonial expansion, the Enlightenment sparked European interest in exotic cultures. Writers glorified the naiveté of "the noble savage," sheltered from the complexities of modern European society. They also showed respect for the great ancient civilizations of the East, whose impressive histories and cultural legacies dated back millennia before the rise of Europe. But their glory was in the distant past, and European writers viewed contemporary Eastern cultures as being in a state of total decline, a historiographic bias that, in addition to the ethnocentric claim of European superiority, is pervasive throughout the early European literature on Indian and other non-Western musics.

English authors, both travelers and colonial administrators, wrote the vast majority of this literature. In 1835, when English became the official language of British India, the language itself became an important agent, shaping Indian scholarship for both European and Indian writers, and establishing a unique dialectical process between Eastern and Western approaches that henceforth characterized scholarship. Just as Latin functioned as the language of scholarship in medieval Europe, providing a common ground for scholarly discourse, English became the language in which both Indian and European scholars addressed an international audience. English supplanted Sanskrit, texts of which become increasingly rare after the late 1700s; Indian-language texts were usually in a vernacular. To this day, English is the primary means of communication between Indians from diverse areas of the subcontinent whose mother tongues are among the countless dialects and different language families. The pragmatic sharing of this common language certainly results in the exchange and sharing of ideas.

Early European scholars

Sir William Jones (1746–1794), a famous judge in Calcutta, made the first significant European scholarly efforts in Indian music. After founding the Asiatic Society of Bengal in 1784, Jones was among the first Europeans to learn Sanskrit and translate key Sanskrit texts. He recognized the close relationship between Sanskrit and classical Greek and Latin, and posited the existence of the Indo-European language family, thereby contributing to the foundation of comparative philology and linguistics. The notion of Indian and Western civilizations sharing a common heritage aroused Western interest in Indian music; from the Western perspective, Indian music was perhaps a surviving relative of the irretrievable musical traditions of classical Western antiquity, and could shed light on them. Jones wrote on a wide range of topics. His article "On the Musical Modes of the Hindus," published in *Asiatic Researches* in 1792, drew scholarly interest toward Indian music by showing that it deserved respect and attention (Tagore 1965:123–160). The article was reprinted several times, and was translated into German in 1802. Jones's scholarly efforts reflected biases in European historical writing, showing interest only in the ancient texts, for example, not in existing practices. This partially reflects the traditional, canonical values of some Indian writers themselves, as evident in their Sanskrit treatises.

Asiatic Researches became the venue for further articles on Indian music, which increased in scope and methodological precision: Francis Fowke's article "On the Vina or Indian Lyre" (1788) is a short but very precise description using increasingly objective methods (Tagore 1965:191–197). Fowke was an early example of the European musician who admired and grew deeply interested in Indian music, one of the many who would later emerge.

The path of "proto-ethnomusicology" among European writers took an interesting turn in the person of Augustus Willard, whose *Treatise on the Music of Hindoostan* (1834) set some remarkable precedents (Tagore 1965:1–122). Apparently, Willard himself learned to play Indian music, an advantage for scholarly methodology and perspective (sometimes called bimusicality) that immediately sets his work apart from all other European efforts before the second half of the twentieth century. Willard was also interested in contemporary practice, not ancient theory. Taking a stance that

English scholarship generally focused on Hindustani music; it was not until 1891 that an important European study of contemporary Karnatak traditions was written.

later became the fundamental credo of modern ethnomusicology, Willard conducted fieldwork with "living professors" and "famous performers" both Hindu and Muslim who, though illiterate, possessed vast amounts of knowledge about music. Finally, Willard's overall tone and outlook on Indian music was generally positive, thus contrasting sharply with the condescension of much European scholarship of the time. Like seminal works in other fields in the past, Willard's book was not well received by his contemporaries, who minimized its contribution or simply ignored it.

Throughout the nineteenth century, European scholarly writing on other topics of interest appeared in Orientalist journals published in Europe and India. Musical instrument studies, translations of historical documents (often only portions of large works), and ethnographies, as well as works on Indian music history, the nature of Indian scales and tuning theory, and Vedic chant were published in this period. General music histories and encyclopedias appeared in Europe written by armchair scholars who, having neither traveled nor experienced for themselves the musical cultures they studied, wrote comprehensive descriptions of non-Western traditions based on the research of others. There were volumes on India, usually drawing heavily on Jones and Willard, as well as on a mélange of Far Eastern, Middle Eastern, African, and New World traditions, in an attempt to write music history from a more universal perspective. Works such as those of William Stafford (1830), François Fétis (1869), and Adrien de La Fage (1844) represent the most complete nineteenth-century collections of world music data.

English scholarship generally focused on Hindustani music; it was not until 1891 that an important European study of contemporary Karnatak traditions was written by Charles Day. Day was a captain in the British army and provided a cogent summary of South Indian music history and theory, ancient and contemporary. He drew comparisons between European and Hindustani music and instruments, and also offered observations on the social aspects of performance. Day's description of classical music as being in a state of decline at the hands of the Muslims reinforced the European historiographic bias that equated the Karnatak tradition with primordial Hindu practices and greater "purity"; this attitude persists today among musicians and some scholars. Filled with tables, transcriptions, and illustrations, Day's study presented the most comprehensive and reliable account of Karnatak music written up until that time, and set new standards for subsequent work.

Indian writers

Around 1800, there appeared a Hindi compilation of ancient and contemporary theory called the *Saṅgītsār*. This work, which presented descriptions of current Hindustani ragas, was the result of a conference of musicians sponsored by Maharaja Pratap Singh of Jaipur (1779–1804), in the Indian tradition of royal patronage and interest in musical scholarship. Mohammad Reza's Persian treatise *Naghmāt-i Āsafī* (1813) continued the scholarly focus on Hindustani raga families but rejected the *rāga/rāgiṇī* classification in favor of a closed system showing clear scalar affinities between family members. His work crystallized ideas that had been first proposed in the *Saṅgītsār*, and set a precedent in establishing *bilāval ṭhāṭ* (a "source scale," identical to Western C major) as the foundation scale to which all ragas relate, representing a shift from the principal D-modal, or Dorian, scale (*grāma*) of earlier theories, and which still remains a part of modern theory.

A treatise published in the mid-nineteenth century in Lucknow, *Ma'dan al-Mūsīqī* 'Mine of Music', represents a significant crossing point of scholarly styles and goals, as well as an amalgam of contemporary music theory and practice. Written around 1860 by Hakim Mohammad Karam Imam, a courtier of Wajid Ali Shah, this text also provides insight into the local history of late-eighteenth-century Lucknow (see translated portions in Vidyarthi 1959).

The East-West dialectical process in nineteenth-century scholarship is clearly exemplified in the contributions of Raja Sourindro Mohun Tagore (1840–1914), a wealthy intellectual who published extensively. Although his goal was to present to the world research that showed Indian music in a positive light, in contrast to the general European tone, he adopted the methods and approaches of European musicologists. His anthology of early European writings is still the single most useful source of early English-language scholarship, providing important examples from the breadth of the field (Tagore 1965); it is also valuable in showing how the origins of modern ethnomusicology predate the alleged founding of the "Berlin School" by at least a century.

In this early stage of the East-West dialectic, authors typically understood either Indian or European music, but not both; this mutual ignorance resulted in distortions and misunderstandings on both sides. Tagore contradicted the stereotype, for he grew up playing Indian music and later studied Western music performance and theory. He had a practical as well as a scholarly bent and established music schools in Bengal for which he wrote elementary handbooks for a variety of instruments. Many such introductory handbooks by Indian authors were published in the late nineteenth century, often including musical notation and illustrations, and aimed mainly at literate amateur musicians. They offer interesting grass-roots insights into late-nineteenth-century musical practice, values, and culture. Allyn Miner's *Sitar and Sarod in the 18th and 19th Centuries* (1993) draws on this interesting literature, which has otherwise received little scholarly attention.

Tagore's scholarly works, as well as the books and instrument collections he donated to individuals and organizations in Europe and North America, influenced Western musicologists. Alexander Ellis's influential article "On the Musical Scales of Various Nations" (1885) was indebted to Tagore's work and resources. Tagore's account of the four categories of musical instruments described in the *Nāṭyaśāstra* laid the foundations for the Sachs-Hornbostel system of instrument classification, which appeared in 1914. His *Saṅgītasārasaṅgraha* 'Theory of Sanskrit Music' (1875), written in Sanskrit, reignited interest in ancient treatises among Indian and European scholars, resulting in translations and critical editions of important treatises and (more commonly) portions of larger texts. B. A. Pringle continued Tagore's function as a catalyst in the East-West dialectic: his *History of Indian Music* (1894) emphasized details of contemporary performance, using both practical musical jargon and Western scholarly methods and citations.

SCHOLARSHIP FROM 1900 TO 1960

Indian scholarship

The most influential early-twentieth-century Indian scholar of Hindustani music was undoubtedly Vishnu Narayan Bhatkhande, who lived from 1860 to 1936 [see INSTITUTIONAL MUSIC EDUCATION: NORTHERN AREA]. Bhatkhande combined an Indian emphasis on reconciling theory and contemporary performance practice with Western methods of fieldwork, data collection, and musical notation (though not actually Western staff notation). His early work, which he published as the four-volume *Hindustānī Saṅgīt-Paddhati* (1910–1932), analyzed raga in terms of both contemporary practices and the ideas of certain sixteenth-century treatises, some of which he had discovered and published himself (whole or in part). He traced the emergence of the modern tradition through history and contended that these treatises were still relevant to modern musical practice, whereas the authoritative *Nāṭyaśāstra* and *Saṅgītaratnākara* were not.

A system of raga classification that Bhatkhande devised and described in many of his works has been very influential. In accord with the South Indian theories he had studied, Bhatkhande based his system on ten scale types (*ṭhāṭ*). The concept of scale types was hardly new to Northern scholarship. Various earlier writers had discussed it (as far back as Vitthala in the sixteenth century), but despite the widespread and adamant criticism leveled at it for being too simplistic and arbitrary, Bhatkhande's system gained wide currency among theorists and performers, both Indian and Western. Indeed, Bhatkhande's influence is evident in much of North Indian scholarship since his time, and his works are considered authoritative by Western scholars.

Bhatkhande traveled extensively and collected enormous amounts of orally transmitted musical repertoire from master performers, including many old and rare compositions. He notated the basic structure of some two thousand examples in *sargam* (Indian sol-fa) notation, which he collected over decades and published in six volumes as *Kramik Pustak-Mālikā* (1920–1937). In this work, Bhatkhande also discusses ragas according to both classical sources and his own views, providing many structural details.

Anthologies of repertoire from both Northern and Southern traditions appeared with increasing frequency during the first half of the twentieth century. Subbarama Diksitar's treatise *Saṅgīta Sampradāya-Pradarśinī* (1904) established notational techniques and presented transcriptions of orally transmitted Karnatak repertoire as well as biographies of important eighteenth- and nineteenth-century musicians. Omkarnath Thakur's *Saṅgītāñjalī* (1938–1962) is the most comprehensive collection of notated traditional Hindustani music, including both compositions and improvisatory models. Among the publications of Vishnu Digambar Paluskar (1872–1931) are collections of compositions, although these do not hold great scholarly significance. Paluskar promoted Indian music, especially among middle-class Indians, by establishing music schools and organizing public concerts. He encouraged a more accessible musical aesthetic that was criticized by more traditional musicians and connoisseurs (Deodhar 1973).

British scholarship

In the early twentieth century, European scholarship was still primarily British and generally retained nineteenth-century orientations, albeit viewing Indian music with increasing respect and insight. Western writers conducting fieldwork in India were usually there already in some colonial capacity, although in this period travel to India with exclusively musical research agendas became increasingly common among scholars. General introductions to Indian music, covering history, theory, and practice, continued to appear (Fox Strangways 1914; Popley 1950). Fox Strangways's study, although based on only eight months of field research, was the most sympathetic, astute, and comprehensive of these. With charts, illustrations, and hundreds of accurate and meaningful musical examples, and written with a keen objective sense, it became a classic of twentieth-century Indian musical scholarship. Fox Strangways was also among the first to warn Indians of the danger to their music posed by Westernization.

General features

Indian and European scholars, such as K. B. Deval, C. S. Ayyar, and Ernest Clement, shared an interest in the mathematical analysis of modal structures and tuning apart from their practical musical context, and often combined these analyses with references to classical texts. Out of this focus grew a small scholarly movement extending through the 1940s (especially with Alain Daniélou) and into the 1960s. Jairazbhoy and Stone's article on intonation in music (1963) still stands as a milestone in this long scholarly heritage. The authors used oscillograph measurements to show a wide range of discrepancies in contemporary intonation and cast doubt on the relevance of the theoretical topic of interval measurement in general.

Some Indian and European writers have also shared a renewal of interest in the philosophical, spiritual, and cosmological aspects of the Indian musical tradition. This branch of study was highly developed in traditional Indian theory, beginning with Matanga's *Bṛhaddeśī*, and was also important in medieval Europe, where it was known as speculative music theory. Twentieth-century studies of speculative music theory vary greatly in their scholarly standards—some are merely vehicles for the subjective views and beliefs of the author—but this renewed emphasis and focus is a significant twentieth-century development. Hazrat Inayat Khan (1882–1926), a Chishti Sufi and musician, wrote many articles and short books that contain his personal glosses on important traditional speculative doctrines from written and oral sources (Khan 1983). His personal mission, apparently the dying wish of his spiritual master, was to communicate his knowledge of Sufism and music to the Western world. He lectured extensively in Europe and North America, and his presentations and writings remained influential among speculative authors through the 1960s and to this day [see MUSIC AND INTERNATIONALIZATION]. Dane Rudhyar, a French composer who settled in the United States in the 1920s, was among the first Europeans to reexamine speculative doctrines, largely from a theosophical perspective, in his *Rebirth of Hindu Music* (1928). Alain Daniélou, who undertook extensive fieldwork in India between 1935 and 1950, included in his studies of raga and instrument tunings speculative perspectives that were generally rejected by subsequent scholars. Although there are indeed problems with his mathematical explications and his use of ancient sources, Daniélou's work should be reassessed for its contribution to the interpretation of speculative doctrines.

SCHOLARSHIP IN THE LATE TWENTIETH CENTURY

Ethnomusicology

In general, toward the end of the twentieth century scholarship has continued with the topics of previous periods but has developed them extensively with new approaches and perspectives (figure 4). Since 1960 contributions by Western and Western-educated ethnomusicologists have become more frequent and prominent. Whether dealing with India or any other world tradition, this ethnomusicological literature has generally tended toward a normative perspective—establishing and describing phenomena that are commonly shared or "normal" within a certain aspect of a musical culture; idiosyncrasies are noted but not emphasized. Since the late eighteenth century, Western scholars have attempted to establish a bird's-eye view of the vast field of Indian music; much of the literature since the 1960s can be viewed as a

When viewed collectively, master's theses and Ph.D. dissertations form probably the most significant body of late-twentieth-century scholarship in Indian music.

FIGURE 4 Some twentieth-century approaches (mainly ethnomusicological) to studying Indian music.

Performance Practice	*History*
Bimusical	Comprehensive surveys
Coauthored	Documenting oral history
Repertoire	Micro-histories
Instrument-centered	Translation/edition
Repertoire-centered	
Theory	*Speculative*
Tuning	Explicating classics
Tala/raga catalogs	Documenting oral traditions
Recording	*Nonclassical Music*
Collective/archiving	Devotional music
Artist discography	Folk music
	Popular music

more objective redrafting of this approach. The primary vehicle of this scholarship is graduate-student writing—master's theses and Ph.D. dissertations. When viewed collectively—whether in their original form or revised as books—such theses and dissertations form probably the most significant body of late-twentieth-century scholarship in Indian music.

Practical performance

A prominent feature of recent ethnomusicological scholarship is the increase in studies of contemporary practice reflecting the performer's perspectives and sensibilities. Indian performing artists themselves, such as T. Vishwanathan (1975) and L. Shankar (1974), have made such valuable contributions. Also contributing to this trend are Western musicians and scholars who have acquired proficiency in the performance of Indian music; the archetypal figure of this group is Jon B. Higgins (1939–1984), who studied and performed Karnatak vocal music (Higgins 1994).

The most interesting and potentially fruitful aspect of this performance-oriented research is coauthored studies that focus specifically on the dialectic between the performing bimusical ethnomusicologist and the artist. These studies depart from the normative stance of earlier research and reflect the complexities of individual artists. The authors aim for a more precise view of a tradition by examining the significance of the individual in both aesthetic and scholarly terms. This scholarly approach toward the Indian artist is analogous to Western musicologists' pattern of focusing on the works of "great composers," not merely surveying Baroque music or Romantic

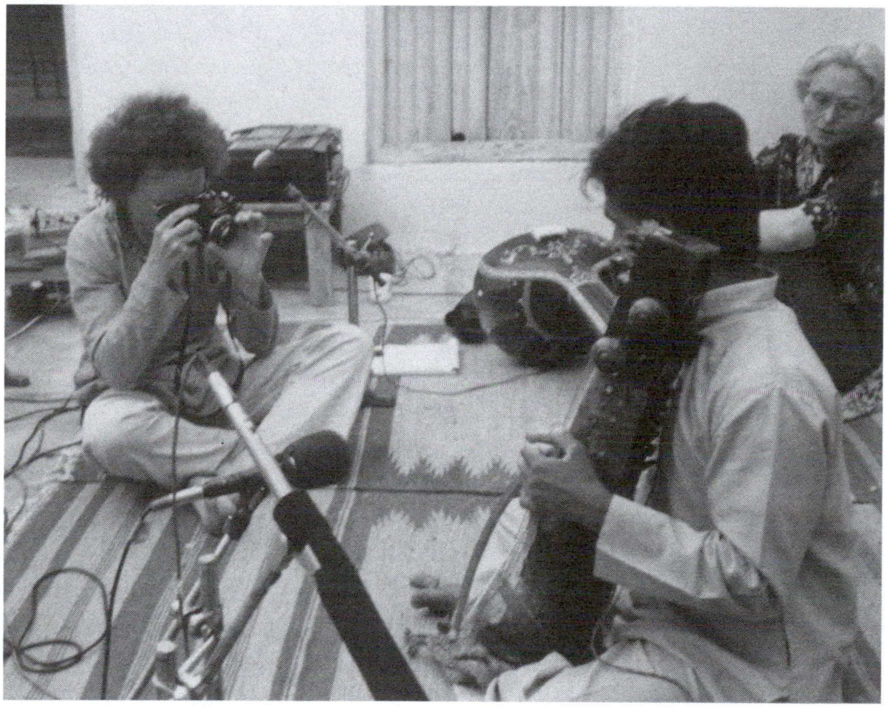

FIGURE 5 Western ethnomusicologists conducting field research with Indian musicians: *above*, James Kippen working with informant Bhupal Ray Choudhuri of the Lucknow tabla *gharānā*, using the Bol Processor system to elicit notes for tabla improvisation, Calcutta 1986; *below*, Joep Bor documenting the *sāraṅgī* 'bowed fiddle', Vrindavan 1984. Photos by James Kippen.

piano repertoire. Neil Sorrell's work with the great *sāraṅgī* 'bowed fiddle' master Ram Narayan exemplifies this approach, which has likewise been adopted in many recent Ph.D. dissertations on Indian as well as other musical cultures (Sorrell and Narayan 1980).

Many studies focus on the history, technique, repertoire, performers, and performance practice of particular instruments or vocal styles (figure 5); to some extent these works are contemporary extensions of the late-nineteenth-century instructional manuals by Indian authors. Like the earlier manuals, current studies on Indian instruments also document oral histories and traditions. They tend not to be coauthored, but often represent the style of a particular individual or lineage. Western and Indian writers and perspectives are fairly equally represented in this branch of scholarship, from which many valuable studies have emerged (Brown 1965; Kippen 1988;

Manuel 1989; T. Sankaran 1994; R. Shankar 1968; L. Shankar 1974; Wade 1984). The six-volume *Saṅgītāñjalī* (1938–1962) by the great Hindustani vocal master Omkarnath Thakur can be viewed as an important contribution to this movement as well.

Studies in nonclassical music

Ethnomusicologists have further extended musical scholarship to include areas outside the realm of art music, contrasting sharply with the classical exclusivity of almost two millennia of musicological scholarship. Several studies have dealt with devotional singing (Beck 1996; Capwell 1986; Qureshi 1986; Slawek 1986, 1988), a vital aspect of Indian musical activity throughout history that remained largely neglected. Vedic recitation has also received ethnomusicological attention (Howard 1986). The vast and rich traditions of Indian folk music, often overlapping with the category of devotional singing, are only beginning to be documented (Deva and Kuckertz 1981; Henry 1988; Thompson 1987), as are the musical traditions of tribal (*ādivāsī*) populations (Babiracki 1991; Wolf 1997). Furthermore, popular music such as Hindi film song (Arnold 1991) and other genres are also now within the purview of musical scholars (Baily and Oliver 1988; Manuel 1993).

Speculative and historical studies

The revival of speculative music theory in the early part of this century has continued in later decades, with the examination of Indian doctrines figuring prominently in general studies of the topic by popular Western authors such as Peter Hamel (1984) and Joachim Berendt (1987—directly influenced by Hazrat Inayat Khan). Prem Lata Sharma's contributions are more erudite and focus exclusively on India; her translation (with R. K. Shringy) of *Saṅgītaratnākara* (1978–1989) includes valuable and extensive glosses on the long speculative portion of the first chapter, based on traditional Indian sources and perspectives. Suresh Chandra Dey's *The Quest for Music Divine* (1990) surveys the topic from the perspective of the Indian scholarly tradition. Much recent scholarship on this topic comes from disciplines other than musicology, such as philosophy, religion, and Indian literature.

Meanwhile, primarily historical studies have appeared that build on the work of earlier scholars. Both Indian and Western authors have regularly published comprehensive music histories. Bhatkhande's historical work was a particularly influential contribution; other important Indian authors include R. Ayyangar (1972), O. C. Gangoly (1989), O. Goswami (1957), Swami Prajnanananda (1981), and P. Sambamurthy (1963–1973). Among the important Western scholars of Indian music history are Emmie te Nijenhuis (1992), Harold Powers (1980), Lewis Rowell (1992), and Richard Widdess (1995).

Harold Powers (1965) points out the differing scholarly standards of Western and Indian writing on Indian music. He expresses Western readers' criticisms of certain aspects of Indian scholarship, such as insufficient documentation of references and the assumption of familiarity with early sources. The author explains that these criticisms reflect both a Western scholarly bias and the nature of traditional Indian scholarship: in the latter, scholarly protocol assumes knowledge of important texts and considers general references to previous writers sufficient, making fully documented citations unnecessary. Powers notes that medieval Western scholarship made the same assumptions. These factors have led to occasional East-West conflicts that are usually the result of varying or incompatible standards on both sides. A common bias among South Asian and Western scholars is the great attention paid to Sanskrit sources; studies of Persian and Urdu sources are comparatively few and present an open field for further research.

Another form of historical study is the translation of musical sources, begun in the late nineteenth and early twentieth centuries and continued by both Indian and European scholars such as Alain Daniélou (1959), Manomohan Ghosh (1951–1961), C. Kunhan Raja (1945), Prem Lata Sharma and R. K. Shringy (1978–1989), and Emmie te Nijenhuis (1992). Throughout the twentieth century, Indian scholars have continued to produce authoritative and critical editions of Sanskrit sources in the original Sanskrit; although most important treatises have now been edited and published, much work remains to be done. Some scholars have focused on a narrow historical period or on the history of a particular region or musical lineage (*gharānā*), often drawing considerably upon oral histories for which the scholarly studies serve as documentation. Indian authors, and occasionally musicians, have realized the value of this work and made significant contributions, such as Vilayat Hussain Khan's *Saṅgīt-gyoṇ ke saṃsmaraṇ* (1959). Musical studies focusing on other topics, particularly instrument-based studies, can contribute to the documentation of oral history and tradition as well. Daniel Neuman's *The Life of Music in North India* (1980) is an interesting consolidation of various *gharānā* histories, offering a general view of the social structure of the professional Hindustani musical milieu. Wim Van der Meer (1980) presents an excellent survey of Hindustani music in the twentieth century with effective treatment of various aspects of history, musical structure, and performance practice.

Sound recording, archives, and journals

As in all areas of musicology, the development of recording technology marks a new era in the study of Indian music. The implications of this development are vast, and scholars have yet to appreciate them fully or to realize their potential even partially. The historical perspective that early-twentieth-century sound recordings afford can hardly be overstated. Sorting through the accumulated documentation (wax cylinders, vinyl records, and cassette tapes) of almost a century of recorded Indian music in all its variety and complexity—Karnatak, Hindustani, and regional styles, and the individual styles of masters, students, innovators, and mediocre amateurs—is surely a task that will occupy scholars in future centuries. Sound recordings have facilitated the study of transmission, musical change, stylistic features, raga and tala definitions, compositions, and improvisational processes in ways hitherto impossible. Scholarly archives of Indian music exist in the West at universities and in private collections, and in India at the American Institute of Indian Studies and the Sangeet Natak Akademi in Delhi, and the National Centre for the Performing Arts in Bombay, among others. But vast archives remain in private hands and are generally inaccessible to the public, such as the vaults of record companies and of the state-run All India Radio, and private connoisseur collections. Although Kinnear has performed important discographical work (1985, 1994), systematic documentation and preservation of huge, historically significant collections are urgently needed. Awareness of this enormous research area recently emerged when in 1990 the Society of Indian Record Collectors was formed in Bombay to preserve, promote, and research collections of recorded Indian music. Furthermore, recording companies regularly produce reissues of portions of this legacy, though as a commercial and not a scholarly enterprise.

Finally, in addition to the steady production of academic dissertations and the publication of books on Indian music, significant articles appear regularly in Western ethnomusicology journals, particularly *Asian Music*. Prominent journals in English

Throughout the twentieth century, Indian scholars have continued to produce authoritative and critical editions of Sanskrit sources in the original Sanskrit; although most important treatises have now been edited and published, much work remains to be done.

devoted exclusively to Indian music include the *Journal of the Music Academy, Madras*, the *Journal of the Indian Musicological Society*, the *Indian Music Journal*, the *Sangeet Natak Akademi Bulletin*, and *Bansuri*.

REFERENCES

Arnold, Alison. 1991. "Hindi Filmī Gīt: On the History of Commercial Indian Popular Music." Ph.D. dissertation, University of Illinois at Urbana-Champaign.

Ayyangar, Rangaramanuja. 1972. *The History of South Indian Music: From Vedic Times to the Present.* Madras: Author.

Babiracki, Carol. 1991. "Musical and Cultural Interaction in Tribal India: The *Karam* Repertory of the Mundas of Chotanagpur." Ph.D. dissertation, University of Illinois at Urbana-Champaign.

Baily, John, and Paul Oliver, eds. 1988. *Popular Music* 7(2). "South Asia and the West" issue.

Beck, Guy. 1996. "Vaiṣṇav Music in the Braj Region of North India." *Journal of Vaiṣṇav Studies* 4(2):115–147.

Berendt, Joachim. 1987. *Nada Brahman: Music and the Landscape of Consciousness.* Rochester, Vt.: Inner Traditions.

Bhagyalekshmy, S. 1991. *Lakshanagrandhas in Music.* Trivandrum: CBH Publications.

Bhatkhande, Vishnu Narayan. 1981 [1910–1932]. *Hindustānī Saṅgīt-Paddhati.* 4 vols. Hathras: Sangeet Karyalaya.

———. 1978–1982 [1920–1937]. *Kramik Pustak-Mālikā.* 6 vols. Hathras: Sangeet Karyalaya.

Bor, Joep. 1988. "The Rise of Ethnomusicology: Sources on Indian Music c.1780–c.1890." *Yearbook for Traditional Music* 20:51–73.

Brown, Robert. 1965. "The *Mrdanga*: A Study of Drumming in South India." Ph.D. dissertation, University of California at Los Angeles.

Capwell, Charles. 1986. *Music of the Bauls of Bengal.* Kent, Ohio: Kent State University Press.

Daniélou, Alain. 1959. *Textes des Purāṇa sur la Théorie Musicale.* Pondicherry: Institut Français d'Indologie.

Day, Charles. 1974 [1891]. *The Music and Musical Instruments of Southern India and the Deccan.* Delhi: B. R. Publishing.

Deodhar, B. R. 1973. "Pandit Vishnu Digambar in His Younger Days." *Journal of the Indian Musicological Society* 4(2):21–51.

Deva, Chaitanya, and Josef Kuckertz. 1981. *Bhārūḍ, Vāghyā-muraḷi, and the Ḍaff-gān of the Deccan: Studies in the Regional Folk Music of the Deccan.* Munich: Musikverlag Emil Katzbilcher.

Dey, Suresh Chandra. 1990. *The Quest for Music Divine.* Delhi: Ashish.

Ellis, Alexander J. 1885. "On the Musical Scales of Various Nations." *Journal of the Society of Arts* 32:485–527.

Fétis, François. 1869. *Histoire générale de la musique: depuis les temps les plus anciens jusqu'à nos jours.* Vol. 2. Paris: Firmin Didot Frères, Fils et Cie.

Fox Strangways, Arthur. 1965 [1914]. *The Music of Hindoostan.* Oxford: Clarendon Press.

Gangoly, Ordhendra Coomar. 1989 [1934]. *Ragas and Raginis.* New Delhi: Munshiram Manoharlal.

Ghosh, Manomohan, trans. 1951–1961. *Nāṭyaśāstra.* 2 vols. Calcutta: Asiatic Society.

Goswami, O. 1957. *The Story of Indian Music: Its Growth and Synthesis.* Bombay: Asia Publications.

Hamel, Peter M. 1984. *Through Music to the Self.* Berne: Scherz Verlag.

Henry, Edward. 1988. *Chant the Names of God.* San Diego: University of San Diego Press.

Higgins, Jon B. 1994. *The Music of Bharata Natyam.* Sittingbourne, Kent: Asia Publishers.

Howard, Wayne. 1986. *Veda Recitation in Vārāṇasī.* Delhi: Motilal Banarsidass.

Jairazbhoy, Nazir, and A. W. Stone. 1963. "Intonation in Present-Day North Indian Classical Music." *Bulletin of the School of Oriental and African Studies* 26(1):119–132.

Khan, Hazrat Inayat. 1983. *The Music of Life.* Santa Fe: Omega Press.

Khan, Vilayat Hussain. 1959. *Saṅgīt-gyoṇ ke saṃsmaraṇ.* New Delhi: Sangeet Natak Akademi.

Kinnear, Michael. 1985. *A Discography of Hindustani and Karnatic Music.* Westport, Conn.: Greenwood Press.

———. 1994. *The Gramophone Company's First Indian Recordings 1899–1908.* Bombay: Popular Prakashan.

Kippen, James. 1988. *The Tabla of Lucknow: A Cultural Analysis of a Musical Tradition.* Cambridge: Cambridge University Press.

La Fage, J. Adrien de. 1844. *Histoire générale de la musique et de la danse,* vol. 1. Paris: Au Comptoir des Imprimeurs Unis.

Manuel, Peter. 1989. *Thumri in Historical and Stylistic Perspectives.* Delhi: Motilal Banarsidass.

———. 1993. *Cassette Culture: Popular Music and Technology in North India.* Chicago: Chicago University Press.

Miner, Allyn. 1993. *Sitar and Sarod in the 18th and 19th Centuries.* Wilhelmshaven, Germany: Florian Noetzel Verlag.

Neuman, Daniel. 1980. *The Life of Music in North India: The Organization of an Artistic Tradition.* Detroit: Wayne State University Press.

Nijenhuis, Emmie te. 1992. *Saṅgītaśiromaṇi: A Medieval Handbook of Indian Music.* Leiden and New York: E. J. Brill.

Popley, Herbert. 1950. *The Music of India.* Calcutta: YMCA Publishers.

Powers, Harold. 1965. "Indian Music and the English Language: A Review Essay." *Ethnomusicology* 9:1–12.

———. 1980. "India." *The New Grove Dictionary of Music and Musicians,* ed. Stanley Sadie. London: Macmillan.

Prajnanananda, Swami. 1981 [1960]. *The Historical Study of Indian Music.* New Delhi: Munshiram Manoharlal.

Pringle, B. A. 1962 [1894]. *The History of Indian Music.* Delhi: Susil Gupta.

Qureshi, Regula Burckhardt. 1986. *Sufi Music of India and Pakistan: Sound, Context, and Meaning in Qawwali.* Cambridge: Cambridge University Press.

Raja, C. Kunhan, trans. 1945. *Saṅgītaratnākara of Śārṅgadeva,* vol. 1, chap. 1. Madras: Adyar Library.

Rowell, Lewis. 1992. *Music and Musical Thought in Early India.* Chicago: University of Chicago Press.

Rudhyar, Dane. 1928. *The Rebirth of Hindu Music.* Madras: Theosophical Publishing House.

Said, Edward W. 1978. *Orientalism.* New York: Torch Books.

Sambamurthy, Pichu. 1963–1973. *South Indian Music.* 6 vols. Madras: Indian Music Publishing House.

Sankaran, Trichy. 1994. *The Rhythmic Principles and Practice of South Indian Drumming.* Toronto: Lalith Publishers.

Shankar, L. 1974. "The Art of Violin Accompaniment in South Indian Classical Music." Ph.D. dissertation, Wesleyan University.

Shankar, Ravi. 1968. *My Music, My Life.* New York: Simon & Schuster.

Shirali, Vishnudass. 1977. *Sargam: An Introduction to Indian Music.* New Delhi: Abhinav Publishers.

Shringy, R. K., and Prem Lata Sharma. 1978–1989. *Saṅgītaratnākara of Śārṅgadeva: Sanskrit Text and English Translation with Comments and Notes.* Vol. 1, Delhi: Motilal Banarsidass; vol. 2, New Delhi: Munshiram Manoharlal.

Slawek, Stephen M. 1986. "Kirtan: A Study of the Sonic Manifestations of the Divine in the Popular Hindu Culture of Banāras." Ph.D. dissertation, University of Illinois at Urbana-Champaign.

———. 1988. "Popular *Kīrtan* in Benares: Some 'Great' Aspects of a Little Tradition." *Ethnomusicology* 32(2):77–92.

Sorrell, Neil, and Ram Narayan. 1980. *Indian Music in Performance: A Practical Introduction.* Manchester: University of Manchester Press.

Stafford, William. 1830. *A History of Music.* Edinburgh: Constable and Co.

Tagore, Sourindro Mohun. 1965 [1875]. *Hindu Music from Various Authors.* Varanasi: Chowkhamba Sanskrit Series Office.

Thakur, Omkarnath. 1938–1962. *Saṅgītâñjalī.* Vol. 1 (Lahore: 1938, 2nd ed. 1959), vol. 2 (Hathras: 1954), vols. 3–6 (Varanasi: 1955, 1957, 1958, 1962), vols. 7 and 8, unpublished manuscript.

Thompson, Gordon. 1987. "Music and Values in Gujarati-Speaking Western India." Ph.D. dissertation, University of California, Los Angeles.

Van der Meer, Wim. 1980. *Hindustani Music in the Twentieth Century.* The Hague: Martinus Nijhoff.

Vidyarthi, Govind. 1959a. "Melody through the Centuries." *Sangeet Natak Akademi Bulletin* 11/12:13–26 [transl. of portion of *Ma'dan-ul-Mūsīqī* 'Mine of Music', c. 1860].

———. 1959b. "Effects of Raga and Mannerism in Singing." *Sangeet Natak Akademi Bulletin* 13/14:6–14 [trans. of portion of *Ma'dan-ul-Mūsīqī* (Mine of Music), c. 1860].

Viswanathan, Tanjore. 1975. "Rāga Ālāpana in South Indian Music." Ph.D. dissertation, Wesleyan University.

Wade, Bonnie. 1984. *Khyal: Creativity within North India's Classical Music Tradition.* Cambridge: Cambridge University Press.

Widdess, Richard. 1995. *The Ragas of Early Indian Music.* Oxford: Clarendon Press.

Wolf, Richard. 1997. "Of God and Death: Music in Ritual and Everyday Life. A Musical Ethnography of the Kotas of South India." Ph.D. dissertation, University of Illinois at Urbana-Champaign.

Part 2
Issues and Processes

The world of South Asian music and dance expresses the diverse cultures, societies, economies, religions, history, and politics of this geographical area. To penetrate this world, to gain an understanding of South Asia's performing arts, we must ask questions not only about the music itself but about the musicians, the audiences, the performance contexts, the modes of learning, the impact of modern technology and communications, and much more. The issues and processes addressed here, grouped within broad areas such as music in religion and ritual or music learning and transmission, reflect questions asked by scholars, students, and performers, as well as the topics they consider important. These discussions open up for us the world of music and dance in South Asia; they also remind us that other topics remain unexplored and other questions unanswered.

In Indian cinema, producers highlight the juxtaposition of modernity and tradition by drawing on historical, religious, and mythological themes to create popular films and film songs. *Sant Tukaram* (Prabhat Films, 1936), on the life of a sixteenth-century Marathi poet-saint (shown here in the film lyric booklet), attracted huge crowds to cinemas throughout India. Photo courtesy Alison Arnold.

The Classical Traditions

As in the West, classical art music in South Asia has been passed down through many generations of performers, and has become a music based on ancient practices yet encompassing modern ideas. Unlike its Western counterpart, classical music in India gradually diverged into two separate streams from the thirteenth century on, resulting in today's Hindustani musical tradition in the north and Karnatak tradition in the south. Both these Indian musical systems have highly developed theories, musical forms, performance contexts, and stylistic lineages that pass on practical knowledge orally. Musicians from the two traditions occasionally perform together, integrating performance styles and genres; for the most part, however, the two classical traditions remain separate, cultivated by artists and students devoted to maintaining their musical heritage.

The tabla drum pair is a fundamental component of most Hindustani vocal and instrumental music ensembles. The tabla player Bikram Ghosh of Calcutta, who studied with his father and guru, Pandit Shankar Ghosh, performs regularly as a soloist and as an accompanist for major Hindustani artists, including Pandit Ravi Shankar and Ustad Ali Akhbar Khan. Photo by Greg Plachta, courtesy Music of the World.

Hindustani Raga

George Ruckert
Richard Widdess

The essence of what is meant by the term *rāga* (a Sanskrit word) in Indian music is latent in much of the rest of the world's music. In its broadest sense, the word refers to the "color," and more specifically the emotion or mood produced by a particular combination or sequence of pitches. Etymologically, the word is related to *raṅga* 'color'; a Sanskrit saying from classical times is often quoted: *rañjayati iti ragaḥ* 'that which tinges the mind with color is a raga'. Throughout history and in most cultures musical experience has been clearly tied to emotional meaning and affect. From the earliest writers on music to those of the present day, discussion of mood and color and the production of emotion in music has often been a starting point. The ancient Greeks related states of mind to their modal theory; the Chinese connected music with Confucian ideals of serene harmony with nature; the Indonesians refer to the unique color of each gamelan's sound; the West Asians to their multicolored *maqām*; Western medieval composers talked of melodic color, and Baroque composers thought in terms of *Affektion;* the early twentieth-century Russian composers Nikolay Rimsky-Korsakov and Alexander Skryabin had their famous color theories; and in modern music we have "the blues" at the same time that computer microchips are transforming sound instantly into color patterns.

WHAT IS A RAGA?

In a technical sense, raga can be described as lying on the continuum between a scale and a mode, encompassing both straight, emotionally neutral lines of ascent and descent and a fixed song or melody full of feeling. In their abstract form, most ragas lie somewhere between these two extremes: in terms of the scale, the performer is permitted to move freely between the raga notes without the rigors of following tune patterns; in fixed compositions, however, the performer must keep to the rigid confines of a melodic grid. Most musicians spend their time in the midground fulfilling the ecstatic possibilities of compositions and dealing with the restrictions of a raga, for in this middle area they can find and exploit most of the tonal possibilities that are typical of all ragas. Tonal characteristics include transilience in the scale (ascending or descending patterns of five, six, or seven tones); observing tonal centers as well as strong and weak notes (*vādī-samvādī* and *alpatva-bahutva* relationships; see

"Theoretical Terms" below); controlling the microtonal tuning; concentrating on the emotional effect; remaining within a given range; starting and ending sections on the correct note; resting at the correct places; and, perhaps most important of all, observing the subtle melodic ornaments and features of the raga that traditionally characterize it. (If the various restrictions are glided over or ignored, mature artists consider the "picture of the raga" faulty and carelessly executed.)

We still face the question, What is a raga? Simply, it is "some combination of notes which charms the mind and produces the moods of love, joy, pathos, heroism, and peace" (Ali Akbar Khan, personal communication). Such a definition actually belongs to no particular culture. However, a North Indian classical raga is a musical complex with a great history and significant spiritual implications, with extramusical associations regarding time, personality, and mood, and which, as it is iterated again and again, runs the gamut of tonal structure from simple scale to fully formed composition. A raga performance may be a huge structure, permitting large-scale expansions in time and melodic variation; or it may be quite small and confining, with no more than a short exposition of its delicate miniaturism. The realization of a raga through performance reveals the nature of the balances of pitch and mood inherent in it. Any single performance may or may not faithfully portray its character and potential affect. Even in the hands of a master musician, one raga may take repeated renderings to reveal its seemingly endless charm and developmental possibilities. For a less experienced musician, singing or playing any raga is fraught with pitfalls as one attempts to avoid such errors as bringing in other ragas of similar pitch content, introducing wrong balances or tunings, neutralizing or destroying the mood, or blurring the differences among ragas by subjecting them all to the same sort of development. The understanding of the movement of a raga is gained through years of association with a teacher, and the student practices hundreds of compositions in order to develop the discernment and understanding of how ragas differ one from another as well as the ability to realize all the possibilities within a single one.

When we hear the term *rāga*, several visual images may come to mind: a sitar player and a tabla player sitting on an oriental carpet in the concert hall, blazing away at a breakneck tempo; a detailed medieval miniature painting in the Persian style depicting a prince and his lady in a flowery garden; a solitary vocalist, accompanying himself on a stringed drone instrument, humbly going about his daily meditative music practice. Each image conveys an important facet of the elusive musical pattern called a raga—a kind of personal musical inquiry into pitch and rhythm that has come to be enhanced with courtly refinements and which has gathered to itself important extramusical and spiritual associations. It is also a devotional yoga nurtured on Indian soil and at the same time the musical substance of public concerts and recordings produced for the entertainment of audiences worldwide. It is a vehicle for the beautiful expression of breathtaking virtuosity, intoxicated flights of fancy, and profound feeling. And there are no perfect models, for ragas are never rendered twice the same way.

To restate the musical parameters, a raga is an abstract, tonally centered combination of pitches, often as simple as a scale but more often a series of melodic motives within a scale; in a few cases, these can add up to a complete composition—a song, for example—with fixed melodic contours and rhythmic implications. Some ragas use a series of motives that may span a range of from three to ten notes, while others are conceived of as full-blown melodies. In the former case (by far the most prevalent) the performer combines and rearranges the motives when rendering the raga; in the latter case (more common in folk melodies and in certain ragas of the classical tradition) a larger contiguous melody is fragmented in the rendering. In general, the word *rāga* implies a set of performance practices by which these abstract melodic kernels are revealed in formulaic patterns. In this sense, a raga is a map a musician follows in his or her creation of a musical performance: a catalog of melodic movements that the artist unfolds, details, and expands while following a traditional performance format that has been passed down orally from teacher to student.

Musical practice has been evolving in India for more than three thousand years, and the origins of raga date back to the chanting of the Vedas, the scriptures of the Aryans, who settled in modern India's Ganges River plain, probably moving from original settlements in the Indus Valley, in about 1500 B.C. The four Vedas (the Ṛgveda, Sāmaveda, Yajurveda, and Atharvaveda) form an oral tradition maintained and performed by specialists, the priests of the Brahmin caste. The hymns that make up the Sāmaveda were chanted on the seven notes of the diatonic scale, later named Sa, Re, Ga, Ma, Pa, Dha, and Ni. Scholars suggest that the Vedas may also have absorbed melodies of pre-Aryan origin (Tarlekar 1985). Classical Indian music inherited many features of these Vedic foundations: it is an oral tradition largely of monophony with spiritual dimensions whose theory and practice have been maintained and developed by specialists over the centuries. A central part of the theoretical evolution has been the grammatization of the melodic concepts collectively known as raga.

The pool of musical theory and melodies, eventually classified under the raga system, is immense in terms of diversity both of character and context, having developed over such a great time span and containing vastly differing cultural admixtures. Because of the wide variety of sources, it remains difficult to come up with a simple and satisfactory definition of raga. When direct description becomes elusive, metaphors of water recur continually in the speech of musicians describing ragas: "This raga is a swift-moving stream; that one a deep lake; another a majestic river; and overall, the music is a vast ocean." Besides the Vedic systems of musical thought, the music of the dance and theater played a central role in the formation of early melodic theorizing. Regional musical styles, including what we might now term folk songs, have always teemed with great variety in India and have been sung in the hundreds of languages and dialects. Ever since the fifth-century treatise of Matanga, the *Bṛhaddeśī*, this vast literature of regional music has been acknowledged as vital to the classical traditions, and has continued to inform them. To make sense of this very profusion of melodic types was at the heart of the early theoretical systems.

There are four broadly based areas from which the ancient and modern ideas and practices of raga must be discussed. First, there are the many extramusical associations that have always been germane to the spiritual and cosmic understanding of music in India. These include the religious bases, as well as time and mood associations, natural cosmologies, and poetic and visual images suggested by the music. Second, there is a vast theory of raga pitch configurations that details the scales, tonal centers, and principal movements in a terminology that has much in common with both early Greek and Western medieval theory. Third, there are the more pragmatic dimensions of raga, which result from the observation of practice throughout the centuries—in short, raga seen through performance styles. And fourth—though for a trained musician primarily—is the tradition of passing on the technique and literature of raga through the *guru-śiṣya paramparā* (teacher-student teaching tradition), a grasp of which is essential to understanding the ethos and balance of the first three. In this article reference is made to two ragas in particular, *jaunpurī* and *darbārī kānaḍā*, to show how these components interrelate. Preceding these sections is a general introduction to the terms used in Hindustani raga theory.

THEORETICAL TERMS AND CONCEPTS IN THE HINDUSTANI RAGA TRADITION

Despite the number of theoretical works available, a definitive statement of raga theory in the Hindustani tradition does not exist. Of course the practice is definitive, but this varies in detail from one *gharānā* 'stylistic school' to another; attempts to encapsulate or conceptualize the practice in words are a secondary phenomenon. Nevertheless, a number of generally accepted basic concepts can be identified. Terms for these concepts have generally been adapted from the Sanskrit theoretical tradition, often with some modification of meaning to reflect changes in both system and practice since ancient or medieval times.

Śruti and *svara*

Fundamental to raga theory is the distinction between *śruti*, the infinite gradations of pitch that the voice (and most Indian melodic instruments) can produce, and *svara*, the selected pitches from which scales, ragas, and melodies are constructed. *Śruti* means that which is audible, in the sense of the smallest perceptible increment of pitch. The earliest treatises (the *Nāṭyaśāstra* and the *Dattilam*) laid down the number of *śruti* in the octave, or rather, "heptad" (*saptak*) as twenty-two. This number is still accepted in principle, although it is of doubtful relevance to modern practice. Infinite gradations of pitch are employed in the decorative or expressive inflection of each *svara*, and in different ragas the same *svara* may be given a microtonally higher or lower intonation (*uccār* 'pronunciation'). Such inflections and intonations may help to distinguish one raga from another, but cannot be reduced to a rigid system.

As in Karnatak music, there are seven scale degrees (*svara*) to the octave; they have Sanskrit names (see figure 1), of which the abbreviations (Sa, Re, Ga, Ma, Pa, Dha, Ni) are used as a solmization or "oral notation." Sa is the tonic (*kharaj*), and Pa is always a perfect fifth above the tonic, if it is present in the raga; both pitches may be included in the drone, but if Pa is not present in the raga, it may be replaced in the drone by Ma or Ni. The other pitches are movable. In their basic (*śuddh*) positions, the *svara* approximate the Western major scale; in addition Re, Ga, Dha, and Ni may be flatted by a half tone (more or less, depending on context), and Ma may be similarly sharped, to give twelve notationally equally spaced positions (*svara-sthān*) in the octave. (See "A sampling of Hindustani ragas in letter notation" below for a description of the Hindustani notation system.)

Ṭhāṭ and raga

Different selections of the twelve *svara-sthān* provide the basic scales (*ṭhāṭ*) of Hindustani music. Theoretical systems have almost always been based on seven-note scales; Bhatkhande's system of ten heptatonic *ṭhāṭ* is the most successful such system for Hindustani music, but it is important to remember that such systems are derived from the ragas as performed in practice, not the reverse. Thus individual ragas may diverge from the *ṭhāṭ* to which they are theoretically assigned by taking fewer than seven pitches or by taking both positions of the same pitch (*śuddh* 'natural' and *komal* 'flatted' or *tīvra* 'sharped'). The scale of a raga is often stated theoretically in both ascending (*āroh*) and descending (*avaroh*) forms, since different pitches may appear in ascending and descending contexts; the order of pitches may deviate from strict scale order, in which case they are *vakra* 'crooked'.

A raga is a mode, as that term is currently understood in ethnomusicology: a concept operating between the domains of "scale" and "tune." It is not a tune, because an infinite number of tunes can be based on the same raga; it is not a scale, because numerous ragas can be based on the same scale. A raga is distinguished from a scale, and from other ragas based on the same scale, by its unique array of melodic features, which give rise to a unique aesthetic sentiment (*rasa*). Whereas the analyst might define a raga in terms of a basic scale and the different functions of its constituent degrees, to the performer it is an aesthetic whole, identified mainly by its melodic motifs or phrases.

Still important to musicians today is the "time theory": each raga is to be sung at a specific time, in one of the eight divisions of the day and night, or one of the six seasons of the year.

Vādī and *samvādī*

From an analytical perspective, an important feature of many ragas is the relative degree of importance or emphasis given to different pitches. Normally at least two pitches in any one raga are made prominent by being sounded clearly and frequently, whereas other pitches will be passed over more lightly or occur only in limited contexts. In many ragas, two prominent pitches are found a perfect fourth or fifth apart, balancing one another in the lower and upper halves of the scale. One pitch of such a consonant pair may be more prominent than the other, in which case it will be regarded as the *vādī* 'speaker', while the other is termed the *samvādī* 'co-speaker, consonant'. Other relatively strong pitches may be termed *anuvādī* 'assonant', while *vivādī* 'dissonant' refers to a note foreign to the basic scale that is used judiciously in certain phrases. Related terms are *alpatva* and *bahutva*, denoting the "weakness" and "strength" of particular pitches. Even a relatively weak (*alpa*) pitch, one that is not prolonged or otherwise emphasized and that appears only in limited contexts, may be essential to the character and identity of the raga. Thus, two ragas may be identical in scalar material, but the different disposition of *vādī, samvādī*, and other emphasized and nonemphasized pitches will give rise to (or result from) different melodic phrases and distinct tonal and aesthetic identities.

The theory of *vādī* and *samvādī* is problematic, however, in that there are often more than two emphasized pitches in a raga, and hence more than two pitches that could theoretically be identified as the *vādī-samvādī* pair. For example, the tonic and fifth (Sa and Pa) may be important points of repose, while other pitches (such as Ga and Ni) are emphasized during the course of the melody. There is no infallible rule by which the *vādī* may be identified, unless it is given overwhelming prominence by the performer. More commonly, there is an interplay of emphases on different pitches in different phrases or stages of improvisation. Practice is thus considerably more flexible than the theory that has been derived from it (or imposed on it).

The theoretical *vādī* nevertheless has an important role in relation to the time of performance of the raga (see below).

Motives and phrases

From the performer's perspective, a raga is identified less by scale and individual features such as emphasized tones than by the phrases and motives that belong to it and from which all melodies or improvisations are constructed. A basic outline of the raga is called *calan* 'way of moving'; *pakaḍ* 'catch' means a particular motive or phrase that encapsulates the identity of the raga. A distinction is sometimes made between phrases that emphasize the lower part of the scale (*pūrvāṅg*) and those that emphasize the upper part (*uttarāṅg*). Some motifs may be common to a group or "family" (*kula*) of ragas, although the members of such a family need not all use the same basic scale; thus the motive Sa re ga re Sa (C–D♭–E♭–D♭–C) occurs in both *miyāṅ kī ṭoḍī* and *bilāskhānī ṭoḍī*, but the scales of these ragas are respectively C–D♭–E♭–F♯–G–A♭–B–C and C–D♭–E♭–F–G–A♭–B♭–C. Some ragas include an "echo" or "shadow" (*chāyā*), a phrase reminiscent of a different raga, and some are composite ragas that combine phrases from two or more independent ragas; however, as noted above, the inadvertent introduction of a phrase from a different raga is regarded as a gross error. The practitioner must learn to distinguish each raga from similar ragas with which it might be unintentionally confused: the aesthetic impact of each raga depends on the preservation of its unique melodic identity (*svarūp*).

Other features

Many other features might be cited as distinctive to particular ragas. A particular *svara* may be ornamented in a particular manner or given an especially high or low intonation. One raga may be suitable for fast, vigorous melodies emphasizing the upper register, and another for slow, contemplative melodies emphasizing the low register. Some ragas are considered to be serious (*gambhīr*) in character and therefore suitable for *ālāp, dhrupad*, or *khyāl*; others are light (*halkā*) and suitable for *ṭhumrī* and other semiclassical genres.

The quasi-emotional effect of a raga on the listener is sometimes defined with reference to the classical theory of *rasa* (literally 'juice', 'flavor', or 'essence'), according to which the connoisseur (*rasika*) derives enjoyment from savoring the mood (*bhāva*) portrayed by the performer. Nine aesthetic "flavors" are traditionally identified: love (*śṛṅgāra*), heroism (*vīra*), disgust (*vībhatsa*), anger (*raudra*), mirth (*hāsya*), terror (*bhayānaka*), compassion (*karuṇa*), wonder (*adbhuta*) and peace (*śānta*); a tenth, devotion (*bhakti*), is sometimes added (see figure 2). Theorists or musicians may describe a particular raga as evoking one or more of these "flavors," but such descriptions are subjective, not systematized; in any case the aesthetic effect of each raga is unique and cannot be completely defined in such terms.

Traditionally, ragas were believed to have magical or therapeutic powers, and to exist as divine beings whose presence or blessings were invoked by their performance. Still important to musicians today is the "time theory": each raga is to be sung at a specific time, in one of the eight divisions (*pahar*) of the day and night, or one of the six seasons (*ṛtu*) of the year. According to Bhatkhande and other theorists, the daily cycle of ragas is correlated with scale type and with the position of the *vādī*. The latter is in the lower half of the scale in evening ragas, in the upper half in morning ragas. A progression of scale types can be seen in both morning and evening ragas; and ragas for dawn or dusk (*sandhiprakāś* ragas) often reflect the transition between day and night by using both *śuddh* 'natural' and *tīvra* 'sharped' forms of the fourth degree (Ma, that is, F and F♯). In practice, there are exceptions to these theoretical correlations; but musicians tend to observe the traditional timings at least approximately, and in the correct sequence. One rarely hears a morning raga in the evening or vice versa—or even an early evening raga after a late evening raga.

EXTRAMUSICAL ASSOCIATIONS OF RAGAS

To refer to the cosmic and natural imagery associated with Indian musical traditions as extramusical is to at once betray an outsider's orientation. Those familiar with Indian scholarship know the predilection of early Indian philosophical writers for classifying and organizing their knowledge with endless taxonomic lists that included intricately worked cosmologies covering the remotest corners of theology, philosophy, and natural science. For example, a recent edition of the beacon thirteenth-century musical treatise *Saṅgītaratnākara* (Shringy and Sharma 1978) begins with no less than a hundred pages explaining the relationships of sound, celestial sources, and the human body. Lewis Rowell, in his essential study of Sanskrit writings on music, refers to this in condensed fashion (Rowell 1992:6):

> The most powerful and generally accepted ontological conception of music is rooted in a profound cultural metaphor, in which the emanation of vocal sound from deep within the human body has been linked with a process of creation as a "bringing forth" of the divine substance that lies at the heart of our innermost being.

Modern Indian musicians and theorists tend to suspend comment on the practical importance of this type of metaphysical elaboration; however, far from a refutation, such silence usually only hides great reverence for the infinite possibilities of music and a profound respect for the forefathers of the tradition, even if the specifics of the ancient and detailed lists mystify most modern musicians and music lovers. Contemporary practitioners' more casual inquiry into the past does not invalidate their veneration: at the very heart of the tradition lies a reverential sense of the sanctity of antiquity. In music, as in other areas of Indian tradition, old is infinite. Old is good. Old is true.

A second aspect of the larger, more cosmic idea of raga is the notion that the rendering itself is considered a spiritual practice, the practitioner a yogi whose discipline consists of meditatively managing a devotional musical process. The unfolding of the raga is often likened to that of a flower opening or seed awakening and growing. Although this dimension of raga belongs properly to the discussion of performance practice below, it should be noted that the ultimate nature of this musical practice is considered by many to have the lofty personal goal of *mokṣa*—liberation, salvation, and release. Hence the musician practices a multifaceted role: beyond his or her worldly duties as a performer and entertainer, he or she is on a very personal spiritual path, in which the ragas are the mantras, the sacred formulae of meditation. The musician has taken a role of priest and *guni* 'learned one', who maintains a sacred literature and storehouse of technique, as suggested in the words of the legendary instrumentalist Allauddin Khan (Dhar-Chowdhury 1982:41):

> Do you know what true music is? To a musician, music should be the Supreme Deity who will be worshipped with the eagerness of an undivided mind, and tears shall be his ritual ingredients.

A central idea in the cosmology is the sacredness of sound itself (a concept that derives from Vedic thought); *sruti* 'hearing' the scriptures was considered as important as actually understanding them. Indeed, due to the archaic language, poetic constructions, and formulaic permutations of the verses, the meaning of any given Vedic recitation could easily be lost on everyone but its professional reciter. From ancient times, sound (*nāda*) itself has been looked on as a manifestation of the divine, and has been regarded as *Nāda-brahman* 'the language of God'. A recital of a raga still begins with this principle in mind (Shringy and Sharma 1978:108–109):

> We worship *Nāda-brahman,* that incomparable bliss, which is immanent in all the creatures as intelligence and is manifest in the phenomenon of this universe.

Thus was the learning of the ancient writers summarized in the famous thirteenth-century treatise *Saṅgītaratnākara*. Sarngadeva, its author, drew on a written theoretical tradition, already at least a thousand years old, that provided him with detail in its descriptions and, more important, flexibility in its guidelines, thus enabling the tradition to accommodate future additions to the literature and practice of music.

FIGURE 1 Notes and their associated colors, animals, and gods, according to the first-century treatise *Nāradīyaśikṣā.*

Name of Note	Color	Source	Patron
Ṣaḍja (Sa)	lotus colored	six parts of the body	Brahma
Ṛṣabha (Re)	parrot colored	bull	Agni
Gāndhāra (Ga)	golden	goat	Soma
Madhyama (Ma)	jasmine colored	curlew	Vishnu
Pañcama (Pa)	black	cuckoo	Brahma
Dhaivata (Dha)	yellow	horse	Kshatriyas (warriors)
Niṣāda (Ni)	all the above	deer	Yakshas (demons)

One of the earliest pieces of writing devoted to music was the first-century *Nāradīyaśikṣā* (Banerji 1983), a short treatise on the chanting of the Sāmaveda that associates the seven pitches (generally accepted as a diatonic scale, probably the medieval Dorian mode) with colors, animal sounds, and gods (or other patrons) (figure 1).

Since there was no necessity to develop the concept of absolute pitch at this time, exemplified by such later notions as the Western A = 440 cycles per second, these relationships must be understood as relative pitches. The natural associations of pitches in the *Nāradīyaśikṣā* was a tradition that was greatly augmented by later writers. By A.D. 1500, there were several such systematic cosmologies in circulation, often with contradictory color and natural associations. (For a comparative chart, see te Nijenhuis 1993:6)

Mood: The theory of rasa

The most important of the early treatises that include discussions of music is the *Nāṭyaśāstra*, which is attributed to a scholar named Bharata who lived during the early centuries of the Christian era. Though dealing primarily with the dramatic arts, it included chapters on the combined arts of singing, instrumental music, and movement (dance and drama), calling them *saṅgīt*, a word used by later authors to refer to music alone. In the course of trying to correct perceived excesses in sacred-drama performance practice, Bharata described the dramatic and musical arts in great detail. In chapter 6 of the *Nāṭyaśāstra*, he codified the aesthetic nature of the arts of *saṅgīt* into a theory of *rasa* (Sanskrit, 'juice', 'sap'), which is essentially a list of eight primary moods (Rangacharya 1986:39) (figure 2).

The similarities between figure 1 and figure 2 are striking, in associating pitch with colors and deities on the one hand, and moods on the other. Abhinavagupta, a later commentator (eleventh century), added a ninth *rasa*: *śānta* 'peace', stating that a dramatic performance would be complete if it included the eight *rasa* and left the audience with the feeling of peace. The concept of the *nava rasa*, the classical "nine moods," has been a central aesthetic feature of the performing arts ever since.

FIGURE 2 The eight moods (*rasa*) and their associated colors and deities as listed in the *Nāṭyaśāstra*.

Rasa	Translation	Color	Deity
śṛṅgāra	love	dark blue	Vishnu
hāsya	humor	white	Pramatha
raudra	anger	red	Rudra
karuṇa	compassion	pigeon color	Yama
vīra	valor	yellowish	Mahendra
adbhuta	wonder	yellow	Brahma
vībhatsa	disgust	blue	Mahakala
bhayānaka	fear	dark	Kala

Perhaps for ease of classification, writers assigned relationships to ragas according to their male and female aesthetic qualities, grouping them into families with husbands, wives, sons, and grandsons.

But the moods of Bharata and Abhinavagupta were designed to describe dramatic arts and dance; musicians used only a portion of this list to identify the moods of a raga. Thus one finds no angry ragas, or disgusting, fearful, or wondrous ones (or rather, every raga is filled with wonder). The dramatic effect of performance in one of the latter *rasa* can certainly be enhanced by music, but there are no specific ragas that embody them. Love, compassion, laughter, valor, and peace: these are the moods the classical sources use to describe raga affect.

Musicians today also normally use several other words to describe raga moods. Among these are *bhakti* 'devotion', the more pietistic aspect of the *śṛṅgāra* 'love' mood. The link between bhakti and *śṛṅgāra* is age old in Indian philosophy, personified in the love-play (*līlā*) of Lord Krishna and the milkmaids of Vrindavan, a favorite metaphor of the bhakti poets of the fifteenth through seventeenth centuries. Their poetry is frequently used in song texts, and this playful ambiguity of mood, a union of divine and erotic love, is a favorite of musicians.

Tyāga 'renunciation' is used to describe those ragas suited to personal devotions. Often a musician will suggest that only certain compositions within a raga convey strong elements of bhakti and/or *tyāga;* they may also maintain that the sincere feelings of these two moods cannot be conveyed in concert situations, owing to the conflict of private devotion with public entertainment. The word *chamatkāri* 'marvelousness' describes the effect of wonder or surprise achieved by a raga rendition in which a certain note or phrase is delayed and then presented with special care as a sudden revelation. In addition, ragas are described in terms of their basic nature (*prakrit*): either *gambhīr* 'solemn' or *chanchal* 'restless'. Of our chosen examples, *rāg darbārī kānaḍā* is considered to be a *gambhīr* raga; it is played in the late evening, and its moods are those of devotion, peace, pathos, and heroism. A regal quality, here spoken of as "heroism," can be inferred from the name *darbārī kānaḍā* 'Southern court'; the raga was said to have been a composition of the famous Tansen of the grand court of the sixteenth-century Mughal Akbar the Great. *Jaunpurī* is less grand, although it is still devotional, and is rendered in the late morning. Its moods are pathos and love.

In their personal vocabularies, most musicians no doubt use many recurring terms to explicate the emotional content of particular ragas. Figure 3 presents an overview of ancient and modern words that give a general feeling for the way modern musicians categorize the emotional content of the ragas.

Mood	Translation
gambhīr	serious, solemn
chanchal	restless, flighty
bhaktī	devotion, devotional love
śṛṅgāra	romantic love, eroticism
karuṇa	compassion, sadness
śānta	peace
hāsya	comical, laughter
vīra	heroism, valor
tyāga	renunciation, sacrifice
chamatkāri	marvelousness, surprise

FIGURE 3 Common words used to describe the emotional content of a raga.

Gender and time associations

From a group of treatises written between the seventh and eleventh centuries (the *Saṅgītmakaranda*, *Panchamasārasamhitā*, *Nāṭyalochana*, and *Sarasvatīhṛdayālaṅkāra*), we can see that writers had started to classify ragas according to male and female qualities, to assign them to particular times of day, and to give them specific ritual functions (Gangoly 1989:21–31). A great number of the melodies listed are simply so many names to modern musicians—it is important to note that the ancients did not supply us with the pitch content. Nevertheless, from this time period we do begin to hear the names of the ragas still current today: *bhairav, bilāval, bhupāla, shrī, sāranga, kāmbhōjī*, and the like.

Perhaps for ease of classification, these writers assigned relationships to the ragas according to their male and female aesthetic qualities, grouping them into families with husbands, wives, sons, and grandsons. These came to be called *parivār* 'family' groupings and were quite popular in the early medieval period. Six primary male melodies (ragas) were each paired with five or six wives (*rāgiṇī*), making up a core group of thirty to thirty-six melodies that could be related to times of day, different seasons of the year, and festive functions, as well as to moods and colors. These raga personifications often became quite elaborately symbolic in character. Poetic descriptions (*dhyāna*) were written about such ragas, as for example the following regal sixteenth-century description of *rāg mālkauṅs*, from Rajasthan (Ebeling 1973:118):

> A golden crest is on his head; various sorts of ornaments glitter (on him); an auspicious lion-throne has been arranged (for him); in front of him stands a woman like gold, who has taken *pān* [betel leaf] from a most elegant *pān*-box and felicitates him with it. Behind him a female friend waves a fly-whisk. He is in a house of gold; everything is covered with gold. Happily he eats betel. His body is said to be like gold. His mind is happy—the *Malakosa rāg.*

We have no medieval descriptions specifically mentioning *rāg darbārī kānaḍā* or *rāg jaunpuri*. The following is one for a variant, *rāg kanada,* which captures some of the royal quality of *darbārī kānaḍā* (Kaufman 1968:500):

> Kanada is an impressive regal figure holding a sword in one hand and a tusk of an elephant in the other. The gods and a host of bards are always singing his praises.

By the end of the medieval period, the tradition of associating particular extramusical ideas with particular ragas had become systematized, though the system also encompassed many local variations; many painters produced visual images of ragas grouped in family series called *rāgmālā* 'garlands of ragas', which could comprise as many as a hundred miniature paintings [see RAGMALA PAINTING]. These delightful visual raga associations have always fascinated music lovers, but in the process of their elaboration during this period practical musicians seem to have been left quite far behind. Today many who become enchanted by the magic of these often exquisite miniatures are disappointed when they find that modern musicians have difficulty understanding the aesthetics and associated visual representations of earlier music.

ANCIENT WRITERS AND PITCH THEORY

The *Nāradīyaśikṣā*, the *Nāṭyaśāstra* (first to second centuries, mentioned above in connection with *rasa* theory) and a companion treatise, the *Dattilam*, also provide us with our first extensive look at early "pure" music theory (Banerji 1983; Rangacharya 1986; Lath 1978). In them, the word *rāga* is not used to describe melodic formats; in fact, the word does not even appear in a musical treatise until the *Bṛhaddeśī*, possibly of the ninth century. Nevertheless, the characteristics of a number of melodic types (*jāti*) are expounded on, and these clearly are prototypical of the scale varieties later identified as ragas. Bharata, the legendary author of the *Nāṭyaśāstra*, illustrated his two basic scale classes (*grāma*) by comparing the precise tuning of two arched harps (*vina*); he noted the relationships of the fifth intervals when he induced slight changes in one of the tunings. His experiment has resulted in volumes of controversial literature over the centuries, both on the exact nature of these early scales and the significance of his microtonal tunings (*śruti*).

The fact that Bharata used a harp to explain his theory helps us understand how musicians of his era thought. In playing a harp, which has strings tuned in diatonic pitch sequence, the importance of the interlocking scales (*murchhana*) is quite important: any string may be taken as the starting point for a new scale in which the order of whole and half steps is thus changed. In the same way as the Western medieval modes are successive permutations of each other, interlocking scales have continued to play an important role in the generation and interrelationships of ragas. Furthermore, they are an important aspect of performance practice: they are not realized in the same way as modulated polyphonic music, and yet they create important tonal variety within the raga by aurally suggesting alternative "tonic" notes.

Also, one cannot infer that a drone, such an essential feature of modern Indian classical music, was then in use, for although some of a harp's strings could have been plucked as drones, there does not appear to have been an imperative to return to the fundamental tone (a fixed Sa, *do*, or "tonic"). Bharata in fact described a number of possible final tones in each scale type. The drone, and hence the fundamental tone ("tonic") in its modern sense, became an essential theoretical and practical feature only in the medieval period, when plucked lutes with stopped strings had long superseded harps as the preferred stringed instruments. The *tānpūrā* (*tambūrā*), the stringed drone instrument common to the modern classical ensemble, does not appear as a regular feature in musical iconography until the seventeenth century. During the medieval period there would continue a turning away from the harp-based organizational theories of Bharata and their implied complex system of tuning.

In Bharata's time, a *jāti* system based on two scales, the *sa grāma* and the *ma grāma*, generated other related scales. The basic scale, *sa grāma*, was the same as the Western medieval Dorian mode, nearly the intervallic equivalent of a scale generated on the white keys of a piano from D to D. This is essentially the scale used for the modern-day *rāg kāfī*. In Bharata's *ma grāma*, the tuning of notes of the same name is changed slightly, generating a scale with which ragas in the modern *bāgeshrī* family may have affinities. The resulting scale system was much like the medieval modes of the West, which also interlocked in a similar fashion and were associated with different moods.

Bharata further stated that all these scales were more than simple lists of notes in ascending or descending order: each scale had dominant notes, strong notes, and weak notes. And within each scale were tones recommended as beginning and ending tones for compositions. Additionally, ideas of consonance (*samvādī*, the intervals of a fourth or a fifth) and dissonance (*vivādī*, the interval of a second) were important in early theoretical conceptions and continue to distinguish one raga from another. In *darbārī kānaḍā*, for instance, the *vādī* is Re and the *samvādī* is Pa, whereas in *jaunpurī*, the pairing is Dha and Ga. This is consistent with the usual registration of the two, for it is generally held that morning ragas have their dominant notes in the upper tetrachord (*uttarāng*, Ma to Sa), whereas evening ragas have theirs in the lower tetrachord (*pūrvāng*, Sa to Pa). In actual practice, however, these rules allow for a lot of variation, due to the sprawling growth and "intermarriage" in the raga literature. Often it is impossible to know what the *vādī-samvādī* relationship is in a raga by simply hearing, as expressed in the words of the master musician Ustad Ali Akbar Khan (personal communication):

> Each raga is like a small state. There is a king (*vādī*) who rules with the help of his prime minister (*samvādī*). But all rulers are different. In this state the ruler is

strong, in that one the council makes decisions for the king; in a third the king sleeps all day and the prime minister takes all the money. So you cannot know a raga simply by stating the *vādī-saṃvādī.*

We can see that many ancient characteristics have been carried over into the modern concepts of raga. When we look at the early treatises, we can find the terminology and endless lists confusing, for there are often many undefined terms, unexplained possibilities, and puzzling variations. For example, Bharata states that the final note (*nyāsa*) can come in twenty-one ways (Rangacharya 1986:121), but does not explain how. And there are of course no notated examples.

The author of the *Bṛhaddeśī*, Matanga, was the first musicological writer to use the word *rāga* for what Bharata had called *jāti*. (Sometimes his work is dated in the fifth century.) He did not make much of introducing its use, which suggests that it was in widespread circulation. His purpose was to include under the theoretical umbrella of classical music (*śāstrīya saṅgīt*) regional music and the music of "women, children, cowherds, and kings" (Sharma et al. 1992:5). We gather from his descriptions that this regional (*deśī*) music was primarily in the form of songs—what we would now call folk songs, as opposed to the sacred or dramatic music described by earlier writers. He noted the existence of transilient scale patterns of five, six, or seven notes. Matanga also introduced the term *varṇa*, referring to four kinds of melodic motion: upward (*āroh*), downward (*avaroh*), stable (*sthāī*), and meandering (*saṇcāri*). Matanga's role in India was similar to that of Pope Gregory (who was actually a figurehead for his musical scholars): both examined an existing body of literature and classified it, thereby creating a foundation for later theory—the world of raga on one hand, Gregorian chant on the other.

The great treatise *Saṅgītaratnākara*, of the 1200s, stands out as one of the last writings on the ancient theory in which no distinction is made between the two modern schools we now call North Indian and South Indian, Hindustani and Karnatak music. The *Saṅgītaratnākara* is a classic summation of early theory, which conveys a stronger feeling for the individual ragas themselves and the types of compositions based on them. Some of the vaguer concepts of Bharata become clear in the *Saṅgītaratnākara*, which goes further in the elaboration of its ideas and gives many musical examples. It is clear that the author, Sarngadeva, was working with a theoretical palette that included the twelve modern pitches and described the scales in terms of melodic types (*jāti*), which omitted notes. These were the three types described by Matanga, pentatonic (*auḍav*), hexatonic (*sharav*), and heptatonic (*saṃpūrṇ*). In other words, ragas could be made up of five, six, or seven notes, in ascending or descending patterns; these could also be combined, making nine possibilities in all.

Rāg darbārī kānaḍā is said to be a *saṃpūrṇ jāti*, that is, with all seven notes in its ascent and descent. The elaborate descending scale pattern is not straight but rather *vakra chal* 'crooked movement', following a sinuous path. A straight descent—Sa ni dha Pa ma ga Ri Sa—would be considered a violation or "breaking" of the raga. *Jaunpurī* permits this straight descent of tones but omits the minor third in ascent; hence it has a hexatonic-heptatonic scale pattern (*sharav-saṃpūrṇ jāti*) (figure 4).

The *Saṅgītaratnākara* clarifies the concept of the three registers alluded to by earlier writers, and suggests features of the notation system that are still in common use: a lower register (*mandra*), indicated with a dot under the note; the middle one (*madhyam*), without any marking on the note; and the high register (*tār*), with the dot above the note. Many types of compositions are described, and quite a few notated—although the skeletal rhythmic simplicity of this notation suggests a sing-song regularity in the music that is undoubtedly misleading. Nevertheless, this beacon treatise effectively carries the ancient, flexible principles of raga into the medieval

During the eighteenth and nineteenth centuries, the specifics of the Great Tradition of ancient Sanskrit theory became less and less a part of music practice.

FIGURE 4 The ascending and descending scale patterns of *rāg darbārī kānaḍā* and *rāg jaunpurī.*

rāg darbārī kānaḍā
Ascent: Sa Re ^{ma}ga — ma Pa ^{ni}dha — ni Ṡa
Descent: Ṡa Ṙe ni Ṡa Ṙe ^{ni}dha — niPa ni ma Pa ni ^{ma}ga — Re Sa Re Sa

rāg jaunpurī
Ascent: Sa Re ma Pa dha ni Ṡa
Descent: Ṡa Ṙe ġaṘe Ṡa ni dha Pa ma ga Re Sa

period and ultimately to us. It was a primary reference point for many writers during the next five hundred years.

RAGA IN MEDIEVAL INDIA

In the eleventh century, just before Sarngadeva's era, Islamic conversions and the broad impact of West Asian culture began to have their effect on India. By the time of the generation following Sarngadev, the Ghazni (Turkish and Afghani) court of Allauddin Khilji (1293) was established in Delhi. Although the exact nature of the musical contributions of Khilji's famous court musicians, Gopal Nayak and Amir Khusrau, may be difficult to trace, clearly a new style emerged after this time, born of ancient Indian roots but with new practical ramifications—the accents and instruments of western Asia.

Medieval theorists still felt it important to build their models on the writings of the ancients as summarized by Sarngadev. They carried forth the old ideas and copied out the taxonomies, and the *parivār* system of raga classification enjoyed great popularity in the artistic and courtly imagination. However, for these writers the archaisms of ancient theory and the realities of contemporary practice were problematic; they remain so to this day. This rift was exacerbated by the cultural changes sweeping North India, as many of the most important patrons of the arts were Muslim, especially after the founding of the Mughal court in Delhi-Agra in the sixteenth century. Mughal artists set the style trends in musical presentation. At the same time that West Asian fashions were a part of court life, the traditions that these regal emperors nevertheless became immersed in for diversion and edification—and which they ultimately absorbed so thoroughly—were largely Hindu in origin. In the important spiritual realm (ever intertwined with music in India), the Hindu bhakti movement emphasized a personal devotion expressed in common languages as against a formal kind of religion presided over by a Sanskritized priesthood. A mystic branch of Islam, Sufism, also seized on the intoxicated spirit in the poetic and musical expression of a similar fervor to bend the orthodoxy of Islam toward a more tolerant and personal religion; this appealed strongly to many musicians. If Matanga in the ninth century first argued for the incorporation of the *deśī* music into the classical theory, eight hundred years later it was again the song of the people that clamored to gain entry into the sacred spaces of the musical canon. It is to the credit of the ancient theorists that there was room for these new ideas.

Raga classification always lay at the heart of the theorists' reaction to changes in musical practice. Relating ragas to one another in family organizations (the *parivār* system) was convenient, practical, and useful for teaching. The legendary musician in the great Mughal emperor Akbar's court, Miyan Tansen, subscribed to the grouping of the Hanuman school, one of four (or more) scholarly traditions (*mat*): *Shiv-mat, Kallinath-mat, Hanuman-mat, Bharat-mat*, and so on. In the Hanuman *mat*, the six male ragas were *hindol, shrī, bhairav, megh, mālkauns*, and *dīpak*. Also in the late 1500s, the respected theorist Pundarika Vitthala suggested the list should include *hindol, shrī, bhairav, deshkār, naṭ*, and *naṭ-narāyan*; the last three ragas of the two lists are different, which makes but one illustration of the frequent disparities among classification systems. Furthermore, it is often difficult to understand the bases for such classifications. Should all morning ragas relate to *rāg bhairav* because of their similar time? Or should ragas be related by mood or pitch content? During the medieval period, music theorists started to think in terms of parent scales based solely on pitch. Ramamatya, writing in 1550, departs from the husband-wife associations in favor of father (*janaka*) scales and their offspring (*bhāsā*). In a second, later treatise by Pundarika Vitthala, nineteen parent scales are suggested.

In the seventeenth century, the separation into Northern and Southern musical styles—which had been present in the preceding centuries due to the overlay of Persian social and artistic conventions in the North—became theoretically established with the writings of Venkatamakhi, a South Indian [see KARNATAK RAGA]. This system was eventually accepted as the theoretical basis for modern Karnatak music, but the response to it has been mixed in the North. Many musicians today see it as an objective, comprehensive structure relating scales that otherwise have no logical relationship to any existing Northern system. Others use the system to find new combinations of notes, generating other new or long-forgotten ragas. Venkatamakhi's creation of two successive minor seconds in his scale system (Sa ri Ri and Pa dha Dha) was uncommon in raga literature; this, along with the sweeping away of the emotional and old family associations, was enough to render the novel system suspect to many theorists and musicians. In addition, the perennial veneration of old ideas, so basic to India, makes many musicians wary of new systems, even one like this, now nearly four hundred years old.

Other seven-tone scale systems have been proposed, such as the thirty-two-*ṭhāṭ* 'framework' system (Jairazbhoy 1995:46–47, 181–185), which systematically configures all possible combinations of sharps and flats (but only one form of each per scale) starting with a "natural" (Western major) scale. It, too, has had limited acceptance, for similar reasons: all such systems grow from mathematical permutations of the notes, and not out of a response to the musical literature.

THEORY AND PRACTICE IN RECENT CENTURIES

During the eighteenth and nineteenth centuries, the specifics of the Great Tradition of ancient Sanskrit theory became less and less a part of music practice. Part of the reason was pragmatism: why would a Muslim musician want to spend his time learning Sanskrit, an archaic language of the Hindus, when he himself was master of a living tradition within which an Islamic voice had been prominent for several hundred years? Moreover, a literature in Persian was accumulating, some of it translations of Sanskrit source materials. More immediately, it was the practice to incorporate the lessons of the ancients into the texts of special songs about music, in which the history and theory became the topic of the songs, rather than for musicians to explain these to their students. Such song texts have been used for centuries as an educational tool by the inner circle of teachers and students; although the texts are not elaborate, they serve as springboards for discussion. As late as the 1860s, we can see that theory played a backseat role for the practical musician, as seen in this description of a lesson with the Hindu vocal master Balkrishna Bua (Deodhar 1973):

> The students got the [lessons] at the guru's residence in the morning, and more often at night. All of them, the juniors and the seniors, learnt together simultaneously. They were not permitted to sit comfortably, but had to sit in the kneeling position in a semicircle in front of the guru, seniors to the fore and juniors to the rear. Guru-ji would teach the compositions but rarely, if ever, tell the name of the raga. It was not in vogue in those days to state the rules of the raga, the ascent and descent scale patterns, the prominent scale pitches (*vādī-samvādī*), etc. Theory, latent in practice, was not analytically conceived as a separate entity to be taught to the students. They learned whatever the teacher taught, and writing the lesson was taboo. No one could ask questions, and if one were so bold as to do so, one courted expulsion from the house.

With the twentieth century came a new perspective on the ancient musical traditions. The noted musicologist, lawyer, and educator Vishnu Narayan Bhatkhaṇḍe looked toward the future of India and saw a need for a simpler, less cumbersome, more practical approach to theoretical matters. The age-old gulf between practice and theory still persisted, as well as the break with the written traditions of the past that had started in the medieval period and had become more strident in the eighteenth century. And looking around him, Bhatkhande saw that musicians of his era were as reluctant to part with the techniques of their craft as they were incapable of explaining the theoretical bases for them. He deemed these attitudes to be fragile postures for the maintenance of the illustrious tradition. Wishing to save the music from getting crushed by the steamroller of the emerging new world order that India was intent on joining, he developed a comprehensive, streamlined new theory and a new basis for raga classification. He collected six volumes of songs from many sources, as reference depositories for the ragas. He wrote books explaining his theoretical ideas and composed songs for students that explained the characteristics of the music (*lakśaṇa gīt*). He also opened schools throughout North India to teach the basics of music.

Most important among Bhatkhande's theoretical contributions is his system of ten *ṭhāṭ*, which has had wide acceptance. Today they are memorized by every student of Hindustani music. The virtue of his system is its simplicity; it is easily learned. He took ten common ragas and made seven-tone (heptatonic) scales in which every pitch was neutral with respect to directional implications; every scale, as a whole, was devoid of emotional or temporal associations. It is easy to see that the ragas *darbārī kānaḍā* and *jaunpurī* are related to Bhatkhande's *āsāvarī ṭhāṭ*; the basic pitch collection is the same (figure 5).

The difficulties of this system are the same ones that have plagued musicians since at least the time of Matanga (ninth century): the corpus of ragas is so vast and disparate that to relate it to ten framework scales inevitably creates a host of anomalies
TRACK 1 and ambiguities. The common ragas *bhūpālī* and *kāmod*, for example, with the pitches Sa Re Ga Pa Dha Ṡa and Sa Re ma Pa Dha Ni Ṡa (with Ma and Ga in descent), respectively, could be classified in *kalyāṇ* or *bilāval ṭhāṭ* (musicians generally relate them to *kalyāṇ*). Other ragas, such as *ahīr bhairav* (Sa re Ga ma Pa Dha ni Sa), seem to sit astride more than one *ṭhāṭ*.

Many musicians and scholars have still not embraced Bhatkhande's theories and methods, sensing in them a compromise that fully encompasses neither the ancient

FIGURE 5 The ten scale types (*ṭhāṭ*) of Bhatkhande.

Kalyāṇ	Sa	Re	Ga	Ma	Pa	Dha	Ni	Ṡa	
Bilāval	Sa	Re	Ga	ma	Pa	Dha	Ni	Ṡa	(Western major scale)
Khamāj	Sa	Re	Ga	ma	Pa	Dha	ni	Ṡa	
Kāfī	Sa	Re	ga	ma	Pa	Dha	ni	Ṡa	
Āsāvarī	Sa	Re	ga	ma	Pa	dha	ni	Ṡa	(Western natural minor scale)
Bhairavī	Sa	re	ga	ma	Pa	dha	ni	Ṡa	
Bhairav	Sa	re	Ga	ma	Pa	dha	Ni	Ṡa	
Toḍī	Sa	re	ga	Ma	Pa	dha	Ni	Ṡa	
Pūrvī	Sa	re	Ga	Ma	Pa	dha	Ni	Ṡa	
Mārvā	Sa	re	Ga	Ma	Pa	Dha	Ni	Ṡa	

theoretical contributions nor the traditional ways of thinking of trained artists. Some who reject the *ṭhāṭ* theory prefer raga family groupings, whether based on common melodic ideas or seasonal and mood affinities.

In summary, it would be a mistake to think that there is today one Hindustani raga theory or classification system to which all musicians subscribe. The ancient writers talked of time and emotional qualities, pitch-content classifications, and strong- and weak-note attributes of melodic configurations that may have run the gamut from simple scale formations to extended compositions. In essence, it is the same today. A student is instructed to keep in mind the characteristics that theoretically describe a raga (see "Theoretical Terms" above) when he or she chooses one to perform. The modern teacher is likely to emphasize a few of these as he or she imparts the compositions in a particular raga to the student over time.

A sampling of Hindustani ragas in letter notation

The letter notation system for Indian music, here adapted to Roman letters, employs the abbreviated Sanskrit pitch names. An initial upper-case letter indicates the higher form of a note (*tīvra*), while an initial lower-case letter indicates the lower form of the note (*komal*). Since there is only one Sa and Pa (always spelled with initial capitals), the twelve notes of the chromatic scale, here compared with a scale starting on the Western C, can be rendered as below. Indian classical music is usually thought of as being in three registers—low, middle, and high. A dot above the pitch name indicates the upper register, a dot below indicates the lower register, and the middle register has no dots.

Sa	re	Re	ga	Ga	ma	Ma	Pa	dha	Dha	ni	Ni	Ṡa
C	D♭	D	E♭	E	F	F♯	G	A♭	A	B♭	B	C

The Hindustani ragas presented in figure 6 are grouped to show structural similarities in their ascending and descending scale patterns. Ragas of *sandhiprakāś* (literally 'the meeting of the light') are those traditionally performed at dawn and dusk. These ragas (see figure 6*a*) often have the augmented second between the second and third degrees of the scale (re to Ga) and then again between the sixth and seventh degrees (dha to Ni). In the morning, the natural fourth (ma) is stronger than the raised fourth (Ma); in the evening, the opposite is true.

RAGA PERFORMANCE

Tuning the notes

In sitting to play or sing a raga, the musician first turns his or her attention to the tuning of the pitches of the particular raga. For the serious musician, this is a meditative process that continues with great intensity throughout the rendering. It is often mystifying for an uninitiated listener to watch as a performer takes great care in get-

It is often mystifying for an uninitiated listener to watch as a performer takes great care in getting the tuning of the instruments correct before the performance begins.

FIGURE 6 A selective list of Hindustani ragas, presented in Indian letter notation and grouped according to scale structure.

a. Ragas of *sandhiprakāś*:

Dawn ragas:

bhairav

Sa re Ga ma Pa dha Ni Ṡa   Ṡa Ni dha Pa Pa dha Pa ma Ga ma Pa Ga ma re Sa

ahīr bhairav

Sa re Ga ma Pa Dha ni Ṡa   Ṡa ni Dha ni Dha Pa Dha Ga Pa ma Ga ma re Sa Ḍha ṇi re Sa

rāmkalī

Ni Sa Ga ma Pa Ma Pa dha Pa dha Ni Ṡa   Ṡa Ni dha Pa Ma Pa Ga ma re Sa

TRACK 2 *bairāgī*

Sa re ma Pa ni Ṡa   Ṡa ni Pa ma re Sa

Sunset ragas:

pūriyā dhanāshrī

Ṇi re Ga Ma Pa Ma dha Ni Ṡa   Ṡa Ni dha Pa Ma dha ṙe Ni dha Pa Ma Ga Ma re Ga re Sa

pūrvī

Ṇi re Ga ma Ga re Ga Ma Pa Ma dha Ni Ṡa   Ṡa Ni dha Pa Ma Pa Ma Ga   Ma Ga re Sa

nārāyaṇī

Ṇi Sa Ga Ma Pa Ni Ṡa   Ṡa Ni Pa Ma Ga Ma Ga re Sa

mārvā

Ṇi re Ga Ma Dha Ni ṙe   ṙe Ni Dha Ma Ga re Ṇi Ḍha re Sa

b. Four ragas of the *bilāval* family primarily use tones of the Western major scale.

Morning ragas:

alhaiyā bilāval

Ṇi Sa Ga Re Ga Pa Dha Ni Ṡa   Ṡa Ni Dha ni Dha Pa Dha ma Ga Re Ga ma Pa ma Ga Re Sa

devgirī bilāval

Sa Ṇi Ḋha Sa Re Ga ma Ga Re Ga Pa   Pa Dha Ni Ṡa   Ṡa Ni Dha Pa ma Ga ma Ga Re Sa

Evening ragas:

durgā

Sa Re ma Pa Dha Ṡa   Ṡa Dha Pa ma Re Sa

hemant

Sa Ga ma Dha Ni Ṡa   Ṡa Ni Dha Pa Dha Ni Pa Dha ma Pa Ga Ga ma Re Sa

(continued)

FIGURE 6 *(continued)* A selective list of Hindustani ragas, presented in Indian letter notation and grouped according to scale structure.

c. Four ragas of the *āsāvarī* family primarily use tones of the Western natural minor scale.

Morning ragas:

āsāvarī

Sa Re ma Pa dha Ṡa   Ṡa ni dha Pa ma ga Re Sa

jaunpurī

Sa Re ma Pa dha ni Ṡa   Ṡa Ṙe ġa Ṙe Ṡa ni dha Pa ma ga Re Sa

Evening ragas:

darbārī kānaḍā

Sa Re ma ga ma Pa ni dha ni Ṡa   Ṡa Ṙe ni Ṡa Ṙe dha ni Pa ni ma Pa ni ga Re Sa Re Sa

aḍānā

Sa Re ma Pa dha ni Ṡa   Ṡa ni dha Pa ni Pa ga ma Re Sa

d. Four ragas have similar ascent and descent patterns but use different forms of the pitches.

bhīmpalāsī

ṇi Sa ga ma Pa ni Ṡa   Ṡa ni Dha Pa ma ga Re Sa

paṭdīp

Ṇi Sa ga ma Pa Ni Ṡa   Ṡa Ni Dha Pa ma ga Re Sa

multānī

Ṇi Sa ga Ma Pa Ni Ṡa   Ṡa Ni dha Pa Ma ga re Sa

madhuvanti

Ṇi Sa ga Ma Pa Ni Ṡa   Ṡa Ni Dha Pa Ma ga Re Sa

e. The following three ragas are traditionally associated with the rainy season.

megh

Sa Re ma Pa ni Ṡa   Ṡa ni Pa ma Re Sa

deś

Sa Re ma Pa Ni Ṡa   Ṡa ni Dha Pa ma Ga Re Sa

TRACK 3 *miyāṅ malhār*

Sa Re Pa ma Pa .ma Pa ni Dha Ni Ṡa   Ṡa ni Pa ma Pa Dha Pa ga ma Re Sa

ting the tuning of the instruments correct before the performance begins ("Why didn't they take care of that backstage?"), or stopping suddenly midway to make adjustments, bringing the momentum to a halt. In a similar manner, right in the middle of a performance, a musician will often return to the simple intonation of the tonic note, Sa, to reestablish this prime point of reference. Again, to a new listener, this will most likely seem to halt or mar the onward flow and developmental sense of the performance. To the performer, however, it is a return to, a reminder of, the essence of what he or she is trying to create; a performance without such returns may well be viewed as careless. Tuning the notes of the raga is metaphorical, as the musician puts himself in tune with the raga, which is of course regarded as a vehicle for sacred exploration and realization.

Another aspect of tuning is the microtonal nature of the shadings certain ragas require. In *darbārī kānaḍā*, these microtones (*śruti*) are critical to the correct rendering of the raga. The notes Ga and Dha in *darbārī kānaḍā* are not found in the

Western tempered-tuning system. Both are flatter (microtonally lower) than their minor-third and minor-sixth counterparts in Western scales. The third is in fact considerably flatter, but what makes them so different is that both are rendered with a slow and controlled wavering called *āndolan.* Unlike the more rapid vibrato of Western music, the undulations of *āndolan* clearly expose degrees of flatness that would certainly be considered out of tune in a Western minor scale. Correct performance of these waverings is a mark of virtuosity to which most Hindustani musicians aspire.

The performer thus takes great care with the microtonal tuning in the music; it is essential to both getting the raga's aural persona correct and to its proper rendering. This is "natural," which is similar to Pythagorean, tuning; nevertheless the basic twelve pitches remain similar in the Western and Hindustani systems, tempered tuning notwithstanding. Hence, one hears the tempered harmonium (a Western reed instrument similar in mechanics to an accordion) accompanying many classical singers in performance; but one rarely hears a harmonium solo, for the instrument is incapable of the finesse of slide, ornament, and pitch control, and exactness of intonation that are expected. Instruments of the classical tradition are constructed with attention given to the variable placement of the twelve pitches and the ability to slide between them. In modern performance, however, one does often hear the *santūr,* the hammered dulcimer, and other instruments such as the saxophone and even the piano which, despite their limitations, are capable of rendering other aspects of raga—even though they restrict the performer's ability to execute slides and ornaments.

Composition in a raga

How does one learn to perform a raga? The ways of approaching the performance are almost as varied as the elusive raga concept itself. The most common way of imparting a raga to a student is by teaching a fixed composition in it. Compositions are in fact a kind of catalogue of a raga's configurations; one ordinarily learns many compositions in a given raga before one really grasps the movements within it. The fact that one "knows" a few ragas will help in rapidly assimilating others, but one must still practice each composition over and over again until it becomes suggestive of raga movement.

From ancient times, musicians have rendered ragas in two ways—with meter (*nibaddh*) and without meter (*anibaddh*) (literally 'bound' and 'unbound'). Metered compositions have a tala framework, in modern times always marked by an accompanying tabla or *pakhāvaj* drums. There are two unmetered, unaccompanied (*anibaddh*) instrumental forms, *ālāp* and *joṛ.* The former has no ostensible rhythmic pulse; the latter has a pulse but no recurring meter or accent pattern [see HINDUSTANI INSTRUMENTAL MUSIC]. Some teachers will teach *ālāp* as a fixed composition with a looser sense of phrasing but will insist on the relative durations of the pitches, which are necessary for a meaningful musical statement. More commonly, the student will learn compositional skills in *anibaddh* forms only after prolonged studies of *nibaddh* ones.

In the words of the modern sarod master Ali Akbar Khan (Ruckert 1991:4):

> *Ālāp* is like, you go someplace nice for a visit—like you go to France for a vacation. Then you come home and write a letter or tell your friend about where you were—where you stayed, what you did, what you saw, what you ate—like that, the memory of the compositions comes in the *ālāp.*

Simply stated, the fixed compositions are respected as the repository of a raga's configurations. As a snapshot of a family member provides a visual identification of the person, a given composition shows the main details and outlines of the raga. But an old photo album will show many shots of that person in a variety of situations and at different ages in life, thus giving a more profound impression of the person's background, personality, and character. In the same way, a musician who knows many compositions in a raga, or "has a large photo album," will be highly esteemed by his peers or juniors. Collecting compositions from one's teacher, from visiting artists, from recordings, and from concerts—from any source the student can find—yields rewards in the form of a depth of understanding of how a given raga behaves in different musical situations, rhythms, registers, and stages of development.

Compositions in the *dhrupad* tradition are considered a historical watershed concerning conceptions of raga. The word's etymology helps us to understand this position of respect: it is a combination of *dhruva* 'fixed' and *pad* 'verse'. Thus, a *dhrupad* composition was a fixed setting of a song text that was itself a metrical construction, often with as many as four stanzas [see HINDUSTANI VOCAL MUSIC]. A singer would sing each precomposed stanza the same way each time, respecting the composition in the same way a Western singer renders a Schubert song faithfully at every recital. In this way the melodic course of individual compositions became embedded in the minds of musicians, and the songs themselves came to be regarded as authoritative repositories of a raga's melodic characteristics.

The *dhrupad* tradition was in sharp contrast to the other prevailing vocal style, the *khyāl*, compositions in which style varied greatly from one tradition (*gharānā*) to another. In some styles, the composition (*cīz* literally 'thing') is a minimal part of the presentation, often only one or two lines, which are then repeated and freely embroidered with ornamentation. One song is often adapted to fit alternate talas, which involves changing the length of the lines or adjusting the long and short notes to fit the new metric scheme. The compositions are frequently used in this way as springboards for an artist's improvisatory skills with *alankār* 'ornament', *vistār* 'expansion', and *tān* 'melodic runs'. In some *khyāl* styles—notably those of Gwalior, Agra, and Jaipur—the compositions themselves may be more elaborate and held in high regard for their individual melodic, rhythmic, and poetic merit, thus becoming, as in the *dhrupad* style, focal points in a presentation. Indeed, compositions of the Gwalior school have especially high merit in the eyes of many musicians today.

It follows that not all compositions carry the same weight as bearers of the images of raga; besides the issue of style, consideration of factors such as the age, composer, source, dissemination, and purity of rendering of a composition is also part of the discussion. A venerable old song in a raga can sometimes be fine as an individual composition but may no longer convey the feeling of the raga as it is rendered in contemporary practice. In such a case, it would have to be recomposed and adjusted in order to fit a master's conception of the true picture of the raga. On the other hand, if it is said to be a song by one of the greatly admired musicians of the past, it may be rendered intact in spite of its archaic qualities. Since it is common for a composer to sign his name to a song text, it is sometimes easy to identify such old compositions, although the oral tradition can play some tricks with the authority of the original songs, and it is sometimes difficult to say who composed a melody even though the identity of the poet is known.

In any *gharānā*, there is usually a repository of from five to ten compositions that form the basis of that *gharānā*'s conceptions of a given raga. Individual musicians of this school may know many other compositions in that raga of a more peripheral nature, more like personal acquisitions that do not carry the full weight of the *gharānā*'s knowledge and endorsement. Time is often the test: if a composition is rendered for three or more generations, it becomes clearly labeled *gharānādār* 'of the *gharānā*'. Some songs and compositions are widespread in several *gharānā* as well as

As in cooking, a younger artist is likely to stay close to the "recipes," while a mature one will feel freer to innovate and blend, in an interplay of learning, experience, and personality.

over several generations; widespread circulation may give them authority as repositories of the raga's true image.

The personal authority and experience of the performer must also be taken into account. Musicians will typically say, "To hear such-and-such raga, you must listen to so-and-so"; for ragas, though they bear a *gharānā* coat of arms, are truly products of personal research and practice, and have become individually identified with the foremost interpreters. An artist who renders a raga throughout the course of a lifetime will almost invariably change his or her perspectives, presumably adding depth and refining the delivery over the years. The picture of the raga will thus undergo a slow metamorphosis, and anyone clinging to fixed ideas of the identities of *āroh-avaroh*, *vādī-samvādī*, and other characteristics as described in "Theoretical Terms" above (which lag behind performance practice), will definitely be confused by unexpected changes in balance and emphasis. As the same artist renders the raga over and over, the colors change slightly each time, as they do in the famous legend of the nineteenth-century sitarist who was said to have played the same raga for his royal patron on fifty successive evenings, each evening bringing out a new shade.

Raga realization

Starting with a basic conception founded on the knowledge of fixed compositions, an artist builds a raga in performance according to compositional maps provided by his teacher and style. These may be carefully plotted beforehand, or arrived at very spontaneously in performance. As in cooking, a younger artist is likely to stay close to the "recipes," while a mature one will feel freer to innovate and blend, in an interplay of learning, experience, and personality. In this tradition, the greatest artists have often spent vast amounts of formative time first following the precomposed routes—the prodigies, eccentrics, and geniuses notwithstanding.

The way a raga is developed in performance is spoken of in terms of its *baṛhat* 'growth'. In the *dhrupad* tradition, an artist begins with an *ālāp,* an "improvised" invocational unfolding of the raga, first without rhythm and then slowly introducing a pulse that gradually increases in tempo to a fast conclusion, usually in a lax duple meter. Although musicians would be reluctant to admit or follow any strictly imposed meter, in some presentations of the *ālāp* a drummer may even tap a downbeat in slow duple rhythm. In the *khyāl style,* the unmetered section is played over a drumbeat that is often very slow (each beat can be four to five seconds in length) and the melodic materials may relate only loosely to this pulse. This overall pattern of raga presentation—starting with slow and abstract movement and proceeding through a section of slow rhythm that grows more metrical as it accelerates to a presto conclusion—is typical of the *baṛhat* in many Indian styles. Teachers use various metaphors to explain it, ranging from a seed growing to the act of love. The management of this unfolding—for it is a careful process in which any stray note emphases can easily distort the balanced picture of the raga—is an artistic tour de force for a mature musician. In past generations, some musicians specialized in only this part of a performance, and left the *nibaddh* sections to other artists. There are many tales of connoisseurs leaving the performance hall after the *ālāp*, although this is rarely seen today. The implication would of course be that the subsequent sections of the performance would be caught up with the less lofty musical values of accompanied-performance genres—rhythmic games, demonstrations of speed, virtuosity, and stamina—the mere hoopla of entertainment, as opposed to the artistic manipulation of a raga's growth. Indeed, during these lively second parts, it is true that fidelity to the raga can often be left behind in the speed and musical bravado.

In our example, *rāg darbārī kānaḍā,* the microtonal pitches, pauses, and irregular ascending and descending scale patterns dictate a slow and deliberate approach to the raga's unfolding. If these melodic subtleties are attempted at fast speeds, the curves and tunings must be compromised in order to accommodate the velocity. True, *darbārī kānaḍā* is sometimes played today in fast tempos, but older musicians would look on this as infidelity to the true spirit of the raga; in former times it was paired with the similar raga, *aḍānā,* which is usually rendered only in faster speeds. *Jaunpurī,* in contrast, is more flexible and allows for both slow and fast movements; quick tempos with dazzling melodic runs are common in its concluding sections.

Senior artists in both the *dhrupad* and *khyāl* traditions speak of the process of rendering a raga in metered sections also using the term *baṛhat*: namely, that the compositional materials should be generated from and related to the composition on which the performance is centered. Therefore, the image of the raga itself will change according to the composition, which is why the sitarist in the story could play the same raga night after night, each time turning a new page in the collected set of images of one musical format. Now musicians of the older generation smile sadly, often with bitterness mixed with resignation, when they speak of the deterioration of this compositional integrity in the music of the younger musicians. "They are using the same spices for every dish!" they will exclaim. "Everything tastes the same! What has become of the raga? I'll tell you: there is absolutely no raga at all!" In essence, the older musicians are referring to two things: first, that every raga is being put through the same developmental processes, when tradition would suggest that the subtleties of each raga and each composition within it demand highly individual treatment; and second, that the imperious demands of the modern concert hall require that the musician present every raga according to the kind of modern entertainment values that put fidelity to the image of the raga in second place.

Two other aspects of raga are the compass of performance and the shadows (*chāyā*) of related ragas. There are "large" ragas and "small" ragas. Big ones such as *imān kalyāṅ, deś, bhairav,* and *pūriyā dhanāshrī* allow the musician to present many different movements and shadings of color, and have huge compositional repertoires within them. Smaller ones, such as *sāwani kalyāṅ, dhulia malhār,* and *bahāduri toḍī,* may have a restricted delicacy of motion that will not endure extended development. They are like miniatures that must be handled carefully in performance lest they break. For a modern audience to hear one of these ragas is a rare treat, even though, ironically enough, the bulk of the raga repertoire is made up of just such smaller gems.

There may be hundreds of ragas with similar notes, as for instance, those in *khamāj ṭhāṭ.* When an artist is rendering a raga in that scale, he must take great pains to avoid the shadows (*chāyā*) of the many others that might be suggested if he uses prolongations and sequences not suggested by that particular raga's tradition. This would be termed playing out of the raga or "breaking" the raga, and is as much of a sin as introducing notes not within the raga or playing out of tune.

Many are the legends and stories still repeated that warn performers to be respectful of the confines and purity of the raga. One of the most famous is the traditional story of the demigod singer Narada, told here in the words of the author:

> One day Narada was taken to heaven by Lord Vishnu. They entered a room in which there were many graceful and beautiful statues, but each had some defect, marred features or lost limbs. "Who has wrought this terrible destruction?" cried Narada in anguish. "It is you, Narada. These are the ragas. By your insensitive and mindless singing you have ruined many of these beautiful works of art. You must have more respect and sing them correctly." Narada was flushed with horror and vowed to mend his careless ways.

The teaching tradition

To convey any kind of true conception of raga, the transmission of the raga tradition through the *guru-śiṣya paramparā* must be mentioned. In India, the study of music has been primarily the realm of professionals and of those willing and able to devote long hours to practicing. It has never been a common activity among the population at large, although casual interest increased from the 1800s on, following the Western tradition of gifted amateurism in the arts (the foremost example being young ladies studying piano).

Since it is not a written tradition, Indian musical practice must be taught orally. Such an expenditure of energy is not to be undertaken lightly. A teacher does not wish to spend long hours of underpaid time with a young student who, after five years, decides that he or she has had enough and wishes to do something else. Therefore, a traditional period of lax initiation, typically lasting two years, begins the process of learning from a master. During this time, the student hears the lessons of others and helps with the household chores, to get used to the rhythm of the master's lifestyle—but with no direct training from the master. After this period, if the student wishes to continue, a formal initiation takes place in which the student's education—in effect, his or her life—is entrusted to the master in a form of discipleship. A symbolic thread is tied around the student's wrist (*guru-bandh*), and the student's family pledges a monetary gift to the teacher [see The Classical Master-Disciple Tradition]. This bond is for life, and is a solemn trust on the part of teacher and student. Thus, by the time he receives his first lesson, the student has already undergone a test for sincerity. One often hears of such initiation periods today; such stories can be a shock to Western students looking for a teacher and expecting immediate contact and help on the road to perfecting their technical skills. Often they react negatively to the "closed door." But it is an ideal of commitment to the music and devotion to the teacher, and hence to the tradition and to music itself, which is revealed in the very first notes of a raga.

The teacher may give a composition in which the framework and balance of the notes accords readily with popular conceptions of the raga. Or it might be a singular composition in which the features of the raga are barely discernible. The student may not be able to understand which is which without clarification by the teacher. The concepts, patterns, and compositional styles of raga development take years to transmit and years to master. The teacher must be there at every step of the way to breathe life into the process, or else the student can wander astray into the many pitfalls of religious delirium, dry intellectualism, frustrated expression, vapid technical displays, or the distractions of public adulation. It is often a painful learning process, and it should come as no surprise that just as the Western word *disciple* is related to "discipline," the Sanskrit word for scripture and learning, *śāstra,* is etymologically related to the word for punishment.

Musicians say that a raga comes *guru mukh se* 'from the mouth of the guru'.

From the student's point of view this is indeed where the ragas come from. They may be written in books, heard in concerts and recordings, or exchanged between friends. These are by no means invalid forms of communication and learning. However, from the teacher's mouth or playing comes the repeated exposure, the patient correcting, and the sure path through the confusion. An ability to imitate is a great asset to the student, for he or she will spend hours doing just that until the teacher is satisfied with the accuracy, the ornamentation, and the feeling. Is this path the only path? For the student who wishes to walk this traditional route, it might as well be, for the other alternatives are not available to her or him in the long years of endless training. The student gives up a certain personal freedom of speculation and free expression but receives in return, through his or her devotion to the teacher, the nectar of the tradition and the flowering of his or her own music. Someone asked an old musician in a recent interview on Indian television what a true guru was. He said simply, "A guru gives blood."

Nevertheless, it is true that teaching everywhere is changing and opening up in the modern era. For those wishing to begin to learn the lore of raga and its development, there are teachers living all over the globe. Courses are taught in universities, and there are conservatories in India and abroad for those who wish to immerse themselves in the study of the music. A spate of literature about raga and its practice has been published in the last two decades, and the immediate future promises a good deal more. The most important new factors are the electronic media, especially sound recordings, which can be played over and over again to isolate the details of raga melodic and rhythmic configuration by master musicians. Whereas older musicians originally reacted with some horror over this facile imitation of the old system of learning, it is now becoming accepted that these recordings, which are so readily available, do provide a viable tool for repeated exposure and thorough learning. Teachers themselves are instructing the students to seek out this or that recording for its wealth of material from this or that tradition. As the ancients held to be the case, the *saṇgīt sāgar* 'ocean of music' is wide and deep enough to sustain the surface ripples of inevitable changes in style and practice.

REFERENCES

Banerji, Suresh, trans. 1983. *Nāradīyaśikṣā.* Calcutta: Ravindrabharati Visvavidhyalaya.

Bhātkhande, Vishnu Narayan. 1981 [1910–1932]. *Hindustānī Saṅgīt-Paddhati.* 4 vols. Hathras: Sangeet Karyalaya.

———. 1978–1982 [1920–1937]. *Kramik Pustak Mālikā.* 6 vols. Hathras: Sangeet Karyalaya.

———. 1971 [1917]. "A Short Historical Survey of the Music of Upper India." *Journal of the Indian Musicological Society* 2:1–43.

———. 1972 [written 1930]. "A Comparative Study of Some of the Leading Musical Systems of the 15th, 16th, 17th, and 18th Centuries." *Journal of the Indian Musicological Society* 3:1–61.

Daniélou, Alain. 1980. *The Ragas of North Indian Music.* New Delhi: Munshiram Manoharlal.

Deodhar, B. R. 1973. "Pdt. Vishnu Digambar Paluskar in His Younger Days." *Journal of the Indian Musicological Society* 4(2):21–51.

Dhar-Chowdhury, Sisirkona. 1982. "Acharya Allauddin Khansahib." *Journal of the Department of Instrumental Music.* Calcutta: Rabindra Bharati University.

Deva, B. C. 1981. *The Music of India: A Scientific Study.* Delhi: Munshiram Manoharlal.

———. 1986. *Indian Music.* New Delhi: Indian Council for Cultural Relations.

Gangoly, O. C. 1989 [1935]. *Ragas and Raginis.* Delhi: Munshiram Manoharlal.

Gautam, M. R. 1980. *The Musical Heritage of India.* New Delhi: Abhinav Publications.

———. 1987. "The Concept of Rāga in Hindustāni Music." In *Aspects of Indian Music,* ed. Sumati Mutatkar, 13–18. New Delhi: Sangeet Natak Akademi.

———. 1989. *Evolution of Raga and Tala in Indian Music.* New Delhi: Munshiram Manoharlal.

Jairazbhoy, Nazir A. 1995 [1971]. *The Rāgs of North Indian Music: Their Structure and Evolution.* Bombay: Popular Prakashan. With audio cassette.

Jairazbhoy, Nazir A., and A. W. Stone. 1963.

"Intonation in Present-Day North Indian Classical Music." *Bulletin of the School of Oriental and African Studies* 26(1):119–132.

Kaufmann, Walter. 1968. *The Ragas of North India.* Bloomington: Indiana University Press.

Lath, Mukund. 1978. *A Study of Dattilam.* New Delhi: Impex India.

Levy, Mark. 1982. *Intonation in North Indian Music: A Select Comparison of Theories with Contemporary Practice.* New Delhi: Biblia Impex.

Moutal, P. 1991a. *Hindustani Ragas Index.* New Delhi: Munshiram Manoharlal.

———. 1991b. *A Comparative Survey of Selected Hindustani Ragas Based on Contemporary Practice.* New Delhi: Munshiram Manoharlal.

Nijenhuis, Emmie te, ed. 1974. *Indian Music, History and Structure.* Leiden: Brill.

———. 1993. *The Saṅgītaśiromani.* Boston: Brill Academic Publishers, Inc.

Powers, Harold S. 1970. "An Historical and Comparative Approach to the Classification of Rāgas." *Selected Reports in Ethnomusicology* 1(3):1–78.

———. 1976. "The Structure of Musical Meaning: A View from Banaras." *Perspectives of New Music* 14(2)–15(1):308–334.

———. 1981a. "India, Subcontinent of." In *The New Grove Dictionary of Music and Musicians*, ed. Stanley Sadie. London: Macmillan.

———. 1981b. "Mode." In *The New Grove Dictionary of Music and Musicians*, ed. Stanley Sadie. London: Macmillan.

———. 1992. "Reinterpretations of Tradition in Hindustani Music: Omkarnath Thakur contra Vishnu Narayan Bhatkhande." In *The Traditional Indian Theory and Practice of Music and Dance*, ed. J. Katz, 9–51. Leiden: Brill.

Prajnanananda, Swami. 1973. *Historical Development of Indian Music.* Calcutta: Mukhopadhyay.

Ranade, Ashok. 1990. *Hindustani Classical Music: Keywords and Concepts.* New Delhi: Promilla & Co.

Rangacharya, Adya. 1986. *Natyasastra.* Bangalore: IBH Prakashana.

Ratanjankar, S. N. 1952. "Raga Expression in Hindustani Music." *Journal of the Music Academy, Madras* 23:52–61.

Rowell, Lewis. 1981. "Early Indian Musical Speculation and the Theory of Melody." *Journal of Music Theory* 25(2):217–244.

———. 1992. *Music and Musical Thought in Early India.* Chicago: University of Chicago Press.

Ruckert, George. 1991. *Introduction to the Classical Music of North India.* St. Louis: East Bay Books—MMB Music, Inc.

Shankar, Ravi. 1968. *My Music, My Life.* New York: Simon & Schuster.

Sharma, Prem Lata, et al., eds. 1992. *Brihaddesi of Sri Matanga Muni.* New Delhi: Indira Gandhi Centre for the Arts, with Motilal Banarsidass.

Shringy, R. K., and Prem Lata Sharma, trans. 1978–1989. *Saṅgītaratnākara of Śārṅgadeva.* Vol. 1, Delhi: Motilal Banarsidass; vol. 2, New Delhi: Munshiram Manoharlal.

Subbha Rao, B. 1993 [1956–1966]. *Raga Nidhi: A Comparative Study of Hindustani and Carnatic Ragas.* Madras: The Music Academy.

Tarlekar, G. H., et al. 1985. *The Saman Chants.* New Delhi: Indian Musicological Society.

Thakur, Omkarnath. 1938–1962. *Saṅgītāñjalī.* 6 vols. Vol. 1, Lahore; vol. 2, Hathras; vols. 3-6, Banaras.

Van der Meer, Wim. 1980. *Hindustani Music in the 20th Century.* The Hague: M. Nijhoff; New Delhi: Allied Publishers.

Wade, Bonnie. 1979. *Music in India: The Classical Traditions.* Englewood Cliffs, N. J.: Prentice-Hall.

Widdess, D. R. 1983. "Indian Music." *The New Oxford Companion to Music.* Oxford: Oxford University Press.

———. 1995. *The Rāgas of Early Indian Music: Modes, Melodies and Musical Notations from the Gupta Period to c. 1250.* Oxford: Clarendon.

Karnatak Raga

Gayathri Rajapur Kassebaum

In Karnatak music, the term *rāga* encompasses the concepts of scale, mode, tonal system, melodic motifs and themes, microtones, ornaments, and improvisation within a three-octave range. In South India, raga is a major resource for composed (*kalpita*) and improvised (*kalpana*) classical music; it is also a foundation for nonclassical devotional songs (*bhajana*), storytelling traditions such as *harikathā*, temple music, dance music, and light classical music. Versions of ragas appear in film music, and some genres of folk music incorporate traces of ragas.

South India is distinct from the North in its physical, geographical, and cultural makeup, including its musical culture. Karnatak music is the art music common to all four South Indian states—Andhra Pradesh (Telugu-speaking), Karnataka (Kannada-speaking), Kerala (Malayalam-speaking) and Tamil Nadu (Tamil-speaking)—as well as to northern Sri Lanka, where a Tamil-speaking population is concentrated. These regions share the theory and performance practice of Karnatak raga. Compared with northern Hindustani raga performance, southern ragas are shorter on improvisation (*ālāpana*), and the ornamentation is more rapid.

Historically, the southern area made contact with the outside world through maritime trade; it remained more or less isolated from the overland invasions from Asia minor that periodically changed and reshaped North India. This relative isolation led to distinct styles of architecture and music, dance and drama. Oral tradition, however, transmitted by students of composers and performers, provides evidence that musicians were mobile. Interaction between North and South Indian performers took place through the royal courts, particularly those of Tanjore (now Thanjavur) and Mysore, where musicians of both traditions received patronage. The two performing traditions exhibit evidence of borrowing and adopting ragas.

RAGA CHARACTERISTICS

Tonal relationships and melodic movement in Karnatak raga are linear and horizontal in contrast to the harmonic and vertical relationships central to Western classical music. South Indian raga evolved over centuries, its distinct character established by the thirteenth century. Throughout its history, composers and performers have been

Ragas are associated not only with a mood or passion, but also with a time of day.

continually creating and recreating ragas through composition and improvisation. The term *rāga* is used in a variety of ways; its meaning is both abstract and elusive.

One meaning of *rāga* is color. Like color, raga has many shades, as many as there are performers. Composers and performers define and redefine specific named ragas. They base these definitions in part on the experience of performing and acquiring musical knowledge from their teachers.

The word *rāga* is derived from the root *rañj*, which means being affected, moved, or delighted. The term thus expresses wide ranges of emotion: feeling, intensity, passion, love, and beauty. It refers to the performance and experience that both informed and not-so-informed listeners share. Ragas *āsāvēri* and *punnāgavarāli,* for example, evoke melancholy, *kīravāni* and *vasanta* ragas evoke serenity, and *nīlāmbari* and *yadukulakāmbhōjī* feelings of devotion. Lakshmana Pillai, a Karnatak performer, wrote in 1912: "Each raga comes and goes with its store of smiles or tears, of passion or pathos, its noble and lofty impulses, and leaves its mark on the mind of the hearer" (Popley 1966:66).

Ragas are associated not only with a mood or passion, but also with a time of day. In theory, a particular raga should be performed at a prescribed time of day or night. This time theory may have derived from the daily routine in Indian households, which is marked by auspicious and inauspicious periods for carrying out particular activities (Popley 1966). Musicians have traditionally believed that performing ragas at a certain time of the day not only increases their auspiciousness but also erases inauspiciousness and brings good luck.

In present-day South Indian concerts, musicians accept the time theory of raga and its principles, but do not diligently practice it. Some traces exist in the theatrical traditions of *kathakaḷi* (in Kerala), *yakṣagāna* (in Karnataka), and *terukkūttu* (in Tamil Nadu), where performers sing certain ragas as background accompaniment for particular mythological characters, to evoke emotions associated with a certain time of day. In *nāgasvaram* 'double-reed pipe' ensembles, players still follow the practice of performing particular ragas at specific hours for temple rituals.

SPECIFIC MEANINGS IN PRESENT-DAY PRACTICE

With every performance, a musician re-creates an individual raga out of melodic material that has specific sound characteristics, melodic shapes and ornaments, and that generates specific moods and emotions. Each individual raga has a definite character, an individual identity, and a name.

The word raga also means improvisation on a melodic entity. In Karnatak music, the term *ālāpana* refers to improvising on a particular raga; however, in the South Indian music world, raga also means nonmetered improvisation. Musicians often refer to the *ālāpana* section of a performance as "raga."

Karnatak ragas consist of pitches (*svara*) arranged in characteristic ascending (*ārōhaṇa*) and descending (*avarōhaṇa*) patterns forming scales. The scale patterns may employ stepwise or oblique motion, a combination of both steps and leaps, or other permutations and combinations.

Each raga has prescribed functional tones. These include a tonal center (*jīva svara*), final tone (*nyāsa*), initial tone (*graha*), weak tones (*alpatva*), passing tones (*bhāśāṅga*), and ornamented tones (*gamaka*), which include a wide range of shakes, turns, slides, and long pure tones (*dīrgha śuddha svara*). Musicians bring out the essence of raga (*bhāva*) by employing characteristic motives (*saṇcāra*) derived from the thematic stock of tonal clusters (*prayōga*). A drone, consisting of the tonic, fifth, and sometimes fourth scale degrees, serves to enhance the microtonal inflections (*śruti*) of the raga, and provides a constant pitch reminder throughout the performance (Neuman 1980; Row 1977).

The raga is a tonal framework with defined individual pitches, characteristic ornaments, and microtonal variations. These characteristics guide performers as they spontaneously create melodic patterns (Rowell 1992).

COMPONENTS OF KARNATAK RAGA

As in a recipe, where certain ingredients are essential, so in South Indian raga, certain sonic elements must be present for a correct performance. These elements are primordial sound (*nāda*), tonal system (*svara*), pitch (*śruti*), scale, ornaments (*gamaka*), and important tones. These individual elements contribute to shaping the South Indian raga (figure 1).

Primordial sound (*nāda*)

South Indian music culture distinguishes between the concepts of organized, cultivated sound (*nāda*), and noncultivated, ordinary sound (*śabda*). The cultivation of *nāda*, one of the basic components of raga, is a much-respected concept in Karnatak tradition. The realization of *nāda* is a crucial aim of composer-performers of the past and present. However, the sound that is audible to human ears is only a fraction of primordial sound. The musician-performer's ultimate aim is not only to perfect the technique of sound production, but to experience, realize, or be united with the primordial, latent sound housed within the human body. Performers often communicate this abstract concept to students when teaching raga performance (figure 2).

Tonal system (*svara*)

The Karnatak tonal system includes seven basic pitches, expressed by sol-fa syllables that represent Sanskrit words: Sa (*ṣaḍja*), Ri (*ṛṣabha*), Ga (*gāndhāra*), Ma (*madhyama*), Pa (*pañcama*), Dha or Da (*dhaivata*), and Ni (*niṣāda*). The tonic (Sa) and the dominant (Pa) are stable tones and remain unchanged in the tonal system. The remaining five tones (Ri, Ga, Ma, Dha, Ni) can be raised (*tīvra* 'sharp') or lowered (*śuddha* 'flat'), making twelve tones in the octave scale. The present-day Karnatak raga system includes another four enharmonic tones: Ga (as the third degree Ri_2),

FIGURE 1 Components of a Karnatak raga.

Term	*Types*
Nāda	sound
Svara	seven, twelve, and sixteen tones in the octave
Śruti	pitch, drone, microtone, and intonation
Scale	ascending (*ārōhaṇa*) and descending (*avarōhaṇa*); interval structure, ornaments (*gamaka*), and tonal hierarchy (*vādi, samvādi,* and *anuvādi*)

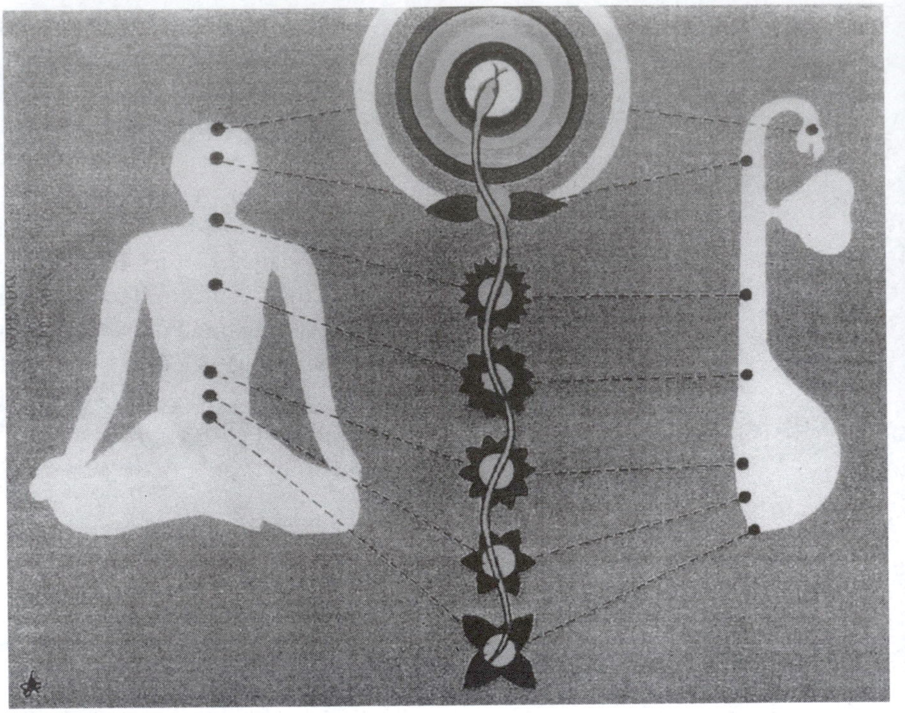

FIGURE 2 A yogic concept of energy and sound centers allied with the sound production of the voice and instruments. From Anantapadmanabhan 1954, plate 4. Published with permission.

Ri_3 (as the fourth degree Ga_1), Ni (as the tenth degree Dha_2), and Dha_3 (as the eleventh degree Ni_1). The octave thus has twelve pitches but sixteen different names (figure 3).

Meanings and contexts of the term *śruti*

Another important component of raga is *śruti*. The word *śruti* appears in both musical and philosophical works in India, connoting what is heard or received. One specific meaning of the word *śruti* is drone. In present-day performance practice, the drone consists of the fundamental tonic pitch (*ādhāra ṣaḍja*), the upper tonic (*tāra ṣaḍja*), and the fifth scale degree (*pañcama*), inclusive of its harmonic series. Occasionally a performer shifts the fundamental tone Sa to the pitch of the fourth scale degree (Ma), raising the fundamental by a fourth in order to expand the octave for certain ragas or to emphasize aspects of a raga in a higher range.

In Karnatak music, the main performer selects the fundamental pitch (*śruti*) according to his or her vocal or instrumental range, and tunes the drone accordingly. The melodic and rhythmic accompanists are then obliged to tune their instruments to the fundamental pitch of the principal performer. This flexible, unfixed pitch (*śruti*) is an important characteristic of the South Indian performing tradition.

A third use of the term *śruti* is to denote microtones. The delicate microtonal inflections are among the elements that make Karnatak ragas different from Hindustani ragas. Furthermore, the twelve intervals in the octave are uneven, and this tonal phenomenon distinguishes Indian music from the Western musical scale. The number of microtones is theoretically uncountable, but performers believe that a trained musician can hear twenty-two *śruti* in an octave (see figure 3). Karnatak ragas have various kinds of tonal inflections and shades that give them shape and character.

A performer also uses the term *śruti* to communicate that his or her instrument is in tune with the drone, as well as with the individual tones and intervals of the raga being performed. In this sense, "being in *śruti*" is a very important component of raga performance.

FIGURE 3 *Svara* and *śruti*: *a*, seven-tone scale system showing Karnatak tones (*svara*), Karnatak syllables, and corresponding Western sol-fa syllables; *b*, expanded twelve-tone scale system showing Karnatak syllables (subscripts indicate *śuddha* 'flat' and *tīvra* 'sharp'), Western equivalent pitches (taking C as the fundamental pitch), and Karnatak/Western enharmonic tones; *c*, Karnatak syllables for the twenty-two unequal scale divisions (*śruti*), with the closest corresponding Western pitches (taking C as the fundamental pitch).

a

1	2	3	4	5	6	7
Ṣaḍja	*Ṛṣabha*	*Gāndhāra*	*Madhyama*	*Pañcama*	*Dhaivata*	*Niṣāda*
Stable				Stable		
Sa	Ri	Ga	Ma	Pa	Dha	Ni
do	re	mi	fa	so	la	ti

b

1	2	3	4	5	6	7	8	9	10	11	12
Sa	Ri$_1$	Ri$_2$	Ga$_1$	Ga$_2$	Ma$_1$	Ma$_2$	Pa	Dha$_1$	Dha$_2$	Ni$_1$	Ni$_2$
C	D♭	D	E♭	E	F	F♯	G	A♭	A	B♭	B
		Ga	Ri$_3$						Ni	Dha$_3$	
		E♭♭	D♯						B♭♭	A♯	

c

S	R$_1$R$_2$	R$_3$R$_4$	G$_1$G$_2$	G$_3$G$_4$	M$_1$	M$_2$M$_3$	M$_4$P	D$_1$D$_2$	D$_3$D$_4$	N$_1$N$_2$	N$_3$N$_4$
C	D♭	D	E♭	E	F	F♯	G	A♭	A	B♭	B

Raga as scale

The contemporary raga consists of an ascending and descending scale pattern. Both ascent (*ārōhaṇa*) and descent (*avarōhaṇa*) must have at least five tones, although some rare ragas have only four tones in either ascent or descent. Raga performance uses the scale pitches but does not present pure scales. A particular raga melody moves in tonal clusters (*saṇcāra*), which act as reference points as a performer explores the tonal material of the raga. Scales provide a tonal boundary and establish rules for melodic performance, rules to which all performers adhere. Typical scale features also help listeners identify ragas.

Interval structure

The interval structure of a raga scale is a basic identifying feature. The important TRACK 4 Karnatak raga *śankarābharaṇa,* often performed in present-day concerts, resembles the Western major scale in its interval structure. In South Indian sol-fa syllables, its scale is Sa Ri$_2$ Ga$_2$ Ma$_1$ Pa Dha$_2$ Ni$_2$ Sa, equivalent to the Western scale tones C–D–E–F–G–A–B–C. The tones Ma$_1$ and Dha$_2$, regarded as flat and sharp in Karnatak music, are considered natural tones (F and A) in the Western system.

Ornamentation (*gamaka*)

Ornamentation (*gamaka*) is essential in Karnatak raga performance. In the broadest sense, *gamaka* encompasses controlled shaking, articulating, sliding, glottal stops, and other vocal or instrumental manipulation. In the Karnatak music tradition, musicians do not conceive of the tone of certain pitches (*svara*) separately from their ornament (*gamaka*). When two ragas have the same scale pitches, the integrally associated ornamentation of certain tones serves to differentiate between the two (Kassebaum 1987). Beyond this distinction, performers also personalize their style by employing ornaments in particular ways for certain tones. This leads to considerable differences in individual styles of singing or playing a raga.

Performers perceive ornaments as part of a raga. Since the performance tradition does not stipulate particular ornamentation for each raga, performers use *gamaka* in a very personal way to express the flavor (*bhāva*) of a raga, to communicate their own feelings, and to evoke emotions in their audience. Students can learn ornaments only from the teacher who has guarded and preserved the technique as a treasure, express-

The integral nature of ornaments in Karnatak raga performance distinguishes it from Hindustani music, in which performers much prefer pure tones and slides to widely ornamented tones.

ing a style of singing raga. Only the ardent and talented students are capable of absorbing the complexities of raga ornaments. The best become master performers and preservers of the guru's raga-performing tradition.

Ornaments (gamaka)

Writers on music from the seventeenth century onward have variously classified *gamaka* into groups ranging from six to twenty-two. Classification schemes of fifteen (*pañcadaśa gamaka*) and ten (*daśavidha gamaka*) became the most widely known. In each scheme, writers assigned each ornament a name and a notational symbol. From the performer's point of view, ornaments generally fall into two broad types: oscillations or shakes (*kampita*); and accents, slides (*jāru*), and glottal stops. Oscillations between two tones range from two shakes to as many as fifteen or more, depending on the raga and the performer's style. Distinct types of *kampita* include three oscillations combined with glottal stops and four or more oscillations combined with wide tonal leaps. There are also many forms of tonal accents and glottal stops. *Rāga śankarābharaṇa* illustrates the complexity of ornaments in Karnatak music.

Ornaments in rāga śankarābharaṇa

Rāga śankarābharaṇa appears in many ancient raga classification systems as well as the relatively recent seventeenth-century theoretical scheme of Venkatamakhi (see below). *Śankara* is another name for the major Hindu deity Shiva; *ābharaṇa* is the name of the serpent that he wears as a neck ornament, which is associated with this raga. All the major and minor Karnatak composers have created compositions in this raga. In concerts, musicians often perform it as an *ālāpana* before a composed piece (*kriti*), as well as in its elaborate form of improvisation (*rāgam-tānam-pallavi*).

Śankarābharaṇa is notable for all its tones (besides Sa and Pa) having some kind of ornament in performance (*jāru* 'quick slide type', *kampita* 'oscillating type', and combinations of accents and glottal stops). Performers ornament the tones Ri_2, Ga_2, Ma_1, Dha_2, and Ni_2, providing different ornaments in ascent and descent (figure 4): thus the direction of a raga melody determines the kind of ornament a tone is given.

In ascent, the second scale degree Ri_2 (D) and sixth degree Dha_2 (A) receive wide ornaments (*kampita*), stretching from their lower to upper neighboring tones before landing on the principal tone (Sa Ga_2 Ri_2 or C–E–D; Pa Sa Dha_2 or G–C–A). The third scale degree Ga_2 (E) and seventh degree Ni_2 (B) receive similar kinds of ornaments (*kampita*), both moving from the lower neighboring tone to the principal tone. The fourth scale degree Ma_1 (F) is artfully oscillated with its lower neighboring tone (Ga_2 Ma_1 Ga_2 Ma_1 or E–F–E–F).

In descent, there are both oscillating (*kampita*) and slide (*jāru*) ornaments combined with a glottal stop. The seventh scale degree Ni_2 (B) starts from the upper neighboring tone and oscillates between two tones (Sa Ni_2 Sa Ni_2 or C–B–C–B), whereas the sixth degree Dha_2 (A) and second degree Ri_2 (D) combine a slide with a glottal stop (Sa Dha_2 Ni_2 or C–A–B, and Ma_1 Ri_2 Ga_2 or F–D–E). The fourth scale

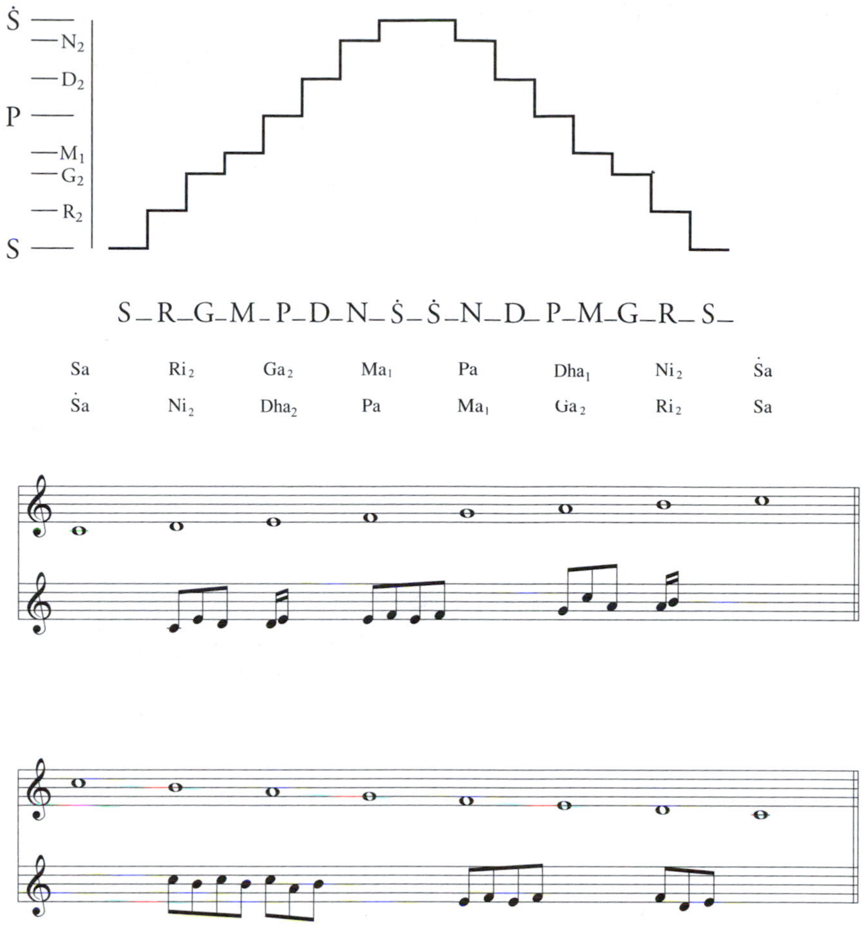

FIGURE 4 Ascending and descending scale of *rāga śankarābharaṇa*: in graphic representation and in Indian solfège, showing interval structure with subscripts; the ornamentation (*gamaka*) integral to the scale pitches is shown in Western notation.

degree Ma_1 has the same ornament as in the ascent. The integral nature of ornaments in Karnatak raga performance distinguishes it from Hindustani music, in which performers much prefer pure tones and slides to widely ornamented tones.

Tonal hierarchy in raga

In all ragas, certain pitches are more important than others, comparable to the role of tonic and dominant pitches in Western music. The most important tone is the *vādi* or *jīva svara* 'soul tone'. Its counterpart is the *samvādi*, a perfect fifth or fourth away from the soul tone. Usually in raga performance, tones a half step from the soul tone are considered *vivādi* 'dissonant' tones. Another tone class is *anuvādi* 'assonant' tones. These help to bring out the essence of the raga, and may be used frequently in some ragas but not in others. Certain tones in a raga are considered weak tones, and are not given prominence. A raga's initial tone (*graha*), final tone (*nyāsa*), and highest tone (*tāra*) also play an important role in shaping the melodic performance. Performers do not usually verbalize tonal hierarchy, but learn it from practicing ragas and imitating the teacher.

Tonal hierarchy in rāga śankarābharaṇa

Rāga śankarābharaṇa provides an illustration of tonal hierarchy: the second, sixth, and fourth scale degrees (Ri_2, Dha_2, Ma_1) are the important tones. Pitch Ri_2 is the predominant *vādi* or *jīva svara*, and Dha_2 is the *samvādi*, a fifth apart from the *vādi*. The fourth degree Ma_1 is hierarchically important, and many characteristic melodic phrases include this tone. Ma_1 may be considered the assonant (*anuvādi*) of *rāga śankarābharaṇa*.

FIGURE 5 Important and ornamented tones in *rāga śankarābharaṇa: vādi* 'soul tone', *samvādi*, *anuvādi* 'assonant', and unornamented tones or tones with accents and slides.

Western scale	C	D	E	F	G	A	B
Rāga śankarābharaṇa	Sa	Ri_2	Ga_2	Ma_1	Pa	Dha_2	Ni_2
Stable tones	X				X		
Vādi with *gamaka*		X					
Samvādi with *gamaka*						X	
Anuvādi with *gamaka*				X			
Unornamented tones, accents, slides			X				X

To balance the ornamented tones, performers sometimes sound the third degree Ga_2 and seventh degree Ni_2 as long held tones. The fundamental tone (Sa) and fifth degree (Pa) are the stable tones; musicians may slide onto them from either the lower or upper neighboring tones but never ornament them with oscillations (*kampita*). *Rāga śankarābharaṇa* has no weak tones (figure 5).

HISTORICAL BACKGROUND

Indian music has its roots in the chanting of metered sacred verses (Sāmaveda). Priests in Vedic times (1500–600 B.C.) sang these sacred chants with tonal inflections and prescribed melodic direction. Present-day raga similarly has prescribed melodic direction, but raga has evolved into a "melody type."

Around the ninth century of the common era, raga seems to have become a separate entity. The author Matanga described raga in his treatise *Bṛhaddeśī* as a collection of pitches, comparing it with a village (*grāma*), a collection of people.

In his *Saṅgītaratnākara*, the thirteenth-century author Sarngadeva introduced the term *jāti*, meaning not only an assemblage of pitches but a scale type with defined characters. The *jāti* was able to generate ragas if the fundamental tone (Sa) was moved to different pitches in the octave scale. The author described two species of ragas with defined interval structures, known as *ṣaḍja grāma* and *madhyama grāma*, as "generating" ragas. This concept of source (or major) scales, and derived (or minor) scales existed in South India long before this time: ancient Tamil musicians of the fourth and fifth centuries, for example, classified ragas as *paṇ* (source) and *tiram* (derived).

Theoretical works on Indian music confirm that what we hear as raga in present-day practice dates back to around the fifteenth century. The fundamental tone Sa became established as the tonic for the whole tonal system. Around the same time, a continuous drone provider was introduced to reinforce the Sa as the fundamental tone and thus stabilize the melodic system (Rowell 1992).

Raga and the Hindu devotional (*bhakti*) movement

In the fifteenth century a great saint, Purandara Dasa, lived in what is now Karnataka state, propagating the concept of surrendering oneself to the divine energy (*bhakti*). Purandara Dasa used raga with his vernacular Kannada texts as a medium to convey *bhakti* concepts to the common people, since the existing Sanskrit texts reached only the literate few, not the unlettered masses. In the process, Purandara Dasa also systematized Karnatak musical practice. He is well known for developing a method of teaching Karnatak ragas to students, a model still used today, with some added components [see KARNATAK VOCAL AND INSTRUMENTAL MUSIC].

Karnatak raga classification

Since the fifteenth century, South Indian theoreticians, much influenced by the

Sanskrit language structure, classified ragas according to a logical and formulaic framework. These writers considered ragas with certain defined characteristics as source (*mēḷa*) ragas. Such ragas served as source material not only for improvising and creating abundant melodic patterns, but for creating other ragas through a process of shifting the tonic (*mūrccanā*) to other scale tones. Scales built on different scale degrees resulted in new scales with different interval structures, called derived ragas.

Venkatamakhi devised a grand scheme for categorizing ragas in his seventeenth-century theoretical work *Caturdaṇḍī Prakāśikā*. He incorporated many features of previous systems and perfected the formula that served neatly as a framework. According to Venkatamakhi's system, there are seventy-two *mēḷa* ragas, and each *mēḷa* has the potential of generating many more ragas. Musicians proudly accept Venkatamakhi's classification as a theoretical system in present-day Karnatak music, but performers do not study the system directly. In practice they learn ragas (both source and derived) from their teachers as clusters of tonal patterns in the form of compositions.

Parent ragas (janaka) *and derived ragas* (janya)

Venkatamakhi divided Karnatak ragas into two categories: (1) parent raga (*janaka, mēḷa,* or *mēḷakarta*), and (2) derived raga (*janya*). The parent raga must adhere to three distinct features: first, the raga must consist of all seven notes (Sa, Ri, Ga, Ma, Pa, Dha, Ni) both in ascent and descent; second, the tones must move in stepwise order, without skips or change of direction; and third, the interval structure must be the same in ascent and descent.

Śankarābharaṇa is a parent raga in Venkatamakhi's scheme. Its ascent and descent have the same seven tones, in stepwise order (see figure 4).

Many derived ragas have existed for centuries, but a few contemporary South Indian composers continue to create new ones. A lively debate on the newly invented ragas appears in Indian newspapers, magazines, and in music conferences. One way of legitimizing a new raga is through scholarly discourse substantiated with musical demonstrations.

Derived ragas can have many varied characteristics. They often take an irregular (*vakra* 'crooked') motion, either in ascent or descent or in both. Some derived ragas take extra tones not belonging to the raga structure. Others are pentatonic, taking five tones both in ascent and descent, or have a hexatonic, six-tone scale. Derived ragas may take an oblique pattern in ascent, and six or seven tones in descent. There are infinite possibilities for producing *janya* ragas (figure 6).

Oral tradition

While theoreticians were constructing a classification system in the seventeenth and eighteenth centuries, composers and performers were simultaneously preserving the raga tradition in their composing, performing, and teaching. Both source and derived ragas existed for centuries before the theoretical system was devised.

Even to this day the performance tradition (*sampradāya*) preserves ragas in compositions (*kriti* and *kīrtana*) and in medleys or garlands of ragas (*rāgamālikā*). Different singing styles prevail among performers, depending on the lineage of major composers or of the composers' disciples (*śiṣya*). Performing traditions follow the raga models of the three major eighteenth-century composers' lineages, those of Muttusvami Diksitar, Syama Sastri, and Tyagaraja. Karnatak musicians greatly revere these three composers for their different interpretations of a single raga. Many disciples of these major composers have contributed to raga development through their own compositions.

Karnatak music consists of two major kinds of repertoire: composed music and music improvised during a performance. Raga and its components are essential for both.

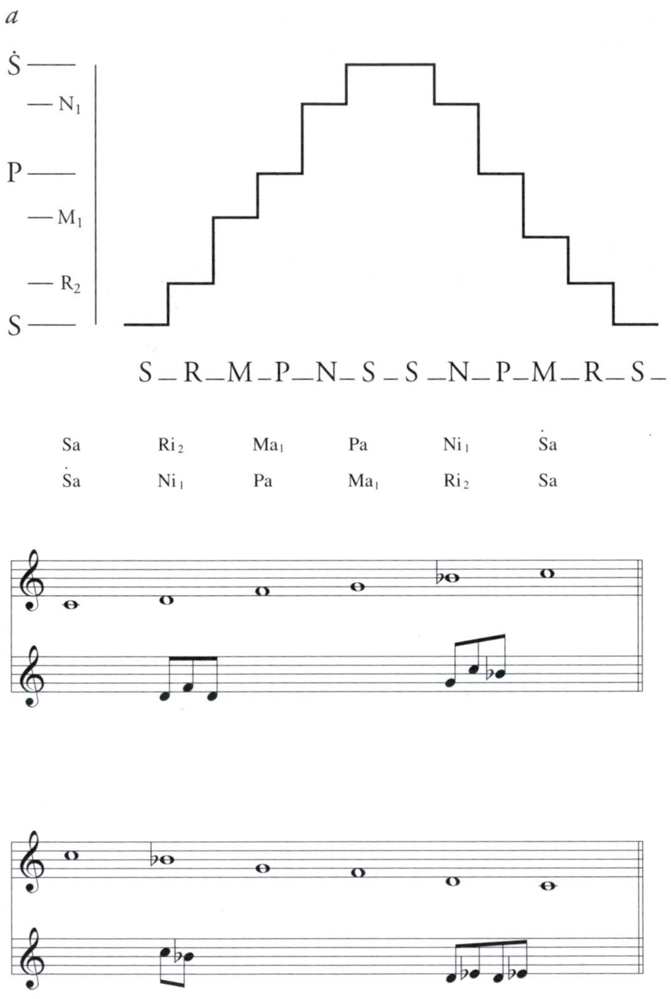

FIGURE 6 Derived (*janya*) ragas: *a*, five-tone *madhyamāvati* and *b*, *rāga pūrvikalyāṇi* with an irregular six-tone ascent and seven-tone descent, shown in graphic representation and Karnatak sol-fa syllables; the ornamentation (*gamaka*) integral to the scale pitches is shown in Western notation.

RAGA IN IMPROVISED FORMS

Karnatak music consists of two major kinds of repertoire: composed music (*kalpita saṅgīta*) and music improvised during a performance (*kalpana saṅgīta*). Raga and its components are essential for both. Composed music embraces a variety of compositional forms. Improvised music, identified as *kalpana saṅgīta* or *manōdharma saṅgīta* 'music of imagination' (terms coined by the musicologist P. Sambamurthy in the early twentieth century), encompasses several types: unmetered improvisation on a raga (*ālāpana*), improvisation on a section of a composition (*niraval* or *sāhitya prastāra*), improvisation using solfège within the time cycle (*svara kalpana*), and nonmetered improvisation on a Sanskrit poem (*śloka*), Tamil poem (*viruttam*), or Telugu poem (*sīsapada*).

FIGURE 6 (*continued*) Derived (*janya*) ragas: *a*, five-tone *madhyamāvati* and *b*, *rāga pūrvikalyāṇi* with an irregular six-tone ascent and seven-tone descent, shown in graphic representation and Karnatak sol-fa syllables; the ornamentation (*gamaka*) integral to the scale pitches is shown in Western notation.

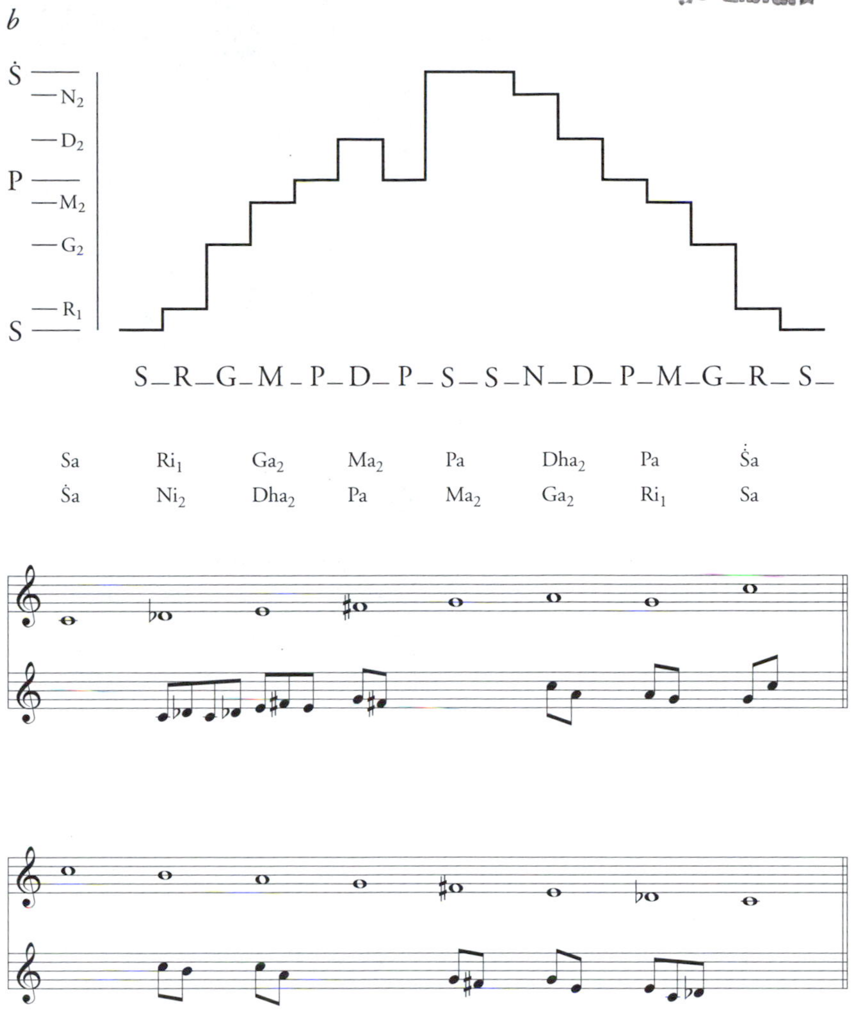

FIGURE 7 Sangita Kalanidhi T. Brinda (d. 1996), a well-known Karnatak vocalist and exponent of *ālāpana*. 1978. Photo by Joseph Thaikkuttathil, used with permission.

Ālāpana is a rhythmically free improvisation performed within the framework of a raga [see KARNATAK VOCAL AND INSTRUMENTAL MUSIC and CD track 4]. The performer's objective in performing *ālāpana* is twofold: to reveal the "essence" of the raga, and to create melodic patterns related to the ascent and descent of the raga scale. A vocalist uses neither text nor sol-fa syllables, only meaningless vocal syllables, and closely follows the raga's characteristics such as interval structure, ornaments, and tonal hierarchy. A well-known Karnatak vocalist and exponent of *ālāpana* was Sangita Kalanidhi T. Brinda (figure 7). Instrumentalists such as the revered flute player T. Viswanathan (figure 8) also perform *ālāpana*, using articulations appropriate to their instrument that closely imitate the vocal syllables.

In *sāhitya prastāra* or *niraval*, improvisation on a section of a *kriti* composition, the performer retains the composed text and tala cycle, but creates melodic variations within the tala structure for which knowledge of and strict adherence to raga idioms is essential.

Another form of raga improvisation, *kalpana svara* or *svara kalpana*, employs solfège and often follows *niraval* in a *kriti* performance. A musician performs solfège improvisation within the framework of a particular tala cycle, and employs raga idioms as in *niraval*.

A vocalist usually sings a Sanskrit, Tamil, or Telugu poem toward the end of a concert by improvising in a *rāgamālikā* 'garland of ragas'. This is nonmetered improvisation similar to *ālāpana*, in which the performer uses the text freely to bring out the essence of the raga and the meaning of the text.

FIGURE 8 Sangita Kalanidhi T. Viswanathan playing the South Indian flute, c. 1992. Photo by Nancy Wooltz, used with permission.

There are three varieties of improvised music, usually performed in sequence: *rāgam-tānam-pallavi*. In this context, the word "raga" (*rāgam*) refers to the nonmetered improvisation *ālāpana,* which is usually longer than the typically brief *ālāpana* preceding a *kriti* composition. The biographies of great nineteenth- and twentieth-century performers such as Pallavi Gopala Ayyar and Maha Vaidyanatha Ayyar show how much concert time they devoted to the performance of *rāgam-tānam-pallavi,* and how well known they were as experts at improvisation.

TRACK 5 *Tānam,* also known as *ghana* 'weight, dignity' or *madhyama kāla* 'medium speed', is nonmetered improvisation with a definite pulse. Vocalists articulate the pulse by singing vocables *anan-tam-tvam*, or *nan-tam-nom* (Sanskrit, 'endless thou') in deep tones. On stringed and wind instruments such as vina, *goṭṭuvādyam*, violin, and flute, musicians employ special plucking, bowing, or lipping techniques to produce the vocable sounds. It is possible to perform *tānam* in any raga, but five in particular—*nāṭa, gauḷa, ārabhi, varāḷi,* and *śrī*—are called *ghana* ragas, and performers often use them to explore *tānam*.

Pallavi is a precomposed piece usually set within one tala cycle. While improvising, a performer retains the basic compositional structure throughout the performance and creates skillful melodic patterns on the original raga or in a garland of ragas.

Learning and performing

To perform *ālāpana* and other forms of improvisation, a student must thoroughly learn the idioms of the raga on which the improvisation will be based. The student
TRACK 6 needs to learn compositions in several genres (*varṇam*, *kriti*, and *padam*, for example) based on one particular raga to grasp fully all of that raga's complexities. Teachers present these compositions to students in levels of increasing difficulty.

Karnatak music is taught aurally. Although twentieth-century composers notate their works in *svara* notation (solfège), the written form is little more than an aid to memorization that has already taken place. Notation serves to assist recall for future reference. Students learn primarily through listening and imitating, not through direct teaching of *ālāpana* (Viswanathan 1977). A teacher may impart, with or without sung sol-fa syllables, short raga phrases as independent units to be imitated but not closely memorized. However, listening and practice may be considered the most important parts of the learning process in the Karnatak tradition. The student listens to the teacher play or sing during lessons and performances, and also listens to performances of other musicians. Through these processes the student develops a mental model of a raga idiom inclusive of all the components of raga. The student further increases competency in performing ragas by learning a large repertoire of composed forms. The ability to improvise evolves naturally, without special effort; at some point in the process the student becomes competent to perform *ālāpana*.

A competent performer has mastered the elements of raga—sense of pitch (*śruti*), sense of time (*laya*), ornaments (*gamaka*), dynamics, aesthetic judgment, use of tones, and voice quality—and is capable of expressing mood and feeling in musical performance. The musician must be in harmony with all these elements, and must have mastered all the vocal or instrumental techniques necessary to perform raga effectively.

Voice quality is an important aspect of vocal *ālāpana* performance. Karnatak performers and audiences highly regard a gifted voice, but also prize a trained voice capable of producing all the techniques required in raga performance. Of the two, mastery of technique is more highly valued: older singers continue to be respected as raga *ālāpana* performers, even if their vocal timbre is no longer youthful.

Within the Karnatak performance tradition, musicians are expected to feel and communicate bhakti (devotion) and *rasa* 'mood'. The two elements of feeling and communicating are not so much separate or independent as complementary. Since mood and feeling are complex and subjective—and to a degree culturally determined, learned, and responded to—perhaps individuals can learn and experience them only through performance (figure 9).

Many generations of South Indian performer-composers have created compositions as a learning tool, and have taught them to their disciples. The disciple absorbs the complexities of ragas both formally, through these excercises, and informally, by spending much time in the teacher's presence and offering personal services to the guru and his or her family. The guru first accepts the student, who must show competence in musicianship (the ability to improvise "on" and "in" a raga) and imbibe other musical behavior and etiquette. Only then does the guru accept the student as a full-fledged disciple (*śiṣya*). The new disciple seeks to gain respect and status as a performer by pleasing first the teacher and then audiences, connoisseurs, and music lovers.

As an experienced performer, the student shoulders the responsibility of preserving and disseminating the guru's musical (raga) style and tradition. Musical lineages through hereditary and nonhereditary musicians have survived and thrived in this manner for centuries.

The normal performing ensemble includes a main performer, the ever-present drone, and an accompanying melodic instrument—vina or violin. The accompanying instrument quite literally follows the principal melodic part, although players occasionally modify melodic phrases, producing a heterophonic texture.

In the past, vina players performed not only as solo instrumentalists but often as accompanists in vocal *ālāpana* performance. After its introduction into Indian classical music in the 1830s, the Western violin proved to be more appropriate as an accompanying instrument because of its flexibility and volume. In South Indian concerts today, the violin is almost always the accompanying instrument for vocal or instrumental *ālāpana* performance.

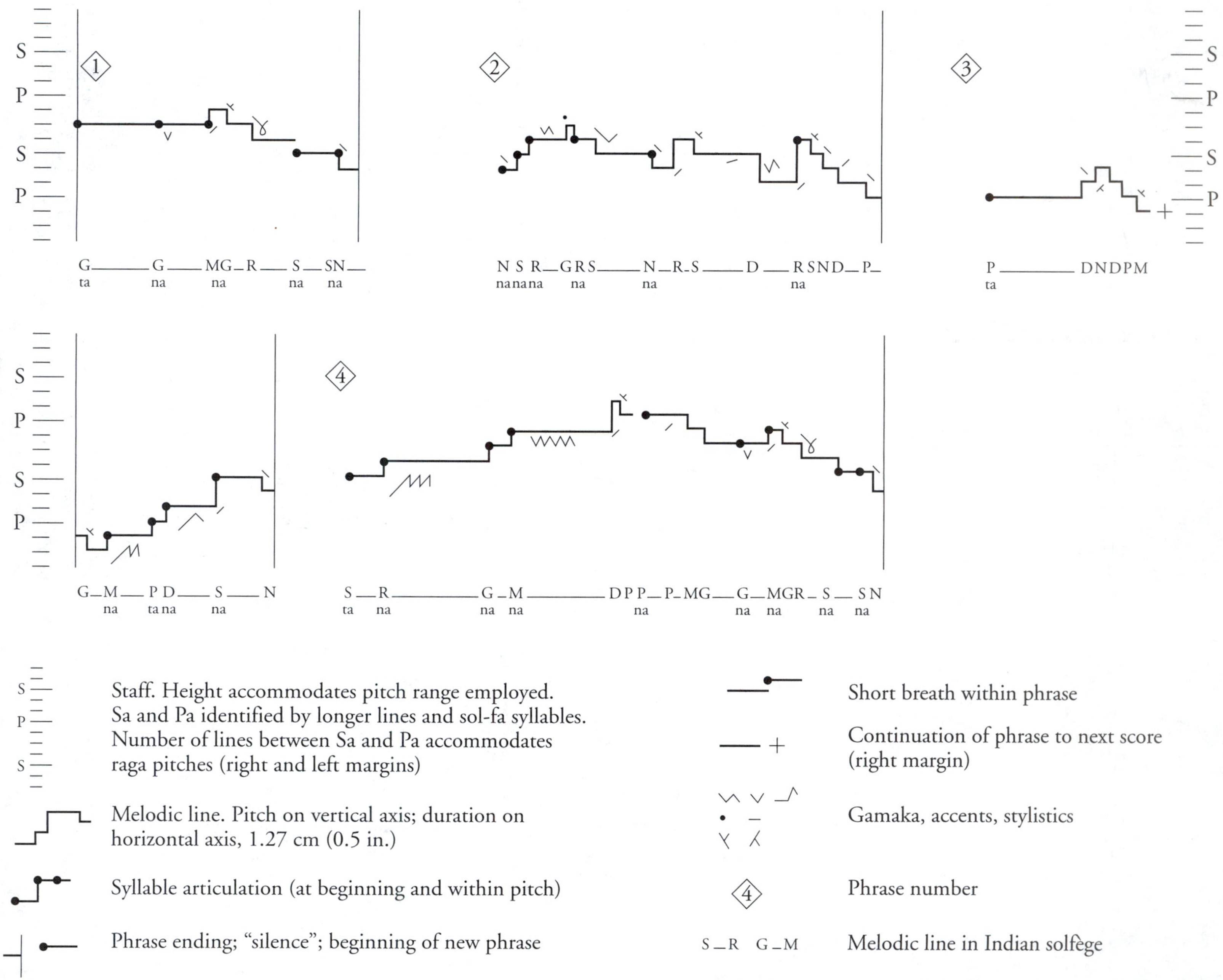

FIGURE 9 Four phrases of an *ālāpana* performance in *rāga śankarābharaṇa* by T. Viswanathan (Viswanathan 1973). Transcription by Gayathri Rajapur Kassebaum.

Raga improvisation and gender

Before the 1920s, *ālāpana* performers were predominantly men. However, women musicians who belonged to certain communities with long musical lineages were exponents of the most challenging compositions (*padam* and *jāvaḷi*) that epitomize the raga essence [see SOCIAL ORGANIZATION OF MUSIC AND MUSICIANS: SOUTHERN AREA]. They performed in musical gatherings and in temples, but never on the concert stage. In the early 1920s, female pioneers (the legendary Vina Dhanammal, Coimbatore Tayi, Dhanakoti, Bhavani, and a few others) revolutionized musical practice by performing ragas and compositions on the concert stage (in both purely musical and dance events). They paved the way for the many prominent female concert musicians of today (Sankaran n.d.).

In present-day practice, entry into the Karnatak music world as a performer is open to nonhereditary, nonlineage musicians; it also cuts across the barriers of caste, class, and gender. However, the challenge of performing raga with sensitivity, imagination, and skill, which demands lifelong dedication, remains as in the past.

RAGA IN *PERIYA MĒḶAM* ENSEMBLE PERFORMANCE

Hindu temples in South India were centers for all the arts including music and dance from the ninth to the nineteenth centuries (Thapar 1966). From the time of the Vijayanagar empire (fourteenth to seventeenth centuries) most South Indian temples have had a processional ensemble called *periya mēḷam*. This major ensemble consists of a double-reed melody instrument (*nāgasvaram*), a double-headed drum (*tavil*) played with thimbles and stick, a cymbal (*tāḷam*) that serves as a time keeper, and either a double-reed drone instrument (*ottu*) with a single finger hole, or a bellowed reed-box drone (*śruti peṭṭi*).

The *nāgasvaram* has its own repertoire for temple ritual functions. Its presence is also required for household rituals, especially traditional marriage ceremonies of the higher castes. *Nāgasvaram* players strictly follow the raga idioms when performing Karnatak compositions. Performers are known for their extended *ālāpana* improvisations on major Karnatak ragas as well as rare ragas, and in the past performers have played one raga for many hours without repeating a single phrase. Since the 1930s this practice has declined considerably.

In contrast to the Karnatak concert music tradition, in which *ālāpana* improvisation is unaccompanied, in the *nāgasvaram* tradition the *tavil* usually provides rhythmic accompaniment for *ālāpana*. The drum also plays rhythmic interludes during the major sections of the *ālāpana*. Since *nāgasvaram* playing demands constant breath control and players must perform long hours in the temple rituals, the accompanying drum in *ālāpana* provides some relief for the instrumentalist. The special ritual status of the *tavil* may have brought about the tradition of accompanying *ālāpana* with a drum.

The *periya mēḷam* ensemble is not considered part of the Karnatak concert tradition, although voluntary music associations have invited *nāgasvaram* performers to give Karnatak concerts. The *nāgasvaram* has nevertheless had considerable influence on Karnatak musicians of the twentieth century. Senior Karnatak musicians and South Indian classical music connoisseurs still celebrate legendary *nāgasvaram* players and their elaborate *ālāpana* performances (Terada 1992).

Not all *periya mēḷam* musicians in South India are trained Karnatak musicians. In such ensembles attached to small town and village temples of Karnataka, hereditary *nāgasvaram* musicians do not always perform extended *ālāpana*, but rather play a combination of classical compositions and film tunes.

RAGA IN DANCE AND DRAMA

The minor ensemble (*cinna mēḷam*) provides music accompaniment for dance. Before 1800, South Indian temples and courts patronized the ensemble. The female dancers dedicated their life to dance and music, undergoing arduous training to become expert dancers. What was once considered an art practiced among only a few families and preserved and propagated by hereditary artists has now become a popular art form in which nonhereditary members of all communities participate. Two female dancers, the legendary T. Balasaraswati and Rukmini Devi, the founder of the Kalakshetra school of music, dance, and allied arts in Madras in the late 1940s, were responsible for reviving and propagating dance. Since this time the dance form has become known as *bharata nāṭyam* 'dance art of the sage Bharata', and the music accompanying the dance is Karnatak classical music based on raga and tala. *Bharata nāṭyam* has its own repertoire, but some raga-based compositions are common to both Karnatak concert music and dance (*svarajati, varṇam, padam, jāvaḷi*, and *tillāna*).

The *bharata nāṭyam* ensemble consists of a principal dancer and an accompanying ensemble. A typical dance ensemble consists of two melody instruments (Indian flute and clarinet, or vina and *goṭṭuvādyam*), rhythm instrument (*mridangam*), string drone (*tambūrā*), two vocalists (male, female, or both), and the dance teacher (*naṭṭuvanār*), who recites the drum syllables (*solkaṭṭu*) and plays the cymbal (*tāḷam*) (Higgins 1993).

One of the vocalists usually sings a Sanskrit, Telugu, or Tamil poem (*śloka*) in the form of nonmetered *ālāpana*. As the singer conveys the text, the dancer conveys its meaning through *abhinaya*, a form of dancing using hand gestures and facial expressions to convey moods and symbolize actions.

In the early centuries of the common era, the sage Bharata defined and discussed *gīta* 'song', *vādya* 'instruments', and *nṛtya* 'dance' as integral components of Indian music in his treatise on music, dance, and drama—the *Nāṭyaśāstra*. Thus in that ancient period South Indian music and dance were already closely connected, as they have been ever since, and raga has become an important element of both.

Raga in theater traditions

The theater traditions of the Southern regions include *kathakaḷi* and *kuchipuḍi*, dance dramas of Kerala and Andhra Pradesh, respectively, and three different *yakṣagāna* traditions of Karnataka—Northern, South Kannada, and Mysore. All of these drama traditions deal with mythological stories; actors wear elaborate costumes, masks, headdresses, and makeup. In each, ragas are an essential part of the musical element. Both *kathakaḷi* and *kuchipuḍi* employ Karnatak ragas, although in *kathakaḷi* their names differ from those used in the Karnatak concert tradition.

The music of the *yakṣagāna* theater in northern Karnataka, popularly known as *doḍāta* 'big play', uses ragas mostly from the Hindustani tradition, but also some tunes based on Karnatak ragas. Prior to the reorganization of the states in independent India, northern Karnataka was part of the Bombay Presidency, and was thus influenced by Marathi culture. Historically the Bahmani dynasty of the Deccan (1347–1526) ruled this land, and Hindustani music traditions were widespread.

The southern Kannada *yakṣagāna* tradition is distinct for its use of stylized costumes and its alternation of singing with spoken dialogue. The actors sing melodies relating to both Karnatak and Hindustani raga traditions, in free verse as well as in composed songs.

The southern Mysore village tradition of *yakṣagāna*, although employing compositions performed in raga, emphasizes acting and conveying the role of the mythological figure. In the process, musicians and singers do not strictly follow traditional raga structure but mix Karnatak elements with film songs and folk tunes.

RAGA IN NONCLASSICAL TRADITIONS

There exists a demarcation, expressed by musicians and listeners alike, between music performed in the concert hall or temple that adheres to the strict rules of raga, and music rendered for devotional gatherings, narrative stories, or other contexts, which may depart from these rules. Classical and nonclassical music have close affinities. Both share textual themes in compositions, tala cycles, and most importantly, raga structure. The distinction between the classical and nonclassical is often blurred, and depends on the performance context.

Nonclassical music based on raga structure includes devotional or love poems, group devotional singing (*bhajana*), and *harikathā,* the narration of Hindu epics, mythology, or the lives of saints that integrates drama, music, dance, and humor.

Raga in devotional poetry and song

Musicians have popularized *aṣṭapadi*, Sanskrit metered poems from the North Indian poet Jayadeva's twelfth-century work *Gīta Govinda*, both in Karnatak and Hindustani ragas [see RELIGIOUS AND DEVOTIONAL MUSIC]. Singers also perform Tamil poetry in Karnatak ragas, notably hymns and devotional songs created by saints on their pilgrimages. The Tamil Shaivite poet-saints known as Nāyanārs composed *tēvāram* hymns between the second and eighth centuries. Manikkavasagar composed passionate love poems to Shiva called *tiruvāsakam*. From the seventh to ninth centuries, the Āḷvār poet-saints composed *nālāyira-prabandam* songs to the deity Vishnu, and the fifteenth-century poet-saint Arunagirinadar composed a genre of Tamil poems called *tiruppugaḻ* to the deity Murugan (Powers 1980). The sects of Shiva, Vishnu, Murugan, and Krishna have different myths and rituals, but they share a common heritage of linguistic idioms, attitudes of devotion (bhakti), and religious themes that is alive today (Ramanujan 1981). A Tamil music association (Tamil Iśai Saṅgam) established in 1942 has popularized these raga-based songs in recent years, and thereby promoted Tamil musical culture.

In the Kannada-speaking areas of South India, another type of devotional composition is popular. Songs of god (*devaranāma*) are compositions by the fourteenth-century poet-saint Purandara Dasa and other saints (*dāsakūta*) and are venerated by both classical and nonclassical musicians. Purandara Dasa's song texts are in vernacular Kannada. The composer originally intended them as a means of popularizing devotion, and of reaching both the literate and the nonliterate masses. Singers usually sang them in nonclassical music contexts and devotional gatherings, and gave primary attention to the text, not always observing the rules of raga. In contemporary musical practice, musicians set Purandara Dasa's songs in classical Karnatak and Hindustani ragas, and both professional and amateur singers perform them in formal concerts as well as in nonclassical music gatherings.

In the Telugu language of Andhra Pradesh, devotional poems by the sixteenth-century composer Annamacharya are popular among well-known classical concert artists. Also sung in Karnatak ragas are the Telugu song cycles *divyanāma saṅkīrtana* of Tyagaraja (1767–1847). These song compositions are in both rare and popular Karnatak ragas; performances take place only in devotional settings.

Three philosophers, Sankara (eighth century), Madhwa (tenth century), and Ramanuja (thirteenth century), along with their disciples and other anonymous poets, composed devotional poetry for daily Hindu worship. These songs constitute a large repertoire set in Karnatak and Hindustani ragas. Religious groups sing these songs and verses as group songs in temples or religious gatherings. Classical musicians

Among the popular film subjects of the early talkie era were the lives of Indian saints, and film-music directors/composers based their songs for these films on classical ragas.

have popularized these devotional songs by recording them on cassettes, and by performing them toward the end of a concert. Both the Madras Music Academy and music societies (*sabhā*) recognize this category of nonclassical music. Besides live performance and cassette recordings, these songs can also be heard on the nationalized All India Radio.

Group singing (*bhajana*) is the most characteristic form of music making in the Hindu devotional (bhakti) movement. *Bhajana* includes group performance of both songs and dance, in praise of the principal Hindu deities. Both trained Karnatak musicians and amateur musicians perform in singing groups (Singer 1972).

Group members usually sing in leader-chorus format; a leader initiates the melody, generally based on a raga, and the chorus repeats the leader's melodic phrases. The song melody is short, and the leader repeats the same melody for successive verses. Most devotional songs are metered, although groups may include solo performance of nonmetered verses. A trained voice is not essential for participation in amateur groups. However, some singers have outstanding voices and a three-octave range (devotional songs usually have a one-octave span). More men participate in *bhajana* groups than women, although women have become more prominent since the mid-1980s. Various castes perform *bhajana*. Not all groups follow classical raga rules, but all sing melodies related to raga.

Raga in storytelling with music and dance (*harikathā*)

Harikathā is an art form demanding knowledge of raga and of Karnatak musical structure, dance, speech, diction, and dramatic technique. The *harikathā* tradition—popular storytelling combined with music and dance—originated in Maharashtra, where performers were known as *kīrtanakāra* (singers of *kīrtana* 'devotional song'). The recitation of mythological narratives was long popular in South India, but toward the end of the nineteenth century a *harikathā* performer named Ramachandra Bua traveled south to the Tamil region. Krishna Bhagavatar, an exponent of Karnatak music living in Tanjore, mastered this art after leaving Bua, and created the South Indian *harikathā* style. Thereafter the tradition of singing in raga, dancing with tala, and narrating stories with clear diction and humor to sustain the attention of the audience spread throughout the southern area.

The main aim of *harikathā* performance is to communicate with nonliterate and literate audiences. Earlier in the twentieth century, well-known *harikathā* performers always had a sound knowledge of Karnatak music. Some were established Karnatak musicians and composers who became professional *harikathā* performers. Today a few fine performers keep this performance tradition alive. They use classical Karnatak as well as Hindustani ragas for the short composed songs they intersperse through their narratives, and they are capable of singing elaborate improvisation (*ālāpana*) on these ragas.

RAGA AND LIGHT CLASSICAL MUSIC

In Karnatak music the distinction among classical, light classical, and devotional is not so clearly marked as in the Hindustani tradition. No single genre or group of songs neatly fits into a category called light classical music, a term that may refer to a genre such as devotional hymns (*tēvāram, tiruppugaḻ,* and so on), to ragas borrowed from the Hindustani tradition for the singing of devotional poetry, or to compositions in traditional ragas with romantic or erotic texts. It may also be used to refer to the repertoire of an ensemble that performs devotional music in traditional ragas and talas, and comprises a solo singer and a small accompanying ensemble including violin, vina, flute, sitar, guitar, and *mridangam.*

Performance context plays an important role in identifying music in this category. For example, the last portion of a Karnatak concert usually consists of devotional songs, Sanskrit *śloka,* or Tamil *viruttam.* Karnatak vocalists sing these in nonmetered improvisation, often in a *rāgamālikā* 'garland of ragas' from Karnatak and Hindustani sources. Performers and audiences tend to view these as light classical music.

The dance and music forms *padam, jāvaḷi,* and *tillāna* straddle the line between classical and light classical. These compositions differ from the classical *kriti* composition in their texts; *padam* and *jāvaḷi* portray love and romantic themes rather than purely devotional ones, whereas *tillāna* is a fast, rhythmic piece with a short text. The composers express the feeling of being deeply in love with the deity (*madhura bhāva*), aspiring to be united with the deity as the lover with the loved one. These human emotions, which the classical dancer conveys, are romantic on the surface but have a deeper spiritual meaning. From the point of view of the text, these musical forms that deal with romantic, erotic, human love may be considered light classical, comparable to the Hindustani light classical genres *ṭhumrī* and ghazal. However, the exponents of *padam* and *jāvaḷi,* who are highly trained hereditary Karnatak musicians, bring out the essence (*bhāva*) of the raga in their performances. In a musical sense, these genres are thus part of the authentic Karnatak raga tradition and may be considered classical.

Raga in film songs

Early South Indian sound films of the 1930s incorporated songs composed in Karnatak ragas. In addition to professional actor-singers, a few well-known male and female Karnatak vocalists became film actors and actresses. Among the popular film subjects of the early talkie era were the lives of Indian saints. Film-music directors/composers based their songs for these films on classical ragas such as *bhairavī, kāmbhōjī,* and *ketāragoula*; contemporary traditionally trained musicians composed the lyrics. Some of these songs were nonmetered poems; others were metered songs.

In the 1940s, advances in recording technology enabled film sound technicians to record the sound separately from the image, and the technique of "playback" singing was introduced. Singers recorded songs in a studio, and actors merely had to mouth the words in front of the camera (Manuel 1993). Playback singers in South Indian cinema of the 1940s and 1950s, such as M. S. Subbulakshmi, Maduri Mani Ayyar, and M. L. Vasantakumari, were classical musicians who had received traditional training with a guru. Some became well known as film playback artists. These Karnatak vocalists performed classical music concerts, but their audiences demanded that they also sing popular film songs. In the 1990s, some playback singers still perform Karnatak music concerts, which are extremely popular, attracting thousands of people. The Karnatak vocalist Yesudas has gained popularity, performing both for films and in traditional Karnatak concerts [see FILM MUSIC: SOUTHERN AREA].

One main distinction between raga-based film songs and Karnatak music is voice quality. In classical singing, a deep and open voice is desired, with explicit ornaments and strict adherence to raga rules. In film singing, the voice tends to be softer and higher pitched. Singers develop more "head" tones, use microphones to manipulate the voice quality, and may deviate from the strict rules of raga.

Many film songs produced since the 1970s are no longer raga-based melodies, but a synthesis of Indian and non-Indian musical elements. Although some music directors are knowledgeable about Karnatak music, most have the capacity and desire to combine Indian music with tunes from Greece, the Middle East, or Latin America. They employ orchestras combining traditional Indian instruments with guitars, mandolins, keyboards, and other non-Indian instruments.

RAGA IN SRI LANKA

Sri Lankan society comprises Theravada Buddhists, who constitute 69 percent of the population; a large minority of Hindu Tamils (approximately 23 percent) residing in the Northern Province; and small groups of Muslims, Moors, and the descendants of Dutch and Portuguese colonists known as Burghers. The aboriginal population, the Vedda, lives in remote hill country and has its own distinct musical culture. There is a long historical and musical connection between the Tamils of Sri Lanka and those of Tamil Nadu in South India. Tamil musicians in the Jaffna area of northern Sri Lanka perform Karnatak ragas. For three decades or more, students from Sri Lanka have attended Tamil Nadu music institutions to learn Karnatak music (Berberich 1974). *Nāgasvaram* music in temples and domestic rituals plays an important role in the Tamil music culture of Sri Lanka, as in South India. Sri Lanka also imports cassette recordings of *bharata nāṭyam* dance music, devotional music, and film songs performed by well-known South Indian artists.

Tamil culture has been significantly disrupted by the ethnic strife and violence in Sri Lanka during the past decade. At present, it is difficult to ascertain to what extent Karnatak raga performance continues to flourish.

REFERENCES

Anantapadmanabhan, C. S. 1954. *The Veena: Its Technique, Theory and Practice.* New Delhi: Gana Vidya Bharati.

Berberich, Frank. 1974. "The Tavil: Construction, Technique and Context in Present-Day Jaffna." M.A. thesis, University of Hawaii.

Higgins, Jon B. 1993. *The Music of Bharata Nāṭyam,* New Delhi: Oxford and IBH Publishing.

Jairazbhoy, Nazir A. 1995. *The Ragas of North Indian Music: Their Structure and Evolution.* Rev. ed. Bombay: Popular Prakashan.

Kassebaum, Gayathri R. 1975. "Gamaka in Alapana Performance in Karnatic Music." M.A. thesis, University of Hawaii.

———. 1987. "Improvisation in Alapana Performance: A Comparative View of Raga Shankarabharana." *Yearbook for Traditional Music* 19:45–64.

Manuel, Peter. 1993. *Cassette Culture: Popular Music and Technology in North India.* Chicago: University of Chicago Press.

Neuman, Daniel M. 1980. *The Life of Music in North India: The Organization of an Artistic Tradition.* Detroit: Wayne State University Press.

Popley, Herbert A. 1966. *The Music of India.* 3rd ed. New Delhi: Y.M.C.A. Publishing House.

Powers, Harold. 1980. "India, Subcontinent of." In *The New Grove Dictionary of Music and Musicians,* ed. Stanley Sadie. London: Macmillan.

Ramanujan, A. K. 1981. *Hymns for the Drowning: Poems for Viṣhṇu by Nammāḷvār.* Princeton, N.J.: Princeton University Press.

Row, Peter. 1977. "The Device of Modulation in Hindustani Art Music." *Essays in Arts and Sciences* 6(1):104–20.

Rowell, Lewis. 1992. *Music and Musical Thought in Early India.* Chicago: University of Chicago Press.

Sambamurthy, P. 1973. *South Indian Music Book,* vol. III. 7th ed. Madras: The Indian Music Publishing House.

Sankaran, T. N.d. "The Life of Music in South India." Unpublished manuscript.

Singer, Milton. 1972. *When a Great Tradition Modernizes: An Anthropological Approach to Indian Civilization.* New York: Praeger.

Terada, Yoshitaka. 1992. "Multiple Interpretations of a Charismatic Individual: The Case of the Great Nagasvaram Musician T. N. Rajaratnam Pillai." Ph.D. dissertation, University of Washington.

Thapar, Romila. 1966. *The History of India*, vol. 1. Baltimore: Penguin.

Vatsyayan, Kapila. 1980. "India: Dance." In *The New Grove Dictionary of Music and Musicians,* ed. Stanley Sadie. London: Macmillan.

Viswanathan, T. 1973. *Pallavi South India Flute Music*. Nonesuch Explorer Series H-72052. LP disk.

———. 1975. "Raga Ālāpana in South Indian Music." Ph.D. dissertation, Wesleyan University.

———. 1977. "The Analysis of Rāga Ālāpana in South Indian Music." *Journal of Asian Music* IX(1):13–71.

Hindustani Tala

James R. Kippen

Principles of Tala and Their Terminology
The *Pakhāvaj*
The Tabla
Recent Developments in Indian Rhythm
Sources and Further Reading

The modern meaning of the word *tāḷa* is twofold: first, the North and South Indian systems of rhythm as a whole; second, a specific metric cycle. Rhythm and meter govern all music involving drums, whether folk, popular, or classical. Since the tala system of meter and rhythm is a complex theoretical concept, its scope may be more easily understood through a study of its practical applications in modern drumming traditions.

Drums have always been an indispensable part of Indian musical traditions. They exist in a vast variety of shapes, sizes, and styles; they are struck with sticks, hands, and fingers, and are played sitting, standing, and dancing. The rest of the world marvels at the depth of this percussive art and wonders at the technical brilliance of players whose fingers and hands ripple over drumheads to produce a rich vocabulary of sounds in rapid, exhilarating bursts.

Hindu religious lore holds that the dance of Shiva, in his role as Nataraja, represents the movement of the universe; in one of his two right arms he holds a small hourglass-shaped drum (*ḍamaru*), which still today can be heard accompanying dancing monkeys and bears and can be found in tourist shops. In his hand, the drum symbolizes the audible space that fills the universe, the sound of creative energy [see VISUAL SOURCES]. So rhythm and drums are manifestations of basic Hindu beliefs.

Tala as a theoretical concept, found in ancient treatises such as the *Nāṭyaśāstra* of Bharata (c. 200 B.C.–A.D. 200), is a complex issue bound up with sophisticated philosophical musings on the nature of time. In the second century C.E., the word evidently had two specific meanings: the system of rhythm as a whole, and a physical gesture in which the left hand slaps down on the right hand (or the left knee). This movement was just one of eight gestures designed to mark the temporal structure of rhythmic music; others included counts on the finger and waves of the hand. One of the most notable features of any modern performance of North Indian music is the use of such actions to mark the divisions of specific metric cycles, though the practice is not quite so prevalent as in South India, where most of the audience joins in the process.

Writings on music from Vedic times (c. 1500–600 B.C.) commonly expressed time through circular imagery—the wheel of the chariot, the sun, the eye, the cycle of human life. In turn, cultural ideas about time manifested themselves in the musical phenomenon of metric cycles. By the time Sarngadeva compiled the *Saṅgītaratnākara* (c. A.D. 1240) no fewer than 120 *deśī* talas had been catalogued. *Deśī* implies these were regional rhythmic patterns organized in cyclic form. The cyclical disposition of time is therefore another link between modern and ancient practices.

In addition to hand gestures and metric cycles, another ancient rhythmic feature that continues in modern practice is the use of syllables as onomatopoeic references to drummed sounds. These syllables (*bol*) function as an oral notation by differentiating among various qualities of sound and can also be written down. Though the syllabic notation of early music treatises does not correspond predictably with modern drumming, at least a sense of historical continuity comes through the ongoing concept of verbal-musical correlation.

Aspects of the ancient system, as reflected in the *tāladaśaprāṇa* 'ten breaths of tala', form the underpinning of the rhythmic system of South India (see below). However, they are invoked only by modern Hindustani music theorists and remain largely meaningless to performers in the North.

In North India, drums both accompany other instruments and play solo. There are many different styles of accompaniment, depending on the nature of the performance: dance, vocal, or instrumental (that is, in which instruments assume the lead melodic role). In a performance, there are different levels of interaction among drummers—from the passive marking of a metric cycle to soloistic interludes and musical tugs of war for rhythmic supremacy. The classical traditions of two drums—the *pakhāvaj* and tabla—serve here to introduce North Indian tala, as both a rhythmic system and a specific metric cycle.

PRINCIPLES OF TALA AND THEIR TERMINOLOGY

The root meaning of the word *tāḷa* is linked to clapping. The gestures developed in ancient times served as a method of indicating the structure of a fixed period of time that would repeat cyclically—a metric cycle. The gestures essentially marked segments of the cycle. The segmentation of the cycle has always remained the primary description of a tala in the Karnatak system of South India, but North Indian (Hindustani) performance, which began to follow different organizational principles in about the 1300s, has departed from this system in a significant way. Over the past few centuries, individual talas in the North gradually became associated with configurative patterns of drumming, to the point that a specific pattern—and not the clapping structure itself—is the primary description of a tala. Ask any tabla player what the structure of, say, the seven-beat *rūpak tāl* is, and the musician will recite a set of onomatopoeic syllables that correspond to strokes on the drumheads: *tin tiṅ na dhin na dhin na*. The drummer may well indicate its gestural pattern simultaneously—wave on beat 1, 2, 3, clap on beat 4, 5, clap on beat 6, 7—but generally the gestures are dispensable, whereas the drummed pattern is not.

Lay

Lay, another important concept relating to musical time, also has two meanings, which correspond to notions of rhythm and tempo. A musician is said to be *laydār* if he demonstrates exemplary rhythmic command. *Laykārī* denotes a part of a performance dominated by rhythmic play, particularly complex rhythms. Thus *lay* is a fundamental term for rhythm in the Western sense of "timing." In its second meaning, "tempo," the word is usually qualified by one of three terms: slow (*vilambit lay*), medium (*madhya lay*), and fast (*drut lay*). The prefix *ati* 'very' before *vilambit* or *drut* conveys a greater sense of the extremes of tempo.

The tala cycle

Āvartan (sometimes *āvart*) is the term for one cycle of a tala. The root meaning of the word is "rotation." A tala cycle contains a fixed number of beats (*mātrā*). The term *mātrā* also denotes the duration between two beats, in the same way that a quarter-note represents both the beat and a relative duration. Each cycle is segmented into smaller divisions (*vibhāg*), and these divisions may comprise an equal or unequal number of beats. For example, *rūpak tāl* has seven beats, divided unequally into three divisions: three beats plus two beats plus two beats, or 3+2+2.

The first beat of any tala (and therefore the first beat of the first *vibhāg* division) is called *sam.* Subsequent divisions of the tala cycle are called a clap (*tālī*) if the gesture on their first beat is a clap, or empty (*kh̲ālī*) if a wave of the hand indicates their first beat. Players tend to equate *tālī* with an accented pattern and *kh̲ālī* with an unaccented one, as in poetic meter, but there are far too many examples of drummed patterns whose natural stresses do not correlate with this architecture for this generalization to be valid.

The notational symbols for *sam* and *kh̲ālī* are *X* and *O* respectively. Since *sam* is usually considered the first clapped division (*tālī*), subsequent clapped divisions are numbered 2, 3, and so on. This notation can result in confusion when the first beat of the tala is *kh̲ālī,* as in seven-beat *rūpak tāl.* The following pattern (*ṭhekā*) for *rūpak tāl* shows the correct notation:

O	tin	tin	nā
2	dhin	nā	
3	dhin	nā	

which is more commonly, but incorrectly, notated with the clap (X) on the first beat, as:

X	tin	tin	nā
2	dhin	nā	
3	dhin	nā	

The pattern for sixteen-beat *tīntāl* more clearly exemplifies the notational convention of *sam*, *tālī*, and *kh̲ālī*; *tīntāl* has four equal divisions of the sixteen beats, marked on beats 1, 5, 9, and 13 with X (clap), 2 (clap), O (wave), 3 (clap).

X	dhā	dhin	dhin	dhā
2	dhā	dhin	dhin	dhā
O	dhā	tin	tin	tā
3	tā	dhin	dhin	dhā

The position of the word *tāl* in Indian tala names is purely conventional: *tīntāl* is a single word, while *rūpak tāl* are two separate words.

Rhythmic divisions

Many terms exist for the rhythmic divisions of a beat, known in Western music as triplets, quadruplets, quintuplets, septuplets, and so on. A ratio of one event (drum stroke) per beat (1/1) is called equal time (*barābar lay*), two events per beat (1/2) is two times (*dūguṇ*), three events is three times (*tīguṇ*), and so on. Cross-rhythms are fractional ratios, and the most common are *paun* (1/0.75), *savāī* (1/1.25), *deṛhī* (1/1.5), *paune do* (1/1.75), and *ḍhāī guṇ* (1/2.5) (figure 1).

Some musicians prefer to use generic terms to describe rhythmic divisions:

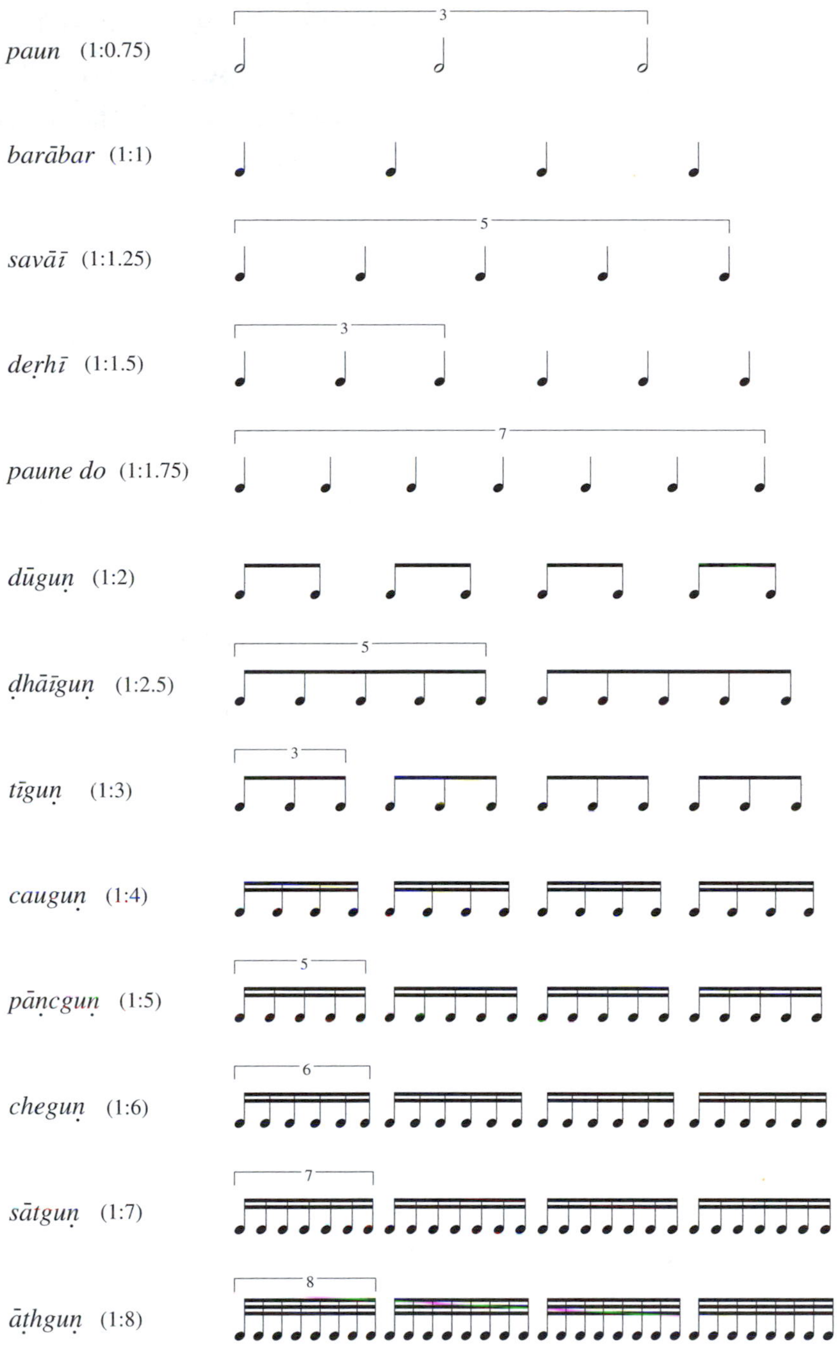

FIGURE 1 The main rhythmic divisions in Hindustani music.

barābar can indicate duple time, whether two, four, eight, or sixteen events per beat; *āṛī* may refer to triple time and its multiples; *kuāṛī,* to fives; and *viāṛī,* to sevens. Less technical, but equally effective, is the term *jhūlnā* 'swinging' for sevens.

The word for *measure* or *meter* (*chand*) describes rhythmic groupings that appear as a result of a consistent pattern of accents. *Rūpak chand* is the name given to the seven-beat grouping stressing the first, fourth, and sixth events in the pattern, mirroring the internal divisions of *rūpak tāl.* Yet *chand* can be used more broadly for any regularly recurring rhythmic pattern, whether or not it conforms to the pattern of a tala. In general, musicians who have studied theory separately from practice (as in a music school) will know all the technical terms, whereas those less conversant with theory will opt for metaphorical descriptions of rhythm [see INSTITUTIONAL MUSIC EDUCATION: NORTHERN AREA].

For India, the general rule should be that nothing is as old as it seems; though ancient and modern drums are superficially similar, there is no way of determining whether they are essentially the same.

THE *PAKHĀVAJ*

Few writings in English discuss the *pakhāvaj* 'barrel drum', and most books in Indian languages do little more than provide notations of talas and drumming pieces. Most musicians and scholars assume the instrument to be ancient, and point to two-thousand-year-old Indian temple carvings of figures playing barrel-shaped drums similar in appearance to the *pakhāvaj* (figure 2). The word *pakhāvaj* comes from two Sanskrit terms, *pakśa* 'side' and *āvaja* 'instrument, drum'. The *āvaja* occurs in the thirteenth-century treatise *Saṅgītaratnākara* (chap. 6, verse 1077), as do "drummed" syllables such as *tā, dīn, thuṅ,* and *nā*. Yet for India, the general rule should be that nothing is as old as it seems; though ancient and modern drums are superficially similar, there is no way of determining whether they are essentially the same, or if the techniques used in playing them are comparable. The *pakhāvaj* has evolved over time, as have its musical function, repertoire, and technique. It probably crystalized into its current form, in all these respects, within the past four hundred years.

The North Indian *pakhāvaj* (figure 3) shares many traits with its cousin the South Indian *mridangam*. Indeed, an alternative name for *pakhāvaj* is *mridang*. It is a double-headed barrel drum just over 60 centimeters long (no size is standard). The smaller head measures about 18 centimeters in diameter, the larger about 23 centimeters. Each head is made from a circular piece of treated goatskin, partly covered by a second skin that is trimmed away to form a rim around its circumference. Both

FIGURE 2 Temple carving of a dancer accompanied by two musicians playing double-headed barrel drums, Khajuraho. Photo by Gordon Arnold, 1983.

FIGURE 3 Detail from "The Dance of Krishna" showing drummers playing *pakhāvaj*, *naqqārā*, and *ḍholak*, played somewhat unusually with a stick. *Sūr-Sāgar* manuscript of Surdas, Rajasthan, Mewar, mid-1600s. Courtesy Vinod Krishna Kanoria, Patna.

skins are laced to a ring that fits tightly over the neck of the barrel. The heads are then laced together with a long strip of hide. The smaller has a layered black spot (*siyāhī*), about 10 centimeters in diameter, made of paste and iron filings (each maker jealously guards his own recipe). This spot provides pitch and resonance. The drummer can adjust the pitch by altering the tension of the head, either by moving cylindrical wooden wedges under the lacing or by tapping on the ring around the drumhead with a hammer or stone. The *pakhāvaj* is tuned to the tonic pitch Sa (equivalent to *do* in the Western sol-fa system; see HINDUSTANI RAGA) chosen for the performance. It most frequently hovers around C♯ below middle C. Since tuning two heads connected by the same straps would prove virtually impossible, the drummer prepares the larger head for playing by making a temporary spot from fresh dough (flour and water) and pressing this onto the skin. The drummer can adjust and flatten the size and shape until the required resonance and pitch are achieved.

The player (*pakhāvajī*) sits on the ground. The drum also rests on the ground, and is usually wedged with a rolled-up shawl for stability (though stands do exist). Most commonly the left hand plays the larger head, producing two basic sounds: (1) a low, booming resonance produced by a ricochet of the whole hand, known by the drum syllables *ga* or *ge* (the aspiration and ending vowel can change according to stress or context); or (2) a slap of the hand that sticks to the drumhead, called *kat* or *ke*. Resonating sounds on the left drumhead are said to be open (*khulā*) and nonresonating sounds closed (*band*). The right hand produces a greater variety of strokes, which are of three kinds: (1) *tā* or *nā*, which produce the tonic pitch, using either the whole hand or the index finger to ricochet from the rim while another part of the hand or finger touches the drumhead at the edge of the black spot to filter out unwanted harmonics; (2) *din* or *thuṅ*, a pitch a minor seventh below the tonic (Re in the lower octave), where the four fingers ricochet off the drumhead; and (3) nonresonating strokes in which the fingers or palm stick to the drumhead (strokes with the fingers are called *tit, te,* or *ṭe,* and fluttering strokes of the palm, *dere*). Strokes involving both the right hand and the left abound; the most important are *dhā,* produced by *ge* and *tā, dhit* (*ge* + *tit*), and *dhere* (*ge* + *dere*).

Drum syllables constitute an oral notation that aids teaching and memory and serves as a mode of performance. Yet a drummer's fluency in using them comes from an intuitive understanding of the contexts in which they are used; there is no one-to-one correlation between a stroke and a syllable: strokes may have many different names, and one name can imply many different strokes. In some contexts, *gā* and *kā* can even represent the right-hand stroke more commonly known as *tā.* Only years of study and practice can clarify this system.

Pakhāvaj talas

The talas most closely associated with the *pakhāvaj* repertoire are those found in the *dhrupad* vocal genre. First is *cautāl* (occasionally called *cārtāl*), whose rhythmic cycle comprises twelve beats in six equal divisions, with *k̲h̲ālī* counts on the second and fourth divisions. The pattern for *cautāl* is:

X	dhā		dhā		O	din		tā	
2	ki	ṭa	dhā		O	din		tā	
3	ti	ṭe	ka	tā	4	ga	dī	gi	na

The feel of the tala is really three sections of four beats, with the second section being a variant of the first. The third section features the most common sequence of syllables, *tiṭe katā gadī gina,* a sequence that functions as a cadential unit in playing *pakhāvaj.* The same phrase, whose two syllables per beat propel the tala forward and round into the next cycle, also occurs in two other common talas: the seven-beat *tīvrā tāl,* which has no *k̲h̲ālī:*

X	dhā		din		tā
2	ti	ṭe	ka	tā	
3	ga	dī	gi	nā	

and the ten-beat *śūltāl:*

X	dhā		dhā		O	din		tā	
2	ki	ṭa	dhā		3	ti	ṭe	ka	tā
O	ga	dī	gi	na					

The patterns for *tīvrā* and *śūl* talas are clearly related to or even derived from that of *cautāl,* but no single, indisputable version of a pattern emerges. In many versions, the syllables (and sometimes the structure of the clapping) differ, and in most traditions the pattern also varies with the tempo.

The variability of tala and drum-pattern structures raises an important issue about tala in North India as opposed to South India. Karnatak concepts of tala are rigid and highly systematic; all possible rhythmic cycles are derived by calculation from the available structural parameters [see KARNATAK TALA]. The Hindustani system is entirely unsystematic and nebulous—which suggests that it arose organically through performance, not as the result of a theoretical scheme.

Another common tala associated with the vocal genre *dhrupad* is the fourteen-beat *dhamār* (the long dashes indicate silence):

X	kat	dhe	ṭe	dhe ṭe
2	dhā	—		
O	kat	te	ṭe	
3	te	ṭe	tā	—

Dhamār illustrates how the structure of these patterns can contradict the gestural architecture of the tala. Whereas the tala's divisions suggest 5 + 2 + 3 + 4 (clap, clap, wave, clap), the pattern for *dhamār* is configured as a largely open seven-beat pattern of resonating drum strokes, mirroring itself with a seven-beat closed pattern without resonating strokes.

Thousands of talas exist in theory. Hardly any of these are widely known, and for *pakhāvaj* only the four given above feature with any regularity. Many lesser-known talas carry the names of gods: *brahma tāl* (fourteen beats), *lakshmī tāl* (eighteen), *gaṇeśa tāl* (eighteen). Some configurations are bound to mystical-number symbolism (*brahma tāl* has a clap, a wave, two claps, a wave, three claps, a wave, four claps, a wave; Brahma is the creator of the world, one of the trinity of deities, with Vishnu the preserver and Shiva the destroyer, and some say this pattern expresses the expansion of creation itself). However, players and theorists interpret *pakhāvaj* inconsistently.

Pakhāvaj repertoires

Generically, a *pakhāvaj* composition is called a *paran*. There is no structural consistency among pieces termed *paran*, so clearly the word does not indicate a particular pattern or formula. Other terms for composition include *mukhṛā* and *mohrā*, though there are examples of these two forms in which the drum syllables and phrasal structures are identical to pieces called *paran*. Two features that differentiate *mukhṛā* and *mohrā* from *paran* are their inclusion of a cadential formula (*tīyā*) and their use as a concluding section of a performance.

The following is a *paran* composition in twelve-beat *cautāl*, notated with two events per beat (*dūguṇ*) over two tala cycles:

X	dhā	—	na	dhi		O	ki	ṭa	dhā	ge
2	ti	ṭe	kra	dhā		O	ti	ṭe	dhā	ge
3	ti	ṭe	ka	tā		4	ga	dī	gi	na
X	nā	ti	ṭe	tā		O	ge	na	dhā	ge
2	ti	ṭe	kra	dhā		O	ti	ṭe	dhā	ge
3	ti	ṭe	ka	tā		4	ga	dī	gi	na

The composition may be viewed in two halves, with the second repeating a substantial portion of the first. In performance, a drummer would repeat this composition several times; each time, the density of the syllables would increase proportionately from two events per beat to three, four, six, eight, and even further, depending on the initial tempo and the drummer's technical capabilities. With three events per beat, the notation for the beginning of the composition is as given below. Since the rhythmic ratio has been increased to 3:2, the composition will no longer fit two cycles (twenty-four beats), but will last only sixteen beats. Therefore the drummer repeats the piece three times, so its ending coincides with the end of a tala cycle (3 times 16 equals 4 times the twelve-beat cycle).

X	dhā — na	dhi ki ṭa		O	dhā ge ti	ṭe kra dhā
2	ti ṭe dhā	ge ti ṭe		O	ka tā ga	di ge na

The drummer's role is to mirror the soloist's rhythms with appropriately improvised patterns. A good accompanist will enhance the overall sensation of continuity and growth; an overzealous accompanist may dominate and distract.

This composition challenges the listener's sense of rhythm from the outset, because the natural accents within the patterns, primarily the composite strokes featuring the phoneme /dh/, are now occurring at different points in relation to the beat. The sensation of shifting accents, of one thing accelerating proportionately yet in perfect relation to another, is one of the essential aesthetic underpinnings of Hindustani drumming.

Many *paraṅ,* and all *mukhṛā* and *mohrā,* include a cadential formula called a *tīyā* (Sanskrit *tri* 'three', *tṛtīya* 'third'). The word *tīyā* implies threes and denotes a pattern played three times. The drummer calculates the last syllable of the final statement of the pattern to coincide with an important point in the cycle, most frequently the first beat. The following *mukhṛā* is designed to conclude the *paran* given above. It begins with the same syllables, and for convenience is notated with two events per beat, though as a finale it would ordinarily be played at a much higher density:

X	dhā	—	na	dhi	O	ki	ṭa	dhā	ge
2	thuṅ	—	thuṅ	—	O	nā	ge	ti	ṭe
3	ti	ṭe	kra	dhet	4	—	tā	gadī	gina
X	ti	ṭe	ka	tā	O	tiṭe	katā	gadī	gina
2	dhā	—	—	—	O	tiṭe	katā	gadī	gina
3	dhā	—	—	—	4	tiṭe	katā	gadī	gina
X	dhā								

Extended structures also exist, some being *paran* of extraordinary length and complexity. Yet the most common extended structure is the most fascinating because it demonstrates a remarkable capacity to integrate musical and arithmetic ideas. This structure is the *cakkardār,* a term implying something that goes round in circles. A *cakkardār* is a *paran* played three times, calculated to conclude on the first beat of the tala. The chosen *paran* need not include a cadential formula, though most do; so when the drummer plays a *paran* three times, the cadential pattern appears nine times. A multitude of arithmetic solutions exist, but one formula deserves special mention: the *farmāiśī* 'requested' *cakkardār.* In the *farmāiśī* composition, a *paran* that includes a cadential pattern is played three times: the first time, the drummer plays the *tīyā* so that the first of its parts ends on beat 1 of the tala cycle; the second time, the second part of the *tīyā* ends on beat 1; the third and final time, the third and concluding part of the *tīyā* ends on beat 1. The following is an example. Here, each statement of the *paran* lasts thirty-nine beats, including a seven-beat cadential pattern (*kat —, tā —, kra dhet, — tā, tiṭe katā, gadī gina, dhā—*). The *cakkardār* is thus 117 beats (39 times 3). A two-beat gap (in parentheses) that separates the statements must be added in for a total of 39 + 2 + 39 + 2 + 39 = 121 beats: precisely ten cycles of the twelve-beat *cautāl,* plus one for the first beat of the next cycle.

X	dhira	kiṭa	tak	dhi	O	ki	ṭa	kat	—
2	dhi	ṭa	dhi	ṭa	O	tira	kiṭa	tak	tā
3	kat	—	dhet	tat	4	—	tā	kra	dhet
X	—	tā	tiṭe	katā	O	gadī	gina	dhet	—
2	tā	dhet	—	tā	O	kat	—	tā	—
3	kra	dhet	—	tā	4	tiṭe	katā	gadī	gina
X	dhā	—	kat	—	O	tā	—	kra	dhet
2	—	tā	tiṭe	katā	O	gadī	gina	dhā	—
3	kat	—	tā	—	4	kra	dhet	—	tā
X	tiṭe	katā	gadī	gina	O	dhā	—	(—	—
2	—	—)							

The whole thirty-nine-beat pattern (shown above) is played three times.

A *farmāiśī cakkardār* may begin not just on the first beat of the tala, but anywhere in the cycle. Traditionally, drummers have been expected to demonstrate command over these formulas. If a patron makes a specific request (*farmāiś*) for a *cakradār* beginning on the third beat of *cautāl,* the drummer will immediately oblige.

Pakhāvaj **accompaniment**

Traditionally the *pakhāvaj* has always accompanied compositions in the vocal or instrumental genre *dhrupad.* However, even well into the late 1800s, the *pakhāvaj* was widely used to accompany compositions in another vocal genre, *khyāl,* and in *kathak* dance. Now its exposure in India is more restricted because of the popularity of the tabla, which is used for every genre except *dhrupad.*

In the performance of a *dhrupad,* a singer (or the player of a *bīn* 'stick zither') introduces a composition following an extended, unaccompanied, and unmetered section known as the *ālāp.* This composition is nearly always in ten-beat *cautāl;* subsequent compositions are frequently in different talas. It is common for the singer to clap the tala throughout the performance, and this action can help the audience follow the metrical cycle, since the drummer may not spend much time playing the drum pattern. During the statement of the vocal composition, the drummer is expected to play *paran.* The effect is one of growing excitement and power as the drummed patterns ripple beneath the slow and stately melodic framework.

After presenting the composition in full (perhaps with several parts), the soloist embarks on textual variation and elaboration. The general rule is that as the performance progresses, these variations become faster, longer, and more rhythmically intricate. The drummer's role is to mirror the soloist's rhythms with appropriately improvised patterns. A good accompanist will enhance the overall sensation of continuity and growth; an overzealous accompanist may dominate and distract.

Between improvisational sections, the drummer often relies on sequences of rapidly drummed syllables drawn from compositions called *relā* (or *paṛāl*). These are usually short fragments, designed to provide variation. The *relā* sequence below, notated as a cycle of *cautāl,* is normally played at a much greater speed and density:

X	dhā —	kiṭa	taki	ṭata	O	kā —	kiṭa	dhuma	kiṭa
2	taki	ṭata	kā—	kiṭa	O	dhuma	kiṭa	taki	ṭata
3	kā —	kiṭa	taka	dhuma	4	tiṭe	katā	gadī	gina

By constantly spinning variations, the drummer can show off his technique and keep the excitement simmering before launching into the next series of variations with the singer.

ga– ṇa nā– tha ga– ṇa– pa– ti ga– ṇe– śa lam– bo– da– ra so– haiṅ
bhu– jā cā– ra e– ka dan– ta can– dra–ma la– lā– ṭa rā– je
brah– mā viś– nū ma– he– śa tā– la de dhu– ru– pa– da gā– veṅ
a– ti vi– ci– tra ga– ṇa nā– tha ā– ja mi– ra– dan– ga baj– jā– veṅ

FIGURE 4 A Ganesh *paran.*

Pakhāvaj traditions

The *pakhāvaj* has a booming, majestic sound that inspires awe. It is easy to see why, according to legend, the instrument was used to tame wild elephants in the court. Part of its mystique may also stem from the tradition of beginning solo performances on it with the recitation of special *paran,* which mix drum syllables with Sanskrit prayers and other invocations. First, the drummer recites the *paran,* then he plays a representation of it on his drum, reiterating the rhythm and drawing on syllables that most closely match the syllabic content of the text. Figure 4 presents the opening phrases of a *paran* to Shiva's son Ganesh, the elephant-headed god who symbolizes knowledge, wisdom, and good fortune. A Ganesh *paran* is thus a particularly appropriate invocation before an artistic presentation.

gaṇa nātha gaṇapati gaṇeśa lambodara sohaiṅ
bhujā cāra eka danta candrama lalāṭa rāje
brahmā viśnū maheśa tāla de dhrupada gāveṅ
ati vicitra gaṇa nātha āja miradanga bajjāveṅ

Ganesh, the protector, leader, and lord of the Gaṇas [the army of Shiva], large-bellied, presents a grand sight,
with four arms, one tooth, and the moon on his forehead.
Brahma, Vishnu, and Mahesh, keeping tala, are singing *dhrupad.*
Today the lord of the Gaṇas is playing the *mridang* in a strangely wondrous way.

Little information exists on the family or teaching lineages of *pakhāvaj* players. Traditionally the regions of eastern Uttar Pradesh (Ayodhya, Banaras) and Bihar (Darbhanga), and the old court cities of Madhya Pradesh and Maharashtra, have had larger concentrations of these musicians, many of whom come from drumming families. Major North Indian players of the twentieth century have included Purushottam Das (from Rajasthan, but based in Delhi), Ram Shankar Das "Pagal Das" ("Mad Das," from Ayodhya), and Raja Chatrapati Singh of Bijna (near Jhansi in Uttar Pradesh). Purushottam Das has been acclaimed for the beauty of his sound and the quality of his accompaniments for *dhrupad* singing. "Pagal Das" has written about the *pakhāvaj,* and has upheld the mystical tradition of the drum and its supernatural power; he has claimed to have cured severe stammering by feeding individuals with dough taken from a drum on which he has played special, magical *paran* that unlock the tongue—a story that has probably appeared many times throughout history. Raja Chatrapati Singh (figure 5), an aristocrat and brilliant mathematician, has been pro-

FIGURE 5 Raja Chatrapati Singh of Bijna with *pakhāvaj*. Photo courtesy of Peter Pannke.

ductive in rediscovering rare talas; he has repeatedly presented performances in which the most complicated arithmetic formulas unfold in some of the most unusual tala structures. In one performance, he progressed from the twelve-beat *cautāl* through thirteen-, fourteen-, fifteen-, sixteen-, seventeen-, and eighteen-beat talas, playing special *paran* and *cakkardār* in each before effecting a metric modulation that allowed him to start over again at a faster tempo. Raja Chatrapati Singh has contributed greatly to the expansion of the modern *pakhāvaj* repertoire.

Most modern *pakhāvaj* players trace at least part of their musical inheritance to one of two nineteenth-century figures: Nana Panse of Maharashtra and the legendary Kudau Singh Maharaj (?1815–1910) of Uttar Pradesh. Kudau Singh earned acclaim by performing at the courts of North India, including important occasions like the coronation of Wajid Ali Shah of Lucknow (1847). He is said to have defeated all other *pakhāvaj* players in musical battle, to have tamed rogue elephants, to have been awarded an elephant and one thousand rupees for his recitation of a Ganesh *paran*, and to have received the princely sum of 12,000 rupees for composing a *paran* that pleased a patron: the "twelve thousand" (*bārah hazārī*) *paran*, which musicians still know and play.

THE TABLA

Evolution of the tabla

According to a popular legend, the poet-musician Amir Khusrau (1253–1325) invented the tabla by cutting a *pakhāvaj* in half to form the two-piece instrument that has become the most popular and widespread symbol of North Indian percussion. Yet pictorial evidence for the tabla emerges only from about 1745 onward, and the structure of the drums seems to change frequently until the early 1800s, when something recognizable as the modern instrument appeared. The *Muraqqa'-i Dihlī* 'Delhi Album', a contemporary view of musical life, genres, musicians, and instruments at the court of Emperor Muhammad Shah written in 1738, makes no mention of the tabla. The oldest hereditary lineage of tabla players traces its ancestry to Sudhar Khan Dharhi of Delhi, who probably flourished in the middle third of the 1700s. We can therefore assume with some degree of certainty that the tabla itself emerged in the early 1740s [see MUSICAL INSTRUMENTS: NORTHERN AREA].

Traditionally, most tabla players have been Muslims from hereditary occupational specialist families of low social status. Since the turn of the twentieth century, the tabla has reigned supreme and has steadily risen in social prestige.

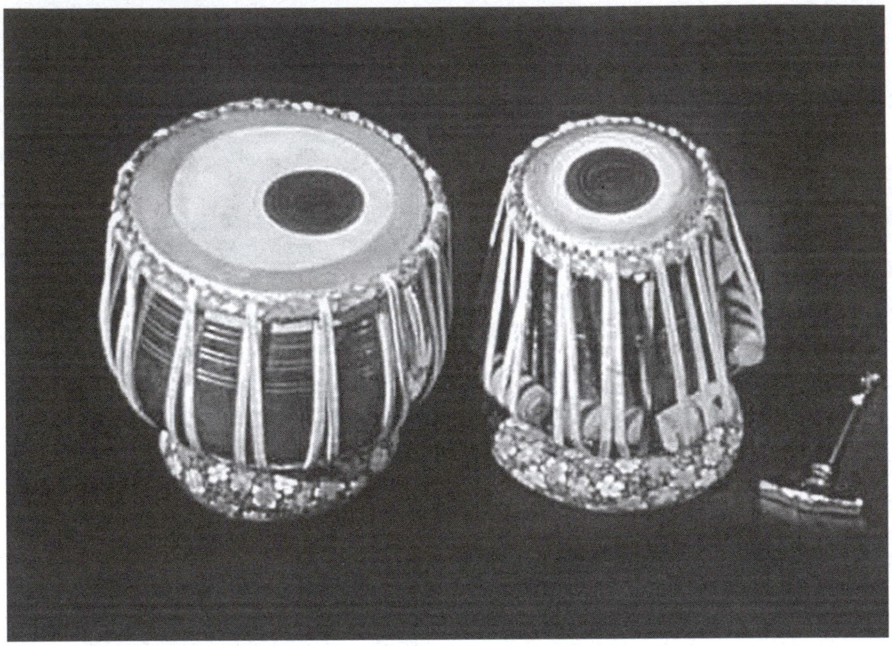

FIGURE 6 The tabla drum pair: the left drum (*bāyāṅ*) and the right drum (*dāhinā*). Photo by Eric Parker.

The term *tablā* derives from an Arabic word for drum, *ṯabl*. It consists of two drums, known most commonly as the right (*dāhinā*) and left (*bāyāṅ*) drums (figure 6). The right drum has a slightly flared, closed cylindrical body carved from a single block of wood, the narrower end of which is partly hollowed. Its organological relationship to the *pakhāvaj* is undeniable, and it looks to all intents and purposes as if a *pakhāvaj* has indeed been chopped in half. The left drum is quite distinct, being a modified hemispherical kettledrum, commonly made of copper or brass. One can still find left drums made of clay, and this hints at their possible origin in the *naqqārā*, two shallow hemispherical clay kettledrums played with sticks (see figure 3). Rather than dough, the left drum has a permanent black spot (*siyāhī*) placed off center. The left drum, unlike the right, is not tuned precisely, but is adjusted to produce a low, resonating boom.

Whereas the *pakhāvaj* was played mainly by high-caste Hindus and sometimes even by the nobility, the tabla has had a more common identity. If Sudhar Khan Dharhi was indeed a member of the first tabla-playing family, then our clue to the drum's low status comes from the word *ḍhaṛhī* itself, denoting a type of low-class Muslim minstrel. In general, the minstrel was closely associated with female dancers, called nautch girls (*nāc*) by the British. This term is misleading, since the British rulers tended to group prostitutes with high-class courtesans, who had considerable skills in the arts of music, dance, and poetry. The British ethos profoundly affected the emerging middle classes, particularly in the latter half of the 1800s, when the

FIGURE 7 The singer Tasrih al-Aqvam with *ḍholak*, 1825. Reproduction by permission of the British Library, Oriental and India Office Collections.

English language and a Western education marked an important road to success. Tabla players were regarded as social pariahs—a stigma difficult to shake off. Even today, the tabla has some distasteful connotations in more puritanical social circles.

Traditionally, most tabla players have been Muslims from hereditary occupational specialist families of low social status. Since about the 1870s, the quasi-caste term Mīrāsī has replaced the term Ḍhaṛhī. The Hindu Kathak caste from eastern Uttar Pradesh (particularly Banaras), members of which have traditionally shared the same occupation as the Mīrāsī, has provided the only non-Muslim hereditary clan of tabla players. The *Ma'dan al-Mūsīqī* 'Mine of Music' of Hakim Muhammad Karam Imam (late 1850s) lists the names of many early players who appeared at the Lucknow court. It is highly likely that the repertoire and playing of the tabla have always been strongly influenced by those of the *naqqārā* 'kettledrum', the *pakhāvaj*, and a cylindrical drum known as the *ḍholak* (figure 7), which can all be seen providing accompaniment to vocal and instrumental music in paintings from the 1700s and 1800s.

For much of its early history, the tabla primarily accompanied *kathak* dance and courtesans' songs, particularly *ṭhumrī* and associated genres. Many photographs show players standing to play drums tied about their waists, or bound in cloth (figure 8). By the late 1800s, the tabla was becoming the principal percussive accompaniment for *khyāl* and for the sitar and sarod traditions. Yet the *pakhāvaj* and the *ḍholak* completely disappeared from these genres only at the turn of the twentieth century. Since then, the tabla has reigned supreme and has steadily risen in social prestige, first because it has taken on a greater role in the modern instrumental ensemble, and second because increasing numbers of nonhereditary high-caste Hindu musicians have become eminent performers on it.

FIGURE 8 Players of the *sārangī* and tabla, standing with their instruments bound about them, accompanying female dancers, 1860s. Photo reproduced by permission of the British Library, Oriental and India Office Collections.

Sound and technique

Essentially, the range of sounds that can be made on the *pakhāvaj* can be produced on the heads of the tabla. There are two major differences in the playing traditions: first, lighter finger strokes predominate on the tabla, whereas on the *pakhāvaj*, heavier two- and three-finger strokes and full-handed strokes are more common; second, the left tabla drum can be made to produce a much wider range of sounds.

On the left head of the *pakhāvaj*, one basic resonant sound is possible, and no variation in pitch can be effected because of the use of fresh dough. So the sound *ge* is produced with all four fingers and the palm bouncing off the head. The left tabla drum has no dough, and thus the wrist can rest on the skin, apply pressure, and slide around to vary the pitch before and/or after the finger has struck the skin. (The black spot's being off center lets the player move his wrist in a greater range.) In addition, more rapid sequences of strokes are possible because individual fingers strike alternately; when combined with the possibility of adding inflection to the drum's resonance, a wide range of pitch and stress contours can be achieved. The results can be as subtle as the sound of the human voice.

The quintessential tabla sound is *tā* (or *nā*) on the right drum. A similar sound is played on the *pakhāvaj* with the full hand, yet on the tabla it is produced with the index finger ricocheting off the rim. It is characterized by a sharp crack. A more refined version of the same pitch, one that explores a different set of harmonics, is played by the same finger on the inner portion of the head between the rim and the black spot. The difference is an important one in the tabla aesthetic: tabla players differentiate between strokes played on the rim (*kinār* or *cāṅṭī*) and in the middle (*sūr* or *maidān;* an alternative nomenclature exists for all recognized parts of the drums). The predominance of, or preference for, one or the other can be a distinguishing stylistic trait.

Tabla talas

Sixteen-beat tīntāl

The most commonly occurring tala in Hindustani music is *tīntāl*, comprising sixteen beats divided into four equal divisions. The usual version of the drumming pattern—called *ṭhekā* in tabla playing—that appears in books on Indian music is given in the subsection on the tala cycle. In that version, the syllable *dhā* dominates. Yet most musicians, when asked to recite the pattern, will say:

X	nā	dhin	dhin	nā
2	nā	dhin	dhin	nā
O	nā	tin	tin	nā
3	nā	dhin	dhin	nā

Some musicians will use the *dhā* version in slow tempo and the *nā* version (or some combination of the two) in fast tempo. Regardless, the *dhā* version more accurately reflects the way drummers think of the pattern because it clearly identifies the drum stroke *ge* on the left drum, identified by the phoneme /dh/. But the *ṭhekā* seems to contradict the clap-wave (*tālī-k͟hālī*) structure of the tala: on beat 9, the gesture is the unstressed wave while the syllable is the emphatic *dhā*, and on beat 13, where the stressed clap returns, the syllable is the less emphatic *tā* (*nā*). It has been suggested that despite the sometimes conflicting theoretical-gestural structure of the tala, the drumming reflects four balanced phrases that feature a three-beat upbeat to a stressed downbeat. So instead of thinking in terms of *DHĀ dhin dhin dhā* (on beats 1 to 4), as many theorists would have us do, we should really think of the phrases as *dhin dhin dhā DHĀ* (beats 2 to 5). The "empty" wave on beat 9 thus becomes more an anticipatory signal, indicating that the next grouping (beats 10 through 13) is unstressed. The logic of this phrasing makes sense to the listener too, because Indian musicians tell audiences and students to listen for the return of the *ge* stroke on beat 14 as a means of locating where the music is with respect to the tala cycle. (The left drum stroke *ge* in combination with the right drum stroke *tin* results in *dhin.*) Beat 14 then becomes linked to the next stressed beat, the all-important beat 1.

Looking once again at the *tīntāl* pattern, we see an immediate difference between its simple drum-syllable vocabulary and the more complex *pakhāvaj* talas.

X	dhā	dhin	dhin	dhā
2	dhā	dhin	dhin	dhā
O	dhā	tin	tin	tā
3	tā	dhin	dhin	dhā

Apart from the inclusion or omission of the left drum, only two strokes are used: *tā,* played on the rim, and *tin* (otherwise known as *tā* or *nā*), on the inner drumhead. This fact, plus the phrasal structure of the pattern, suggest that the origins of *tīntāl* lie in patterns found in folk or semiclassical genres whose aesthetic is based far more strongly on what might best be termed a groove. Indeed, nineteenth-century music manuals refer to *tīntāl* as *qawwālī tāl.* (The term *tīntāl*—sometimes called *tritāl*—appears to date from the second half of the nineteenth century.) The Sufi vocal genre qawwali, known for its rhythmic grooves, influenced the classical *khyāl. Khyāl* compositions from the 1700s feature what we know now as *tīntāl.* The earliest compositions for sitar, the *masītk͟h͟ānī gat* from the mid-1700s, are configured in sixteen beats. *Tīntāl* therefore probably emerged in the early to mid-1700s. It has always dominated instrumental music and fast-tempo *khyāl,* just as it has dominated performance on tabla. Until the current generation, tabla players only rarely performed solo in any pattern other than *tīntāl.*

Other talas

If *khyāl* was influenced by the light-classical music of qawwalis, then it was also undoubtedly influenced by, and was largely an imitation of, the classical *dhrupad.* Therefore, not surprisingly, *khyāl* adopted twelve-beat *cautāl,* the gestural structure of the characteristic *dhrupad* tala, for its own slow compositions. Yet since performers of *dhrupad* were almost certainly disinclined to share their tradition with outsiders, *khyāl* singers and their accompanists needed to develop a modified accompaniment, one that would function like that of its *pakhāvaj* counterpart while being distinct from it. The result was twelve-beat *ektāl,* a pattern that almost entirely contradicts the gestural structure of *cautāl,* because its inherent phrase and stress structures do not coincide with those of its parent. Some musicians substitute the syllable *tin* for *tū.*

X	dhin	dhin	O	dhā ge	tira kiṭa
2	tū	nā	O	kat	tā
3	dhā ge	tira kiṭa	4	dhin	nā

The pattern is better understood as two six-beat phrases, the second of which in large part mirrors the first (some musicians substitute the syllable *tin* for *tū*):

X	dhin	dhin	O	dhā ge	tira kiṭa	2	tū	nā
O	kat	tā	3	dhā ge	tira kiṭa	4	dhin	nā

In medium and fast speeds, the pattern has an almost dancelike quality, a kind of

When one thinks of Hindustani music, one often thinks of improvisation, but many musicians in North India claim their performances contain little improvisation. Most of what is played will have been preconceived and thoroughly practiced.

cross-rhythmic groove, whose origins may once again have been rooted in folk and semiclassical drumming patterns. That groove is now only implicit in fast-tempo versions, yet the extremes of fast and slow tempos encountered in twentieth-century musical performance were probably rare or nonexistent in previous centuries. In some modern styles of *khyāl,* to present one cycle of twelve-beat *ektāl* can take almost a minute. In other words, slow-tempo *ektāl* has been slowed down greatly during the twentieth century.

Though all talas can be played on tabla, those specifically associated with the instrument are modified versions of *tīntāl* and *ektāl.* The tabla's equivalent of the *pakhāvaj* ten-beat *śūltāl* is *jhaptāl*:

X	dhin	nā	2	dhin	dhin	nā
O	tin	nā	3	dhin	dhin	nā

Jhaptāl is clearly indebted to *tīntāl* and has the same four structural divisions. Seven-beat *rūpak tāl* (cited above) is also modeled on the drum strokes of *tīntāl* and is the tabla's answer to *tīvrā.*

For playing the tabla, only one version of the seven-, ten-, and twelve-beat cycles is available; yet this is not true for fourteen- and sixteen-beat talas, each of which has several versions. These structures seem to have arisen in response to the genre each accompanies. *Tīntāl* itself is associated both with medium and fast compositions in *khyāl* and with instrumental compositions such as *masītkhānī, razākhānī,* and *firozkhānī gat.* Yet *tīntāl* is not played with slow *khyāl* in sixteen beats, except in *tīntāl* performances by the school of Jaipur and Alladiya Khan; these were probably performed faster a century ago. Instead, *tilvāṛā* is used: its structure is the same as for *tīntāl,* and its syllables draw on both *tīntāl* and *ektāl*:

X	dhā	tira kiṭa	dhin	dhin
2	dhā	dhā ge	tin	tin
O	tā	tira kiṭa	dhin	dhin
3	dhā	dhā ge	dhin	dhin

Two versions of *tīntāl* accompany the *ṭhumrī* vocal genre: first, *panjābī tāl* (sometimes called *sitārkhānī* when used with instrumental compositions influenced by *ṭhumrī*):

X	dhā	ge dhin	— nā	dhā
2	dhā	ge dhin	— nā	dhā
O	dhā	ge tin	— nā	tā
3	tā	ge dhin	— nā	dhā

and second, *cancār tāl*:

X	dhā	—	dhin	—
2	dhā	dhā	tin	—
O	tā	—	tin	—
3	dhā	dhā	dhin	—

Three fourteen-beat talas are commonly used in playing tabla. Slow *khyāl* is accompanied by *jhūmrā*:

X	dhin	— dhā	ṭira kiṭa	
2	dhin	dhin	dhā ge	tira kiṭa
O	tin	— tā	tira kiṭa	
3	dhin	dhin	dhā ge	tira kiṭa

Faster *khyāl* compositions resort to *āṛācautāl*, an extended version of *ektāl* (hence the reference to the *pakhāvaj* equivalent, *cautāl*):

X	dhin	tira kiṭa	2	dhin	nā
O	tū	nā	3	kat	tā
O	tira kiṭa	dhin	4	nā	dhin
O	dhin	nā			

And in *ṭhumrī*, the fourteen-beat tala *dīpcandī* is employed. Confusingly, it is sometimes also called *cāṅcar*, being just a compressed version of its sixteen-beat counterpart:

X	dhā	dhin	—	
2	dhā	dhā	tin	—
O	tā	tin	—	
3	dhā	dhā	dhin	—

Dādrā has a six-beat cycle used for a style of *ṭhumrī* set specifically in this tala. It too is indebted to the syllables of *tīntāl*:

X	dhā	dhin	nā
O	dhā	tin	nā

Dādrā is sometimes used for lighter and more popular genres, such as ghazal, *gīt*, and film songs. Even more common here, though, is the eight-beat *kaharvā*. Many drum-pattern types come under the general rubric of *kaharvā*, and all represent essentially a different kind of groove. The most common pattern of stresses for *kaharvā tāl* is 3 + 3 + 2, with heavier accents on the first and third subgroups :

X	dhā	dhin	nā	tin
O	nā	ka	dhin	nā

Tabla repertoires

Theme and variations

When one thinks of Hindustani music, one often thinks of improvisation, but many musicians in North India claim their performances contain little improvisation. This is true of most solo tabla playing. Performers have great autonomy in the choice of repertoire. They may well decide on the spur of the moment to improvise on some material in a way not previously thought of, but most of what is played will have been preconceived and thoroughly practiced. This is true even of tiny flourishes inserted before the first beat of the tala (*mukhṛā*): though they appear to be improvised, their consistency and frequent repetition suggests they are mostly memorized patterns. Theme-and-variation compositions offer the player an opportunity to improvise on a rhythmic phrase of strokes; but equally the player may have rehearsed hundreds of variations, and may simply choose from what is already prepared.

There are many types of theme-and-variation compositions, but most fundamental to the training of tabla players is *qā'ida* (Hindi *kāydā*), from an Arabic word meaning "rules" or "system." All tabla students begin with this composition; it continues as a staple of training at all levels, and in most styles of playing it features prominently in solo performance. In its simplest form, *qā'ida* is a phrase that reflects itself, as in this well-known piece from Delhi:

dhā dhā	ti ṭe	dhā dhā	tī nā
tā tā	ti ṭe	dhā dhā	dhī nā

The pattern is elementary and square, employing few syllables: *dhā*, the indispensable right-left combination of *tā* and *ge*; *ti ṭe*, the middle and index fingers playing crisp, dry strokes on the center of the right drum's black spot; *tī* (*tū* in some styles), the low-pitched ricochet on the right drum. Correlations are clear between voiced strokes (*dhā*, *dhī*) and unvoiced (*tā*, *tī*), and whereas the first phrase moves from voiced to unvoiced, its reflection moves back from unvoiced to voiced. The swing between these polarities is important—from phrases dominated by open, resonating strokes on the left drum to phrases with closed, nonresonating strokes. In a general sense, they reflect the swing from the first beat of the tala to the wave (on beat 9) of the *tīntāl* cycle, whose foursquare metric arrangement is ideal for the presentation and development of the rhythmic phrases of the *qā'ida*. The original model for *qā'ida* may well have been a form called *laggī*, commonly used when accompanying *ṭhumrī* and other light vocal styles, and bearing traits similar to those of the *qā'ida* as given above.

Qā'ida probably first appeared during the 1800s, and was almost certainly a short theme like the one above. The twentieth century has seen an expansion of the *qā'ida* concept to ever larger and more complex themes, some with multiple layers in a variety of stroke densities. Even so, the best-known classical models developed in the early years of the twentieth century, like the following, which was composed by the famous Delhi tabla player Natthu Khan (1875–1940):

X	dhā ti	ṭe dhā	ti ṭe	dhā dhā
2	ti ṭe	dhā ge	tī nā	ke nā
O	tā ti	ṭe tā	ti ṭe	dhā dhā
3	ti ṭe	dhā ge	dhī nā	ge nā

Doubled in density from two events per beat to four, this *qā'ida* might simply be played twice per tala cycle; yet it would be more commonly expanded into four phrases, matching the four-division structure of *tīntāl:*

X	dhāti ṭedhā	tiṭe dhādhā	tiṭe dhāge	dhīnā gena
2	dhāti ṭedhā	tiṭe dhādhā	tiṭe dhāge	tīnā kena
O	tāti ṭetā	tiṭe tātā	tiṭe tāke	tīnā kena
3	dhāti ṭedhā	tiṭe dhādhā	tiṭe dhāge	dhīnā gena

With these patterns established as the fundamental structure, the tabla player begins to expand (*prastār* or *vistār*) into variations. The rules for improvisation are rarely explicit; students just copy their masters, much as infants copy their parents' speech, learning to be independent as they gain competence. However, three facts are clear: (1) only syllables used in the theme are permissible in the variations; (2) at the end of the first half of the fundamental structure, a fragment of the original phrase must conclude the variation (minimally this might be *tiṭe dhāge tīnā kena*); (3) whatever is played in the first half must be reflected in the second with the appropriate open-closed (resonating-nonresonating) transformations of strokes. Numerous aesthetic and technical considerations distinguish a good variation from a bad one. Improvisation on a *qā'ida* is a skill that takes time to develop.

Some of Natthu Khan's own variations were quite simple:

dhā— —dhā tiṭe dhādhā tiṭe dhāge dhīnā genā

However, other strategies may involve the permutation (*palṭā* literally 'inverted') of segments of the phrase, the substitution of syllables (like replacing *dhādhā* with *tiṭe*), and the repetition of small segments (*bal*). The following is an example of the latter technique:

X	dhāti	ṭedhā	tiṭe	dhādhā	tiṭe —dhā		tiṭe	dhādhā
2	tiṭe	—dhā	tiṭe	dhādhā	tiṭe dhāge		tīnā	kena
O	tāti	ṭetā	tiṭe	tātā	tiṭe —tā		tiṭe	tātā
3	tiṭe	—dhā	tiṭe	dhādhā	tiṭe dhāge		dhīnā	gena

In performance, a tabla player may present just a few variations or a great many, but averaging eight to twelve. The sequence would conclude with a cadential formula (*tihāī*) constructed out of phrases from the *qā'ida*. The *tihāī* is to the tabla what the *tīyā* is to the *pakhāvaj*: a thrice-repeated phrase, designed to end on the first beat of the tala.

TRACK 7 Similar techniques pervade the remaining theme-and-variation compositions, including a slow introduction that frequently opens a performance (*peshkār*) and different forms of what is most commonly called *relā*. In some styles of drumming, *relā* comprises sequences of rapid strokes, like *tira kiṭa taka* and *dhira dhira giṛa naga*, which are designed to be played at lightning speeds. In other styles, the composition is more subtle: the basic structure (*ṭhā* literally 'place, station') is a simple rhythmic idea, maintained as an outline in the *relā* as the drummer uses rapid strokes to fill the gaps. This realization is evident in the simple Lucknow *relā* in figure 9.

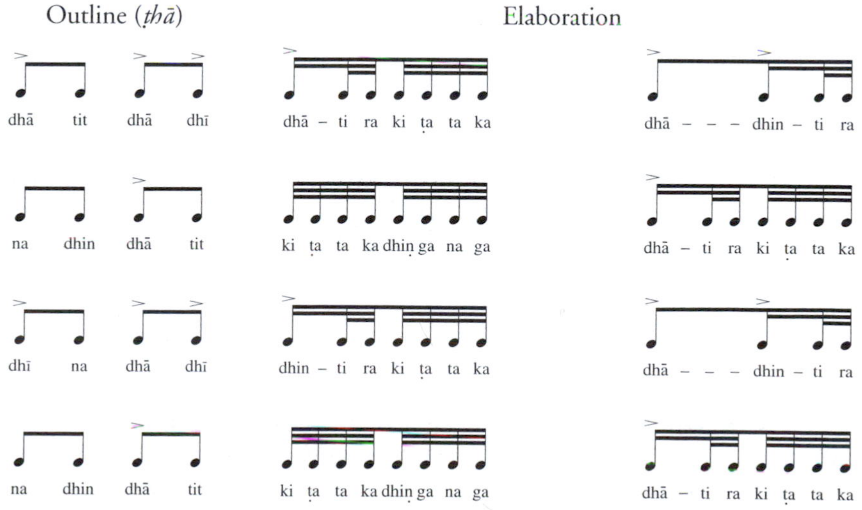

FIGURE 9 *Relā* of the Lucknow tabla tradition, showing the outline (*ṭhā*) subsequently filled in with rapidly drummed strokes.

In Indian artistic traditions, knowledge can be considered wealth. It can function quite literally as wealth when a bride's family gives sets of compositions to the groom's family as part of a dowry.

Fixed compositions

In Indian artistic traditions, knowledge can be considered wealth. It can function quite literally as wealth when a bride's family gives sets of compositions to the groom's family as part of a dowry (the dowry system, though ruled illegal in 1961, is still practiced). Those compositions may represent the knowledge of a tradition going back several generations, and musicians would not give them away lightly. Examples of dowries in the past have included fifty *gat* or one hundred *paran*.

If the fixed *pakhāvaj* composition par excellence is the *paran*, then for the tabla it is the *gat* 'movement, gait'. Just as the word *paran* can signify any number of structures, so too can *gat*. The modern *gat* is both fixed and extended; the earliest examples are simple two-part phrases, which almost certainly influenced the *qā'ida*'s development into a more complex and extended form around 1900. Certain types of simple *gat* must once have been patterns designed for variation, and would probably be mistaken for *qā'ida* nowadays. In some remaining styles of *gat,* variation is possible, but these usually mix two types of composition, as in *gat-qā'ida.*

The following are three compositional strategies involving *gat.*

1. The varied two-part *gat.* The composition from Lucknow shown below bears a striking resemblance to the *paran* given above in the section on *pakhāvaj* repertoire. In alternative versions of this *gat,* the phrase *dhī ne dhī nā ge na* is replaced with *ka tā ga dī gi na*, making it even closer to the *pakhāvaj* model. Here, the second half of the composition reflects the first half, with slight variation at the beginning of the repetition.

X	dhā — —	ge nā ga	ta ki ṭa	ge nā ga
2	dhā tra ka	dhi ki ṭa	dhī ne dhī	nā ge na
O	nā gi na	nā gi na	ta ki ṭa	ge nā ga
3	dhā tra ka	dhi ki ṭa	dhī ne dhī	nā ge na

2. The four-part *gat.* In this style, each phrase concludes in an identical manner. In this Lucknow composition, the second line offers a permutation of the first, whereas the other lines are unrelated. Alternative approaches may include the setting of one or more lines in different densities of syllables:

X	giṛa	naga	tiṭe	tiṭe	giṛa naga	dhīṅga naga
2	tiṭe	giṛa	naga	tiṭe	giṛa naga	dhīṅga naga
O	dhā—	giṛa	naga	dhā—	giṛa naga	dhīṅga naga
3	dhira	dhira	dhira	dhira	giṛa naga	dhīṅga naga

3. *Akāl gat. Akāl,* literally 'untimely, premature', signifies a *gat* that ends before the first beat of the tala. In common practice, *dhā* is never the final syllable; rather, *kat* or *dīṅ* feature prominently, as in this *gat* from Lucknow:

X	dha	—	—	dīṅ	—	ga	dīṅ	—
2	nā	gi	na	nā	gi	na	dhi	ne
O	ta	ki	ṭa	dhā	ti	ṭe	dhi	ne
3	dhā	dhā	ghe	ge	nā	ga	tā	—
X	tin	na	tā	tin	na	tā	tin	ne
2	tin	ne	nā	rā	—	na	dhi	ne
O	ta	ki	ṭa	dhā	ti	ṭe	nā	nā
3	kiṭa	taka	dhira	dhira	kiṭa	taka	dīṅ	—

The phrase structure is less bound to the divisions of the tala (*vibhāg*) than in the other kinds of *gat* encountered above, and though some repetition occurs, the general logic seems to be to add segments that simply sound good and work technically. This additive style is sometimes called the progressive *gat,* and phrases may be made to finish before, on, or even after the first beat of the tala. These are technical showpieces, played rapidly; connoisseurs earnestly anticipate and appreciate them.

Borrowings

It has already been seen that many fixed compositions for tabla owe their origins to *pakhāvaj* pieces. Including *pakhāvaj* strokes (such as *tiṭe katā gadī gena, dhāge tiṭe gadī gena,* and even *dhuma kiṭa*) in tabla pieces is a prime indicator of borrowing. Some compositions are direct translations, and others were merely inspired by *pakhāvaj* repertoire and technique. Yet it is entirely possible that successful tabla compositions found their way back into *pakhāvaj* practice. In general, any tabla piece modeled on a *pakhāvaj paran* without a cadential formula is termed a *gat* (or the term *paran* might even be retained in some traditions), while one modeled on a *paran* with a cadential formula is termed a *ṭukṛā.* The following is a short example of the latter:

X	dhiṭe	dhiṭe	dhāge	tiṭe	kradhā	tiṭe	dhāge	tiṭe
2	dhāge	nadhā	gadī	gena	nāge	tiṭe	katā	katā
O	katā	—dhā	dīntā	katā	dhā—	katā	katā	—dhā
3	dīntā	katā	dhā—	katā	katā — dhā		dīntā	katā
X	dhā							

Kathak dance repertoire has been a rich source of material for the tabla. *Paran* and *ṭukṛā* abound in dance, often with elaborate cadential formulas, some of which are designed to accompany the dancer as she or he pirouettes nine times, or three times nine. The logic of *kathak* syllables is really the logic of the *pakhāvaj,* not of the tabla; owing to a number of sociocultural differences among regions of North India, some tabla traditions adapted *pakhāvaj* and *kathak* ideas more readily than others.

The tabla tradition has always been most flexible and adaptable, absorbing not only *pakhāvaj* and *kathak*-dance elements, but also the techniques and repertoire of the two other drums used formerly in classical and semiclassical performance: the *ḍholak* 'cylindrical drum' and the *naqqārā* 'kettledrums'. The main reason for the demise of these drums has been the phenomenal rise of the tabla. Traces of their patterns of strokes permeate modern performance on the tabla: the *dhātiṭe* element of *qā'ida* originates in the *ḍholak* tradition, as do *ghege nāga* and *nāgina nāgina* strokes, used frequently in *gat*; *naqqārā* practice gave rise to the *dhīnā genā* and *tīnā kenā* elements in *qā'ida,* and to the *giṛa naga* strokes found in *gat.* Where the *ḍholak* and the *naqqārā* once dominated (essentially Delhi and western Uttar Pradesh), the combined influences of these drums resulted in a rich body of *qā'ida,* featuring the *dhātiṭe* plus *dhīnā genā* syllables. The *pakhāvaj* dominated in eastern Uttar Pradesh, giving rise to a greater body of *paran*-inspired fixed compositions. Some centers, such as Lucknow (widely known for its *kathak* tradition), felt strong influences from both directions, and the result was an unusually rich repertoire of tabla *gat* that show strong influences from all three drums.

Tabla accompaniment

Being multifaceted, the tabla is naturally ubiquitous in North India. It accompanies all kinds of music from folk to classical, including dance, instrumental, and vocal genres. The only tradition from which it is absent is the *dhrupad,* a vocal genre. The role of the tabla changes greatly in each genre it accompanies.

Vocal music

In *khyāl,* the tabla plays the part of timekeeper. The soloist grants little opportunity for rhythmic exchange, and only with the presentation of a fast composition would a tabla player have two or three tala cycles to present a short, fixed composition. Yet there is an art to vocal accompaniment that eludes many, and it lies in the subtlety of presenting the drumming pattern and the ability to fill small gaps with fitting flourishes of strokes that maintain the mood and momentum created by the singer.

The same is true for *ṭhumrī,* though here, near the end of a piece, the tabla player has a chance to play short, composed sequences (*laggī*) at high speed. Whatever the tala of a composition, the final section shifts into moderately fast *tīn-tāl.*

Dance

Opportunities for short tabla solos abound in modern *kathak* (allowing for the dancer's changing costumes, taking brief breaks, and other such interruptions), yet in this context the tabla player mainly shadows the dancer. Most of a dance performance comprises set pieces, such as *paran* and *ṭukṛā*: often, the dancer first recites the dance syllables (*bol* literally *paṛhant* 'reading'), and then dances this rhythm. The drummer will offer the drumming pattern as an accompaniment to the recitation, to verify the rhythmic character of the dance and ensure that it fits with the tala; then the drummer will accompany the dancer's movements with the syllables of the piece.

In expressive dance, which enacts a story or creates a caricature, the role of the tabla is often more subtle: the drummer uses many rhythmic devices to accompany different movements (such as the characteristic walks of the Hindu deities Radha or Krishna), or to suggest programmatic effects (such as running water, thunder, a stone being thrown, a pot breaking).

Instrumental music

Much evidence suggests that even in the early 1900s the role of the tabla in instrumental accompaniment resembled that in vocal music. Yet as the tabla has gained social prestige and musical importance, so has its role expanded from mere timekeeper to contributor in the creative process. This change came with Allauddin Khan, who began a kind of ritualized exchange or question-answer (*savāl-javāb*) between soloist and accompanist: whatever the soloist played rhythmically, the accompanist would be expected to mimic, and the segments would progress from long to short, finally merging in a frenetic, melodic-percussive joint conclusion (figure 10). Allauddin's son Ali Akbar Khan and his disciple Ravi Shankar continued this trend. Shankar developed a style of presentation that, during the raga, allowed the accompanist to perform several solo segments, each lasting only a few cycles. This style of performance, alternating between focus on the drummer and focus on the soloist, is now the norm.

FIGURE 10 Allauddin Khan (sarod) with the great Banaras tabla player Kanthe Maharaj in a pose that epitomizes the modern tendency toward greater rapport between soloist and accompanist. Photo courtesy Ali Akbar College of Music, San Rafael, California.

Tabla-playing traditions

The first family to specialize in tabla playing was that of Sudhar Khan Dharhi of Delhi, probably beginning in the 1740s. Sudhar Khan belonged to an endogamous clan of lower-class Shia Muslims who had converted from Hinduism to Islam at some indeterminate point in the past—a strategy aimed at social mobility and patronage from wealthy Muslim courts. Delhi was a thriving cultural center in the early 1700s, and the reign of Emperor Muhammad Shah (1719–1748) had seen lavish court patronage of music, even after the sack of the city in 1739. Yet Delhi around 1750 was in economic turmoil, and many musicians began turning toward local courts, such as Jhajjar to the west of Delhi and Faizabad-Lucknow to the east. Evidence suggests that Shia Muslims from the Delhi tabla-playing clan migrated to these centers in the 1760s or 1770s.

The court of Nawab Asaf ud-Daula moved, on his accession in 1775, from Faizabad to Lucknow. Until his death (1797), Lucknow witnessed massive investment in the arts and architecture. In this climate, Bakhshu Khan Dharhi established himself as one of the greatest tabla players of his age and the head of a breakaway lineage. During the first half of the 1700s, tabla players who had previously migrated to Jhajjar moved to Lucknow, so abundant were the opportunities for patronage.

Around that time, both the Delhi and Lucknow families spawned new traditions of tabla playing. Each taught Sunni Muslim students: in Lucknow, Bakhshu Khan and his son Mammu Khan taught Haji Vilayat Ali Khan of Farrukhabad, a village in western Uttar Pradesh; in Delhi, Sudhar Khan's great-grandson Shitab Khan taught the brothers Kallu and Miru Khan of Ajrara, a village near Meerut and Delhi. Ram Sahai, a Hindu from Banaras, learned from the Jhajjar lineage in Lucknow. A further lineage, seemingly unconnected to any of these, developed in Lahore (in the Punjab), probably as a Muslim branch of a Hindu *pakhāvaj* tradition.

Each drumming tradition developed its own distinct style of playing (*bāj*). The Delhi style, inspired by the *naqqārā* and the *ḍholak,* featured delicate fingerstrokes, ideal for the presentation and development of theme-and-variation compositions. Delhi *gat* tended to avoid *pakhāvaj*-style strokes, and favored playing on the rim. The Ajrara style was similar, though its players had a greater tendency to use the ring finger on the right tabla drum to supplement Delhi's use of the index and middle fingers. As for repertoire, many traditional Ajrara compositions are set in triple time. Lucknow and Farrukhabad pieces featured a strong mix of rim and inner-drumhead

Within the world of classical musicians, being associated with a *gharānā* 'family, clan' conveys a sense of prestige, since it implies a long musical pedigree.

FIGURE 11 Ahmad Jan Thirakva, possibly the greatest tabla player of the twentieth century. Photo courtesy Sangeet Natak Academy, New Delhi.

syllables and were well known for the variety and complexity of their *gat.* Haji Vilayat Ali Khan was particularly famous as a composer, and many of his compositions survive. The Banaras and Punjab styles owed much of their technique and repertoire to the *pakhāvaj*; later, however, the Punjab tradition appears to have adopted some features of the Delhi style.

There has been a tendency to think of tabla styles as either Western (*pachvāṅ,* that is, Delhi and Ajrara) or Eastern (*pūrab,* that is, Lucknow, Farrukhabad, and Banaras). This categorization is misleading, since it fails to differentiate style beyond a general tendency either to avoid or include *pakhāvaj* technique and repertoire. Furthermore, the name Purab is commonly used to denote another tradition stemming from Munir Khan (?1870s–1938), who was said to have learned to play the tabla from Ajrara drummers. Purab is also sometimes called Laliyana (another village near Meerut), continuing the trend of naming traditions after their founders' ancestral homes.

Around 1900, tabla players began calling their traditions *gharānā* 'family, clan'. *Khyāl* singers first used the term in the late 1800s to identify their families as having common traits: distinct and unique musical styles, family cores of at least three generations, charismatic and famous personalities, and a living authority as leader (*khalīfa*). Tabla players, realizing their families had the same basic ingredients, adopted this strategy to help raise drummers' social prestige by emulating the social organization of solo singers. Within the world of classical musicians, being associated with a *gharānā* conveys a sense of prestige, since it implies a long musical pedigree.

The twentieth century has seen many great tabla players rise to prominence. In 1926, Abid Husain Khan of Lucknow (1867–1936) became the first professor of tabla at the Bhatkhande Music College of Lucknow. His contemporary was the great tabla player Natthu Khan of Delhi (1875–1940). Ahmad Jan Thirakva (?1880s–1976) achieved an unprecedented level of fame for his technical prowess and compositional skills (figure 11); he was known, too, for his rivalry with Habibuddin Khan of Ajrara (1899–1972). Alla Rakha of Lahore (Punjab *gharānā,* b. 1919) and Kishan Maharaj of Banaras (Banaras *gharānā,* b. 1923) have been notable for their extraordinary rhythmic inventiveness. Yet as the century has progressed, more and more nonhereditary musicians have established themselves, now easily outnumbering the hereditary musicians within the tabla *gharānā* system.

RECENT DEVELOPMENTS IN INDIAN RHYTHM

New talas

The sixteen-beat *tīntāl* has long dominated Hindustani music, especially in performance on tabla. However, in recent decades influential musicians, particularly Ravi Shankar and Ali Akbar Khan, have stimulated an interest in alternative talas, an interest that has filtered through to the solo tabla repertoire. Most material designed to be played in alternative talas derives from preexisting *tīntāl* models. For instance, the varied two-part *gat* notated above in *tīntāl* is easily transformed into a ten-beat *jhaptāl* by the addition of a single phrase (in parentheses below) and the repetition of the phrase *dhā tra ka, dhi ki ṭa*:

X	dhā — —	ge nā ga	
2	ta ki ṭa	ge nā ga	dhā tra ka
O	dhi ki ṭa	dhī ne dhī	
3	nā ge na	nā gi na	nā gi na
X	ta ki ṭa	ge nā ga	
2	dhā tra ka	dhi ki ṭa	(ghin — nā
O	rā — na)	dhā tra ka	
3	dhi ki ṭa	dhī ne dhī	nā ge na

Similar additions and subtractions can result in all manner of possibilities, and there are few restrictions, since musicians appear to pay little regard to maintaining the divisional structure (*vibhāg*) of a tala; rather, they consider a tala primarily a number of beats, not a subdivided structure.

Around 1900, musicians showed considerable interest in searching out older, complex talas. The personal notebooks of Abid Husain Khan bear this out. Masit Khan of Farrukhabad modeled his own invention, *nasruk tāl*, on an older, rare *pakhāvaj* tala called *nishorūk*. He kept neither the drum syllables nor the structural division, just the target of nine beats. *Nishorūk tāl*:

X	dhin	na	ki ṭa	ta ka
2	dhu ma	ki ṭa	ta ki	ṭa ta
3	kā			

became *nasruk tāl*:

X	dhī		nā	
O	dhī	na	kat	
2	dhī—	—kra	dhī nā	
3	dhā	ge	dhī nā	kat tā

Fractional talas are a twentieth-century novelty. Latif Ahmad Khan of Delhi (1941–1990) created a tala of five and a quarter beats. The logic for its construction was a division of three beats, a division of three half-beats, and a final division of three quarter-beats. In his Hindi textbook on the tabla, entitled *Tāl Prakāsh,* Bhagvat Sharan Sharma notated *kalāvatī tāl* (1981); this structure was apparently created to match a *gat* in nine and a half beats composed by the Bombay All India Radio sitarist Baburao Kulkarni:

X	dhī —	nā —	
2	dhī —	dhī —	nā —
O	tī —	nā —	
3	dhī nā	dhin tira	kiṭa

The final division features *dhī nā dhin* as eighth notes and *tira kiṭa* as sixteenth notes.

There are no limits to creativity in inventing talas. Players increasingly produce imaginative new formulas and dig up obscure talas no one else has managed to find.

New trends in drumming

TRACK 7

Paralleling the movement toward different and more complex talas is a general movement toward increasingly complex rhythmic play (*laykārī*). The solos of Ahmad Jan Thirakva, arguably the greatest tabla player of the twentieth century, exhibit an almost complete absence of complex rhythmic divisions; his playing is foursquare, with phrases that rarely defy the divisional structure of *tīntāl.* Such an approach would be unusual nowadays, since the aesthetic of drumming has shifted to complex rhythms, often at the expense of compositional integrity. Where substance and rhythmic complexity combine (for instance in the playing of Alla Rakha), the result can be as mind-boggling as it is exhilarating.

Alla Rakha's son, the modern superstar Zakir Hussain (b. 1951), has been largely responsible for experimentation with jazz and pop fusion, as with the group Shakti. The percussionist Trilok Gurtu has created his own worldbeat-jazz fusion drumming approach, involving the tabla as a component of his sound. Jerry Leake has scored compositions for drum set based on tabla drumming. The tabla has also found its way into contemporary art music, as in *Stedman Doubles* for clarinet and percussion (1956, revised 1968) by the British composer Peter Maxwell Davies. In *Lahara* (1977), the percussionist Bob Becker scored elements of the repertoire of his teacher, Sharda Sahai of Banaras, for solo drum with accompaniment by drone and melodic instruments (*lahrā* is the cyclical melody used to accompany a tabla solo). Becker has written for tabla solo and Western percussion in *Palta* (1982) and for drum solo imitating tabla in *Mudra* (1990).

Tabla ensembles first appeared under the tutelage of the Calcutta teacher Jnan Prakash Ghosh, and his student Shankar Ghosh continued the trend. The material featured multiple tablas playing the same pieces, various sounds in counterpoint, heightened use of verbal drum-syllable presentations as an art in itself, and the tuning of several right-tabla drums to form a pitch row (*tablā tarang*). (In extreme cases, other musicians have used *tablā tarang* to perform ragas.) The tabla-ensemble concept is being continued and developed in North America by Ritesh Das and his Toronto Tabla Ensemble.

SOURCES AND FURTHER READING

Little has been written on the *pakhāvaj,* and recordings of solo performances are rare. An exception is Raja Chatrapati Singh (1989), whose recitations and performances became legendary in his lifetime. In accompaniment, the *pakhāvaj* can be heard on the vocal *dhrupad* recordings featuring members of the Dagar or Mallick families.

Noteworthy literature exists on the tabla, much in Indian languages. In English, Rebecca Stewart's doctoral dissertation (1974) laid the foundation for modern studies of tabla. Stewart investigated the technical origins of various stylistic schools and analyzed the repertoire and the structure of individual types of composition in detail. Robert Gottlieb (1993) has provided recordings and extensive transcriptions of six tabla solos representing the *gharānā* traditions of Delhi (Inam Ali Khan), Farrukhabad (Keramatullah Khan), Lucknow (Wajid Husain Khan), Banaras (Kishan Maharaj), Ajrara (Habibuddin Khan), and Punjab (Alla Rakha). James R. Kippen (1988) has offered a cultural analysis of the Lucknow tabla *gharānā* through a study that focused on its *khalīfā,* Afaq Husain Khan (1930–1990), and its repertoire; both Afaq Husain and his son Ilmas Husain Khan provide solos on accompanying cassette. Kippen (1988, 1989) and Daniel Neuman (1990) have provided information on the social organization of tabla players. David Roach (1972) and Frances Shepherd (1976) have written on the Banaras tradition, and Gert-Matthias Wegner (1982) has covered the Laliyana *gharānā.* Both Shepherd and Wegner notate extensive repertoires.

Commercial recordings of solo tabla playing abound on LP disk, cassette, and compact disc; most of the twentieth-century masters mentioned above are represented as both accompanists and soloists. Of particular interest are LP recordings of Ahmad Jan Thirakva performing with his contemporaries such as Amir Hussain Khan (Laliyana-Purab *gharānā*; 1968, 1969). On cassette are fascinating performances by Keramatullah Khan (?1980s), Afaq Husain Khan (1991), and Shanta Prasad (Banaras *gharānā*; 1988). The number of compact-disc recordings is growing rapidly. Notable among them are those of Nizamuddin Khan (Laliyana-Purab; 1994) and Kishan Maharaj (1993). Alla Rakha has made many solo recordings (1989) and duets with his son Zakir Hussain (?1980s, 1991). Zakir Hussain (1987) and Swapan Chaudhuri (Lucknow *gharānā*; 1993a, 1993b) both live in California and have produced solo recordings of excellent quality, as has Anindo Chatterjee (Calcutta, a student of Jnan Prakash Ghosh; 1992).

REFERENCES

Bor, Joep, and Philippe Bruguiere. 1992. *Masters of Raga.* Berlin: Haus der Kulturen der Welt.

Chatterjee, Anindo. 1992. *Anindo and His Tabla.* Audiorec ACCD 1016–7. Compact disc.

Chaudhuri, Swapan. 1993a. *The Majestic Tabla of Swapan Chaudhuri.* Chhanda Dhara SNCD 71093. Compact disc.

———. 1993b. *The Soul of Tabla.* Interworld Music CD 809092. Compact disc.

Husain Khan, Ustad Afaq. 1991. *Tabla Lahara.* Concord Records 05023. Audio cassette.

Gottlieb, Robert S. 1993. *Solo Tabla Drumming of North India: Its Repertoire, Styles, and Performance Practices.* 2 vols. with cassettes. Delhi: Motilal Banarasidass.

Hussain, Zakir. 1987. *Zakir Hussain and Sultan Khan.* Chhanda Dhara SNCD 4487. Compact disc.

Hussain, Zakir, and Alla Rakha. 1991. *Indian Night Live Stuttgart '88: Memorable Tabla Duet.* Chhanda Dhara SNCD 70891. Compact disc.

Khan, Keramatullah. ?1980s. *Tabla Solo.* Electrogand EBI 0322 133. Audio cassette.

Khan, Nizamuddin. 1994. *Ustad Nizamuddin Khan.* India Music Archive IAM CD 1014. Compact disc.

Kippen, James R. 1988. *The Tabla of Lucknow: A Cultural Analysis of a Musical Tradition.* Cambridge: Cambridge University Press.

———. 1989. "Changes in the Social Status of Tabla Players." *Journal of the Indian Musicological Society* 20(1,2):37–46.

Maharaj, Kishan. 1993. *Brilliancy and Oldest Tradition: Tabla Solo and Duet (with Kumar Bose).* Chhanda Dhara SNCD 70493. Compact disc.

Neuman, Daniel M. 1990. *The Life of Music in North India: The Organization of an Artistic Tradition,* 2nd ed. Chicago: University of Chicago Press.

Prasad, Pandit Shamta. 1988. *Tabla Lahara.* Concord Records 05015. Audio cassette.

Rakha, Alla. 1989. *The "Ultimate" in Taal-Vidya: Solo Masterpieces in Teentaal and Jhaptaal.* Magnasound D4H10079. Compact disc.

Rakha, Alla, and Zakir Hussain. ?1980s. *Together.* Magnasound C4H10241. Compact disc.

———1991. *Maestro's Choice: Alla Rakha and Zakir Hussain.* Music Today A19013. Compact disc.

Roach, David. 1972. "The Benares Bāj—The *Tablā* Tradition of a North Indian City." *Asian Music* 3(2):29–41.

Sharma, Bhagvat Sharan. 1981. *Tāl Prakāś.* Hathras: Sangeet Karyalaya. Hindi.

Shepherd, Frances. 1976. "Tabla and the Benares Gharana." Ph.D. dissertation, Wesleyan University.

Singh, Raja Chatrapati. 1989. *Masters of Tala: Pakhawaj Solo.* Wergo SM1075–50. Compact disc.

Stewart, Rebecca M. 1974. "The Tablā in Perspective." Ph.D. dissertation, University of California, Los Angeles.

Thirakva, Ahmad Jan, and Amir Hussain Khan. 1968. *Great Percussion Masters.* Gramophone Company of India MOAE 5007. LP disk.

———. 1969. *Rhythms of India Tabla Recital: Ustad Ahmed Jan Thirakwa and Ustad Amir Hussain Khan.* Gramophone Company of India EASD 1335. LP disk.

Wegner, Gert-Matthias. 1982. *Die Tablā im Gharānā des Ustād Munir Khān (Laliyānā).* Hamburg: Verlag der Musikalienhandlung Karl Dieter Wagner.

Karnatak Tala

David Paul Nelson

The Sanskrit word *tāḷa* covers the whole subject of musical meter in Indian music. A tala is a metrical framework, or structure of beats, within which pieces of music are composed and performed. In South India, as in the northern area, modern talas are cyclic; that is, a piece of music has the same repeating metrical structure from beginning to end. In this way, South Indian talas are analogous to meters in Western music. There are important differences between talas and meters, however. Talas may be much longer. One Karnatak tala is twenty-nine beats long, and in performance each cycle takes up to forty-five seconds, much longer than any Western meter. Another difference concerns accentual structure. In Western 3/4 time, every measure of this meter has the same downbeat accent: *one*–two–three—a strong beat followed by two weak beats. South Indian talas have no inherently strong or weak beats; instead, accents are the result of the shape of phrases.

Possibly the most striking feature of a tala is that it is not written down. It is counted gesturally, by clapping, waving, and touching the fingers sequentially to the other hand or thigh. In Western music, a measure of 3/4 time is written on paper with staves, clefs, notes, and rests, but in performance it is not usually counted aloud; a three-beat tala, however, is counted using visible gestures: a clap, a clap, and a wave (palm upward), or a clap, a touch of the pinkie (little finger) to the other hand or the thigh, and a touch of the thumb to the other hand or the thigh. The gestures that count talas are not chosen randomly but have been passed from teacher to student in an evolving transmission going back more than two thousand years.

For South Indian musicians, the human voice is the main vehicle for music. The archetypal musician is a singer who expresses with voice and hands all three of the essential features of music: melody (raga), text (*sāhityam*), and rhythmic structure (tala). All Karnatak musicians, including drummers, begin their studies by singing; many drummers who have not formally studied singing learn to sing quite well over the course of their careers. Even students of drumming can speak their rhythmic phrases so that their hands are free to show the tala.

Musicians learn the sung or spoken phrases and the gestures together, concentrating sometimes more on the sequence of the gestures, sometimes on the shapes of the phrases. The ability to feel the phrase and the beat moving together gives musicians confidence because they can sense immediately whether a phrase is properly synchronized with the beat, and if not, how to make the necessary correction. This confidence is the basis of the rhythmic improvisation for which South Indian musicians are famous.

During a performance of Karnatak music, one or more of the on-stage musicians keeps the tala, as performing the gestures is called. This is normal practice; the tala is as much a part of the music as the raga or the text. Informed listeners enthusiastically clap out the tala beats along with the performers, making Karnatak music participatory to an extent not common in Western concerts. Listeners who keep the tala find that their movements enhance their understanding, and therefore enjoyment, of the music. By uniting their visual, auditory, and tactile senses in attending to the music, they access a level of detail not far removed from that which the musicians are experiencing. This sort of "dancing in place" is comparable with finger snapping or foot tapping in jazz, another music in which energetic rhythms inspire listeners to move with the musicians.

TALA HAND GESTURES

Karnatak musicians count time by clapping (one hand moving up and down against the other), touching the fingers on the hand or thigh, and turning the palm up in a hand wave. These types of gestures, called *kriyā*, are the only ones used to reckon talas in modern times; older musical texts list several others, but none continues to be used. Gestures fall into two general categories: sounded like the clap (*taṭṭu*); and unsounded like the finger count and hand wave (*vīccu*). In performance, both categories are likely to be audible, though the clap is clearly the dominant sound. *Kriyā* belongs to a group of rhythm-related concepts that have come to be known as *tāḷa-daṣaprāṇa* 'ten life-breaths of tala'. These are *kriyā, anga, jāti, kāla, kaḷai, graha* (*eḍuppu*), *laya, yati, prastara,* and *mārga*. Most theoretical treatises from Bharata's *Nāṭyaśāstra* onward discuss at least some of them, and this article covers the first nine.

The gestures function somewhat differently in the three types of tala in current use. These types—*sūlādi sapta tāḷa*, the *cāpu tāḷa*, and the *tiruppugaḻ tāḷa*—represent the influences of music theory, folk music, and ancient hymnody respectively.

THE PRIMORDIAL SEVEN TALAS

The composer and musicologist Purandara Dasa (1484–1564) codified the theory of his day into exercises still used by musicians. His scheme, called *sūlādi sapta tāḷa* 'primordial seven talas', employs three groupings of gestures, called *anga*: the *laghu*, made up of a clap followed by counts on the fingers, the *drutam*, a clap followed by a wave of the hand, and the *anudrutam*, a solitary clap. These gestures are normally made with one hand striking the other hand or the thigh. Only the *laghu* may have different numbers of beats; the *drutam* is always two beats long, and the *anudrutam* is always one beat. Each grouping is assigned a symbol: for the *laghu*, a vertical line (I); for the *drutam*, a circle (O); and for the *anudrutam*, a half-circle (◡).

The primordial seven talas are made up of groupings arranged in the following ways (each arrangement represents one cycle of the given tala):

dhruva tāḷa: *laghu* + *drutam* + *laghu* + *laghu* (I O I I)
maṭya tāḷa: *laghu* + *drutam* + *laghu* (I O I)
āṭa tāḷa: *laghu* + *laghu* + *drutam* + *drutam* (I I O O)
jhampā tāḷa: *laghu* + *anudrutam* + *drutam* (I ◡ O)
tripuṭa tāḷa: *laghu* + *drutam* + *drutam* (I O O)
rūpaka tāḷa: *drutam* + *laghu* (O I)
ēka tāḷa: *laghu* (I)

FIGURE 1 A nine-beat (*sankīrṇa jāti*) *laghu*, showing the appropriate gesture for each beat.

1	2	3	4	5	6	7	8	9
clap	pinkie	ring	middle	index	thumb	pinkie	ring	middle

The number of beats in a *laghu* depends on which of the five possible families (*jāti*) of rhythm it belongs to:

caturaśra jāti, four beats
tiśra jāti, three beats
miśra jāti, seven beats
khaṇḍa jāti, five beats
sankīrṇa jāti, nine beats

A four-beat *laghu* is counted as follows: clap, pinkie, ring finger, middle finger. Finger counts always start with the pinkie touching the thigh or palm of the other hand, then the ring finger, and so on. For the seven- or nine-beat *laghu*, which have more beats than a musician has fingers on one hand, the finger counts (starting on beat 2 following the clap) return to the pinkie for beat seven, and so on. Figure 1 shows a nine-beat *laghu.*

In any given tala structure, the *laghu* is always the same length. For example, a cycle of five-beat *laghu dhruva tāḷa* has three *laghu* (*laghu* + *drutam* + *laghu* + *laghu*), each of which is five beats long, so the cycle's total number of beats is seventeen (5 + 2 + 5 + 5). We can calculate how long any cycle is by knowing the name of its family (the number of beats in its *laghu*) and its structure (the name of the tala). The shortest possible tala in Purandara Dasa's scheme is three-beat *laghu ēka tāḷa*, with a single *laghu* of three beats. The longest possible tala is nine-beat *laghu dhruva tāḷa*, with twenty-nine beats (9 + 2 + 9 + 9).

The result of combining the seven tala structures with the five classes of rhythm is that each tala structure has five possible numbers of beats per cycle, producing thirty-five different talas. Using *tripuṭa tāḷa* (*laghu* + *drutam* + *drutam*) as an example, the following five cycles are possible:

four-beat *laghu tripuṭa tāḷa*: 4 + 2 + 2, or eight beats per cycle
three-beat *laghu tripuṭa tāḷa*: 3 + 2 + 2, or seven beats per cycle
seven-beat *laghu tripuṭa tāḷa*: 7 + 2 + 2, or eleven beats per cycle
five-beat *laghu tripuṭa tāḷa*: 5 + 2 + 2, or nine beats per cycle
nine-beat *laghu tripuṭa tāḷa*: 9 + 2 + 2, or thirteen beats per cycle

The order in which the classes of rhythm are listed, with their numerical values, raises important questions. Why are they not arranged in ascending order of three, four, five, seven, and nine? or in descending order? Why are there no classes of six and eight? Perhaps most interesting of all: why is three the smallest number among them? What happened to two?

For answers, we must turn to ancient sources. In the oldest known treatise that refers to Indian music, the *Nāṭyaśāstra* (c. 200 B.C.–A.D. 200), only certain talas were accepted as legitimate for sacred music. Though that music bore little, if any, relation to modern South Indian music, present-day Karnatak musicians place great value on connections with ancient times, and consequently some traces of ancient theoretical ideas survive. Talas acceptable at the time of the *Nāṭyaśāstra* were based on the numbers four (*caturaśra* 'four-sided') and three (*tryaśra* 'three-sided'). These names suggest that early Indian notions of tala incorporated a kind of spatial character. Such notions would explain the absence of a tala based on two, since three is the smallest number of sides that can enclose a space.

As centuries passed and the scope of acceptable influences broadened, other talas became legitimate. Eventually, seven (*miśra* 'mixed'), five (*khaṇḍa* 'broken'), and nine (*sankīrṇa* 'all mixed up') entered the realm of legitimacy. Purandara Dasa's scheme preserves this historical order of acceptance.

Purandara Dasa did not invent these talas or the symbols used for the groupings of gestures; they can be found in ancient music-theory texts. By looking at these old books, it is impossible to know just how a tala would have been used in the music, since the songs were not written down. Purandara Dasa's contribution was to compose musical exercises for all seven and to teach these to his students, who in turn taught them to their students, and so on. Because musicians have continued to use these exercises since his time, they may represent an accurate picture of how talas were used as far back as the 1500s.

The thirty-five-tala scheme is a mainstay of Karnatak musical pedagogy, and musicians sometimes use its less common talas to create short, strenuous compositions called *pallavi*. But musicians regularly use few of the talas listed within it. In fact, only the following five are in common use:

five-beat *laghu āṭa tāḷa*, a fourteen-beat cycle (figure 2*a*)
seven-beat *laghu jhampā tāḷa*, a ten-beat cycle (figure 2*b*)
four-beat *laghu tripuṭa tāḷa*, the formal name for the eight-beat *ādi tāḷa* (figure 2*c*)
four-beat *laghu rūpaka tāḷa*, a six-beat cycle (figure 2*d*) almost always counted as three beats (figure 2*d′*)
three-beat *laghu ēka tāḷa*, a three-beat cycle (figure 2*e*)

One of these talas, four-beat *laghu rūpaka tāḷa*, presents an interesting case of a tala with two identities. Within Purandara Dasa's scheme, it should be counted as two plus four, with a clap and wave (*drutam*), followed by a clap and three counts (four-beat *laghu*) (figure 2*d*). In practice, though, it is only rarely counted this way. It is virtually always counted as a three-beat cycle: a clap (*anudrutam*) followed by a clap and a wave (*drutam*) (figure 2*d′*). Even in slow-tempo *rūpaka tāḷa,* in which the normal practice is two counts per beat, musicians use the three-beat mode of counting.

In Purandara Dasa's time, *rūpaka tāḷa* was possibly counted as a six-beat cycle. It may have existed as a widely used three-beat cycle, and Purandara Dasa wanted to include it in his scheme. To fit into the seven-tala system, it had to include a *laghu* so it could be varied according to the classes of rhythms. However, Purandara Dasa may have reasoned that calling it a six-beat cycle with claps on beats 1 and 3 (for the *drutam* and *laghu*) would be similar enough to a three-beat cycle with claps on beats 1 and 2 that musicians would accept it as equivalent. They would not have to change their *rūpaka tāḷa* performance, and he would have his generative tala cycle. A third possibility is that by custom over time, a three-beat count has replaced the more theoretically proper six-beat count.

The beat in the primordial seven talas

Purandara Dasa's legacy is largely oral. Every student of Karnatak music learns to play or sing his set of exercises (*alankara*) in all seven talas, and all learn his thirty-five-tala scheme. Any student can count out the longest and the shortest cycle (*āvarta*). Even though he did not write a text, musicians are in general agreement about the essential features of his system.

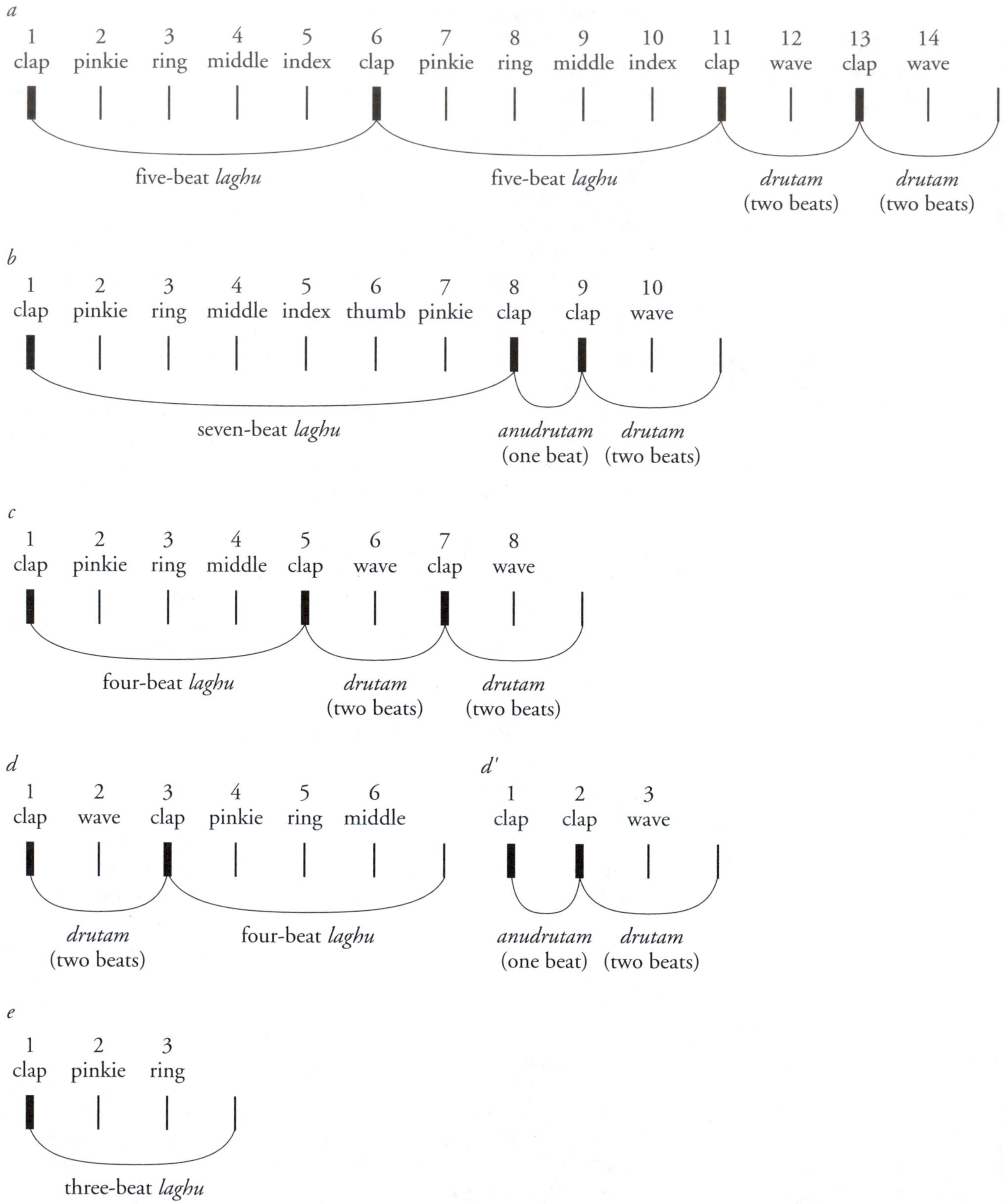

FIGURE 2 The five most commonly used talas in Purandara Dasa's seven-tala scheme, showing gestures and gesture groupings: *a*, five-beat *laghu āṭa tāḷa*; *b*, seven-beat *laghu jhampā tāḷa*; *c*, four-beat *laghu tripuṭa tāḷa* (*ādi tāḷa*); *d*, four-beat *laghu rūpaka tāḷa* and *d′*, as usually counted; *e*, three-beat *laghu ēka tāḷa*.

Since his day, musicians and musicologists have given much attention to the internal structure of the beat (*akṣara*), a subject at which Purandara Dasa's exercises only hint. Karnatak musicians think of beats as syllabic groups (*mātrā*). This idea is not new; an old Indian music text defines a beat as "the length of time it takes to speak five short syllables." As an example of this kind of thinking, try speaking the four-syllable phrase *take it Toni* four times, clapping on the first syllable each time. The syllabic groups help make the beats move evenly. These groups usually have four

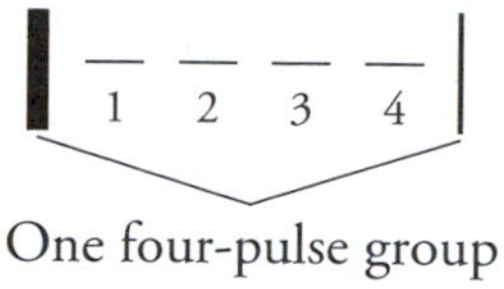

FIGURE 3 One tala beat subdivided into a four-pulse group; the dashes show potential notes or rests.

syllables, or pulses. There are no strong or weak pulses, but each syllable may be stressed, sounded, or silent, depending on the musical phrase, as in *TAKE it Toni, TAKE it Toni, TAKE it Toni, TAKE it Toni,* or in *take it TOni, take it TOni, take it TOni, take it TOni.* Rests or silent pulses can substitute for any of the syllables. A short dash (–) representing the omitted syllable signifies a rest the same length as the syllable. So the phrase still has four pulses, but the second one is silent: *take – Toni, take – Toni, take – Toni, take – Toni.* Since any of the syllables may fall out in favor of a rest, it will perhaps be more helpful to call these groups pulse groups. Figure 3 shows a beat with a four-pulse group. The dashes indicate potential notes or syllables.

Although four is the most common pulse group of a beat, there are other possibilities: three, five, seven, and nine. These are the same numbers that make up the *laghu* in the thirty-five-tala scheme; when used to describe the pulse group that subdivides a beat, they are called *gati* 'way of walking'. To get a sense of the effect of different subdivisions of the beat, try the following phrases the same way as before. Speak each phrase several times, clapping on the first syllable every time:

three-pulse group: ||take| To|ni ||take| To|ni
four-pulse group: ||take| it| To|ni ||take| it| To|ni
five-pulse group: ||take| it| to| To|ni ||take| it| to| To|ni
seven-pulse group: ||take| it| o|ver| to| To|ni ||take| it| o|ver| to| To|ni
nine-pulse group: ||take| all| of| it| o|ver| to| To|ni ||take| all| of| it| o|ver| to| To|ni

A tala that makes use of only one pulse group per beat is called a one-count (*oru kaḷai*) tala. Figure 4*a* shows the most common tala, the eight-beat cycle known as *ādi* 'ancient, primordial' *tāḷa*, as a one-count tala with one four-pulse group per beat. The beats are numbered, and the gestures are shown in the top lines. The dashes between the lines represent the four pulses in each beat, totaling thirty-two pulses per cycle.

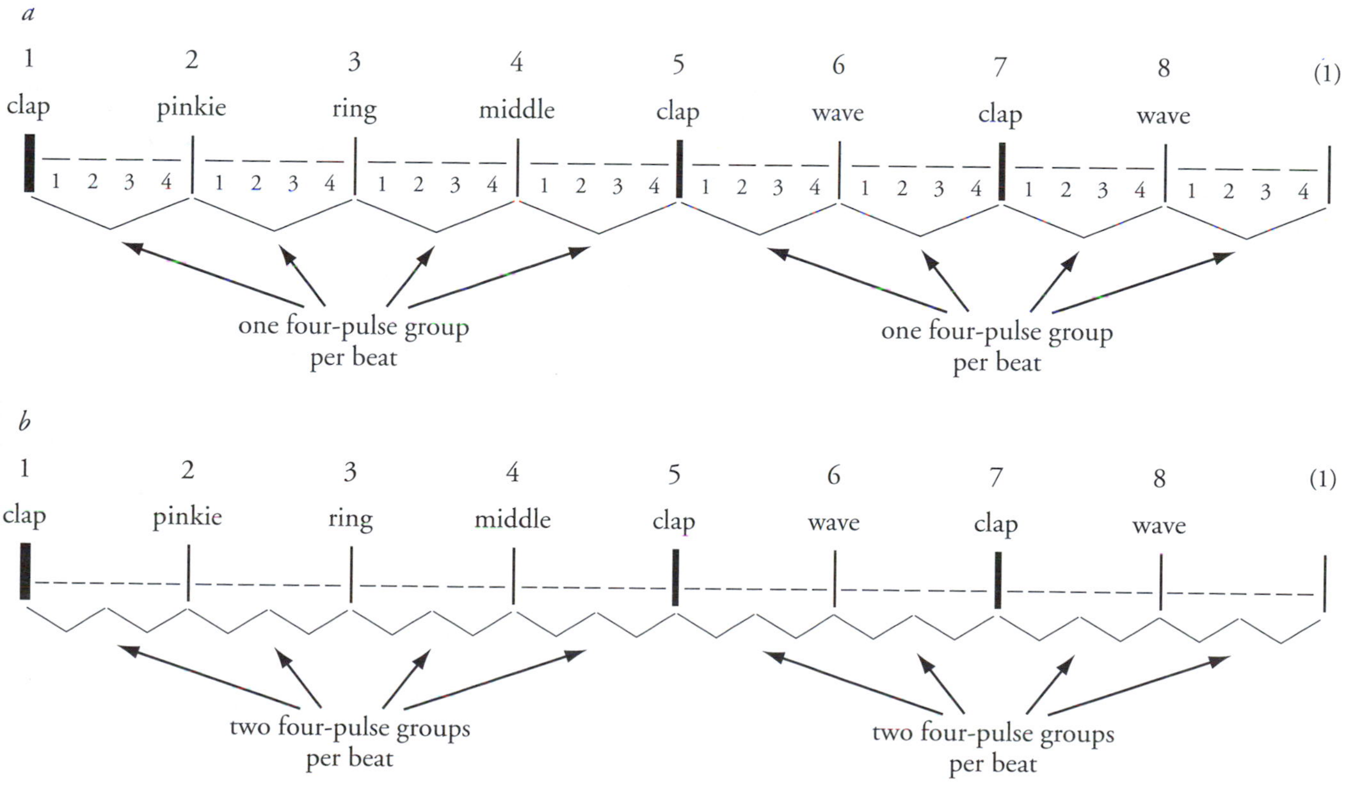

FIGURE 4 Two versions of eight-beat *ādi tāḷa*: *a*, one-count (*oru kaḷai*), showing one pulse group of four pulses per beat, played at a rate of 72 to 120 a minute; *b*, two-count (*reṇḍu kaḷai*), showing two pulse groups of four pulses each per beat, played at a rate of 36 to 60 a minute.

More than one pulse group may occur in each beat, producing a long cycle. In *ādi tāḷa*, for instance, there can be two pulse groups per beat, as in figure 4*b*. This is called two-count (*reṇḍu kaḷai*) *ādi tāḷa*. As one might expect, a cycle of two-count *ādi tāḷa* takes twice as long as a cycle of one-count *ādi tāḷa*. Though both versions have eight beats, the two-count version has sixty-four pulses (twice as many), and these move at more or less the same rate as those in the one-count version. A musician composing a slow, stately, serious song will often use a two-count tala.

An understanding of pulse groups can be helpful in following the tala at a concert of Karnatak music. A listener who knows that *ādi tāḷa* is an eight-beat cycle may notice that the musicians count twice on each beat in some songs and only once in others. Double counting is a nearly universal habit of performance in two-count talas. A cycle of *ādi tāḷa* is always eight beats, but musicians find it convenient to mark both the first and second pulse groups of each beat, giving the appearance that they are counting a sixteen-beat cycle.

THE *CĀPU* TALAS

Karnatak music probably absorbed the *cāpu* talas from folk music or other nonclassical traditions. These talas are characterized by simpler gestures and much shorter cycles than those of the primordial seven talas. *Miśra cāpu tāḷa,* a seven-beat cycle and by far the most frequently used *cāpu* tala, is counted by claps with the palm up on beats 1 and 2, followed by claps with the palm down on beats 4 and 6 (figure 5*a*). *Khaṇḍa cāpu*, five beats long, is counted by three claps with the palm down on beats 1, 3, and 4 (figure 5*b*).

Since the gestures used in the *cāpu* talas are not grouped into the three divisions (*drutam, anudrutam,* and *laghu*), there is some flexibility in how people use the hand while counting them. In *miśra cāpu*, the clap on the second beat may be left out, making the gestures for this tala identical to those of the *rūpak tāl* of North Indian music. In *khaṇḍa cāpu*, the first clap may be with the palm up or down, though it is normally consistent once established. In general, musicians use the same gestures their teachers use.

Cāpu talas often move more quickly than those in the seven-tala scheme, so notions of pulse group and double counting do not usually apply. Normally, two comfortably pronounced syllables or pulses fit into each beat. Though these talas are much shorter than others, they are not less important. Musicians and composers favor them, and some of the most stately and beautiful Karnatak songs are set in *miśra cāpu tāḷa.*

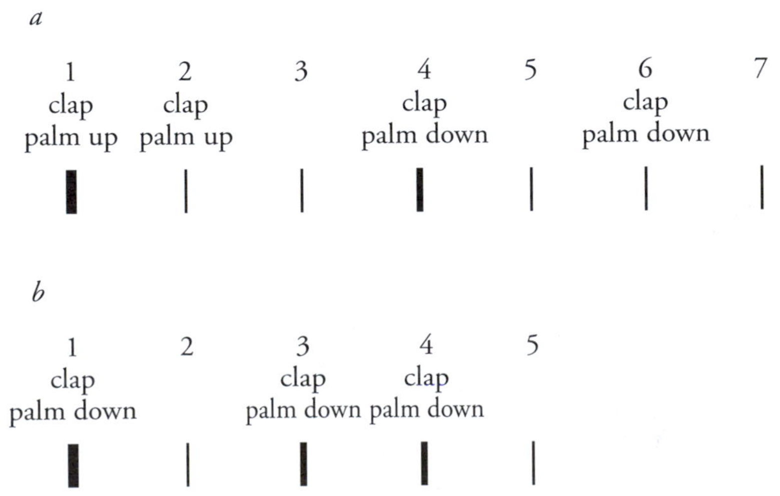

FIGURE 5 Two *cāpu* talas: *a*, *miśra cāpu tāḷa*, seven beats; *b*, *khaṇḍa cāpu tāḷa*, five beats. For the first two claps in *miśra cāpu tāḷa*, the palm is up; for the last two, it is down.

FIGURE 6 First line of a *tiruppugal̲* by Arunagirinadar (sixteenth century), showing tala beats as they are normally reckoned.

clap	clap	clap	clap	clap	pinkie	ring	middle	index
kā – di	mō – di	vā –	dā – ḍu	nū –	kaṭ –	ṭri ḍu	vō –	rum –
1 2 3	1 2 3	1 2	1 2 3	1 2	1 2	1 2	1 2	1 2

THE *TIRUPPUGAL̲* TALAS

The sixteenth-century composer Arunagirinadar left a body of devotional songs that have become popular among South Indian musicians. These songs, known as *tiruppugal̲*, are performed without any improvisatory elaboration and almost always near the end of a concert. The tala in which a *tiruppugal̲* is performed usually matches the syllabic content of the text exactly. The number of syllables in these texts does not necessarily conform to the number of syllables in modern talas, and syllables are often counted with nonstandard gestures. Figure 6 shows a *tiruppugal̲* text line of twenty-one syllables or pulses, arranged according to a 3 + 3 + 2 + 3 + 2 + 2 + 2 + 2 + 2 accentual pattern and repeated in every line of the song. Modern musicians apply claps and counts that fit this scheme, including a convenient 3 + 3 + 5 + 10 hand pattern, though it does not match any of the primordial seven talas or the *cāpu* talas.

Many musicians feel that this connection between tala and syllabic structure reveals something about the original meaning of tala. Modern musicians, however, have only the sketchiest information about how these songs would have sounded in Arunagirinadar's time. The performance of *tiruppugal̲* seems to represent modern Karnatak musicians' desire to establish a link with antiquity, rather than a continuous flow of material from the past.

TALA AND MUSICAL STRUCTURE

The setting of a musical text (*sāhityam*) within a tala adds a vibrant aspect that is missing in the discussion of tala as pure structure. Animated by poetry, a tala becomes a charged field of demands and possibilities.

The most commonly encountered Karnatak vocal and instrumental form is the *kriti.* It usually has three distinct sections: *pallavi, anupallavi,* and *caraṇam* [see KARNATAK VOCAL AND INSTRUMENTIAL MUSIC]. The *pallavi* is usually the shortest, lasting from two to four or five tala cycles. In figure 7, it is four cycles long; to sing it once takes less than ten seconds. The *anupallavi* is usually about the same length, but may end with a passage of text or solfège in double tempo. The *caraṇam,* the last and longest section, often echoes the melody of the *anupallavi* toward its end and usually repeats its double-time passage, if there was one. A vocalist repeatedly sings all these text lines, offering progressively elaborate variations (*saṅgati*).

The earlier discussion of tala structure established four or eight pulses as the "size" of a beat, measured in spoken groups of short syllables. The sung syllables of a *kriti* move at half that speed for two reasons. First, the composer, who is almost always a singer, wants to be sure the words of the song are understood. Second, Karnatak songs are highly melismatic: a single syllable of text may be sung to several musical notes.

In Karnatak music, this kind of ornamentation is part of a song, but within strict rhythmic boundaries marked by the structure of the talas and pulse groups. Figure 8*a* shows the counts and pulses of the first section (*pallavi*) of a stately and popular *kriti* by Muttusvami Diksitar, *Mīnākṣī mēmudam;* the song is set in two-count *ādi tāḷa*, with eight beats and sixty-four pulses. There are only eight text syllables in the first cycle. A vocalist will sing these syllables to an elaborate, melismatic melody regulated by the pulse groups, shown as dashed lines below the text.

The most important point in a Karnatak tala is the point at which a text begins.

FIGURE 7 First section (*pallavi*) of *Paridāna mīcitē*, a *kriti* by Patnam Subramania Ayyar (1845–1902), in *bilahari rāga, khaṇḍa cāpu tāḷa*, showing the rhythmic setting of the text.

1	2	3	4	5
clap		clap	clap	
pa	ri	dā	–	na

1	2	3	4	5
clap		clap	clap	
mī	–	ci	tē	–

1	2	3	4	5
clap		clap	clap	
bā	–	len	–	du

1	2	3	4	5
clap		clap	clap	
vē	–	–	–	–

The most important point in a tala is the point at which a text begins (*eḍuppu*). This is most commonly on the first beat (*sam*) or within the first two beats, but it can also be just before the first beat. Figure 9 shows a two-count beat, with the most common starting points. Different sections of a song may start at different points within the tala cycle. Even within a section, the start of one line of text may differ from that of the next. In figure 8*b*, the beginning of the third and last section (*caraṇam*) of *Mīnākṣī mēmudam*, the starting point has shifted from beat 1 to beat $1\frac{1}{2}$.

Another important point in a tala cycle is the resolution (*arudi*). In long, slow talas such as two-count *ādi tāḷa*, if a text does not start on the first beat (which weakens the rhythmic force of that beat), a composer will often set the text so that a strong rhythmic resolution point occurs somewhere in the middle of the cycle. This point helps to anchor such a slow cycle. In figure 8*b*, it is on beat 5, and coincides with the syllable *yē*. In shorter cycles such as the seven-beat *miśra cāpu*, it coincides with the first beat of a later cycle. The start and the resolution are important targets in melodic and rhythmic improvisation.

Karnatak composers use other devices to generate rhythmic interest within their songs. One of these is to include a passage with a lot of words and few ornaments at the end of a section. In *Mīnākṣī mēmudam*, the composer has added such a passage at the end of the *caraṇam* (figure 8*c*). The starting point for this passage has returned to

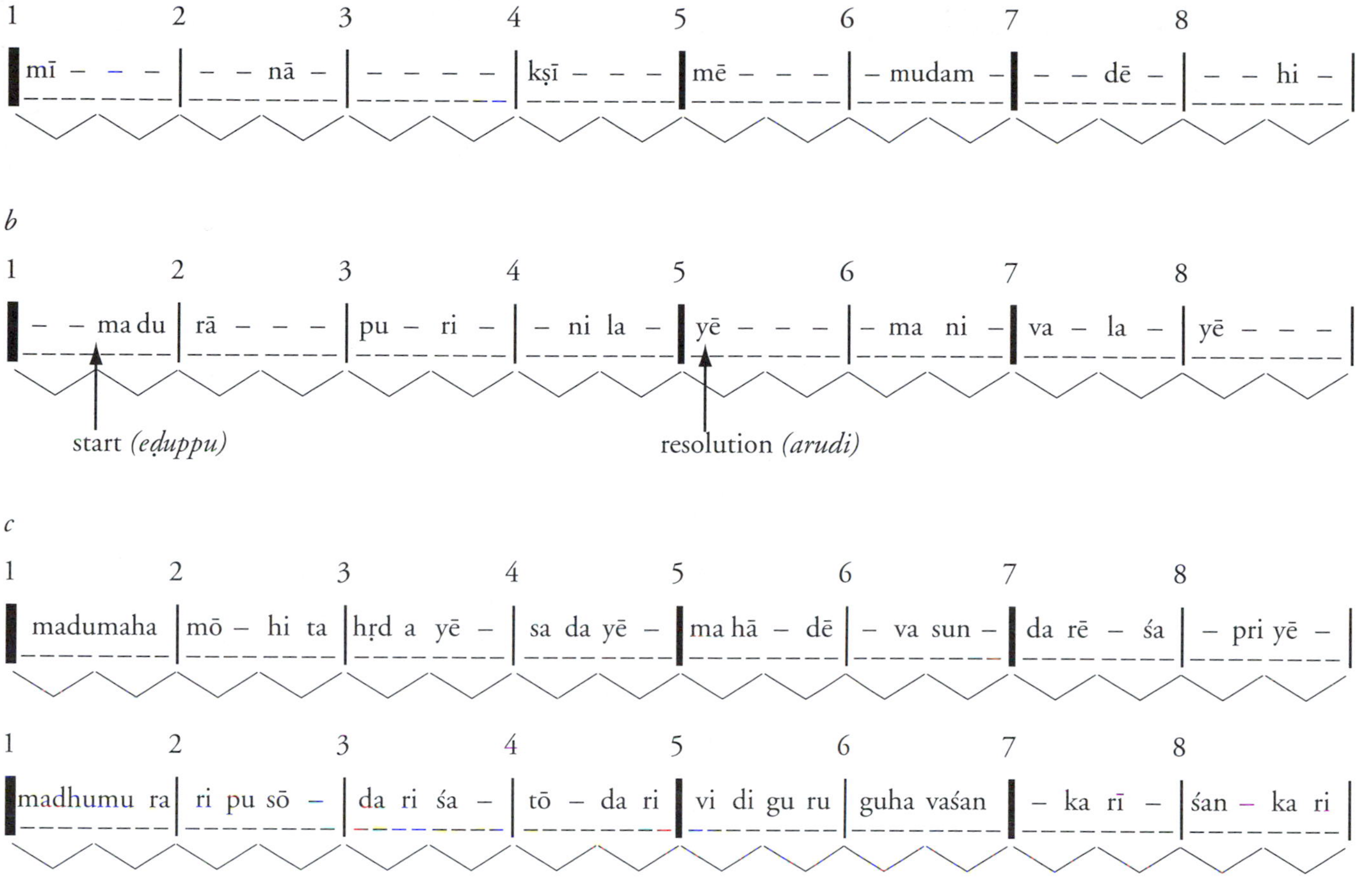

FIGURE 8 Excerpts from *Mīnākṣī mēmudam*, a *kriti* by Muttusvami Diksitar (1775–1835): *a*, first line of the first section (*pallavi*); *b*, first line of the third section (*caraṇam*), showing the starting point (*eḍuppu*) and the resolution point (*arudi*) of the text in the tala cycle; *c*, end of the third section (*caraṇam*). Each sung syllable occurs every two pulses. Thus, within each numbered section (1, 2, and so on) representing one beat, each text syllable or dash (representing the absence of a syllable or a continuation of the previous syllable) is aligned with two short dashes (representing pulses) on the line beneath.

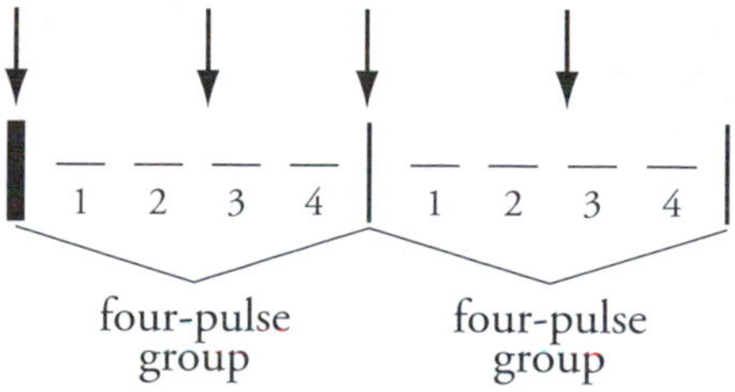

FIGURE 9 A two-count tala beat with eight pulses, showing the most common textual starting points at pulses 1, 3, 5, and 7.

the first beat. Because these passages have more words, they generate rhythmic momentum that effectively balances the much slower, heavily ornamented textual movement in the earlier parts of the song.

Another device for generating rhythmic interest is rhythmic shape (*yati*), the repetition of a musical idea in progressively shorter statements, progressively longer statements, or some combination of the two. These shapes occur at all levels of musical structure, but they are easiest to demonstrate at the level of the phrase. The text in figure 10*a*, an example of the cow's-tail shape (*gopucca yati*), follows an orderly reduction. Each stage of the reduction is a meaningful Sanskrit expression. The reverse of cow's tail is river mouth (*srotovaha*), as shown in the next example from the same song (figure 10*b*). Again, each of the stages is a meaningful expression.

Other rhythmic shapes include the hourglass (*damaru yati*), named for the shape of the drum played by the god Shiva. The hourglass moves from long to short, then from short to long. Its opposite, *mridanga*, named for the barrel-shaped drum *mridangam*, is wider in the middle than at the ends. Two other shapes, all-the-same (*sama*) and random (*visama*), complete the six possibilities Karnatak musicians use. Rhythmic shape is a powerful tool in melodic and rhythmic improvisation, and in composition.

Tala and rhythmic improvisation

Several times during a concert, Karnatak musicians extend songs by improvising on them. Some of this improvisation occurs during an unmetered introduction before the song (and therefore the tala) begins, and does not concern us here. But three types of rhythmic improvisation take place within the tala. Two of these, *niraval* and

FIGURE 10 Excerpts from *Tyāgarāja yoga vaibhavam*, a *kriti* by Muttusvami Diksitar (1775–1835) in *ānandabhairavi rāga*, *rūpaka tāḷa*: *a*, end of the first section, showing a long-to-short pattern (*gopucca yati*); *b*, end of second section, showing a short-to-long pattern (*srotovaha yati*).

a

tyāgarāja yoga vaibhavam
agarāja yoga vaibhavam
rāja yoga vaibhavam
vaibhavam
bhavam
vam

b

śam
prakāśam
svarūpa prakāśam
tattva svarūpa prakāśam
sakala tattva svarūpa prakāśam
śiva śakty ādi sakala tattva svarūpa prakāśam

svara kalpana, involve melodic ideas as well as rhythmic ones. The third is the drum solo (*tani āvartanam*; see below), which happens in only one song per concert.

In *niraval,* the singer improvises on the melody of a text line while leaving the rhythmic setting of the words constant. The singer may choose any line from any section of the song for its lyrical and textual richness. Since *niraval* involves melodic elaboration on a text, singers most often utilize it, but it can also be used effectively by sensitive instrumentalists.

A musician usually begins *niraval* slowly, so that the text is clearly understandable. As the performance gathers in intensity, its focus shifts away from the words and more toward the melodic line; each text syllable may take on florid ornaments. This ornamentation progresses until the actual syllables are all but unintelligible. The increased density of notes, as in all forms of Karnatak improvisation, takes place without an increase in the speed of the tala. South Indian musicians double the number of notes per beat, say from four pulses to eight, and strictly maintain one tempo throughout a song, including its improvised sections. This approach provides a contrast with Hindustani music, in which musicians speed up the tala at later stages of a composition.

At the densest stage of *niraval,* the musician introduces *svara kalpana*, an improvisation that uses sol-fa syllables instead of words. Imagine a jazz singer scat-singing with the syllables *do re mi fa so la ti do* instead of the made-up syllables one usually hears. Now imagine that every one of these solfège phrases resolves by returning to the first words of the song, and you will have an idea of *svara kalpana*. Like *niraval,* this improvisation begins in a slow tempo; it gathers momentum and intensity as the musicians trade phrases. Solfège improvisation may be brief (just a few phrases), or it may go on for as long as musicians keep thinking of ideas.

In solfège improvisation, musicians adopt two broad rhythmic strategies. Some, preferring not to think much about complicated rhythms, let their notes flow with the pulse of the tala. This approach is called time flow (*sarvalaghu*). More rhythmically energetic musicians work out patterns and designs that generate great tension with the tala. This approach is called calculation (*kaṇakku*). Either method can go too far. Sometimes avoidance of rhythmic complexity is an excuse for not developing strong rhythmic control (*laya*). At the other extreme, too much complexity results in rhythmic gymnastics at the expense of beauty. The best Karnatak improvisers make judicious use of both approaches, using time flow to draw attention to beautiful melodic ideas and calculation to reveal aesthetic aspects of rhythmic order.

Musical forms and conventions

The *kriti* is the form most likely to be expanded and decorated by improvisation, but it is not the only musical form used in Karnatak music. Two other genres, concert études (*varṇam* 'color') and songs accompanying classical dance, provide examples of the relationship between tala and musical structure.

Classical études

The *varṇam* is an important form in the study of raga. A *varṇam* has little text, and elaborate ornaments and phrases provide the essential features of its raga. The best compositions are rich enough sources of musical insight that musicians learn them early in their musical careers and continue to practice them.

Because the *varṇam* has the character of an extremely sophisticated étude, musicians often experiment with its rhythm. A musician might perform a *varṇam* in an extremely slow tempo at one concert, at twice that speed at the next concert, and with each section in a different tempo at a third concert. Only the musician's imagination, taste, and willingness limit such an approach. This kind of flexibility does not exist when the same performer sings a *kriti*, for each *kriti* has its appropriate tempo (*kālapramana*), and musicians are strict about keeping it.

The manner of performing a *varṇam* is a matter of personal preference and learned style. Some musicians, disapproving of overtly rhythmic manipulation, do not teach their students these approaches. But nothing prevents rhythmically adventuresome students from working out how to perform them. Conversely, teachers who stress rhythmic knowledge (*laya gñānam*) are likely to encourage their students, even those who lack the interest or capacity for it, in such efforts.

Songs accompanying classical dance

Bharata nāṭyam, South India's classical dance, has its own literature of music and its own relationship with tala. In it, the dancer interprets or acts out the text. A rare dancer may be gifted enough to improvise such an interpretation, but the performance is usually precomposed or choreographed by a master (*naṭṭuvanār*) and layered over the song, which may have been composed centuries earlier.

Choreographed material in classical dance is of two general types: pure, or noninterpretive (*nritta*), and interpretive (*nritya*). Noninterpretive dance sections of a performance are made up of rhythmically energetic patterns of movement (*aḍavu*) emphasizing drumlike footwork, leaps, and other physically demanding movements. Highly percussive footwork provides a distinct rhythmic counterpoint to the tala, which the accompanist plays on cymbals (*tāḷam*), and to the text. In keeping with South Indian use of the voice as the fundamental musical vehicle, classical dancers use spoken syllables as a verbal notation for their footwork, in much the same way that Indian drummers use syllables as a notation for drumming.

TALA AND THE DRUMMER

The main percussion instrument of South India is the *mridangam*, a double-headed barrel-shaped drum made from a hollowed-out piece of jackwood about 60 centimeters long. Its heads are made from the hides of goats, cows, and buffaloes, and its right head (for a right-handed player) is precisely tunable thanks to the addition of a semipermanent tuning paste. The left head, also tunable to an extent but not so precisely, provides a low, booming sound. The *mridangam* is played with the fingers and palms and can produce about twenty distinct sounds. Other South Indian percussion instruments include a lizardskin frame drum (*kañjīrā*), and a tuned clay pot (*ghaṭam*); these are the secondary drums most often used (figure 11). Players of these instruments usually begin as *mridangam* students and change at some later time.

Karnatak musicians and audiences are extremely forgiving of mistakes caught in time to abort and restart, but they become unsympathetic if a musician actually completes an improvisation on the wrong beat.

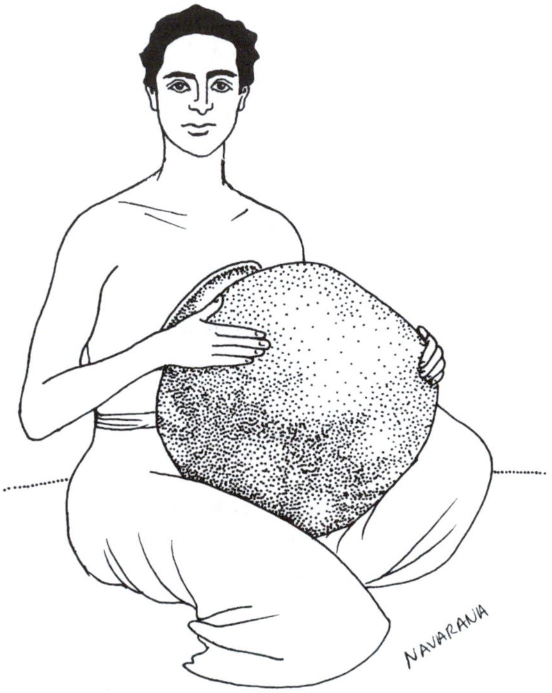

FIGURE 11 Drummer with clay pot (*ghaṭam*). Drawing by Navarana, 1996. Used by permission. Courtesy David Reck.

Whatever the instrument, the technique is challenging, but this is only the first hurdle for Karnatak drummers; they must also master the arts of accompaniment and playing solo. Until about the 1980s, all drummers were men; even now, few women have developed concert-level proficiency.

Learning the fundamentals

A *mridangam* player's training usually begins at an early age; many drummers report having started at the age of six or seven. A child may begin studies with a parent, a relative who is a drummer, or, if the child shows early interest and no family member plays, with a local teacher.

A student's first lesson is an important occasion for the family. The parents of a Hindu student accompany the child to the Hindu temple, where they give offerings to Ganesha, the elephant-headed god worshiped as the lord of beginnings and remover of obstacles, seeking his help in making a good beginning. Then, after making offerings to the family's chosen deity, they go to the teacher's house. All students begin their training by making offerings (*guru-pūjā*) of fruit, flowers, incense, and money to the teacher. The student touches the teacher's feet and formally asks for blessing and instruction. Only after these formalities are over does the first lesson begin.

The bond between teacher (guru) and student (*śiṣya*) is a powerful one that lasts as long as both of them live. The student considers the teacher's musical authority to be absolute and would not dream of questioning it. The student is not a slave to the teacher, but independent thought is thoroughly discouraged, at least in the early years of training. In some cases, unquestioning receptivity results in a continuity of style unheard of in the West. Under certain circumstances, such as changing residence or furthering study, students may change teachers, but they do so with care and trepidation. In any case, musicians always recall their first teacher with special regard.

The early lessons are the same, regardless of the teacher or the student's age. These lessons, on the *ta di tom nam* series, introduce fundamental strokes and patterns that will form the core of the drummer's technique as both player and teacher.

From the beginning, *mridangam* students learn two approaches to the patterns they receive. Naturally, they must learn to play them properly. They must also recite them in syllables (*śolkaṭṭu*), a kind of drum language of spoken syllables bound together by a tala. Every stroke has its corresponding syllable; the student learns the stroke and the syllable together. When the teacher says, "play *ta*," there is no doubt that the teacher means an open-palmed slap on the left drumhead. Likewise *di, tom, nam,* and other syllables signify particular strokes on the drum.

A student learns quickly that a stroke may be indicated by more than one syllable, depending on the way it combines with other strokes. In the pattern *ta ka TA ri KI ṭa ta KA,* the capitalized syllables refer to the same stroke, which is taught as *di* in the first lesson. At first glance, this may appear puzzling; on the one hand, every stroke has its own syllable; on the other, a particular stroke may be indicated by different syllables, as in this example.

Some Indian drummers have tried to change the drum-syllable system so that a given stroke is always represented by the same syllable, but their efforts have not gained widespread favor. Most drummers feel that the strokes are combined into patterns designed for fast playing according to a logic of the hand. Some movements combine more easily than others. In the same way, the corresponding spoken patterns are designed for fast reciting according to a logic of the tongue. Because the spoken and played patterns are learned together, students absorb their parallel structures without difficulty. Figure 12 shows typical drum-syllable phrases for some of the most common rhythmic groupings.

Practicing syllables is an extremely powerful tool, since it frees the hands for tala keeping. By reciting the patterns vocally and simultaneously keeping the tala, students walk a razor's edge: too much concentration on the phrases causes the tala to falter; too much concentration on the tala and the syllables break up. In either case, the student is quickly aware of the error and knows there is more work to do to master the pattern.

The awareness that the pattern and the tala are not synchronized is an important safeguard against mistakes in performance. Karnatak musicians and audiences are extremely forgiving of mistakes caught in time to abort and restart, but they become unsympathetic if a musician actually completes an improvisation on the wrong beat. In the words of one drummer, "Everybody makes mistakes, but you have to minimize the response time as much as possible. All's well that ends well."

The necessity that a student of drumming learn flawless tala keeping leads the teacher to use every occasion as an opportunity for teaching. The teacher may direct an advanced student to sit on the concert stage during the teacher's performance to help prepare the drums. Sitting in an inconspicuous place but not out of the teacher's line of sight, the student keeps the tala (does the hand gestures) throughout the concert. The student would probably do so anyhow, but the pressure of doing it in sight of the audience and the teacher guarantees an attentive performance (figure 13).

FIGURE 12 Some commonly used spoken drum-syllable (*śolkaṭṭu*) patterns.

one syllable	ta, di
two syllables	ta ka, ki ṭa, jo ṇu, di mi
three syllables	ta ki ṭa, ta da ri, ta jo ṇu,
four syllables	ta ka di mi, ta ka jo ṇu, ki ṭa taka
five syllables	ta ka ta ki ṭa, ta din gi ṇa tom
six syllables	ta ka ta ka di mi ta ri ki ṭa ta ka ta din — gi ṇa tom
seven syllables	ta ka di mi ta ki ṭa ta ki ṭa ta ka jo ṇu ta — din — gi ṇa tom
eight syllables	ta ka di mi ta ka jo ṇu ta ka ta ri ki ṭa ta ka ta din — gi — ṇa — tom
nine syllables	ta ka di mi ta ka ta ki ṭa ta ka di ku ta di ki ṭa tom ta — din — gi — ṇa — tom

Drummers need to make rhythmic control a matter of unshakable physical confidence. They frequently accompany solo instrumentalists whose hands are not free and therefore cannot show the tala. This is not a problem when a drummer knows a particular song, but if this is not the case, or if the other instrumentalist engages in rhythmic improvisation, the drummer must reckon the tala alone. To some extent in these cases, drummers and gifted instrumentalists can internalize the tala, but most transfer tala keeping to the feet and legs. In other words, musicians make up leg and foot movements that correspond to various talas so that they need not depend on somebody else to keep the tala.

FIGURE 13 The great *mridangam* master Palghat Mani Ayyar (1912–1981) in concert with Alathur Srinivasa Ayyar. An unidentified student sits to the drummer's left on stage. 1970. Photo © Carol S. Reck.

Rhythmic steadiness is also necessary for solo playing. As described below, Karnatak drummers invent cadential patterns that can generate tremendous tension within the tala. These are often so difficult to execute in synchronization with the tala that drummers must practice them intensively before trying them in public. When they perform, another musician (who probably does not know the design in question) will keep the tala. Since it is nearly certain that the drummer's sense of rhythm is slightly different from that of the tala keeper, the drummer must be extraordinarily alert to avoid a mishap. If the tala slows down or speeds up, he must adjust his pace accordingly.

Four basic talas

Once the *ta di tom nam* series is completed, a *mridangam* student's course of study moves through four talas: *ādi tāḷa*, of eight beats (see figure 2*c*); *rūpaka tāḷa*, of three beats (see figure 2*d′*); *miśra cāpu*, of seven beats (see figure 5*a*), and *khaṇḍa cāpu*, of five beats (see figure 5*b*). In each tala, the structure of the lessons is a drum solo (*tani āvartanam*) in paradigmatic form. The first lessons comprise material appropriate for the beginning of a solo, the more advanced lessons reveal aspects of rhythmic form and development, and the final lessons demonstrate how a solo should end.

Time flow

At all these stages, a student learns two fundamental aspects of rhythmic form: time flow (*sarvalaghu*) and calculation (*kaṇakku*). Time flow includes all the repeating patterns and quasi-melodic figures drummers use to reinforce the flow of the tala. Karnatak drummers devise their time-flow figures as much for their pleasing sound as for their rhythmic effect. A listener will find it relatively easy to keep the tala during sections that emphasize this kind of playing. These patterns may be compared with others found in drumming throughout the world: the ride cymbal patterns used by jazz drummers, the complex yet flowing patterns of African-Latin drummers, and the patterns employed by players of the Irish frame drum (*bodhran*) are all analogous to the time flow of Karnatak drummers.

Time-flow patterns are sometimes called by the North Indian term for drummed pattern, *ṭhekā*, though they are used more flexibly than their North Indian counterparts in tabla playing. For tabla players, the *ṭhekā* represents one cycle of the tala; Karnatak musicians use the hands to keep the tala, so this is not the drummer's job. Every musician in a Karnatak ensemble is equally responsible for keeping the tala.

Karnatak drummers use different time-flow patterns for different tempi (*kāla*). Figure 14*a* shows one cycle of a slow-tempo (*vilamba kāla*) pattern often used at the early stages of a song or solo in eight-beat *ādi tāḷa*. As if to emphasize the inherent dignity of the tala, slow-tempo patterns accent only the first and third pulses of the pulse group in a slow, regular flow.

A typical medium-tempo (*madhyama kāla*) pattern for the same tala might look like the one in figure 14*b*. Both the slow- and medium-tempo examples require two pulse groups for each statement of the time-flow pattern. But although the first figure moves squarely with the pulse groups, the second is arranged so that it does not. In medium tempo, any of a group's pulses may be accented, drawing more attention to the pattern than to the tala. The following pattern's eight pulses are laid out in a three-three-two pattern:

(ta na ta) (din — ta) (din —)

Such a figure would be called syncopated in Western music, but Karnatak music requires no such naming, since every pulse of a beat has the same weight. Even if the

The kind of conscious thinking that goes into inventing these rhythmic compositions sets Karnatak drummers apart from percussionists in most other musical traditions.

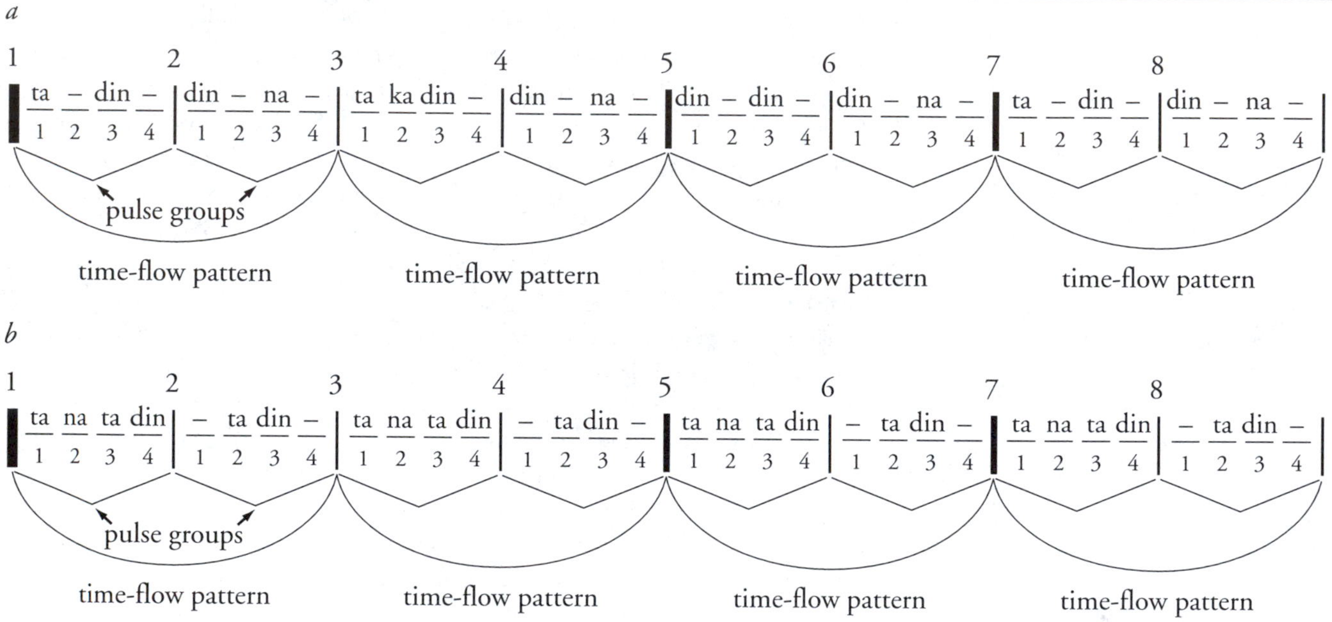

FIGURE 14 Some common time-flow patterns (*sarvalaghu*) for *ādi tāḷa*: *a*, slow tempo, four pulses per beat; *b*, medium tempo, four pulses per beat.

drummer shifts to a different pulse-shape, for example to three or five pulses per beat, the flow patterns of the new shape will share the twin characteristics of the time-flow approach: an easy relationship with the beat and tala structure and a pleasing sound. Pulse shifting is an important device for Karnatak drummers, who use it sparingly in accompaniment to generate tension with the song. They make extensive use of it in solos, sometimes playing long sections in three or four of the pulse-shapes in a single solo.

Rhythmic design

Calculation (*kaṇakku*), the second approach to rhythmic form a student must master, is the study of generative principles that have something in common with mathematical formulas. These principles enable a drummer to create the intricate cadential designs called *mōrā* and *kōrvai*. A listener may know that one of these designs is unfolding by noticing that the tala has suddenly become hard to follow. Some sort of rhythmic shape emerges, but its relationship with the beat seems tense. When it resolves, informed listeners, including the other performers, may nod their approval or briefly applaud.

The kind of conscious thinking that goes into inventing these rhythmic compositions sets Karnatak drummers apart from percussionists in most other musical traditions. The use of the intellect to compose music for drumming is encouraged and actively cultivated among South Indian drummers. A teacher may give a student a *mōrā* or *kōrvai* for one tala and assign its recomposition for other talas, requiring the student to shorten a thirty-two-pulse *mōrā* to twenty-eight pulses, or lengthen it to thirty-six pulses, and so on.

The effect on the student's mind is one of creative destabilization. No material is fixed, but can be transformed to fit circumstances. As the student's mind becomes accustomed to the fluidity of rhythmic structures, it goes beyond the first stage, permutation and combination (*prastāra*) of known material, into a state in which really new material arises. As is true of all music, the most important criteria for beauty in a rhythmic composition are intuitive and indescribable. The drummer and the informed listener inwardly "know" when something is aesthetically satisfying. In addition to creativity, a South Indian drummer has the additional ability to justify a composition in terms of its formal and arithmetical order.

The *mōrā* is the fundamental cadential design pervading all forms of tala-bound Karnatak music. It may end sections of songs, sections of classical-dance compositions, and solfège improvisations. It serves several functions in drum solos. It is analogous in form and function to the *tihāī* of Hindustani music, which melodic soloists and tabla players use. Countless *mōrā* are in use, but they share an inner, germinal form.

A *mōrā* consists of two types of material: a phrase stated three times and a gap (*kārvai*) separating the statements. Figure 15*a* presents the same time-flow pattern as figure 14*a* in its first four beats, with a *mōrā* on beats 5 to 8. The *mōrā* is a sixteen-pulse example, with groups of 4 + 2 + 4 + 2 + 4. *Ta ka di na* is the four-pulse triple statement, and *tam* — is the two-pulse gap. The final *tam* coincides with the start of the song (usually, as in this case, on beat 1); it is not, strictly speaking, part of the cadential design, but serves to release the tension generated by the preceding material. It may be helpful to think of the final *tam* as a punctuation mark—like a period—that ends a statement without being included in it.

The statement and the gap are different types of material. The statement must state something, and it has to comprise at least one syllable. The gap, however, may exist only as potential. In a particular case, its value may be zero, as in figure 15*b*, a *mōrā* that appears to consist of a five-pulse figure (*ta din gi ṇa tom*) stated three times with no gap at all. But a Karnatak drummer might play a series of designs like this one, expanding the gap each time in a kind of motivic development. The next *mōrā* in the series might expand the gap to one pulse, as in figure 15*c*, with subsequent patterns continuing to increase the gap.

The designs of *mōrā* may be quite elaborate. A drummer could play the three *ta din gi ṇa tom* designs mentioned above in sequence. In this case, each small design would become one of the statements in a compound design, with a zero-value gap. Figure 16 demonstrates that the three statements of a *mōrā* do not have to have the same duration but may make a rhythmic shape (*yati*) by expanding or contracting in an orderly way. In figure 16, the statements go from fifteen pulses (5 + 0 + 5 + 0 + 5) to seventeen (5 + 1 + 5 + 1 + 5) to nineteen (5 + 2 + 5 + 2 + 5)—an example of expansion (*srotovaha yati*). This structure could also be reversed to form a reduction (*gopucca yati*).

From this idea, myriad variations develop. The *mōrā* is an extraordinary generative device that has enabled every generation of Karnatak musicians to create fresh cadential material.

The other main cadential design, the *kōrvai*, is not nearly so pervasive as the *mōrā*. Its use is mainly confined to the drum solo, though rhythmically adventuresome singers and instrumentalists use it, set to a melody, in their solfège improvisations. It is also used in choreography.

There are only two requirements for a rhythmic structure to be called a *kōrvai:* it must have at least two parts, and the terminal part must be in the *mōrā* form.

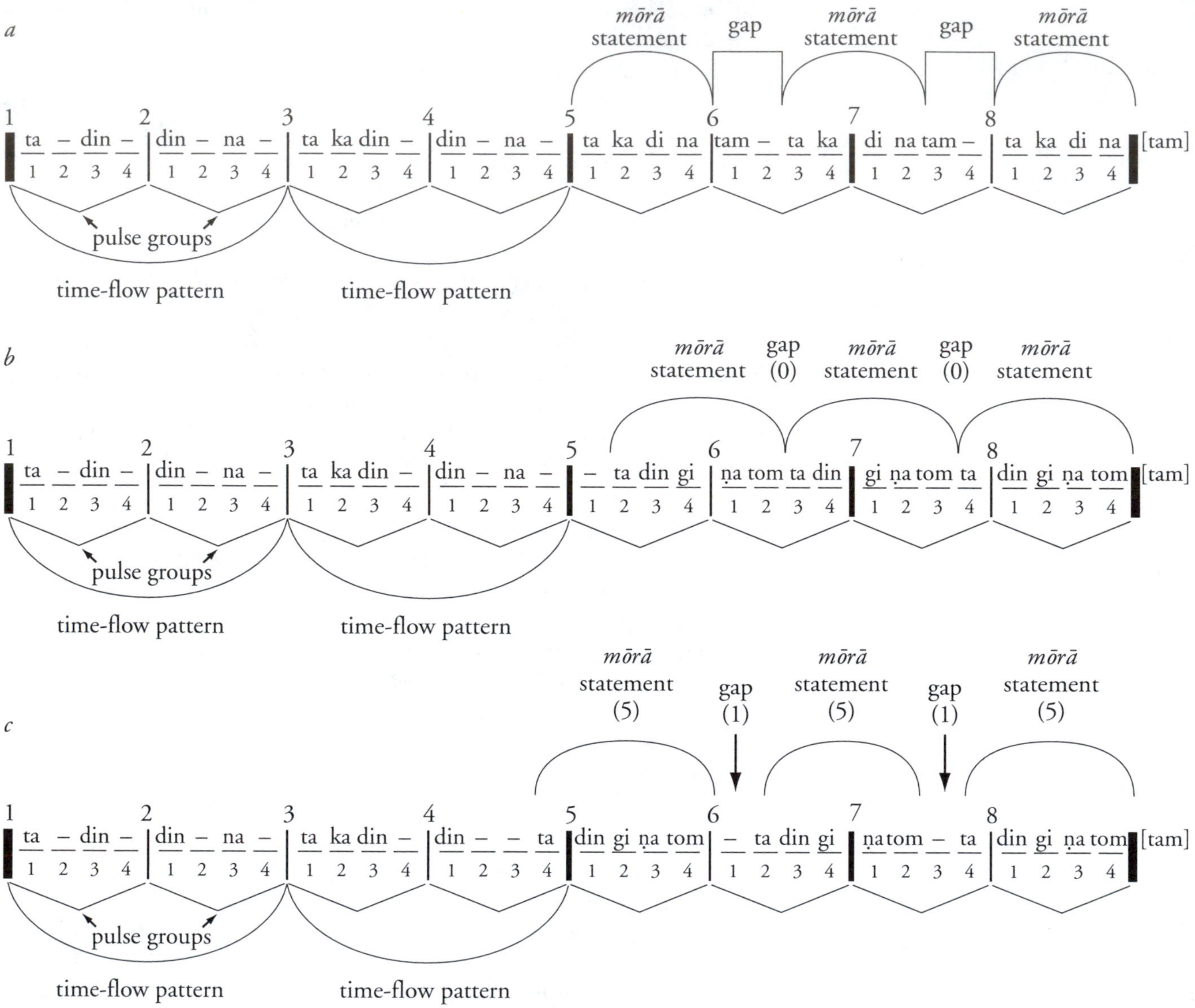

FIGURE 15 Some simple cadential designs (*mōrā*) in beats 5–8 of *ādi tāḷa*; *a*, sixteen pulses; *b*, fifteen pulses; *c*, seventeen pulses.

Drummers most often play a *kōrvai* three times in succession, though they may play a long *kōrvai* just once. Figure 17 shows a *kōrvai* with an hourglass (*damaru yati*) design; its introductory section moves from long phrases to short, whereas its *mōrā* proceeds from short to long. The composer created this design to fit neatly into a tala, as is characteristic of the *kōrvai.* In this case, its sixty-four pulses fit perfectly into eight-beat *ādi tāḷa,* no matter how many pulse groups per beat. A *kōrvai* is almost always precomposed; only rarely does a drummer create a fully formed *kōrvai* in the middle of a concert. A typical drummer uses dozens of *kōrvai*; some have been handed down by the guru or other respected elders, and some are self-designed.

Drummers design *kōrvai* with a wide range of aesthetic criteria in mind. Some drummers compose them so that they are immediately understandable and create little tension with the tala. Others favor concealment and the element of surprise. Some insist on strict arithmetical symmetry within and among the parts. Others value integrity of particular phrases more highly than numerical precision. A *kōrvai* does not have to begin in any particular place in the tala cycle. The only absolute requirement is that its end must resolve perfectly at the point in the tala cycle when the text begins (*eḍuppu*).

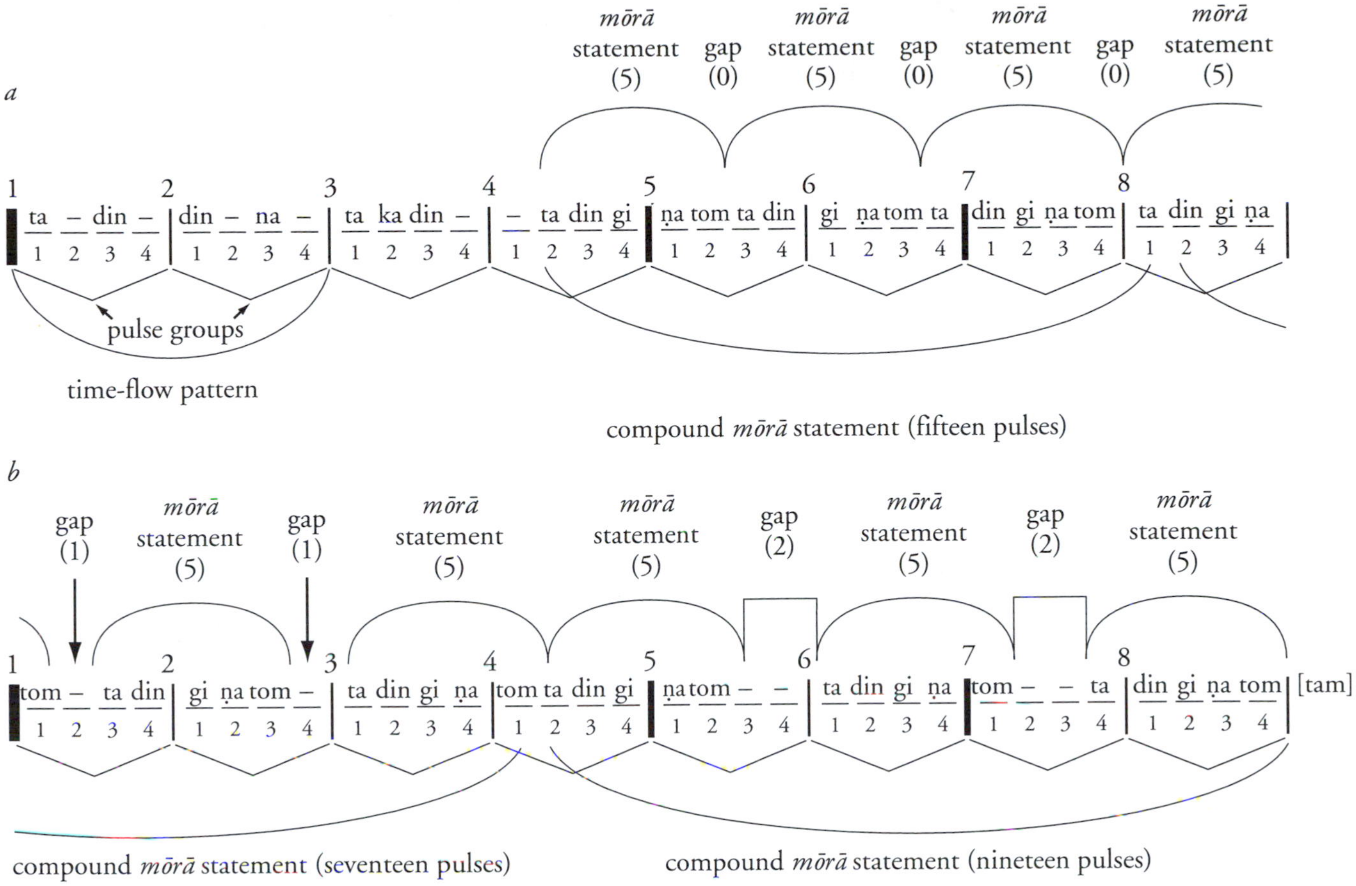

FIGURE 16 A compound cadential design (*mōrā*) of fifty-one pulses within two cycles of *ādi tāḷa*, comprising shorter to longer statements of the pulses.

Graduation day: The *arangētram*

When the teacher feels that a student has mastered enough of the above-mentioned material to play in public, he arranges a coming-out concert (*arangētram*). The other performers are often the teacher's peers and may include the teacher himself. Its purpose is to showcase the student in an emotionally supportive and musically high-caliber context. This concert is an important rite of passage; in the words of one well-known drummer, "There are certain dates that you don't forget in your life: your birthdate, your wedding date, your *arangētram*." Afterward, the drummer may continue studying, but on a different basis. His concentration now moves to developing accompaniment and playing as a solo concert artist on his own.

The drummer as concert artist

Accompaniment

A drummer spends about 90 percent of his career accompanying other musicians, and does it without notation or any absolute course of action. Given this fact, it may seem surprising that teachers almost never teach the art of accompaniment formally. Drummers are expected to absorb the principles of effective accompaniment by listening: first to the teacher, then to other senior drummers. A bewildered drummer may ask the teacher, "What should I play?" In the context of a lesson, such a question would prompt a specific response. Asked about accompaniment, however, the teacher might answer, "Play like the music," or "Play *ādi tāḷa*," or something equally unspecific.

Every drummer finds an individual path to accompaniment, much as every jazz drummer does. Some tend toward flashy displays and excess, while others adopt a reserved style. Drummers learn that some musicians like to be accompanied in an

An extended drum solo may be said to be improvised much as a conversation is improvised: the words and the grammar are familiar, but the exact expression is a function of a situation.

FIGURE 17 An *ādi tāḷa* cadential design (*kōrvai*), exhibiting a long-short-long shape (*damaru yati*).

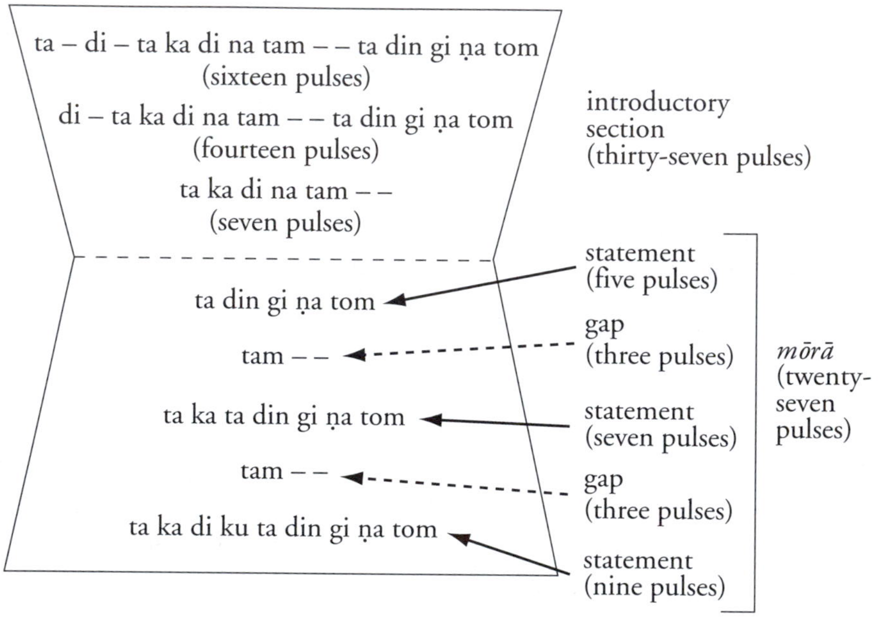

aggressive style (loud, dominating, energetic), whereas others prefer a lighter, quieter approach. They also learn that their preferred style of accompanying makes their music more compatible with that of some musicians than with that of others. Most important, they learn that all those years of deferring to the teacher's wishes have not destroyed their individuality.

The drum solo

TRACK 8 Once in every concert, the drummer plays an extended solo (*tani āvartanam*), an opportunity to demonstrate creativity, and without any direct reference to the music that preceded it. This solo may take from two to twenty minutes, depending on the situation. The drummer does not usually know beforehand in which piece the solo will occur, and in this sense the solo is improvised; however, the soloistic material and approach are part of a familiar vocabulary. So the solo may be said to be improvised much as a conversation is improvised: the words and the grammar are familiar, but the exact expression is a function of the situation.

In general, experienced listeners can track the development of a solo by following the progression of its time-flow patterns. These evolve from sparsely articulated, slow-tempo figures at the beginning, through medium-tempo figures in the middle, to extremely dense patterns (*paran*) toward the end.

In the original tempo of the solo, the drummer punctuates the time-flow patterns with more densely articulated figures, usually at the ends of cycles. At the outset, such phrases do not necessarily herald a cadential design (*mōrā* or *kōrvai*), but once a particular design has come to the drummer's mind, a phrase from it may serve to end cycles, then half- and quarter-cycles, even individual beats, until the drummer decides to play the whole pattern. After playing a cadential design, the drummer may return to the original tempo to set up another design or continue to the next section. Most often, the drummer will play an elaborate *kōrvai* before moving on to the medium-tempo section.

In the medium-tempo section (as in the slow-tempo section), the drummer sets up a cadential design by introducing its phrases into the time-flow patterns. Typically the longest section of the solo, this includes any pulse shifting the drummer wishes to do.

If more than one percussionist performs in a concert, each one in turn plays all the previous material, with the *mridangam* player signaling the changes of the sections. Just before the final section of the solo, two or more percussionists usually play a trading section (*koraippu*), in which they take turns playing sets of phrases of exactly the same length, usually generating tension with the tala structure. A trading section based on seven (*miśra koraippu*) is often performed in the eight-beat *ādi tāḷa.* In the first stage, each percussionist plays eight seven-pulse phrases, as in figure 18*a.* To end on the first beat of this cycle (a thirty-two-pulse one), the player begins the fifty-six-pulse group after eight pulses and takes two tala cycles to complete the pattern. Each percussionist in turn waits for eight pulses, then plays the eight seven-pulse phrases.

In the second stage, the traded figure is reduced to four seven-pulse phrases. For this twenty-eight-pulse group to end at the point of the start, it begins after four pulses and takes only one tala cycle to complete (figure 18*b*). The third stage follows the same pattern: two seven-pulse phrases begin after two pulses and last a half-cycle (figure 18*c*). In the final stage, one seven-pulse phrase follows one silent pulse and lasts just a quarter-cycle (figure 18*d*).

At this point, all the percussionists who have been trading come together in unison to play the terminal section. Because the length of the solo is not predetermined, this section is highly stylized so that the musicians playing melody instruments know when to rejoin the percussionists. It comprises three principal elements: *paran*, the big (*periya*) *mōrā*, and a final *kōrvai.*

The *paran,* a densely articulated pattern, is included more for its percussive force than for its rhythmic interest. Played energetically and on the high end of the dynamic range, it typically remains close to the tala structure, generating momentum toward the big cadential design (*mōrā*), which all the musicians immediately recognize as the next-to-last composition in the solo. On hearing it, they know that the solo will end after one more *kōrvai,* which usually fits neatly into the tala, and is always played three times. At the end of the third statement, the other musicians join the drummer and finish the song.

FURTHER LISTENING AND READING

Of the many available recordings of Karnatak singing, Ramnad Krishnan's *Vidwan* (1968) and *Jon Higgins* (1970) are both noteworthy. Vidwan presents one of South India's greatest singers with a sensitive ensemble of accompanists; the main item is a *rāgam-tānam-pallavi* performance that features a lively solo by two drummers. Jon Higgins's recording features the first convincing non-Indian performer of Karnatak vocal music, and presents songs in six different talas.

Three compact discs on the Music of the World label present different aspects of Karnatak instrumental music and drumming. *Sunada* (1992) and *Laya Vinyās* (1990) feature the same pair of musicians, the vina player Karaikudi S. Subramaniam, and drummer Trichy S. Sankaran. The former, which includes extensive, helpful liner

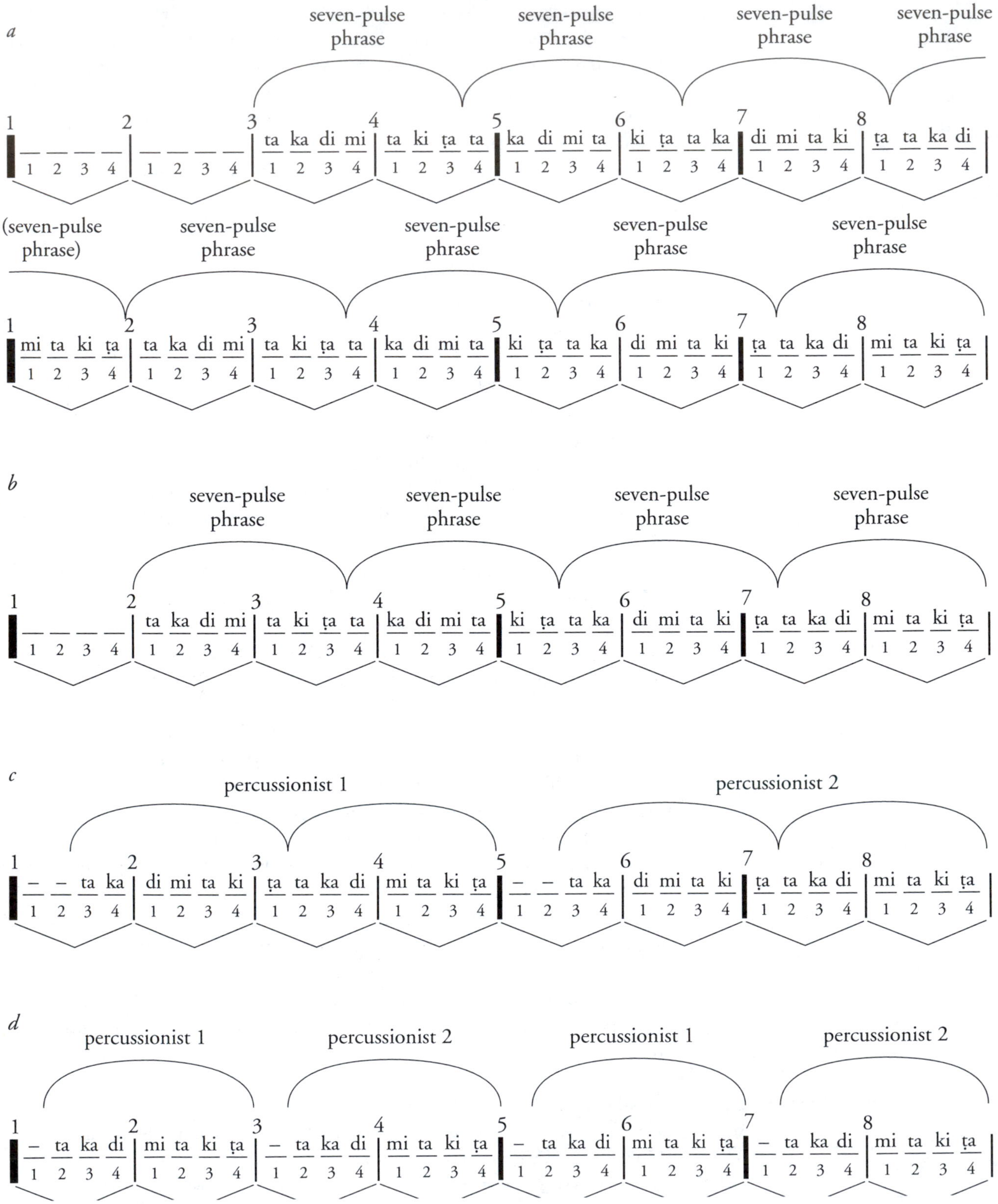

FIGURE 18 Four stages of a trading section based on seven (*miśra koraippu*) in eight-beat *ādi tāḷa*: *a*, first stage, showing the eight-pulse rest and the fifty-six-pulse set of phrases; *b*, second stage, showing the four-pulse rest and the twenty-eight-pulse set of phrases; *c*, third stage, showing the two-pulse rest and the fourteen-pulse set of phrases; *d*, fourth stage, showing the one-pulse rest and the seven-pulse phrase.

notes, provides a good survey of musical styles featuring the *mridangam* as an accompaniment to the soft, subtle sound of the vina. Its companion recording, *Laya Vinyās*, features the *mridangam* as a solo instrument. On the third CD recording, entitled *Vadya Lahari* (1992), the violinist A. Kanyakumari leads an innovative ensemble combining relatively soft-sounding chamber instruments (violin, vina) with much louder temple music instruments (*nāgasvaram* and *tavil*). A drum "solo" features both *mridangam* and *tavil*, instruments only rarely played together.

Books on subjects related to Karnatak tala can be divided into two groups—those dealing with music theory and those dealing specifically with drumming. Lath (1978) and Sambamurthy (1963–1969) fall into the former category; their writings are useful as reference material, and cover all facets of Karnatak music. In the second category, Sankaran (1994) and Sarma (1969) both provide background information on tala theory, but their main focus is drumming pedagogy. Both have developed drum-stroke notations: Sarma's is an attempt to equate drum syllables with specific strokes, whereas Sankaran's is graphical. Brown (1965) also deals with pedagogy, but from the point of view of the student. He uses yet another stroke notation, developed during his study under the *mridangam* player T. Ranganathan. Nelson (1991) surveys five styles of *mridangam* playing, including full transcriptions in the Ranganathan-Brown system, detailed analyses of all five drum solos, and interviews with the drummers.

REFERENCES

Brown, Robert E. 1965. "The *Mrdanga:* A Study of Drumming in South India." Ph.D. dissertation, University of California, Los Angeles.

Higgins, Jon B. c. 1970. *Jon Higgins.* Gramophone Company of India CDNF 147728. Compact disc.

Kanyakumari, A. 1992. *Vadya Lahari.* Music of the World CDT 125. Compact disc.

Krishnan, Ramnad. 1968. *Vidwan.* Elektra/Nonesuch Explorer Series 9-72023-2. Compact disc.

Lath, Mukund. 1978. *A Study of Dattilam.* Delhi: Impex India.

Nelson, David P. 1991. "*Mr̥daṅgam* Mind: The *Tani Āvartanam* in *Karṇāṭak* Music." Ph.D. dissertation, Wesleyan University.

Sambamurthy, Pichu. 1963–1973. *South Indian Music.* 6 vols. Madras: Indian Music Publishing House.

Sankaran, Trichy. 1994. *The Rhythmic Principles and Practice of South Indian Drumming.* Toronto: Lalith Publishers.

Sarma, Harihara. 1969. *The Art of Mridhangam.* Madras: Sri Jaya Ganesh Talavadya Vidyalaya.

Subramaniam, Karaikudi S., and Trichy S. Sankaran. 1990. *Laya Vinyās.* Music of the World CDT120. Compact disc.

———. 1992. *Sunada.* Music of the World CDT 127. Compact disc.

Hindustani Vocal Music

Bonnie C. Wade

Dhrupad
Dhamār
Khyāl
Light Classical Genres
Ṭhumrī
Dādrā
Ghazal

Several generalizations emerge from the study of Hindustani—North Indian—vocal genres. First, vocal music has been the most significant type of music in India from ancient times; only in the late twentieth century has instrumental performance risen to its present state of artistic development and popularity with classical-music audiences. Second, the development of instrumental music cannot be separated from that of vocal music. This cultural fact and value underscores eight further generalizations about Hindustani vocal music.

1. Vocal genres performed at the present time have a long history, beginning in the 1500s or earlier.

2. Over time, as local traditions have affected the more widely shared classical repertoires, new genres have emerged. Each successive new infusion, initially considered light music, has gradually become more classical, with the oldest vocal genre, *dhrupad*, becoming the epitome of classicism. Use of the terms *classical* and *light classical* to describe genres performed today reflects a continuation of that process (Prajnanananda 1981).

3. Only four classical and light classical genres—*dhrupad, khyāl* (also commonly transliterated as *khayāl*), *ṭhumrī,* and ghazal—have dominated the history of North Indian vocal performance. This discussion considers two other frequently performed genres, *tarānā* and *dādrā.* Concerts featuring any of these genres often include performance of other "light" vocal forms, such as the regional song genres *ṭappā* (from Banaras, based on a Punjabi folk song), *Rabindrasaṅgīt* (from Bengal), and *pad* (from Maharashtra).

4. Since the 1700s, these four main genres have coexisted rather than replacing each other in historical succession (Meer 1980; Wade 1987). *Khyāl* has been the preeminent form in concerts throughout the twentieth century.

5. Each of the four main genres consists of a brief composition complemented by improvisation. The compositions themselves are not radically different from genre to genre, although they are often associated with and thus represent a particular genre. It is misleading to think of a Hindustani composition as a "fixed" entity, to be performed exactly as a composer intended it to sound (Wade 1973). Even the most widely known songs by the most respected singer-composers only provide a basis for

flexible interpretation and improvisation: a raga, a tala, and a text, which together provide the basic materials for improvisation.

6. Two aspects of performance—the way the singer uses the composition and the nature of the singer's improvisation—most clearly distinguish one genre from another.

7. The performing ensemble and the musical roles of its members are also important differences among the genres.

8. The context in which each genre developed and the sociomusical identity of the singers are important aids to understanding Hindustani vocal music (Powers 1979, 1980).

DHRUPAD

Dhrupad is today considered the most serious Hindustani vocal form. Evoking images of elegance and grandeur, it demands from its singers a deep knowledge of raga and a thoroughgoing competence in vocal rhythmic improvisation. A lengthy vocal exposition of the melodic mode precedes the composition, and rhythmic play within the meter of the song concludes the performance.

History of the genre

In the early 1500s, North India was divided into princely realms, and a variety of vocal genres existed. At that time, the *dhrupad* may have been widespread in the Indo-Gangetic plain. Historical accounts associate it mostly with Gwalior, a kingdom then ruled by an important patron of music, Man Singh Tomar (r. 1486–1516). Due to the remarkable artistry of singers employed in his court, *dhrupad* emerged as a genre whose roots lay in, but encompassed more than, the historical and widely known *prabandha,* the form it replaced in importance. *Dhrupad* was an immediately accessible genre, with compositions in the oldest and best-known ragas as well as in more locally familiar ragas. Unlike earlier classical vocal music, which had texts in the scholarly and religious language Sanskrit, *dhrupad* used texts in the vernacular Hindi language of the area. Also in contrast to earlier classical songs, its texts eschewed classical poetic meters, and were unconstricted by the demands of metrical versification. A new era in Hindustani classical music had begun.

Dhrupad was not merely a court-based genre. Singers of the bhakti devotional movement used this form, creating thousands of songs about the love of the milkmaid Radha for the elusive, flirtatious deity Krishna, an incarnation of the god Vishnu. Listeners understood the allegorical message: as Radha loved and sought Krishna, all humankind should seek the love of God. Religious mendicants sang devotional *dhrupad,* accompanying themselves on the vina, and a temple-based repertoire developed.

The *dhrupad* genre spread quickly to courts outside Gwalior. By 1550, it was part of the culture of the Mughal courts, where both lower-ranking Indian musicians and famous singers trained in Gwalior and employed at the court of Emperor Akbar (r. 1556–1605) performed it. *Dhrupad* became preeminent among Hindustani vocal forms, and reigned as the vocal genre of choice in regional courts of North and Central India and in the imperial courts in Delhi and Agra. The first Mughal sovereign to prefer newer, "lighter" styles of music was Muhammad Shah (r. 1719–1748), under whose patronage the vocal form *khyāl* gained acceptance into the mainstream of classical music. By Muhammad Shah's time, *dhrupad* had probably become the rather solemn and extremely serious genre known to twentieth-century audiences. Although concerts featuring *dhrupad* are now rare—with few performers, teachers, and students compared with those of *khyāl*—the prestige of the genre among classical forms remains undiminished.

The precise form and character of *dhrupad* in the 1500s and immediately thereafter is unclear. Pictorial evidence provides some details of the court-based *dhrupad* ensemble over time. In the 1500s, this ensemble included one singer, or a pair of singers, who kept the tala (showed the rhythmic cycle) with motions of the hands and sang to the accompaniment of the *rudra vīṇā* 'stick zither'. This instrument was still part of the accompaniment in seventeenth-century paintings, but the ensemble had otherwise changed: a *tambūr* 'long-necked, plucked lute' played a continuous drone, and the *pakhāvaj* 'barrel drum' provided rhythmic accompaniment, much like the ensemble of the present day. In the 1700s, players of vinas began to assert their musical independence, with the result that the vina (now called *bīn*) is no longer part of the *dhrupad* ensemble. The complete modern ensemble for a performance of *dhrupad* consists of the singer(s), the keeper of the drone, and the drummer.

From surviving examples of *prabandha* (the predecessors of *dhrupad*), scholars have deduced characteristics that show similarities with those of *dhrupad* and other, more modern, Indian vocal forms (Rowell 1992:274–281). *Prabandha* had multiple sections; in the early history of the genre, *dhrupad* had three sections, whose number increased to four in the late 1800s (Srivastava 1980:31, 60). The performance of *prabandha* followed a sectionalized sequence, with changes of pace delineating some sections (from metered to unmetered music, for example) or shifts between meaningful text and meaningless syllables (vocables). Texts of *prabandha* featured two-syllable rhymes; those of *dhrupad* do also, as in the words *gyānī, bānī, jānī,* and *siyānī* in the text of figure 1 (see below).

Surviving *dhrupad* texts of the late 1400s and 1500s by the greatest singers of the age (Tansen, Nayak Bakshu, and others) show a song form that could address a god or a goddess, laud a king, express feelings of intimate romantic love, describe a season, transmit musicological knowledge, or deal with a metaphysical or religious concept (figure 1):

> Kauna bharama bhūle ho mana gyānī?
> Bujhata rāga akshara budha bānī,
>
> Anjānī kachu na jānī.
> Jānī na jāta, vidyā bahuta siyānī.
>
> In what delusion have you lost yourself, O knowing mind?
> Though you know ragas and words and meanings of speech,
>
> The Primal Sound [the unknown] cannot be known.
> So deep is the knowledge, it cannot be grasped.

Conventionally, the first section of a piece is called its *sthāī,* and its second section is called its *aṅtarā.* As is frequently the case, in this example each section is a couplet.

Dhrupad in performance

The hallmark of *dhrupad* today is raga, the melodic mode, which the most respected Hindustani musicians—whom Indians consider repositories of traditional knowledge—present in its clearest and purest form both in improvisation and in composition. (Until the mid-twentieth century, a singer of *khyāl* often went to a singer of *dhrupad* to learn ragas.) The performance of *dhrupad* emphasizes raga, and in a present-day concert its performance, lasting forty to sixty minutes, begins with a lengthy improvisation (*ālāp*) on the raga of the *dhrupad* that will follow. Only after fully

FIGURE 1 The *dhrupad* composition "Kauna bharama bhūle" and improvisation on the text of the *sthāī*, as sung by N. Zahiruddin and N. Faiyazuddin Dagar. In *rāg miyāṅ kī toḍī*, twelve-beat *cautāl*. Transcription by Rajna Klaser, from Dagar Brothers 1988. Large commas are breath marks; short, wavy lines indicate ornamentation.

(continued)

introducing the scale and melodic motifs of the raga does the singer present the composition and develop it with further improvisation (Widdess 1981).

Melodic improvisation **(ālāp)**

Accompanied only by a *tambūrā,* which continuously sounds a drone, the vocalist (usually male) begins the improvised melody, at first focusing on introducing the melodic mode and presenting with intense concentration the musical traits of the chosen raga. If there are two vocalists, they share the role of soloist, taking turns singing. Initially intoning a prolonged tonic (Sa) in their middle register (the middle C at the beginning of figure 2), the singers bring the audience into their concentration. Then progressing slowly, they sing with thoughtful attention each pitch of the raga, each connection to the next pitch, each characteristic melodic turn, and any significant ornamentation. As they establish the mood and the traits of the raga, they give correct emphasis to its proper tones. The rhythm at this point is free, unmetered, changing, and unstructured by words, as the singers use vocables such as *na* and *re.*

The artist often succeeds in creating a suspenseful, climactic, exhilarating feeling of arrival at the upper tonic.

FIGURE 1 (*continued*) The *dhrupad* composition "Kauna bharama bhūle" and improvisation on the text of the *sthāī*, as sung by N. Zahiruddin and N. Faiyazuddin Dagar. In *rāg miyāṅ kī toḍī*, twelve-beat *cautāl*. Transcription by Rajna Klaser, from Dagar Brothers 1988. Large commas are breath marks; short, wavy lines indicate ornamentation.

Departing from the tonic, the singers explore the adjacent pitches, mostly down into the lower tetrachord (*maṅdra*) but ideally as far as the lower tonic (Sa). (If two singers frequently perform together, one may cultivate a lower vocal range.) Musical phrases emerge as the singers return briefly to the middle tonic with a recurring melodic formula (*mohṛā*) that serves to finish a melodic thought. When the singers

FIGURE 1 (*continued*) The *dhrupad* composition "Kauna bharama bhūle" and improvisation on the text of the *sthāī*, as sung by N. Zahiruddin and N. Faiyazuddin Dagar. In *rāg miyāṅ kī toḍī*, twelve-beat *cautāl*. Transcription by Rajna Klaser, from Dagar Brothers 1988. Large commas are breath marks; short, wavy lines indicate ornamentation.

are satisfied that they have sufficiently explored the lower register, they focus on the middle (*madhya*) register, and then gradually move to the high (*tār*) register. The artist often succeeds in creating a suspenseful, climactic, exhilarating feeling of arrival at the upper tonic (Sa). But that feeling may not last, because the best singers take the improvisation even higher, until they reach the fourth or fifth scale degree (Ma or Pa)

FIGURE 2 Beginning of a *dhrupad ālāp* improvisation, representing the first two minutes of a performance by N. Zahiruddin and N. Faiyazuddin Dagar. In *rāg miyāṅ kī toḍī*. Transcription by Rajna Klaser, from Dagar Brothers 1988.

FIGURE 3 *Nom-tom ālāp* as sung by N. Zahiruddin and N. Faiyazuddin Dagar. In *rāg miyāṅ kī toḍī.* Transcription by Rajna Klaser, from Dagar Brothers 1988.

of the high register. The ideal of sustaining musicality across such a wide vocal range puts extraordinary vocal demands on singers of improvised introductions, and it may be one reason for the custom that allows vocal duos to perform *dhrupad.*

Rhythmic improvisation (nom-tom ālāp)

Gradually (and perhaps unnoticeably to listeners), the speed of the singing increases through the melodic improvisation. Melodic phrases increasingly encompass more tones. Having fully imparted the melodic aspects of the raga, the singer permits the musical element of rhythm to take on more prominence. Without pausing, he shifts into a portion of the introduction called *nom-tom ālāp*. He initiates a definite pulse by enunciating repeated vocables on repeated pitches (figure 3). The rhythm does not necessarily remain regular; in fact, rhythmic groupings can be quite irregular, drawing attention to the element of rhythm itself.

Dhrupad *composition*

When the vocalist wishes to end the unmetered melodic section, he subtly communicates with the drummer playing the *pakhāvaj,* who has remained silent: the moment has arrived for presenting the *dhrupad* composition. The drummer joins the performance because the composition is set to a tala (metric cycle); in Hindustani classical music, accompaniment on drums always indicates metered music.

Composers of *dhrupad* have always drawn on a large number of ragas, but they have not always used a large number of talas. Theoretical treatises of the 1600s show that performances of *dhrupad* in that period employed many talas; however, performances of the 1990s use five talas, of which two—*cautāl,* with a cycle of twelve beats (in figure 1, each bar delineates one cycle of this tala), and *jhaptāl,* with a cycle of ten beats—are preeminent.

Until the early twentieth century, the performance of *dhrupad* by a full ensemble may have comprised four sections (*sthāī, aṅtarā, saṅcārī,* and *ābhog*), but performers nowadays usually sing only the first two, both of which are short, consisting of two, three, or four textual phrases. One distinction between these two sections lies in their relative tonal registers: *sthāī* melodies often remain mostly in the lower half of the middle register and a few pitches below the middle tonic, and the *aṅtarā* ascends in its first phrase to the upper tonic. The song in figure 1 is a lesson in reality, varying the characteristic form: the *sthāī* ascends to the upper tonic in the first phrase, albeit more gradually than the ascent in the *aṅtarā* (see cycle 10). The *aṅtarā* composition permits smooth linkage back to the beginning of the *sthāī* (cycle 14), in terms of both the melody and the place in the metric cycle. Thus, the performance of the *sthāī* and the *aṅtarā* is cyclical.

Most Hindustani compositions, including *dhrupad,* do not begin on the first count of the tala. Many begin halfway through the metric cycle, as in figure 1. The soloist sets the speed for the drummer by singing the first notes of the song alone, and the drum enters on count 1. The short, beginning phrase of the *sthāī* ("Kauna bharama bhūle" in figure 1), presented from the midpoint of one tala cycle to the midpoint of the next, provides a convenient cadential formula for further repetitions of the *sthāī.*

The artist presents the entire composed *sthāī,* often, as in figure 1, repeating the first phrase in the process. Then the singer has the option of either presenting the *aṅtarā* immediately (in figure 1, tala cycle 10) or delaying its presentation by using the text of the *sthāī* as a vehicle for a newly improvised melody. Whenever the vocalist introduces the *aṅtarā,* he uses its initial phrase, like that of the *sthāī,* as a cadential formula; however, performers spend far more time improvising on the text of the *sthāī* than on that of the *aṅtarā.* See the return to the *sthāī* in figure 1, at the end of cycle 14.

Improvisation on the composition

What most distinguishes the performance of *dhrupad* from that of other Hindustani vocal genres is the nature of the improvisation following the composition: specifically, its primarily rhythmic orientation. The singer must always articulate the composition clearly; but expressing the meaning of the text through melodic improvisation is far less important than using the text for rhythmic purposes (*bolbānt*) (see tala cycles 17 to the end of figure 1). The singer may alter a single word, two words, or a phrase, thereby changing the speed (*laykārī*), creating syncopated rhythms, or making patterns against the regular beats of the tala. All the while, the improvised melody must remain true to the raga of the composition. Few singers of other genres can match the rhythmic skill of *dhrupad* singers (*dhrupadīyā*).

Dhrupad performances also contrast with those of other vocal genres in terms of the drummer's role. He does not have to play the rhythmic pattern that constantly enunciates the tala (*ṭhekā*), as in *khyāl* and other more recent genres; rather, he is a partner in the rhythmic improvisation. He may play complex patterns, and these may or may not conform with the vocalist's rhythm-oriented improvisation. He may be silent just when listeners expect percussive emphasis on a beat, or he may try the extremely challenging technique of simultaneously improvising the same rhythm as the vocalist. This kind of drumming may have its roots in the early practice of the singer's keeping the tala, in the period before the *pakhāvaj* player became part of the ensemble.

Unless the singers mark the subdivisions and beats of the tala with their hands in the traditional visual manner [see HINDUSTANI TALA], the performance gives the audience no indication of the metric pattern. This is an instance of connoisseurship in Hindustani music aiding the listener: being able to keep track of the tala—not

Despite periodic cries of distress about the role of *khyāl* in the dissolution of "pure" classical music, it became in the 1800s, and remains, the most frequently performed genre of Hindustani classical vocal music.

only feeling the rhythmic play within it but also anticipating the finish of an improvisational unit on a cadential count 1 (*sam*)—can greatly enhance enjoyment of the artists' improvisations.

DHAMĀR

Dhamār is a name sometimes given to *dhrupad*-like compositions composed and performed for the Hindu spring festival of Holī. They differ from *dhrupad* primarily in their tala: *dhamār tāl* is a cycle of fourteen beats, with irregular subdivisions of 5 + 2 + 3 + 4 beats. Conceived to show off this tala, the texts of *dhamār* display a playful lilt as they joke about Krishna's flirtations. The performance of *dhamār* is appropriate for the fun of Holī, when Indians delight in splashing one another with red powder or liquid, relishing the sexual symbolism of the color and the splashing.

KHYĀL

In Hindustani concerts, *khyāl* is the most frequently performed classical form of singing. Considered a lyrical and flexible genre, it begins with the vocal presentation of a brief composition. The singer then draws on several kinds of improvisation while presenting a raga and reveals musical creativity while displaying increasing vocal virtuosity.

History of the genre

Khyāl was developed to maturity after *dhrupad* and is second in prestige among the Hindustani vocal genres. Legend credits a royal patron of the 1400s, Sultan Husain Sharqi (r. 1458–1477) of Jaunpur, with the creation of a genre by that name. Though its relationship to the *khyāl* of today is dubious, it was probably one of numerous popular regional genres that surfaced in classical music only when a royal patron brought it into an influential cultural sphere; in the case of *khyāl,* the patron who did this was another Mughal sovereign, Muhammad Shah (r. 1719–1748).

Historical lore has linked *khyāl* with several persons: Nyamat Khan, who played *bīn* and sang *dhrupad* in Muhammad Shah's court (and was a descendant of the great singer Tansen); Nyamat Khan's students; and singers of the Muslim religious form qawwali and an undefined genre called *khyāl.* According to tradition, Nyamat Khan chafed at his subordinate position as an instrumental accompanist and left his post. Wanting to create a livelier musical fashion than the then-ponderous *dhrupad*, he integrated into a new improvisational genre some elements of qawwali style (probably the florid, rapid melodic runs called *tān*) with traditional compositional forms. Instead of performing, he composed songs (under the pen name Sadarang) and trained two young boys, who themselves eventually became masterly artists. Muhammad Shah invited the young men to sing and offered them positions at court. Only later did he learn that the new musical genre was Nyamat Khan's innovation. The story has a happy ending: Muhammad Shah permitted Nyamat Khan to be a

FIGURE 4 The renowned Hindustani vocalist Veena Sahasrabuddhe, with *tambūrā*, performing at the New Delhi home of Pandit Ravi Shankar on the occasion of his seventy-second birthday, 1992. Photo by Stephen Slawek.

soloist on the vina (*bīn*), and the new genre, performed by top-ranking musicians (Kalāvant), joined the other genres of court-approved music.

In the waning years of the Mughal empire, *khyāl* became more classicized as musicians disseminated it throughout North India, seeking new patrons. Despite periodic cries of distress about its role in the dissolution of "pure" classical music, it became in the 1800s, and remains, the most frequently performed genre of Hindustani classical vocal music (Wade 1984). Moreover, *khyāl* performances are generally identified not by the genre but by the raga being performed, unlike performances of other vocal genres.

Khyāl in performance

Khyāl differs noticeably from *dhrupad* in the hierarchy of musicians' roles within an ensemble, which consists of the featured soloist(s), an accompanist on a melody-producing instrument, a drummer, and one or two accompanists on *tambūrā* (from the 1700s to the mid-1800s, the singers were exclusively male, but since then the number of female artists has increased) (figure 4).

Khyāl is primarily a solo vocal genre, although male duos, usually family members who learned music together, have performed it. As in *dhrupad,* where two soloists might sing the composition and the cadential phrase together, the singers of *khyāl* divide the improvisation between them, jointly performing only one melodic solo line. Another possible vocalist might be a supporting singer, an aspiring young artist engaging in traditional performance-centered training. The player of the stringed drone (often the same person as the supporting singer) will be a trusted disciple whose nameless role is an honored position. (Conforming to the Western custom of announcing all the performers' names, concert organizers nowadays sometimes acknowledge the *tambūrā* player.) There the similarities to the *dhrupad* ensemble end.

The melody-producing instrument in a *khyāl* ensemble is a bowed lute (either *sāraṅgī* or violin), or a harmonium (a small, portable reed organ), or both. The melodic accompanist is subordinate to the vocalist in every way. The accompanist's role is to complement the vocal line and provide continuity between breathing pauses by playing slight variations a split second behind the soloist's improvisation. The player may repeat either phrasal endings for continuity during short breaks or (should the soloist desire to rest) whole phrases during longer breaks. Some vocalists autocratically denounce accompanists, claiming that the player of the *sāraṅgī* is poorly trained, does not know the ragas, and depends on the soloists for musical creativity. In fact, in the history of *khyāl,* there has been considerable upward mobility from player of *sāraṅgī* to vocalist.

The primary reasons for the hierarchy among performers are sociocultural. The *sāraṅgī* was associated in the 1800s with light music. It provided accompaniment for female singers and dancers; indeed, its tonal quality blends beautifully with that of the female voice. Some of the female singers and dancers—even the most accomplished artists, patronized in a court-related context or by wealthy landowners—offered both sexual and musical entertainment. Their accompanists acquired their social and cultural stigma. Only from the mid-1920s would some male vocalists sing with *sāraṅgī* players, but soon thereafter the full complement of *sāraṅgī* with tabla and stringed drone became the standard ensemble. In the past few decades, the number of *sāraṅgī* players has been decreasing, for few young musicians are learning to play it; there would seem to be more interest in the *sāraṅgī* among Western musicians seriously involved in Indian classical music.

The use of the harmonium is probably a twentieth-century practice, one that has received some criticism. Objections by purists focus not so much on sociocultural factors as on the fixed tempered tuning of the instrument, which does not allow the intonational flexibility that is a hallmark of Hindustani music. In practice, players and audiences can effectively ignore the problematic fixed pitches because of the harmonium's low dynamic level.

The drummer in the *khyāl* ensemble also occupies a clearly subordinate position: he keeps the tala by repeating the *ṭhekā*. This role contrasts sharply with that of the tabla in accompanying dance and performing light music. In the performance of *khyāl*, the inclusion of a drum solo usually indicates that a special musical relationship exists between the singer and percussionist. The reasons for this subordinate position are unclear. Perhaps the drummer's role of playing the tala came into existence to contrast the performance of *khyāl* with that of both *dhrupad* and light music; perhaps singers thought a drummer who would just keep the tala would provide better balance for the greater variety of melodic improvisation in *khyāl*; perhaps performers of *khyāl* whose status was below that of performers of *dhrupad* wished to assert the superiority of their position.

Khyāl **composition**

The common terms for Hindustani composition are *bandiś,* which denotes both vocal and instrumental compositions, and *cīz,* generally referring to vocal composition. *Khyāl* compositions, though similar to those of *dhrupad,* are shorter, having only two sections, the *sthāī* and the *aṅtarā* (Wade 1973). The *sthāī* presents the essential musical elements of the particular raga in which the song is composed, and it remains within the middle octave of the vocalist's range. The melody of the *aṅtarā* ascends to the upper-octave tonic (Sa), and even rises into the upper-octave register before descending to link with the melody of the *sthāī.* The initial phrases of the *sthāī* and the *aṅtarā,* known as the *mukhṛā,* provide the material for cadences throughout the improvisation.

Compositions fall into two categories depending on the speed of their performance: slow or medium-speed songs (*baṛā* 'large' *khyāl*) and fast songs (*choṭā* 'small' *khyāl*). The performance of a *khyāl* usually consists of a *baṛā khyāl* followed without break by a *choṭā khyāl,* usually in the same raga but a different tala. However, a principle of the performance of *khyāl* is that the basic speed of the tala gradually increases. By the end of a *choṭā khyāl,* the singing is often spectacularly fast.

TRACK 1

The point where the composition occurs in the vocal performance differs radically between *khyāl* and *dhrupad*: except in performances by singers of the Agra *gharānā* 'musical lineage', no lengthy unmetered *ālāp* precedes the singing of a *khyāl* composition. Instead, singers introduce the pitches of the raga using vocables, and they rarely rise above the fifth pitch (Pa) of the middle octave. The melody of this brief, unmetered introduction, which only occasionally lasts as long as five minutes, is often merely an anticipation of the melody of the composition. After the introduction, the singer immediately renders the first phrase of the song to set the tempo for the drummer. From that moment on, the performance is "in tala" (metered). The drummer does not wait long on stage before entering the performance.

The manner in which singers present the composition in the performance of a *baṛā khyāl* differs from artist to artist. Before settling down to lengthy improvisation on the text of the *sthāī,* a singer may present the *sthāī* and the *aṅtarā* together or with improvisation between them. The singer may choose not to perform the *aṅtarā* at all. Presentation of the *baṛā khyāl* composition usually takes no more than four minutes, but the whole performance lasts anywhere from twenty to forty minutes. If a *choṭā khyāl* follows the *baṛā khyāl,* this section lasts only about three to five of the total minutes. Here, the singer presents and reiterates the composition much more straightforwardly.

A composition is not a fixed work, and artists do not have to perform it in a specific manner. Singers have transmitted songs orally for generations with the understanding that in performance other singers will not reproduce the songs exactly. Two renditions of the same song can be so different as to share only the raga and the text. The vocalist chooses whether to perform a *baṛā khyāl* in an initially slow or medium speed (the actual speed is relative), and occasionally selects a tala different from that usually performed with the composition.

The texts of *khyāl* treat more or less the same set of topics as the texts of *dhrupad,* but they are generally spoken of as light, rather than ponderous. They are rich in symbolism and imagery. They may express views on life or religious devotion, either Hindu or Muslim. Some concern the Hindu Lord Krishna, whereas others express the synthesis of religious cultures that marks North Indian music, as does the following example. (The first reference to God is the Indian Muslim form of address, "*Allāh sāhab,*" but the second reference, to "the beauty of the Supreme Lord," is Hindu.)

> *Allāh sāhab*, the all-graceful God, is sitting on his throne.
> One feels wonderful beholding the beauty of the Supreme Lord.

The first line of this text is the *sthāī,* and the second is the *aṅtarā.*

Khyāl texts may describe seasons or shower praise on patrons; they may lavish attention on divine or human love, in sorrow (due to the absence of a loved one) or in joy (over union with a lover). Most texts, whether sung by a man or a woman, speak from the woman's point of view:

> Oh my mother, my anklets are jingling, so I know my husband has come.
> It has been four days since he came; all my heart's sadness has gone.

As in *dhrupad,* the texts of *khyāl* become vehicles for improvisation rather than deeply meaningful entities to be explored expressively. Singers sometimes place so little stress on the text that the words can be hard to understand; or they may use the words solely for rhythmic articulation.

Khyāl improvisation

Khyāl further contrasts with *dhrupad* in having a greater variety of improvisational types from which an artist can choose. This trait explains the name *khyāl,* glossable as 'imagination'. Six types of improvisation are usually associated with the genre: *bolālāp, nom-tom, bolbānt*, two kinds of *tān* (*ākār* and *boltān*), and *sargam.* The first two occur only in *baṛā khyāl,* but the other four occur in both *baṛā* and *choṭā khyāl.*

A singer draws on these improvisational choices in structuring the performance of a *khyāl.* The order in which the singer performs different types of improvisation, following the initial presentation of the composition, is characteristic of Hindustani classical music in general: attention first to melody, then to rhythm, then to speed. When adhering strictly to these principles, a singer will perform *khyāl* in the following order of events: composition, *bolālāp, bolbānt, boltān, tān.* In practice, however, as the tempo begins to accelerate, singers introduce improvised passages of any type in any order, according to their imagination and creativity. Furthermore, an artist may use *sargam* at any point in the improvisation of *khyāl.*

The use of improvisation differs in the two types of *khyāl* performance, *baṛā* and *choṭā.* In the slower one, *baṛā khyāl,* an artist usually covers the range of improvisational possibilities, ideally giving full attention to all musical elements—-melody, rhythm, and speed. In *choṭā khyāl,* the artist satisfies the melodic aspect mostly by

> The purpose of an improvised section is for the singer to reveal the raga by establishing its mood and showing its traits, gradually but systematically.

repeating the composition many times, employing improvisation to emphasize rhythm and speed. To fulfill the ideal of giving attention to all three musical elements, vocalists rarely perform *choṭā khyāl* as an independent piece; artists might even replace it with a highly rhythmic genre, *tarānā* (discussed below).

Initial improvised section using text (bolālāp)

After presenting a *khyāl* composition in an exceptionally slow tempo, an artist proceeds to a formal, lengthy, improvised section (*ālāp*). For this, the singer employs text (*bol*) as introduced in the composition, hence the term *bolālāp*. The purpose of the improvised section, as in *dhrupad*, is for the singer to reveal the raga by establishing its mood and showing its traits, gradually but systematically. The melodic line in figure 5 shows a singer's exploration of tones from the initial phrase (*mukhṛā*) of the *sthāī*. The text of this example is translated "You came early in the morning and uttered a blessing." It repeats "came early" (*bhore hī āye*) in an ascending melody suggestive of the rising sun and of the singer's rising in the early morning.

Unlike that in *dhrupad*, the *ālāp* in *khyāl* is metered, for the drummer continues playing the tala after the presentation of the composition. Most vocalists downplay the meter, however, by seeking a rhythmically free, floating melody. They slur consonants in the text so as not to constrict the rhythm, except when they intend to do so. Because the tempo is so slow, the drummer plays not only the rhythmic pattern (*ṭhekā*) of the tala, but subdivisions of the tala count as well (see the bracketed beats,

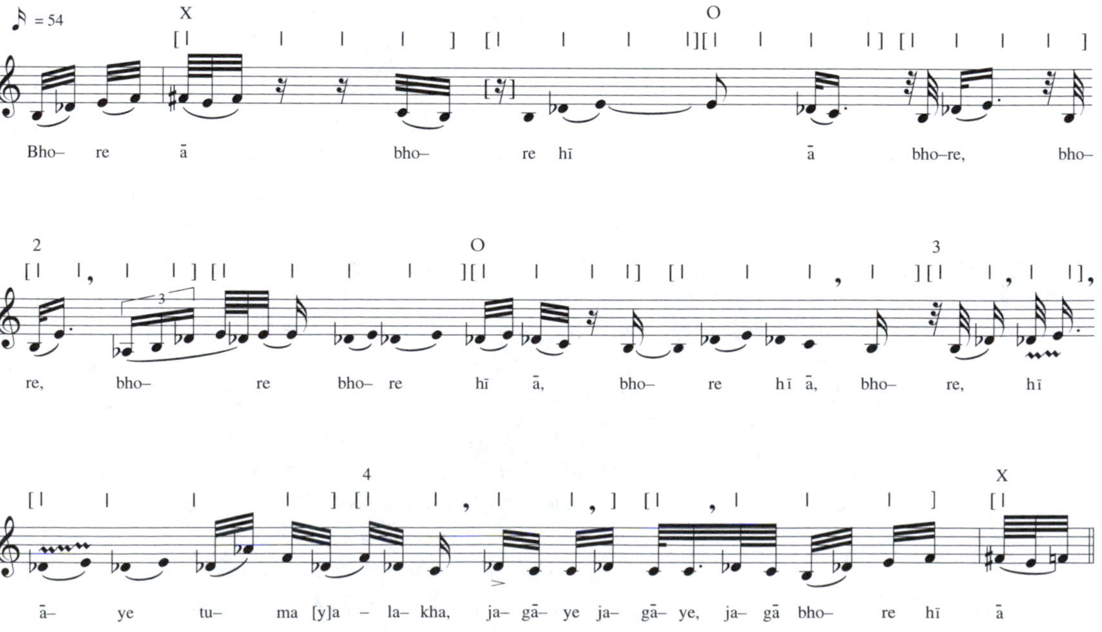

FIGURE 5 "Bhore hī āye," a *bolālāp*, sung by Dipali Nag (Agra *gharānā*) in slow-tempo *baṛā khyāl*. In *rāg lalit*, twelve-beat *ektāl*. Transcription by Bonnie C. Wade, from All India Radio broadcast, New Delhi, 1969. (Bracketed lines indicate subdivisions of a beat.)

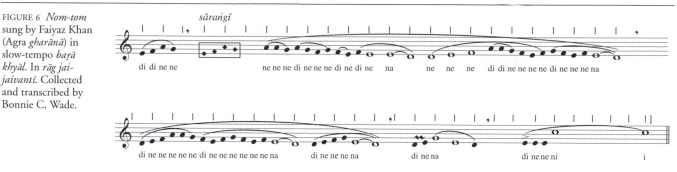

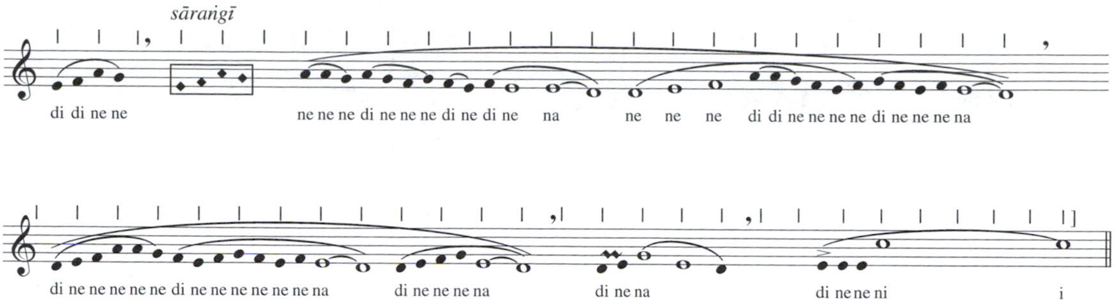

FIGURE 6 *Nom-tom* sung by Faiyaz Khan (Agra *gharānā*) in slow-tempo *baṛā khyāl*. In *rāg jaijaivantī*. Collected and transcribed by Bonnie C. Wade.

each with four subdivisions, in figure 5). The performers emphasize the tala only at the cadences of improvised sections, using the *mukhṛā* as a cadential formula or perhaps additional text immediately before the cadential *bhore hī* text, as in figure 5.

If the performance of a *baṛā khyāl* begins in medium speed, the melodic improvisation may be less exhaustive; to some extent, however, the artist will still explore the tonal registers and the raga.

Rhythmic improvisation

Highly rhythmic improvisation sung on vocables (*nom-tom*) draws attention to rhythm through the repetition of tones or syllables, through particular ornamentation, or by other means. *Nom-tom* refers to a passage consisting of emphatic ornamentation on each successive tone with repeated tones, which give the music a rhythmic punch. This kind of singing "with *zor*" (forcefully) would be typical in *khyāl*, in contrast to the presentation of a whole section of systematic *nom-tom* as in *dhrupad*. Shifting rhythmic combinations are characteristic of *nom-tom* (figure 6). After the repetition of the initial phrase by the *sāraṅgī* (boxed in figure 6), the vocal melody has a grouping of three notes sung to the vocables *ne ne ne,* then a group of four (*di ne ne ne*), then of two (*di ne*), and then a longer grouping.

Bolbānt is a type of improvisation that uses the text (*bol*) for rhythmic play. Though *bolbānt* predominates in *dhrupad*, few singers of *khyāl* exploit it beyond fairly simple patterns of syncopation, with one syllable per tone. Only singers with particularly good control of tala cultivate daring rhythmic play (*laykārī*). In figure 7, *bolbānt* on the text *sagarī raina meṅ jāge* 'awake the whole night' imparts a feeling of restlessness.

Fast melodic improvisation (tān)

Fast, virtuosic melodic figures (*tān*) are the hallmark of the vocal style of *khyāl*. Such melodic improvisation varies in shape, range, and numerous other ways. *Tān* may be clear "like a string of pearls" or ornamented so heavily that the tones are indistinguishable from one another. A *tān* can be entirely descending or entirely ascending, or it can have the shape of a roller coaster, constantly covering a range of tones. It may contain a series of tones sustained by a fast vibrato, creating an illusion of speed with ornamentation rather than with real melodic motion. It may even employ musical elements not characteristic of the raga, moving slightly "out of the raga."

A vocalist may sing fast melodic patterns on vowels (*ākār tān*) unattached to any word. In figure 8, following the *mukhṛā* textual phrase *bāje jha* 'make your anklets jingle', the singer imitates this sound with three such melodic patterns. Singers can also use the vowels of textual syllables (*bol*), thereby creating *boltān*. In figure 9, quick melodic patterns on *o* of the name *Udho* and *u* of *tum* 'you' keep the text intact. As in this example, a singer may improvise a *boltān* that employs textual syllables for rhythmic interest without turning the improvisation into a *bolbānt*. Some

FIGURE 7 "Sagarī raine meṅ jāge," a *bolbānt,* as sung by Faiyaz Khan (Agra *gharānā*) in fast-tempo *choṭā khyāl.* In *rāg jaijaivantī,* sixteen-beat *tīntāl.* Collected and transcribed by Bonnie C. Wade.

singers become known for singing fast melodic patterns, perhaps a *tān* of a certain shape, whereas others dislike them and sing only a minimal number.

Sol-fa syllables (sargam)

Sargam is the term for Indian sol-fa syllables (Sa, Re, Ga, Ma, Pa, Dha, Ni), based on the names of the first four syllables. *Sargam* in *khyāl* refers to improvised passages using the sol-fa syllables. Vocalists use these passages in different contexts. Most artists employ them when doubling or quadrupling the speed of the singing in relation to the tala counts. Singers also use *sargam* in rhythmic improvisation *(bolbānt)*, and a few artists mix the syllables with the words of the composition in such passages. Figure 10 demonstrates the mixture of these possibilities. Some singers render slow, expressive passages using *sargam* syllables.

The use of sol-fa syllables in vocal music is an ancient Indian practice, cultivated widely in some South Indian vocal genres. In Hindustani music, some traditional singers of *khyāl* adamantly refuse to include *sargam* in their performances, considering them a technique for practice rather than performance.

Stylistic schools of performance

All singers of *khyāl* foster the general traits as described above, but individuals and groups of musicians have cultivated distinct ways of performing. These family traditions or stylistic schools (*gharānā*) promote styles that have become increasingly important, as the traditional system of teaching and learning has given way to broader musical education.

Most singers of *khyāl* belong to the *gharānā* system, the organization of musicians and musical knowledge that developed through the history of this genre in par-

FIGURE 8 "Bāje jha," an *ākār tān,* as sung by Kishori Amonkar (Alladiya Khan *gharānā*) in medium-tempo *baṛā khyāl.* In *rāg jaunpurī,* sixteen-beat *tīntāl.* Transcription by Bonnie C. Wade, from Amonkar 1967.

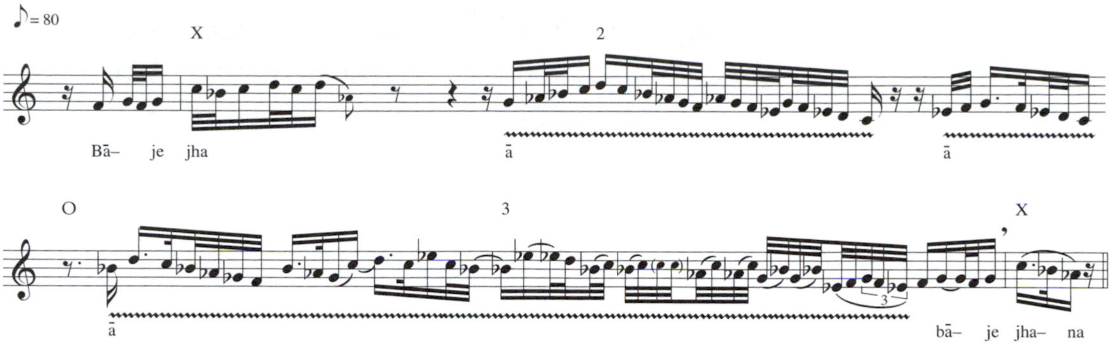

ticular. The social and musical conditions under which *khyāl* evolved spawned the styles of *gharānā,* conditions (including the diverse vocal genres) that preceded it, the different family musical traditions fostered within it, and the system of patronage of Hindustan court singers, reaching from Gwalior in present-day Madhya Pradesh to Patiala in northwestern Punjab (Wade 1984). The Agra *gharānā,* for instance, owes its heavily *dhrupad*-like style (with full-blown *ālāp* preceding the composition) to the fact that the early members of the group were singers of *dhrupad;* even when this stylistic school became noted for *khyāl,* its singers continued to perform both genres. In so doing, these singers have continually asserted their claim both to the musical tradition of highest cultural value and to the highest rank in the social sphere of musicians. Fully comfortable in their standing in the tradition, several Agra singers have been composers of original *khyāl* songs.

The same factors—cultural value, social status among musicians, and musical value—are significant in the development of the Kirana *gharānā* style of *khyāl.* Its founders belonged to a family of accompanists on the *sāraṅgī,* performers accorded low social status among musicians. Since they accompanied singers of *khyāl,* they had access to soloists' musical knowledge, which proved to be their means of elevating their status—culturally, socially, and musically. Two famous Kirana singers, Abdul Karim Khan and Abdul Wahid Khan (1976), chose to emphasize melody and raga from among the musical options available in *khyāl*—the aspects of Hindustani music accorded the highest musical value. Furthermore, in the light of the hierarchy of

FIGURE 9 "Udho tum ho," a *boltān,* as sung by Vinayakrao Patwardhan (of the Gwalior *gharānā*) in slow-tempo *baṛā khyāl.* In *rāg anandi kedar,* twelve-beat *ektāl.* Transcription by Bonnie C. Wade, from Patwardhan 1976. Each pair of brackets indicates one beat.

In the 1800s, light classical vocal genres burgeoned in the northern part of the subcontinent. These genres have remained important.

FIGURE 10 "Gumānī, Jāga," a *sargam* passage, as sung by Abdul Wahid Khan (Kirana *gharānā*) in slow-tempo *baṛā khyāl*. In *rāg multānī*, sixteen-beat *tīntāl*. Transcription by Bonnie C. Wade, from Khan 1976.

musical values, Kirana singers within the *gharānā* system use traditional musical material—compositions and ragas—as if to assert their place within tradition rather than to call attention to any departure from it.

With the present shift away from *gharānā* affiliation and toward emphasis on individual artistry, and with singers feeling free to combine aspects of several styles to create their own style, *khyāl* continues as a flexible yet vital genre of Hindustani classical music.

Tarānā

Occasionally vocalists complement the performance of *baṛā khyāl* with a genre called *tarānā,* which has a South Indian counterpart, *tillāna* [see KARNATAK VOCAL AND INSTRUMENTAL MUSIC]. As *tarānā* requires skill in rhythmic manipulation (*laykārī*) and the ability to sing syllables rapidly, few *khyāl* singers perform this lively, fast-tempo genre.

The text of the composition most clearly distinguishes *tarānā* from *chotā khyāl. Tarānā* uses mostly vocables, particularly phrases such as *u dana dim, diradira,* and *tom ta na na,* which permit crisp and quick rhythmic enunciation. Occasionally a *tarānā* includes a Persian-language couplet, revealing its historical link to Indo-Muslim culture and music, notably Sufi songs of qawwali singers and songs accompanying North Indian *kathak* dance.

Tarānā syllables derive from three other sources. Vocalists employ *sargam* syllables for rhythmic improvisation. They also use dance-movement syllables from the *kathak* tradition and percussion-stroke syllables for tabla accompaniment to *kathak* and *khyāl,* all of which they render melodically in the sparkling *tarānā* style.

LIGHT CLASSICAL GENRES

In the 1800s, vocal genres burgeoned in the northern part of the subcontinent. These genres have remained important. Cultivated at first in particular locales and for particular audiences, they spread throughout the northern regions, and in the twentieth century they entered the musical mainstream. Without exception, these new genres—*ṭhumrī, dādrā,* and ghazal—are considered light classical, contrasting with the more serious *khyāl* and *dhrupad.* History has repeated itself, for the early singers of *khyāl* had to struggle to earn respect in the world of classical music when singers of *dhrupad* denounced *khyāl* as light music.

Why were (and are) these genres considered light? One suggested reason is that the talas that composers use for them are simpler and less weighty than those used for *khyāl* and *dhrupad* compositions. Another suggestion concerns the texts, which are altogether romantic, emphasizing the explicit, tantalizing, sensual language of love, rather than the devotional expression of Radha's love for Krishna found in *khyāl* and *dhrupad* texts. Furthermore, these light genres have been associated with women and were the core reportoire of courtesan singers until film songs became dominant. By far the most important difference between classical and light classical music, however, concerns the most valued of all aspects of South Asian classical music: raga. These genres are light largely because their singers are less rigorous in adhering to the raga than they are when performing *khyāl* or *dhrupad.*

ṬHUMRĪ

Ṭhumrī is the best-known example of the light classical vocal genres because it is performed in diverse contexts. These include classical-music concerts, which often conclude with a light piece; *kathak* dance performances, in which *ṭhumrī* is the basis for interpretive dance; and vocal concerts devoted almost exclusively to *ṭhumrī.* This genre is also a full-fledged instrumental genre. Like compositions in other light classical genres, a *ṭhumrī* is not always composed in a specific raga. Even when it is, improvisers may depart from the raga.

History of the genre

The history of *ṭhumrī* is similar to those of *dhrupad* and *khyāl* (Manuel 1986). Cultivated for some time as folk-style music and in songs accompanying courtesan dancers, *ṭhumrī* developed as the music for the emerging *kathak* style of dance from about 1770 to 1870. Contemporary popular accounts most frequently associated the genre with the ruler of the princely state of Oudh (Avadh), Nawab Wajid Ali Shah of Lucknow (r. 1847–1856), who elevated *ṭhumrī* to a court genre by lavishing personal patronage on excellent musicians who performed and refined it. These singers were exclusively women. The prevalent musical type was *bandiś ṭhumrī*—light, lively songs, emphasizing ingenious rhythmic manipulation of the text in fast tempo. *Sāraṅgī* and tabla players accompanied the singer-dancers.

After 1857, the British moved the nawab from Lucknow to Calcutta, but primarily female musicians continued to cultivate the genre in Lucknow and in nearby Banaras. The social context in which *ṭhumrī* flourished was a refined world of pleasure, where wealthy landowners sought company, sexual favors, and entertainment from female vocalists, who were often quite well trained. Many Western and Indian writers have described this context as disreputable prostitution, but it gave skilled and cultured courtesans the chance to earn high cultural status performing for private gatherings of connoisseurs, either in their salons or in the homes of their noble or landowner patrons.

Toward the end of the 1800s, as South Asia was reorganized under the British raj, a new middle class emerged consisting largely of civil servants, lawyers, teachers, doctors, and certain merchants and landlords. This class extended the source of patronage for classical music beyond the courts of those few princely states whose rulers continued to care about the traditional arts. In the realm of light classical music, however, *ṭhumrī* remained the domain of an increasingly stigmatized courtesan society, whose sensuous fine arts were scorned by those who adopted the values of Western education. After the democratization of landownership in the 1950s, patrons of *ṭhumrī* singers could no longer support their lifestyle, and courtesans sank to a low social position. The rubric *singing girl* took on entirely negative connotations, and male singers—including performers of *khyāl*—took over the artistic singing of *ṭhumrī*. By then, *khyāl* had effectively absorbed the fast and lively *bandiś ṭhumrī* in the form of the short, fast *choṭā khyāl* section. Also, some players of *sāraṅgī*, whose musical education had been in the courtesans' salons, had become prominent singers of *khyāl:* in this way *ṭhumrī* became a part of most *khyāl* singers' repertoires. It also came to exist apart from dance, and a more classicized form, *bol banāo ṭhumrī*, developed.

The new *ṭhumrī*, which remains the *ṭhumrī* heard today, featured a slower tempo and an emphasis on a leisurely, meaningful rendering of the feelings expressed in the text—an important difference between *ṭhumrī* and *khyāl*. The two styles of *ṭhumrī* correspond to—and emerged from—the two dance styles of *kathak*: the fast, rhythmic style of pure dance (*nritta*) and the slow, declamatory style of expressive dance (*nritya*). *Ṭhumrī* continues to be associated with women, if only through its textual "voice." A full performing ensemble will still probably include a *sāraṅgī* player and certainly a string drone and a tabla, but the singer is likely to provide accompaniment on a harmonium. The recent addition of harmonium to the *khyāl* ensemble shows the influence of the *ṭhumrī* ensemble.

Texts of *ṭhumrī*

Not surprisingly, *ṭhumrī* texts are romantic. Some refer to Krishna and his amorous pranks, or to the beloved, who may or may not be Krishna. Other texts are unequivocally romantic, and they contain no allegorical suggestions. Pangs of longing, the desperation of separation, a mind distracted by unrequited love—such emotions, as expressed in these texts, create an immediate and intensely personal impact: "I've been smitten by the scimitar of love; my lover has left, how can I go on? We've played the game of love together. I lost, and she won" (Manuel 1989:117).

Ṭhumrī in performance

Like all other Hindustani vocal forms, *ṭhumrī* compositions are short. Each consists of a *sthāī* and one or more *aṅtarā*, usually with the same registral contrast of middle octave and upper octave, as with *khyāl*. In examples that have more than one *aṅtarā*, the performer sings the additional text to approximately the same melody. *Ṭhumrī* compositions in ragas are likely to use one of a fairly discrete set—*khamāj, pīlū, bhairavī,* and *kāfī* especially. These preferred ragas feature two pitches varying the same tone within the scale, mostly a raised pitch in the ascending scale and a lowered pitch in descent (pitches 7 and flat 7 in *khamāj,* for example). Even if the raga does not have this trait, singers will exploit this sort of melodic play.

Ṭhumrī compositions also employ a certain group of talas—*jat, dīpcandī, panjābī, kaharvā,* and *dādrā.* Singers use tala flexibly, for different performers may sing the same composition in different talas, and the same singer may even do so on different occasions.

Clearly the most important aspect of a *ṭhumrī* composition is the text, and the most important aspect of its performance is the exploitation of the emotional meaning conveyed by the words. Because of this emphasis, there is a greater sense of repertoire in *ṭhumrī* than in *khyāl* or *dhrupad,* and listeners and artists tend to have favorite compositions. They refer to *ṭhumrī* compositions by the first line of the text, whereas they identify *dhrupad* and *khyāl* by the raga. Also of great importance, and characteristic of the genre, is the declamatory rhythmic style resulting from the emphasis on the text.

A brief rendition of "Nāhak lāe gavana morā" 'Unjustly they've brought me to my village' by the illustrious singer Girija Devi shows how the performance of a *ṭhumrī* (figure 11 shows the *sthāī* only) is structured. The song is in *rāg bhairavī* and *dīpcandī tāl* of fourteen counts (a cycle of 3 + 4 + 3 + 4 beats).

> Nāhak lāe gavan(va) morā,
> Ab to saiyāṇ videśva chā (morā).
>
> Kahtī chabīle sovat ras bhas bhāe;
> Bīt jātī jobanva morā.
>
> Unjustly they've brought me to my village,
> And now my lover has gone away.
>
> His heart has settled with his other wife;
> My full breasts are aging.

To set the speed of the tala counts, the singer improvises briefly on the syllables *a, a, ena,* then begins the *sthāī* section with the words "nāhak lāe gavanva." As in all Hindustani vocal music, final consonants and even some internal consonants of words often become full syllables, as in "nāhaka" for "nāhak" and "gavanava" for "gavanva." The player of the tabla joins the phrase on count 1 of the first cycle of the tala, on the syllable *va* of *gavan.* The first musical phrase (sung to "nāhak lāe gavanva") constitutes the cadential phrase (*mukhṛā*), which the singer performs at the end of every musical unit using the *sthāī* text. Both melody and text repeat. During repetitions, a performer will improvise slight melodic variations, and will separate, link, or repeat units of text for emotional effect, displaying expressive artistry, as in the treatment of the words *nāhak* 'unjustly' and *gavana* 'village'. At will, a performer can add a vocable such as *re* without disturbing the meaning.

Ṭhumrī singing features characteristic vocal passages or ornamentation, such as a dynamic swell on the highest tone of a word and quick, light trills. Singers also employ rapid melodic passages (*tān*). During a performance, the *sāraṅgī* and tabla players may offer brief solos. Those of the *sāraṅgī* in particular are short, lasting only the remainder of one tala after the cadential phrase, as in the eighth tala cycle of figure 11.

The tabla solo, however, is a distinctive event called *laggī,* a *ṭhumrī*-dance feature

Clearly the most important aspect of a *ṭhumrī* composition is the text, and the most important aspect of its performance is the exploitation of the emotional meaning conveyed by the words.

FIGURE 11 The *ṭhumrī* "Nāhak lāe gavana morā," as sung by Girija Devi. In *rāg bhairavī*, fourteen-beat *dīpcandī tāl*. After a transcription by Peter Manuel (Manuel 1989). Published by permission of Motilal Banarsidass and Peter Manuel.

that persists in vocal *ṭhumrī*. In what may seem an entirely abrupt manner, the tabla launches into a splash of virtuosity, playing at double or quadruple the speed of the established tala counts, in an eight- or sixteen-count tala. Either the singing stops during this section and the harmonium or *sāraṅgī* repeats the melody of the first section, or the vocalist sings that melody, effectively fulfilling the role of marking beats. However, the vocalist might instead sing rather drifting melodic passages, which contrast strangely with the ferocity of the tabla, or she may even sing a few rapid passages that would have seemed out of place in the slower vocal improvisation. Basically, the *laggī* gives the tabla relief from the tedious role of keeping the tala. An extended per-

FIGURE 11 (*continued*) The *ṭhumrī* "Nāhak lāe gavana morā," as sung by Girija Devi. In *rāg bhairavī,* fourteen-beat *dīpcandī tāl.* After a transcription by Peter Manuel (Manuel 1989). Published by permission of Motilal Banarsidass and Peter Manuel.

formance may include several *laggī,* providing contrast with the slow, soulful, text-oriented singing. The performance may end climactically with a *laggī* polished off with the drummed cadence called *tihāī,* a quick rhythmic pattern played three times and ending on count 1. This leads back to the leisurely pace of the *ṭhumrī* song that is then concluded.

DĀDRĀ

Dādrā is the name of a six-count tala that is common in *ṭhumrī* compositions. A group of other light classical songs composed in *dādra, kaharvā* (eight counts), or a few other talas, and performed in medium tempo or faster with an emphasis on rhythm, have acquired the name *dādrā.* In present-day concerts, singers sometimes follow the performance of a *ṭhumrī* with that of a *dādrā,* thereby accelerating the pace of the music, as in the *baṛā* and *choṭā khyāl* sequence.

Like the texts of *ṭhumrī,* the texts of *dādrā* are about the pangs and joys of love, and in performance the singer emphasizes them. But this genre differs from *ṭhumrī* in several ways other than tempo. *Dādrā* admits considerable flexibility in structural terms; melodies may be precomposed or improvised. Many are simply light classical renditions of folk songs in local Hindi dialects, Braj Bhasha and Bhojpuri. *Dādrā* is more likely than *ṭhumrī* to have more than one stanza, and a Hindi text may contain stanzas in Urdu, the Persianized form of Hindi that is the official language of Pakistan and used widely in India.

GHAZAL

One other light classical form, ghazal, is popular throughout much of North India. Distinctively, the texts of ghazals are all in Urdu, and they are associated specifically with Indo-Islamic culture.

History of the genre

Growing from Persian roots, the ghazal poetic form has been cultivated in South Asia for several centuries as an art song. Ghazals by the revered thirteenth-century Indo-Muslim poet Amir Khusrau have remained in the repertoire (Manuel 1988–1989). Like *ṭhumrī,* ghazals flourished in nineteenth-century Lucknow and were performed largely for private musical entertainment by courtesans, often accompanied by dancing. The light classical ghazal was brought to a peak in the mid-twentieth century by Begum Akhtar (d. 1974), a vocalist whose recordings are still widely available. Nowadays, ghazals serve as film music, and a form of the genre is widely distributed on recordings.

Ghazal texts

It is the music rather than the poetry that gives ghazals the designation light classical (Qureshi 1990). Whereas the texts of *dhrupad, khyāl,* and *ṭhumrī* are prose-poems of a flexible nature, the texts of ghazals are true poetry that is performed to light classical Hindustani music. When set to a raga, the text will be a light one, expressing amorous sentiments. In Indo-Muslim culture, respect for and cultivation of the poetic word derives ultimately from the supremacy of the word of God as revealed in the Qur'ān. Reinforced by Sufi tradition since the 1200s, poetry has been the medium of choice for intensely expressive communication. As an art, poetry is characterized by high formal and aesthetic standards. The texts of ghazals feature poetic meter, rhythmic patterns, and a set structure. The prevailing theme is unfulfilled love, as in the text of figure 12, by the great poet Ghalib (1797–1869); in that emphasis, ghazals do not differ greatly from other Hindustani vocal forms. But the texts contain many symbolic references and exploit metaphors that enrich the language and resonate deeply with Indo-Muslim culture.

The nuclear structural unit of ghazal is the couplet. Each couplet is thematically complete and self-contained in meaning. The first line of each couplet is completed or answered by the second line. All second lines in a poem rhyme, providing a close link from beginning to end. In addition, the first line of the first couplet of a poem ends in that same rhyme, resulting in the scheme *aa, ba, ca, da.* The first couplets of "Yeh na thī hamārī qismat" (pronounced *qisumat* in performance; see figure 12) demonstrate this structure (translated by Aditya Behl):

> Yeh na thī hamārī qismat keh viṣāl-e yār hotā;
> Agar aur jīte rehte yahī intizār hotā.
>
> Koī mere dil se puche, tere tīr-e nīm-kash ko.
> Yeh <u>kh</u>alish kahāṇ se hotī jo jigar ke pār hotā?
>
> It was not our good fortune to enjoy union with the beloved;
> If we had continued to live, there would still be this waiting.
>
> Someone should ask about the arrow in my heart, half-buried, sent by you.
> Why would there be this torment, if it had passed all the way through?

Each text is set to one of several meters, consisting of patterns of long and short syllables. When it comes to adjusting the poetic meter to the musical tala, considerable variety of interpretation can theoretically result, as singers allocate different musical lengths to long syllables at the beginnings of phrases and to short syllables at the ends of phrases. In practice, however, performers favor certain adjustments of poetic meters, and usually perform ghazals in simpler talas such as *kaharvā* or *dhumālī* of

FIGURE 12 First couplet of the ghazal "Ye na thī hamārī qismat" as sung by Begum Akhtar. Transcription by Rajna Klaser, from Akhtar and Rafi 1968.

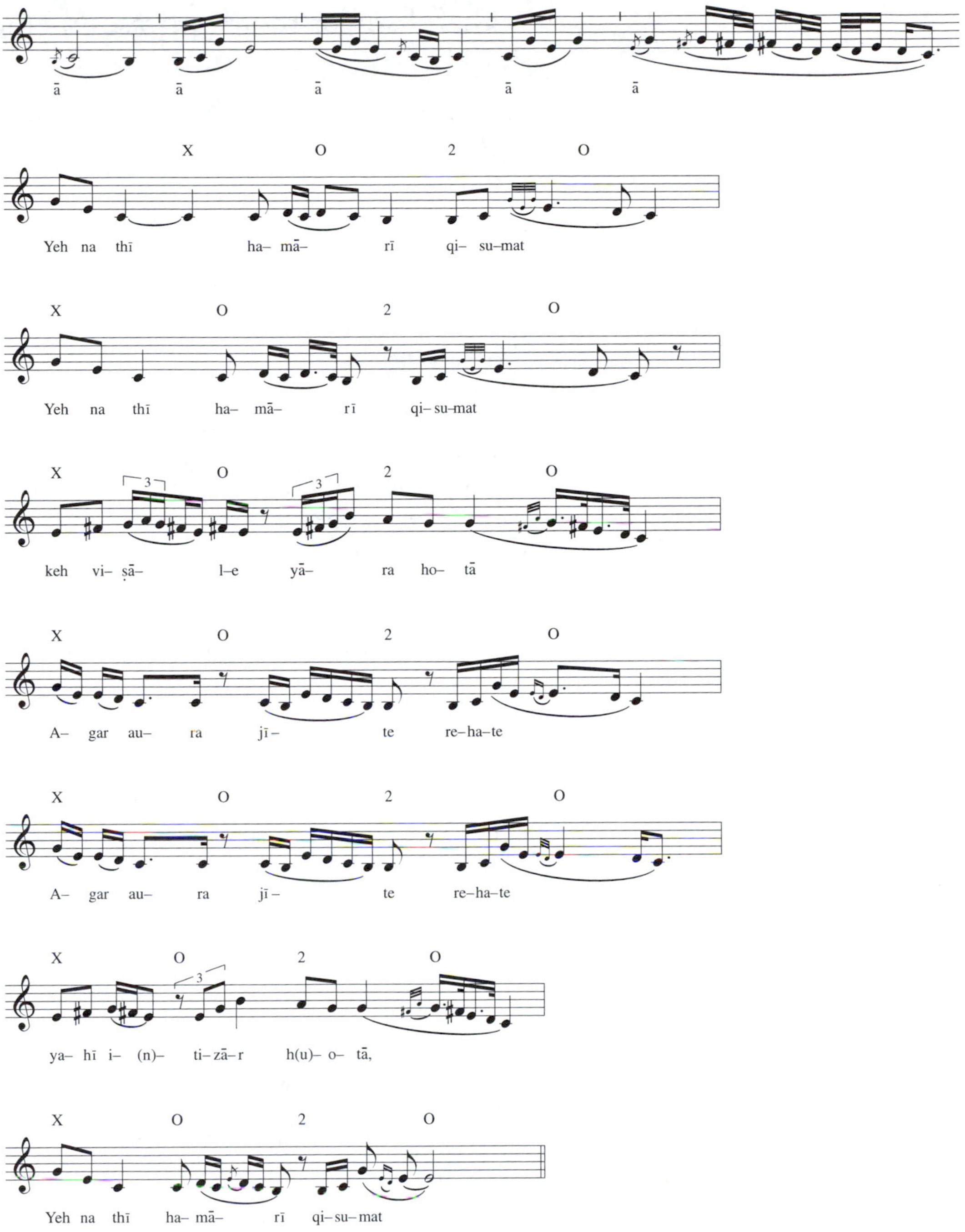

eight counts (see figure 12) and *dādrā* of six counts; less often used are *rūpak tāl* of seven counts and *jhaptāl* of ten counts.

Musical setting

Melodically, the setting of the poem is straightforward. Both lines of the initial couplet are set to a *sthāī*-register line of melody. Contrast is then achieved by melodic setting in the higher *aṅtarā* range. To set off all the nonrhyming lines from the rhyming lines, the first line of each successive couplet is typically sung to an *aṅtarā*-range melody, then the second, rhyming line returns to the *sthāī* range.

A ghazal singer molds phrases melodically and rhythmically and even draws on facial miming and gestures to enhance the expression and to engage the audience in a dialogue.

Ghazal in performance

Performers sing the text of ghazals at a pace slower than that of speech, and they take care to maintain the integrity of the poem, whose mood the music activates. Though improvising less than in *ṭhumrī,* for example, a singer molds phrases melodically and rhythmically and even draws on facial miming and gestures to enhance the expression and to engage the audience in a dialogue. Since the poem often addresses or refers to a beloved other, and since the singer, as in *ṭhumrī,* is traditionally female in front of a male audience, the listener becomes the character of the beloved in the poem, addressed by the singer in an almost intimate manner.

The ensemble that performs ghazals consists of a tabla and either a *sāraṅgī* and a harmonium or (sometimes) two harmoniums. As in *ṭhumrī,* the tabla has the opportunity to play brief solos in *laggī* sections. In the performance of "Yeh na thī hamārī qismat" (first couplet notated in figure 12), a *laggī* section follows each successive couplet.

In several musical ways, the pop and film-music versions of ghazals differ from the light classical genre and impart an entirely different effect. What remains is the fundamental basis of all ghazals: the poetic meter and the Urdu language. Distributed with raging success to a predominantly Hindu mass audience, ghazals show that music can overcome the central cleavage of Indian society, that between Hindu and Muslim cultures.

REFERENCES

Akhtar, Begum, and Mohammed Rafi. 1968. *Ghalib—Portrait of a Genius: A Ghalib Centenary Presentation.* Gramophone Company of India EMI ECSD 2404. LP disk, reissued as compact disc.

Amonkar, Kishori. 1967. *Kishori Amonkar.* Gramophone Company of India ECLP 2326. LP disk.

Dagar Brothers. 1988. *Dagar Brothers: Raga Miyan ki Todi.* Jecklin Disco JD628-2. Compact disc.

Khan, Abdul Wahid. 1976. *Great Master, Great Music: Ustad Abdul Wahid Khan.* Gramophone Company of India ECLP 2541. LP disk.

Manuel, Peter. 1986. "The Evolution of Modern Thumri." *Ethnomusicology* 30(3):470–490.

———. 1988–1989. "A Historical Survey of the Urdu Gazal-Song in India." *Asian Music* 20(1):93–113.

———. 1989. *Ṭhumrī in Historical and Stylistic Perspectives.* Delhi: Motilal Banarsidass.

Meer, Wim Van Der. 1980. *Hindustani Music in the Twentieth Century.* New Delhi: Allied Publishers.

Patwardhan, Vinayakrao. 1976. *In Memoriam: Pt.*[Pandit] *Vinayakrao Patwardhan.* Gramophone Company of India ECLP 2766. LP disk.

Powers, Harold. 1979. "Classical Music, Cultural Roots, and Colonial Rule: An Indic Musicologist Looks at the Muslim World." *Asian Music* 12(1):5–39.

———. 1980. "India, Subcontinent of." In *The New Grove Dictionary of Music and Musicians,* ed. Stanley Sadie. London: Macmillan.

Prajnanananda, Swami. 1981. *A Historical Study of Indian Music.* Delhi: Munshiram Manoharlal.

Qureshi, Regula. 1990. "Musical Gesture and Extra-Musical Meaning: Words and Music in the Urdu Ghazal." *Journal of the American Musicological Society* 43(3):457–497.

Rowell, Lewis. 1992. *Music and Musical Thought*

in Early India. Chicago: University of Chicago Press.

Srivastava, Indurama. 1980 [1977]. *Dhrupada: A Study of Its Origin, Historical Development, Structure and Present State*. Delhi: Motilal Banarsidass.

Wade, Bonnie C. 1973. "Chīz in Khyāl: The Traditional Composition in the Improvised Performance." *Ethnomusicology* 17(3):443–459.

———. 1984. *Khyal: Creativity within North India's Classical Music Tradition*. Cambridge: Cambridge University Press.

———. 1987 [1979]. *Music in India: The Classical Traditions*. New Delhi: Manohar Publications.

Widdess, Richard. 1981. "Aspects of Form in North Indian *Ālāp* and *Dhrupad*." In *Music and Tradition: Essays on Asian and Other Musics Presented to Lawrence Picken*, ed. D. R. Widdess and R. F. Wolpert, 143–181. Cambridge: Cambridge University Press.

Hindustani Instrumental Music

Stephen Slawek

***Gat* Forms and Styles**
Improvisation
Performance Contexts and Program Design
Performers

Instrumental music within the North Indian classical tradition ranges from the manipulation of improvisational models to the repetition of relatively unchanging compositions. In contrast to the South Indian tradition, it is possible to think of classical instrumental music in the North as a somewhat autonomous repertoire independent of the vocal tradition. Why this is so can only be speculated on, for the historical record relating to North Indian instrumental traditions is far from complete. In the North Indian situation, however, sitar music may sound autonomous in comparison with Hindustani vocal music, but in reality practically all the elements of sitar performance practice have vocal sources or counterparts.

Particular Hindustani classical instruments can be linked with particular musical styles through genres, idioms, and musical functions. The repertoires of wind instruments such as the *bāṅsurī* 'bamboo flute' and the *śahnāī* 'double-reed instrument' share stylistic features that differ in some ways from those of repertoires of stringed instruments such as the sitar or sarod. Instruments such as the *bīn* 'fretted stick zither' whose development was associated with the Mughal courts and, in particular, the *dhrupad* vocal genre, for example, are confined to a musical idiom directly related to *dhrupad*. More obvious are the different musical functions of instruments, which affect the characteristic playing styles: the *tānpūrā* serves specifically as a drone instrument; the tabla usually serves as percussive accompaniment; and the harmonium is used almost exclusively to provide accompaniment for vocal music. Genre, idiom, and musical function thus play a prominent role in North Indian instrumental music styles.

The predominant instrumental style of the twentieth century is that associated with the sitar and sarod, the two most popular Hindustani musical instruments. Of the two the sitar is older, dating back at least to the mid-eighteenth century, and appears to have been the instrument for which the core repertoire of classical compositions was created. The sarod, a modified version of the Afghani *rabāb* 'short-necked lute', did not appear until the mid-1800s. Its repertoire drew heavily on existing repertoires of the sitar and of the earlier Indian *rabāb*. Compositions for these instruments were called *gat*, and musicians commonly speak of the *gat* style (*gat śailī*) when addressing sitar and sarod music. Another common term for this musical style is *tantrakārī aṅg*; *tantra* refers to a stringed instrument, thus *tantrakārī* means "of the string players," and *aṅg* in this context means "style."

The tremendous importance of *gat* in Hindustani instrumental performance renders it a logical starting point for the discussion of composition and improvisation in North Indian instrumental music. The common English definition of *gat* is "composition"; however, there is a qualitative difference between the Western notion of a composition and the Indian concept of *gat*. The Hindi term *gat* derives from the Sanskrit word *gatī*, which refers to a way of moving, and as described below, a particular rhythmic flow is often an important factor in determining the character of a *gat*. An abstract but potentially useful way of thinking about *gat* is as a syntactic equivalent of the raga concept. Just as a raga can be understood as a set of melodic rules and possibilities that a musician can realize in countless ways, so can a *gat* be viewed as a means of moving musically through time in accordance with certain rules a performer can interpret in a variety of ways. Thus *gat* expresses a musical process as much as if not more than a product. In Western art music the terms *genre* and *piece* provide a comparable distinction; genre—for example, the sonata—is the more abstract category indicating a structure, and piece represents a fixed composition in that genre. The concept of *gat* exists clearly at the level of genre, for there are several different categories of *gat*, but not so clearly at the level of piece. It is true that certain *gat* have fixed content, like Western compositions, but there are equally as many—if not more—that constantly undergo change and variation in performance.

GAT FORMS AND STYLES

Current stylistic schools (*gharānā*) of instrumental music draw heavily on sitar and sarod music of the eighteenth and nineteenth centuries in their compositions and improvisations. But the instrumental tradition has not been immune to change, and a comparison of early twentieth century recorded examples and performances in the 1990s shows that tempo ranges have increased, more emphasis is placed on virtuosic scalar improvisations, and technical variety and difficulty have increased.

Instrumental *gat* forms in current practice include most *gat* forms that evolved during the eighteenth and nineteenth centuries, twentieth-century modifications of these, and recent innovations. Indian musicians prize rare and ancient musical materials, and those who perform pre-twentieth-century *gat* forms—thus holding them in their possession—accrue considerable prestige. In talking about their music, musicians may consequently exaggerate the age of their repertoires. The few surviving historical sources on eighteenth- and nineteenth-century Indian instrumental music mention at least two *gat* forms, the *firozkhānī gat* and the *amīrkhānī gat*, which have by now disappeared or been combined with other *gat* forms, or may still exist in the repertoires of only a small number of living musicians. *Firozkhānī gat* presumably represents a tradition extending back to Firoz Khan of Delhi, the son of Khusrau Khan, who reportedly brought the sitar's forerunner, the Persian three-stringed *setār*, from Kashmir in the early eighteenth century (Miner 1993). *Amīrkhānī gat* takes its name from Amir Khan, nephew and disciple of Amrit Sen, a famous sitarist who moved from Delhi to Jaipur in the mid-eighteenth century. Amir Khan eventually settled in Gwalior, where the *amīrkhānī gat* gained prominence.

Masītkhānī gat

The oldest *gat* form in the current repertoire that maintains some degree of continuity with its historical form is the *masītkhānī gat*. Traditional musicians attribute this form to Masit Khan, believed to have been both a contemporary of Niyamat Khan (also known as Sadarang), the most famous musician at the Delhi court of Muhammad Shah (1719–1748) and a direct descendant of Tansen, the legendary

FIGURE 1 Comparison of an early-twentieth-century *masītkhānī gat* with a late-twentieth-century slow *gat,* both in *tīntāl*: *a,* segment of a *masītkhānī gat* performance in *rāg bhūp kalyāṇ* by the sitarist Barkat Ullah Khan, 1904–1905 (78-rpm recording, Gramophone Company of India 17373; rereleased Pathé 62); *b,* segment of a slow *gat* performance in *rāg chārūkauns* by Pandit Ravi Shankar, c. 1990, based on the older style (live performance at the University of Texas at Austin). Notated by Stephen Slawek.

master musician of the court of Akbar (1562–1607). Traditional musicians place Masit Khan either in the lineage of *rabāb* players extending back to Tansen's son Bilas Khan, or in the *bīn* 'stick zither' players' lineage of Tansen's daughter Sarasvati Devi. Hindustani instrumentalists usually credit Masit Khan with substantial contributions to the sitar repertoire, claiming that he drew on both the earlier vocal genre *dhrupad* and the newly created vocal genre *baṛā khyāl* (fashioned by Niyamat Khan) in creating this new style of sitar music [see HINDUSTANI VOCAL MUSIC].

The *masītkhānī gat* became a widely practiced form of raga elaboration among Delhi sitarists in the second half of the eighteenth century; in the nineteenth century it became known as *pacchvā bāj* 'Western playing style', Delhi *bāj,* or *masītkhānī bāj.* A group of instrumentalists belonging to the Seniyā lineage of Tansen settled in Jaipur (about one hundred miles southwest of Delhi) in the late eighteenth century, and contributed to the proliferation of this playing style. The earliest extant recorded example of a *masītkhānī gat* is a 78-rpm sitar recording, made by William Sinkler Darby on his 1904–1905 recording tour, of Barkat Ullah Khan playing *rāg bhūp kalyāṇ* (Kinnear 1994:21, 142). Barkat Ullah Khan belonged to the branch of the Seniyā lineage that had moved to Jaipur. Scholars generally regard this rendition of the *masītkhānī gat* as representative of the old "Western playing style." Figure 1*a* contains notation of a brief segment from this recorded example; figure 1*b* comprises a short segment from a recent sitar performance by Pandit Ravi Shankar of a modern *vilambit* 'slow' *gat* based on this style. A comparison of the two examples reveals some of the many changes undergone by the *masītkhānī gat* in this century.

Several aspects of musical construction and general style stand out in these examples. A continuity is apparent in the general approach to phrasing, for both performers structure the melody in similar ways within the sixteen-beat rhythmic cycle of *tīntāl.* Both *gat* begin on the twelfth beat of the cycle, and both incorporate a rhythmic pattern of right-hand strokes that begins on the twelfth beat of the cycle (believed to have been created by Masit Khan):

s-s-1-s-s-1-1-(1)-1-1-s-s-1-s-s-1-1-1-1-1
(l = one beat, s = half beat, (1) = the first beat of the cycle)

The older example, however, contains fewer and less extensive melismas than the recent example: the incorporation of complex, technically challenging melismas (*mīṇḍ*) into *masītkhānī gat* is a twentieth-century development that instrumentalists have carried to extraordinary dimensions. The execution of *mīṇḍ* on the sitar requires pinpoint accuracy in producing pitch changes by pulling the playing wire across the fret, effectively increasing or decreasing the wire tension and creating a continuous rise or fall in pitch. The technique is similar to pitch bending in Western pop guitar styles, but the possible range and the degree of ornamentation is much greater. Some sitarists manage to alter the pitch by as much as a minor sixth. Lastly, figure 1*a* contains the first few improvisations of the performance played by Barkat Ullah Khan, then called *toḍā* (today referred to as *tān*). In a late-twentieth-century performance such fast improvisations at the beginning of a slow *gat* would be unusual, as current practice favors gradual development (*vistār*) of the *gat* with a variety of improvisatory strategies employed, usually starting with very slow pacing and working toward dense, rapidly flowing bravura passages.

Both North and South Indian classical musicians employ contrast of tessitura to distinguish discrete musical phrases of a composition. The North Indian instrumental *masītkhānī gat,* which usually comprises three relatively independent musical phrases—*sthāī, manjhā,* and *aṅtarā*—is no exception. A performer first introduces the *sthāī* phrase, which in sixteen-beat *tīntāl* typically begins on the twelfth beat (as in figure 1*a–b*). Performers use the section from beat twelve to the first beat of the tala cycle (*mukhṛā*)—independently of the *sthāī* phrase—as a point of departure for or to return from improvisation. The *manjhā* has the same rhythmic phrasing as the *sthāī,* but usually descends to the register below the tonic. Its *mukhṛā* section usually varies slightly from that of the *sthāī* and can similarly serve to lead into improvisation. The *aṅtarā* phrase commonly comprises two linked subphrases, the first ascending to a cadence on the upper tonic and the second descending either to the tonic pitch or to a pitch that leads logically to the beginning of the *sthāī.* Some *aṅtarā* phrases are one tala cycle in length, like the *sthāī* and *manjhā,* but many take two cycles. Usually only the first subphrase has an effective *mukhṛā.* Performers often use it as a point of departure and return for melodic improvisation in the higher tonal regions.

Razākhānī gat

The *razākhānī gat* developed during the nineteenth century apparently around pre-

Instrumentalists of the twentieth century recognize the historical importance of "Western" and "Eastern" styles (of Delhi and of towns farther east, respectively), but commonly specialize in neither one, preferring to gain competency in many different genres and playing styles.

sent-day Lucknow, southeast of Delhi. Like the *masītkhānī gat,* the *razākhānī gat* takes its name from its creator, Ghulam Raza Khan, a sitarist popular within the aristocratic culture of Lucknow and a favorite musician at the court of Nawab Wajid Ali Shah, ruler of the princely state of Oudh from 1847 to 1856. The new *gat* style contrasted with the earlier *masītkhānī gat* in its faster performance tempo; musicians also regarded it as less serious, since it drew upon vocal genres such as *ṭhumrī* and ghazal, which were part of the repertoire of courtesans and dancers at the royal court. These genres were characterized by a liberal treatment of raga, often incorporating pitches and melodic movements untypical of the raga being performed, and by romantic sentiments embedded in the texts and symbolically realized in elaborately embellished melodies. The Indian system of musical aesthetics also affected the new *gat*'s reputation—for faster speed or pacing is generally associated with levity and a frivolous attitude.

Recent research by the sitarist and scholar Allyn Miner has shown that Ghulam Raza Khan was not the only nineteenth-century musician responsible for the creation of a new *gat* style for the sitar that contrasted with the "Western style" (Miner 1993:120–121). Many musicians in Tansen's lineage, including Basat Khan and Pyar Khan, played a fast *gat* style that together with *razākhānī* style became known as the *purab bāj,* or Eastern playing style, named after the towns and villages to the east of Delhi where these musicians lived. Instrumentalists of the twentieth century recognize the historical importance of "Western" and "Eastern" styles, but commonly specialize in neither one, preferring to gain competency in many different genres and playing styles. It is possibly this situation that led musicians to the present simpler method of categorizing and naming the various types of *gat*. Twentieth-century *razākhānī* style appears to have subsumed the *gat* types of the nineteenth-century Eastern style; its present diversity of characteristics has led many musicians today to speak of these *gat* simply as *madhya* 'medium', *madhya-drut* 'medium-fast', or *drut* 'fast', avoiding any implied attribution to a nineteenth-century musician. As noted above, musicians today also appear to be shying away from using *masītkhānī gat* as a classificatory term, preferring to replace it with *vilambit* 'slow' *gat.* It is doubtful that any *gat* performed in the 1990s are actually compositions by either Masit Khan or Ghulam Raza Khan. Hence, with consideration given to historical accuracy, the increasingly common practice of naming a *gat* according to its performance tempo or the tala in which it is set is preferable to ascribing its authorship to obscure musicians whose precise musical creations are probably irretrievably lost.

Although *razākhānī gat* lacked the kind of standardization of structure found in the *masītkhānī gat,* the most common *razākhānī gat* started on the seventh beat of the sixteen-beat *tīntāl.* As performed today, these *gat* may also contain a *manjhā* phrase and usually have an *aṅtarā* in two sections, like the *masītkhānī gat*. The modern *drut* 'fast' *gat* composition may start on any beat of the tala, and fast *gat* in talas other than the common *tīntāl* have become popular. The challenge for the composer (who is

FIGURE 2 Rhythmic cadences (*mukhṛā*) of five fast *gat,* leading to the first beat of the *tīntāl* rhythmic cycle. Taught to Stephen Slawek by Pandit Ravi Shankar; notated by Stephen Slawek.

usually the performer or the student of a performer) is to shape the melody in such a way as to highlight key raga phrases, while its rhythmic setting accentuates the rhythmic motion of the tala—the basic "groove"set up by tala subdivisions and by stress and accent. Generally, composers construct the rhythmic setting by linking together small units of conventional stroking patterns to match the length of the tala cycle. Given the lack of standardization and the expanded scope for rhythmic diversity in *drut gat,* the composition's musical charm could be said to derive largely from rhythmic tensions within the composition and from the way these resolve on the first beat of the tala. Figure 2 contains selected *mukhṛā* of several *drut gat*, illustrating a variety of rhythmic patterns leading to the first beat of the tala.

Miscellaneous *gat* types

In addition to the slow and fast *gat* types most commonly encountered in current practice (based on the *masītkhānī* and *razākhānī* styles), several other *gat* forms exist that resist categorization. Some emphasize a particular musical element such as a type of ornament (*zamzamā gat*, a type of composition incorporating profuse trills, is such a form), a kind of melodic phrasing associated with a certain improvisational technique (*tān kī gat,* for example, which includes rapid scalar passages), or a particular kind of structure (*do muhī gat* spans at least two tala cycles and includes two ways of approaching the first beat of the tala). Other *gat* forms are linked to various traditions of the eighteenth or nineteenth centuries.

One *gat* type with a credible connection to the eighteenth century that is now performed by a limited group of musicians is the *firozkhānī gat*. Some musicians believe that Firoz Khan—possibly Masit Khan's father—produced compositions for the sitar that gained some popularity in the eighteenth century. He eventually left Delhi and settled in Rohilkhand, a small kingdom of Pathans (from Afghanistan) northeast of Delhi, where he reportedly influenced musicians who played the Afghani *rabāb* (Miner 1993:205–208). This tradition evolved into a major sarod tradition of the nineteenth and twentieth centuries, the *gharānā* 'stylistic school' of

Ustad Ghulam Ali Khan. Some musicians in this lineage continue to play *gat* they call *firozkhānī gat.* As they generally perform these *gat* in a medium to medium-fast tempo, the compositions can easily be mistaken for typical *razākhānī gat,* but it is an interesting possibility that they embody a form that originated with the sitar and survives only among a few sarod players.

Another class of *gat* that has carried the plucked string-instrument playing style (*tantrakārī aṅg*) of the eighteenth and nineteenth centuries into the twentieth century includes compositions set to difficult or unusual talas. During the last sixty years, Ustad Ali Akbar Khan and Pandit Ravi Shankar especially have popularized *gat* set to tala containing odd numbers of beats such as *cārtāl kī savārī* (eleven beats divided four - four - three), or even fractional beats, such as *upa tāl jhampak* (eight and a half beats divided 2 - 3 - 2 - 1 1/2). Along with other musicians, they have also popularized *gat* in more common talas such as seven-beat *rūpak,* ten-beat *jhaptāl,* twelve-beat *ektāl,* and fourteen-beat *āṛācautāl. Gat* performance in *rūpak* or *jhaptāl* is usually at slow to medium tempos, and in *ektāl* or *āṛā cautāl* is generally medium-fast or fast. These *gat* are still less common than *tīntāl gat,* however, and are more difficult to perform for most players.

One further kind of *gat* serves to bridge the tempo gap in instrumental performance from fast to very fast. Musicians sometimes call these compositions *atī* 'very' *drut gat.* They are distinct in usually having only one note per stroke per beat, compared with the common two-stroke beat division of slow and fast *gat.* Typically, these short *gat* lead directly to an improvisatory section known as a *jhālā* (see below).

Light classical instrumental compositions

Hindustani instrumental concerts commonly conclude with a less serious light classical piece. The *gat* compositions that constitute the themes of these lighter concert items often differ from the idiomatic *gat* styles of the sitar and sarod. Three factors in particular distinguish these *gat* as a separate genre. First is the sources of melodic materials, which range from a special class of raga (*ṭhumrī aṅg* raga) to melodies supposedly rooted in regional folk tunes (*dhun*). The *ṭhumrī aṅg* ragas include *bhairavī, bihārī, deś, gārā, khamāj, māñjh khamāj, pahārī, pīlū,* and others. Musicians refer to some of these (especially *bihārī, gārā,* and *pahārī*) as *dhunī* ragas, indicating their probable origin in regional melodies. The second factor distinguishing these light-classical *gat* is the kinds of tala to which they are generally set. Some talas such as *kaharvā* (eight beats) and *dādrā* (six beats) are common in folk traditions; others, including *dīpcandī* (fourteen beats in slow or medium speed) and *addhā* (a syncopated sixteen-beat tala), are associated with the vocal *ṭhumrī* tradition. The third distinguishing factor is the stroke patterns instrumentalists use in performing these *gat.* They generally originate in the rhythmic patterns of a common folk tune, a particular tala, or a vocal text, such as that of a *ṭhumrī.*

Compositions in imitation of vocal styles

Several developments in the modern instrumental styles of North India have served to reinforce the intimate link between vocal and instrumental music. These include the move to soloist status by some *sāraṅgī* 'unfretted bowed fiddle' players and the emergence of the bamboo flute and violin as solo instruments. The *sāraṅgī* and violin are capable of closely imitating vocal melody; Indians regard the bamboo flute as an instrument particularly close to the human voice, since both produce sound with an unrestricted stream of air, that is, with human breath. There has also been a conscious effort by sarodists, sitarists, and other players of plucked instruments to incorporate the musical materials of North Indian vocal music more directly into their stock of musical resources. Along with this trend of strengthening the resemblance of instrumental performance practice to vocal performance, new approaches to the composition and improvisational elaboration of instrumental *gat* have emerged.

The term *gāyakī aṅg* (literally 'singing style') generally refers to the elements of vocal music incorporated in instrumental practice, but can mean different things to different musicians. It serves the useful purpose of distinguishing twentieth-century innovations in North Indian instrumental music from the more idiomatic plucked-string playing style (*tantrakārī aṅg*), as discussed above. A more specific connotation of the term occurs among Imdad Khan *gharānā* musicians, who since the 1950s have developed a new approach to the sitar repertoire that emphasizes imitation of *khyāl* vocal music [see HINDUSTANI VOCAL MUSIC]. These musicians call their style the *gāyakī aṅg*; this narrower use of the term has also gained some currency in common discourse about music.

Khyāl ***style***

A number of different manifestations of *gāyakī aṅg* appear on North Indian concert stages. The current musical repertoires of the *sāraṅgī*, violin, bamboo flute, and *śahnāī* are unrelated to the core repertoire of stringed instruments (*tantrakārī aṅg*). Musicians specializing in these wind instruments or violin generally model their performances on *khyāl* structure and speak of playing in the *khyāl aṅg*. The exposition of a raga in this manner of performance commences with a few minutes of unaccompanied *ālāp*—a slow-paced, unmetered, and nonpulsed style of improvisation—which then overlaps with the beginning of the composition, when the tabla joins in to maintain the tala cycle. Musicians playing in this style favor the slow twelve-beat *ektāl*, but sometimes employ other talas associated with *baṛā khyāl* (slow or medium-tempo songs). The composition is often an instrumental rendition of a *baṛā khyāl*, and thus a more accurate term than *gat*—which refers to textless instrumental compositions—would be *bandiś* 'the artful combination of text, melody, and tala'. However some musicians prefer to call it *gat* because the *bandiś* is receiving an instrumental rendition.

The composition differs in several ways from a slow *gat*. Typical *masītkhānī* phrasing is absent, and plectrum strokes occur in place of the *bandiś* text syllables, creating a more lyrical flow in the melodic phrasing. Also, as with *baṛā khyāl*, articulations tend to occur off the beat, for the *khyāl* aesthetic strives to create a sense of liberation from the tala while maintaining its integrity. Finally, the bipartite *sthāī–aṅtarā* form of the *baṛā khyāl* replaces the tripartite *sthāī–manjhā–aṅtarā* structure of the slow *gat*.

As in vocal *khyāl* performance, where a fast-tempo composition (*choṭā khyāl*) commonly follows the slow-tempo *baṛā khyāl*, in instrumental performances modeled on *khyāl* a fast *bandiś* usually follows a slow one. The fast composition is a relatively faithful instrumental rendition of a particular *choṭā khyāl*. In comparison with a fast sarod or sitar *gat*, the instrumental rendition of a *choṭā khyāl* incorporates fewer articulations and more melisma. As in the slow *bandiś*, musicians articulate the places where text syllables occurred in the original composition.

A mid-twentieth-century development in the plucked stringed instrument repertoire is the *khyāl aṅg gat*. These *gat* differ from the instrumental *khyāl aṅg* of the bowed and wind instruments, however, which Indian musicians consider closer to the voice. Plucked-string players generally model a slow *gat* in *khyāl* style on the basic structure of a *masītkhānī gat*, only preceded by a truncated *khyāl ālāp* introduction in especially slow tempo. The *gat* composition itself incorporates profuse melismas but in other respects conforms to the general style of the modern slow *gat* as elaborated above. In practice, the modern slow *gat* style owes much to the influence of vocal *khyāl*; the distinguishing features of *khyāl aṅg gat* remain the improvisational elabora-

The musicians of the Imdad Khan *gharānā* have excelled at transferring vocal repertoire to their sitar repertoire, and will often sing a vocal composition at some point in their instrumental performance.

FIGURE 3 Singing style (*gāyakī aṅg*) in a fast instrumental *gat* in *rāg khamāj*, *tīntāl* rhythmic cycle. Live performance on sitar by Shujaat Khan; notated by Stephen Slawek.

tion and the concentrated effort of plucked-string players to incorporate key aspects of the *baṛā khyāl* style into the elaboration of a raga without losing the central features of the autonomous *gat*.

TRACK 3

Plucked-string players generally use a vocal composition (*bandiś*) as the basis of a *khyāl aṅg* fast *gat*. Depending on how faithfully the instrumentalist reproduces the original *choṭā khyāl*, the resulting *gat* either matches closely a bowed instrument's rendition, as described above, or includes some stroking patterns more idiomatic of plucked instruments. Additional articulations are sometimes necessary in the attempt to transfer the vocal composition into a plucked-string idiom because of the limited sustaining capability of the sitar and sarod. The musicians of the Imdad Khan *gharānā* have excelled at making such transfers from the vocal repertoire to their sitar repertoire, and will often sing the vocal composition that forms the basis of their fast *gat* at some point in their performance. The *gāyakī aṅg* fast *gat* in *rāg khamāj* presented in figure 3 clearly displays a more lyrical character than the stroke-oriented plucked-string-instrument style of fast *gat*.

Dhrupad *style*

The repertoire of the *rudra vīṇā* 'stick zither' and *surbahār* 'large sitar-like plucked lute' provides another manifestation of *gāyakī aṅg* in Hindustani instrumental music. These instruments, along with the *rabāb* and *sursiṅgār*—which are no longer played as classical instruments—were associated with the *dhrupad* genre of vocal music. *Dhrupad* predates *khyāl*; its heyday was the sixteenth through the eighteenth centuries, and it fell out of favor as *khyāl*'s popularity increased in the nineteenth and twentieth centuries. *Dhrupad* has nevertheless maintained its high status within Hindustani musical culture and is generally considered the repository of the most authentic raga forms. It has enjoyed a degree of resurgent interest since the 1970s, but this renewed interest unfortunately arose too late to ensure the continued viability of the *rabāb* and *sursiṅgār* for instrumental performance. Even the *rudra vīṇā*, once considered the king of all stringed instruments, is dangerously close to extinction.

In *dhrupad*-based instrumental performances, musicians may refer to the *dhrupad* composition as *gat*, although they would probably be aware of the anachronism since the instrumental *gat* tradition arose well over a century after the establishment of *dhrupad* style. In contemporary practice, a full-fledged *ālāp* precedes the composition, which occupies a relatively short performance time compared with the *ālāp*.

Distinguishing features of *dhrupad*-based *gat* include characteristic talas to which compositions are set, restricted ornamentation, a strong link between articulation and the pulsation of tala beats, medium-slow tempo, and improvisations stressing rhythmic manipulations such as syncopations, cross-rhythms, and counter-rhythms. The talas associated with *dhrupad* include (among others) *tīvrā, śūltāl, cautāl*, and *dhamār* (seven, ten, twelve, and fourteen beats, respectively). In *dhrupad* performance, the *pakhāvaj* 'barrel drum' is the drum of choice, although some musicians in the twentieth century have used a tabla tuned an octave lower than normal in imitation of the *pakhāvaj*. The *dhrupad* style is well known for its avoidance of sprightly ornaments such as trills and fast mordents and its emphasis on slow glissandi (*mīṇḍ*) and heavy shakes (*gamak*). Melodic progression in inexorable lockstep with the articulation of the tala beats further reinforces *dhrupad*'s austere, bold effect. On plucked-string instruments, musicians play strokes that generally coincide with the drummer's articulation of the rhythmic cycle.

Ṭhumrī *style*

One other important vocal style that instrumentalists have adapted in recent years is the *ṭhumrī* (see Manuel 1989:160–191). Ghulam Raza Khan (after whom *Razā<u>kh</u>ānī gat* is named) drew inspiration from the *ṭhumrī* he heard at the court of Wajid Ali Shah in the mid-1800s. This might suggest that its use in instrumental music is an old practice, but the *ṭhumrī* of the nineteenth century differs from that of the late twentieth century, and consequently a modern *ṭhumrī aṅg gat* will differ from Ghulam Raza Khan's innovations. In current practice, all Hindustani instruments play in *ṭhumrī* style, except those specifically associated with *dhrupad* (*rudra vīṇā* and *surbahār*).

The term *ṭhumrī aṅg*, like *khyāl aṅg*, may refer to a particular approach to *gat* elaboration or to direct transferral of an actual *ṭhumrī* composition to instrumental performance. In the former, a musician might choose to develop a slow *gat* in the *ṭhumrī aṅg*, and generally does so when performing slow *gat* in ragas such as *bhairavī, pīlū, gārā, khamāj*, and *kāfī*. Also similar to *khyāl aṅg*, the *ṭhumrī aṅg* slow *gat* may be based on the traditional phrase-structure of the *masīt<u>kh</u>ānī* style; its distinguishing feature as *ṭhumrī aṅg* is its method of elaboration rather than its actual composition.

The typical method of improvising in vocal *ṭhumrī* is *bol banāo*: the vocalist creates short melismatic melodic phrases based on the song text syllables. The concept of *bol banāo* influences the manner in which an instrumentalist improvises on a *ṭhumrī aṅg gat*. Raga elaboration proceeds less according to note-by-note progression, as in *khyāl aṅg*, and more by motivic elaboration. In *ṭhumrī aṅg gat* musicians often incorporate *rāgmālā* 'raga garland', the practice of making abrupt modulations to different ragas. During the course of elaborating melodic motives of the primary raga, the musician begins the *rāgmālā* by playing a key motive of a different raga. The instrumentalist generally introduces scale patterns or important phrases of various ragas, often returning to the composition's *mukhṛā* 'cadential phrase' in the primary raga after each contrasting raga or group of ragas. Another variation process musicians use in *ṭhumrī aṅg gat* improvisation is changing scale types while maintaining the melodic contours of the primary raga's key motives. Musicians indicate their intention to draw upon these improvisational methods by adding the prefix *miśra* to the name of the primary raga (for example, *miśra khamāj, miśra bhairavī, miśra pīlū*).

Following the elaboration of melodic motives, instrumentalists generally launch into the kinds of rapidly moving improvisations (*tān*) more correctly associated with the *khyāl aṅg*. Here, instrumentalists are asserting a kind of musical license, as *tān* are not generally an important part of the vocal *ṭhumrī*, although they are by no means entirely absent from it.

A *ṭhumrī aṅg gat* that attempts direct transferral of a vocal composition to instruments constitutes a different musical piece. Phrasing and articulation originate in a texted vocal composition, as in *dhun* (see above), not in the stroking pattern of the *masītkhānī* or *razākhānī* playing style. In *ṭhumrī aṅg*, an instrumentalist might recreate "true" *bol banāo* based on the text of the original melody. One noteworthy aspect of performance practice in such a *gat* is the potential change of tala toward the end of the performance. The musician selects the primary tala from the group associated with the *ṭhumrī* tradition, but ends by shifting to a fast quadruple meter, possibly sixteen-beat *tīntāl*, while the tabla accompanist plays a syncopated, lilting, fast improvisation called *laggī*—typical of vocal *ṭhumrī*.

IMPROVISATION

Hindustani musicians speak of improvisation as the heart and soul of their music; it is a complex topic covering a wide range of musical phenomena. The *ālāp-joṛ-jhālā* sequence that precedes performance of a *gat* constitutes a form of improvisation that qualifies as a genre in itself. Improvisation exists even within the *gat* composition, as a performer subjects the composition to continuous variation in a process called *gat vistār* 'expansion'. More wide-ranging improvisations such as *tān*, *toḍā*, and *tihāī* occupy the majority of performance time after the beginning of the *gat*.

Ālāp-joṛ-jhālā

Ālāp is one of the oldest surviving performance practices in Indian music. Its current manner of performance is compatible with the description of *ālāp* found in the thirteenth-century treatise *Saṅgītaratnākara* [see THEORETICAL TREATISES]. The modern instrumental *ālāp*—an expansive exploration of possible tonal combinations within a raga—is directly related to the vocal *ālāp* preceding a *dhrupad* composition, known as *rāg-ālāp* or *vistār-ālāp*. The vocal *dhrupad ālāp* consists of two large sections [see HINDUSTANI VOCAL MUSIC]. The first, performed at a slow pace with no continuous or stable rhythmic pulsation, originally had four subsections—*sthāī*, *antarā*, *sañcārī*, and *ābhog*—although current performers usually sing only the first two; each subsection is characterized by a different registral emphasis. The second section, *nom-tom*, increases the general pace of activity while confining the improvised melody to a stable pulsation.

The instrumental *ālāp* follows the vocal model relatively closely, but certain differences provide it with its own idiomatic character. As instrumentalists focus on successively lower pitches of the raga below the middle tonic in the first major section of *ālāp*, the range of their instruments can limit this exploration. For example, the lowest pitch on a sitar strung in the manner devised by Ustad Vilayat Khan is one octave below the middle tonic, but sitarists who follow the stringing and tuning method devised by Pandit Ravi Shankar extend the bass register one further octave lower and thus have the option of including within the *sthāī* section an extensive foray into the bass register. Following this initial descent, the *ālāp* progresses up the instrumental range. Vocalists normally focus their melodic elaboration (*vistār*) on each successive note in the ascent of the raga being performed. After elaborating one or a few notes, the instrumentalist often returns to the middle tonic pitch sounding a conventional, briefly pulsed motif referred to as *sam dikhānā* 'to show the first beat of the tala cycle (*sam*)' or *mohrā*. The *sthāī* section of instrumental *ālāp* thus consists of a series of melodic elaborations, each one terminated with the return to the middle tonic.

The *antarā* begins after elaboration of all scale degrees in the middle octave. A typical *ālāp antarā* begins on either the fourth or fifth scale degree, briefly descends, possibly to the third scale degree, then leaps upward to the upper octave tonic. The instrumentalist gives this pitch quite a deliberate and sustained sound. *Antarā* performance continues with further melodic elaboration of raga pitches in the upper octave range, until a descent to the middle tonic terminates this phase. The *saṅcārī* briefly revisits the key features of the raga in all registers, and the *ābhog* recapitulates the *aṅtarā*, but at a quicker pace, adding forceful leaps and heavy shaking ornaments (*gamak*) before ending with a final motif (*mohrā*) on the tonic pitch.

Indian plucked-string instruments usually include a set of drone strings (*cikārī*) strung alongside the principal melody-playing strings. The number of drone strings varies with the instrument, but most instruments normally include two strings tuned to the tonic and its upper octave. Throughout the nonpulsed *ālāp* section, the performer sounds the drone strings just prior to a stroke on a melody string to help establish the tonic and to maintain correct intonation. In the next, pulsed section
TRACK 2 (*joṛ*), the instrumentalist sounds the drone strings in balanced alternation with strokes on the melody strings. The drone thus becomes important in establishing the stability of pulsation throughout the *joṛ*. Bowed string instruments and wind instruments, in contrast, accomplish the pulsation effect with stress and accent, in a manner similar to vocal *nom-tom* performance.

Musicians consider the *joṛ* of contemporary instrumental music to be part of the *rudra vīṇā*'s legacy. Traditionalists have attempted to transfer the playing techniques and austere restraint of the *dhrupad* aesthetic to their contemporary instrumental *joṛ*. In playing melodic phrases these musicians emphasize a persistent stroking in one direction followed by brief periods of repose that revert back to the melodic string–drone string alternation. The *joṛ* tempo starts slightly faster than the ending pace of the nonpulsed *ālāp* and increases gradually. More dramatic tempo changes separate subsections of the *joṛ*, each of which typically terminates with a final motif (*mohrā*) as in *ālāp*. Instrumentalists maintain the restrained approach to ornamentation characteristic of *dhrupad* throughout the *joṛ* section, although they employ a more varied selection of ornaments, including various cutting (*krintan*) and "hammer on" (*sparś*) techniques similar to left-hand articulations of Western guitarists.

Musicians also believe that the final section, *jhālā*, originated in the music of the *rudra vīṇā*. The drone strings in *jhālā* become more pronounced as the performer strikes them in clusters of strokes. Though tradition does not mandate it, musicians tend to keep a recurrent period of sixteen beats throughout the section. They link various patterns made up of a melody stroke followed by one, two, three, or four drone strokes to make up the sixteen. Alternatively, in what is called *ultā* 'inverted' *jhālā*, the performer sounds the drone strings first and then the melody string once or several times.

In contemporary performance practice, several schools of musical thought have drifted away from the original *dhrupad* aesthetic. These musicians play *ālāp* and *joṛ* with greater abandon and less systematization. Most modern musicians conclude the nonpulsed *ālāp* after the *aṅtarā* section, for the *saṅcārī* and *ābhog* sections have become archaic features, understood by few musicians and seldom included in performances. Virtuosity replaces restraint, especially in the pulsed *joṛ*. Even within the *ālāp*, displays of virtuosity in playing *mīṇḍ* and other extended ornaments reveal a modern aesthetic that has little to do with the austerity of the *dhrupad* tradition. Although the *jhālā* would conclude a traditional *ālāp-joṛ-jhālā* in the *rudra vīṇā* tradition, modern instrumental styles emphasizing virtuosity add a final section of rapidly moving scalar passages (*tān*). The performer uses back-and-forth stroking to sound one note per stroke and intersperses portamento techniques, conceiving and executing technically amazing feats of melodic creativity.

Other types of improvisation

Musicians employ a wide variety of improvisational skills in developing the relatively

Monumental feats of calculated improvisation are more commonly found in Hindustani instrumental music than in the vocal traditions.

short *gat* theme into a large-scale performance form. Until about 1930, the generic name for instrumental improvisations within a *gat* was *toḍā*. Some performers continue to use the term *toḍā* in this sense to refer to any instrumental improvisation within a *gat*. For many others, the term *toḍā* now connotes a more limited corpus of improvisational phenomena, specifically improvisations consisting predominantly of double strokes per note. The term these performers use for more diverse improvisational possibilities is *tān,* because of its connection with the *khyāl* vocal genre, in which intense experimentation in melodic improvisation gave rise to various types of improvisational practices (*tān*). Instrumentalists use a host of other terms to identify such practices, but little standardization exists. Two terms that do enjoy some consistency of meaning among the majority of practitioners are *upaj* and *tihāī. Upaj* refers to improvisational passages in general, and musicians often use it as an umbrella term to provide a taxonomic shelter for improvisations that otherwise would be difficult to classify. *Tihāī* is a specific kind of improvisation that ends a *tān*, a *toḍā*, or an *upaj*. It may also stand alone as a self-contained improvisation. In either case, it contains a motive played three times, usually creating a good deal of rhythmic tension that is resolved in a final articulation. A *tihāī* generally ends immediately before the opening section (*mukhṛā*) of a *gat sthāī* or on the first beat of the tala cycle.

TRACK 3 The word *tān* 'to spread, expand, or develop' like many other Indian musical terms has both a general and a specific meaning. Broadly speaking, *tān* can imply any kind of improvisation within a particular raga, that is, any melodic gesture that extends the organic structure of a raga in performance. More specifically, *tān* denotes rapidly moving bravura passages. In twentieth-century practice, musicians usually link the word to a descriptive modifier such as *chūṭ tān, sapāṭ tān, gamak tān,* and so forth. These designations derive from some persistent feature of the *tān* improvisation such as the inclusion of wide interval leaps (*chūṭ,* from *chūṭnā* 'to be left behind') or a heavy shake (*gamak*). Beyond a few common types—*gamak tān* or *sapāṭ tān* (scalar runs covering a range of an octave or more in straight ascent and descent)—there is little standardization of this terminology, although musicians commonly group improvisations of a particular *tān* type together in performance.

Musicians also commonly label classes of *tān* according to their rhythmic character [see HINDUSTANI TALA]. A *tān* whose density (number of notes per beat) matches that of the tempo (*laya*) of the tala would be *ṭhāh guṇ tān*; one at double the speed of the basic tempo would be *du guṇ*; and so forth up to *nau guṇ* (nine times the basic tempo) and *bārah guṇ* (twelve times the basic tempo), if the original tempo is slow enough to allow them.

All *tān* improvisations that exploit a strict rhythmic relationship with the tala are considered *laykārī* 'rhythmic manipulation'. Instrumentalists commonly use *laykārī* in performance to order their sequence of *tān* improvisations, proceeding from less dense to more dense, faster-moving ones. The general concept of *laykārī* also encompasses the creation of rhythmic patterns (*chand*). Plucked-instrument players learn a

FIGURE 4 *Farmāiśī tihāī* improvisation in *rāg tilak kāmod* and *tīntāl* rhythmic cycle, comprising a *tān* (A) followed by three repetitions of a melodic motive (B) repeated three times, forming the pattern 3[A + 3(3B)]. Taught to Stephen Slawek by Pandit Ravi Shankar; notated by Stephen Slawek.

stock repertoire of plectrum patterns (*bol* or *mizrāb*) for use in *tān* improvisations, and a special class of instrumental *tān* (*bol tān*) incorporates much rhythmic patterning by stress, accent, and duration of plectrum strokes.

The *tihāī,* an improvised motive repeated three times, can be anything from a simple cadential pattern lasting a few beats to a complex, large-scale structure spanning several tala cycles. Simpler *tihāī* are of two types: *damdār* 'with breath', having a rest between repetitions of the phrase, and *bedam* 'without breath', in which rests do not occur. *Cakkardār* 'circuitous, complicated' *tihāī* are larger structures that incorporate *tihāī* within *tihāī.* Thus, each part of the thrice-played phrase is a *tihāī* in itself. An even more rarefied structure exists with the *farmāiśī tihāī.* This type of *tihāī* generally includes a *tān* followed by an internal *tihāī* that together form the basic material to be extended into a "super"-*tihāī.* The musician accomplishes the expansion to a full structure in the following way: (1) presentation, with the end of the first part of the internal *tihāī* falling on the 'first beat of the tala cycle' (*sam*) the (2) repetition, with the end of the second part of the internal *tihāī* falling on *sam*; (3) second repetition, with the end of the third part of the internal *tihāī* falling on *sam*, concluding the entire *farmāiśī.* This structure can be summarized as 3[A + 3(B)], where A represents the *tān* and B the internal *tihāī* motive that is repeated three times. Figure 4 exemplifies a further refinement of the *farmāiśī* concept. This *farmāiśī tihāī* in *rāg tilak kāmod* inflates the internal *tihāī* to yet another level, resulting in a structure that conforms to the expression 3[A + 3(3B)]. In figure 4, brackets surround the first occurrence of the melodic material that constitutes the (3B) segment of this expression. Such syntactical nesting practices tend to produce extreme levels of rhythmic tension during their execution, with a musical catharsis occurring at the end of the structure on the first beat of the tala cycle. Monumental feats of calculated improvisation such as these are more commonly found in Hindustani instrumental music than in the vocal traditions.

A single *toḍā* improvisation exhibits a more diverse set of rhythmic durations than does a single *tān* of most varieties. The distinguishing mark of *toḍā,* for most

FIGURE 5 Some common plectrum-stroke syllables (*bol*) of *toḍā* improvisation.

a. da diri diri diri da diri da ra da ra diri diri da- rda -r da (16 beats)
b. da dir da da- -r da da ra da ra diri dir da- rda -r da (16 beats)
c. da diri da diri da diri da diri da ra diri diri da rda -r da
diri diri da da- -r da da- -r da da — diri da- rda -r da (32 beats)

On sitar:
da = inward stroke
ra = outward stroke
diri = da + ra at double speed
r = a shortened ra

On sarod:
da = downward stroke
ra = upward stroke with the plectrum (*java*) held between the thumb and index finger, similar to the way a guitarist grasps a pick

musicians, is the inclusion of many double-stroke notes. The right-hand stroke pattern *diri* produces this effect, and the stroke patterns for *toḍā* contain many *diri*, along with other patterns such as *dirā-rdā* and *dā-rdā-rdā*. Figure 5 shows a few extended plectrum-stroke patterns that commonly serve as a rhythmic base for *toḍā* improvisations.

Association between improvisation and genre

The kinds of improvisation associated with a Hindustani music genre partially determine its inherent character. For example, virtuosic displays of *sapāṭ tān* are more characteristic of *khyāl* performance than of *dhrupad* or *ṭhumrī*. *Gamak tān*, though allowed within a *khyāl* performance, are more closely linked with *dhrupad* performance, and certainly not expected in *ṭhumrī*. When an instrumentalist performs a raga in a *khyāl aṅg*, *dhrupad aṅg*, or *ṭhumrī aṅg gat*, part of what guides the musician's explorations is a knowledge of the appropriate kinds of improvisation associated with the genre being performed. Also of importance to the musician is the proper use of ornamentation. An instrumentalist wishing to associate *ālāp* performance with a *dhrupad* origin avoids rapid turns and trills more typical of the *khyāl* and *ṭhumrī* styles, and concentrates on *mīṇḍ* 'complex melismas' and moderately paced turns.

The most varied improvisations in instrumental music occur in the slow *gat*. Here a musician may draw on the improvisational techniques of *ālāp* and *joṛ*, on all the varieties of *tān* discussed above, and on all the various types of *tihāī*. *Jhālā* is the only improvisational type that rarely appears in the slow *gat*. In the eighteenth and nineteenth centuries, musicians used *jhālā* to conclude the older slow-paced *masītkhānī gat*; contemporary musicians usually incorporate it in a fast *gat*. Similarly, while *toḍā* may appear in the slow *gat*, current practice favors its inclusion in the fast *gat*, often following the presentation of *tān*. *Tān* improvisation generally requires a lot of left-hand finger work, for the musician plays only one note per right-hand stroke. Since *toḍā* improvisation has two strokes per note, the left hand can move at a relatively slower pace, and musicians can thus play this at faster speeds. As the tempo increases during contemporary instrumental *gat* performances, musicians often resort to *toḍā* once they reach a tempo that prohibits *tān*. In all varieties of *gat*, *tān* improvisations increase in length and *tihāī* become more complex as the performance progresses.

PERFORMANCE CONTEXTS AND PROGRAM DESIGN

Performances of Hindustani instrumental music occur within the same contexts as those of classical vocal genres. These range from small, intimate private recitals (*jalsā* or *mehfil*) to large public events called *saṅgīt sammelan* or *samāroh* 'music conference', rivaling Western rock and jazz festivals in size. Many Indian concert stages now follow the Western proscenium model, especially in large cities such as Bombay, New Delhi, and Calcutta, but also in smaller cities like Jaipur and Banaras. Prior to the twentieth century, musicians typically performed for a patron, invited guests, and other musicians in the patron's music room. Listeners were generally knowledgeable about music and freely offered vocal expressions and gestures of appreciation and encouragement throughout a performance. The more formal separation of performer and audience in the twentieth century has led to a dampening of the traditional performer-audience dynamic.

Concert programs

The concert hall venue has also had an impact on the items musicians choose to include in their performances. Concert programs have become more formalized during the course of the twentieth century. Musicians develop personalized plans of action during a program rather than following a generally accepted order of performance. This personal approach contributes to the artist's identity as an individual within a particular tradition. Instrumentalists, especially those who perform outside South Asia, have experimented with concert-program format more than have vocalists; a possible reason for this may be that instrumentalists are in greater demand on the international circuit, and thus have done more to modify their typical concert programs to suit Western expectations.

Whether it takes place in a concert hall or in a more intimate setting, a Hindustani instrumental performance consists of ragas. The genres in which a musician chooses to elaborate each raga primarily determine the order of events in a program. The performer usually elaborates the first raga with a complete *ālāp-joṛ-jhālā* followed by slow and fast *gat*. Typically, the next raga includes only an abbreviated *ālāp* followed by *gat*, possibly another slow-fast sequence, or just a medium-tempo *gat*. Additional short *ālāp* and one or more *gat* in a particular raga may follow, or the performance may conclude with a *ṭhumrī aṅg* raga or *dhun*. In this kind of concert program, the musician usually gives the greatest amount of time and attention to the first raga and less time to succeeding ragas.

The typical concert program of Pandit Ravi Shankar exemplifies ways in which modern artists have satisfied both traditional expectations of concert content and exigencies of the modern international concert-hall venue with innovative approaches to programming. Shankar, along with Ustad Ali Akbar Khan, can be credited with opening the doors of the international market to other Indian musicians [see MUSIC AND INTERNATIONALIZATION]. He usually begins his programs in Western countries with an *ālāp-joṛ-jhālā* sequence shorter than would be considered the norm in an Indian concert. He follows this with a medium-tempo *gat* in the same raga, often in seven-beat *rūpak* tala. (Performances in India by other instrumentalists more commonly begin with a substantial *ālāp-joṛ-jhālā*, followed by slow and fast *gat*—all in the same raga.) Shankar usually chooses to play as his second item a slow *gat* in sixteen-beat *tīntāl* in a different raga, which he concludes with a fast *gat*, often in twelve-beat *ektāl*, complete with a virtuosic *jhālā*. After an intermission, he might then play a third raga with a more extended *ālāp-joṛ-jhālā* followed by a medium tempo *gat*, or possibly an abbreviated *ālāp* followed by a *gat*. This post-intermission raga is an optional item in Shankar's program plan, which he includes or excludes depending on his and/or the audience's mood.

Shankar normally concludes a performance with a *ṭhumrī aṅg gat*, possibly incorporating a succession of ragas (*rāgmālā*), followed by a fast *gat*. He often asks his

Ravi Shankar and Ali Akbar Khan have not only propagated Indian music far beyond India's borders, but have expanded the horizons of their respective instrumental idioms, sitar and sarod.

tabla accompanist to play a short solo between the two *gat* to increase audience enthusiasm before the virtuosic ending. The conclusion of the fast *gat* often includes a musical duel (*savāl-javāb* 'question-answer') in which the soloist challenges the accompanist to match wits and construct rhythmic responses to his melodic statements. Modern audiences have come to expect this question–answer section within a performance. The *savāl-javāb* style developed and popularized by Ravi Shankar and Ali Akbar Khan often progresses in arithmetically shrinking segments, leading to a spiraling climax of rapid volleys back and forth between the soloist and accompanist.

PERFORMERS

Both Ustad Ali Akbar Khan and Pandit Ravi Shankar belong to the Maihar *gharānā* 'stylistic school', one of the most influential instrumental styles of the twentieth century. The *gharānā* is named after their teacher, the late Ustad Sangitacharya Allauddin Khan of the Maihar court, who was Ali Akbar Khan's father. The Maihar *gharānā* is also known as the Senī Baba Allauddin *gharānā; Senī* indicates the connection to the lineage of Tansen, as Allauddin Khan's principal teacher, Wazir Khan of the Rampur court, was thought by many to be a direct descendant of Tansen. Allauddin Khan, a well-known virtuoso performer on the sarod and violin, played many other instruments as well, and besides receiving recognition as a master musician gained fame as a pedagogue when his two most famous students—his son Ali Akbar and his disciple Ravi Shankar—became internationally acclaimed artists (figure 6). Among Allauddin's other students, his daughter, Annapurna Devi, is a renowned *surbahār* player even though she shuns the public concert stage; Sharan Rani Bakhleval, who studied with both Allauddin Khan and Ali Akbar Khan, is

FIGURE 6 The late Sangitacharya Allauddin Khan (*center*) performing left-handed on the sarod, accompanied on tabla by Shanta Prasad (*far left*), on sarod by his son Ali Akbar (*far right*), and on sitar by Ravi Shankar (*left*), c. 1938. Photo courtesy Pandit Ravi Shankar.

FIGURE 7 Ustad Shujaat Khan, son of Ustad Vilayat Khan of the Imdad Khan *gharānā*, 1995. Musicians of the Imdad Khan *gharānā* often sing the vocal basis of their music in performance, hence the microphone placed at mouth level. Photo by Stephen Slawek.

notable as one of only a few women who specialize in the sarod. The late Pandit Nikhil Banerjee, who was one of India's greatest exponents of the sitar, received his initial training on that instrument from his father, Jitendra Nath Banerjee, before completing his advanced studies with Allauddin Khan, Ali Akbar Khan, and Annapurna Devi.

Pannalal Ghosh, another of Allauddin Khan's students, introduced the North Indian bamboo flute to the concert stage. Pandit Hari Prasad Chaurasia received much of his later training from Annapurna Devi and became a virtuoso flute player in Ghosh's footsteps. The students of these flute players and other musicians who studied with Allauddin Khan include hundreds of professional and amateur performers who carry on the tradition consolidated by Allauddin Khan. Ravi Shankar and Ali Akbar Khan have not only propagated Indian music far beyond India's borders, but have expanded the horizons of their respective instrumental idioms, sitar and sarod. They have combined these instruments in concert performance, popularizing the instrumental duet form (*jugalbandī*). They have also combined them with non-Indian instruments, creating concertos for sitar and Western orchestra, experimental ensemble music using Western instruments from popular and jazz idioms, and experimental pieces drawing upon other Asian traditions (Slawek 1991:173).

Another extremely influential twentieth-century lineage of musicians is the Imdad Khan *gharānā*. Imdad Khan was the most famous sitar player at the turn of the century, employed by Sourindro Mohun Tagore, an influential member of the famous Tagore family of Bengal who actively promoted the study and promulgation of classical music during British rule (1857–1947) [see MUSIC AND NATIONALISM]. Ustad Imdad Khan's sons, Ustads Enayat and Wahid Khan, his grandsons Ustads Vilayat and Imrat Khan, and great-grandsons Ustads Shujaat (figure 7), Irshad, Nishat, and Hidayat Khan, are or were all recognized virtuoso exponents of the sitar and/or *surbahār*. Ustads Rais Khan and Shahid Parvez are more distantly related to Imdad Khan but are equally well known as great sitar virtuosos. Arvind Parikh and Budhaditya Mukherjee are two other prominent musicians who belong to this *gharānā* through discipular relationships.

FIGURE 8 Ustad Amjad Ali Khan, doyen of the instrumental Gwalior *gharānā,* with his sarod, 1992. Photo by Stephen Slawek.

The sitar style of the Imdad Khan *gharānā* has attained immense popularity; the school has become famous particularly for its approach to *khyāl aṅg* on the sitar. Musicians of this school generally favor playing medium-fast and fast *gat* based on existing vocal compositions (*choṭā khyāl*), not on plucked-string playing style (*tantrakārī aṅg*). Their performances generally commence with an extensive *ālāp-joṛ-jhālā,* as would most performances on stringed instruments, but they are equally likely to follow the solo *ālāp* section with a *khyāl aṅg* fast *gat* or a slow *masītk͟hānī gat.* They favor playing in sixteen-beat *tīntāl,* and also in other *khyāl aṅg* talas such as seven-beat *rūpak.* Their lyrical approach to the instrument is most apparent in *ṭhumrī aṅg* compositions.

At the end of the twentieth century both the Imdad Khan and the Maihar stylistic schools occupy positions in the Hindustani musical universe equal to or surpassing those of the *masītk͟hānī* and *razāk͟hānī bāj* at the end of the nineteenth century. Less extensive lineages of musicians include the Gwalior *gharānā,* whose foremost exponent is Ustad Amjad Ali Khan, and the surviving extension of the nineteenth-century Jaipur Seniyā sitar *gharānā,* the lineage of the late Ustad Mushtaq Ali Khan. Mushtaq Ali Khan's father studied with Ustad Barkat Ullah Khan, whose rendition of a *masītk͟hānī gat* in *rāg bhūpālī* appears in figure 1. The most prominent disciple of Mushtaq Ali Khan is Professor Devbrata Chaudhuri of Delhi University.

Ustad Amjad Ali Khan (figure 8) is recognized today as a leading figure in Hindustani instrumental music. He has developed innovative approaches to *gat* construction and has contributed toward amalgamating the North and South Indian classical traditions by performing duets with South Indian musicians. He is the son of Ustad Hafiz Ali Khan, who studied with Rampur's famous Wazir Khan at the same time as Allauddin Khan. Since Hafiz Ali Khan was employed in the maharaja of Gwalior's court throughout most of his musical career, musicians in his lineage now refer to their tradition as the Gwalior *gharānā.* However, he was also a direct descendant of Ghulam Ali Khan, considered an important figure in the early history of the sarod. The other senior artist who can claim a legitimate connection to Ghulam Ali

FIGURE 9 Musicians at a party given by India's first president, Rajender Prasad, following the 1952 Music Conference of Bharatiya Kala Kendra, arranged by Ravi Shankar. From bottom left (seated): Nisar Hussain Khan, Ahmad Jan Thirakva, Hafiz Ali Khan, Mushtaq Hussain Khan, Omkarnath Thakur, President Rajender Prasad, Kesar Bai Kerkar, Allauddin Khan, Kanthe Maharaj, Govind Rao Bharanpurkar, and Mirashi Bua. Second row from left: All India Radio staff artist, unidentified, Keramatullah Khan, Radhika Mohan Maitra, Ilyas Khan, Bismillah Khan, Kishan Maharaj, Altaf Hussain Khurjawale, Ravi Shankar, Ali Akbar Khan, Vilayat Khan, Vinayak Narayan Patwardhan, Narayan Rao Vyas. Third row: four unidentified musicians, Munne Khan (tabla), B. R. Deodhar, Jnan Prakash Ghosh, four unidentified musicians. Fourth row: unidentified, Vinay Chandra Maudgalaya, three unidentified musicians. Photo courtesy Pandit Ravi Shankar.

Khan's lineage is Buddhadev Das Gupta, who received his training on the sarod from the late Radhika Mohan Maitra.

The *dhrupad* vina tradition has survived in the late twentieth century principally through Ustad Zia Mohinuddin Dagar (died c. 1989) and Ustad Asad Ali Khan. Two great modern masters of the *vicitra vīṇā* 'plucked zither'—an instrument on which musicians have played both the older *dhrupad aṅg* and newer *khyāl aṅg* styles of instrumental music—are Ustad Abdul Aziz Khan, who was active in the early twentieth century, and the late Dr. Lalmani Misra, the former dean of the Faculty of Fine Arts at Banaras Hindu University. Misra's son, Gopal Shankar Misra, carries on his father's contributions to the *vicitra vīṇā* repertoire. Pandit Brij Bhushan Kabra and Pandit Vishwa Mohan Bhatt, the latter a disciple of Pandit Ravi Shankar, have translated the slide technique of the *vicitra vīṇā* to the Western guitar modified by the addition of sympathetic and drone strings.

The *khyāl aṅg* approach on bowed instruments has reached its highest levels of mastery in the playing of Pandit Ram Narayan, V. G. Jog, and Dr. N. Rajam. Pandit Ram Narayan raised the status of the *sāraṅgī* (bowed fiddle) to that of a solo instrument on the modern concert stage. V. G. Jog and Dr. N. Rajam are both violinists, the latter a prominent disciple of Pandit Omkarnath Thakur (founder of the Music College at Banaras Hindu University) who has taken the Indian version of the Western violin to levels of technical achievement equal to those of the greatest Western violin virtuosos.

Several other instruments have risen to solo status on the concert stage during the twentieth century. The *khyāl aṅg* on the *śahnāī* 'double-reed instrument' arose through the efforts of Ustad Bismillah Khan of Banaras (pictured among many other luminaries of the Hindustani music world in figure 9). A younger *śahnāī* player, Daya Shankar Misra, also of Banaras, has ensured that the instrument will continue its solo status in the Hindustani performance tradition. The Kashmiri *santūr* 'hammered dulcimer' has also become a concert instrument primarily through the internationally acclaimed performances and recordings of Pandit Shiv Kumar Sharma.

The preponderance of male musicians reflects a gender imbalance that has existed in the instrumental traditions of North India throughout history. Playing musical instruments was in the past an activity engaged in primarily by men, but although the imbalance persists even today, the proportion of women instrumentalists has increased dramatically since the mid-twentieth century. Women are also beginning to appear as competent artists on instruments such as the tabla and *sāraṅgī* that had tra-

Playing musical instruments was in the past an activity engaged in primarily by men, but although the imbalance persists even today, the proportion of women instrumentalists has increased dramatically since the mid-twentieth century.

ditionally been assigned exclusively to males. With both women and men devoting an abundance of talent to creative music making on North Indian instruments, and a formidable niche existing for its performance on the international stage, Hindustani instrumental music enjoys a secure position in world music as it enters the next millennium.

REFERENCES

Kinnear, Michael. 1994. *The Gramophone Company's First Indian Recordings 1899–1908.* Bombay: Popular Prakashan.

Manuel, Peter. 1989. *Ṭhumrī in Historical and Stylistic Perspectives.* Delhi: Motilal Banarsidass.

Miner, Allyn. 1993. *Sitar and Sarod in the 18th and 19th Centuries.* Intercultural Music Studies 5. Wilhelmshaven: Florian Noetzel.

Shringy, R. K., and Prem Lata Sharma. 1978. *Saṅgīta Ratnākara of Śārṅgadeva,* vol. 1. Delhi: Motilal Banarsidass.

Slawek, Stephen. 1987. *Sitār Technique in Nibaddh Forms.* Delhi: Motilal Banarsidass.

———. 1991. "Ravi Shankar as Mediator between a Traditional Music and Modernity." In *Ethnomusicology and Modern Music History,* ed. Stephen Blum, Philip V. Bohlman, and Daniel M. Neuman, 161–180. Urbana: University of Illinois Press.

Karnatak Vocal and Instrumental Music

Amy Catlin

Performance Contexts
Institutions for Music Education
Media Spinoffs
Genres
Composers
Performers and Performance Style

The term *Karnatak* refers to the classical music tradition of South India (Andhra Pradesh, Karnataka, Kerala, and Tamil Nadu), which has developed independently from the Hindustani tradition of the North at least since the sixteenth century. Karnatak vocal and instrumental music together form the subject matter of this article, as they have developed in close association. Karnatak forms, styles, and contexts are virtually indistinguishable for vocalists and instrumentalists, with few exceptions. Raga improvisation by singers and instrumentalists follows the same basic patterns. And since the vast majority of compositions have texts, Karnatak musicians can either sing them with words or play them instrumentally without words.

Karnatak music is a highly sophisticated art form strongly rooted in the devotional (bhakti) tradition of Hinduism. Virtually every musical event participates in that historical and spiritual context. Whether deities are praised or invoked or spiritual principles enunciated, music and devotionalism are inseparably linked, and both musicians and devotees see music as one path to spiritual enlightenment. The most influential Karnatak composers were saint-singers or religious figures who dedicated their entire lives to musical devotionalism. The following *kriti* song text by South India's most important composer, the saint-singer Tyagaraja (1767–1847), expresses the belief in music's mystic powers:

> The breath of life joins the inner fire to form Om [sacred sound] and the seven notes.
> Shiva's pleasure in playing the *vīṇā* [lute] is the consciousness Tyagaraja adores.

When a musician neglects this spiritual element, traditionalists consider it a failing deserving of private or public criticism.

The Karnatak term for composer, *vāggeyakāra* 'word-song-maker', indicates the fundamental importance of the verbal text in every composition. Ideally, a composer creates both lyrics and melody at the same time. Musical settings of devotional texts dominate the range of musical genres, whether they are performed vocally or instrumentally. Performances frequently take place in cities, towns, and villages of South India, as well as Sri Lanka. Emigrés from these regions also support Karnatak classical

Karnatak classical music developed principally with the support of royal and other wealthy patrons as well as the Hindu temple system.

music in the major cities of North India, the Persian Gulf, Malaysia, Singapore, Australia, Europe, and the Americas.

PERFORMANCE CONTEXTS

Karnatak classical music developed principally with the support of royal and other wealthy patrons as well as the Hindu temple system. Traditional performance contexts included the court, the temple, and the home altar. In this century, the contexts of Karnatak musical performance have expanded to encompass the public concert hall and the mass media. An examination of these contexts provides an introduction to the subsequent discussion of Karnatak genres and composers.

Temple

The temple has long been a locus for classical music performance, in processions, rituals, concerts, and festivals. Processions that circumambulate the temple must begin with the *mangaḷa vādyam* 'auspicious musical instruments', including the *nāgasvaram* 'double-reed aerophone' and *tavil* 'barrel drum'. The resounding timbre of this ensemble sanctifies the entire space it penetrates. The same ensemble performs for rituals within the precincts of the temple. A few temples have integral stone pillars that produce musical tones when struck and can be played both rhythmically and melodically, but these are not regarded as standard temple instruments [see MUSICAL INSTRUMENTS: SOUTHERN AREA].

Temples frequently sponsor concerts to celebrate religious festivals or to commemorate the birthday of a local composer. These usually take place within the temple hall or within temporary structures erected adjacent to the temple, and feature a variety of instruments as well as vocalists. Occasionally temples conduct special noncalendrical religious events such as musical marathons within the temple compounds, sometimes as offerings for specific goals such as world peace. These concerts range in length from all night to three days.

Musico-religious festivals honoring great Karnatak composers occur throughout the year, according to the date in the Hindu calendar on which the composer was born. Temples also commemorate the death anniversaries of singer-composers who reached the fourth and final stage of life for upper-caste Hindus (*sannyāsin*). Celebrations of both birth and death anniversaries take place for the "Musical Trinity"—Tyagaraja and his contemporaries Muttusvami Diksitar and Syama Sastri—and the temple is a major venue for such events.

Tyagaraja festival

One of the best-known temple observances featuring Karnatak music is the annual Tyagaraja *ārādhana* 'worship' held in Tiruvaiyaru, Tamil Nadu, commemorating the self-prophesied death during meditation (*samādhi*) of the saint-singer Tyagaraja in

January 1847 [see SOCIAL ORGANIZATION OF MUSIC AND MUSICIANS: SOUTHERN AREA]. According to popular belief, within hours of his death Tyagaraja appeared to a disciple in a dream, informing the disciple that his soul would first conduct a pilgrimage to certain temples before finally reaching the Lord at the beginning of the following week. For this reason, the date of the observations is usually six days after his death date. As Tyagaraja also prophesied, annual remembrances by his disciples expanded (in 1907) to include performances of his music. These remembrances took place near the *brindāvanam,* a 1-meter structure within which a holy basil plant grows and that was erected over the place where he instructed his followers to inter his body in salt in the meditating posture—the customary burial for a *samādhi.* The present temple was completed in 1927 on the same site; it was donated by a female singer of the *dēvadāsi* community of hereditary temple dancers, Bangalore Nagaratnammal, who had learned Tyagaraja's music from one of his second-generation disciples.

During the three-day festival, priests conduct special rituals (*uñcavritti*), singing for alms in the streets as Tyagaraja had done to avoid seeking royal patronage. Other rituals include processions around the temple carrying Tyagaraja's image and the bathing of the black stone statue of Tyagaraja in various sacred substances (*abhishēka*). An important musical component of the festival is a choral performance of five of Tyagaraja's vocal compositions (*kriti*) led by some of South India's most prominent musicians. This performance of the *pañcaratna* 'five jewels', as festival organizers have named these compositions, affirms the relationship between the essentially soloistic classical-music tradition and the communally sung devotional song (*bhajana* or *kīrtana*). Other performances comprise complete, unembellished renditions of Tyagaraja's compositions by a series of soloists and accompanists.

Besides observances for the Karnatak Trinity—Tyagaraja, Diksitar, and Sastri—a three-day festival has memorialized the saint-singer Purandara Dasa of Karnataka, the "father of Karnatak music" (1484–1564), since 1971. First held in Hampi (Vijayanagar) at the suggestion of His Highness Sri Jayachamarajendra Wodeyar, the former maharaja of Mysore, this festival was moved in 1988 to the Hanuman temple in Mulubagilu, an important center for the transmission of Purandara Dasa's compositions near Bangalore, Karnataka. South Indians celebrate Purandara Dasa festivals in other parts of India as well as in the diaspora; as fostered by Kannada-speaking associations, these festivals emphasize less ritual activity and more attention to music and dance performance. Similar annual functions commemorate Svati Tirunal, the great composer and former maharaja of Travancore, Kerala, whose music especially honors the various forms of the goddess. As with Tyagaraja's memorials, group singing is often a feature of these observances, and organizers encourage both amateur and professional musicians to perform as soloists.

FIGURE 1 Sarasvati holding a vina. Painting by L. Kondiah Raju. Photo by Amy Catlin, 1977.

The home

The home is an important context for creating and hearing classical music, through rituals, lessons, and practice. Daily *pūjā* 'worship' rituals may involve singing and playing music as an act of devotion and offering to the deity, particularly in musical families. Music making is often part of annual observances such as the *sarasvatī pūjā,* when a priest blesses all instruments of learning—including books, pens, and musical instruments—in honor of Sarasvati, the goddess of learning, music, and the arts (figure 1).

For music lessons, a teacher may travel to students' homes, or students may go to the teacher's home, where the teacher's own children may also receive lessons. The teacher usually performs a ritual to Ganesha, the elephant-headed god of beginnings, before the first lesson. Lessons and practicing frequently take place in close proximity to religious artifacts such as images of deities or important saint-composers, which enhances the devotional mood.

House concerts for invited guests are another context for enjoying Karnatak music. For larger rituals or celebrations with invited guests, such as weddings or sixtieth-birthday observances, families may rent a hall (*maṇḍapam*), either a permanent structure sometimes connected to a hotel, or a temporary one constructed of cane poles lashed together and covered with woven palm-leaf mats. They hire the auspicious *nāgasvaram-tavil* 'double-reed pipe and drum' ensemble to play for such events, often announcing the occasion and purifying the space by playing in procession around the hall.

Public concerts

The public concert is now the most prevalent context for live performance of Karnatak music. At the end of the nineteenth century, musicians began traveling to urban centers, especially Madras, seeking performance contexts to make up for the lost patronage of the royal courts and the declining patronage of the aristocracy. These former court musicians performed either for wealthy patrons residing in Madras or in free public concerts (*kaccēri* 'court') to establish their musical proficiency. Their repertoire consisted mainly of improvisational genres, although a format balancing composition and improvisation established around the 1930s has now become standard. Since about 1900, music societies (*saṅgīta sabhā*) have been the principal organizers of public concerts, by subscription and/or admission charge. They make arrangements with the musicians, publicize the event, solicit patrons and advertisers for souvenir program booklets, sell tickets, pay the expenses including hall rental and artists' fees, and award honorific titles and prizes to deserving musicians.

Although organizers produce concerts year round, the most popular season in Madras (the most musically active South Indian city) is winter (December–January) when the weather is most pleasant. During this time, called "the music festival season" or simply "the season," each society presents numerous music and/or dance concerts. In the 1994–1995 season, a total of thirty-nine organizations presented concerts, ranging from four to 112 events per society. The total number of musical events from 1 November to 5 February was 1,275. The increase in music societies and concerts over the previous year's figures (thirty-six societies and 1,124 programs) was typical of a trend that has lasted through the entire twentieth century, reflecting the population growth of Madras, which now numbers over 5 million. Karnatak music societies and performers are similarly increasing in Bangalore, Mysore, Vijayawada, Calcutta, Bombay, and Delhi; audiences seem smaller, but perhaps they are increasingly spread thin by the plethora of events (Aslesha 1995).

Probably the most prestigious patron of concerts, and well known throughout India, is the Madras Music Academy, founded in 1928 with surplus funds from the Fifth All-India Music Conference held in Madras in 1927. Its annual music festival features not only concerts, but also a conference on music and dance conducted by eminent scholars and musicians. These are mostly Indian, but some foreign guests are always included. The annual Madras Music Academy Journal publishes the conference papers. Another major venue for concerts is the Mysore Chowdiah Hall in Bangalore, shaped like the unique seven-stringed violin for which the violinist Mysore T. Chowdiah (1895–1967) was famous.

In all live performance contexts, Karnatak music audiences actively participate in the performance. They delight in visibly and vocally expressing enjoyment, appreciation, and spiritual upliftment by clapping and counting the tala metrical cycles on fingers, legs, and hands. Musicians, who also count for each other when the situation permits, take this as a sign of encouragement.

INSTITUTIONS FOR MUSIC EDUCATION

Professional musicians almost always integrate teaching with performing careers, teaching either privately or in an institution. Music schools train students from early childhood through adulthood. Graduates may then attend music colleges to study for performance degrees in Karnatak music, or university music departments for B.A., B. Mus., and M.A. degrees. The Telugu musicologist P. Sambamurthy (1901–1974), who received training in comparative musicology from Curt Sachs in Germany, founded the first such program at Madras University in 1937, which now grants the Ph.D. This program enabled a series of musicologists from Madras University to study abroad and earn Ph.D. degrees in ethnomusicology, the first being the flute virtuoso Tanjavur Viswanathan, now a professor of ethnomusicology at Wesleyan University in Connecticut. University programs tend to focus heavily on Karnatak music performance and theory rather than music history. Although group instruction is the norm, some institutions such as Kalakshetra in Adayar, Madras, emulate the traditional *guru-śiṣya* 'master-disciple' individual-lesson format. Brihaddhvani, also in Madras, conducts research and training in Karnatak music based on a world-music perspective [see INSTITUTIONAL MUSIC EDUCATION: SOUTHERN AREA].

MEDIA SPINOFFS

Since the earliest days of audio recording, India's music has been the subject of recording for research as well as commercial purposes. Europeans made wax-cylinder recordings of Karnatak classical music at the beginning of the twentieth century, followed by other forms of field recording devices. Commercial 78-rpm and 33-rpm discs, audio cassettes, and CDs of Karnatak music produced by Indian as well as foreign companies, sometimes in collaboration, have continuously supplied an active marketplace. Filmmakers have similarly documented the visual component on film and videocassette. Many older commercial and private recordings reside in private collections and institutional archives in India and abroad. One extensive archive of Karnatak music exists in Madras, run by an organization named Sampradaya 'tradition', which also documents and arranges musical and educational events.

The national and local All India Radio stations and the national television network present Karnatak music regularly, particularly in the four South Indian states. Commercial films occasionally make use of themes involving Karnatak music and musicians, and classically trained musicians have always worked in the film industry composing and recording film scores. These scores usually propel the music into nonclassical realms in combination with Indian and Western pop idioms.

Regional-language and English publications provide a lively forum for the discussion of Karnatak musical life. In newspapers, music is a favorite subject for debate, as attested to by the daily reviews of concerts and by cartoons on musical topics. People frequently rent billboard space to proclaim a position in a current musical debate. Publishers print a steady stream of books about music as well as editions of musical notation from the past and present. *Śruti* is a monthly magazine in English devoted entirely to Karnatak classical music and dance. Its editors present a wide variety of historical and contemporary topics. They also take an active part in the musical life of Madras by conducting research on topics of current interest such as the decline in *rāgam-tānam-pallavi* singing, and by organizing efforts to counteract disturbing trends (as when they founded a musical society devoted to *pallavi* performance).

GENRES

With a few exceptions, Karnatak melodic genres are identical for vocalists and instrumentalists. It is thus not uncommon for a singer to teach an instrumentalist, and vice

Musicians teach the art of improvising within composed forms, at least to a certain extent, since the ability to improvise is equally important as the mastery of a large repertoire of compositions.

versa. As main performers, both present essentially the same ragas, talas, and texted compositions, although instrumentalists omit the texts. Percussionists perform a variety of rhythmic genres both as accompanists and soloists. Singers may perform similar pieces vocally in a spoken rhythmic system called *konakkoḷ*, akin to the dance master's spoken syllables (*jati*); these may also provide rhythmic accompaniment during a concert. Musicians teach all genres orally in a systematic manner, with the aid of syllabic notation for more complex pieces. They also teach the art of improvising within these composed forms, at least to a certain extent, since the ability to improvise is equally important as the mastery of a large repertoire of compositions (over ten thousand compositions are currently available in print).

Unmetered melodic improvisation

The basis of all Karnatak melodic music is the raga, or melodic mode, of which there are several hundred in use today. Singers and instrumentalists perform melodic improvisations on a particular raga, as a pulseless, unmetered prelude to a composition in the same raga. These preludes serve to introduce the raga, and are called *ālāpana,* a Sanskrit word meaning "to speak, address, discourse, communicate." The *ālāpana* preceding the major composition in a concert may last forty-five minutes or more, whereas those introducing other compositions are proportionately shorter.

TRACK 4 The main principle of *ālāpana* is development. The exposition of the raga gradually unfolds in a series of spontaneously constructed statements within a coherent overall structure. The artist must interpret the raga's various colors, moods, and nuances, while holding the audience's attention from one statement or section to the next. Few ironclad rules exist for developing *ālāpana*, but performers generally follow certain commonly shared principles. These include the exploration of the low, middle, and high registers, improvisation on particular tones, the introduction of fast scale passages, and a conclusion on the fundamental tone Sa.

One typical design of a major *ālāpana* is for the performer to begin in the middle register, and then proceed to the lower and higher registers. As in all the sections, the fundamental note of the raga, to which the drone instrument is tuned, is the point of repose and conclusion. After an introductory "thumbnail sketch" (*akṣiptika* literally 'tossing outward'), in which the performer presents several characteristic raga phrases, the improvisation takes place in three or four stages. The first stage is mostly in a slow tempo, beginning with the gradual introduction of typical melodic motifs in the middle register and followed by development of the salient melodic features in the lower register. The second stage is in a medium tempo and centered on the middle register, with occasional flights to other registers. Again, the unique character of the raga is sought after, with emphasis on certain notes, contours, ornaments, and moods associated with the raga. The third stage, also in a medium tempo, concentrates on reaching and developing the upper register, while the fourth stage consists of rapid passages. This concluding section presents the most comprehensive melodic statements throughout the three registers, with many phrases beginning and returning to the same note after full-octave excursions that may cross two registers. The final approach to the central drone tone is usually in slower tempo, from the lower register.

Karnatak singers do not use meaningful text in vocal *ālāpana,* rather vocalizations. They choose vowels and syllables such as *ta*, *da*, *ri*, *na*, and *tom*, or may use the name of a deity. In instrumental performance, the main artist mirrors the vocal syllables on his or her instrument. A drone instrument accompanies *ālāpana,* and an optional melody instrument may echo and imitate the soloist's phrases. Soloists generally allow the melodic accompanist, usually a violin player, to perform an entire *ālāpana* solo of shorter duration following their own *ālāpana*.

TRACK 1-5 A second type of raga improvisation, *tānam,* employs an intermittent pulse created by the repetition of single notes and short melodic units. A vocalist performs *tānam* using syllables such as *ta*, *nom*, and *tom*, also heard occasionally in *ālāpana.* Each phrase increases in energy until the pulse dissolves, followed by a relaxing pause and resumption of the same process using different pitches. Up to the early twentieth century, this genre used to occur in performances of important ragas (with great scope for development and improvisation) between the *ālāpana* and the composition that followed. Musicians now perform it mainly within the *rāgam-tānam-pallavi* and *tāḷamālikā* genres (see below). *Tānam* is very similar to the Hindustani *nom-tom ālāp* in its use of syllables and intermittent pulsation during exploration of the raga. Paccimiriyam Adiyappayya (b. 1730), resident court musician at Tanjavur, systematized the rules for improvising *ālāpana, tānam,* and *pallavi* (see below).

A third form of raga improvisation in free rhythm is the melodic declamation of poetic texts, called *viruttam* or *padyam.* These texts may be verses (*śloka*) in Sanskrit or poetry or prose in vernacular languages. In this improvisational form, the performer usually begins each line in a chanted syllabic style and concludes with melismatic flourishes. Musicians often use the *rāgamālikā* technique, progressing from one raga to another.

Compositions

The earliest known examples of notated compositions are the seventh-century stone inscriptions of instructional instrumental pieces found near Pudukkottai, Tamil Nadu. The pieces demonstrate the melodic capabilities of various ragas in a manner similar to the more systematic technique of raga development (*svaraprastāra*) first described in writing by Sarngadeva in the thirteenth-century treatise *Saṅgītaratnākara.* A king (probably the Pallava emperor Mahendravarman I, c. 600–630) provided the inscriptions for students of the seven-stringed vina, most likely a kind of harp. The notation consists of thirty-eight lines divided horizontally into seven sections, each labeled with a different raga name and containing from four to seven lines. The notation employs the seven note names, as in today's syllabic notation system of Sa, Ri, Ga, Ma, Pa, Dha, and Ni, but also with varying vowels Si, Su, and Se. The musicologist P. Sambamurthy (1973b) and others presumed that the changing vowels in the note names indicated microtonal changes in pitch level, but Widdess has proposed a more sophisticated theory, namely that the vowels were indicators of relativity and directionality (Widdess 1979). Others have interpreted the vowel changes as rhythmic indicators (Kuppuswamy and Hariharan 1986). Scholars have interpreted dots above the note names to indicate a change in octave, as today, or an ornament. The final inscription indicates that the notes may be played in "either eight or seven," perhaps referring to metrical cycles of eight and seven beats.

During the seventh to ninth centuries, three Tamil saints—Tirujnanasambandar, Appar, and Sundaramurti Nayanar—created what are believed to be the oldest extant

FIGURE 2 Sri Purandara Dasa. Painting by S. Rajam. Photo by Amy Catlin, 1977.

musical compositions in India. These rhythmic Tamil poems to Shiva, known as the *tēvāram*, were sung to particular melodies in ancient ragas called *paṇ*. In the eighteenth century, a hereditary community of professional temple singers known as Oduvars recast the melodies, which have been preserved in oral tradition ever since. Nowadays performers sometimes include *tēvāram* in Karnatak music concerts [see RELIGIOUS AND DEVOTIONAL MUSIC: SOUTHERN AREA].

The genre that has most influenced the modern Karnatak repertoire is the Telugu *kīrtana*, especially those works composed by the three "Tallapakam" composers of the fifteenth and sixteenth centuries: Annamacharya (1408–1503), his son Pedda Tirumalayyangar, and his grandson Tallapakam Chinnayya. Previously the *kīrtana* had consisted of only two alternating sections, *pallavi* and *caraṇam*. The Tallapakam compositions were the first written works to comprise three parts—*pallavi, anupallavi,* and *caraṇam*. This tripartite structure has dominated Karnatak composition ever since. Inscriptions on three thousand copper plates preserve the texts and raga names of some twenty thousand pieces, but unfortunately not the original melodies.

The next major composer to use the three-part *pallavi-anupallavi-caraṇam* form was the seventeenth-century Bhadrachala Ramadas, who was followed by many more composers in the eighteenth and nineteenth centuries. The most notable of these were the Karnatak Trinity (see "Composers" below) who also elevated the text-dominated *kīrtana* into today's musically refined *kriti*. Group *kīrtana* singing, in which a leader sings each line for a chorus to repeat, is still an important spiritual exercise. Some *kīrtana* have only two sections, the opening *pallavi* and the subsequent *caraṇam*, which may be a single verse or a series of verses. Whether in two sections or three, musicians perform the refrain-like *pallavi* after each *caraṇam* of the *kīrtana*.

The Kannada compositions of Purandara Dasa (1484–1564) follow this two-part structure. Singers often include his devotional songs in concerts of Karnatak music, but there is no way to confirm the authenticity of the melodies. Purandara Dasa was a wealthy diamond merchant of Karnataka who abandoned his riches to become a mendicant religious singer (figure 2). He is called the father of Karnatak music partly because he is credited with composing many exercise pieces that Karnatak music students still use today. These exercises, *svarāvali* and *alaṅkāra,* are systematic repetitions of patterns throughout the three octave registers, practiced in different ragas and talas. The many song compositions credited to Purandara Dasa include *piḷḷari gīta*, beginners' songs about Ganesha, and *sañcāri gīta* that demonstrate the main phrases of elementary ragas, interspersed with vocables such as *a iya, ti iya, a iyam*.

Karnatak musicians include in their classical concerts many other forms of religious music still sung in Hindu temples, such as the *tiruppugaḻ* 'holy praise' hymns of Arunagirinadar (sixteenth century), with their vast array of talas, and the *tiruvaruṭpā,* hymns to the deity by the nineteenth-century singer Ramalingasvami.

Varṇam

The *varṇam* is a type of lengthy, academic, multipart composition that explores the melodic and emotional range of a major raga and incorporates note patterns believed to be very old. Karnatak musicians play or sing the *varṇam* as a study at the commencement of a concert, often in two different speeds. The composition contains three texted sections—*pallavi, anupallavi,* and *caraṇam*—and sometimes a fourth, concluding section called *anubandham*. Singers perform *citta svara*, nontexted sections with sol-fa syllables: the first (*muktai svara*) follows the *pallavi*; the second (*ettugaḍa svara*) occurs in the *caraṇam* and comprises passages of increasing length and complexity that return to a refrain theme. *Ettugaḍa* (literally 'deceiving and jumping') *svara* sections are essentially composed models for improvised solfège passages (*kalpana svara*). There are two kinds of *varṇam*: the concert or *tāna varṇam,* which makes use of many passages in the *tānam* style, and the dance or *pada varṇam. Varṇam* texts are relatively short, spaced throughout the piece by lengthy melismas. They may be devotional, erotic, musicological, or panegyric. *Varṇam* is demanding to perform, and only a few hundred compositions exist, due to their difficulty.

Paccimiriyam Adiyappayya (b. 1730), a vina player and the guru of Syama Sastri, composed the most famous *tāna varṇam,* "Viri boni," in *bhairavī rāg, āṭa tāḷa.* In the well-known *varṇam* "Valaci vācci," which pleads to Lord Venkatesvara for recognition, the composer Patnam Subramania Ayyar (1845–1902) uses *rāgamālikā* 'melody in a series of ragas'. Rather than finding strongly contrasting ragas for his series, the composer changes the melody subtly from one closely related raga to another: the *pallavi* is in *kedaram,* the *anupallavi* is in *śankarābharaṇam,* the *muktai svara* begins in *kalyāṇi* and concludes in *bēgaḍa,* the *caraṇam* is in *kāmbhōjī,* and the final *citta svara* progress from *yadukulakāmbhōjī* to *bilahari* to *mōhanam,* ending with a contrast in the ninth and final raga, the auspicious *śrī.* There is considerable freedom in the way such compositions are performed. For example, in one performance of this *varṇam,* the renowned singer M. D. Ramanathan sang in the customary two speeds and then, in an unusual practice, added his own *kalpana svara* in *kēdāra rāga,* after which the violin accompanist created his own *svara* improvisations (Lieberman and Catlin 1994). Other *rāgamālikā varṇam* compositions are in the five "weighty" (*ghana*) ragas (*nāṭa, gauḷa, ārabhi, varāḷi, śrī*), as in Tyagaraja's *pañcaratna* 'five jewels' *kriti,* and in other raga groupings.

Rāgam-tānam-pallavi

At the time of the Trinity (mid-eighteenth to mid-nineteenth centuries), musical virtuosity resided principally in the hands of *pallavi* improvisational musicians, who competed against each other for royal patronage and favors in court musical contests. TRACK 5 Each *pallavi* singer presented an exposition of the raga in *rāgam* and *tānam* sections, then performed variations on a texted musical theme (*pallavi*). The theme itself had to be composed according to specific rules that are still followed today. Most important is its two-part structure. The first part begins with the melody's approach (*purvaṅga*) to the "arrival point" (*ar̲uti, muḍivu*), which must always occur on a strong beat of the rhythmic cycle and on the same pitch as the beginning note of the *pallavi* theme, or a fourth or a fifth away from it. A rest follows this moment of arrival. The second part of the theme (*uttaraṅga*) leads smoothly back again to the beginning of the *pallavi* theme by ending one note below the starting note. After repeating the theme a few times, a performer alters it according to a series of variational techniques, which include the following:

1. *saṅgati*: embellishments, sometimes highlighting aspects of the text and other times developing nuances in the raga. These gradually increase the dimensions of the melodic contours until the performer reaches a satisfying conclusion.
2. *niraval*: improvisations in which the original theme's text and its rhythm remain constant but the performer forsakes the melodic contours in favor of a more recitational style, smoothing out the melody and transferring it to different levels. Musicians may incorporate wide-spanning melodic flourishes into these phrases. These again gradually extend higher and higher in pitch, until the performer creates a feeling of completion.
3. *anulōma-pratilōma*: variations by augmentation and diminution in which the melody is first presented four times slower than normal, then at half speed, then at normal speed, and finally at double and quadruple speed. In *pratilōma*, the

Soloists usually indicate the tala with hand gestures while concentrating their gaze on the percussionists—partly to help the audience to visualize the tala counts, partly to assist the percussionist, and partly to demonstrate appreciation of the accompanists' talents, skills, and knowledge.

melody remains constant but the clapping of the metrical cycle by the soloist is doubled and quadrupled. A reversal of this is *vilōma anulōma/pratilōma*, in which the process slows the theme or the meter.

4. *gatibhēda*: metrical subdivisions in which the basic pulse of the meter subdivides into three, five, seven, or nine.
5. *kalpana svara*: improvisations in which the performer creates untexted melodic patterns that constantly return to the beginning of the *pallavi* theme at its correct place in the metric cycle. Vocalists sing these melodies to the *svara* note names. The melodies gradually increase in length, becoming more and more complex yet always returning to the familiar theme.
6. *rāgamālikā*: 'garland of ragas' variations, in which the musician presents the theme in one raga after another. The soloist begins by introducing phrases in each new raga successively, often using the *svara* note names in the case of a singer. The performer then refashions the original *pallavi* theme in each raga, sometimes revealing the name of the raga in the sung text.
7. *tāḷamālikā:* 'garland of talas' variations, through which the musician adapts the *pallavi* theme as he or she plays or sings it in a series of different metrical cycles.

Rāgamālikā

Musicians employ the *rāgamālikā* 'garland of ragas' technique, presenting several different ragas sequentially, not only in *pallavi* but in other genres as well. Composers have also created *pallavi* compositions in *rāgamālikā* form, with a text to identify each raga. The technique dates back at least to the medieval period, for pieces from this time called *kadambaka* 'collection' have indications for different raga names from verse to verse. The technique assumed the name *mālikā* at a later date, possibly to suggest the garland of blossoms strung together as an offering to wreathe the statue of a divinity or an honored person. Implicit in the idea of a garland is a circular form, returning to and concluding with the initial raga, although performers do not always follow this in practice. Because of the relative ease of migrating from one raga to another on South Indian instruments without retuning, the process has remained quite prevalent in Karnatak music.

Vocalists sing the unmetered *śloka* and *padyam* forms frequently as *rāgamālikā,* and audiences find them especially appealing when the text includes the name of each raga woven into the poetry. Since raga names are frequently highly suggestive of poetic and religious imagery, this technique can create double meaning, aside from merely identifying the raga. Instrumentalists often perform *ālāpana* and *tānam* genres in *rāgamālikā* form, particularly on the vina and using the five "weighty" ragas (*ghana rāga pañcaka*).

Over a hundred compositions make use of *rāgamālikā* by stringing together multiple ragas in the same piece; examples include the sixteen-raga *kriti* by the nineteenth-century composer Tiruvottiyur Tyagayyar and the nine-raga *varṇam* by

Patnam Subramania Ayyar. Longer compositions in the *rāgamālikā* structure include the seventy-two *mēḷa rāgamālikā* of Maha Vaidyanatha Ayyar (1844–1893), in which the composer employs each of the seventy-two scale types (*mēḷakarta*) sequentially in a two-hour piece (Sastri 1937). Ramasvami Diksitar composed a *rāgatāḷamālikā* using all talas in the 108-tala system and 108 ragas, each raga and tala named in the text. The piece takes about three hours to perform, which makes it the longest composition in Indian classical music.

At the conclusion of these variations, the percussion accompanists perform a lengthy *tani āvartanam.* This series of precomposed and improvised solos and dialogues provides reference to the rhythmic properties of the *pallavi* theme and concludes with several climactic pieces. Soloists usually indicate the tala with hand gestures while concentrating their gaze on the percussionists—partly to help the audience to visualize the tala counts, partly to assist the percussionist, and partly to demonstrate involvement and appreciation of the accompanists' talents, skills, and knowledge.

Kriti

TRACK 6 The *kriti* is the standard compositional form of the modern period and dates from the early nineteenth century. Beginning with the Trinity composers, Karnatak musicians and composers have combined *pallavi* improvisational techniques with the composition and performance of *kriti* devotional songs (Catlin 1985).

The lion's share of the Karnatak concert repertoire consists of the three-part *kriti*, a highly evolved musical genre distilled from its *kīrtana* predecessor. The three composed sections begin with the *pallavi*, which has one or two text lines and is often in the middle-octave register of the melodic range. The second section (*anupallavi*) begins with notes related to the beginning of the *pallavi*, and frequently contrasts with it by proceeding into a somewhat higher register. This second section is either the same length as the first or twice as long. The third composed section (*caraṇam*) consists of single or multiple verses set to a third melody, sometimes with a return to the *anupallavi* melody in the conclusion. The final *caraṇam* text often concludes with the composer's signature, either an actual name or a pen name such as "devotee of Rama." After each section, performers repeat the first line of the *pallavi* as a refrain, and composers may enhance this transition by having the text of the last *caraṇam* line lead into the first *pallavi* line.

Kriti texts are predominantly spiritual in nature, although there are some examples of didactic or other subjects. Of over ten thousand in current usage, most texts are in the Telugu language, followed by Sanskrit, Tamil, and Kannada (Kuppuswami and Hariharan 1981). *Kriti* texts also exist in Malayalam, Hindi, and combined languages. The vast majority are in the eight-beat metric cycle, *ādi tāḷa*, which allows the maximum freedom for rhythmic improvisation. The *kriti* repertoire consists of compositions in over four hundred ragas.

Padam, jāvaḷi, tillāna

The *padam* is a love song derived from the dance repertoire; composers have adapted the form for musical concerts by presenting more melodic variety than would usually be found in a danced rendition. The form has a particular association with the seventeenth-century composer Ksetrayya, but prior to this time Purandara Dasa and other composers created *padam* compositions. *Padam* poetry is similar to *ṭhumrī* texts in Hindustani music, in which the writer posits a metaphorical link between love of the divine beloved, usually Krishna, and love of the worldly beloved. *Padam* texts portray three characters: the heroine, longing for union; her elusive hero; and her female friend, who advises her on her conduct. Many connoisseurs interpret these characters as representing the soul longing for the Divine, with guidance from a spiritual preceptor. *Padam* songs are usually slow and somewhat serious, with an emphasis on the text, and usually appear in the latter portion of a concert.

The *jāvaḷi* is a secular, erotic song that arose in the nineteenth century, named for a type of erotic poetry in the Kannada language. The jesting, colloquial texts lack the spiritual dimension of the *padam. Jāvaḷi* melodies are in medium or slow tempo, and performers can take liberties in their treatment of the raga. They may introduce occasional melodic phrases that are outside the raga, which would not normally be permitted in Karnatak music except in the *rāgamālikā.* Svati Tirunal was an early *jāvaḷi* composer.

The *tillāna* is another lively nonsacred form closely associated with dance. The *tillāna* is a counterpart of the North Indian *tarānā,* whose text is said to be derived from Sufi mystic syllables. *Tillāna* texts are nonlexical tongue twisters based on drum syllables and other euphonious sounds. Rhythmic patterns are playful, with many syncopations and surprises. Like the *jāvaḷi,* the *tillāna* often concludes a Karnatak concert, followed by the sanctifying *mangaḷam,* a short ending piece usually in the auspicious *madhyamāvati rāga.*

COMPOSERS

The modern period of composition began with the Trinity musicians: Tyagaraja (1767–1847), Muttusvami Diksitar (1775–1835), and Syama Sastri (1762–1827). The works of these three composers form the core of modern Karnatak music; up to the present day, a vast number of subsequent composers have continued to use forms perfected by the Trinity and their colleagues, including many concert artists who perform their own compositions. Such composers trace their musical lineage to one or more members of the Trinity through the *guru śiṣya paramparā* 'master-disciple lineage'.

Tyagaraja, Muttusvami Diksitar, and Syama Sastri were all born in the town of Tiruvarur in Tanjavur. Their shared goal was to unite the devotional path (*bhakti yoga*) with the refinements of musical devotion (*nāda yoga*) by perfecting the musical and poetic aspects of the *kriti* form. Many of the Trinity's *kriti* compositions were notated during their lifetime, unlike the custom of earlier times when, though song texts and raga names were sometimes written down, oral tradition transmitted most musical creations. Each of these composers had a unique style: Diksitar's learned and majestic music has been compared to the coconut, difficult to penetrate, but the enjoyment inside well worth the struggle. Syama Sastri's music, like the banana, is covered in a protective jacket but is easy to enjoy after that is removed. Tyagaraja's music is, like the grape, immediately accessible and pleasurable without effort.

FIGURE 3 Sri Tyagaraja. Painting by S. Rajam. Photo by Amy Catlin, 1977.

Tyagaraja

Tyagaraja was a Telugu Brahmin whose ancestors had migrated from present-day Andhra Pradesh in the seventeenth century, during the declining years of the Vijayanagar empire (figure 3). The Telugu Nāyaks had acquired power in Tanjavur by that time, and were great patrons of learning and the arts. Tyagaraja's ancestors were Vaidika Brahmins, priests and purveyors of Sanskritic knowledge; for example, his father recited the Ramayana for his royal patrons at the Tanjavur court. They belonged to the Smarta sect, which recognized five great manifestations of the divine Brahma: Shiva, Vishnu (and his avatars, including Rama), the Goddess, Ganapati, and Surya. Smarta Brahmins were largely responsible for the Sanskritization of local bhakti traditions in the South, and Tyagaraja likewise classicized the musical expression of bhakti devotion and its emotional states. His parents named him for the dancing ascetic form of Shiva called Tyagaraja 'King of Renunciation', the temple deity in his natal town of Tiruvarur. (There is some evidence that he may have been born in Tiruvaiyaru, but the standard belief is that he was born in Tiruvarur.) Like his father, Tyagaraja's personal deity was Rama, and both were initiates in the Rama mantra that causes the speaker to "cross the sea of rebirths." As a follower of *nāmasiddhanta*, the recitation of holy names as a path to enlightenment, the composer is believed to have chanted Rama's name in a six-syllable mantra a total of 960 million times during his lifetime. This practice achieved the intended result, for Tyagaraja received visions of Rama several times and spontaneously sang new *kriti* while in those ecstatic states. The first such vision, brief but intense, occurred when he had completed the ten-millionth repetition. Details of Tyagaraja's life remain in oral tradition; some scholars consider many of these speculative (Jackson 1994).

Tyagaraja taught freely throughout his life, welcoming students to his home, but refused the court *pallavi* singers who insisted on improvising variations on his *kriti* (Mudaliar 1892). In 1785, he performed for the Pudukkottai court and is said to have caused an unlit lamp to burst into flame by his singing of a fire-producing raga. From as early as 1802, he declined invitations to perform for the Tanjavur king, an aspect of his personality regarded as a mark of his saintliness. In the same year, after twenty years' tutelage, he performed twice for the Tanjavur court musicians in the home of his music guru, Sonti Venkatramanayya, also a Tanjavur court musician. He traveled to Kancipuram in 1839 to honor an invitation to sing for the head of a religious center, a composer and saintly scholar who had been his father's schoolmate. En route he sang new *kriti* compositions as offerings at the temples he visited, just as he frequently did in Tanjavur. Beyond these excursions he performed only at home and while conducting processions for alms collection in the streets of Tiruvaiyaru as a means of supporting his household and feeding his students without resorting to princely patronage. Two of his disciples, a father and son of Saurashtran descent (originally from a region of Gujarat)—Walajapet Venkatarama Bhagavatar and Walajapet Krishnasvami Bhagavatar, respectively—wrote biographies of Tyagaraja and notated his compositions on palm-leaf manuscripts and in notebooks. A Saurashtran association in Madurai preserves these Walajapet manuscripts along with numerous volumes that belonged to Tyagaraja, some inherited from his grandfather, a vina player at the Tanjavur court, and many from his guru. Five of his disciples became composers, and about twenty became notable performers. Some notated his compositions, many of which were later published, although some published collections contain only his texts. Many of his major disciples taught their own disciples, thus preserving Tyagaraja's legacy of over seven hundred *kriti* compositions.

Tyagaraja's *kriti* compositions follow a logical tripartite structure in which the *pallavi* (P) states a musical and textual idea, the *anupallavi* (A) develops it, and the *caraṇam* (C) extends it still further. In some cases the musical idea dominates, in others the textual idea takes the foreground, or else there is a balance between them. A return to the *pallavi* (sometimes preceded by the *anupallavi*) as a refrain at the conclusion of each section serves to reiterate the central idea of the *kriti*. The tripartite form can be expressed as P, A P, C (A) P (commas indicate a break in the singing, a drum cadence, or possibly a cycle or two of solo drumming).

Another important innovation attributed to Tyagaraja is the incorporation of composed melodic variations (*saṅgati*) on the vocal melody lines. This innovation further distinguishes the *kriti* from its *kīrtana* predecessor. Each variation becomes slightly more complex than the previous one. Some emphasize particular ideas in the text, and others illuminate different facets of the raga.

Tyagaraja composed many *kriti* on the subject of musical sound (*nāda*) as a divine art. "Nādatanum aniśam" in *citrañjani rāga* is an example of this type of *kriti*, addressed to the god Shiva. It praises the Sāmaveda, the most musical of the four

Muttusvami Diksitar is the first Indian musician known to have been trained in the Western violin and, according to some scholars, the first to play the violin in Karnatak music.

Vedas, traditionally considered to be the source of music. The text mentions one of Shiva's aspects, "destroyer of time and death (*kāla*)" (Raghavan 1981) (translation by Hartmut Scharfe):

Pallavi:
Nādatanum aniśam śankaran
Namāmi me manasā śirasā
Anupallavi:
Modakara-nigamottama-Sāma-
Veda-sāram vāram vāram
Caraṇam:
Sadyojātādi-pañca-vaktraja-
sa ri ga ma pa dha ni-vara-sapta-svara-
Vidyā-lolam vidalita-kālam
Vimala-hrdaya-Tyāgarāja-pālam

Pallavi:
To the source of musical sound, Lord Shankara (Shiva),
I constantly bow my mind and bow my head.
Anupallavi:
To the exhilarating and greatest among Vedas,
The Sāmaveda, I bow repeatedly.
Caraṇam:
To Sadyojata and the other forms of Shiva, all five,
From whose mouths are born Sa Ri Ga Ma Pa Dha and Ni, his seven chosen tones
In whose knowledge he constantly sways, he who makes death and time explode,
To pure-hearted Tyagaraja's protector.
(Repeat *pallavi*)

A rendition of this *kriti* sung in 1964 by Voleti Venkatesvarlu (1928–1989), a much-honored singer from Voleti, Andhra Pradesh, exhibits many features typical of *kriti* performance, including types of improvisation (figure 4). First, the singer introduces a few *saṅgati* in the two melody lines of the *pallavi* section, which serve to express aspects of the text. He varies and thus emphasizes the word *aniśam* 'constantly'; then subtly expands the phrase *manasā śirasā* up one note, underscoring the concept of devotion to music in both mind and body. Second, the melodic accompanist (violin) supports the singer in unison or heterophonically, while the rhythmic accompanists (*mridangam* and *morsing* 'mouth harp') play patterns that support the rhythm of the song text and provide the recurrent metrical cycle. The *tambūrā* 'drone lute'

FIGURE 4 "Nādatanum aniśam," *kriti* by Tyagaraja in *citrañjani rāg*, *ādi tāla*, as sung by Voleti Venkatesvarlu. Recorded by Nazir Jairazbhoy, 1964, transcribed by Amy Catlin.

provides a smoothly undulating fundamental pitch and its fifth. On completing the composed *kriti*, Venkatesvarlu sings *svara kalpana* improvisations using the note names instead of text, and returns to the incipit "Nādatanum..." after each improvisation. Finally, the percussion accompanists become dual soloists in a concluding *tani āvartanam* 'percussion solo' improvisation based on memorized rhythmic compositions.

FIGURE 5 Sri Muttusvami Diksitar. Painting by S. Rajam. Photo by Amy Catlin, 1977.

Muttusvami Diksitar

Muttusvami Diksitar (1776–1835) was the son of the prolific composer Ramasvami Diksitar (1735–1817). Like Tyagaraja, he was a Smarta Brahmin, but from the Tamil-speaking rather than the Telugu-speaking community (figure 5). He believed in the unity of all existence with the Supreme Being, and praised all Hindu deities. His *kriti* compositions exhibit a sublime intellectual and spiritual dignity, and most of his song texts are in praise of deities. His works include twenty-five pieces to Ganesha, the elephant-headed god of beginnings, and many to the Goddess, in whose cult he was an initiate.

Diksitar's life began in Tiruvarur, where he and his father before him were devotees of the dancing Shiva idol in the Tyagaraja temple. They both organized and composed music that the temple still uses today for its services, processions, and festivals. Like Tyagaraja, Diksitar eschewed the patronage of royal courts and lived a life of poverty. A prominent Mudaliar family (translators to the English governor) took an interest in Ramasvami Diksitar and his three young musician sons, and brought the Diksitars to its estates outside Madras in Manali about 1800. They stayed for many years, during which time they were introduced to English band music. Muttusvami composed Sanskrit texts to many English band tunes, including one on the goddess Sarasvati to the tune of "God Save the King." Chinnayya Mudaliar arranged for the

Sarasākaye	O you, having a beautiful form
rasākaye	O you, charm incarnate
sakāye	O you, the embodiment of knowledge
āye	Come [expressing affection]
sa	To cease
prakāsam	Illumination
svarupa prakāsam	Illuminating the true form
sakala tattva svarupa prakāsam	Illuminating exactly thus the entire true form
Siva saktyādi sakala tattva svarupa prakāsam	The true form of Shiva and Shakti and the rest are illuminated exactly thus.

FIGURE 6 Text phrases of Muttusvami Diksitar's *kriti* "Tyagaraja yoga vaibhavam" in two rhythmic shapes (*yati*): *Top*, cow's tail *yati*; *bottom*, river *yati*. An alternate translation of *sakāye* is "O you, Parvati, with Sarasvati and Lakshmi."

youngest Diksitar brother, Balusvami, to study the Western violin for three years; he later adapted the instrument to Indian music. He is the first Indian musician known to have been trained in this way, and the first to play the violin in Karnatak music (others attribute this accomplishment to his contemporary, Vadivelu Pillai, of the Tanjavur Quartette). During this period, the Diksitars were introduced to a yogi who led Muttusvami to Banaras on a five-year pilgrimage. Muttusvami's preference for slow tempos and languorous ornaments and the austere mood of his compositions have led some to believe his pieces reflect the influence of Hindustani *dhrupad*, which he is presumed to have heard while in the North.

Upon his return to Manali, while meditating in a temple, Diksitar received a vision of the temple deity in the guise of an elderly man. He immediately composed his first set of eight *kriti* to Sanskrit texts. Each used a different Sanskrit declension of Kumara, the god of that temple, also known as Guha. In this way Diksitar acquired his signature name (*mudra*) of Guruguha, meaning "teacher Guha." Before returning to Tiruvarur, he spent four years studying with a composer who taught him the unity of all being and the practice of singing the divine name. The remainder of his life was a constant pilgrimage.

Diksitar's *kriti* texts are primarily in Sanskrit, of which he was a great master. He embellished his texts with many euphonious rhymes. He favored the *svarakṣara* literary device, in which the composer weaves *svara* note names into the text, and the melody coincides with the actual note being named. A Western parallel to this practice is the song "Do, Re, Mi" by Rodgers and Hammerstein, which begins with the line "Doe, a deer, a female deer," the word "Doe" being sung on the sol-fa syllable *do*. Similarly, the second line "Ray, a drop of golden sun" gives the word "Ray" on the syllable *re*, and so forth.

Many poetic features adorn Diksitar's texts, such as the use of *yati*, the rhythmic shape of a group of phrases. Diksitar's *kriti* "Tyāgarāja yoga vaibhavam" in *ānandabhairavi rāga* and *rūpaka tāḷa* illustrates the "cow's tail" and "river" shapes, in which even the most reduced text line is still meaningful, if obscure (figure 6).

Diksitar created many *kriti* cycles, which unite five to nine compositions on a particular theme. He dedicated one such cycle to the five *linga* (the generative symbol of Shiva) found in the Tiruvarur temple, each representing a different element: earth, air, fire, water, and ether. He composed another cycle, the *navagraha* 'nine planets', to the heavenly bodies depicted in the Tiruvarur temple's inner courtyard, seven of which were associated with the days of the week. Replete with astrological and mantric knowledge, in which Diksitar was deeply educated, these pieces were intended to cure an illness contracted by one of the main temple musicians at Tiruvarur. Diksitar had diagnosed him on the basis of his horoscope and instructed him to play the pieces regularly; in the end he was cured. Vocalists often sing these pieces individually in concert, observing the assigned weekday. For example, the late M. D.

FIGURE 7 "Budham āśrayāmi," *kriti* by Muttusvami Diksitar in *rāga nātakurañji, jhampā tāḷa*: *a*, as published in Diksitar 1977 [1904]:779, transcribed by Amy Catlin; *b*, as sung by M. D. Ramanathan in 1978, published in Lieberman and Catlin 1994, transcribed without performed ornamentation by Amy Catlin.

TRACK 6 Ramanathan sang "Budham āśrayāmi" 'Taking Refuge in Budha (Mercury)' in a house concert that took place on a Wednesday, the piece being dedicated to Mercury, Wednesday's planet (Lieberman and Catlin 1994). The piece as notated and published (Diksitar 1963–1983, 4:779) bears only a rough resemblance to its performance by M. D. Ramanathan (figure 7). This divergence is typical of the effects of oral tradition and individual creativity on transmission.

Diksitar composed over six hundred *kriti* in a vast array of ragas, including many rare ones. He thus created an archival resource for otherwise forgotten ragas. Diksitar's *kriti* compositions contrast with Tyagaraja's in their variety of melodies: within a *kriti* performance, musicians sometimes skip Tyagaraja *caraṇam* verses because they are set to the same melody, whereas singers must perform all Diksitar's verses, since the music changes for each.

Unlike his father, Muttusvami Diksitar was not particularly partial to the *rāgamālikā* form, but he did compose two important such works. One is a *kriti* employing fourteen ragas. The *pallavi* and *anupallavi* sections contain the first six ragas, which repeat in reverse order. The eight remaining ragas occur in the *caraṇam* and then again in reverse order, after which the *pallavi* returns in the first raga. The second *rāgamālikā kriti* honors the ten incarnations of the god Vishnu and contains ten ragas.

On his many pilgrimages Diksitar composed *kriti* to commemorate each new temple, shrine, and encounter with the divine. Each such piece gives detailed information about the location, the temple, its architecture, the deity enshrined, its sculptural form, associated myths and legends, mantras, folk beliefs, customs, and food offered to the deity. His texts thus contain vast amounts of esoteric knowledge, and may require considerable explanation to be fully understood. However, his pieces are elegant and full of serenity; while Tyagaraja's *kriti* compositions offer a colorful and emotion-laden experience, Diksitar's are more consistently majestic in mood.

Diksitar's best-known piece is "Vātāpi gaṇapatim bhaje ham," a lively composition in the *hamsadhvani* raga, created by his father. Chinnasvami Mudaliar (1893) attributes the meaning of the raga name to the mythical *hamsa* 'swan', capable of separating water from milk, but V. Raghavan and others (1975) believe its name derives from an *advaita* 'nondualist' mantra asserting the unity of the individual spirit with the Supreme Soul. The song describes and praises the stone statue of the elephant-headed deity Ganesh, also known as Ganapati, which was brought to Tamil Nadu from Vatapi in northern Karnataka (Catlin 1980, 1991). The *caraṇam* contains a

There was a certain stigma attached to professional musicianship: since Bharata's second-century treatise, the *Nāṭyaśāstra*, all performers had been classified Shudras, the lowest social class—a stigma that the achievements of the Trinity eventually lifted.

concluding section in *madhyamakāla sāhitya* 'middle speed text', meaning a faster setting of the words, for which Diksitar is especially known (Sambamurthy 1973a:146–147). This short Sanskrit *kriti* has become the most popular item for beginning a Karnatak concert, following a tradition established by Maha Vaidyanatha Iyer at the turn of the twentieth century, including the *saṅgati* variations that he is believed to have added to the piece (figure 8). Other compositions to Lord Ganapati, remover of obstacles and blesser of all beginnings, may also begin a concert, although the choice is not limited to compositions to Ganapati (explanatory information is added in brackets):

> *Pallavi:*
> I praise the Ganapati from Vatapi,
> The elephant-faced giver of boons,
> *Anupallavi:*
> Whose feet are worshiped by ghosts and others,
> The support of the universe of living beings and spirits,
> Devoid of passion, to whom yogis bow down,
> Creator of the world, averter of obstacles,
> Worshiped by the sage of old [Agastya, sixth–seventh centuries], who was born in a pot,
> Residing in the middle of the [Tantric] triangle,
> *Caraṇam:*
> Worshiped greatly by Vishnu and others,
> Enshrined in the *mūlādhāra kṣetra* [in Tiruvarur],
> Having as its essence the embodiment of the four levels of speech, the highest and the others,
> Whose trunk is curved into the form of the sacred syllable *om,*
> Always having the crescent moon at his forehead,
> With the sugarcane staff held in his left hand,
> Who holds the pomegranate/citron noose-like in his lotus hand,
> Without blemish, shaped like a giant,
> Whose round form is pleasing to Shiva's son, *guruguha* [the composer's signature],
> Who is decorated by the raga named *hamsadhvani.*

After Maha Vaidyanatha Ayyar, other performers continued to develop their own *saṅgati* variations for the piece. Figure 8 provides examples of such variations on the first line of "Vātāpi gaṇapatim bhaje ham," as taught by K. R. Lakshmi at Madras University in 1977; these are for the most part distinct from Maha Vaidyanatha Ayyar's, for which notations attributed to him have been published (Sambamurthy 1967a:1–4, reprinted in Catlin 1980:302–305). Both sets exemplify the second type of *saṅgati* mentioned above, which develops the musical materials inherent in the raga as opposed to emphasizing important words in the text. In this

FIGURE 8 *Saṅgati* variations on the first line of "Vātāpi gaṇapatim bhaje ham," *kriti* by Muttusvami Diksitar in *hamsadhvani rāga, ādi tāḷa*, as taught by K. R. Lakshmi at Madras University, 1977. Transcribed by Amy Catlin.

example, *Vātāpi* is the word on which the melody is developed, although it refers merely to the name of the site where the statue was found. The variations follow the ideal model, proceeding gradually in a coherent manner from simple to complex, and from the lower to upper vocal range.

Diksitar's two younger brothers, Chinnasvami (1778–1823) and Balusvami (1786–1858), enjoyed a career as a singing duo, virtually originating the practice of *jōḍippaṭṭu*, 'paired soloists'. When Chinnasvami died, Balusvami conducted a pilgrimage and stopped in Ettayapuram, where the local king, captivated by his violin playing, appointed him court musician. Balusvami later adopted his brother's grandson Subbarama (1839–1906) and brought him to Ettayapuram for his education. Subbarama became one of India's greatest musicologists. The musicologist Chinnasvami Mudaliar, who published many compositions by the Trinity in Western staff notation, inspired much of Subbarama's early publication and work (Mudaliar 1892).

Subbarama Diksitar published the monumental seventeen-hundred-page opus entitled *Saṅgīta Sampradāya-Pradarśini* 'On the Music Tradition', which contains seventy-six biographies of musical figures from the time of Sarngadeva (thirteenth century) to his own contemporaries. The two-volume work encompasses information on performance practice, extensive notated music of Venkatamakhi, Ramasvami, and Muttusvami Diksitar, and over a hundred works by other composers, including himself.

Syama Sastri

Syama Sastri (1762–1827) was the son of a Brahmin priest whose ancestors had for centuries been associated with a golden statue of the goddess Kamakshi (figure 9).

FIGURE 9 Sri Syama Sastri. Painting by S. Rajam. Photo by Amy Catlin, 1977.

According to legend, attendants carrying the statue wandered throughout South India after the fall of Vijayanagar in 1565 seeking a permanent temple for the idol. They eventually enshrined the statue in the Tiruvarur temple in 1739, where it was housed until 1781, during which time Syama Sastri was born. In 1783, the Kamakshi Amman temple was built to house the statue, and Syama Sastri's father was granted an estate and landholdings. For this reason, Syama Sastri did not suffer the poverty to which the other two Trinity members subjected themselves, nor did he need to seek patronage from the court. As temple priest, Syama Sastri's father sang the liturgy following the ragas appropriate to the time of day; Syama Sastri performed the same function. His family did not encourage him to become a musician, as that was not the family profession. Furthermore, there was a certain stigma attached to professional musicianship: since Bharata's second century *Nāṭyaśāstra*, all performers had been classified Shudras, the lowest social class—a stigma that the achievements of the Trinity eventually lifted.

Like Tyagaraja, who first received musical knowledge from a visiting *sanyāsi* 'ascetic', and Diksitar, who first studied music for four years with a yogi-composer, Syama Sastri was first introduced to raga and tala by a visiting ascetic, who spent four months training him. Afterward, the swami returned to Banaras, advising his student to listen to the great Paccimiriyam Adiyappayya of the Tanjavur court, but not to study with him. At age eighteen, Syama Sastri thus became friends with the great composer and evidently learned a great deal from him.

Syama Sastri's compositions are the least well known of the Trinity's works, largely because he did not have many students, but also because they are rhythmically complex and difficult to perform. Only about forty of the three hundred compositions attributed to him have survived. Most are *kriti* with Telugu texts, but some are in Sanskrit and Tamil. He also composed a few *varṇam*, and the *svarajāti*, a didactic form that he perfected. One of the three *svarajāti* he composed contains eight *caraṇam*, each beginning on a successively higher note of the scale. Another has a dramatic *makuṭam* 'crown' of concluding rhythmic passages in five, seven, and nine beats. Syama Sastri also devised the *svara sahitya*, a compositional technique in which a composed *svara* section later reappears with text (Sambamurthy 1973a:144).

Syama Sastri's *kriti* compositions are notable for their highly rhythmic qualities and an individual melodic lyricism. The texts are largely in adoration of the Mother Goddess, including one set of nine compositions to the goddess Minakshi of Madurai. When Sastri sang them in front of the idol, according to legend, the goddess responded visibly, earning him temple honors. One piece in his *Navaratnamālikā* 'Garland of Nine Gems' is in the *vilōma cāpu* 'reverse seven-beat' *tāḷa,* which he was the first to use in compositions (figure 10). A translation of the Telugu text shows Syama Sastri's typically personal and emotional relationship with the goddess, as if she were his own mother (Catlin 1980: 208–209):

Pallavi:
Nannu brōvu lalita vēgamē cāla
Ninnu nera nammi unna vāḍa gadā
Anupallavi:
Ninnu vinā evaru unnāru gati janani
Ati vēgamē vachi
Caraṇam 1:
Parāku cēyakane vachi kripa salpa rādā
Mora vinā rādā
Parā sakti gīrvāna vandita
Padā nī bhaktuḍanu amma santatamunu

na– nnu brō– vu la– li– tā vē– ga– mē

FIGURE 10 "Nannu brōvu lalitā," *kriti* by Syama Sastri in *lalitha rāga, vilōma cāpu tāḷa.* Published in Vidya 1948:40; transcribed by Amy Catlin.

Caraṇam 4:
Sūmērū madhya nilaye
Syāma Krishna sodhare kaumarī
Ūmā Śrī Mīnākṣamma Śankari
Mahārājñi rakṣimba samayamide
Pallavi:
Oh Goddess Lalita, quickly protect me!
Am I not the one who remains completely faithful to you,
You who are the vine that grants all boons?
Anupallavi:
Oh Mother, I have no refuge apart from you.
Come quickly!
Caraṇam 1:
Can't you stop neglecting me and come show me your favor?
Can't you listen to my plaint?
Supreme Goddess, worshiped by learned persons,
Mother, I am always your devotee.
Caraṇam 4:
You who stay in the high mountains of the north,
The virgin sister of Lord Krishna,
Uma (Goddess of Dawn), Goddess Minakshi, Giver of Boons,
Protect me now, Great Queen.

Like the other Trinity members, Syama Sastri composed in both well-known ragas and rare ones. He is credited with perfecting the *ānandabhairavi rāga.* Syama Sastri composed in unusual and intricate talas, and indicated that some pieces may be performed in more than one tala.

Syama Sastri was a gifted performer, but like his colleagues in the Trinity he rarely performed outside his own religious environment. According to oral tradition passed on to the musicologist P. Sambamurthy from his own guru, one exception was a performance at the request of the Tanjavur maharaja. The renowned Andhra musician from the Bobbili court, Kesavayya, had challenged the musical primacy of the maharaja's realm. Syama Sastri agreed to defend the Tanjavur court's reputation by submitting to a musical contest. He won by repeating the challenger's *pallavi* in the 128-beat *simhananda tāḷa*, and then outdoing him with a *pallavi* in the *sārabhandananda tāḷa* of seventy-nine beats consisting of four cycles of nineteen and three-quarter beats (Sambamurthy 1962:95–101).

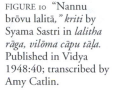

FIGURE 11 Maharaja Svati Tirunal. Painting by S. Rajam. Photo by Amy Catlin, 1977.

Svati Tirunal

Svati Tirunal (1813–1846), the maharaja of Travancore (in present-day Kerala), was a brilliant composer and patron of music whose vast accomplishments belie his short lifespan (figure 11). His stature is in many ways comparable to that of the Trinity composers. To his credit are approximately four hundred compositions, including two hundred Sanskrit *kriti* as well as twenty-three *varṇam*, sixty-seven *padam,* and six *tillānā* in various South Indian languages. He also composed thirty-eight works with Hindustani (combined Urdu and Hindi) texts in North Indian musical forms such as *dhrupad, khyāl, ṭappā, bhajana,* and *tarānā.* At his court, he patronized artists from all over India, including some fifty resident musicians, both Hindustani and

Regional stylistic qualities once differentiated Karnatak music in each of the four South Indian states and languages where it is performed.

Karnatak. Anglo-Indians provided English music, using portable organs and other "exotic" instruments. With the demise of the great patron of the Tanjavur court, King Sarabhoji, in 1832, many great musicians came from Tanjavur to Svati Tirunal's court. Among these was the yogi Merusvami, an adept in both Hindustani and Karnatak systems, who became Svati Tirunal's principal guru.

Svati Tirunal's *kriti* compositions are in two structural types, one with a *pallavi* section followed by two or more *caraṇam*, and a second type with *pallavi, anupallavi*, and three *caraṇam*. In the latter form, each *caraṇam* is rendered in a different speed, from slow tempo to medium (double) to fast (quadruple) tempo. The *kriti* contain many musical embellishments, such as the use of *citta svara* (composed solfège passages), *solkaṭṭu* (spoken drum syllables), and *svarākṣara* (double-meanings of *svara* names in the song texts). His *Navaratnamālikā* 'Garland of Nine Gems' song cycle contains nine *kriti*, each describing a different form of bhakti devotion. Another series of nine pieces is his *Navarātri Kīrtana* 'Nine Night Songs' celebrating each night of the Hindu Navrātrī festival with a different song. Formerly, singers performed these *kriti* to Sarasvati and Parvati in groups, but in modern times soloists have rendered them.

Tirunal's lyrics are regarded as highly sophisticated poetry: they usually identify the composer with the signature "Padmanabha," the name of his principal deity, an incarnation of Vishnu. Svati Tirunal addressed most of his compositions to Vishnu or his incarnations, such as Rama, Krishna, or Narasimha, in addition to Padmanabha. Other songs honor Shiva, Parvati, and other major deities, usually invoked to provide blessings to Padmanabha's followers. A scholarly debate continues over the authorship of compositions attributed to Svati Tirunal; some authors argue that his court musician, Vadivelu Pillai, composed at least some if not many of these works.

Svati Tirunal is credited with introducing Karnatak style into the music of Kerala, blending its elaborate techniques with the existing *sōpāna* style. *Sōpāna* was a minimally ornamented slow melodic style without *svara* singing, employed in compositions sung on the steps (*sōpāna*) leading up to the deity. After his death, Tirunal's successors at court returned to the more familiar compositions in *sōpāna* style and all but forgot his compositions. Since he did not train any disciples, his tradition survived only through his court musicians, especially the *nāgasvaram* masters. The publication of some notated Tirunal compositions beginning in 1916 accompanied a gradual revival of interest, and performances of his works have steadily increased since that time (Ayyar 1975).

PERFORMERS AND PERFORMANCE STYLE

Regional stylistic qualities once differentiated Karnatak music in each of the four South Indian states and language areas where it is performed. Karnatak music originated in Karnataka, was developed by Andhra musicians—from whom the compositional repertoire derives—and flourished principally in Tamil Nadu during the eighteenth and nineteenth centuries. These factors all contributed to its stylistic growth and diversity. Most distinctive stylistic traits related to particular lineages, schools, or traditions (*sampradāya*) handed down from teacher to disciple and often hailing from a former court center that patronized music. Today, each tradition emphasizes its own composers, compositions, and genres as well as certain stylistic traits. But since many performers nowadays study in more than one tradition or listen to other performers, cross-fertilization often occurs, and it has thus become very difficult to associate specific stylistic traits neatly with each region. Certainly the ornate, rigorous, and robust style of Tamil Nadu, largely the result of inheriting the Tanjavur court style, has influenced performance in the other regions. Yet the contrasting gentleness, simplicity, and individual freedom characteristic of other styles still exists among many Tamil artists. The Tamil Iśai Movement that began in the 1940s championed the cause of Tamil-language composition, causing a revival of many Tamil compositional genres such as *tevāram* hymns. Kerala retains some of its distinctiveness in rendering dance music and other musical genres unique to the region, especially the temple songs in *sōpāna* style such as the *aṣṭapadī* that have their own smoothly curving rather than ornamental melodic style. Some feel, however, that the unique Kerala flavor has nearly disappeared in concert music, including the *kriti* of their native prince, Svati Tirunal, in favor of the stylistic features imported from Tamil Nadu (Pattabhiraman 1994). Each region continues to foster composers who wrote in the local language, whether Kannada, Tamil, Telugu, or Malayalam.

Besides the many performance traditions, stylistic traits unique to an individual artist are referred to as that artist's *bāni* 'style'. These may eventually persist in succeeding generations and become integral to the artist's tradition. Many contemporary performers' unique individual styles have permanently influenced their musical descendants.

Several foreign artists have also become solo concert performers, including the late Jon Higgins, an American vocalist, and Ludwig Pesch, a German flutist. In general, the style of Karnatak music is most homogeneous in and around Madras, the most active center and prime inheritor of the Tanjavur style. But the Karnatak tradition is in a constant state of evolution, influenced by individual creativity and the effects of general cultural and social trends, while always retaining a strong allegiance to the past. It is this heritage, coupled with the conflicts and tensions between tradition and modernization, that gives the music some of its most interesting areas of discourse.

Vocal music

Karnatak singers use a unique method of vocal production in order to create the timbres that have aesthetic appeal in the tradition. Women sing in an unmixed chest voice with a high larynx, to produce a strong, focused tone capable of very rapid note passages. Men may adopt more flexibility in vocal timbre and may even employ a relaxed larynx, especially among lower voices, although higher voice types are sometimes criticized as "crooning." Head voice and falsetto are taboo in either gender. The microphone has become mandatory equipment for the Karnatak singer, and has had a significant effect on voice production in this century. Formerly, the finest voices were those that could project clearly in open settings; today, the microphone enables those with less forceful voices to be heard.

The enunciation and musical expression of texts is an important stylistic element for singers, since texted vocal compositions form the foundation of Karnatak music. In general, critics will never fault a singer for overclarity of text. Rather, the reverse is often the case, particularly when vocalists sing in a nonnative language—most typically when a Tamil-speaking vocalist sings in Telugu—since the majority of singers are Tamils, and Telugu remains the classical language for Karnatak music. Some illustrious vocalists today have distinctive personal styles, such as M. Balamurali Krishna, whose light and rounded voice has an enormous range and capacity for rapid passagework and ornamentation. The unmixed chest voice and sweet tone of M. S. Subbulakshmi is usually regarded as the ideal for women.

Most soloists in Karnatak music are vocalists, and Madras is the center where all singers and instrumentalists must "prove themselves." The Madras music scene is a highly competitive arena, since senior vocalists abound and relatively few occasions are open to young vocalists. Sometimes a singer will begin performing as an accompanist to a guru, singing in unison or at the octave or responding to designated phrases by singing invited passages alone, usually while strumming the *tambūrā* 'drone lute' in the background. There are many vocal duos, usually siblings of the same gender who share the roles of soloist and accompanist equally on stage. According to popular belief, this tradition, called *jōḍippaṭṭu*, began with two brothers of the composer Muttusvami Diksitar (see above). Tyagaraja also paired his disciples for learning and performing. Prominent sibling pairs include the twins B. V. Raman and B. V. Lakshmanan and the Bombay Sisters, C. Saroja and C. Lalitha. Such duos sing compositions simultaneously in unison, breaking occasionally into octaves, but take turns when improvising.

Instrumental music

There are two basic categories of instrumentalists: soloists and accompanists. Like vocal artists, players of melody instruments are normally soloists (with the exception of the violin, the standard melodic accompaniment), whereas percussionists are nearly always accompanists. Occasional "twins," or duos of soloists playing the same instrument, occur in various instrumental categories. Frequently, these players actually are siblings, such as the Sikkil Sisters, flutists; the Tiruppambaram Brothers, *nāgasvaram* artists; the A. K. C. Brothers (A. K. C. Natarajan), clarinetists; and various violin pairs. When a duo shares the stage, the two perform compositions in unison or octaves and also trade solo and accompanying roles.

Instrumental and/or vocal ensembles sometimes assemble to perform concerts of Karnatak compositions in unison. This tradition of *vādya vrinda* 'orchestra' and *gāyaka vrinda* 'chorus' is an ancient one, though it is rarely excercised in the twentieth century. At such concerts, musicians can improvise during solo interludes.

The vina is the most venerated instrument in Karnatak music; it is often called the *sarasvatī vīṇā* after the goddess of music, dance, and knowledge (figure 12). In recent years, however, it has attracted smaller audiences than singers or other instruments. Some stylistic developments in Tamil Nadu have revived its popularity, such as the use of the contact microphone pioneered by the brilliant vina player the late S. Balachander. This enabled him to prolong tones and produce ornaments (*gamaka*) of unusual duration after a single pluck of the string, which he characterized as the *gāyaki aṅg* 'vocal style'. And such importance is attached to vocal music that any instrumentalist who can evoke a vocal quality will inevitably receive praise. Balachander's personal playing style was virtuosic and aggressive as well as innovative. In contrast, another Tanjavur-style vina player, Tanjavur K. P. Sivanandam, has a gentle, pure style that adheres faithfully to tradition. Thus two musicians of the same performance tradition have vastly different personal styles. This can even occur among disciples of the same guru. Karnataka and Andhra Pradesh have produced numerous contemporary vina artists, particularly women; Kerala has produced relatively few.

Most vina players use wire plectra worn on the fingers of the right hand to increase the clarity of attack, giving a more metallic tone color. Some prefer a more

FIGURE 12 Karnatak ensemble at the South Indian Music Academy, Lakewood, California, c. 1990, with (*left to right*) Poovalur Srinivasan (*mridangam*), K. R. Subramaniam (flute), Geetha Ramanthan (vina), Santhi Ayyar (*tambūrā*), and Srikanth Venkatraman (violin). Photo courtesy Amy Catlin.

subtle attack and pluck only with the fingernails or with the fleshy fingertip, following the style of the venerated Vina Dhanammal. Many players use a contact microphone; others rely on normal microphones.

Today's primary exponent of the *goṭṭuvādyam*, a fretless "slide" vina with sympathetic strings, is Ravikiran, initially from Karnataka but raised in Madras, who renamed the instrument *citravīṇā* (figure 13). Performers usually play the instrument by stopping the strings with the left hand using a polished wooden, glass, or metal rod; Ravikiran uses Teflon. His smooth, melodious, sensitive style has made him very popular and caused something of a renewal of interest in this mellifluous instrument.

The stringed instrument most prevalent in Karnatak music today is the Western violin, but tuned to fifths and octaves rather than open fifths. Mysore Chowdiah devised a seven-stringed violin in which the upper three strings were doubled at the

FIGURE 13 Chitravina Ravikiran, with *citravīṇā* and Teflon *goṭṭu*. Photo by Mark Humphrey, 1994.

One recent arrival in Karnatak concerts is the mandolin, actually an adapted electric version of the mandolin with four double courses of strings.

lower octave, but other musicians did not adopt the instrument. L. Subramaniam plays a five-stringed violin that includes a lower viola-like register. His brother L. Shankar has created a double-necked electric violin with two separate sets of strings.

Violinists normally begin their careers as accompanists to solo artists and gradually work up to solo status. Even among Karnatak violinists who have achieved solo status, most continue to function as accompanists as well. Violin duos are frequent between father and child, between siblings, and between husband and wife, with an occasional violin trio appearing on stage.

One recent arrival in Karnatak concerts is the mandolin, actually an adapted electric version of the mandolin with four double courses of strings. Mandolin U. Srinivas of Andhra Pradesh was the originator of this instrument and has trained other performers. His brother Rajesh and his cousin U. P. Raju now also give solo concerts. Other stringed instruments that have acquired solo status include the viola (which also serves as accompaniment), the cello, and the *dilrubā*, a bowed North Indian relative of the *sāraṅgī*.

The flute (*vēṇu* or *kuḻal*) has long been a very popular Karnatak instrument. Its playing style has undergone a radical transformation in the twentieth century due to the influence of the late T. R. Mahalingam, known as "Mali" (d. 1985). His innovative style influenced a majority of today's South Indian flute players, particularly in Tamil Nadu and Karnataka, where he lived for many years. Mali introduced new lipping and fingering techniques, as well as a new preference for the lower register and a haunting ability to imitate the human voice. His musicianship was consummate, including mathematically precise rhythm. His use of silence was as eloquent as his mastery of timbre. His musical expressiveness evoked profound emotion in his listeners. He often planned entire concerts by selecting a passage of notes that would become transformed when played in different ragas and compositions.

The double-reed *nāgasvaram* retains its preeminence in ritual functions as the melody instrument of the sanctifying *periya mēḷam* 'big ensemble', and enjoyed some popularity a few years ago as a concert instrument. Music organizations have since sponsored very few concerts by *nāgasvaram* artists. The dearth of exceptional players equal to those of the previous generation may be the cause of this situation, or its result. One new *nāgasvaram* duo is remarkable in two ways: first, it is a husband-wife team (Sheik Mahaboob Shobani and Khalishabi Mahaboob), and women *nāgasvaram* players are a rarity; and second, they are Muslims. The vast majority of Karnatak musicians are Hindu, but a few Karnatak musicians are Christians, and one pocket of Muslim *nāgasvaram* and *tavil* players has existed in Andhra Pradesh for quite some time (Jairazbhoy 1980:151). *Nāgasvaram* and *tavil* players maintain a repertoire of compositions without texts called *mallāri*, which they play at the beginning of a procession in accelerating tempi, starting on different subdivisions of the beat (Terada 1992:104–105).

With regard to rarer aerophones, there are several soloists and duos on the clarinet, an instrument first adopted in the nineteenth century from European bands in India, as well as saxophonists and even professional whistlers. The harmonium, a hand-pumped reed organ brought to India by nineteenth-century missionaries, has also appeared occasionally in the Karnatak concert world, as well as its transistorized descendant, the electronic organ or Casio.

The *mridangam* is the principal rhythmic accompaniment for Karnatak music, a double-headed wooden barrel drum played with the bare hands and fingers. Other accompanying rhythmic instruments include the *ghaṭam* 'clay pot', the *kañjīrā* 'lizard-skin tambourine', and the *morsing* 'mouth harp'. Sometimes several rhythmic accompanists perform with a soloist; occasionally, percussion players perform an entire concert of both unison and solo compositions and improvisations normally reserved for the *tani āvartanam* 'percussion solo'.

REFERENCES

Aslesha, Ram. 1995. "The Mad, Mad, Madras Season: Supply-Demand Equation Worsens." *Śruti* 125 (February):25–28.

Ayyar, S. Venkita Subramonia. 1975. *Swati Tirunal and His Music*. Trivandrum: College Book House.

Brown, Robert E. 1965. "The Mrdanga: A Study of Drumming in South India." 2 vols. Ph.D. dissertation, University of California at Los Angeles.

Catlin, Amy. 1980. "Variability and Change in Three Karṇāṭak Kritis: A Study of South Indian Classical Music." Ph.D. dissertation, Brown University.

———. 1985. "Pallavi and Kriti of Karnatak Music: Evolutionary Processes and Survival Strategies." *National Centre for the Performing Arts Journal* 14(1):26–44.

———. 1991. "'Vatapi Ganapatim': Sculptural, Poetic, and Musical Texts in a Hymn to Ganesa." In *Ganesh: Studies of an Asian God*, ed. Robert L. Brown, 141–169. Albany: State University of New York Press.

Diksitar, Subbarama. 1963–1983 [1904]. *Sangīta Sampradāya Pradarṣiṇi*. 5 vols. Madras: The Music Academy.

Jackson, William J. 1991. *Tyagaraja: Life and Lyrics*. Madras: Oxford University Press.

———. 1994. *Tyāgarāja and the Renewal of Tradition: Translations and Reflections*. New Delhi: Motilal Banarsidass.

Jairazbhoy, Nazir A. 1980. "The South Asian Oboe Reconsidered." *Ethnomusicology* 24(1):147–156.

———. 1997. *Karnatak Music of Andhra*. Voleti Venkatesvarlu, voice; R. Subba Rao, vina; K. Kannan, flute; Anavarupu Gopalam, *mridangam, morsing*; Yella Venkatesvara Rao, *mridangam*; N. C. H. Krishnamacharyulu, violin; D. Pandurangaraju, violin; A. Gopalan, *ghaṭam*. Van Nuys, Calif.: Apsara Media for Intercultural Education. Audio cassette.

Kuppuswamy, Gowri, and M. Hariharan. 1981. *Index of Songs in South Indian Music*. Delhi: B. R. Publishing Corporation.

———. 1986. "A New Theory on the Kudumiyamalai Inscription." In *Kudumiyamalai Inscription in Music*, ed. V. Premlatha, 63–69. Madurai: n.p.

Lieberman, Fredric, and Amy Catlin. 1994. *South Indian Classical Music House Concert with M. D. Ramanathan, vocalist, T. N. Krishnan, violin, and Umayalpuram Sivaraman, mridangam*. Van Nuys, Calif.: Apsara Media for Intercultural Education. Video cassette.

Mudaliar, A. M. Chinnaswami. 1892–1893. *Oriental Music in European Notation*. Madras: Ave Maria Press. Reprinted, ed. P. Sambamurthy. Madras: Tamil Nadu Eyal Isai Nataka Manram, n.d.

Pattabhiraman, N. 1994. "Carnatic Music During the Decade: How It Was Ten Years Ago." *Śruti* 125 (July):21–37 (excerpted from the original six-part series in *Śruti* 3, December 1983).

Pattabhiraman, N., T. T. Narendran, and Jayalakshmi Balakrishnan. 1983–1984. "Carnatic Music Today," 6-part series. *Śruti* 3 (part 1: Dec. 1983), 4 (part 2: Jan.–Feb. 1984), 7 (part 3: May 1984), 8, 9, 10 (part 4: June–Aug. 1984), 11 (part 5: Sept. 1984), N/A (part 6: n.d.).

Nijenhuis, Emmie te. 1974. *Indian Music: History and Structure*. Leiden: E. J. Brill.

Raghavan, V., ed. 1975. *Muttuswami Dikshitar*. Bombay: *National Centre for the Performing Arts Quarterly Journal* [special September issue].

Raghavan, V., and C. Ramanujacari. 1981. *The Spiritual Heritage of Tyāgarāja*. Madras: Sri Ramakrishna Math.

Rajagopalan, N. 1990. *A Garland (Biographical Dictionary of Carnatic Composers and Musicians)*. Bombay: Bharatiya Vidya Bhavan.

Sambamurthy, P. 1952–1971. *A Dictionary of South Indian Music and Musicians*. 3 vols. Madras: Indian Music Publishing House.

———. 1962–1970. *Great Composers*. 2 vols. Madras: Indian Music Publishing House.

———. 1967a. *Kīrtana Sāgaram*, vol. 4, 2nd rev. enl. ed. Madras: Indian Publishing House.

———. 1967b. *The Flute*. Madras: Indian Music Publishing House.

———. 1973a. *South Indian Music*, book 3. Madras: Indian Music Publishing House.

———. 1973b. "Kudumiyamalai Inscription." *Bulletin of the Institute of Traditional Cultures*, 85–91.

———. 1975. *South Indian Music*, book 6. Madras: Indian Music Publishing House.

Sastri, S. Subrahmanya, ed. 1937. *The Mela-Raga-Malika of Maha Vaidyanatha Sivan* (Iyer). Adyar: The Adyar Library.

Śruti: South Indian Classical Music and Dance Monthly. Madras: P. N. Sundaresan.

Terada, Yoshitaka. 1992. "Musical Interpretations of a Charismatic Individual: The Case of the Great *Nagasvaram* Musician, T. N. Rajarattinam Pillai." Ph.D. dissertation, Wesleyan University.

Vidya, S. 1948. *Kritis of Syama Sastri*, vol. 3. Madras: C. S. Iyer.

Viswanathan, Tanjore. 1974. "Raga Alapana in South Indian Music." Ph.D. dissertation, Wesleyan University.

Who's Who of Indian Musicians. 1968. New Delhi: Sangeet Natak Akademi.

Widdess, Richard. 1979. "The Kuḍumiyāmalai Inscription: A Source of Early Indian Music in Notation." *Musica Asiatica* 2:115–150.

———. 1995. *The Ragas of Early Indian Music: Modes, Melodies, and Musical Notations from the Gupta Period to c. 1250*. Oxford: Clarendon Press; New York: Oxford University Press.

Music in Religion and Ritual

Religion may be considered the basis of most music and dance in South Asia. Artists typically perform to honor deities, saints, spirits, and other religious beings, whether or not the context is specifically religious. The most important life-cycle rituals, celebrating births, marriages, and deaths, incorporate singing or chanting. Seasonal festivals typically include vocal and instrumental performance, and often dance as well.

All the world's major religions are to be found here: Hindus form the majority in India and Nepal, as do Muslims in Afghanistan, Pakistan, and Bangladesh, and Buddhists in Bhutan and Sri Lanka. Christians, Sikhs, Jains, and others live as significant minorities in specific regions of the subcontinent. For most of these religious groups, music is essential to worship, and Hindus, Buddhists, Jains, Sikhs, Sufis, and Christians all have their own forms of devotional singing. Among Muslims and Vedic priests, chanting is a supreme mode of expression. Tribal groups respect and honor ancestors through song. In all South Asian religious and ritual contexts, music and chant function above all to increase spiritual awareness; in some, their powers move beyond spiritual awakening to create ecstatic states of trance.

Parmar Khorabai Baghubhai, a Saurashtran bhajan singer, accompanies himself on the *rāmsāgar* drone lute, together with (*left*, barely visible) *ḍholak* drum and (*right*) *mañjīrā* finger-cymbal players. Rajkot, Gujarat, 1996. Photo by Amy Catlin.

Vedic Chant

Wayne Howard

The Four Vedas and Their Milieu
Transmission and Memorization
The Recited Vedas
The Sāmaveda

THE FOUR VEDAS AND THEIR MILIEU

The four Vedas—Ṛgveda, Yajurveda, Sāmaveda, Atharvaveda—are the canonical religious and cultural texts of the light-skinned Aryans (Indo-European-speaking people from the Iranian plateau) who arrived in the Indian subcontinent from the northwest around 1800 B.C. These four canonical collections comprise the earliest Hindu sacred writings. The oldest Vedic text, the Ṛgveda (*veda* 'knowledge') is a compilation of 1,028 metrical hymns encompassing 10,462 verses in praise of the early Hindu gods. It was first compiled in what is now Pakistan, though many of the events described in it occurred farther west, in such places as Bactria, in northeast Afghanistan (Parpola 1988). The Yajurveda is a collection of sacrificial formulas and prayers in two formats—with and without prose commentary. The Sāmaveda is a collection of verses, most of them also occurring in the Ṛgveda, and hundreds of chants utilizing these verses as textual sources. The Atharvaveda is essentially a book of magical formulas and spells (Renou 1971).

On arriving in northwest India, the Vedic Aryans came into conflict with a darker-skinned people variously called Dāsa, Dasyu, and Paṇi in the Ṛgveda. The Dāsas were Aryans who had entered the subcontinent around 2000 B.C., also from the northwest, and had interbred with the indigenous (probably Dravidian) people of the Harappan civilization in the Indus Valley. Over time, the Dāsas and the Vedic Aryans intermarried, and their religions became amalgamated. The Dāsa gods Varuna and Rudra, for example, were adopted as Vedic deities, and Dravidian words made their way into the Vedic lexicon.

The *agnicayana* rite and the Sāmaveda

As the Vedic Aryans spread eastward, additional acculturations occurred. The Aryans adopted the large Dravidian fire-containing altar in the shape of a bird with outstretched wings, which became the centerpiece of the rite known as *agnicayana* 'the piling [of bricks for an altar] of fire'. The altar had five layers of bricks, each layer forming a mosaic. On its completion, at preordained sites around it, priests sang selected hymns from the Sāmaveda, the musical Veda consisting of thousands of notated melodies. The Sāmavedic chants are miniature musical mosaics, consisting of standard phrases from a pool of three hundred or more. Howard (1977:115–124, 289–362) suggests that this Veda had its origin in pre-Vedic times, and that each brick of the altar may have been laid down to the accompaniment of one of these formulas. If this conjecture is true, then the Sāmaveda is musically the oldest Veda, its components dating back to Harappan civilization. The melodies or melodic fragments were eventually adapted to the texts of the Ṛgveda; only seventy-five verses of the Sāmaveda cannot be traced back to the Ṛgveda.

Music of soma *sacrifices*

The *agnicayana* was an independent ritual that could be solemnized with *soma*. In this ritual, priests presented gifts in honor of Vedic deities, chief among them being *soma*, which the priests poured into the fire (*agni*). Certain rewards, including prosperity, male offspring, or abundance of cattle, were believed to accrue from performing a Vedic ritual, and *soma* sacrifices were considered the most efficacious religious acts of the Vedic Aryans (Renou 1971:104–112).

Soma is the intoxicating liquid obtained by pressing the stalks of the *soma* plant. During the sacrifices, the priests and Vedic gods consume this liquid. *Soma* sacrifices are perhaps the world's most complex rituals; during them, the recitations and chants appear in secret forms known only to certain qualified priests. For instance, the Sāmaveda chants occur in large combinations of chants (*stotra)*, some of which make great use of the *gāyatra* melody, the most sacred chant of the Sāmaveda (Howard 1987). In some combinations of these, the words of the central portion of the *gāyatra* are replaced by *ō* vowels, representing the sacred syllable *ōm*. Originally an affirmative particle of pre-Vedic (Dravidian) origin, this sacred syllable later, in the Upanishads, came to symbolize god almighty, the supreme power and mystery. This unexpressed chant (*aniruktagāna*) occurs in other combinations.

The *soma* cult, with other Vedic Aryan customs, eventually spread over the entire subcontinent. The earliest Vedic traditions in South India, including those of the Nambudiri Vedic priests in Kerala (who preserve some of the oldest forms of Vedic recitation and chant), came from Uttar Pradesh, and traveled southward through Madhya Pradesh and along the west coast.

TRANSMISSION AND MEMORIZATION

Members of the highest, priestly caste of Hindus, called Brahmins, teach the Vedas. Every Brahmin follows one Vedic tradition, and belongs to the school of his Veda, though in India, Brahmins commonly master two, or indeed all four Vedas. They memorize the sacred words and transmit them orally along with the Vedic accents (symbolized by the notation found in Sanskrit manuscripts) from father to son or from teacher to pupil, as priests have passed them down for millennia. Errors in recitation are strenuously avoided, as they are thought to bring catastrophe.

Pandits (learned Brahmins) have evolved a system of checks and balances to insure that not even the smallest element of recitation is lost or contaminated. Many reciters have the ability to declaim lengthy texts according to various mnemonic formulas (*vikṛti*) that specify changes of both spelling and accent. In a practical representation of the traditional eight mnemonic patterns, lowercase letters (*a, b, c,* and so on) symbolize each word of a verse, a slash (/) separates groupings of words, a double slash (//) indicates endings of verses, and the particle *iti* 'thus' marks the final word of a verse or half-verse. Each pattern has a name (Howard 1986:121–151):

TRACK 9

1. *jaṭā* 'braid': abbaab / bccbbc / cddccd / deedde / and so on. Two words of a verse entwine, just as two strands of hair entwine to form a tress.

2. *mālā* 'garland'. This pattern has two forms:
   a. *kramamālā* 'ordered garland': ab / h *iti* h / bc / hg / cd / gf . . . / fg / dc / gh / cb / h *iti* h / ba //. Forward movement from the beginning of each half-verse in two-word groups alternates with backward movement from the end of the half-verse, with each two-word group presented in reverse order.
   b. *puṣpamālā* 'garland of flowers': ab / ba / ab / bc / cb / bc / cd / dc / cd / and so on. The two-word units entwine, just as a garland is constructed by a process involving reversal of entwined stems.
3. *śikhā* 'topknot': abbaabc / bccbbcd / cddccde / and so on. This is the same as the *jaṭā* pattern, with an additional word in each grouping, just as the hair is bound and encircles the top of the head, with the end of one strand left over after each circle.
4. *rekhā* 'row': ab / ba / ab / bcd / dcb / bc / cd / defg / gfed / and so on. The words are deposited in a series of straight lines.
5. *dhvaja* 'flag': ab /p *iti* p / bc / op / cd / no / . . . / op / bc / p *iti* p / ab //. This resembles *kramamālā,* except that the two-word groups are not reversed in the backward movement, and the pattern consists of movement from the beginning and end of the verse, not the half-verse.
6. *daṇḍa* 'staff': ab / ba / ab / bc / cba / ab / bc / cd / dcba / . . . / ab / bc / cd / de / ef / fg / gh / hi / ihgfedcba. This pattern takes shape little by little, until the completed scheme (all the words of the verse in reverse order) is presented, just as a staff emerges slowly as a piece of wood is whittled away.
7. *ratha* 'chariot': ab / ef / ij / mn / ba / fe / ji / nm / . . . / dcba / hgfe / lkji / ponm / and so on. The four quarter-verses—more or less equal divisions of a complete verse—are analogous to the four wheels of a chariot: each quarter-verse takes shape according to the *daṇḍa* pattern.
8. *ghana* 'bell': abbaabccbaabc / bccbbcddcbbcd / cddccdeedccde / and so on. Each group of three words is treated as one rings a bell, by swinging it to and fro.

One of the most frequently performed patterns, though not one of the eight *vikṛti*, is the *krama* 'progression', which has the form ab / bc / cd / de /, and so on. A pandit who has mastered the bell, the braid, and the progression is called *ghanapāṭhī.*

THE RECITED VEDAS

Notation for the recited Vedas exists in Sanskrit manuscripts housed in archives and libraries in India and elsewhere. The India Office Library in London, for example, houses manuscripts containing Vedic notation that were collected by A. C. Burnell. Precisely when these were written down or by whom is not known, but printed editions of Vedic notation have appeared in the twentieth century, such as the Sāmavedic chants performed at Vedic sacrifices (Ramanatha Dikshita 1969) and those sung outside the sacrificial arena (Narayanaswami 1958).

Traditional notation for the recited Vedas consists of the Vedic texts with accent marks that indicate how to recite syllables. The principal accent is raised (*udātta*) and has no written mark. The accent that normally precedes the raised accent is not raised (*anudātta*); a horizontal line below the syllable designates this accent. The sounded (*svarita*) accent is transitional, marking the shift from a raised accent to an unraised or to a multitude (*pracaya*) of accentless syllables. A vertical line above a syllable indicates the sounded accent, but the multitude has no sign. Notation for the opening verse of the Ṛgveda illustrates the four accents, symbolized by their first letter.

| | | |

agnim īḷe purohitam yajñasya devam ṛtvijam /
A U SP AUSP A U S AU AUS

| |

hotāram ratnadhātamam //
USP P A US P

I praise Agni, put at the head of sacrificial worship, god, priest,
hotṛ, distributing great riches.

This mantra likens the Vedic fire god, Agni, to the chief Ṛgveda priest of the Vedic sacrifices, the *hotṛ*.

Since the meaning of *udātta* is "raised," one might expect this accent to be sung to a high pitch. However, in an analysis of Ṛgvedic hymns sung by Brahmins with ancestral roots in the western Indian state of Maharashtra, it was found that more than 70 percent of "raised" accents were sung on a middle pitch, not a high one (Howard 1986:30–92). Also contrary to expectations, 59 percent of unraised accents were sung to a high pitch, not a low one.

Nambudiri recitation

In 1961, the Vedic scholar J. F. Staal claimed that the Nambudiri Brahmins of Kerala in southwest India preserved certain recitations in which they sang a high tone for the raised accent (Staal 1961). This assertion contradicted the tradition of Brahmins in Maharashtra and other parts of India, who recite the *udātta* on a middle pitch. The Nambudiri described their recitation with the high-pitch *udātta* as having
TRACK 9 *jaṭāmātrā*, the temporal values (*mātrā*) of their braid pattern (*jaṭā*). Scholars visited a Ṛgvedic seminary in Trichur, Kerala, to test this theory. They found that reciters produced the highest tone not only for the raised accent, but for all four accents, and thus did not distinguish them by pitch. This trait proved that the Nambudiri have not preserved the high-pitch *udātta* but have their own manner of reciting the braid pattern. These Kerala Brahmins also have a manner of performance different from the usual solo-reciter format common elsewhere, with two male singers facing each other and partially concealing their faces with their hands (figure 1).

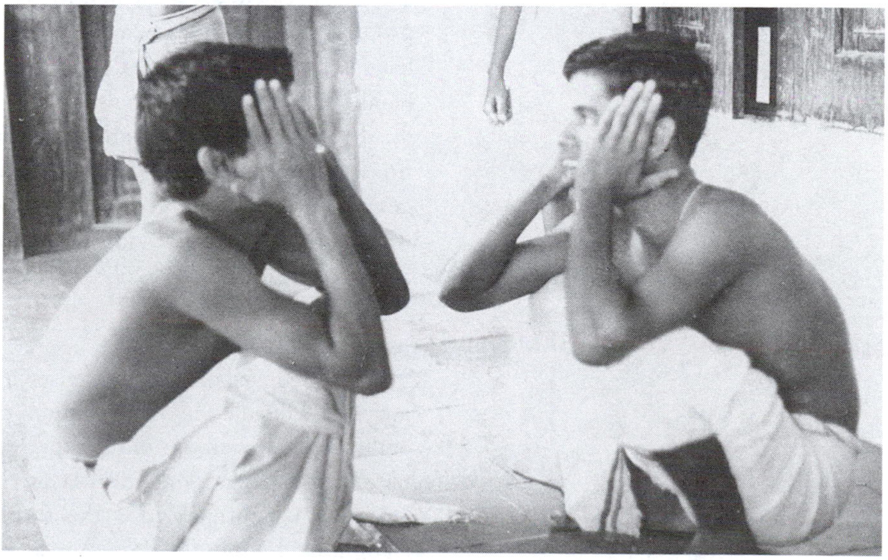

FIGURE 1 Nambudiri Brahmins in Trichur, Kerala, recite the Ṛgveda with specific rhythms (*jaṭāmātrā*), 1971. Photo by Wayne Howard.

The chanted Veda, the Sāmaveda, contains probably the world's oldest notated melodies.

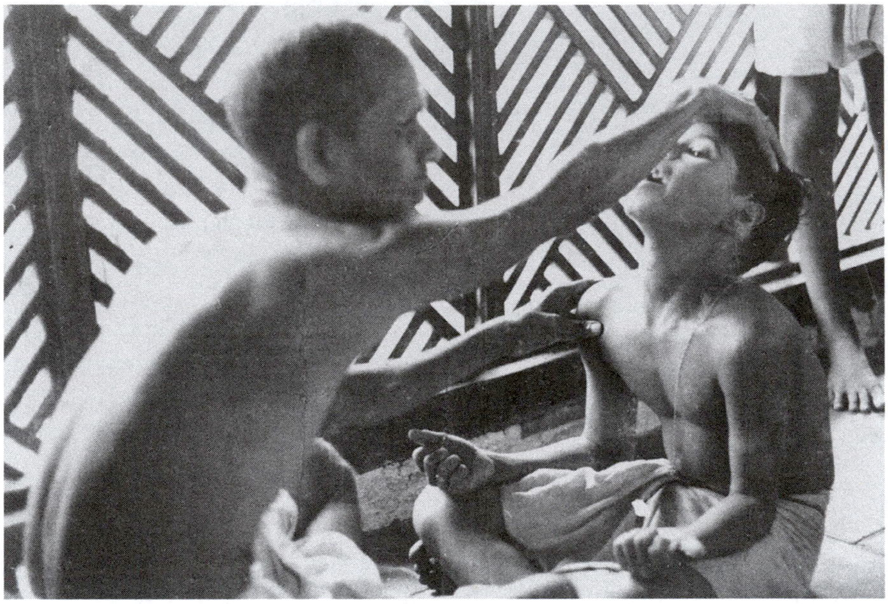

FIGURE 2 By pushing a student's head backward, a Nambudiri Brahmin tutor teaches the raised accent (*udātta*) in Nambudiri Ṛgvedic recitation. Trichur, Kerala, 1971. Photo by Wayne Howard.

Ṛgvedic positions of the hands

When Vedic reciters sing, they make hand gestures (*mudrā*) that coincide with the vocal accent patterns. The Nambudiri teacher emphasizes the accents to his pupil by pushing the student's head up for the raised accent (figure 2), down for the unraised accent, and sideways for the transitional sounded accent. The Nambudiris use a high-position hand gesture when reciting a middle-pitch *udātta*. The four gestures are: hand up for the raised accent (*udātta*), hand down for the unraised accent (*anudātta*), hand to the right for the transitional sounded accent (*svarita*), and hand to the left for the "multitude" of accentless syllables (*pracaya*). Not one of the Ṛgvedic recitations still practiced makes use of a high-pitched raised accent except under special circumstances (as in Nambudiri *jaṭāmātrā*). This situation raises the question whether in normal conditions the *udātta*, the principal accent, has ever been sung to a high pitch (Howard 1982:27–92; 1986:93–109).

THE SĀMAVEDA

The chanted Veda, the Sāmaveda, contains probably the world's oldest notated melodies. Like the Ṛgvedic recitation, the Sāmavedic chants have been passed down orally to the present day though they are also preserved in manuscript form. This is not to say that all styles of Sāmavedic chanting—of which there are a dozen or so—are of equal antiquity. Of the three existing schools of Sāmavedic chanting (Jaiminīya, Kauthuma, Rāṇāyanīya), the Jaiminīya preserves the oldest tradition.

Within any school are communities of Brahmins whose traditions have older origins than those of other communities.

A case study: The village of Puthucode

Some four hundred years ago in the village of Puthucode in Palghat District, Kerala, Nambudiri Brahmins of the Jaiminīya school served the raja (Rajagopalan and Howard 1989). But an instance of alleged impropriety on the ruler's part angered the Nambudiris, causing them to leave the raja's service. One of the raja's ministers assured his master that he could bring Brahmins of equal or greater learning from the Tanjore district of Tamil Nadu. The minister traveled there and brought back several Brahmins, for whom he built houses and temples in the Tamil style. Among the immigrants were Sāmavedic scholars belonging to the Kauthuma school, who settled in Puthucode and other villages.

Until the late 1940s, Palghat had schools teaching both Sāmaveda and Yajurveda, and a college for the study of Sanskrit. During the Great Depression of the 1930s, finding jobs as priests became increasingly difficult for Vedic pandits, and they began encouraging their children to enter other professions. The Vedic schools closed, and the Sanskrit College became an ordinary school. Vedic learning had already started to decline under British rule in the 1800s. The rajas' support of Vedic studies had stopped when the British took over Palghat and pensioned off its rulers. Vedic scholars then had to depend on local landlords' patronage, and performances of Vedic rituals in which the Sāmaveda plays an important part virtually ceased. Since domestic rituals could be conducted by priests who knew only representative chants, Sāmavedic chanting declined even more. Barring two or three old people, no priests now follow this old style perfectly, for corruptions have crept into their chant. Some Sāmavedic pandits in Palghat even began sending their sons back to Tanjore District to learn Rāmaṇṇa, a style of chanting that began there some two hundred fifty years ago.

The *Rāmaṇṇa* style of chanting

The famous eighteenth-century Sāmavedic scholar Ramanatha Srauti, affectionately called Rāmaṇṇa, originated a style of chanting based on the Puthucode style, but more melodic. His style gradually spread throughout Tanjore and adjoining districts, as the rulers of Tanjore approved its teaching only in the Vedic schools. Today, this style is the strongest Sāmavedic tradition in India, practiced throughout South India and as far north as Banaras.

Numerical notation

Rāmaṇṇa-style chanters use a numerical notation peculiar to the Kauthuma school (Howard 1977:29–75), though it is also followed by some Rāṇāyanīyas. This system uses five basic numbers, 1 through 5, to denote the thumb and fingers of the right hand. Numbers 6, 7, and 11 occasionally appear, and may be later additions to the notation: the number 7, for instance, is a symbol for 2 followed by 1 on the same syllable. The numbers designate the hand gestures (*mudrā*) that all Sāmavedic chanters use as they chant, not the tones of a scale. The gestures in turn represent the melodic motifs and phrases that make up the chant. The five basic hand gestures, different and distinct from the Ṛgvedic gestures, are as follows:

1. The thumb (the first finger) is held above the forefinger (index finger).
2. The thumb touches the middle joint of the forefinger.
3. The thumb touches the middle joint of the middle finger.
4. The thumb touches the middle joint of the ring finger.
5. The thumb touches the middle joint of the little finger.

The thumb is "high," and the little finger "low," because of the manner in which the singer sits: his legs are crossed, and his right hand rests, thumb uppermost, on his right knee. Hand gesture 2, however, does not necessarily signify a motif, tone, or phrase higher than gesture 3. (A circumflex placed above a number calls for special hand gestures not found in the foregoing list.)

The actual musical interpretation of a chant depends on several factors, including the arrangement of numbers and the length of vowels. In Kauthuma numerical notation, the numbers placed above and within the text lines symbolize the hand gestures. Numbers within the text line mark specific melodic motifs or phrases that the chanter must intone at that point, motifs that the numbers written above the text line cannot designate. Numbers within the text line belong to the syllable they follow and usually call for longer, more ornate motifs than superscript numbers. When notated in the text, a number may or may not increase the temporal unit of the preceding syllable (Howard 1988:17–42). The letter *r* placed over some syllables with long vowels indicates that these are long syllables, with a temporal value of two units. Long syllables without a superscript *r*, called prolated or augmented, have three units. Short syllables have only one.

Melodic adaptations of words

One of the most striking features of the Sāmavedic chants is the change that the words undergo when adapted to melody. The twentieth chant of the Sāmaveda, based on a verse in praise of Agni, illustrates this. The example below presents the text, its form when recited melodically, and an English translation. The recited form modifies all the words of the chant except the first: the second word, *te,* becomes *tau*; the third word, *agna*, becomes *hognāi*; and so on. The recited form includes extraneous material (*stobha*) inserted between two consecutive words or even between the syllables of one word, as in the addition of *au ho vā* in the ninth word.

namas te agna ojase gṛṇanti deva kṛṣṭayaḥ /
amair amitram ardaya

4 5 r 4 5 1 2 1 3 5 1 7
namas tau / hognāi / ojasā3̂i / gṛṇā2̂ntā234i de / vā kṛṣṭayā2̄ḥ /

1 2 1 3 5r r 2 31111
amāye3̂ḥ / ā2̂mā234 au ho vā / tram ardâyā2345 //

For strength, O Agni, god, men sing songs of adoration to you:
through terror, scatter the enemy.

In the recited version, the slashes demarcate the sections of the chant, showing not only where the reciter should take a breath, but also where one standard phrase ends and another begins. About three hundred of these melodic formulas exist; to form several thousand chants, they undergo various combinations and permutations.

Figure 3 presents a transcription of a performance of the twentieth chant of the Sāmaveda in Rāmaṇṇa style by a member of the Kauthuma school. The numerical notation appears beneath the text. One temporal unit is equivalent to a sixteenth note, though timekeeping in the Sāmavedic chants is relative: one unit may have a certain duration on one syllable and be shorter or longer on a different syllable (Rowell 1977). The comma in the musical notation is equivalent to the slash in the text line, which indicates separate word groupings.

FIGURE 3 The twentieth chant of the Sāmaveda, as sung in the Rāmaṇṇa style by Sri Sesadri Sastrigal of Madras, 1971. Transcription by Wayne Howard.

REFERENCES

Howard, Wayne. 1977. *Sāmavedic Chant.* New Haven and London: Yale University Press.

———. 1982. "Music and Accentuation in Vedic Literature." *The World of Music* 24(3):23–34.

———. 1986. *Veda Recitation in Vārāṇasī.* Delhi: Motilal Banarsidass.

———. 1987. "The Body of the Bodiless Gāyatra." *Indo-Iranian Journal* 30:161–173.

———, ed. 1988. *Mātrālakṣaṇam: Text, Translation, Extracts from the Commentary, and Notes, Including References to Two Oral Traditions of South India.* New Delhi: Indira Gandhi National Centre for the Arts; Delhi: Motilal Banarsidass.

Narayanaswami, R., ed. 1958. *Grāmageyagāna—Ārangakagāna* (Village Chant Book—Forest Chant Book). Pardi: Svadhyayamandala. [Sāmaveda melodies]

Parpola, Asko. 1988. "The Coming of the Aryans to Iran and India and the Cultural and Ethnic Identity of the Dāsas." *Studia Orientalia* 64:195–302.

Rajagopalan, L. S., and Wayne Howard. 1989. "A Report on the Prācheena Kauthuma Sāmaveda of Palghat." *Journal of the Indian Musicological Society* 20(1–2):5–16.

Ramanatha Dikshita, A. N., ed. 1969. *Ūhagānam—Ūhyagānam* (Modified Chant Book—Modified Secret Chant Book). Varanasi: Banaras Hindu University Press. [Sāmaveda melodies]

Renou, Louis. 1971. *Vedic India,* trans. Philip Spratt. Delhi: Indological Book House.

Rowell, Lewis. 1977. "Abhinavagupta, Augustine, Time and Music." *Journal of the Indian Musicological Society* 13(2):18–36.

Staal, J. Fritz. 1961. *Nambudiri Veda Recitation.* The Hague: Mouton.

Religious and Devotional Music: Northern Area

Guy Beck

Hindu Music
Islamic Music
Sikh Music
Buddhist Music
Christian Music

In India, the performance of music (*sangīt*) has nearly always been associated with divine experience, beginning with chants uttered by the seers and sages of Vedic times (c. 4000–600 B.C.). Thus most Indian music is religious in content or function. Even the classical music traditions—the refined, frequently nonsectarian ensemble music of the sovereign courts, produced by settled, professional, highly skilled musicians—had their roots in devotional music. The development of classical music often followed its own course, shaped by the preferences of patrons, individual artistry and improvisation, and even foreign influences. Purely religious music, in contrast, was always more conservative, with great attention given to preserving established liturgical patterns within specific devotional lineages. But just as church music laid the groundwork for the evolving classical tradition in the West, so in India the religious music of the various bhakti or devotional movements, along with the musical styles inherited from the ancient period, provided raw materials for the polished classical music heard today, both the northern Hindustani and southern Karnatak traditions. Karnatak music emerged from the devotional songs and hymns of the great Vaishnavite and Shaivite saints performed in the temples and shrines of Vijayanagar, Tanjavur, Srirangam, Tirupati, and Cidambaram. What became known in succeeding centuries as Hindustani classical music developed primarily from the temple vocal form known as *dhrupad* and from the elaborate bhajan music performed by Vaishnavite singers in the northern region of Braj.

This survey identifies the most important and enduring forms of Hindu music in northern areas of India. Although some of these types of music have indeed become popular today—even commercial successes—in modified form, this article emphasizes those traditions that have remained within religious or ritualistic contexts. Short summaries of the devotional music of Indian Islam, Sikhism, Buddhism, and Christianity follow.

HINDU MUSIC

The performance of Hindu religious music in India is rooted in theoretical principles related to the notion of sacred sound in the Hindu tradition. The ancient and sacred scriptures of the Vedas and Upanishads (c. third to first millenium B.C.) are said to have been heard by sages in trance and to embody the eternal primeval sound that brought about the creation of the cosmos; the Supreme Absolute of the universe, Brahman, is accordingly composed of this elemental sound, known as Śabda-Brahman. Yet sacred sound was even more often identified as Nāda-Brahman, or causal sound, in Sanskrit musicological treatises and by advanced yogis and saintly musicians. Singers of Indian music today, whether Hindu or Muslim, generally acknowledge Nāda-Brahman as the underlying foundation of all musical sound (Beck 1993). Music is closely associated as well with the Hindu gods themselves, for example, with the goddess Sarasvati, who plays the vina; with Krishna, who plays the flute; and with Shiva, who plays a drum during the phase of cosmic creation.

Hindu religious and devotional music reflects a basic aesthetic principle, namely, the Upanishadic notion that Brahman, the Supreme Truth, is full of bliss and emotional taste or pleasure (*rasa*). God as supreme deity—whether Vishnu, Shiva, or Shakti—is taken to be the fountainhead and source of all pleasure, and according to some of the traditions, extremely fond of music. If the music is dedicated in the spirit of bhakti, or love of God, the musician or devotee is said to gain the association of God. The emotional experience of both singers and listeners may vary according to the melody and the lyrics but certainly brings about a sense of communal harmony: thus the great attention given to preserving the different musical repertoires.

The most popular Hindu deities are believed to have touched down on northern ground when they appeared on earth, specifically in the modern state of Uttar Pradesh. Braj, a region south of New Delhi that includes Vrindaban and Mathura, is the place where Krishna was born and spent his youth. Ayodhya, a city to the northeast, is where Rama took birth; from it he ruled India (Bhārata) for many years. Shiva, having lived in the Himalayas, settled down in Banaras, near the bank of the Ganges River. All these locales became in time particular focal points where devotional music was seriously cultivated for purposes of sectarian definition and continuity.

The main lineages

The Gauḍīya and Vallabha sectarian lineages (*sampradāya*) are the most influential and widespread movements associated with the worship of Krishna, each having contributed to the spread of Vaishnav devotional music from their start in Bengal and Braj, respectively, to the whole of India and even abroad. There are several other important Krishna lineages, also found within the Braj area. Based in Ayodhya, the Ramanandi order worships Rama and has promulgated Rama bhajans in various styles. Devotional songs in honor of Shiva have been especially prominent in Banaras, home of the most important temple of Shiva in the form of Vishvanatha; the *bheṇṭ,* a category of devotional songs to the Mother Goddess (Kali, Durga, Vaishno Devi), has a panregional circulation.

These sacred locations are all in Hindi-speaking areas; thus the most common language of northern devotional music is Hindi, and especially its dialects, Braj Bhasha and Avadhi. Close linguistic cousins such as Gujarati, Bengali, Punjabi, Marathi, and Rajasthani are also used but less frequently. Two languages cultivated from the fifteenth to the seventeenth centuries specifically for the purpose of devotional singing were Braj Bhasha and Brajbuli, a hybrid of Braj Bhasha and Maithili in northeastern India. The majority of northern religious poetry is composed in these two languages, but Bengali follows close behind, and collections of old manuscripts are still being discovered.

Archaic forms of the religious and devotional music of northern India are still alive in the many temples, shrines, and domestic chapels that endure in the villages and endless countryside. Sectarian musicians, whether settled or itinerant, lay or monastic, perform this devotional music. Although containing prayers and hymns sung in Sanskrit, modeled on Vedic chants, devotional music is sung mostly in the vernacular languages (bhakti *gīt*). This music came into its own during the medieval period (1300–1550) and early modern period (1550–1750), when the bhakti movements swept over the entire subcontinent from the south, preaching the adoration of a personal deity (Perera 1988). The northern Sant (saint) tradition, worshiping the impersonal Absolute, also influenced and was influenced by the bhakti tradition, and contributed many songs to the repertoire, particularly in Hindi.

Performance practices

Devotional singing is simple and straightforward, with the utmost importance placed on the words as they communicate religious messages and narratives. Melody and rhythm are important, but devotional singers normally deplore musical virtuosity for its own sake, in contrast with the classical Hindustani and Karnatak traditions, which emphasize improvisation and technical mastery. A large variety of musical styles and forms exist, and no single formula has ever been mandated by custom to the exclusion of others. Musicians and religious leaders thus freely compose religious and devotional songs.

In terms of logistical arrangement, most religious music is a group endeavor, with a choir seated close to a lead singer (figure 1). The exception is standing groups appearing in temples, public spaces, or in procession to sing the names of God (*nām-kīrtan*). The lead singer reads from a published volume of lyrics or a handwritten ledger and frequently accompanies himself on the harmonium, a small version of the upright portable reed organ that originated with Christian missionaries. Chorus members repeat the leader's words line by line in unison, although in some cases the leader may sing solo throughout a song or with occasional group refrains. Besides the harmonium, the most common instruments include pairs of hand cymbals (*kartāl* or *jhāñjh*) and drums such as the tabla, the *pakhāvaj* 'barrel drum', the *ḍholak* (cylindrical drum used also in folk music), and the *khole* 'clay barrel drum'. Along with bowed lutes (*sāraṅgī* or *esrāj*), various other types of percussion instruments sometimes accompany devotional singing, including bells, clappers, and tambourines. A long-

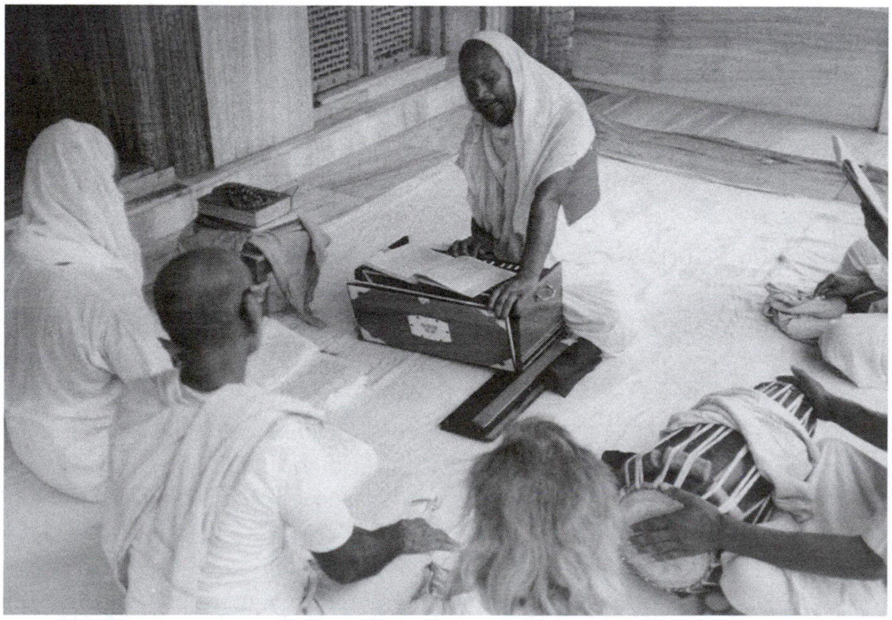

FIGURE 1 Hindu devotional singing group: the lead singer (*mukhiyā*) is Sri Rup Kishor Das, of the Nimbārka sect, Vrindavan. Photo by Guy Beck, 1992.

necked lute (*tānpūrā*) or a *śruti* box, a reed instrument with limited tones used more in Karnatak music, may also provide a background drone.

Medieval and early modern periods (1300–1750)

In the twelfth century, a new kind of Sanskrit poem emerged that greatly influenced medieval composers of religious and devotional songs in the vernacular languages. The *Gīta Govinda* of Jayadeva depicted the pastimes of the Hindu deities Radha and Krishna, and was saturated with the fervent devotional theism of an earlier Hindu sacred text, the *Bhāgavata Purāṇa*. Although respecting the standards for court poetry of the day, the poem contained, in its sung portions, poetic innovations in Sanskrit that were quickly applied to Prakritic (non-Sanskritic) regional dialects. These included changes in meter and a redistribution of long and short syllables. Nearly all forms of devotional music in India were affected, from the singing of simple bhajans to the complex vocal traditions of both Hindustani and Karnatak classical music (Prajnanananda 1973).

For the next few hundred years, the most conspicuous northern devotional music was Vaishnav, especially Krishnaite. Shaivite traditions were more prominent in the south, and Shakta (goddess worship) traditions were at their height in Bengal, Bangladesh, parts of Kashmir, and Kerala in the south. As distinct from the Sant traditions, which worshiped Brahman (God) without attributes (*nirguṇa*), the Vaishnavs addressed Brahman as "with attributes" (*saguṇa*). Many poets did not distinguish clearly between these two representations, yet most became readily identified with a theological preference in their native language. In praise of Krishna, for example, Sur Das addressed the deity as Sri Nathji in Hindi (figure 2), Tukaram and Namdev addressed him as Vitthala in Marathi, Mira Bai invoked him as Giridhara Gopala in Rajasthani and Hindi, and Vidyapati called him Madhava in Brajbuli. Shankardev venerated Krishna in Assamese; Chandidas depicted Radha and Krishna in Bengali; Ramprasad composed songs to the goddess Kali in Bengali; and Tulsi Das venerated Rama in Avadhi (Raghavan 1966).

These religious preferences, however, are noticeable only in the lyrics. From a musical perspective, similarities outweigh differences; listeners cannot infer a song's doctrinal message from the type of tune or rhythm employed if they do not understand the language. There is no clear musical distinction comparable to that between

FIGURE 2 Sur Das sings for Krishna. Poster illustration. Printed by S. S. Brijbasi and Sons, Bombay.

The Braj region of Uttar Pradesh is the historical center of North Indian religious traditions. Within the various bhakti lineages represented there, it is still possible to sample and chart the development of devotional music genres.

Catholic plainchant and Protestant chorales in the West, for example. In Indian music, all of the different religious traditions—whether Vaishnav, Shaivite, Shakta, or in praise of Brahman with attributes or without attributes—drew on evolving patterns of classical raga and tala structures. Only a very seasoned listener could distinguish subtle differences in theology from the singing and performing styles.

The various types of classically based devotional music of the northern bhakti traditions are known by specific names, such as *Vishṇupad* 'Vaishnav *dhrupad*-style songs', *havelī saṅgīt* 'temple music of the Vallabha tradition', *samāj gāyan* 'collective singing,' *abhaṅg* 'Marathi devotional song', *kīrtan* 'praise song', *shabd kīrtan* 'Sikh song', and *padāvali kīrtan* 'refined Bengali devotional music' (Slawek 1996). The genres of *havelī saṅgīt, samāj gāyan,* and *padāvali kīrtan,* performed in a style related to the classical *dhrupad* and *dhamār* genres, with lyrics describing Krishna's attributes and pastimes, continued to play an extremely important role in five or six major Vaishnav lineages that were once or still are headquartered in Braj, the actual birthplace of *dhrupad,* or in Bengal. Secluded conclaves of singers representing these original groups still employ pristine and even archaic forms of classical ragas and talas in northern areas and parts of Rajasthan, Maharashtra, Gujarat, Madhya Pradesh, Uttar Pradesh, Bengal, and Bangladesh. In Bengal and Bangladesh, singers consider *padāvali kīrtan* the most cultured form of religious music. The singing of the names of God (as in Sita Rama, Hare Krishna, Hare Rama, Radhe Shyam, Jai Mata Di, and so on) is popular everywhere in India and is called *nām kīrtan, nagara kīrtan,* or *nām saṅkīrtan*. The *abhaṅg* is specific to Maharashtra and Gujarat, whereas the *shabd kīrtan* refers to the music of the Sikh tradition.

Braj region: Classically based group singing

The Braj region of Uttar Pradesh is the historical center of northern religious traditions (Beck 1996). Within the various bhakti lineages represented there, it is still possible to sample and chart the development over many years of devotional music genres (Saksena 1990).

As the oldest Hindustani classical vocal form, *dhrupad* has been linked to the *prabandha* compositions mentioned in earlier Sanskrit treatises (c. thirteenth-century). As a kind of parent to several religious and classical forms, *dhrupad* generally means the formal, slow, four-section vocal rendition of a poem using the pure form of a raga, usually set in twelve-beat *cautāl* or fourteen-beat *dhamār* tala (Gupt 1982). Since most devotional poems contained at least four lines, there was a natural division into the four parts of *sthāī, aṅtarā, saṅcārī,* and *ābhog*. Singers performed classical *dhrupad* wherever they received patronage from the ruling elite, and the genre spread beyond northern India to Nepal, Bangladesh, and Pakistan.

In the medieval Vaishnav devotional forms of *havelī saṅgīt* and *samāj gāyan,* the performance was also very slow and austere, but faster tempo sections punctuated the long sets of descriptive lyrics. *Havelī saṅgīt* placed less emphasis on the long introductory raga elaborations and rhythmic permutations found in the Hindustani tradition. This temple music, formerly known as *kīrtan* within the Vallabha tradition, acquired the name *havelī saṅgīt* among the public, via All India Radio as recently as the 1950s. Now the term is more commonly applied to the music of the Vallabha Vaishnav tradition.

Havelī saṅgīt 'music of the Lord's house' originated in Braj in the early sixteenth century as part of worship in the temple of Sri Nathji or Lord of Govardhan (Krishna), who appeared to Vallabhacharya around 1495. *Havelī saṅgīt* actually refers to the music performed in the *havelī* temples ('house' or 'mansion' in Persian) that predominates in Rajasthan, where the icon of Sri Nathji was moved in 1672 to avoid Muslim persecution. Since then, devotees have strictly maintained a continuous tradition of temple music, including exact prescriptions and times of day for raga performances (Gaston 1994).

The poet-musicians who worshiped the original deity of Sri Nathji at Govardhan in Braj were collectively known as the Aṣṭachāp, eight prolific composers who each ended their poems with their *chāp*, or signature: Kumbhan Das (c. 1469–1584), Sur Das (c. 1478–1580), Paramananda Das (c. 1494–1585), Krishna Das (c. 1497–1580), Govinda Swami (c. 1506–1586), Chitswami (c. 1517–1586), Chaturbhuj Das (c. 1531–1586), and Nanda Das (c. 1534–1584). According to tradition, Sri Vitthalnath (c. 1516–1586), Vallabha's second son, introduced an elaborate liturgical system that included special songs for eight different times of the day, song cycles for the many annual festivals of the tradition, and various musical instruments as part of the musical service. All eight composers wrote volumes of poetry, but Sur Das became the most famous, writing the largest collection of verses, *Sūr-Sāgar* (Hawley 1984; Sur Das 1989). Performers today sing some of his songs in a faster tempo and lighter mood; the original performances were assuredly in the more elegant *dhrupad* style.

Nowadays more people in northern India are becoming familiar with *havelī saṅgīt* and sponsor its preservation, despite its transmission within a closed lineage. It is the best-known genre of music to originate in Braj and has spread to Gujarat, Rajasthan, and Maharashtra (including Bombay). Vallabhite *kīrtan* singers such as Vittal Das Bapodara, Gokul Utsav Maharaj, and Askaran Sharma have acquired a panregional audience through recordings.

The Braj region: Congregational singing

The other, less well-known tradition of Braj devotional music is *samāj gāyan*. This is a type of collective responsorial singing similar to *havelī saṅgīt*, yet different in that it is not so strictly raga based and employs many specific tunes that defy classification. Unlike the *havelī saṅgīt*, in which the musicians and singers are usually quite distinct from the rest of the seated congregation, the singing in *samāj gāyan* is shared more equally by the leader and the congregation. Its most unusual aspect is its interactive nature, requiring the presence of at least two responsorial singers (*jhelā*) to reiterate each line of the lead singer (*mukhiyā*), along with a variety of special phrases, exclamations (*erī hā*, *erī maī*, and so on), and hand gestures (figure 3). The accompanying instruments, as in *havelī saṅgīt*, are the double-headed barrel drum (*pakhāvaj*) (sometimes replaced by the tabla), hand cymbals (*kartāl* or *jhāñjh*), and harmonium, with occasionally a string drone (*tānpūrā*) and a bowed lute (*sāraṅgī* or *esrāj*).

The still thriving *samāj gāyan* is at the heart of three important but lesser-known Vaishnav sects of North India, the Nimbārka, Haridāsī, and Rādhāvallabha, all of which emerged from the Radha-Krishna worship tradition in Braj. All three still emphasize congregational singing in their current religious practices. Nimbārka, the Vaishnav tradition originating with Sri Nimbarkacharya in the twelfth century,

FIGURE 3 Responsorial singers (*jhelā*) in collective responsorial singing (*samāj gāyan*), led by Sri Krishna Caitanya Bhatta, Vrindavan. Photo by Guy Beck, 1993.

affirms that Krishna first taught *samāj gāyan* to the legendary sage Narada in heaven, and that it was passed down the chain of disciples to Sri Nimbarkacharya. Famous poets of song texts within this tradition include Sri Bhatta (c. 1500–1600), regarded as the first Braj Bhasha poet among Vaishnav groups, who wrote the classic *Yugal-Śatak,* and his disciple Sri Harivyasdevacharya (1550–1630), author of the *Mahāvāṇī,* the main hymnal of the sect, which contains songs for twenty festivals from spring (*vasant*) through the October–November festival of lights (Divālī).

The Haridāsī sect was founded by Swami Haridas (c. 1535–1595), the "father of Hindustani music," allegedly an expert *dhrupad* singer and musician as well as the teacher of Miyan Tansen (c. 1520–1590), court singer of Emperor Akbar. As in the other traditions, the songs of the Haridāsī sect are entirely in Braj Bhasha and focus on the love sports of Radha and Krishna in Vrindavan. (TRACK 10) The text of figure 4 describes the beautiful face and eyes of Syama (Krishna). A group of ascetic disciples follow a succession of eight leaders. Haridas's main poetical work, *Kelimāla,* contains the names of particular ragas above each of its 110 verses (Shastri 1982). Among all the groups performing *samāj gāyan,* this sect follows the most rigid calendar, singing verses from their standardized hymnal, *Samāj-Śṛṅkhalā,* in various ragas and talas on fixed days of the lunar year (Shastri 1988).

The third sect, the Rādhāvallabha, founded by Sri Hit Harivansh (1502–1552), claims to have practiced *samāj gāyan* continually since its inception. Hit Harivansh's main work in Braj Bhasha, *Hita-Caurāsi,* consists of eighty-four prescribed verses in various ragas. The present hymnal of this group, *Śrī Rādhāvallabhjī kā Varṣotsav,* is the largest of all such anthologies and contains poems by many other authors.

Despite the absence of musical notation in the songbooks of these traditions, congregations of singers follow a familiar, orally established pattern of melody and rhythm, without improvisation. There are almost no published transcriptions of *samāj gāyan* songs, although a few published collections of *havelī saṅgīt* with Indian *sargam* notation do exist. The *dhrupad* compositions of Tansen are said to be the oldest existing notated Indian songs, and probably reflect existing forms of *samāj gāyan* and *havelī saṅgīt.* In contrast, the familiar ragas of the current Hindustani classical tradition that appear in these Vaishnav songbooks differ significantly from the living traditions, suggesting the possibility of unknown or archaic ragas (Saksena 1990).

Su- bha- ga- va- ra- ṇa ta- na śyā- ma ma- no- ha- ra
sun- da- ra nai- na vi- śā- la o sa- ja- ni

FIGURE 4 Excerpt from a responsorial song of the Haridāsī sect, recorded in Vrindavan, 1992. Transcription by Guy Beck.

Banaras

A very important composer of religious songs in northern India was Tulsi Das (1532–1623), who lived in Banaras in eastern Uttar Pradesh most of his life. Venerated for his celebrated *Rāmcaritmānas*, a Hindi retelling of the Rama story, Tulsi Das wrote some of the most enduring devotional songs in praise of Rama (Raghavan 1966).

A related form of devotional music emerged from the Sant tradition of the Natha Yogis and Siddhas. Saints including Kabir, Dadu, and others composed bhajans addressing the formless Brahman (*nirguṇa*) instead of a personal deity with attributes (*saguṇa*). They are sometimes referred to as Nirgunis, or devotees of the *nirguṇa* Brahman. The many songs of Kabir (c. 1370–1448), a Muslim weaver of Banaras who became a Hindu saint, are central to the Kabir Panth, or sect. He regarded Rama and the Muslim Allah (God) as one and the same. Dadu (1554–1603), born in Gujarat but living mostly in Rajasthan, wrote *nirguṇa* bhajans celebrated within the Dadu sect.

Western India

In Maharashtra, Saint Tukaram (1608–1649) founded an order of householder devotees known as Varkarīs, and wrote hundreds of songs in Marathi known as *abhaṅg*, devoted to Panduranga (Vitthala). Other Marathi saints, Eknath and Nandu, wrote many *abhaṅg* that are still influential in western and northwestern India today (Paintal 1971).

Northeastern India

The Gauḍīya sect is a Vaishnav tradition of the northeastern region prominent for its performances of refined Bengali devotional music (*padāvali kīrtan*) and for singing the names of God (*nām kīrtan*). This movement, inaugurated by Sri Chaitanya Mahaprabhu (1484–1533), preached universal love of God through public singing expressing fervent devotion to Radha and Krishna. Groups of Vaishnav devotees incorporated refrains consisting of various names of God (Hare Krishna, Hare Rama, Hari bol) sung to simple melodies as a means of spiritual outreach, in performances during street processions, and in standing ensembles.

The immediate disciples of Chaitanya also sang devotional songs of Vidyapati (1352–1448), Chandidas (c. 1390–1450), and Jayadeva (c. 1100), laying the foundation for the more refined form of *kīrtan* called *padāvali kīrtan* or *pālā kīrtan*. Based on the model of the slower *dhrupad* of Vrindaban and Mathura, the *padāvali kīrtan* was formally introduced in Bengali under the direction of Narottam Das at Kheturi (in present-day Bangladesh) around 1583. *Pālā kīrtan* consists of extended narrative song texts describing the pastimes of Krishna and his Braj associates, with musical portions set to melodies associated with classical ragas and set to specialized talas that are related in form (though not in name) to Hindustani rhythms. Singers use the clay drum (*khole*) along with hand cymbals, flutes, and various kinds of bowed lutes as accompaniment. Although this music now survives mostly in villages of West Bengal and Bangladesh, several universities in Calcutta and elsewhere offer instruction by respected masters. Famous *padāvali kīrtan* practitioners include Nanda Kishore Das

Bhajan, an informal, loosely organized devotional music, has found increasing popularity in recent times among the masses all over the northern regions, including Nepal. It is probably the most ubiquitous genre of Indian religious music.

and the late Rathin Ghosh, whose large *kīrtan* ensemble has performed all over India; women *kīrtan* singers such as Radharani and Chabi Bandyopadhyay have also achieved considerable success (Chakrabarty 1988).

The later modern period (1750–present)

The Hindu Renaissance of the nineteenth century witnessed the birth of several new forms of religious expression, not the least of which were new musical forms. The Brahmo Samaj movement, originated in 1828 by Ram Mohan Roy, employed as part of its communal gatherings new devotional songs in Sanskrit and Bengali that were modeled on Vedic chants and old Hindi *dhrupad*-style songs. The tradition continued with the Tagore family, particularly Rabindranath Tagore (1861–1941), who contributed greatly to the stock of Bengali devotional songs. Much of his music—*Rabindra saṅgīt*—is of a humanistic nature, yet many beautiful songs express deep devotion and philosophical insight. They continue to be used in the worship services of the Brahmo Samaj. Tagore took his initial inspiration from the Vaishnav songs of Vidyapati and Chandidas and blended songs of the Bāul sect, folk songs, classical *dhrupad* vocal techniques, and Sanskrit religious songs together with his refined Bengali lyricism into a totally new genre of northern music. Women singers such as Kanika Bandyopadhyay and Sucitra Mitra have made definitive recordings of *Rabindra saṅgīt* (Ray 1985).

Bhajan

Bhajan, an informal, loosely organized devotional music, has found increasing popularity in recent times among the masses all over the northern regions, including Nepal. It is probably the most ubiquitous genre of Indian religious music (Henry 1988). Bhajan is directly related to the word *bhakti*, or devotion to God, and to a popular word for God, *bhagvān*. It shares with them both the common Sanskrit root *bhaj* 'to share, partake of' (as in a ritual), and is an important component of *pūjā*, the worship of images or icons.

Bhajan performance has earned mass appeal because of its relative simplicity, and has become the most identifiable feature of Hindu religious gatherings and worship worldwide. Performances vary widely, and may take place almost anywhere or anytime, indoors or outdoors, lasting from an hour to several days, and involving from two people to several thousand.

Whereas other traditional styles of religious music often require separate seating arrangements for men and women on the floor, the informal bhajan may not adhere to such social customs. Bhajan performances can consist of male, female, or mixed gatherings; on special occasions enclosed tentlike structures (*paṇḍal*) are constructed and used for extended time periods. Various monastic sects in India and abroad have established regular bhajan sessions (daily, weekly, or otherwise) at their monasteries, and lay associations organize bhajan singing for devotees of particular religious lineages. The Swaminarayan movement in Gujarat encompasses both of these features.

As the earlier bhakti movements affirmed class egalitarianism, religious music developing later provided occasions open to people of different social strata. The bhajan session was distinct from other Hindu occasions in fostering informal social relations based on mutual respect, in which everyone sits, sings, and eats together without regard to caste, gender, or religious viewpoint.

A typical session starts with the recitation of "Om," followed by invocatory prayers in Sanskrit in honor of a guru or deity, divine names such as Jai Govinda, Jai Radhe, Hari Narayan, or Jai Sri Ram, and a sequence of specific songs in a preferred or random order. Sanskrit prayers or short sermons may punctuate the event. Eventually a formal worship ceremony (*āratī*) occurs during which the congregation rises and devotees make offerings of food, flowers, incense, and lamps to the deities. These items are usually distributed as sacraments to everyone at the end of the session.

Bhajan song texts vary from complex structures to simple litanies containing several divine names, refrains, or the constant repetition of a single name. The song repertoire draws mostly from medieval saintly compositions, only simplified, and constantly acquires new compositions or arrangements, as in the growing popularity of Sai Baba bhajans. The rhythms are mostly up-tempo, avoiding the slower talas found in classical music. The most popular rhythm is *kaharvā*, an eight-beat tala corresponding to a lilting 4/4 cut time. Other favorite rhythmic cycles are *tīntāl*, with sixteen beats, serving as a straight 4/4 time, and *dādrā*, a six-beat tala corresponding to 3/4 or 6/8.

The partly improvised solo bhajan has emerged in the twentieth century as a formidable item on the concert stage, due to the efforts of such celebrated classical musicians as V. D. Paluskar (d. 1931); his son D. V. Paluskar (d. 1955), singer of the famous bhajan "Raghupati Rāghava" 'In praise of Rama, leader of the Raghu dynasty'; Omkarnath Thakur (d. 1967); M. S. Subbulakshmi; Bhimsen Joshi, famous for "Jo Bhaje Hari ko Sadā" 'One who always worships Lord Vishnu'; Pandit Jasraj; and others. Most classical artists have a stock of these stage bhajans for use as concluding items or encores in live performances or cassette recordings. Perhaps the most beloved of the hymns and religious songs of the medieval bhakti saints and musicians in the northern regions have been the Krishna bhajans of the songstress Mira Bai (c. 1450–1550). These are still sung all over India and abroad wherever Hindus congregate, and have achieved the greatest commercial success in recent times through the recordings of M. S. Subbalakshmi and others.

More recently—since 1980—the pop bhajan, partly influenced by the Urdu pop ghazal, has achieved great success through the singers Anup Jalota, Pankaj Udhas, and Hari Om Sharan, along with the film bhajan sung by playback singers Lata Mangeshkar, Mukesh, Manna Dey, and others [see POPULAR ARTISTS AND THEIR AUDIENCES; FILM MUSIC: NORTHERN AREA]. Even the film version of *āratī*, a type of bhajan used in worship, is now widely used in temple *pūjā* sessions. The greater population consequently has access to enormous resources in the form of recorded songs, films, radio broadcasts, television programs, and live performances, which can stimulate and enhance private worship (Manuel 1993).

North Indian forms of religious and devotional music saturate the movements of modern saints such as Swami Sivananda, Anandamayi Ma, Sri Aurobindo, and Srila A. C. Bhaktivedanta Swami Prabhupada, among many others. Purely religious music, especially singing the names of God, has developed a significant Western following due to the preaching efforts of Swami Bhaktivedanta and the ISKCON (Hare Krishna) movement he started in 1965 in the United States. Westerners also participate in devotional songs and bhajans when performed in movements such as the 3HO (Sikhs, followers of Yogi Bhajan), the Ramakrishna movement, the Divine Life Society, and the Self-Realization Fellowship.

ISLAMIC MUSIC

Despite the general prohibition against music in official Islamic doctrine and practice, various forms of what may be considered Muslim devotional music are found in South Asia. The omnipresent cantillation of the verses of the Qur'ān, though resembling music in several ways, is not regarded by Muslims as music per se. Indo-Muslim music may be either liturgical (Arabic verses chanted or performed in assemblies or on Muslim holidays) or nonliturgical (vernacular songs, mostly Urdu, sung in religious assemblies and accompanied by instruments), the latter derivative of Hindu classical (raga-based) forms and folk music. The qawwali is the most professionally "musical" form of Muslim nonliturgical music in South Asia, and is associated with the Chishti movement of Sufi mystics, going back to Amir Khusrau in the thirteenth century.

This particular Sufi order, rather than proscribing music as most other orders do, elevates music to the level of divine contemplation. Qawwali music involves group singing of Sufi poems and ghazals in the Urdu language, often at a tomb or shrine of a Sufi saint and led by a principal singer accompanied by harmonium and percussion. This singing is based on structured melodies and group refrains but also contains improvisation with melismatic passagework and rapid coloratura resembling the Hindustani *khyāl* genre. The late Nusrat Fateh Ali Khan made qawwali singing a commercial success in films and recordings, and is famous in the West.

The Shia and Sunni branches of Islam each have their own form of nonliturgical music in South Asia. In expressing mourning for their martyr Husayn, grandson of the Prophet Muhammad, Shia Muslims have developed *majlis* 'assembly', a passionate form of devotional music that includes chest beating and exists wherever Shiite Islam has flourished, particularly Lucknow and Hyderabad. The Sunni *milād* 'birthday', hymns of praise to God in celebration of the Prophet's birthday, is more orthodox in tenor and more widespread, especially among women; it is the least sophisticated musically and is, unlike the other nonliturgical forms, divorced from professionalism.

Indo-Muslim music continues to grow and pervades South Asia through films, radio, recordings, and public performances, especially of qawwali and ghazal. In addition, the domestic and educational spheres provide venues for the transmission of these musical traditions [see PAKISTAN: MUSIC, THE STATE, AND ISLAM; PAKISTAN: DEVOTIONAL MUSIC].

SIKH MUSIC

Sikh music is the most prominent of the so-called non-Hindu musical traditions. Guru Nanak (1469–1539), the founder and first guru of the Sikh tradition, addressed the nameless and formless Brahman as Sat Nam, or True Name. He stressed the unity of God regardless of religious affiliation and caste by using all names interchangeably, such as Rama, Govind, Hari. Guru Nanak traveled widely and preached his simple devotional message of *nirguṇa* bhakti through the medium of song. His companion, Mardana, would accompany him on the *rabāb*, a bowed lute similar to a *sāraṅgī*. Nanak's many songs, along with those of Kabir, Namdev, other bhakti saints and Sikh gurus among the famous ten gurus, were compiled into a large hymnal known as the Guru Granth Sahib. A standard script was fashioned for the Sikh songs called Gurumukhi, but the language was close to Braj Bhasha and Punjabi. A volume that is used today among the Sikhs in their temples (gurdwaras) is called Guruvani, and contains a selection of the most important songs drawn from the Guru Granth Sahib.

The Sikhs developed a devotional music based on classical ragas and talas, yet lighter in mood, called *shabd kīrtan*. They employ musicians in their worship centers who accompany the singing mostly on tabla and harmonium, sometimes daily but especially during sacred occasions. The Golden Temple in Amritsar in Punjab is the headquarters of Sikhism, and maintains a twenty-four-hour nonstop *shabd kīrtan* performance. Though originating in Punjab, Sikhism and *shabd kīrtan* are found all over South Asia wherever Sikhs congregate. Some singers like Bhai Harbans Singh have achieved considerable renown as performers and recording artists [see NORTHWEST INDIA: PUNJAB].

BUDDHIST MUSIC

Buddhism and Buddhist music in South Asia are now generally found only in the extreme northern and southern regions. In former times, art and music were considered sensual in early Buddhism, but the community gradually developed a monastic routine of chanting the Pali Canon along with instrumental music (sounds), punctuating the daily schedules. This has now all but disappeared in India, with the more liberal, theistic Mahayana tradition surviving in Nepal, Bhutan, Sikkim, Ladakh, and Tibet in the North, and the conservative Theravada tradition in Sri Lanka in the South. Theravada Buddhism is much more austere, with almost no sacred music; Mahayana Buddhism, particularly its ritualistic branch of Vajrayana, maintains a unique vocal art of intonation accompanied by cymbals and other percussive instruments [see HIMALAYAN REGIONS: TIBETAN CULTURE IN SOUTH ASIA; SRI LANKA].

CHRISTIAN MUSIC

As Christianity penetrated South Asia, it was influenced by Indian music in its devotional expression. The Jesuits in Goa and the British Protestants throughout North India attempted to syncretize European hymn singing with Hindu bhajans; several different editions of Christian hymns in Hindi and other Indian languages came into use. A recent example is the song "Jesus Is My Lord" ("Prabhu Nām Jesu Nām") in *Madhur-Vani* by Sister Louisa Machedo (Bombay: Sangeet Abhinay Academy, 1983). As was already mentioned, Christian missionaries originally brought the harmonium to South Asia. Despite widespread overlapping of traditions, Christian hymns are still performed in English and other European languages in the Western manner at many churches and cathedrals in the cities of the North.

REFERENCES

Beck, Guy L. 1993. *Sonic Theology: Hinduism and Sacred Sound.* Columbia: University of South Carolina Press.

———. 1996. "Vaiṣṇava Music in the Braj Region of North India." *Journal of Vaiṣṇava Studies* 4(2):115–147.

Bhattadevacaryaji. 1992 [1500s]. *Yugal-Śatak*, ed. Brajvallabh Saran. Vrindavan: Sri Sarvesvara Karyalaya.

Chakrabarty, Ramakanta. 1988. "Vaiṣṇava Kīrtan in Bengal." In *The Music of Bengal: Essays in Contemporary Perspective*, ed. Jayasri Banerjee, 12–30. Bombay and Baroda: Indian Musicological Society. Reprinted in *Journal of Vaiṣṇava Studies* 4(2) 1996:179–199.

Gaston, Anne-Marie. 1994. "Continuity and Tradition in the Music of Nāthdvāra: A Participant Observer's View." In *The Idea of Rajasthan: Explorations in Regional Identity*, ed. Karine Schomer, Joan Erdman, Deryck Lodrick, and Lloyd Rudolph, vol. 1, 238–277. Columbia, Mo.: South Asia Publications.

Goswami, Hit Harivansh. 1989 [1500s]. *Hita-Caurāsi*, ed. Lalitacaran Goswami. Vrindavan: Venu Prakashan.

Goswami, Lalitacaran, ed. 1978–1980. *Śrī Rādhāvallabhjī kāa Varṣotsav*. 3 vols. Vrindavan: Sri Radhavallabha Mandira Vaishnava Committee.

Gupt, Bharat. 1982. "Origin of Dhruvapada and

Krishna Bhakti in Brijabhasha." *Sangeet Natak* 64/65:55–63.

Haridas, Swami. 1982 [1500s]. *Kelimāla*, ed. Govinda Saran Shastri. Vrindavan: Swami Haridas Seva Samsthan.

Harivyasdevacharya. 1975 [?1500s]. *Mahāvāṇī*, ed. Govinda Saran Shastri. Vrindavan: Sri Nimbark Prakashan Trust.

Hawley, John S. 1984. *Sūr Dās: Poet, Singer, Saint*. Seattle: University of Washington Press.

Henry, Edward O. 1988. *Chant the Names of God: Music and Culture in Bhojpuri-Speaking India*. San Diego: San Diego State University Press.

Manuel, Peter. 1993. *Cassette Culture: Popular Music and Technology in North India*. Chicago: University of Chicago Press.

Paintal, Ajit Singh. 1971. "The Nature and Place of Music in Sikh Devotional Music and Its Affinity with Hindustani Classical Music." Ph.D. dissertation, University of Delhi.

Perera, E. S. 1988. "Bhakti Movement and Indian Music Tradition during the Middle Ages." In *Viśvabhārati Annals*, New Series I *On Music*, ed. Nimaisadhan Bose, 60–67. Bolpur: Shantiniketan Research Publications.

Prajnanananda, Swami. 1973. *Historical Development of Indian Music*. Calcutta: Firma KLM.

Qureshi, Regula B. 1972. "Indo-Muslim Religious Music: An Overview." *Asian Music* 3:15–22.

———. 1981. "Islamic Music in an Indian Environment: The Shiʿa Majlis." *Ethnomusicology* 25:41–71.

———. 1986. *Sufi Music of India and Pakistan: Sound, Context and Meaning in Qawwali*. Cambridge: Cambridge University Press.

Raghavan, V. 1966. *The Great Integrators: The Saint-Singers of India*. Delhi: Ministry of Information and Broadcasting.

Ray, Sukumar. 1985. *Music of Eastern India*. Calcutta: Firma KLM.

Saksena, Rakesh B. 1990. *Madhya-Yugin Vaiṣṇava Sampradāyoṅ meṅ Saṅgīt* (Music in the Madhya-Yugin Vaishnav tradition). New Delhi: Radha Publications (Hindi).

Shastri, Govinda Saran, ed. 1988. *Samāj-Sṛṅkhalā*. Vrindavan: Sri Swami Haridas Seva Samsthan.

Slawek, Steven. 1996. "The Definition of Kirtan: An Historical and Geographical Perspective." *Journal of Vaiṣṇava Studies* 4(2):57–113.

Sur Das. 1989 [sixteenth century]. *Sūr-Sāgar*, ed. Balmukund Caturvedi. Mathura: Gopala Pustakalaya.

Thompson, Gordon. 1987. "Music and Values in Gujarati-Speaking Western India." Ph.D. dissertation. University of California, Los Angeles.

Religious and Devotional Music: Southern Area

William Jackson

Religious feelings have run deep and steady in South India from time immemorial to the present day, and South Indians have expressed these feelings in a variety of musical forms and styles. Every neighborhood or village has its aged shrine or temple, its saint's burial place (*samādhi*), and its holy site, such as a tree with stone carvings near its trunk. Housewives keep little altars in their kitchens and teach their children the songs of saints. Hindu religious traditions, including rituals, customs, sacred images, and stories, pervade everyday life and all the arts. On every street and lane, Hindus sing in worship of the goddess in her many forms and in praise of the deities Shiva and Murugan, and offer flowers to incarnations of Vishnu such as Rama and Krishna. About three-quarters of India's people are Hindu, though *Hindu* is an umbrella term that covers a rich variety of identities.

Besides hearing the sounds of Hindu religious life, listeners hear Muslims chanting their call to prayer throughout villages and city streets five times a day, and notice the musical presence of other minority groups, such as Jains and Christians, which are also part of the cultural landscape.

Devotional music has flourished in capitals and temple towns. Musical styles and traditions of teacher-pupil succession (*sampradāya*) developed in centers of devotional music including Machilipatnam and Vizianagara on the eastern coast and Tirupati (in recent times, also Hyderabad) in Andhra Pradesh; Kanchipuram, Madras, Srirangam, and Madurai in Tamil Nadu; Mysore and Bangalore in Karnataka; and Trivandrum and Ernakulam in Kerala. During the last Hindu empire, that of Vijayanagar (1335–1565), the city of Hampi, or Vijayanagara, on the Tungabhadra River was an imporant cultural center in the Kannada area. Afterward, Tanjavur (also called Tanjore) in Tamil Nadu became a great center.

TAMIL MUSICAL TRADITIONS

South Indian music has its roots in ancient times, with contributions branching from different communities and cultural groups. The oldest evidence of religious musical traditions in the South is mostly connected with Tamil Nadu. Shamanic music and dance are depicted in *Paripāṭal*, a sixth-century anthology of Tamil poetry: "The shaman . . . with his flute, and horn, and other small musical instruments . . . dances

The beginnings of all Hindu and Buddhist chanting were probably the daily chanting by proto-Brahmin families more than five thousand years ago.

on the hills" (Ramanujan 1981:112–115). Shamanic chants and rhythmic movements of trance date back to prehistoric times; around the world, the shaman is the original "technician of the sacred" and user of powerful rhythms and songs (Rothenberg 1968) [see MUSIC AND TRANCE].

Tamil culture has always been eclectic, with court and folk elements, tribal and caste, city and village mixing and producing a complexity of expressions. Already in the Classical Tamil period of Cankam literature (supported by Pandya Dynasty kings in the first to fourth centuries), music and dance were significant themes, and composers set some long Cankam poems to music. Tradition holds that thirteen musicians publicly performed these pieces. The fifth-century Tamil classic *Cilappatikāram* 'The Tale of an Anklet', an epic by Ilanko Atikal, is also full of musical lore. The author dramatized the power of melody with the subtle musical misunderstandings that set the plot in motion: the interpretation of one series of notes to mean disagreement and of another series of notes to mean disloyalty, changes two lovers' lives forever.

An important strand of South Indian religious tradition is the devotional (bhakti) music of the *tēvāram* 'Garland of the Divine' lyrics sung by Shiva devotees (Peterson 1989). The *tēvāram* is a collection of 8,284 verses of sung Tamil devotional poetry composed by three poet-saints: Appar, Cuntarar, and Tirujnana Sambandhar (seventh to ninth centuries). Musicologists have retrieved or reconstructed the twenty-three original melodic patterns (*paṇ*), and have established their relations to modern Karnatak ragas. For the past ten centuries, professional singers have chanted these songs in the daily liturgy of Tamil Shiva temples.

The *tēvāram* songs, together with the *Divya Prabandham* 'Sacred Collection' of four thousand Tamil verses composed by twelve saints devoted to Vishnu (including Andal and Nammalvar), give evidence of early devotional music in South India. They are examples of a significant shift that occurred in Hindu culture between the sixth and ninth centuries. This shift is in part associated with the Tamil-area bhakti movement involving Āḷvārs (Vishnu devotees) and Nāyanārs (Shiva devotees), singer-saints who lived during the first millennium.

The Āḷvārs and Nāyanārs were intensely devotional seekers and ecstatics who made pilgrimages to shrines that served as sacred attractions at geographic points across the South. They sang their songs to deities whose images graced sanctums of temples and ancient holy places (*tīrtha*), often at rivers and mountains, and their songs were preserved as inspired utterances of praise: "Saints' pilgrimages and celebratory songs about hundreds of holy places mapped the country much as the king's institutions did; they literally sang places into existence" (Ramanujan 1981:107). The hymns of the *tēvāram* reflect a creative synthesis of mutually enriching Dravidian and Aryan-Sanskritic elements.

By accompanying their poetry with unforgettable music, these wandering saints attracted enthusiastic followers to join them in singing, and the musical element has enabled their poetry to remain a vibrant part of peoples' lives. Unlike the Brahmin priests (who used Sanskrit in Vedic rituals and learning), these musician-saints used local languages to express religious ideas, just as Buddhists and Jains had been doing. These early songs in colloquial form, such as Andal's songs of love for Krishna, were an inspiration to composers in other regions of India. In the spring, young women still sing Andal's songs. Over the centuries, singers have transmitted these songs orally and have revived them again and again. Listeners can still hear singers chanting the ancient *tēvāram* songs and *Divya Prabandham* verses in South Indian temples.

Ancient Vaishnava chanting today

In the Thousand-Pillared Hall of the great Srirangam Temple, located on a large island in the Kaveri River just outside Trichy, Vaishnava chanters annually perform the 1,102 Tamil verses of the *Tiruvaymoḻi* (a part of the *Divya Prabandham* collection) for ten days. One of the names of Vishnu in this temple is Emperor of All Musicians. During the recitation, the Gates of Heaven, at the north end of the temple, are open to pilgrims who come to listen. *Tiruvaymoḻi,* which internal evidence suggests originated with the intention that it be sung and danced, is the expression of Nammalvar's yearning for oneness with Vishnu. This was the first vernacular (non-Sanskrit) work in Hindu literature to be accepted as revealed scripture. It may also be the first to be chanted in both home and temple worship and by both men and women of all castes of the Shrivaishnava community (Vishnu devotees). Singing the *Divya Prabandham,* including the *Tiruvaymoḻi,* grew more popular among Shrivaishnavas after 1950, in part because of performances on radio, TV, and cassettes. Since then, musicians have set some Āḷvār lyrics to traditional Karnatak ragas for temple and concert performances (Narayanan 1994).

SANSKRIT MUSICAL TRADITIONS

Other roots of religious music in the South involve Sanskrit, the language of Aryans who migrated south during the first millennium B.C. Aryan language and culture contributed values and mediums of expression to Dravidian culture and artistic outlook. The earliest examples of Sanskrit religious verse (*mantra*) are the Vedas, the sacred texts of the early Aryans, chanted in prayer for rites and on religious occasions (Staal 1961).

The beginnings of all Hindu and Buddhist chanting were probably the daily chanting by proto-Brahmin families more than five thousand years ago. In Aryan society, the Brahmins were the priestly caste, responsible for maintaining religious rites and literature. Their commitment to perpetuating oral traditions was a matter of family identity and religious priority, and so Vedic chanting endured. Chanters gradually transformed plain Vedic chant, with its three-note syllabic melody, into a more complex chanting of the Sāmaveda with trills and melismatic graces [see VEDIC CHANT]. Wives of Sāmavedic priests sang the more intricate parts, including melodies of the *soma yāga,* an elaborate Vedic sacrifice, that required skillful performers. The Yajurveda mentions the long-necked lute (vina) as accompanying vocal recitation during sacrifices. Orthodox Hindus have traditionally considered Sāmavedic chant the source of later Indian music.

The Ramayana, the oldest parts of which were composed in the middle of the sixth century B.C., was set to music in ancient times and performed as a musical narrative. This epic poem tells the story of the righteous king Rama, an incarnation of Lord Vishnu, who battles demonic forces to win back his wife, Sita. As the epic spread to Java, Bali, Thailand, Cambodia, and elsewhere, performers adapted it using local languages and musical systems. In the original Sanskrit, the typical verse-pattern is the *śloka,* invented by Valmiki, the epic's author. Later musical forms, like the *sto-*

tra, the *kālakṣēpam* (see the last section of this article), and the bhajan, use *śloka* verses set to music.

Some musical genres, including devotional poems, lullabies of Perialvar (a ninth-century Āḷvār), and songs associated with festivals, dances, and games, blend the Sanskrit language and other materials. Great composers of later centuries, such as Purandara Dasa and Tyagaraja, often wove elements of old folk songs, proverbs, rhymes, and rhythms into more fully shaped and polished works. Such echoing of familiar pieces and conventional wisdom is characteristic of Karnatak musical creativity.

Jayadeva, a twelfth-century Brahmin from Orissa, composed the poem *Gīta Govinda* 'Love Song of the Dark Lord', an innovative masterpiece synthesizing Sanskrit lyrics containing playful sounds (such as internal rhymes and alliteration) and Dravidian or regional language patterns of rhythm and rhyme (Siegel 1990). This work seamlessly combines physical love's imagery and spiritual longing's depths in soulful beauty. The refrain (*druva*) and stanzas (*caraṇam*) of its eight-stanza form (*aṣṭapadī*) set the pattern for the structure of *kīrtana,* also involving a refrain (*pallavi*) and stanzas (*caraṇam*)—a structure developed by Haridāsa singers of Karnataka in and after the 1300s. (Haridāsas were itinerant Vishnu devotees who sang songs of devotion, criticizing social ills, hypocrisy, and excessive worldliness; they endeavored to bring scriptural stories to life.) Singers have performed the *Gīta Govinda* at Jagannātha Temple in Puri every day for almost five hundred years. Similarly, over the centuries, performers of classical Indian dance (*bharata nāṭyam*) have danced the *Gīta Govinda* with graceful gestures evoking erotic yearning. During the 1930s, a revival of classical dance occurred, and Brahmin women took up the art. Since then, dancers have only occasionally performed the *Gīta Govinda* in concert.

CONSERVATIVE SANSKRIT MUSICAL TREATISES AND INNOVATIONS

In century after century, Indian musicologists wrote treatises to update the written theory of music (Ayyangar 1972). Sarngadeva's treatise *Saṅgītaratnākara* 'Ocean of Music', of the 1200s, summed up and carried forward the cumulative tradition first documented in Bharata's *Nāṭyaśāstra*, bridging ancient and later music. The *Saṅgītaratnākara* is one classic source among many speaking of God as the embodiment of music and of music as an integration of science, art, and yoga that offers both Hindu musicians and listeners a way to spiritual liberation. The treatise describes the *rasika* as the enjoyer of aesthetic bliss; with devotion (bhakti) and spiritual wisdom (*jñāna*), this knower of music resonates deeply with the divine vibrations that are the basis of the universe. For centuries, Hindu musicians have envisioned Shiva and other forms of God as the musical shimmering of cosmic consciousness, a mysterious harmony, deep and pervasive. Vidyaranya (1300s), Ramamatya (1500s), Venkatamakhi (1600s), and Subbarama Diksitar (1839–1906) also wrote treatises updating the theory of music in South India [see SCHOLARSHIP SINCE 1300]. Even conservative musical traditions are not static. They can be lively, responsive, changing as life does, reflecting the human being's mind-body impulses and processes (Prusinkiewicz et al. 1989).

Sanskrit had a stabilizing effect, providing a timeless ideal in the form of written treatises, while regional dynamics and historical change stirred innovations. Though musical authorities in South India developed new systems of classifying ragas, culminating in the seventy-two-scale (*mēḷakarta*) system of Venkatamakhi in the seventeenth century, the conservatism of southern Hindus precluded drastic change. Such conservatism possibly stemmed from a fear that the whole traditional way of life and religious identity would be threatened if uncontrollable change intruded. Because of the conservatism of Hindu social customs, with close-knit cultural ties and birth-group communities, Muslim influence was weak, even though Muslim rulers at times controlled areas of South India, and some of them supported the arts. Southern India's musical traditions have resisted the influx of foreign elements in general, except those that were orthodox Hindu, such as the influence of Marāṭhā rule in eighteenth- and nineteenth-century Tanjore. Custodians of Brahmin culture accepted these readily as part of the unifying Sanskritic legacy (Seetha 1981).

TEMPLE DANCERS AND MUSICIANS

Periods of temple building changed the South Indian landscape in the ninth, tenth, and eleventh centuries, caused by devotional enthusiasm and royal ambitions. Religious and royal authorities attached young girls trained in music and dance to each great temple to perform before its deity. Such women, called *dēvadāsi* 'the deity's female servant', were recruited from many castes and were supported by the temple, and thus indirectly by the king. Rajaraja, the Chola king who reigned from 985 to 1016, assigned four hundred *dēvadāsi* to the great Shiva temple he built in Tanjore. Southern temples often feature pillars carved with images of these women holding musical instruments or caught in alluring dance postures and gestures (figure 1).

The *dēvadāsi* nurtured and promoted musical knowledge for centuries. They were often temple courtesans. In good times, as during the reign of the sixteenth-century Vijayanagar emperor Krishnadevaraya, society honored and respected them; in bad times, society mistreated and exploited them. Because they were ritually married to the temple deity, they were auspicious in the South Indian customary view, which holds that one married to God need never fear becoming a widow. *Dēvadāsi* women trained their daughters to be *dēvadāsi* also, to carry on the traditional arts of graceful melody and rhythmic gesture. Sons became musicians and dance instructors, keeping the disciplines of music and dance alive. Some of today's great musicians are descendants of *dēvadāsi* families.

BHAKTI DEVOTIONAL MUSIC AND POET-SAINTS

Combining a long-enduring artistry of music and lyricism with intense enthusiasm, South Indian musical devotion has earned a pan-Indian reputation as a source of religious fervor and inspired musical expression. According to old beliefs, the South is the source of India-wide Hindu passion for God. A well-known Sanskrit verse depicts devotion (bhakti) as a lovely woman born in the South who gains strength and maturity in the middle regions and migrates to the North, to live there rejuvenated and in full flower.

Like North Indian music, Karnatak compositions embody a unity of feeling and thought brought about in part by the theory of the nine emotional moods (*rasa*): yearning love, compassion, courage, comedy, wonder, anger, fear, disgust, peace. In Karnatak theory, a vital emotional mood shapes the theme of a song; in practice, devotional music often evokes the mood of yearning love.

According to Hindu belief, the songs of the poet-saints are records of their feelings and thoughts, and people who sing them faithfully embody anew the religious experiences and utterances by voicing them. The following devotional text is an example of bhakti poetry from the fifteenth-century Telugu *Bhāgavata Purāṇa*, chapter VII, verse 150 (Potana 1981, I, p. 711; translated by William Jackson).

FIGURE 1 A temple pillar in Hampi, Karnataka, showing a *dēvadāsi* dancing. Photo by William Jackson, 1992.

Mandāra makaranda mādhuryamuna dēlu madhupambu vōvunē madanamulaku?
Nirmala mandākinīvīcikala dūgu rāyanca canune taranginulaku?
Lalitara sālapalla vakhadiyai cokku kōyila cērunē kuṭajamulaku?
Būrṇēndu candrika sphurita cakōrakam barugunē sāndra nīhara mulaku?
Nambujōdara divya pādāravinda cintanāmrita pānaviśēṣamatta
Cittamērītinitarambu jēra nērcu? Vinutaguṇaśila maṭalu vēyu nēla?

Song was the easiest, most natural, and most pleasurable way to long for, reach out toward, and revel in experiences of ecstasy and surrender to the loving Lord, whether conceived as Allah or as Rama.

Would a bee who lives on honey from the blossoms of the Coral Tree [Mandara tree in Vishnu's heaven] ever fly to the bitter dhattura plant?
Would the king of swans who knows the breeze-swayed currents of pure Mandakini Lake prefer paltry brooks?
Would the cuckoo bird who loves to eat tender sprouts of mango feel drawn to a Kutaja tree [wild jasmine plant]?
Would a *cakravāka* bird who flourishes touched by subtle moonbeams want to go and bathe in the harsh saltwater of the sea?
Would a mind euphoric from drinking the spiritual nectar of thinking about God leave that for anything lower? Why talk such nonsense?

Bhakti is experiential seeking and spiritual exercises cultivating desire for union with the divine. With its drive toward vision, its songs of longing, and its moments of exaltation in finally tasting vision, it has ancient roots. The Vedic verse "I saw the Cosmic Person (*Puruṣa*)" is not so different from "I saw Rama" or "I saw Krishna" in the verse refrains of Purandara Dasa (1500s), Ramadas (1600s), Tyagaraja (1767–1847), and most other bhakti saints (figure 2). Singer-saints dramatized this seeking and tasting of visionary bliss by singing their songs.

Some bhakti poets emphasized the value of sincere spontaneity over artificial form and pompous elaboration. Basava of the Virashaiva sect (Shiva devotees), a Kannada poet of the 1100s, wrote, "I'll sing as I love." Rather than follow external rules, he wanted to make his heart's momentary feelings a kind of music. Perhaps the

FIGURE 2 Tyagaraja (*seated, right*) envisions Lord Rama and his entourage. Painting by S. Ramachandra Rao, 1931. Location unknown.

Virashaiva disapproval of symbols and images of God was influenced by Islam. Some Virashaiva stances, such as colloquial utterance, antiritualism, anticasteism, and the desire to relate directly to the deity, appear in lyrics of later bhakti singers, such as Purandara Dasa and Tyagaraja. Following Basava's path of love for Shiva in Kannada-speaking areas (now known as the state of Karnataka), members of sects, called Lingāyat saints, sang Virashaiva verses (*vacana*). Farther south, the fifteenth-century saint Arunagirinadar composed hymns praising Lord Murugan, a Hindu deity.

Haridāsa singers and *kīrtana*

Haridāsa singers such as Narahari Tirtha (1300s) and Sripadaraya (1400s) in Kannada-speaking regions began singing *kīrtana* songs in their vernacular language. The term *kīrtana* here refers to a song form composed of a refrain (*pallavi*) and up to ten verses (*caraṇam*). It can also serve in a more general sense to refer to devotional singing by a leader with a collective response, and can encompass other forms of devotional music. In Karnataka and other parts of India during the latter half of the 1400s, collective devotional singing became a popular practice. Some Hindus consider the Bengali saint Chaitanya (1486–1533), who traveled to the South, the originator of collective *kīrtana* chanting. He popularized the practice, and from then on, worship became more of a social endeavor. Besides family worship at home, individual worship in the temple, and annual festival celebrations with worship, frequent *kīrtana*-singing sessions took place that were open to a variety of communities in villages and towns. Bhakti egalitarian ideals ameliorated and softened rigid prejudices about castes, criticizing these prejudices as inapplicable to spiritual life. Sufis (Muslim mystics) and the Hindu men and women who espouse bhakti have expressed their spiritual ideas and feelings through music and dance. Song was the easiest, most natural, and most pleasurable way to long for, reach out toward, and revel in experiences of ecstasy and surrender to the loving Lord, whether conceived as Allah or as Rama.

The specific *kīrtana* genre that became popular in the 1400s and 1500s flourished in the creative piety of Kannada-language Haridāsa composers such as Vyasaraya and Purandara Dasa. Itinerant Haridāsas, devotees of the school of the great Vaishnava teacher Madhvacharya, were a vital part of the Vijayanagar empire (1336–1565), which covered much of the South (Ranade 1989).

The Telugu composer Tallapakka Annamacharya (b. 1424), the official devotional songmaster at the Tirupati Temple, sacred to pilgrims from all over India, had composed thousands of Telugu *kīrtana* songs while Purandara Dasa was still a youth. According to legend, the two met, and Annamacharya invited the younger devotee to join him in singing praise. Both composed music and lyrics. Devotees and singers of later generations remember them for their saintly lives and honor them as spiritual giants (figure 3).

FIGURE 3 Typical depictions of Annamacharya (*left*) and Purandara Dasa, commonly used in various publications in South India.

The singer-saint Purandara Dasa (1485–1565) composed thousands of *kīrtana* songs, ranging from the simple *gīta* for beginners to the sophisticated *sūlādi,* which employs a medley of ragas. Later generations honored him with the title "Father of Karnatak Music" [see KARNATAK VOCAL AND INSTRUMENTAL MUSIC, figure 2]. Legends depict him as a once miserly man who, after experiencing a miracle, became one of the wandering Haridāsas. He addressed his songs primarily to Lord Krishna, as in the following *kīrtana* lyrics (after Ramachandra Rao 1985:160; translated by William Jackson). The song has a refrain (*pallavi*) and verse (*caraṇam*) structure, the refrain repeated after each verse.

pallavi Hyānge bareditto pracīnadalli,
Hānge irabeku samsāradalli.
caraṇam 1 Paksi angaladalli bandu katante:
Ākṣaṇadalli hārihūdante. + *pallavi*
caraṇam 2 Nānā pariyali sante naradante,
Nana panthava hiḍidu hōdante. + *pallavi*
caraṇam 3 Makkaḷaḍi mani kaṭṭidante,
Āṭa sākendu aḷisi pōdante. + *pallavi*
caraṇam 4 Vasatikāranu vasati kanḍante:
Hottāriddu horatu hōdante. + *pallavi*
caraṇam 5 Samsāra pāśava nīna biḍisayya,
Kamsāri purandara vithalaraya. + *pallavi*

pallavi Earlier lives have written all the lines,
Which we must follow in subsequent lives.
caraṇam 1 It's like a bird alighting in your courtyard:
It settles, then suddenly flies far away. + *pallavi*
caraṇam 2 Like weekly markets gathering from many paths,
Arriving from different corners, suddenly gone. + *pallavi*
caraṇam 3 Like children who build palaces with care,
Then say "Enough!", demolish them, run elsewhere. + *pallavi*
caraṇam 4 It's like a wanderer finding an inn for the night:
Early morning he gets up and soon is on his way. + *pallavi*
caraṇam 5 Lord Purandara Vithala [an incarnation of Vishnu], destroyer of Kamsa,
Come free me from the bondage of worldly life. + *pallavi*

Verse 5 refers to the story of Krishna (an incarnation of Vishnu) destroying the demonic King Kamsa.

Other bhakti singer-composers

Following in Tallapakka Annamacharya's footsteps, his son and grandson carried on this tradition of composing and singing Telugu *kīrtana* expressing moods of passionate love or espousing spiritual philosophy. Ramadas of Bhadracalam (1600s) also composed many Telugu devotional songs to Lord Rama employing the *kīrtana* form. In South India, singers still perform their works, which represent the values of heartfelt bhakti and enthusiastic musicality. Kanaka Dasa, another contemporary of Purandara Dasa, is also a favorite *kīrtana* composer in Kannada; he was a lower-caste devotee of Krishna, and some of his works insist that a person's depth of devotion is not caste determined.

Ksetrayya (1600s) specialized in composing and singing simple Telugu songs expressing love's longings (*padam*). Dancers often depict the texts of his languorous songs with highly stylized gestures (*abhinaya*). Ksetrayya used intimate idiomatic language and portrayed a variety of lovers' situations, feelings, and moods. In India, the erotic mood is integral to religious music of longing.

The eighteenth-century sage Sadashiva Brahmendra, of Tiruvisanallur in Tamil Nadu, left only a small number of songs, all in Sanskrit, but is nevertheless a well-loved saint-composer of the Kaveri Delta. Remembered as a mysterious sage with yogic powers, a man who wandered naked and was considered liberated while alive, he composed songs that still charm and fascinate listeners. Narayana Tirtha, also from this same time and delta region, composed *The River of Krishna's Sports*, a drama made up of colorful *kīrtana* songs.

Svati Tirunal (d. 1847), of Trivandrum in Kerala, was a Hindu king who composed in a variety of musical forms, including *kīrtana* and *padam* [see KARNATAK VOCAL AND INSTRUMENTAL MUSIC]. Professional musicians in South India often perform his works in concert.

Bhajans for collective singing

The bhajan is an important Indian form of devotional music. Hindus of all communities, and Christians too, sing congregationally in bhajan meetings. The bhajan is simpler in form than the *kriti* and *kīrtana.* It often has fewer words, and thus tends to be the shortest of the three. Mohandas K. Gandhi's favorite bhajan was simply a list of divine names: *Raghupati Rāghava Rāja Rām, Patita Pāvana Sītā Rām ; Ishwar Allah Tere Nām, Subko Sanmati Dē Bhagavān* 'Your name, God, is Rama, protector of your people, uplifter of the fallen, Sita's lord; And Your name is Allah; Lord, please give us a heart of goodness'. Gandhi requested M. S. Subbulakshmi, one of the twentieth century's greatest South Indian singers, to sing bhajans such as this whenever she was in his presence.

Bhajan sessions occur in homes, bhajan halls, or temples and may involve any number of participants, from a handful of family members and neighbors to hundreds or even thousands of community members or pilgrims. The men usually sit on the floor in rows on one side of the meeting place and the women in rows on the other side, before an altar or images of Hindu deities decorated with flowers and incense. Bhajan sessions are often held once or twice a week. On Mahāshivarātri (the new-moon night in February or March), annual all-night bhajans are devoted to Shiva; on Ekādashī (the eleventh day of either two-week period of a lunar month), monthly bhajans are sung to Vishnu.

FIGURE 4 Singers at a bhajan celebration in Tiruvidaimarudur Village, Tamil Nadu, 1990. Photo courtesy Venkatraman Bhagavatar.

At a bhajan session, the singers take turns leading responsorial singing of different songs. Some programs of bhajans are fixed in format; others depend only on the leaders' choice of songs. Singers of bhajans are often accompanied by harmonium, barrel drum (*mridangam*), and small jingling clappers (*ciplā*). In many of the larger halls, microphones and speakers enable leaders to be heard clearly, so that the group can repeat their musical lines in response. The soulful participation of many devoted singers from varied backgrounds is an important aspect of bhajan singing; practitioners believe it promotes peace and harmony. Bhajan texts consist of names of God and are usually so simple that the textual language, whether Hindi, Telugu, Kannada, or Tamil, is irrelevant; people can sing the same songs everywhere in the South, and all can understand them (Singer 1968) (figure 4).

Since at least the 1960s, Sathya Sai Baba, a spiritual teacher based in Andhra Pradesh and Karnataka, has given a boost to bhajan singing, as thousands of his followers enthusiastically gather for sessions in homes and halls in many parts of India. His devotees, from a variety of castes and sectarian backgrounds, have built halls for bhajan singing. There they hold regular meetings, especially on Thursdays and Sundays. Sai Baba's devotees have adopted the practice of *nāgasankīrtana,* the singing

People often say that Tyagaraja is famous for creating new ragas expressing profound moods that the listener tastes immediately, like grapes melting in the mouth.

of bhajans while walking in a procession just before dawn. Other groups also sing and promote bhajans, including the followers of Amrita Mata, probably the most famous living woman guru of Kerala.

The poet-saint Tyagaraja

With Muttusvami Diksitar and Syama Sastri, the other members of the so-called Trinity of South Indian music, Tyagaraja (1767–1847) practiced his art in Tanjavur (figure 5). Marāṭhā kings who ruled Tanjavur in his time encouraged the arts, scholarship, and religion, drawing musicians, poets, singers, and reciters from all regions of South India. Almost two centuries later, in May 1992, UNESCO declared the Tanjavur region a World Heritage Zone to recognize the importance and richness of this meeting place of Tamil, Kannada, Telugu, and Marāṭhā cultures.

The saint Tyagaraja, widely called the Beethoven of South Indian music (partly for his sheer productivity as a composer of large-scale classical works) perfected the

TRACK 11 *kriti* song form. He synthesized ardent devotional music and the subtle sophisticated art music of the courts, composing haunting, innovative masterpieces. He came from a musical family, and was a disciple of a great court musician of the day. Rejecting a king's invitation to play in court and be richly rewarded, he chose a simple life of voluntary poverty and devotion, dedicating his songs only to Lord Rama. Instead of continuing the tradition of composing devotional songs in the rather simple *kīrtana* form or in the *stotra* verse forms of chanted praise, he intensified their artistic quality by composing shorter pieces, often using shorter lyrics than those of existing *kīrtana* to bring out the subtle potential of words and feelings.

Tyagaraja's songs were more complex than most existing devotional songs of his time. Instead of syllabic settings of texts, his compositions had fluid and melismatic

FIGURE 5 The Trinity of South Indian music: *from left,* Muttusvami Diksitar, Tyagaraja, Syama Sastri. Painting by Chitraleka.

melodies. Partly because of his musical genius and the mellifluousness of the Telugu language (called the Italian of the East) in which he sang poignantly of his longing for Lord Rama, Telugu became the language most used in South Indian music and dance. (Though Tyagaraja lived in Tamil-speaking Tanjavur, staying in the village of Tiruvaiyaru most of his life, his native language was Telugu.) The language also became popular because of Telugu court musicians and pandits in Tanjavur, the Southern school of Telugu literature (which flourished under the Nāyak rulers), and lyricists such as Ksetrayya.

Tyagaraja's *kriti Rāga sudhārasa* 'Drink Up the Nectar Called Raga' provides an example of his faith in devotional music, celebrating it as the ultimate vehicle to spiritual realization. The song has a typical three-part structure: *pallavi, anupallavi,* and *caraṇam.* In performance, the first section, *pallavi,* is repeated after each of the other sections in rondo fashion. As part of a pattern to aid memory, the text, in Telugu, typically has first-letter alliteration at the beginning of lines, although not in the example cited below. Such patterns help Karnatak musicians draw on a large repertoire without having to use a written score. The performer, like the reciter of Vedic verses, needs no written notation to repeat the text-and-sound pattern, though published works of the basic notes of many favorite songs do exist (text after Ramanujachari and Raghavan 1981:594–595; translated by William Jackson).

pallavi	Rāga sudhārasa pānamu jesi rajillave o manasā;
anupallavi	Yāga yoga tyāga bhoga phalla mosaṇge;
caraṇam	Sadāśiva mayamagu nādoṇkāra svara—
	Vidulu jīvanmuktulani! Tyāgarāju teliyu. + *pallavi*

pallavi	Drink up the nectar called raga and be joyful, O heart of mine;
anupallavi	Raga gives the fruits of sacrifice and yoga, enjoyment and renunciation;
	Those who know that the musical tones and the primordial OM compose
caraṇam	The body of Shiva—they're liberated souls! And Tyagaraja knows. + *pallavi*

All three members of the Trinity of South Indian music were masters of variations of the *kriti* [see KARNATAK VOCAL AND INSTRUMENTAL MUSIC]. Their compositions became prominent in concerts and religious celebrations. People often say that Tyagaraja is famous for creating new ragas expressing profound moods (*bhāva*) that the listener tastes immediately, like grapes melting in the mouth. Diksitar, who spent much of his life on pilgrimages, is known for his elaborate compositions in ragas well known before his generation; the flavors of his melodies are enjoyed gradually, like a coconut requiring to be cracked before eating. He wrote intricate Sanskrit lyrics praising the goddess Minakshi and other South Indian temple deities. The composer Syama Sastri, a less prolific but soulful devotee of the goddess Kamakshi, is most famous for his rhythmic expression. Hearing his Telugu songs is like peeling a banana, requiring only a little effort. But as musicologists have noted, it was not his flair (nor Tyagaraja's nor Diksitar's) to emphasize one element to the exclusion of others. He blended all three in harmonious wholeness. The totality of melody-rhythm-feeling is inseparably joined with lyrical religious meaning.

South Indians continue to celebrate this musical Trinity. A Tyagaraja Festival takes place each year in Tiruvaiyaru, which has become an all-India event via television and radio broadcasts [see SOCIAL ORGANIZATION OF MUSIC AND MUSICIANS: SOUTHERN AREA]. Other major celebrations center around Diksitar's works, which articulate ritual worship with artistic flourish and profound knowledge. Other annual celebrations take place in various centers of religious culture and honor singer-saints such as Annamacharya (in Tirupati), Ramadas (in Bhadracalam), and Purandara Dasa (in Hampi).

MUSIC SOCIETIES, MODERN MEDIA, AND LOCAL CUSTOMS

Around 1900, lovers of music in South India countered dwindling royal patronage of music by forming public music societies (*sabhā*) to support concert performances. The emphasis of Karnatak music remained religious, but varied audiences of music lovers developed. The Music Academy of Madras and music societies in Rajamundry and Vijayawada in Andhra Pradesh and in Mysore and Bangalore in Karnataka all gathered members and supported musicians as a matter of civic pride and love of Hindu artistry.

All India Radio (A.I.R.) and the national TV network (Doordarshan) present cultural performances of religious music from South India. A.I.R. executives and producers have striven to present to large audiences the best examples of devotional Karnatak music genres. The cinema, too, has been a workplace for composers and performers: many films have religious themes, and popular religious songs sometimes spread among the people from this source. Strict classicists often disapprove of the liberties taken by film-music composers, feeling that flashy novelties and cheap effects threaten conservative disciplines, but some performers display creative virtuosity in old venues and new media, satisfying the needs of both.

Regional Hindu traditions include story narrations with song and dance (*harikathā*), which center on saints' lives or other religious stories told by singing narrators (*bhāgavatar*). The narrator is a popular figure who leads public devotional programs, wearing a colorful turban and a distinctive costume. For years, Banni Bai (c. 1920–c.1990), associated with the honored female musician Bangalore Nagaratnammal, called herself a lady *bhāgavatar* and performed in Tamil Nadu. The *kālakṣēpam* (literally 'time well spent') is a spiritual discourse accompanied by music, a form of teaching and storytelling that has appealed to the masses for decades. Tamilians call Tanjore Krishna Bhagavatar (d. 1903), who was influenced by Maharashtrian performers, the father of modern *kālakṣēpam* (Seetha 1981:226). Today, performers of this art, such as T. S. Balakrishna Sastrigal, record their works on cassettes. Vaishnava devotion leaders in Andhra Pradesh developed the *kuchipuḍi* religious dance-drama. Tamil devotion leaders developed the *bhāgavata mēḷa nāṭaka*, featuring dances on religious themes. Musical plays (*yakṣagāna*) are another form of religious entertainment that aims to educate audiences. Puppet shows and *yakṣagāna* performances involving actors singing and dramatizing epic and other religious narratives are part of the region's heritage [see MUSIC AND DANCE: SOUTHERN AREA].

Festivals, temple functions, and processions often begin with musical performance on double-reed instruments (*nāgasvaram*) accompanied by resonant drums, making sonorous and strongly rhythmic music that pervades the temple and the depths of listeners' minds and hearts. In South Indian temples, an ensemble of *nāgasvaram*, drum (*tavil*), and small cymbals (*tāḷam*) is an essential part of most processions. On many levels, religious music plays an important part in everyday life in South India; without it, life would be drab and tasteless, "like lentils without salt," as South Indians say.

REFERENCES

Atikal, Ilanko 1994 [fifth century]. *The Tale of an Anklet*, ed. and trans. R. Parthasarathy. New York: Columbia University Press.

Ayyangar, R. Rangaramanuja. 1972. *History of South Indian (Carnatic) Music.* Madras: Author.

Higgins, Jon. 1976. "From Prince to Populace: Patronage as a Determinant of Change in South Indian (Karnatak) Music." *Asian Music* 7(2):20–26.

Jackson, William. 1991. *Tyagaraja—Life and Lyrics.* Madras: Oxford University Press.

Janaki, S. S., ed. 1989. *Bibliography of [V. Raghavan's] Writings on Music, Dance.* Madras: Kuppuswami Sastri Institute.

Narayanan, Vasudha. 1994. *The Vernacular Veda.* Columbia: University of South Carolina Press.

Parthasarathy, T. S. 1982. *Music Composers of India.* Madras: C. P. Ramaswami Aiyar Foundation.

Peterson, Indira V. 1984. "The Kriti as an Integrative Cultural Form." *Journal of South Asian Literature* 19(2):165–167.

———. 1989. *Poems to Siva: The Hymns of the Tamil Saints.* Princeton, N.J.: Princeton University Press.

Potana, Bammera. 1981. *Srimad Bhagavatam.* 2 vols. Madras: Balasarasvati Book Depot.

Prusinkiewicz, P., K. Krithivasan, and M. Vijayanarayana. 1989. "Application of L-Systems to Karnatic Music." In *A Perspective in Theoretical Computer Science*, ed. R. Narasimhan, 229–246. Singapore: World Scientific.

Qureshi, Regula. 1972. "Indo-Muslim Religious Music, an Overview." *Asian Music* 3(2):15–22.

———. 1995 [1986]. *Sufi Music of India and Pakistan*. Chicago: University of Chicago Press.

Raghavan, V. 1979. *The Great Integrators: The Singer-Saints of India.* New Delhi: Ministry of Information, Government of India.

Ramachandra Rao, S. K., ed. 1985. *Purandara Sahitya Darshana* (The lyrical vision of Purandara Dasa). Bangalore: Directorate of Kannada and Culture, Government of Karnataka.

Ramanujachari, C., and V. Raghavan. 1981. *The Spiritual Heritage of Tyagaraja,* 3rd ed. Madras: Ramakrishna Matha.

Ramanujan, A. K. 1981. *Hymns for the Drowning.* Princeton, N.J.: Princeton University Press.

Ranade, R. D. 1989. *Pathway to God in Kannada Literature.* Bombay: Bharatiya Vidya Bhavan.

Rothenberg, Jerome, ed. 1968. *Technicians of the Sacred.* New York: Doubleday.

Sambamurthy, P. 1971. *A Dictionary of South Indian Music and Musicians.* Madras: Indian Music Publishing House.

———. 1978 [1962–1970]. *Great Composers* series. Madras: Indian Music Publishing House.

Seetha, S. 1981. *Tanjore as a Seat of Music.* Madras: University of Madras.

Sewell, Robert. 1982 [1900]. *A Forgotten Empire (Vijayanagar).* New Delhi: Asian Educational Services.

Siegel, Lee. 1990. *Sacred and Profane Dimensions of Love in Indian Traditions as Exemplified in the Gītagovinda of Jayadeva.* Delhi: Oxford University Press.

Singer, Milton. 1959. *Traditional India: Structure and Change.* Philadelphia: American Folklore Society.

———, ed. 1968. *Krishna: Myths, Rites, and Attitudes.* Chicago: University of Chicago Press.

Staal, J. Fritz. 1961. *Nambudiri Veda Recitation.* The Hague: Mouton.

Wade, Bonnie. 1979. *Music in India: The Classical Traditions.* Englewood Cliffs, N.J.: Prentice-Hall.

Music in Seasonal and Life-Cycle Rituals

Richard Wolf

Life-Cycle Rituals
Seasonal and Calendrical Rituals
Functions of Music in Seasonal and Life-Cycle Rituals

Father, older brother, younger brother, listen!
Don't sleep in the ceremonial tent! . . .
Dance and chant [the holy words] "Ōly Ōly". . . .
Don't sit there like senseless people!
Father God and Mother Goddess are listening
Let us celebrate that WE ARE THE KOTAS.

—Song of the South Indian Kota tribe, sung at the annual Devr festival

Throughout the Indian subcontinent, music is used to accompany, punctuate, describe, announce, and give definition to rituals. This article discusses the music of calendrical rituals and rites of passage. Ritual music is almost always classified according to its context rather than its style; for this reason, there is a conspicuous focus here on the contexts and meanings of music, rather than on sound qualities. Still, it may be noted that musics of a particular ritual type (such as the wedding) in different regions of South Asia tend to share some sonic features. For example, joyful rites may occasion the performance of dancing and drumming—often at brisk tempos (figure 1). Occasions of sadness might inspire melodically stylized crying; the tempo of music at sad events is likely to be slow; dancing at such sad events (in the rare cases where it is sanctioned) will also probably be slow. Ceremonies relating to the vicissitudes of personal or communal fortune, such as healing rituals or rainmaking ceremonies, may make use of short repetitive pieces to induce spirit possession. These features of performance are not specific to South Asia and thus do not reveal significant information about the character of South Asian ritual musics. To move beyond these generalizations, we must examine individual ceremonial musics in each South Asian subculture.

Although we might attempt to construct a comprehensive list of South Asian ritual types and their associated musics, such a list may not help us to understand what the musics actually mean in these contexts. The first part of this article presents not a comprehensive list but rather a representative sample of ritual music types. The second part attempts to cut across specific traditions and discover some of the common functions and meanings in South Asian life-cycle and seasonal ritual musics.

FIGURE 1 Men and women dance together to the rhythms of the *ḍhol* at an elite Punjabi Muslim wedding in Lahore, 1997. Photo by Richard Wolf.

Ideas about how music "functions" in particular contexts may vary among different sectors of a population, and these functions may change over time (see Tingey 1994, for example). Nevertheless, it may be recognized that a common range of functions and meanings are ascribed to music in life-cycle and seasonal ceremonies in South Asia, whether by scholars studying the region or by participants interpreting their own musical cultures.

The performers of music in South Asian rituals comprise both hired professionals and nonspecialist singers and instrumentalists. Although the men of a musical community may be more frequently hired as musicians, there are many examples of men and women participating together as professional musicians, such as among the Mīrāsīs of the Pakistani Punjab, the Manganihārs of Sindh and Rajasthan, and the Damāis of Nepal. But whether professional or amateur, women tend to be singers rather than instrumentalists; their most salient musical contributions to life-cycle rituals are wedding songs and funeral dirges.

LIFE-CYCLE RITUALS

Among the more controversial uses of music in life-cycle ceremonies is its connection with funerals. Many Hindus and Muslims feel that music (whether singing or playing instruments) is by definition happy or enjoyable and therefore should not be performed during a funeral. High-caste Hindus in South India tend to frown on the use of music at funerals; however, drums, double-reed aerophones, and band instruments are commonly used at funerals of lower caste members. Throughout South Asia it is common for music to be performed at the funeral of a very old person. Reflecting the idea that such funerals are considered to be like weddings, often the same bands play for both occasions (Parry 1994). Laments are commonly sung in honor of the deceased, often by women, and sometimes bhajans are sung to the "departed soul" (Patel 1974). Laments are also sung during segments of dramas and dramatic rituals depicting mourning.

At the other end of the life-cycle spectrum, most South Asian communities celebrate the birth of a child. A male child may be welcomed by singing, rejoicing, and the sound of the *śahnāī* 'double-reed pipe' played by professional musicians, indicating the value both Hindus and Muslims place on male offspring—whereas the birth of a female may be greeted with less enthusiasm, or even mourned. A variety of rituals follow in the days, months, and years after childbirth, and these may call for singing or instrumental music: circumcision for Muslim boys; first application of charcoal (*kājal*) on the eyelids; piercing of the ears; naming of the child; and head shaving (Tewari 1974). Lullabies, which frequently employ repetitive meaningless syllables (in South India, for instance, "*rā rā re,*" "*tā le lo,*" or "*jō jō*"), are common in the subcontinent but are not associated with rituals as such. However, lullabies are sometimes incorporated into dramatic rituals depicting a baby being lulled to sleep, as in the *raṭa yakuma* rituals of Sri Lanka (Sarachchandra 1966).

After childhood a youth may encounter a number of other rites of passage in the journey to adulthood. For male members of thread-wearing Hindu castes, special musics sometimes accompany ceremonies for installing the sacred thread (Tewari 1974). Puberty rites for a girl's menarche may be the occasion for music making, as for instance among Telugu Brahmins, who sing *Gauri kalyāṇam* 'Marriage of the goddess Gauri' at an auspicious time of day. This song is part of the purification rites performed four days after the onset of menstruation (Kapadia 1995).

Before marriage it is common for girls and women to engage in a variety of activities believed to improve their marriage prospects. In some families, girls are encouraged to study classical music and dance; the performance of these arts is often discontinued after marriage. There are also series of prayers and fasts, sometimes incorporated into other seasonal festivals, that are specifically intended to aid in securing a favorable mate. These rites sometimes feature the singing of particular song genres such as the *khānḍana* of southern Gujarat (Patel 1974) or the *tiruppāvai* and *tiruvempāvai* of Tamil Nadu.

Marriage

The details of marriage ceremonies vary widely throughout the subcontinent according to religion, caste, and socioeconomic status. Still, in most communities music is not only desirable but virtually mandatory at weddings (figure 2). Moreover, the positioning of musical pieces in the sequence of rituals is analogous.

The following example of musical practices associated with Tamil Brahmin marriages provides some insight into the role music plays in South Asian marriage ceremonies generally.

Among Tamil Brahmins, marriage songs frequently concern the wedding of Sita or Andal (the female Vaishnavite saint). In Tamil Nadu, as in much of South Asia,

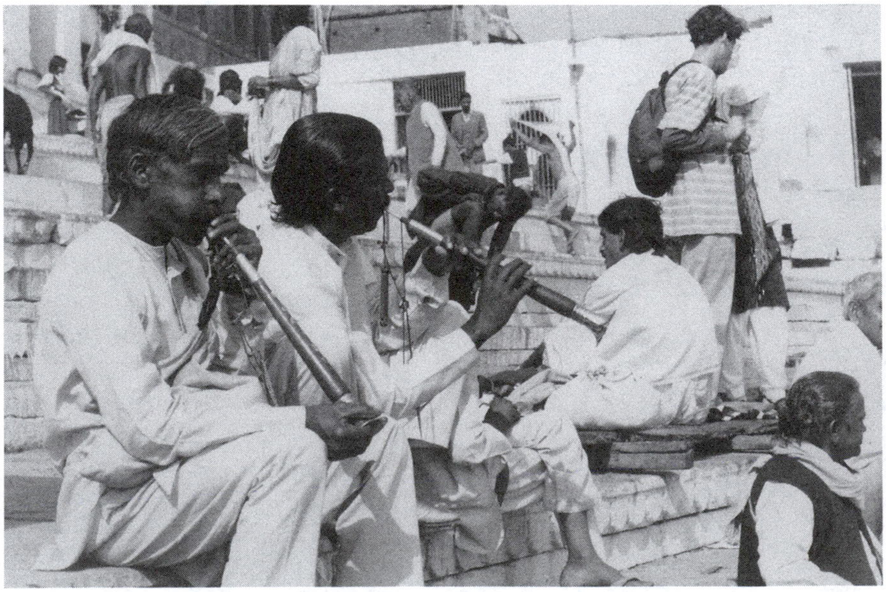

FIGURE 2 *Śahnāī* players performing for a wedding on the ghats (steps) of the Ganges River in Banaras. This picture was taken during wedding season (in this case December 1997), when many such weddings were occurring every day along the river. Photo by Richard Wolf.

marriage rituals have come to be abbreviated in recent times, and few women are preserving the tradition of singing marriage songs. Still, old-fashioned, musically elaborate weddings are still conducted in some Tamil villages.

In the betrothal ceremony, the bridegroom pretends to set out for the holy city of Kasi, where he vows he will remain a celibate and religious man for the rest of his life. The father of the bride stops him and offers the hand of his daughter. The maternal uncles of the bride and groom then provide garlands for the couple to exchange. The song associated with this action is called *mālai māṟṟiṟa pāṭṭu* 'garland exchanging song'. The melody of this song is usually played on the *nāgasvaram* 'double-reed pipe', but it may also be sung. In a later ritual, women surround the bride and groom, who sit on a swing and sing swing songs such as *ūñcal,* set to a slow tempo, and *lāli*, a slightly faster lilting tune in septuple time and in *rāga kuranji*. The *nāgasvaram* plays the same melody.

The wedding proper occurs during a one-and-a-half-hour auspicious period called the *muhurtam*. The bride and groom sit on a plank while the song "Lakṣmi kalyāṇam" 'Lakshmi's wedding' is played or sung. Then at the moment of tying the *tāli*, a necklace signifying marriage, the song is played again and all the instruments (usually *tavil* 'double-headed drums' and *nāgasvaram*) perform together rapidly and loudly—a practice called *kēṭṭi mēḷam* 'loud, thick, robust ensemble' that draws attention to the moment and drowns out inauspicious sounds. The *kēṭṭi mēḷam* is also performed on the most important day of drama productions, and at high points of temple worship, when the deity is in direct communication with the devotees.

In the evening, the couple sings songs and performs the *nalunku*—a custom that allows the bride and groom to interact informally with one another before the wedding night. The bride and groom paint each other's feet with red turmeric paste and calcium hydroxide, joke and play with one another, and sing. This practice is similar to Muslim and North Indian Hindu ceremonies in which red stain made from *meṅhdī* 'myrtle' leaves is applied to the palms and feet, and for which there are also special songs. A ritual called the *pattiyam* follows the *nalunku*: the bride sings of all her wishes and desires, gives the bridegroom betel leaves and areca nuts (*veṟṟilaippākku*) and performs *namaskāram* (prostrates in the manner of praying).

After the *nalunku*, all those present perform *ārati* (clockwise, vertical circling of a flame before an image of the deity) and sing an auspicious concluding song (*mangaḷam*) such as "Śri Rāmacandranukku jeyamangaḷam," a song in *madhyamāvati rāga* composed for the *Rāma nāṭakam* (a Tamil music-dance-drama about the god Rama) by Arunachala Kavirayar. After the wedding, there are also *campanti* songs, in which the family of the groom makes fun of the bride's family and vice versa; this is similar to the *gālī* songs of North India. Although they are intended to be in good fun, these songs sometimes result in arguments between the new in-laws. The last ritual is associated with the couple's first night together *(śānti muhurtam*); this too was once performed with a set of songs. Perhaps not too long after, when the new bride becomes pregnant for the first time, a "morning sickness" song (*macakkaippāṭṭu*) will be sung.

One of the emotional components of North Indian weddings that is less pronounced in the south is the sadness that accompanies the departure of the bride from her natal home. In South India, cross-cousin marriage is prevalent; a consequence of this form of marriage preference is that brides remain in close contact with their natal families. North Indian Hindus, in contrast, do not offer their daughters in marriage to close relatives; in a village setting, this often means the bride moves far away from her natal village. The departure of the bride from the natal home in North India is the occasion for the demonstration of significant grief. Departure songs (*bidāī gīt*) are sung at this time. In Pakistan, among Muslims, the departure of the bride from the home is also considered sad, and one Punjabi player of the *ḍhol* 'barrel drum' suggest-

Holī celebrates the defeat of the mythical ruler Hiranyakasipu by the man-lion incarnation of the god Vishnu. North Indian Hindus commemorate the original celebration of this defeat by building a bonfire and throwing colored powder and water at one another.

ed that the six-beat *dādrā tāl* played for the departure of the bride (*rukhsat*) is in this context a "sad beat."

SEASONAL AND CALENDRICAL RITUALS

Although one may distinguish life-cycle rituals analytically from seasonal rituals, it must be noted that not all of the former are scheduled solely on the basis of biological circumstances. Funerals cannot be planned at all because they must be held almost immediately after a death, but marriages and other auspicious rites are planned: they must be held during auspicious months and at auspicious times. Sometimes the season determines auspiciousness: the rainy season is considered inauspicious in Nepal, therefore marriages and sacred-thread ceremonies are not scheduled during these months (Tingey 1994). Furthermore, calendrical religious festivals and life-cycle ceremonies are sometimes interdependent, as, for example, when a sudden death might render family members or even an entire village ritually unfit to conduct auspicious religious ceremonies.

Not all celebrations that occur annually during particular seasons are necessarily connected with that season. The birthday of Krishna (Kṛshnā Janmāshṭamī in the north or Śrī Jayantī in the south, during August–September) is one such example. Other rituals ostensibly commemorate mythological events, but have come to be associated with seasons. Holī, for instance, celebrates the defeat of the mythical ruler Hiranyakasipu by the man-lion incarnation of the god Vishnu. North Indian Hindus commemorate the original celebration of this defeat by building a bonfire and throwing colored powder and water at one another. Lewd songs sung at this time reflect the temporary loosening of social mores during the festival (Tewari 1991). The philosophical basis for Holī activities is that all bad feelings and jealousy should be dissolved in a bonfire so that life can begin afresh at the new year. Holī has come to be understood as a heralding of spring, but Basant is more directly concerned with the agricultural season of spring.

Solar calendars, lunar calendars, and the seasons

Three major calendars are followed in South Asia: the Gregorian calendar, the Hindu (*Vikram samvat*) calendar, and the Muslim (*Hijrī*) calendar. Although the Hindu calendar is based on the lunar year, it periodically corrects so as to be in phase with the solar year.

The Muslim calendar remains continually out of phase with the solar year, and therefore there is no Muslim calendrical festival that is also seasonal. Some Muslim occasions, including some *ʿurs* 'death anniversary celebrations for saints', are seasonal in that they are scheduled during particular solar months (de Tassy 1995). Others are seasonal in spirit if not in actual performance time: the *ʿurs* of Madholal Husain of Lahore, for example, is considered to be a spring festival even though it is celebrated in different seasons according to the Muslim calendar. Similarly, Shias know that the

Muharram festival attains its greatest impact during the summer months, when the heat makes the pious mystically identify with the thirsty participants in the memorialized battle of Karbala. The Shias devote significant religious sentiments, expressed through melodically rendered poetry (*marṣiya* and *nauḥa*), to mourning the death of Husain, the Prophet Muhammad's grandson, who was killed on the orders of the Ummayad Caliph Yazid in this battle of A.D. 680.

Muslim marriages in Pakistan are scheduled according to seasonal convenience. In the Punjab, the months from September through December are considered favorable. This scheduling is tempered, however, by the calendrical observance of mourning (Muharram) and fasting (Ramadan), and the period between ʿĪdu'l-fiṭr 'breaking of the fast after Ramadan' and ʿĪd-ĕ-aẓḥā 'the commemoration of Abraham's sacrifice', during which weddings are prohibited.

Music itself may be seasonal without necessarily being attached to a seasonal ritual as such, and thus in itself constitutes a type of seasonal ritual. Some songs, for example, are sung during particular months. The themes of these songs are connected with the seasons. The love song genre *caitī* of Uttar Pradesh, or the openly erotic *keśyā* of Rajasthan, for example, are sung in the spring (Raheja and Gold 1994); the *bārahamāsā* can be sung anytime, but it is particularly associated with the rainy season and depicts the separation of husband and wife (Tewari 1974).

Common seasonal and calendrical festivals

During the months of April and May in Tamil Nadu, the fields are bare after the harvest. This is the time for the staging of village dramas such as the *Rāma nāṭakam* or *Ariccantiran nāṭakam* (about the Hindu god Rama or the mythological figure Harishchandra). A stage is set up in the paddy fields; if a Mariyamman (goddess) temple is nearby, the festival for the goddess will incorporate the drama. Characters speak as well as sing their parts.

Mariyamman festivals in Tamil Nadu are scheduled differently according to subregion, but are usually between the months of February and July. Special genres of music and dance are performed during this time, such as *kummi* and *karakam* [see TAMIL NADU]. The analogous goddess in North India is Sitala; her festival is celebrated during the month of Māgh (January–February) (Stutley and Stutley 1984). Special songs are dedicated to this goddess, but multicontextual genres such as *keśyā* are also sung to please her. Women sing these songs in conjunction with worship "both to ward off childhood diseases and to improve community fertility" (Raheja and Gold 1994).

During Āświn (September–October), Hindus of North and South India celebrate Navrātrī 'nine nights', a festival dedicated to the three goddesses Lakshmi, Parvati, and Sarasvati. The festival starts after the new-moon day. In Tamil Nadu, Brahmin women construct dioramas with dolls (*bommai*) of gods, goddesses, and people. Children are dressed in costumes and sent out to invite neighbors, who come, view the exhibit, sing devotional songs, and consume sweets. The ninth day is *sarasvatī pūjā*. All the books, musical instruments, and instruments of one's trade are put in front of an image of Sarasvati, goddess of learning and music, to be blessed. This festival is also celebrated in cities with concert series of classical music. In Gujarat, Navrātrī is an occasion for the *garbā* and *garbī* dances, performed around a clay pot by women and men respectively. This is the end of the rainy season, when crops are becoming ready for harvest.

The festival of lights, Dīpāvalī, is celebrated during Kārtik (October–November). As with Navrātrī, there are no special songs for this festival, but the ritual contexts for devotional singing are diverse. Sometimes children perform the central ritual activities. Tamil Brahmin children aged five to twelve, for example, celebrate by commissioning a local potter to sculpt a clay cow and calf, sowing seeds of nine grains in a clay pot, and taking the figures and pot to dissolve in the river. They sing devotional songs while walking in procession, and afterward young girls dance *kummi*. This ritual is said to ensure bountiful rainfall.

There are many kinds of rituals in South Asia designed to bring rainfall, and inasmuch as rainfall is closely connected with the seasons these too should not be overlooked. The Kotas of the Nilgiri Hills play a sacred repertoire of "god tunes" (*devr koḷ*) on their drums and reed instruments as they encircle the village, making a procession to sites of divine significance around the village (see "Ritual order" below). Rain is said to fall within the boundaries of the village immediately following the ritual (Wolf 1997b). In Gujarat, women go on a procession carrying a clay image of the Vedic god Indra and singing songs to this deity requesting rain.

Muslims celebrate the birthday (*mīlād*) of the Prophet Muhammad with a variety of poetic forms; these are recited tunefully but are not considered "songs" because of Muslim injunctions against "music." In the weeks leading up to the birth date, gatherings of men or women recite *nʿat* 'poems of praise in honor of the Prophet' and *qaṣīda* 'poems in praise of the family of the Prophet'. In Sindh, men sing a genre called *maulūd*: a leader begins a text line and is joined by a chorus in unison; sometimes a question-and-answer form is adopted. The pace of the singing increases as the men sing into the night. The style is sometimes characterized by insistent vocal pulsations. Each Sindhi village has a *maulūd* group that practices throughout the year.

FUNCTIONS OF MUSIC IN SEASONAL AND LIFE-CYCLE RITUALS

Ritual contexts for music in South Asia are diverse, and some widely acknowledged reasons for performing music cut across these contextual divisions.

Announcing an event

Music frequently serves to announce an occasion or an event. There are at least three aspects to the function of announcement: (1) invitation/prohibition, (2) display of status, and (3) demarcation of time.

Invitation and prohibition

Music is often used to invoke or invite deities to an occasion of worship or healing. Sometimes malevolent forces or demons are also summoned, as in Sri Lanka, where a priest invites demons by name to partake of food while his attendants play the drums and chant (Sarachchandra 1966). Demonic forces are called on not to do harm, as in black magic, but to cease their affliction of a sick person. In both North and South India, spirits of the dead—believed responsible for certain illnesses—are similarly implored to leave a sick patient alone.

Equally common is the use of music to invite people to a ceremony. At the beginning of a festival, a loud horn blast, a cascade of drumming, or even rifle shots often announce to neighboring villages and towns that the festivities have begun. Among the Kotas of South India, the sound of all musical instruments playing at once (*ōmayṇ*) and the performance of a particular dance melody (*kālgūc āṭ*) on the drums and double-reeds (*koḷvar*) announce to the neighboring Baḍaga people that their annual god festival (Devr) has commenced. The Baḍagas know from this first sound that they should not enter the nearby Kota village at night for a prescribed number of days; following this, they are invited to an intercommunity day of worship and dance. Similarly, a Kota funeral is announced with a drum beat on a kettledrum (*ērtabaṭk*), followed by a blast on pairs of brass horns (*kob*). Traditionally, neighboring Baḍagas would know that they must attend and provide certain materials (chief among which are sacrificial buffaloes) for the funerals of those Kotas with whom they have established past ritual and economic relations.

The rapid, loud sounding of all instruments at once (*kēṭṭi mēḷam*) also signifies the high point of a ritual or a marriage in South India; during the multiday performance of village dramas such as the *Rāmā nāṭakam*, such use of music marks the moment of crowning the god Rama as king. The event is called *paṭṭāpiṣēkam* (coronation) and occurs on the last day at about 3:00 or 4:00 A.M. Even if people missed other parts of the drama they want to be present at this time, for it signifies a moment of divine vision (*darśan*): spectators worship the actors as embodiments of the gods they are portraying.

Display of status

Patrons commonly employ musicians at festivals and weddings for the purpose of displaying or enhancing their status. In South India, villages compete by attempting to surround their festival premises with a large number of loudspeakers, and also by playing recorded music at the loudest possible volume. At least in the 1980s and early 1990s sheer volume was the criterion, not choice of repertoire, quality of recordings, or quality of loudspeaker system. At weddings in South India, status is measured in part by the fame of the classical musician who plays at the wedding concert. In Nepal, status is sometimes measured by the number of musicians playing at a wedding (Tingey 1994).

Demarcation of time

Another kind of announcement serves to mark off time periods. The most important kind of ensemble in South Asia for performing this function is the *naubat k̲h̲ānā*. The term literally means a building where drums are sounded, but it also refers to the ensemble itself, which usually comprises kettledrums such as *naqqārā* or *tāshā*, cymbals, and sometimes double-reed instruments with conical bores.

In Lucknow, a *naubat k̲h̲ānā* sits across from the *choṭā imāmbāṛā*, a building in which services are held commemorating the martyrdom of Husain and his family (figure 3). The ensemble that plays here consists of a *ḍhol*, a *tāshā*, and a *jhāñjh* 'pair of cymbals' (figure 4). The Shia performers in the ensemble hail from military families and play five times a day: at 6:00 A.M. to announce the first prayer time, then at

FIGURE 3 The *naubat k̲h̲ānā* building across from the *choṭā imāmbāṛā* in Lucknow. Photo by Richard Wolf, 1997.

Hindus normally begin any sequence of musical pieces, whether the context is framed as a ritual or as entertainment, with an item devoted to the elephant-headed god Ganesh, also called Vinayak, the "remover of obstacles."

FIGURE 4 *Jhāñjh* (*left*), *ḍhol* (*center*), and *tāshā* (*right*) players keeping the hours playing "*sain imām ḥusain*" in the *naubat khānā* building in Lucknow, 1997. Photo by Richard Wolf.

jh		jh		jh	jh(r)
		d		d	d
		t		t	t
		/		/	/
sain	i-	mām	ḥu-	sain	ḥaidar
1 . .		2 . .		3 . .	4 . .

jh = single strike of *jhāñjh* cymbals together; (r) indicates prolongation of sound by allowing the rim of one cymbal to touch the face of the other.
d = *ḍhol* stroke
t = *tāshā* stoke
/ = A beat of the hand on the chest in the performance of *mātam* (self-flagellation)
1 . . = Numbers indicate beats; dots show a triple subdivision of each beat.

FIGURE 5 The beat of the *naubat khānā* of Lucknow and the verbal text that players understand the beat to mean. Shias beat their breasts to this rhythm and chant the text during the Muharram festival.

9:00 A.M., 12:00 P.M., 3 P.M., and 6:00 P.M. The performers consciously encode a religious significance into their simple drum beat: the beats stand for the words "*sain imām ḥusain ḥaidar*" 'Religious leader, Husain, Lion' (an epithet for ʿAlī, Husain's father) (figure 5).

Turko-Afghan Muslims from Central Asia had already introduced the instruments and the concept of the *naubat khānā* to the subcontinent by the twelfth century, and by the fourteenth century it had been adopted by Jains (Tingey 1994) and presumably by North Indian Hindus as well. Now it is firmly established within Hindu traditions. In the *havelī* 'house' (in this case, of worship) of Shri Nathji in Nathdvara, Rajasthan, for instance, the *naubat khānā* music "summons the worshipers, generates excitement, and focuses attention on the temple and its celebrants" (Gaston 1997). The musicians who play in this ensemble are called Ḍholīs (a term that generically refers to *ḍhol* players in other parts of South Asia) and are not allowed to enter the *havelī* most days, probably due to their low-caste rank. They perform on the *śahnāī*, *ḍhol*, *naqqārā*, and *dhūmsa* 'double-headed drum'. Music in this *havelī* calls devotees for daily worship at 10:30–11:30 A.M. and 6:30–7:30 P.M. In addition to the diurnal announcement of prayer, each festival occasions the performance of *naubat khānā* music at certain times of the day. The more music, the more important the occasion (Gaston 1997).

In Nepal, the *naubat khānā* is called *pāncai bājā* and is performed by Damāi musicians who are also tailors by profession [see NEPAL]. The ensemble employs a variety of kettledrums, the double-reed *śahnāī*, cymbals, and natural horns, and plays for calendrical cycles of both agricultural and religious festivals and for all Hindu rites of passage. The music is said to be for "divine rather than human consumption" (Tingey 1994).

Not all music performed for the keeping of hours is so sacredly invested or divinely appreciated. In Islam, independent of the shrine or mosque context, drumming may still serve a timekeeping function. For example, *ḍhol* players in Lahore drum every day during Ramadan, the month of fasting, to announce the time when people may break the fast. At the end of the month, the drummers go around and collect money from each neighborhood home, hoping that their services have been appreciated.

Identifying an event

Music may be used not only to announce a particular occasion, but also to delineate more specifically the identity of an event or its constituent parts—to articulate a ritual order, provide distinction between events and between communities, convey contextual specificity and generality, reinforce or create hierarchy, and provide expression for gender distinctions in ritual.

Ritual order

There are at least two ways in which music can articulate the order of a ritual. In one case, particular musical pieces may accompany more primary nonmusical ritual activities that must occur in a specific order. In the other case, a serial performance of musical pieces may itself be the focus of ritual activity.

Both ways of musically articulating a ritual order are found among the Kotas of South India. During funerals, the Kotas perform a number of conventionalized actions such as announcing the demise of the deceased, dressing the corpse within the house, moving the corpse from the house to a bier in the yard, washing and dancing around the corpse, carrying the corpse to the cremation ground, and lighting the pyre. Each of these activities is accompanied by one or more musical pieces, some specifically prescribed, others elective.

TRACK 12

During Devr, the annual ceremony paying homage to the Kota gods, a similar set of melodies is performed on special days at particular times to coincide with other activities such as opening the temple, mixing rice offerings, and collecting materials for a symbolic rethatching of the temple (which is now made of concrete). But there is also a special time set aside on a few of the evenings when twelve special melodies (*devr koḷ* literally 'god tunes') are played, more or less in a fixed order. This is a special time during which the villagers gather and listen to music for music's sake—there are no words to these melodies, and no other activities occur at this time. The Kotas believe their gods appreciate these melodies, which are said to be of divine origin, and some of the melodies help them recall miraculous stories of the gods (Wolf 1997a, 1997b).

Within any sequence of ritual musical pieces, it is common for a particular piece or type of piece to precede all others because of its auspiciousness or because it honors a personage or deity who is supposed to be formally recognized at the beginning of any undertaking. Hindus, for instance, normally begin any sequence of musical pieces, whether the context is framed as a ritual or as entertainment, with an item devoted to the elephant-headed god Ganesh, also called Vinayak, the "remover of obstacles." Manganihār *ḍhol* players in the Sindh province of Pakistan begin their playing at virtually any festival or ritual with a percussion rhythm called *dhamāl* (figure 6). Although *dhamāl* appears in many contexts, the form of the rhythm used at the beginning of a performance is intended to honor the thirteenth-century Sufi "Saint of Saints" (*pīrān-e-pīr*), Sheikh ʿAbdul Qadir Jilani (1088–1166), whose tomb in Baghdad is a popular place of pilgrimage for Indo-Pakistani Muslims.

FIGURE 6 Male visitors (except for close family members) are received outside the village at a rural Muslim wedding near Thatta, in southwestern Sindh, Pakistan, 1997. All male dancing takes place accompanied by a Manganihār performer on the *ḍhol*. Photo by Richard Wolf.

Sometimes song texts are chosen according to the order of a particular ritual. In the Shia observance of Muharram in India and Pakistan, for instance, the texts of *soz* chants are supposed to be chosen according to the day of observance: each day memorializes a particular set of events connected with the battle of Karbala. Sermons (*hadīth*) and *soz* texts tell the stories of the events of each particular day. *Soz* are always mournful in character, recited tunefully—sometimes in classical ragas—and accompanied by a unison chorus or a vocal drone, never with musical instruments (Qureshi 1981). They may be sung by men or by women, but never in ensembles of mixed gender (figure 7).

The narrative order of a story often structures the order of a musical performance in ritual reenactments of epics such as the Ramayana (Blackburn 1997; Lutgendorf 1991). Unlike Muharram, which can be understood as a discrete, dispersed set of ritual events loosely organized around the historical theme of a given day, the reenactment of a Hindu epic often consists of a single ceremony performed over the course of days or weeks. The narration or singing of the story forms the organizing core of the ritual, and may be combined in varying degrees with drama or puppetry. In most South Asian narrative traditions, a few fixed melodies or sequences of pitches are employed for an entire performance; the narrative thus structures the choice of text within the framework of a larger ritual performance, but not necessarily the melody or the rhythm.

Distinction between events

Perhaps the most important, and certainly the most obvious, semiotic function of music in South Asia is to distinguish between culturally opposed types of events: happy and sad, auspicious and inauspicious, or pure and impure. Wedding music is therefore assiduously avoided during a funeral and vice versa (except in the case of the death of a very old person, which is considered auspicious). Sad ragas associated with mourning or death, especially *mukhāri*, should not be played during weddings, either in the ritual music accompanying the ceremony itself or in any concert of classical music that might be staged as part of the reception. Likewise, the music of funeral bands does not include auspicious ragas such as *kalyāṇi*. A drum rhythm rather than a melody usually signifies a funeral in South India; the only nonfunereal context in which such a rhythm is performed is Tamil drama—when a funeral is being depicted.

FIGURE 7 Sikander Johan (center), a noted *soz khvān* (performer of *soz*) in Lucknow, sings with a female chorus, 1997. Photo by Richard Wolf.

Music during funerals is somewhat uncommon in modern-day South Asian Islam, but in northern areas of Pakistan, among the Burusho people, a distinct type of music is still performed, played by a double-reed and drum ensemble known as *harīp*. The special funeral piece is called *toghorā*. This piece is never played during a wedding. Remarkably, however, performers claim the piece is not sad, but celebrates the deceased.

Ethnic and geographical differences

Performers also articulate differences between communities musically. In the days before the partition of India and Pakistan, for example, Mīrāsī hereditary musicians in Multan (in Pakistani Punjab) used to perform different rhythms for the weddings of ordinary Muslims, Sayyids (family of the Prophet Muhammad), and Hindus. Patron families and those within earshot of a wedding would be familiar with this rhythmic code and could distinguish, by the drum beats and the types of drums, what kind of wedding was taking place. A distinguishing feature of Hindu weddings was the use of the *tāshā* drum 'shallow kettledrum'; *tāshā* playing has virtually been abandoned in Punjab since the departure of the Hindus (figure 8).

FIGURE 8 Muhammad Baksh Multani, a Mīrāsī musician from Multan, Punjab (Pakistan), used to play the *tāshā* for Hindu weddings before partition. Here he demonstrates a *tāshā*; the drum shown is about ninety years old. Photo by Richard Wolf, 1997.

Kotas too play different types of musical pieces according to their patrons and the origin of the gods they honor with music. They use a percussion pattern for deities of Hindu origin that is distinct from the three types of pattern they use to honor Kota indigenous deities. In the days when Kotas were patronized by Baḍaga and Toda families, they maintained separate repertoires of melodies for the funerals of each community.

Performers use music not only to reinforce the identity of patron communities but also to create a sense of place. Professional performers on the *ḍhol* and *śahnāī* in Pakistan know (albeit often in reduced form) rhythms and melodies associated with other parts of Pakistan and name musical pieces after their respective places of origin. At weddings, connoisseurs from Lahore might ask a Punjabi drummer to play a rhythm from Peshawar, or perhaps from a city in Punjab such as Sialkot. Drum rhythms played in local ritual contexts come to articulate a musical map of Pakistan as filtered through the performance idiom of a particular local musical subtradition. Some musicians, especially those who live at the geographical border of two or more linguistic and cultural regions, also maintain repertoires of more than one musical subtradition because they play for patrons of more than one community.

The mere presence or absence of music at an occasion cannot reveal to an outsider whether or not the occasion is of great importance within a culture. It is necessary to know how music is valued in the culture, and also exactly what is considered "music."

Music can articulate not only ethnic and geographical differences between communities, but also similarities. Close association between communities is sometimes paralleled by similar musical traditions at festivals. For instance, in Uttar Pradesh "songs sung during life-cycle ceremonies among Brahman, Kshatriya, and Vaisya families are identical, as there is a reciprocal association between these caste groups" (Tewari 1991). In the Nilgiris, the interaction among Kotas, Baḍagas, Iruḷas, and Kurumbas at festival times may also account for some of the similarities in their dance styles and musical traditions. Then again, the musical styles of two communities who do not have a great deal of reciprocal association, such as the Nāyakkars and Aiyankārs of Tamil Nadu, are often markedly different, even if they inhabit the same village and perform the same genres. The *kummi* song style of the Nāyakkars is very different from that of the Aiyankārs.

Specificity versus generality

Repertoires and styles not only differentiate one occasion from another and one patron group from another, they also cut across contexts in complex ways. Some types of music can be used in a variety of public situations; others must be extremely restricted.

The musicologist Carol Tingey (1994) describes three kinds of repertoires among the Damāi musicians of Nepal: a popular repertoire that is not ritually significant but may be used in ritual settings such as processions; context-related pieces that are or were associated with rituals or seasonal activities, but are only loosely connected with these activities in their actual performance today; and a ritual repertoire indispensable for particular ritual activities, and which cannot be played elsewhere.

Folk-dance repertoires tend to be multipurpose: for weddings, for childbirth or circumcision, for welcoming a great personage, for public display on a national holiday, or for performances on television.

Devotional songs are generally appropriate for a variety of occasions and may be sung in various kinds of temples; however, differences exist in the repertoires of specific sects or among Shaivites and Vaishnavites. Hindu devotional songs of a relatively casual nature such as bhajans are also sung outside the temple context, often for social entertainment. Such is not generally the case with laments.

In Muslim South Asia, the praise poem *qaṣīda* is sung in many contexts: at poetry readings (*mushāira*), weddings, social celebrations (such as the retirement of a respected man), death anniversaries of saints (*ʿurs*) and (principally in Punjab) mourning sessions (*majlis*) during Muharram. In contrast, other genres such as *soz* are performed only in the *majlis*. A probable explanation for the different contextual appropriateness of these two genres lies in their nature: the praise of important personages in the *qaṣīda* is suitable for both happy and sad situations, whereas the evocation of sadness in the *soz* is not appropriate for ritual celebrations.

Hierarchy

The presence or absence of music during ritual ceremonies in South Asia may indicate the importance of an occasion. The ubiquity of and necessity for marriage music among Hindus, for example, highlights the emphasis Hindus place on marriage as a final and binding ritual. The Kotas, in contrast, view marriage as a responsibility, not as an end in itself; Kota marriages are simple, and divorce, remarriage, polygamy, and widow remarriage are common. Kotas have developed no special repertoire of wedding pieces and generally abstain from performing music at their own weddings. Although Kotas certainly consider marriage to be important, it is not ranked as highly in their hierarchical scheme as funerals and the annual Devr celebrations. The absence of music is part of a more general cultural pattern in which marriage is not culturally elaborated.

In a different cultural context, the absence of music can signify that one ritual occasion is more profound or more valued than others. Such is the case with the Muharram festival, at which "music" is supposedly banned. In Lahore, any instrumental sounds that can be remotely construed as musical are banned, but in Sindh, drums and *śahnāī* are traditionally used in the Muharram rituals (figure 9). Sindhis refrain from playing music for public entertainment during Muharram, but the status of ritual music is somewhat ambiguous. They all acknowledge that drumming and *śahnāī* playing are forms of "music," but even some of the musicians say that one should not speak of these things as music (*mūsīqī*) per se.

The previous examples indicate that the mere presence or absence of music at an occasion cannot reveal to an outsider whether or not the occasion is of great importance within a culture. It is necessary to know how music is valued in the culture, and also exactly what is considered "music."

Sometimes a hierarchy of rituals can be more subtle than implied by the simple presence-versus-absence model. In the highly elaborate ritual system of the Kotas, the types of pieces performed during the most holy days of the "god ceremony" differ from those performed on previous days. At night on each of the four days preceding the opening of the temple, men and women dance in a peripheral area of the village, where houses are located. This location, in contrast to the central temple area, is a relatively ordinary space in the Kota scheme of things. Only short, relatively simple, unornamented melodies are performed in these ordinary spaces. In the temple area,

FIGURE 9 *Tāshā* players in Hyderabad, Sindh, heat drum skins to tighten them before a performance. These drummers perform only during Muharram. All belong to Sunni families who migrated from India at partition and are members of the Shaikh Siddiqi community. Photo by Richard Wolf, 1997.

FIGURE 10 Men dancing at a rural Muslim wedding near Thatta, in southwestern Sindh, Pakistan, 1997. Photo by Richard Wolf.

after the temple is opened, longer and more elaborate dance pieces are performed, as are the highly esteemed twelve god tunes. Music is but one of a number of elements articulating the hierarchy of the central space and the period of solemn devotion with which it is associated.

Gender

As in South Asian musical culture generally, music and dance function to articulate gender divisions in ritual contexts (figure 10). Examples include the musical celebration of male versus female children in Hindu families (mentioned previously), the different repertoires of wedding songs sung by the bride's and groom's families, and the distinction of male instrumentalists and female lamenters in funerals. However, the same genres may be rendered by either men or women in gender-segregated settings, especially in Muslim contexts such as the *majlis*.

Accomplishing a goal

Music is present in rituals for a variety of reasons; it is often perceived as accomplishing something in support of the goals of the ritual. Such accomplishments include creating auspiciousness, removing evil, inducing trance, promoting healing, and securing a suitable mate.

To create auspiciousness

In many rituals, music is used to create an atmosphere of auspiciousness. This is accomplished in at least two ways: by drowning out inauspicious sounds, and by playing auspicious musical pieces on a set of instruments considered auspicious. An example of the first process is the loud outdoor music of the *tavil* and *nāgasvaram* at South Indian weddings, and particularly the *kēṭṭi mēlam* discussed above. An example of the second process is the auspicious *pāncai bājā* ensemble of Nepal, whose music is said to "generate an aura of well-being and to confer specific blessings at ritually significant times" (Tingey 1994).

It should be mentioned that the auspiciousness of a musical style or repertoire in a Hindu context may be unrelated to whether or not the musicians themselves are considered to be pure or impure. However, inauspicious music played at Hindu funerals is never performed by musicians of high or "pure" ritual status.

To drive away demons or remove evil

In many cases, certain classes of musicians are called on to drive away evil spirits from the body of an individual or from the premises of a festival. When musicians are thus employed as exorcists, the individual afflicted by possession of a demon or spirit of the dead is usually a woman. In Tamil Nadu, one type of musician who acts as an exorcist is the player of the *pampai* drum, a double cylindrical drum (Nabokov 1995). In Sindh, the player of the *alg̲hozah* 'double duct flute' sometimes acts as an exorcist; when he plays a piece called *lehrā*, an afflicted woman spontaneously dances and the infecting spirit is supposed to be chased from her body.

In Nepal, Damāi drummers of the far western and eastern regions of Nepal play music for funerals and during eclipses to protect against forces of evil that may be particularly dangerous at those times. According to Tingey (1994), they create an "auspicious sound barrier" by producing "as much noise as possible." Explanations given for drumming and other loud music at funerals and during ceremonies requiring blood offerings frequently center around discussions of spirits and demons, who are said to be attracted to blood and death.

To induce trance

Short repetitive melodies or drum beats are commonly used to induce trance in certain ritual settings [see MUSIC AND TRANCE]. Possession may be induced not only to drive away spirits, but also to attract spirits or deities whose counsel may be required. Villagers may ask local deities why rain has not come, or why animals have become sick. In ecstatic traditions such as the *teyyam* of Kerala, dancers wear elaborate make-up and dress in the costume of a particular deity; they become possessed by listening to special songs (*uṟaccal tōṟṟam*) consisting of descriptions of the deity's family and birth, physical appearance, and shrines, and by staring into the mirror at their own cosmetic metamorphosis (Freeman 1991).

To promote healing

Music is used in healing rituals, which may or may not involve trance or driving away evil spirits. The tribal groups Beṭṭa Kurumba and Kāṭṭu Nāyakka of the Nilgiris, for example, have special repertoires of antiphonal healing songs. Suspicious of allopathic cures, some members still prefer these traditional cures in cases of serious illnesses.

Music may also perform a prophylactic function. In village circumcision rituals in Sindh, women sing continuously until the wound is healed.

To secure a suitable mate

Hindu women commonly sing devotional songs when performing rituals to ensure the acquisition of a good husband or a male child, or to secure the health and well-being of their families. In some Muslim traditions in northern Pakistan and Brahmin traditions in South India, special songs, music, or chants are reported to accompany the formal consummation of a marriage in order that a boy child will result from the union.

REFERENCES

Blackburn, Stuart. 1997. *Rama Stories and Show Puppets: Kambaṉ's Rāmāyaṇa in Performance.* Delhi: Oxford University Press.

de Tassy, Garcin. 1995. *Music Festivals in India and Other Essays*, trans. and ed. M. Waseem. Delhi: Oxford University Press.

Freeman, John R. 1991. "Purity and Violence: Sacred Power in the Teyyam Worship of Malabar." Ph.D. dissertation, University of Pennsylvania.

Gaston, Anne-Marie. 1997. *Krishna's Musicians: Musicians and Music Making in the Temples of Nathdvara Rajasthan.* New Delhi: Manohar.

Kapadia, Karin. 1995. *Siva and Her Sisters: Gender, Caste, and Class in Rural South India.* Delhi: Oxford University Press.

Lutgendorf, Philip. 1991. *The Life of a Text: Performing the Rāmcaritmānas of Tulsidas.* Berkeley: University of California Press.

Nabokov, Isabelle R. 1995. "'Who are you?' Spirit Discourse in a Tamil World." Ph.D. dissertation, University of California at Berkeley.

Parry, Jonathan P. 1994. *Death in Banaras.* Cambridge: Cambridge University Press.

Patel, Madhubhai. 1974. *Folksongs of Southern Gujarat.* Baroda: Indian Musicological Society.

Qureshi, Regula B. 1981. "Islamic Music in an Indian Environment: The Shiʿa *Majlis.*" *Ethnomusicology* 25(1): 41–71.

Raheja, Gloria G., and Ann G. Gold. 1994. *Listen to the Heron's Words: Reimagining Gender and Kinship in North India.* Berkeley: University of California Press.

Sarachchandra, E. R. 1966. *The Folk Drama of Ceylon*, 2nd ed. Sri Lanka: Department of Cultural Affairs.

Stutley, Margaret, and James Stutley. 1984. *Harper's Dictionary of Hinduism: Its Mythology, Folklore, Philosophy, Literature, and History.* San Francisco: Harper & Row.

Tewari, Laxmi. 1974. "Folk Music of India: Uttar Pradesh." Ph.D. dissertation, Wesleyan University.

———. 1991. *Folk Music of Uttar Pradesh.* International Institute for Comparative Music Studies. Musicaphon BM 55802 ADD. Compact disc with liner notes.

Tingey, Carol. 1994. *Auspicious Music in a Changing Society: The Damāi Musicians of Nepal.* London: School of Oriental and African Studies, University of London.

Wolf, Richard. 1997a. "Of God and Death: Music in Ritual and Everyday Life. A Musical Ethnography of the Kotas of South India." Ph.D. dissertation, University of Illinois at Urbana-Champaign.

———. 1997b. "Rain, God and Unity among the Kotas." In *Blue Mountains Revisited: Cultural Studies on the Nilgiri Hills*, ed. Paul Hockings, 231–292. Delhi: Oxford University Press.

Music and Trance

David Roche

Cross-Cultural Psychoacoustics
Nepali Shamanism
Goddess Spirit Possession
Sufi Ecstasy

In South Asia sound is generally believed to invoke or represent symbolically the unseen power of the universe. Ritual music, the encoded, organized sound for religious ceremonies, is thus a widespread means by which South Asians access or initiate deep levels of spiritual communication. From the ancestor invocations of tribal (*ādivāsī*) elders to the formal liturgy of Vedic priests, from the chanted scriptures of Buddhist monks to the mystical poetry of Sufi singers, from popular Hindu ecstatic group singing to the din of street processions, trance remains an enduring sign of successful connection to a macrocosmic reality. Trance occurs in the form of shamanic journeying, voluntary spirit possession, hyperemotional involuntary possession, or meditative awareness.

The relationship of music and trance phenomena also illuminates social and biological dimensions of culture. Western medical taxonomy provides no clinical or biological definition of trance, but the outward physical appearance of a person in a trance state is generally one of somnambulance accompanied by involuntary motion of eyelids and limbs. In common usage, trance can cover many possible dissociative or "altered states of consciousness," a term coined by psychologists in the 1960s to describe the effects of hallucinogenic drugs on mental and other biological functions. In South Asian cultural terms, trance signifies temporary dissociative states of a voluntary or involuntary nature, explained by the participants as resulting from the visitation of a spiritual entity, for good or ill.

Music accompanies ceremonies or performances in which bodily expressions, such as convulsions and anesthesia, signal dramatic shifts of consciousness. Such musical contexts represent culturally condoned enactments of spiritual metamorphosis. Initiates become the vehicles of divinities, as in the shaman's danced journeys among the Thulung Rai community of eastern Nepal, or they become mediums of divinities, as in the spirit possession of Mīna folk priests (*bhopā*) in southern Rajasthan. In both environments, exorcism, curing, geomancy, and divining follow the intoning of chant and the playing of drums and other percussion.

Involuntary possession of bystanders may occur in both shamanic and spirit-possession ceremonies, but it is in the latter, where musicians and mediums are distinct, that such events occur more commonly. This distinction is emerging as a defining principle in South Asian ethnographic literature: shamanism is identified by voluntary self-induced trance, in which the shaman provides his own musical accompaniment; spirit possession is defined by voluntary trance inducement in a priest or medium accompanied by initiated, ritual musicians who do not themselves become spirit possessed. Both phenomena represent common trance performance contexts. Ecstatic events in which audience members may be overcome by the performance proceedings, as in the case of some Sufi devotional music, are also common. The degree and intensity of trance varies among events and contexts, but lower-class rural and urban populations are more likely to witness and participate fully in trance performances as part of regular religious observances than either rural or urban educated elites in South Asia.

The physiology of trance and the role music plays in trance inducement are both important approaches to an interdisciplinary study of music and trance. The former clinical, scientific approach deals with the variety of trance states, from those that allow extraordinary physical control or unusual feats of physicality and those that involve emotional excess, debilitating and uncontrollable convulsive behavior, and hyperventilation, to those that resemble hypnotic states of meditative focusing. The latter cultural approach studies the role of music in inducing these various trance states. The scientific vocabulary of clinical hypnosis allows certain parallels to be drawn between hypnosis and South Asian trance that help to clarify the crucial relationship between music and trance.

CROSS-CULTURAL PSYCHOACOUSTICS

Certain psychoacoustic experiments indicate music's profound biological effect on humans cross-culturally. These include the hearing of frequencies, highlighting confusion inherent in locating certain musical intervals, the neural processing of pitches close to each other, and the musical memory of Parkinson's syndrome patients. The literature of Western medical practice includes references and case studies clearly recognizing these sonic and psychoacoustic phenomena, but usually casting them in a negative light as part of disease symptomatology. In South Asia, an alternative, positive model has existed for millennia. The conscious use of psychoacoustic phenomena—part of the oral wisdom passed down through generations within ethnic and cultural groups and formalized in the sacred technologies of religious ceremonialism—brings powerful nuances to ritual musical performance practice. The sensory overload common to celebrations in the typical urban Hindu temple, for example, represents the daily manifestation of attentiveness to stimuli evident to even the most casual observer: the din of brass bells and large drums, the reflected flashes from oil lamp flames and sputtering fluorescent lights, the overpowering clouds of incense smoke, the crush of devotees to view the central icon at the auspicious moment, the taste of blessed offerings, and the wafting fragrance of flower garlands. When the soundscape also involves ritually encoded music, as it does in shamanic, spirit possession, and ecstatic ceremonial performances, it can represent both a contributing factor to and an evocative symbol of transcendance. It can simultaneously be a modality for hypnotic trance inducement, both of devotees and priests.

NEPALI SHAMANISM

A Nepali shaman is most commonly referred to as *dhāmi, garau,* or *jhāṇkri,* or one of many other specific local names. A shaman is the privileged lineal or spiritual descendant of all preceding shamans. He (or more rarely she) is an intermediary with training in diagnosing and treating illnesses, a spiritual doctor with certification in oral traditions of healing. Learning from the sacred texts and technologies of forebears, the shaman comes to his or her craft either by heredity or by avocation. In some instances, a child saved from a life-threatening illness by shamanic intervention becomes a suitable candidate for apprenticeship to the shaman's and the presiding divinity's lineage.

Music making is one of the central techniques employed in ceremonies involving healing (which may or may not include soul journeying, exorcism, or spirit possession) and plays a major role in establishing rapport between shaman and client, as well as between shaman and spirit world. Some scholars argue that music induces trance, but the complexity of various trance or altered psychological states militates against unrigorous use of such a sweeping term as inducement. Its general usage implies a uniformly successful one-to-one correspondence—that when the initiated shaman plays a musical code on a sacred musical instrument, possession automatically follows. The establishment of shaman-client rapport, for example, is central to the induction (Desjarlais 1992; Hitchcock and Jones 1994; Maskarinec 1995; Tingey 1994).

The shaman requires ritual regalia to practice this healing art, including a specially consecrated frame drum and a belt or bandolier of brass bells. The frame drum is the locus of musical power. Through its historic existence as the shaman's preferred instrument, not only among Nepali communities but also among some East Asian, Arctic, and North American peoples, the frame drum is symbolic of the vast geographic region in which Asian shamanism exists or has existed as a unitary cultural pattern. The typical double-headed frame drum (*ḍhyāṅgro*) used by the *puimbo* shaman of the Sunuwars in eastern Nepal is approximately 48 centimeters in circumference, covered with deer- or goatskin, with overlapped edges secured by knotted sinew. Between the skins and the hazelwood frame, porcupine quills form an internal rim to prevent the skin from overstretching when loose. The frame drum has a 30-centimeter-long handle carefully carved with iconic figures representing a nexus of symbols including spiritual guides, cosmological features, and magic numerology. The shaman attaches to the handle red and white cloth ribbons offered by the client. Each side of the drum has ritual paintings representing land markings; the sun, moon, and stars; a trident (pan–South Asian symbol of power, now often identified with the Hindu deity Shiva); and crosses. The shaman strikes the drum with a wand-like drumstick in the shape of a serpent.

A shamanic healing session is premised on the belief that divine intercession will occur during the course of a night (the most common time for performance). The shaman gains access to a portal of communication by the proper rendition of specific drum codes and chants, which results in trance. Following the preparation of an altar and the proper placement of ritual paraphernalia such as an oil lamp, a winnowing tray with husked rice and/or corn kernels, and a clay incense cup, a typical healing session begins with the shaman seated, chanting prayers in Sunuwari while steadily beating his drum. The shaman's assistants, the client and family, and possibly other lineage members are normally present at a trance session. From the standpoint of psychoacoustics, it is the encompassing ring of partials set in motion by the beater striking against the drum skin that carries the greatest importance in inducing a trance state. Rapid drumming, in which the echo of the partials is not allowed to decay but is maintained and shaped continuously as a wave, is an effective agent. As the strike tone beats on steadily, the echo of the partials is heard as a fluctuating "wow" by the shaman, his head close to the drum. The undulation of this wow bears little resemblance to the regular beating, though it is entirely controlled by the intensity of that beating, the tension of the drum skin, and the acoustic properties of skin and drum frame (thickness, shape, size, and resonance of the wood). When a healing session occurs inside a home, the acoustical properties of the room may also influence the psychological states of all present.

Rapport based on culturally defined expectations represents probably the greatest initial agent in trance induction, but the psychoacoustic signaling of the drumming, plus the chant coding in the form of the shaman's opening Sunuwari prayers, deepens it. The moment of the shaman's dramatic catharsis arrives with violent shaking leading to a standing dance, the shaman all the while chanting and drumming to the spirit guides while assistants crash cymbals and blow a conch shell. The ringing partials of all these instruments bounce off the walls, obliterating the silence and acoustically doming the proceedings. After fifteen minutes, the shaman's first trance passes and he falls to his knees, exhausted. After recovering and identifying an offended spirit, the shaman initiates subsequent ceremonial acts utilizing the ritual paraphernalia. The spectators continually ask for news from the spirit world, including the welfare of recently deceased relatives, while the shaman ministers to his client, whose health has been compromised by malevolent spirits. Two or more trance sessions may occur during the remaining hours of the night, before the entire exorcism concludes at sunrise.

GODDESS SPIRIT POSSESSION

A second music and trance performance practice exists, from the western Himalayas in the north to Cape Comorin (Kanyakumari) at the southern tip of India. Originating with non-Brahmanic social groups, the common features of this ceremonial repertoire include spirit possession of priests or mediums by a local or regional goddess (*devī*), processions celebrating agricultural fertility, animal sacrifice (real or symbolic), ritual music performed exclusively by initiated musicians (usually male), and the use of iconic musical instruments. The percussion instrument of choice is frequently an hourglass pressure drum. The family of such drums used for contemporary goddess ceremonies includes the double-headed, hourglass-shaped drum characterized by tension ligatures that bind the two goatskin heads with continuous V-lacing from the edge of one hooped head, around its circumference, to the other. The long tension ligatures are bound at the drum's waist with a belt that keeps them taut. Such drums are held in the hand, under the upper arm, or attached to the top of the seated musicians' feet, and are struck by hand, with a curved drumstick, or a combination of the two.

Northern area

In the Garhwali- and Kumaoni-speaking districts of Uttar Pradesh, adjacent to western Nepal, celebrants of goddess-invoking rituals may refer to the goddess as Devi. This Brahminic designation for the South Asian Great Goddess is often identified with Durga (Shakti in Tantra traditions) or other regionally prominent, virgin warrior goddesses. Sometimes Garhwali-speaking followers call her Mata Durga Bhavani, signifying a wrathful mother goddess figure (Berreman 1963; Chandola 1977). Most closely identified with her ceremonies in these districts are the *huḍki* 'hourglass drum', played by Bājgī (tailor caste) or other artisan-caste musicians, and the spirit possession of a female dancer of the Nāī (barber caste) or other artisan caste, specifically during the prophetic and/or exorcistic "black night" session (*kalrātra*) or night of the new moon. Central to the ceremony in Garhwal is the use of particular drum codes specifying movements within the ceremony itself. In a client's home or village temple, a caste-designated priest chants, and assistants drum and sound a brass percussion plate (*thālī*) to invoke the goddess. As the hereditarily selected female dancer performs, she intones a magical recitative that must be interpreted by village priests. Spirit possession signifies the goddess's presence, and the goddess then dances in the body of the possessed woman to a second rhythmic pattern. Later, when the priest addresses the goddess directly and she answers in a kind

In South Asian belief, drums are one of the main ritual devices for evoking possessing spirits. Processions to these spirits, invariably accompanied by percussion ensembles, often culminate in spirit possession not only of priests or mediums but also of susceptible bystanders.

of heightened speech through the medium of the dancer, the musicians employ another percussion pattern. Finally, at the conclusion of such a session, they use a fourth pattern, along with an appropriately contrasting chant text, to indicate the departure of the goddess. Particular song texts and rhythmic patterns specifically identify local goddesses. Drummers can draw on a variety of rhythmic patterns, depending on the mood displayed by the goddess through the dancer's actions.

TRACK 13

Equally theatrical events involving spirit possession by a goddess exist in southern Rajasthan among the Mīna *ādivāsī.* Hourglass drums (*ḍhāk*), accompanied by a brass percussion plate (*thālī*), represent the iconic drum of choice. The musical-performance aspect of a trance ceremony here is the chanting of a lengthy origin-myth narrative, rather than spirit-possessed trance dancing. Formulaic strophes set to two- and three-pitch chant melodies, over a rhythmic cycle of thirty-two beats, recount the return of Devi Ambav to this region after a devastating famine. Miracle chants, featuring episodes filled with such shamanic themes as passage to the underworld, geysers of blood and milk, the felling of cosmic trees from which ritual objects are constructed, and the marshaling of benevolent spirits to counteract evil predators, culminate in spirit possession of the leading *bhopā* priests by the goddess and her cohort, the bailiff Bheru. The resonance of the chanting and percussion help to establish hypnotic standing waves in the confined and acoustically hard surfaced "gods' house" (*devrā*), a rectangular, room-sized enclosed temple, and contribute to an atmosphere essential to the induction of a trance state. Spirit possession for the Mīna also occurs outside the *devrā,* during ritual events such as the monsoon-season pilgrimage drama known as *Gavrī.* In this event, initiated actors may become possessed by the goddess at climactic moments (figure 1).

FIGURE 1 A ceremonial pilgrimage drama in southern Rajasthan, 1982. To the left, Mīna priests (*bhopā*) chant, encircling a portable shrine to the goddess (*devī*); to the right, an actor playing the role of a robber becomes possessed. Photo © 1982 by David Roche.

FIGURE 2 A ritually anesthetized, skewered mendicant participates in a street procession marking the beginning of a pilgrimage in downtown Madras, 1968. Photo © 1968 by David Roche.

Southern area

In the South Indian state of Tamil Nadu, similar spirit-possession ceremonies are common (Beck 1982; Blackburn 1988; Frasca 1990; Hiltebeitel 1991; Moffatt 1979). Those involving the hourglass drum as the central iconic instrument in goddess worship are widespread. The *uḍakkai* drum (with many variant pronunciations and spellings) has long been associated with the followers of the Tamil Great Goddess, Mariyamman. The sacred power of percussion instruments in general has a long history in this region, dating from early Cankam-period literature (first to third centuries) that describes residual forces lying inert inside drums, awaiting release—like the genie of Aladdin's lamp. These forces may only be tapped at ceremonially prescribed auspicious moments of performance. In South Asian belief, drums are one of the main ritual devices for evoking possessing spirits. Processions to these spirits, invariably accompanied by percussion ensembles, often culminate in spirit possession not only of priests or mediums but also of susceptible bystanders. This is an example of psychoacoustically induced "mass hysteria," the temporary physical symptoms of which appear to be transmitted socially. These symptoms include fainting, dizziness, weakness, and seizurelike spasmodic motions, and are triggered by an as-yet-undefined set of agents, of which the belief system and/or physiological response to sound cues may be crucial. Acts of self-mortification, such as the skewering of flesh or firewalking, also appear commonly in processions or during ritual-music performances throughout the Dravidian-language regions of India (figure 2) and the Indian diaspora [see RÉUNION ISLAND]. In Sri Lanka, so-called demon dancing represents yet another manifestation of the relationship of music, dance, and religious theater to trance states in this region (Kapferer 1991). Sinhalese exorcism ceremonies are complex performances that illuminate the cultural basis underlying cosmological beliefs.

SUFI ECSTASY

Attention to psychoacoustics as a means of accessing otherwise inaccessible states of consciousness shapes belief systems at every level of South Asian life. Though rooted in village expressions, belief in the evocative power of music to alter consciousness continues to nourish more elite expressions across social barriers of religious sectarianism, caste, and class. Indeed, the fourteenth-century *Fawaʿid al-fuʿad* 'Morals of the Heart', a record of the conversations of the great Indian Sufi mystic, Nizamuddin Auliya (1242–1325) of Delhi, contains a singularly revealing passage that may serve as a concise summation of beliefs regarding the place of trance in the practice of ceremonial music. The passage is broadly applicable to many South Asian religious music traditions, though located in this case precisely within the canons of Sufism. Describing the *samaʿ* 'assembly for the audition of ecstatic devotional music', Sheikh Nizamuddin Auliya reportedly said (Currie 1992:121):

> In listening, the devotee experiences a sense of spiritual bliss which may be manifest as celestial lights, mystical states, and physical effects. Each of these derives from three worlds: the present world, the angelic sphere, and the potential realm, this last being intermediate between the first two. And these three manifestations of spiritual bliss may occur in one of three places: the spirits, the hearts, or the bodily limbs. At first, celestial lights descend from the angelic sphere on the spirits, then mystical states descend from the potential realm on the hearts, and finally physical effects from the physical world alight on the bodily limbs. In other words, during the state induced by listening to music, celestial lights descend from the angelic sphere upon the spirits. What subsequently appear in the heart are called mystical states, because it is from the potential realm that they descend on the hearts. Next, crying, movement, and agitation appear, and they are called physical effects because they alight from the present world on the bodily limbs.

There may be no clearer statement in the spiritual literature of South Asia so succinctly charting a relationship between hearing music and the subsequent arrival of the trance state.

REFERENCES

Auliya, Nizamuddin. 1992. *Fawaʿid al-fuʿad* (Morals of the heart), translated and annotated by Bruce B. Lawrence. Mahwah, N.J.: Paulist Press.

Beck, Brenda E. F. 1982. *The Three Twins: The Telling of a South Indian Folk Epic.* Bloomington: Indiana University Press.

Berreman, Gerald. 1963. *Hindus of the Himalayas.* Berkeley: University of California Press.

Blackburn, Stuart. 1988. *Singing of Birth and Death: Texts in Performance.* Philadelphia: University of Pennsylvania Press.

Chandola, Anoop. 1977. *Folk Drumming in the Himalayas: A Linguistic Approach to Music.* New York: AMS Press.

Currie, P. M. 1992. *The Shrine and Cult of Muʿīn al-dīn Chishtī of Ajmer.* Delhi: Oxford University Press.

Desjarlais, Robert R. 1992. *Body and Emotion: The Aesthetics of Illness and Healing in the Nepal Himalayas.* Philadelphia: University of Pennsylvania Press.

Feldhaus, Anne. 1995. *Water and Womanhood: Religious Meanings of Rivers in Maharashtra.* New York: Oxford University Press.

Frasca, Richard A. 1990. *The Theatre of the Mahābhārata: Terukkūttu Performances in South India.* Honolulu: University of Hawaii Press.

Hiltebeitel, Alf. 1991. *The Cult of Draupadī,* vol. 2: *On Hindu Ritual and the Goddess.* Chicago: University of Chicago Press.

Hitchcock, John T., and Rex L. Jones, eds. 1994. *Spirit Possession in the Nepal Himalayas.* New Delhi: Vikas Publishing House.

Kapferer, Bruce. 1991. *A Celebration of Demons: Exorcism and Aesthetics of Healing in Sri Lanka.* Providence, R.I., and Washington, D.C.: Berg and Smithsonian Institution Press.

Maskarinec, Gregory G. 1995. *The Rulings of the Night: An Ethnography of Nepalese Shaman Oral Texts.* Madison: University of Wisconsin Press.

Moffatt, Michael. 1979. *An Untouchable Community in South India.* Princeton, N.J.: Princeton University Press.

Roche, David. 1996. "Devi Amba's Drum: Mina Miracle Chant and the Ritual Ostinato of Spirit-Possession Ritual Performance in Southern Rajasthan." Ph.D. dissertation, University of California at Berkeley.

Tingey, Carol. 1994. *Auspicious Music in a Changing Society: The Damāi Musicians of Nepal.* London: School of Oriental and African Studies.

Musical Material Culture

South Asia is home to a wealth of sources relating to its musical cultures, ranging from ancient treatises to modern sound recordings and from sculptures, paintings, and photographs to musical instruments. Each of these sources allows us to expand our knowledge of South Asian music and music making. The focus of this section is visual sources and musical instruments; written sources are treated separately in the introduction to this volume, and references to modern sound recordings can be found in the concluding Guide to Recordings. Visual documentation is an invaluable resource for understanding South Asian music history, as there was little notated music and no recorded sound before the end of the nineteenth century. Mughal miniatures, *rāgmālā* paintings, and Jain manuscripts are among the varied, extant works of art. And surviving musical instruments together with the ways they have been classified are particularly revealing about the nature of music and musical thought in South Asian cultures.

Ustad Umrao Bundu Khan plays the bowed *sāraṅgī*, stopping the three main playing strings with the base of the fingernails. Karachi, Pakistan, 1975. Photo by Nazir Jairazbhoy.

Visual Sources

Bonnie C. Wade

The Sources
Iconography
Iconology
Organology
Musicology

In India, the depiction of musical sound—and its frequent partner, dance movement—abounds in many media: sculpture and bas-reliefs, pottery, wall paintings and drawings, palm leaves, cloth, paper, prints, and photographs. In some periods, visualized music making has been intimately linked with the related arts of literature, theater, dance, and architecture; it provides a remarkable source for considering the visual items as works of art, the contexts in and for which the art was created, the content of the artistic depiction, and the creators themselves.

Context and content are discussed in this article from the perspectives of four scholarly fields: iconography, iconology, organology, and musicology. The distinctions among these fields, for which visual sources have provided invaluable evidence in the study of Indian music, are primarily a matter of emphasis. A piece of sculpture, a painting, or a photograph can serve many purposes. When compared with a sufficient sampling of similar artifacts, it can be matched to complementary and confirming textual material, or to other visual media.

THE SOURCES

Visual sources of music and dance in South Asia abound throughout the subcontinent and over millennia. Contemporaneous with the cave paintings of Europe, Paleolithic or Stone Age cave paintings in several parts of India (including present-day Maharashtra and Andhra Pradesh) provide the earliest sources, depicting dance formations still common today among some groups and drums of several shapes (Vatsyayan 1982:10). In the urban civilization of Mohenjo Daro and Harappa (which flourished in the area of present-day Pakistan) motifs of dancers prevail in drawings on pottery and in the form of bronze, stone, and pottery figurines from the Neolithic period (c. 2400–2000 B.C.) (Kramrisch 1965, figs. 1–4).

In the early centuries of the common era, treatises such as Bharata's *Nāṭyaśāstra* enunciated the significant and enduring South Asian concept of the interrelationship of all the arts—literature and drama, architecture, sculpture, painting, music, and dance [see THEORETICAL TREATISES]. Theoreticians expressed the content of art in terms of the presentation of feelings and emotive states (*bhāva*) and the consequent

FIGURE 1 Bas-relief of female dancer with female instrumental ensemble. Pavaya, c. fifth century. *Top left*, a drummer plays *mṛdang*; *top center*, a player claps or plays a hand-held cymbal; *middle row left*, a woman plays a horizontal flute; *middle right*, drummer (instrument identified as "similar to the modern *tāshā*"); *bottom left*, player of an ovoid, short-necked lute with seven pegs (instrument identified as *citrā vīṇā*); *bottom right*, player of an arched harp (*vipañcī vīṇā*) (Mishra 1973: caption for Illustration 9). Photo copyright American Institute of Indian Studies, New Delhi.

evocation of those feelings in the spectator (*rasa*). The most abundant early evidence about music and its performance occurs not in visual form but in words—in the Vedas and in other sacred texts composed by about 400 B.C., and in plays and stories of the Golden Era (between A.D. 300 and 500).

Murals on the walls of Buddhist caves, and bas-reliefs from the second to sixth centuries, provide the most important visual documentation of surviving practices of music and dance. Paintings in the Ajanta caves in Maharashtra depict the use of drums and hand-held cymbals to accompany dance and also depict ensembles playing stringed and wind instruments. In figure 1, a bas-relief from around the 400s in Pavaya, Madhya Pradesh, a female dancer is surrounded by an ensemble of wind, stringed, and percussion instruments [see CLASSIFICATION OF MUSICAL INSTRUMENTS]. Dating from between the eighth and eleventh centuries, paintings on walls at Ellora, near Ajanta, are an equally important visual source; these include the dancing Shiva (Nataraja), destined to become a powerfully meaningful icon and to be produced in every conceivable artistic medium (see figure 2). The Chola dynasty of South India (ninth through eleventh centuries) produced stone and bronze sculptures and temple-wall paintings, the former illustrating the movements of dances in a technical way, the latter showing scenes of music and dance. Eleventh-century sculpted dance poses provide striking cultural continuity with those described centuries earlier in the great treatise on drama, dance, and music known as the *Nāṭyaśāstra*. Sculptures also show singers using their hands in a way suggestive of keeping the tala, the rhythmic cycle (Vatsyayan 1982:41).

From the eighth century—but with gathering momentum from the twelfth century—many new genres emerged in the visual media, as was the case in literature, music, and dance. Regional and even local (*deśī*) styles blossomed, complementing

FIGURE 2 Shiva as Lord of the Dance (Nataraja). Tamil Nadu, Chola period, late eleventh century. Copper alloy, diameter 57 cm. Metropolitan Museum of Art, New York (gift of R. H. Ellsworth Ltd., in honor of Susan Dillon, 1987).

the classical (*mārga*) norms of the Indian arts. Painting predominated among visual media; regional schools of painting flourished. In the northern area particularly, diverse styles provide evidence about music and dance. These include the "Eastern style" of paintings, on book covers and palm-leaf manuscripts (especially from the 1100s through the 1300s); a "Western Indian style," encompassing manuscript miniatures by writers of the Jain religion and paintings on Hindu Vaishnav themes (especially from the 1300s to the 1500s); Sultanate, Deccani, and Mughal styles (Wade 1997) influenced by Persian miniature painting (1400s to 1700s) (see figures 3, 4, 5); and several local styles of the sixteenth through early nineteenth centuries such as Basohli and Kishangarhi. In South India there were fewer styles, but some schools of painting arose, as exemplified by such works as the miniatures produced in the Mysore district for the twelfth-century Hoysala dynasty and the murals painted in Vijayanagar (in Karnataka), Andhra Pradesh, Tamil Nadu, and Kerala between the sixteenth and nineteenth centuries. There was also a "Southern" style of painting in the eighteenth- and early-nineteenth-century kingdom of Tanjore (now Tanjavur). Finally, many paintings from the 1700s and 1800s—mostly done for British patrons—were in a style called Company School.

A set of thirty-six prints etched in the 1790s by a Flemish artist, François Baltazard Solvyns, and printed in a folio edition between 1808 and 1812 constitute a unique source. Embedded in a set of 288 plates that Solvyns produced with an ethnographic approach covering castes, costumes, vehicles, festivals, and other Hindu categories, the folios about music provide the first systematic portrayal of Indian instruments (Hardgrave and Slawek 1997). Photographs are the most recent visual source used in the scholarly study of Indian music.

ICONOGRAPHY

The term *iconography* literally refers to the study of the conventional, emblematic nature of visual items that evoke symbolic meanings (see Zimmer 1962). Indian art is replete with musical icons; some are imbued with sacred meaning, others come out of secular culture. Among the most potent and sacred of Indian icons is Nataraja (*naṭa* 'dance', *rāja* 'lord'), a form of Shiva, the deity of music, dance, and theater, often cast in bronze (figure 2). Encircled by symbols of universal continuity—a halo of flames, space, and time—Shiva stands poised in the perfect equilibrium of a mystic dancer. The small hourglass-shaped drum in his uplifted right hand represents the audible space that fills the universe, which causes sound to issue forth at the first moment of creation. Shiva appears as the essence of ordered movement and the ultimate embodiment of rhythm.

A second perennial icon of Indian music is the vina, a principal melodic instrument from ancient times. During the Vedic period (1500–600 B.C.), a set of correspondences was outlined between the divine vina, the body, and the ordinary wooden vina in at least one sacred text (Rowell 1992:115). The vina—in such a philosophical context—is not to be taken as a particular instrument, but rather as a generic term for "stringed instrument." Sculptures and paintings depict numerous divine personages with some kind of vina, notably Parvati (the wife of Shiva), Ganesh (Shiva's elephant-headed son and a patron of the performing arts), and Narada (the bringer of music from heaven to earth). Most frequently depicted with the vina in the form of a stick zither is Sarasvati, the goddess of music, as illustrated in a painting from a Jain palm-leaf manuscript of the 1100s (reproduced in Flora 1987, plate 2). The vina of sixteenth-century North India was the accompanying instrument of choice for Hindu musicians who wandered the countryside singing devotional songs in praise of Krishna and other deities. In some Mughal-style paintings of the sixteenth- and seventeenth-century Muslim courts, the vina was an icon for the religious expression of Hindu holy men (figure 3). In other Mughal paintings, its inclusion evoked less a religious connotation than an acknowledgment of Indian musical performance—as opposed to Western or Central Asian musical performance—in Mughal court culture (see figure 4).

A more secular North Indian musical icon, from around the 1200s, was the *naubat*, an ensemble of drums, cymbals, trumpets, and double-reed instruments that symbolized the ruler's authority—an association well known throughout Asia. Even if the ruler was not present (and in Mughal-style painting, he frequently was not), the image of the *naubat* reminded viewers of his authority just as resoundingly as the live ensemble would have proclaimed it to its listeners. An illustration from a copy of the chronicle of the reign of Akbar (*Akbarnāma*) shows the ensemble pounding and blasting away during festivities for the birth of Akbar's heir, which is depicted as taking place near the mother's quarters (figure 4). Astrologers at the top of the illustration calculate the child's horoscope. Female drummers and singers accompany two female dancers. The father of the child does not appear—but for knowledgeable viewers he is amply represented by the noise of the *naubat.*

From about 1600, a unique genre of painting developed called *rāgmālā* 'garland of ragas', not in the centrally powerful Mughal culture but in the princely fiefdoms of North and Central India. These paintings bring together in visual form the verbal imagery of poetry with the mood and sentiment of traditional ragas (see

Questions arise about the purpose of an artistic item; about the patron who causes its creation; about the audience that experiences it. Iconology includes the wealth of meanings in a depiction of music and dance performance in Indian art.

FIGURE 3 A Hindu holy man (*center*) with a vina (stick zither) is being greeted with reverence. From the manuscript *Yog vashisht*, 1603. Chester Beatty Museum and Gallery of Oriental Art, Dublin.

Waldschmidt and Waldschmidt 1962). They are the quintessential example of icons; by far the most attention regarding Indian music in art has been paid to the iconographical study of *rāgmāla*, in several regional styles [see RAGMALA PAINTING].

ICONOLOGY

The term *iconography* is frequently applied to a type of study that is more properly called *iconology*. Moving beyond individual musical icons and to the nature of all icons, iconology leads also to the study of broader contextual considerations. Questions arise about the purpose of an artistic item; about the patron who causes its creation; about the audience that experiences it. Iconology thus includes all the

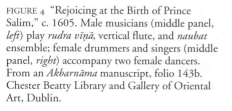

FIGURE 4 "Rejoicing at the Birth of Prince Salim," c. 1605. Male musicians (middle panel, *left*) play *rudra vīṇā*, vertical flute, and *naubat* ensemble; female drummers and singers (middle panel, *right*) accompany two female dancers. From an *Akbarnāma* manuscript, folio 143b. Chester Beatty Library and Gallery of Oriental Art, Dublin.

wealth of meanings in any depiction of the performance of music and dance in Indian art, iconic or otherwise—understanding that "meaning" will always require exploration of numerous types of sources besides the artistic depiction itself. Iconological study further encompasses the issue of interpretation; beyond the representational face value of a work of art, iconology deals with questions of function and style, such as aesthetic considerations resulting in distorted proportions of an instrument. A few examples will demonstrate the richness of the musical iconology of Indian art, and the kind of sources needed for the study of its context and meaning.

Textual correspondence

The emperor Akbar (r. 1556–1605), for whom the Mughal style of painting was created, sits prominently and unmistakably in the seat of power at the top center of figure 5 as the patron of the painting. This miniature illustration in the imperial manuscript of the chronicle of his reign (the *Akbarnāma*) is burgeoning with meanings that the courtly viewers of this book would have fully understood. The picture depicts a happy occasion: Akbar is hearing the news of the birth, at last, of a healthy heir to his throne. But the painting is essentially political, providing assurance of the continuity of the Mughal dynasty. The folio illustrates text that corroborates details of the pictorial content, including the name of the fortunate bearer of the news (who was richly rewarded) and a brief description of the consequent celebration. Contemporary textual accounts of other royal births confirm that the custom of celebrating a prince's birth with festivities throughout the court was traditional. (Celebrations on the birth of a princess were held by the women only.)

FIGURE 5 "News of Salim's Birth Being Brought to Akbar," c. 1590. *Center left*, a bowed-lute player and women playing frame drums and vertical flute accompany two female dancers; *lower left*, male *naqqārā* drummers and *śahnāī* player accompany male sword dancers; *bottom center*, female singer and male *huṛuk* drummer. From an *Akbarnāma* manuscript, folio 79. © The Board of Trustees of the Victoria & Albert Museum, London.

Textual accounts rarely contain much detail about music and dance, but references to entertainment in prose sources affirm that they were a significant element in most celebrations. Music and dance consume most of the pictorial space of figure 5, evoking sounds and patterns of rhythmic movement that courtly viewers of the illustration could easily "hear" and feel from the experience of their lives. Because of the lack of textual information about music and dance, viewers today need this visual illustration to complement the prose account. Two of the three musical groupings portrayed in figure 5 may be considered reliable, since there is a sufficient number of similar paintings of other celebrations to see consistency. Female musicians playing tambourine (*dā'irā*) and vertical flute (*nā'ī*), and perhaps also a male musician playing a bowed lute (*ghīchak*), accompany two female dancers wearing Central Asian dress. Male musicians playing small kettledrums (*naqqārā*) and a double-reed instrument (*śahnāī*) accompany two male dancers brandishing swords.

Figure 5 is a scene type in Mughal painting; but as in every individual rendition of a raga in classical music, each specific version of the type differs at the level of detail. The third set of musicians in the painting illustrates this kind of difference: at the bottom center stand a male drummer and a female singer accompanying herself with a pair of small, hand-held cymbals (*tāla*). From details in contemporary writing, these musicians can be identified as being of the *huṛukīyā* community, named after the kind of drum involved, the hourglass *huṛuk*. Contemporary writings and the work of historians afford certain historical facts suggesting an interpretive explanation for the presence of the *huṛukīyā* in this painting: they were musicians whose repertoire was associated with the Rajput tradition of the mother (a princess) of this particular newborn prince. Without the presence of those musicians at the celebration, the mother would have been completely ignored in the memories of the event. There is another meaning in the marginalized position of those musicians, who stand as far from the center of activity as the boundary of the scene permits: Akbar's practice of marrying the daughters of his Indian allies was nothing new in the subcontinent, but his respect for the traditions of his non-Muslim, non-Mughal wives set precedents. Unlike the practice in mixed marriages of earlier Indian Muslim princes, Akbar's non-Muslim wives (Rajput and other) did not have to convert to Islam and could otherwise maintain their accustomed lifestyles. That his policy of tolerance was controversial is suggested by the uncertainty expressed in the figures of the *huṛukīyā* musicians in this particular celebratory scene.

Documentation of musical contexts and performers

Mughal paintings tell us that music was as vital a part of everyday life in the imperial household as the contexts for making music were many and varied. Every morning, the sovereign's *naubat* awakened him and the other members of the imperial residence with a concert. The sound of the same trumpets, double-reed instruments, and drums likewise announced the arrival of any important visitor and the beginning of the requisite daily court sessions. Drums and double-reed instruments accompanied polo games. Signaling instruments, usually trumpets and kettledrums, sounded in battle, and due to the Central Asian Mughal conquest of the subcontinent, battles—and thus paintings of battles—were numerous. Musicians and dancers were a ubiquitous element in elaborate festivities marking significant personal and political events. These included celebrations of the circumcision of imperial princes, nuptial parties and processions, military victories, and receptions in honor of significant courtiers and external visitors. Notably, painted scenes marking a new Mughal sovereign's accession to the throne are not festive; a lutenist and his accompanist playing a frame drum typically stand on the sidelines in relative quiet. These scenes are hardly distinguishable from depictions of day-to-day court sessions, during which a small ensemble performed in the background while business was conducted.

Visual sources provide important information about musicians and dancers in different contexts. The context of the performance determined gender, for example. In Mughal culture, musicians who played in formal court sessions were male (whether Indian or West Asian), but informal male celebrations called for both female and male dancers and musicians. Women of the imperial family lived in residential quarters separate from those of men; prose accounts indicate that the women

Women of the imperial family lived in residential quarters separate from those of men; prose accounts indicate that the women maintained household ensembles of women musicians, but few paintings give details.

maintained household ensembles of women musicians, but few paintings give details. Ensembles comprising both men and women are noteworthy and require specific contextual explanation; in the case of two of the *huṛukīyā* musicians in figure 5, the mix of genders is due to their being from a particular professional musical community in Indian society; the pair may well be related by blood or marriage.

Historical context can sometimes aid in the explanation of instruments in ensembles. A fascinating example is the presence of the West Asian vertical flute (*nā'ī*) in dance and other ensembles in Indian paintings (see figure 5). In ancient Indian sculpture and painting, flutes are horizontal, not vertical. Such sources frequently show women playing them in accompaniment to dancing (see figure 1); however, from the bhakti period of North Indian religious history (fifteenth and sixteenth centuries), the Indian transverse flute emerged as a male-gendered instrument, a sacred and sexual icon seen as the enticing instrument of the sometimes mischievous deity Krishna, whose playing attracted women's devotion. Perhaps because the transverse flute had assumed this meaning, women shown in Indian paintings of the 1500s played vertical flutes. In figure 5, one of the non-Indian women musicians plays a vertical flute, a West Asian aerophone important in Indo-Muslim culture for several previous centuries, according to evidence in the writing of the revered thirteenth-century Indo-Muslim writer Amir Khusrau (Sarmadee 1976:245). The appearance of vertical flutes in sixteenth-century Indian paintings (as in the male vina-flute duo pictured in figure 4) suggests wide adoption of the vertical flute in Indian music. Both the vertical flute and horizontal flute thereafter disappeared from the "classical" performance of music until the twentieth century.

ORGANOLOGY

Visual media have always been an important store of information for the scholarly study of musical instruments (organology), since few historical instruments have survived the extreme climatic conditions of the South Asian subcontinent. As the organologist Reis Flora points out (1987), consideration of all possible visual media is necessary to obtain comprehensive information both on the existence and spread of musical instruments, and on their dating.

For information on ancient instruments, sculptural evidence is crucial. Two instrument types important in India in the Buddhist period (second century B.C. to eighth century of the common era) illustrate this point: ovoid, short-necked lutes, and arched harps (see figure 1). The ovoid, short-necked lutes in bas-reliefs document the migration of this West Asian instrumental type into other parts of Asia. It has remained prominent in East, Central, and West Asia, but has disappeared from India. Discussions of modal theory in early Sanskrit treatises confirm the historical significance of the arched harp. By the 1200s, both the arched harp and the ovoid lute had disappeared from sculpture. Only the arched harp survives—-in the music of a tribal group in Madhya Pradesh (Knight 1985).

Certain Indian instruments have received much organological study. Scholars have paid great attention to the history of vinas of the stick-zither type, for example, which first appeared in visual evidence from the 600s. Important in music theory after the ancient period and gaining gradually in iconographical significance, the vina has been important in both Hindustani and Karnatak music, though the instruments used in North India (the stick zither of figure 3) and South India (the long-necked lute) differ structurally (Deva 1978; Flora 1987; Marcel-Dubois 1941) [see MUSICAL INSTRUMENTS, both articles]. Another ancient and continuously important instrument that has been the subject of focused study is the double-headed barrel drum, the *mridangam* (Brown 1965).

Studies of modern instruments—the Hindustani sitar and sarod (Miner 1990, 1993), the *sāraṅgī* (Bor 1987), the tabla (Stewart 1974; Kippen 1988), and the Karnatak vina (Subramaniam 1985)—have all drawn deeply from an abundant store of visual sources. A painting in the regional Kishangarhi style (of Rajasthan) produced between 1760 and 1766 entitled *A Moonlight Music Party* (Lalit Kala Academy, New Delhi) provides important historical documentation, as it depicts male musicians entertaining a patron on a terrace in the cool of the evening by accompanying a female dancer on tabla and *sāraṅgī*. Instrumental studies are ethnomusicological in nature, tracing not only the morphological development of the instruments, but such issues as their place in music culture and in culture generally, the effect of patronage on instrumental tradition, the status and musical contribution of performers, and the instrumental repertoire and performance practice. A painting such as *A Moonlight Musical Party* addresses just such questions.

In studying the history of modern instruments, other visual sources—photographs of ensembles and particular musicians—are valuable. In *The Report of the Second All-India Music Conference, 1918,* for instance, Allyn Miner found a superb photo of the sitarist Inayat Khan (d. 1938) and his instrument (Miner 1990:47). In his study of the *sāraṅgī,* Joep Bor used visual sources from different periods to provide historical depth: a photograph of a female dancer performing in Lucknow accompanied by two *sāraṅgī* players and a tabla player; an East India Company–style painting, *Nautch in a European Mansion*, from Delhi about 1820; and a painting from the princely state of Bundi, from about 1780, *Prince and Child Watching a Young Kathak Dancer* (Bor 1987:141, 91, 103 respectively).

MUSICOLOGY

The study of visual sources, which has long aided the scholarly study of Western classical music, is increasingly useful in the study of Indian and other musical traditions. Paintings from the Mughal period, for instance, provide a rich source in tracing the influence of West Asian culture in North India and therefore the development of today's Hindustani classical music. Since notated music from historical times does not exist, it is impossible to be certain just what listeners in the past heard. For that reason, visual sources are all the more significant, even for fairly basic information.

A case in point is the practice of keeping a continuous drone throughout a performance of classical music, in both North and South Indian traditions. An occasional reiteration of a pitch referent is probably an old practice in Indian music, kept on a one-stringed folk instrument, a tuned drum, a flute, or some other instrument. Not until the 1500s in *rāgmālā* paintings and the early 1600s in Mughal paintings is there a clear depiction of a drone being produced continuously to underpin vocal melody on an instrument specifically devoted to this musical role, as is the case with the *tambūrā* today. Iconography, iconology, organology, and musicology all intersect in attempts to explain the adoption of the continuous drone, from the culturally hege-

FIGURE 6 "Akbar Hears a Petition," c. 1604. *Bottom center*, a musician holds a long-necked lute. Dispersed from an *Akbarnāma* manuscript. Freer Gallery of Art, Smithsonian Institution, Washington, D.C.

monic Mughal court to the present. In both *rāgmālā* and Mughal paintings, two particular instruments are foci of this historic event: the stick-zither type of vina called *rudra vīṇā* (the ancestor of the modern Hindustani *bīn*) and the West Asian long-necked lute called *tambūr*.

In secular contexts, such as sessions of Akbar's formal court, the *rudra vīṇā* was an accompanying instrument for one or two singers. Paintings show the player of the vina or the *bīn* ordinarily using both hands, presumably producing melody and not drone. In 1603, toward the end of Akbar's reign, an illustration in the manuscript *Yog Vashisht* (probably produced for Akbar's heir, Jahangir) pictures the Hindu yogi as

FIGURE 7 "Prince Dara Shukoh in a Garden." *Bottom right*, a singer accompanies himself on the *tambūr*. Royal Album No. 7, folio 7. Chester Beatty Museum and Gallery of Oriental Art, Dublin.

Krishna with the Hindu musical icon, the vina (see figure 3). The holy man accompanies himself, supporting the instrument entirely with his body, plucking with one hand and using the free hand to gesture with his song. Although the *rudra vīṇā* was not being used to produce a continuous drone in sixteenth-century vocal genres at court, it did serve that function for songs of religious devotion—that is, the songs of the bhakti cults.

Many *rāgmālā* paintings show a one-gourd version of the stick zither being played with one hand in a position indicating the keeping of a referential pitch, a practice quite probably typical of regional classical musical styles before classical musicians at the Mughal court adopted it (Wade 1996). Paintings of musical performance in Mughal courtly contexts do not show musicians using the *rudra vīṇā* to keep a continuous drone. Instead, organological tracking of the vina in paintings from the 1560s to the 1660s reveals a gradual increase in its use as an independent melody instrument, acquiring along the way more strings, more frets, and larger gourd resonators. Not until after 1750 did players take an independent role, and it

The West Asian long-necked plucked lute called *tambūr* appears in Indian paintings of the pre-Mughal and early Mughal periods as a melody-producing instrument. Then suddenly, in numerous paintings from the time of Jahangir (r. 1605–1627), the *tambūr* is depicted as a drone instrument.

was probably well into the 1800s before they shook off their function as accompanists to vocalists.

The West Asian long-necked plucked lute called *tambūr* appears in Indian paintings of the pre-Mughal and Mughal periods as a melody-producing instrument. Paintings of Akbar's time (mid to late sixteenth century) suggest its use as a solo melodic instrument, either featured with a percussionist playing a frame drum (*dā'irā*) or played by a musician alone. In figure 6, a musician holding up a long-necked lute stands with others at a gate, seeking entrance to the court. The face of the bowl is a light wood, with a contrasting dark wood on the underside. The norm seems to have been three or four strings, and even the tiniest of drawings show frets.

The long-necked lute does not seem to have been a prominent melody-producing instrument in the culture of Akbar's court, though it was present. Paintings indicate that its popular use in West Asia as a member of stringed ensembles was not continued in India. They further reveal that another West Asian plucked lute, the *rebāb*, was by far the preferred plucked lute at court. These factors may contribute to the explanation of the emergence of the *tambūr* in a new musical role—the official keeper of the drone.

Not in a single painting of the Akbar period, but then suddenly, in numerous paintings from the time of Akbar's son and successor Jahangir (r. 1605–1627), the *tambūr* is depicted as a drone instrument. Light and delicate, still dressed with frets for making melodies, the *tambūr* shifts to a new position over the musician's left shoulder, permitting easy access for the continuous plucking of drone-producing strings (figure 7). The instrument is so light and so easily balanced over the shoulder that the singer need not even support it fully under the bowl; his fingers make a small gesture with the song. Without drum accompaniment, the singer can easily keep the tala with the characteristic finger counts [see HINDUSTANI TALA]. In time, the *tambūr* lost its useless frets, grew to larger proportions, and became the drone-producing instrument (*tambūrā* or *tānpūrā*) of modern Hindustani classical music.

REFERENCES

Basham, Arthur L. 1954. *The Wonder That Was India*. New York: Grove Press.

Bor, Joep. 1987. *The Voice of the Sarangi: An Illustrated History of Bowing in India*. Bombay: National Centre for the Performing Arts. [*NCPA Quarterly Journal* 15(3, 4) and 16(1).]

Brown, Robert. 1965. "The Mṛdaṅga: A Study of Drumming in South India." 2 vols. Ph.D. dissertation, University of California at Los Angeles.

Deva, B. Chaitanya. 1978. *Musical Instruments of India*. Calcutta: Firma KLM.

Flora, Reis. 1987. "Miniature Paintings: Important Sources for Music History." *Asian Music* 18(2):196–230.

Hardgrave, Robert L. Jr., and Stephen M. Slawek. 1997. *Musical Instruments of Northern India: Eighteenth-Century Portraits by Balthazard Solvyns*. New Delhi: Manohar. First published in *Asian Music* 20(1) (1988):1–92.

Kippen, James. 1988. *The Tabla of Lucknow: A Cultural Analysis of a Musical Tradition*. Cambridge: Cambridge University Press.

Knight, Roderic. 1985. "The Harp in India Today." *Ethnomusicology* 29(1):19–28.

Kramrisch, Stella. 1965. *The Art of India through the Ages,* 3rd ed. London: Phaidon.

Marcel-Dubois, Claude. 1941. *Les instruments de musique de l'Inde ancienne.* Paris: Presses Universitaires de France.

Miner, Allyn. 1990. "The Sitar: An Overview of Change." *The World of Music* 32(2):27–57.

———. 1993. *Sitar and Sarod in the Eighteenth and Nineteenth Centuries.* Wilhelmshaven, Germany: Florian Noetzel Verlag; Delhi: Motilal Banarsidass, 1997.

Mishra, Lalmani. 1973. *Bhāratīya Saṅgīt Vādhya* [Indian musical instruments]. New Delhi: Bharatiya Jnanpith.

Rowell, Lewis. 1992. *Music and Musical Thought in Early India.* Chicago: University of Chicago Press.

Sarmadee, Shahab. 1976. "About Music and Amir Khusrau's Own Writings on Music." In *Life, Times, and Works of Amir Khusrau Dehlavi: Seventh Centenary,* 241–269. New Delhi: Shri Hasnuddin Ahmad for the National Amir Khusrau Society.

Stewart, Rebecca. 1974. "The Tablā in Perspective." Ph.D. dissertation, University of California at Los Angeles.

Subramaniam, Karaikudi S. 1985. "An Introduction to the Vina." *Asian Music* 16(2):7–82.

Tarlekar, G. H., and Nalini Tarlekar. 1972. *Musical Instruments in Indian Sculpture.* Pune: Pune Vidyarthi Griha Prakashan.

Vatsyayan, Kapila. 1982. *Dance in Indian Painting.* Atlantic Highlands, N.J.: Humanities Press.

Wade, Bonnie C. 1990. "The Meeting of Musical Cultures in the 16th-Century Court of the Mughal Akbar." *The World of Music* 32(2):3–25.

———. 1996. "Performing the Drone in Hindustani Classical Music: What Mughal Paintings Show Us to Hear." *The World of Music* 38(2):41–67.

———. 1998. *Imaging Sound: An Ethnomusicological Study of Music, Art, and Culture in Mughal India.* Chicago: University of Chicago Press.

Waldschmidt, Ernst, and Rose L. Waldschmidt. 1962. *Miniatures of Musical Inspiration.* Bombay: Popular Prakashan.

Zimmer, Heinrich. 1962. *Myths and Symbols in Indian Art and Civilization,* ed. Joseph Campbell. New York: Harper & Row.

Rāgmālā Painting

John Andrew Greig

Patronage and the Development of *Rāgmālā* Painting
The Divine Element
***Rāgmālā* Paintings and Emotions**
Classification Systems
***Rāgmālā* Painting and Music**

Rāgmālā paintings are visual interpretations of classical South Asian ragas that have been among the most popular South Asian art forms since the fifteenth century. In the earliest paintings, ragas were given human or divine form, and by the sixteenth century they were envisioned in human situations. The Sanskrit term *rāgcitrā* 'raga-icon' is used interchangeably with *rāgmālā* for this ambitious attempt at fusing a fine art and a performing art. Raga icons were almost always produced in a structured set, hence the term *rāgmālā* 'raga-garland', which implies that the depicted ragas are linked like beads in a necklace.

Initially, these raga visualizations appeared in Sanskrit music treatises, where they may well have served as meditative preparations for raga performances. Later treatises in Sanskrit and other South Asian languages often included anthropomorphic descriptions of ragas, typically placing them in human situations intended to convey a particular emotional content. These descriptive passages are the basis for the *rāgmālā* paintings and account for a certain consistency in the painting traditions. They act as the link between the musical and visual arts; the *rāgmālā* paintings thus synthesize three art forms—music, painting, and poetry.

PATRONAGE AND THE DEVELOPMENT OF *RĀGMĀLĀ* PAINTING

The earliest extant *rāgmālā* illustrations are in a palm-leaf manuscript of the *Kalpa Sūtra*, a Jain hagiography from western India, dated 1475 (Nawab 1956). No other examples of the art form survive from the fifteenth century, but *rāgmālā* painting thereafter clearly benefited from the introduction of paper and more advanced Islamic painting and publishing techniques. From the sixteenth century well into the nineteenth, artists generally produced small paintings, uniform in size and style and easily handled and kept together. Each *rāgmālā* painting depicted one raga only; they were typically collected into albums of several dozen folios, most commonly thirty-six and forty-two. Individual paintings of ragas were rare. Commissioning a set of paintings required considerable financial resources and sophistication from a patron, which both stimulated and limited the production of *rāgmālā* paintings.

The genre of *rāgmālā* painting reached its apogee in the artists' workshops in the princely feudal states of Rajasthan, Central India, the Deccan plateau, the Gangetic valley, and (most important) the Himalayan foothills, where styles of Pahari painting such as the Kangra school originated. These paintings were most often vignettes of a patron's aristocratic milieu, sometimes mixed with borrowed thematic material such as from the South Asian fine art tradition of courtly love. Kangra *rāgmālā* paintings often drew heavily on the popular *nāyaka nāyikā* 'hero heroine' theme of women in love found in South Asian literature, dance, and painting, and the related Krishna-Radha love story (Randhawa 1971:15f). With the decline of the princely states during British rule in the nineteenth and early twentieth centuries, *rāgmālā* painting became gradually less vibrant, virtually ceasing to be a living art.

THE DIVINE ELEMENT

Since Vedic times (1500–600 B.C.), music or sound (*nāda*) has been considered divine in the South Asian Great Tradition, and the practice of music a path to self-realization (*sāddhanā*). In this context, a raga was conceived of as a minor divinity (*devatā*), and a raga performance ideally began with a verbal meditation, that is, a raga visualization (*rāgdhyāna*). Sanskrit musicological treatises contained the first written raga visualizations. The earliest extant text is the *Rāgasāgara* attributed to Narada and Dattila, some time between the second and eighth centuries. In his ninth-century treatise, *Bṛhaddeśī,* Matanga assigned grammatically feminine names to some ragas and implied a gender-based distinction between *purusha* 'male' and *strī* 'female' ragas. The *Saṅgītopaniṣad-sāroddhāra*, written in 1324 by a Jain scholar, Sudhakalasa, describes raga visualizations that closely resemble the Jain pantheon. Later raga visualizations drew from the popular Hindu stories of Krishna and his amorous adventures with the milkmaids. An illustration of *rāgiṇī megh malhār* depicts Krishna playing a vina in the rain while dancing with two female musicians. The stormy background of this painting enhances its eroticism, for thunderstorms are considered to have aphrodisiac power in South Asia [see SCHOLARSHIP SINCE 1300, figure 3].

RĀGMĀLĀ PAINTINGS AND EMOTIONS

A raga defined as female and depicted as a woman came to be called *rāgiṇī*, the grammatically feminine form of *rāg*. The codification of the division into 'male' and 'female' ragas was a necessary step in creating raga visualizations that expressed human emotions. Perhaps because emotions become more apparent in the context of human situations and relationships, *rāgmālā* paintings soon came to depict characters in situations and scenes. These emotional contexts reflected the codified emotions (*rasa* literally 'flavor') common to South Asian theories of music, drama, dance, and literature. The eight codified emotions that appeared in Bharata's *Nāṭyaśāstra* (c. 200 B.C.–A.D. 200) were: *śṛṅgāra*, erotic; *hāsya*, comic; *karuṇa*, compassionate; *raudra*, furious, *vīra*, heroic, *bhayānaka*, terrible; *vībhatsa*, odious; and *adbhuta*, wondrous (Rowell 1992:329). By the time of Abhinavagupta (eleventh century) in the late classical period, a ninth emotion, *bhakti*, or religious devotion, had been added (Raghavan 1967:18). Gangoly has suggested that the emphasis on an emotional situation explains why sculpture, a medium better suited to depicting iconography than context, was not used to depict ragas (Gangoly 1948:100). Furthermore, *rāgmālā* painting arose in the medieval milieu when the art of sculpture was in eclipse, and when bhakti (Hindu) and Sufi (Muslim) devotional cults were congruent religious movements that stressed an emotional relationship with God.

CLASSIFICATION SYSTEMS

From the beginning of the sixteenth century, scholars commonly classified male and female ragas into systems patterned on the family. Art historians often use the term *rāgmālā* to refer to the practice of grouping a series of paintings based on written raga visualizations (*rāgdhyāna*) into extended families composed of one male (raga) and five or six females (*rāgiṇī*).

Writers have also employed the terms *parivār* and *mat* in connection with a musical classification system that groups male and female ragas in a family-like arrangement. *Parivār* 'family' has been used to refer specifically to the structure of a classification system at least since Pundarika Vitthala's *Rāgamālā*, a Sanskrit treatise written in 1576. *Mat* 'opinion' implies an attribution of a system to a particular author or theoretician, almost always apocryphal. By the seventeenth century, contemporaneous musicology such as the Sanskrit treatise *Saṅgītadarpaṇa* (c. 1625) and the Persian-language *Tuḥfat al-Hind* (1664) commonly recognized four *mat*, attributed to Hanuman, Kallinatha, Somesvara, and Bharata. Of these four, only the *Hanumāna* system is the basis of existing sets of *rāgmālā* paintings.

Virtually all family-based classification systems share some characteristics. Common to all systems is the initial division into six main ragas, generally believed to have first emanated from the five mouths of Shiva plus that of his consort Parvati. Regardless of the system, the six ragas have the same names, and each male raga has five or six wives (*rāgiṇī*). Similarities end with the names of the wives, however. In some systems, authors include additional *rāg* and *rāgiṇī* names conceptualized as sons (*putra*) and daughters-in law (*bharyā*). (The systems presented in figures 2–4 do not include such additional names due to their wide variations in different sources.) Some elaborate family systems were quite populous; the Kshemakarna classification, for example, totalled eighty-six ragas and wives. The major systems typically comprised a more modest thirty-six: six ragas and thirty (six times five) wives.

The early sixteenth-century *Mān Kutūhal*, a music text (no longer extant) written for a great patron of music, Raja Man Singh of Gwalior (r. 1487–1516), set forth a family system of six ragas, each with five wives and eight sons (except *rāg śrī*, which had six and nine respectively) (figure 1). The *Mān Kutūhal* system was the basis for the *Rāgamālā* (1570) by Kshemakarna (sometimes known as Meshakarna). This work was among the most important *rāgmālā* texts in the eighteenth-century Pahari painting tradition of the Himalayan foothills. The *Mān Kutūhal* system was also echoed at the end of the *Ādi Granth Sāhib*, the 1604 revision of the Sikh holy book better known as the *Guru Granth Sāhib*.

A second system, generally referred to as the Painters' system, had obscure origins but was very popular among painters of the princely state of Rajasthan, especially Jaipur, as well as in the Hindi-speaking belt of North India (figure 2). It first appeared in sets of *rāgmālā* paintings dating from the second half of the sixteenth century, and became increasingly popular in the eighteenth and nineteenth centuries. This family system included six ragas, each with five wives. Many raga names in the Painters' system also appear in the *Mān Kutūhal* system, but many more in the former are recognizable to modern musicians.

One of the oldest and most obscure systems used in *rāgmālā* painting is the *Hanumāna mat,* attributed to Hanuman, a legendary musicologist none of whose works has survived (figure 3). This system appears in musical works of the seventeenth century, most notably the *Tuḥfat al-Hind.*

Classification systems based on scale type came to replace the family systems as a means of classifying and organizing ragas. In Karnatak musicology this occurred in the seventeenth century. Family systems lasted longer in North India, but they too fell into disuse. Written descriptions of ragas (*rāgdhyāna*) nevertheless survived virtually unchanged for centuries, as evident in descriptions of *rāg bhairav* from nearly one thousand years of Sanskrit texts (Kaufmann 1965). Raga visualizations and anachronistic family associations appear even today. The following verse from a mod-

FIGURE 1 The *Mān Kutūhal* raga classification, based on a family (*parivār*) system of raga classification, compiled by the author from a Persian-language translation of the *Mān Kutūhal, Rāg Darpan*, and compared with Kshemakarna's system in *Rāgamālā* (Gangoly 1948, app. 15) and the *Ādi Granth Sāhib*, the Sikh holy book. Name variations and deviations appear in parentheses.

Rāga Bhairava	
Five *Rāgiṇī*	*Baṅgālī (Vanṅgalī)*
	Bhairavī
	Velāvalī (Bilāvalī)
	Punyakī (Baṅkī)
	Snehakī
Rāga Mālakauśa	
Five *Rāgiṇī*	*Gauṇḍa (Gauḍakrī, Guṇakrī)*
	Kannaḍī (Gandhāriṇī, Gandhārī)
	Mālaśri
	Śivarī (Śrīhaṭhī)
	Āndhreyakī (Āndhiyālī) or Dhanāśrī
Rāga Hindola	
Five *Rāgiṇī*	*Tilaṇgī (Bhūpālī)*
	Devagirī
	Vasantī
	Śindhūrī
	Ābhirī
Rāga Dīpaka	
Five *Rāgiṇī*	*Kamodinī*
	Patamañjarī
	Toḍī
	Gurjarī
	Kāheli (Kalyāṇa, Kampilī, Kaccelī, Sārangī)
Rāga Śri	
Six *Rāgiṇī*	*Vairātī (Vārārī)*
	Karṇāṭakī
	Sāverī
	Gauṛī
	Rāmakrī
	Saindhavī
Rāga Megha	
Five *Rāgiṇī*	*Mallārī*
	Soraṭhī
	Āsāvarī
	Kāmakshanī (Kokaṇī)
	Mukuṭavānī (Gauṇḍmallārī, Suhavī)

ern music textbook used at Banaras Hindu University describes *rāgiṇī toḍī* (Basu n.d.:25).

> A snow-white lady, with saffron and camphor scented body, playing on the vīṇā, is wandering about in a forest, where her music is attracting the wild deer.

This verse would aptly describe typical paintings of *rāgiṇī toḍī*. One such illustration, dating from around 1725, portrays a woman playing the vina, a common long-

Rāgmālā painting clearly reflected a society with the resources and leisure to pursue aestheticism.

FIGURE 2 The Painters' system of raga classification employing a family (*parivār*) arrangement of six ragas each with five wives (*rāgiṇī*). Based on Ebeling 1973:18.

Rāga Bhairava		*Rāga Dīpaka*	
Five *Rāgiṇī*	*Bhairavī*	Five *Rāgiṇī*	*Dhanāśrī*
	Naṭa		*Vasanta*
	Mālaśrī		*Kannaḍa*
	Paṭamañjarī		*Vairvaṭi*
	Lalita		*Pūrvī (Desvarāṭī)*
Rāga Mālakauśa		*Rāga Śri*	
Five *Rāgiṇī*	*Gauṛī*	Five *Rāgiṇī*	*Pancama*
	Khambahavatī		*Kāmoda (Kāmodanī)*
	Mālavī		*Seṭmallār*
	Rāmakalī		*Āsāvarī*
	Guṇakalī		*Kedārā*
Rāga Hindola		*Rāga Megha*	
Five *Rāgiṇī*	*Bilāvala*	Five *Rāgiṇī*	*Gurjarī*
	Ṭoḍī		*Gauṛamallārī*
	Desakha		*Kakubha*
	Devagandhāra		*Vibhāsa*
	Madhumādhavī		*Baṅgāla*

FIGURE 3 The *Hanumāna mat*, an obscure raga classification system attributed to a musicologist named Hanuman, which serves as the basis for several sets of *rāgmālā* paintings. Based on Gangoly 1948, app. 33.

Rāga Bhairava		*Rāga Dīpaka*	
Five *Rāgiṇī*	*Madhymādī*	Five *Rāgiṇī*	*Kedārī*
	Bhairavī		*Kānnaḍā*
	Vāṅgālī		*Deśī*
	Varāṭikā		*Kāmodī*
	Saindhavī		*Nāṭikā*
Rāga Mālakauśa		*Rāga Śri*	
Five *Rāgiṇī*	*Ṭoḍī*	Five *Rāgiṇī*	*Vasantī*
	Khaṃvāvatī		*Mālavī*
	Gaurī		*Mālaśrī*
	Guṇakrī		*Dhanāsikā*
	Kakubhā		*Āsāvarī*
Rāga Hindola		*Rāga Megha*	
Five *Rāgiṇī*	*Velāvalī*	Five *Rāgiṇī*	*Mallārī*
	Rāmakrī		*Deśakārī*
	Deśakhya		*Bhūpālī*
	Paṭamañjarī		*Gurjarī*
	Lalita		*Taṅka*

FIGURE 4 *Todi Rahini, Woman with a Vina beside a Pool in the Forest Attracting Deer* (miniature of *rāgiṇī toḍī*). Bundi, Rajasthan, c. 1725. Opaque watercolor on paper, 18.2 × 12.1 cm. Museum of Fine Arts, Boston (gift of John Goelet).

necked lute of the period, while surrounded by deer and other animals of the forest (figure 4).

RĀGMĀLĀ PAINTING AND MUSIC

The relationship between raga music and the *rāgmālā* paintings would seem central to an inquiry into this fine art form. However, this question seems not to have occupied the thinking of the painters: both poetic raga visualizations and raga classifications rarely make any reference to distinctly musical elements.

South Asian painting, music, and poetry share a common thread through their references to standardized emotions (*rasa*), which were codified in Bharata's *Nāṭyaśāstra* in association with the performing arts of drama, dance, and music. These codified emotions began appearing in the aesthetics of poetry in the fifth century, and by the advent of *rāgmālā* painting, music, poetry, and design all typically employed references to them. The artistic rendition of emotion in South Asia, whatever the medium, relied heavily on traditional and formal codifications.

These formalisms link *rāgmālā* painting with other art forms, yet no study to date has found a direct connection between music and painting. Of the five major publications on *rāgmālā* painting, the earliest views the connection as tenuous and figurative (Gangoly 1948), the study by the Waldschmidts (1967) dismisses it, and that by Dahmen-Dallapiccola (1975) ignores the question completely. Ebeling looked for but found no surface correlation between colors, scales, and affect (Ebeling 1973). Interestingly, Ebeling states that "the manner in which the iconography of a certain raga or ragini is treated in paintings, produced by different painters at different times in different workshops and/or localities, provokes the analogy of the musical performance of a raga" (1973:15). In the most recent of the five studies, Powers develops this theme by comparing the performance of a raga, which involves a musician's creative manipulation of a set of musical ideas, scales, scalar motions, melodic motives, and so on, with an artist's rendition of a *rāgmālā* painting, in which the artist manipulates compulsory visual motifs traditionally associated with the raga or *rāgiṇī* (Powers 1980). Powers connects raga music and *rāgmālā* painting by demonstrating that both depend on the variation of conventional elements within recognizable limits (1980:475).

Whether or not *rāgmālā* painting was truly a multimedia art form that combined the creative elements of music, painting, and literature, it clearly reflected a society with the resources and leisure to pursue pure aestheticism, as is underscored by its popularity and princely patronage. *Rāgmālā* painting stands as one of the more fascinating experiments in combined artistic genres, one that focused a microscope on the highly refined society and culture that nurtured it.

REFERENCES

Basu, Sivendranath. n.d. *Music Text Book (B.H.U.): Saṅgīta Praveśikā.* 2 vols. Varanasi: Banaras Hindu University (in Hindi, Sanskrit, and English).

Dahmen-Dallapiccola, Anna L. 1975. *Ragamala-Miniaturen von 1475 bis 1700.* Wiesbaden: Otto Harrassowitz.

Ebeling, Klaus. 1973. *Ragamala Painting.* Basel: Ravi Kumar.

Gangoly, Ordhendra C. 1948 [1935]. *Rāgas and Rāgiṇīs.* Bombay: Nalanda Publications [reprint of vol. 1 of the 1935 edition].

Kaufmann, Walter. 1965. "Rasa, Rāgamālā and Performance Times in North Indian Rāgas." *Ethnomusicology* 9(3):272–291.

———. 1968. *The Ragas of North India.* Bloomington: Indiana University Press.

Nawab, Sarabhai M. 1956. *Masterpieces of the Kalpasutra Paintings.* Ahmedabad: [Pvt. publ.].

Pal, Pratapaditya. 1967. *Rāgmālā Paintings in the Museum of Fine Arts, Boston.* Boston: Museum of Fine Arts.

Powers, Harold. 1980. "Illustrated Inventories of Indian Rāgamālā Painting." *Journal of the American Oriental Society* 100(4):473–493.

Raghavan, V. 1967. *The Number of Rasa-s* [sic]. Madras: Adyar Library.

Randhawa, M. S. 1971. *Kangra Rāgmālā Paintings.* New Delhi: National Museum.

Rowell, Lewis. 1992. *Music and Musical Thought in Early India.* Chicago: University of Chicago Press.

Stooke, Herbert J., and Kare Khandalavala. 1953. *The Laud Ragmala Miniatures: A Study in Indian Painting and Music.* Oxford: Bruno Cassirer.

Waldschmidt, Ernst, and Rose L. Waldschmidt. 1967. *Miniatures of Musical Inspiration in the Berlin Museum of Indian Art. Part 1: Ragamala Pictures from the Western Himalayan Promontory.* Bombay: Popular Prakashan.

Classification of Musical Instruments

Reis Flora

Musical Instruments in the Indus Valley Culture
Ancient Lithophones in Eastern India
Classification in the *Nāṭyaśāstra*
Classification in Tamil Literature
Classification in Buddhist Texts

The classification of musical instruments has a long history in India. The different systems have been based on various methods and parameters. Five systems of taxonomy, for instance, are to be found in the *Nāṭyaśāstra*, a famous Sanskrit treatise on drama, dance, and music c. 200 B.C.–A.D. 200 [see THEORETICAL TREATISES]. One of these systems, which appears to have greatly influenced the Western theory of organology, classifies musical instruments into four groups according to four primary sources of vibration: strings, membranes, solid material such as wooden clappers or metal cymbals, and air. This article discusses these remarkably diverse methods of classification.

Data on classification from two other ancient Indian traditions are also presented: early Tamil literature (primarily the *Cankam* literature of the first through the fourth centuries and the fifth-century epic *Cilappatikāram* 'The Tale of an Anklet'), and Buddhist texts. A basic knowledge of classification systems in these early written traditions sheds light on various aspects of performance practice in ancient and contemporary times. It also gives the reader a point of reference for evaluating classification systems found in later Indian traditions.

The first evidence of musical instruments in South Asia comes from the ancient culture of the Indus Valley, in the northwest (c. 2500–2000 B.C.), and from a rare type of ancient musical instrument discovered only recently in the eastern Indian state of Orissa, tentatively dated c. 1000 B.C. Together, these two sources illustrate the importance of geography as a parameter in organology: the geographical distribution of musical instruments increases our comprehension of larger cultural patterns, after an appropriate classification and inventory of data has been established.

MUSICAL INSTRUMENTS IN THE INDUS VALLEY CULTURE

It is reasonable to conjecture that musical instruments representing the four categories identified in the *Nāṭyaśāstra* had already been in use among the people of the fertile Indus river valley for over two millennia. The Indus Valley civilization flourished c. 2500–2000 B.C. The two largest cities were Harappa and Mohenjo Daro, in the present-day Pakistani provinces of Punjab and Sindh, respectively. Excavated artifacts indicate the use of spherical clay pellet rattles and simple small vessel flutes in

The early distribution pattern of musical idiophones (percussion instruments) across the subcontinent tentatively suggests an east-west polarity in ancient South Asian culture.

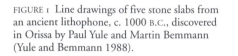

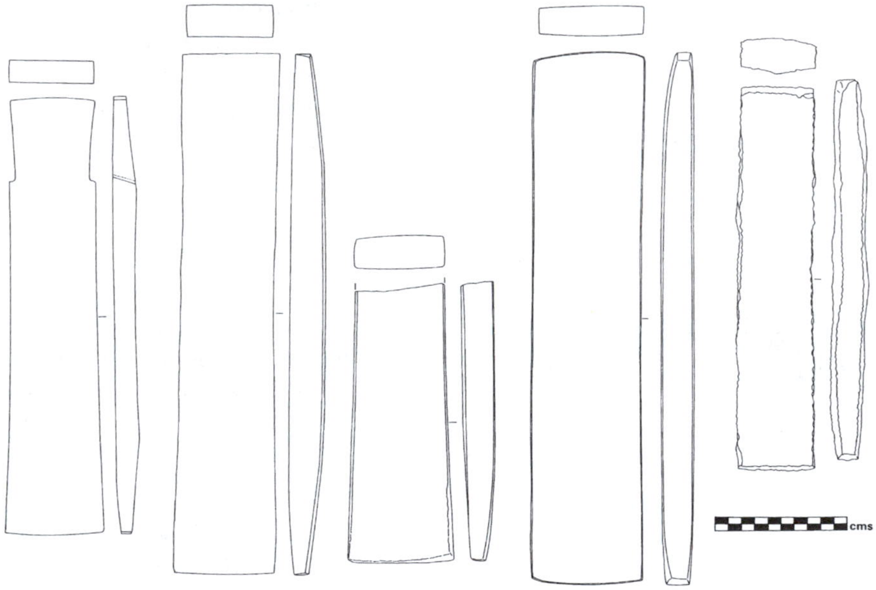

FIGURE 1 Line drawings of five stone slabs from an ancient lithophone, c. 1000 B.C., discovered in Orissa by Paul Yule and Martin Bemmann (Yule and Bemmann 1988).

this ancient culture. Iconographic data suggest that harps and drums may also have been played during this time. Whether musical instruments were organized locally into a classification system during this era is not known.

ANCIENT LITHOPHONES IN EASTERN INDIA

In the 1980s, the archeologists Paul Yule and Martin Bemmann reported on the discovery of an ancient lithophone (a series of resonant stone slabs) at the Sankarjang site in the highlands of Orissa, west of Cuttack, near Bhubaneshwar (Yule and Bemmann 1988). The set, from c. 1000 B.C., consists of twenty relatively large rectangular basalt slabs, carefully shaped, most of them carefully polished (figure 1). When struck, the slabs sound different pitches. The use of ancient lithophones named *goong lu* in mainland Southeast Asia and southern China, from approximately the same period and earlier, is apparently not a coincidence, the authors point out. The stone artifacts from Orissa appear to belong to a notably different cultural milieu than the musical instruments of the Indus Valley people.

The early distribution pattern of musical idiophones across the subcontinent tentatively suggests an east-west polarity in ancient South Asian culture, although data from the Indus Valley predate those from Orissa by more than a millennium. Musical instruments classified later in the *Nāṭyaśāstra* as consisting of solid material are found in both the Indus Valley culture and in first-millennium-B.C. Orissa. Nonetheless, a vast difference exists between the types of instruments within the same classification found on opposite sides of the subcontinent: for example, the small spherical clay pellet rattles of the Indus area, with diameters of between 2 and 5.6 centimeters, and the Orissan lithophone of polished basalt slabs ranging from 16.3 to 40.6 centimeters in length, from 5.9 to 9.7 centimeters in width, and from 1.8 to 3.8 centimeters in thickness. Furthermore, the pellet rattles may have links further west in Mesopotamia and ancient northern Iran (Flora 1999), and the lithophones may have links further east in Vietnam (Ngô Dông Hai 1988).

CLASSIFICATION IN THE *NĀṬYAŚĀSTRA*

The *Nāṭyaśāstra*, the ancient treatise on drama, dance, and music attributed to Bharata, contains data in the first six verses of Chapter 28 and in key passages in chapters 31and 33 that suggest four distinct methods for classifying musical instruments were current in Indian antiquity, as well as a broad conceptual view (figure 2). The first classification system described in the text is based implicitly on the mode of sound production, as noted above—stretched strings, membranes, solid materials, and air. The second method classifies instruments according to three musical functions—namely, whether an instrument is used primarily to play melody or rhythm, or to mark meter and tempo.

The third method couples an ensemble with each of the three basic character types of Sanskrit drama—high, medium, and ordinary ("low") characters. The fourth method assigns musical instruments to either a major or minor class according to the relative complexity of their construction. Instruments of the major class, those of complex construction, are generally associated with relatively complex styles of performance, whereas those of the minor class, by comparison simpler in construction, are associated with relatively simple styles of performance.

Overarching these four methods of classification is a markedly different broad conceptual view about musical instruments. This view identifies the human body as the origin of musical sound and calls the body the musical instrument compared to which all other musical instruments are secondary.

The human body as an instrument

The human body is identified as a musical instrument in the *Nāṭyaśāstra* (Chapter 33) with the term *gātra vīṇā* (literally, 'body instrument'). According to this passage, music first emanates from the body through various musical pitches, which are then passed on to musical instruments. Such a view clearly implies a primary position for

FIGURE 2 Five Indian classification systems for musical instruments, based primarily on the *Nāṭyaśāstra* (c. 200 B.C.–A.D. 200).

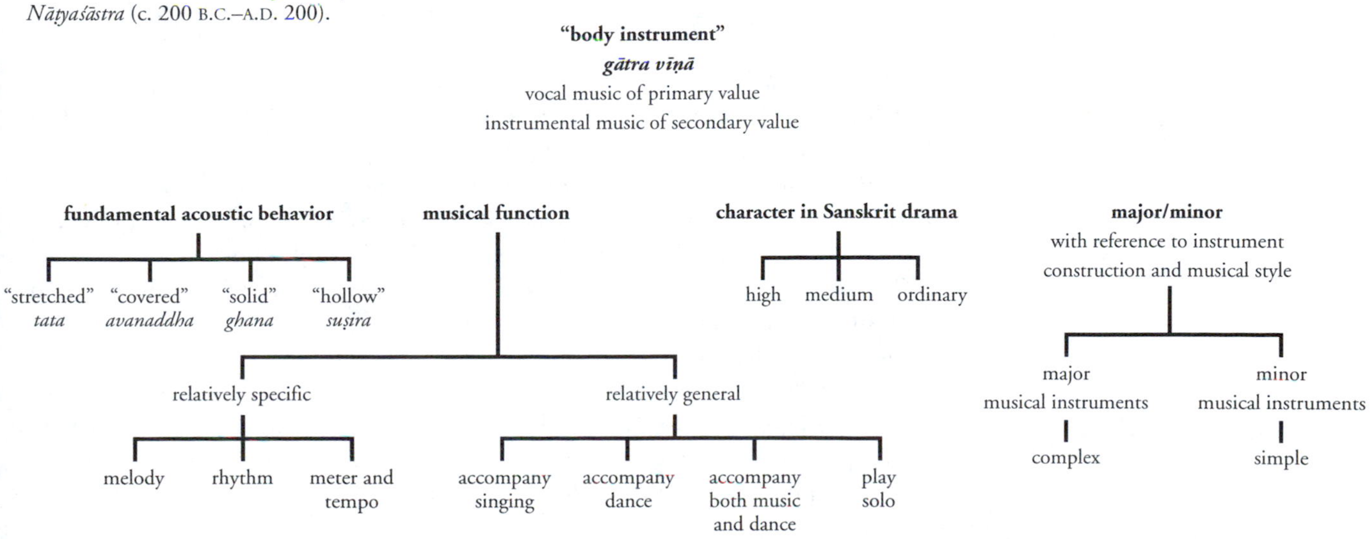

vocal music. This high esteem for the voice is also implied in Chapter 28, where singers are mentioned first as part of the *kutapa* or melody ensemble.

In this context the treatise ranks all other musical instruments secondary, regardless of their relative position in any of the four classification methods discussed below. This early view of the supremacy of vocal music over instrumental music persists in India down to the present, in the two classical systems of Hindustani and Karnatak music and also in numerous regional and folk genres.

Method of sound production

The first classification system mentioned in the *Nāṭyaśāstra* (Chapter 28) presents four categories of instruments based on method of sound production: (1) *tata vādya*, stringed instruments with something "extended" or "stretched" from one point to another, as on a hunting bow; (2) *avanaddha vādya*, instruments that have something "bound on" or are "covered," that is, drums; (3) *ghana vādya*, instruments that are "solid," such as bells, cymbals, gongs, or clappers; and (4) *suṣira vādya*, wind instruments "having a good tube or channel," or that are "hollow." The vibrating entities that produce the sound are a taut string, a taut membrane, solid material, and the air inside a tube or vessel.

Fundamental acoustic behavior is also the basis of the well-known classification method published by Erich M. von Hornbostel and Curt Sachs in 1914. Their four primary categories are idiophones (percussion), membranophones (drums), chordophones (strings), and aerophones (wind instruments). The four-part system presented in the *Nāṭyaśāstra* may have been unknown to Hornbostel and Sachs. They based their system on a method published by Victor-Charles Mahillon of Brussels in 1878. Details of the transfer of an ancient Indian classification system into modern European intellectual tradition through Mahillon, who seemingly drew his basic ideas from publications by Raja Sourindro Mohun Tagore of Calcutta with only indirect acknowledgment, are difficult to unravel. Recently, Nazir Jairazbhoy has published valuable comments and research on this important topic (Jairazbhoy 1990).

The order in which the four basic instrument families are presented in Chapter 28 of the *Nāṭyaśāstra* would appear to reflect a hierarchy among types of instruments in Indian antiquity. Stringed instruments are identified first; drums, idiophones, and wind instruments follow in sequence. This same order is maintained in subsequent sections of the *Nāṭyaśāstra* text (later in Chapter 28, and then in Chapter 33).

Musical function

The second classification method presented in Chapter 28 of the *Nāṭyaśāstra*, based on musical function, corroborates the hierarchy noted above. Instruments are initially grouped into two ensembles: first, stringed instruments with a flute—an ensemble that is associated with a singer—and second, drums. The clear implication here is that instruments are divided according to whether their role is melodic or rhythmic. Two different stringed instruments and the transverse flute have a melodic role, and the drums have a rhythmic role. Iconography suggests that the stringed instruments are an arched harp and a plucked lute.

In Chapter 31 of the same work, another type of musical instrument is identified as being responsible for a third musical function: marking the meter and tempo of a performance. This instrument is the *tāla,* belonging to the "solid" category. Significantly, data about the instrument appears at the beginning of an extensive discussion on meter.

Melody and rhythm

In ancient Sanskrit drama, an ensemble known as *kutapa* comprised three different types of musician: a singer, the singer's assistants, and players of melodic instruments. The singer's assistants marked the meter and tempo with small metal cymbals (*tāla*). Musicians of the third group played the two stringed instruments and the flute, as mentioned above. During a drama, a singer may well have performed melodies without text, perhaps to establish a mood, in addition to song texts. Musicians playing the stringed instruments and flute most likely rendered vocal melodies at some points, and may have ornamented or varied the vocal line as well. Finally, each of these musicians may also have played their own idiomatic instrumental melodies.

Another ensemble of various types of drum was known as *avanaddha varga,* which no doubt provided rhythmic accompaniment for the melody ensemble. These two ensembles generally performed together in a Sanskrit drama, but either ensemble could be given more prominence in different parts of a play.

A sandstone relief from Pavaya, near Gwalior in northern India, and dating from the fifth or sixth century, shows these two ensembles functioning together to accompany dance [see VISUAL SOURCES, figure 1]. In this relief a singer and the assistants playing *tāla* are not depicted. Five female musicians and a dancer are performing for a patron and her two attendants. The dancer is noticeably larger than any of the other figures and is placed in the center, suggesting that dance is the focus of the scene. In the foreground to the right, a musician is seated comfortably on a large cushion or mat, playing an arched harp. To the left, also seated on a cushion or mat, a second musician plays a relatively large plucked lute. Within the context of the whole scene, the position of the two chordophones in the foreground implies a higher status for instruments of the *tata* category.

Depicted immediately above the lute player is a (damaged) figure playing a relatively large transverse flute, probably made of naturally hollow bamboo. This musician, along with those playing the arched harp and plucked lute, make up the *kutapa* melodic ensemble.

The top row of figures consists of a musician playing a set of three drums (to the left) and the patron, with an attendant on either side of her. The drum set consists of a large double-headed horizontal drum positioned immediately before the drummer (with only a drumhead visible, to the player's right), and two vertical drums a little further in front. The figure shown above the harpist may be playing another type of drum, a clay pot covered by a membrane. In this scene, the set of three drums and the pot drum make up the *avanaddha varga* rhythmic ensemble.

Meter and tempo

To illustrate the third musical function—marking meter and tempo—it is useful to consider the function of a pair of small hand cymbals of bell metal known today as *tāḷam* in Tamil, a prominent language of South India. This instrument is an essential component of the well-known *periya mēḷam* ensemble of Karnatak music. This auspicious ensemble generally consists of two large double-reed instruments (*nāgasvaram*), drums (*tavil*), a pair of *tāḷam*, and a drone instrument. The ensemble performs during morning and evening worship (*pūjā*) at Hindu temples, for various festive occasions, and at public concerts. During a performance, the *tāḷam* player enters only after the unmetered introduction, when the meter commences.

Drummers reinforce the metric pattern, but they also play many different rhythmic patterns for interest and variety, using a variety of strokes. The player of the *tāḷam,* in distinct contrast, marks appropriate pulses of the meter without change or elaboration. This cymbal player uses two strokes, an open ringing stroke and a damped stroke. In *ādi tāḷa*, for example, which is a Karnatak meter of eight beats,

Present-day musical performance in South India clearly illustrates the long-established theoretical classification of musical instruments according to the three musical functions: melody, rhythm, and meter.

the musician on the *tāḷam* plays the following pattern ("–" indicates no stroke): open – – – open damped open damped. The *tāḷam* player repeats this pattern continuously until the end of the performance. The time-keeping or metric role of the *tāḷam* in the *periya mēḷam* ensemble today appears to be identical to the function assigned to the *tāla* idiophone in the *Nāṭyaśāstra*.

Another instance of the durability of this early musical function may be observed in the performance of Karnatak vocal music in South India today. Hand gestures by a musician and by many members of the audience fulfill the essential function of keeping the metrical pattern. These gestures consist of an audible clap, or a slap on the thigh, and an obligatory wave of the hand on the appropriate beat. The eight-beat *ādi tāḷa* pattern is indicated: clap 2 3 4 clap wave clap wave, where beats 2, 3, and 4 are articulated by touching the tip of the little finger, ring finger, and middle finger respectively to the tip of the thumb [see KARNATAK TALA]. The musical function of hand gestures during a Karnatak vocal performance is identical both to the function of a pair of *tāḷam* in the *periya mēḷam* ensemble and to the *tāla* as noted approximately two millennia ago in the *Nāṭyaśāstra*.

Present-day musical performance in South India clearly illustrates the long-established theoretical classification of musical instruments according to the three musical functions. In a *periya mēḷam* performance, the *nāgasvaram* (aerophone), *tavil* (membranophone), and *tāḷam* (idiophone) perform the melody, rhythm, and meter respectively. Similarly, during a performance of Karnatak vocal music, the singer, *mridangam,* and hand gestures provide the melody, rhythm, and meter respectively. In this latter example, the "body instrument" of the *Nāṭyaśāstra* performs two of the three musical functions, melody and time keeping.

Accompaniment and solo performance

The Indian musicologist P. Sambamurthy has noted another early method of classification according to function, in the *Saṅgītaratnākara*, c. A.D. 1250 (Sambamurthy 1967:17). This system is based not on relatively specific musical functions, as in the *Nāṭyaśāstra,* but rather on four very general roles assumed by musicians and their instruments during a performance. Three categories identify instruments used to accompany singing, to accompany dance, and for solo playing. The fourth category identifies instruments used to accompany both vocal music and dance. Sambamurthy names an instrument for each category; respectively, the violin, clarinet, *sarasvatī vīṇā,* and *mridangam*. One might infer from this classification that certain instruments were uniquely associated with each of the four categories.

The ensemble that accompanies *kathakaḷi* dance dramas in Kerala today provides an example of such categorization. This ensemble consists of two drums and two idiophones (a flat gong and a pair of thick cymbals). Their loud, outdoor sound is perfectly suited to the *kathakaḷi* genre. Two male vocalists play the idiophones and sing in a loud style, required in order to project in outdoor contexts without the aid of amplification. This ensemble of four musicians would not be appropriate for an indoor performance of refined vocal music in a court environment.

The four categories mentioned in the *Saṅgītaratnākara* should not be interpreted as mutually exclusive. An ancient Indian harp or lute, or a sophisticated drum, could usefully have been played in each of the categories. In Hindustani music today, both the sitar and tabla are solo instruments but are also used to accompany *kathak* dance; and tabla is a familiar accompaniment for solo vocalists or instrumentalists. Similarly in South India, the *sarasvatī vīṇā* and the *mridangam* are both played as solo instruments and also used to accompany dance; the *mridangam* also accompanies solo vocalists or instrumentalists. In these instances, markedly different styles of performance characterize solo performances, dance accompaniments, and vocal accompaniments. Expert drummers must be skilled in all three styles.

Three categories of character in Sanskrit drama

The third method of classification in Chapter 28 of the *Nāṭyaśāstra* informs us that ensembles are associated with different types of character in a drama—high, medium, and ordinary characters—and that these ensembles are located at different places on stage during a performance. Further details are not available in the text. Though the data linking musical ensembles with basic categories of characters in a drama is only very general, it may foreshadow later developments.

In South Asia, certain musical instruments have very strong associations with certain Hindu deities. In these cases their meaning and symbolism are deeply grounded in local ideas and values, and the respective classification as membranophone, chordophone, or aerophone does not account for the essential significance. A link may well exist between musical instruments associated with character types in Sanskrit drama on the one hand and musical instruments associated with deities in Indian culture on the other. The latter may be an extension of the former.

Several instruments illustrate this association with Indian deities. The small hourglass-shaped pellet drum (*ḍamaru*) is an emblem of Shiva. The sound of this drum, in conjunction with the dance of Shiva, symbolizes the continuous rhythm of the universe, from the most extensive cycle of time imaginable to the smallest rhythmic unit audible. In iconography, a *ḍamaru* is often shown held by one of Shiva's right hands.

The modern South Indian *sarasvatī vīṇā* (commonly called vina), which today is the most important stringed instrument in that region, is one of the symbols of the goddess of learning, speech, and music, as the name suggests. Sarasvati is a patron deity of musicians. Not only is mastering this instrument considered a pinnacle by those wishing to master musical performance techniques, the *sarasvatī vīṇā* also symbolizes acoustic knowledge at the highest level.

Yet another example is the transverse bamboo flute associated with Krishna, a manifestation of Vishnu, the deity of preservation. This association of Krishna, the young cowherd of the great Gangetic plain near Mathura, with flute playing evokes images of an idyllic pastoral existence, of idealized village life in India. Krishna is well known for his amorous activities; he plays the flute to attract the attention of milkmaids. The flute thus also carries an association with fecundity.

The major/minor system

The fourth and final classification system in the *Nāṭyaśāstra* (Chapter 33) divides stringed instruments, drums, and wind instruments into two classes—major and minor (idiophones are not included). The major class comprises a primary group of instruments, the minor class a secondary group of instruments. Based on the instruments categorized in these groups, major and minor identify complex and simple musical instruments respectively, and by extension correspondingly complex and simple styles of performance.

In the case of drums, the treatise indicates a direct link between the relative complexity of a membranophone and its corresponding musical style. A similar link is not clearly demonstrated for stringed and wind instruments, but it is reasonable to deduce such a link.

Considering first the drums, the text lists three important aspects of performance practice associated with "major" drums that are not associated with "minor" drums. The first is the use of sophisticated hand and finger strokes with the major drums; these are outlined in some detail. Second is a method of drum notation using syllables, which is common in India today; the third is the performance of complex patterns and styles.

These three techniques for major drums, as noted in the *Nāṭyaśāstra,* are indispensable components of the complex performance styles associated with particular Indian drums today, especially the two major drums of Hindustani and Karnatak music, the tabla and *mridangam,* respectively. The present-day use of these techniques is witness to the long continuity and enduring vigor of remarkably complex drumming traditions in South Asia.

In comparison, the minor drums noted in the treatise are valued only for "the depth of sound from their slackness and extensive surface" (Chapter 33). Also, they are "played with a view to time and occasion [in a play]" (Chapter 33, brackets as in M. Ghosh's translation). This difference suggests that the minor drums were used only intermittently, for special effects; in contrast, the major drums would have been played more extensively.

The *Nāṭyaśāstra* does not contain a list of names of drums, but mentions that a "hundred varieties" of drum were extant at the time. Even if this number is somewhat inflated, it still alludes to a very impressive variety. Many of these drums were probably associated with various *deśī* traditions.

Four chordophones are mentioned in Chapter 33, two identified as belonging to the major class (the *vipañcī vīṇā* and the *citrā vīṇā*) and two given secondary status (the *kacchapī* and the *ghoṣaka*). The *vipañcī vīṇā* is known to have been an arched harp with nine strings that was played with a plectrum, the *citrā vīṇā* an arched harp with seven strings played by hand. In construction and performance techniques, both of these harps are examples of relative complexity.

The identities and musical roles of the two minor stringed instruments are comparatively unclear. Nevertheless, by analogy with the drums that are mentiond in Chapter 33, it is reasonable to assume that the two minor stringed instruments were less sophisticated in their construction than the two harps, and consequently filled minor musical roles in Sanskrit drama performances.

In the *suṣira* or aerophone group, the bamboo flute (*vaṃśa*) is the only instrument assigned to the major class. The minor class includes two other aerophones, the conch-shell trumpet (*śaṅkh*) and a long, straight trumpet known as *tuṇḍakinī.* As part of the melodic ensemble, the flute would probably have had more extensive use during a drama performance. The two other wind instruments would likely have been reserved for special effects at certain moments, as is implied in Chapter 33.

CLASSIFICATION IN TAMIL LITERATURE

Early musicological treatises written in Tamil and known to us through various later commentaries have been lost. However, written data on musical instruments from the earliest Tamil period are found in *Cankam* literature (from the first to the fourth centuries), which consists of several anthologies of poetry. The famous

Cilappatikāram 'The Tale of an Anklet' of the fifth century also contains significant quantities of information about music and musical instruments.

An early Tamil classification of musical instruments comprises five categories; N. Chengalvarayan (1935–1936) mentions four of these: "leather instruments" (*tole karuvi*); instruments "with holes" (*tuḷai karuvi*); "stringed instruments" (*narampu karuvi*); and "throat instruments" (*mitatru karuvi*); S. Ramanathan (1974) adds a fifth category, "brass instruments" (*kancha karuvi*). These represent membranophones, aerophones, chordophones, the human voice, and idiophones respectively, and are comparable to the five categories of the *Nāṭyaśāstra*. Deva (1978) notes that the Tamil word *karuvi* has the more general meaning of "tool," but in a musical context signifies an instrument.

The term "throat instrument" (*mitatru karuvi*) indicates a local transformation of the phrase "body instrument" (*gātra vīṇā*), used to signify a vocalist in the *Nāṭyaśāstra*; however, Chengalvarayan suggests it may refer to an instrument that "simply helps the vocal music." Such an instrument might be the small brass cymbals that are used in the performance of many devotional vocal genres in India today. If "throat instrument" refers to small brass cymbals in this classification, the "solid" instruments (*ghana vādya*) of the *Nāṭyaśāstra* would be represented by two categories in Tamil literature.

A variety of names for musical instruments appears in Tamil literature. These include over thirty different names for drums, several stringed instruments (especially harps of twenty-one, nineteen, fourteen, and seven strings), flutes made from different materials (bamboo, several varieties of solid wood, and bronze), and cymbals. For a single instrument type, the greatest variety is found, in descending order, among drums, stringed instruments, and flutes.

The scholar V. P. Raman claims that in Tamil literature, "percussion instruments [drums] were further divided into several categories depending upon the time and manner of their use" (Raman 1966). He does not give any further information, however. It is possible that early Tamil literature may record one or two additional methods of classification not previously noted in the *Nāṭyaśāstra*, but further research is needed.

CLASSIFICATION IN BUDDHIST TEXTS

The classification system in Buddhist texts, known as *pañcatūrya nāda*, consists of five categories. The term *pañca* means "five," the term *nāda*, "sound." *Tūrya* may mean "musical instrument" in general or a particular type of musical instrument, depending on the context. It may also mean an ensemble of instruments (*tūryaugha*). Thus, *pañcatūrya nāda* may be translated as "the sound of five instruments" or "the sound of five [types of] instrument." The ethnomusicologist Ter Ellingson has observed that Buddhist sources often define the term *pañcatūrya nāda* vaguely, and that in Tibetan tradition *tūrya* always means "cymbals" (Ellingson 1979:159).

The five categories of the Buddhist system are *ātata*, *vitata*, *ātatavitata*, *ghana*, and *suṣira*. Categories four and five (*ghana* and *suṣira*) are identical to two of the categories found in Chapter 28 of the *Nāṭyaśāstra*, which identify idiophones and aerophones, respectively. The meaning of the first three categories is less clear, and has been interpreted differently in various written sources (Seneviratna 1979:49–51). The term *tata,* which is common to all three categories, designates stringed instruments in the first system in the *Nāṭyaśāstra.*

One interpretation of the instrument categories in Buddhist texts is based on morphology. According to this view *ātata* refers to a single-headed drum, *vitata* to a double-headed drum. It is conceivable that the unidentified third term (*ātatavitata*), which combines the first two terms, might indicate a set of two or more different

It is possible that early Tamil literature may record one or two additional methods of classification not previously noted in the *Nāṭyaśāstra*, but further research is needed.

types of drum. In the dance scene from Pavaya, for instance, we have already noted a single drummer playing a set of three drums consisting of one double-headed and two single-headed drums.

Another interpretation is based on the method of playing a drum. In this view, *ātata* refers to a drum played by hand, *vitata* to drumming with a stick. If these two categories are combined, the third grouping may refer to a drummer playing one drum head with the hand and the other with a stick. The medieval *bherī* of India and the large *ḍhol* of Rajasthan and other parts of India today are both double-headed drums played in this manner.

A third interpretation, noted by Anuradha Seneviratna (citing the view of C. Sivaramamurti), identifies *ātatavitata* as a "stringed drum," also known as a "plucked drum." The *ānandalaharī* and *gopīyantra* of Bengal are also contemporary examples of this possibility (figure 3) [see WEST BENGAL AND BANGLADESH].

According to Sanskrit dictionaries, the prefix "*ā*" suggests something stretched

FIGURE 3 *Left, gopīyantra; right,* a Bāul from Bengal playing a *gopīyantra* and a small kettle-drum (*ḍugi*) (Daniélou 1978:109). © Bärenreiter Verlag Kassel.

between two points, like the taut string of a hunting bow. The prefix "*vi*" suggests something stretched as a cover. These two definitions clearly account for the first two categories mentioned in the *Nāṭyaśāstra*, namely stringed instruments and drums. The combination of a string stretched between two points and a stretched skin drumhead is clearly exemplified in the stringed drum, and is thus a reasonable interpretation of the *ātatavitata* category.

Although the taut membrane of a drumhead quickly comes to mind for *vitata*, a stretched membrane is also used to cover the resonator of certain stringed instruments. In this fourth interpretation, the combination of *ātata* and *vitata* would seem an apt description for certain types of lute (the bowed *pena* of Manipur and the plucked Kashmiri *rabāb,* for example) and for the arched harp or bow harp of ancient India, in which multiple taut strings were stretched from an arched wooden neck to a boat-shaped resonator covered with skin [see MUSICAL INSTRUMENTS: NORTHERN AREA, figure 6]. This description is also apt for the arched harp of ancient India, as already noted in the representation from Pavaya, had a resonator covered with leather. Other similar instruments used today are the *bīṇ bājā* of central India (Knight 1985) and the Burmese arched harp (*saùṅ*) [see BURMA, in the Southeast Asia volume], which show clear historical connections to the arched harps of ancient India.

Of the four interpretations noted for the category *ātatavitata*—set of drums; drum played with one stick and one hand; stringed or plucked drum; chordophone with membrane-covered resonator—the third is perhaps the most consistent and reasonable. Basically, a stringed drum is a string stretched between two points and attached at one of them to a membrane stretched to cover a circular opening, as with the *gopīyantra*. In the case of the Bengali *ānandalaharī,* a string, doubled back on itself, is attached to stretched membranes at both ends. One membrane is much larger than the other (Dick 1984). (For an investigation of the acoustic behavior of plucked drums, see Picken 1981.)

Throughout the history of Buddhist culture, each interpretation could conceivably have been valid at a different time and place in South Asia, depending on local circumstances. In contemporary times, the drumming context in Buddhist music, as currently practiced by the *hēvisi pūjā* ensemble of Sri Lanka, illustrates the second interpretation above: *ātata, vitata,* and *ātatavitata,* referring to playing a drum by hand, with a stick, and as a combination of the two, respectively. Stringed instruments do not have a place in this ensemble of drums, cymbals, and a reedpipe. The *gâṭa bera* is a double-headed barrel drum played by hand, illustrating the *ātata* category. The *tammâṭṭa,* consisting of a pair of medium-size kettledrums played with two sticks, belongs to the *vitata* category. The *daule*, a double-headed cylindrical drum played by hand and with a stick, illustrates the *ātatavitata* category. Large cymbals known as *tālampoṭa* and a type of small oboe known as *horanâva* complete this ensemble of five sounds.

The *pañcatūrya nāda* system may relate to relatively specific performance situations. It does not appear to define a consistent classification method in the strict sense, as does the first system of the *Nāṭyaśāstra*. The flexibility of *pañcatūrya nāda* allows it to be applied variously and inconsistently. As performance circumstances changed, the specific meaning of *pañcatūrya nāda* would change. According to this view, the concept functioned not as a classification method per se, but rather as a flexible prescriptive guideline for musical instrument ensembles.

REFERENCES

Chengalvarayan, N. 1935–1936. "Music and Musical Instruments of the Ancient Tamils." *Quarterly Journal of the Mythic Society* 26 (New Series):73–90.

Daniélou, Alain. 1978. *Südasien. Musikgeschichte in Bildern* 1:4. Leipzig: VEB Deutscher Verlag für Musik.

Deva, B. Chaitanya. 1978. *Musical Instruments of India: Their History and Development.* Calcutta: Firma KLM Private Ltd.; 2nd ed. 1987. New Delhi: Munshiram Manoharlal.

Dick, Alastair. 1984. "Ānandalaharī." In *The New Grove Dictionary of Musical Instruments*, ed. Stanley Sadie. London: Macmillan.

Ellingson, Terry J. 1979. "The Mandala of Sound: Concepts and Sound Structures in Tibetan Ritual Music," 2 vols. Ph.D. dissertation, University of Wisconsin–Madison.

Flora, Reis. 1988. "Music Archaeological Data from the Indus Valley Civilization, c. 2400–1700 B.C." In *The Archaeology of Early Music Cultures, Third International Meeting of the ICTM Study Group on Music Archaeology*, ed. Ellen Hickmann and David Hughes, 207–221. Bonn: Verlag für Systematische Musikwissenschaft.

———. 1999. "Music Archaeological Data for Culture Contact between Sumer and the Greater Indus Area, c. 2500–2000 B.C.: An Introductory Study." In *Hearing the Past: Essays in Historical Ethnomusicology and the Archaeology of Sound*, ed. Ann Buckley. Liège: Université de Liège Presse.

Ghosh, Manomohan, ed. and trans. 1961. *The Nāṭyaśāstra*, vol. 2 (chaps. 28–36). Calcutta: The Asiatic Society.

Hornbostel, Erich M. von, and Curt Sachs. [1914] 1961. "Classification of Musical Instruments, Translated from the Original German by Anthony Baines and Klaus P. Wachsmann." *Galpin Society Journal* 14:3–29.

Jairazbhoy, Nazir A. 1990. "The Beginnings of Organology and Ethnomusicology in the West: V. Mahillon, A. Ellis, and S. M. Tagore." *Selected Reports in Ethnomusicology* 8:67–80.

Kartomi, Margaret J. 1990. *On Concepts and Classifications of Musical Instruments.* Chicago: University of Chicago Press.

Kaufmann, Walter. 1981. *Altindien. Musikgeschichte in Bildern* 2:8. Leipzig: VEB Deutscher Verlag für Musik.

Knight, Roderic. 1985. "The Harp in India Today." *Ethnomusicology* 29(1):9–28.

Mahillon, Victor-Charles. 1878. "Catalogue descriptif et analytique du Musée Instrumental du Conservatoire Royal de Bruxelles, précédé d'un essai de classification méthodique de tous les instruments anciens et modernes." *Annuaire du Conservatoire Royal de Musique de Bruxelles, 2e Année*:81–256.

Ngô Dông Hai. 1988. "The Vietnamese Lithophone: An Ancient Percussion Instrument." *Archaeologia Musicalis* 1/88:51.

Picken, Lawrence. 1981. "The 'Plucked' Drums: *Gopī yantra* and *ānanda laharī*." *Musica Asiatica* 3:29–33.

Raman, V. P. 1966. "The Music of the Ancient Tamils." *Tamil Culture* 12:203–21. Reprinted in *Readings on Indian Music*, ed. Gowrie Kuppuswamy and M. Hariharan, 80–99. Trivandrum: College Book House, 1979.

Ramanathan, Subrahmanya. 1974. "Music in Cilappatikaaram." Ph.D. dissertation, Wesleyan University.

Sambamurthy, P. 1967. *The Flute*, 3rd ed. Madras: Indian Music Publishing House.

Seneviratna, Anuradha. 1979. "*Pañcatūrya Nāda* and the *Hēwisi Pūjā*." *Ethnomusicology* 23(1):49–56.

Yule, Paul, and Martin Bemmann. 1988. "Lithophones from Orissa—The Earliest Musical Instruments from India?" *Archaeologia Musicalis* 1/88:46–50. In German, *ibid.*:41–46.

Musical Instruments: Northern Area

Allyn Miner

Hindustani Instruments
Folk Music Instruments
Film Music and Popular Music Instruments

Musical instruments in South Asia reflect the complex political and social history of the region. Some instruments are traceable to early periods through texts and iconography; others are more recent, having been brought to the subcontinent by successive waves of settlers from the Middle East and Europe. Oral, written, and visual sources tell a fascinating story of musical continuity and change, as musicians have appropriated or modified instruments to accommodate changing musical demands. Each instrument has its own story of physical origins and development and a colorful history of changing musical uses, offering a window into the musical and cultural conditions of its time.

Hindustani music, the art music of the North, was nurtured in temples and in the elite environment of the Hindu and Indo-Persian courts from the fourteenth to the eighteenth centuries. As court patronage faltered during the British era (eighteenth to mid-twentieth centuries), urban centers offered new public venues for instrumental performance. In the 1990s, Hindustani musicians perform in concert halls, schools, and homes in the urban centers of North India as well as in Pakistan, Afghanistan, Bangladesh, and Nepal. Radio, television, and cassette recordings carry the music of prominent Hindustani musicians all over the subcontinent. In the last three decades, touring musicians and teachers have traveled abroad, giving performances and introducing Hindustani instrumental music to many parts of the world.

Away from the cities, linguistic and regional histories define folk music practices that thrive in an amazing diversity of forms in South Asia. Instruments differ in name, shape, and usage from region to region. Yet the continuity across regions is often as striking as the variance.

HINDUSTANI INSTRUMENTS

Instruments perform several functions in the various genres of Hindustani music. Some provide a drone background to vocal and instrumental performances. Others sound the repeating melodic line that sustains the rhythmic cycles of dance and drum performances. Musicians use some instruments to play the melodies that shadow and accompany vocal performances and others to specialize in the vast and intricate solo repertoire. Musicians consider the concert solo the zenith of instrumental playing,

One of the most ubiquitous stringed instruments in Hindustani music is the *tambūrā*, which provides a drone background to all vocal and instrumental performance.

although most instruments have served in accompaniment roles at various times in their history.

Stringed instruments (chordophones)

Drones

One of the most ubiquitous stringed instruments in Hindustani music is the *tambūrā* (or *tānpūrā*), which provides a drone background to all vocal and instrumental performance. This long-necked unfretted lute comprises a gourd cut through its stem, to which is fitted a wooden "face" and a long hollow wooden neck. A platform bridge with a rounded surface, and threads placed on the bridge surface under the strings, help give the instrument a sound rich in overtones. The *tambūrā* is found in a variety of sizes, the largest for accompanying male vocalists and the smallest for accompanying instrumentalists. It typically has four or five strings, tuned to the tonic and the fourth or fifth scale degree, and sometimes another prominent interval. It is held vertically and plucked, to sound the constant tonal grounding essential to the singer or instrumentalist. In concert performances, a student of the principal performer often plays it, or a junior musician willing to provide the respectful service and honor of being a background presence on the stage.

The *tambūrā* is most likely a modification of the *tambūr* (or *tanbūr*), a long-necked fretted lute of Middle Eastern origin used as a solo melody instrument in the medieval Indian courts (see VISUAL SOURCES). As a drone it first appears in seventeenth-century Mughal paintings, and may reflect changes in performance practices. Drone instruments are uniquely associated with South Asian musical traditions.

Another instrument some vocalists use is the *svarmaṇḍal* (Sanskrit: 'circle of notes'). The singer strums and plucks this box zither as background filler to a vocal performance. Its playing position is either on the lap or upright against the chest. The term *svarmaṇḍal* appears in texts from about the fifteenth century. The instrument is probably a derivative of the *qānūn*, a Persian trapezoidal zither used in medieval Indo-Persian courts, and by extension a relative of the similar Indian zither, the *santūr*.

Bīn

In almost all melody stringed instruments in North India, elements of structural or musical inspiration can be traced to the *bīn* (North Indian vina, or *rudra vīṇā*), the premier melody instrument of the North Indian royal courts from the fifteenth to eighteenth centuries. The *bīn* is a stick zither, an instrument type with a long and illustrious history in India, often used as an iconographical symbol of music. It has two large gourd resonators attached below each end of a straight, hollow bamboo or wooden body. A platform bridge and prominent raised frets allow the player to deflect the four metal melody strings and produce several intervals from each fret

FIGURE 1 *Bīn* (stick zither), played by Asad Ali Khan. Collection Daniel M. Neuman.

position. The *bīn* player holds the instrument diagonally across the body with one gourd resting on the left shoulder, and strikes the melody strings with downward strokes of the wire plectrums on the first and second fingers of the right hand. The little finger is used to sound three side drone strings with upward strokes of the nail.

The *bīn* reached its modern form and its musical zenith in the Mughal period. It appears in many paintings through the eighteenth century in both indoor and outdoor settings, played by men and women, in solo and accompaniment roles. It was the premier carrier of the instrumental version of the *dhrupad* repertoire and techniques, the elite court genre of the time. Associated with Tantric-yogic austerities as well as with concert music, the *bīn* also carried a reputation of religious and mystical potency. Highly trained lineage specialists who developed this repertoire ranked at the top of the court hierarchy. In the early nineteenth century, however, the *bīn* declined in popularity as the *khyāl* genre developed, and the more versatile and less intimidating sitar eclipsed its preeminence. The *bīn* became all but obsolete, barely surviving today as a concert instrument, although relatives of the *bīn* exist as folk instruments in various regions of India. There is only one active Hindustani performer, Asad Ali Khan of Delhi (figure 1). The *bīn's* legacy survives in the techniques and repertoire that the sitar and many other North Indian stringed instruments inherited from it.

A classical instrument structurally close to the *bīn* is the *vicitra vīṇā* 'marvelous vina'. Constructed like a *bīn*, it has a broad fretless wooden body, sometimes shaped into a peacock's body at the bridge end. It rests on its resonating gourds on the floor, and the player slides a glass ball over the strings with one hand and plucks the strings with the other, using wire plectra. The *vicitra vīṇā* shares its repertoire with the sitar

FIGURE 2 Sitar, played by Ravi Shankar. Photo by Marianne Barcellona, 1980s.

and the sarod. Credit for the instrument's invention goes to a twentieth-century musician, Abdul Aziz Khan of Indore, who might have based his instrument on the similar South Indian *goṭṭuvādyam*. There are few active concert performers of the *vicitra vīṇā* at this time.

Sitar

The sitar is one of the premier concert instruments of Hindustani music, and is India's most famous contribution to world music culture (figure 2). The sitar's structure—a half-gourd body, wooden face, and long, hollow wooden neck—is similar to that of the *tambūrā*; the two instruments probably have a common ancestry. The standard sitar has twenty arched metal frets tied to the neck with nylon thread, which are movable to different scale positions. The sitar has six or seven main strings that run over the main platform bridge and thirteen sympathetic strings running under the frets and resting on a small bridge of their own. The instrument's unique sound depends on several structural features, many inherited from the *bīn*. The long wide neck and the position of the playing strings to one side allows the player to pull the main melody string precisely across the arched metal frets, sounding portamentos of up to a fifth interval on each fret. The curved top surface of the platform bridge (a design inherited from the *bīn*) facilitates a long sustained sound. A pointed wire plectrum (*mizrāb*) worn on the right hand forefinger makes fast rhythmic work possible.

Sitars are made in various centers of North India, Nepal, Pakistan, and Bangladesh, but two styles of concert sitar, developed in Calcutta, have now become standard. They represent the two stylistic schools that dominate professional sitar playing. The elaborately inlaid and carved sitar of the Ravi Shankar style has a second

FIGURE 3 "Karva Dance." Nautch dance group, with (*from left*) tabla, *sāraṅgī*, sitar, and dancer. From *Seventy-Two Paintings Depicting Trades and Crafts in Cutch, 1856*. By permission of the British Library, IOL Add. Or. 1520.

gourd resonator behind the upper neck, and seven playing strings, including bronze strings pitched to a bass range. The smaller and less ornamented sitar of the Vilayat Khan style has a different tuning configuration of six strings, reaching only one octave below the middle tonic. The stringing styles reflect the musical preferences of the two schools, the former emphasizing its *dhrupad* and *bīn* origins, and the latter its *khyāl* and vocal influences.

Oral and textual evidence indicate that an eighteenth-century musician named Khusrau Khan may have first brought the sitar to Delhi from Kashmir in the form of the small Persian three-stringed *setār*. A written source of 1739 first mentions the sitar in the city, where a volatile political environment and an enthusiasm for music and poetry combined to create the conditions for musical innovation (Khan 1989:76). Later, a tendency to attribute early histories to modern instruments in India led to a mistaken popular belief that the famous fourteenth-century court poet and musician Amir Khusrau was responsible for introducing the sitar to India.

The sitar was quickly adopted for use as accompaniment to song and dance (figure 3). Professional musicians created a solo music for it comprising compositions (*gat*) and improvisations (*toḍā*), which combined features of *dhrupad* and *khyāl* music with patterns suited to the specific capabilities of the sitar [see HINDUSTANI INSTRUMENTAL MUSIC]. By the mid-nineteenth century, it was North India's most popular instrument, played by both amateurs and professionals in a range of musical genres. Today, the sitar still has a broad range of uses, from classical concerts to light music ensembles, dance accompaniment to film orchestras. With the accompaniment of tabla drums, the sitar has virtually become a musical emblem of India (Miner 1993).

Surbahār *and related instruments*

The sitar's closest relative is the *surbahār* (literally 'springtime of notes'), larger in all its dimensions and tuned a fourth or a fifth below the sitar. Its invention was the product of a nineteenth-century revival of interest in *dhrupad* music; it was designed

The sarod is one of North India's most prominent concert instruments today, played by numerous virtuosi from several stylistic schools.

FIGURE 4 *Isrāj* (long-necked bowed lute), played by Chandrika Prasad Dubey (Roychowdhury 1929:38–39). By permission of the British Library, IOL T 12824.

to recapture the sound of the *bīn*. Its deep tone and capacity for long pulls on the strings make it especially suited for playing the intricate, nonmetered introductory section of a *dhrupad* performance (*ālāp*). A number of sitar players own and play the *surbahār*, but few use it for stage performances. Sitar player Imrat Khan and his son, Irshad Khan, are noted concert performers on this instrument.

The bowed *isrāj* combines elements of the sitar and the *sāraṅgī*: the long neck of a small sitar, and a small-waisted, skin-covered wooden body (figure 4). The instrument often has European-style mechanical tuning pegs, a sign of the British era in which it was invented. The *isrāj* is held vertically and played with a Western-style bow, giving a delicate resonant sound. It had some currency through the mid-twentieth century but was not suited to virtuosity, and is now rare. The *isrāj* is sometimes used in eastern India to accompany *Rabindra saṅgīt,* the songs of the Bengali poet Rabindranath Tagore.

Instruments similar to the *isrāj* include the *dilrubā* (literally 'heart-ravishing'), which is somewhat larger and has a square body reminiscent of the *sāraṅgī*. An imaginative version of the *isrāj* was the *tāus* 'peacock', now obsolete, on which a wooden neck and head of a peacock was attached, the neck of the instrument becoming the peacock's tail. Another is the *tār śahnāī* 'string *śahnāī*', an *isrāj* with a metal soundbox and bell fixed to the instrument's face. The amplified sound has a loud nasal quality not unlike that of a double-reed *śahnāī* (see below). This instrument is occasionally used in film and radio ensembles.

Sarod and related instruments

The sarod (Arabic 'music') is one of North India's most prominent concert instruments today, played by numerous virtuosi from several stylistic schools (figure 5). It is a short fretless plucked lute with a deep-waisted body that narrows gradually into the neck. The lower portion of the body is skin-covered and the upper portion and fingerboard is faced with a shiny metal plate. As with the *bīn,* sitar, and *surbahār,* the player sits with legs crossed and holds the instrument across the lap. The left-hand fingernails press the metal strings and slide along the metal fingerboard to produce sustained tones and portamento, while the right hand strikes the strings with a triangular coconut-shell plectrum (*javā*). The sarod's sound ranges from deep and resonant to bright and percussive.

The sarod appeared in India in the early nineteenth century as a modified version of the Afghani *rabāb*, which was played in the Afghani-populated areas east of Delhi. The *rabāb* is still an important instrument in Afghanistan and in parts of Pakistan and Kashmir (figure 6). During the second half of the nineteenth century, descendants of *rabāb* player and Afghani trader Ghulam Bandagi Khan gave the instrument the metal strings and metal plate that define the modern sarod. The modifications allowed more sustained tones and the capacity to produce the minute ornamentations of *dhrupad* and *khyāl*-influenced music.

FIGURE 5 Sarod, played by Ali Akbar Khan, with drone accompaniment played by Allyn Miner, 1990. Photo by Kamal Bakshi.

Sarod music originally derived from the percussive, lively tunes of the Afghani *rabāb*, and the music of the Indian or *dhrupad rabāb*, an important instrument in the Mughal courts. Today, the sarod shares its repertoire with the sitar, but has contributed its own techniques, especially rhythmic work, to instrumental performance style. Two lineages currently dominate sarod playing. The Ghulam Bandagi lineage is represented most prominently by his descendant Amjad Ali Khan of Delhi. The sarod tradition of Allauddin Khan (1881–1972) is represented by his son Ali Akbar Khan. The two schools use sarods of different dimensions and tunings, and distinguish themselves from each other stylistically. The musical lineage of Allauddin Khan, who was one of the most prolific teachers of his time, is shared by players of various instruments. The sarod is currently thriving in the hands of many young virtuosi who are experimenting with a range of stylistic possibilities.

A few hybrid instruments have been based on the sarod. The *candrasārang* of Allauddin Khan, which is still played by a few of his students, has the neck of a small sarod and the deep-waisted body of the folk lute *sārindā,* and is played with a bow. The sarod player Kaukabh Khan invented the *sarod-banjo* on a trip to Europe, when he removed the frets from a banjo, covered the neck with a metal plate, and played it like a sarod.

FIGURE 6 Afghani *rabāb* (plucked lute). Kashmir, 1970s. Copyright Sangeet Natak Akademi, New Delhi.

The Indian or *dhrupad rabāb*, now extinct, was a long-necked fretless lute with gut strings, round skin-covered body, and distinctive protruding barbs or collar at the base of the neck. Its immediate predecessor was clearly the Persian court *rabāb*, although barbed lutes are seen in paintings and reliefs dating several hundred years earlier in India. The *rabāb* provided the same sort of musical inspiration to the sarod as the *bīn* did to the sitar. It was highly regarded in the Mughal court, and Akbar's legendary musician Tansen (late sixteenth century) played it, as did his descendants and other luminaries in centers across North India. It is depicted in numerous miniature paintings through the nineteenth century. This *rabāb* became virtually obsolete by the beginning of the twentieth century, but like the *bīn*, it left its musical legacy in the repertoire and techniques of the sarod and other instruments.

A nineteenth-century modification of this *rabāb* was the *sursiṅgār* (literally 'ornament of notes'), in which the skin cover was replaced by a wooden face, and the gut strings by metal. The *sursingār* had a sweet tone particularly suited to improvised raga introduction *(ālāp)*, but it did not survive past the mid-twentieth century.

FIGURE 7 *Sāraṅgī* (bowed fiddle), played by Inder Lal Dhandra. Collection Joep Bor.

Sāraṅgī

North India's peerless bowed chordophone is the *sāraṅgī*, existing in a wide range of shapes and sizes, and employed in both classical and folk musics (figure 7). It has survived many phases of Hindustani music's colorful history, but is now used relatively infrequently in concerts (Bor 1986–1987). The concert *sāraṅgī* is carved from a single block of wood, has a waisted skin-covered belly, a short wide fretless neck, three main playing strings made of gut, and as many as thirty-six sympathetic strings. It is held vertically, resting on the floor, and is played with an arched bow held in an underhand grip. The left hand stops the gut melody strings with the base of the nails and cuticles of three or four fingers. The *sāraṅgī* has a soulful resonant sound.

The origin of the *sāraṅgī* is unclear, but the name appears in Indian texts dating as early as the eleventh century (Bor 1986–1987:51), and sixteenth-century descriptions detail more or less its modern form. In the eighteenth and nineteenth centuries, numerous players provided accompaniments to virtually all song, dance, and drum performances, and gave solo performances as well. The great *sāraṅgī* players were thus competent in all the vocal genres and were among the most respected musicians of their times.

Unfortunately, the social stigma attached to courtesan singers and dancers during the British period extended to their accompanists and their instruments. Increasingly, potential *sāraṅgī* players opted for vocal music or other instruments. But the *sāraṅgī* has survived and has been revitalized as a solo instrument, notably by Ram Narayan in the last three decades. Other players and promoters have also made efforts to maintain its presence on the concert stage. Although its accompaniment role has largely been usurped by the harmonium (see below), some vocalists prefer *sāraṅgī* accompaniment. There is no longer a stigma attached to the *sāraṅgī*, and one hopes that this unique and beautiful instrument will regain its deserved position as one of the prominent instruments of Hindustani music.

Violin

Europeans brought the violin to India, and according to popular belief a prominent South Indian musician, Balusvami Diksitar of Madras, adopted it in the nineteenth century. The violin became one of the most important instruments of Karnatak music. It has played a lesser role in Hindustani music, but is nevertheless a standard classical instrument with several well-known players. Hindustani violinists may accompany *khyāl* singers or play a solo repertoire shared with the sitar and sarod. Indian-made instruments differ somewhat in construction and sound from Western violins; prominent players often obtain Western instruments and modify them according to their needs. An example of extreme customization is the electric double-necked violin played by L. Shankar.

Both North and South Indian violin players usually hold the instrument with the nut pointed downward resting on the foot, to allow the left hand to slide freely on the fingerboard. Some violinists, however, hold it upright in the Western position; the famous sarod player Allauddin Khan played violin in this way. It is tuned in fourths or fifths, and to a somewhat lower pitch than the Western violin. Sizable violin sections figure prominently in film music orchestras (see below).

Santūr

The *santūr*, similar to the American hammered dulcimer, is a box zither with parallel front and back, and sides at forty-five degree angles to the longer front (figure 8). The concert *santūr* has one hundred or more strings that rest on twenty-five moveable bridges, positioned parallel to the sides of the instrument. On one side the strings are attached to metal pegs, tuned with a tuning key. The *santūr* sits on the player's lap,

FIGURE 8 *Santūr* (hammered dulcimer) and tabla, played by Shiv Kumar Sharma and Shafaat Ahmad Khan, respectively. By permission of Shiv Kumar Sharma.

and is struck with light wooden hammers. Characteristic of Indian playing styles is a tremolo created by allowing a hammer to bounce on a string. The *santūr* has a particularly echo-like resonance, and a sound ranging from delicate and ethereal to forcefully percussive.

The predecessor of the *santūr* was probably the *qānūn,* an Iranian box zither that appeared in medieval India as a Persian court music instrument. This plucked zither disappeared from Indian court music, but the Persian hammered dulcimer (*santūr*) became an important instrument in Kashmir, where musicians adopted it for use in the Persian-derived Sufi music (*ṣūfyāna mūsīqī*) (Pacholczyk 1996). Shiv Kumar Sharma (b. 1933), a native of Jammu, is credited with bringing the *santūr* to the concert stage. The *santūr* has become one of Hindustani music's most popular instruments, and is regularly used in film and popular music ensembles.

Guitar

A Western instrument that has only recently come to be accepted as a serious concert instrument in India is the slide or Hawaiian guitar. Guitars have been known and used in India since the nineteenth century, and have been standard members of film and light music ensembles for several decades. The concert guitar has both sympathetic and drone strings. Current concert guitarists belong to the Allauddin Khan stylistic lineage, and their musical repertoire is the same as that of the sitar and sarod.

Wind instruments (aerophones)

The bamboo side-blown flute, *bāṅsurī* (Hindi *bāṅs* 'bamboo'), is also a relatively recent classical concert instrument, although it has an ancient history in both folk and art music (figure 9). It has long-standing mythological associations in Hindu South Asia as the instrument of the young god Krishna, who enthralled his devotees with its sweet call. The Hindustani concert flute is a bamboo tube closed at one end, with seven keyless fingerholes used to produce portamento and microtonal nuances. Skilled players achieve a mellow tone and a voice-like fluidity. Pannalal Ghosh of

> Ubiquitous in North India as accompaniment to most classical and nonclassical vocal music and dance is the harmonium, a free-reed keyboard instrument brought to India from Europe in the nineteenth century.

FIGURE 9 Ronu Majumdar, *bāṅsurī* player, warming up for a performance in Jaipur, 1992. Photo by Stephen Slawek.

Bombay, a disciple of Allauddin Khan, successfully introduced the large bamboo flute to the concert stage in the 1950s. The most famous current player is Hari Prasad Chaurasia, whose rich tone and contemporary style has set the standard for modern Hindustani flute players.

The *śahnāī* is the North Indian shawm or oboe (figure 10). A double cane reed attaches to a thin metal tube that is inserted in the top of the wooden body. The body is slightly flared, and has a metal bell-shaped lower end and fingerholes without keys. The ancestor of this instrument was the Persian *surnā* or *surnāy,* part of the outdoor court ensemble (*naubat*) in medieval North India that performed at specific times and events. With its singular, strident sound, the *śahnāī* is an essential part of Indian weddings and other auspicious events and processions, both in real life and in film sequences.

Bismillah Khan of Banaras (b. 1908) brought the *śahnāī* to the concert stage, and applied sophisticated fingering and blowing techniques to produce the nuances of classical music. In concert, a *śahnāī* ensemble often accompanies the *śahnāī* soloist, with at least one player providing a background drone, and one or two others shadowing the melody of the main player. The tabla completes the ensemble, although the traditional drum for *śahnāī* accompaniment is a pair of small hand-played kettledrums (*khurḍak, ḍukkaṛ,* or *ḍuggī*), possibly remnants of the *naubat.*

Ubiquitous in North India as accompaniment to most classical and nonclassical vocal music and dance is the harmonium, a free-reed keyboard instrument brought

FIGURE 10 Daya Shankar's *śahnāī* ensemble performing at the home of Ravi Shankar in New Delhi on the occasion of Shankar's seventy-second birthday, 1992. Photo by Stephen Slawek.

to India from Europe in the nineteenth century. The instrument box measures about 60 by 30 by 23 centimeters. The player, seated on the ground, pumps the back of the harmonium, which opens as a bellows with one hand while the other plays the keyboard. It has a range of about three octaves. The number of instructional books that appeared in the late nineteenth and early twentieth centuries attests to the early popularity of this instrument. It quickly assumed the function of the *sāraṅgī* in concert music, providing accompaniment to vocal performances. Purists and theoreticians argued that it was unsuited to Hindustani music, and banned its use on All India Radio in 1940. Some restrictions remained until 1980, when the ban was lifted. Despite the fact that its tonal capabilities are limited to the twelve half-steps of the Western octave, the harmonium is pervasive throughout the northern regions of South Asia and is used by both professionals and amateurs in classical vocal, film, and light genres. Some harmonium players have gained reputations for excellence in accompaniment and even for solo work.

Drums (membranophones)

The tabla is the principal drum of North Indian classical, light-classical, and film musics. The tabla set consists of two hand-played drums: a slightly tapering, cylindrical wooden tabla or *dāhinā* 'right', and a kettledrum-shaped metal or clay *bāyāṅ* 'left' (see figure 8). The goatskin heads, like those of the *pakhāvaj* barrel drum on which they were modeled, are double layered around the edge and have a black weight spot *(siyāhī* 'ink') at the center of the tabla and off center on the *bāyāṅ*. Leather straps, laced through a leather hoop at the rim, attach the heads to the body of each drum, and wooden dowels placed between the straps and the body further tighten the right drumhead. The player tunes the drums by tapping the dowels and the hoops with a light hammer. The right drum is tuned more precisely than the left, to the tonic or fifth of the scale, and produces a clear ringing tone. Different finger and hand strokes can produce a variety of sounds. The *bāyāṅ* has a deep, resonant, imprecisely pitched tone, and is modulated by pressure from the heel of the hand on the skin. Sizes and styles of right and left drums differ, depending on the genre of music to be accompanied and the tabla player's style and preference.

The tabla, whose name derives from *ṭabl*, an Arabic term for drum, appears in Indian drawings and Hindi references from the late eighteenth century (Singh

1910–1912, 2:70–71). The *tablā-bāyāṅ* pair is possibly a combination of originally separate hand-played drums (*nagāṛā*) from the medieval *naubat* traditions (Dick 1984:492–93). The main sources of tabla techniques were the *naubat* instruments; its other predecessors were the *ḍholak* cylindrical drum and the *pakhāvaj* barrel drum.

The tabla repertoire encompasses a wide range of rhythmic materials and styles developed for accompanying specific genres and for solo playing [see HINDUSTANI TALA]. During its early history, the tabla was closely associated with courtesan dance, and it still has a close musical relationship with classical *kathak* dance. As in other South Asian drum traditions, right- and left-hand strokes and their combinations are expressed by a vocabulary of spoken syllables, which are used in both teaching and performance. Performance traditions attribute the oldest style of tabla playing to Delhi. Later stylistic schools emerged from Lucknow, Banaras, and a number of other centers of North India, from which the tabla lineages (*bāj* or *gharānā*) acquired their names in the nineteenth and twentieth centuries. Today, players often identify with one *gharānā* but adopt compositions and techniques from others. Tabla training is extensive and involves many years of concentrated instruction.

In the last few decades, tabla players have moved into more prominent roles, often sharing equal solo time with instrumental soloists. This springs partly from the performance style of Allauddin Khan and his disciples, who have encouraged musical interaction with the tabla. Zakir Hussain, a star tabla player of the 1990s, has reached large audiences in India and abroad with his virtuoso performances of classical and fusion music. Audiences around the world now recognize the bright and expressive sound of the tabla.

The preeminent drum of premodern North India was the *pakhāvaj* or *mṛdang*, which was used to accompany the elite singers and instrumentalists of the medieval courts. The *pakhāvaj* is also believed to have carried ritual potency, and some of its compositions employ devotional or mystical formulae. *Pakhāvaj* players today accompany *dhrupad* performances and *kathak* dance, and occasionally give solo performances; indeed the *pakhāvaj* still holds a position of esteem in the world of Hindustani drumming [see HINDUSTANI TALA, figure 5].

The *pakhāvaj* is a barrel-shaped, double-headed drum held horizontally on the lap or resting on the floor and played with the hands and fingers. It has a deep, resonant, dignified sound, and is made in a range of sizes, the better instruments being the larger. The heads are constructed with a second layer of skin overlaid around the edge. A hard black weight spot covers the center of the smaller right-hand head. A dough of flour and water is prepared for the larger left head and applied by the player before each performance. The heads are strapped to the body by leather thongs, laced between two hoops on the rims, and fine-tuned by tapping the rims with a hammer.

Percussion instruments (idiophones)

Small cymbals, called *tāla* in Sanskrit musicological texts, were used in art music through the medieval period to express emphatic beats of the tala metrical cycle. In some medieval texts, authors describe the cymbal pair as symbolic of Shiva-Shakti, the male-female duality of nature (Sastri 1986:636). The North Indian *mañjīrā* 'finger cymbals' are no longer used in classical music, but accompany *kathak* dance as well as individual or group Hindu and Sikh devotional songs. The sound of the *mañjīrā*, along with that of temple bells, has come to symbolize Hindu devotion in film music.

The *jaltarang* 'water waves' is a set of porcelain bowls filled with different levels of water and played by striking the edges with bamboo sticks. Mentioned in Indian musical texts from at least the seventeenth century, the instrument had a minor presence in court music and some currency as an art instrument in the late nineteenth century. The *jaltarang* is not a concert instrument today but appears in film and radio ensembles.

FOLK MUSIC INSTRUMENTS

The rich variety of narrative song and dance traditions in South Asia is reflected in the multiplicity of instruments across and within its regions. Instrumentation is specific to each genre within the many types of rural music, including women's domestic songs, men's participatory music, music performed by mendicants and hereditary specialists, and entertainment and dance music performed by professionals in public venues.

Stringed instruments

Drones

The predominant association of drone instruments in nonclassical music is with Hindu devotional singing, in which drones provide tonal and rhythmic accompaniment. Indian films and popular graphics frequently link specific drone instruments with religious mendicants and devotees.

The widely known *ektār* 'one string', which is found across the northern regions, is a drone lute consisting of a gourd resonator covered with skin, through which a bamboo neck is inserted. The single string stretches from a tuning peg in the neck across a bridge on the skin to the protruding bamboo at the other end (Baloch 1975:12–13). Other lute-type drones resemble the small-sized classical *tambūrā*, and are constructed of gourd and wood or entirely of wood. Two such drones are the *tambūrī*, played by pilgrim devotees of the Maharashtran poet-saint Tukaram, and the *cautārā* used by devotional singers in Rajasthan.

Another kind of single-string drone has a cylindrical metal, wood, or gourd resonator and an externally attached bamboo stick. The *tuntune* of Maharashtra has a cylindrical resonator covered on the bottom with skin, to which one end of the metal string is attached. The bamboo neck is bolted to the side of the resonator, and a tuning peg holds the other end of the string. The *gopīyantra* (or *gopīyantro*, also called *ektārā*) of Bengal and Orissa has a forked bamboo frame nailed to the sides of the resonator that holds the tuning peg and the centrally positioned string [see CLASSIFICATION OF MUSICAL INSTRUMENTS, figure 3]. This drone has a particular association with mystical singers of the Vaishnavite Bāul sect; the player squeezes the frame while plucking the string, producing distinctive liquid tone variations characteristic of lively Bāul music (Capwell 1986:89–93).

A related instrument used by the Bāuls and other specialist singers across northern and central India provides a nonpitched but highly variable sound that cannot provide a sustained drone but gives distinctive rhythmic accompaniment to narrative song genres. It is known variously as *khamak* (Bengali), *premtāl* (Hindi), *conkā* (Marathi), *dundhukī* (Orissa), and *tokara* (Assam) (Deva 1993:101; Ray 1988:46). The instrument consists of a small drum open at one end, with a metal string attached to the center of the skin that extends through the drum cylinder and is tied at the other end to a block or a second, tiny drum. The player holds the larger drum body under the arm, and with the same hand holds the block and flexes the wrist, varying the tension on the string, while the other hand plucks the string with a plectrum.

Plucked melody instruments

The *king* of Jammu and Kashmir and the *jantar* of Rajasthan and northwest India are stick zithers clearly related to the North Indian *bīn* and probably to its earlier ancestor, the *kinnarī vīṇā* described in medieval musicological texts (Sastri 1986,

Unfretted plucked lutes are widespread across the northern regions of rural South Asia. Most clearly derive from Central and West Asian lutes but have been a part of South Asian musical culture for several hundred years.

FIGURE 11 *Deśī* sitar of Gujarat, played by Sri Karsan Yadav at the Bhakti Sangit Festival in Somnath, 1981. Copyright Sangeet Natak Akademi, New Delhi.

3:389–396). These stick zithers consist of a bamboo or wooden bar with prominent wood and metal frets and two or three large resonator gourds. They are held diagonally in front of the body. In Rajasthan, a specific group of professional ballad singers plays the *jantar*.

Rural members of the sitar family exist in northern and western India. The Kashmiri *setār* is a small, thin-necked, wooden lute with tied-gut frets closely resembling the Iranian *setār,* from which it obviously derives. In Gujarat, the *deśī* 'folk' sitar is larger and longer than its classical counterpart, with a wide neck and double courses of strings that are strummed and used for limited melodic work (figure 11).

Unfretted plucked lutes are widespread across the northern regions of rural South Asia. Most clearly derive from Central and West Asian lutes but have been a part of South Asian musical culture for several hundred years. Various instruments have names derived from the Arabic-Persian *dutār* 'two-string'. The *dotārā* of Bengal, famous for its use by the Bāul sect, has four strings and is played like a small sarod. It has a round, skin-covered wooden belly tapering into the neck, which is sometimes covered with a metal or glass sheet. Urban music stores in Bengal sell a standardized version that is also used in film-studio productions. The *dutār* of Afghanistan is a long-necked fretted lute (Jenkins and Olsen 1976:24–27). The *dotāro* of western India is an unrelated instrument; it resembles the drone *ektār*, with a bamboo neck inserted through the side of a cylindrical resonator (Bhowmik and Jani 1990:148).

Long-necked plucked lutes of Pakistan and Afghanistan include the fretless *damburā* (*dhambura, danburo*) of Central Asian origin, and the *tambūr*, a fretted lute also found in Iran and other areas of the Middle East that was once part of the Indo-Persian court ensembles in India.

The *rabāb* is an important instrument of art and regional music in Afghanistan. A short-necked waisted lute with a deep body, the *rabāb* has six gut playing strings, sympathetic strings, and three or four gut frets tied onto the wide wooden fingerboard. It was common in parts of North India until it was modified into the sarod in the nineteenth century (see above). Nowadays it is played in northwestern Pakistan and Kashmir to accompany folk singing and dance.

Bowed melody instruments

Bowed lutes are common throughout the northern area. Short-necked fiddles, made out of a single block of wood, are especially numerous in Rajasthan and northwest India, Pakistan, and Afghanistan. Spike fiddles—instruments in which the neck pierces the body and the neck and body are of different materials—are also found in various regions. Most numerous among bowed lutes are varieties of *sāraṅgī* and *sārindā.* Each occurs in an array of sizes and shapes, and with many different names.

The term *sāraṅgī* is sometimes used as a generic term for Indian fiddle. In Rajasthan, specific *sāraṅgī* types are identified with professional groups whose caste occupation is narrative singing and entertainment (Sorrell 1984:295–296). The *gujarātan* and *sindhī sāraṅgī* of the Laṅgā musicians are small, whereas those played by Mīrāsī performers are closer in size to the concert *sāraṅgī*. The Jogis of Uttar Pradesh use concert-style *sāraṅgī* to accompany their bhajans, singing of god in the ineffable (*nirguṇ*) form (Henry 1988:162–163). The *sāraṅgī*'s variety and use make it one of the most important instruments in South Asia.

The *sārindā* has a distinctive deep-waisted double belly and a deep, arched back. The upper portion is large and uncovered, with distinct downward-pointed barbs or a crescent-moon shape; the smaller lower portion is skin covered. The *sārindā* is similar to the *sāraṅgī* in its vertical playing position, but differs in its sole use as a folk instrument. Varieties of *sārindā*, with related names such as *surindā, sarān*, and *sarāng*, are found in southern Afghanistan, Pakistan, and North India.

The *kamaicā*, used by the Manganihār group of professional singers in Rajasthan, is a long-necked, bowed lute with a skin-covered body. It is similar in shape to, and appears to be a bowed version of the *dhrupad rabāb* (see "Sarod and related instruments" above). The Persian *kamanche*, or *ghīchak*, is a spike fiddle once used in the medieval Indo-Persian courts and still found in Afghanistan (Jenkins and Olsen 1976:41).

Bhopā ballad singers in Rajasthan play the *rāvaṇahatthā* 'hand of Ravana', a spike fiddle made of a skin-covered coconut-shell resonator and bamboo body. The horsehair playing string is positioned to the side of the body, and sympathetic strings attach to long, protruding tuning pegs. The player holds the instrument almost horizontally, with the resonator against the chest. Similar instruments of eastern and northeastern India made with a coconut resonator and a bamboo neck are called *bānam* (Orissa), *kenrā* (Bihar), and *pena* (Manipur) (Kothari 1968:69, 75). *Cikārā* or *cakārā* are names of both short-necked and spike fiddles in Madhya Pradesh, Rajasthan, and Kashmir (Kothari 1968:70).

Wind instruments

The conch (*śaṅkh*) gives the auspicious signal at junctures in religious rituals at temples and in homes. In early Indian history it signaled the start of battle. Today, animal horns and various metal or bone horns and trumpets also have limited melodic roles in tribal and village South Asia in temple, processional, and group-dance functions.

Flutes and double-reed shawms are widespread melody instruments of the wind family. Vertical bamboo flutes exist throughout South Asia. The wooden *nāṛ* of Sindh (Pakistan) and Rajasthan is blown obliquely through the end, and the player may
TRACK 14 hum a drone while playing. The *algojā* (*alghozā*) and *satāra* or *pāwā* of Rajasthan and Gujarat (Kothari 1968:62) are end-blown flutes played in pairs by shepherd communities. The player blows both instruments at the same time; on the *algojā* pair the melody is sounded simultaneously on both flutes; on the *satāra* one flute produces the melody and the other serves as a drone. Side-blown bamboo flutes, typically named *vaṅsī* or *baṅsī* 'bamboo', are usually associated with herding communities.

The snake charmer in South Asia plays a single-reed hornpipe (*bīn* or *puṅgī*). This consists of a blow tube inserted into a gourd, the lower end of which holds a single reed and extends into two pipes with finger holes [see TRANSMISSION OF NONCLASSICAL TRADITIONS, figure 1]. In the Sindh region of Pakistan, this instrument, called *murlī* (Sanskrit 'flute'), was developed into a solo instrument for popular and classical musics (Baloch 1975:58–59).

Bagpipes survive as a legacy of the British presence, and are occasionally seen in street band and processional groups. An indigenous version, the *maśak* (Persian 'water-bag'), is played by one specific *bhopā* community of Rajasthan.

Rural and tribal shawms—double-reed aerophones with a conical or cylindrical bore and a metal or wooden bell—were introduced to India from the Middle East. They are widespread throughout the subcontinent, and are used in temple ritual functions and processions. Their names are of West Asian derivation: *śahnāī, surnāī, tūtī* (Persian 'parrot'), and *mohurī* (*mahurī, mohorī*; possibly Persian 'affection').

Drums

The most prevalent drums in South Asia are double-headed cylindrical or barrel drums. The *ḍholak* is a medium-size barrel drum widespread throughout the northern regions. Its two heads of equal size are single skins fastened to leather hoops that are laced across the body with cotton cord. The tuning is not precise, although a resin or paste affixed to the inside of the skin gives the left head a lower pitch. The player places the *ḍholak* on the lap or floor when sitting down, and suspends it from the neck or ties it around the waist when standing. Drummers produce a variety of sounds with hand strokes on the rim and center of the heads. The delicate single-finger strokes of the right hand, and the pitch variation created when the heel of the hand presses on the left head, may be gifts of the *ḍholak* to tabla playing style. The *ḍholak* accompanied professional vocal and instrumental music and dance into the nineteenth century, but was gradually replaced in those roles by the tabla. Nowadays it accompanies devotional and regional musics, and women often play it to accompany domestic songs celebrating births and weddings, a function also depicted in pre-twentieth-century sources. The film and popular music industries regularly employ the *ḍholak* as the epitome of a folk sound.

The *ḍhol,* and the *kham* of Tripura are large, cylindrical drums played by hand or sticks of differing thicknesses. Varieties exist all over the northern regions for outdoor events and processions, announcements, and dances.

Regional varieties of the classical *pakhāvaj*, barrel-shaped drums smaller at one end, may carry an elaborate and highly developed repertoire, and are used to accompany song and dance. Such drums include the *khol* of Bengal and eastern regions and the *pung* of Manipur.

Hourglass-shaped or waisted drums with skins laced to both heads are widespread in South Asia. The *ḍamaru* is famous in Hindu mythology as the drum played by Shiva in his cosmic dance, and is thus symbolic of Shiva. The small *ḍamaru* is a signature drum of some street performers, particularly monkey trainers, who signal their presence and performances with its sharp sound [see MUSIC AND THEATER, figure 2]. It has strings with knots that strike the heads when the player quickly rotates the drum. Drummers strike the larger *huḍukka* with the hand or a stick, and squeeze laces connecting the two drumheads to produce variable pitched sounds. Varieties of this musical drum are found especially in western, central, and eastern India and are used to accompany folk dances, narrative performances, and theater.

Two basic types of frame drums are widespread. The first is a small single-headed, hand-played drum (*kañjarī*) used by specialists across North India both for accompaniment and solo performance. The second type is a larger frame drum with wood or metal frames, played by hand, stick, or a combination of both. A common name for the latter is *ḍaf,* derived from the Persian drum of that name.

Stick-played kettledrums may have clay, wood, or metal bowls. The *nagāṛā, tāś,* and the larger *bher* are descendants of the Arabic-Persian kettledrums that made up the processional ensembles of the Indo-Persian courts. The *nagāṛā* or *naqqāṛā* has a loud sound and accompanies temple ceremonies and group dances. Drummers play the *nagāṛā* pair in various folk contexts, in film music, and in the *nauṭaṅkī* street theater of Uttar Pradesh (Tewari 1974:155; Hansen 1992:210–13). Two-piece sets of *nagāṛā* might have inspired the *tablā-bāyāṇ* pairing.

Clappers and cymbals

The simplest of idiophones, sticks, and clappers are common instruments in devotional song and dance contexts. A dancer's pair of sticks struck against another dancer's is a central feature of the stick dance (*ḍāṇḍiā rās*) of Gujarat. The *kartāl* is a pair of wooden or iron clappers, sometimes with metal platelets attached, played with one hand. *Cimṭā* 'tongs' are two flat iron bars about 30 centimeters long, with metal platelets attached along their length and joined at one end. Players sound them by clashing the bars together with one hand. These instruments have a particular association with bardic and mendicant traditions. Film and popular media often depict religious mendicants holding the single-string drone (*ektārā*) in one hand and the *kartāl* or *cimṭā* in the other.

The small finger-cymbal pair, *mañjīrā*, is widely used in devotional and dance genres. Larger cymbal pairs, such as the *tāl* of Rajasthan and Uttar Pradesh and the *jhāñjh* of Orissa and Gujarat, are used in folk dance and song traditions in all the northern regions.

FILM MUSIC AND POPULAR MUSIC INSTRUMENTS

Dwarfing Hindustani music in audience size and recording-industry output are the urban popular music genres. These include Hindi film music (*filmī gānā*), Muslim and Hindu devotional and popular musics (qawwali, bhajan, *kīrtan*), and nonclassical songs in regional languages (*gīt*). Except in street bands that play for weddings and processional functions, instruments generally serve as background for the lyrics. They are nevertheless important in setting ambience and texture. Styles and instrumentation vary within each genre, and may borrow from folk, light-classical, and Western rock and pop musics.

The Indian film industry is the largest in the world, and virtually all Indian popular films are musicals [see FILM MUSIC]. The orchestration of contemporary film songs is often elaborate, consisting of large ensembles with an eclectic assortment of instruments. Film studio orchestras draw upon the entire range of both Hindustani instruments and nonclassical and Western instruments. Most numerous among instruments from South Asian folk traditions are drums, especially the *ḍholak* 'barrel drum' and stick-played *naqqārā* 'kettledrums', which provide programmatic background sounds for action and dance sequences. Because of their use in film scores, some instrumental sounds have become identified with specific dramatic situations: the *sāraṅgī* 'bowed lute' is associated with sad or tragic situations (an association with which *sāraṅgī* players are understandably unhappy); the double-reed *śahnāī* invariably accompanies wedding and birth celebrations; sitar and sarod enhance traditional Indian settings; and the flute is sometimes emphasized in rural or pastoral scenes.

Film-music directors have included Western instruments in their orchestras since the early years of sound film in the 1930s. In the first few decades, film orchestras included the accordion, mandolin, Hawaiian guitar, clarinet, and conga drums. The South Asian banjo is a type of autoharp used in film and light genres. Since the 1950s, violin sections have provided high, soaring interludes and cascading runs. Electronic keyboards, synthesizers, and electronic rhythm tracks have become common studio equipment since the 1980s (Arnold 1991; Manuel 1988).

In urban and rural areas of North India, Bangladesh, and Pakistan, colorful, uniformed street bands lead wedding processions and provide color and sound at various festive occasions. Specialized ensembles include *śahnāī* bands, bagpipe bands, and, most prominently, brass bands. Brass bands in North India may consist of trumpets, cornets, clarinets, euphoniums, valve trombones, baritone horns, saxophones, the stick-played *ḍhol* 'cylindrical drum', snare drums, bass drums, and cymbals. They

In urban and rural areas of North India, Bangladesh, and Pakistan, colorful, uniformed street bands lead wedding processions and provide color and sound at various festive occasions.

play a repertoire of film songs, marches, folk tunes, and light classical pieces (Booth 1990; Henry 1988:220).

REFERENCES

Arnold, Alison E., 1991. "Hindi Filmī Gīt: On the History of Commercial Indian Popular Music." Ph.D. dissertation, University of Illinois at Urbana-Champaign.

Baloch, Nabi B. K. B. 1975. *Musical Instruments of the Lower Indus Valley of Sind,* 2nd ed. Hyderabad, Sind: Zeb Adabi Markaz.

Bandyopadhyaya, Shripada. 1980. *Musical Instruments of India (With Forty-Six Rare Illustrations).* Varanasi and Delhi: Chaukhambha Orientalia.

Bhowmik, Swarnakamal, and Mudrika Jani. 1990. *The Heritage of Musical Instruments (A Catalogue of Musical Instruments in the Museums of Gujarat).* Vadodara: Department of Museums.

Booth, Gregory D. 1990. "Brass Bands: Tradition, Change, and the Mass Media in Indian Wedding Music." *Ethnomusicology* 34(2):245–262.

Bor, Joep. 1986–1987. "The Voice of the Sarangi: An Illustrated History of Bowing in India." *National Centre for the Performing Arts Quarterly Journal* 15(3 & 4);16(1).

———, and Philippe Bruguière. 1992. *Masters of Raga.* Berlin: Haus der Kulturen der Welt.

Capwell, Charles. 1986. *The Music of the Bauls of Bengal.* Kent, Ohio: Kent State University Press.

Day, Charles R. 1974 [1891]. *The Music and Musical Instruments of Southern India and the Deccan.* Delhi: B. R. Publishing Corporation.

Deva, B. Chaitanya. 1978. *Musical Instruments of India: Their History and Development.* Calcutta: Firma KLM.

———. 1993. *Musical Instruments,* 3rd reprint. New Delhi: National Book Trust.

Dick, Alastair. 1984. "Tablā." In *The New Grove Dictionary of Musical Instruments,* ed. Stanley Sadie. London: Macmillan.

Flora, Reis. 1995. "Styles of the *śahnāī* in Recent Decades: From *naubat* to *gāyakī aṅg.*" *Yearbook for Traditional Music* 27:52–75.

Garg, Lakshminarayan. 1978. *Hamare Sangeet Ratna,* 3rd ed. Hathras: Sangeet Karyalaya.

Hansen, Kathryn. 1992. *Grounds for Play: The Nautanki Theatre of North India.* Berkeley: University of California Press.

Henry, Edward O. 1988. *Chant the Names of God: Musical Culture in Bhojpuri-Speaking India.* San Diego: San Diego State University.

Jenkins, Jean, and Poul Rovsing Olsen. 1976. *Music and Musical Instruments in the World of Islam.* London: Horniman Museum.

Khan, Dargah Quli. 1989 [1739]. *Muraqqa'-e-Delhi: The Mughal Capital in Muhammad Shah's Time,* trans. Chander Shekhar and Shama Mitra Chenoy. Delhi: Deputy Publication.

Kippen, James. 1988. *The Tabla of Lucknow: A Cultural Analysis of a Musical Tradition.* Cambridge and New York: Cambridge University Press.

Kothari, Komal S. 1968. *Indian Folk Musical Instruments.* New Delhi: Sangeet Natak Akademi.

Krishnaswamy, S. 1971. *Musical Instruments of India.* Boston: Crescendo.

Manuel, Peter. 1988. *Popular Musics of the Non-Western World: An Introductory Survey.* New York and Oxford: Oxford University Press.

———. 1993. *Cassette Culture: Popular Music and Technology in North India.* Chicago: University of Chicago Press.

Miner, Allyn. 1993. *Sitar and Sarod in the 18th and 19th Centuries.* Wilhelmshaven: Florian Noetzal Verlag; Delhi: Motilal Banarsidass, 1997.

Pacholczyk, Jozef. 1996. *Ṣūfyāna Mūsīqī: The Classical Music of Kashmir.* Berlin: Verlag für Wissenschaft und Bildung.

Ray, Sukumar. 1988. *Folk-Music of Eastern India: With Special Reference to Bengal.* Shimla: Indian Institute of Advanced Study.

Roychowdhury, Harendra K. 1929. *The Musicians of India (Illustrated),* part 1. Ramgopalpur: Author.

Sachs, Curt. 1968 [1940]. *The History of Musical Instruments.* New York, London: W. W. Norton.

Sastri, S. Subrahmanya, ed. 1986. *Saṅgītaratnākara of Śārṅgadeva*, 2nd rev. ed., vol. 3. Madras: Adyar Library.

Shankar, Ravi. 1968. *My Music, My Life.* New York: Simon & Schuster.

Singh, Sawai Pratap Maharaj. 1910–1912. *Saṅgītsār.* 7 parts. Pune: Poona Gayan Samaj.

Slawek, Stephen. 1987. *Sitar Technique in Nibaddh Forms.* Delhi: Motilal Banarsidass.

Solis, Theodore. 1970. "The Sarod." M.A. thesis, University of Hawaii.

Sorrell, Neil. 1984. "Sāraṅgī." In *The New Grove Dictionary of Musical Instruments,* ed. Stanley Sadie. London: Macmillan.

———, and Ram Narayan. 1980. *Indian Music in Performance: A Practical Introduction.* New York: New York University Press.

Tagore, Sourindro M. 1976 [1875]. *Yantra Kosha or A Treasury of the Musical Instruments of Ancient and of Modern India, and of Various Other Countries.* New York: American Musicological Society.

Tewari, Laxmi G. 1974. "Folk Music of India: Uttar Pradesh." Ph.D. dissertation, Wesleyan University.

Musical Instruments: Southern Area

David B. Reck

Karnatak Concert Instruments
Temple and Dance Music Instruments
Folk Instruments
Popular and Film Music Instruments

The musical instruments of South India and Sri Lanka share a common history with those of the North. They play similar roles as artifacts within society, and function in closely related musical traditions within a diverse yet remarkably unified cultural environment. Instruments in the two areas have much in common: the bamboo flute, associated with Krishna; the snake charmer mesmerizing his tame cobras by piping on his double clarinet of gourd and reed; the four categories of instruments in Bharata's treatise on drama, the *Nāṭyaśāstra* (c. 200 B.C.–A.D. 200); wandering minstrels playing single-stringed, gourd and bamboo drones; hereditary musician castes associated with specific genres and instruments; and classical musicians performing on elaborate string instruments and sophisticatedly engineered drums.

Yet differences persist. Instruments may have different names in southern Dravidian languages—Telugu, Tamil, Malayalam, Kannada, Tulu, or Sinhalese—or may have names phonetically modified from Sanskrit roots. In the South, the northern *bāṅsurī* 'bamboo flute' is known variously as the Tamil *kuḻal,* the Sanskrit *vēṇu,* the English flute, or the Sinhalese *vasdaṇda.* The snake charmer's double clarinet, known as *puṅgī* in the North, may be called the *nāgasvaram* (literally 'snake notes') in Andhra Pradesh and the *mākuṭi* or *pambatti-kuḻal* 'snake-folk's flute' in Tamil Nadu (Dournon and Helffer 1984; Dick 1984).

In addition, over the centuries Southern musicians have adapted Northern musical instruments, modifying shapes and sounds to fit their taste. Indians view these instruments, which include the *nāgasvaram* 'double-reed pipe' (different from the snake charmer's pipe of the same name in Andhra Pradesh), the *sarasvatī vīṇā* 'plucked lute', and the *ceṇṭa* and *mridangam* drums, as typical of the South, in spite of their North Indian ancestry (Reck 1968–1994). Finally, the southern peninsula has experienced far less exposure to the instruments of Afghanistan, Persia, Central Asia, or other Islamic regions, as the South was never part of the Mughal empire. It remained predominantly Hindu, with small Muslim and Christian minorities. Sri Lanka is predominantly Buddhist, with a substantial (Tamil) Hindu minority.

The association between specific musical instruments and caste is particularly strong in the South. The *pullavān vīṇā* 'folk fiddle', for example, is played by the Puḷḷavas, who are astrologers, healers, and priests of the serpent cult as well as singers and musicians. In Kerala, hereditary temple drummers say that those outside the Mārār or Pothuval hereditary castes may learn to play the cylindrical *ceṇṭa*, but the music "will never really be in their blood" (Reck 1968–1994).

South India and Sri Lanka have several unique types of ensemble, especially in temple or ritual contexts. These include the *pañcavādyam* 'temple drum ensemble' in Kerala, the *periya mēḷam* 'large drum and double-reed ensemble' of temples and rites of passage in Karnataka, Andhra Pradesh, and Tamil Nadu, and the *hēvisi* of Buddhist ceremonies in Kandy and elsewhere in Sri Lanka. Many such orchestras contain twenty or more players.

In spite of its reputation for conservatism, the South readily adopted European instruments such the violin, clarinet, mandolin, and guitar. Some South Indian musicians combine Northern instruments such as the sitar, tabla, or *śahnāī* 'double reed aerophone' with Southern classical music instruments, in concerts referred to as *jugalbandī*.

The role of instruments and their physical characteristics, their playing technique, and the musicians who create music on them are interconnected with musical style and genre. Four broad categories of South Indian and Sri Lankan musical traditions can thus serve as the basis for a discussion of musical instruments: the Karnatak classical concert-music tradition; temple and dance traditions; folk music; and popular music generated by the movie industry.

KARNATAK CONCERT INSTRUMENTS

Karnatak music, the high art music of the concert stage in South India and Sri Lanka, is also played by ensembles in temples, at weddings and other ritual occasions, and to accompany classical dance.

In classical concerts in both Southern and Northern areas, musicians play their instruments sitting more or less cross-legged on a stage or platform. Performers may hold their instruments in their hands, set them on the floor, or cradle them in some way on their lap, against their foot or leg, or on their thigh. Musicians in outdoor processions and in some dance and temple traditions such as *kathakaḷi* and *kṛshṇāṭṭam* stand; but under no circumstances do traditional Karnatak musicians sit on chairs, as musicians do in Europe. However, most musicians in India's cinema recording studios do sit on chairs.

The voice is the primary instrument of Karnatak music, and well over half of all Karnatak concerts feature a singer as the main artist. Except for a handful of modern pieces, there are almost no purely instrumental compositions. The massive repertoire comprises composed songs—devotional poetry set to melodies—that forms the basis of any performance, vocal or instrumental. The greatest compliment a Karnatak instrumentalist can receive is that he or she makes the instrument "sound like the human voice."

In India the four common categories of instruments (*vādya*) follow the ancient system described in the *Nāṭyaśāstra* [see CLASSIFICATION OF MUSICAL INSTRUMENTS], based on the way sound is produced: *tata vādya* (strings, or chordophones), *suṣira vādya* (winds, or aerophones), *avanaddha vādya* (drums, or membranophones), *ghana vādya* (solids, or idiophones). However, in South Indian classical music, instruments may also be classified according to their function within the musical texture; there are five functional layers, each with a different role in the music:

1. The featured solo melody (sometimes a duet)
2. The melodic accompaniment, which supports the solo melody and alternates with it in improvisations
3. The constant background *śruti* (drone)

4. The percussion accompaniment
5. The time-keeping cymbals (in temple and dance music)

Solo melody instruments

The Western violin and the Indian bamboo flute (*kuḻal*) are by far the most popular Karnatak solo instruments, but concerts may feature a variety of other principal instruments: the South Indian *vīṇā* 'fretted, plucked lute', the *goṭṭuvādyam* 'fretless vina played with a slide', the *jaltarangam* 'set of struck porcelain bowls', or the *nāgasvaram* 'large double-reed pipe', as well as increasingly popular European instruments such as the clarinet, saxophone, mandolin, guitar, harmonium, or electronic keyboard. In many present-day concerts, instruments are heavily amplified, many with contact microphones. Since the mid-1970s, however, some music societies have sponsored concerts without microphones, to promote pure acoustic sound.

Violin

The European violin, technically a short-necked bowed lute, was adopted almost two hundred years ago during the British colonial era. South Indian musicians quickly realized its adaptability to Indian music (the fretless fingerboard permits slides and ornaments, and its sustained tone has a pre-eminently vocal quality) and they developed their own playing techniques.

The violinist, seated on the floor, holds the instrument firmly between the shoulder or chest and the heel of the foot. The violin is tuned to the tonal center (Sa) and its fifth (Pa), for example, G–d–g–d′, so the open strings can be touched by the bow frequently as drone notes. The left hand combines the virtuosic fingering of European playing technique with a quick sliding motion of one finger along the unfretted neck, permitting subtle intonation and the complex swoops, curves, and oscillations of ornamentation (*gamaka*). South Indian violinists tend to play long tones purely, without the vibrato so typical of Western violin playing. Also, by pressing the bow on the playing strings, they achieve a piercing, nasal timbre strikingly different from the common European violin sound.

Viṇā

The South Indian vina (*vīṇā*)—sometimes called *sarasvatī vīṇā* after the Hindu goddess of learning and music, Sarasvati—evolved from medieval prototypes to its current form about four hundred years ago. It is a long-necked plucked lute with a thick hollow neck and large resonator, both laboriously chiseled from jackwood logs. A natural gourd (today commonly made of papier-maché or fiberglass), attached under the neck, rests near the musician's knee for ease in playing, and provides extra resonance (figure 1).

The vina typically has finely crafted decorations. A carved dragon's head protrudes from the curving end of the neck; the pegs are large and finely turned; and ivory, deer horn, or plastic trim etched with floral designs covers all joints, and forms two rosettes with tiny multiple sound holes on the top plank (Diagram Group 1976: 219). A slightly convex brass plate, conforming to a generic Indian design, tops a table-like bridge (figure 2). When the player plucks the melody strings, they vibrate against the bridge surface to create a rich blend of harmonics and the "nasal" sound characteristic of much of India's music.

Chromatic brass frets are set in black wax that is scalloped to allow room for finger movement to press and pull the strings. The variable string tension thus created is a primary technique for achieving glides and ornaments. The vina has seven strings, four main playing strings tuned to a male vocal range in alternating fifth and tonic degrees (for example, B″–E′–B′–E) and three drone strings (tuned tonic, fifth, tonic,

FIGURE 1 The *sarasvatī vīṇā* played by Kalpakam Swaminathan, Madras. Photo by Carol S. Reck, 1969/1970.

as for example E–B–e) strung across a small curved side bridge. Traditionally the vina player uses only two fingers of the left hand for sliding from fret to fret or for stopping and pulling the strings. Wearing plectrums on the right-hand fingertips, the musician plucks with downward strokes of the index and middle fingers in alternation, while the little finger brushes the drone strings in an upward motion.

A rich literature and mythology relate to the vina. According to legend, the instrument symbolizes the body of the goddess Sarasvati (the frets representing her ribs, for example), and specific points on the instrument are connected with each *cakra* 'psychic center' of yoga meditation. In a connection with Hindu mythology, the monkey god Hanuman and the demon king Ravana (the villain of the epic Ramayana) are believed to have been great virtuosi.

FIGURE 2 The bridge of the *sarasvatī vīṇā*, showing its convex top. The curved brass bridge (also convex) supporting the drone strings leans against the main bridge. Photo © 1997 Carol S. Reck.

Western fretted stringed instruments, including the guitar and mandolin, have entered the South Asian environment through Indian film music and pop music of both East and West.

Goṭṭuvādyam

The *goṭṭuvādyam* is a fretless vina played by sliding a polished stone or hardwood tube along one of the strings with the left hand, increasing and decreasing the string's vibrating length, and by plucking the string with the right hand. The instrument lies horizontally on the floor before the musician. The *goṭṭuvādyam*, which is related to the North Indian *vicitra vīṇā* and is unlike most South Indian instruments, may have as many as thirteen sympathetic strings set under the playing strings. Its chief melody string is a double course, two strings that are tuned an octave apart, giving it a strong sound not unlike that of the American twelve-stringed guitar (Sambamurthy 1952–1971, 2:201).

Electric guitar, mandolin

Western fretted stringed instruments, including the guitar and mandolin, have entered the South Asian environment through Indian film music and pop music of both East and West. Audiences have responded enthusiastically to a generation of gifted musicians playing these instruments with great speed and virtuosity.

Flute

The transverse flute has a relatively simple construction; it is a bamboo tube a little over 30 centimeters long with a blow-hole and seven finger holes. Related to bamboo flutes throughout the subcontinent, the South Indian *kuḻal*, also called *vēṇu* or flute, has its finger holes burned and drilled to produce the scale of *rāga harikambhōji* (equivalent to the Western major scale with a flat seventh). With adjustment of the embouchure and an elaborate system of half-hole fingering, the musician can produce all the many scales and subtle ornaments of the raga system. Each flute has a specific tonal center (pitch Sa), and to change the tonic pitch a flute player must play a different flute. The bamboo flute is associated with the Hindu god Krishna, and is an important instrument in music for dance and dance drama exploring the mythology of this deity.

Clarinet, saxophone

These are the only two European wind instruments that Karnatak musicians have adopted. As concert instruments both seem to emulate the double-reed *nāgasvaram* in sound and style, and the clarinet may also be part of ensembles providing music for classical dance. Both appear in the ragtag urban street bands (based upon the European military marching band) that play cinema music in wedding and other kinds of processions.

Jaltarangam

Xylophones and/or metallophones are common in Africa, Indonesia, Burma, Thailand, and elsewhere, but tuned idiophones are exceedingly rare in South Asia.

The *jaltarangam* is an exception. It consists of a set of Chinese porcelain bowls, graduated in size, that are placed in a semicircle around the player. The musician tunes the bowls to a raga scale by filling them with water to different levels, keeping a pitcher or flask handy for tuning (Krishnaswamy 1971:69–70). The musician then plays by hitting the rim of the bowls with chopstick-size bamboo sticks, agitating the water to achieve ornaments, and playing fast repeated notes to create the effect of sustained tones.

Melodic accompanying instruments

The violin is almost exclusively the instrument of choice today for the melodic accompaniment of Karnatak music, regardless of whether the soloist is a vocalist or instrumentalist. Violinists are consequently well trained and highly experienced in the techniques and nuances of accompaniment; even the most famous violin virtuosi accompany other artists in addition to their own solo performances.

Occasionally, when the featured soloist is an instrumentalist, a duplicate of the solo instrument provides melodic accompaniment. Thus a vina may accompany a solo vina, or one or two *nāgasvaram* players may accompany a principal *nāgasvaram* artist.

Drone (*śruti*) instruments

Some solo melody instruments such as the vina and violin are tuned so that their open strings sounding the tonic and fifth can serve as drone strings; however, most classical music concerts include one or more instruments that provide a continuous drone (*śruti*). In the wider context of South Asian music, drone instruments form a unique and important family.

Tambūrā

The South Indian long-necked lute, *tambūrā,* differs from its northern counterpart in several ways. Like the *sarasvatī vīṇā,* its hollow neck and resonator are chiseled out and shaped from single pieces of jackwood, in contrast to the northern *tambūrā,* which commonly uses a gourd resonator. In North India, the *tambūrā* tends to have relatively simple ornamentation, but in the South its finishwork and ornamentation duplicate those of the vina—lacking only the frets and the dragon's head. Four turned pegs hold the strings at the squared end of the neck.

The southern *tambūrā* has four steel or brass strings tuned according to the soloist's tonal center in the following pattern: fifth (Pa)–upper tonal center (Sa)–upper tonal center (Sa)–lower tonal center (Sa) (for example, G–c–c–C). The player plucks the strings in this order (Sambamurthy n.d.:17–19), and often in a long-short-short-long rhythm entirely unrelated to the tempo or tala of the music. The objective is to provide a continuous background "wall" of sound.

The low bench-like bridge of the instrument, carved from a hardwood like ebony or rosewood, has a convex top, as on the vina. A silk thread (*jīva* 'life') is inserted between each string and the bridge surface at just the right point (figure 3), creating a rich blend of overtones on each string in addition to the fundamental, and dramatically increasing the length of the string's vibration.

Śruti peṭṭi

The *śruti peṭṭi* or *śruti* box (literally 'drone box') is a small reed organ without a keyboard. The hinged sides open up to form a bellows operated by the player's hand. At the top the lid opens to reveal three or more disks; by rotating the hole in each disk over chambers containing tuned brass reeds (similar to those in an accordion or harmonica), the musician can set the drone notes to a variety of tonal centers.

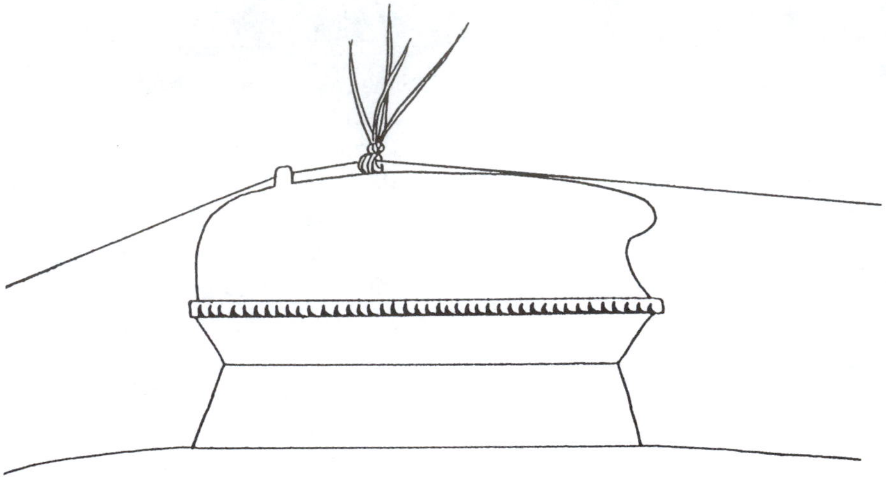

FIGURE 3 Side view of the *tambūrā* bridge with a convex top and the string *jīva* beneath a playing string. Drawing by Navarana, 1997. Used by permission. Courtesy David Reck.

The electronic *śruti peṭṭi,* invented in the late twentieth century, duplicates the reed organ sound and shape of the original. Another model duplicates the sound of the plucked *tambūrā.* The instrument is capable of fine tuning within the entire spectrum of an octave, and runs on electricity or batteries (thus avoiding the frequent surges of India's electricity). It sounds automatically when turned on, eliminating the need for a player.

Percussion accompaniment

Mridangam

The *mridangam* is a barrel-shaped double-headed drum with a jackwood body (figure 4). Its technically complex, multilayered leather heads produce as many as twenty different sounds when played with different combinations of fingers and parts of the hands. The *mridangam* functions as the chief accompanying percussion instrument in Karnatak music, its role and status similar to the tabla in northern regions. In performances with additional percussion accompanists, the *mridangam* player is in charge, signaling nonverbally when each can begin and stop playing, choosing which precomposed patterns the group will play together, and setting the structure of the percussion solo (*tani āvartanam*).

Like the vina, the *mridangam* has a documented history stretching back at least two thousand years (Tarlekar and Tarlekar 1972:59). Its name may derive from the Sanskrit words *mṛd* 'mud' and *anga* 'limb', thus denoting a "body of clay"; the name of the contemporary Bengali drum *khol* has the same meaning. The *Nāṭyaśāstra* 'Treatise on Drama' (200 B.C.–A.D. 200) and the thirteenth-century *Saṅgītaratnākara* 'Jewel Mine of Music' describe another feature still in use today: the application of a tuning paste to the drumheads. The present-day mixture of rice flour, ash, and other ingredients has evolved from early pastes of river mud and cow dung. The *Saṅgītaratnākara* also mentions many-layered drumheads, which are still in use today.

The *mridangam*'s two drumheads use four different types of skin (goat, calf, cow, and water buffalo). Both heads have a goatskin base covering the entire opening. The left head has two layers of buffalo hide stretched over this, with a circle cut out of their centers. The drummer presses a damp blob of cream of wheat (farina)—now sometimes replaced by silicon caulk—within the circle before each performance, resulting in a rich booming bass sound. This left head is not tuned to a specific pitch. The right head has a layer of calfskin placed around the rim over the goatskin base, and then a layer of stretched cowhide with a circle cut out in the center. Reeds of broom straw or fine gravel are inserted between the goatskin and the cowhide, result-

FIGURE 4 Children in a music school in Madras playing the *mridangam*. Photo by Carol S. Reck, 1969/1970.

ing in a slight buzzing timbre. Within the cut-out circle a shiny "black spot" is built up from a mixture of boiled rice flour and finely ground iron slag. Each of the black spot's forty or fifty layers is dried and polished, providing the drumhead with a slightly metallic ringing sound that emphasizes the tonal center and its fifth.

Lacings of buffalo leather thongs or nylon webbing run the length of the drum and are attached to the rim at either end. The right head is tuned to the main artist's tonal center or tonic. The drummer fine-tunes the *mridangam* by hammering on the rim with a stone and/or prying small dowels under the lacing, thus tightening or loosening the heads. The drummer needs different sizes of drums to cover the various vocal and instrumental ranges of Karnatak musicians.

The patron god of *mridangam* players is the great bull Nandi, an animal associated with the Hindu god Shiva. In many South Indian temples a massive sculpted Nandi of polished stone sits facing the inner sanctum of the shrine of Shiva.

Kañjīrā

The *kañjīrā* is a small, round frame drum about 20 centimeters in diameter. The hoop is 5 or 6 centimeters deep and carved from a single piece of jackwood. A lizard or snakeskin head is glued to the rim, and dampened in performance for tuning. Metal jangles (occasionally heavy old English colonial coins) are mounted into the rim.

The musician holds the *kañjīrā* in the left hand and plays with the fingers of the right hand, alternating with and responding to the *mridangam* rhythms in Karnatak concerts. Most *mridangam* players can also play *kañjīrā*, although there are a few *kañjīrā* specialists.

Ghaṭam

This large, narrow-mouthed clay water pot is an important idiophone in the large Karnatak percussion ensemble. The *ghaṭam* player alternates with and responds to the *mridangam* player's lead. The *ghaṭam,* with its distinctive metallic sound, is the favorite instrument for duets with the drum. The water pot comes in different sizes, each tuned to a different tonic pitch.

In contrast with the "sizzle" or "splash" of Western cymbals and their Turkish archetypes, Indian cymbals have bell-like ringing tones.

The *ghaṭam* player holds the instrument in the lap, and sometimes rotates its mouth—usually facing upward and away from the player—against the chest to achieve a muffled timbre. The player strikes the clay pot on different parts of its body and mouth with all fingers of both hands, achieving different sonorities. Rhythmically, the *ghaṭam* shares the tradition and repertoire of the *mridangam.*

Morsing (murcing)

The *morsing* is a metal mouth harp (also described as a jew's harp) with a long vibrating tongue set in a pear-shaped rim. Players use instruments of different tunings to match the tonic pitch of the main artist in concert.

The musician holds the instrument with one hand at the mouth, and plucks the tuned metallic tongue with a finger from the other hand. By changing the size and shape of the mouth cavity with the larynx and tongue, the musician sounds different overtones of the fundamental pitch, as does the *mridangam* player by hitting different sections of the multilayered drumhead with different finger strokes. Because South Indian musicians have recognized this acoustical connection between *morsing* and *mridangam*, Karnatak music is the one cultural context in which the mouth harp has the status of a classical-music instrument.

Time-keeping instruments

Tāḷam

Tāḷam is the generic name for a matched pair of small, circular hand cymbals of brass, bronze, or other bell metal. In contrast with the "sizzle" or "splash" of Western cymbals and their Turkish archetypes, Indian cymbals have bell-like ringing tones. They vary in diameter from 2 to 7 centimeters, are somewhat thick, and most have a "boss" (that is, a bulge) in the middle. The cymbal player holds the *tāḷam* by a connecting string braided through a hole in their centers.

In the *bharata nāṭyam, kuchipuḍi,* and *mōhini āṭṭam* dance traditions, in bhajan religious group singing, and in the *periya mēḷam* pipe and drum ensemble, time-keeping by metallic percussion is integral to the music. When a Karnatak classical-music concert incorporates music from these traditions, the ensemble may include *tāḷam* cymbals to mark time.

Hands

In Karnatak music concerts hand clapping and finger counts serve to keep the tala [see KARNATAK TALA]. This human-hand idiophone is an essential part of a South Indian classical music performance, although American or European audience members unfamiliar with the practice may find it distracting.

FIGURE 5 Members of the *periya mēḷam* ensemble playing in a temple in Kanchipuram, Tamil Nadu. The instruments are *tavil* (*left*) and *nāgasvaram* (*right*). Photo by David B. Reck, 1969/1970.

TEMPLE AND DANCE MUSIC INSTRUMENTS

Periya mēḷam

The *periya mēḷam* 'big band' is a temple ensemble consisting of the double-reed *nāgasvaram,* the double-reed *ottu* drone (or alternately the *śruti peṭṭi*), the *tavil* drum, and the *tāḷam* hand cymbals common throughout Hindu South India and among the Tamils of Sri Lanka (figure 5). There are often two or more of each instrument. Inside a Hindu temple, the ensemble fulfills the functions of the pipe organ in European churches, and South Indians consider its sound highly auspicious. Outside the temple, the *periya mēḷam* ensemble performs in a variety of ritual or ceremonial contexts, such as weddings and street processions with images of Hindu gods. The ensemble also adds luster to openings of stores, buildings, fairs, political campaigns, and concert series. In terms of melody and meter, the ensemble falls within the repertoire and style of Karnatak classical music, often appearing on the classical concert stage. Recently there has been experimentation combining instruments of the *periya mēḷam* with other classical music instruments.

Nāgasvaram

The large (60-to-90-centimeter-long) double-reed *nāgasvaram* (literally 'snake-notes') has a penetrating, saxophone-like sound considered—like that of the *periya mēḷam*—highly auspicious by South Indians (see figure 5). Its conical wooden tube has seven finger holes and a flaring wooden bell. It is the leading instrument of the *periya mēḷam* ensemble: since c. 1940, players sit when performing indoors with the ensemble and stand when playing outdoors. Before this period, *nāgasvaram* players always had to stand [see SOCIAL ORGANIZATION OF MUSIC AND MUSICIANS: SOUTHERN AREA]. The *nāgasvaram* is related to the smaller *śahnāī* of the northern regions.

The *nāgasvaram* playing technique includes circular breathing, in which the player inflates the cheeks to keep a constant source of air, making possible a continuous sound without breaks for breath. Players produce various raga scales, bends, and ornaments through half-hole fingering and lip control of the flexible double reed, which results in wide variations of pitch and dynamics (Sambamurthy 1952–1971, 3:106–108).

Ottu

The *ottu* is a double-reed instrument 60 centimeters or more in length. It provides drone notes for the *nāgasvaram,* whose shape and size it duplicates. The *ottu* has no finger holes, but has several tuning holes on its underside, all but one of which the player blocks with wax for tuning to different tonic notes. Since the 1960s, the *śruti peṭṭi* 'bellows reed organ' has replaced the *ottu.*

Tavil

The *tavil* is a double-headed barrel drum with a penetrating, brittle sound. Two contributing factors to this sound are the tightness of the stretched skin heads—a tuning paste of powder that has been sanctified by a temple ritual and mixed with oil is applied to the center of the left head—and the hard plaster thimbles worn on the fingers of the player's right hand, together with a drumstick held in the left. One or more *tavil* accompany the double-reed *nāgasvaram* in the *periya mēḷam* ensemble. In outdoor temple performances or processions, players carry the drums held up by means of cloth straps over their shoulders. In indoor concerts, seated performers place their drums on the floor.

The *tavil* relates historically to the North Indian *ḍhol,* which also accompanies a double-reed instrument, the *śahnāī.* Linguistically the *tavil* relates to the Arabic-Turkish *davul.*

Cinna mēḷam

The ensemble that accompanies *bharata nāṭyam* classical dance is called *cinna mēḷam* 'little band'. It consists of one or more voices, violin, *tambūrā* 'string drone' or *śruti peṭṭi* 'drone reed organ', and *mridangam* drum, with the addition of *kuḻal* 'bamboo flute', *tāḷam* 'hand cymbals' (all these instruments are discussed above), and sometimes a European clarinet.

Pañcavādyam

The *pañcavādyam* 'five instruments' is a major ensemble connected with Hindu temples in Kerala, southwest India. Primarily percussive in sound, and drawing upon its own complex rhythmic tradition, this large ensemble of twenty or more players includes the original 'five instruments': hourglass-shaped *timila* drums, the *iṭaykka* 'small variable tension drum', the *maddaḷam* 'barrel drum', the *iḻatāḷam* 'ringing hand cymbals', and the *kompā* 'curved trumpet', as well as the *ceṅṅala* 'gong', the *śaṅkha* 'conch shell trumpet', and occasionally the oboe (called *kuḻal,* which is also the term used for flute). The trumpets and other wind instruments play a percussive role in the ensemble rather than a melodic one.

Members of the Mārār caste are specialists in playing *pañcavādyam* drums [see KERALA]. In the famous Puram Festival at Trichur each year, multiple *pañcavādyam* orchestras slowly converge in an all-night procession through the streets surrounding the temple. Eventually dozens of decorated elephants follow for the spectacular culminating ritual and fireworks.

FIGURE 6 A group of *timila* drummers in a *pañcavādyam* orchestra in Trichur, 1969/1970. One end of a *maddaḷam* drum can be seen at the left. Photo © Carol S. Reck 1982.

Timila

The *timila* drum has an elongated hourglass shape a little less than 90 centimeters in length, with calfskin heads mounted on bamboo hoops at both ends. A player can tune the drum by adjusting the "W" lacing connecting the bamboo hoops. Standing drummers hold the *timila* diagonally in front of them with a fabric strap, playing rhythms on the upper head with the hands (figure 6). Both the drum's shape and its playing position point to a possible connection with African drums, across the Arabian Sea, a lineage that probably relates to the hourglass-shaped *iṭaykka* as well.

Maddaḷam

The *maddaḷam* or *śuddha* 'pure' *maddaḷam* is a barrel-shaped double-headed drum with layered composite heads and tuning paste, like the large *mridangam*, to which it is related. The musician plays standing, with the drum held horizontally slightly below the waist and tied with a fabric strap over the shoulders. The drummer plays the left and right drumheads with fingers and hands but with the fingers of the right hand encased in plaster thimbles, as with *tavil* players, producing a penetrating metallic sound.

The *maddaḷam* is also the principal drum in the dance-theater forms *kathakaḷi* and *kūṭiyāṭṭam* in Kerala and *yakṣagāna* in Karnataka.

Iṭaykka

The *iṭaykka* has an hourglass-shaped body; it is held by a strap over the musician's left shoulder. The drumheads, attached to bamboo hoops, extend over the shell-faces, and lacing connects the two. The drummer squeezes the lacing with the left hand to achieve variable tension, and produces a variety of pitches by striking the front drumhead with a small wooden or horn stick slightly curved at the end.

The *iṭaykka* is associated with the Mārār and Pothuval castes and in addition to its role in the *pañcavādyam* ensemble is also used in other temple and devotional musical genres in Kerala. In *kathakaḷi* dance dramas, its delicate melodic sound accompanies the appearance of female characters on stage.

Kompà

Also known in Sanskrit as the *śṛṅga,* the *kompà,* a semicircular trumpet with a conical bore, is played in temples throughout South India and Sri Lanka (figure 7). Performers play in pairs, with instruments tuned to the tonic and fifth degrees (Sa and Pa). *Kompà* players participate not only in the *pañcavādyam* ensemble but in the *ceṇṭa mēḷam* temple ritual ensemble, and they also perform *kompà pāṭṭu* '*kompà* song', military band music, and village signaling. In Sri Lanka, the *kompà* is part of both Hindu and Buddhist ceremonial music; its shape has evolved over time; and a number of coiled varieties exist, as well as the double crescent found in *hēvisi* Buddhist temple bands.

FIGURE 7 The *kompà* section of a *pañcavādyam* orchestra, Trichur, 1969/1970. Photo by Carol S. Reck.

Śaṅkha

The *śaṅkha* 'conch-shell trumpet' has an association with Hindu, Buddhist, and animist religions that dates back thousands of years. South Asians consider its penetrating sound the most auspicious of all instrumental sounds, perhaps because of its natural origin in the sea. The instrument marks key moments in such contexts as temple worship, weddings, warfare, and coronations. The blowing of the conch accompanied ancient epic heroes (as described in the Mahabharata) as they rode into battle in chariots. In the first Indian-Pakistan war (1948), Indian newspapers reported that conch blowing preceded the first attack by an Indian armored division.

To craft the *śaṅkha,* instrument makers slice off the pointed end of the shell and sometimes add a silver mouthpiece, thus providing an opening to the spiraling conical tube inside the shell. According to myth, the instrument was one of many important objects that emerged during the gods' primordial Churning of the Ocean of Milk (in the Ramayana and Mahabharata epics), and it became symbolic of the Hindu god Vishnu as well as the Buddha and earthly kings and emperors.

Kuḻal

Kuḻal is the ancient Tamil term for flute, but South Indians use the word interchangeably for flutes, double-reed oboes, and single-reed clarinets. The double-reed

A famous Malayalam proverb calls the *ceṇṭa* "the king of instruments," and Keralites associate its sound with Kerala's jungles, rice fields, and palm trees as well as with the regional culture.

FIGURE 8 A *ceṇṭa* player on stage next to an actor in a *yakṣagāna* performance near Mangalore, 1969/1970. Photo © Carol S. Reck 1982.

kuḻal is a small conical-bore oboe similar to the Northern *śahnāī* type, which exists throughout South Asia, Central and West Asia, and North Africa. The pipe has eight finger holes, a thumb hole, and a conical bell. Its reed is made of a squashed piece of cane attached to a round disk through which a tube passes that enters the pipe. As is common in Asian double-reed instruments, the entire reed vibrates freely within the musician's mouth cavity. (In contrast, the double reed of the European oboe is held between the player's lips.)

Ceṇṭa mēḷam

The *ceṇṭa mēḷam,* named after the *ceṇṭa* drum, is a ritual ensemble played during temple ceremonies in Kerala. The instruments include the *ceṇṭa* 'cylindrical drum', *iḷatāḷam* 'ringing cymbals', *kuḻal* pipes, and *kompà* trumpets; an ensemble may consist of a large number of each. The annual Puram Festival in Trichur employs a *ceṇṭa mēḷam* of over fifty musicians.

Ceṇṭa

Resembling the European military field drum, the *ceṇṭa* is a double-headed cylindrical drum that a standing drummer holds vertically with a fabric strap passing over his shoulders (figure 8). The drumheads are made of calfskin, the upper playing head a single layer, the bottom head a composite of six or seven glued layers, decreasing in diameter. A bamboo or metal hoop secures each leather head, and rope braces connect the two hoops. The specialized performance tradition includes complex drum strokes and patterns played with sticks or with stick and fingers in combination.

A famous Malayalam proverb calls the *ceṇṭa* "the king of instruments" (Sambamurthy, personal communication 1969), and Keralites associate its sound with Kerala's jungles, rice fields, and palm trees as well as with the regional culture. Besides its use in *ceṇṭa mēḷam,* the *ceṇṭa* is a principal drum in *kathakaḷi* and *kṛshṇāṭṭam* dance dramas, *tāyampaka* temple music, *muṭiyettu* ritual dance (associated with the goddess Bhagavati cult), *yakṣagāna* drama, and in firewalking ceremonies, ritual trance, and possession. Its powerful ringing tone can carry for a mile or more: in *kathakaḷi* dance dramas the *ceṇṭa* player "announces" a performance by drumming at the outdoor venue for an hour beforehand. The playing tradition, like most temple drumming traditions in Kerala, is associated with the Mārār and Pothuval castes [see KERALA].

Kathakaḷi

The *kathakaḷi* classical dance-drama ensemble features a solo singer, backup singer(s), the *śuddha maddaḷam* 'barrel drum' (essentially the same as the *maddaḷam*), the cylindrical *cenṭa* drum, the delicate *iṭaykka* hourglass drum, the *ceṅṅala* 'bell metal gong', and the *iḷatāḷam* 'ringing hand cymbals'. The singers play the latter two instruments. All musicians stand on the stage throughout the dance-drama performance.

The *ceṅṅala* is a small flat gong of Kerala that singers use to mark time, not only in *kathakaḷi* but also in *kṛshṇāṭṭam* dance drama and *sōpānam saṅgītam* vocal music. It is made of bell metal and struck with a short thick wooden stick. Players either suspend the gong from a string held by the hand (for a bright, ringing sound) or place it on the forearm (for a more muffled sound). It is also used to accompany Tantric rituals.

The *iḷatāḷam* is the Kerala version of paired hand cymbals, of bossed bell metal or brass. Each cymbal is approximately 15 centimeters in diameter and half a centimeter thick. The cymbals have two basic sounds: a prolonged ringing produced by a crash of the cymbals followed by the rims touching gently; and a damped sound created by striking the cymbals together and then holding them together face to face. *Iḷatāḷam* cymbals are an essential part of temple music in Kerala, and are also used to mark time in *kathakaḷi* and *kṛshṇāṭṭam* dance dramas and in *tōlpavakuthu* shadow-puppet plays.

FIGURE 9 The *miḻāvà* of the *kūṭiyāṭṭam* dance drama, Kerala. Drawing by Navarana, 1997. Used by permission. Courtesy David Reck.

Kūṭiyāṭṭam

Kūṭiyāṭṭam is a rare form of Sanskrit dance drama [see MUSIC AND DANCE: SOUTHERN AREA]. It is nearly a thousand years old, and is performed by the Cākyār and Nambiyār castes of Kerala. The form, closely related to the dramatic arts described in Bharata's *Nāṭyaśāstra* (a treatise from the first and second centuries), uses a singer/narrator and an ensemble of five types of instrument: two massive *miḻāvu* 'pot drums' that dominate the rear stage, the *kuḻiṭṭāḷam* 'bronze ringing cymbal' played by the singer, the *iḍakku* 'small hourglass tension drum', the *kompà* 'curved semicircular trumpet' and the *kuḻal* 'double-reed pipe'. The *śaṅkha* 'conch shell trumpet' is blown at auspicious moments in the drama (Raja 1964:10).

The *miḻāvà* drum is a large elongated copper pot about 90 centimeters high set upright in a small round stand (figure 9). The mouth of the pot is covered with a taut skin drumhead. The musician sits on a stool behind the drum and plays with both hands, producing a sharp, metallic sound. The spectacle of the two *miḻāvu* drums dominating the stage behind the elaborately costumed dancers is a unique feature of *kūṭiyāṭṭam*.

Hēvisi

The *hēvisi* ensemble provides music for Buddhist rituals in Sri Lankan temples. Its instruments are the *horanâva* 'small oboe', which plays simple melodic patterns defining the time, place, and occasion, and two types of drum. On the double-headed cylindrical drum (*daule*), drummers play ostinato cyclical rhythms, and on the paired small kettledrums (*tammâṭṭa*) they play rhythmic elaborations [see SRI LANKA]. In ritual processions in the hill country and as accompaniment to the Kandyan sacred processional dance, the drummers wear spectacular headdresses and breastplates and dance as they play.

The *horanâva* is a small quadruple-reed pipe on the model of the North Indian double-reed *śahnāī*. It has open finger holes and a high, penetrating sound.

The *daule* is a large cylindrical drum with double heads of deer- or calfskin. Standing or dancing drummers suspend the *daule* by a cloth from their shoulders. Also called *davula* or *davul,* the drum is related to the Tamil *tavil,* described earlier, and like the *tavil* it is played with the fingers of the right hand but with a stick in the left hand. Prior to the twentieth century, drummers used the *daule* and a smaller version, the *ana bera*, for signaling and for calling attention to announcements by public criers because of the great carrying power of the drums' sound.

The *tammâṭṭa* is a pair of wooden kettledrums suspended from the musician's hips and played with two cane sticks with hoop ends. In Buddhist processions the *tammâṭṭa* players move in formalized steps to the rhythm of their drums, the left hand playing punctuating ostinatos, the right playing complicated variations. Occasionally the drummers show their skill by drumming with their elbows and forearms as well as their sticks.

The *gâṭa bera* is the most important drum of Kandyan dance and Buddhist ritual. It is a relatively narrow double-headed barrel drum slung horizontally over the chest of the standing player, and varies in length from about 45 to 60 centimeters. Interestingly, drum makers often fit the drum size to the player's physical size. The high ringing sound of the right drumhead results from its tightly stretched skin (of a monkey's stomach), while the left head, made of oxhide, produces a muffled sound. In Hindu mythology, the *gâta bera* was built on orders from the god Brahma, with its two heads representing the sun and moon, and the bulge in the middle of its body representing the earth. Besides its importance in Kandyan dance, the drum signals the inauguration of important temple rituals and provides elaborate accompaniment for the three-day epic dance drama *kohomba-kankāriya*.

Bhajana

Group devotional singing as an act of worship (*bhajana*) incorporates various instruments from classical and folk traditions played by participant devotees. These may include a violin, *mridangam* or tabla, *kañjīrā* 'tambourine', harmonium, *tambūrā* and/or *śruti peṭṭi* 'drones', and a variety of time-keeping *tāḷam* 'ringing hand cymbals' and rhythmic clackers.

The harmonium is part of the legacy of nineteenth-century Christian missionaries. It is a small portable reed organ played with the right hand of the musician while the left operates the bellows by pulling shut then releasing the back of the instrument. Players "fake" ornaments—their subtle intonation is impossible on the fixed-pitch reeds—by blurring together adjacent notes on the keyboard, much as jazz pianists "fudge" blues notes on the piano. Perhaps because of the awkwardness of its equal temperament, and a Southern preference for the violin, the harmonium has not achieved the popularity it has as an accompanying instrument to Hindustani vocalists. Its appearance as a solo instrument in Karnatak music today is extremely rare. Karnatak musicians began using the instrument in the 1930s, but musicologists were horrified and tried to ban its use in concert halls and on the radio. In the South it now functions mainly as an accompaniment to *bhajana* singing, folk and light music, and vernacular theater. The much more flexible electronic keyboard synthesizer, used in film music, may yet emerge as a replacement.

Bhajana cekkalu is a pair of wooden clappers with metal jangles. Like the *cekkai* or *kartāḷa* of Tamil Nadu or the *ciplā* of elsewhere in the South, the Andhra Pradesh clappers may be rounded or oblong, sometimes having an animal or fish motif or shape. Musicians often clack together a pair between the fingers and thumb of one hand, each component mounted on a finger ring.

The *jālra* or *kaimaṇi* in Kerala are thin flat cymbals made of copper or bell metal, about 10 centimeters in diameter and connected by a string running through their centers. They mark time both in *bhajana* and in folk dance.

Other temple instruments

Ancient Hindu and Buddhist temple archives provide lists of instruments to be used in ritual contexts. Most describe the instruments as *pañçavādyam* 'five instruments' or *pañcamahāśabda* 'five great sounds'. The Brahadamba temple in Pudukkottai, however, lists eighteen string, wind, and percussion instruments (*aṣṭadasavādya*), and the scholarly text *Viveka Cuḍāmaṇi* describes a band of no less than twenty-six different types of drums (Sambamurthy 1959:25). Two of the many temple instruments are described here.

The *pañcamukha vādyam* 'five-faced instrument' is a huge drum with a pot-like body made of a sacred mixture of five metals. On its top side, instead of the usual single neck and mouth of a pot drum, it has five necks with circular openings. Two layers of cowskin cover the central opening, making this a composite drumhead similar to that of the *mridangam*. The other four slightly smaller necks arranged around this each have a single goatskin covering. The drumheads are tuned to different pitches, and played with the musician's hands (Sambamurthy 1959:25–27).

Musical stone pillars are another remarkable musical instrument found in temples dating from the fourteenth to the seventeenth centuries, ranging from the ruins of the great city of Vijayanagar, Andhra Pradesh, to the still functioning temple of Meenakshi in Madurai, southern Tamil Nadu. All traditional Hindu temples had "thousand-pillared halls," which were large pavilions for classical music and dance performance, and perhaps sacred theater as well. Clusters of slender, finely polished musical pillars, rising from floor to ceiling and precisely tuned to scales of a specific raga, were carved from a single piece of stone in one corner of these halls.

It is unclear in what context these pillars were played, but they were certainly struck with mallets or sticks, or perhaps slapped with the hands as they are by tourist guides today. The musicologist P. Sambamurthy suggests that performers played solo music on them as well as dance accompaniments, but no written or oral record remains of their actual use in the past (Sambamurthy 1952–1971).

FOLK INSTRUMENTS

Like the northern part of the subcontinent, South India and Sri Lanka have an extraordinary variety of folk instruments. These include bamboo cane fiddles with half a coconut shell as a resonator topped with pigskin, wooden or clay tambourines, drums and clackers of every shape and size, the snake charmer's double clarinet, the single-stringed plucked lute (*ekanāda*) with bamboo shaft and gourd, tiny hourglass drum rattles (*ḍamaru*), and a group of instruments such as the clarinet, harmonium, or double-reed pipes that have infiltrated from cultivated or classical traditions. A few characteristic folk instruments are presented below.

The *geṭṭuvādyam* 'twig instrument' is like a small multistringed *sarasvatī vīṇā*. It has only four strings tuned in double courses to tonic and fifth (Sa and Pa), and functions as a rhythmic drone instrument. The seated player places the instrument on the floor in front of him, and beats patterns on the open strings with two chopstick-like sticks.

The *pullavān kuḍam* and *pullavān vīṇā* are two instruments of the Puḷḷavas, a caste of astrologers, healers, priests, and minstrels of the ritual music associated with the snake cult of Kerala (figure 10). The *pullavān vīṇā* is a small fiddle with a lizard-skin top on its soundbox and a single string of vine. In household and other rituals it is played with *tāḷam* 'small bell cymbals' and the *pullavān kuḍam* 'Puḷḷava pot', a variable-tension plucked chordophone related to similar North Indian instruments such as the Bengali *ānandalaharī* and the North American washtub bass.

The *pullavān kuḍam* has a single gut string that players pluck with snapping percussive rhythms as they alternately stretch and loosen it to produce different pitches. A large clay pot, its mouth covered with leather, forms the resonator, which the play-

Musical stone pillars are another remarkable musical instrument found in temples dating from the fourteenth to the seventeenth centuries. It is unclear in what context these pillars were played, but they were certainly struck with mallets or sticks, or perhaps slapped with the hands as they are by tourist guides today.

FIGURE 10 A ritual in Cheruthuruthy, Kerala. Instruments (left to right) are the *pullavān kuḍam,* the *tāḷam* (cymbals), and the *pullavān vīṇā* (fiddle), and another *pullavān kuḍam.* Photo by Carol S. Reck, 1969/1970.

er holds in the lap under one arm. The string is anchored from a hole in the middle of the leather-covered mouth, and stretches to the end of a narrow board projecting on the ground in front of the player. By swaying or moving the pot forward or backward with the arm, players vary the tension of the string to provide accompaniment for their song.

Ekanāda 'one-sound' is the South Indian term for a single-stringed drone instrument made of a gourd attached to a bamboo shaft (*ektār* in the North) and plucked by wandering minstrels and religious mendicants to accompany their songs.

The *mukhavīṇā* 'mouth vina' is a small oboe of Tamil Nadu that may be accompanied by the *dhankī* 'kettledrum' or a folk *mridangam* and the *śruti upaṅga* 'drone bagpipe'. The combination of small double-reed pipe and drums is common in festive and ceremonial folk music throughout the South. The *mukhavīṇā* was part of the *bharata nāṭyam* dance ensemble until replaced by the clarinet early in this century. Among the Kota people and other tribals of the Nilgiri Hills, northwest Tamil Nadu, the oboe is called the *koḷ,* and players perform with *tabeteke* drums and *kompȧ* trumpets. In Sri Lanka the quadruple-reed *horanâva* is played in a variety of festive contexts.

The *buguri* is an end-blown, obliquely held trumpet of the Toda and Baḍaga peoples of the Nilgiri Hills, Tamil Nadu. These tribal groups play it to accompany songs and to perform solos. It is made from thin cane, has finger holes, and may have a buffalo horn or metal bell at the end. Because of its finger holes the *buguri* contrasts

FIGURE 11 A drummer plays a set of *burburi* in the foreground while another plays a large *ḍamaru*, Andhra Pradesh, 1969/1970. Photo © Carol S. Reck.

sharply with the metallic trumpets found elsewhere in India, which can produce only the fundamental and overtones of the tube. It is similar to the cornett family of horns with finger holes popular in sixteenth- and seventeenth-century Europe and the later English folk horn known as the serpent.

The *bummâḍiya* is a Sri Lankan drum used in sowing and harvest rituals in the Kandy region. Its body is a bulbous clay pot up to 75 centimeters high with a base and short flaring neck culminating in an iguana-skin drumhead. It is slung by a strap across the shoulder and played by the drummer diagonally.

The *tamukku* is a pair of small kettledrums of Tamil Nadu that are sometimes slung on the back of a sacred bull in temple processions. In Sri Lankan Buddhist ritual the instrument is called the *tammâṭṭa,* as noted above. Also of ritual significance in South India is a pair of small cylindrical drums held horizontally one on top of the other in front of the musician's chest. An example is the *burburi* of Andhra Pradesh and Karnataka, played in festivities for the goddess of smallpox, Mariyamman (figure 11).

The *pirai* (or *parai*) of Tamil Nadu and Andhra Pradesh are pairs of shallow drums with handles. The musician carries the pair on a frame projecting out from the forehead, and beats them with small sticks for rituals worshiping Mariyamman and other village deities. Each drum is made with a continuous metal band, the drumhead of one forming a circle to represent the sun (*sūrya pirai*), the other forming a rough crescent representing the moon (*candra pirai*).

The *kokkara* of Kerala is a scraper made from a sheet of iron rolled into a tube about 135 centimeters long, with its edges raised and serrated. Specialists of the Pulaya and Kanikar castes scrape the serrated edge rhythmically using another metal scraper (*śuktivāḍya*). Its sound is essential for rites of sorcery and witchcraft.

The *villādi vādyam* 'bow instrument' of Tamil Nadu, named after *vil* or *villu* 'bow', is unusual in having several components and requiring a group of performers (figure 12). Its primary sound comes from a musical bow 2 to 2.5 meters long fitted with a string of taut leather. From one to five players alternately beat rhythms on the stretched string with pairs of sticks, while the group leader gives a religious discourse

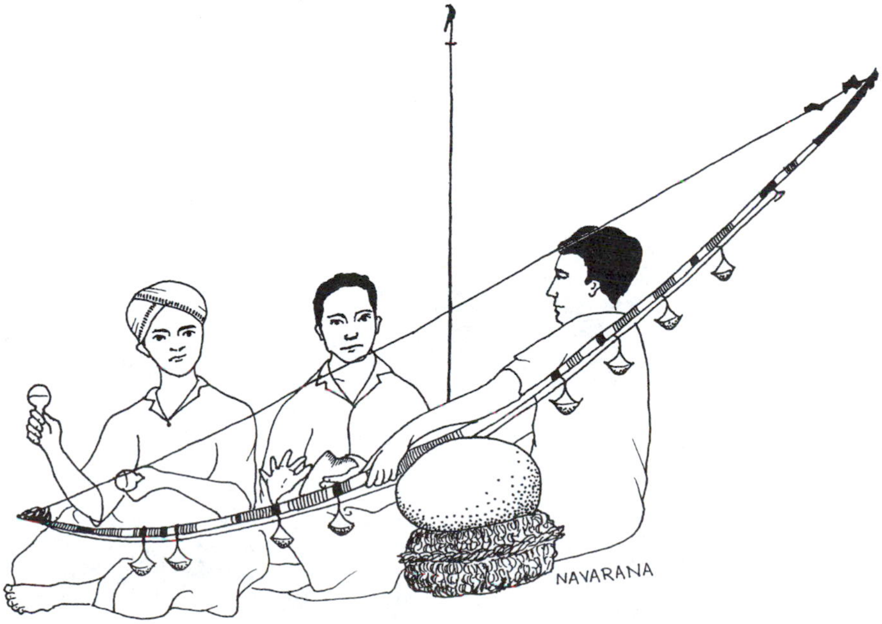

FIGURE 12 The *villādi vādyam* of Tamil Nadu. Drawing by Navarana, 1997. Used by permission. Courtesy David Reck.

TRACK 15 and sings appropriate songs (*villuppāṭṭu* 'bow songs') or verses from holy texts (Kothari 1968:26). The middle of the wooden bow rests on a pot (*ghaṭam* or *kudam*) that another percussionist beats with two rubber pads. Other instruments in the group, called a '*villu* party', are the *uḍukkai* 'hourglass drum', the *daru tāḷam* or *kaṭṭai* 'oblong wooden clappers', and the *tāḷam* or *jālra* 'small ringing cymbals'.

POPULAR AND FILM MUSIC INSTRUMENTS

The predominant music played today on the radio or television, in coffee shops and restaurants, and in homes is popular music in the various southern languages—Sinhalese, Tamil, Malayalam, Telugu, and Kannada—as well as in Hindi. A majority of Indian pop songs, called "cine music" or cine *pāṭṭu,* comes from movies, virtually all of which are musicals.

Over the past few decades, film music composers (called "music directors") have employed instruments from many world music traditions as well as those of South Asia for their song accompaniments. Violin sections, Fender bass, electric guitars, keyboard synthesizers, Western kettledrums, trumpets, piano, bird whistles, drum machines, conga drums, bongos, maracas and other American percussion, accordion, and harmonica coexist with tabla, sitar, vina, *sāraṅgī, tambūrā, ḍholak,* and other indigenous instruments.

South Indian music directors combine North Indian and South Indian styles, folk and classical, and Eastern and Western instruments with ease in what has been called a stylistic musical *masālā,* a spicy stew of styles and sounds with syncretic characteristics all of its own. This use of an extraordinarily wide variety of instruments in India's pop music contrasts quite sharply with the relatively static and inherently conservative approach to instrumental combinations in American and European rock, pop, and jazz genres. Such a fact would suggest that culture has now certainly moved beyond the stereotypical "dynamic West" and "unchanging East."

In live concert performances of cine music, musicians may play on an eclectic selection of the many instruments used in recording studios. In street processions for temples or weddings, a different type of band may also play the latest popular tunes. These are street bands modeled on the British military bands of the colonial era. From eight to twenty or more musicians, in quasi-Western band uniforms, play clarinets, saxophones, trumpets, trombones, horns, baritones, and even sousaphones, to the jackhammer rhythms of snare, field, and bass drums (Flaes 1993:23). The instruments are entirely European while the music, mostly melodic unison with percussion, is South Asian. Sri Lankans and South Indians, through movies and popular music, are increasingly aware of instruments from outside their traditional cultures, and continue a long pattern of adapting foreign instruments for their own use in a variety of musical contexts.

REFERENCES

Diagram Group. 1976. *Musical Instruments of the World: An Illustrated Encyclopedia.* London: Paddington.

Dick, Alastair. 1984. "Pūṅgī." In *The New Grove Dictionary of Musical Instruments,* ed. Stanley Sadie. London: Macmillan.

Dournon, Geneviève, and Mireille Helffer. 1984. "Bāṅsurī." In *The New Grove Dictionary of Musical Instruments,* ed. Stanley Sadie. London: Macmillan.

Flaes, Rob B. 1993. *Bewogen koper.* Amsterdam: Uitgeverij De Balie.

Jenkins, Jean L. 1970. *Musical Instruments, Horniman Museum, London.* London: Inner London Education Authority.

Kothari, Komal S. 1968. *Indian Folk Musical Instruments.* New Delhi: Sangeet Natak Akademi.

Krishnaswamy, S. 1971. *Musical Instruments of India.* Boston: Crescendo.

Raja, K. Kunjunni. 1964. *Kutiyattam: An Introduction.* New Delhi: Sangeet Natak Akademi.

Reck, David B. 1968–1994. Field notes. Unpublished.

Sambamurthy, P. 1952–1971. *A Dictionary of South Indian Music and Musicians.* 3 vols. Madras: Indian Music.

———. 1959. *Laya Vadyas.* New Delhi: All India Handicraft Board.

———. n.d. *Sruti Vadyas.* New Delhi: All India Handicraft Board.

Tarlekar, G. H., and Nalini Tarlekar. 1972. *Musical Instruments in Indian Sculpture.* Pune: Pune Vidyarthi Griha Prakashan.

Music and Social Organization

Soloists, accompanists, professional artists, hereditary musicians, street performers, poet-singers, temple dancers, shamans . . . the world of South Asian musicians is a complex network of individuals, all identifiable in terms of social position and musical role. But who are these individuals? To what social communities do they belong? How do they interact? In what contexts do they sing and dance? How does their social status affect their performance practice, patronage, and transmission to future generations? And who are the listeners and patrons of South Asian music? What is their role in current musical performance?

Such questions provide the starting point for our inquiry into the social organization of music and musicians. As the answers lead to further questions, we begin to understand the rich diversity and the dynamic nature of music as it exists today in South Asian society.

A Nacnī woman dances the *mardānā jhumar* 'men's jhumar' with men at the Ind festival, Lacharagarh, Bihar, 1984. In Indian villages, music and dance often take place in gender-segregated contexts, but professional female performers are exceptional. Nacnī 'dancing women' live as the goddess Radha, devoted to music and dance and also to a *rasika* 'male partner' both on and off stage. Although they live literally "outside society," their peformances are considered auspicious at village weddings, festivals, and all-night entertainments. Photo by Carol Babiracki.

The Social Organization of Music and Musicians: Northern Area

Robert Ollikkala

Classical Music and Musicians
Women and Light Classical Music
Historical Background
The Teaching Tradition
Social and Musical Hierarchy
Artists and Training in the Late Twentieth Century

The social organization of music and musicians in the northern parts of South Asia, the ways musicians relate to each other and to the larger community, as in much of the world, involves appropriate behavior, practice techniques, performance norms, training systems, and relationships between students and teachers, performers and patrons. Especially in North India, certain musical genres, styles, and instruments—and the musicians who perform them—are considered more important and prestigious than others. Respect, status, and financial remuneration are linked to this hierarchy. Sound and social structures in North India are inextricably related, and an appreciation of Indian music is incomplete without a knowledge of the social environment that nurtures and molds it.

CLASSICAL MUSIC AND MUSICIANS

Scholars and native performers generally classify Indian music according to four basic categories: classical, light classical, folk/tribal, and popular/film. The focus in this article is the world of North Indian classical music and the derivative style commonly known as light classical. Classical music is the most prestigious, revered, and successfully publicized internationally. The closest parallel indigenous terms are: *śāstrīya saṅgīt* 'scientific, academic music and dance', and *mārga saṅgīt* 'music governed by the rules of raga and tala', which contrast with *deśī saṅgīt,* referring to folk and regional music that is less stringent regarding raga and tala. When foreigners speak about Indian music, they are usually referring to North Indian (Hindustani) or South Indian (Karnatak) classical traditions, which are more familiar due to the worldwide concert performances of classical artists [see MUSIC AND INTERNATIONALIZATION].

Classical music in India, as in the West, is part of a "Great Tradition" (Singer 1972) and has received intellectual support over the centuries from musical scholarship and philosophical treatises dating back to Bharata's *Nāṭyaśāstra* (second century B.C.–second century C.E.), as well as financial support from royal, aristocratic, and middle-class patrons. It is abstract, intellectually and emotionally demanding, and associated with spiritual values. Years of training are necessary to become an accomplished performer—or even a knowledgeable listener—and, at least until the mid-twentieth century, it has been a largely male tradition characterized by male teachers and performers entertaining male aficionados.

Throughout Indian history, and particularly since the nineteenth century, male master musicians have guided devoted disciples into a life focused on classical music. The many years of training require arduous practice as an intense discipline (*riyāz*), both secular and spiritual. The raga-based melodic improvisation in which these musicians excel requires prodigious technique and knowledge; stringent rules, although negotiated, delineate the bounds that allow each raga to remain distinct, hence "pure." Rhythmic tala cycles are similarly demanding. By the nineteenth century, Muslim family lineages guided and controlled most of the approaches to, and orientations in, classical-music knowledge and style. These family lineages (*khāndān*) developed into a limited number of stylistic schools (*gharānā*), each representing a discrete bloodline dating back at least three generations and an identifiable musical style (Neuman 1980). Throughout the nineteenth and twentieth centuries, the *gharānā* has been a source of knowledge and a stamp of musical approval required for professional success. *Khāndān* musicians do not limit their disciples to male lineage members as in the past, but it is common knowledge that they may well reveal musical secrets only to a favorite son or nephew. Even today, this nineteenth-century system forms the basis for classical music's norms and values.

WOMEN AND LIGHT CLASSICAL MUSIC

Professional women musicians—often as well trained and knowledgeable as their male counterparts—have also played a role in the history of Indian music [see WOMEN AND MUSIC]. From the nineteenth to the mid-twentieth centuries, female musicians were not respected Muslim begums or Hindu *devī*—women playing the traditional domestic roles—but rather women who followed an inherited professional role. These women of the *tawāif* social category, commonly addressed as *bāī* or *bāī-jī*, were an essential component of the social fabric; they were respected for their skills in the arts of singing and dancing but also looked down upon for the intimate relations they commonly maintained with their male patrons. Upper-class men typically led two lives, spending the early part of the evening with their families and the later part with these female entertainers and courtesans, whom they supported financially. Respectable women were largely confined to the home and did not sing in public, whereas virtually all professional female singers circulated freely in the social, male-dominated realm.

Women musicians often entered into the same master-disciple relationships as their male musical counterparts, but only as students. They carried out their daily practice (*riyāz*) with equal devotion and dedication, but together with their teachers and their patrons they understood that their role was limited to singing in the derivative light classical style, a subcategory of classical music. Most scholars, performers, and aficionados generally acknowledge that light classical music is more sensual and less stringent in raga and tala requirements than its "pure" classical counterpart. Performers frequently combine lighter ragas, rendering them less pure by comparison. Also, whereas classical texts are usually sacred or spiritual, light classical texts commonly imply both sacred and sensual innuendos. There are no female-based stylistic schools (*gharānā*), and no such schools for light classical music. Famous female singers claim affiliation with male lineages through their teacher. Historically the great classical vocal forms—*dhrupad*, *dhamār*, and later *khyāl*—developed in Delhi, the center of the powerful Mughal empire, between the sixteenth and nineteenth centuries. Light classical forms such as *ṭhumrī*, *dādrā*, and ghazal, sung by the professional female singers of the era, developed in the important regional court of Lucknow in the nineteenth century [see HINDUSTANI VOCAL MUSIC].

FIGURE 1 A *tawāif* sings and dances, accompanied by tabla and harmonium (partly visible), Karachi, 1978. Photo by Nazir Jairazbhoy.

Up to the mid-twentieth century, the only female professional musicians were of the *bāī* or *tawāif* social category, as stated above (figure 1). These women followed an inherited role and filled significant positions in the largely Muslim court culture. Considered a necessary addition to all court social occasions, they developed the light classical style from its inception in the nineteenth century until its appropriation by the middle class some time after independence in 1947. They were so knowledgeable regarding social graces that aristocratic families sent their young men to them for social polishing. Under the Muslim feudal court system their positions were secure; with the demise of the courts, however, and the rise of British rule and the spread of British values (including Victorian morality), *bāī* women were soon no longer recognized as artists but branded as prostitutes. With approaching independence, the rise of a Hindu middle class only made their demise more certain, for the new rulers, like the British by whom they had been influenced, had no sympathy for the old Muslim court structure and its traditions. When the nationalized radio refused to broadcast their singing from the early 1950s on, their fate was sealed. Although some were able to begin singing careers as a begum or *devī*, many disappeared from public view, others married and no longer sang, and still others turned to prostitution. Their vast contribution to Indian music has until recently been largely ignored (Ollikkala 1997:8–153; Rao 1990:31–39; Oldenburg 1990:259–288). Much of the Indian middle class is embarrassed by the morality that *tawāif* women adopted, and descendants of these entertainers have frequently altered their lineages to hide connections even with famous female singers.

HISTORICAL BACKGROUND

The social status, role, and organization of musicians in South Asia have developed within one of the oldest and best documented civilizations known to humankind. A well-established urban culture, the evidence of which lies in extensive archeological ruins, already existed in the period c. 2800–1500 B.C., particularly at two sites, Harappa and Mohenjo Daro, located in the Indus valley in what is now Pakistan. Since that time, three major invasions overtook the indigenous population and dominated the region: the Aryans, followed by the Muslims (particularly Afghans and Persians) from Central Asia, and finally the British. Each invasion resulted in major changes in the social structure and a new cultural layer added to the whole. Today, all the impressions left by these events coexist and form the dynamics, generally peaceful and stable but often marred by hostile violence and extreme volatility, that constitute the reality of modern India, Pakistan, and Bangladesh. India today remains troubled by continuous border tensions with Pakistan and by occasional violent Muslim/Hindu and Hindu/Sikh confrontations within its borders. Prior to the separation of Pakistan from India, approximately 30 percent of South Asia's population was Muslim; today, the vast majority of Indians are Hindus (82 percent), but Muslims still account for 11 percent, with the remainder largely Sikhs (2 percent), Christians (2 percent), Buddhists, Jains, and Zoroastrians.

The Aryans

The first wave of invasions on the subcontinent occurred between 2000 and 600 B.C., as nomadic horsemen and warriors from the Asian steppes, known as Aryans, gradually arrived and assumed social rank high above all the indigenous people, much as did the medieval Normans in England. Many scholars believe that the caste system, a complex method of social organization that has dominated the region for two millennia, resulted from these invaders' establishing their dominance over all aspects of life. Under the caste system, people inherit from their parents their place in the social and spiritual hierarchy, their occupation, and their level of sacred purity.

Upward mobility is rarely an option in this life, but is rather deferred and promised for one's next life, for those who adhere to their inherited social and spiritual duties (*dharma*). Spiritual ascent toward absolute purity may take thousands of reincarnations, but ends with liberation (*mokṣa*) from the cycle of rebirth. The caste system, with its secular and spiritual rewards and duties, has formed one of the most effective barriers to social change that any society has experienced. Despite its official ban in 1947, the caste system in India continues to affect many aspects of society. The acceptance of inherited roles in the musical realm—manifest in the *gharānā* system and the *bāī* heritage in the nineteenth century—has been part of this long-standing emphasis on the importance of lineage and inherited professional roles.

Islam

The second, Muslim wave of invasions actually came in three parts. The first was brief, temporary incursions immediately after the founding of Islam (seventh to ninth centuries), followed by more wide-reaching and permanent settlements (twelfth to sixteenth centuries), and culminating in the establishment of the Mughal empire (1526–1707), which lasted in weakened form until the establishment of the British *rāj* 'rule' in 1818. The Mughals conquered the northern half of the subcontinent and established a sociopolitical system that was strikingly different from that in the south. In the musical realm, two related yet separate musical systems developed from the thirteenth century on: the northern Hindustani and southern Karnatak styles. North Indian classical music as it is now known developed from the sixteenth to the mid-nineteenth centuries, including the primary musical genres, the most important instruments, and most extant ragas and talas. The patrons were largely Mughal kings, but even the most independent of the unconquered Hindu rulers followed their lead in musical matters, and the centers of patronage were the royal courts (*darbār*). From the mid-nineteenth century to the present day, many major Hindustani musicians have been Muslims, often from Hindu families long converted to Islam.

The British

The final major cultural overlay in India came with the establishment of British colonial rule in the nineteenth century. The British rulers attempted to dominate most aspects of Indian life and, like the Muslim rulers, to establish their superiority. Unlike the Muslims, however, their lack of familiarity with (or sympathy for) the Indian musical system deterred them from directly influencing musical developments. Nevertheless their abolition of both Muslim and Hindu courts (and hence court patronage), and their Victorian morality, which led to the devaluation of professional women's artistic contributions, substantially altered musical life and even, though to a lesser extent, the sound of Indian music.

Independence

The success of the independence struggle in 1947 immediately brought with it important sociocultural readjustments. The British, who handed over the reins of power largely to a rapidly expanding Hindu middle class, trained in a British-style educational system and fluent in English, had laid the groundwork for a "Hindu Revival." The new Hindu politicians and administrators were eager to reestablish Indian control. The educated and titled Muslims, who had dominated much of the region during the seven centuries preceding British rule, had been largely left out of the power hierarchy, which had led to their own struggle for an independent Muslim state.

The "Hindu Revival" introduced many changes in the artistic realm that contin-

Hindus have always viewed music as a spiritual vehicle, as in the devotional singing of bhajans or the use of mantras for meditation, whereas orthodox Muslims have acknowledged the power of music but expressed the fear that its "intoxication" may lead devotees away from Allah (God).

ue to have an important influence on contemporary music and musical life. These have included the development of conservatories where middle-class boys and girls receive training in the traditional arts including classical music [see INSTITUTIONAL MUSIC EDUCATION]; the introduction of nonhereditary Hindu musicians into the *gharānā* system previously monopolized by Muslim families [see CLASSICAL MASTER-DISCIPLE TRADITIONS); the replacement of *bāī* entertainers by respectable, middle-class female performers; the associated demise of *ṭhumrī* and ghazal and their transition to substantially altered but widely enjoyed pop genres sung by middle-class male and female performers; and the replacement of court patronage by government agencies, private arts organizations, and concert halls.

THE TEACHING TRADITION

Virtually all successful professional classical performers still receive training in the traditional manner, through the master-student tradition (Hindu *guru-śiṣya,* Muslim *ustād-śāgird*). Despite the development of modern music schools and university music departments since independence, where young men and women from nonmusical families can learn the basic concepts and tools required for Indian classical music performance, most performers believe in the notion of musical inheritance (Neuman 1980:50–58).

The terms *guru-śiṣya* and *ustād-śāgird* are frequently used interchangeably, yet their cultural roots reflect a subtle but important difference. Hindus use the Hindi term *guru* to refer to a teacher, but also a spiritual guide; a *śiṣya* is a spiritual disciple. The term *ustād*, for Muslims, refers to a master of any craft, in this case music; the *śāgird* is a devoted and hard-working student. The discrepancy highlights a long-standing difference between the two religious communities: Hindus have always viewed music as a spiritual vehicle, as in the devotional singing of bhajans or the use of mantras for meditation, whereas orthodox Muslims have acknowledged the power of music but expressed the fear that its "intoxication" may lead devotees away from Allah (God). For Muslims in general, music is thus generally not an acknowledged component of worship, although the Sufis have always used music and dance in their devotional expression [see RELIGIOUS AND DEVOTIONAL MUSIC; PAKISTAN: DEVOTIONAL MUSIC]. The historic model is the sixteenth-century musician Tansen, a Hindu who converted to Islam and worked as a professional musician in the court of the greatest Mughal emperor, Akbar. Virtually all classical instrumental lineages trace their heritage, often via a circuitous route, back to the great Tansen and his descendants. The spiritual (hence Hindu) model is Tyagaraja, the eighteenth-century South Indian singer-saint who sang only for the glory of God and refused to accept court patronage. In present-day practice, many Muslim musicians adopt something of a spiritual attitude in their professions, while both Hindus and Muslims may exhibit a secular approach.

The traditional Indian student (*śāgird* or *śiṣya*) is by Western standards an unusually devoted follower. Until recent decades, students lived with their teachers for many years, and those who were not family members were virtually adopted into the family as sons. Since this arrangement placed a great burden on the teacher—in terms of finances, time, and household readjustments—he would not allow a student to become a disciple until the student had demonstrated true dedication to the art. Once a student was adopted into the musical family, a formal ceremony (*gaṇḍā bandhan*) sealed the relationship between student and master. Students did not pay money for lessons, but frequently offered gifts to their teacher, and at times acted as servants, getting food or water for guests or arranging travel plans. At a more advanced stage they became accompanists in performance. In living with their musical guides, they absorbed the entire musical atmosphere and way of life, surrounded by musical sounds, lessons, conversations about music, and financial negotiations. The relationship was one of discipline, love, and devotion both to the teacher and the art.

Indian musicians today fondly refer to times past, when musicians were free to develop their art working under the secure patronage of a noble in his court. That same patronage also enabled them to maintain the distinctive training system. Today musicians try as best they can to re-create some of that atmosphere for their own followers, but are frequently stifled by a faster pace of life and the replacement of court patronage by hectic touring schedules and a large roster of students. Students rarely live with their teachers, but rather come for a number of lessons each week. In many cases money now exchanges hands, for most teachers depend on tuition fees to make a living. Yet there are still situations in which that special one-to-one relationship is maintained, in which lessons are free, and in which the master transmits more than mere knowledge of raga and tala. For many students the love and devotion to the teacher still remains, and the repeated memories of a bygone era are enough to help capture at least some of the intangible magic that makes the art, and the learning experience, transcendent. This teaching system is still effective, for virtually all major contemporary performers have been nurtured by this heritage.

Gharānā

In its most limiting sense the term *gharānā* refers to three specific requirements: a direct family lineage of at least three generations; a notable founding figure in the past and at least one active and respected living member; and an identifiable musical style. Neuman (1978:186–222; 1980) has traced the term *gharānā* to the nineteenth century. He proposes that family traditions arose as an adaptive strategy for musicians who were losing the support of court patronage and were consequently forced to seek employment as performers and teachers in the rapidly developing larger cities. The identification with a well-respected family tradition gave a musician entering the new labor force a competitive edge and a stamp of authority and accomplishment that preceded his own work. This was particularly crucial in Indian society, where the importance of lineage has long been emphasized. The *gharānā* institution also enabled musicians initially to limit the competition, for masters trained mostly family members and thus protected lineage stylistic and performance secrets. In the early twentieth century, master musicians began accepting nonhereditary students out of financial necessity. Many of these were Hindus and would form an important musical component of the postindependence Hindu Revival. The *gharānā* is still extremely important today, and musicians often consider a performer's lineage as important as his or her ability to perform, if not more so. Indeed, musicians and aficionados often argue as to whether or not a particular lineage satisfies all the requirements of and can be called a true *gharānā*.

FIGURE 2 Zia Mohinuddin Dagar playing the vina (*right*), accompanied on *pakhāvaj* by Maharaja Chatrapati Singh (*left*) and an unknown *tambūrā* player, Banaras Hindu University, 1981. Photo by Stephen Slawek.

A *gharānā* usually takes the name of the city or region in which it was founded or centered, and occasionally the name of a founding member. In the realm of classical vocal music, the oldest, preeminent and most austere genre, *dhrupad*, is dominated by the Dagar family, whose musical style and lineage is known as the Dagar *bānī* (figure 2). The most popular type of classical vocal music, *khyāl*, is the specialty of some six to eight primary lineages, mostly identified by place names, including Agra, Delhi, Gwalior, Kirana, Patiala, and Sahsawan/Rampur. In the realm of instrumental music, virtually all soloists trace their families back to Tansen, hence there is really only one instrumental lineage, the Seniya *gharānā*. However, performers follow one of two branches: that of Tansen's daughter Sarasvati and that of his son Bilas Khan. Since all solo instrumentalists are by and large part of the same *gharānā*, social and musical distinctions are frequently based on student-teacher connections with famous masters such as the sitar virtuoso Ravi Shankar or the sarod master Ali Akbar Khan.

Bāj

Over the past few decades many scholars and solo musicians have claimed that *gharānā* implies only soloist lineages, and that tabla traditions, for example, should be called *bāj* instead—a less reputable term referring to musical style but not family heritage. Accompanists and other scholars have refuted this claim. This is not a trivial discussion, for the acknowledgment of *gharānā* status is an issue of repute and social placement, which connects to some rather volatile and sensitive issues in the musical community and among its supporters.

Accompanists have traditionally been looked down upon not only because soloists were considered to be greater artists, but also because accompanists frequently made a living by playing for *bāī* entertainers as well as for *gharānā* musicians in the courts. *Sāraṅgī* 'bowed fiddle' players in particular, who provided melodic accompaniment by shadowing and imitating the vocal line, were often the teachers of *bāī* women. They, like tabla players (the rhythmic accompanists), worked and lived in the same cultural milieu, and thus suffered the same moral stigma. The modern repercussions of this situation form a current issue, not a historic one. Tabla and *sāraṅgī* players, like *bāī* descendants, are still reluctant to speak about the lives of their ancestors for fear of losing their hard-won social positions. One Western scholar, James Kippen, an accomplished tabla player, was refused a room for rent in the early

1980s when the owner found out that his tabla teacher might occasionally come to visit him and possibly play tabla; the owner of the Lucknow apartment feared that his neighbors would think ill of him if they heard tabla playing, or saw accompanists and dancers coming and going (Kippen 1988:87–88).

Two major social groups developed into vocal *gharānā* in the nineteenth century: the Kalāvants and the Mīrāsīs (Neuman 1978:186–222). The former, the more prestigious group, consisted of musicians from pure vocal-soloist lineages. The latter was composed of accompanists generally descended from rural folk musicians. In the twentieth century, the emphasis on lineage purity has severely hampered the descendants of Kalāvants, for the work available to soloists in the modern age of jet transportation and computerized communication is limited. As in the West, a handful of outstanding artists can perform most major concerts. Mīrāsīs have fared much better, for their social network is larger and their skills as accompanists and soloists have made them much more adaptable to contemporary circumstances. At the All India Radio station in Delhi, a soloist is hired for a specific type of single concert, but an accompanist is needed for every performance (Neuman 1980). There are consequently far more permanent staff artists who are accompanists (and hence Mīrāsīs) than soloists; the latter often find full-time employment as administrators rather than as musicians.

SOCIAL AND MUSICAL HIERARCHY

For millennia, the social organization of Indian civilization has involved social hierarchy and distinction; the social organization of musicians is no exception. The most pervasive, obvious, and best publicized manifestation of this hierarchy is the caste system discussed above. In the musical realm, male classical musicians have benefited from *gharānā* status, pure solo lineages being more highly esteemed than accompanist traditions. Particularly outstanding artists can nevertheless raise the status of lesser lineages, especially by reinterpreting genealogy to emphasize solo heritage (even if there are accompanists in the family history). Among vocalists, *dhrupad* specialists do not sing what they consider to be lesser genres, such as the more popular *khyāl*. Until the mid-twentieth century, *khyāl gharānā* musicians generally did not sing light classical music on stage, with the exception of *ṭhumrī*, for this would lower their reputation. Nowadays most *khyāl* singers commonly end their performances with a light closing piece.

Traditionally, accompanists have been supportive of and subordinated to soloists; Neuman (1980) has described their different roles as artisans (accompanists) and artists (soloists). This distinction assumes that each soloist is a uniquely gifted individual, while an accompanist is just one of a pool who can readily be replaced by another. On tour, accompanists until recently (and to a certain extent today) played the role of assistants, running errands for the soloist in return for the payment of expenses plus a small retainer. On stage, soloists sit at the front and center, accompanists to the side or behind. The soloist makes most of the musical decisions, and has traditionally been advertised as the performer, sometimes with no mention of the accompanists.

Over the past few decades the hierarchy has changed, greatly affected by Indian musicians touring abroad, particularly in the West. Since the international renown and popularity earned by sitarist Ravi Shankar in the 1960s, many Indian performers have toured in the United States, Europe, and Asia, and many have held permanent or temporary positions in universities and conservatories abroad [see MUSIC AND INTERNATIONALIZATION]. Accompanists in particular have benefited from this foreign exposure, for from the outset Western audiences (particularly the youth),

As in the West, great artists have as much status and earning power as other established professionals, including doctors, lawyers, and politicians.

unaware of Indian norms and entranced by rhythm as much as melody, have praised and given equal status to tabla players. As a result, tabla players both in India and abroad now receive greater fame and financial remuneration than in the past. Concert programs, cassette cards, and compact disc covers now include the names, and at times the photographs, of both soloists and accompanists. The tabla player Zakir Hussain, son of the famous Alla Rakha, accompanies virtually all the major Hindustani artists. He gets equal billing and is as famous and as great an audience attraction as the soloist. Like some other famous tabla and *sāraṅgī* players, Zakir Hussain also plays the occasional solo concert, or in his case performs a duet with his father. Such virtuosic duets (*jugalbandī*) between two soloists, two tabla players, or more frequently a tabla player and an instrumental soloist, are particularly appealing to today's mixed concert audiences of both aficionados and newcomers, both in India and abroad.

The "Hindu Revival" has also affected prestige and hierarchy among musicians. Despite the difficulty in generalizing about India's complex society of nearly 940 million people, some scholars have demonstrated that the return of Hindu dominance after independence (1947) has drastically altered the music world (Qureshi 1991). Many Hindu musicians feel that they have reclaimed a sacred musical heritage that was taken over by India's Muslims during the six centuries of Muslim rule. Hindus from the newly empowered middle class have studied diligently with Muslim musicians; especially noteworthy among these are pandits Vishnu Narayan Bhatkhande and Vishnu Digambar Paluskar. Many Hindus now excel in the classical idioms that were once the sole inheritance of Muslim lineages. Furthermore, although Indian musicians do not generally become involved in politics, Indian politicians are certainly aware of the social and cultural resources and national distinction represented by international touring artists, whether Muslim or Hindu. According to Neuman, only two musical cultures have successfully exported themselves internationally—the classical idioms of Europe and India.

ARTISTS AND TRAINING IN THE LATE TWENTIETH CENTURY

During the first half of this century, two Hindu music reformers in particular, Vishnu Narayan Bhatkhande and Vishnu Digambar Paluskar, rescued Indian music and dance from the disrepute into which it had fallen through association with the *bāī* tradition. These men founded music schools where middle-class children from respectable, nonhereditary families could study the traditional arts with well-established performers and teachers [see INSTITUTIONAL MUSIC EDUCATION: NORTHERN AREA]. For Hindu girls such training has become an important requirement for marriage eligibility. This situation contrasts markedly with that of previous generations, when respectable Hindu families would never have considered musical training for their daughters. Parents of Muslim girls generally remain unwilling to give them formal musical education. Both Indian and foreign scholars acknowledge the great benefits of such Western-based institutions, not their success in training the next generation of top performers, rather their success in creating a large and knowledgeable listening public—the future patrons of the arts.

Most Indian students in colleges and conservatories, who represent the future concertgoing public, are now from the middle class. This sector of society has successfully replaced the court patronage of the nineteenth century. Indian artists today tour their nation and the globe by jet, some performing the same program in Delhi and Chicago in a single week. At least to some degree they are their own masters, commanding fees according to their reputations and setting their own touring schedules; they are no longer subject to the whims of a single patron. With the demise of the court system and the establishment of democracy, musicians of some accomplishment are now of the same class as their patrons, and can lead quite comfortable lives. As in the West, great artists have as much status and earning power as other established professionals, including doctors, lawyers, and politicians.

The leading artists today are products of the *gharānā* system. They have spent many years in the traditional student-teacher relationship, but since lifestyles now differ and audiences in the late twentieth century are more heterogeneous than those for which their forebears performed, the extensive training is consequently adapted to accommodate the reality that they encounter. Some students study individually with their teachers while simultaneously attending college; others study with famous artists at established, privately funded institutions such as the Bharatiya Kala Kendra in Delhi.

The *gharānā* system and the student-teacher tradition have continued because they are both extremely functional and effective and also adaptable. The social world around them has altered dramatically during the twentieth century, but these core characteristics of social organization among classical musicians have remained largely intact. Perhaps as a result, so too have the core musical characteristics and the sound of North Indian classical music.

The continuity of light classical music as cultivated within the *bāī* tradition seems less likely. Most classically oriented female singers today, including those from both traditional and nontraditional backgrounds, prefer to sing the more prestigious *khyāl* than the light classical *ṭhumrī*. The pop ghazal generally bears little resemblance to its traditional light classical counterpart, and most popular artists who specialize in this genre are middle-class professionals who have not benefited from extensive classical training. Some *bāī* women, who in the 1950s married into respectable families and became begums, continued to sing light classical music. A few of these, like the great Begum Akhtar, taught several female students (predominantly middle-class Hindus) in the traditional manner (Ollikkala 1997:45–50). But these cases are quite rare, and the possibility of these middle-class students' being able and willing to pass on their musical heritage is questionable. The great *bāī* singers of the past were not blessed with *gharānā* prestige, and contemporary female singers who have studied with such women are reluctant to speak about many aspects of the *bāī* tradition because of the stigma that still adheres to the female tradition. Although the current position of Hindustani classical music appears to be secure both within India and abroad, the future of the light classical idiom is less certain.

REFERENCES

Kippen, James. 1988. *The Tabla of Lucknow: A Cultural Analysis of a Musical Tradition*. Cambridge: Cambridge University Press.

Neuman, Daniel. 1978. "*Gharanas*: The Rise of Musical 'Houses' in Delhi and Neighboring Cities." In *Eight Urban Musical Cultures: Tradition and Change*, ed. Bruno Nettl, 186–222. Urbana: University of Illinois Press.

———. 1980. *The Life of Music in North India: The Organization of an Artistic Tradition*. Detroit: Wayne State University Press.

Oldenburg, Veena Talwar. 1990. "Lifestyle as Resistance: The Case of the Courtesans of Lucknow, India." *Feminist Studies* 16(2):259–288.

Ollikkala, Robert. 1997. "Concerning Begum Akhtar, Queen of Ghazal." Ph.D. dissertation, University of Illinois at Urbana-Champaign.

Qureshi, Regula. 1991. "Whose Music? Sources and Contexts in Indic Musicology." In *Comparative Musicology and Anthropology of Music: Essays on the History of Ethnomusicology*, ed. Bruno Nettl and Philip Bohlman, 152–168. Chicago: University of Chicago Press.

Rao, Vidya. 1990. "Thumri as Feminine Voice." *Economic and Political Weekly*, 28 April, 31–39.

Singer, Milton. 1972. *When a Great Tradition Modernizes*. New York: Praeger.

The Social Organization of Music and Musicians: Southern Area

T. Sankaran
Matthew Allen

The Tyagaraja Festival
Gender and Invisibility
Caste and Music
Gender, Caste, and Musical Performance
A History of Social Organization in the Tyagaraja Festival

South India has many kinds of music, each socially organized in a different manner. A comprehensive study of this topic would have to consider a myriad of people and situations: Anglo-Indian musicians in the recording studios of the Madras film industry, tribal communities in the Nilgiri Hills, an urban Muslim neighborhood in Coimbatore, a fishing village where the vast Godavari River delta in Andhra Pradesh meets the sea, one of the many Christian churches in the west coast state of Kerala, Kuruvar gypsy musicians who migrate throughout the region, or a folk-dance group sponsored by scholars from a university in Madurai—to mention a few.

This article examines the social organization of musicians in South India as reflected in one event, the Tyagaraja *ārādhana*, the annual death-anniversary celebration in honor of the revered composer Tyagaraja (1767–1847). Thousands of musicians appear at this huge annual celebration, men and women from different social communities and performance traditions. They include performers in the Karnatak art-music tradition—ubiquitous in the concert halls of South India today—as well as two closely related performance traditions sharing the Karnatak musical language of raga and tala: the *periya mēḷam* instrumental tradition of Hindu temple ritual music, and the music ensemble (formerly known as *cinna mēḷam*) that accompanies the South Indian classical dance form *bharata nāṭyam*.

The dynamic nature of the Tyagaraja *ārādhana*, which takes place over three days each January, in the town of Tiruvaiyaru, Tanjavur District, in Tamil Nadu, facilitates the study of two parameters at the heart of India's changing social organization: gender and caste. Attention to these two central parameters illuminates other aspects of social organization such as the patronage, presentation, and transmission of music, and people's attitudes about music, musicians, and music making. In locating caste and gender relations within the history of the Tyagaraja celebration, this article provides an account of the roles played by two important transitional figures: Sri Malaikottai Govindasvami Pillai (1879–1931) and Srimati (Smt.) Bangalore Nagaratnammal (1878–1952). Their lives and work clearly illustrate changes in the gender and caste organization of South Indian musicians in the twentieth century.

The typical Karnatak concert can give the impression of a wonderful if occasionally strained marriage of devotion and virtuosity.

THE TYAGARAJA FESTIVAL

Madras to Tiruvaiyaru

Departing from Madras's Central Station, the Cōl̲an Express bound for Tanjavur passes slowly (despite its name) through the hot arid countryside toward the seacoast and the temple town of Cidambaram, the South Indian center of the Shiva Nataraja (king of dance) cult. Passing Cidambaram, the train enters the lush, rice-growing Kaveri River delta, the heartland of South Indian kings from the ninth to the nineteenth centuries.

Once in Tanjavur, a visitor traveling from Madras can see the magnificent Cōl̲a-era Brihadisvara Shiva temple and the Sarasvati Mahal, former palace of the Telugu and Maratha rajas who ruled from 1532 to 1855. A bus then leaves for the brief ride to the town of Tiruvaiyaru, site of the well-known Pancanadisvara Shiva temple. During the festival, thousands of musicians as well as Karnatak music connoisseurs and aficionados (*rasika*) arrive from all over India and abroad, swelling the town's population. The crowds snake down the narrow streets toward the area where the afternoon music performances are about to begin. Sitting on a straw mat, the first-time observer can note similarities and differences between musical performances here and Karnatak concerts (*kaccēri*, from the Urdu 'court of law') such as those of the late-December "music season" in Madras.

The Karnatak concert today

In a typical Karnatak concert, the main artist sits in the middle of a stage, with a melodic accompanist, usually a violinist, to his or her left, and a rhythmic accompanist playing the double-headed *mridangam* 'barrel drum', to the right. A person seated behind the main artist, often a senior student (*śiṣya*), provides the melodic drone (*śruti*) by playing the *tambūrā* 'long-necked lute'; if the main performer is a vocalist, the drone player also often sings in a supporting capacity. The relationship between the performers appears to be quite collegial, but the main artist seated in the middle has the status of first among equals. This person engages the accompanists beforehand, and then onstage manifests a variety of leadership roles, such as determining the compositions to be performed, initiating and concluding the various genres of improvisation, and indicating to the other musicians when their solo turn has come. Concert etiquette requires the violinist and drummer to remain mindful of supporting the soloist, but these musicians take their turns showing virtuosity in raga *ālāpana* 'unmetered exposition of the raga' and *tani āvartanam* 'drum solo', respectively. They also respond to the improvisatory initiatives of the main artist during genres like *svara kalpana*, melodic and rhythmic improvisation using Karnatak sol-fa syllables. The eminent violinist Lalgudi Jayaraman, who has served in both roles during his long career, has published a list of desiderata for soloists and accompanists that is instructive (figure 1).

FIGURE 1 Desirable attributes for soloists and accompanists (Jayaraman 1986:31).

Soloist	Accompanist
1. Mastery over the instrument	1. Pleasant temperament
2. Musical ability	2. Cooperative teamwork
3. Original approach and style	3. Supportive role
4. Creativity	4. Self-control
5. Effortless-seeming presentation	5. Alertness
6. Concert management	6. Adaptability to different styles
7. Leadership quality	7. Restraint
8. Rich repertoire	8. Time consciousness
9. Understanding of the lyric and its mood	9. Interaction

The typical Karnatak concert can give the impression of a wonderful if occasionally strained marriage of devotion and virtuosity. The major genre of Karnatak music, the *kriti*, invariably has a devotional text (*sāhitya*), but many connoisseurs feel that the audience should perceive the words and their meaning as subsidiary to the musical virtuosity of the accomplished professional performers.

Performance at the Tyagaraja festival

The festival ensembles in Tiruvaiyaru are identical to those of the typical Karnatak concert in comprising one main artist (occasionally two) flanked by accompanists. Similarly, in both contexts many women vocalists participate, although far fewer women instrumentalists than men. But significant differences are evident as well—in the broader, inclusive nature of the Tiruvaiyaru ensembles, and in the festival's focus not on virtuosity but on devotion. Performers of all ages and skill levels participate, from the greatest concert artists (*vidvān*) to young beginners. Each group of musicians plays only one or two songs (nowadays invariably Tyagaraja compositions) in a brief and straightforward manner, with little of the expansive improvisation or competitive playing in a standard Karnatak concert. Some musicians who have accompanied a solo artist in one performance appear soon after as soloists in their own right.

One of the authors (M. Allen), a young first-time observer of the festival, views the event as a primarily devotional experience and an inclusive, participatory celebration of a great composer. The senior author (T. Sankaran) has attended the Tyagaraja *ārādhana* for over half a century; attending the event still reminds him of the long struggle of women like his own grandmother, Vina Dhanammal (1867–1938), to achieve full participation in the festival. Festival organizers excluded her on the basis of gender, despite the fact that virtually the entire male musical establishment held her in high regard as evidenced by her inclusion in a 1911 photograph alongside prominent male artists (at that time an extremely rare phenomenon). As an older, native South Indian watching the crowd, T. Sankaran can readily ascertain the social background and religious affiliation of most people at the festival. He recalls relationships between Brahmin and non-Brahmin musicians he has known, and thinks of his wife's grand-uncle, the violinist Malaikottai Govindasvami Pillai, who had to make excruciatingly difficult choices in his desire to honor Tyagaraja. To this veteran observer, musical performance has largely come uncoupled from gender and caste considerations during his lifetime, but strong resonances remain of conflict and cooperation, hierarchy and intimacy, between humans of different genders and social classes.

GENDER AND INVISIBILITY

Women and men from different geographic regions and social communities have contributed to the history of South Indian music, yet Indian women's role both in music and other expressive traditions remains largely unrecorded (see, however, Post 1989). Fleeting anecdotal references to women affirm not only their participation in music but the strong influence of their artistic excellence and character on their contemporary communities, including their male colleagues. In the sixteenth century, for example, Purandara Dasa desired to see and hear the dance and music of a renowned unnamed *dēvadāsi* 'female servant of god' at Pandarpur, and in appreciation of her talents presented her with a bracelet of rare beauty. In the nineteenth century, the *dēvadāsi* Tiruvarur Kamalam was a renowned dancer, musician, and student of the composer Muttusvami Diksitar (1776–1835), to whom, according to some accounts, she in turn taught dance music.

What little is known about such women usually comes from biographical accounts of the men whose lives they influenced. In some cases scholarship by and about women performers and composers has been published but later deliberately altered, in effect erased. In 1887, Orientalist scholars printed a new edition of a mid-eighteenth-century work by a *dēvadāsi* composer of the Tanjavur court, Muddupalani, entitled *Radhika Santwanam* 'Appeasing Radha'. The publishers, however, omitted the prologue, in which the author introduced herself and discussed her matrilineal descent and her life at the court of Raja Pratap Singh (1739–1763), thus concealing the author's gender. Bangalore Nagaratnammal, a musician of the *dēvadāsi* community, located the manuscript and reprinted it in 1910 in its complete form. Government authorities immediately seized and banned her edition. Clandestine copies circulated until the ban was lifted in 1947. An accurate (and legal) reprint of the 1910 edition appeared in 1952, and yet a team of feminist literary scholars report that they had difficulty locating a copy when preparing an anthology of Indian women writers in the 1980s (Tharu and Lalitha 1991:1–12).

The lack or suppression of documentation on women's participation in music results partly from the particular caste (social class) of virtually all female dancers and musicians in temples and courts from possibly as early as the Cōḻa period (c. ninth to eleventh centuries) to the 1930s. Young girls who were born or adopted into this caste received training in music, dance, and ritual activities in order to become *dēvadāsi*; they were married to a Hindu temple deity and dedicated to a life of service (Kersenboom 1987; Marglin 1985; Srinivasan 1984). There were two important consequences: first, due to her divine marriage, a *dēvadāsi* could not marry a human husband—though she might have children either with her patron or through adoption; second, because her husband was divine, she could not become a widow—and therefore avoided the profound inauspiciousness of that state in the Hindu world [see WOMEN AND MUSIC].

CASTE AND MUSIC

The state of intercaste relations in South Indian music around 1900 might be characterized as intimacy within hierarchy. This subject is perhaps the most contentious a student will encounter in the study of South Indian music. In the history of caste relations, many individuals have certainly reached across sometimes formidable caste boundaries to form deep and lasting friendships.

In discussing musician castes in South India, a dual scheme of Brahmin and non-Brahmin is a more accurate framework than the overarching four classes (*varṇa*) of Hindu society (Brahmin 'priest', Kshatriya 'warrior', Vaishya 'merchant', and Shudra 'menial'). The primary South Indian musician communities reflect this basic duality of social background, which is in some respects analogous to the dynamic between Hindu and Muslim communities in the social organization of North Indian music (Qureshi 1991).

The non-Brahmin musician community

There are many non-Brahmin social communities in South India; the particular community to which the *dēvadāsi* belonged, comprising two hereditarily linked subgroups, produced the great majority of non-Brahmin musicians and dancers in South India for the last several hundred years. Eminent composers from this community have included Muttuttandavar (seventeenth century), one of the first composers of the *kriti* genre, and the four brothers known as the Tanjavur Quartette, a great nineteenth-century family of composers and dance masters (Sankaran 1982).

Up to the mid-twentieth century, people referred to musicians of this community as *mēḷakkāran*, a generally derogatory term meaning doer or maker of the musical ensemble (*mēḷam*). In 1948, the year after *dēvadāsi* dedication was legally outlawed in Tamil Nadu, the non-Brahmin musician community adopted the new caste name of Iśai Veḷḷāḷar 'Music Cultivators'. Veḷḷāḷar is the name of a large and well-respected non-Brahmin South Indian caste group that includes many occupational specialties. Many male musicians of the community also appended the Veḷḷāḷar caste suffix Piḷḷai to their given names.

The performance ensembles of the community's two branches were traditionally known as the *cinna mēḷam* 'small ensemble' of temple and court dance, comprising the female dancer, her male dance master, and accompanying musicians; and the *periya mēḷam* 'large ensemble' for temple ritual music, centered around the *nāgasvaram* 'large double-reed instrument' and the *tavil* 'double-headed drum'. According to some scholars, the dance ensemble was named *cinna mēḷam* because of the small double-reed *mukhavīṇā* that used to be part of the ensemble, and the *periya mēḷam* took its name from the larger double-reed *nāgasvaram*. Others believe *periya* connoted a higher, and *cinna* a lower, status (Srinivasan 1984).

In the late twentieth century, both *cinna mēḷam* and *periya mēḷam* ensembles perform on the public stage. The *periya mēḷam* has also retained its original temple ritual context, but a social reform movement culminating in the 1930s severed the *cinna mēḷam* dance from its temple roots. In a profound social transformation, *dēvadāsi* dancers were replaced by upper-caste women—notably, of the Brahmin community—who had hitherto completely shunned the professional performance of either music or dance. Many eminent male dance masters of the *cinna mēḷam* community continued as teachers to these new Brahmin women students (Srinivasan 1984; Arudra 1986–1987; Allen 1997).

The Brahmin musician community

Men from many different Brahmin subcommunities—Ayyars (Smarta Brahmins) and Ayyangars (Vaishnavite Brahmins) are today especially prominent (Jackson 1991:30)—have played a central role in Karnatak music throughout its history, whereas Brahmin women entered the professional practice of music and dance in numbers beginning only in the 1930s. Purandara Dasa and the three men canonized as the "Trinity" of Karnatak composers—Tyagaraja, Syama Sastri (1762–1827), and Muttusvami Diksitar—were all Brahmins. Furthermore countless outstanding composers and vocalists (and some accompanists), have come from Brahmin backgrounds. Young men of this community are traditionally highly educated and enter many professions, outside as well as in the arts.

During the Tanjavur court period, from the sixteenth to the nineteenth centuries, Telugu-, Kannada-, and Maratha-speaking Brahmin families were prominent immigrants to the Tanjavur region, joining the indigenous Tamil-speaking Brahmins. The Tanjavur rulers, who depended on and valued the priestly, artistic, and administrative expertise of this community, often gave them lands and houses. In addition to providing musical performers and composers, Brahmin scholars developed the theo-

The Brahmin community considered animal skin and saliva polluting substances, and accordingly did not train their children to play drums or aerophones.

retical discussion of Karnatak music in published treatises. This occupational activity continues in modified form today, as most contemporary scholars and critics—as well as patrons—of Karnatak music come from various branches of the Brahmin community (Singer 1972; Jackson 1991, 1994).

GENDER, CASTE, AND MUSICAL PERFORMANCE

Since the beginning of the twentieth century, profound changes have taken place in the gender and caste organization of music and musicians. The structure of musical performance in South India is quite different today than it was a century ago, whether a Karnatak concert, the Tyagaraja festival, a *bharata nāṭyam* dance performance, or a *periya mēḷam* temple ensemble performance.

Women's and men's music

In significant respects, women's and men's musical performance practices in the 1990s are similar: male and female main artists present both vocal and instrumental concerts, and melodic accompanists are of both genders, though now as always women percussionists are few in number. The Karnatak concert repertoire, genres of improvisation, and the on-stage relationship between soloist and accompanists are virtually identical whether the performers are male or female. In the early twentieth century, however, performances by men and women were quite distinct. Male artists engaged in intellectual acrobatics in the *rāgam-tānam-pallavi* genre (extensive melodic and rhythmic improvisations on a brief composed musical phrase) that occupied the major portion of a concert. In the previous century male performances were inevitably competitive; the main artist and his sidemen hurled challenges back and forth, aiming to show up the adversary's weak points.

In the early twentieth century, Brahmin and non-Brahmin male performers in fact measured their musical competence largely by their expertise in the *rāgam-tānam-pallavi* genre. Legendary encounters between an expert court musician (*āsthāna vidvān*) and a visiting challenger made and broke careers. Men sang with different accompanists on different occasions, and group rehearsals prior to a concert were virtually unknown. Available biographical accounts of eminent nineteenth-century musicians testify that although men honed their skills on *rāgam-tānam-pallavi*, they had relatively small repertoires of *kriti* compositions compared to their female counterparts.

Around 1900, professional women musicians came only from the *mēḷakkāran* community referred to above, and almost no Brahmin women musicians performed in public before the 1930s. At the beginning of the century, women musicians were mostly singers, with a few instrumental performers, mainly on the vina. They often performed with the same accompanists (frequently their male relatives) throughout their careers (Sankaran 1986). Sisters led many of the famous female groups, mixing unison and octave singing; in the early decades of this century "Dhanam's Daughters"

(Smt. Lakshmiratnammal and Smt. Rajalakshmiammal, the elder two of Smt. Vina Dhanammal's four daughters) and the Enadi Sisters were prominent, and in the next generation, the sisters Smt. T. Brinda and Smt. T. Muktha, granddaughters of Dhanammal, who performed with their violinist sister Smt. T. Abhiramisundari from the 1930s to the 1960s. Such women's performances exhibited cooperation rather than competition. Programs were well rehearsed, and comprised many items including *kriti* compositions and song genres from the *cinna mēḷam* repertoire (*padam* and *jāvaḷi*). Before 1930 few women performed the rhythmically based improvisatory forms in *rāgam-tānam-pallavi*; women musicians did however excel in raga *ālāpana*, a melodic improvisation that introduces and develops raga outside the confines of tala, leading to a composition in that raga.

Caste relations in music

As noted above, members of the two major South Indian sociomusical communities, Brahmin and non-Brahmin, have had long and intimate histories of interaction and have developed profound respect for each other. The composer Muttusvami Diksitar, for example, one of the Brahmin "Trinity," had a long-lasting relationship with the Tanjavur Quartette, the four non-Brahmin brothers to whom he gave musical instruction, and from whom many believe he learned a great deal about dance music. His succession of students (*śiṣya paramparā*), all of whom learned his compositions and passed them down to the next generation, includes both Brahmin and non-Brahmin pupils. A more recent example is the relationship between the non-Brahmin violinist Malaikottai Govindasvami Pillai (1879–1931) and his beloved Brahmin student "Papa" K. S. Venkatarama Ayyar (1901–1972) (see below).

Caste and instrumental specialization

The materials used to make musical instruments were important considerations socially as well as musically in the early 1900s. The Brahmin community considered animal skin and saliva polluting substances, and accordingly did not train their children to play drums or aerophones such as the *kuḻal* 'bamboo flute' or *nāgasvaram*. Almost all percussion accompanists c. 1900 were thus non-Brahmins. The earliest reference to a Brahmin *mridangam* player known to the authors is a 1915 photograph of the *cinna kaṭci* 'small faction' of Tyagaraja festival organizers, at Tiruvaiyaru (see figure 2). The first great Brahmin *mridangam* player was Palghat Mani Ayyar, born in 1912. The first great Brahmin flutist, Sarabha Sastri (1872–1904), was the disciple of a non-Brahmin flute player, Natesa Pillai, also a renowned *nāgasvaram* temple performer. Such prohibitions did not affect other instruments. Both sociomusical communities have played the vina since the Nāyaka period (1500s) and the European violin since its introduction to South India by the British in the late eighteenth century; gradually the violin became the primary melodic accompanying instrument for Karnatak music. The first two great South Indian violinists were Balusvami Diksitar (1785–1858), brother of Muttusvami Diksitar, and Vadivelu Pillai (1810–1847), the youngest brother in the Tanjavur Quartette.

At the turn of the twentieth century, *periya mēḷam* and *cinna mēḷam* (the *nāgasvaram* and dance ensembles, respectively) were exclusively spheres of non-Brahmin performance, although Brahmins composed much dance music from the seventeenth to the nineteenth centuries, and a few Brahmin dance teachers in the nineteenth century have been documented. Brahmins and non-Brahmins did, however, wholeheartedly participate together in the Karnatak court (and later concert-hall) tradition. Performances by mixed-caste ensembles were common, though markers of caste status such as first garlanding Brahmin musicians (even a Brahmin accompanist before a non-Brahmin soloist) were observed. During the twentieth century, the former *cinna mēḷam* dance-music tradition has become *bharata nāṭyam*, a largely Brahmin dance practice, but the *periya mēḷam* has substantially retained its non-Brahmin sociomusical makeup. Saliva and animal skin are no longer barriers to the performance of aerophones or membranophones by any community; however, very few Brahmins have as yet taken up the study of *nāgasvaram* or *tavil*, the instruments of the *periya mēḷam*.

A HISTORY OF SOCIAL ORGANIZATION IN THE TYAGARAJA FESTIVAL

Music in Tanjavur

Tanjavur District, the home of the Tyagaraja *ārādhana*, earned its reputation as the seat of the emergent Karnatak music culture due to the patronage of successive kings from the sixteenth century on (Seetha 1981). Beginning with Sevappa Nayak in 1532, Telugu-speaking governors or viceroys (*nāyaka*) from the embattled Vijanayagar empire in the Deccan (to the north) moved south and assumed the rule of Tanjavur. Many Telugu- and Kannada-speaking musicians followed, their descendants becoming central to the development of Karnatak composition and practice. The Telugu rulers patronized both Sanskrit and Telugu at court, as did the succeeding Marāṭhā rulers from the 1670s to 1855. Marāṭhā musicians who immigrated to Tanjavur at that time also made strong contributions to South Indian music, notably in *bhajana sampradāya* 'group devotional singing', and the immensely popular late-nineteenth- and early-twentieth-century genre of musical-religious discourse, *harikathā*, performed by Brahmin singers called *bhāgavatar*.

The musical practices that evolved in the Tanjavur district incorporated profound influences from other parts of South India alongside ancient Tamil indigenous musical traditions. The Tamil language received on balance relatively little patronage from Tanjavur's Telugu and Marāṭhā rulers, a situation not addressed directly until the 1940s by the Tamil Iśai 'Tamil Music' movement (Nambi Arooran 1980) and the concurrent recognition of such Tamil composers as Gopalakrishna Bharati and Papanasam Sivan. Of the "Trinity" of Karnatak composers, Tyagaraja and Syama Sastri came from immigrant Telugu-speaking families. All three composers were born in the Tanjavur district town of Tiruvarur, yet all three—including Muttusvami Diksitar, born into a Tamil-speaking family—wrote almost all their musical compositions in Telugu or Sanskrit.

Early years of the Tyagaraja festival

After Tyagaraja's passing in 1847, some of his disciples (*śiṣya*) would come to his gravesite at Tiruvaiyaru on the anniversary of his death each January. The commemorations were at first extremely simple; the disciples would pray, sing some songs, and return home. As Tyagaraja's lineage of students and students' students multiplied, more musicians came to the site to offer their worship. About sixty years after Tyagaraja's death, the commemoration became institutionalized, due to the efforts of two Brahmin brothers from the village of Tillaisthanam, adjacent to Tiruvaiyaru. These brothers, Narasimha Bhagavatar and Panju Ayyar, collected sufficient money and food to feed the Brahmins who would assemble for the rites. Narasimha Bhagavatar, a disciple's disciple of Tyagaraja, also published a major edition of Tyagaraja's *kriti* compositions and a biographical account of the composer, in 1908 (Jackson 1991:7–8).

This early commemoration focused on two major activities. The first was *santarppaṇa* 'feeding Brahmins on a large scale', in which the Tillaisthanam brothers imitated a traditional practice of kings and other patrons who wished to accumulate spiritual merit by acts of charity toward Brahmins. Historically, large gifts such as lands and houses were also common; the well-known Patinaintu Maṇṭapam, a set of fifteen solidly built houses on the outskirts of Tiruvaiyaru, are testimony to this practice, given by a Tanjavur raja to a group of Brahmins that included Tyagaraja's forebears.

The second essential activity in commemoration of Tyagaraja's death was and is the *uñcavritti bhajana*. Since about 1910, male musicians and devotees (women musicians did not participate until the mid-1960s) have met at "Tyagaraja's house" at dawn on the anniversary, and carried a framed portrait of the composer as they walk in procession through the town streets. They go from house to house singing group bhajans and gleaning handfuls of rice as alms, a process called *uñcavritti*. This constitutes homage by imitation, as Tyagaraja is well known for having refused royal patronage, preferring instead to beg for food to support his family and his large number of disciples. After an hour or so the gleaners arrive at the shrine (*samādhi*) where Tyagaraja is believed to have died, and priests perform a series of religious rituals (*pūjā*). In the early years, the assembled Brahmins were then given lunch.

The Tillaisthanam brothers disagreed over financial accounts after the first year's celebration, and split into separate factions (*kaṭci*). The group led by the elder brother, Narasimha Bhagavatar, became known as the *periya kaṭci* 'large faction', while the younger Panju Ayyar formed the *cinna kaṭci* 'small faction' (figure 2). Not until 1939 were the two factions reunited. The *cinna kaṭci* remained throughout its history the exclusive preserve of Brahmin males, but the *periya kaṭci* soon embraced many non-Brahmin musicians, prominent among them the violinist Malaikottai Govindasvami Pillai.

Malaikottai Govindasvami Pillai

Govindasvami Pillai (1879–1931) was born into a family of hereditary non-Brahmin musicians in a small village near the city of Tirucirappalli (Trichy). His primary guru was Lalgudi Kodandapani Pillai, a musician about whom little is known. By the age of twenty Govindasvami was receiving accolades for his violin technique and musicianship from his fellow violinists. By 1910 he had become a celebrity, the most popular and highest-paid Karnatak violinist of his day, proficient as both soloist and accompanist.

Around 1910 Govindasvami Pillai took over the responsibility of organizing the *periya kaṭci* activities (see above), after its founder Narasimha Bhagavatar passed away. Not only did Govindasvami immediately assume financial responsibility for feeding the Brahmins—which he regarded as the crucial element of the festival—he also changed the dates of the *periya kaṭci*'s five-day celebration so that it would overlap only one day with that of the *cinna kaṭci* (the two had formerly been celebrated over

FIGURE 2 The *cinna kaṭci* (small faction), 1915. President Lakshmanachariar sits in an ornate wooden chair, center back. The faction's founder, Tillaisthanam Panju Ayyar (wearing a diagonal upper cloth), sits second from left, back row. Mylattur Krishna Ayyar, a Brahmin *mridangam* player, sits on the floor, second from right. Photo courtesy T. Sankaran.

The 1930s were a time of both nationalist agitation and fierce, caste-based political debate in Tamil Nadu, a debate that had profound repercussions on the performing arts and on the artists themselves.

the same five days). Thus the assembled Brahmins were now fed for nine consecutive days, instead of five.

Govindasvami Pillai earned great respect in the Brahmin community for his strict observation of the rules of caste decorum, as for example his feeding of the Brahmins and his relationship with his Brahmin student, "Papa" K. S. Venkatarama Ayyar, whom he always fed in orthodox style, unseen and untouched by polluting eyes or hands. He observed the caste rules even though this at times demeaned his own kin, and also meant receiving respect often tinged with condescension.

In his stewardship of the *periya kaṭci,* Govindasvami Pillai consistently acted in defense of prevailing social orthodoxies, which sometimes dismayed and humiliated musicians from his own community. *Nāgasvaram* artists were at that time low on the social scale, and were allowed to perform at the festival standing only. Even a bosom friend of Govindasvami, the eminent *nāgasvaram* player Madurai Ponnusvami Pillai, was refused a seat and left in a huff, feeling insulted. Govindasvami Pillai supported the prohibition on women musicians' participation with equal conviction. How he felt about the tightrope he walked between social communities in his attempts to facilitate the yearly homage to a composer he revered is simply not known.

Govindasvami Pillai handed over responsibility for the *periya kaṭci* to the Tiruvilimilalai brothers (Subramania Pillai and Natarajasundaram Pillai), eminent *nāgasvaram* musicians, in 1930, the year before he died. He had distinguished himself through his music, and his selfless and wholehearted service to the memory of Tyagaraja. In the years after his death, the major outdoor Brahmin feeding became a cosmopolitan feeding for all social communities; *nāgasvaram* artists challenged and struck down the custom requiring them to stand while performing; and women moved by stages into the center of the commemoration activities (see "Developments in the 1960s").

Bangalore Nagaratnammal

Into the history of the exclusively male commemoration of Tyagaraja stepped, in 1921, a woman musician of *dēvadāsi* background, Bangalore Nagaratnammal (1878–1952). Like her contemporary Govindasvami Pillai, Nagaratnammal was a tremendously successful performer who had dedicated her heart and her considerable resources to the Tyagaraja festival. Nagaratnammal was born in Mysore and studied as a child with the violinist Bangalore Munusvami Appa of the Tyagaraja discipular lineage. Her vocal debut (*arangēṟṟam*) took place in Mysore in 1892. A catalogue of her performances between 1905 and 1934 lists 1,235 concerts in 116 different cities. Thanks to her spartan discipline, she was able to surmount many hurdles; for example, she designed a portable *tambūrā* for herself and carried it during her many journeys throughout India and Ceylon (now Sri Lanka).

Nagaratnammal built a comfortable house in the Georgetown section of Madras, a neighborhood where many musicians lived in the early twentieth century.

In October 1921 she received a letter from her guru, Bidaram Krishnappa, who had just been on a pilgrimage to Tiruvaiyaru. His heart was torn in two by the ecstasy of *darśan* 'vision' of Tyagaraja's shrine and the agony of seeing the sepulcher's dilapidated condition and unsanitary surroundings. Krishnappa ordained Nagaratnammal to dedicate herself to its renovation. She immediately took the train to Tiruvaiyaru to see for herself the unsanitary ruins maintained by Tyagaraja's worshipers.

Nagaratnammal focused all her energies on the speedy renovation and consecration of a shrine to the composer. At Trichy she met Govindasvami Pillai, who found her a sculptor to make stone images of the composer and of the deity Hanuman for the shrine. Descendants of the last Maratha raja of Tanjavur exchanged their lands at the site with those already purchased by Nagaratnammal, which helped her shape an auditorium with a large seating capacity. Consecration of the newly renovated shrine took place in 1925 (Sankaran 1984:16), and as owner of the land Bangalore Nagaratnammal was in a position to deliver her coup de grace to male chauvinists: "Now we women have a platform to commence singing." The *periya* and *cinna* factions still forbade women's participation at that time, but Nagaratnammal organized and conducted her own "women's faction" until 1939, when the various groups were reunited. Women then began to sing in the music performances during the *ārādhana*, but it was still over twenty more years before women began participating in the *uñcavritti bhajana* and the Tyagaraja *pañcaratna* 'five gems' *kriti* group singing as well.

Bangalore Nagaratnammal continued her intimate involvement with the Tyagaraja *ārādhana* until her death in 1952. She established the Bangalore Nagaratnammal Trust to ensure that after her death the property would be maintained properly and cleanly and that observances would be appropriately conducted and open to people of all communities. In her will, written in 1949, she insisted that her mausoleum be positioned close to Tyagaraja's shrine, to enable her always to have *darśan* 'sight' of the composer. The carpenters who build the temporary performance platform for the festival every year obey this injunction by placing it so that Tyagaraja and his great female devotee can have direct visual contact in perpetuity.

Developments in the 1930s and 1940s

The seating of nāgasvaram *'oboe' and* tavil *'drum' performers*

The 1930s and early 1940s saw several momentous developments in the festival's organization. Non-Brahmin and Brahmin musicians together celebrated Tyagaraja's memory, but markers of caste status remained in place through the 1930s and became increasingly galling to the non-Brahmin participants. This decade was a time of both nationalist agitation and fierce, caste-based political debate in Tamil Nadu, a debate that had profound repercussions on the performing arts and on the artists themselves. In Tanjavur district, the Tamil non-Brahmin politician E. V. Ramasvami Naicker (1879–1973), nicknamed by his supporters Periyar 'The Great One', criticized Brahmin musicians for "monopolizing the field of music" and deplored the "lack of self-respect among non-Brahmin musicians" (Nambi Arooran 1980:255).

A crucial moment for the Tyagaraja *ārādhana* came in 1939, when *nāgasvaram* performers and their *tavil* accompanists won the right to sit during their performances. These musicians had moved beyond the temple ritual context in the early twentieth century and had begun playing concerts, but upper-caste patrons did not allow them to perform seated, sometimes—as in the southern Tirunelveli district—insisting that *nāgasvaram* players perform naked from the waist up as in *periya mēḷam* temple ritual performance. T. N. Rajarattinam Pillai (1898–1956), the most famous *nāgasvaram vidvān* of this century, achieved a great breakthrough with his personal crusade to cross hitherto forbidden social boundaries, when he obtained permission in 1939 to perform on the stage at Tiruvaiyaru in sitting position, after intense negotiations with festival organizers (Terada 1992:260).

The Indian government broadcasting service, founded in 1932 and given its present name, All India Radio, in 1936, began relaying musical programs from the Tyagaraja *ārādhana* in 1939, providing exposure throughout India and eventually abroad. In the same year, the *periya* and *cinna* factions rejoined ranks, agreeing that the newly christened Tyāgabrahma Mahōtsava Sabhā 'Tyagaraja Great Festival Society' would have two secretaries, one Brahmin and one non-Brahmin. After this time, the festival changed from a five-day to a three-day celebration.

Evolution of the anniversary to its current form

In the early 1940s, organizers added a new musical component to the celebrations that quickly became an institution and is now an essential part of all Tyagaraja festivals around the world: the *pañcaratna* 'five gems' *kriti* compositions of Tyagaraja. During the 1940 Tyagaraja festival in Tiruvaiyaru, "Harikesanallur Muthiah Bhagavatar [a highly respected singer and religious speaker] told his colleagues that he considered five of the *kritis* of Tyagaraja to be *pañca ratna* [five gems] and suggested that steps be taken to present them at the *ārādhana*" (Krishnamurti 1995:4–5). At the time, not all five compositions were well known, and the two secretaries of the united organization, Musiri Subramania Ayyar and Tiruvilimilalai Subramania Pillai, carried out research over the next year to assemble complete texts and skeletal melodic arrangements (*pāṭhāntara*) for the newly constituted set of "gems." At the 1941 festival different groups of musicians sang each of the five compositions; within a few years it became customary for one large group of musicians—until 1964, all male—to sing all five *kriti* compositions, in a set sequence.

Once the five "gems" became a staple of the celebrations, the sequence of events on Tyagaraja's death anniversary morning had substantially reached the form in which it endures today. Early in the morning, the *uñcavritti bhajana* takes place as discussed earlier, the devotees arriving at the shrine with Tyagaraja's portrait at 8:00 A.M. after walking from the composer's house. Following the decoration of a stone image of the composer and a series of rituals accompanied by *nāgasvaram*, a group of singers and instrumental accompanists perform the five Tyagaraja compositions from 9:00 to 10:30 A.M., seated facing each other in two rows perpendicular to the shrine. *Nāgasvaram* and *tavil* players seated on the dais then perform sacred, auspicious music (*mangaḷa iśai*) from 10:30 to noon, at which time all adjourn for the public mass feeding. Around 2:00 P.M. musical performances resume, and continue through the afternoon into the night. The day ends with a final ritual at the shrine and a procession, at about 10:00 P.M., taking the portrait back through the streets of Tiruvaiyaru to Tyagaraja's house. During this procession, which sometimes lasts until the early morning, the group sings Tyagaraja's songs in praise of divine names (*divyanāma kīrtana*), and the *periya mēḷam* musicians provide further sacred music.

Developments in the 1960s

An important encounter took place in January 1961 or 1962 that led to a more equitable relationship between Brahmin and non-Brahmin musicians at Tiruvaiyaru. In previous years, in the morning on the anniversary day, a mostly Brahmin group of vocalists would sing the five *kriti* compositions with the *nāgasvaram* performers sitting and listening to them. Immediately following, the *nāgasvaram* musicians would begin playing for the prelunch forenoon session, and the Brahmins would get up and leave. Finally, in 1961 or 1962, some of the *nāgasvaram* and *tavil* performers stopped playing and asked the Brahmins to pay them the courtesy of listening to their performance. The Brahmins would not stay and listen, so in response the *nāgasvaram* players refused to accompany the evening procession back to Tyagaraja's house, during which *nāgasvaram* music is considered absolutely essential. With no *nāgasvaram* musicians willing to play, the evening procession was canceled that year. However, at the next year's festival—and thereafter—the singers remained seated and listened to the *nāgasvaram* performance after finishing their five Tyagaraja compositions.

In January 1964, a group of eminent women vocalists—Smt. M. S. Subbulakshmi, Smt. T. Brinda, and Smt. T. Muktha—boldly "gate-crashed" the *uñcavritti* and *pañca ratna* groups, in which women had not previously been permitted to perform, opening the floodgates for women's full participation in the future. The Madras newspaper *Hindu*, in its coverage of that year's Tyagaraja festival, printed a large photo showing the women participating in the *uñcavritti* procession with a caption saying simply, "Prominent musicians, including . . . M. S. Subbulakshmi, taking part in the *Uñcavritti Bhajan* procession . . ." In an accompanying article, the *Hindu*'s (male) correspondent wrote matter-of-factly that women musicians had joined the *uñcavritti bhajana* and had taken part in the singing of the *pañcaratna kriti* compositions, without commenting on the fact that this was the first time in history they had done so.

REFERENCES

Allen, Matthew. 1997. "Rewriting the Script for South Indian Dance." *TDR (The Drama Review)*, 41(3):63–100.

Arudra. 1986–1987. "The Transformation of a Traditional Dance." *Śruti* 27/28:17–36.

Catlin, Amy. 1985. "*Pallavi* and *Kriti* of Karnatak Music: Evolutionary Processes and Survival Strategies." *Journal of the National Centre for the Performing Arts, Bombay*, XIV(1):26–44.

Jackson, William J. 1991. *Tyagaraja: Life and Lyrics*. Madras: Oxford University Press.

———. 1994. *Tyagaraja and the Renewal of Tradition: Translations and Reflections*. Delhi: Motilal Banarsidass.

Jayaraman, Lalgudi G. 1986. "The Violin in Carnatic Music." *Kalakshetra Quarterly* VIII(1–2): 28–34.

Kersenboom, Saskia. 1987. *Nityasumangali: Devadasi Tradition in South India*. Delhi: Motilal Banarsidass.

Krishnamurti, Calcutta K. S. 1995. Response, Letters to the Editor Column. *Śruti* 128:4–5.

Marglin, Frédérique. 1985. *Wives of the God-King: The Rituals of the Devadasis of Puri*. Oxford: Oxford University Press.

Menon, Raghava R. 1982. Foreword to *Indian Classical Music and Sikh Kirtan*, by Gobind Singh Mansukhani. New Delhi: Oxford & IBH Publishing.

Nambi Arooran, K. 1980. *Tamil Renaissance and Dravidian Nationalism 1905–1944*. Madurai: Koodal Publishers.

Parthasarathy, T. S. 1975. "Contemporaries and Disciples of Sri Muthuswami Dikshitar." *Birth Bi-Centenary of Sri Muthuswami Dikshitar*. Special issue of *Journal of the Indian Musicological Society* VI(3):28–32. Baroda: Indian Musicological Society.

Post, Jennifer. 1989. "Professional Women in Indian Music: The Death of the Courtesan Tradition." In *Women and Music in Cross-Cultural Perspective*, ed. Ellen Koskoff, 97–109. Urbana: University of Illinois Press.

Qureshi, Regula. 1991. "Whose Music? Sources and Contexts in Indic Musicology." In *Comparative Musicology and the Anthropology of Music*, ed. Bruno Nettl and Philip Bohlman, 152–168. Chicago: University of Chicago Press.

Sankaran, T. 1975. "The Nagaswaram Tradition Systematised by Ramaswami Dikshitar." *Birth Bi-Centenary of Sri Muthuswami Dikshitar*. Special issue of *Journal of the Indian Musicological Society* VI(3):16–21. Baroda: Indian Musicological Society.

———. 1982. "Last of the Tanjore Quartette." In *Glimpses of Indian Music*, ed. Gowry Kuppuswamy and M. Hariharan, 206–09. Delhi: Sundeep Prakashn.

———. 1984. "Bangalore Nagaratnammal: A Devadasi True." *Śruti* 4:14–16.

———. 1986. "Women Singers." *Kalakshetra Quarterly* VIII(1-2):58–65.

———. 1989. "Fiddle Govindaswamy Pillai (1879–1931): A Prince among Musicians." *Śruti* 55:19–25.

Sastri, H. Ramachandra. 1986. "Winds of Change." *Kalakshetra Quarterly* VIII(1–2):35–36.

Seetha, S. 1981. *Tanjore as a Seat of Music during the 17th, 18th and 19th Centuries*. Madras: University of Madras.

Singer, Milton. 1972. *When a Great Tradition Modernizes: An Anthropological Approach to Indian Civilization*. New York: Praeger.

Srinivasan, Amrit. 1984. "Temple 'Prostitution' and Community Reform: An Examination of the Ethnographic, Historical and Textual Context of the Devadasi of Tamil Nadu, South India." Ph.D. dissertation, Cambridge University.

Terada, Yoshitaka. 1992. "Multiple Interpretations of a Charismatic Individual: The Case of the Great Nagasvaram Musician T. N. Rajarattinam Pillai." Ph.D. dissertation, University of Washington.

Tharu, Susie, and K. Lalitha. 1991. *Women Writing in India: 600 B.C. to the Present. Volume I: 600 B.C. to the Early 20th Century*. New York: The Feminist Press at the City University of New York.

Regional Caste Artists and Their Patrons

Gordon R. Thompson

Patrons and Clients
Traditional South Asia
Modern South Asia

In South Asia, "folk" performers are generally considered to be both rural and regional. Social circumstances at birth determine their ascribed status. Among the numerous kinds of folk performers that exist throughout the subcontinent, some of the best-documented examples are highlighted in the present discussion.

Two basic observations concerning South Asian music culture are in order. First, musical differences between regions, as between rural and urban areas, are significant and meaningful. Second, birthright is paramount in defining roles for musicians, bards, and dancers; this is one of the ways in which much of the past has survived into the present, in spite of the fundamental changes that have taken place in the twentieth century. This article is organized into two sections, on the traditional and the modern, but it illustrates the continuity between performers of the past and those of more recent years.

An overlay of familial, linguistic, geographic, economic, political, and racial groups—each with at least some of its own customs and traditions—defines the cultural landscape of the subcontinent. Like Europe, South Asia is a patchwork of peoples speaking different languages and following local customs. Moreover, Bengalis, Gujaratis, Kashmiris, Punjabis, Tamils, and numerous other peoples with politically and linguistically marked and geographically linked identities also all have identifiable musical cultures, exhibiting characteristic genres, rhythms, melodies, and concepts of sound. Nevertheless, regionally associated performance styles are really those of the individuals living there. A state such as West Bengal, for example, has many different social groups, and it is the individuals within these social groups who create and sanction elements of musical style.

A related principle is the contrast between musical traditions in urban and rural areas. The classical Hindustani and Karnatak traditions of the northern and southern subcontinent, for example, are largely urban phenomena, and urban artists and patrons foster, develop, and exchange musical ideas in cities like Bombay, Calcutta, Delhi, Karachi, Lahore, and Madras. The cosmopolitan musical styles that have resulted from such exchanges are consequently more consistent among themselves than are regional musical styles. In fact, part of the contrast between folk, or regional, and classical music lies precisely in the heterogeneity of the former and the homo-

Musicians in rural and regional South Asia have traditionally existed as clients, enmeshed within a complex web of rights and obligations with their patrons.

geneity of the latter, although this was always prone to modification. As provincial musicians migrated to the cities in search of work, they shed much of their *deśī* 'regional' style and at the same time infused the classical tradition with new ideas.

The second given—that status is ascribed according to the social circumstances of one's birth (essentially, caste)—is fundamental to much South Asian scholarship. It is not unique to the Indian subcontinent, but historically South Asians, particularly Hindus, have refined the concept and developed sophisticated philosophical and religious explanations of the caste system. The two most important South Asian and Hindu social constructs are *varṇa* 'class' and *jāti* 'caste'. *Varṇa* broadly refers to a commonality of birth and occupation, and includes four main groups: Shudra (artisan), Vaishya (merchant), Kshatriya (warrior), and Brahmin (priest). *Jāti* is the specific social group into which one is born, and implies both an immediate and distant sense of kinship. A Laṅgā, for example, belonging to a caste of musicians in northwestern India, has caste fellows in Sindh, Punjab, Rajasthan, Gujarat, Madhya Pradesh, and Uttar Pradesh, indeed in most of the northern subcontinent. All Laṅgās (known in some areas as Laṅghās) have a distant sense of blood relationship, though they also have subcaste structures in the specific region where they live, through which they relate to other specific groups such as those with which they intermarry.

The *varṇa* system, a societal structure dating from Aryan Vedic society of the second millennium B.C., does not cover all sectors of South Asian society; it excludes tribal peoples and common laborers. And the institution of caste is far from rigid. Though some castes have maintained the same occupation for centuries, others have clearly changed theirs. Artists who have found their skills to be stepping stones to higher status have moved ranks. In turn, other castes have taken their old places, sometimes even assuming the name of the previous holders of the occupation—especially if that name had become directly associated with the occupation. Some caste musicians, especially hereditary performers such as the Laṅgās, are Muslims who pass down their performance traditions from one generation to another within the family. Caste is not a feature of Islam—indeed Islam is fundamentally egalitarian—but Hindu musicians who converted to Islam over the previous millennium have maintained much of their family structure.

PATRONS AND CLIENTS

Musicians in rural and regional South Asia have traditionally existed as clients, enmeshed within a complex web of rights and obligations with their patrons. This relationship has apparently never been static; from generation to generation, the clients' fortunes have waxed and waned. Invaders have destroyed cultural environments, replaced them with new priorities; then they have themselves been supplanted. Musicians have moved on, seeking better payment and recognition. In some instances, the lure of a more affluent patron has compelled a change in repertoire or style, often of residence; the offspring further diversify by developing new performance media. The latter situation is increasingly the case in the late twentieth century, with increased communication and travel. Some musicians give up their profession altogether when they have achieved a comfortable rank, and their status or role is assumed by others in the struggle to fill cultural niches.

Just as music may function on a deeper level than mere entertainment, performers likewise create more than artistry; they are part of a cultural ritual enacted for a select audience. Performers participate in the audience-selection process when they provide symbolic communication for their audience members that requires an informed community for proper interpretation. In South Asia, a bard will exclude verses in coded language when performing for a potentially uncomprehending audience. A musician's performance can only transcend the mundane and technical level of virtuosity when the listener knows and comprehends the repertoire. Similarly, an audience ignorant of the intended meaning of a dancer's gestures will misinterpret or reinterpret her performance. Thus, a performance in its cultural context is a measure of its audience's membership. Knowing how to respond, what to request, and when to request it (or even just demonstrating an interest), contributes to a community's recognition of itself. Cultural performances are not the only measure of membership in a community, but they nevertheless contribute to a complex, expressive web of belonging.

TRADITIONAL SOUTH ASIA

Historical accounts of music on the subcontinent suggest continuity between the past and the present, and yield some generalizations concerning South Asia's traditional musical culture and present-day practice. First, regional musical styles have played an important part in the culture for more than a millennium. Second, feudal states and temples were important patrons of music until 1947, when the independent republics of India and Pakistan were formed. Third, the role of the performing artist has often been hereditary. And fourth, social mechanisms were in place for the transmission of musical skills and knowledge from one generation to the next.

The major epic tales of ancient India mention communities of musicians (Gandharvas), dancers (Apsaras), and bards (Cāraṇs), suggesting how well established they were in South Asian cultural life. In the Mahabharata, one of Hinduism's principal literary sources, these celestial performers entertain the gods and goddesses. The earliest known treatise on drama, Bharata's *Nāṭyaśāstra* (c. 200 B.C.–200 C.E.), has significant sections on dance and music and, like the epics, provides a picture of musical life on the subcontinent two millennia ago. The authors (presumably several authors contributed to the work over the centuries) define musicians by their role in an ensemble and by their knowledge and ability. To acquire these, a performer needs both instruction and a means of financial support during the educational process. Both men and women became dancers and musicians. Furthermore, in the closing chapter of the *Nāṭyaśāstra*, Bharata relates the story of how he himself handed down the tradition of drama to his sons, certainly suggesting that performance was a hereditary art. In twentieth-century practice, *kūṭiyāṭṭam*, a temple drama of Kerala, is one of many examples of South Asian music and dance performed by hereditary artists; *kūṭiyāṭṭam* is performed by Cākyārs and Nangiyārs (Nair 1978).

The *Jātaka* stories, about Siddhartha Gautama in the period before he became the Buddha, are roughly contemporaneous with the *Nāṭyaśāstra*. This collection contains a tale describing the Buddha incarnated as a musician. In the tale, the Buddha appears as a young man named Guttila, who takes a student, Musila. The student irreverently challenges his teacher's superiority, and even goes as far as to demand his position as chief royal musician. A harp competition ensues, and the humble Guttila miraculously wins because of the divine help he receives when a heavenly Apsara appears, dancing to his music. Notably, the story reveals that government patronage and the music teacher-student relationship have deep roots.

In the *Bṛhaddeśī,* from the second half of the first millennium, Matanga documented the period's South Asian regional traditions. He made a distinction between *deśī* 'provincial' and *mārga* 'canonic' ragas, and drew associations between certain musics and their regional origins; this suggests strongly that even at this early stage, there was already quite a heterogeneous musical style map. Rowell (1992:273) refers to the period of the sixth through the tenth centuries as the "age of *deśī*," when the South Asian cultural map changed, and musicians became aware of and accepted provincial traditions.

Patronage in sacred contexts

In Hinduism, devotees treat gods and goddesses as living entities who themselves function as patrons, most obviously of the daily ritual performances by priests and devotees. But just as royal courts have relied on the labors of farmers and on the taxes on merchants' income, temples have also depended upon the practical and financial support of the communities they serve. In a secular analog, the reciprocal relationship between an aristocratic host and a performer was often described as *yajmānī* (*jajmānī* in common speech), even though a *yajmān* is literally the performer of a religious sacrifice (as in the Yajurveda, the ancient religious text that describes sacrificial rituals). The relationship between the priests who perform rituals and their patrons in the community has commonly been hereditary. Numerous records detail the donations of food and clothing that the Brahmin priests conducting the ceremonies expected to receive.

Temples in many parts of India have often supported whole communities whose main activity was the constant praise of resident deities in music and dance. Most renowned of these were families with hereditary rights and obligations as temple servants. The *devadāsi* tradition in South India, among others, fused human sensuality with the adoration of the divine through dance and music (figure 1) [see WOMEN AND MUSIC]. Even today, as various cultural forces historically and morally redefine traditions in secular terms, nevertheless classical *bharata nāṭyam* dancers, for example, see their ideal performance as intended for a divine audience, although it is being watched by a human one (Kliger 1993).

FIGURE 1 Santabai Jagwali with other *devadāsi* women and male devotees (*jogan*) singing in praise of the goddess Renuka (also known as Yellamma) playing (*left to right*) *cawandgā*, *mañjīrā*, and *ektār*, Haripur, Maharashtra, 1998. Photo by Amy Catlin.

Another example of performers with hereditary ties to temple worship is the *havelī saṅgītkār* 'temple musician' tradition associated with the Vallabhacarya Vaishnavs of northwestern India [see RELIGIOUS AND DEVOTIONAL MUSIC: NORTHERN AREA]. This Hindu sect has maintained temples in the form of mansions (*havelī*) where devotees feed, clothe, and praise Krishna, most often to the accompaniment of music, sometimes with dance and drama. The Brahmin temple musicians perform as part of daily and annual rituals for Krishna, just as secular musicians in the former royal courts used to perform for aristocratic hosts. Another such hereditary group performs the *yakṣagāna* (or *yakṣagāna bayalata*), an elaborate masked and costumed drama with music and dance sponsored by temples in Mysore (Upadhyaya 1978). Other performers of religious ritual music do not belong to any particular
TRACK 15 musician caste, such as the practitioners of the Tamil Nadu *viluppāṭṭu* 'bow song' tradition. Their performances take place on a seasonal basis, and they engage year-round in other occupations (Blackburn 1992).

Muslim shrines have also supported musicians. For example, members of the Laṅgā community announce the hours of prayer at Sufi saints' mausoleums (*dargāh*), places of pilgrimage and worship, by playing the *śahnāī* 'oboe' and the *naqqārā* 'kettledrum' [see also PAKISTAN: DEVOTIONAL MUSIC]. Such performances are probably modeled after those of the musicians who traditionally played at the gates of royal cities such as Jaipur in western India and Hyderabad in south-central India. The relationship of present-day performers to the institution honoring the saint is most often hereditary; from generation to generation, they depend for their income on the living memory of the saint.

The many singers and storytellers who have helped to spread religious ideas throughout the subcontinent have also been caste musicians with sacred patrons. Bhajan singers (*bhajanik*) distinguish themselves not only by their knowledge of devotional hymns and their ability to perform, but also by their personal commitment. Although the typical *bhajanik* may not be from a specific caste or have a hereditary relationship with a particular set of patrons, these devotional singers do form communities and serve a relatively consistent population of worshipers. Storytellers, however, often have a hereditary occupation and inherited patronage relationships. Because of the extensive memorization involved in learning their long, involved stories, including side plots and illuminations, children of storytellers are the most likely candidates for the storyteller role since they hear stories over and over again [see GUJARAT for a description of the *māṇ bhaṭṭ ākhyān* 'storytelling tradition']. Storytellers are often—though not necessarily—Brahmins, and live in every state of India.

Patronage in secular contexts

Secular and sacred patronage patterns have shared many characteristics over the centuries. Common to both is the *yajmānī* (or *jajmānī*) relationship, which involves reciprocal responsibilities between a host and a performer. The term *yajmān* is employed in secular contexts but literally refers to the performer of a Vedic religious sacrifice and is also used to indicate the sponsors of such sacred events. Indeed in some cases, *yajmānī* performers have fulfilled both secular and sacred duties for the same patron. The link between secular sponsors and the performers who received their beneficence has also been hereditary and, in many cases, considered almost a sacred relationship. Furthermore, the patron-client relationship is often part of a chain of relationships in which a client in one context is a patron in another.

India's feudal aristocracy was the most prominent secular patron of the performing arts prior to independence in 1947. Epic tales such as the *Prithvīrājrāso* (Thompson 1992) and the *Ālhā* (Schomer 1992) recount the lives, loves, and fates of

The Rajputs have been one of the most important groups of secular patrons in South Asia. Wherever they established themselves, Rajputs were hosts to a network of castes involved in the performing arts.

FIGURE 2 The Cāraṇ Prabhudua M. Sumi, in Lathi, Saurashtra, Gujarat, 1995. Photo by Amy Catlin.

twelfth-century Rajputs and, not coincidentally, their support of bards and musicians. The sixteenth-century chronicle of Emperor Akbar's reign, the *ʿAin-i Akbarī,* includes a tally of performing artists and their duties at his court. These and other historical sources document some of the extent of royal patronage in the past millennium.

The Rajputs have been one of the most important groups of secular patrons in South Asia. After their appearance on the subcontinent almost two millennia ago, the ancestors of the Rajputs gradually expanded their political, military, and social domination. In the fourteenth to sixteenth centuries, Rajputs controlled vast regions of the western Indo-Gangetic river valley, even during periods when other groups such as the Mughals dominated the major urban centers. Wherever they established themselves, Rajputs were hosts to a network of castes involved in the performing arts.

The wealthiest urban courts in this northwestern region retained several kinds of bards, musicians, and dancers. In Gujarat, two groups of male bards, the Bāroṭs and Cāraṇs, attended to their patron's genealogy and history, respectively (figure 2). Both composed and performed poetry, often with pitch and rhythm; verses related the patron family's heroes and icons, including gods, goddesses, horses, weapons, geography, and other "royal" topics. The Cāraṇs remained the bards of the Rajputs in good times and bad, often accompanying their patrons into battle. In this way they could not only recount the battles of the past, but record the battles of the present, linking past to present and ancestor to descendant. These artists affirmed the values of their hosts. Cāraṇs composed and intoned poetry about the bravery of the Rajputs; Bāroṭs sang tales of Rajput fidelity. Such traditions, in which the performing artists provided more than entertainment for their hosts, helped cement the client-patron bonds, and enabled both parties to continue performing and sponsoring over many generations.

Two groups of male musicians, the Mīrs and Laṅgās, had similar relationships with clients in northwest India. Mīrs were singers and *sāraṅgī* 'short-necked fiddle' players who accompanied visiting artists and also offered musical genres specifically associated with the region. Laṅgās, mentioned above, played the *naqqārā* 'kettledrums' and *śahnāī* 'oboe' (figure 3). They provided the necessary ceremonial music for almost every important state occasion, such as royal births, weddings, funerals, and coronations. Both Laṅgās and Mīrs performed music in styles that either confirmed their hosts as members of the ruling elite (classical music) or connected them with the gods and goddesses who epitomized their patrons' fearlessness and prowess.

Laṅgās were responsible for all music accompanying official events in a royal palace, including the arrival and departure of important personages and the marking of the hours of the day (Kothari 1972). They also played the tabla and *pakhāvaj* 'barrel drum' with the Mīrs' *sāraṅgī,* for visiting artists. The women of these two castes performed devotional and seasonal songs in the secluded quarters of the court females. Women who performed in open court or in private recitals where men were present were most often dancers, although some notable singers were among them.

FIGURE 3 The Laṅgā *sāraṅgī* players and singers Noormohammad Khan and Allauddin Khan, accompanied by (*left*) *ḍholak* drum and (*right*) *kartāl* (wooden clappers), Smithsonian Festival of American Folklife, Washington, D.C., 1976. Photo by Amy Catlin.

Such women came from a variety of low castes and tribes. In this and other parts of northwestern India, these groups and others have sought to establish a network of patron and client relationships (see Jairazbhoy 1977 for a discussion of performing groups in western Rajasthan).

The numerous smaller states and city-states of South Asia (of which there were over two hundred before independence in 1947) repeated the patron-client pattern with variations. Among the less wealthy sectors of society, lower castes have acted as clients. In northwestern India, for example, poorer families of genealogists replaced castes such as the Bāroṭs and the Cāraṇs in the more humble estates. Similarly, lower-ranking musicians (such as the Ḍholī or Ḍhāḍhī castes associated with drumming) might replace better-known musician groups such as the Laṅgās and Mīrs. The pattern for dancers repeats that of the bards and musicians.

The musicians, bards, and dancers of premodern South Asia and the patrons they served formed a broad web held together by a mutual bond. The performers reinforced the values and beliefs of their benefactors. The patrons acknowledged and thus legitimized the activities of their clients. Their mutual reliance, however, began to dissolve with the rise of the middle class and the emergence of a democratic environment.

MODERN SOUTH ASIA

Regional patrons and clients in South Asian countries at the end of the twentieth century live in a cultural environment radically different from that of their forebears. More than any other factor, partition was the most significant contextual change in patronage since the rise of British power in the eighteenth and nineteenth centuries. Millions of people migrated between regions: Muslims in predominantly Hindu areas of India traveled to Pakistan, while Hindus in Pakistan moved to India. Qureshi (1992) has observed that the political and social environments in India and Pakistan have contributed to a stifling of many musical activities in the latter, the exception being religious music such as qawwali (group devotional singing).

Many patrons and performers saw their patronage relationships broken. The extensive rail and road networks that had been built by the British over the previous century enhanced the rapidity and volume of this massive twin exodus. The same transportation system has since continued to speed the dilution of regional identities, as people become accustomed to greater mobility. Today, great distances separate the families of former patrons and clients. How can a bard keep updating the genealogy of a family that now has branches in India, Uganda, England, and Canada?

Moreover, how can any artist continue performing genres whose nature requires an audience conversant with the particular artistic language? In most cases these artists simply cannot continue in the same way; new traditions arise from the broken pieces of the old.

The creation of the republics of India and Pakistan deprived the numerous states and estates of rights and privileges, as the new federal governments sought to establish a sense of nationhood that would transcend provincial identities. Musicians who performed regional genres no longer had access to princely purses; the new state governments faced both diminished revenues and monumental socioeconomic problems. Though some performers managed to hold onto their official music positions, in many cases they remained at 1947 wages. Many others had to find new sources of income, and their art evolved in response to the interests of new patrons, who were often less extravagant members of the middle class. Some abandoned their artistic status and took up unrelated occupations. Among the bards in Gujarat, for example, were individuals who chose to become lawyers and teachers; as they had been used to reciting at court and had often been courtiers, they were well prepared for these professions.

The local languages and dialects of regional musics are another important component of the bond between patron and client that has been weakened in contemporary South Asia, as governments encourage use of a standardized language as a unifying influence. Hindi, Urdu, and English are widely spoken in parts of India and Pakistan, and function as national languages, whereas languages with regional associations such as Punjabi, Gujarati, Bengali, and Telugu have largely become the province of two groups. The first group, an economic underclass of individuals with limited education, often speaks only the regional language well; the second group is comprised of members of the intelligentsia who sometimes speak the regional or local tongue by choice, even though they are perfectly able also to speak the national umbrella-languages.

Artists who relate to patrons in regional languages now find their audiences are generally less wealthy than the old aristocracy and less interested in associations with the past. Their focus on regional genres provides an emotional link with their patrons but simultaneously limits their access to new audiences on a larger national scale. Yet rendering regional material in a national language, no matter how much grammar the languages share, diminishes the symbolic and intrinsic flavor of their presentation. Many regional caste artists have only a basic education, which limits them to menial labor and often isolates them from potential patrons. This is especially true for musicians who have several occupations, who remain at the margins of South Asia's emerging economies.

The impact of urbanization

The development of South Asia's major cities—Bombay, Calcutta, Delhi, Karachi, Madras—has seen the transplantation and transformation of regional cultures, as migrants re-create their provincial origins in new urban environments. In cities, individuals forge new identities as they shoulder greater personal responsibility for survival. The agrarian feudal society of traditional South Asia nurtured a web of relationships and mutual support that cradled families. In the modern monetary economy, an employer rewards an individual's services with cash, not with a promise to return a service or commodity in kind. This system grants economic and social mobility, but it has also contributed significantly to the demise of feudal relationships.

But members of urban social groups have appropriated many of the old hereditary musical roles as avocations. In instances where a hereditary performer is unavailable, a patron may substitute another kind of performer or performance, or may reinvent the original genre and conceptualize "folk" art as performance art. Nothing is more destructive to the identity of a caste musician than a patron's assumption that nonprofessional, nonhereditary musicians can fill that role. Avocational performers on the one hand bring an honest love of the music, dance, or poetry to their activity and preserve aspects of the tradition. On the other hand, they necessarily transform it and thereby hasten the elimination of hereditary performers. This is largely a result of life in the city, where caste musicians may not be available, but where the urban middle class still seeks to re-create a real or mythic rural existence partly through musical patronage. Caste performers who do live in cities may in turn themselves seek new patrons, adopting a new repertoire or modifying an existing repertoire. In the 1980s, for example, some Cāraṇ performers in Bombay modified the traditional festive Gujarati dance form called *ḍāṇḍiā rās* 'stick dance', to create *disko ḍanḍīā*, in which the original dance rhythm is altered to imitate Western disco music [see GUJARAT].

Educational and state institutions are also constantly coopting regional music and dance, and rendering them as classical art. Universities and government cultural agencies, in the context of a democratic and capitalist economy, tend to teach and promote regional art forms as systematized canonical forms. Indeed, the interest taken in the regional performing arts by South Asia's bourgeoisie significantly shapes the identity of these art forms. Moreover, had middle-class scholars not taken an interest in the "folk arts," discussion of regional caste performers would almost certainly be completely historical. Urban patrons of some caste musicians, bards, and dancers now assure performers of at least some support.

Certain underlying assumptions regarding India's perpetuation of caste performers do remain. One is the notion that caste is important; Hindu belief fuels the presumption that performers acquire their talent genetically. You can sing a Bāul song (the Bāuls are a caste of Bengali mendicants), but you cannot sing it as well as a Bāul. Similarly, you can call an exterminator, but will he really do as good a job as a Jogi (one of a North Indian community of performers) who plays the *puṅgī* 'free-reed aerophone', recites a magical mantra, and entices the snake never to return?

The impact of mass media

Regional artists have sought new patrons through the growing variety of telecommunications and recording media. Not surprisingly, these have included national and regional radio and television stations, and cassette producers.

Regional state radio stations walk a fine line between preserving the heritage of provincial culture and acknowledging that it must evolve. Where once there were hundreds of courts supporting localized traditions, there are now tens of radio stations whose directors must attempt to represent broad regions and tastes in their programming. A program director often has to employ a station's limited resources—its contracted musicians—to accompany several different kinds of performer. Radio stations thus help define a region's musical style by their choices of inclusion and exclusion. Commonly, a constant staff of instrumentalists accompany all artists at a radio station, from classical musicians to devotional singers.

Possibly the single greatest cause of the homogenization of South Asia is popular music, and in particular that associated with film. Today, most performers who are not expressly classical include film songs or dance styles in their repertoire. This musical and choreographic pan–South Asian style owes much to the eclectic, if rather Western-flavored, nature of film music.

Caste artists also attempt to reach new patrons through the medium of cassettes. Most markets throughout India and Pakistan contain stalls selling cassettes of regional music. Caste performers remain an important part of most regional traditions,

Nothing is more destructive to the identity of a caste musician than a patron's assumption that nonprofessional, nonhereditary musicians can fill that role.

although their cassettes lie next to those of noncaste musicians. In some cases, the recording artists belong to castes not known for their musicianship and have taken up musical performance as a conscious choice. From an ecological point of view, all of these performers are attempting to appeal to patrons by satisfying a particular inclination. Caste performers bring continuity and tradition to their performances, while noncaste performers may bring stylistic echoes of traditions more directly familiar to patrons.

REFERENCES

Blackburn, Stuart H. 1992. "Context into Text: Performance and Patronage in a Tamil Oral Tradition." In *Arts Patronage in India: Methods, Motives and Markets*, ed. Joan Erdman, 31–45. New Delhi: Manohar Publications.

Jairazbhoy, Nazir. 1977. "Music in Western Rajasthan: Continuity and Change." *Yearbook of the International Folk Music Council* 9: 50–60.

Kliger, George, ed. 1993. *Bharata Natyam in Cultural Perspective*. New Delhi: Manohar/American Institute of Indian Studies.

Kothari, Komal. 1972. *Monograph on Laṅgās: A Folk Musician Caste of Rajasthan*. Borunda, Jodhpur: Rupayan Sansthan.

Nair, D. Appukkuttan. 1978. "Koodiyattom." In *Lesser Known Forms of Performing Arts in India*, ed. Durgadas Mukhopadhyay, 1–4. New Delhi: Sterling Publishers Pvt. Ltd.

Neuman, Daniel M. 1980. *The Life of Music in North India: The Organization of an Artistic Tradition*. Detroit: Wayne State University Press.

Qureshi, Regula. 1992. "Whose Music? Sources and Contexts in Indic Musicology." In *Comparative Musicology and Anthropology of Music: Essays on the History of Ethnomusicology*, ed. Bruno Nettl and Philip Bohlman, 152–168. Chicago: University of Chicago Press.

Rowell, Lewis. 1992. *Music and Musical Thought in Early India*. Chicago: University of Chicago Press.

Schomer, Karine. 1992. "The Audience as Patron: Dramatization and Texture of a Hindi Oral Epic Performance." In *Arts Patronage in India: Methods, Motives and Markets*, ed. Joan Erdman, 47–88. New Delhi: Manohar Publications.

Steward, Julian. 1955. *Theory of Culture Change*. Urbana: University of Illinois Press.

Thompson, Gordon R. 1991. "The Cāraṇs of Gujarat: Caste Identity, Music, and Cultural Change." *Ethnomusicology* 35 (3): 381–391.

———. 1992. "The Bāroṭs of Gujarati-Speaking Western India: Musicianship and Caste Identity." *Asian Music* 24 (1): 1–17.

Upadhyaya, K. S. 1978. "Yakshagana Bayalata." In *Lesser Known Forms of Performing Arts in India*, ed. Durgadas Mukhopadhyay, 70–82. New Delhi: Sterling Publishers Pvt. Ltd.

Women and Music

Jennifer C. Post

History
Dual Roles, Limited Spheres
Musical Genres
Twentieth-Century Performers
Women's Folk Traditions

The diverse social and cultural history of the Indian subcontinent reveals a complex record of women's participation in music. Women's roles are seldom well documented, and in order to learn about their role in musical culture a variety of sources must be consulted. Both women and men have participated in South Asian vocal and instrumental traditions, religious and secular music, and classical and folk genres. Yet until recently, women and men occupied separate spheres in their artistic expression.

Women have played key roles in classical and nonclassical music traditions, beginning with that of the courtesan performing for private patrons, and journeying toward that of the highly respected public performer of today. In villages, women continue to maintain an important social position in relation to life-cycle events through their participation in song. Recent changes in South Asian lifestyles, largely the result of widespread contact with the West through radio, film, and television, have affected both women's and men's musical exposure and interest. The popular music industry has brought *filmī gīt* and other popular music genres into many homes and villages during the last few decades and continues to affect the forms and styles women sing and listen to in both classical and regional music traditions.

HISTORY

Women have taken part in South Asian religious and secular music traditions in distinct ways during every historical period. Their light classical and classical performances before the twentieth century included singing and dancing in temples, private clubs, and royal courts. By the mid-twentieth century they had begun to perform as independent musicians on the concert stage and in recordings, radio, and film.

In the religious sphere, references to women in music before the twentieth century are to *devadāsī* or temple dancers, who danced and sang at Hindu temples beginning as early as the third century B.C. In the *Kāmasūtra* of Vatsyayana (around 200 C.E.) there are references to dancers called *niyukta* who were expected to dance regularly at the temple. Around the ninth century, the clearest and most consistent references to temple dancers begin to appear in literature and inscriptions from Assam, Bengal, Deccan, Karnataka, Kashmir, Orissa, and Rajasthan. *Devadāsī*

The position of women in music is still not equal to that of men, but women have gained status and respect as music and dance performers in many contexts.

women were considered servants of the gods and married to the temple or to an object in the temple, usually a dagger. Since they could never become inauspicious widows, they represented the auspiciousness of a married woman. They were responsible for keeping the temple clean and performing at the temple and in public celebrations. They regularly danced before the deity and performed at both religious festivals and domestic celebrations of the local elite, such as weddings and dedications of household gods (Altekar 1956:183).

In the secular sphere, the earliest reference to the *ganika* 'dancing girl' is found in the Ṛgveda, the oldest text of the Vedic Aryans (c. 1400 B.C.). Subsequent literature, including Bharata Muni's treatise on music and drama, the *Nāṭyaśāstra* (second century B.C. to 2nd century C.E.), the Ramayana and the Mahabharata epics (400 B.C. to 200 C.E.), and the *Kāmasūtra* of Vatsyayana, as well as the dramatic and poetic writings of authors such as Kalidasa (2nd century C.E.), all provide evidence that society expected women to cultivate skills in the arts, especially in vocal and instrumental music and dance. In the Mahabharata, there are references to courtesans who played musical instruments during victory celebrations after a battle. References in the Mahabharata and the *Kāmasūtra* describe professional women who sang and danced in *gosṭhi,* 'clubs for connoisseurs of the arts'. Similarly, Bharata in the *Nāṭyaśāstra* characterizes courtesans as women who were accomplished singers, dancers, and actresses (Chandra 1973:70).

Before the fourth century, nonprofessional women had greater freedom to be involved in music. During the ensuing centuries child marriage became more widely practiced, and the generally low status of women dictated by Muslim rule placed further restrictions on women's opportunities to learn and perform music. When nonprofessional women did take part in music, their performances were separate from those of professional women. In courtly life, women were generally restricted to the court environs and performed only for other women. Thus women's social participation moved more toward the private sphere; courtesans and temple dancers became the sole carriers of the majority of women's music and dance traditions.

During the Muslim occupation of India (1200s–1700s), the practice of court patronage of musicians placed women in a variety of performing roles. The nobility (both male and female patrons) organized music-and-dance events at which courtesans and court-appointed dancing girls performed. In the Muslim and Rajput courts of North India, and as far south as Vijayanagar (now in Karnataka), professional women danced and performed both instrumental and vocal music. Their responsibilities included accompanying the entrance of the ruler in the women's quarters of the imperial households, and performing before him, as well as entertaining at festivals and at the homes of nobles. Sources of this period also contain occasional references to nonprofessional women's musical activities at court.

The adoption of Victorian moralistic attitudes in India during British colonial rule in the nineteenth century affected women's musical roles and contributions, and placed restrictions on professional women's involvement in music. In the late nineteenth century, court and private patronage diminished, as did women's performing opportunities. In addition, growing numbers of Europeans and Indians frowned on performance contexts once occupied by courtesans, who had maintained certain types of musical traditions among women. In 1892, a social-reform movement in Madras sought to prohibit professional music and dance performances. This movement spread throughout India during the first decades of the twentieth century, radically affecting women's participation in music, both sacred and secular, and influencing the passage of several laws banning temple dancing. Between 1910 and 1947 formal bans on the practice of temple dancing took effect in Mysore, Travancore, and Madras, swelling the movement to abolish this once-widespread practice (Marglin 1989).

At the beginning of the twentieth century, some professional women challenged their stigmatized role by altering their performance styles and repertoires. Many changed their performance dress, from the kind of stylized outfit associated with courtesans to more conventional women's clothing; they stopped performing erotic dance movements while singing, lending greater seriousness to the music and eliminating sexual overtones from their performances. As the century progressed, women from professional backgrounds were thus able to move into the once exclusively male realm of high classical music.

Since the middle of the twentieth century, women have had greater opportunities to perform publicly, to learn both vocal and instrumental music, to specialize in a single performance medium, and to be involved in popular music performances. The position of women in music is still not equal to that of men, but women have gained status and respect as music and dance performers in many contexts.

DUAL ROLES, LIMITED SPHERES

Before the mid-twentieth century, professional women were associated with specific social groups, and therefore acquired different names in various parts of the subcontinent. The most common names for women performers include *devadāsī*, *tawāif*, *kanchani*, *kalāvantin*, and *naikin*. The British called them collectively "nautch girls," derived from the Sanskrit word for dance, *nāc*. Until the mid-twentieth century, they performed in the limited spheres of Hindu temples, courts, and private clubs. They were born into specialist communities and/or were connected with hereditary families of musicians or dancers. In North India, some women traced their families to the male-dominated Mīrāsī or Kalāvant musician castes. In both North and South India many women performers came from their own musical specialist communities in which the musical and professional inheritance passed from mother to daughter (Neuman 1980:100).

Professional women were expected to play dual or multiple roles in the social and cultural lives of their patrons. As performers of largely erotic, light classical songs, women acted as performers and courtesans; they performed in Hindu temples yet were also expected to serve (sexually) priests and patrons. Professional women performed at private clubs and in Rajput and Muslim courts, singing and dancing for private patrons, rulers, and members of the court, yet also were expected to demonstrate skills in poetry and art, and to serve nobles and club members. In general, the dual role of professional women as musicians and as courtesans or prostitutes adversely affected their social status; even among hereditary musicians, the overall status of women performers was low. Sometimes even accompanying a female musician negatively affected the status of male musicians as well.

Before the twentieth century, women's musical education took place outside the musical lineage (*gharānā*) system occupied exclusively by men. This highly regarded

FIGURE 1 *Nauṭaṅki* urban folk-theater dancer performing in Banaras, 1978. Photo by Edward O. Henry.

system, which provided a structure for the training and maintenance of essentially all the classical and some of the light classical music in North India, initially existed outside the realm of women's traditions. Instead, women learned music from other women (especially their mothers), and from Mīrāsī and other professional musicians with relatively low social status, particularly accompanists.

In their journey from stigmatized to respected performers, professional women arranged to learn music from hereditary specialists and ultimately became disciples of well-known master musicians. Today, women's names can be found in the teaching lines of the great masters, including Alladiya Khan of the Jaipur *gharānā*, Abdul Karim Khan of the Kirana *gharānā*, and Bade Ghulam Ali Khan of the Patiala *gharānā*.

Since the mid-twentieth century, many nonhereditary women musicians have entered the mainstream through a more broadly developed system of music education and greater family support for women studying music. The mandatory lineage, once a prerequisite for involvement in any classical, light classical, or theatrical media, has been relaxed. As a result, some musicians today do not trace their lineage to a specific musician caste or line, yet have developed highly regarded skills as instrumentalists and vocalists. Nevertheless the increased numbers of women students and performers, especially in South India, reflect a rise in amateur musicianship more than a boom in active professional musicians (L'Armand and L'Armand 1978).

Most female performers have until recently divided their education and performance between the two disciplines of music and dance. Indeed, it is difficult to separate women's participation in music and dance in North India prior to the twentieth century. In South Indian traditions, a close connection between the two continues even today. In a typical court or private club performance, women have been expected to demonstrate multiple artistic skills, and especially to dance while singing. In northern regions the vocal form *ṭhumrī* and the *kathak* dance are closely related, as are the *padam* vocal form and the *bharata nāṭyam* dance of South India.

Women's musical participation is also intertwined with theater. South Asian societies have expected professional women, as entertainers exhibiting grace in performing music and dance and reciting poetry, to demonstrate social and movement skills equivalent to those of a male actor. In some regions, professional women have participated in regional and folk theater (figure 1), often acting in alluring roles and performing erotic songs and dances for entertainment. Until the twentieth century women did not act on stage: men always played female roles.

Women in the twentieth century have had opportunities to perform in public contexts similar to those of men. While their musical options (including repertoire) are still more limited than men's, women vocalists have become well-known performers of light classical songs (*ṭhumrī* and ghazal), and the classical *khyāl*, but not *dhrupad*. Women's names appear in musician rosters at festivals and concerts, in articles, and in books; many play instruments. But their numbers remain considerably smaller than those of men; it is especially rare to see a female accompanist. The instruments women play are almost exclusively stringed instruments; they seldom play wind or percussion instruments.

MUSICAL GENRES

Throughout South Asia, where there are extremes in urban and rural lifestyles, where Islam, Hinduism, Buddhism, Christianity, and other religions all play important roles in everyday life, and where caste and class have played a significant role in the lives of women and men for many generations, numerous musical genres exist. Vocal forms that have been especially popular among women include *khyāl* in the Hindustani classical tradition and *pallavi* and *kriti* in the Karnatak; bhajan and *padam* adopted from the religious sphere; ghazal, *ṭhumrī*, *jāvali*, and *filmī gīt* in the light classical and popular traditions.

Classical and light classical vocal genres

Women entered the classical music sphere in North India first as performers of light classical songs, particularly *ṭhumrī* [see HINDUSTANI VOCAL MUSIC]. Originating in the seventeenth century, *ṭhumrī* was sung in the courts and salons of North India and was especially popular among courtesans (*tawāif*) until the mid-twentieth century. Performers during this time period also used *ṭhumrī* as a vehicle for interpretive dance (*abhinaya*), expressing sentiments as well as scenes with facial, hand, and body movements that added to the interpretation of their typically erotic songs. Even today *ṭhumrī* is one of the most popular genres sung by women (Manuel 1989:65). Another popular form among women is the ghazal, which courtesans often sang in Muslim courts.

There is no historical evidence of women performing the classical *dhrupad* form of the sixteenth- and seventeenth-century Hindu and Muslim courts, but some well-known *ṭhumrī* singers of the late nineteenth and early twentieth centuries did seize the opportunity to perform the later *khyāl* form by arranging to work with some of the great teachers of the period. As a result, women began to perform *khyāl* in public performance contexts beginning in the late nineteenth century (Post 1992:103). While the light classical genre *ṭhumrī* was characterized by a relatively short performance that stressed a romantic text, *khyāl* was a highly regarded classical genre that included extensive improvisation. By the end of the nineteenth century, *khyāl* had enjoyed a place in the courts and on the stage for over a hundred years, so the opportunity to learn and perform this genre allowed women to be more easily accepted into the male-dominated classical performance world. In recent decades, women have become widely accepted as *khyāl* singers throughout North India.

In the twentieth century, South Indian women have earned acclaim for their *kriti* performances. Like *khyāl* in North India, *kriti* is considered the primary classical genre of South Indian vocal music. Unlike some of the lighter classical forms that women also perform, such as *jāvaḷi* and *padam*, *kriti* songs are extended pieces that require a greater degree of improvisation.

Devotional music

Women perform the Hindu devotional song genre, bhajan, in several contexts, including public concert performances by popular North and South Indian female vocalists. Like bhajans, the religious genre *kīrtan* is also performed by women. In another religious sphere, the Bāuls of Bengal often perform religious songs with women in their ensembles. Well-known women soloists accompany their songs on stringed or percussion instruments. Among Muslims, men perform most religious music, but Sunni women regularly sing hymns during the *milād* assemblies, which celebrate the birth of the Prophet Muhammad.

Classical instrumental music

Some of the earliest South Asian literature contains references to women playing musical instruments. Rajput and Mughal miniature paintings from the sixteenth to nineteenth centuries frequently depict women playing instruments, and court records include references to women who played stringed instruments and sometimes percussion. Yet nowadays it is relatively rare for South Asian women to perform classical instrumental music in public. Some women have distinguished themselves as performers on the sarod, sitar, and violin in North India and the vina (plucked lute) in South India, but they are relatively few in number compared with male instrumental-

> References to specific women who performed before the twentieth century are rare, but by the mid-twentieth century women musicians began to be identified as individuals.

ists, who have performed as soloists and accompanists in both North and South India for many generations.

Popular traditions

Current popular-music traditions are highly influenced by the conventions of film music, popular throughout India since the 1940s and 1950s. Film music (*filmī gīt*) is the most widely produced popular music in South Asia, both in the film and recording industries. The Indian cinema typically integrates speech, song, and dance; thus it has been natural for professional women to move into this medium. Women have sung film music since the beginning of Indian sound film in the 1930s, first as actress-singers and later in the 1940s as playback singers [see FILM MUSIC]. Their position in the film industry, like their place in the arts in earlier centuries, has been structured by their desire for social support as performers and their concern regarding the social stigma that surrounds such very public performance practices.

In the popular-music industry, the performances of some professional women who began their careers in the earlier years of this century, such as the ghazals of Begum Akhtar and the film songs of Lata Mangeshkar and her sister, Asha Bhosle, have paved a more comfortable path for women. Popular forms among women include the *dādrā* and ghazal, rendered in a popular style; pop ghazal in particular has played an important role in the music industry in recent years.

Whereas patrons in the nineteenth and early twentieth centuries expected courtesans to perform *ṭhumrī* with interpretive dance gestures, now film music and pop ghazals constitute the primary repertoire of courtesans living in the red light districts of urban India.

TWENTIETH-CENTURY PERFORMERS

References to specific women who performed before the twentieth century are rare, but by the mid-twentieth century women musicians began to be identified as individuals and to be celebrated for their performances of classical music. Sources from the turn of the century describe musical performances of individual women in the salons and courts; literature from the second half of the century discusses women on stage, in films, and on commercial recordings. Women's active involvement in classical and light classical performance has paved the way for their peers and students to continue to provide valuable and innovative interpretation of music in South Asia.

Many, though not all, of the best-known female singers of the twentieth century came from professional families. Some of the earliest singers of this class to be recognized as individual performers were Malka Jan and Gauhar Jan of Calcutta, Zohra Bai of Agra, and Janki Bai of Allahabad. They performed in the courts and private clubs of North India, and also had opportunities to perform publicly on the stage, in early sound films, and on commercial recordings. Their training included singing *ṭhumrī* and dancing, especially with expressive dance gestures. Of these women,

Gauhar Jan earned renown not only for her *ṭhumrī* singing but also for her classical *khyāl*.

As women moved from the private world of the court, the intimate musical gathering (*mehfil*), and the temple into the public-performance sphere in the first half of the twentieth century, they continued to perform as singers and dancers, both as courtesans and as respectable musicians. Among women in classical music, Kesarbai Kerkar has probably received the most public recognition. Born in Goa in 1892, she studied with Ramkrishnabua Vaze and Barkat Ullah Khan, but ultimately was a disciple of Alladiya Khan. She distinguished herself in music for many years as a *khyāl* singer, seldom singing the light classical forms that were more often associated with female vocalists.

Mogubai Kurdikar, born in Goa in 1904, began her professional career dancing and singing (figure 2). When the opportunity arose, she chose to study vocal music with Alladiya Khan and became a highly regarded performer and teacher. Among her successful students is her daughter Kishori Amonkar. Hirabai Barodekar, a student of Abdul Wahid Khan and Abdul Karim Khan, sang on the Marāṭhi stage as well as the concert platform. She distinguished herself both as an actress (she was the first woman to play female lead roles in the Marāṭhi theater) and as a *ṭhumrī* and *khyāl* singer. Gangubai Hangal also played an important role in music during this period. Born in South India but trained in Maharashtra in the Hindustani tradition, she was a disciple of Sawai Gandharva of the Kirana *gharānā* 'musical tradition'. She sang *khyāl*, *ṭhumrī*, and bhajan. Kesarbai Kerkar, Mogubai Kurdikar, Hirabai Barodekar, and Gangubai Hangal each played an important role for women in music by insisting on changes in performance practice and gaining public recognition and respect.

Other North Indian vocalists include Siddeshwari Devi, a highly respected light classical singer born in Varanasi in 1903, and Begum Akhtar, who was born Akhtari Bai Faizabadi in 1914 in Uttar Pradesh. Known as a *ṭhumrī* and ghazal singer, Begum Akhtar studied with Abdul Wahid Khan of the Kirana *gharānā*. Roshanara Begum, born in 1922 in Calcutta, also studied with a Kirana *gharānā* singer, Abdul Karim Khan. Her mother, Chandra Begum, was a singer and disciple of Abdul Haq. Rasoolanbai, born in 1902, was a singer of *ṭhumrī* and the Punjabi-style *ṭappā*. She

FIGURE 2 The North Indian vocalist Mogubai Kurdikar, c. 1976. National Centre for the Performing Arts, Bombay.

studied with Shammu Khan. These women were known more for their light classical singing, especially *ṭhumrī,* than classical performances, but sought to enhance the expressivity of their musical interpretations rather than continuing the tradition of employing erotic dance gestures.

Other women who have been well known as public performers during the twentieth century include Hirabai Barodekar's sister, Sarasvatibai Rane, and Prabha Atre, both students of Suresh Babu Mane and Hirabai Barodekar. Nirmala Devi, Manik Verma, and Parveen Sultana are well known as *ṭhumrī* singers. Lakshmi Shankar, originally from Mysore, was a student of Abdul Rahiman Khan and is respected for her ability to sing in both Karnatak and Hindustani styles; she is especially famous for her *ṭhumrī* and bhajan singing.

In the Karnatak tradition, the performer who has carried the tradition for women for much of the twentieth century is M. S. Subbulakshmi. Born in Madurai, she studied primarily with her mother, Vina Shanmukhavadivu, who was a vina player. M. S. Subbulakshmi has maintained a broad repertoire that includes classical and light classical forms such as *kriti, tillāna,* and *jāvaḷi,* as well as devotional songs. She is probably best known for her bhajan singing. Other women who have distinguished themselves in the Karnatak tradition include D. K. Pattamal, M. L. Vasantakumari, and Vina Dhanammal.

Women instrumentalists in the classical traditions are still relatively rare. One renowned Hindustani sarod player is Sharan Rani Mathur, who began her study as a dancer. She is a disciple of Ustad Allauddin Khan and Ustad Ali Akbar Khan. Annapurna also became well known as an instrumentalist. A sitar and *surbahār* player, she studied with her father, Allauddin Khan.

In the realm of popular music, Lata Mangeshkar is regarded as the most important female film playback singer in the Indian film industry. Daughter of the actor-musician Dinanath Mangeshkar, Lata studied with her father and began her career as a child actress-singer in Marathi films in 1942. Her sister Asha Bhosle has also won great acclaim as a playback artist since the late 1940s, and since that time they have recorded songs as playback artists for thousands of films. They have numerous audio recordings to their credit, and have presented many live performances to teeming audiences around the world. Of the same generation was Geeta Dutt, a popular film singer who performed from the 1940s into the 1960s.

WOMEN'S FOLK TRADITIONS

Village and urban women in South Asia take part in musical events on a regular basis in the family and the neighborhood. Women generally sing songs connected with specific cultural contexts, such as life-cycle songs, seasonal and festival songs, and work songs.

In village and urban neighborhoods, women encounter musical restrictions similar to those experienced by women in the professional music sphere. Most village women do sing and dance, but their songs are limited to certain song genres; they perform primarily among women; and their songs are generally not integrated with men's song traditions.

As in many cultures, South Asian village women contribute musically to their community with life-cycle songs. Both Hindu and Muslim communities have documented wedding songs sung by women for hundreds of years. The wedding cycle includes specific rituals and traditions in which village and, sometimes, professional women participate. Before, during, and after the male-dominated marriage ceremony, women sing songs of joy, songs that tease and taunt, and songs that express the bride's sadness as she moves from her home to the village of her husband's family.

Music at a typical Hindu wedding consists of simultaneous performances by separate social (and gender) groups. While a priest chants, men connected with the groom's party may be engaged in instrumental music, and women of various ages connected with the bride's family sing. In Kangra, Himachal Pradesh, girls and women sing *suhāg* songs for luck and blessing, *gālī* insult songs, bhajans, and ritual songs that relate directly to specific acts performed during the wedding ceremony. *Suhāg* songs express the sadness of departure from the village, and the loss of friendship among girls (Narayan 1986:64).

Boyā dūrā tā desā var tole andā nī
merā naram kalejā toṛe andā nī
dekho dekho saiyo nī mere hāth saje
hāth saie hue nāl mahendivāṅ nī
dekho dekho saiyo nī mere ḍolī chalī
saiyāṅ rondyāṅ mahalāṅ chavāriānde

Father sought and brought a groom from a distant land.
My tender heart is breaking.
Look, look, girlfriends, my hands are decorated,
My hands are decorated with henna.
Look, look, girlfriends, my palanquin is setting off,
My girlfriends weep from the palace balconies.

Birth songs sung by women serve to appease the gods and to invoke health and well-being for a child. Women's singing in celebration of the birth of a son shows the preference for male children in traditional families, for many fewer songs are sung surrounding the birth of a daughter.

Women sing seasonal songs connected with events within the family and agricultural practices in the community. In some regions, a woman sings specific songs to express her feelings about separation from her husband or to celebrate the seasonal return of her married daughters when they visit their maternal family and village.

Village women also sing work songs. The most common in this category are grinding songs and those sung while laboring in the rice fields, transplanting paddy. In Karnataka, Tuluva women sing *pāḍdana* songs in call-and-response form while transplanting paddy. These narrative songs describe the exploits of spirits (*bhūta*) (Claus 1991:137).

FIGURE 3 Ḍholī woman plays a *ḍhol* at the entrance to Bhattiyaniji Devi temple in Jasol, Rajasthan, 1977. Photo by Amy Catlin.

Women and men in tribal villages dance and sing songs at social dances that take place in conjunction with the agricultural seasons. Among the Muṇḍas and Santals of eastern India, women sing and dance together in a tightly formed line while men play the drum or flute and dance separately [see MUSIC AND DANCE: NORTHERN AREA, figure 6]. The *baha* (flower festival), *sohrae* (harvest festival), and *kadam* (karam tree festival) songs constitute the largest repertoire, although there are a number of other smaller social contexts for music and dance. The *baha* or flower festival focuses on fertility and features separate songs for men and women. Dancing and singing, women sing songs with descriptions of their activities and containing images from the natural world (Archer 1974:250).

The trees
The forest
Has decked itself in beauty
I will go for leaf-cups
And make my body
Beautiful with flowers

Women's singing in celebration of the birth of a son shows the preference for male children in traditional families, for many fewer songs are sung surrounding the birth of a daughter.

In the religious sphere, women in many parts of India have embraced a devotional bhakti cult that was established around the eleventh century. South Asian women have found that through bhakti or devotion to a deity, they have direct access to the gods without involving a male priest (figure 3). In both rural and urban areas, singing songs that are both devotional and at times erotic has been popular throughout India as a vehicle for women's musical expression of bhakti. Women, on the one hand, have adopted the practice of bhajan and *kīrtan* singing, especially in neighborhood gatherings in both village and urban contexts. Women's groups that sing bhajans provide religious, musical, and social experiences for their members. On the other hand, the most popular Islamic devotional song form, qawwali, has not been adopted by women except in popular film renditions, which emphasize erotic rather than devotional elements of the text.

REFERENCES

Altekar, A. S. 1956. *The Position of Women in Hindu Civilization.* Banaras: Motilal Banarsidass.

Archer, William G. 1974. *The Hill of Flutes.* Pittsburgh: University of Pittsburgh Press.

———. 1985. *Songs for the Bride: Wedding Rites of Rural India.* New York: Columbia University Press.

Chandra, Moti. 1973. *The World of Courtesans.* Delhi: Vikas Publishing House.

Claus, Peter J. 1991. "Kin Songs." In *Gender, Genre, and Power in South Asian Expressive Traditions,* ed. Arjun Appadurai, Frank Korom, and Margaret Mills, 136–177. Philadelphia: University of Pennyslvania Press.

Dasasarma, Amala. 1993. *Musicians of India: Past and Present Gharanas of Hindustani Music and Genealogies.* Calcutta: Naya Prokash.

Erdman, Joan L. 1978. "The Maharaja's Musicians: The Organization of Cultural Performance at Jaipur in the Nineteenth Century." In *American Studies in the Anthropology of India,* ed. Sylvia Vatuk, 342–367. New Delhi: Manohar.

Imam, Hakim Mohammad Karam. 1959. "Melody through the Centuries." *Sangeet Natak Akademi Bulletin* 11/12:13–26.

L'Armand, Kathleen, and Adrian L'Armand. 1978. "Music in Madras: The Urbanization of a Cultural Tradition." In *Eight Urban Musical Cultures,* ed. Bruno Nettl, 115–145. Urbana: University of Illinois Press.

Manuel, Peter L. 1988. *Popular Musics of the Non-Western World.* New York: Oxford University Press.

———. 1989. *Thumri in Historical and Stylistic Perspectives.* Banaras: Motilal Banarsidass.

Marglin, Frédérique Apffel. 1985. *Wives of the God-King: The Rituals of the Devadasis of Puri.* Delhi: Oxford University Press.

Narayan, Kirin. 1986. "Birds on a Branch: Girlfriends and Wedding Songs in Kangra." *Ethos* 14(1):47–75.

Neuman, Daniel. 1980. *The Life of Music in North India: The Organization of an Artistic Tradition.* Detroit: Wayne State University Press.

Post, Jennifer C. 1982. "Marathi and Konkani Women in Hindustani Music, 1880–1940." Ph.D. dissertation, University of Minnesota.

———. 1992. "Professional Women in Indian Music: The Death of the Courtesan Tradition." In *Women and Music in Cross-Cultural Perspective,* ed. Ellen Koskoff, 97–109. New York: Greenwood Press.

Raghunathji, K. 1884. "Bombay Dancing Girls." *The Indian Antiquary* 13:165–178.

Sharma, Amal Das. 1993. *Musicians of India.* Calcutta: Naya Prokash.

Vatsyayan, Kapila. "In the Performing Arts." In *Indian Women,* ed. Devaki Jain, 291–297. New Delhi: Publications Division, Ministry of Information and Broadcasting.

Wade, Bonnie C. 1972. "Songs of Traditional Wedding Ceremonies in North India." *Yearbook of the International Folk Music Council* 4:57–65.

———. 1984. *Khyal: Creativity within North India's Classical Music Tradition*. Cambridge: Cambridge University Press.

Wade, Bonnie C., and Ann M. Pescatello. 1979. "The Status of Women in the Performing Arts of India and Iberia: Cross-Cultural Perspectives from Historical Accounts and Field Reports." In *The Performing Arts: Music and Dance*, ed. John Blacking and Joanne W. Kealiinohomoku, 119–137. The Hague: Mouton.

Popular Artists and Their Audiences

Gregory D. Booth

The Popular Audience
Popular Artists and Indian Film Culture
Popular Artists and Styles Outside Film Culture
Rock and Pop Artists

The expression *popular artist* in South Asia generally refers to a singer or musician who performs popular, mediated music. Popular artists in the twentieth century may be categorized according to their relationships with various entertainment-industry phenomena or in terms of the geographic location, social identity, and size of the audience that patronizes them and consumes their products. Before the advent of the mass media, some actor-singers in urban theatrical forms achieved exceptional popularity, but their numbers were few and their fame was relatively localized.

FIGURE 1 An Indian popular-music cassette card illustrates the relatively greater emphasis given to the identity of the devotional genre than to the identities of the artists. Courtesy Tips Industries Pvt. Ltd.

Popular artist is used here in three general senses. First, it indicates artists whose appeal is widespread across South Asia and enhanced significantly by heavy mass-media exposure. Linguistic, cultural, and political barriers have tended to limit the number of artists who have achieved such truly supraregional stardom. Second, popular artists are those who perform regularly and professionally for the broadcast media, or for whom the production and sale of recordings are primary sources of income. Such artists are often stars in local, regional, or supraregional terms, but their stardom may be limited to a particular linguistic or devotional community. There are also many musicians who record as soloists for the popular media but have no claim to stardom at any level. As artistic but largely anonymous cogs in the industrial music machine, they may record only occasionally, or solely at the behest of record producers. To illustrate this phenomenon, figure 1 shows an Indian popular-music cassette cover emphasizing the devotional nature of the content; the artists' names appear only in small print at the lower right. The third sense in which "popular" may define a particular artist is its reference to musicians who derive their livelihood from the live performance of a mediated repertoire, in styles dominated by media stars. Any sense of stardom attached to such musicians is confined to a specific locality, city, or region.

The term *popular music* is used in this article to refer to the music performed by these three types of popular artists. In the twentieth century, it is largely either mediated or live music appropriated from media sources. Prior to this time, popular music encompassed well-liked songs and melodies widely disseminated by traveling musicians, mendicants, and musical-theater troupes.

THE POPULAR AUDIENCE

It will be helpful for the purposes of this article to think of South Asian societies in terms of three broad social categories: (1) the elite, a wealthy group composed of large landowning or business families who acquired the trappings of British colonial culture as status symbols in the early twentieth century; (2) the largely urban middle classes, who have sought English-language education and new (predominantly British-style) job skills as a means of upward social and financial mobility; and (3) the lower classes, who have remained tied to vernacular languages and more traditional patterns of behavior. The relative proportion of these groups to the entire society increases respectively; but the middle class, with increasing internal divisions, has absorbed numbers from both other groups. Education levels, income, religious and linguistic identity, and traditional caste affiliation all play a role in these divisions, and yet each familial instance offers a unique perspective on the negotiation of social status. These negotiations have included choices regarding the popular music a family is willing to consume.

Pre-1930 live audiences

Up to the early twentieth century, before the advent of the mass media, live audiences normally consumed popular musics (folk, theatrical, and devotional genres) within the context of fairs, religious celebrations, and life-cycle rituals. The regionally and linguistically specific audiences that attended traditional music drama—-genres such as *nauṭaṅkī* (Uttar Pradesh), *bhavāī* (Gujarat), *jātrā* (Bengal), *tamāśā* (Maharashtra), or the more explicitly religious *līlā* dramas of North India—are the earliest collective audiences. Most of these dramatic forms were outdoor traditions with no controlled consumption processes (tickets, limited access to performances, fixed and enclosed performance spaces), in contrast to nineteenth-century urban theatrical forms (see "Popular artists before the sound-film era," below). Normally villages, prominent individuals, or religious institutions directly sponsored these performances.

The mass audience since 1930

Since the early days of this century, a concert format based partly on European models has developed for the consumption of many popular musics. Initially the concert audience consisted largely of the educated middle and upper-middle classes, who intentionally adopted British social models as a means of demonstrating their upwardly mobile status. More recent rock-pop concerts held in some South Asian countries, especially India, attract a predominantly young, urban, and westward-looking audience.

The audience for recorded music prior to the 1930s comprised members of the South Asian elite classes who could afford the expensive new technology of gramophones. Significant factors in the subsequent growth of the popular music audience were the wide accessibility of inexpensive Japanese gramophones beginning around 1927 and the advent of Indian-language sound films in 1931. Film songs reached the middle and lower classes with ever-greater frequency and intensity via cinema, radio, and popular and street musicians, and permeated South Asian popular culture.

The late-twentieth-century audience consumes popular music in two distinct fashions: through attendance at live performances (with or without tickets), and through the purchase of mediated products (records, cassettes, videotapes). In much of contemporary South Asia, live performances and even mediated products rarely possess precise and exclusively popular, commercial identities. Expressions of devotion, social identity, or prestige are often tightly interwoven in popular-music production and performance. Thus, a free live concert of devotional bhajans in a Hindu temple or of qawwali near a Muslim shrine generally includes music that reflects the influence of the popular media, through repertoire choices, instrumentation, musical style, and choice of artists. In such contexts, performers may occupy dual roles as devotees and popular stars (of whatever status), and the audience similarly and simultaneously worships both their religious and musical idols.

Indirect consumption of popular music through radio, film, and (since the mid-1960s) television has been the dominant phenomenon in South Asian popular culture. The mediated audience has developed along the regional and linguistic lines of earlier premedia audiences. In some cases, political events arising from religious and ethnic conflicts have intensified specific associations between popular artists or styles and particular national, religious, or linguistic audiences. Popular music in South Asia appears increasingly fragmented in the late twentieth century, but Hindi film songs, as consumed on radio and in film, have remained at the core of the mass audience's experience of indigenous popular culture.

POPULAR ARTISTS AND INDIAN FILM CULTURE

Hindi film music stars

Film singers are the most famous popular musicians in South Asia. Audiences throughout the subcontinent have consumed their music in mediated and live forms. The first singers of film songs (*filmī gīt*) were film actors and actresses, such as the actor-singer Kundan Lal Saigal. By 1935, as technology made possible the separate recording of visual and sound sources, film studios increasingly employed trained singers to record the songs. These individuals, later known as playback singers, quickly became the stars of popular music. In the early days of the Hindi film music industry (1931–c. 1945), some actor/actress-singers were also music directors who both composed and sang film songs. Members of this group include Anil Biswas, Saraswati Devi, Ghulam Haider, Pankaj Mullick, and Govindrao Tembe. Most of these artists had received at least some classical music training. Other famous early film singers include the actress-singers Shanta Apte, Shamshad Begum, Noorjehan, Khurshid, Devika Rani, and Suraiya, and the actor-singers Rafique Ghaznavi and Surendranath.

A second generation of Hindi film singers arose in the mid-1940s whose members never acted in films; their role was solely to record songs off screen. The first playback singers were often artists who performed outside the film industry as well and thus had reputations independent of the film-song style and repertoire. Many artists of the 1940s–1950s established extraordinary degrees of popularity and fame as playback singers. The male stars in this group included Manna Dey, Talat Mahmood, Mukesh, Mohammad Rafi, and Kishore Kumar. Female playback singing from 1947 onward was increasingly dominated by two sisters, Lata Mangeshkar (figure 2) and Asha Bhosle. Lata Mangeshkar, who recorded her first major hit songs in 1947 and was still active in the late 1990s, is the most widely heard and the single most famous playback star of the Indian subcontinent. The public reception of her performances created a monolithic concept of popular female vocal style that continues to the present day. Other important female playback stars of the 1950s and 1960s include Geeta Dutt and Suman Kalyanpur.

The playback singers of the Hindi film industry dominated South Asian popular culture through the 1970s. Only in the 1980s were younger singers, especially female singers, able to make careers for themselves. Contemporary stars have maintained the

FIGURE 2 Lata Mangeshkar in a Bombay recording studio, c. 1955. Photo by Harish Bhimani.

vocal styles defined by Bhosle, Mangeshkar, Mukesh, and Rafi, but broad changes in popular culture have meant that none has equaled the prestige achieved by Lata Mangeshkar and her contemporaries. Playback singers of the 1980s and 1990s include the female artists Kavita Krishnamurthi, Anuradha Paudwal, and Alka Yagnik, and the male artists Mohammed Aziz, Nithin Mukesh, Vinod Rathole, and Suresh Wadkar.

The absence of significant competition from other repertoires or media until the 1970s compounded the dominance of film song in South Asian popular culture. Film culture's popularity led to live concert performances by the most famous playback singers, presenting their hits on stage without the intermediary cinematic images, and also to live star shows including both film stars and singers. Concerts by playback artists probably date from the late 1950s. Throughout India and the Indian diaspora, shows featuring playback singers, film stars, dancers, and musicians have become a staple of popular culture. Figure 3 shows an advertisement for a film-star show in the United States. In addition to pictures of the film stars featured, the pictures and names of the playback singers—Alka Yagnik, Ila Arun, Ashwini Bhave, and Bali Brahmbhatt—appear on the bottom row. The latter artist is better known for his Hindi pop releases.

Regional film singers

The dominance of the Hindi cinema led to the labeling of other linguistic cinema industries within India as "regional." The largest regional industries are those that produce Malayalam-, Tamil-, and Telugu-language films; these have popular playback artists comparable to those of the Hindi cinema and possessing similar star status. Notable Telugu film singers include P. Susheela, Ghantasala, and P. Bhanumathi. In the Tamil commercial cinema, Srinivasan, Jikki, A. M. Raja, and Jamunarani all acquired star status in the early 1950s. The careers of S. Janaki and T. M. Soundarajan paralleled those of Lata Mangeshkar and Mohammed Rafi in Hindi cinema during the 1960s. L. R. Ishwari, who specialized in songs that reflected Euro-

Early media stars came from a variety of backgrounds, including the classical tradition, the live stage traditions of western India, the world of courtesans, and the qawwali tradition of Sufi devotional music.

FIGURE 3 Poster for a typical film-culture star show at the Nassau Coliseum, Long Island, New York, 3 September 1994, shows featured actors in the center and featured playback singers at the bottom.

American jazz and pop styles, together with Shushila, Chitra, and, slightly later, S. P. Balasubramanium occupied a dominant position through the 1970s and early 1980s. K. J. Yesudas, whose career and reputation as a popular and classical artist grew steadily through the 1970s, is perhaps the most famous and popular of modern Tamil film singers. Others who sing for Tamil films in the 1990s include Unikrishnan, Manu, Minmini, and Sunanda. Ilayaraja is another very popular composer and singer in the Tamil film world [see POP MUSIC AND AUDIO-CASSETTE TECHNOLOGY: SOUTHERN AREA].

Artists aspiring to popularity and commercial success have relied heavily on the film-song repertoire since the 1940s. A 1995 cassette release of "gramophone songs" provides a contemporary example of this phenomenon from Sri Lanka; the tape contains rerecordings of popular songs from Sri Lankan music drama (*nādagama*) and Indian film songs as well. The cassette cover shows the highly popular vocalist Nandamalini listening (presumably) to one of the songs she will sing on her new release, songs whose original versions were consumed on 78-rpm gramophone records by the middle classes of the 1950s (figure 4). The market for the live repro-

FIGURE 4 A cassette card for Sri Lankan "gramophone songs" recorded by the popular vocalist Nandamalini. Photo courtesy SingLanka Ltd.

duction of film hits remains an important source of income for local singers, pop orchestras, and street bands. Local popular artists perform for all social classes throughout South Asia. Venues may include structured concerts but are more commonly processional or background music for public and private events, especially weddings.

POPULAR ARTISTS AND STYLES OUTSIDE FILM CULTURE

Popular artists before the sound-film era

The dominance of film culture in South Asia was at its most monolithic during the period roughly from 1940 to 1975, when alternative options for a readily accessible and inexpensive commercial popular music were almost nonexistent. Popular artists whose careers have existed independent of the film industry are consequently rare in this period. The most distinctive nonfilm careers in South Asian popular music are either those that were established prior to the film hegemony or those that developed along with the advent of mass-produced audio cassettes in the 1970s. Early media stars came from a variety of backgrounds, including the classical tradition, the live stage traditions of western India, the world of courtesans, and the qawwali tradition of Sufi devotional music. From its earliest years, the Indian recording industry, dominated by the Gramophone Company of India, segmented the popular audience along linguistic lines. The catalogues of South Indian music recorded on the HMV label between 1911 and 1933, for example, include songs in Tamil, Telugu, Sanskrit, Malayalam, and Canarese by a variety of male and female singers.

Nineteenth-century urban theatrical forms produced a small number of identifiable popular artists prior to the advent of the mass media. Marathi *nāṭya saṅgīt* 'musical drama', Parsi musical theater, and in some instances the more rural Marathi folk theater, *tamāśā*, were music and dance dramas performed in permanent, enclosed theaters with controlled access and scheduled, ticketed performances. The level of financial investment in such productions, the accompanying need for marketing efforts on a significant scale, and the resulting large audiences produced artists of popular reputation on a regional scale. Ranade (1986) mentions Marathi actor-singers such as Bhaburao Kolhatkar and Pandit Balkoba Natekar, who were active around the turn of the century. Some Marathi theater artists combined stage and media careers, including such early-twentieth-century stars as Balgandharva and Master Krishnarao Phulambrikar. Lata Mangeshkar's father, Dinanath Mangeshkar, was another celebrated singer and theater-company owner from this tradition. The classical training that these actor-singers possessed created a complex but strongly classical musical identity. Parsi musical theater doubtless produced similarly well-known but probably less classically oriented musicians within the Bombay area. Some *tamāśā* artists may have had local popular reputations based on their regular performances at the Aryabhushan Theater in Pune.

Some of the earliest recording artists in South Asia were women performers who belonged to the professional courtesan class of entertainer (*tawāif*). Gauhar Jan, Malka Jan, and Janki Bai are three such artists whose recordings have recently been rereleased (Spottswood 1993). Perhaps the most important member of this group is Begum Akhtar Faizabadi, whose voice is among the most important in popular South Asian music. During her career (based on live concert performance, radio, and the elite market for LPs) Begum Akhtar sang a variety of light classical genres such as *ṭhumrī, dādrā,* and ghazal. Her performances were extremely well received by the middle and upper classes of India and Pakistan, who sought an accessible but refined alternative to the growing dominance and perceived vulgarity of film song.

Popular classical musicians

Among the many musicians who perform classical music are those whose musical versatility and personal appeal have helped them achieve a high degree of popularity and fame through mediated and live performances. The late vocalist Bade Ghulam Ali Khan (1903–1965) and the mandolin virtuoso U. Srinivas (b. 1969) offer two examples of this phenomenon. Many respected classical vocalists, however, have recorded and performed light classical and/or devotional music genres with much commercial success. Dr. Balamuralikrishna, S. P. Balasubramanium, the Bombay Sisters, Kumar Gandharva, Faiyaz Khan, Maharajapuram Sandanam, M. S. Subbalakshmi, Omkarnath Thakur, and Narayanrao Vyas all made their music readily accessible to a relatively large, mostly middle-class audience. Instrumentalists such as Hariprasad Chaurasia (*bāṅsurī* 'flute'), Kadri Gopalnath (saxophone), Zakir Hussain (tabla), Bismillah Khan (*śahnāī* 'oboe'), Ravi Kiran (Karnatak *goṭṭuvāḍyam* 'lute played with a slide'), A. K. C. Natarajan (clarinet), and Ravi Shankar (sitar) could also be considered popular artists on the basis of their mass appeal and commercial success.

Popular styles and artists since 1970

The cassette revolution of the 1970s significantly expanded the possibilities for direct and indirect popular music consumption [see POP MUSIC AND AUDIO-CASSETTE TECHNOLOGY, both articles]. The relatively inexpensive and durable nature of audiocassettes and cassette players encouraged the production of recordings targeted at markets delineated along linguistic, religious, and regional lines. Commercial recordings and live concerts generally reflect such divisions through their packaging and performance context, respectively. In Sri Lanka, for example, artists such as Amaradeva, Sanant Idrasingha, Edward Jayakori, Gunadasa Kapuge, and Victor Ratnayaka all sing Sinhalese lyrics to a combination of Indian and Sri Lankan melodies and instruments in a style well received by the Sinhalese middle class.

In India, popular musicians who have avoided a primary association with Indian film culture have specialized in particular traditional music genres. The first artists to build popular careers independent of the film industry focused on the romantic/philosophical Urdu-language ghazal and the Hindu devotional bhajan. Artists in both styles have gained recognition by relying on middle-class consumption of recorded cassettes and live concerts. Much of the audience is common to both genres; but there are potentially divisive socioreligious implications associated with the secular but strongly Muslim-inflected ghazal, and the explicitly Hindu devotional bhajan.

Ghazal artists

The careers of two Pakistani musicians, Ghulam Ali and Mehdi Hasan, signaled the beginnings of a career path for artists who wanted popularity without the perceived compromises of the film world. These male singers performed the ghazal—a philosophic or romantic poem in Urdu, organized in couplets, with a specific rhyme scheme [see HINDUSTANI VOCAL MUSIC]—which appealed to audiences that wanted light, easily consumed music without the obvious commerciality of film music. Iqbal Bano is another Pakistani ghazal singer who established her popularity in the early 1970s. Pakistan's commitment to the Urdu language—and perhaps a need to establish an alternative to Indian film songs—provided ghazals with especially strong levels of public and private support.

More popular ghazal singers appeared in the mid-1970s and 1980s. In contrast to the first stars of this genre, who were primarily Pakistani Muslims, many new ghazal stars were Indian Hindus. They sang in styles clearly reminiscent of film-song crooning, and sometimes in a less rigorous Urdu as well. The musical accompaniment similarly reflected the eclectic instrumentation and melodic freedom of film song. The Udhas brothers—Pankaj, Manhar, and Nirmal—were early proponents of this lighter ghazal. Jagjit and Chitra Singh, and the unrelated but stylistically similar Bhupinder and Mitalee Singh, also made family careers from ghazal performance. More recently, the Pakistani singer Ataullah Khan has achieved great success in this field. These performers are appreciated by Asians from a variety of regions as well as the diaspora. The relative refinement of the ghazal style has allowed artists to find a very profitable middle ground between the disparate classical and film genres. Ghazals have been marketed both as mediated products and in public concerts, attended by largely middle-class audiences.

Popular devotional music

Many Hindu ghazal artists have also released recordings of devotional Hindu songs (bhajans). Such performances range from solo virtuoso pieces to congregational songs. Although packaging and song texts are distinctive, modern bhajans are musically similar to ghazals. The inclusion of temple bells, small hand cymbals, or a responsorial chorus are common distinguishing features of the bhajan that replicate the devotional context and performance style. Anup Jalota and Hari Om Sharan have specialized in this style, and the ghazal singer Pankaj Udhas has also recorded many bhajans. Among classical artists who have released popular devotional recordings, Bangalore A. R. Ramani Ammal typified this mid-twentieth-century trend, and Dr. P. B. Srinivas, Dr. Balamuralikrishna, and Dr. S. S. Govindarajan continue the practice in the later twentieth century.

Artists often target specific audiences by focusing their Hindu devotional song recordings on a particular deity or guru, such as Anup Jalota's songs in praise of Shirdi ke Sai Baba. In one sense such recordings are commercial ventures, but they

Since the early 1990s, MTV has proven an especially potent source of inspiration for both young artists and their young audiences. India in particular has become one of the largest MTV audiences in the world.

are also often the artists' personal expressions of devotion. These recordings further illustrate the multileveled nature of South Asian musical culture, and the intersection of religious devotion with both the classical and popular worlds of music, on the part of both artists and audiences. People listen to Hindu devotional tapes in private homes and in temples.

Within an increasingly fragmented audience for popular devotional music, relatively small and usually socially distinct groups support a variety of musical styles and artists. Religion and language are the two important criteria that help distinguish these audience-artist relationships. Following ghazal and bhajan singers, the artists who have the greatest claim to meaningful star status are those of the Muslim ecstatic qawwali tradition [see PAKISTAN: DEVOTIONAL MUSIC]. Qawwāls who sang this music, such as Kaloo Qawwal and Nur Mia Qawwal, were among the earliest commercial recording artists. The best-known qawwali singers of the late twentieth century are the Sabri Brothers (Haji Ghulam Farid and Haji Maqbool Ahmed) and the late Nusrat Fateh Ali Khan (1949–1997), although many other artists, such as Abdul Rahman Kanchwalla and Aziz Mia, record and perform qawwali.

Many other devotional styles are performed by popular artists whose music reaches a geographically and numerically limited audience. Among the most distinctive in terms of content, style, and region are the devotional songs of the Sikh religion (*gurbāṇī*), of which recordings exist by many specialist Punjabi artists, including Harjinder Singh Srinagar Walle and Harinder Singh Faridkot Walle.

Bhangra and other popular folk-music artists

Mediated folk-music styles, strongly influenced by film music and European-American pop, are significant popular musics. The Punjab region is responsible for one of the most widely consumed secular popular musics in India, the folk-based bhangra. Bhujangy is the most popular traditional song and dance troupe that performs in this style. The group performs in exoticized versions of traditional Punjabi costume to the accompaniment of primarily traditional instruments (such as the *ḍhol* 'large barrel drum' and harmonium) [see PUNJAB, figure 1]. In the hands of urbanized expatriate Punjabis such as Malkit Singh (of Birmingham, England), bhangra has also developed into a contemporary pop style. Although many of bhangra's most successful media stars are from the Indian diaspora, the enthusiastic audience for this music includes both young South Asians (both within and beyond South Asia), and young people of European and American descent. Sardool Sikandar and Gurdas Maan are vocalists who appeal to most modern bhangra fans.

Like many other popular "folk" traditions, bhangra clearly exhibits a new urban style with a rural, traditional basis. Earlier popular Punjabi artists such as Surinder Shinda usually sang in a complex and elusive Punjabi, but the simpler lyrics of recent bhangra songs have addressed issues of urbanization and negotiated the complex multicultural identities of many "westernized" Punjabis. In the 1990s, singers often combine bhangra music with rap styles; Precious P. and Deepak Khanzanchi are bhangra stars who have followed this trend toward an increasingly syncretic music.

Other folk-dance musics have also evolved into commercial styles, including the *ḍāṇḍiā rās* and *rās garbā*. These have both retained their original function as group dance musics, and unlike bhangra, have not developed into nightclub music danced to by couples. As such they have produced fewer named artists than has bhangra. Recordings tend to be largely instrumental, and thus highlight few singers. The popular Portuguese-influenced dance form *bailā* is common at social functions and parties in Sri Lanka; artists who may have cultural or hereditary links to Portuguese culture often perform it. M. S. Fernando was an important *bailā* musician in the 1950s–1960s; the unrelated C. T. Fernando is currently prominent. On a local level, popular orchestras can often establish themselves as the preferred group in a given style, and thus achieve some local recognition.

The singer Ila Arun has added a distinctive dimension to the folk/popular spectrum, becoming one of the most popular commercial artists of the mid-1990s. Her career advanced significantly after she made a series of folk-inflected film-song recordings in which her rough, low-pitched voice and vulgar or suggestive lyrics contrasted with the film heroine's high-pitched voice and innocent lyrics. Her recordings and live concerts are widely popular, and emphasize modern arrangements of Rajasthani folk music.

ROCK AND POP ARTISTS

An almost completely separate category of popular artists comprises musicians who have modeled their music and images on Euro-American popular culture. The careers of South Asian rock-pop artists are closely tied to changing attitudes among South Asian youth, the indigenous recording industries, and the growing availability of Euro-American music models either via cassette and compact disc or through improved satellite coverage. Since the early 1990s, MTV has proven an especially potent source of inspiration for both young artists and their young audiences. India in particular has become one of the largest MTV audiences in the world. The number of artists attempting to achieve success in the rock and pop world is growing daily throughout much of the subcontinent.

Global pop in South Asian languages

Major pop hits modeled on American genres but with clear Indian stylistic features, and sung in Hindi, have been appearing at least since the 1970s. One of the first such hits using American rock and pop styles was a Hindi film song by music director R. D. Burman, "Dam māro dam" from the 1971 film *Hare Rama Hare Krishna*. Without a ready market for independent pop music, however, this recording remained a rock-oriented film song. Almost ten years later another pop film song, "Āp jaisā koī," from *Qurbani* 'Sacrifice', earned fame not for its composers, Kalyanji-Anandji, as is typical of film songs, but for its singer, Nazia Hassan, who was born in India but was living in London at the time. Hassan was able to follow up the film song's success with an independent album of Hindi-language pop, *Disco Deewane* 'Disco Madness'. The cassette album was a commercial success, but the audience was not yet large enough to sustain support for such enterprises. Later efforts by Hassan with her brother Zoheb were unsuccessful. Remo Fernandes met with greater success producing Hindi pop in the 1980s, as did Runa Laila, an early pioneer in restructuring traditional South Asian music with rock/pop beats and instruments. An example is Laila's recordings of Muslim devotional classics such as "Shabaz qalandar" with electric guitar and synthesizer band (Laila n.d.).

By the mid-1980s, Sharon Prabhakar and Shweta Shetty among others had achieved renown for Hindi-language versions of international popular styles. Prabhakar often sings in multiple languages, quite likely in order to develop a national rather than a linguistic market. A similar use of standard global pop music with indigenous languages has appeared in Bangladesh, where singers such as Tapan Chaudhuri, Laki Akhand, Azam Khan, and Firoz Shai have pursued solo careers in the late 1980s and early 1990s. Nepal also has its own native-language pop singers, including Anup Mahajan, Dinesh "Leon," Uma Gurung, and Prakash C. Shrestha.

South Asian guitar bands

In addition to mainstream pop music, a louder and more aggressive South Asian rock style developed in the 1970s and 1980s. Artists used steady back-beat rhythms, guitars, synthesizers, and vocals in English and indigenous languages, modified by considerable reverberation. The earliest layer of South Asian rock music developed through the late 1970s, largely in the major cities of India and Pakistan. In general, groups assumed iconoclastic and intellectual postures, often copying the Western styles but performing original music. Bombay's Western aspect and global economic activity may explain the higher number of pop-rock groups in this city than anywhere else in the subcontinent. The Bombay-based band Rock Machine was one early and successful group; the lead singer, Uday Benegal, remains one of India's most popular rock singers.

Most rock groups have religiously, linguistically, and nationally mixed membership, and some include resident Europeans as well as Hindus, Christians, and Muslims. By the mid-1980s, most major Indian cities had at least one professional or semiprofessional rock band, famous among them being Core (Delhi), 13 AD (Cochin), and Shiva (Calcutta). In the 1990s, a number of rock groups are active in Kathmandu, Nepal, including Axe, a four-man guitar band, and the trio Kalind. In Bangladesh, contemporary rock-oriented bands include Feed Back, Renesa, Chimes, and War Faze. Like their contemporaries abroad, these Bengali groups attempt to combine recent trends in international pop-rock music styles and instrumentation with references to their indigenous music culture. They mix standard rock instrumentation with Bengali instruments such as the tabla drums or the one-stringed *ektār*, sing Bengali lyrics, and refer to local issues. Many regularly incorporate Bengali folk melodies in their compositions and performances.

In contrast to northern guitar bands, Sri Lankan pop music incorporates a contemporary version of Portuguese musical features. Groups emphasize synthesizer sounds in addition to guitars, and often employ clearly Latin American instrumental touches such as *timbales* or *tres*. Sri Lankans often simply call pop music "group music"; it is popular among the primarily non-English-speaking working classes.

The rock and pop audience

In major cities, audiences listen to international pop music in European- or American-style nightclubs and discothèques. Hotels also offer venues for popular music consumption; prestige, exclusivity, and novelty are important factors in the success of these locations. In an increasingly liberalized and middle-class urban India, international pop culture and marketing are steering developments in youth culture.

The most recent venues for this music are pubs, rock bars, and cocktail lounges, where this international pop trend of the 1990s has grown phenomenally. The music in such clubs is a mixture of international pop, Hindi film song, and indigenous pop performed by rappers such as Baba Seghal or Kamal Sidhu. Pop artists rearrange film songs with rock or disco beats and synthesizer melodies, and add raps in Hindi and English. Recordings exist on all the major Indian music labels (Venus, Tips, T Series, and so on). Generally these products appeal through a combination of familiarity (old songs) and modernity (new rhythms and instruments) represented by the music itself, rather than by a specific artist's identity or reputation.

South Asian groups and singers have only recently been able to compete technically and technologically with their Western counterparts. A major source of audience appeal has stemmed from the production of music that *sounds* Asian, at least in part, catering to a young audience that does not necessarily seek to reject its Asian heritage but nevertheless seeks the excitement and prestige of Euro-American youth culture. Journalist Arvind Kumar considers the "multifaceted, multilayered" nature of South Asian society: ". . . the youth of Pakistan who might enjoy listening to Western music, but most of all want to express *themselves* [emphasis added] through music. This younger generation is into denims and sneakers, yet never too far from its native music" (Kumar 1992:29).

Unlike the large audiences that appear regularly for foreign touring groups and shows, the audience for indigenous rock music has not grown significantly since the late 1980s. The audiences that choose to listen to the syncretic musical styles or the blatantly imitative ones reflect the conflicting directions of originality and imitation inherent in the South Asian rock and pop scene. While the more sophisticated, perhaps radical, outward-looking college students and intellectuals may patronize artists playing Western rock music, the broadest audience consists of consumers who want to hear Euro-American pop styles in a language they can understand. Alisha Chinai has earned a reputation by catering to the South Asian interest in Madonna, recasting both the image and the music of that global star in South Asian cultural terms and in the Hindi language (Chinai 1989).

Rock concerts, often sponsored by commercial concerns or by colleges, have taken place in most Indian cities. The increased coverage of MTV broadcasts on Indian television, and related marketing exposure means that unlike their predecessors, younger bands such as the MTV-inspired Agni or McGill have found larger audiences willing to support them. Among other things, this increasingly global marketing has resulted in the unlikely phenomenon of an Algerian pop-*rai* artist, Cheb Khaled, achieving success by performing this urban North African popular music in the Hindi language.

REFERENCES

Baily, John, and Paul Oliver, eds. 1988. *Popular Music* 7(2), entire issue on *South Asia and the West.*

Bhimani, Harish. 1995. *In Search of Lata Mangeshkar.* New Delhi: HarperCollins Publishers India Pvt. Ltd.

Chinai, Alisha. 1989. *Madonna-Jaadoo.* Gramophone Company of India CD-PSLP5111. Compact disc.

Hassan, Nazia. ?1980s. *Disco Deewane.* Audio cassette. Label and no. unknown.

Kumar, Arvind. 1992. "Signs of the Times." *India Currents,* Sept., 29.

Laila, Runa. n.d. *Runa Sings Shabaz Qalandar: Non Stop Dhamal.* Double Apple, Apple 1062. Audio cassette.

Manuel, Peter. 1988. *Popular Musics of the Non-Western World.* New York: Oxford University Press.

Pinto, Monaesha. 1989. "Rock, A Bye?" *Playback and Fast Forward,* May, 15–21.

Ranade, Ashok. 1986. *Stage Music of Maharashtra.* New Delhi: Sangeet Natak Akademi.

Spottswood, Richard. 1993. *Vintage Music from India: Early Twentieth Century Classical and Light-Classical Music.* Rounder Records CD 1083. Compact disc.

Music and Nationalism

Charles Capwell

Like many political entities of the present day, the countries of South Asia comprise geographical units that have undergone phases of integration and fragmentation. The modern concept of nationhood came to South Asia in the colonial and postcolonial periods, during which both colonizers and colonized alike, willingly or not, forged national units from disparate ethnic, political, linguistic, and religious groups. Among the tools used to forge these new nations were hundreds of nationalistic songs. Two of these, both by the Bengali poet and Nobel laureate Rabindranath Tagore, eventually became the national anthems of India and Bangladesh.

THE UPRISING AND LOYALIST NATIONALISM

Nationalist feeling against British colonialism in the Indian subcontinent first manifested itself during the nineteenth century as a rising sentiment against a foreign overlord. During the 1857 struggle between the British and the Indians they governed—viewed either as a "Mutiny" or a "first war of independence"—British surveillance of native activities included the collection of song texts in areas of the country where anti-British sentiment was of concern. After the 1857 uprising, when the British Parliament replaced the East India Company as the official governing body of the Indian colonies, the Indian-British relationship was never the same. The British government now viewed the inhabitants of India as subjects of the crown, and Victoria eventually achieved her wish to be invested with the title Empress of India. Her Indian subjects were compelled to seek a political identity that either conformed to or opposed this imperial concept.

The post-1857 development of nationalism divided Indians into two camps, loyalist (pro-British) and independent (pro-Indian). Calcutta became a center for pro-British nationalist activity, as it was the capital of British India until 1911, when the capital was moved to New Delhi. The musical leader of the loyalist camp was clearly Sourindro Mohun Tagore, the most prominent musical scholar of the time by virtue of his wealth and position as well as his learning. Tagore was also typical of those whose nationalism expressed an intense pride in India's cultural heritage, including fervent devotion to the monarchy.

Along with his elder brother Jotindro Mohun Tagore, Sourindro was among the most important patrons of theater and music. His interests led him to establish schools for musical training, and he adopted the colonial model of instruction in an attempt to make musical accomplishment and enjoyment suitable for educated Bengali gentlemen. Explicit in this activity was Sourindro's desire to show that Indian music was an advanced art with a codified theory and technique, as logically and scientifically based as European music and equally suited to pedagogical transmission. In order to assert the value of "native music," however, and to change the Indian elite's low opinion of musical accomplishment, Sourindro Mohun had to use the methods and attitudes of the colonizers.

Contemporary comments reveal this transformation in progress. On August 21, 1873, the *Englishman* reported the following words of H. Woodrow, Director of Public Instruction:

> A few years back . . . one of his [Tagore's] native friends (a very learned man) had told him that "He would sooner see his son dead at his feet than allow him to learn music." . . . Little did he think to see the day when the Bengalis would get over their prejudices and begin to set to learning this branch of the Fine Arts in right earnest.

In a similar vein, a writer for the *Indian Mirror* (February 18, 1877) rhetorically asks:

> Will our European readers believe us when we say that no son could hum a tune, or sing a line in the presence of his father, without seriously insulting the latter . . . . The real credit of having brought life and progress into the music of the land, belongs to Maharaja Joteendro Mohun Tagore and his brother Dr. Saurindro Mohun Tagore.

Finally, an observation made by the one-time protégé of Sourindro, Krishnadhana Bandyopadhyaya, shows the ironic influence of one colonial attitude on the nascent nationalism (Bandyopadhyaya 1875:5–6; emphasis added):

> [A]mong Indians there is a surprising prejudice that "knowledge of music is for princes and fakirs" [and by implication, not for the respectable classes]. But nowadays, *having seen the love of music among European householders,* contemporary Bengalis have begun to have some faith in music.

The proverb Bandyopadhyaya quotes here underscores a traditional Bengali view of music as either an aristocractic indulgence, implying frivolity and debauchery, or a devotional activity meant for those who lived without the cares and duties of ordinary people—not a suitable interest or pastime for the average householder.

Notation

Sourindro Mohun and other loyalists believed that a significant way to improve the status of Indian music was to demonstrate that it was rational, scientific, and therefore capable of being notated. Confronted with the role of notation in European music, with its corollary notions of intervallic, scalar, and rhythmic precision,

Sourindro and friends concluded that notation is an essential component of any advanced musical system. Musical notation thus became a field of nationalistic contention (Clark 1874); ironically, Sourindro Mohun pushed for a Bengali letter notation, devised by his teacher and colleague Kshetramohan Gosvami, while Krishnadhana Bandyopadhyaya received the backing of British educational authorities for Western notation. Sourindro Mohun and his supporters became known as the "nationalist" party (Clark 1874:257) for their adherence to the Bengali notation (Tagore 1965:366, 380):

> Every nation that has a music of its own has also its own system of notation for writing it. Whether that system be an advanced one or not [the music] cannot be correctly expressed in the notation of another nation, however improved and scientific it may be. . . . Every civilized nation that has a music of its own has also a system of notation adapted to the peculiarities of that music.

Interestingly, Sourindro Mohun's view of notation as uniquely national did not interfere with his fervently loyalist stance in the political realm. A conservative Hindu, he wrote a book documenting the historical tradition of Hindu loyalty to the British crown, and dedicated many sumptuously illustrated and decorated books of music to the empress and other members of the royal family. Perhaps the most sumptuous of all was a traditionally illustrated collection of ragas for the Empress Victoria on her jubilee (1887). In the work Sourindro described each of thirty-six ragas in hand-colored lithographs, and presented original songs praising the empress. As they were meant to flatter the empress, Sourindro used Western notation for these songs.

"God Save the Queen"

Sourindro's involvement in the National Anthem Project illustrates his loyalist brand of nationalism. This project resulted in his publishing at his own expense his translation of "God Save the Queen" set to a variety of tunes based on Indian ragas, parodying the original tune of the anthem.

Despite the effort and expense this project cost him, Sourindro Mohun concluded that the anthem was perhaps best left as it was, since the tune was no more alien to many Indians than would be the tunes he created.

Sourindro Mohun was undoubtedly the most active and recognized scholar of his day in the new musical interface between native and colonial cultures, but he was not alone. Other musicians, such as the Maharashtran singer Vishnu Digambar Paluskar, joined him in efforts to "rehabilitate" Indian music as a worthy representative of nationalist aspirations. Paluskar, with his exemplary devotion to music and his stress on moral probity, helped make the institutional study of musical performance acceptable to the growing middle class. As the patronage of princes and landlords declined, the middle class became the mainstay of classical music.

COMMUNAL SENTIMENT

This reformation of Indian attitudes toward Indian music had to take into account the differing opinions and involvement of Hindus and Muslims. The rising awareness of India's greatness in nineteenth-century South Asia, stimulated by Western orientalist research and the nascent middle class, was paired with an awareness of "The Wonder That Was India" (the title of a standard Western text on Indian history)

When King Wajid Ali went into exile in a Calcutta suburb, he took with him many excellent musicians who contributed to the growing importance of Calcutta as a musical center.

(Basham 1968). This wondrous heritage was located primarily in an ancient Hindu past. Moreover, British scholarship in the colonial period fostered an opposition between Hinduism and Islam by attributing the decline of Sanskrit learning to the alien imposition of Perso-Arabic culture by Turkic-speaking rulers.

Musicians and scholars such as Tagore and Kshetramohan Gosvami agreed with Hindu nationalists about the need to revive a great tradition, and also attributed what they considered the regrettable condition of their musical traditions to the imposed, alien Islamic culture. The absence of notation once again plays a role in this issue (Gosvami 1879:85):

> If the practice of notation is so old, then how did we come to lose it? To this we may answer that as India, through time and chance came into the hands of *yavanas* [Muslims], acquaintance with various of our treatises was lost, and by the neglect of Sanskrit treatises, canonic music was also neglected; but the very *yavana* kings, who bore such malice toward Hindu learning, were so far attracted by the excellence of our music that though they abandoned its other parts, they could in no way relinquish its practice, and they initiated the custom of the oral transmission of music. Therefore, on account of its prevalence, over the course of time, this also became the custom for Hindus . . . .

Remarks such as these about the "malice toward Hindu learning" of Muslim kings and their attraction to "the excellence of *our* music" constitute some of the seeds of today's Hindu chauvinistic nationalism. In recent times, to cite a different example, ethnomusicologist Peter Manuel has observed in the North Indian cassette industry an epiphenomenon pairing music and chauvinism—the distribution of recordings of inflammatory anti-Muslim speeches by Hindu nationalist rabble rousers. In particular, a song text on a 1990 Hindi-language cassette incites Hindus to destroy the site of a mosque built by the Mughal Emperor Aurangzeb, which Hindus claim to be the birthplace of Rama (Manuel 1993:252–53):

> The time has come, wake up, young people, and go to Lucknow,
> you must vow to build Ram's temple . . .
> Don't play their farcical game of acting in a courtroom
> Liberate the *janmbhoomi* [birthplace] of the jewel of the house of Raghukul
> If they don't heed your words, whip out your swords . . .
> Face our enemies with courage, now isn't the time for contemplation

But it was a little over a century ago, in the Hindu community, particularly in the seat of colonial government, that the ground was prepared for such expressions of communal enmity (communal in the sense of Hindu-Muslim). Hindu clerks and other intermediaries felt increasingly confident of their influence and power because of their alliance with colonial trade and government. The British and their Hindu partners often viewed Muslims as either uneducated and lower-class—generally the case in Bengal, where many were converts from the lowest castes—or decadent and corrupt, as for example the king of Oudh, Wajid Ali Shah, whom the British deposed in 1857.

When Wajid Ali went into exile in a Calcutta suburb, he took with him many excellent musicians who contributed to the growing importance of Calcutta as a musical center. Yet Hindus always referred to the exiled king—himself a poet, dancer, and musician—as a representative and patron of a light, frivolous style of art that was effeminate and debilitating. They unfavorably contrasted the "light classical" vocal forms (like *ṭhumrī* and ghazal), which employed much embellishment and for which Wajid Ali's court city of Lucknow was famous, with the more austere, manly, profound style of *dhrupad* derived from Hindu devotional expression.

Anti-British sentiment

The British saw little in the character of their Bengali business intermediaries and clerks that conformed to their own concept of virility, despite the manly view of Hindu music. Bengalis acquiesced in this assessment, and the English-language magazine *Modern Review* regularly contained advertisements for bodybuilding programs that would enable India's youth to come to her defense with strong bodies. A band of guerilla patriots epitomized this nationalist physical self-improvement program. They were the heroes of Bankim Chandra Chatterji's famous novel *Anandamath*; in the story, the leader of this band, Bhavan, is asked a question by Mahendra, whom he has just rescued from the British (Chatterji 1941:58–59):

> "Then what makes this difference between the British and the Indian soldier?"
>
> "Because the British soldier would never run away even to save his life. The Indian soldier runs away when he begins to perspire; he seeks cold drinks. . . . British soldiers would not run away even if dozens of cannon balls should fall in their midst. . . . Virtues like these cannot be plucked from trees like ripe fruit. We have to acquire them by patient practice and unyielding perseverance."

Prior to this unflattering comparison between British valor and native shirking of duty, Bhavan had just finished singing a hymn of praise to the Motherland that begins with the salutation "Bande Mātaram!" (Hail, Mother!). Shortly afterward, Bhavan brings Mahendra to his group's ashram headquarters to meet Satya, their holy man and leader, who then proceeds to enlighten Mahendra on their nationalist agenda (Chatterji 1941:62–63):

> Mahendra, following the Mahatma, soon found himself in a spacious room with a high ceiling . . . . Gradually a picture revealed itself to him. It was a gigantic, imposing, resplendent, yes almost living map of India.
>
> "This is our Mother India as she was before the British conquest," the Mahatma said. "Now say *Bande Mataram.*"
>
> "*Bande Mataram,*" Mahendra said with much feeling. . . .
>
> [T]hey entered into a dark tunnel to emerge into another, even darker room. . . . There Mahendra saw a map of India in rags and tears. . . .

"This is what our Mother India is today," the Mahatma said. . . . "Those that talk of winning India's independence by peaceful means do not know the British, I am sure. Please say *Bande Mataram*."

Mahendra shouted *Bande Mataram*, and bowed low in reverence with tears in his eyes.

They went through another dark tunnel and suddenly faced a heavenly light inside another room.

The effulgence of the light was radiating from the map of a golden India—bright, beautiful, full of glory and dignity!

"This is our Mother as she is destined to be," the Mahatma said; and he in turn began to chant *Bande Mataram*.

The text of the nationalist hymn "Bande Mātaram," first published in a Bengali magazine in 1880, rapidly became the rallying cry for independence seekers. It also inspired later nationalist and spiritual leaders like Aurobindo Ghose and Mohandas K. Gandhi. The multitalented artist Rabindranath Tagore first sang the song at a political Congress Party meeting in Calcutta in 1896. His tune, in the Hindustani *rāg deś*, had already been published eleven years earlier in *Balok*, a children's magazine, but that publication had included only the first seven lines because of its difficult classical style (Bhattacharya 1978:79).

The creation of new songs to stir up Indian patriotism developed simultaneously with Sourindro Mohun Tagore's active fostering of "Hindu" music as a loyal subject of the Empire. Sourindro Mohun composed works praising the Imperial Family to demonstrate to the rulers the value of India's music as a possession worthy of admiration, while the nationalist songs, such as "Bande Mātaram," used music to carry a nationalist message effectively and affectively to the colonized mass.

THE PARTITION OF BENGAL AND RABINDRANATH TAGORE

Rabindranath Tagore is not particularly remembered for his political activity in the independence struggle, although he did devote part of his artistic output to the nationalist cause. The 1905 partition of Bengal by India's colonial rulers fired his national pride. This political act was aimed at weakening the demands of the educated, partly Westernized Hindu elite for greater influence in the country's judicial, educational, and political institutions. Prior to this time, Tagore had written twenty-four nationalistic songs, all but two of which had been in the Hindustani classical style. But in 1905 alone he wrote twenty-two more, nearly half of which were set to tunes based on folk songs of the Bāuls, a Bengali religious sect (Ghosha 1962: 178).

Tagore's nationalistic sentiments were intimately tied to his feelings for his own native land. He expressed these in a musical style that he had come to admire while administering his family's country estates in East Bengal, rather than through the music of an alien, though naturalized, Hindustani classical tradition. Tagore not only drew on the music of the Bāuls, but used the sect's name as the title of the book in which he published his new songs. The best known among the collection is "Amar Sonar Bangla" 'My Golden Bengal', which was a natural choice for the national anthem of the newly named Bangladesh when that country (then East Pakistan) was victorious in the 1971 war of independence with West Pakistan.

The text of this song seems an innocuous tribute to the beautiful countryside of Bengal; yet its final verse (author's translation below) contains a sharp metaphor describing how many Indians felt about the way the British destroyed local industries and flooded the market with manufactured goods, especially cloth:

> Whatever wealth a poor man has I will place at your feet,
> I will not buy at another's house a hangman's noose for your necklace.

A lilting tune in compound duple meter conjures up a sweet image of rural Bengal. However, the official Bangladesh national-anthem version exhibits a martial quality. Arrangers have transformed the musical setting, like that of other national tunes in the region, to proclaim the idea of nationhood abroad in a postcolonial musical idiom by using the colonial legacy of harmony, counterpoint, and a military band arrangement.

IQBAL AND NAZRUL ISLAM

The Muslim community in the early twentieth century was more loyalist in its leanings, but nascent sentiment against the British was evolving. The Punjabi poet Muhammad Iqbal, for example, was among those whose nationalist and patriotic poems many Indians sang. According to Riffat Hasan, "Iqbal's *Tārānā-i Hindi* (The Song of India) became the unofficial national anthem of India" (Hasan 1971). Another Indian writer claimed in 1951 that the work "remains to this day the best patriotic poem written by any Indian poet in modern times. It comes nearest, in fact, to a truly non-communal national anthem of India" (Hasan 1971:139).

The Bengali Muslim poet Kazi Nazrul Islam was also an apostle of intercommunal unity in his nationalist poetry. He followed a populist Bengali tradition that recognized the common roots of Bengali culture among both Hindus and Muslims. But as Iqbal veered in his later work toward a concept of Muslim unity transcending state boundaries, Nazrul early in his life became a member of a socialist-oriented group within Congress that was marginal to the mainstream (Rahamana 1972:38).

In 1971, resurgent Bengali nationalism resulted in the war of independence against Pakistan and in the formation of Bangladesh. Rabindranath Tagore's quintessentially Bengali song "Amar Sonar Bangla" was selected as the national anthem. Perhaps the songs of Nazrul Islam could not compete against the poignant association of Tagore's song with the first partition of Bengal in 1905.

MADRAS AND THE NATIONALIST EXAMPLE OF BENGAL

Significant though Bengal was as the source of nationalistic musical expression (Baskaran 1981), the Madras poet Subramania Bharathi began writing nationalistic poems in the same year that Tagore published his Bāul collection (1905). He employed a simple style, and set the texts to versions of Tamil folk tunes. Then, in 1921, "A. S. Sadashiva Rao of Madurai drew pointed attention to the use of popular songs in inspiring nationalist activity in Bengal and advocated a similar usage in Madras" (Baskaran 1981:48).

Once initiated in Madras, the nationalistic song practice grew, and became firmly rooted through regular performances at political rallies and in staged dramas. The connection between the Congress Party and nationalist song was of particular importance in districts it controlled, for it was able to introduce printed books of nationalistic songs into school curricula (Baskaran 1981:54).

Following India's independence, Tagore's "Janaganamana" became the national anthem, thus confirming Bengal's musical precedence in the independence struggle. In fact, India has two national songs, "Janaganamana" and "Bande Mātaram." The latter song had become the national anthem by the time of independence, but some

Following India's independence in 1947, Tagore's song "Janaganamana" became the national anthem, thus confirming Bengal's musical precedence in the independence struggle.

Indians—primarily Muslims—objected to some of its verses, which they considered idolatrous in addressing Mother India as a goddess. Consequently the Congress Party limited it to the first seven verses in 1947 (Tagore's rendition at the 1896 Congress meeting had already confined it to those verses). At the 1947 United Nations meeting in which India participated as an independent nation, Tagore's "Janaganamana" was rendered instrumentally. Thereafter "Janaganamana" became the instrumental anthem, and the opening verses of "Bande Mātaram" became the vocal anthem (Bhattacharya 1978:14–15). These separate instrumental and vocal compositions continue to be the official anthems, although "Janaganamana" is more commonly used.

Sourindro Mohun Tagore, had he lived long enough, might have been surprised, even dismayed, by the dissolution of British hegemony in South Asia and by the proliferation of musical emblems for its previously united components. Nevertheless, his own nationalist aspirations for Indian music would certainly have been satisfied. The music schools for which he provided the first examples now exist throughout the nation, musical sophistication and accomplishment have become respectable, and Indian music has gained international recognition.

REFERENCES

Bandyopadhyaya, Krishnadhana. 1875 [1382]. *Gitasutrasara.* Calcutta: A. Mukharji & Co.

Basham, Arthur L. 1968 [1954]. *The Wonder That Was India: A Survey of the History and Culture of the Indian Sub-Continent before the Coming of the Muslims.* New York: Taplinger.

Baskaran, S[undararaj] Theodore. 1981. *The Message Bearers: The Nationalist Politics and the Entertainment Media in South India 1880–1945.* Madras: Cre–A.

Bhattacharya, Jagadish. 1978. *Bande Mātaram.* Calcutta: Kabi o Kabita Prakasana.

Capwell, Charles. 1991. "Marginality and Musicology in Nineteenth-Century Calcutta: The Case of Sourindro Mohun Tagore." In *Comparative Musicology and Anthropology of Music,* ed. Bruno Nettl and Philip Bohlman, 228–243. Chicago: University of Chicago Press.

Chatterji, Bankim Chandra. 1941. *Dawn over India,* trans. Basanta Koomar Roy. New York: Devin–Adair.

Clark, C. B. 1874. "Bengali Music." *Calcutta Review* LVII/CXVI:243–266.

Ghosha, Shantideva. 1962. *Rabindrasangita* (Songs of Rabindranath). Calcutta: Viswabharati Press.

[Gosvami], Kshetramohan S., trans. 1879. *Saṅgītasāra* (The Essence of Music), 2nd ed. Calcutta: Kaliprasanna Bandyopadhyay.

Harford, Frederick K. 1883. *On the Good That May Result to England and India from the Establishment of "God Save the Queen" as a National Anthem in Her Majesty's Eastern Empire.* London: Richard Bentley and Sons.

Hasan, Riffat. 1971. "The Development of Political Philosophy." In *Iqbal,* ed. Hafeez Malik, 136–158. New York and London: Columbia University Press.

Manuel, Peter. 1993. *Cassette Culture: Popular Music and Technology in North India.* Chicago and London: University of Chicago Press.

Rahamana, Ataura. 1972 [1379]. "*Najrulera rājnaitika o sāmājika cintadhāra.*" In *Najrula samikṣaṇa,* ed. Mohammad Manirujjamana, 36–55. Dacca: Ananda Prakashan.

Tagore, Rabindranath. 1905. *Baul.* n.p.

Tagore, Sourindro M. 1882. *The "National Anthem" Translated into Sanskrit and Bengali Verse and Set to Twelve Varieties of Indian Melody.* Calcutta: the author, printed by I. C. Bose & Co.

———. 1965. "Hindu Music." In *Hindu Music from Various Authors*, 3rd ed., 337–412. Varanasi: Chowkhamba Sanskrit Series Office.

Music Learning and Transmission

The ways people pass on knowledge from one generation to the next tell us much about society and the kind of value it places on learning and transmission, as well as about the nature of relationships between teachers and students. In South Asia, the phenomenon of sound has fascinated music scholars and performers since ancient times. While writers have pondered its essential nature, it has been practitioners who have imparted musical knowledge; thus the spoken word has played a far greater role in musical transmission than the written word. Children learn to sing, play instruments, and dance by seeing, hearing, and practicing. Established lineages of musicians pass on their knowledge and skills orally from master to disciple and father to son. Only since the late nineteeth century have music schools and other institutions arisen, introducing classrooms, standardized curricula, and written texts for music teaching. Likewise, only since that time have musical notation systems been adopted for preserving and teaching indigenous musical traditions.

Children in South Asia learn and practice both music and dance traditions from a young age. Here, young Brahmin boys dance as Radha (*front*) and Krishna (*behind*) in the *rās līlā* dance drama, Vrindavan, Uttar Pradesh, c. 1997. Photo by Kiran Chandra Roy, courtesy Mekhala Natavar.

Institutional Music Education: Northern Area

Andrew Burton Alter

Educational Pathfinders
Influential Twentieth-Century Publications
Institutional Education in the Late Twentieth Century

For many centuries, the master-disciple relationship has been the traditional form of training of classical musicians in the Indian subcontinent. This apprentice system—which continues today—has ensured the primarily oral transmission of musical knowledge through many generations of teachers and students [see THE CLASSICAL MASTER-DISCIPLE TRADITION]. However, since the end of the nineteenth century, various government institutions such as schools and universities have grappled with ways of adapting traditional teaching methods to institutional structures and systems. Oral processes of teaching and master-disciple relationships do not automatically lend themselves to classrooms, blackboards, and textbooks, but the adaptation of traditional teaching to the institutional setting has nevertheless become widespread.

In North India, no one system of music education is dominant through the whole geographical region; educators and performers employ a variety of strategies and approaches in educating their music students. Most musicians regard the idealized traditional teaching system, featuring the master-disciple relationship, as the basic model from which music educators develop their teaching methods. Several key pre-independence figures were in fact influential in molding traditional pedagogy to the institutional setting. Their efforts coincided with general trends of modernization and Westernization that permeated the subcontinent. As in other learned and scholarly disciplines, India not surprisingly adopted Western models of mass education for the field of music. No less influential in this process of institutionalization was the increased publication throughout the early twentieth century of books on the theory and practice of music in languages other than Sanskrit.

EDUCATIONAL PATHFINDERS

Sourindro Mohun Tagore of Bengal

The impulse to create a music teaching institution loosely based on Western models came to fruition first in Calcutta. The former headquarters of the British East India Company and capital of India, Calcutta was an important cultural and economic center where the forces of Westernization and modernization were strong; these forces undoubtedly influenced Raja Sourindro Mohun Tagore (1840–1914) when he founded the Bengal Music School in 1871. This was the first music school of its kind to offer not only diplomas to students, but also awards and titles to eminent musicians. At least five faculty members taught the students at this school using books and notation as teaching aids. Tagore was a keen advocate of Western ideas and fraternized freely with the British intelligentsia. His innovations in instrument construction and his ideas for cross-cultural concerts were part of an approach that was both Indian and British.

Raja Sourindro Mohun Tagore was not the only prominent figure in the arts who espoused Western living. At the end of the nineteenth century, many rulers of the so-called native states of India traveled widely throughout India and Europe and began to adopt Western dress, culinary taste, and decor in their palaces. They also hired Western tutors for their heirs. By 1900, English was the language of the aspiring elite, and for those lower in the Indian social hierarchy Western education began to appeal as a means for social mobility and advancement. Young students increasingly began to study abroad at English universities, and from the mid-1800s on, institutions of learning based on the European model began to spring up throughout India. The British administration fostered this development, initially by setting up the first Indian universities in Calcutta, Bombay, and Madras (all in 1857) and thereafter by providing grant-in-aid programs for the establishment of private colleges.

Sayajirao III of Baroda

One of the most progressive princely rulers with regard to education was the maharaja (or gaekwad) of Baroda (now Vadodara), Sayajirao III (1863–1940). Among the most significant of Sayajirao's innovations was the introduction of compulsory primary education throughout his princely state. He provided generous grants and endowments, ensuring that fees were kept to a minimum in high schools and colleges. Sayajirao's interest in education extended beyond the general curriculum to the field of music, and in 1886 he established the Bharatiya Sangeet Vidyalaya 'Indian Music School'. This school subsequently became the Faculty of Performing Arts at maharaja Sayajirao University of Baroda, founded under his auspices. Many if not all of the Maharaja's court musicians participated in some way at the music school.

Ustad Faiyaz Khan (1881–1950), of the Agra lineage and stylistic school (*gharānā*), was one of the most notable of the Baroda court musicians. He provides an interesting example of the relationship between a Baroda court musician and the maharaja's music school (Nag 1985). Most of Ustad Faiyaz Khan's teaching took place at his own house, where he upheld the traditional master-disciple relationship with his students. The maharaja did not restrict Faiyaz Khan—his most eminent musician—to the music school's classrooms, but let him teach students of his choice in his home. Other Baroda state musicians, for example Ustad Ata Hussain Khan (1899–1980), taught at the music school and earned considerable respect as teachers.

Madhavrao Scindia of Gwalior

Another ruler interested in Western ways and ideas but less concerned with social reform than Sayajirao was Maharaja Madhavrao Scindia of Gwalior (1873–1925). Gwalior, in modern Uttar Pradesh, was one of the richest states in India at the end of the nineteenth century, and was able to support numerous musicians and artisans. Musicians of the Gwalior *gharānā*, which was associated with the state, mostly found employment under the Maharaja and his family. In the early 1900s the maharaja founded the Madho Sangeet Mahavidyalaya 'Madhav Music College' along the lines of the earlier Baroda school. The ruler controlled the performing activities of court musicians both inside and outside the court. Most significant, he instructed seven of his court musicians to learn Indian music notation to use in teaching at his newly established school, a clear departure from traditional teaching methods.

Pandit V. N. Bhatkhande

The maharaja of Gwalior sought help in founding his school from one of the most important twentieth-century figures in Hindustani music, Pandit Vishnu Narayan Bhatkhande (1860–1936). Bhatkhande himself received much of his musical training from the musicians of the Gwalior *gharānā,* and became a friend and musical adviser to the maharaja of Gwalior. Since they both came from the state of Maharashtra, Bhatkhande's cultural affinity with the ruling family enhanced his ability to influence the maharaja.

Bhatkhande was a performing musician of considerable ability, but his scholarly contributions to music remain the achievements for which he is most remembered (Bhatkhande 1981, 1985). He grew up in Bombay, and completed a law degree while maintaining his interest in music. Widely read and widely respected, he was able to promote his vision for music education in North India through numerous publications and personal contacts. His firm belief that Hindustani music had reached a critical point motivated his actions. In his view, only a small minority of the Indian population respected and understood music, which thus risked becoming extinct. Those in the wider public domain who shunned classical music did so mainly because they associated it with decadent court life. Intent on remedying this situation, Bhatkhande sought to spread music appreciation to a broader audience using music publishing and education. He believed that efficient and modern instruction methods in music schools would lend respectability to music and increase the size of the appreciative audience. Notation, expanded and refined, could preserve dying traditions and aid in teaching.

In addition to helping establish the music school in Gwalior, Bhatkhande was instrumental during the 1920s and 1930s in founding music schools in other important urban centers such as Lucknow, Nagpur, and Bombay. His efforts were spurred by a nationalist feeling among the growing middle class, who were beginning to value the cultural significance of Hindustani music. From this social class came students keen to learn part of Indian culture that had been suppressed for over a century under British domination. From the 1930s onward, the number of music institutions in India increased rapidly. Education at all of these early schools was structured on the basis of class instruction, established curricula, and final examinations, a system that had developed out of Tagore's desire for westernization and Bhatkhande's principles of modern music education.

Pandit V. D. Paluskar

Like Bhatkhande, the outstanding musician and fellow member of the Gwalior *gharānā* Pandit Vishnu Digambar Paluskar was equally interested in the advancement of Indian culture and the preservation of music. Both men attended the great music conferences of the early decades of the twentieth century that propagated music revivalist intentions (Misra 1985). Paluskar established the Gandharva Sangeet Mahavidyalaya 'Gandharva Music College' in Lahore in 1901, and opened an affiliated music college in Bombay ten years later. His attitude toward music was closely tied to his strong religious beliefs, and he spent much time toward the end of his life singing only devotional songs and following ascetic Hindu practices. He linked his actions to his desire to rekindle Hindu culture and values. Paluskar's Bombay institution, now called the Akhil Bharatiya Gandharva Sangeet Mahavidyalaya 'All-India Gandharva Music College', has several affiliated institutions. In general, the schedule and teaching method at these institutions follow a curriculum and examination system based on educational principles similar to those in other music institutions in India.

INFLUENTIAL TWENTIETH-CENTURY PUBLICATIONS

The growth in institutional music education at the start of the twentieth century was followed in the 1930s and 1940s by the increased publication of material on music and music theory. Many performing musicians remained illiterate through the first part of the twentieth century, but a growing number of music students and scholars provided a market for these publications. Bhatkhande's own published work, which included collections of compositions as well as theoretical explanations, were the most influential in the Marathi and Hindi languages. They remain an important reference for music educators and students today.

The Sangeet Karyalaya 'Music Bureau', a publishing house specifically organized for the printing of music- and dance-related Hindi publications, was established in 1935. It continues to operate today from Hathras, in Uttar Pradesh, and is still responsible for many of the textbooks and much literature about music printed in Hindi. The Sangeet Karyalaya continues to publish most of Bhatkhande's books.

The Bhatkhande method

Bhatkhande's most influential works appear in two sets of volumes. The first is a lengthy explanation of North Indian music theory contained in four volumes under the title *Bhātkhaṅde Saṅgīt-Śāstra: Hiṅdustānī Saṅgīt-Paddhati* 'Bhatkhande's Musical Works: The Hindustani Music System', first published in Marathi during the 1920s. The second is a collection of musical compositions presented in six volumes entitled *Hiṅdustānī Saṅgīt-Paddhati: Kramik Pustak-Mālikā* 'The Hindustani Music System: Book Series'. This set of volumes was also first published in Marathi before appearing in Hindi during the 1950s. Both sets together are considered to be Bhatkhande's definitive treatise on music theory. While debate continues over the validity of some of his theoretical explanations, there is no doubt that the works have influenced countless musicians, students, and scholars.

The *Saṅgīt-Śāstra* imitates the teaching style of the master-disciple tradition, of which Bhatkhande was a part. The disciple sits at the master's feet, and music is sung and explained through a series of questions and answers. The work explores an exhaustive range of topics in this manner. Primary among these topics are Bhatkhande's parent-scale (*ṭhāṭ*) system of raga classification, his explanation of microtones (*śruti*), his efforts toward a standardized notation system, and his historical discussions of previous writers and treatises. Such a comprehensive treatment of music has attracted critics who question the applicability of his theories to actual music practice as well as certain details of his classification scheme. Nevertheless, the *Saṅgīt-śāstra* has succeeded in providing considerable uniformity in education circles on issues such as notation, parent-scale nomenclature, and conventions of sharp (*tīvra*) and flat (*komal*) note designation. The work has also provided a basis for the standardization of some terminology, although this has always been a vexing question in Hindustani music and remains problematic today.

Bhatkhande's *Kramik Pustak-Mālikā* differs from his *Saṅgīt-śāstra* in several important ways. The six-volume *Kramik Pustak-Mālikā* is a collection of compositions in many ragas. At the beginning of each volume the author presents a short clarification of terminology. Each chapter within each volume deals with a specific raga and begins with a short discussion of the peculiarities of the raga, including the important notes (*vādi* and *samvādi*) and the correct time of day for performance. Bhatkhande provides the ascending and descending scales of the raga as well as a

Many Indian universities have music in their curricula, and music instruction is more common now than it was at the beginning of the twentieth century.

short catch-phrase (*pakar*), then transcribes several compositions in the raga in Hindustani notation (*svarlipi*).

INSTITUTIONAL EDUCATION IN THE LATE TWENTIETH CENTURY

Bhatkhande's publications and his considerable influence on music education in the early twentieth century had far-reaching effects. His own intentions on the matter were quite clear, as the following quotation from an address he delivered to the first All-India Music Conference at Baroda in 1916 suggests (Neuman 1980:200):

> I cannot but hope that in a few years more there will be an easy system for the instruction of our music which will lend itself to mass education. Then will the ambition of India be fulfilled, for then the Indians will have music in the curricula of their Universities and music instruction will be common and universal.

In some respects, Bhatkhande's vision has been achieved. Many Indian universities have music in their curricula, and music instruction is more common now than it was at the beginning of the twentieth century.

Many decades later, however—and with the benefit of hindsight—some scholars and musicians are voicing their concerns about the current direction of music education in India. In spite of the good intentions of educators like Paluskar, Bhatkhande, and others, critics nowadays point to the problems of institutionalized music education and advocate the need for a reappraisal of instruction methods that have developed. The following statement by a present-day scholar and educator, Jayasri Banarjee, is representative of some of these views (Banarjee 1986:11):

> The present profile of Indian classical-music education, one must be frank, does not put up a devilishly splendid picture.... Caught between our regrets for the past and our fears of the future, we have been making do with many an uncertain and unthinking practice in the teaching of our classical music.

Banarjee suggests that the diversity of music instruction in present-day India can be described using three broad institutional categories. The first category includes those situations and institutions that ostensibly follow the master-disciple model [see THE CLASSICAL MASTER-DISCIPLE TRADITION]. The second category includes small, unaffiliated private music organizations that call themselves "schools," and the third includes government-funded universities and statutory institutions. These categories represent a loose generalization that facilitates the discussion of curricular emphases and pedagogic techniques. Music education within universities and statutory institutions, the third category, best represents the culmination of music-education policies that originated with early twentieth-century music scholars and thus receives greater emphasis below.

The master-disciple institutional model

Instruction following the master-disciple tradition can occur privately or under the auspices of an institution, but either system ensures that students receive extensive individual attention from their teacher over a lengthy period of time. The organization of the education system that occurs in this first institutional category depends primarily on two factors: the ideal image of the master-disciple tradition that the system claims to emulate, and the economic viability of maintaining such an ideal. Increasingly from the 1970s onward, individuals and institutions have claimed to follow the ideals of a master-disciple tradition, but the criteria they use for such an assertion are by no means universal. In reality, they follow master-disciple principles in many vague and indirect ways, but with only varying degrees of success. Nevertheless, some notable successes have been achieved (Alter 1994).

Private, unaffiliated music schools

The second category of music instruction that Banarjee discusses in her analysis includes the numerous so-called music schools and colleges in many towns throughout India. The standard of education in these schools and colleges is far from consistent. Teaching generally occurs in group classes and follows a nominal syllabus with various forms of evaluation. In some cases teachers are paid on a commission basis according to the number of students they draw to their classes; consequently, there is no upper limit to these classes. In general, no systematic attempt is made to maintain standards in these institutions. Teachers, administrators, and students create individual approaches to such instruction, and often emulate university teaching with limited success.

University music departments and music schools

The third and final category of instruction within music education encompasses university music departments and faculties and various statutory music schools that receive considerable government funding. Degrees and honors awarded by these institutions have become meaningful documentation of certain levels of achievement. Maharaja Sayajirao University of Baroda, Banaras Hindu University, Delhi University, and Rabindra Bharati in Calcutta, among others, all maintain faculties of performing arts that award music degrees. Similarly, a variety of statutory music schools including the Indira Kala Sangeet Viswavidyalaya 'The Indira University for Arts and Music' in Khairagarh (Madhya Pradesh), the Bhatkhande Sangeet Vidyapeet 'Bhatkhande School of Music' in Lucknow, and the Gandharva Sangeet Mahavidyalaya 'Gandharva Music College' in Bombay all award music degrees to their own students and to students at numerous affiliated institutions.

Each of the major institutions listed above sets its own entrance requirements for a course leading to a degree. An entrance examination and/or audition is a universal requirement. Although age is not always a criterion, the majority of students who enroll are at the postsecondary level and are usually seventeen years of age or older. Two degree systems operate concurrently: one, similar to Western institutions, grants bachelor's, master's, and doctoral degrees; the other designates levels of achievement according to Hindi terminology—*pratham* 'initial or primary', *madhyam* 'intermediate', *viśārad* 'advanced', and *nipuṇ* 'supplementary or final'. The B. Mus. and *viśārad* degrees are roughly equivalent (subject to individual institutional interpretation), as are the M. Mus. and *nipuṇ* degrees. A student's progress from one year to the next within these degree courses depends on passing practical examinations. Each institution's published prospectus clearly states the annual requirements for each course.

All such published curricula list the ragas and talas to be learned during the year, as well as specific requirements regarding the number and type of compositions in various ragas and genres. Students are required to learn these for practical performance and to be able to notate them correctly. In addition, students may learn to write various improvised model patterns and characteristic raga phrases. The list of ragas grows during the successive years of a course, often with specific attention to reviewing ragas from a more theoretical perspective in the final year. In general, education focuses on the soloist's melodic repertoire, although some institutions are now beginning to offer practical instruction in accompaniment instruments such as tabla and *pakhāvaj* 'barrel drum'.

A second curricular component comprises the theoretical and historical subjects to be covered in each year of a course. These range widely from biographical accounts of historical figures to the specific theories of music discussed in important historical treatises. Within these specifications, institutions develop their own progressions and emphases. Students at all institutions are often required at some stage to study Bhatkhande's theoretical works, as well as the theories presented in early Sanskrit music treatises. The emphasis on this aspect of a student's education varies from institution to institution.

Instruction occurs in classes of ten to twenty-five students. Classes are sometimes designated either specifically for practical training or for theory. Even so, the majority of classes emphasize the practical aspects of a student's musical skills. Student schedules include four to five classes per day, each taught by a different teacher and each of approximately fifty minutes' duration. Each class meets either two or three times a week. Generally, teachers explain the intricacies of various ragas and talas from their own individual perspective without specific reference to textbooks.

Practical training in music institutions is largely by rote learning. Each class usually focuses on the intricacies of a particular raga. The teacher sings a phrase, which the students repeat either as a group or individually. In a departure from master-disciple traditions, students often notate phrases as they are sung or soon afterward, and keep this notebook of phrases and compositions with them during all their classes. Teachers rarely make this a formal requirement, but it is now common practice.

From this brief description, it is possible to identify five main features of institutional music education in North India that set it apart from the traditional master-disciple system of training. First, institutionalized education follows structured curricula and syllabi that designate specific ragas and talas for study during any one year. Second, examinations are the basis for awarding degrees. Third, instruction occurs in classes of specific duration in which group teaching is the norm. Fourth, each student's education remains the responsibility of a variety of teachers, not just one master teacher. Finally, institutional education espouses an integrated approach to theoretical and practical training in which musical literacy and academic scholarship are valued. As the debate over the direction and purpose of institutionalized music education in North India continues today, teachers are forging their own adaptive strategies to balance traditional methods of instruction with the constraints of institutionalized education.

REFERENCES

Alter, Andrew B. 1994. "*Gurus, Shishyas* and Educators: Adaptive Strategies in Post-Colonial North Indian Music Institutions." In *Music-Cultures in Contact: Convergences and Collisions*, ed. Stephen Blum and Margaret J. Kartomi, 158–168. Sydney: Gordon and Breach.

———. 1997. "Key Processes in the Oral Transmission of Hindustani Vocal Music." *Journal of the Musicological Society of Australia* 20:61–83.

Banarjee, Jayasri. 1986. "The Methodology of Teaching Indian Classical Music: A Statement on the Problem." *Journal of the Sangeet Natak Akademi* 79:11–48.

Bhatkhande, Vishnu N. 1981 [1932]. *Bhātkhaṅde Saṅgīt-Śāstra: Hiṅdustānī Saṅgīt-Paddhati.* 4 vols. Hindi transl. Sudama Prasad Dube, et al. Hathras: Sangeet Karyalaya.

———. 1985 [1920–1937]. *Hiṅdustānī saṅgīt-paddhati: Kramik Pustak-Mālikā.* 6 vols. Hindi trans. Vaman N. Bhatt, et al. Hathras: Sangeet Karyalaya.

Misra, Susheela. 1985. *Music Makers of the Bhatkhande College of Hindustani Music.* Calcutta: Sangeet Research Academy.

Nag, Deepali. 1985. *Ustad Faiyaaz Khan.* New Delhi: Sangeet Natak Akademi.

Neuman, Daniel M. 1980. *The Life of Music in North India.* Detroit: Wayne State University Press.

Institutional Music Education: Southern Area

N. Ramanathan

Music Education in Schools and Universities
Music Institutions without Exams
Criticisms of Institution-Based Music Education

When music education in India is discussed, art music is usually the subject of reference. This is because systematic methods have been devised and adopted for teaching art music, whereas such systematic methods have been only rarely used in teaching the lighter forms of music or music used in other arts such as dance music. Normally, folk music and devotional music are not taught in formal settings, although there are a few exceptions. Folk music is taught at the Tamil Nadu Government Music College, for example. However, it is usually transmitted and absorbed in an informal manner in its natural settings. Devotional music is learned in the course of religious rituals and congregational singing.

There are, broadly speaking, two systems of art music recognized in India, South Indian or Karnatak (Carnatic or Karnatic as the British rulers spelled it) music and North Indian or Hindustani music. The southern area includes the four southern states of India: Andhra Pradesh, Tamil Nadu, Karnataka, and Kerala, as well as the Union territory of Pondicherry and the nation of Sri Lanka. In Sri Lanka, South Indian music is cultivated in the north, which is inhabited chiefly by Tamil-speaking people; Yazhpanam (Jaffna) is the main urban center. In the south, with the center at Colombo, it is the North Indian system that is popular.

The South Indian system is also taught and practiced elsewhere outside southern India. Institutions big and small teach Karnatak music throughout northern India, for example in the cities of Bombay, Delhi, and Calcutta, as well as in other parts of the world such as Singapore, Malaysia, South Africa, Australia, Europe, the United States, Mauritius, and the Persian Gulf countries—in other words, wherever there is a sizable South Indian population.

The North Indian, or Hindustani, system is also taught and practiced in other regions. In the south, Hindustani music is taught at a few schools, especially in Karnataka, Andhra Pradesh, and southern Sri Lanka. Although Hindustani music is studied in the south by people of both southern and northern origins, in the northern region it is chiefly those of southern origin who learn Karnatak music.

Finally, a number of institutions in the south offer training in Western music as well. Some of these prepare students for graded examinations conducted by institu-

Although Hindustani music is studied in the south by people of both southern and northern origins, in the northern region it is chiefly those of southern origin who learn Karnatak music.

tions like Trinity College, in the United Kingdom. (Only education in South Indian music is considered in what follows.)

MUSIC EDUCATION IN SCHOOLS AND UNIVERSITIES

Music education consists primarily of training in musical performance and the transmission of knowledge—theoretical understanding—about music. Normally, theoretical knowledge is imparted only in an institutional setting. In private training, theory is rarely taught, unless the teacher happens also to be a musicologist.

A music school is a place for teaching and learning music that is open to the public and has been set up by an organization that selects and appoints teachers. The institution's administration collects fees from students and obtains funds and grants from various other sources; it pays the teachers, cares for the musical instruments, builds up a library, and maintains the building and other facilities. The curriculum is usually drafted by a board consisting of experts on the subject, and the students are tested for proficiency by an examining board. Those judged as having successfully completed the course of study are awarded certificates referred to variously as degrees, diplomas, certificates, titles, and so on.

Music schools vary with respect to each of the above aspects of institutional education, as the following discussion indicates.

Degrees

A degree can be awarded only by a university to students enrolled in its music department or in one of its affiliated colleges. A university may also award a diploma or certificate. Some twenty-six universities currently offer education in South Indian music: five in Andhra Pradesh, three in Karnataka, two in Kerala, one in Pondicherry, seven in Tamil Nadu, four in Sri Lanka, and one each in the northern cities of Delhi, Banaras, Khairagarh, and Bombay. Almost all these universities have courses leading to a degree; in a few, diploma courses alone are offered.

Some universities have their own music departments and at the same time also govern courses taught in affiliated colleges; examples are Andhra University and the University of Madras. Some, such as Annamalai University and Tamil University, in Tamil Nadu, and Padmavathi Mahila Vishvavidyalaya in Andhra Pradesh, have no affiliated colleges. There are also universities like the Madurai Kamaraja (Tamil Nadu) and Nagarjuna University (Andhra Pradesh) that have no music departments but do have affiliated colleges running courses in music.

Various degrees are usually offered: the bachelor of arts (B.A.) and three graduate degrees—the master of arts (M.A.), master of philosophy (M.Phil.), and doctor of philosophy (Ph.D.). Requirements for these degrees in terms of course divisions and number of courses are similar to those prescribed in other disciplines, such as the social sciences, languages, and the hard sciences.

Certificates, diplomas, and titles

These usually represent short-term courses that may be conducted by universities (such as Kerala University and Sri Venkateswara University) or by examining boards set up or approved by the education departments of state governments (as in Tamil Nadu and Karnataka) or national governments (as in Sri Lanka, where the North Ceylon Oriental Music Society functions). In some cases the content of a university diploma course may almost equal that of the university degree. The difference between the two courses, in such cases, normally consists of a lower eligibility requirement for admission to the diploma course, and the absence of the kind of additional nonmusical courses—such as the study of languages—required for the degree.

Usually, institutions that conduct courses to prepare students for state or national examinations are themselves run by the state (for example, the Tamil Nadu Government Music College in Madras) or are recognized by the state government (the Teachers' College of Music of the Music Academy, also in Madras). In Andhra Pradesh, the state government runs a number of music "schools" that offer four-year certificate courses, and a number of music "colleges" that have the four-year certificate and a two-year diploma course as well. Very recently, these have become part of Telugu University, Hyderabad.

Examinations are also conducted independently by government bodies, and no institutions formally prepare students to take them (examples include the lower- and higher-grade Tamil Nadu state examinations and the junior, senior, and *vidwāth* 'advanced performance' levels of the Karnataka exams). Students taking these exams may be learning music privately from an individual teacher or may be enrolled in a music school but studying some other courses in music.

A private institution such as the Tamil-Isai Kalloori and Kalakshetra in Madras may also conduct its own examination and award a certificate.

Curriculum

Institutions of music education vary in terms of the course content, but a broad overview of the practical and theoretical elements that constitute the typical curriculum is possible. The performance syllabus is based primarily on music as it is played at a typical Karnatak concert. Theory consists of analyzing and understanding this music, its elements, the musical forms in practice, their history, and so on.

The practical curriculum

The contents of the practical syllabus can be divided roughly into six groups:

1. *Svara* exercises (singing and playing melodic passages using the Indian sol-fa syllables Sa, Ri, Ga, Ma, Pa, Dha, Ni) and simple songs with meaningful devotional texts and/or *svara* syllables, intended to inculcate a basic sense of music and tala. (These have no place in the typical concert.)
2. Compositions mastered in the second stage of training and presented in concert today, such as *varṇam*, *kriti*, the *svarajāti* of Syama Sastri, and the *ghana rāga pañcaratna* 'five weighty compositions' of Tyagaraja [see KARNATAK VOCAL AND INSTRUMENTAL MUSIC].
3. Areas of improvisation (*manodharma*), including *ālāpana*, *tānam*, *niraval*, and *svara kalpana* [see KARNATAK RAGA].
4. Groups of song compositions on a common theme or deity: for example, *navagraha kriti* 'songs on the nine houses (planets) in their deified form' and *kovur pañcaratna* 'five songs on the deity' of the main temple at Kovur, near Madras.

5. Classical compositions whose original tunes have been lost, but which are sung to melodies composed by later musicians; examples are the songs of Annamacharya, Purandara Dasa, and Muttuttandavar.
6. Songs used in conjunction with other art forms and for social activities. These include songs used in dance, such as *jāvaḷi*, *padam*, and *tillāna*; songs used in congregational singing (bhajans), such as the *utsava-sampradāya-kīrtana*; and songs used in music dramas such as the *Gīta Govinda* of Jayadeva, *Kṛshṇalīlātaraṅgiṇī* of Narayanatirtha, and *Naukācaritram* of Tyagaraja.

With regard to course content, we should note that institutions in southern states usually include songs either peculiar to that particular region or set in the language of that state. South Indian compositions were traditionally set to texts in Sanskrit, Telugu (Andhra Pradesh), Tamil (Tamil Nadu), and Kannada (Karnataka). Songs in Malayalam (of Kerala) are a recent addition.

In practical music training, students are expected to choose one area of specialization from the variety offered—voice, vina, violin, flute, *nāgasvaram* 'large oboe', and so on. But the course content is the same regardless of the option chosen, since in the Karnatak system the music is broadly the same whether one chooses to render it vocally or instrumentally. Many schools expect instrumental students to learn the music vocally first before playing it on their instruments, to enable them to express the "vocal" nature of the music through the instruments. The process of "culturing the voice" is also built into the practical training and not treated separately. Because of the vocal training required of instrumental students, some schools reduce the course content for students learning instrumental music.

Drums and other rhythm instruments, such as the *mridangam* 'barrel drum', *tavil* 'cylindrical drum', *kañjīrā* 'tamborine', and *ghaṭam* 'clay pot' are nonmelodic and hence require a different syllabus. The institutions in which they are taught are relatively few; a degree course in these instruments is offered by only one institution, Telugu University in Andhra Pradesh. Institutions offering courses in the *nāgasvaram*, however, invariably include courses for the *tavil* drum as well.

The music theory curriculum

The contents of current music theory curricula may be listed as follows:

1. General introduction to music, South Indian music in particular.
2. The melodic aspect: concepts like *nāda*, *svara*, and raga, with their classifications—that is, the features identifying different ragas [see KARNATAK RAGA].
3. Meter and rhythm elements of tala, and *laya* [see KARNATAK TALA].
4. Song text: alliteration and other structural features; theme content; signature of the composer (*mudra*).
5. Musical forms: *gītam*, *varṇam*, *kriti*, *ālāpana,* and so on.
6. Biographies, musical contributions, and musical styles of the important composers.
7. Notation.
8. Musical instruments: classification, construction, tuning, and playing techniques.
9. History: early musical systems, music treatises, and other literary and nonliterary sources.
10. Aesthetics: the aim of music, concert form, merits and faults in singing and playing.

11. Other musical systems: Hindustani music; Western music (including staff notation); and comparative studies.
12. Music in other arts and spheres: dance, dance drama, *harikathā*; devotion; occupations; and religious and social functions, such as temple worship and marriage.
13. Music and other disciplines: physics (acoustics); psychology; and anthropology.

Above the master's level, in the M.Phil. and Ph.D. courses the main focus of study is on research tools and methods, with the primary emphasis on thesis writing. Only a minimal number of additional courses is required.

Administration and funding

In India, universities and their affiliated colleges get financial assistance not only from state governments but also from the University Grants Commission, a body of the central government. This body lays down norms for the salaries disbursed by the state to the various levels of faculty, and also offers funding for research students and faculty research projects. (As a result, university teachers normally draw somewhat better salaries than their counterparts in the state-run nonuniversity institutions.)

The Grants Commission also prescribes norms with regard to the educational qualifications for faculty appointments; for example, the master of philosophy is the prerequisite for the lowest faculty level, lecturer. For music and other fine arts, the Grants Commission has made an exception whereby a performing musician (or practicing artist) from a respected tradition, although not in possession of a university degree, can be considered for appointment to a faculty.

Some university administrations permit teachers employed in schools and colleges to pursue degree courses without regular attendance in classes. They are referred to as "teacher candidates" or part-time students. There is also one rare instance of a "distance education" program offering a B.A. in music. The Institute of Correspondence Education of the University of Madras offers this course, providing students with study materials in the form of audio recordings and printed notes. These materials are supplemented with short sessions of personal instruction, although the program does not require attendance at these sessions. This course has helped many to acquire a degree in music, from teachers and people employed in other professions to married women who do not work outside the home.

Materials

For most diploma and degree courses, written textbooks for theory and books of notated songs are available in various languages. In recent years, audio cassette tapes of music lessons have been released to aid in the study of music at both early and advanced stages (as for instance, lessons on *ālāpana*). The practice of publishing graded music instruction books began in the late nineteenth century, but those of Professor P. Sambamurthy have dominated the institutional scene since the 1930s and have influenced the form and content of all subsequent books. In fact, Sambamurthy's contribution has been phenomenal, not only to the world of books but to the entire process whereby the discipline of music has been introduced into the educational institutions of South India. No discussion of the subject would be complete without reference to him.

Professor Sambamurthy devoted himself to music education at the university level, beginning in the late 1920s. In 1937, he joined the faculty of the Department of Indian Music at the University of Madras, and assumed the position of department head, which he held for twenty-five years. He was also a central figure in the organization of music departments at various other universities and nonuniversity

South Indian music requires learning under a single teacher, and even within an institution the single teacher–student relationship, not the institution-student relationship, still prevails.

institutions in both the south and the north, involved in framing syllabi, selecting faculty, and conducting examinations. He was instrumental in establishing a school for teaching instrument making, as well as compiling several books of notated compositions. He wrote on diverse aspects of music theory, in particular on elements of Karnatak music, as well as on composers, musicians, instrument construction and playing techniques, folk music, the teaching of music, Western music, and the history of music. He even set up the Indian Music Publishing House, which published most of his books. Ironically, he himself never studied music at any school—he had studied law—nor did he ever acquire any diploma or degree in music. But due to his position at the University of Madras, and to his appointments as visiting professor at other universities, he came to be known popularly as Professor Sambamurthy. Even after his retirement in 1961, he continued to be active in music administration until his death in 1973. Syllabi framed by him, and the books he wrote in English and Tamil, continue to be followed to this day in many schools.

Placement

In the South Indian context, young women have formed a large proportion of music students at universities and music schools. Until recently, the assumption was made that because they intended to marry, they would have no need of employment outside the home. Since job opportunities for students who have successfully completed music courses are few (as are those available for students in other disciplines such as the humanities or the social sciences), more young women have taken these courses than young men.

The primary employment opportunities for music students are teaching posts in the music schools themselves. A few find employment at other types of institutions that deal with music and the other arts, such as broadcasting stations (All India Radio) and television studios (Doordarshan), and with government agencies instituted for the preservation and propagation of music. Some take up self-employment as private teachers, or perform in film-music orchestras. Generally, among artists in the South Indian system, very few are able to sustain themselves purely on the income from concerts. Only rarely do music school or university students become concert performers, although there are instances of performing musicians attending an institution to acquire a diploma or degree in music.

MUSIC INSTITUTIONS WITHOUT EXAMS

The institutional setup discussed above refers only to schools that provide instruction covering a specific syllabus and whose students are tested for their proficiency by a board of examiners and awarded degree certificates. Quite different are those schools set up by music theaters (*sabhā*), or by individual musicians, that impart training in performance only. A few of these also assist students in preparing to take certain government examinations "privately" (see above). The teachers at these schools are usually successful concert musicians past their prime, artists who are not able to rely completely on concert performances for their livelihood, or musicians who never really made it to the stage. Music schools run by theaters are found mainly in Tamil Nadu, Sri Lanka (Jaffna), and Karnataka. Normally these classes are run on the theater premises. Occasionally, music theaters also organize short-term advanced courses taught by eminent musicians, perhaps on compositions of a particular composer such as Syama Sastri, or on a genre such as the *rāgam-tānam-pallavi*.

In institutions run by an individual musician, the teachers are usually a group consisting of the musician and some senior students. (Women musicians still make up only a small minority of Karnatak artists, and none has yet established an institution; see THE SOCIAL ORGANIZATION OF MUSIC AND MUSICIANS: SOUTHERN AREA.) The students are mainly schoolchildren, and as a result the classes are conducted on weekends and before or after school hours. In the music world, these institutions occupy a middle position between the *guru-śiṣya* 'master-disciple' system and syllabus-and-exam-oriented schools. Of the three systems, the last group has not generally commanded the same respect from the general public as the others; the reasons for this lack of regard are discussed at some length below.

CRITICISMS OF INSTITUTION-BASED MUSIC EDUCATION

The most common criticism of institutional music education is that not only has no concert artist ever been shaped by it, but also the system is incapable of achieving such a goal. It is said that these institutions produce only "trained ears," not artists, such that students develop into knowledgeable listeners, not good performers.

But these are sweeping generalizations. It is difficult to identify the various factors that go into shaping a successful artist. Not all students under the tutelage of a "guru" succeed as concert artists, and the successful student is not always the one whom the guru has regarded as most promising.

These schools have rarely benefited from a clear definition of goals and roles. Are they expected to shape concert artists? Should all institutions set this as their goal? Among the different kinds of institutions, the distinction between those functioning within a university and others that do not fall within such a system has also not been clearly thought out. Although justifiably emphasizing the "research" approach, universities have not been uncompromising in maintaining standards of musicianship. Quite often this has been due to the appointment of faculty members who hold degrees but are not skilled performers. Nonuniversity institutions, which should be concentrating fully on performance, seem to burden their students with too much theory, and also promote the misconception that principles of *manodharma* 'improvisation' can be imbibed through constant listening and exposure, rather than through instruction. Teachers have generally avoided training students in improvisation, yet it is this skill that makes a successful concert artist.

Another charge leveled against institutions is that they place priority on completing the syllabus rather than on monitoring the progress of each student. However, this is unavoidable, since institutions have necessarily to operate within a time-bound framework aimed at achieving specific targets. Admittedly, in such a framework regular monitoring, and strict standards for evaluating progress should also be enforced.

Within the institutional system no individual school has been able to develop a single homogeneous musical personality. South Indian music requires learning under a single teacher, and even within an institution the single teacher–student relationship, not the institution–student relationship, still prevails. There are any number of instances of a student learning from the same teacher both officially in the institution as well as unofficially at his home. With teachers on the faculty drawn from different musical traditions, the setting is totally heterogeneous. Thus differences exist among teachers in terms of teaching methods employed, the manner of rendering musical compositions, the conception of raga, and so on. The very first faculty members appointed to an institution no doubt came from noninstitutional backgrounds; everywhere, the process of transition toward integration has only just begun, and it will be a decade or two before any institution develops a consistent musical personality. At present these schools are only the sum of their parts, nothing more.

If one looks at the situation dispassionately in the Indian context there is really no need for institutional training of performing musicians, since classical music must be learned from a single teacher in the master-disciple tradition. It is only when one seeks knowledge "about" music—in other words, when one wishes to understand the music and its history—that one really needs the help of an institution. A university is certainly expected to provide academic knowledge of any subject or art; and in such academic settings, the teaching of performance does indeed become necessary, since the personal experience of producing music is truly a prerequisite for knowing "about" music. Schools have come into existence to teach music perhaps because of a social need. Through the creation of such institutions, society makes "learning music" available to everyone, regardless of caste, creed, or sex, and at affordable rates. Finally, it must be said that the weaknesses of institutions have been due more to individual failures than to flaws in the system itself.

REFERENCES

Deva, B. C. 1990. *Indian Music*. Delhi: Indian Council for Cultural Relations.

Music Academy, Madras: Diary 1988–89. 1988. Madras: Music Academy.

Pesch, Ludwig. 1999. *The Illustrated Companion to South Indian Classical Music*. Delhi: Oxford University Press.

Rangaramanuja Ayyangar, R. 1972. *History of South Indian (Carnatic) Music: From Vedic Times to the Present*. Madras: Author.

Sambamurthy, P. 1949–1968. *South Indian Music*, 6 vols. Madras: Indian Music Publishing House.

Srinivasa Iyer, P. S. 1937. *Articles on Carnatic Music*. Tirupapuliyur: Kamala Press.

The Classical Master-Disciple Tradition

Stephen Slawek

For over two thousand years, India's traditions have been transmitted from one generation to the next by means of a very formal institution, the *guru-śiṣya paramparā* 'master-disciple succession'. In Vedic times (c. 1500–500 B.C.), the guru was conceived of essentially as a spiritual teacher whose role was to guide his students toward an understanding of the true nature of existence by imparting to them the knowledge of the Vedic tradition. Students lived with the guru in the institution of the *gurukul* 'household of the guru', complete with attached living spaces for his students. This became so common a practice that even in the West notions of the *guru-śiṣya* relationship are embedded in the everyday vocabulary of the English language, based on the ancient conception of what a guru was. The layperson understands guru as a spiritual guide, a religious mystic, and regards his devoted followers more as disciples than as students. Gurus who fit the ancient description of the concept continue to thrive in Hindu society, but the meaning of guru has been generalized. In India today, a guru is a special kind of teacher, but is not necessarily a religious teacher. Traditions of literature, painting, music, dance, medicine, astronomy, astrology, philosophy, and more have all been codified into bodies of knowledge that get passed on by gurus to their students.

THE GURU

Although the guru system has come to be ingrained in the secular traditions of knowledge, many of the original ideas regarding the guru's godlike status persist. A respectful term of address to one's guru adds the word *deva* 'god' to form the honorific *gurudeva*. Other compound words incorporating guru suggest the degree to which the guru concept permeates Indian culture. The *Oxford Hindi–English Dictionary* defines *gurujan* as "venerable or eminent persons; elders." Members of the Sikh religion worship at temples that are called *gurudvāra* 'the guru's residence'. Pupils honor their gurus on *gurupūrṅimā*, celebrated on the day of the full moon of the month of Asāṛh (June–July). Every week, Indians are reminded of the guru concept on Thursday, which is known in Hindi as Guruvār, often translated as "the guru's day."

In the first century B.C., the Indian poet Asvaghosa, a contemporary of King Kaniska of the Kuṣāṣa dynasty, wrote his *Gurupañcāśikā* 'Fifty Verses of Guru-

> Music gurus, like ancient religious gurus, receive respect not only from their pupils but from their pupils' parents and other close family members. They are often regarded as transcendent individuals, set apart from society in general by their special knowledge.

Devotion'. A few of Asvaghosa's verses (Asvaghosa 1975) provide a glimpse of the status of the guru in ancient India. (Although Asvaghosa wrote within a Buddhist tradition, his instructions pertaining to a disciple's attitude toward his or her guru were the same within the Hindu tradition.)

> (3)
> Three times each day with supreme faith you must show the respect you have for your Guru who teaches you (the tantric path), by pressing your palms together, offering a maṣḍala as well as flowers and prostrating (touching) your head to his feet.
>
> (4)
> A disciple with sense should not accept as his Guru someone who lacks compassion or who is angersome, vicious or arrogant, possessive, or undisciplined or boasts of his knowledge.
>
> (8)
> (A Guru should be) stable (in his actions), cultivated (in his speech), wise, patient and honest. He should neither conceal his shortcomings nor pretend to possess qualities he lacks. He should be an expert in the meanings (of the tantra) and in its ritual procedures (of medicine and turning back obstacles). Also he should have loving compassion and a complete knowledge of the scriptures.
>
> (10)
> Having become the disciple of such a protecting (Guru), should you then despise him from your heart, you will reap continual suffering as if you had disparaged all the Buddhas.
>
> (11)
> If you are so foolish as to despise your Guru, you will contract contagious diseases and those caused by harmful spirits. You will die (a horrible death caused) by demons, plagues or poison.
>
> (17)
> It has been taught that for the Guru to whom you have pledged your word of honour (to visualise as one with your meditational deity), you should willingly sacrifice your wife, children and even your life, although these are not (easy) to give away. Is there need to mention your fleeting wealth?
>
> (46)
> What need is there to say much more? Do whatever pleases your Guru and avoid doing anything he would not like. Be diligent in both of these.

As Asvaghosa's verses make abundantly clear, the guru occupied a privileged position in the relationship with his students. The exalted position of the guru persists even today, especially in the classical music and dance traditions. This is partly a result of the oral nature of these traditions, in which the material to be transmitted from teacher to student exists, for the most part, only in the teacher's memory, and a student must "do whatever pleases the guru" to ensure continued access to this storehouse of knowledge. In addition to the superordinate position of the guru relative to his disciples, there are several other aspects of the *guru-śiṣya paramparā* of ancient India that continue to influence how Indians view the relationship of music teachers and their students.

In his comprehensive inquiry into the nature and place of the guru in ancient Indian religious tradition, Jan Gonda writes that it was as natural for a person seeking knowledge to have a guru as it was for him to have parents. The guru was to transmit his knowledge only to his resident pupils or sons. Knowledge was not to be made available to the general public. Students began their studies with a guru only after submitting themselves to an elaborate initiation ceremony (*upanayana*), which included tying a girdle around the student's waist that signified a protective umbilical cord. The guru had a sacred obligation to pass on his knowledge, otherwise, it was felt, the universe would fall into decay and chaos would ensue. As such, gurus were not to receive remuneration for their work. Rather than being paid tuition, a guru would receive a gift (*dakṣiṇā*) from the student (Gonda 1965:230–234). Several ancient Hindu and Buddhist texts call for a probationary, or testing period before which a guru should not accept a pupil (1965:253).

Music gurus, like ancient religious gurus, receive respect not only from their pupils but from their pupils' parents and other close family members. They are often regarded as transcendent individuals, set apart from society in general by their special knowledge. Music, moreover, has enjoyed a privileged position in Hindu society since ancient times. Philosophers and aestheticians alike within the Hindu tradition have attributed mystical powers to music; thus those who are capable of performing music are likewise invested with spiritual powers. Music gurus protect their knowledge and ensure that the most valued materials in their repertoires are revealed to only the most dedicated and worthy of their students. Many musicians continue the tradition of the thread-tying ceremony (*gaṇḍā bandhan*), symbolizing the binding of the student to the guru, an obvious connection with the ancient *upanayana* ceremony of the Brahminic tradition. In the mythic past, music gurus accepted their pupils into their homes like family members, providing room and board in return only for their pupils' respect and the opportunity to teach their tradition, thus keeping the music alive. Those musicians who can afford to do so continue this practice of the *gurukul* today, but changing socioeconomic conditions in India, especially since independence, have greatly diminished this aspect of the musical tradition. Likewise, teaching free of any tuition is becoming a rarity in modern India, although there are still music gurus who receive only *guru dakṣiṇā*. Even among those who charge tuition, however, it is still a common practice to subject their students to a lengthy probationary period to test their worthiness. During this time, a guru might insist on teaching only mechanical exercises to the new student, delaying for a considerable time the teaching of any performable materials.

THE MASTER-DISCIPLE TRADITION IN MUSLIM CULTURE

The classical tradition of music in North India has existed in both Hindu and Muslim cultural spheres from approximately the thirteenth century until the present. The concept of guru is associated particularly with the Hindu sphere, which has sustained the classical tradition through centuries of oppression and adversity. But a master-disciple tradition incorporating the core features of the Hindu *guru-śiṣya paramparā* also exists in the Muslim sphere. Here, the analogous terms are *ustād-*

śāgird. Ustād is a word of Persian origin that, like guru, means teacher. In India, the word *ustād* has gained a more specific connotation as a teacher and master musician of the classical music tradition. Brian Silver (1976) has traced the development of this more specific meaning of *ustād* and has delineated the characteristics that constitute the quality of being an *ustād*—such as dedication to practice, simplicity and honesty (*sādagī*), and service to one's family and *gharānā*—all of which are collectively referred to as *ustādī.* There also exists a religious-disciple tradition that parallels the Hindu *guru-śiṣya paramparā.* Silver notes that, as in the Hindu sphere, spiritual overtones also pervade the relationship of the music teacher and his student in the Muslim sphere. Speaking of his own sitar teacher, Silver (1976:39) states:

> Ghulam Husain Khan takes his obligations to his shāgirds not only as a musical relationship, but as a spiritual and very personal one as well. Certain features of his preceptive philosophy are similar to those of the Sūfī *ṭarīqā* (path), in which the relationship between *shaikh* and *murīd* often parallels that of ustād and shāgird. The aspect of trial and testing by the ustād shaikh [sic] has already been mentioned, as has the aspect of *suḥbat* (literally, company, but in Sūfism, spiritual conversation), in which ustād and shāgird become well acquainted through extensive conversations and long periods of time spent in each other's company.

From this description of the *ustād-śāgird* relationship, it is apparent that the social relationship of classical-music teacher and pupil in the Muslim sphere is very similar to that in the Hindu sphere. Indeed, the relationships are so similar that it is not unusual to find Hindu students learning from a Muslim *ustād* and Muslim students learning from a Hindu *guru.* For example, Ravi Shankar, a Hindu, studied with the Muslim Ustad Baba Allauddin Khan; also, one of his own disciples is Ustad Shamim Ahmad. Arvind Parikh, a Hindu, is one of the senior students of Ustad Vilayat Khan. Likewise, Mogubai Kurdikar, a female Hindu vocalist popular in the mid-twentieth century and the mother and teacher of Kishori Amonkar (now one of the most popular female vocalists of North India), studied with the famous founder of the Atrauli *gharānā,* Ustad Alladiya Khan. Pandit Malik Arjun Mansur, a Hindu, studied with Alladiya Khan's sons, Manji Khan and Bhurji Khan.

Within the Hindu sphere, two other terms are associated with the status of the guru: *paṇḍit* and *ācārya.* Both of these words indicate a learned individual who is entirely capable and qualified to serve also as a guru. In the musical world, master musicians are often given the informal title *saṅgītācārya,* 'one who has vast knowledge of music'. While the components of this compound word come from Sanskrit, the language of Brahminic Hinduism, some Muslim musicians have adopted the title or applied it to their teachers. Pandit, another Sanskrit word that has found its way into the English language, also denotes a male who has attained a superlative state of learnedness. Like guru, *paṇḍit* has a more specific meaning, with religious overtones in addition to its generalized meaning, as the term was originally applied only to learned Brahmins. Today, *paṇḍit* has acquired specific associations within the classical-music realm. Hindu musicians use it as a title indicating that a musician has been recognized for achieving a high level of competence within the tradition.

Daniel M. Neuman, in his cogent remarks concerning the manner in which the terms *ustād* and *guru* are deployed in social discourse, notes that although he uses the terms interchangeably in his own writing, there is a fine distinction to be drawn in the ways Indian musicians use the terms. *Ustād* is frequently appended as a title to a Muslim musician's name, whereas guru is never used as a title by a Hindu. Rather, Hindus use the word *paṇḍit.* Neuman reasons that these usages reflect the fact that Muslims professionalized the occupation of musician, but Hindus did not (1980:44).

Pupils, obviously, do not enjoy the kind of status bestowed by such titles; nonetheless, pupils are referred to by a number of terms. Most common are *śiṣya*, *śāgird*, and *chelā*. The associations of these terms relate more to the distinction between Hindu and Muslim spheres than to any nuanced difference in the relationship with the teacher. *Śiṣya* is a word more directly associated with the Hindu guru, *śāgird* with the Muslim *ustād*. *Chelā*, interestingly, mediates between the two spheres, as both *śiṣya* and *śāgird* may also be referred to as *chelā*.

SEEKING A GURU: TWO CASES

The fondness Indian musicians have for anecdotes about interactions of gurus and their disciples attests to the special place that the *guru-śiṣya paramparā* occupies in the culture of classical music. A few representative tales can shed much light on the nature of the *guru-śiṣya paramparā* as it has functioned in the twentieth century. Two prominent musicians of the late nineteenth and twentieth centuries, Pandit Balkrishnabuwa Ichalkaranjikar (1849–1926) and Ustad Allauddin Khan (c. 1869?–1972) relate stories from their musical training that have much in common. Both succeeded in finding their true guru only after several episodes of truncated study with musicians who, for one reason or other, would prematurely discontinue teaching them. Both Balkrishnabuwa and Allauddin also endured hardships difficult to imagine in their pursuit of a musical education. Both were initially rejected by their future gurus; and both were brought back through some kind of supernatural experience. In Balkrishnabuwa's case, at the end of nearly a month of fasting and meditating at the temple of the goddess Kali he fell into a stupor in which he dreamed that he was visited by the goddess (in the form of his previous teacher's wife, who had prohibited her husband from teaching Balkrishnabuwa!). She instructed him to go to Banaras, where he would find Joshibuwa, the musician whom he had wished to accept as his guru. B. R. Deodhar (1993:10) relates what happened next:

> Balkrishna recovered a little from the fit of extreme exhaustion. He felt a little refreshed and somewhat stronger because of the visitation of the goddess. He once again prayed to the goddess . . . and straightway set off on the journey to Kashi (another name for Benares). Not far from the town he met a stranger who enquired after him and to Balkrishna's amazement gave him five rupees and some clothes. He was convinced that the blessings of the goddess had caused a favourable change in his fortunes. When he reached Kashi he was told that Joshibuwa had arrived there a couple of days before him and was staying in the Angre Mansion. Balkrishna went to see him at 3.30 in the afternoon. Joshibuwa had just got up from his afternoon nap and was about to prepare his *buti* (a ball of hemp or *cannabis* and other substances). He civilly enquired about Balkrishna and asked him to prepare his *buti*. Balkrishna had prudently brought along the *cannabis* with him. Joshibuwa was pleased and said to him, "The past is past—I am now going to teach you music." He took out and tuned the tanpura and taught Balkrishna, by way of an auspicious beginning, a composition pertaining to Lord Rama. Balkrishna, greatly delighted, stayed with his guru and devotedly began ministering to his needs. After a fortnight's stay in Kashi, Joshibuwa made preparations to return to Gwalior. He was apparently keen on taking his disciple with him but was in an awkward position because he did not have enough money to cover the fare of both of them. Balkrishna said, "Sir, you go ahead. I shall follow you within a few days." Joshibuwa's parting words were, "Come quickly so that I can keep the promise I have given to make you a musician. I shall not feel 'free' otherwise."

There is a saying among Indian musicians that characterizes those musicians who guard their knowledge zealously as "teaching with a closed fist."

> Balkrishna collected enough money for the journey by giving concerts in Kashi and finally arrived at Gwalior. By diligently serving his guru, Balkrishna had already won over Joshibuwa. The latter started teaching Balkrishna in all seriousness. The tuition started early in the morning and would go on 3 or 4 hours until it was time for Joshibuwa to go for his bath. Balkrishna used to officiate for his guru so far as novices were concerned so that he could practise and polish what he had learnt. After the morning instructions were over it became Balkrishna's practice to have his bath and then set out on his round to collect food (given as alms) for his meal. This routine continued unchanged for some six years.

Ustad Allauddin Khan began his pursuit of a musical education at an early age by running away from home. The precise dates of events in Allauddin Khan's life are unknown. In an interview conducted by B. R. Deodhar in 1948, Khan stated that he was born in 1869 in the village of Shivpur in Tripura (now in Bangladesh). It is possible that this date is inaccurate by as much as a decade, as Khan's own account of his life corresponds better with some key dates that Khan himself remembered in the interview if the year of his birth is delayed to 1879. It is known that he studied vocal music for seven years with Pandit Nanu Gopal, and that he was about fifteen when Gopal died. He spent a few years learning various instruments, including the violin and clarinet, with Habudatta, the brother of Swami Vivekananda, a spiritual guru whose teachings were known in the West. When Khan was approximately eighteen years old, he had the opportunity of performing in the house of a local *zamīndār* 'landowner', Jagatkishore. There, he heard Ustad Ahmed Ali Khan perform on the sarod (short-necked plucked lute) and, as Deodhar (1993:110) recounts, was completely captivated by the music:

> As the first notes struck me, I felt a shudder pass through me. Time and space were forgotten. I was captivated by those notes. Khansaheb played the *sarod* for three hours. As soon as he had finished I fell at his feet right there, in that big gathering. Khansaheb told me to get up. I said I would not let go of his feet unless he accepted me as a pupil and taught me to play the *sarod*. Jagatkishore intervened, and mainly because of his intervention, Khansaheb promised to teach me and I got up from my prostrate position. Jagatkishore, too was exceedingly pleased with the sarod playing. He immediately issued orders to his servants to procure various things such as black thread (which is to be tied around the wrist of a formally initiated student), flowers, clothes, etc. The material was brought into the hall. Jagatkishore gave Rs. 400 and the new clothes to Khansaheb and presented a first-rate sarod to me and the black thread was ceremonially tied around my wrist.

Ahmed Ali Khan turned out to be less than the ideal guru for Allauddin Khan. There is a saying among Indian musicians that characterizes those musicians who guard their knowledge zealously as "teaching with a closed fist." Deodhar's brief biographical sketch of Allauddin Khan provides some insight into such a teacher (1993:112):

> Khansaheb declined to take me beyond the primary level. If hard pressed, he would occasionally teach me a set piece in some raga but carefully refrained from teaching me any refined or advanced technique. But, since I had heard him on innumerable occasions, I acquired a fair idea of what he was doing. One day, while I was doing the *alapi* in *Darbari Kanada*, he made an unexpected appearance and heard the notes from outside. He angrily kicked the door open and shouted, "Stop playing that instrument; you are to practise only the compositions I have taught you. You are not to touch anything else until I choose to teach it to you." He was convinced that I had purloined his art merely by listening to him. From that day onwards, his manner became distinctly cold towards me.

Ustad Ahmed Ali Khan eventually discontinued teaching Allauddin Khan and set him loose. This occurred while Allauddin happened to be staying with Ahmed Ali's father in the princely state of Rampur. Rampur was famous in the late nineteenth century as a place of great musical activity. Over five hundred musicians were employed at the palace of the ruler, the *navāb* of the state. Of these, Ustad Wazir Khan was regarded as the chief musician of the court, and Allauddin Khan now set out to become his disciple. However, it would not be easy to gain an audience with the great musician, as Wazir Khan lived in princely style, and it was not possible for a commoner to approach the musician directly. Allauddin himself related to Deodhar the depths of his despair at the prospect of failing to be accepted as Wazir Khan's student (1993:114):

> Whenever Ustadji emerged from his house I would salute him but why should he turn his head to look at a penniless student like me! Finally, I could not bear it any longer. I lost interest in life. I underwent privations, subsisted on food which is provided to beggars by charitable institutions, made everybody at home unhappy just to become a good singer. . . . I cried that whole night. The next morning I bought two rupees' worth of opium, resolved to eat it after *namaj* (prayers) that evening to commit suicide.

Luckily, the *maulavī* 'Muslim cleric' of the mosque Allauddin prayed at saw that Allauddin Khan was upset and inquired as to what was wrong. After hearing his story, the holy man concocted a plan by which Allauddin could get the attention of the *navāb*: he was to stand in front of the *navāb*'s vehicle whenever the opportunity presented itself and deliver a petition declaring Allauddin's intense desire to become a disciple of Wazir Khan. Eventually, Allauddin was able to do just that, and the *navāb*, impressed with the young man's persistence, invited him to the palace to test his musical achievements (Deodhar 1993:115):

> While Nawabsaheb was putting my knowledge to the test the entire coterie of court musicians had gathered there. Nawabsaheb was very pleased. I begged him to make me a shagird of Vazir Khan. Nawabsaheb sent a car to fetch Vazir Khan to the palace there and then. A sum of one thousand rupees, clothes and other gifts were given to him and the black thread was duly tied around my wrist. Before doing so, Ustad Vazir Khan made me take the following vow: "I shall not visit the houses of dancing girls or take food at their houses or teach them music." It was only after I had repeated these words that he tied the thread.

Although Wazir Khan had accepted Allauddin as a disciple, a full two years passed before he granted a session to the eager and dedicated student. It was not until he had received the news that Allauddin's second wife, feeling abandoned by a husband more interested in music than in her, had tried to commit suicide several times, and had recently died of a heart attack (recall Asvaghosa's verses!) that he realized Allauddin's extreme devotion to music and decided to teach him the classical ragas (Deodhar 1993:119).

> Ustad Vazir Khan began giving me instruction during his strolls in the garden with one hand resting on my shoulder. This went on for four or five years during which I acquired a mass of knowledge. One day Ustadji called me to his side and told me that I had learnt enough. I should travel all over, give concerts and listen to other great singers in the country. That would make me a perfectly accomplished musician.

Allauddin Khan had not wasted his time at the Rampur court during the two years he waited to receive instruction from Wazir Khan. He was appointed to the court orchestra, developed friendships with numerous musicians there, and held frequent musical soirees in his room that would go late into the night, assiduously adding to his musical knowledge by notating the compositions he heard performed at these sessions.

ON BEING A *ŚIṢYA*

From these anecdotes, it is apparent that the master-disciple system of transmitting Indian classical music is a special relationship involving the transmission of music within complex modes of social interaction and hierarchical structures. The relationship is built on an element of exchange: the guru gives the *śiṣya* musical knowledge; the *śiṣya* gives the guru devotion and lifelong gratitude. Additionally, a strong emotional bond naturally develops between the guru and the *śiṣya*. Even today, as the traditional structure of the *guru-śiṣya paramparā* is undermined by modern life-styles, *śiṣya* still are accepted almost as family members within the household of the guru.

My guru, Pandit Ravi Shankar, has told me many times that I am like a son to him; and my daughters regard him as they would their natural grandfather. Receiving his blessing is important sustenance for my own music-making efforts. Even though I have been performing on the sitar since 1970, and was initiated as Ravi Shankar's disciple in 1977, I still feel musically energized when I get the opportunity to meet with him and learn a new raga or some new compositions in a raga that I first studied with him twenty years ago. Although no individual can profess to know another's inner feelings, I feel confident that my own experience of being a disciple of a master musician of India has much in common with the experiences of others who have assumed the role of *śiṣya*.

The pedagogical method of the *guru-śiṣya paramparā* has always been based on rote learning. Although rudimentary forms of written notation now exist in the classical traditions, the process of teaching is still purely oral/aural. A student may notate traditional compositions and even model improvisations taught to him/her by the guru, but this is usually done only after committing the musical material to short-term memory within the context of a lesson. In the past, a *śiṣya* would learn much simply by being within earshot of the guru. The Indian tradition is famous for emphasizing long practice sessions as a basic part of a musician's training. Most musicians claim to have endured a period in the early years of their study during which they would practice as many as fifteen hours each day. Even seasoned veterans often practice several hours each day, or spend several hours a day teaching a small group of students. With so much musical activity going on in a guru's household, it is easy to see how a perceptive student would absorb a substantial amount of musical knowledge in an informal manner.

For many musicians, it is no longer possible to provide room and board for students. Thus students no longer have the opportunity for the kind of saturation experience that the students of the nineteenth century enjoyed. Yet the notion of the ideal *guru-śiṣya* relationship remains, and students often spend long evenings at their guru's house, or learn in small groups that receive instruction for several hours at a time. My own experience as a *śiṣya* of Pandit Ravi Shankar has been one of feast or famine. My training took place over many years, starting with a period of about six weeks during which I met with him about ten hours a week. I was already an accomplished performer on the sitar, having studied for seven years under Dr. Lalmani Misra. My training with Dr. Misra combined the traditional *guru-śiṣya* method with modern conservatory-style training, as he was a professor of instrumental music at the Banaras Hindu University. Nevertheless, I needed to return to basic exercises when I first started learning from Ravi Shankar, as his approach to technique was very different from Dr. Misra's. Still, I progressed rapidly, and he taught me a great deal in those first six weeks.

Ravi Shankar is a celebrity and has been circling the globe as a stage artist since he first joined his elder brother Uday Shankar's dance troupe in the 1930s. Much of the instruction I have received from him has been in hotel rooms; in cars, trains, and airplanes; during evening walks; and even on the stage, when I have assisted him on sitar in a few performances or have provided *tānpūrā* drone lute accompaniment in countless others. My musical development during the long periods of time between opportunities to receive *tālīm* 'training' from him was greatly facilitated by the use of tape recordings of *tālīm* sessions. I am not alone in resorting to modern recording technology as a substitute for the kind of "immersion learning" that students of the past experienced. The cassette recorder has become a standard accessory in the musical paraphernalia of many students of Indian music. Taping a class is done, of course, only with the guru's permission. In my case, Ravi Shankar restricted my taping at times, and always insisted that I use the tapes only for my own learning. He himself has kept a recorded copy of all of my lesson tapes for his personal library. He will make these available to selected students as he chooses in the future.

THE *GHARĀNĀ*

The *guru-śiṣya paramparā* is the core of the larger sociomusical structure known as *gharānā* in North Indian music. A similar but by no means equivalent concept in South Indian classical music is the *sampradāya*. *Gharānā* is a loose term that usually refers to a group of musicians who share lineal linkages and a particular musical style. Most *gharānā* are named after the place of origin of their musical style. Among the major *gharānā* of Hindustani music are the Agra, Gwalior, Atrauli, Patiala, and Kirana vocal *gharānā*, and the Imdadkhan and Maihar instrumental *gharānā*. The musicians mentioned above were important figures in two of these *gharānā*: Balkrishnabuwa Ichalkaranjikar was a key figure in preserving the music of the Gwalior tradition within the teaching line of Hassu Khan. It is interesting that this line within the Gwalior *gharānā* consists almost entirely of Hindus from Maharashtra. Allauddin Khan is recognized as the fountainhead of the Maihar *gharānā*. Both the Maharashtran Hindu branch of the Gwalior *gharānā* and the Maihar *gharānā* have made significant contributions to the present state of Hindustani music. The Gwalior *gharānā* Hindus have helped solidify the place of music in postindependence Indian society; the Maihar *gharānā* musicians pioneered in the internationalization of Indian music.

> Both Ali Akbar Khan and Ravi Shankar have spread Indian music beyond India's borders by devoting much of their adult lives to concertizing around the world, building audiences that continue to support the concert tours of other Indian musicians who are following the trail of these two luminaries of the Maihar *gharānā.*

One of Balkrishna's most important students was Pandit Vishnu Digambar Paluskar (1872–1931). Paluskar was a fervent nationalist and believed that India's classical-music tradition was part of a Hindu cultural heritage that needed to be reclaimed from the Muslim cultural sphere, within which music had thrived for several hundred years. To advance his ideas, Paluskar set out to educate Hindu students in the theory and practice of Indian classical music. Among his many students were such noteworthy individuals as B. R. Deodhar, Omkarnath Thakur, Shankar Shripad Borus, Narayanrao Vyas, and Vinayakrao Patwardhan. Paluskar conceived the idea of establishing a network of music conservatories throughout the major cities of North India. The first was established in Lahore in 1901. Later, a school that was to become the main campus was opened in Bombay. These music schools were all named Gandharva Mahavidyalaya. They provided a social milieu within which children of respectable Hindu families could learn Indian music and be awarded degrees in recognition of their accomplishments [see INSTITUTIONAL MUSIC EDUCATION: NORTHERN AREA]. Omkarnath Thakur eventually was recruited by the Banaras Hindu University to establish the Music College within the Faculty of Fine Arts at that institution. Today, this branch of the Gwalior *gharānā* can boast of several musicians who have carried their tradition to the highest levels of musical accomplishment and fame. Two who have released several recordings and toured internationally are Veena Sahasrabuddhe, daughter of Shankar Borus, and the virtuoso violinist Dr. N. Rajam, who studied with Omkarnath Thakur. Pandit Balwant Rae Bhatt was another of Omkarnath Thakur's students. Bhatt is a prolific composer, has published hundreds of notated compositions for use in music conservatories, and was the vocal teacher of the musicologist Harold S. Powers, who has written extensively on the Hindustani raga tradition.

Saṅgītācārya Baba Allauddin Khan shared Paluskar's desire to spread the classical music of India to a larger audience. He taught many students during his tenure as chief court musician in the Hindu princely state of Maihar, in what is now Madhya Pradesh. His most famous protegés include his son and daughter, Ustad Ali Akbar Khan and Annapurna Devi, and Pandit Ravi Shankar. Allauddin Khan was also the guru of Pandit Nikhil Banerjee, a sitarist of international fame whose career was cut short by a heart attack in 1986, and Sharan Rani Bakhleval, one of the few women who have succeeded in pursuing a career in instrumental music. Ali Akbar's son Ashish, who plays sarod, and Ravi Shankar's daughter Anoushka, a young and talented sitar player who is just beginning her career as a performer, will continue the association of the Maihar *gharānā* with the families of Allauddin Khan and Ravi Shankar. The Maihar *gharānā* has produced many other stellar musicians of the Hindustani tradition, many of whom are known internationally. Pandit Hari Prasad Chaurasia, a virtuoso on the Indian bamboo flute, had advanced training from Annapurna Devi. Vishwa Mohan Bhatt, who studied with his older brother Shashi Mohan (who studied with Ravi Shankar) and with Ravi Shankar, has attracted an international audience with his soaring improvisations on his modified slide guitar, which he calls *mohan vīṇā*. Both Ali Akbar Khan and Ravi Shankar have spread Indian music beyond India's borders by devoting much of their adult lives to concertizing around the world, building audiences that continue to support the concert tours of other Indian musicians who are following the trail of these two luminaries of the Maihar *gharānā*.

The future of the *gharānā* system is the future of the *guru-śiṣya paramparā*. The exigencies of survival in a world that is changing ever faster have been very hard on classical musicians in India. As Silver (1976:28) has noted:

> Today, few musicians can make a comfortable living by performance alone, and life is filled with such pressures and anxieties that some traditional ustāds have either abandoned musical careers altogether, or at least have discouraged their children from becoming musicians, preferring instead to educate them for more "respectable" and stable careers. Those who have elected to continue their musical tradition, or gharānā, have had to modify, to some extent, the traditional roles of the ustād.

REFERENCES

Asvaghosa. 1975. *Fifty Verses of Guru-Devotion* (*"Gurupañcāśikā," "La-ma nga chu-pa"*) . Trans. Bureau of the Library of Tibetan Works and Archives. Dharamsala, Himachal Pradesh: Library of Tibetan Works and Archives.

Deodhar, B. R. 1993. *Pillars of Hindustani Music*. Bombay: Popular Prakashan.

Gonda, Jan. 1965. *Change and Continuity in Indian Religious Tradition*. The Hague: Mouton.

Neuman, Daniel M. 1980. *The Life of Music in North India*. Detroit: Wayne State University Press.

Silver, Brian. 1976. "On Becoming an Ustād: Six Life Sketches in the Evolution of a Gharānā." *Asian Music* 7(2):27–50.

Transmission of Nonclassical Traditions

Ashok D. Ranade

Prestige of the "Word"
Oral/Aural Transmission
The Coexistence of Oral and Written Traditions
The Guru
Ritualism
Multiplicity of Communicators

In the Indian context, as to some extent in all major Asian contexts, nonclassical traditions of music are generally described as regional and tribal. However, dividing Indian traditions into five musical streams—art (or classical), popular, devotional, folk, and tribal—provides a better understanding of the Indian response to musical performance. In this scheme, nonclassical music traditions would comprise the four categories of music other than art music. This article focuses on the process of musical transmission in devotional, folk, and tribal musics.

Various general features pertaining to the transmission of devotional, folk, and tribal musics can be identified. Principally, the transmission of music can be distinguished from the larger process of cultural communication. Both transmission and communication are processes for conveying the ideas, skills, and experiences of one person, group, or society to another. However, transmission aims at creating as a consequence another agency to carry on the practice of the skills being transmitted.

Certain features of musical transmission serve to differentiate devotional, folk, and tribal musics from the art music of India. These three musical categories are commonly distinguished from art music as being less under the influence of urbanization. Furthermore, because urbanization relies heavily on writing, ultimately the written or printed word emerges as the main if not the sole avenue of transmission. In contrast, nonclassical traditions are generally transmitted through what is broadly described as oral tradition. In fact, oral tradition is held to be their *sine qua non,* permitting transmission of the entire body of musical structures and experiential molds accompanying them.

Two other common features of devotional, folk, and tribal musics keep them apart from art music. First, compared with art music the other three assume a broader definition of music: in the latter, music can be placed anywhere on a continuum from mere sound production to song. Second, song in these three categories may be music oriented, dance oriented, or drama oriented; within the music-oriented class, songs may have a melodic or rhythmic focus. The very concepts of "music" and "song" in the three nonclassical musical categories differ radically from those in art music. The following discussion of the transmission process identifies the general features that separate India's tribal, folk, and devotional music from its art music, as well as specific technical features within particular genres.

PRESTIGE OF THE "WORD"

Perhaps the most important and easily discernible feature of devotional, folk, and tribal music is the significance attached to words. When a word is written it is transformed, and the transformation is achieved with the help of accepted signs known as letters. Indian culture, on account of the primary importance given to oral tradition, holds the word in high regard in its unwritten form.

A prominent example of this feature is the high regard for and comprehensive practice of mantra incantation. *Mantra* is broadly defined as a cluster of meaningful or meaningless syllables intended as a formula of prayer to any deity or supernatural power or as a formula of meditation. In chanting such a formula an individual may or may not seek to achieve a practical goal, ethical or otherwise. In general, there are two overarching aims of mantra recitation: securing the desired and avoiding the unwanted. A significant portion of music in the three categories involves mantras. Following ancient practice, some mantras are metrical and meant to be recited aloud, such as the Ṛgvedic hymns composed by various Vedic seers. A second variety is couched in prose and intended to be muttered in low tones, as in the Yajurveda formulations, whereas a third is metrical and meant to be chanted to melodies as, for example, the Samavedic hymns [see VEDIC CHANT]. Mantras are taught by a qualified person to another individual after certain preconditions have been fulfilled. The related acts of transmission are preceded and succeeded by rituals that ensure effective transmission. Examples of such rituals are propitiatory incantations in tribal life-cycle observances, snake charming, and snakebite cures in the folk category, often accompanied by instrumental performance (figure 1), and the incantation or recitation of the names of God in devotional genres. Participation at various levels, according to the requirements of the occasion, is the main avenue of transmission. Through participation, which may involve such actions as hand clapping, joining the hands in supplication, or reciting the deity's name, the nonverbalized norms of performance are absorbed.

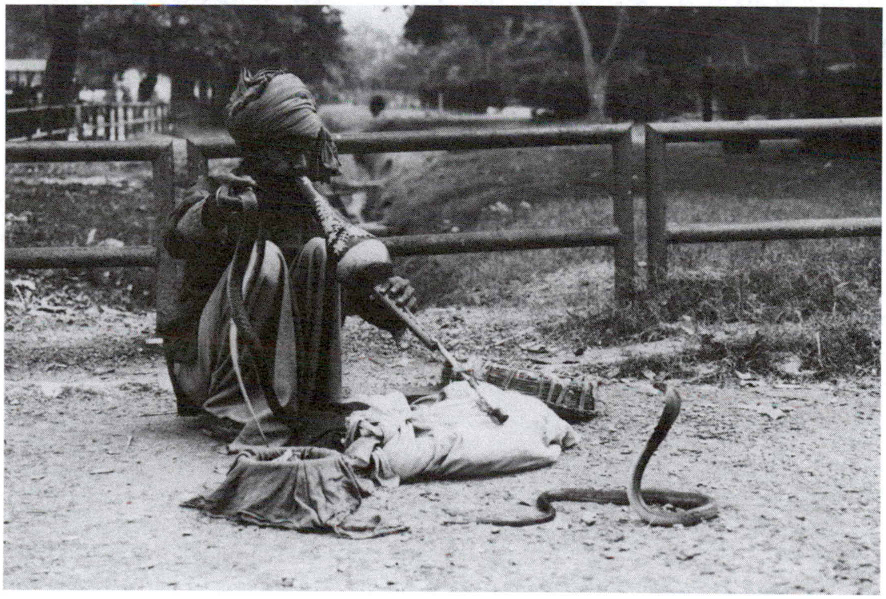

FIGURE 1 Snake charmer playing *puṅgī* (also called *bīn*) in Delhi, 1992. Photo by Stephen Slawek.

ORAL/AURAL TRANSMISSION

Articulation (the production of sound) and hearing (the reception of sound) are physiologically interdependent processes, and oral tradition heightens their mutual dependence by insisting on the importance of the receiver's role as a listener. A critical distinction is made between hearing and listening, and thereby between the hearer and the listener. One major factor that distinguishes listening from hearing is attention.

If the oral nature of music is exemplified by acts of speaking and singing, its aural aspect is made concrete by the audience. In the three categories of nonclassical music under discussion, the audience is held in veneration—although to varying degrees. The audience's contribution in all music-related processes is praised. Certainly the oral/aural identity of oral tradition in India has led to the high status enjoyed by the audience. The critical value of audience response has been recognized in India since antiquity. The sage Bharata, in the *Nāṭyaśāstra* (c. 200 B.C.–A.D. 200), acknowledges the contribution of audience response to the quality and success of a performance by enumerating the ways and means in which the audience registers its approval or disapproval. Within Indian culture, the qualifications of a good auditor are mentioned with clarity and firmness. Norms of behavior for audiences are also laid down. Indian scholars today generally believe that such observations made in this ancient treatise can greatly enhance the study of nonelite traditions such as folk music genres.

In folk, tribal, and devotional music, listening is encouraged as an obligatory strategy, even if due to age or the lack of previous or adequate exposure, the receiver is unable to *understand* the nature and import of the proceedings. Performers, for example, often bring children with them to carry out manual chores such as handling property, collecting alms after the performances, and feeding the animals, but also so that the children can listen. They may also ask prospective performers to keep the rhythm, join in the refrains, or play simple instruments (idiophones, for example), which establishes for them a more direct musical connection with the tradition. Such exposure, interspersed with the intent listening involved in following musical cues during a performance, is also part of the transmission process.

THE COEXISTENCE OF ORAL AND WRITTEN TRADITIONS

Oral traditions do not exclude writing and written material, even nonclassical traditions. Indian culture does not regard the oral and the written as mutually exclusive. In nonclassical traditions, the process of writing is thought to reduce the potency and quality of certain items, and a dependence on writing and silent reading is expected to dilute the performer's mastery over the material. However, this does not mean that nothing at all is written down. In fact, choices are made about what is and what is not to be written down. Further, reference to the written is not forbidden but placed in a carefully constructed procedural chain. The Vasudevs, for example, are itinerant singers of auspicious songs of the Vaishnav cult in Maharashtra; they keep their corpus of songs in notebooks called *bād*, which they pass on within the family lineage and regard as sacred, to be kept away from general view. Another example is the Kalgi-turra of Madhya Pradesh, who perform music dramas involving question-and-answer competitions among parties owing loyalties to different sects. The competing parties carry large texts with them from village to village. These texts (*pothi*) have been ceremoniously bound together, and are reverentially stored and respectfully consulted.

THE GURU

The emergence of the guru as an institution, and the supremacy of this master musician-teacher in the transmission of Indian music, result from the importance of oral tradition in this culture. The guru transforms mere words into meaningful directions, converts information into knowledge, and replaces isolated facts with a coherent whole. He makes many decisions about the method, timing, depth, and rigor of his teaching (master musicians are predominantly male), according to the capacity of the trainee. For example, to organize a performance of *bharata nat,* a theater genre of the tribal peoples in the Bastar region of Madhya Pradesh, a Naṭ (theater) guru is invited to train those hopeful of becoming performers. For weeks he trains the participants for the selected play, following a rigorous schedule. The village takes care of all his needs and provides resources in the form of paddy, rice, or money. The performance, which involves face painting and masks as well as a handwritten script (*champu*), naturally requires a central controlling force, which is aptly provided by the Naṭguru. Among the highly musical Santals of West Bengal and adjoining areas, *dasae* is a vocal form named after the festival that precedes the worship of the goddess Durga. Members of the community who have been initiated by a guru sing these "songs" as a test of the merit they have acquired. The songs are invitations to various spirits to possess the singers as a result of their effective rendering. The guru in this case not only teaches but also tests the trainee.

The *sūtra*

Broadly speaking, *sūtra* may be defined as a versified prescription, a concise technical sentence used as a memorized rule. A well-circulated definition of the *sūtra* reads (in translation) as follows: *sūtra* is known to the knowledgeable as consisting of few syllables, unambiguous, an embodiment of essence, interpretable from varied aspects, not interpolated, and free from censure. The content and form of musical traditions are preserved and passed on through *sūtra* prescriptions. The *sūtra,* however, is hardly ever entirely self-explanatory. Explanation and interpretation are necessary for its understanding. In oral tradition this is achieved through discussions based on a *sūtra.* Discussions vary in intensity, variety, and depth according to the qualification (*adhikār*) of the discussant. With his disciples, a guru does not so much discuss as maintain a dialogue generally in question-and-answer form. In response to a disciple's question, a guru may begin by quoting a *sūtra,* which he then goes on to explain by replying to additional questions that he deems valid and permissible. Thus a kind of catechism appears to be the standard format for communication between guru and disciple.

To use a *sūtra* is to transmit an idea in seed form that will be processed and expanded later as a result of interaction between participating personalities. The question-and-answer format is well suited for communication designed to exchange ideas, influences, and experiences. That it should find a place in the formation of many genres should not come as a surprise. In the devotional category, for instance, members of the Jogira and Kabira sects in northern India, who owe allegiance to Saint Kabir and the older Nath cult respectively, travel from village to village organizing singing parties in which they throw metaphysical riddles in song form at each other, vying for supremacy as performers and philosophers. On the occasion of Holī, a festival in which participants smear colors on each other, these parties entertain as well as spread didactic messages. Through an agile combination of composing and extempore performing skills, they pass on their lore, their songs (often including references to contemporary matters). Thus rivalry and revelry go hand in hand. The *manch,* a form of musical theater in Madhya Pradesh, features dialogues composed in question-and-answer format. Performances are all-night ventures, attesting to the efficacy of the format and the effectiveness of the practitioners.

Musical influences, experiences, and materials are transmitted through a process that can best be described as musical accretion. Instrumental pieces, songs, stylistic elements, or technical formulas are absorbed gradually, sometimes over a period of years.

Memory

Sūtra formulas function as a means of focusing the intellect, and are therefore to be memorized and expected to surface as and when required, to bring about the progressive enrichment of knowledge and experience while allowing adequate scope for the particular moment, event, or feeling. If the *sūtra* represents the relatively constant element in any experience, then memory and recall, which affect the *sūtra*, represent the variable element. This process ensures the essential dynamism of the act of transmission as part of the wider process of communication.

Mnemonic aids, the methods of employing them, and the contexts in which they are employed are invaluable components of the transmission process. These include repetition and chanting aloud, but also the deliberate and well-controlled use of nonverbal elements. For example, in the *manch* performances mentioned above, actors deliver the last lines of their dialogues to the accompaniment of specific, repeated, and sonorous strokes on the *ḍholak* 'double-headed drum'.

RITUALISM

In practice, South Asian oral tradition involves elements of ritualism. Whatever the particular performance practice or genre, there are deliberate rituals before, after, and sometimes during the performance itself. Ritualistic acts that take place before include, for example, remembering one's guru or deity, doing *namaste* (greeting with palms together) to the performing space, or bowing to the audience, instruments, or sacred objects; similar respects are paid to the deity, guru, or elder audience members after the performance and occasionally at ecstatic moments during the performance, when someone may lie prostrate in front of the performer or may dance as in a trance. The ritualism particularizes the oral tradition itself by bringing into play multiple aspects of life and assigning them definite roles. The oral tradition, and therefore the performance taking place within it, becomes more "real" because a firmer relationship with other areas of life is thus established. The physiomental action through which ritualism seeks to operate is known as *saṅskār* (literally 'mental impression'). This term has great prestige in oral tradition, especially since the goals of oral tradition include not merely the conveying of information but also the transmission of knowledge and the communication of experience.

Ritualism is also expected to carry out the twin tasks of registering an impact on the conscious and effecting a permeation of the unconscious. To help in this psychocultural maneuver, activities indirectly or loosely connected with performance are intently explored. Ritual activities are often, but not necessarily, sacred. In oral tradition, no human activity can be totally realized through recourse to intelligibility, rationality, and objectivity. In order to grapple with the totality of reality, it is essential to accept the legitimacy of emotion, contradiction, and subjectivity. This is what the comprehensive role of ritualism in oral tradition seeks to achieve.

The processes of song creation and performance preparation for a particular occasion are often collective activities that not only ensure transmission of the concerned musical lore to a group rather than to an individual, but also involve ritual activities. The performing group ensures the continued involvement of the community in the creative process over a period of time, and invokes the sanction of the sacred by such acts as beginning regular rehearsals with salutations to the gurus and deities. In Mathura (a major center of Krishna worship in Uttar Pradesh), for example, various performing groups (*akhāṛā*) with fierce loyalties to gurus or locales compose and rehearse songs in secret throughout the year with the aim of performing them in public for the annual Holi festival. The songs (*choupai*) are presented by parties of poets, dancers, and musicians, all of whom have been involved to varying degrees in creating them over a long period.

MULTIPLICITY OF COMMUNICATORS

The oral tradition encompasses a considerable variety of communicators or performers, each with a specific task allotted to him or her. Naturally, each type of communicator has developed skills and methods appropriate for the tasks he or she undertakes. In the related transmission processes, these get reflected in many ways. Transmission occurs through a multiplicity of communicative channels—movement, dress, language, emotion, prose/poetry, dance, for example—even when, for all practical purposes, the general activity or the genre involved is mainly "musical." In many song forms, for example, the textual content is delivered in prose and is then followed by a sung rendition, with appropriate gestures, thus involving two other communicative channels (prose and gesture) besides singing. Many nonclassical songs, musical dramas, and other musical performances have a story attached to them. These stories are usually accessible to members of a cultural group through different channels. A story may be conveyed in one musical category such as a song, and then retold in a different category such as a dance or drama.

As already indicated, the effects of oral tradition on transmission in the nonclassical music traditions constitute only half the story. Other more technical items play a role.

Centrality of performance

Beyond the consequences of the oral-transmission process considered so far, the centrality of performance in the musical expressions under examination must be stressed. An understanding of the features of nonelite musical expressions requires actual "doing"—observation with participation. Appreciation from a distance or a detached observation without any participation whatsoever are almost entirely ruled out. No doubt different levels of participation and involvement are possible, but simple passive reception of the performing stimulus is almost nil, and is never present to the extent imaginable in art music. Unlike the case in art music, scholarly endeavors of magnitude are rarely associated with the *musical* aspects of the nonelite expressions. In other words, it is not possible to read/write/talk about them, touching their essence or core, *without* performing (according to the established norms). The transmission of performing ideas through nonperforming channels is extremely suspect in nonelite musical expressions.

Musical accretion

Musical influences, experiences, and materials are transmitted through a process that can best be described as musical accretion. Instrumental pieces, songs, stylistic elements, or technical formulas, for example, are not transmitted at one time but are absorbed by the subject gradually, sometimes over a period of years, and at no set pace (except in extenuating circumstances such as religious compulsions or orders from authorities). Song rhythms may be grasped first followed later by melody, gesture, literature, and other aspects of a song. A possible scenario for this manner of transmission begins with initial exposure to performances at a very early age: a child, reclining on its mother's lap or perched on its father's or elder brother's shoulders, is a spectator, perhaps clapping, admiring, and joining in choruses in a half-hearted and mumbling manner. A few years later, the child is allotted a task, such as holding or arranging items or carrying messages. Doing simple imitations follows until the youth becomes a knowing participant in developing the multifaceted performance. Receiving the material is a process of slow, gradual, and often unconscious absorption. The training and rehearsing centers (*akhāṛā*) of many folk performing genres are places for such unconscious transmission, as are the youth dormitories of tribal societies.

Economical use of variation

The element of variation appears to have been used sparingly in nonclassical music traditions. Variation is used here in the sense of avoidance of repetition, search for novelty, and desire to impress by being different or original. In the music-, dance-, and drama-oriented songs in the three categories of devotional, folk, and tribal musics, variation is not given undue importance. In fact, concepts such as originality, creativity, and modernity seem to have been relegated to the background, with more attention paid to authenticity, propriety, and effectiveness. Hence it is logical that repetition and stylization are accepted, and stereotypes as well as stock responses are regarded as legitimate. Marriage songs of the Santals, for example, are known as *bapla* 'marriage'. The tribe passes on the tunes with the help of meaningless syllables (*tahareta*), since the tunes will not be changed but the texts may be. Variation is expected in the text according to the parties or persons involved. Another manifestation of this tendency is to keep one tune unchanged for all successive stanzas of a long composition. *Powada*, a genre of heroic ballads practiced in Maharashtra, even today uses this strategy to narrate hero stories. With a slight modification in the strategy, the same song is used in two different contexts: *don,* a song form of the Santals named specifically after a dance, is performed as part of the marriage ceremony; the same song is also performed in other contexts, except in the months of December and January, which may contain auspicious days for marriages. Variation in this instance is effected in the function associated with the song. A similar case is the *ṭīpaṇī*, a work song sung lustily by women in Gujarat, particularly when they are hired to level newly laid earthen floors in temples and other buildings [see GUJARAT]. The women hold wooden poles in their hands and rhythmically pound the ground with them (figure 2). The songs they sing are the same Krishna songs sung during the *garbā* dance festival, but the songs' function has changed.

Affinity with nature

The relationship between music and nature is prominent in regional music traditions, not so much in the form of an aesthetic response to nature, as in descriptions of natural beauty, but rather in response to the natural cycles of birth and death, day and night, and the seasons. The music and dance of the three categories makes reference to the world of animals, insects, and birds, thus showing a special affinity with nature. The music is transmitted as a part of daily life; it does not remain an external repertoire of pieces to be transmitted through formal procedures. In the northern state of Madhya Pradesh, for example, dance songs are named after the animals and birds of that state, such as the lion, peacock, deer, serpent, buffalo, cock, cuckoo, par-

FIGURE 2 *Ṭīpaṇī* women's dance performed by Corī women, accompanied by *śahnāī* and *ḍholak*. Corwad, Gujarat, 1995. Photo by Amy Catlin.

rot, elephant, python, horse, lizard, goat, monkey, bee, and bear. Since the participatory activity of performing these dance songs represents a learning process and group dancing is an enjoyable activity, musical transmission becomes a natural, automatic process within the culture. The *choumasa* and *barmasa* songs, describing the four months of the rainy season and the full year respectively, are other instances of the same spirit of closeness to nature expressed through music; they are also transmitted unobtrusively. These and other such links with nature make musical processes more organic.

Structural features

Textual features of devotional, folk, and tribal songs are significant because they facilitate memorization by performers and at the same time provide aural interest for the listener. For example, assonance, alliteration, and rhymes (especially end-rhymes) play an extremely important role, creating patterns of sound that are by themselves attractive to the ear and are felt with an unmatched immediacy. They also generate a rhythm of expectancy and fulfillment among listeners, who thus become participants in the performance.

Distribution of choral and solo singing also constitutes an important structural component, although admittedly this is closely connected with the presentational aspect of songs. In *jindua,* a song genre of the Punjab, one performer sings a stanza and others join in with the chorus line, interjecting the seemingly meaningless words "*āhā, āhā.*" A common *jindua* theme is the beloved's plea to the lover not to leave her, and yet the song's presentation is a judicious distribution of choral and solo elements ensuring accessibility—an essential precondition for transmission. The wider the involvement, the easier the transmission of the song corpus. In *rūf,* a women's dance song in Kashmir, parties of women face each other in semicircles, swaying as they sing without accompaniment. Two or more choral groups sing in alternation, an arrangement that ensures close coordination [see KASHMIR]. *Dhalo,* a women's dance song genre in Goa, exemplifies the same phenomenon [see GOA]. Women form parties arranged in close semicircular ranks facing each other, and sing in question-and-answer format. Young and old alike can participate freely. Those sitting in the audience obviously absorb the lore, and the processes of participation and transmission merge.

Chakri, a religious and secular song form of Kashmir, incorporates into a solo-chorus structure a patterned use of musical instruments. The participants perform

Perhaps the strongest aid in the transmission of devotional, folk, and tribal music in South Asia is the long-standing tradition of musician families in which exposure, assimilation, and direct teaching play time-honored roles.

sitting down (women now also perform a secular form), and all sing the refrain to the accompaniment of instruments such as the *ghada* 'clay pitcher drum', *ghuṅghrū* 'metal bells tied to the feet', and *tumbaknarī* 'goblet-shaped clay drum'. When the main singer sings his solo stanza, the chorus and instruments are silent, thus musically framing the stanza. This structure is important for the transmission of the song content.

A *yakṣagāna* folk drama performance in Karnataka includes dance and music, the material both memorized and improvised [see MUSIC AND THEATER, figure 4; MUSIC AND DANCE: SOUTHERN AREA]. The characters learn the songs by heart and improvise the prose dialogues. Since the dialogues are based on the songs, the main content of the two remains the same; the improvised dialogues vary in every performance according to the abilities of the actors involved. Many theatrical forms in India are constructed in a similar manner.

Widely understood metaphors are sometimes employed in structuring songs. Among the Santals, for example, a charm song known as *jan* tells of a sorcerer driving away a tiger from a person suffering from a malady. Another Santal charm song, addressed to the goddess Mansa, describes the charm working from the forehead downward, the song text line always the same except for the body part. Listeners know what to expect, as the age-old formula of the human body as symbol comes into play. They can easily guess the sequence of the lines, based on human anatomy, and the repetitive nature of the song text makes it relatively easy to memorize: "See the power of the goddess Rohini, O sister: The charm has come down from the hair to the forehead, the charm has come down from the forehead to the stomach, the charm has come down from the stomach to the waist, the charm has come down from the waist to the water, and finally it has come down to the ocean."

Family traditions

Perhaps the strongest aid in the transmission of devotional, folk, and tribal music in South Asia is the long-standing tradition of musician families in which exposure, assimilation, and direct (and sometimes minimal) teaching play time-honored roles. Such performing castes are numerous in India. In Rajasthan and the Malwa region, for example, performing castes include the Bhavāī, Ḍholī, Ḍhāḍhī, Mīrāsī, Manganihār, Phadali, Kalāvant, Kanchni, Laṅgā, Naṭ, Nāth, Patar, Qawwāl and Rawal (figure 3). In central Punjab in Pakistan, families of professional musicians include the Bharain, Dāstāngoh, Garvi Valin, Jafri, Kanjri, Khusrā, Malang-fakir, Mīrāsī, Qureshi, and Tawāif. Similar families carry on devotional music traditions, and even musical theater traditions thrive on transmission from one generation to another. Family traditions are also part of the larger network of the patronage (*jajmānī*) system, in which performing services are exchanged for monetary rewards and other forms of recompense, which also helps with the continuity of musical traditions.

FIGURE 3 The Laṅgā musician Gane Khan playing *sāraṅgī* while training Bundu Khan, a young Laṅgā, Barnava village, Rajasthan, 1978. Photo by Amy Catlin.

In the Kutch region of Gujarat, a kind of bird whistle is played dexterously by the tribal people. During the course of an interview, I asked a main player how he had taught his son the complicated blowing technique. After many reluctant turns in the conversation he took up a straw I was using to sip a cold drink, filled a glass with water, and started blowing into it; when the pace of the upsurging bubbles satisfied him he said, "I tell him to practice this to my satisfaction before allowing him to touch the whistle!" In a similar attempt to elicit a response from a folk *sāraṅgī* player about the age at which he began teaching his son, I was eventually told by the player, "He was *that* small . . . [he] was just able to hold his head. I used to sit him in my lap and play the *sāraṅgī*. He used to fall asleep and I continued to play."

REFERENCES

Bhattacharya, Sudhibhushan. 1968. *Ethnomusicology and India*. Calcutta: Indian Publications.

Garg, Lakshminarayan, ed. 1966. *Loksaṅgīt Aṅk* [Folk Music Volume]. *Saṅgīt* series. Hathras: Sangeet Karyalaya.

Lath, Mukund. 1979. "Why Study Ancient Musical Texts?" *Quarterly Journal of the National Centre for the Performing Arts* 8(2).

Parmar, Shyam. 1974. "Prelude to Ethnomusicology in India." *Folklore* 12(1):20–29.

Ranade, Ashok. 1983. "Researches in Folk Performing Arts: Aims, Objectives, and Relevance." *Quarterly Journal of the National Centre for the Performing Arts* 12(4):36–40.

———. 1984. "Categories of Music." *Quarterly Journal of the National Centre for the Performing Arts* 14(4):6–19.

Music, Drama, and Dance

Music, drama, and dance have been closely associated in South Asia for over two millennia. Since the time of the *Nāṭyaśāstra* (200 B.C.–200 A.D.), the earliest known treatise on the performing arts of South Asia, music has been used to accompany myriad forms of dance and drama. Each of these forms is a distinctive expression of a particular culture and society—from the meaningful gestures of classical dance to the suggestive movements of rural folk theater; from the choreographed, costumed performances of popular dance troupes to the lively, traditional expressions of village festival dances; and from musical dramas that propagate religious beliefs to devil dances that cure the sick. And now at the turn of the millennium, even as new hybrid forms are created on urban dance floors and cinema screens, the millions of women and men living in villages and towns throughout the subcontinent still find meaningful expression in their own dance, drama, and music—both as participants and observers.

The major classical dance style of North India is *kathak*. The *kathak* dancer Archana Joglekar holds a dance pose signifying "waiting," with her right-hand gesture indicating "holding a veil." She wears the traditional long, flowing skirt (*ghāghrā*) and fitted blouse (*colī*). Bombay, 1996. Photo by Gautam Rajadhyaksha.

Music and Theater

Ashok D. Ranade

Theatrical Categories
India
Pakistan
Bangladesh
Afghanistan
Bhutan
Nepal
Sri Lanka

Theater in South Asia is a complex phenomenon, for throughout the region the concept of performance, and hence the notion of theater, has been shaped by many different forces. To understand the resulting diverse theatrical developments, many quite unlike what developed in the West, one needs to refer not to the Greek philosopher Aristotle and his poetics but to Bharata and his Sanskrit treatise on music and drama, the *Nāṭyaśāstra* [see THEORETICAL TREATISES], as well as to the enormous diversity of peoples and cultures of South Asia. These inhabitants include Mongoloid, Mediterranean, Negrito, and Proto-Austroloid peoples. Their languages fall into four distinct linguistic families—Indo-Iranian, Dravidian, Austro-Asiatic, and Sino-Tibetan—and their respective societies have developed in distinctive modes, such as the intricate web of the caste system, which operates irrespective of religion, race, or language. Among their religious practices, both major and minor world religions are represented, including Hinduism, Islam, Christianity, Sikhism, Buddhism, Jainism, and Judaism.

Due to constraints imposed by religious beliefs, theater often appears in disguise or indirectly. For example, puppet drama, narrative storytelling, religious epic presentations, and comic improvisations on festive occasions are all forms of theater in South Asia. In addition, the South Asian sensibility seems to be intrinsically composite, thus challenging efforts to classify performances as musical theater. An abundance of genres adds to the difficulty, for many of these remain undocumented to this day. By a rough estimate, there are more than one thousand forms currently in circulation throughout the region.

THEATRICAL CATEGORIES

Theatrical performances in South Asia can for the most part be grouped into five categories: primitive, folk, ritual/religious/ceremonial, popular/commercial/professional, and art/experimental/amateur. There are of course conceptual variations, differences in historical placement, and infinite overlaps in reference to particular genres. And yet, the five categories underscore theatrical features and dynamics of the region that in some instances contrast with generally prevailing academic perspectives on South Asian theater.

FIGURE 1 A Naṭ acrobat performing at the Smithsonian Festival of American Folklife Mela. Washington, D.C., 1985. Photo by Amy Catlin.

It is essential to note that these categories are structural and experiential, and are not defined by the producer. The term *structural* refers to an arrangement of theatrical components and deployment of forces related to specific presentations. The term *experiential* points to the ultimate intended and emerging experience that the concerned presentations aim to provide. Thus an urban production depending for its effectiveness on body actions, harsh timbres, nonlinguistic sounds, and unclassifiable emotions would be classified as primitive, whereas a tribal ritualistic presentation in which kingship is symbolized with towering headgear would be described as art/experimental. Each category is a legitimate expression and enables a valid theatrical experience.

Primitive theater

This category of musical theater relies on nonlinguistic communicating agents such as movements, gestures, property items, and sounds. Jugglers, animal tamers, acrobats, magicians, and shamans are typical main agents for such theatrical performances (figure 1). These artists present mostly combinations of dance, drama, and music—although, in this context, of course, dance is understood as any deviation from a steady bodily state, drama as any deviation from everyday, mundane behavior, and music as any arrangement of sounds, even those generally thought of as nonmusical.

From a psychological perspective, primitive theater does not purposely aim to create, develop, or elaborate any classifiable feeling or emotion. Its goal is to generate a mental state that is charged with emotion rather than to enlighten the mind with intellectual stimulation. Unaccountable fear and a feeling of awe and admiration are perhaps the ever-present responses to primitive theater.

To a great extent, the audience for such performances is not passive. Auditors are participants, and varying responsibilities are assigned to them according to predefined cultural norms.

Primitive theater is highly symbolic, ritualistic, and inspired, influenced as well as permeated by a mythic spirit. Mythology is therefore a primary constituent of such performances. Animals and even supernatural phenomena are considered potential active agents in structuring theatrical presentations. Performance is at the center of this theatrical category, and no textual, linguistic, or scholarly activity can replace the primitive theater.

Folk theater

The folk category is narrower than the primitive but enjoys a greater focusing of theatrical forces. Folk theater, better termed folk drama, is the presentation of a story enacted by characters according to the accepted conventions of a particular cultural group.

Even though presentations continue to be composite, individual components are more easily identifiable, have specific qualities, and make particular, noticeable contributions. There is a greater sense of arrangement or composition in the folk category than in the primitive. Language and literary sensibility are allowed more scope.

A significant feature of folk theater is that it responds to three of the great cycles of human life—birth and death, day and night, and the seasons. Folk theater, like folk music, is pervaded by a spirit of nostalgia for the fast-disappearing or long-alienated rural ethos. Much of South Asia is mainly agricultural, with most of the land located in the monsoon belt, a fact easily discerned in the array of genres, song themes, associated functions, and rituals accompanying or framing the presentations.

The folk category recognizes both cultural conventions and family customs as forces shaping performances. Through such forces a performance acquires a framework of its own as a reference. Consequently a comparison between two or more performances and performers is both conceivable and possible, a minimal precondition for movement toward artistic acts as normally understood. Instead of the fundamental but rather undifferentiated psychological state at which primitive theater aims, folk theater is unambiguously didactic and recreational. It prefers to refer to morality rather than to ethics. It has a close relationship with particular religions, cults, creeds, and philosophies. Needless to say, myths and not mythology guide the proceedings.

Unlike primitive theater, in which listeners are generally participants, folk theater attracts a genuine audience, and performers receive individual recognition for their special skills and achievements. Hence both the formation and continuation of performing castes and their place in the patronage hierarchy are ensured. This is of great significance, for such individual recognition leads to family traditions of acting.

Features of the folk-theater performance tradition are verbalized; some are even written down, and although they may not be accessible to the general public, they could in the future be the basis of a scholarly tradition.

Folk theatricals often use, highlight, and develop plots instead of mere stories or themes. This element of craftsmanship leads to the origin and evolution of institutions known as composers, writers/playwrights, directors (or gurus), and actors.

The category of folk theater is specifically associated with the geographical, historical, religious, and cultural backgrounds of specific cultural groups. To this extent it becomes directly identifiable as a voice of a particular people; both presentation formats and the wide appeal the presentations enjoy reflect this cultural tie.

Religious theater

Religion in South Asia enjoys a preeminent position in society. Islam, Hinduism, Buddhism, Jainism, Christianity, and animism (typically mixed with other religions) all have long traditions in the area and are widely distributed. All the major religions are also divided into many sects and cults. A mind-boggling variety of religious centers and places of worship dot the landscape. Religion being a life-enveloping concept in South Asia, theatrical genres are influenced by it both directly and indirectly. Many aspects of theater reflect this fact—subjects, themes, symbolism, textual sources, and stylistic abundance.

Fairs and festivals organized in connection with various deities, saints, or major devotees are celebrated occasions for performances of religious theater, though related performances can take place in other contexts. Productions are overtly religious, though they often voice the secular or earthly/mundane cravings, desires, and demands of the common man. Religion and the religious sphere are used as occasions for irrepressible sorties into the domain of everyday life. Indeed, this sanctified freedom from the constraining aspects of religion is one of the main attractions of religious theater for the general populace. Throughout South Asia, an impressive array of genres has emerged based on the basic philosophical tenets of the religions concerned (Varadpande 1983).

A major feature of religious theater is the extensive use of versification to convey all kinds of content. Information, knowledge, insights, and worldly wisdom presented in verse form all find a place in this category. The various verse forms are simple to remember as well as to apply, and in the great spread of religious ideas, this unerring choice between prose and poetry has been an important force for shaping the dramatic impulse. The Indian epic tales of the Ramayana and the Mahabharata in their many versions have been the mainstay of many religious theater genres, and the easy and almost archetypal versifications of the epics are well known.

Religious theater performances do not place a great premium on originality, novelty, creativity, or other such values. Their emphasis is on the intensity of passions aroused through the combined power of religious and theatrical associations. Theatrical occasions enable the audience to work out its collective and often undefined tensions; propitiation, worship, repentance, grateful prayers, intense emotional and often cathartic outbursts, and other such stock responses typically characterize performances. Frequently, it is frenzied participation rather than aesthetic appreciation that is elicited.

This category of religious theater is a "total" theater, invoking all sensory powers. It is also collective: the crowd or mob psychology takes hold. From among the five categories, folk and religious theater could easily be described as eminent examples of the totality of theatrical vision. They appeal not only to many senses, but also to many strata of society simultaneously.

Art theater

The first and most important feature of art theater is its very separation from all other forms of theater in South Asia. It aims at being artistic or aesthetic, and its performers try to carve out their own territories by keeping their traditions distinctive. Toward this end, art theater has developed with determination and method. With notable tenacity, a scholarly tradition has also grown up in which theatrical activity is analyzed in all its various aspects. A strong written body of work exists alongside the performance tradition, and codification is valued. Emphasis is also placed on training, appreciation, and criticism.

This category of theater has been the one most fundamentally reshaped by Western colonization. Industrialization, urbanization, and the advent of Westernized education are all factors that have affected art theater deeply. Debates about modernity, authenticity, and self-identity have assumed greater relevance in this category than in any other, and such intellectual discussion accounts for the comparatively wider accessibility to "outsiders" of art theater than of other types of theater.

Art theater in general has very limited appeal in rural societies. This fact seems to generate fierce loyalty among its practitioners, giving rise to movements, manifestos, schools, and other such activist manifestations. Intermittently, the category appears to make claims to the universality of art and to an aesthetic validity that can transcend geographical and cultural boundaries.

This category is eclectic; producers and performers will typically pick up concepts, performing strategies, presentation formats, and the like from any other theater category. Whenever ideas are borrowed, however, art-theater personnel feel compelled to back up the assimilating ventures with some aesthetic reasoning. This aesthetic sanction has an immense legitimizing capacity. In many ways, such personnel also try to sublimate what they borrow as, for example, when they radically change superstitions or primitive religious beliefs. The scholarly tradition surrounding art theater seriously and persistently seeks rational or theoretical explanations for everything that the category values or rejects; it verbalizes concepts, considers ideas to be focally important, and propagates them.

The development of present-day art theater has moved through three phases: folklike religious presentation, music drama, and prose play. Music has been so integral to theatrical performance in South Asia that many genres, even today, follow the convention of seating the musicians on stage during a performance. This arrangement has been on the decline in art theater, although occasionally it is deliberately included as an act of experimentalism.

Instant sense gratification is an immediate goal for popular plays. Producers often add gimmicks or technical tricks to attract attention, seeking to stimulate the eye before the ear.

Popular theater

The most obvious feature of popular theater is the extreme eagerness of its producers to provide the "people" with what they are reported to like. Topical themes, fashionable presentations, and an innate attraction to anything novel (which does not always mean modern) characterize popular theater. Its main goal is to offer pleasure and entertainment.

Of all the five theater categories, the popular is the most inclined toward the structure and operation of an industry. The primary consideration of producers is what sells. Market forces, supply and demand, imitation of the successful, and a desire to seek the security of brand names and other image-building devices assume importance.

It also has the most heterogeneous audience, and so popular theater producers are keen on formulating and following success formulas to ensure that they produce what a majority of people like most. It is sometimes described as a category targeting the "lowest common denominator" in audiences.

Instant sense gratification is an immediate goal for popular plays. Producers often add gimmicks or technical tricks to attract attention, seeking to stimulate the eye before the ear.

Popular theater is noticeably accommodative and borrows from every possible source, indigenous and foreign. Unlike in art theater, the reasons put forward by producers for such eclecticism are not artistic or aesthetic, but largely relate to pleasing the public.

INDIA

Sanskrit theater, with its remarkable sophistication, flourished in ancient India, but had ceased to exist effectively by the tenth century, when regional voices began to be heard. With the legendary and real contributions of Ashvaghosha (A.D. 100), Bhasa, Sudraka, Kalidasa, and Bhavabhuti, among others, the Sanskrit tradition continued to remain in view beyond this time as a model to be deviated from or followed. However, the most influential legacy of the tradition is the *Nāṭyaśāstra* of Bharata Muni, dating from about 200 B.C.–A.D. 200. The work is at once a treatise, a manual, and a compendium. Along with the *rasa* theory of aesthetics in the arts, the *Nāṭyaśāstra* has percolated into all theatrical expression in India, whether consciously or otherwise. However, it is widely accepted that the *kūṭiyāṭṭam*, a dance drama of Kerala, is the only genre performed today that closely approximates the dramatic model laid down by Bharata.

In South Asia, India is perhaps the only country in which all five theatrical categories have flourished over many centuries (unless one equates the art theater with the modern, urban, Western-oriented, British-inspired stage play).

Jugglers, acrobats, magicians, animal tamers, and wrestlers have existed from earliest times (figure 2), as have rituals and ceremonial performances involving role

FIGURE 2 Monkey trainer playing *ḍamaru* in Delhi, 1992. Photo by Stephen Slawek.

playing, collective expression, dialogues, mask wearing, and stylized dancing. These and other such features are found in tribal life today, and thus reveal the long continuity of primitive theater traditions in South Asia. Three examples suggest the variety of this category today: the courting dance of females of the Gadaba tribe in the Nicobar islands, a tribal dance enacting seasonal changes and agricultural operations in Tamil Nadu, and the marriage dance of the Baro Nagas, which includes masked presentations and comic interventions by a jester.

Dramatic narrations—that is, character-oriented recitations—have been in vogue since Vedic times. Secular in spirit and voicing the concerns of the Indian people, these belong to the folk-drama category: performances always represent a particular cultural and linguistic group, and each Indian region has its own distinctive array of folk dramas. Some well-established examples are *tamāśā* in Maharashtra, *bhavāī* in Gujarat, *bhand-jashna* in Kashmir, *caviṭṭunāṭakam* (practiced by Christians) in Kerala (figure 3), *nauṭaṅkī* in Uttar Pradesh, and *bidesia* in Bihar.

FIGURE 3 *Cāviṭṭunāṭakam* performance of the Charlemagne story. Kunjali, Kerala, 1990. Photo by Amy Catlin.

FIGURE 4 *Mūdalapāyā yakṣagāna* dancer in the role of Ravana. Hampi, Karnataka, 1993. Photo by Amy Catlin.

Given the religious spirit of India's original inhabitants, as well as of those who later chose to make India their home, religious theater assumed great importance. Even after Islam had transformed Indian culture by the tenth century, religious theater continued. Among the reasons for this were the bhakti cult (with its doctrine of *avatar* 'incarnation') that flourished all over the country and its mainstay, the Vaishnav Krishna–centered movement that actively employed the performing arts. Also, the Muslims in India remained less puritanical than their brethren elsewhere. Religious theater in each of the major linguistic areas had its own character, leading to an immense array of genres and formats. The following genres are representative: *bhavana* and *ojapali* in Assam, *jātrā* in Bengal, *jātrā* and *pala* in Orissa, *vidhināṭak* in Andhra Pradesh, *kūṭiyāṭṭam* in Kerala, and *yakṣagāna* in Karnataka (figure 4).

The categories of art and popular theater had their respective historical correspondences. As understood today, however, they are a product of postindependence India. Each Indian region responded to modern stimuli in accordance with its own cultural dynamics, and the history of modern theater differs in chronology, quality, and quantity from region to region. However, certain characteristics of the modern theater stand out irrespective of region: plays are in local languages, even though their early developmental stages were inspired by Sanskrit and Western classics; themes are selected for contemporary relevance; play scripts are more structured than those in the folk category, with a greater use of prose; costumes, set design, and lighting assume aesthetic importance; attention is paid to the unity of time and action; the acting and audience areas occupy separate spaces; performances take place in enclosed/sheltered acting areas, preferably in auditoriums; a curtain divides the proscenium arch stage and the audience; audience size is regulated by ticket sales; and theater management attends to publicity and reviewing.

Bombay and Calcutta have long been active centers for theater performance; other places are now also becoming prominent. The scene is full of possibilities, as new playwrights, actors, and directors struggle to make their mark, although television—like cinema in the 1930s—threatens to draw audiences away from the theater. Since independence, institutes established to promote theater have become more active, and some autonomous bodies have dedicated themselves to this purpose. In addition, the central and state governments have become more involved in theater development. Amateur groups, university drama departments, competitions for amateur and professional groups, and awards and grants to individuals and institutions have all provided more opportunities. Training institutes have been founded, and opportunities on the "small screen" have also made theater more attractive to a greater number of people.

PAKISTAN

Pakistan and India share a cultural history that dates back to the Indus Valley civilization, c. 2500–1600 B.C. However, since Pakistan came into existence, at partition in 1947, the nation's identification with Islamic ideology has restricted the country's cultural freedom. Pakistan's cultural identity, including its theatrical traditions, is shaped by such factors as a strongly patriarchal family organization, limited freedom for women, a severe stratification of society, a Western orientation among the affluent, a less influential middle class, and the slow spread of modern education.

Muslim culture in the Middle East has frowned on the performing arts, but Islam in India soon assumed its own identity. Theater in Pakistan did not have to look to the Arab or Persian traditions for inspiration. With Urdu as its national language, Pakistan drew on two theatrical sources: Bengali theater (as it had existed prior to 1971, when East Pakistan broke away to form the new nation of Bangladesh) and the Urdu/Persian theater that came to fruition in Wajid Ali's court in 1855. Wajid Ali, the ruler of the princely state of Oudh (near Lucknow) and a patron of both Hindu and Muslim art, nurtured *kathak* dance and supported a dramatic spectacle known as *Indrasabha*. The court poet Agha Hasan ("Amanat") wrote this musical dance drama based on the love story of a fairy and a prince. The drama, entirely in verse, was picked up by Parsi theater companies in Bombay that produced Urdu plays in India, presenting their own versions of *Indrasabha.* These companies toured Pakistan with great success, and also performed in Sri Lanka and in Southeast Asia.

This Urdu theater was secular, as is evident in the plays of Agha Hashr (1876–1935), the other major playwright in the tradition. Hashr wrote *Sita Banwas*, on a theme from the Ramayana; *Bilwa Mangal*, on a social theme; *Rustom-o-Sohrab*, from the Persian epic love story of the same name; as well as adaptations of Shakespeare. In lavish productions, the Parsi theater made free use of elements of folk drama, including a wide variety of music ranging from vocal recitation and song to dance music, dialogue in rhymes and verses, and the participation of a large and heterogeneous audience. Actors' voices were extremely loud, the emotional content was dependent on stock phrases and responses, and the use of trick scenes to produce astonishment was an accepted theatrical practice. The genre became known as the "Parsi musical," as other writers created works in a similar vein, borrowing from Persian legends and Hindu mythological sources. Among these playwrights were Raunak Banarasi, Narain Prasad Betab, Munshi Mohammad "Dil," Man Zarif, Ahsan Lucknowvi, and Vinayak Prasad Talib.

After independence, college drama clubs became the pioneers of a new Pakistani theater when they staged both Urdu and English plays. Imtiaz Ali Taj (1900–1970), whose *Anarkali* (1922) became a classic, represented a link between Indian and Pakistani forms of Urdu theater. In 1956, the Pakistan Arts Council helped establish a theater in Lahore, and also helped produce plays. In Karachi, the older Parsi theatrical style current in Bombay and Calcutta continued for a while. Also in 1956, the Arts Council provided active assistance when the Karachi Theater was formed under the direction of Sigrid Nyberg Kahle, the German wife of a diplomat; Khwaja Moinuddin and Zia Mohyeddin were its major playwrights. After Ms. Kahle left, the Avant Garde Arts Theater came into being. Ali Ahemad, who had previously produced children's plays in Lahore, moved to Karachi and established both the Avant Garde Theater and Natak, an allied institute for teaching drama. Besides adapting Molière, Beckett, and other Western playwrights, he forged new ground by producing plays that satirized Western imperialism and neocolonial regimes.

Art theater in Pakistan suffers from a lack of longstanding professional theater groups. Amateur clubs in cities like Karachi, Lahore, and Rawalpindi, however, stage plays on an occasional basis. Lahore has a comparatively stronger history of theater productions, for an open-air theater, built by a Mr. Sondhi in 1942, has facilitated such activities. Among the "hot themes" that have proved appealing are Agha Babar's adaptation of Nikolai Gogol's *Inspector General* (Rawalpindi, 1961), Naseer Sahmasi's interpretation of an aristocratic family's plight in Delhi, and Khwaja Moinuddin's comic depiction of refugees. These plays reflect a movement to break away from dramas based on stock responses. Influential writers include the actor-playwright Rafi Pir, who was trained in Berlin in the 1930s and has contributed much with his versatility and professionalism, and Saadat Hassan Manto (1912–1955), whose radio plays, short stories, and features are notable for their theatrical absurdity, realism, and moving dialogue. Since 1968, some theatrical groups have begun touring the country with their productions. Furthermore, state awards have been instituted. In the art-theater category, many more Urdu plays have been written than have actually been produced on stage.

In Pakistan, fortune-tellers with parrots, snake charmers, mendicants (*jogī*), and wandering medicine men present one-man theater performances—the latter two often including reptiles and other animals.

Considering the terrain, the proportion of tribal peoples, and the village-based economy in Pakistan, it is no wonder that the primitive and folk categories of theater are flourishing. Fortune-tellers with parrots, snake charmers, mendicants (*jogī*), and wandering medicine men present one-man theater performances—the latter two often including reptiles and other animals. In the *chili-gari-ai* (literally 'juniper and goat') ritual, performed in the Astor Valley of the Northern Areas, a goat, children selected for piety, and juniper-over-a-fire are given roles in a purifying ritual typical of the primitive theater category. Acrobatic performers from the Tharparkar area are notable for their skilled movements with a pitcher that they carry in their hands and also use as a wind instrument. The *thari* horse-dance from Multan in the desert area of Punjab is theatrical. Also in Punjab, the *bhand* performance and puppet theater are part of the folk drama of Pakistan.

BANGLADESH

The cultural identity of Bangladesh (East Pakistan prior to nationhood in 1971) is closely linked with that of West Bengal, formerly its other half, now a contiguous Indian state. The theater landscape indeed results from the development of Bengali theater as a totality, encompassing both regions, now politically in two different nations.

Agriculture being the mainstay of the land, folk drama functions as the predominant form of theatrical expression. *Jātrā* 'procession' is the chief genre, a composite presentation of dance, music, and drama flexibly employed to propagate the Vaishnav cult of Hinduism. The religious bias was strong until the nineteenth century, when moral didacticism slowly took over, in turn replaced in more recent decades by a secular orientation. After the advent of the modern urban proscenium-stage tradition, *jātrā* adopted scenic displays as well as acting and writing concepts imported from the West by the upper middle class. *Jātrā* groups are highly organized and operate as an industry; the owner, director, actor, prompter, technician, and so on have well-defined roles, with specific tasks. Performances are long and loud, but well constructed for the desired effect. The form remains relevant today due to its ability to communicate to heterogeneous audiences, its character of the *vivek* (literally 'conscience') who comments on and joins in the drama at will, its musical orchestration (blending native and foreign instruments), and its performance style, which mixes a modern format with a traditional manner of execution.

The present capital of Bangladesh, Dhaka, was the first seat of the modern urban theater movement in South Asia, which began in the nineteenth century. This urban theater voiced the concerns of the growing middle class. Until partition in 1947, Calcutta and Dhaka shared many views and positions on Indian and Bengali problems. After partition, when Bengal was divided into East and West and East Bengal became a province of Pakistan, women began appearing on the stage, coacting as it was then known. In the University of Dhaka, amateur activity took root.

Western and other theatrical influences, including that of Japanese theater, had their impact. Furthermore, experimental theater took risks, such as staging plays by the Swedish dramatist August Strindberg (1849–1912) in the *jātrā* style. The liberation movement gave theater new motivation and momentum, and many new theater groups were founded during the 1970s including the Aranyak, Bahubachan, Nagorik, Dacca Drama, and Kathak. Centers other than Dhaka are now emerging as Bangladesh takes its place on the international theater map.

AFGHANISTAN

The earliest mention of the word Afghan (*avagana*), by the Indian astronomer Varahamihir in A.D. 600, reflects the close historical link between Afghanistan and India. The country was formerly known as Gandhara; Buddhism flourished there until the fifth century. The main cultural influences on the country have been Persian, Indian, and Central Asian.

Only 8 percent of the population is urban, the remainder being farmers or nomads. Outside the main cities, Afghan society is tribal in composition and lifestyle. Theater in the modern sense came into existence only since the 1960s; the first plays were adaptations of Western classics, followed by works often on contemporary problems. Folk singing, Indian music, and Western music have each in turn influenced theater in Afghanistan. On account of Afghanistan's long ties with India, it is no surprise that North Indian classical music secured a following in the country, as did Hindi film music prior to the ban on all music and dance by the Taliban movement in the 1990s [see MUSIC AND THE STATE].

BHUTAN

The kingdom of Bhutan is tucked away in the Himalayan ranges with Tibet to the north, India to the south and east, and Sikkim to the west. A central mountain range divides the country, the western portion inhabited by people of Tibetan origin, the eastern area populated by Assamese descendents. Northern Bhutan, with valleys 3,600–5,500 meters above sea level and heavy rainfall, and southern Bhutan, also with high annual rainfall and dense forests, both have low population density, whereas the fertile valleys of central Bhutan have moderate rain and are comparatively well populated. Following four centuries of Tibetan rule (with British influence in the nineteenth century) the country became a British protectorate in 1910 before gaining independence in 1949. Today, the nation's relation to India is defined by a treaty that guarantees its independence, with India guiding its foreign relations and supplying aid.

The Bhutanese, though largely Buddhist, have maintained links with the earlier, "natural" religious faith. People of Assamese origin are greatly influenced by Hinduism, and a strong Nepalese presence also stresses Hindu leanings. The main theatrical event in Bhutan belongs to the primitive category. Participants in the annual archery competitions wear colorful clothes, and are encouraged by richly attired girls, who dance intermittently. To the accompaniment of *ḍhol* 'large cylindrical drum' and *tutari* 'high-pitched horn', dancers wearing long robes and animal and bird masks execute heroic dances.

NEPAL

The kingdom of Nepal is situated in the Himalayas, with India to the south and west, Tibet to the north, and Sikkim to the east. Some of the world's most rugged mountain ranges are found in Nepal, where nearly 75 percent of the land is mountainous. Over the centuries, massive migrations of Mongoloid groups from Tibet, and Indo-Aryans from India, have produced considerable ethnic, linguistic, and religious diversity. By the sixteenth century, Nepal was ruled by high-caste Hindus who favored an isolationist stance. Gradually however, local nobles gathered influence and power, and in the 1950s the monarchy established a cabinet system of government; the accompanying religious tolerance, political conservatism, and cultural accommodation are reflected in Nepal's theatrical traditions.

The following fairs and festivals (*jātrā*) associated with various deities exemplify typical Nepalese theatrical elements that blur the borders between primitive, folk, and religious expressions: the Bhairav *jātrā*, a buffalo sacrifice and dance; the Macchindra *jātrā*, a procession of the idol with celebrations; the Indra *jātrā*, the setting up of a tall wooden column with masked dancing and a procession of virgins; and the Holī festival, complete with the erection of a pillar, color throwing, and revelry. The Sherpa dance drama *mani-rimdu* is another example of a religious/folk presentation. Lasting over three days, this outdoor spectacle is designed to assert the superiority of Buddhism over other religions. The ritualistic setting up of a flagpole, group dances, improvised comic skits, masked dances, and singing are the main features. Modern theatrical activities are confined to Kathmandu, the political and cultural nerve center of Nepal.

SRI LANKA

Located off the southern tip of India, this island country won independence from Great Britain in 1948 and changed its name from Ceylon to the Republic of Sri Lanka in 1972. The island is linked to India through the great Indian epic, the Ramayana, as the seat of the demon king Ravana. Frequent references to it in Buddhist literature suggest the early introduction of Buddhism. The Indian emperor Ashoka (c. 269–232 B.C.) propagated the religion in Sri Lanka, although the earlier animistic religion survived. Hinduism, especially Brahminism, flourished later, and South Indian Chola and Pandya dynastic rule from the tenth century onward enabled Shaivism to take firm root. By the sixteenth century, as the Portuguese and Dutch managed to secure footholds in Sri Lanka, Christianity also made its presence felt, and it continued to do as the British entered the stage in 1796 and colonized the country in 1802.

Literary drama developed late in Sri Lanka, since Buddhist monks shunned theater. However, influences from South India, as well as indigenous traditions prevalent from pre-Buddhist times and the multireligious, multiracial character of Sri Lanka, soon led to the crystallization of a distinctive theater.

Many Sri Lankan theater forms include dance. The devil dance, for example, is a form in which music, dance, and spectacle are all combined to cure a person suffering from disease, bad luck, or insanity. The chief exorcist plays the role of the demon king Vesamuni. For this all-male dance, each performer is dressed to suggest a half-male, half-female character. Bells, drums, choral singing, flaming torches, whirling and energetic movements (including leaps and dives), and masks complete the theatrical experience. *Sanni yakku*, another curing dance, has some humorous (including female) impersonations.

Kandyan dance, in contrast, is more sophisticated, with four varieties: *panteru, naiyadi, udekki*, and *ves*. The genre is reminiscent of the South Indian *kathakaḷi* tradition in artistry as well as in its intricate structure. Besides the four major varieties there are eighteen other styles employing animal motifs such as the elephant, monkey, and peacock. Early manifestations of the dance were based on Hindu mythology, especially the Ramayana. However, thematic sources were soon extended to include legends of kings and other tales. Royal patronage in Kandy enhanced the quality of the dance to such an extent that even the Buddhist authorities admitted it in their tributary rituals. The dress of the male Kandyan dancer is designed to dazzle and promote an atmosphere of royal splendor and authority. His headdress is impressive, as are his leaps and swirls. While narrating a story, the dancer acts and dances. During the annual *perahēra* celebration, dancers move in procession to the Temple of Buddha's Tooth where they successfully create a theater of opulence permeated with devotion.

Four other genres of masked folk drama are *pasu, sokari, kolam,* and *nādagama*. *Pasu* is a Roman Catholic passion play originating in the Jaffna area in the late nineteenth century. It sometimes uses life-size statues. *Sokari*, perhaps the oldest performance genre in Sri Lanka, is a devotional music-drama dedicated to the goddess Pattini on the occasion of the Sinhalese New Year. In *kolam* the dancers wear brightly painted and intricately carved wooden masks to represent a series of characters including a king, a demon, a deity, a hunter, animals, and birds. Using strong and deliberately distorted movements, the dancers present secular stories during the annual, all-night performances. The fourth genre, *nādagama,* is today viewed as the first creative departure from the conventional processional displays, group dances, ritual performances, and choruses that dominate the Sinhalese performing tradition. The folk drama has intoned verse dialogues and minimal prose; songs; scripts that include improvisation; religious, mythological, and contemporary themes; and a leader who directs the proceedings.

Modern theater made its entry into Colombo in the nineteenth century, its immediate inspiration provided by touring Parsi musical troupes from India. The amalgam of music, dance, pageantry, and the proscenium stage resulted in a genre called *nurti,* which edged out the indigenous *nādagama*. Although C. Don Bastian's *nurti* of 1884 (based on Shakespeare's *Romeo and Juliet*) was the first, the works of playwright John de Silva (1857–1922) proved immensely popular. The Arya Subadha Natya Sabha and Vijay Ranga Sabha were two major institutes that fostered the new genre. The *nurti* prospered until sound cinema nudged out the form in the 1930s.

The 1920s saw the emergence of a new brand of playwrighting, named after the main protagonist, Eddie Jayamma. The Jayamma plays, as they were known, were unabashed satires on high society in Colombo. In the 1940s, university students were active in promoting prose plays and adaptations of plays by such dramatists as Molière, Oscar Wilde, and Anton Chekhov. In 1956, Ediriwira Sarachandra dramatized Buddhist Jataka tales employing native folk genres, including *nadagama* and *sokari*. Thus realistic theater and folk-related modern drama both became firmly established in Sri Lanka.

REFERENCES

Goonatilleka, M. H. 1984. *Nadagama: The First Sri Lankan Theatre.* Delhi: Sri Satguru Publishers.

Martin, Banham, ed. 1988. *The Cambridge Guide to World Theatre*, pp. 747–749. Cambridge: Cambridge University Press.

Mukhopadhyay, Durgadas, ed. 1978. *Lesser Known Forms of Performing Arts in India.* New Delhi: Sterling Publishers.

Raha, Kironmoy. 1980. *Bengali Theatre.* Repr. ed. New Delhi: National Book Trust.

Ranade, Ashok D. 1986. *Stage Music of Maharashtra.* New Delhi: Sangeet Natak Akademi.

Rangacharya, Adya. 1971. *The Indian Theatre.* New Delhi: National Book Trust.

The Reader's Encyclopedia of World Drama. 1970. London: Methuen.

Varadpande, M. L. 1983. *Religion and Theatre.* New Delhi: Abhinav Publications.

Vatsyayan, Kapila. 1980. *Traditional Indian Theatre: Multiple Streams.* New Delhi: National Book Trust.

Music and Dance: Northern Area

Mekhala Devi Natavar

Classical Dance Styles
Dance Dramas
North Indian Folk Dance
Nepal
Bangladesh
Pakistan
Afghanistan

Dance performances in South Asia frequently combine dance, music, poetry, and drama. The definitive treatise on performance, dating from the early centuries of the Common Era, is Bharata's *Nāṭyaśāstra.* It describes dance as consisting of three main elements: *nāṭya* 'the dramatic', *nṛtta* 'pure dance', and *nṛtya* 'sentiment or mood conveyed through expression (*abhinaya*)'. The Sāmaveda, from the even earlier Vedic period (1500–600 B.C.), introduces the terms *mārga,* referring to the classical system and thus to sacred or classical dance, and *deśī,* meaning regional music, and applied to dancing for pleasure or folk dance. Twentieth-century scholars have classified South Asian dance and music into four main categories: classical, light classical, devotional, and popular or folk. More often than not, however, these categories overlap.

The classical dance forms, though originating from folk traditions, are in general more stylized, and are often performed by one or more professional artists for an urban, sophisticated audience. Classical dance performance implies a performer and an audience—an entertainer and the entertained—whereas folk dances are often participatory, performed by people for their own enjoyment. Classical dancers spend years training under a revered master in the hereditary lineage of a particular dance style, whereas folk performers may be either trained or untrained dancers from the community, or professional performers. Men and women usually specialize in their own genres of music and dance, only occasionally performing together. Furthermore, tribal cultures allow mixing of genders in community dances and festivals, while Hindu and Muslim cultures tend to keep them separate.

Women's domain has traditionally been the home, and most women have restricted their dancing to female company within the home or temple. Within the last few decades, it has become customary in some urban centers for school-age girls to dance in cultural shows; only a handful choose dance performance or teaching as a profession. Before this century, women who performed publicly either belonged to low castes or were courtesans. Most castes still prohibit their women from dancing in the company of men, as this carries the stigma of moral laxity. Men still commonly play female roles in dance and dance dramas, an ancient tradition mentioned even in the Mahabharata epic. Cross-dressers often add a comic element to performance as they dance and behave flamboyantly. Usually these men are simply imitating women, but the most extreme example, the transsexual or transvestite Hijras, are devotees of the Mother Goddess who live permanently as women and earn their livelihood by singing and dancing on occasions such as weddings and the birth of a son (Nanda 1990).

In India, much dance performance is devotional in content and intent. Krishna and his consort Radha are the inspiration of innumerable dances all over the country; the deities Shiva and Devi have inspired other dance forms. Dance is also related to ritual and magic. Shamans, as priests and medicine men, interact with the supernatural in mystical ceremonies. Through the power of dance they fight sickness and exorcise evil spirits or forces. Movements that grow progressively frenzied, leading to trance and culminating in the collapse of the performer, are important components of most mystical dances. Sometimes in such ceremonies, the sacrifice of a goat or other animal is part of the ritual process.

CLASSICAL DANCE STYLES

Kathak

Kathak is the major classical dance style of North India (figure 1). Derived from the Sanskrit word *kathā* 'story', the dance was born in the temple, where it gradually developed as a pantomime to accompany the recitation of professional storytellers (*kathakkaṛ*). These wandering minstrels traveled the countryside captivating audiences with their tales of valor, love, and the divine, as their descendants do today.

FIGURE 1 Madan Maharaj, a male *kathak* dancer of the Jaipur *gharānā*. Jaipur, Rajasthan, 1981. Photo courtesy Mekhala Devi Natavar.

The bhakti or devotional cult that flourished during the Hindu Renaissance of the fifteenth and sixteenth centuries influenced all the arts including dance. The expressive, narrative repertoire of *kathak* largely revolves around incidents in the life of the divine cowherd Krishna, his consort Radha, and the milkmaids (*gopī*) of Vrindavan, Krishna's birthplace. Dance ballets and passages of mimetic dance depicting their loveplay—a metaphor for the divine union of the human soul with its supreme source—are a vital part of the *kathak* tradition. In addition to its religious role, *kathak* was a source of entertainment in the courts of North India and was patronized by both Hindu and Muslim rulers. The Mughal emperors (sixteenth to eighteenth centuries) are believed to have brought to their courts Persian dancing girls who were influenced by *kathak* and contributed to its technical refinement. With its stylized gestures, sensuous quality, vigorous and intricate footwork, and speedy pirouettes, *kathak* represents a synthesis of the dance forms of Persia and Central Asia and the folk and classical styles of India.

Until India's independence from Great Britain in 1947, feudal lords and kings employed dancers and musicians in their courts. Dancers performed according to the occasion and interest of the patron; the *kathak* style was thus varied and flexible. Traditional performances took place for small groups of connoisseurs, who enjoyed being close to the solo dancer in order to appreciate the subtleties of facial expression and hand gesture, as well as the rhythmic complexities of the footwork. Devotional *kathak* performance still takes place in temples and at religious festivals, to please the gods as well as to entertain and educate the temple-going public, but patronage during the twentieth century has largely shifted from the temples and courts to government and the elite sectors of society. Private gatherings (*mehfil*) have given way to large proscenium-stage events. In the course of this shift, the *kathak* style has changed. *Kathak* has come to stress technique and broad movements and to offer duets and group numbers. The style's reputation has changed as well. It had fallen into disrepute due to its association with prostitution, especially during the British colonialist regime. However, in recent decades, Indian movies such as the Hindi production *Jhanak Jhanak Payal Baje* (1955), which portrayed *kathak* dance not as cheap nautch associated with brothels but as art and devotion within the realm of popular Indian culture, have been important in reestablishing its respectability, even if exaggerated or vulgar.

A *kathak* performance today consists of three main sections: the invocation, the pure dance recital, and at least one expressive dance. This is true for all three of the main styles (*gharānā*) in which *kathak* dancers specialize: Jaipur, Lucknow, and Banaras, named after the city where each style developed. The dancer begins the invocation by coming on stage and offering respects to the guru and musicians seated to the side. Creating a devotional atmosphere, the dancer depicts the deity and the devotee through hand gestures and facial expressions, invoking the Hindu gods: Ganesh, Sarasvati, Brahma, Vishnu, Shiva, or Shakti. In Muslim settings, a *salāmī* 'salutation' replaces the prayer. Following the invocation is the *nṛtta*, a long section of pure dance of great technical virtuosity, which has become the trademark of *kathak* dance. The dancer begins slowly and gracefully by moving the neck, eyebrows, and
TRACK-16 wrists in a sequence called *thāt*. The dancer recites mnemonic syllables (*bol*) and interprets these during sections such as *toṛā*, *tukṛā*, and *paran* (short technical exercises) that are punctuated by abrupt stops in clearly defined positions, usually with a sharp turn of the head. The dance technique stresses turns and footwork. Speedy pirouettes (*chakkar*) can number from one to 108 turns, but are most commonly arranged in multiples of three. The dancers, who wear between one and two hundred bells (*ghuṅghrū*) tied to each ankle, end the *nṛtta* section with the ultimate display of rhythm and timing in footwork sequences called *tatkār*, slapping their bare feet on the ground in various rhythms and tempos to reproduce the tabla drum patterns.

The dancer may close the recital with a dance rendition of a *ṭhumrī* or ghazal, devotional or romantic songs. In this final section of expressive dance, the performer depicts emotions often connected with Radha-Krishna themes, with storytelling gestures, sweeping turns, and natural facial expressions.

An ensemble of musicians accompanies a *kathak* dancer, playing the melody (*nagmā*) on the harmonium and the rhythm (tala) on tabla drums. Other accompanying instruments include the *pakhāvaj* 'double-headed drum', sitar, flute, and *sāraṅgī* 'bowed fiddle'. At least one vocalist sings and calls out the dance syllables to accompany the dancer's movements. The most common tala is the sixteen-beat *tīntāl*, though more advanced dancers perform complicated dances to *jhaptāl* (ten beats) and *dhamār tāl* (fourteen beats). The dancers and musicians often play with rhythms in a spontaneous manner, especially in the pure dance section, as improvisation is considered one of the most exciting aspects of live *kathak* performance.

Manipuri dance

Manipur, a state in far northeastern India, is the home of the Meiteis, originally followers of the Brātya tantric religion who worship Shiva and the Mother Goddess. The main dances of these people are the *lai hāroba* and the *rās līlā*. Their similar techniques have led some people to believe that *rās līlā* developed from *lai hāroba;* however, the music and costumes are noticeably different. Manipuri dance is known for its expression of moods and sentiments through graceful body movements. These take years of training to perfect. The female dance form (*lāsya*) is slow, smooth, and fluid, conveying a sense of the perfect harmony of the entire body and consisting of turns and half-turns. The male dance (*tāndava*) is swift and vigorous, distinguished by leaps and squatting positions. The male dancer simultaneously plays a *pung* 'double-headed drum' strapped around his neck. The *pung* and other varieties of drums are essential to the dances, along with flutes, conch shells, and a trumpetlike horn. Stringed instruments such as the *isrāj* 'fretted, bowed long-necked lute' and the *tambūrā* 'unfretted, plucked long-necked lute' (used as a drone), as well as the *pena* 'unfretted bowed chordophone', provide the main melody, with *khartāl* 'cymbals' adding to the rhythmic accompaniment. The most commonly used talas are *tanchep* (four beats), *menkup* (six beats), and *rajniel* (seven beats).

The *rās līlā* is a stylized dance form that originated in the early eighteenth century. According to one legend, it was revealed in a dream to King Bhagyachandra of Manipur (r. 1764–1789), who consecrated a temple and dedicated his daughter to dance the role of Radha there (Misra 1984). Several varieties of *rās līlā* exist in Manipur and are performed by trained women dancers: *basant rās* 'springtime pastimes', about the love quarrels of Radha and Krishna, takes place at the full moon in March–April. The light, spirited *kunj rās,* depicting the divine couple's ideal love in the groves of Vrindavan, is performed during the Hindu Dussehrā festival in the fall. On a full-moon night in the same season, the *mahā rās* 'great circle dance' explores the pain of separation when Krishna abandons Radha. Other *rās līlā* dances include *divā rās*, performed only during the day; *nitya rās*, performed on any day of the year; *nātnā rās,* portraying Krishna sporting with the milkmaids; and *ashta-gopī-ashta-shyām rās*, the springtime dance with eight milkmaids (*gopī*) and eight Krishnas. The *rās* follows a set pattern, beginning with the entrance of Krishna dancing, followed by Radha dancing. They then dance together until one or the other decides not to dance—which leads to a quarrel. After some cajoling they dance again, this time with the milkmaids. A devotional prayer describing the pure love of Radha and the milkmaids for their lord ends the *rās*. A male chorus sings the songs of Krishna; women vocalists sing Radha's songs. *Rās* performances also contain passages of pure dance accompanied by instrumental music.

DANCE DRAMAS

Rās līlā of Braj

In contrast to the classical *rās līlā* dance of Manipur, the *rās līlā* of Braj, Uttar Pradesh, is a devotional dance drama performed by prepubescent Brahmin boys, who play all the roles—Krishna, Radha, and the milkmaids. For the duration of the *līlā*, devotee audience members consider the characters synonymous with the deity and his divine consorts. The *rās līlā* consists of two distinct parts. The first, *rās*, is the reenactment of the original, transcendental, eternal circle dance that Krishna performs in the moonlight with Radha and the milkmaids. Krishna performs short *kathak* dance sequences (*natavarī*), while the milkmaids dance in a circle around him. He then circles the stage twirling on his knees in the grand peacock dance and dressed with a peacock-feather fanned skirt (figure 2). The second part, *līlā,* is the dramatic episode, a one-act play depicting one of Lord Krishna's childhood pastimes, whether playing with his friends, killing demons, or stealing butter and the damsels' hearts. A troupe leader (*rāsādhārī*) sings songs by fifteenth-century poet-saints such as Sur Das, written in the poetic Braj Bhasha dialect of Hindi. He also narrates and plays the harmonium, while an ensemble of older troupe members, also playing adult roles, accompany him on the tabla and *khartāl* 'cymbals'.

FIGURE 2 The Krishna peacock dance of the *rās līlā* dance drama of Braj, Uttar Pradesh. 1986. Photo courtesy Chadwyck-Healey Ltd. and the Consortium for Drama and Media in Higher Education.

Rām Līlā of Ramnagar

The *rām līlā* is a religious musical drama about Lord Rama's life. Based on the *Rāmcaritmānas*, a long poem composed by the poet-saint Tulsi Das in the Awadhi dialect of Hindi, the *rām līlā* reenacts the adventures of Rama. Dance is not a significant part of the play, which consists mainly of chanted and sung passages from Tulsi Das's text interspersed with song, drama, and spectacle. Originating in the seventeenth century, the drama has been presented on a grand scale since the nineteenth century, when the royal family of Banaras began to sponsor the event at Ramnagar. It takes place every fall for the nine days leading up to the Hindu festival of Dussehrā,

North Indian folk dances have myriad themes, ranging from life experiences and occupations to ritual prayer and spiritual ecstasy.

FIGURE 3 Dancer-singer performing in the *nauṭaṅkī* 'urban folk theater' production *Baram Bābā ke Śṛṅgār*, accompanied by (*left to right*) *śahnāī*, harmonium, *ḍholak*, and *nagāṛā*. Banaras, 1978. Photo by Edward O. Henry.

which celebrates Rama's killing the demon Ravana; it is watched by an audience of hundreds of thousands of devotees. Nightly performances take place in different locations in Ramnagar to achieve a spatial geographic sense of the story.

Nauṭaṅkī

Nauṭaṅkī, a folk theater tradition of northern India, is known for its ribald and generally secular presentations (Hansen 1992). It is very popular with both villagers and working-class city migrants. Troupe members are mostly low-caste professionals recruited from cities and towns who travel throughout the countryside performing at fairs. Their presentations draw material from both Hindu and Muslim cultures. Performers neither praise nor invoke particular deities but may present Hindu religious stories to express morality, the concepts of good and evil, appropriate behavior for the different genders, and even spiritual issues. Islamic romances such as that of Laila Majnun are popular. Lively music with kettledrums (*nagāṛā*), pulsating double-headed drums (*ḍholak*), and high-pitched double-reed instruments (*śahnāī*) takes precedence over acting, dancing, and the other visual elements of the drama. For the large crowds of people who sit under the stars on three sides of the open stage, the vocal element of the performance is very important, as they often cannot see clearly. Performers must sing, narrate, or act out the text loudly (figure 3).

Chau

Chau is a traditional dance drama form performed by men during the great spring

FIGURE 4 Final tableau of a *puruliā chau* dance with Durga slaying the demon: (*left to right*) Ganesh, goddess, lion, Durga, demon, goddess, unidentified male. Nawadih village, Ranchi District, Bihar, 1984. Photo by Carol Babiracki.

festivals in four major centers of East India. *Puruliā chau*, noted for its acrobatic fighting movements, takes place in West Bengal and Bihar, and depicts stories from the great Hindu epics: the Ramayana, the Mahabharata, and the Puranas. Dancers and musicians who are all farmers perform the lively dance at night in front of the village shrine. It takes place during a spring festival dedicated to Shiva and the sun god, and again a few months later during the extreme summer heat when the farmers have little work to do. There are believed to be hundreds of such *chau* groups. The dancers wear masks and large ornaments on their heads, and *ghuṅghrū* ankle bells (figure 4). Musicians accompany the dancers on the *dhamsa* 'large kettledrum', *ḍhol* 'large double-headed drum', *śahnāī*, and *kartāl*.

The *serāikela chau* of Bihar, known for its sophisticated style, and the *jhargram chau* of West Bengal also employ masks, whereas the *māyurbhanj chāu* of Orissa does not. Members of the royal family of the Singhbum princely state patronized and performed *serāikela chau* during the annual spring festival of Chaitra Prarva and passed down the art from one generation to the next. With as many as eighty troupes currently active, male dancers of other castes can now take part. The main dance during this festival honors Ardhanarishvara, a composite of Shiva and Parvati, and is a prayer for a good harvest. Many of the more than sixty dances depict nature and animal themes or people such as hunters and boatmen; others enact events from the three great Hindu epics (figure 5). Most dances are only fifty years old, but the fighting movements reflect techniques used by the *serāikela* 'soldiers' of long ago. These short dances take place under a canopied stage, with presentations lasting all night long during the festival. The dancers wear thin masks of clay, paper, and cloth and ankle bells. The accompanying instruments are the *ḍhol, nagārā, śahnāī,* harmonium, and *bāṅsī* flute.

NORTH INDIAN FOLK DANCE

Folk dances have myriad themes, ranging from life experiences and occupations to ritual prayer and spiritual ecstasy. They may be secular and revolve around seasonal cycles such as celebrations of good rains and harvests, or may be part of religious festivals. There are dances to welcome guests, to invoke the spirits of fertility, and to depict everyday tasks like sowing, harvesting, winnowing, rowing a boat, fishing, hunting, and fighting. Some require elaborate costumes and masks. Most common

FIGURE 5 *Serāikela chau* dance of the battle between Duryodhana and Urbhanga, warriors of the Mahabharata. Seraika town, Singhbum District, Bihar, 1984. Photo by Carol Babiracki.

are dances performed at important life-cycle rituals such as the birth of a child, puberty, initiation, courtship, betrothal, and death—all significant events for the family and the immediate community. Weddings, which usually take place at the bride's home, abound in song and dance and begin weeks before the final marriage ritual takes place.

Some dances can be performed anywhere, while others must be performed in a specific location such as a shrine or holy place. The community participates collectively in folk and tribal dances, using basic formations such as lines, circles, arcs, or columns. When men and women dance together they generally form separate lines facing each other or alternate in the formation. Occasionally the group encourages a single dancer to demonstrate virtuosity by dancing in the center. Acrobatic skills are necessary in some dances: these include leaps, jumps, cartwheels, multiple spins, balancing objects such as pots or poles on the head, twirling a tray on one raised finger, hopping between bamboo sticks on the floor, using stilts, or making a pyramid formation as a group. Indian dances emphasize the hands and feet. Hands often tell a story, and like the stamping of the feet can be used to sustain rhythm with clapping, finger snapping, or playing drums, cymbals, sticks, or brass pots. Dancers usually tie *ghuṅghrū* 'small brass bells' on their ankles for rhythmic effect.

Jammu and Kashmir

Festive folk songs in Jammu and Kashmir include *rūf,* a simple springtime song and dance performed by two lines of women facing each other, and *hikat*, danced and sung by youthful girls and boys. The latter is a modification of a game played by children: the participants form pairs, hold each other by extending their arms in front, and lean back and twirl, gripping each other's wrists.

Among the nomadic peoples of Kashmir, the men of the Wattal tribe perform circle dances at specific times and locations. They wear colorful robes and conical caps adorned with shells and beads. The dancers begin slowly and gradually build up to jumps and leaps, to the accompaniment of drumming and singing.

Pāther refers to popular folk theater. *Jashan pāther* takes place on the anniversary of a Sufi saint's death (*ʿurs*) and is performed by professional itinerant minstrels. *Bānde pāther*, performed by male professionals (*bhānd* or *bhagat*), combines acting, mime, acrobatic dance, song, music, and witty dialogue in a play with loosely con-

FIGURE 6 Male *bhānd* performers in Srinagar, Kashmir, 1978: *top,* costumed actors; *bottom, bhānd* musicians playing (*left to right*) *surnāi, ḍholak,* and frame drum. Photos by John Emigh, courtesy Amy Catlin.

nected stories [see KASHMIR]. The oppression suffered by Kashmiris over time is a popular theme. Dancers wear masks and costumes to portray animals such as deer and tigers (figure 6, upper photo). The *surnāī* 'double-reed oboe', a frame drum, and a *ḍholak* accompany the performers (figure 6, lower photo).

Dances from the hills of Jammu have more in common with those of Himachal Pradesh than those of Kashmir. The villagers dance the *kud* dance to offer thanks and praises to the village deity (Gram Devata). At the end of the fall corn harvest, everyone gathers around a bonfire, and singing dancers follow musicians playing drums, flutes, and horns. Forming a circle, pairs of dancers take turns dancing in the center.

Himachal Pradesh

Northern parts of the state are influenced by Tibetan culture, and the performance of the *singhi* or "snow-lion" dance to ensure peace and prosperity reflects Buddhist

The bhangra dance has spread internationally to Indian cultural occasions and even discos in the United Kingdom, the United States, and Canada, and its popularity has led to bhangra competitions attracting thousands.

thought. Hindu devotional festivities take place, but most dance and song is associated with agriculture and seasonal changes. The Gaddi peasants of Chamba district sing poignant love songs of separation and songs about domestic life. Often, men dance energetically while women, fully adorned, act as spectators. Songs and dances may last for days, as in the Tushimig, a forty-five-day festival organized by unmarried girls.

At Renuka Lake, in Sirmur, an annual fair honors the sacrifice of Renuka, who was killed by her son Parasurama, the battle-axe-wielding incarnation of Vishnu. The highlight of the fair is the *parāsa* dance, named after the *parāsu* 'battle-axe' that the male dancers carry. Women also participate, adding a gentle aspect to this rather martial dance.

In the Kulu valley—where no festive occasion takes place without song and dance—Dussehrā, the autumn Hindu festival honoring Lord Rama, is the most important. Festivities last for several days, and villagers parade images of Lord Raghunath from various temples to a central place where they sing and dance all night long.

Punjab

Lively music and dance forms are characteristic of the fertile agricultural state of Punjab. Punjabi men of all castes dance the vigorous, spontaneous, and often comic bhangra, especially during the harvest festival (Baisākhī). Dancers, decked out in colorful costumes and turbans, form a semicircle, and individuals take turns showing off in the middle. They squat, leap, perform balancing tricks and acrobatic feats, and form pyramids by climbing on each other while reciting witty couplets (*bolī*) and shouting "oai-Oai," "bale-Bale," and "uh-hah." A *ḍhol* 'large cylindrical drum' or *ḍholak* 'barrel drum' player accompanies the dancing, striking the drum with sticks for a loud effect. The bhangra dance has spread internationally to Indian cultural occasions and even discos in the United Kingdom, the United States, and Canada, and its popularity has led to bhangra competitions attracting thousands [see NORTHWEST INDIA: PUNJAB].

The *giddhā* is the female counterpart of the bhangra, generally performed to celebrate a good harvest, the arrival of the rainy season, or the birth of a child. Women dance in a group, singing and clapping as individuals or pairs move into the center to dance. In one variation called the *kiklī*, pairs of dancers hold hands and twirl.

Haryana

The leading dance of Haryana is *dhamyal*, also called *daph* after the frame drum that the male dancers play. Men alone or with women perform the dance at harvesttime, singing songs of valor or love. Popular women's dances are the *lahū* and *holī*, both performed in springtime. When sowing in the fields is over, women dance the *lahū* in two groups, singing songs consisting of witty questions and retorts. Girls dance the *holī* in a circle, and clap and sing humorous songs of satire and contemporary events, while one or two may take turns dancing in the center.

Uttar Pradesh

In the mountain tract of Garhwal, men and women dance at two of the most important shrines in India: Kedarnath, dedicated to Shiva, and Badrinath, dedicated to Vishnu. Together they perform the *kedar,* swaying gracefully while holding a cloth in the left hand and a *chamar* 'sacred whisk' in the right hand. Among the Kumaon people, men wielding swords and shields dance the energetic *choliya* during weddings, as they process to the bride's house. Tribal peoples (*ādivāsī*) and pastoral nomads of the same hilly regions, such as the Mongoloid Bhotiya community, have ritual dances; they perform the *dhurang* one year after a person's death in order to free the deceased's soul from evil spirits. Dancers hold swords and dance in a circle, using martial movements.

In the rich, fertile plains along the Ganges river, largely agricultural communities celebrate the harvest with dance and music. In the southeastern Mirzapur district, men perform a ritual dance called *karam,* connected with the fertility cult. They offer worship to Karam Devta in the form of a fresh tree branch. The village men dance vigorously, accompanied by loud drumming and led by the village priest, who may fall into a trance at the end of the ceremony.

In the Braj region, the colorful and lively dances of Holī (springtime) last for a full month. Each village has its own version. Ribald men and veiled women dance together, often in procession through the town, and throw colored powder on each other or dance with sticks of varying lengths, the women sometimes striking the men on their shins or their shielded heads. The dances are reminiscent of Lord Krishna's dances with the *gopī* milkmaids, and the songs are permeated by an atmosphere of spiritual eroticism.

Rajasthan [see RAJASTHAN]

Gujarat

The two main dance genres of Gujarat are *garbā* and *rās*. Women perform *garbā* in honor of the Mother Goddess during the Navrātrī 'Nine nights' festival. Under the autumn moon, women sing, clap, and perform a simple circular dance while balancing perforated earthen pots with lighted lamps on their heads. They are accompanied by a male *ḍhol* player in the center. When men join in, the dance is known as *garbī.* The *rās* dance also takes place during Navrātrī, particularly in the Saurashtra region. Men mainly perform *rās* to devotional songs dedicated to the Mother Goddess, Amba, and Lord Krishna, who is believed to have originally performed the *rās.* Women and people of all ages and classes may join in the dancing, which becomes *ḍāṇḍiā rās* 'stick dance' when they hold sticks or rods in their hands.

Similarly for recreation and on festive occasions, Dang tribal men and women of the south dance the *dangi,* which culminates in the women standing on the men's shoulders, forming a pyramid, while continuing to dance.

Koli women workers in Saurashtra perform a functional dance called *ṭīpaṇī.* The dancers stamp their feet and beat the floor with a long wooden stick with bells tied to the top, creating rhythmic patterns as they engage in the tedious work of building a house.

Differing slightly from the folk drama of Rajasthan, the Gujarati *bhavāī* consists of a series of short comic sequences. Professional male performers from certain communities dress up and dance, act, sing, juggle, and perform acrobatic feats to amuse their audiences.

FIGURE 7 Muṇḍas dancing at the Ind (or Indi) festival, a multiethnic, regional annual festival to the god Indra. Gumla District, Bihar, 1984. Photo by Carol Babiracki.

Bihar

Bihar has one of the largest tribal (*ādivāsī*) populations in India. Villages often have an open place, usually surrounded by trees, set apart for dancing by men and women. Men play drums while women dance to songs and dances that describe pastoral scenes such as the picking of indigo, the harvesting of grain, and humorous themes such as the quarrels of co-wives. Men's dances often depict scenes of animal hunting. Men and women of the Oraon tribe often dance together in close-knit formations, singing songs celebrating the seasons. The Muṇḍas, some 20 percent of whom have converted to Christianity, are among India's earliest inhabitants (figure 7). They have revived group dances, called bhajan dances, only within the last twenty-five years. Tribal populations including the Oraon, Santal, and Ho have maintained a continuous tradition of communal dancing unsegregated by gender. Male drummers play *nagārā* 'kettledrums' and *rabga*, *ḍholak,* and *mandar* 'double-headed drums'; men also play bamboo flutes and various kinds of cymbals. Santals represent the largest tribe in Bihar, and like other tribal groups they have seasonal dances for the various events of the agricultural, ritual, and festival calendars. Many dances of the Ho tribe are dedicated to the spirits of their ancestors. Their dances are also related to sowing and harvesting crops, wedding celebrations, or the New Year. In spring, Ho women dance the *mangala ghat* while carrying pots, to the pounding of huge drums by the men.

Sikkim

Sikkim shares much of the same traditional Buddhist culture with Tibet. Women have their own folk dances, but men tend to perform religious dances as devotional offerings. In hundreds of monasteries, monks perform *cham* dances in open courtyards (see "Arunachal Pradesh" below), especially during Tibetan and Sikkimese New Year celebrations and festivals honoring specific guardian deities. The most common Buddhist dance theme is the destruction of evil as depicted in the black-hat dance (*shanag*); through the mystic language of the initiated, the performance reveals how one can attain the highest realm by eliminating the negative forces in life.

West Bengal

When the Bengali saint Chaitanya (1484–1533) spread the Gaudiya Vaishnav sect of Hinduism throughout Bengal in the early sixteenth century, a vibrant devotional music tradition called *kīrtan* was begun. Vaishnav devotees continue to chant and dance *nagar kīrtan* in praise of Krishna through the streets, playing double-headed, laced drums (*mridang*) and cymbals (*khartāl*).

The Bāul sect of Bengal draws spiritual inspiration from four major sources: Islam, the mystic Sufism, the devotional path (bhakti) of Vaishnavism, and Hindu-Buddhist Tantric philosophy. This sect of wandering minstrels make their living strumming a one-stringed plucked lute (*ektārā*), playing a simple drum (*ḍugi*), and singing and dancing ecstatically.

In the villages, men perform the springtime dance called *bolan* at the Gajan festival in honor of Shiva. At the same festival, a masked performer wielding a sword dances the *kālī nāch* dedicated to the goddess Kali (Shiva's consort), often ending in a trancelike or prophetic state. In Bengal's most important festival, Durga Pūjā, devotees worship painted clay images of the mother goddess as they dance to the incessant pounding of drums.

Jātrā has been a popular dance drama of Bengal for hundreds of years. The traditional themes derived from the stories of Radha and Krishna; during the freedom movements leading to partition in 1947 and the founding of Bangladesh (formerly East Bengal) in 1971, patriotic and sociological themes were common in *jātrā* performances.

Assam

Shankardev, a poet-saint of the fifteenth and sixteenth centuries, founded a devotional dance tradition in Assam called *satriya*. Vaishnav men depict episodes from Lord Krishna's life in the play of Gopal (*Kelī Gopāl*), accompanied by the *khol* drum, cymbals, and singing. The performance leads from Krishna's childhood pastimes to the *mahā rās nritya* 'great *rās* dance', in which Krishna dances with the *gopī* milkmaids. The *ankia nat*, a ritual dance-drama form, is also attributed to Shankardev. Celibate male members of monasteries (*sattra*) perform this drama, led by a *sūtradhār* 'narrator' who also dances. The plays about Krishna or Rama combine acting, dancing, singing, and dialogue in a language that combines Maithili, Assamese, and some Sanskrit verses.

Deodhani is a ritual dance in honor of the serpent goddess Manasa. An unmarried female dancer sways in a seated position, twirling her head in a frenzied manner until she becomes possessed by the spirit of the goddess and collapses. *Behula*, another dance connected to the serpent goddess, recounts the story of Behula, who fought the wrath of Manasa to bring her dead husband back to life. A male performer in female attire recounts the story with dance and serpentine movements, supported by a pair of drummers.

Of the many secular Assamese folk dances associated with seasons and occupations, the popular *bihu* dance takes place during the month after harvesting in mid-April. Men and women of all backgrounds dance in a circle or in separate parallel rows without mixing the sexes, to the accompaniment of drums and pipes.

Tripura

Many of the dances from this tiny northeastern state revolve around the daily lives of its nineteen tribal populations. Dances may relate to catching birds and insects, hunting animals, and harvesting. In ritual ceremonies such as the Maimata festival, men and women sing and dance to the accompaniment of *pung* drums and *sarinala* 'bowed stringed instrument'. Villagers at this festival offer new rice to Lakshmi, the Hindu goddess of fortune, and show through their dance movements the entire rice-cultivation process.

Lai hāroba, combining ritual, folk, and classical elements, is one of the most significant aspects of Manipuri culture. The *lai hāroba* dances, each with a specific purpose, depict the Manipuri version of the world's creation.

Manipur

The classical "Manipuri" dance style and the *rās* dance evolved from folk dances of Manipur. *Lai hāroba*, combining ritual, folk, and classical elements, is one of the most significant aspects of Manipuri culture. The main dancers are traditional high priestesses (*maibi*) and priests (*maiba*), who are acknowledged to be specially chosen by the divinities to honor them through the dance (Vatsyayan 1976:133). They perform a wide range of mystical dances at specific times of year before shrines dedicated to gods and deified heroes. The dances, each with a specific purpose, depict the Manipuri version of the world's creation.

Sankīrtan, an extension of the devotional singing and dancing of Chaitanya's Vaishnav sect in Bengal, exists in two varieties. In *khartāl cholom,* dancers use cymbals with long red tassels, and in *pung cholom*, dancers play *pung* drums held on by a long strap behind the neck. Both are energetic dances performed by men who play their instruments as they leap and do dazzling barrel turns in the air. Another example of acrobatic drum dances takes place during the springtime festival of Holī, also famous for a variety of celebratory dances. These are particularly spectacular at the temple of Govindji, an important center of religious life in Imphal, the capital of Manipur. Holī dances include the *thabal chongbi*, a simple dance popular among boys and girls of all castes because they can mix freely and stay out all night. They step and sway while holding hands and singing.

Thang-ta is a martial dance drama performed by young men with swords and shields that was a favorite of the former kings of Manipur. Another form of dance theater is *gop rās* or *sanjenba*, in which professional prepubescent boys perform stories exclusively about Krishna. Only a few adults participate, taking the adult roles. Like Tripura, Manipur also has a sizable tribal population and many joint men and women's dances.

Arunachal Pradesh, Meghalaya, Mizoram, and Nagaland

These states, all predominantly tribal, are known for war dances that display techniques of combat and hunting. Men dress in hide armor and black fiber cloaks and hats, brandishing swords and shouting war cries. In Nagaland, men use spears for the *tushokuko* war dance.

A popular dance among girls in Mizoram is called the *cheraw.* They skip and hop nimbly over bamboo poles, which other kneeling girls hold with both hands and knock rhythmically on the ground. The Khasi tribals of Meghalaya celebrate with song and dance when the paddy is ripe for threshing.

Arunachal Pradesh borders Bhutan and Tibet and is heavily influenced by Buddhism. Tribes such as the Khampas, Khamptis, Monpas, and Sherdukpens perform dances, dance dramas, pantomimes, and operas based on Buddhist legends. Dancers can train in the Tibetan style at special facilities. They make masks representing demons and animals from the Buddhist tradition, and perform the symbolic dances called *cham*, mostly in monasteries during festival times. Musicians with long trumpets, drums, and cymbals accompany the dancing, along with seated monks chanting Buddhist verses. The black-hat dance (*shanag*) is the only monastic dance performed without masks. *Ngonpae don*, a ritual dance of the hunters, depicts Vajrapani, a bodyguard of the Buddha. In the *sha cham* dance of the Sacred Stag, the Lord of Death sends his messenger in the form of a stag. Skeletons appear as servants of the Lord of the Cemeteries in *thoko gari cham*.

NEPAL

Among the people of Nepal, a Himalayan kingdom influenced by both Indian and Tibetan cultures, music and dance are a necessary part of religious ceremonies and family occasions. One of three great festivals held in Kathmandu, the capital, is the Indra Jātrā, which includes a masked dance drama, *mahākālī pyakhan*. The festival takes place for a week in September at the end of the rainy season, and honors the Hindu god of rain. The tradition belongs to the Newaris, the original settlers of the Kathmandu valley, who still make up half its population. A troupe of over a dozen male performers and musicians, mostly goldsmiths, silversmiths, and farmers, present the dance drama. It depicts a story based on the third part of the *Devī Mahātmya,* a religious text praising the Mother Goddess in which the three goddesses—Mahalakshmi, Kumari, and Mahakali (one of the nine incarnations of the goddess Durga)—defeat the demons Shumbha and Nishumbha. The dancers don masks of varied shapes and colors made of clay and paper topped with heavy metal crowns signifying particular characters and personalities, and perform without dialogue or singing. Accompanying musicians play the *jhyāli* 'cymbals', *pashchima* 'double-headed drum', *mwali* 'double-reed wind instrument', and *kahan* 'horn'.

Several kinds of *lakhe* dance also take place at the Indra Jātrā festival. Other dances depict the legend of Lakhe, a notorious Newari demon who runs through the streets of Kathmandu kidnapping children daily. The *lakhe* dancers play the dyers (Chhipa), who sheltered the demon when the king of Nepal ordered him captured.

BANGLADESH

As the former eastern section of undivided Bengal, today's Muslim-ruled Bangladesh has strong cultural and linguistic ties with India's West Bengal. Congregational chanting associated with the lives and activities of Krishna and of Sri Chaitanya (*padāvalī kīrtan*) is popular, as are theatrical renditions of Krishna's pastimes with the milkmaids (*kṛshṇa līlā*). Young boys play all the parts, singing, dancing, and acting before large crowds of villagers. Another favorite entertainment in rural areas is *jātrā* musical theater, with its spoken dialogue, song, music, and dancing. Colorfully dressed and made-up male performers offer varied material on religious and historical themes, performing all night long on raised outdoor stages. A musical ensemble sits near the stage, in which Western instruments such as the saxophone, trumpet, clarinet, violin, and harmonium are combined with local instruments such as the *jhāñjh* 'large cymbals', *khanjanī* 'small cymbals', *mañjīrā* 'brass bells', and the *ḍholak* 'barrel drum'.

In the 1930s, Rabindranath Tagore introduced the *nṛtya-nāṭya,* generally considered to be at the highest artistic level of any dance drama in Bangladesh. Performances take place in urban centers on a plain proscenium stage; dancers present the stories through pantomime, singers sing the dialogue, and choruses and instrumentalists accompany them.

The majority Muslims of Bangladesh have their own dance dramas (*jārigān*), the first of which was a commemoration of a tragic massacre of Muslims over a thousand years ago. Now, in addition to exploring secular and political themes, the dramas also tell religious stories. The leader (*bayati*) tells the story through narration and song, and occasionally sways, crouches, and swings both hands to signal the chorus of eight to ten to sing a fast tempo refrain (*dhuā*). Waving colored handkerchiefs in their hands, the chorus members circle the leader in a performance called *jāri-nṛtya*.

PAKISTAN

Music is a significant part of religious and domestic life, but those who perform professionally are often considered of low social status. A hereditary caste of musicians known in Pakistan, Iran, and northwest India as Mīrāsī, makes its livelihood by dancing, singing, playing instruments, and impersonating women [see PAKISTAN: PUNJAB]. Mīrāsī women entertain their female superiors through song and dance, accompanying themselves on the *ḍhol*. The men play a variety of instruments including drums (*ḍhol, naqqārā, ḍholak, duff*), bells (*ghuṅghrū*), wooden clappers (*chaprī*), lutes (*sārindā, rabāb*), and reed pipes (*bīn, śahnāī*). These professional musicians perform at life-cycle ceremonies associated with birth, circumcision, marriage, and death.

Contexts for nonprofessional music and dance performance include agricultural fairs or festivals associated with the anniversaries of Muslim saints. Men dance in a circle accompanied by drums and shawms, occasionally going into the middle to dance individually or in pairs. Among the conservative Pashtuns of the North West Frontier Province, men sing Pashto poetry, play the *ḍhol* and *śahnāī*, and perform the *ḳhattak* dance in men's gathering places (*hujra*). The *jamalo* dance of the Sindhi community in southeastern Pakistan is similar to the call-and-response forms found in northwest India. The Punjabi community in the east enjoys a lively and relatively unrestricted song and dance tradition. As in the Punjab state of India, men dance the bhangra and women enjoy the *giddhā* dance.

AFGHANISTAN

The Islamic state of Afghanistan encourages neither dance nor music. Dance is considered amoral and potentially dangerous and is therefore restricted, especially for women. Young dancing boys have traditionally provided entertainment [see MUSIC AND GENDER, figure 2]. In the twentieth century, some religious or national feast-day celebrations, and weddings particularly, have included public dancing. The *atan* 'round dance' of the Pashtuns, with its male and female variations, is now the national dance. In public outdoor performances, men dance in a circle and vocalists sing nonrhyming couplets (*landay*) on general topics such as love and war, accompanied by the *ḍhol, surnāī, sārindā, and rubāb*. Although the singers and instrumentalists are male, it is mostly women who compose the poetic verses.

The Afghan Turkmen have one principal male dance, a circular pastoral dance with shepherd's staffs. As part of wedding festivities, women dance individually and as a group in a round dance. The Uzbeks frequently combine music and dance, with the *damburā* player indicating the tempo to the dancer. In the isolated northern mountain region of Badakhshan, the Tajiks perform satirical folk dramas about everyday life and masked dances in which they imitate animals.

REFERENCES

Dance and Music in South Asian Drama: Chhau, Mahakali Pyakhan, and Yakshagana. 1983. Report of Asian Traditional Performing Arts (ATPA) [III], 1981. Tokyo: The Japan Foundation.

Folk Dances of India. 1956. Publications Division, Ministry of Information and Broadcasting, Government of India.

Hansen, Kathryn. 1992. *Grounds for Play: The Nautanki Theatre of North India.* Berkeley and Los Angeles: University of California Press.

Khokar, Mohan. 1987. *Dancing for Themselves: Folk, Tribal, and Ritual Dance of India.* New Delhi: Himalayan Books.

Misra, Susheela. 1989. *Invitation to Indian Dances.* New Delhi: Gulab Vazirani for Arnold Publishers (India).

Nanda, Serena. 1990. *Neither Man nor Woman: The Hijras of India.* Belmont, Calif.: Wadsworth.

Vatsyayan, Kapila. 1976. *Traditions of Indian Folk Dance.* New Delhi: Indian Book Co.

———. 1980. "India, VII: Dance." In *The New Grove Dictionary of Music and Musicians*, ed. Stanley Sadie. London: Macmillan.

Music and Dance: Southern Area

Saskia Kersenboom
Mekhala Devi Natavar

The Origin of *Nāṭya*
The Karnatak Tradition
Kerala
Karnataka
Andhra Pradesh
Tamil Nadu
Orissa
Karnatak Dance Today

THE ORIGIN OF *NĀṬYA*

> "The *Nāṭyaveda* was composed by me so that it would apportion good and bad luck."

Thus Brahma, the supreme god of Hinduism, patiently explains in the *Nāṭyaśāstra* the true nature of *nāṭya*, its universal relevance, aim, and validity (Ghosh 1967, I:105). The term *nāṭya* encompasses the three worlds of existence: the worlds of the gods, of mortals, and of antigods and their allies. Brahma himself distilled four different sensory essences from the four Vedas, the holy texts of eternal knowledge from Vedic times (1500–600 B.C.) that give their name to the early period, and fused them into *nāṭya*. From the hymns of the Ṛgveda he took recitation, from the liturgy of the Sāmaveda he took song, from the formulaic Yajurveda he took drama, and from the magical Atharvaveda he took taste. Brahma revealed all this to the sage Bharata in the form of a manual, the *Nāṭyaśāstra*, which was compiled in the early centuries C.E. (Ghosh 1967). Bharata in his turn taught *nāṭya*—music, dance, and drama—to his one hundred sons. To this day, as in ancient times, words, sounds, forms, and actions are inextricably intertwined in traditional South Indian theater. The presentation of a drama missing either song or dance would be unimaginable. To a great extent, dance *is* drama, and drama *is* dance; both emerge from sound, from musical structure and sensibility, as ever fresh as the human psyche itself.

The performance of *nāṭya*

Ancient Indian music treatises drove home the ambivalent character of *nāṭya*: it is powerful, capable of generating good luck and bad luck—dealing as it does with the divine—and thus is potentially dangerous. Not only is it dangerous in itself, but it is surrounded by danger. For human beings to manipulate these forces is not an easy task; it requires the training, skill, and experience of professionals to interact with the three worlds. *Nāṭya* can therefore take place only with meticulous care and alert protection. A mistake or flaw could bring great danger instead of well-being. Potentially envious spirits must first be pacified, grudging antigods must be charmed. Every facet of the performance is crucial: the stage, the stage props, the text, the diction, the

The mythological world of love and war comes alive in the evening darkness, lit by the huge stage lamp, resounding with the recitation, the loud drumming, and the Karnatak melodies.

music, the movements, the makeup, and the elaborate costumes. For this reason, the dressing room is considered to be a place of ritual importance. The stone on which the paste for makeup is prepared is worshiped before it is used. Then, with makeup, ornaments, and body paint, characters are created. The dressing room is like the womb whence they are born into the actual, physical shape of the divine (Bruin 1994; Nambiar 1981?).

Validity

An occasion for *nāṭya* invites the gods to descend to the playground of this world and enter the bodies of human actors, who empty and open themselves up as "vessels" to receive the divine contents. The relatively short *nāṭya* performance is an intense interaction between gods, mankind, and other sentient beings; it is a nourishing experience, a "tasting" of the three worlds. Such tasting is called *rasa*, and the legendary Bharata distinguished eight "tastes of being" in his musical treatise: the "erotic," encompassing the "comic"; the "furious," encompassing the "pathetic"; the "heroic," encompassing the "marvelous"; and the "odious," encompassing the "terrible." All verbal, musical, and physical training of actors ultimately amounts to the study of *rasa*.

THE KARNATAK TRADITION

South Indians have considered *nāṭya* of vital importance since the earliest times. Artists have been passing on performance practices for some two millennia, resulting in the variety of South Indian drama, music, and dance we know today. These traditions are rooted in the Dravidian languages of Tamil, Kannada, Telugu, and Malayalam, whose grammars were formulated from the third century B.C. It was in the fifteenth and sixteenth centuries that these artistic practices began to be identified as Karnatak, or South Indian, in contrast to the North Indian, or Hindustani, traditions.

Music played a leading role in forming a distinct Karnatak ethos. Around 1500, the saint-singer and composer Purandara Dasa (1484–1564) codified basic musical scales and vocal training. The court of Vijayanagar, a medieval Hindu stronghold, gladly accepted this basic course, and since that time it has served as the training method for both vocal and instrumental music. After the fall of Vijayanagara in the mid-1500s, that court's function as normative center for the arts was taken over by the courts of Tanjore (now Tanjavur) and Trivandrum further south. Poetry, music, and dance flourished once again. Around 1800, four brothers (the so-called Tanjavur Quartette) codified basic dance training much as Purandara Dasa had done for music. They designed an ideal suite (*mārgam* 'path') for dance concerts that survives today. The brothers themselves studied with the greatest Karnatak musicians and composers of the time: Syama Sastri, Muttusvami Diksitar, Tyagaraja, and Svati Tirunal. In this milieu, music and dance developed degrees of refinement that still stand out as quintessentially "classical." Various layers of culture and society may generate, at any time, a vitality that is usually described in the West as "classical." Foreign traditions that are assigned Western labels such as "classical" and "folk" should therefore be understood only as flexible dimensions of one and the same phenomenon, transforming incessantly.

Apart from variation due to external factors such as region, audience, and performance function, Karnatak tradition varies according to the performers' perspective. For example, the distinction between the lyrical, introspective theme of love and the heroic struggle between good and evil has existed in South Indian performing arts since the oldest Tamil sources on music. Two thousand years ago bards "of the small lute" performed love songs (the ancient category of *akam*), whereas songs of victory and fame (the *puṛam* category) usually belonged to the repertoire of bards "of the large lute." Such a distinction persists today in the small band (*cinna mēḷam*) and large band (*periya mēḷam*) that support Tamil temple rituals and the rites of passage in society. This lyrical versus heroic distinction has also generated contrasting dance and drama themes, performances, performers, and contexts throughout South India.

KERALA

Kūṭiyāṭṭam

Of all theatrical forms in India, *kūṭiyāṭṭam* remains closest to the dramatic tradition of Bharata's *Nāṭyaśāstra*. That such a model Sanskrit theater should survive in such excellent state, so far removed from its original cradle in North India (birthplace of such famous Sanskrit dramatists as Kalidasa and Harsa), is quite remarkable. And yet Vedic recitation also survives in this southwestern state, which is home to Syrian Christians, Jews from Cochin, Muslims, and even communists with their legends. Among the many immigrants who settled in Kerala and found its people and cultures open to their ideas and ritual traditions were the Nambudiri Brahmins. Together with the local Nāyars and Cākyārs, the Nambudiris blended Sanskrit and Malayalam traditions into ritual theater forms that were soon firmly established in the precincts of Hindu temples. Even today, temple walls provide safe protection for the auspicious content of the stories enacted, such as the heroic exploits from the great Hindu epics, the Ramayana and the Mahabharata. The great Vadakkunathan temple in Trichur, for example, has an ancient *kūttambalam* 'drama hall' that closely follows the prescriptions for a playhouse given by Bharata.

The characters and the structure of *kūṭiyāṭṭam* plays are also consistent with the ancient manual on drama. Even the performers' makeup conforms to Bharata's advice: heroes and kings are covered with slightly reddish paint; princes like Arjuna and Rama are green; aborigines, antigods, demons, and demonesses are black; and the face of the ferocious adversary-hero Ravana shines pure red. Huge, complex crowns reveal the nature of the heroic characters, and pith balls worn on the tip of the nose, symbolic of warts or disfigurations, adorn characters like Ravana; both add to the elaborate grammar of identities.

The mythological world of love and war comes alive in the evening darkness, lit by the huge stage lamp, resounding with the recitation, the loud drumming, and the Karnatak melodies (Ramanujan 1985). In this safe temple milieu, both women and men can perform *nāṭya*. The ritual dramas echo ancient cults and practices still found outside the temple walls. Fierce village gods and sophisticated martial arts practitioners also seem to be in attendance, peeping over the shoulders of all present.

—Saskia Kersenboom

Kūṭiyāṭṭam, the oldest form of classical Sanskrit theater still performed in Kerala, and possibly the oldest continuously performed dramatic form in all of India, is closely

FIGURE 1 *Kūṭiyāṭṭam* dance drama of Kerala, performed at the Asia Society in New York. Photo courtesy the Asia Society.

associated with temple life and religious rituals. Before the twentieth century, the performance was confined to temple compounds, where it served as a visual sacrifice to the temple deity. The actors and actresses are members of the temple castes in Kerala; the male roles are enacted by Cākyārs, female roles by Nangiyārs (women of the Nambiyār caste) (Richmond 1990:90).

Though the plays are written and sung in both Sanskrit and Prakrit (ancient Indic language or languages), it is the local language, Malayalam, that is used for the improvised prose passages spoken by humorous characters such as the royal clown (*vidūṣaka*), who relates the thematic development of the text.

Performances usually take place on auspicious days in the temple calendar and may last for several nights. They begin and end with elaborate invocatory rituals: lighting an oil lamp with three wicks (representing Brahma, Vishnu, and Shiva) at the beginning and extinguishing it at the end, and offering flowers, water, Sanskrit prayers, and special drumming The actual dance drama begins with *puṛappāṭu,* during which an actor performs movements behind a curtain. This is followed by *nirvāhaṇa*, the entrance of the first character, who relates details about his personal history and the story itself (Richmond 1990). The characters are identifiable by their costumes, ornaments, and headdresses, all of which have symbolic meanings. Throughout the drama, there is more emphasis on the actors' individual interpretations of their characters' nuances and points of view than on ensemble playing or the structure of the play. The acting style blends symbolic gestures (with heavy use of hands, face, and eyes), stylized physical movements, and chanted dialogue and verses. Nambiyārs sitting at the rear of the stage play large *miḻāvā* 'leather-headed pot drums' to keep the tala and set the mood; to the left of the stage a Nangiyār may sing verses, accompanied by a Cākyār playing tiny cymbals (figure 1).

—MEKHALA NATAVAR

Besides *kūṭiyāṭṭam*, the performing arts in Kerala's temples include the singing of the *Gīta Govinda* of Jayadeva, *cākyār* 'solo actor-storyteller' performances, *rāmanāṭṭam* 'dance drama on the life of Rama', *kṛshṇāṭṭam* 'dance drama on the life of Krishna', *mōhini āṭṭam* 'solo dance of the divine temptress', and the spectacular and best-known of Kerala's theater forms, *kathakaḷi*. The latter takes place outdoors or in modest shrines to local heroes who attained divine status through their miraculous deeds or prowess in hunting, or in war. These are the *teyyam* 'gods' and *bhūtam* 'spirits' whose fame or notoriety have spread through the region and who demand worship through *nāṭya*.

—SASKIA KERSENBOOM

Teyyam

Teyyam is a ritualistic form of worship of folk and tribal gods, goddesses, and benevolent or malevolent spirits. With poetry, music, dance, and drama, the ornately costumed performers present stories about festivals, deities, and local shrines. In the worship ritual, the *teyyam* 'gods' and *bhūtam* 'spirits' themselves appear as dancers, made to look huge and formidable with masks and headgear. They are impressive as they dance, and they speak as oracles or become possessed. These gods and spirits help the village and protect the inhabitants, making the fields fertile and curing the sick. Each community and subcaste has its own shrine, which allows it to keep in touch with the powerful gods—and especially goddesses—of the region.

Kūttu

Kūttu (also known as *cākyār kūttu*), the predecessor of *kūṭiyāṭṭam*, was a dramatic performance by members of the Cākyār community, who embellished their narrations from the epics and Puranas by employing suggestive facial expressions and hand gestures. A narrator would act out the roles of the various characters, accompanied by a Nangiyār woman playing small brass cymbals and a male Nambiyār playing the *miḻāvå* drum.

—MEKHALA DEVI NATAVAR

Rāmanāṭṭam

The dance drama *rāmanāṭṭam* portrayed the life of Rama. Like *kṛshṇāṭṭam,* it took place over a period of eight nights. It differed from the Krishna dance drama in its use of the vernacular Malayalam instead of literary Sanskrit. In the seventeenth century, *rāmanāṭṭam* performances took place outside temple walls, and thus were open to the lower castes, prohibited from seeing *kṛshṇāṭṭam* within the temple grounds. Also, in *rāmanāṭṭam* no masks were used, singers were employed in addition to the dancers, and the musical accompaniment included the *ceṇṭa* 'double-headed cylindrical drum'. The enormous popularity of *rāmanāṭṭam* encouraged new plays on broader mythological and sacred themes, which in turn led to the development of *kathakaḷi* (Massey 1989:44–45).

—MEKHALA DEVI NATAVAR

Kṛshṇaṭṭam

The devotional dance drama *kṛshṇāṭṭam*, which also predates *kathakaḷi*, utilizes an elaborate and stylized language of facial expressions, hand gestures, and body movements. Cycles of eight plays based on the exploits of Lord Krishna are performed on eight successive nights. Devotional songs of the Vaishnav tradition (with texts mostly in Sanskrit) are interspersed with dance sequences that function as vehicles "for establishing devotional union with Lord Krsna" (Zarrilli 1990a:309). Characters can be recognized by their elaborate makeup and costumes; some, such as animals and demons, appear with painted wooden masks (figure 2).

—MEKHALA DEVI NATAVAR

The young *kathakaḷi* student must undergo a unique course of massages designed to readjust his body, in order to prepare it for years of intensive training.

FIGURE 2 *Kṛshṇāṭṭam* devotional dance drama performance at the Asia Society, New York. Photo courtesy the Asia Society.

Mōhini āṭṭam

Mōhini āṭṭam, a semiclassical dance dedicated to the goddess Mohini, is traditionally performed by women, although it is often taught by men. This dance style may have originated in the sixteenth century, inspired by the spread of Vaishnavism in India. In dancing *mōhini āṭṭam*, devotees worship Lord Vishnu as Mohini, the enchantress: according to Hindu mythology, the god assumed this guise to distract the demons and allow the gods to carry off the elixir of life (*amrita*) from the churning of the oceans. The dances express divine love and devotion to Vishnu or his chief incarnation, Krishna. Due to its sensual, fluid movements, *mōhini āṭṭam* became associated with erotic indulgence during the nineteenth century and the beginning of the twentieth century, before it was revived and was again taught in dance academies, beginning in the 1950s.

In the majority of *mōhini āṭṭam* performances, a female soloist moves gracefully using circular motions, stylized hand gestures, and delicate footwork to enhance her expression of emotion (*bhāva*); in recent times, group dances have also taken place. Dancers use light makeup—yellow and pink facial paste, black eye liner, and lip reddener. A simple white jacket and white sari are worn, and white jasmine flowers adorn the hair.

As in *bharata nāṭyam*, the *mōhini āṭṭam* performance begins with an invocatory pure dance, followed by *jatisvaram*, *varṇam* (a combination of pure and expressive dance), *padam*, and *tillāna* (a pure dance sequence meant to display the technical artistry of the dancer). The dances utilize four main types of dance steps (*aḍavu*) and are performed to Karnatak music consisting of sung lyrics composed in Manipravala, a mixture of Sanskrit and Malayalam. The dancer usually sings, although the accompanying group includes a singer (Massey 1989:67). Musicians play the *mridangam* and violin and on occasion the *iṭaykka* 'small hourglass drum', instruments that have replaced the earlier *toppi maddaḷam* 'barrel drum' and vina. The tempo is usually slow or moderate.

—Mekhala Devi Natavar

FIGURE 3 The dramatic makeup and headgear of a *satvik* character in the traditional male dance drama, *kathakaḷi*, in a Kerala Kalamandalam performance in New York. Photo by Clifford R. Jones, courtesy the Asia Society.

Kathakaḷi

Kathakaḷi, the classically influenced dance drama of Kerala, joins five forms of artistic expression in one performance genre. *Kathakaḷi* performers, traditionally all male, dance (*nṛtta*) and act out scenes using a codified language of gesture (*nāṭya*) to interpret poetic texts (*sāhitya*), which are usually based on the Puranic stories (Hindu sacred texts) and the Mahabharata and Ramayana epics. Karnatak music (*saṅgīta*), the fourth form of expression, is an integral part of the performance. The main accompaniment is provided by two vocalists singing the text and two percussionists playing the *maddaḷam* 'double-headed barrel drum', which is strapped horizontally across the musician's thighs; the *ceṇṭa* 'double-headed cylindrical drum', usually played with two curved sticks; and the *iṭaykka* 'small hourglass drum'. A conch shell is sounded at the entry of certain characters.

To enhance the visual effect of the dramatic movements, the fifth, pictorial component (*cittram*) is achieved by the use of colorful makeup and elaborate costumes. The makeup for *kathakaḷi*, which can take up to four hours to apply, is the most extensive of all Indian classical dance and dance-drama forms. Actors' faces are painted various colors to denote one of three major character types: *satvik* (divine, noble, heroic, generous, refined), *rājasik* (passionate, greedy, vain, antiheroic), and *tāmasik* (evil, cruel, vicious) (Samson 1987:128). The faces of *satvik* characters, for example, have a green base, a religious marking on the forehead, and a layered, curved white frame (*chutti*) around the lower jaw (figure 3). The lips are a brilliant red, and heavy black lines extend past the eyebrows, calling attention to the reddened eyeballs. Other characters can be identified by the color and type of the beard (white for divine beings, black for hunters and robbers, red for extremely cruel and evil characters), by the application of white bulbs on the nose and forehead (for *rājasik* characters), and by the size and color of their crowns (figure 4). Female roles are played by men wearing a head scarf over a topknot that leans to one side, and makeup consisting only of lip reddener and eye and brow liner. The costumes likewise differ according to role; *satvik* and *rājasik* characters, for example, wear red upper jackets and white pajamas covered by long white skirts with orange and black stripes.

FIGURE 4 *Rājasik* character wearing white bulbs on his nose and forehead, in a Kerala Kalamandalam performance of the *kathakaḷi* dance drama, New York. Photo by Clifford R. Jones, courtesy the Asia Society.

A *kathakaḷi* performer must be skilled in both acting and dance in order to portray the character he embodies. The dance aspect can be divided into pure dance patterns, which take place at the beginnings and endings of performances, and dramatic dance, which may imitate a peacock or depict a battle. Pure dance sequences use no vocalization, whereas dramatic dance sequences usually combine dance with dialogue to bring the epic stories to life. The element of *abhinaya* 'expression' is important in *kathakaḷi* technique, and the performer evokes moods (*bhāva*) through dances that vary in rhythm, movement style, speed, and choreography. This is achieved in "three stages: (a) word-to-word synchronisation, (b) interpretation of the full line, and (c) abhinaya of the dancer following the singer" (Zarrilli 1990b:28).

The young *kathakaḷi* student must undergo a unique course of massages designed to readjust his body, in order to prepare it for years of intensive training (Vatsyayan 1974:26–28). The body is exercised in its entirety, from the quivering lower eyelids to the upturned toes. The dancer follows geometric patterns (rectangular and square for walks, diagonal and circular for vigorous scenes) in both movement and body stance. *Kathakaḷi* has four basic footwork patterns performed at three different speeds. In the basic wide stance (*maṇḍala sthāna*), for example, the feet are spread apart and parallel, the bent knees are bowed out with the outer soles of the feet touching the ground and the inner sides and big toe lifted off the ground. In walking, one foot meets the other before stepping forward and to the side again. The hands, tracing geometric patterns, including diagonals, are followed by the eyes. The torso is used as one unit, often in a fluid circling motion. Leg extensions, spirals, jumps, and leaps are performed to a given rhythmic cycle (tala) in the pure dance portions. Variations of the twenty-four main hand gestures (*hasta*), which communicate both facts and moods, are exaggerated by the use of long silver extensions worn on the fingers. Perhaps the most distinguishing feature of *kathakaḷi* technique, however, is the prominence given to the use of facial muscles, in particular the movement of the eyebrows, eyeballs, lower eyelids, and cheeks (Zarrilli 1990b:338).

Dancers use various methods for entrances and exits. They may enter the stage from the side (with or without a curtain), from the audience, or from behind a curtain held by two associates. The curtain can simply be dropped; or it can be lowered slightly, to give the audience a partial glimpse of the character; or the actor can manipulate the curtain, moving it from side to side or up and down to reveal parts of himself, until he shows his entire being.

—Mekhala Devi Natavar

Tuḷḷal

Tuḷḷal (literally 'jumping') is a dance drama popular with the general public for, unlike those of *kūṭiyāṭṭam*, *kṛshṇāṭṭam*, *mōhini āṭṭam*, and *kathakaḷi*, its poetic text based on the Hindu epics is sung in the local vernacular Malayalam rather than in Sanskrit. Originally choreographed and written two centuries ago by Kunjan Nambiar, a court drummer and poet, *tuḷḷal* is performed by a solo dancer accompanied by two musicians, one playing the *maddaḷam* 'double-headed drum' and the other playing small cymbals. Both musicians sing along with the dancer; they stand slightly behind him during the performance. Of the three kinds of *tuḷḷal*, *oṭṭan* is more popular than *paṛayan* and *sīthangan,* which have simpler costumes. The actor needs neither curtains for his entries and exits nor a formal stage for his presentation; the only stage prop he requires is the lighted brass lamp common in the performing arts of Kerala. The dancer enthralls the audience with a fast-paced, two-hour performance in which he may sing over a thousand couplets while enacting various emotions (*rasa*) such as anger, pathos, valor, humor, and devotion. The strong movements require an agile body and years of rigorous training. The makeup and jewelry are similar to that used in *kathakaḷi,* with the dancer's face painted yellow and blue, his eyes black and his lips red. The costume consists of a series of white skirts, a pearl-bedecked breastplate, colorful tassels, necklaces, bracelets, amulets, and a small, brightly decorated golden crown.

—Mekhala Devi Natavar

KARNATAKA

The three worlds of existence—of gods, mortals, and antigods—are made present literally everywhere, all through the year, according to a ritual calendar that marks daily, weekly, monthly, and seasonal occasions for *nāṭya*. The "belt" of *teyyam* shrines proceeds north from Kerala into southern Karnataka, the gods claiming thousands of such platforms to halt, reside, rest, be feasted, and receive worship. Along with it runs the belt of elaborate drama forms, emerging from the same necessity for gods and

FIGURE 5 The character Karna, played by P. Rajagopal in the *kaṭṭaikkūttu* dance drama *Karna moksham*. Photo courtesy Hanne de Bruin.

men to meet. The Karnataka dance drama *yakṣagāna* 'song of the *yakṣa*', like *kuchipuḍi* of neighboring Andhra Pradesh and *kaṭṭaikkūttu* in Tamil Nadu (figure 5), is very close to the model of the *Nāṭyaṣāstra* but for its stage. Indeed, the actors perform in a space that has been ritually cleansed and demarcated in the village, opposite the village temple or even in its courtyard, but otherwise bearing little resemblance to the *kūttambalam* of *kūṭiyāṭṭam*. Perhaps for this reason women traditionally do not perform in these dramas outside the temple; their roles are taken by male transvestites.

—SASKIA KERSENBOOM

Yakṣagāna

Yakṣagāna, a colorful dance drama performed by temple-sponsored troupes especially during the six-month performance season, is based on episodes from the major epic stories. Its origins lie both in Sanskrit literature and theater and in Kannada literature, ritual music, and dance. The repertoire comprises some sixty plays based on the Ramayana, the Mahabharata, and the *Bhāgavata Purāṇa*. The *yakṣagāna* drama is performed in the open air, sometimes on a raised platform, and is directed and conducted by the *bhāgavatar*, who also plays the finger cymbals, recites, and sings. The musical ensemble includes two drummers (on *maddaḷam* and *ceṇṭa*), and a harmonium player. The actors perform scripted or improvised dialogues; the *bhāgavatar* sets the context for the dramatic scene.

The *yakṣagāna* performers wear spectacular costumes, makeup, and headdresses according to their character type. The basic face color for heroes, for example, is pink-yellow, with a large red, white, or black *tilaka* 'ornamental mark' on the forehead, while the basic makeup color for demons is red and green or red and black (Vatsyayan 1980b:42–43). On their heads, some characters wear crowns as in *kathakaḷi*, but the heroes wear elaborately tied turbans (figure 6) [see MUSIC AND THEATER, figure 4].

Tāl-maddale

Tāl-maddale (literally 'cymbal and double-headed barrel drum' is a narrative drama that is believed to be the predecessor of *yakṣagāna*. A seated actor-dancer, called the

FIGURE 6 *Yakṣagāna* performers rehearsing a martial scene before a performance at Banaras Hindu University, 1982. Photo by Stephen Slawek.

The traditional *kuchipuḍi* dance drama is still presented as a dramatic form of worship by male devotees from Brahmin families in the village of Kuchipudi, but *kuchipuḍi* performance has now become popular as an expressive solo classical dance form.

bhāgavata, performs a narrative without the use of costumes or makeup. He may be accompanied by associates (*arthadharī*).

—Mekhala Devi Natavar

These and other dance-drama forms—*yakṣagāna* (Karnataka), *kathakaḷi* (Kerala), *kuchipuḍi* and *bhāgavata melām* (Andhra Pradesh), and *kaṭṭaikkūttu* (Tamil Nadu)—were created from the sixteenth century onward, when the regional literatures of Kannada, Malayalam, Telugu, and Tamil were developed in South India. Their stories are from the great Hindu epics, the Mahabharata and the Ramayana, not in the Sanskrit original but in the local language and in their locally known versions. Regional heroes, saints, and local gods and goddesses are favorite characters that demand their place next to the heroes of the Sanskrit epics. The preference for certain themes prevails in particular drama traditions. The story of Draupadi, the wife of the five Pandava princes, for example, is common in *kaṭṭaikkūttu* performances. Three elements of the story in particular—the plight of Draupadi in the court of the Kauravas, who try to disrobe her; Lord Krishna coming to her rescue and lengthening her sari cloth infinitely; and her final revenge, with all its gory details—empower many village audiences in eastern Karnataka, southern Andhra Pradesh, and northern and southern Arcot in Tamil Nadu.

Such theater forms are performed in villages by itinerant professionals who know their audiences completely and who take into consideration audience preferences. Interaction with the public is extremely important. Performers develop the classical role of the buffoon (*vidūṣaka*) to a maximum. His comments and jokes challenge the audience to respond, to choose sides, and to identify deeply with the characters such that individual spectators may enter into a state of possession. *Nāṭya* is auspicious, and South Indians believe it is good for villages to be immersed in its world from time to time, although the function, form, and power ascribed to the various *nāṭya* forms differ. Those dramas performed as part of temple rituals during festivals are considered very powerful. Others offered in a more spontaneous, free setting are less so. Examples of the latter include forms of street theater such as *vīthināṭaka* (Andhra Pradesh), *oṭṭan tuḷḷal* (Kerala), and *terukkūttu* (Tamil Nadu), which bear close resemblance to the temple forms.

—Saskia Kersenboom

ANDHRA PRADESH

Kuchipuḍi

Kuchipuḍi is an example of a *nāṭya* tradition that derives its name from a "center of excellence": the little village of Kuchipudi in Andhra Pradesh renowned for its performing arts. Brahmin boys were trained in the arts of singing and dancing as performed by female dancers in Hindu temples. Whereas the temple walls protected the female dancers while they performed *bhamakalapam*, these young boys were allowed to perform as itinerant drama troupes in the villages around Kuchipudi. Their repertoire and staging techniques drew on the long history of Dravidian performing arts, including the multimedia rendering of traditional texts. The boys performed their Telugu *kuchipuḍi* repertoire with spoken recitation, song, and dance, this threefold expression of the Telugu language following a similar division in Tamil known as *muttamil*. Furthermore, myriad textual genres were produced in practically all regional languages; all can be considered *prabandham* (literally 'composition'). From a modest tenth-century classification comprising thirty-six genres, *prabandham* expanded to ninety-six genres by the sixteenth century, and to 248 in the nineteenth century. Such stupendous growth can be understood only as a massive penetration to all layers of society and everywhere in the southern peninsula.

The dramatic forms of *kuchipuḍi* and *bhāgavata melām* depend heavily on the *yakṣagāna* tradition of Karnataka, but they do not employ mythological costumes or makeup. The love for grandeur rather takes the form of silk, brocade, jewelry, and gold; actors portray their characters in a relatively realistic manner. Important innovations have emerged in the musical component of this art; the *kīrtana* structure, which shapes dance compositions like *padam, jāvaḷi,* and *pada varṇam,* has become the independent genre known today in Karnatak music [see KARNATAK VOCAL AND INSTRUMENTAL MUSIC].

—SASKIA KERSENBOOM

Though some place its origin back as early as the third century B.C., *kuchipuḍi* has developed considerably over the past three hundred years. Siddhendra Yogi, a Telugu Brahmin and devotee of Lord Krishna, has been called the founder of this dance drama as it is known today. He popularized and redefined the form, and his play about Krishna was performed by young Brahmin men and boys of Kuchelapuram (later called Kuchipudi), on the Krishna river. The play was such a success that its popularity spread to other villages, which likewise performed it for religious festivals. *Kuchipuḍi* dramas are based on Hindu religious epics, the preliminary sung verses presented in Sanskrit and the text dialogues performed in the vernacular Telugu.

The traditional dance drama is still presented as a dramatic form of worship by male devotees from Brahmin families in the village of Kuchipudi, but *kuchipuḍi* performance, with its mimetic action, recitation, singing, and dancing, has now become popular as an expressive solo classical dance form, deemphasizing the dramatic aspect. *Kuchipuḍi* dance is lively and expressive, and its style is sensual and delicate, without losing the strength of poise and purpose. Dancers use a deep squatting position with knees turned out, and statuesque poses are distributed throughout the dance. The costume for female dancers, who nowadays dominate and sometimes play male parts in *kuchipuḍi* dramas, is usually silk minisaris much like those worn by *bharata nāṭyam* dancers. Male dancers may perform bare chested with a colorful wrapped dhoti. Jewelry consists of armlets, necklaces, and golden belts. Although no crown is used, women don head ornaments and adorn their long plaits with more jewelry and flowers. Solo *kuchipuḍi* dancers do not wear heavy makeup, but important characters in the dance drama may be distinguished by their makeup and costumes. Performers wear ankle bells, and must be familiar with Telugu and Sanskrit since they also provide the vocal music (Massey 1989:28). They are accompanied by a chief musician (*sūtradhāra*) who keeps the beat with a pair of brass cymbals, recites the dance syllables, and tells the story. An accompanying ensemble composed of a violinist, a clarinetist, and a *mridangam* drummer plays Karnatak music (Swann 1990:173).

In recent years, many of the solo dances and dramas in *kuchipuḍi* style are seen on proscenium stages, although some dance dramas still take place on temporary stages in the open air. Preliminary stage rituals are presented for all to view, followed by the entry of the musicians; then the principal actors introduce themselves by performing a song-and-dance sequence called *daru,* chosen from a corpus of about eighty such sequences, depending on the identity of the character. Of the many individual dances, the most popular is that in which the dancer manipulates a brass plate with her feet while dancing and balancing a pot of water on her head.

—Mekhala Devi Natavar

TAMIL NADU

After the fall of the cultural stronghold Vijayanagar in 1565, a large-scale exodus of scholarly, musical, and dramatic talent moved south from Andhra Pradesh to Tamil Nadu. The Tamil Chola country, bathed by the waters of the Kaveri river and dotted with ancient temples like the shrines in Tiruvarur and Tanjavur, would now serve as these groups' new home, where they were protected by the royal patronage of the Tanjavur court. For a great many *kuchipuḍi* performers, their final stopover in Andhra Pradesh was Melattur, whence *bhāgavata melām* actors later followed a similarly successful path when they moved south into Tamil Nadu.

Tamil music has always featured the solo female form of *nāṭya*, both in the past within the privacy of the temple and the royal court, and in recent decades on the public concert platform. Two thousand years ago, female bards (*virali* and *pāṭini*) danced and sang Tamil poetry. The first great Tamil epic, the *Cilappatikāram* 'The Tale of the Anklet', speaks of the highly sophisticated courtesan Madhavi. Centuries later, courtesans known as *dēvadāsi* took part in rituals performed for the god-kings in temples, and as *rājadāsi* performed for human kings in the royal courts. Their presence, as well as their arts, were considered auspicious, destroying the effects of the "evil eye." Radiant, beautiful, and bedecked with brilliant jewelry, they asserted the strength of life over death. (figure 7).

FIGURE 7 A *dēvadāsi* of Tanjore (now Tanjavur), 1900. Photo courtesy Saskia Kersenboom.

Apart from daily ritual tasks in the inner sanctum of the temple, the *dēvadāsi* participated in festival rituals involving the temple's entire corps of priests and musicians, who surrounded the processional image on its journey outside the temple walls into the village. On such occasions the temple courtesans could be heard and seen singing and dancing village forms such as the stick dance (*kōlāṭṭam*), the clap dance (*kaikkottikkali*), boat songs (*ōṭam*), and swing songs (*uñjal*). When the procession stopped for a moment to allow the god, mounted on a throne in a pavilion, to relax, the *dēvadāsi* dancers would perform a dance concert (*nāṭya kaccēri*) for the deity as if he were a king in court. Such a concert resembles the concert suite now considered classical. It incorporates the best of South Indian lyrical poetry, music, and drama, expressing love that bespeaks a strength other than heroism on the battlefield or victory of good over evil. Such *nāṭya* performance is a form of bhakti devotion: a melting and total surrender to become part of the Divine, dissolving the boundaries of the Self.

Sometimes temple dancers performed in festival dramas such as the romantic *kuravanji,* in which a gypsy plays an important role as go-between. When the ritual retinue left the temple grounds, the performers intermixed their own dances with village traditions that sought to create auspiciousness for the villagers. Processional forms such as *karakam* 'pot dance', *kāvaṭi* 'dancing under the yoke of ritual offerings', and the merrymaking of the *kutirai* horse dance belong to the tumultuous, exuberant atmosphere of festival ritual (figure 8). The boundaries dividing ritual, folk, and sophisticated or "classical" were thus very flexible, possibly because the main purpose of performance was the auspicious effect, not an artistic one.

—Saskia Kersenboom

FIGURE 8 Dancers of the Om Periyaswami troupe balance pots on their heads. Madurai, Tamil Nadu, 1984. Photo by Amy Catlin.

Kuravanji

This South Indian folk dance is traditionally performed by young women of the Kurava hill tribe, a nomadic gypsy people of whom the men are snake charmers, acrobats, and tumblers, and the women usually fortune-tellers (Massey 1989:35–37). The legends of this noncaste tribe revolve around fortune-telling and romantic episodes, and the women interpret these stories in the *kuravanji* dance. Generally from six to eight dancers perform, with lively and sometimes passionate movements. The length of the performance varies according to the context. Many of the dances are performed for the god Shiva, although at least one honors Vishnu. In recent years, *kuravanji* dancers have tended to be men dressed as women, and dance groups try to outdo each other in dancing and singing about the superior qualities of their own gods (Massey 1989:37).

ORISSA

Oḍissi, a major classical dance form of India, has its roots in the temples of Orissa on the eastern coast of the subcontinent. To judge from archaeological evidence, it may have originated over a thousand years ago, developing into the present "reconstructed" form that was codified in the 1950s. As a regional variety of dance, *oḍissi* is mentioned in several ancient treatises based on the canons of the *Nāṭyaśāstra*, especially Maheshwar Mahapatra's *Abhinaya Chandrika* (c. sixteenth century), which defines the main principles of the dance: the division into *nṛtta* 'pure dance', *nṛtya* 'dance with emotion', and *nāṭya* 'dramatic dance'; and the classification of *tāṅḍava* and *lāsya*, the masculine and feminine aspects respectively (Mishra 1989:51–52; Vatsyayan 1974:34–35). Until recently the dance was performed by female temple dancers (*mahāri*) who were restricted to performing within the temple precincts. They rendered expressive narratives usually based on Vaishnav literature, while imitating the poses of dancing figures carved on temple walls, such as those at Bhubaneshwar, Puri, Kapileshwar, and in the great dancing hall of the Sun Temple at Konarak. Young male dancers (*gotipua*) dressed and performed like their female counterparts, but had to leave the temple at the age of eighteen, when they often became dance teachers.

Poetry plays a vital role in *oḍissi* dance. The most popular text enacted by *oḍissi* dancers has been the *Gīta Govinda*, a set of twenty-four devotional, lyrical Sanskrit

In a performance of *oḍissi*, the dancer begins with a slow invocatory dance, offering flowers and obeisance to the earth.

FIGURE 9 The *oḍissi* dancer Sanjukta Panigrahi in the *tribhaṅga* pose. Photo courtesy the Asia Society.

poems (*aṣṭapadī*) composed in the twelfth century by the Krishna devotee Jayadeva. Dances set to this and other texts inspired by Vaishnav philosophy constitute the *oḍissi* repertoire. The divine love of Radha and Krishna, as well as descriptions of the ten incarnations of Vishnu, are the themes most commonly portrayed. Even in today's performances, statues of Lord Jagannath (Krishna), his sister Subhadra, and his brother Balarama are present onstage.

In a performance of *oḍissi*, the dancer begins with a slow invocatory dance (*maṅgalācaraṇ*), offering flowers (*pushpāñjali*) and obeisance to the earth (*raṅgbhūmi pranām*). The music throughout the performance includes both Hindustani and Karnatak ragas, and is generally played by the North Indian *pakhāvaj* 'barrel drum', flute, sitar, violin, finger cymbals, harmonium, and *svarmaṇḍal* 'box zither' (Mishra 1989:53–54). To the accompaniment of sung Sanskrit verses, the dancer then prays to her favorite deity, the most popular being Lord Jagannath, present in iconic form on an elevated platform (if performed onstage). This is followed by salutations made to the gods (Ganesh in particular), the guru, and the audience. The next item, *batu*, is pure dance, but is inspired by Tantric worship and performed in honor of Shiva in his terrifying aspects as Batukeshwar Bhairava (Patnaik 1971:87; Samson 1987:111). *Batu* builds in tempo and prepares the dancer for *svara pallavi*. Here the dancer's movements illustrate and elaborate on the melody and rhythm. After these pure dance items, the performance focuses on *abhinaya*—demonstrations of emotions in music and sung verses, especially those of the poet-saint Jayadeva's love song *Gīta Govinda*. The concluding item is the *mokṣa nata*, the dance of liberation, which represents one of the four major aims of life, according to Hindu thought. It is a pure dance performed in fast tempo to the recitation of rhythmic drum syllables played on the *mardala* drum, usually by the guru (Samson 1987:111).

Oḍissi dancing is soft, graceful, lyrical, and sensual in both theme and movement. The technique can be divided into *samabhaṅga*, *abhaṅga*, and *tribhaṅga* positions. *Samabhaṅga* refers to a square body position with the spine straight, the weight divided evenly between the legs, and the arms upraised to the sides with elbows bent. In *abhaṅga*, the body's weight shifts unevenly from side to side through deep leg bends, with the knees and feet turned outward, causing one hip or the other to extend sideways. *Tribhaṅga* (literally 'three bends) is the most distinctive position of *oḍissi*, and is to be seen in numerous temple sculptures; it involves the curvaceous bending of the body in three places, with the head and hips deflecting in the opposite direction of the torso (figure 9). The arms are used to frame the body, while hand gestures (*mudrā*) similar to those used in *bharata nāṭyam* and facial gestures (*abhinaya*) focusing on expressions of the eye are used in conjunction with the various postures to express specific moods, emotions, and stories. The bare feet can be moved in several positions called *pada bheda*. The entire body moves like a wave as it shifts weight both in walks and statuesque posturing. Slow turns in a deep knee stance are occasionally incorporated, particularly in pure dance sequences.

Male *oḍissi* dancers wear a dhoti, with a long, thin, folded *dupatta* draped over one shoulder and tucked into a wide belt at the waist. Female dancers wear a comfortably draped and heavily pleated silk sari that is sewn from the waist down to allow maximum movement in executing deep knee bends. The matching sari blouse is further covered with a light veil, tied on the side of the waist and sometimes tucked under the heavy waist belt. The head ornament, earrings, wrist bangles, armlets, necklaces, and heavy, wide belt are usually of silver. The hair is tied in a bun and covered with an elaborate decoration that peaks at the top like a temple tower and includes several concentric wrapped garlands of white flowers. The makeup consists of reddened lips, and eyes and eyebrows elongated and accentuated by dark black liner. The forehead is decorated with a large red vermilion dot. As in other classical dance forms, dancers wear ankle bells and female dancers apply a red liquid (*alta*) to the palms, fingertips, and soles of the feet to mark their auspiciousness.

—Mekhala Devi Natavar

KARNATAK DANCE TODAY

Village dances, temple rituals, and great festivals continue with all pomp, but since the middle of the twentieth century the *dēvadāsi* have disappeared from the public horizon. In independent India, the ritual status of female *nāṭya* artists has been transformed into the secular status of lay performers on proscenium stages dependent on the box office. Fresh boundaries have been drawn between regional manifestations of the older traditional continuum. Now Kerala proudly presents *mōhini āṭṭam*, Andhra Pradesh presents female *kuchipuḍi*, and Tamil Nadu claims *bharata nāṭyam*. The dancers are no longer temple dancers—*ambalavāsi* in Kerala; *bhogam*, *kalavantulu*, or *sani* in Andhra Pradesh; *basavi* or *dēvadāsi* in Karnataka and Tamil Nadu—but upper-middle-class college girls, students, and even housewives, who often pursue "classical dance" as a status symbol.

—Saskia Kersenboom

Bharata nāṭyam

Internationally recognized as the quintessential dance of India, *bharata nāṭyam*, the classical dance style of Tamil Nadu, was variously referred to prior to this century as *sadir kacheri* or *dasi āṭṭam*. Some translate the name as "the dance of Bharat (India)," while others insist it derives from Bharata, the sage who authored the ancient treatise on the performing arts, the *Nāṭyaśāstra*. Still others believe it to be "an acronym of the first syllables of bhava (expression), raga (melody) and tala (rhythm) summing up the three pillars upon which the style rests" (Samson 1987:29). *Bharata nāṭyam* is lively and energetic, graceful and expressive, stylized and statuesque.

FIGURE 10 The *bharata nāṭyam* dancer Leena Pallivathucal poses as Manmathan, a character similar to Cupid, shooting an arrow to pierce the heart of the beloved with erotic love. Irvine, California, 1998. Photo courtesy George Pallivathucal.

Originally performed as part of temple rituals and processions by female temple servants (*dēvadāsi*), *bharata nāṭyam* remains rooted in Hinduism. Religious import is apparent not only in the dance technique, with many of the poses imitating those of deities and figures in sculptural reliefs in Hindu temples, but also in Hindu philosophy and stories from the epics and Puranas (Hindu sacred texts).

This highly codified dance style gives equal weight to pure dance technique (*nṛtta*) and to dramatic or mimetic dance (*nṛtya*), in which verses are interpreted by the dancer. The *nṛitya* aspect requires knowledge of the stories being interpreted as well as knowledge of the technique of *abhinaya*, the portrayal of moods and emotions, predominantly through the eyes and face but enhanced by appropriate hand positions and body movements (figure 10). Dancers, who are usually female, train for many years under the tutelage of teachers (*naṭṭuvanār*). According to Bharata Muni's *Nāṭyaṣāstra*, *bharata nāṭyam* divides the body into major and minor limbs, as well as upper and lower halves, all of which are utilized. The ten major body positions described in the text *Abhinaya Darpana* include half-sitting, full-sitting (a squatting position on the toes with knees spread outward to the sides), and knees dropping to the floor (Samson 1987:30). Equal attention is given to exercises for the legs, torso, hands, fingers, arms, head, and eyes. Of the many elaborate arm positions that frame the body in symmetrical lines, the most common in *bharata nāṭyam* is outstretched arms at shoulder level. The footwork patterns are not so complex as in the North Indian dance style *kathak*, but the hand and finger positions are detailed and specific, each one having a name and a meaning. The *nṛtta* technique entails "the systematic buildup of adavus, a series of static positions linked to form movement" (Samson 1987:34). These include difficult postures, turns, jumps, slides, squats, the stretching of limbs, and foot and hand combinations, all practiced preferably in slow, medium, and fast tempos.

The female dancer wears a heavy silk and brocade-bordered costume sewn in the design of a pleated sari draped over a silk blouse. Her hair is plaited and adorned with bunches of white jasmine flowers. The traditional jewelry consists of head ornaments, earrings, a choker, a longer necklace with a pendant in the middle, gold bracelets, and a wide gold belt covered with gems. She wears bells attached to a wide leather strip on each ankle. Her fingertips, toes, and soles are tinged red as an auspicious marking. The makeup is natural with eyes accentuated and lengthened by dark eyeliner, and a red dot (*tilak* or *biṅdī*) decorates the forehead.

The extensive repertoire of a typical *bharata nāṭyam* performance by a solo dancer begins with an *alārippu*, an invocatory pure dance without sung verses performed to the rhythm of a *mridangam* drum. This is followed by another pure dance sequence to a musical composition called *jātisvaram*. In *śabdam*, the dancer intersperses pure dance with the mimed interpretion of sung verses to a musical composition in Karnatak style. Perhaps the most complex and compelling dance, the *varṇam*, combines both *nṛtta* and *nṛtya* aspects of the dance. In *varṇam* the dancer works closely with the singer and the drummer, weaving dance compositions in differing tempos to the syllables recited by the *naṭṭuvanār* and the drummer, and interpreting the theme being sung through improvisations. This dance is followed by *abhinaya padam* and *jāvaḷi*, interpretive dances on lyrical passages set to music. *Tillāna*, the statuesque and exciting conclusion to a recital, is a purely abstract dance piece performed to a musical composition set in a specific raga and tala. The dancer displays her virtuosic skill in movement and footwork, as drum syllables are sung in ever-escalating tempos. Beginning with the eyes, the movement shifts to the neck and proceeds to the shoulder, torso, arms, and finally to the legs. The body makes geometric patterns in space, tracing circles and diagonals in the air and on the floor. The performance ends with the recitation of a Sanskrit religious couplet. *Bharata nāṭyam* performances may also include invocatory dances called *pushpāñjali* 'an offering of flowers', *kautuvam*, *aṣṭapadī* (on a verse from the poet-saint Jayadeva's *Gīta Govinda*), or *kīrtana*, which combines pure and interpretive dance techniques.

The dancer is accompanied by a *naṭṭuvanār*, who plays the cymbals, calls out the mnemonic rhythmic syllables of the dance, and may sing, as well as a singer and a *mridangam* player, who maintains the pace and supports the dancer rhythmically. The accompanying ensemble also usually includes violin, flute, vina, and *tambūrā* 'string drone'.

—Mekhala Devi Natavar

The modern term *bharata nāṭyam* merges all levels of time, place, performer, and audience; it represents a pan-Indian claim to classical dance, based on the foundations laid down in Bharata's ancient treatise. In the 1930s, dance "reformers" deliberately and selfconciously re-created this dance form in an effort to erase the perceived stigma associated with earlier dance practice and to create legitimacy both for the new dance and for the community of dancers. Today *bharata nāṭyam* has many aspects. Scholarly research on the *Nāṭyaśāstra* has led to innovations that would surprise even Bharata. Dance dramas, thematic concerts, and archeological reconstructions form the inspiration for myriad dance scholars, attending and presenting lecture demonstrations in the many dance festivals, conferences, and international seminars (Gaston 1991).

—SASKIA KERSENBOOM

REFERENCES

de Bruin, Hanne. 1994. "*Kaṭṭaikkūttu,* The Flexibility of a South Indian Theatre Tradition." Ph.D. dissertation, University of Leiden.

Gaston, Anne-Marie. 1991. "Dance and the Hindu Woman: Bharata Natyam Re-ritualized." In *Roles and Rituals for Hindu Women*, ed. Julia Leslie, 149–173. London: Pinter Publishers.

Ghosh, Manmohan., ed. 1967. *Nāṭyaśāstra* (Sanskrit text and translation). Calcutta: Granthalaya.

Kersenboom, Saskia. 1995. *Word, Sound, Image—The Life of the Tamil Text.* Oxford: Washington, Berg Publishers.

———. 1998. [1984]. *Nityasumangali, Devadasi Tradition in South India*, 2nd ed. Delhi: Motilal Banarsidass.

Massey, Reginald, and Jamila Massey. 1989. *The Dances of India: A General Survey and Dancers' Guide*. London: Tricolour Books.

Mishra, Susheela. 1989. *Invitation to Indian Dances.* Bootle, Merseyside: Lucas Books.

Nambiar, Balan. 1981? "Gods and Ghosts, Teyyam and Bhuta rituals." *Marg* 34(3): 63–75.

Patnaik, D. N. 1971. *Odissi Dance.* Bhubaneswar: Orissa Sangeet Natak Akademi.

Ramanujan, A. K. 1985. *Poems of Love and War: From the Eight Anthologies and the Ten Long Poems of Classical Tamil.* New York: Columbia University Press.

Richmond, Farley P. 1990. "*Kūṭiyāṭṭam.*" In *Indian Theatre: Traditions of Performance,* ed. Farley P. Richmond, Darius L. Swann, and Phillip B. Zarrilli, 87–117. Honolulu: University of Hawaii Press.

Richmond, Farley P., Darius L. Swann, and Phillip B. Zarrilli, eds. 1990. *Indian Theatre: Traditions of Performance*. Honolulu: University of Hawaii Press.

Samson, Leela. 1987. *Rhythm in Joy: Classical Indian Dance Traditions*. New Delhi: Lustre Press Private Ltd.

Swann, Darius L. 1990. "The Devotional Traditions: Introduction." In *Indian Theatre: Traditions of Performance,* ed. Farley P. Richmond, Darius L. Swann, and Phillip B. Zarrilli, 169–176. Honolulu: University of Hawaii Press.

Vatsyayan, Kapila. 1974. *Indian Classical Dance.* New Delhi: Ministry of Information and Broadcasting.

———. 1980. *Traditional Indian Theatre, Multiple Streams.* New Delhi: National Book Trust.

Zarrilli, Phillip B. 1990a. "Dance-Dramas and Dramatic Dances: Introduction." In *Indian Theatre: Traditions of Performance,* ed. Farley P. Richmond, Darius L. Swann, and Phillip B. Zarrilli, 307–314. Honolulu: University of Hawaii Press.

———. 1990b. "*Kathakaḷi.*" In *Indian Theatre: Traditions of Performance,* ed. Farley P. Richmond, Darius L. Swann, and Phillip B. Zarrilli, 315–357. Honolulu: University of Hawaii Press.

Ranjit
PRESENTS
SAIGAL
KHURSHID
in
Tansen
JAYANT DE
तानसेन
1943

Mass Media and Contemporary Musical Exchange

At each stage in the advance of technology, the Indian subcontinent has made a vital and creative contribution. Its engagement with the West's march to modernity has resulted in indigenous gramophone records, silent films, electrical recording, radio, sound films, magnetic tape recording, television, hi-fi stereo, audio cassettes, video cassettes, compact discs, digital video discs, satellite TV, the Internet, and more. Such media—as elsewhere in the world—have made rapid communication, widespread distribution of musical forms, and the lively international exchange of mediated products commonplace. They have also encouraged new industries, new popular genres, and new mass markets. India, for example, has become home to the largest film industry in the world, and produces hundreds of films and thousands of film songs every year. While South Asia has experienced commercialism, capitalism, consumerism, and standardization, its mass media have in recent decades been able to give many performing artists a powerful voice in the modern world of South Asia and beyond, a voice they might not otherwise have had.

Many Indian films of the 1930s and 1940s presented familiar mythological, historical, or devotional themes to audiences nationwide, but in the new and exciting cinematic form. This lyric-booklet cover portrays the film actor–singer K. L. Saigal as the hero Tansen in Ranjit Movietone's 1943 production on the renowned court musician of the sixteenth-century Mughal emperor Akbar. Saigal and his heroine Khurshid sang thirteen songs in the film, some of which have become "evergreen hits." Photo courtesy Alison Arnold.

Music Broadcasting, Recording, and Archives

Brian Q. Silver

Broadcasting of Indian Music
Commercial Recordings
Archives

The capability of electronic media to amplify, transmit, and record musical sound has radically transformed the nature of Indian music performance and its propagation. To begin with, broadcast and recording technology have contributed to an extension of Indian music's accessibility for a potentially unlimited audience. Thanks to recording, Indian musical performance is no longer limited to being a momentary phenomenon, captured only in fading memory; a performance of Indian music can now become a concrete, permanent artifact, subject to continued and repeated reexamination over short and long periods of time. Recording has contributed to an unprecedented codification of an improvisational music that traditionally had no full-scale notation. At the same time, it has promoted an expansion of the scope and expressive possibilities of that music through more widespread dispersal, which promotes cross-fertilization. Recordings have served as invaluable tools to musicians for self-assessment and the improvement of their own musical skills. They have also provided precise documentation of the traditions of past masters, as well as a source of new ideas for musicians to study the techniques and approaches of other (often competing) musicians, allowing them to incorporate such techniques into their own performance styles. Certain classical artists have been able virtually to duplicate styles of other musical traditions (*gharānā*) without any direct study within those traditions, even identifying themselves explicitly as exponents of the traditions (the disciples of the late vocalist Amir Khan, for example).

The development of these electronic technologies has come at a critical juncture in the modern era, which began with the loss of traditional court and temple patronage for musicians from the mid-nineteenth century on. Much has been written about the shift from elite royal and aristocratic audiences and private patronage to public sources of income (Neuman 1970). Of greater relevance here is the fact that as the royal and regional court audiences were disappearing, new audiences were created both in large public halls, even stadiums, where hearing the subtleties of Indian music was assisted by amplification, and among radio listeners scattered over a vast broadcast area covered by short- and medium-wave frequencies. (Most recently, FM is now being introduced in South Asia.) To extend accessibility even further, any listener with a gramophone player (and later, sound-reproduction systems) could duplicate the experience of hearing a particular performance of a raga by a classical artist through the medium of recorded sound—initially the 78-rpm disk, then the LP (and marginally the EP), then the cassette, and now the CD.

What follows is a brief survey of the state of these technologies at the end of the twentieth century as they relate to the classical music of South Asia.

BROADCASTING OF INDIAN MUSIC

Each of the state-run radio networks of South Asia—All India Radio, Pakistan Broadcasting Corporation, and Radio Bangladesh—includes classical music in its broadcasts, continuing the nationalist tradition begun early in the century of celebrating the classical heritage in the face of the colonialist occupiers. For decades one of the most prestigious honors a musician could receive in India was an invitation to perform on the *National Programme of Music*, broadcast nationwide on All India Radio for ninety minutes at 9:30 P.M. on Saturday nights; this has now been changed to an hour on both Saturday and Sunday nights at 10:00 P.M. Local stations in many cities broadcast classical music two to four times a day in order to accommodate the full daily time cycle of ragas. At the radio station a musician will record (often by contract once a month) a morning, evening, and night raga, usually at one sitting, for broadcast at some later date.

Although employment with the national All India Radio provided an important source of income for musicians following Indian independence, with the consequent loss of courtly patronage, radio performance is currently of secondary importance, both in prestige and in renumeration. More highly esteemed by both upcoming and established musicians are concert appearances, particularly now that independent radio broadcast channels transmit a strongly youth-oriented pablum of popular music and deejay chatter, complete with telephone calls from listeners. As the percentage of broadcast time devoted to film music increased over the past few decades, the prominence of classical music began to fade. But All India Radio still professes a commitment to classical music. One result of this commitment is the Radio Sangeet Sammelan 'radio music gathering' program that runs for six weeks in November and December with nightly hour-long broadcasts at 10:00 P.M. originating in different Indian cities.

Some efforts are being made in South Asian countries to include dignified programming of classical music performances on national government-run television. Certainly a well-staged *mehfil* 'concert sitting' in a traditional context can be more engaging experientially on video broadcast than on radio. The international commercial satellite networks have yet to incorporate classical music into their programming.

COMMERCIAL RECORDINGS

The current offering of commercial compact-disc recordings of Indian music reflects nearly an entire century of rich musical development. With Indian classical music recognized as one of the world's great traditions, listeners at the end of the 1990s have the option of hearing historic performances as well as renditions by a wide range of contemporary performers of varying stature.

In historical terms, it is worth noting that hundreds upon hundreds of 78-rpm recordings of classical music, featuring some of the nation's greatest artists, were produced in India in the first half of this century. Recognizing a significant market, European companies developed a thriving record industry under a variety of labels, most notably those under the umbrella of the Gramophone Company of England (initially the Gramophone Company Ltd. in England), which began producing recordings at the beginning of the twentieth century and has continued to survive all the changes in recording technology (Joshi 1988). A substantial portion of the early material has been reissued on CD. The discovery of a full set of mint-condition masters in the EMI archives in London greatly helped this task in the 1980s. Indian companies initially lagged behind Western firms in the indigenous production of compact discs—as they did earlier with LP recordings—but there is now in India a thriving industry offering both budget and full-price CDs. A large portion of the extensive Gramophone Company of India catalogue (with registered trademarks EMI and HMV "His Master's Voice") consists of reissues of earlier recordings. The Indian market also encompasses other former vinyl disk companies such as Inreco and Polydor, the Madras-based Sangeetha and AUM, and a new generation of CD companies including Magnasound, T-Series, and Venus.

One particularly interesting development in the release of Indian classical music CDs is the mainstream marketing venture undertaken by Music Today, a subsidiary of the hugely successful Indian magazine *India Today* (a kind of subcontinental equivalent of *Time* or *Newsweek*). Music Today has released dozens of cassettes and CDs and publishes weekly full-page advertisements of the company's latest releases in each issue of the magazine. The material is sometimes explicitly classical, as in the "Great Masters" series, or it may be somewhat disguised in the form of compilations for specific moods, times of day, seasons, or devotional purposes that are adaptations of classical performances, but omit the possibly intimidating terminology of raga and tala.

Unlike in Bangladesh where the production of classical music CDs—or even LPs—is rare, Pakistan until recently has had a comparatively healthy tradition of classical music recording. EMI Pakistan was purchased in the early 1990s by a consortium that apparently chose to deemphasize the company's considerable classical music catalogue. This was an unfortunate development for numerous recordings by some of the century's greatest vocal and instrumental masters were no longer available, including two very significant historical series that had been released on LP and cassette: the first (*Ragamala* 'garland of ragas') documented in detail with both spoken explanation and sung performance a hundred basic ragas in ten volumes, and the second (*Gharanon ki Gayaki* 'the song of the traditional stylistic schools') presented eighty substantial selections by Pakistan's leading vocalists in twenty volumes. Among the holdings in EMI Pakistan's rich archive of master tapes, these two series at the very least deserve to be rereleased on CD as two of the most important recorded documents of the twentieth century.

Indian music is well represented in current CD catalogues in the West. These recordings can be traced to earlier 78-rpm and LP productions that emerged mid-century as a result of three developments in particular: first, an interest in Indian music as an extension of the folk revival of the 1950s; second, a more sophisticated exploration of Indian musical theory by such classical composers as Henry Cowell and Alan Hovhaness and such jazz innovators as John Coltrane and Miles Davis; and third, the Beatles' embrace of Ravi Shankar and the consequent appearance of Shankar as a musical icon in a broad range of contexts (Farrell 1997) [see MUSIC AND INTERNATIONALIZATION]. At one point in the late 1960s, there were more than 350 LP recordings of Indian music available in the West. That number plunged precipitously in the 1970s and 1980s, but with the development of interest in world music in the late 1980s and 1990s, once again hundreds of CDs of the music of India are available.

A number of companies outside India now specialize exclusively in Indian classical music releases. Chhandha Dhara in Germany, Navras Records in England, Omi Music in Canada, and Oriental Records in the U.S. all have large catalogues of CDs; smaller companies such as India Archive Music in New York, Moment Records (founded by Zakir Hussain) in California, and Makar Records in France also have significant catalogues. In addition, individual artists such as Ali Akbar Khan and G. S. Sachdev have released their own CDs, now that marketing is facilitated by the Internet.

The mainstream Western classical label Nimbus, based in England, has a solid line of front-rank Indian classical artists. Numerous world music labels based in France—Ocora, Auvidis, and Chant du Monde being the most prominent—have substantial Indian offerings. The audiophile label Water Lily Acoustics, founded in California by the Sri Lankan Kavi Alexander, includes in its offerings both pure classical recordings as well as fusion efforts—one of which won a prestigious Grammy award—by such Eastern and Western instrumentalists as Vishwa Mohan Bhatt and Ry Cooder [for selected titles, see A GUIDE TO RECORDINGS].

In the West, CDs were traditionally marketed through conventional record and CD outlets (Tower, HMV, and Virgin among the international chains), as well as through specialized shops such as the Ali Akbar Khan College store in California and Indian grocery stores throughout the United States and England. Today the Internet has opened new avenues of access to Indian recordings, both via mainstream CD dealers and specialists in marketing Indian products. A Web search of appropriate keywords (raga, sitar, tabla) and artists' names brings up a rich selection of available recordings.

ARCHIVES

The state-run radio broadcasting systems of India, Pakistan, and Bangladesh maintain the most extensive archives of Indian classical music, the first two possessing enormous quantities of old recordings by nationally known artists dating back to Indian independence in 1947 and even earlier. The case of Radio Bangladesh is more complex, since Bangladesh did not become an independent country until 1971. Generally speaking, such archives are not accessible to anyone outside the broadcasting establishment, although All India Radio has released a number of tapes in the form of commercial LPs and CDs, initially through the Gramophone Company of India, and currently plans further releases.

Institutional archives in India (the Sangeet Natak Akademi in New Delhi, the National Center for Performing Arts in Bombay, and the Sangeet Research Academy in Calcutta, to name a few) and Pakistan (such as Lok Virsa in Islamabad and the All Pakistan Music Conference and the Sanjan Nagar Institute in Lahore) have extensive holdings. In a category of its own is the Archives and Research Center for Ethnomusicology in the greater metropolitan area of Delhi, which functions as a branch of the Chicago-based American Institute of Indian Studies; its express function is to serve as broadly as possible as a repository for duplicate research tapes from both South Asian and Western scholars, but it also collects commercial recordings and copies of recordings from collectors' private holdings.

A comprehensive survey of holdings in institutional archives in Europe and the United States is problematic, for none specializes exclusively in South Asian music. The Institute for Comparative Musical Documentation in Berlin, run for decades by the late Alain Daniélou, is now defunct: rights to its archives, which supplied the master tapes for a number of commercial recordings of Indian music released under the aegis of UNESCO, were in litigation in 1999.

The World Music Institute in New York and numerous museums (such as the Fogg Art Museum at Harvard and the Freer Gallery of Art and the Arthur M. Sackler Gallery in Washington, D.C.) and universities (including Wesleyan University in Connecticut, the University of Washington at Seattle, and U.C.L.A.) have substantial bodies of archival material in the form of recordings of concerts sponsored by these institutions. These recordings are precluded by contract from being released commer-

One wonders what lost and forgotten musical treasures—particularly by some of the lesser-known and less fashionable masters—may yet be discovered in the dim light of some dusty warehouse or cluttered attic.

cially. Most universities with either a strong South Asian studies program or an ethnomusicological specialization in Indian music have their own collection of musical materials. The James A. Rubin collection at Harvard is a noteworthy research archive, housing hundreds of hours of live recordings of Karnatak music made over a thirty-year period at major annual South Indian music festivals.

Personal collections, both in South Asia and the West represent significant resources. Individual collectors in India are linked by the Indian Society of Record Collectors, based in Bombay, which publishes a newsletter and holds monthly listening sessions to hear and discuss treasures from the past, usually old 78-rpm recordings. Notable collectors in Pakistan include M. Lutfullah in Karachi, who is legendary for the extent of his holdings and the precision of his catalogue. Internet resources include such Web pages as the "Toronto gharana." Various collectors throughout the United States trade tapes on a regular basis.

One area of archival interest that deserves to be explored and documented is the personal collections maintained by students, both Eastern and Western, or teachers and performers of Indian music. Raga Records in the United States, for example, has released a number of concert recordings of the late sitarist Nikhil Banerjee that were gleaned from his students' private collections.

In the 1970s and 1980s, various recordings of such luminaries as the late vocalist Kesarbai Kerkar, apparently made from amateurs' ad hoc recordings of concert performances dating from the 1950s, were released on cassette in India. Unreleased tapes in the vaults of the aforementioned commercial record, cassette, and CD companies no doubt constitute in the aggregate an archive of considerable importance. One wonders what lost and forgotten musical treasures—particularly by some of the lesser-known and less fashionable masters—may yet be discovered in the dim light of some dusty warehouse or cluttered attic. One might add that since the majority of such recordings are on reel-to-reel tape that will ultimately deteriorate, a concerted effort to locate, catalogue, and (when appropriate) rerecord these holdings would significantly enhance—for the benefit of the next millennium—the already substantial recorded documentation of Indian classical music in the twentieth century.

REFERENCES

Barnett, Elise B. 1975. *A Discography of the Art Music of India*. Ann Arbor, Mich.: Society for Ethnomusicology.

Farrell, Gerry. 1997. *Indian Music and the West*. Oxford: Clarendon.

Joshi, G. N. 1988. "A Concise History of the Phonograph Industry in India." *Popular Music* 7(2):147–156.

Kinnear, Michael S. 1985. *A Discography of Hindustani and Karnatic Music*. Westport, Conn.: Greenwood Press.

———. 1994. *The Gramophone Company's First Indian Recordings, 1899–1908*. Bombay: Popular Prakashan.

Neuman, Daniel. 1980. *The Life of Music in North India: The Organization of an Artistic Tradition*. Detroit: Wayne State University Press.

Silver, Brian Q. 1996. "Another Musical Universe: The American Recording Industry and Indian Music, 1955–1965." In *Seminar on Indian Music and the West* [ed. Arvind Parekh], 225–236. Bombay: Sangeet Research Academy.

Film Music: Northern Area

Alison Arnold

Early Film Songs
Film-Song Genres
Studio Musicians and Orchestras
Film Music Directors
Playback Singers
Film Music in the Late Twentieth Century

The Indian film industry produces more feature films than that of any other country in the world—over nine hundred per year in the early 1990s. Virtually all these films contain songs and dances, and such musical extravaganzas constitute a major form of entertainment for the Indian population. The songs represent a significant category of Indian popular music, and are marketed independently on cassette recordings and broadcast on radio and TV. In North India, the Hindi film and its songs dominate regional-language markets both in absolute numbers and in stylistic influence. Produced in Bombay, the center of Hindi film production nicknamed "Bollywood" (the Bombay Hollywood), they are the focus of this article. Feature-film production in Pakistan and Bangladesh, which grew in the 1950s and 1960s, has remained closely modeled on the commercial Indian music and dance forms—as reflected in the Lollywood Top Ten (a film-song hit parade in Lahore), named after Bollywood (Gul 1995). In Afghanistan, a state film corporation was established in the 1960s, and theaters showed mostly Hindi, Egyptian, and Iranian films. The Soviet invasion of 1979 ushered in a period of reduced filmmaking and disrupted film exhibition (Armes 1987:127–133, 190).

Film songs (*filmī gīt*) were India's first mass-produced, mass-marketed music. The major film companies of the 1930s and 1940s recorded songs performed by their own actor- and actress-singers accompanied by small orchestras of Indian and Western instruments, and the Gramophone Company (HMV) began rerecording and releasing the songs on 78-rpm records. With widespread distribution of the films, these songs rapidly achieved popularity with Indian audiences; both film and record production expanded to keep pace with demand. Commercial filmmakers, independent film-music directors, studio orchestras, "playback" (ghost) singers, magnetic sound-recording technology, LP records, and a national film distribution network all helped to make the production of film songs a highly commercial music industry.

Unlike many other forms of pop music around the world, Indian film song is not the personal expression of its performers. Songs are created by a production team led by a film-music director/composer to fit a specific cinematic situation. The playback singer who records the song in a studio, like the film actor who performs before

Early film producers and music directors used songs to embellish and enhance the story line and heighten the film's emotional appeal, rather than to move the plot forward.

the camera, must express the screen character's emotion through his or her voice. The lyricist composes words to match the story narrative, although film-song lyrics tend to have broader meanings relevant to the diverse audiences who listen to them both in movie theaters and in their daily lives. Many South Asians accept the unrealistic cinematic world that spawned these songs and enjoy them as a uniquely South Asian brand of modern pop music.

EARLY FILM SONGS

The race to produce the first sound feature film in India was won by Ardeshir Irani, whose Imperial Film Company released *Alam Ara* 'Light of the World' in Bombay in March 1931. This film contained at least seven songs (Arnold 1991:4). *Alam Ara* was a popular stage play of the time, and like many such others included songs and dances; Irani's dramatist adapted both its dialogue and songs for the screen. Many of the early talkies were similarly based on musical stage dramas—whose popularity they soon eclipsed as Indian audiences flocked to movie houses. In this early period, the film songs performed by the film actors and actresses were recorded simultaneously with the picture, using the "single-system" camera then available. The song "Dede khudā ke nāmse," sung by W. M. Khan in the role of a fakir in *Alam Ara,* became perhaps the first "hit" film song, and its circulation—"it was hummed and heard everywhere in Bombay at the time"—heralded the widespread dissemination film songs came to enjoy in later years ("Irani" 1956).

In the early 1930s, a film song was a recorded performance in which one or two actors accompanied by a small instrumental ensemble sang precomposed lyrics sung in "light classical" style. The film producer, and possibly also the screenwriter, would determine the number and placement of songs within the film narrative; the music director would choose the raga (melodic mode) most appropriate to each particular song situation, often selecting an existing classical or light-classical melody in that raga. The songs were generally two to three minutes in length and in a strophic refrain-verse form (in some cases with the traditional *sthāī-antarā* structure), or in through-composed form (Arnold 1991:65–74). The screenwriter, like the Indian stage playwright, usually made up song lyrics to fit a melodic composition. According to the late Vishram Bedekar, a screenwriter with Prabhat Films in Pune in the 1930s and 1940s, it was Hindi film-music directors in Bombay who first "freed film songs from the trammels of fossilized classical compositions" by asking the songwriter to provide the lyrics first, thus allowing them to create new song melodies to fit the words (Arnold, personal communication).

Early film producers and music directors used songs to embellish and enhance the story line and heighten the film's emotional appeal, rather than to move the plot forward—as did some music directors in later decades. For the predominantly mythological, historical, and devotional films of the time, they selected song themes that typically celebrated festivals, praised God or deities, expressed affection or

FIGURE 1 The actor-singer Kundan Lal Saigal sings into the microphone for a radio recording, in a scene from the Hindi film *Dushman* 'The Enemy' (referring to tuberculosis), 1939. Film still courtesy Alison Arnold.

romantic love, or identified occupational or social roles (begging songs, for example). Some filmmakers experimented with a new "social" category of films set in the present, such as family dramas, romances, and crime stories. These productions opened the way for music directors to break out of traditional musical molds and create a new film-song genre applicable to the new technological medium and to a diverse and widespread audience.

The vocal style of the early film singers contrasts sharply with that of later artists. Many early sound film actors and actresses were former stage artists, and some actresses were courtesan singers and dancers. All were accustomed to projecting the singing voice, to using melodic ornamentation, and to exercising a certain rhythmic freedom. Women generally sang in a low to middle range, and their vocal styles varied from a coarse, husky quality typical of trained singers such as Zohrabai, Bibbo, and Shamshad Begum to a lighter, more natural voice common among actresses without vocal training, such as Durga Khote and Shanta Apte. Among the early male film singers, with their characteristically strong, full voices, one actor-singer arose who has been credited with introducing a new soft, crooning vocal style: Kundan Lal Saigal, of the New Theatres Film Company in Calcutta (figure 1). Saigal's vocal quality was well-suited to the microphone, and it was widely adopted by playback singers in the 1940s and 1950s (see below).

FILM-SONG GENRES

Film songs, which represent an enormous category within the South Asian popular music market, are usually grouped in record catalogues and on store shelves according to language—Hindi, Gujarati, Marathi, Bengali, and so on. Songs in these languages can be further subdivided according to musical form and style, somewhat along the lines of native musical genres; the most common genre is a "mainstream" format common to film songs in any cinematic situation. For particular film scenes portraying situations that in real life would incorporate musical performance, music directors have in some instances provided modern film-song versions of traditional song genres. These include film bhajans, ghazals, qawwalis, and folk songs.

The "mainstream" design of the majority of Indian film songs—an alternating refrain-verse structure based loosely on the *sthāī-antarā* form of *khyāl, ṭhumrī,* and other native vocal forms [see HINDUSTANI VOCAL MUSIC]—became the standard film-song format in the late 1940s and remained so. Songs of this "mainstream" type generally begin with an instrumental (occasionally vocal) introduction, and always have instrumental interludes between the verses. Like all Indian film-song forms, the refrain-verse type includes recognizeably Indian musical elements: scale patterns reminiscent of raga scales, a dominant melody supported by rhythm, and vocal ornamentation. It may also encompass Western harmony and other musical characteristics, or styles drawn from any source, native or foreign, known to the music director through live performance or from recordings and considered appropriate to the individual song composition.

The popular devotional bhajan, ubiquitous among the majority Hindu population in India and prevalent also among Sikhs and other religious groups, has been commonly included in Hindu-oriented commercial films, particularly up to and during the "golden age of melody" (1950s–1960s). As in real-life contexts, film bhajans offer praise to Hindu deities and may be solo, group, or solo-group responsorial songs. They are often sung in a Hindu temple or a worship area within a home. Some film bhajans have traditional harmonium, hand-cymbal, and tabla accompaniment, whereas others have a larger orchestral backing but may still emphasize the small-ensemble instruments. Bhajan lyrics tend to emphasize Sanskritized language (Garg 1972), which in Hindi cinema contrasts with the Hindustani (a mixture of Hindi and Urdu vocabulary) commonly used in dialogues. Film bhajans do not generally deviate far from the devotional mood traditionally evoked by these songs.

The film ghazal was especially popular during the heyday of romantic film songs before the cinematic trend toward action-packed thrillers in the 1970s. It retained the poetic Urdu couplet form and the *sthāī-aṅtarā* structure of the traditional ghazal, but diverged in its instrumental accompaniment (usually a large orchestra of Indian and Western instruments), addition of harmony to the solo melody line, omission of vocal and drum improvisation (replaced by composed instrumental interludes), and occasional use of sentimental or even vulgar lyrics. In the 1970s two Pakistani singers, Mehdi Hasan and Ghulam Ali, popularized a modern, nonfilm pop ghazal, "the first popular-music idiom to achieve mass popularity independent of the cinema" (Manuel 1993:103). From that time on, the film ghazal has beaten a gradual retreat from the film-song repertoire, although present-day versions still appear (see below).

Film representations of qawwali, the Sufi devotional song form, have appeared in Muslim social and historical film productions, with secular or religious gatherings of "filmi" characters replacing the traditional religious performance context of the Sufi shrine and the traditional hereditary qawwal singers. Screen performances are often showy and dramatic, unlike the sincere expression of traditional qawwals, and feature female groups (as in "Sharmā ke kyūṅ" from *Chaudhvin ka Chand,* 1960; see Arnold 1991:151–152, 379–380) as well as the traditional male gatherings. Film qawwalis omit improvisation and include nontraditional instruments along with the usual *ḍholak* and harmonium, but tend to follow the basic qawwali musical structure of *sthāī-aṅtarā-sthāī,* the characteristic poetic rhyme scheme, and the stirring rhythmic accompaniment (Qureshi 1986).

India's regional music traditions provide film composers with a wealth of material on which to draw inspiration for film folk songs, from festival and seasonal music to life-cycle and work songs. Many Indian films include rural scenes with costumed groups performing choreographed song-and-dance numbers (figure 2); some composers choose styles from particular Indian regions, others create generic "village" music. Film folk songs are generally rhythmic in character and in a moderate to fast tempo. They have a refrain-verse structure and a syllabic text setting, and are sung by a single- or mixed-gender playback chorus.

FIGURE 2 The actress-dancer Vijayantimala and chorus perform a film folk dance in *Madhumati* (1958). Film still courtesy Alison Arnold.

STUDIO MUSICIANS AND ORCHESTRAS

Film music directors hire studio musicians based on their needs for a particular film song. All musicians are freelance and belong to the Cine Musicians Association, which grades its members according to their performance level, determined after an initial test: extra special group, special group, grade A, and grade B. The higher-ranked musicians receive higher rates of pay, but lower ranks may receive more playing opportunities, since low-budget film music directors can often afford to pay grade B artists only. In the 1980s, extra-special group musicians might have received 300 rupees for one song recording (four hours work), whereas B-grade artists would have received around 100 rupees.

Music directors can hire players of virtually any Indian or Western instrument they might choose. Studio orchestras generally include a basic Western symphony orchestra with strings, winds, percussion, and brass instruments, as well as electronic keyboard and synthesizers, plus Indian instruments appropriate to the particular song (figure 3). As in past decades, music directors often incorporate traditional instrumentation when orchestrating film versions of native song genres, such as harmonium and *ḍholak* for film qawwalis and regional drums and percussion for film folk songs.

Studio orchestras have grown from ensembles of two or three musicians playing harmonium, tabla, and sometimes *sāraṅgī*, in the first year or two of Indian sound film (1931–1932), to over one hundred members in the 1950s and 1960s. To the typical light classical ensemble, early film song composers soon added Western violin, cello, mandolin, piano, organ, clarinet, and even saxophone (figure 4), as well as other Indian instruments including sitar and *bāṅsurī* 'bamboo flute' (Arnold 1988, figure 1). The larger orchestra provided a greater variety of timbre and depth of sound. Musicians were in plentiful supply, especially in Bombay and Pune, where many were from neighboring Goa (then under Portuguese rule) and had been taught Western music in schools there. When the old film studios broke up in the late 1940s, the new independent film makers and film music directors increased the size of the accompanying orchestra dramatically, as a measure of prestige and success in an increasingly competitive market. Naushad Ali and the musical duo Shankar-Jaikishen were among the first music directors to employ a hundred studio musicians for their

Naushad Ali and the musical duo Shankar-Jaikishen were among the first music directors to employ a hundred studio musicians for their film-song recordings.

FIGURE 3 Pandit Hari Prasad Chaurasia plays flute (*bāṅsurī*) in a film-song recording session at Mehboob Studios, Bombay, 1983. Photo by Gordon Arnold.

film-song recordings, featuring large string sections in their long instrumental introductions and interludes. Smaller studio orchestras have been more common in recent years, as technology and synthesized sounds have come to play a more important role.

FILM MUSIC DIRECTORS

Throughout the history of Indian sound film, most music directors have been trained musicians or singers; the vast majority have been men. In the 1930s, the music directors at all three northern centers of film production—Pune, Bombay, and Calcutta—were almost entirely male: those at Prabhat Film Company in Pune were all singers (Govindrao Tembe and Master Krishnarao were traditionally trained classical vocalists). Among the music directors at New Theaters in Calcutta, Rai Chand Boral was a tabla player, Timir Baran a sarod student of Allauddin Khan, and Pankaj Mullick a renowned vocalist. When the first woman director, Saraswati Devi, joined Bombay Talkies Film Company in 1935, she was ostracized by her own Parsi community for her involvement in the film industry. Cinema had inherited the social stigma attached to the Indian stage and classical dance in the early twentieth century, and few women were willing subject themselves to rejection by their families and by society in general (Arnold 1991:112–114; Kinikar 1983). After changing her name from Khurshid Minocher-Homji to Saraswati Devi, she pursued her career as a successful film music director until 1950. The film music industry has nevertheless remained male dominated.

FIGURE 4 Musicians playing Western instruments perform as radio artists in a scene from the film *Dushman* 'The Enemy' (1939); *from left*, standing: violin, double bass, violin, saxophone; seated: piano, two cellos. Film still courtesy Alison Arnold.

The film music director is the creative force behind the production of all music for a film, including the background music, songs, and dance compositions (Arnold 1998). The music director creates the song melody, envisions the final recorded product, and oversees the process by which this is reached. The process requires a production team including a lyricist, singer(s), studio musicians, music assistants, sound recording engineers, and sound editor, each member of which makes his or her contribution to the song recording. Up until the 1950s, music directors such as Khemchand Prakash, Naushad Ali, and Vasant Desai typically employed music assistants, but their workload allowed them time to mold each individual song, and even to teach the song to the singer before the recording date. As Indian film production rapidly increased, successful music directors of the 1950s and 1960s such as the director duos Shankar-Jaikishen, Kalyanji-Anandji, and Lakshmikant-Pyarelal had far less time to devote to each song (figure 5). These music directors relied on the same coterie of playback artists, singers whose experience enabled them to deliver quickly and precisely just what the director requested. Many directors also relied on musical assistants able and willing to orchestrate songs, notate parts for the studio musicians, and conduct the studio orchestra (figure 6).

FIGURE 5 The film music directors Pyarelal (*left*) and Lakshmikant (*right*) in Mehboob Studios, Bombay, 1983. Photo by Alison Arnold.

One of the most popular and successful music directors and singers of the 1970s to 1990s was Rahul Dev Burman (1939–1994), the son of the film music director Sachin Dev Burman (1906–1975). Known as "R. D.," the younger Burman studied sarod with the renowned Ustad Ali Akbar Khan when he first moved to Bombay in the late 1950s, and began his film music career assisting his father with such films as *Pyaasa* 'Thirst' (1957), *Guide* (1965), and *Aradhana* 'Adoration' (1969), all of which became prominent box-office hits. His first successful independent film songs were those for *Teesri Manzil* 'Third Floor' (1966). Gradually R. D. developed his own style, creating a new fusion of Western rock and jazz with Indian melodies. With such songs as "Dam Maro Dam" for *Hare Rama Hare Krishna* 'O Rama! O Krishna!' (1971), R. D. Burman became one of the top Hindi film music directors. He was also among a small number of music directors, including C. Ramchandra, Hemant Kumar, and in the 1990s Anu Malik and Kamal Hassan, who have sung playback for their own song compositions. Since R. D.'s untimely death in 1994 at the age of fifty-four, singers (especially his wife, the famous playback singer Asha Bhosle) have

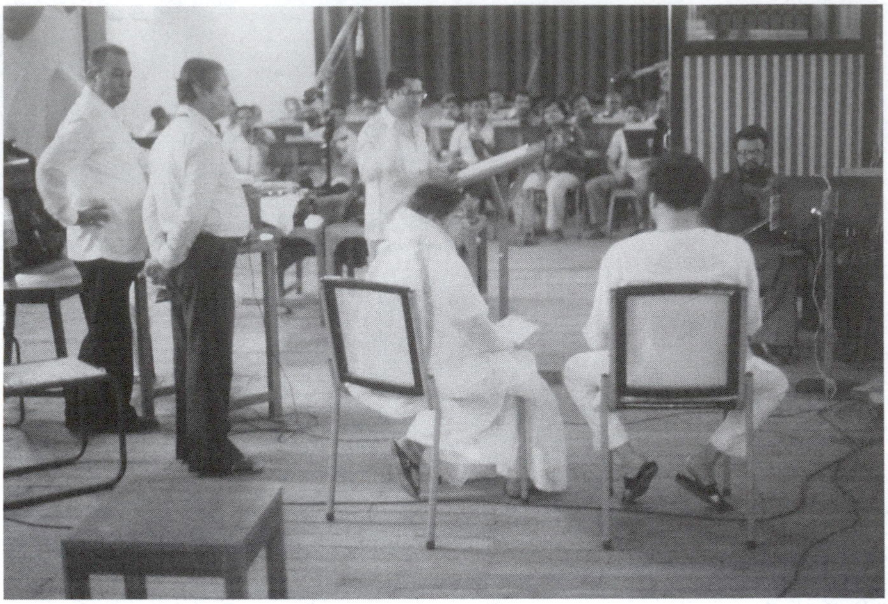

FIGURE 6 Lata Mangeshkar (seated, *center*) and music director R. D. Burman (seated, *right*) in the Film Center recording studio, Bombay, with R. D.'s assistant conducting the orchestra from the music stand, 1983. Photo by Gordon Arnold.

performed his songs in public concerts, and his compositions continue to appear on recordings (Burman 1997; Kohli 1997a and b).

PLAYBACK SINGERS

"Playback singing" is the term used in the Indian film industry to refer to dubbing voice-overs in film songs. Professional singers record the songs, which are then inserted into a film sound track and matched to the frames showing the actors mouthing the lyrics. At the film shooting, the song recording is played back through loudspeakers to ensure correct timing by the screen artist, hence the term *playback.* Indian music directors introduced this process as soon as film technology made separate recording of sound and film possible, in the late 1930s. Prior to that, film actors and actresses had to sing their own songs for the single-system camera. To the Western viewer, hearing the same few singing voices emanating from different screen characters in successive films might seem absurd; however, to Indian audiences the "willing suspension of disbelief" is an accepted part of the escapist entertainment of commercial cinema.

The most famous and respected female playback singer in the history of Indian cinema is Lata Mangeshkar (figure 7), the daughter of a Marathi stage actor-singer and traveling-theater owner. She sang her first Marathi playback song in 1942 (Arnold forthcoming), having studied vocal music with a succession of teachers. She received training from film music directors in the art of Hindi film singing (microphone technique, expression of song lyrics, and so on), and even studied Hindustani and Sanskrit diction with scholars (Bhimani 1995:128–134). In the 1940s Lata Mangeshkar's light, high-pitched voice contrasted markedly with the lower, strong vocal style then in vogue among film actress-singers (Shamshad Begum, Zohrabai, and Noorjehan, for example), and the success and popularity of her songs led music directors to use her voice in film after film (Kabir and Snell 1994). Along with her sisters Asha Bhosle, Usha Mangeshkar, and Meena Mangeshkar, and a few other singers including Geeta Dutt and Suman Kalyanpur, Lata Mangeshkar came to dominate Hindi film playback singing; she recorded in many other languages as well. Her thousands of song recordings over six decades have won her numerous awards, including a citation in the *Guinness Book of World Records* for having recorded the greatest number of songs. Most recently—in 1999—the prestigious Padma

FIGURE 7 Lata Mangeshkar performs on stage at an outdoor concert in Sholapur, Maharashtra, 1983. Photo by Gordon Arnold.

Vibhushan award, one of India's highest national honors, was bestowed on her by the president of India.

From the 1950s to the 1970s, the popular male playback artists were Mohammad Rafi, Mukesh, Talat Mahmood, Kishore Kumar, Manna Dey, and Mahendra Kapoor, each with his own talents and preferred styles. All had been influenced by the soft, crooning style popularized by Kundan Lal Saigal. Talat Mehmood (d. 1998) earned renown for singing film ghazals; Kishore Kumar (d. 1987) was popular for his flamboyant acting style and lively playback singing; and Manna Dey sang many bhajans and romantic songs in which he drew on his classical training. Since the 1970s, playback singers and song composers have generally not studied classical music, although all playback artists consider some vocal training essential to their careers.

FILM MUSIC IN THE LATE TWENTIETH CENTURY

Film-song production in the 1990s has seesawed in response to Indian film production. Commercial films soared to highest-ever levels in the early 1990s, reaching 938 feature films in 1994, then sank to late 1970s levels within the next few years (only 697 films were made in 1997) (Da Cunha 1998). Various factors have contributed to the decline in film production: higher entertainment taxes have raised ticket prices, resulting in dwindling audiences; the cinema has faced increasing competition from cable television, a relatively cheap alternative entertainment; production costs, such as fees to star actors, have become exorbitantly high; video piracy has remained rampant; and foreign-film imports have increased and are attracting larger audiences. Beyond the film industry, nonfilm Indian pop music, which spread widely in the 1970s with the arrival of audio-cassette technology, has become a strongly competitive force within the popular-music market (Manuel 1993). Yet despite the downward trend for films and film songs—and despite the criticism that Indian film songs continue to draw from various sources (Chatterjee 1995, for example)—the film-music industry continues to attract young music directors, lyricists, playback singers, and musicians. Film songs today are reaching ever larger Indian audiences worldwide, whether via the Internet, satellite TV, audio and video cassettes, video compact discs (VCDs), or digital video discs (DVDs).

Instant communications, worldwide markets, and international travel—all fac-

In the last decade of the twentieth century, the current pool of playback singers is significantly greater than during the previous few decades.

tors affecting life in South Asia at the end of the twentieth century—have increased the speed with which foreign and native musical ideas and styles find their way into Indian film songs. Hindi film music directors in the 1990s, like those of earlier decades, draw on the latest popular music styles and sounds from the West. Three examples are *Aflatoon* (1998), in which the music directors Dilip Sen and Sameer Sen employed the rap genre; *Gupt* (1997), in which the music director Viju Shah explored techno; and the hip-hop songs by Anu Malik featured in *Ishq* (1998). Music directors also incorporate Indian and diasporic Indian pop sounds such as bhangra, as in "Hai bada anari rabba," sung by Udit Narayan and Alka Yagnik in *Shapath* (1997), and dandiya, as in the slow-paced "Chale hum do jān sair ko" sung by Kumar Sanu and Ravindra Sathe in *Yugpurush* (1997). Yet as the new millennium approaches, music directors continue to draw stylistic inspiration from traditional Indian music genres as well. These include Sufi qawwali, in "Terī jawānī baḍī mast mast hai" by the directors Sajid-Wajid in *Pyar Kiya To Darna Kya* (1998) and in the "rock-n-roll-cum-qawwali-cum-Macarena song" by Jatin-Lalit entitled "Jo honā hai" in *Pyar To Hona Hi Tha* (1998); folk-music styles—especially those with Punjabi rhythms—as in songs from the 1998 films *Achanak* (music directors Dilip Sen and Sameer Sen) and *Bade Miyan Chote Miyan* (music director Viju Shah); and even the romantic ghazal, as in Uttam Singh's "Chiṭhī na koī sandesh," sung separately by Jagjit Singh and Lata Mangeshkar in *Dushman* (1998).

Indian versions of Western songs are not new to Indian film music. Examples range from "Gore gore o bāṅke chore," C. Ramchandra's 1950 takeoff on the Latin song "Chico Chico from Puerto Rico" in *Samadhi*, to "I Love You, Āte jāte pyār kiyā," Raamlaxman's version of Stevie Wonder's "I Just Called to Say I Love You" from the 1990 film *Maine Pyar Kiya*. In the 1990s—copyright laws aside—music directors have continued to imitate their favorite compositions. Among recent examples are the composer duo Jatin-Lalit's "Chhad zid karnā" in the film *Piya Kiya To Darna Kya* (1998), a version of the album-title song "I've Been Waiting" by the British band Stereo Nation (members are the former bhangra artist Tarsame "Taz" Singh and the Jamaican-born Kendell Smith); and Dilip Sen and Sameer Sen's "Mere liye to fit lūt gayā" in *Zulmi* (1999), their version of "Sexy Eyes" by the Danish female pop singer Whigfield (Music Reviews 1999).

In addition to the East-West connections mentioned above, the late twentieth century is seeing continued if not increased links between South and North Indian film music. Separate regional film industries developed in these two areas in the early decades of sound film, due to differences in language and culture, but musical connections are present in terms of stylistic influence and personnel—especially playback singers working in both the South and the North. For example, the recent success of the Tamil film music director A. R. Rehman in achieving widespread popularity in the world of Hindi film music is now possibly opening doors to new South-North relationships and collaborations. All five of Rehman's songs for the 1998 film *Dil Se* found their way onto Planet Bollywood's *Top 30 Songs of 1998*, with one—"Chal chaiya chaiya" sung by Sukhinder Singh and Sapna Awasthi—taking the number-one position (Planet Bollywood 1999).

In the last decade of the twentieth century, the current pool of playback singers (at least within the Hindi film industry) is significantly greater than during the previous few decades. Along with film music directors, actors, and actresses, these once-invisible performers are increasingly in the limelight as they appear in multi-star stage shows before national and international audiences. The film music directors themselves are experimenting with new musical ideas as they blend the new with the old, and the native with the foreign, and the people of South Asia are responding to this widening spectrum of entertainment available to them. Although film production in the 1990s has declined, creative forces within the film music industry remain vibrant and ready to face the changing, competitive arena of the twenty-first century.

REFERENCES

Armes, Roy. 1987. *Third World Film Making and the West.* Berkeley: University of California Press.

Arnold, Alison. 1988. "Popular Film Song in India: A Case of Mass-Market Musical Eclecticism." *Popular Music* 7(2):177–188.

———. 1991. "Hindi Filmī Gīt: On the History of Commercial Indian Popular Music." Ph.D. dissertation, University of Illinois at Urbana-Champaign.

———. 1998. "Film Musicals: Bollywood Film Musicals." *The International Encyclopedia of Dance.* Oxford: Oxford University Press.

———. Forthcoming. "Naushad Ali." *The New Grove Dictionary of Music and Musicians*, ed. Stanley Sadie. London: Macmillan. [Also "India, Film Music," "Bhosle, Asha," "Mangeshkar, Lata," "Mukesh," and "Rafi, Mohammad."]

Bhimani, Harish. 1995. *In Search of Lata Mangeshkar.* New Delhi: Indus, HarperCollins Publishers India.

Burman, Rahul Dev. 1997. *Immortal R. D. Burman: His Own Voice.* Polygram CDF 201. Compact disc.

Chatterjee, Partha. 1995. "A Bit of Song and Dance." In *Frames of Mind: Reflections on Indian Cinema*, ed. Aruna Vasudev, 197–218. New Delhi: UBS Publishers' Distributors Ltd.

Da Cunha, Uma. 1998. "India." *Variety International Film Guide*, ed. Peter Cowie, 174–178. London: Andre Deutsch; Hollywood: Samuel French Trade.

Das Gupta, Chidananda. 1991. *The Painted Face: Studies in India's Popular Cinema.* New Delhi: Roli Books Pvt. Ltd.

Garg, Lakshminarayan, ed. 1972. *Filmī bhajan aṅk* (Film bhajan volume). Hathras; Sangīt Karyalaya. In Hindi.

Gul, Aijaz. 1995. "Pakistan." *Variety International Film Guide,* ed. Peter Cowie, 246–248. London: Andre Deutsch; Hollywood: Samuel French Trade.

"Irani—Pioneer Who Gave Tongue to Indian Screen." 1956. *Indian Talkie 1931–'56: Silver Jubilee Souvenir,* 23–24. Bombay: Film Federation of India.

Kabir, Nasreen, and Rupert Snell. 1994. "Bollywood Nights: The Voices behind the Stars." *World Music: The Rough Guide*, eds. Simon Broughton et al., 219–222. London: Rough Guides (Penguin).

Kinikar, Shashikant. 1983. "Lasting Lady, Khurshid-Saraswati." *Cinema Vision India* II(2):70–73.

Kohli, Sanjeev, comp. 1997a. *Greatest Hits of the 70's.* Gramophone Company of India Ltd. CDF 130136. Compact disc.

———, comp. 1997b. *Greatest Hits of the 80's.* Gramophone Company of India Ltd. CDF 130118. Compact disc.

Manuel, Peter. 1993. *Cassette Culture: Popular Music and Technology in North India.* Chicago: University of Chicago Press.

Marre, Jeremy, and Hannah Charlton. 1985. "There'll Always Be Stars in the Sky: The Indian Film Music Phenomenon," in *Beats of the Heart: Popular Music of the World*, by Jeremy Marre, 137–154. New York: Pantheon.

Music Reviews. 1999. Virtual Communications Pvt. Ltd. Available at http://www.indiabollywood.com/musicreview

Planet Bollywood. 1999. *Top 30 Songs of 1998.* Available at http://www.indolink.com/bollywood/Library/topSongs.html

Qureshi, Regula. 1986. *Sufi Music of India and Pakistan: Sound, Context, and Meaning in Qawwali.* New York: Cambridge University Press.

Film Music: Southern Area

Paul D. Greene

Early Film Music
Film Music after Independence
Ilaiyaraja
Film Music in the 1990s

In South India, the film industry is the leading source of popular music. Centered in Madras, a handful of film companies produce most of the popular songs in the Tamil, Telugu, Malayalam, and Kannada languages. To South Indian audiences, film music is much more than just music they hear at the movies. Every film is a musical, and the songs from the films are continuously played over the radio and through playback technology (primarily audio cassette players). Film songs are heard on buses, in general stores, in homes and tea shops, and during festivals. In fact, it is almost impossible to walk through a South Indian village, town, or city today without hearing such film songs.

For South Indians, the function of musical media such as cassette players is not to separate the music from the films, but rather to allow listeners to draw the film worlds deeper into their daily lives. Song, drama, and dance have always been experienced together, as integrated modes of expression in the performance traditions of the region (Manuel 1988a:160). Beeman (1981:83) observes that Indian cinema audiences do not experience a sharp "psychological break," or a lack of verisimilitude, when characters suddenly burst into song to the accompaniment of an invisible orchestra. Furthermore, catchy film tunes often become folk songs, another South Indian "mass medium" (Baskaran 1981:46). As songs become part of daily life, they often retain meanings from the cinematic narrative. Songs about agricultural labor (for example, from the Tamil film *Vivasāyi* 'Farmer' of 1967) are sung as work songs (Greene 1995:239–249). Songs concerning Hindu devotion (for example, from *Karagāṭṭakkāraṅ* 'Karagam Dancer' of 1989) become part of devotional festivals (Greene in press). In the case of a successful film, audience members not only identify with the characters, but also make a connection between the world in the film and their own, real way of life (Dickey 1993:67–68). Memorable tunes facilitate this connecting, and help audiences draw the celluloid worlds into their lives.

EARLY FILM MUSIC

For centuries, traditions of musical dance-drama flourished, such as the classical *kathakaḷi* dramas of Kerala and the folk *terukkūttu* dramas of Tamil Nadu, which dramatized tales from Hindu mythology, long before the advent of film technology. In the late nineteenth century, a renaissance of these traditions took place. Drama companies arose in which actors sang and danced, and the playwrights composed music. Cinema entered this cultural niche, long occupied by musical drama, and eventually came to replace many traditions (Marre 1992). Even the remarkable length of Indian films—typically more than three hours—can be traced to drama performances, which often lasted several hours, or even all night.

Western silent films were first screened in South India in Madras, at some point in the early 1900s (Mohan 1994:19). In 1916, the first silent films were produced there, and music was immediately combined with the new medium by adding musical variety acts that performed before or after screenings (Baskaran 1981:99). The first sound film in any South Indian language was *Kālidās,* which was produced in 1931 in Bombay. In *Kālidās,* each main character speaks in a different Indian language. Although few other polylingual films were produced, *Kālidās* does attest to the fact that the Indian film experience is, to an extent, polylingual. Occasionally, South Indians attend films that are not in their primary language or dialect, such as the Hindi film *Pyāsa* (Sarkar 1975:108). Accordingly, visual and musical cues are especially important to articulate the narrative. *Galavarishi*, produced in Bombay in 1932, was the first sound film entirely in a South Indian language (Tamil).

Early South Indian cinema followed traditions of musical theater in its emphasis on mythology; the combination of spoken dialogue and songs; the use of Karnatak (South Indian classical) music; and the incorporation of dance. Actors in films are shown dancing to songs in a syncretic dance style called *disco,* which fuses classical, Western, and folk elements (Manuel 1988a:161). But unlike musical drama companies, early film producers separated the roles of screenwriter and music director. Music directors such as S. V. Venkatraman and G. Ramanathan developed a "light classical" style based on simplified Karnatak forms, ragas, talas, and performance techniques, to be performed on vina, sitar, sarod, violin, harmonium, tabla, and *mridangam.* The light classical style generally involved less melodic variation than the usual Karnatak performance, and more repetition of catchy tunes.

At the time of the first sound films, a radio network and a small recording industry had already developed in the region, and gramophone technology facilitated the marketing of stage songs (Mohan 1994:53). The first film songs immediately took on a life outside the cinema, and were heard in homes, streets, and markets; they became powerful tools in promoting the films. For this reason, songs were designed to be beautiful and memorable as well as appropriate to the cinematic context. To this day, film songs reach potential moviegoers through many media, including radio, cassettes, LPs, and CDs.

In the 1930s, all actors were also singers; but starting in the 1940s, some music directors began to separate the two roles. They hired "playback singers" to perform the vocal lines, and the actors then just mouthed the words. By the 1950s, playback singers had completely replaced actor-singers. Accompanying this shift was a shift in vocal style, from a loud, strident, open-throated style typical of live musical dramas to a less ornate style that was smoother and clearer. The new singer specialists explored a greater pitch range, and cultivated a slightly more nasal "crooning style" (Mohan 1994:61).

FILM MUSIC AFTER INDEPENDENCE

During the 1940s, an increasing number of South Indian films were social dramas, rather than stories based on mythology. Despite British censoring, these social dramas reflected a rising awareness of issues of caste reform and nationalism (Baskaran 1981:19). This preponderance of social dramas continued even after India's revolutionary movement had achieved independence for India from Great Britain in 1947.

But this was a period when filmmakers were searching for genres with a more broad-based appeal. They were working to develop an international audience for their films; promoting them throughout the Soviet Union, Africa, and Asia; and were turning toward more spectacular and "escapist" formulas (Baskaran 1981:150) such as S. S. Vasan's dazzling *Chandralekha* (1948) (Dickey 1993:54). At this time they also began to develop non-Brahmin, anti-North, pro-Tamil themes that appealed to South Indians of many social classes.

Music directors participated in the turn toward the spectacular by increasing the size of the orchestras accompanying film songs. In the 1950s, 1960s, and 1970s, these songs placed increasing emphasis on the orchestra, and also included more non-Indian instruments. Mohan (1994:63) identifies an aesthetic shift that occurred during this period: "Orchestral music in the song is conceived [no longer] as an accompaniment but as a homogeneous whole with the words. The situations and imageries expressed in the words of the song are mirrored and translated in the orchestral parts to an extent that the orchestra transcends the conventional accompanying role; by 'restating' and complementing the lyrical sentiments, it becomes inseparable from the words." The larger film orchestras also afforded composers a greater variety of timbres to work with and made films even less dependent on language for effective expression.

During the 1960s and 1970s, music directors took inspiration from Hollywood and from Western classical music, and combined Western elements with Karnatak music to form a style known as "light music." Film orchestras were expanded to include piano, clarinet, cello, saxophone, vibraphone, xylophone, mandolin, horns, and conga. M. S. Viswanathan (known as "Mellisai Mannan" 'King of Light Music'), T. K. Ramamurthy, and others worked with Western tempered tunings and chordal harmonies (see Manuel 1988b:183–184). Some filmmakers and directors simply copied Western pop tunes and Hollywood thriller sound tracks, especially those of James Bond movies. Others combined Western and Indian cinematic and musical elements in more sophisticated and creative ways, employing Western counterpoint and tonal modulations, and capitalizing on the new timbral resources of the expanded orchestra.

ILAIYARAJA

In the 1980s and early 1990s, the music director Ilaiyaraja was the leader of the film-music industry. With the success of his first film score, *Annakkiḷi* 'The Dove' in 1976, he launched a music directing career that would centralize expressive control in the hands of a music director to an unprecedented extent, and effect a deep integration of South Indian folk, Karnatak, and Western classical musics (Mohan 1994:115–120). Ilaiyaraja, who was from a farm household, was exposed to Tamil folk songs at an early age (Mohan 1994:106–107) and was able to instill in his sound tracks an authentic folk quality. He brought folk instruments into the film orchestra, including the *nāgasvaram, uṟumi, uḍukkai, muṅgoose, sēgaṇḍi, gaṭasiṇgāri, tuntina,* and conch (Mohan 1994:117). He also developed a strong command of Karnatak music (as represented by his *Rāja Pārvai* 'Kingly Vision' of 1981, and by *Salangai Oli* 'Sound of Dancing Bells,' 1982) and of Western compositional techniques (as, for example, in *Priya,* 1978) (Mohan 1994:120–122). He pioneered in bringing electronic music technology into film music, integrating rhythm boxes, MIDI, guitar, electronic keyboards, and synthesizers with an orchestra of fifty performers (as in *Vīrā* 'Hero,' 1994). His deep understanding of so many different styles of music allowed him to create syncretic pieces of music combining very different musical idioms in unified, coherent musical statements. In his album *How to Name It,* he fuses Bach partitas and fugues with the Karnatak *pallavi-anupallavi* form, and Karnatak ragas and performance techniques with Western Baroque musical textures. His music appeals to villagers listening for folk rhythms, cosmopolitan urbanites listening for "modern" electronic sounds, and Karnatak music aficionados listening to the raga, all at once.

FILM MUSIC IN THE 1990S

In the 1990s, music directors such as A. R. Rehman have been taking film music in a more cosmopolitan and international direction, drawing on a greater variety of musical styles from around the world; however, their works are sometimes less unified musically than those of Ilaiyaraja. Sound tracks increasingly contain abrupt juxtapositions of styles and musics, including rap (as in *Kadhalan* 'The Lover,' 1994), jazz (*Duet,* 1994), Karnatak music, and older Indian film styles. Film characters occasionally find themselves in media-saturated settings, listening to boom boxes or moving through abruptly changing soundscapes. Characters often live in cosmopolitan South Indian cities and sport fashions that are a mix of Western, Indian, and other styles. An example is the movie *Prema Desam,* a montage-narrative of rap, reggae, synthesizer atmosphere music, break dancing, the music of the Algerian pop star Khaled, and African-American hairstyles. The film star Prabhu Deva is often called "the Michael Jackson of South India" for his break-dancing talent (as in *Merupu Kallalu).* As films have come to emphasize such cosmopolitan visual spectacles, sound tracks increasingly celebrate the spectacle of intriguing, global sounds more as montages than as unified musical statements.

Such film representations are becoming more common at a time when musical and cultural flows have accelerated and become more multidirectional. Not only is MTV bringing rap and other world popular musics to South India, but South Indian music is also making an unprecedented impact elsewhere. Starting with A. R. Rehman's *Roja* (1993), South Indian film songs have been translated into Hindi and marketed in North India, where they have substantially influenced music. And as the South Indian film-music industry responds to global flows of popular musics, it also shapes and influences them; today South Indian music directors, like characters in films, live amid a cosmopolitan whirlwind of sounds, styles, and trends that they, like the moviegoer, must both make sense of and participate in.

Accompanying these changes in technology and culture may be more ambivalent attitudes toward the West, toward technology, and toward modernism. As the lives of Indian audience members themselves become increasingly affected, even permeated, by advances in technology and cosmopolitanism, old dichotomies such as "traditional" versus "modern" and "Indian" versus "Western" have begun to break down. Hariharan (1995) suggests that this may make it more difficult to employ archetypal characters and formula plots in films, since many of the images, symbols, and circumstances that once seemed quintessentially "good" or "bad" now seem ambiguous. For example, it has been a trope in Indian films that when characters are influenced by Western culture, they are turning their backs on "good" traditional values, especially in the areas of family responsibility and sexual conduct. Audiences may find that such black-and-white distinctions oversimplify the ways in which "Western" and "traditional" elements now interact in their lives. Perhaps as a result, films of the late 1990s have increasingly sought popular appeal through voyeuristic spectacle and the sensuous celebration of exciting sounds, rather than (or in addition to) archetypal plots and characters.

Over the seven-decade history of film music, accompanying orchestras have become larger and more important, and music directors have had at their disposal a growing arsenal of timbres and musical styles. Whereas the catchy tune is a means by which audiences connect film worlds to their cultural lives, the musical accompani-

In the 1990s, music directors such as A. R. Rehman have been taking film music in a more cosmopolitan and international direction, drawing on a greater variety of musical styles from around the world.

ment to these tunes has been a timbral space in which South Indians have reflected on issues of identity, tradition, modernity, technology, cosmopolitanism, and Westernization. As South Indians have reflected on these issues, music directors have added Western chordal harmonies and progressions to the light Karnatak accompaniment of the tunes, as well as South Indian folk instruments, synthesizers, and musical montages of the whole world's sounds. Although production of this music is highly centralized—it is controlled by only a handful of film companies and music directors—the music is highly eclectic in style (Arnold 1988), and through the timbral richness of its new orchestra it represents and engages a changed, culturally diverse world.

REFERENCES

Arnold, Alison E. 1988. "Popular Film Song in India—A Case of Mass Market Musical Eclecticism." *Popular Music* 7(2):177–188.

Baskaran, Theodore S. 1981. *The Message Bearers: The Nationalist Politics and the Entertainment Media in South India 1880–1945.* Madras: Cre-A:.

Beeman, William O. 1981. "The Use of Music in Popular Film: East and West." *Indian International Centre Quarterly* 8(1):77–87.

Dickey, Sara. 1993. *Cinema and the Urban Poor in South India.* New Delhi: Foundation Books.

Greene, Paul D. 1995. "Cassettes in Culture: Emotion, Politics, and Performance in Rural Tamil Nadu." Ph.D. dissertation, University of Pennsylvania.

———. In press. "Sound Engineering in a Tamil Village: Playing Audio Cassettes as Devotional Performance." *Ethnomusicology* 44.

Hariharan, K. 1995. "Who Is the Bad Guy? Commercial Cinema in the South." In *Frames of Mind: Reflections on Indian Cinema,* ed. Aruna Vasudev, 191–196. New Delhi: UBS Publishers' Distributors Ltd.

Manuel, Peter. 1988a. "Popular Music in India: 1901-86." *Popular Music* 7(2):157–176.

———. 1988b. "South Asia." In *Popular Musics of the Non-Western World,* ed. Peter Manuel, pp. 171–197. Oxford: Oxford University Press.

Marre, Jeremy. 1992. *There'll Always Be Stars in the Sky.* Newton, N.J.: Harcourt Films. Video cassette.

Mohan, Anuradha. 1994. "Ilaiyaraja: Composer as Phenomenon in Tamil Film Culture." M.A. thesis, Wesleyan University.

Sarkar, Kobita. 1975. *Indian Cinema Today: An Analysis.* New Delhi: Sterling.

Pop Music and Audio-Cassette Technology: Northern Area

Peter Manuel

Ghazal and Bhajan
Regional Musics
Cassettes and Sociopolitical Movements
The Impact of Cassettes

The spread of cassette technology in the late 1970s and early 1980s had a dramatic effect on popular music in South Asia. The commercial-music industry that had previously emerged in India had been highly centralized, being organized primarily around the production of films and records. Factors such as the high cost of records, record production, and record-playing technology had enabled a small coterie of producers to dominate the entire subcontinent's commercial-music industry (Joshi 1988). Partly because most consumers could not afford radios or phonographs but could occasionally buy cinema tickets, mass-mediated popular music from the arrival of sound film (in 1931) to the 1970s consisted mostly of Hindi-Urdu film music, produced largely in Bombay studios and disseminated throughout much of North India. During this period, the film-music industry itself was remarkably centralized, being dominated by the multinational EMI (operating under the logo HMV, "His Master's Voice"). Further, most film songs were produced by a handful of music directors and vocalists. Though regional-language films and film songs also flourished, these tended to imitate the Bombay Hindi-film style. As a result, although the output of the film-music industry was prodigious and sophisticated, it cannot be said to have represented the linguistic and stylistic diversity of the subcontinent's music.

Import restrictions and other factors initially delayed the introduction of audio cassettes in India, but in the early 1980s the growth of the local bourgeoisie, remittances and imports from gulf-state workers, and the liberalization of the national economy precipitated the massive spread of cassette technology throughout the area. Cassettes soon proved to be much better suited to South Asian conditions than records or compact discs. Unlike records and phonographs, tapes and tape-players are cheap, durable, and portable, and are easily powered by batteries. They are widely accessible to lower-class consumers, including those otherwise lacking electricity. Perhaps most important, the production of cassette recordings is much cheaper than the manufacture of records (not to mention CDs). Accordingly, in the early 1980s, several hundred producers of cassettes emerged in North India, recording and marketing a bewildering variety of local folk musics and folk-pop hybrids. Most of these producers are cottage companies, operating on shoestring budgets, recording local folk singers for local consumers. A few, such as New Delhi's T-Series, have developed

As cassette players spread among the upper and middle classes, the new style of ghazal came to be disseminated primarily via cassettes, and was thus the first pan-regional pop-music genre to enjoy mass distribution independent of films.

into financial giants. Meanwhile, alongside the "legitimate" cassette industry has emerged a vast nationwide network of pirate producers marketing cheap, unauthorized copies of hit cassettes. Although cassette piracy is illegal, prosecution of offenders is irregular, and the practice has bankrupted many legitimate producers.

With the introduction of cassettes, the size, structure, and output of the music industry changed markedly. Production of vinyl records declined, and by 1990 India had become the world's second-largest producer of cassettes, surpassed only by the United States. HMV's virtual monopoly of the music industry ended with the emergence of new rivals like T-Series, Venus, myriad smaller producers, and multinationals like CBS and Polygram. Though sales of film music increased in the recording market, they soon came to be surpassed by sales of nonfilm music. Thus, while cassettes have brought film music into remote villages, they have served to disseminate regional music, giving consumers the ability to choose from a broader variety of recorded-music styles. As a result, commercial music in South Asia has become richer and more diverse (Manuel 1993).

GHAZAL AND BHAJAN

The transformation of the South Asian music industry occurred roughly between 1977 and 1985. The first years of this period were a transitional stage, marked by the emergence of a simplified and commercial-song version of the Urdu ghazal, an Arabic- and Persian-derived poetic form consisting of thematically independent couplets set to a strict meter and rhyme scheme. For several centuries in North India, singers and especially courtesans have sung ghazals as refined light classical pieces. In the mid-twentieth century, film-style renditions of ghazals became popular, although they declined in the 1970s as film music became more oriented toward disco-style Western pop. By the middle of the decade, Pakistani singers Mehdi Hasan and Ghulam Ali were popularizing a new style of ghazal, aimed primarily at bourgeois listeners who, though unfamiliar with classical music, enjoyed the aristocratic associations and languid melodies of the ghazal. Such Indian singers as Pankaj Udhas, Anup Jalota, and Jagjit and Chitra Singh followed the trend with an even more accessible style of ghazal, using simplified Urdu and emphasizing catchy refrains rather than sophisticated improvisations. (As local journalists quipped, "Pop goes the ghazal.") Most purist connoisseurs of the light classical ghazal think little of the current style of singing and choice of poetry, but the renewed popularity of the Indo-Muslim ghazal remains a symbol of Hindu-Muslim syncretism in a period marked by vicious religious conflicts. HMV and its emergent rivals saw the pop ghazal as a means to outflank pirate producers, whose distorted and tinny-sounding tapes may satisfy lower-class film-music audiences, but are inadequate for the smooth and silky timbres of the pop ghazal. As cassette players spread among the upper and middle classes, the new style of ghazal came to be disseminated primarily via cassettes, and was thus the first pan-regional pop-music genre to enjoy mass distribution independent of films.

FIGURE 1 Rajasthani Hindu devotional songs (bhajans), showing musicians with barrel drum (*ḍholak*) and harmonium; the singer, Ghulam Rasool, is a Muslim. Cassette card, late 1980s. Yuki R–0254.

In the wake of the ghazal vogue, cassettes came to serve as the medium for a great variety of devotional music genres. Most prominent among these was a modernized version of the bhajan (a generic term for Hindu devotional song), as sung by professional solo vocalists with standard light classical instrumental accompaniment (primarily tabla and harmonium). In the early 1980s, cassettes of such bhajans by Hari Om Sharan, Anup Jalota, Pankaj Udhas, and others came to rival pop ghazals in sales while tapping essentially the same market—the pan-regional, Hindi-speaking North Indian middle class. Cassettes of qawwalis (an Indo-Muslim Urdu devotional song form) also proliferated, even as live performances of the genre declined.

In the early and mid-1980s, as cassette ownership further spread throughout rural and lower-class communities, local producers began recording and marketing a much broader range of devotional-music cassettes. Many of these have consisted of specialized devotional genres, sung in local languages and dedicated to local deities or celebrating local festivals. Thus, in the state of Maharashtra, one finds numerous cassettes of hymns (*abhang*) dedicated to the local deity Vitthal, while in the Punjab, Sikh devotional hymns called *kīrtan* are particularly popular. Personnel on such recordings often consists only of a singer, who also plays harmonium, and an accompanist playing *ḍholak* 'barrel drum' (figure 1).

Aside from casual listening, such cassettes serve multiple purposes. Temple priests may play them over loudspeakers to attract devotees (and entertain the gods), and lay listeners may play them to memorize popular prayers, like the *Hanumān chālīsā* 'Forty Verses to Hanuman'. Some tapes guide listeners through prayer rituals (*pūjā*), interspersing spoken instructions with musical interludes, thereby enabling devotees to conduct domestic ceremonies without hiring a local pandit. Throughout North India, cassettes have also become vital media for transmitting long narrative Hindu folktales (*kathā*). Producers, for their part, find that tapes of devotional music enjoy more sustained sales than those of other pop-music genres.

REGIONAL MUSICS

FIGURE 2 *The Tale of Bhakt Prahlad,* a North Indian folk music-drama (*nauṭaṅkī*). Cassette card, late 1980s. Rama 511.

Perhaps the largest category of cassette-based popular music consists of secular folk songs rendered in a more or less traditional style. Before cassettes, commercial recordings of many of these genres did not exist, whether because producers did not consider songs in regional dialects to be commercially viable, or, in the case of lengthy narrative epics or dramatic genres like the North Indian Hindi folk music-drama *nauṭaṅkī* (figure 2), because such performances could not be captured on three-minute records. Local cottage producers of cassettes, however, have energetically responded to and stimulated local demand by marketing a variety of products. Most of these consist of traditional genres or newly composed songs in traditional style, often using stock melodies. In some cases, producers modernize the sound by supplementing the customary accompaniment (harmonium and barrel drum) with synthesizers, clarinets, and other instruments. Tastes in and attitudes toward such innovations differ: some rural listeners evidently prefer the traditional instrumentation, which can be recorded quickly and inexpensively; urbanized listeners generally prefer the slicker, more commercial, and often heavily orchestrated sound of film music, which some producers of cassettes try to imitate. Quite often, folk singers set texts in local dialects to melodies of familiar film songs, incurring the scorn of purist folklorists but satisfying the audiences' demand for music that is at once modern and yet recognizably local.

Although film music, ghazals, and Hindi-language bhajans are popular throughout North India, regional-language cassettes best illustrate the diversity of contemporary South Asian music. The music of the Punjab, a large and fertile region straddling India and Pakistan, is particularly dynamic and has been invigorated by urbanization, contacts with emigrants, and perhaps above all, the arrival of cassettes. Cassettes have provided a new medium of expression for artists like Gurdas Maan, whose songs combine local folk rhythms and melodies with modern instrumentation and lyrics dramatizing the modernization of Punjabi society. Such stylized Punjabi folk songs are generically called bhangra, though they have little in common with the traditional rustic genre of that name. They are especially popular among urban Punjabi youth. Their style has evolved in tandem with that of the more Westernized pop bhangra of British-based émigrés, which freely incorporates elements of disco, dancehall reggae, and techno-pop, while retaining an unmistakable Punjabi flavor [see MUSIC AND THE SOUTH ASIAN DIASPORA: THE UNITED KINGDOM].

Cassette-based music in Gujarat is equally cosmopolitan and lively, especially the modernized versions of the *garbā* and *rās* songs that accompany animated social dancing during the Hindu Navrātrī 'Nine-Nights' festival. In Maharashtra, Marathi-language cassettes feature devotional songs to local deities, pop versions of fishermen's songs (*koli*), film-style renditions of folk and semiclassical *lāvṇi* songs, and bawdy ditties called *popat.* In West Bengal and Bangladesh, the most popular genres are songs of the poet-musician Rabindranath Tagore (1861–1941), called *Rabindra saṅgit*; the more contemporary-sounding *ādhunik gīt* (literally 'modern song'); other Bengali folk songs such as *polli gīt*; and tapes of *jātrā* folk plays. Throughout much of North India, Hindi-language, "non-filmi" pop songs constitute another growing market, in which Hindi covers of current Western pop songs play a large part.

Elsewhere in the subcontinent, regional-language musics disseminated on cassette tend to remain closer to their folk roots. Particularly popular in Rajasthan are tapes of ballads (*kathā*), in which epic tales of saints, gods, and heroes are narrated in repetitive, stock melodies with sparse instrumentation. In Bihar and eastern Uttar Pradesh, cassettes of similar narrative ballads, called *birahā,* are widely marketed, typically setting texts in the Bhojpuri dialect to medleys of tunes from Hindi films and local genres. The Braj region south of Delhi also hosts a lively cassette scene, consisting especially of *rasiyā*, often ribald songs about Krishna the cowherd, or about male-female relationships in general. Other places such as Garhwal and Himachal Pradesh (which the music industry had previously ignored) also sustain substantial cassette-based music cultures. Finally, English-language Indian pop has garnered its own shelf space in urban music stores catering to the Westernized middle and upper classes.

The process of recording

Folk-music recording projects originate in various ways. Typically, a producer commissions a lyricist to compose verses on a selected topic, such as hymns to a deity or a saint whose annual festival is approaching. The producer will contact musicians—usually one or more singers, and harmonium and *ḍholak* players—and the lead singer may set the lyrics to familiar tunes derived from folk tradition or films. The recording usually takes place in an urban studio that may be rather makeshift by Western standards, but is usually adequate for local purposes. Power outages frequently cause delays, obliging musicians and technicians to sit around for hours sipping tea while waiting for the electricity to come back on.

Eventually the producer sends his finished master tape to a local workshop—perhaps a tiny, dimly lit back room somewhere—where young men assemble blank cassettes and make copies, often on rickety, locally made, one-to-four duplicators. The new releases are then distributed, either by truck or by bullock cart, to vendors throughout the targeted region. The state-run All India Radio rarely broadcasts folk-music cassettes, for film music and live performances of folk and classical music continue to dominate its airwaves. Nevertheless, even without the publicity afforded by airplay, new cassettes make themselves known by word of mouth and by booming amplification from loudspeakers at vendors' stalls. A cheaply produced folk-music cassette may turn a profit if vendors sell more than two or three thousand copies. As elsewhere, most releases lose money, but particularly catchy tapes, such as the 1989 recycling of the Punjabi ditty "Tūtuk Tūtuk," can become runaway hits, with hundreds of thousands of copies sold. Local manufacturers also produce inexpensive tape players, often in collaboration with Japanese multinationals.

Song texts

Unlike film songs, most of which deal exclusively with sentimental love, the texts of cassette-based regional songs treat a wide variety of themes. Most of these portray ordinary people in typical situations, relating, for example, the frustrations of the young bride, the merriment of local festivals, or the vicissitudes of modernization and urbanization. Particularly popular among cassettes aimed at lower-class male listeners are ribald, spicy songs such as *rasiyā,* narrating titillating encounters or fantasies and often using thinly veiled erotic metaphors or double-entendres. Many elders, women, and folk-music connoisseurs see these cassettes as cheap and vulgar, but their defenders point out that eroticism has always enjoyed a place in traditional Hindu culture, whether in the form of Krishnaite love poetry, sensual sculptures in temples, or the well-known book depicting erotic love, the *Kāmasūtra*. Most such songs develop conventional themes, often involving the customary flirtation between the young man and his elder brother's wife, or the amorous dalliance of the cowherd-deity Krishna with local peasant girls. In many cases, they whimsically dramatize the social and sexual tensions of rural life as perceived by village women (but often as composed and sung by a man). The following typical Braj folk song, loosely associated with the regional Hindu divinity Languriya, comments sardonically on the effects of modernization and film culture:

Naī-naī "fashion" kī jogin ne ye bigāṛo lānguriā;
Pāni bharan ko maiṅ calūṅ to pīche cal de lānguriā.
Mere man meṅ aisī-aisī āve kuā meṅḍhakelūṅ;
Gobar thāpan maiṅ calūṅ to pīche calde lānguriā.
Mere man aisī-aisī āve gobar meṅ thāpūṅ;
Rasoī tapan ko maiṅ calūṅ to pīche āve lānguriā.
Mere man meṅ aisī-aisī āve belan se mārūṅ.

These modern girls have ruined our menfolk;
I go to fetch water, and this guy follows me.
I'd like to push him into the well;
When I collect dung [for fuel], he's behind me.
I'd like to cake him up with manure;
When I go to the hot kitchen, he trails me.
I feel like whacking him with a rolling pin.

Whether such songs are enjoyed or disparaged, the cassette boom has revitalized folk-song traditions, stimulating interest and productivity and providing media outlets for local performers who would not otherwise be represented in mass-mediated music.

CASSETTES AND SOCIOPOLITICAL MOVEMENTS

Cassettes have also come to play important roles as vehicles for sociopolitical movements. Since they are cheap, easily duplicated, independent of corporate finance, and resistant to state censorship, cassettes can constitute an ideal "people's medium," able

Unlike television, cinema, and radio in India, cassettes are decentralized and democratic in ownership, usage, and production. They offer unprecedented opportunities for diverse communities and interest groups to make their voices heard.

to bypass the "old media" of cinema and television. A few progressive grassroots groups have distributed cassettes of sociopolitical songs and speeches. One such organization is Jagori, a feminist group based in New Delhi; among its activities are producing and disseminating cassette-recorded versions of songs, set to familiar tunes, urging women to challenge the chauvinist traditions and abuse they endure. Separatist movements in Kashmir and the Punjab have produced cassettes of militant songs, distributed via informal networks of retailers and activists.

Since 1989, the major political parties have produced their own propaganda cassettes of songs and speeches, which party supporters reproduce and distribute nationwide. Particularly controversial in North India have been cassettes produced by the militant Hindu movement that has arisen since the late 1980s. These tapes, containing firebrand speeches inciting hatred against the nation's Muslim minority, are regarded by journalists as having played a crucial role in provoking communal riots and massacres in which thousands of lives (mostly Muslim) were lost. Like the Kashmiri and Punjabi separatist tapes, these cassettes were banned by the Indian government, but nevertheless circulated widely. Their impact illustrates how cassettes, as a grassroots medium, are just as likely to be used to foment bigotry and intolerance as they are to promote liberation and enlightenment.

THE IMPACT OF CASSETTES

The effects of the cassette boom in South Asia have been dramatic and complex. The most obvious consequence has been the decentralization and democratization of the music industry. Once dominated by Hindi film music as produced by a few composers and singers, the South Asian commercial music scene now includes several hundred cassette-production businesses of various sizes, marketing an unprecedented variety of musics oriented toward diverse classes, religions, and regions. Cassettes have thus played a role in revitalizing folk-music styles, strengthening local traditions otherwise threatened by Hindi-film culture, and spawning the emergence of dynamic syncretic musics that reflect the changing values of a modernizing society. At the same time, cassettes illustrate how new technologies can reinforce not only modernity but also traditional beliefs and arts. Since cassettes are resistant to both state censorship and upper-class aesthetics, it may be inevitable that much of the new cassette-based music consists of cheaply produced lewd ditties rather than slick and sophisticated artworks. Meanwhile, the communal violence incited by Hindu militant tapes has led some commentators to lament publicly that cassettes were ever invented.

Regardless of their mixed effects, cassettes are here to stay. Indeed, they are typical of the sorts of new micromedia—like computer networks, videos, and fax machines—that are revolutionizing global communications. Unlike television, cinema, and radio in India, cassettes are decentralized and democratic in ownership, usage, and production. They offer unprecedented opportunities for diverse communities and interest groups to make their voices heard. Their spread in South Asia illustrates how a new technology can influence not only the structure, but also the content, of the mass media. In this process, cassettes challenge the social order as they provide opportunities for group and individual self-expression.

REFERENCES

Hartman, Paul, B. R. Patil, and Anita Dighe. 1989. *The Mass Media and Village Life: An Indian Study.* New Delhi: Sage.

Joshi, G. N. 1988. "A Concise History of the Phonograph Industry in India." *Popular Music* 7(2):147–156.

Manuel, Peter. 1993. *Cassette Culture: Popular Music and Technology in North India.* Chicago: University of Chicago Press.

Pop Music and Audio-Cassette Technology: Southern Area

Paul D. Greene

Production and Distribution
Shelf Categories and Genres of Cassette Music
Cassettes in a Tamil Village

Audio-cassette technology has sparked an explosion of diversity in the popular musics of South India and Sri Lanka. The production of cassettes is much cheaper than the production of other mass media, notably films, CDs, and LPs, so small-scale or medium-scale producers can compete successfully with large companies, offering diverse, specialized genres for specific markets (Manuel 1993). Cassettes serve as sounding boards for voices that cannot find expression through other media, including voices of villagers, religious minorities, and political activists.

Such diversity of musical genres allows popular music to permeate modern culture. Cassettes can be played back and amplified for specific purposes. Beyond South Asia, popular-music cassettes are a growing part of cultural life in Bedouin Egypt (Abu-Lughod 1989), Afghanistan (Mills 1991), Java (Sutton 1985), and elsewhere. In South India and Sri Lanka, cassettes inspire devotional sentiments, offer pleasing sounds to the gods, create atmosphere for social interaction, and remind listeners of distant places. They offer unprecedented control over sound. To assess their impact, it is important to study how cassettes become part of culture.

Tamil Nadu has been the focus of most research, partly because the cities of Madras and Madurai are important centers for cassette production. Producers make many Telugu and Malayalam cassettes there, and musicians such as the popular artists Yesudas and A. R. Rehman produce songs in Madras that become hits in other South Indian states. Extensive research remains to be done on cassette production and use outside Tamil Nadu.

PRODUCTION AND DISTRIBUTION

Cassette production is much less centralized than other musical media. Studios exist in many cities, including Madras, Madurai, Colombo, Kozhikode, Bangalore, and Hyderabad. Engineers record musicians on a multitrack tape master and commonly add synthesized sounds, reverberation, and echo effects, even to folk products. They then send the master to a duplication ("loop-bin") facility that produces hundreds of copies at a time. In addition, individuals, merchants, and organizations hire dubbing stations to produce customized tapes of selected pieces.

Cassette stores can be found in cities, towns, and a few villages. Village and city-based sound-service businesses rent out audio cassettes and playback and amplification equipment for events such as marriages, meetings, and religious festivals (except devotional festivals of Sri Lankan Buddhism). These businesses bring contemporary music from cities into villages. Together with radio, cinema, and regional buses that continuously play film-music cassettes, they are musical conduits or cultural brokers.

SHELF CATEGORIES AND GENRES OF CASSETTE MUSIC

Cassette-store managers classify cassettes on display shelves by commercial categories such as film (cine), folk (*kirāmiya*), devotional (bhakti), and classical (Karnatak). These categories correspond to patterns of use, such as devotion or diversion. Within each category is an explosion of regionally specific genres and cassette-related cultural practices.

Film music

The largest percentage of recorded music bought, sold, and heard in the south comes from Indian and Sri Lankan films. Film music is ubiquitous in public culture. It is broadcast at meetings, marriages, festivals, and other events. Amplified film songs signal to a village or neighborhood that an important public event is about to occur. Most film-song cassettes feature six to nine songs popularized through movies. Few actors actually sing; on screen, they mouth words sung by studio musicians called playback singers. Both cine music and films have a turnover rate of about four months.

From the mid-1970s onward the music director Isaignani Ilaiyaraja has dominated the South Indian film industry. His popularity is due both to his village heritage and to his ability to combine folk-music elements with Western classical, Western pop, and South Indian classical music (Laul 1988). In 1993, the Madras-based A. R. Rehman came to prominence with the all-India hit movie *Roja*, and he is replacing Ilaiyaraja as the most popular South Indian music director. Rehman develops a new, cosmopolitan sound through his command of a wide variety of Western pop idioms, which he combines with Karnatak music. At present, Ilaiyaraja's music remains popular in villages, and Rehman's music captures the cities and finds popularity in North India.

Though cassette technology seems not to inspire greater diversity in film music, it does allow individuals to customize their film-music listening. In many villages, "classic" film songs from the 1950s, 1960s, and 1970s are revived through cassettes, making the villages popular-music time capsules. Such songs usually foreground a playback singer's voice against a backdrop of light Karnatak instrumentation, including harmonium, vina, tabla, and *mridangam* 'double-headed drum'. In Tamil Nadu, the most popular old film songs are those from films featuring the actor-turned-politician M. G. Ramachandran (figure 1).

FIGURE 1 This Tamil film music cassette features songs from movies starring the actor-turned-politician M. G. Ramachandran. The cassette title, *Folk Songs from Tamil Films*, indicates the actor's film role as a villager; the song recordings are film songs, not folk songs. Cassette card, 1993. Raja Recording Company.

Boundaries between film and folk music are fluid. Film-music directors draw on folk music, and village musicians turn film songs into folk songs. Cassettes allow villagers to select film songs for themselves, play them until they learn them, and then sing them as work songs. Such singers often alter rhythms, adopt a call-and-response form, and improvise new words to reflect their own contexts (Greene 1995: 235–249).

Folk music

The shelf category of "folk music" is an extension of the term in its usual sense. Here the term refers to recorded music categorized as such by distributors and identified by villagers as directly derived from music they produce.

Before the 1980s, when audio-cassette technology became commonplace in

FIGURE 2 Tamil folk music, *Maṉ Vācam* 'Fragrance of the Soil', produced by Pushpavanam Kuppuswamy. Cassette card, 1990. Indu Music IMR 1545.

India, folk music was virtually absent in the mass media, except for occasional adaptations in film music. In the late 1990s, hundreds of folk genres have become popular. Producing this music is a new breed of popular culture producer: music directors who are folklore popularists, such as the folk singer and scholar Pushpavanam Kuppuswamy, the singer and professor Vijayalakshmi Nanavitakrishnan of Madurai Kamaraj University, and S. Balan of Sri Ramji Cassettes, Madurai. These researchers travel to villages with tape recorders and seek out new songs, styles, and genres in villagers' lullabies, work songs, devotional music, and street dramas. They then return to urban studios, hire musicians, and rework the songs for popular consumption.

As these researchers combine commercial interests with the goal of celebrating folklore, they spark debates among villagers and folklorists concerning the authenticity of their products. Critics call them fakelorists, exploiters of village culture. Yet people in cities and villages alike play such cassettes of folk music, and many villagers find in these commercial products the "fragrance of the soil" (*maṉ vācam*), referring to the village (figure 2). For villagers who have moved to cities or abroad, folk cassettes are reminders of rural life.

Popular-folk cassettes began as a commercial extension of professional folk music. Cassettes first popularized music of professional and semiprofessional folk singers, targeting villages and cities in the musicians' performance circuits. Genres include the nondramatic, often devotional, Tamil song form *temmāngu pāṭṭu*, featuring a solo voice accompanied by percussion. Cassettes also popularize music of street dramas performed by amateur and professional musicians on special occasions. With the accompaniment of drums, rattles, and cymbals, genres like the Tamil *terukkūttu pāṭṭu* represent entertaining situations, dialogues, or disputes. Villagers play cassettes of such music for evening entertainment. In Andhra Pradesh, musicians perform drum music (*maro dandorā*) before public announcements, and cassettes of such music now serve similar functions. In Sri Lanka, cassettes popularize the musical tradition of *bailā*, a festive Sinhalese dance dating back to the 1300s and incorporating Portuguese rhythms and instruments. Some professional musicians popularize political agendas through cassettes, such as the Telugu folk singer Gaddar, who voices socialist concerns.

Cassettes popularize nonprofessional folk genres, though recordings feature studio professionals. For the commercial market, producers record highly energetic devotional traditions like the Tamil bow song (*vilppāṭṭu*) and drum song (*uṭukkai pāṭṭu*). They abridge performances that normally last several hours or days to fit on a single cassette. Some villagers say abridged performances inspire devotional sentiment, but are not so moving as live performances. Folk lullabies, such as the Tamil mother's *tālāṭṭu*, appear on cassette recordings and are occasionally played in village homes. Other cassette genres include humorous, often ribald dialogues rooted in and sometimes mocking village life. Some folklore popularists study the music of aboriginal peoples in South India and Sri Lanka and produce and market studio versions of it.

Devotional music

South Indians and Sri Lankans listen to a wide variety of devotional cassette music. Cassettes offer recitations of Sanskrit texts performed in Karnatak ragas to the accompaniment of the string drone (*tambūrā*), tabla, and other classical instruments. Some Hindus play these recordings while performing ritual devotion (*pūjā*).

Many Hindus believe that Karnatak music is sacred and auspicious (*maṅgaḷa*), a pleasing offering to the gods. Tamil Hindus traditionally hire instrumentalists to play the *nāgasvaram* 'double-reed aerophone' for marriages, ritual devotions, and house-opening and ear-piercing ceremonies. In Andhra Pradesh and Kerala, musicians sing

Sanskrit texts in Karnatak ragas for such functions. Throughout South India, people play cassettes of Karnatak music on such occasions as an offering to the gods. To offer good wishes before important ceremonies, Sinhalese Buddhists sometimes play cassettes of blessing songs (*jayamaṅgaḷa gâṭa*) performed by young girls in Sinhalese classical style (*parani gī*). If a priest is unavailable, Sinhalese Buddhists may play cassette recitations of sutras on occasions of death or to confer blessings on a house or a new venture.

Cassettes popularize Hindu and Buddhist devotional music that highlights a singer's voice to the accompaniment of classical instruments, like the *nāgasvaram*, tabla, vina, cymbals (*tāḷam*), flute, and synthesized sounds. The singers Yesudas, S. Govindarajan, K. Veeramani, and L. R. Eswari produce songs in several South Indian languages, some in Karnatak forms and others in forms of five or more stanzas. Some song texts address deities directly; others are more philosophical, offering wisdom about gods and the world.

Besides Hindu and Buddhist music, cassettes make possible the dissemination of devotional music of other religions such as Islam and Christianity, in both light classical and Karnatak styles. Christians, especially in Kerala and Tamil Nadu, listen to devotional-music recordings at home, most commonly during "solitary prayer."

Miscellaneous recordings

Cassettes marketed mostly by Music India Ltd. (better known as MIL) bring Western pop music to young cosmopolitan listeners. Cassettes offer the recited advice of Osho Rajneesh, Sai Baba, and other gurus to the accompaniment of soft sounds, such as those of a drone (*tambūrā*) or samples of natural sounds. Organizations that sponsor Karnatak music (*sabhā*) increasingly record and archive performances on cassette. Entrepreneurs target special concerns with cassettes that help listeners quit smoking or learn ragas.

Political parties and labor unions use audio-cassette technology to promote propaganda. Typically, party propagandists rent and drive an *autoriksha,* a small motor vehicle equipped with playback and amplification equipment. They broadcast speeches, amplifying leaders' voices to create larger-than-life images. Drawing on archives of recorded speeches, they select those appropriate for each discursive moment of a political campaign.

In the 1980s and 1990s, *gāna,* a new genre of folk music, emerged among youths in Tamil urban settings, especially universities. *Gāna* musicians borrow melodies from cassette recordings of cine, folk, and devotional songs, to which they compose new words. Students compose these songs in their quarters, inventing lyrics concerning student life, and beating rhythms on buckets and tabletops. Cassette technology allows such amateur musicians to play back popular songs frequently enough to learn them, and since the melodies are already popularized on cassettes, *gāna* songs rapidly find an audience. Through the cassette-based borrowing of tunes, urban youths thus piggyback *gāna* onto pop melodies to reach a mass audience.

CASSETTES IN A TAMIL VILLAGE

Throughout South India and Sri Lanka, villagers use cassettes in diverse ways and to varying extents. In the village I call Icaikurichi, tea-stall owners, sound-service businesspeople, and home listeners chiefly manage cassette technology (Greene 1995). Icaikurichi is a village of four thousand in the Tanjavur district of Tamil Nadu, where the chief industry is growing rice. The population is almost entirely Hindu, and the village supports a small Brahmin community, a dominant non-Brahmin community (Kaḷḷar), and three Harijan communities (lowest castes, formerly referred to as

Cassettes make musical offerings to the gods affordable for villagers who cannot hire live musicians, thereby allowing them to conduct marriages with prestige and perhaps the gods' blessings.

untouchables). The village connects with other villages and cities through buses, motorbikes, radios, and cassettes. Prerecorded cassettes are available in shops in the city of Tanjavur, 28 kilometers away, and local production is possible at a nearby dubbing station.

Open-air tea stalls broadcast cassettes continuously during the day. Villagers stop for tea before going to the fields in the morning and after work in the evening. Tea stalls amplify cassette sounds into streets and residences. Stall managers offer cassette music according to villagers' shared needs at each time of day. In the morning, as villagers perform devotions to deities and prepare for work, tea stalls broadcast auspicious Karnatak music, followed by popular devotional music. In the evening, villagers seek diversion and relaxation, so tea stalls broadcast film music (including old film songs) and folk music.

Five sound-service businesses provide audio-cassette technology for events such as marriages, house openings, ear piercings, and pilgrimages. Cassettes make musical offerings to the gods affordable for villagers who cannot hire live musicians, thereby allowing them to conduct marriages with prestige and perhaps the gods' blessings. Low-budget pilgrims rent cassette equipment for buses, or mount it on bicycles, broadcasting devotional music during their journey. Sound-service businesses thus offer access to auspicious, devotion-inspiring, or entertaining music appropriate for specific events through affordable cassette technology.

During an annual festival to the local deity Muttumariyamma, the temple committee hires sound-service businesses to mount loudspeakers throughout Icaikurichi and broadcast a program of devotional and other musics to the whole village (figure 3). Affordable playback technology has allowed the committee to extend the festival

FIGURE 3 Loudspeakers mounted on Muruka temple (upper right corner of roof) in Mullikkulam, Madurai district, Tamil Nadu (as on the Muttamariyamma temple), amplifying cassette music to the village. Photo by Paul D. Greene, 1994.

from two days to fifteen. The festival now includes cassette songs about the goddess, live performances, ritual devotions, and other events. A growing, collective effort, it inspires villagewide devotion and solidarity as it structures cultural and political life. Thus, cassettes offer not only open access to valuable sounds, but also new ways to centralize power and influence.

REFERENCES

Abu-Lughod, Lila. 1989. "Bedouins, Cassettes and Technologies of Public Culture." *Middle East Report* 159:7–11, 47.

Greene, Paul D. 1995. "Cassettes in Culture: Emotion, Politics, and Performance in Rural Tamil Nadu." Ph.D. dissertation, University of Pennsylvania.

Laul, Brian. 1988. "Ilaiya Raaja: Nothing but Success." *Playback and Fast Forward*, July, 80–83.

Manuel, Peter. 1993. *Cassette Culture: Popular Music and Technology in North India.* Chicago: University of Chicago Press.

Mills, Margaret. 1991. "Gender and Verbal Performance Style in Afghanistan." In *Gender, Genre, and Power in South Asian Expressive Traditions*, ed. Arjun Appadurai, Frank Korom, and Margaret Mills, 56–77. Philadelphia: University of Pennsylvania Press.

Sutton, R. Anderson. 1985. "Commercial Cassette Recordings of Traditional Music in Java: Implications for Performers and Scholars." *The World of Music* 32(3):23–46.

Music and Internationalization

Gerry Farrell

Background
Historical Perspectives
Journeys to the West
Effects of Internationalization on Indian Music
Contemporary Trends

BACKGROUND

The music of South Asia, particularly that of the Indian classical-music traditions, has evolved a unique relationship with the West: it "is the only major system outside the West that has succeeded in maintaining its traditions largely unmarked by the West . . . and that has journeyed away from its cultural home to be welcomed elsewhere" (Neuman 1990:17). This very strength of tradition accounts in part for the success Indian music has enjoyed in the West. On the one hand, Western audiences have related to the complexity and musical integrity of Indian music as similar to their own classical systems; on the other hand, Indian music and musicians represent an exotic culture, communicating an attractive ambience both mystical and aesthetic, and well suited to Western expectations.

In turn, the West has had a significant impact on Indian music and musicians. Western technologies have altered the face of Indian music. The recording of musical sounds came early to India (1902), and became an important source of income for traditional musicians at a time when patronage from the royal courts was in terminal decline. The gramophone brought certain forms of music, notably the music of courtesans, out of the obscurity of their traditional milieus and into the mass market, first in India and then abroad. This technology had other implications. At first, the capacity of 78-rpm disks meant that musicians had to adapt Indian musical forms to suit; but with the introduction of LPs, and then CDs, Indian musicians lengthened their recorded performances. The film industry in India created a hugely influential popular-music form, now known as film song (*filmī gīt*), which incorporates elements from both traditional Indian music and Western music, and has become the major popular music of the South Asian diaspora.

Beginning in the 1950s, Indian classical music became an international music, mainly due to the efforts of Ravi Shankar, the central figure in the twentieth-century globalization of Indian music. Countless Indian musicians have since made the journey west, and have been active as performers, instrumental teachers, and professors. Such artists include the Hindustani instrumentalists Ali Akbar Khan and Amjad Ali Khan (sarod), Nikhil Banerjee and Imrat Khan (sitar), Ram Narayan (*sāraṅgī* 'bowed lute'), Zakir Hussain (tabla), and the Karnatak artists T. Viswanathan (flute), T.

Ranganathan (*mridangam* 'barrel drum'), and M. S. Subbulakshmi (voice). Many universities in the United States and Europe offer classes in Indian music taught by Indian teachers. In the Rotterdam Conservatory, for example, it is possible to take a five-year bachelor's degree in Indian music. As a central field of ethnomusicological study, Indian music has generated an extensive literature in the English language. And because of the size of the South Asian community resident in the West—particularly in the United Kingdom (see map 3)—the availability of South Asian musical recordings has increased, ranging from the classical music of North and South India to a variety of regional and popular musics.

The internationalization of Indian music has resulted in many collaborations in the West between Indian musicians and Western musicians, in the fields of classical music, jazz, and popular music. These collaborations include concertos for sitar and orchestra, Indian jazz groups, and sitar-flavored mass-media pop. South Asian music in all its myriad forms is now established as a significant strand of the cultural fabric of Western musical life.

Though the twentieth century has witnessed the establishment of Indian music as a global cultural phenomenon, the interaction between Indian musicians and the West has a longer history that stretches back into the 1800s. A contextualization of this history permits greater understanding of contemporary developments.

HISTORICAL PERSPECTIVES

Interaction occurred between Western explorers and Indian musicians in the 1500s and 1600s, but not until the eighteenth century did Western scholars start to take a wider and more sustained interest in Indian music (Bor 1988). Toward the end of that century, some Orientalists, including the famous philologist Sir William Jones, carried out serious studies of Indian music. Then, in 1834, Captain A. N. Willard published an important treatise on Indian music, drawn mainly from observations of contemporary performances. For exotic mementos of a sojourn in the East, European residents collected and arranged Indian songs known as Hindustani airs (one published collection is Bird 1789). Throughout the 1800s, Western scholars showed an interest in certain aspects of Indian music, notably in notation, intonation, and tuning (Clements 1913, 1920, 1923; Day 1891). The question of whether Western harmonic concepts could be applied to Indian music was a topic that occupied the minds of Indian and Western scholars. Two important Indian musicologists, Sourindro Mohun Tagore and A. Chinnasvami Mudaliar, wrote substantial works on the applicability of harmony and staff notation to Indian music. Such matters were of central musical and intellectual importance in India in the 1800s, and reflected the wider interaction (and sometimes friction) between the cultures of India and the West. For example, in 1874, S. M. Tagore clashed with the inspector of schools in Bengal, C. B. Clarke, over which notation, Western or Indian, was more appropriate for music education in schools. Acrimoniously pursued in the pages of the Calcutta press, the debate divided Western and Indian musicians alike (Capwell 1986, 1991).

Despite the genuine interest of some in Indian music, the opinion of most Westerners was that Indian music was little better than noise, without structure or melodic interest—a savage and unruly music. This attitude changed slowly, even as Indian music and musicians became increasingly visible in the West.

South Asian musicians have been traveling to perform in the West since the 1800s. Their reasons for being so far from home varied, as did the contexts in which they performed. Nautches (entertainments provided by female Indian dancers) were favorite attractions at imperial exhibitions that took place in London and elsewhere in the mid-1800s. Such events, including the "Indian Villages in London" Exhibition (1876), displayed India's peoples and cultures like living museum exhibits, shocking and delighting Western onlookers. Nautch girls became symbols of the mysterious and sensual East, alluring but morally dangerous. They became favorite figures in Western popular culture and were portrayed in operas and ballets, of which one of the most famous was Marius Petipa's ballet *La Bayadère* in 1877, with music by Léon Minkus (Bor and Bruguiere 1992). Indians who came to the West to study Western music included the great musician Inayat Khan's brother, Dr. A. M. Pathan, who studied at the Royal Academy of Music in London; on returning to India, he set up a school of Western music in Baroda, central India.

Also in the 1800s, other, less formal music making by Indians occurred in the West. In London and other large cities, a shifting population of Indian sailors, known as lascars, often jumped ship and lived in poverty in slum housing near the docks. They brought with them their music, and performed in pubs and on the streets. The East London missionary Joseph Salter wrote vivid accounts of such music making between 1870 and 1895. Behind the Royal Sovereign, a pub in Shadwell, he once found that "the chief attraction was round a turbaned musician who with his *sitar* was chanting an Eastern melody in which his hearers seemed much interested" (1895:21). Salter also noted that whole neighborhoods of East London had become populated by Indians—so many that "an Indian colony might have been seen transplanted from the Ganges to the Thames, with language, religion, habits and customs intact" (1895:17). At least one Indian, the Bengali A. Chauriya, performed in that period as a music-hall artist in London (Farrell 1997).

Although Indian musicians were present in the West during the late 1800s, in the twentieth century they started making the journey westward in far greater numbers. They came to bring the musical culture of India to the West and to make it more comprehensible to Western listeners. It was also in the twentieth century that Indian music and musicians started to have an impact on Western popular culture, culminating in the sitar explosion of the 1960s.

JOURNEYS TO THE WEST

Figures of particular importance in introducing Indian music to the Western world in the first half of the twentieth century were the great Bengali poet, educator, and musician Rabindranath Tagore (1861–1941), the Sufi mystic Hazrat Inayat Khan (1882–1927), the innovative Indian dancer Uday Shankar (1900–1977), and the sitarist Ravi Shankar (b. 1920).

Rabindranath Tagore

Tagore, "the most important link between India and the West" (Bor and Bruguiere 1992:39), is a major figure in world literature. He was awarded the Nobel Prize for literature in 1913 and accepted a knighthood in 1915 (which he resigned in 1919, protesting the methods adopted for repressing disturbances in the Punjab). Born in Calcutta, Tagore received much of his early education in England. He became well known as a singer and composed more than two thousand songs, known as the *Rabindra saṅgīt* (Rabindra songs). Tagore was keenly interested in Irish, Scottish, and English folk and popular music; for his own compositions, he drew on these and on Indian classical and folk music. In synthesizing these diverse musical elements, he created a new song genre.

Tagore's influence on the West's perception of Indian music and culture cannot be underestimated. He traveled widely in the West throughout his life, promoting Indian culture and espousing political independence for India. His meeting with the young Englishman Leonard Elmhirst in 1921 proved particularly significant in introducing to the West the teaching and performance of Indian music. After working with Tagore in Santiniketan (Tagore's ashram-university in West Bengal), Elmhirst returned to England, where he established Dartington Hall, an educational institution which, through Elmhirst's connections with Tagore, became a focus for Indian music and art from the 1930s on. The contiguous Dartington College became one of the first educational institutions in Britain where Indian music could be studied, and many eminent Indian musicians, including Imrat Khan and Latif Ahmad Khan, later taught there.

Though Tagore was not primarily known in the West for his performances of Indian music, his achievement in acting as cultural ambassador and raising the profile of Indian art ensured that Indian music would become established in the West as a symbol of India's highest cultural achievements.

Inayat Khan

Perhaps the most influential Indian musician to go to the West in the early 1900s was Inayat Khan. A vocalist, vina player, and sitarist, he hailed from Baroda (now Vadodara), and his family had many connections with the West and Western music. His brother, Dr. A. M. Pathan, had set up a school of Western music in Baroda after studying in London, and his grandfather Maula Baksh, a renowned *bīn* 'plucked zither' player, had been invited to perform at the World's Columbian Exposition in Chicago in 1893, but did not attend. A photograph of musicians from the Baroda vocal music school (*gāyanśālā*) in the early twentieth century shows a mixture of Indian and Western musical instruments, including two large upright harmoniums. As a young man under his brother's influence, Inayat Khan wrote instruction manuals for harmonium and violin.

In 1910, Inayat Khan traveled with members of his family to the United States, where they performed as the Royal Musicians of Hindustan. A small but growing number of Americans were already showing interest in Indian music, philosophy, and mysticism, fueled by the widespread belief in the imminent appearance of a world teacher (Khan 1979:553, 585). Inayat Khan came to preach the message of Sufism through music, a medium he believed to be both mystical and universal. He was well received at Columbia University in New York City, where he gave a lecture and demonstrated the structure of Indian music. The head of the music department, Dr. P. M.C. Rybner, commented on the scientific nature of Indian music theory. Inayat Khan soon found himself initiated into the world of popular orientalism, when he traveled extensively across the United States with the exotic dancer Ruth St. Denis (1877–1968), whose performances mixed superficial elements of Indian, Egyptian, and Japanese dances. The Royal Musicians of Hindustan were little more than living props in her shows, and were both amused and dismayed when audiences—unable to distinguish between tuning up and playing—applauded the tuning. The connection with popular culture and the misunderstandings that arose between Western audiences and Indian musicians have been ever-present threads in the encounters between Indian music and the West. As late as 1971, the audience at the Concert for Bangladesh in Canada applauded Ali Akbar Khan and Ravi Shankar after the musicians tuned up; Shankar gently corrected them.

After performing in the United States, Inayat Khan traveled to Europe. Again he was well received, particularly in France and Russia, where he came to the attention of important composers of the day such as Debussy and Skryabin, who praised the subtlety and emotion of his music. When he returned to India, Inayat Khan left behind disciples of both Sufism and Indian music. Likewise, during his period in the West he himself had experimented with Western music, working in Russia with Sergei Tolstoy to harmonize Indian songs.

Inayat's cousin Ali Khan also studied Western singing, his brother Maheboob studied composition with Edmond Bailly; and his son Hidayat went on to become a

Ravi Shankar is the only South Asian musician to have become a household name in the West.

composer of Western music (Khan 1979; Massey and Massey 1993). However, Inayat Khan's encounter with the West was not an entirely satisfactory experience, and in his later writings he advocated, somewhat conservatively, controlling the spread of Indian music within strict boundaries of audiences' musical taste and education. He remains a central figure in the history of the internationalization of Indian music.

Uday Shankar

As a dancer, Uday Shankar crossed the boundaries between Indian and Western art forms. His troupe of musicians included such giants of Indian music as Ustad Allauddin Khan and Uday's younger brother Ravi Shankar, who would become the central figure in Indian music's passage to the West later in the century.

Uday had no formal training in Indian classical dance. In his early life, he had not planned to become a professional dancer but had gone to London to study art. In 1924, the Russian ballerina Anna Pavlova saw him dance in an Indian ballet organized by his father in London (Shankar 1968:63). Her enthusiasm for his performance resulted in an artistic collaboration between Pavlova and Shankar. The Radha-Krishna duet was one of their most famous creations. After touring the United States with Pavlova in 1929, Uday returned to India and formed his own troupe, mixing various forms of Indian dance including *kathak, kathakaḷi,* and *manipurī* in new choreographies [see MUSIC AND DANCE]. Uday's younger brother Ravi both danced and played instruments in the troupe. The group performed in Paris in 1930, and went on to tour the United States, receiving excellent reviews. Uday created new kinds of Indian dance and music from traditional forms and instruments (Shankar 1968), innovations that proved highly successful with Western audiences and presented a simultaneously traditional and modernized image of Indian culture.

Uday returned to India and set up a cultural center in Almora, North India, with Western financial help—particularly from the Elmhirsts of Dartington Hall. Though this venture proved to be short lived, the impact of Uday Shankar's work in the West was far reaching, not least because his brother Ravi returned in the 1950s to become the most important musician in the subsequent internationalization of Indian music.

Ravi Shankar

Ravi Shankar is the only South Asian musician to have become a household name in the West (figure 1). It was through him that the sitar became the best-known Indian instrument and a symbol of Indian music in general. After touring with his brother Uday, Ravi Shankar spent years studying the sitar in Maihar with Allauddin Khan. He nevertheless maintained his connections with the West, and in 1951 met the violinist Yehudi Menuhin, who became an important supporter of Indian music. Shankar was invited to perform in New York in 1955, but was unable to go; in his

FIGURE 1 Ravi Shankar, the world-renowned sitar player, has had a profound impact on the West's perception of Indian music. Abhiman Kaushal is playing the string drone (*tānpūrā*). Photo by Stephen Slawek, 1990 .

place he sent Ali Akbar Khan, the sarod virtuoso and the son of Allauddin Khan, who went on to become another great representative of Indian music in the West (figure 2). In 1956, Shankar returned to the West, first to Europe and then to the United States. In his autobiography *My Music, My Life*, he relates that European audiences gave him a warm reception. He was equally well received in the United States, where his reception led him to begin plans to establish an institute. His school for Indian music, Kinnara, opened in 1967, and ran for a few years (Shankar 1968:88–89).

In the early 1960s, Shankar became a familiar figure on the concert circuit in both Europe and America. In his concerts, he always explained to his audience the structure of the music he was to play: the North Indian ragas (melodic configurations) and talas (rhythmic cycles). He saw his role not only as a performer, but also as an educator, teaching Westerners about Indian music and culture. He forbade smok-

FIGURE 2 Ali Akbar Khan, the celebrated sarod player and founder of the Ali Akbar College of Music in California. James Pomerantz is playing the string drone (*tānpūrā*). Photo by Stephen Slawek, 1993.

ing and drinking at his concerts, and always demanded that audiences listen quietly and attentively. In this way, he linked Indian classical music with the norms and respect that Western audiences accord their own classical music.

Shankar has also been an innovator. He has worked with a variety of Western musicians from the worlds of classical music, jazz, and popular music. He has also worked on numerous film scores and has composed two concertos for sitar and orchestra, both of which received their first performances under the baton of Zubin Mehta. Within the sphere of Indian classical music, Ravi Shankar experimented with mixing North and South Indian elements in his performances.

Shankar is probably best known in the West for his connection with the Beatles, and particularly with George Harrison, who became his pupil in the mid-1960s. The Beatles occasionally used a sitar in their recordings, and Ravi Shankar's music influenced theirs. This, in turn, led to an interest in Indian music within the burgeoning hippie culture of the time, an effect Shankar called the "great sitar explosion." Shankar was critical of this sudden interest in Indian music within Western popular culture and the erroneous connections made between Indian music and taking drugs. Nevertheless, by 1970, Ravi Shankar and his tabla player, Alla Rakha, were performing to huge adulatory crowds at events such as the Monterey Pop Festival. Indian music had never had, and has never since had, such a high profile in the popular culture of the West (Farrell 1988, 1997).

Ravi Shankar's performances in the West had a profound effect on Western perceptions of Indian music. Shankar was a pioneer and a catalyst in popularizing Indian music in the West as a major non-Western form of classical music to be enjoyed and appreciated. He opened doors for the hundreds of other Indian musicians who have become regulars on concert calendars in major Western cities, and who have taught at music schools and universities throughout the Western world.

EFFECTS OF INTERNATIONALIZATION ON INDIAN MUSIC

Due to the efforts of Shankar and others, Indian music has gradually become established as an international music in the West, particularly in the United States. In 1961, the ethnomusicologist Robert Brown started a program in South Indian music performance at Wesleyan University in Connecticut. Like Ravi Shankar, Ali Akbar Khan founded in California in the 1960s an Indian music school, the Ali Akbar College of Music, which continues to train students from all over the world (Slawek 1993) (figure 3).

FIGURE 3 Ali Akbar Khan teaching at the Ali Akbar College of Music, San Rafael, California, 1990. Photo by Stephen Slawek.

Increasing numbers of South Asian musicians have traveled to the West since the 1950s, and inevitably this contact has affected Indian music back in India. The influence of Western technology has greatly influenced Indian music since the 1970s, when the rise of the cassette industry revolutionized the production and distribution of regional and popular musics in North India (Manuel 1994).

Performance practices

Apart from the more obvious impact of film and recording technology on musicians' lives, Western technology has also affected musical performance practices all over the Indian subcontinent. Since the 1930s, microphones and amplification systems have been commonplace in the Indian film industry, and musicians have become used to performing with amplification and in the kind of large auditoriums typical of Western concert environments. Some critics in India argue that these changes have weakened the vocal delivery of singers, who have become used to the extra volume of sound that electronic amplification provides. Also, the conventions of the Western concert, which takes place mainly in the evening and within a prescribed space of time, have affected Indian classical music performance. Critics and more traditionally minded musicians have opined that Indian musicians in India now perform a smaller range of ragas because of the predominance of evening recitals along the lines of Western performances. Musicians who wish to follow the tradition linking raga performance with specific times of day feel restricted by the Western-style concert format. Though all-night concerts still occur in India, they are probably less common than in earlier times. Restriction to an evening schedule limits traditional musicians to the performance of evening ragas within a two-to-three-hour framework. This aspect of the internationalization on South Asian musical practices remains largely unresearched, yet a large amount of anecdotal evidence suggests that both musicians and audiences feel it has been significant.

Social effects

In the social realm in India, enhanced status has been conferred on musicians who have performed in the West, and a cultural premium is typically placed on the experience of playing or teaching abroad (Neuman 1990). Known as "foreign-returned" musicians, these artists often capitalize on their Western experiences to rise quickly within the hierarchy of the musical world back home. The implication is that if musicians have been accepted in the West, they must be superior and worthy of attention. However, Neuman has also observed that success gained by an Indian musician in the West is not always replicated in India. Accompanists in particular can receive praise and celebration equal to that of soloists, only to return to their traditional lower status back home—which can result in social and musical friction. Despite the history of their exposure to Indian music, Western audiences still like to view South Asian performers as something exotic and rare. This is largely a Western cultural construct—a modern version of notions of the mysterious East. The social implications of internationalization have not been researched extensively by ethnomusicologists, yet they are important aspects of the interaction between South Asian music and the West.

CONTEMPORARY TRENDS

The late twentieth century has seen new developments in the internationalization of South Asian music. South Asian communities are well established outside the Indian

In the social realm in India, enhanced status has been conferred on musicians who have performed in the West, and a cultural premium is typically placed on the experience of playing or teaching abroad.

subcontinent, particularly in Britain and North America. A result of this development is that many musical genres from India, Pakistan, and Bangladesh have become part of the cultural fabric of the West. Popular forms such as bhangra have become the musical voice of South Asian youth in the United Kingdom and elsewhere, mixing elements from Punjabi folk genres, Indian film song, and Western pop (Banerji 1988; Baumann 1990). Bhangra has also developed into new forms by being synthesized with African-American genres such as rap; an example is the work of the British artist Apache Indian (b. 1968).

The growing South Asian communities in the West have paved the way for artists from the subcontinent such as Nusrat Fateh Ali Khan, the great singer of Sufi devotional music (qawwali), who before his death in 1997 was performing before large audiences in prestigious venues. He also worked with rock artists such as Peter Gabriel, developing new musical vehicles to express the sentiments of Sufi devotional song.

These developments mark a new phase of the story of South Asian music in the West. Traditional forms of music from the Indian subcontinent are now part of the everyday soundscape of many large Western cities, and second and third generations of South Asian immigrants are creating new musics. While drawing on the strength of South Asian traditions, these new musics are the specific products of the new social and cultural contexts.

REFERENCES

Banerji, Sabita. 1988. "Ghazals to Bhangra in Great Britain." *Popular Music* 7(2):207–13.

Baumann, Gerd. 1990. "The Re-Invention of *Bhangra:* Social Change and Aesthetic Shifts in a Punjabi Music in Britain." *The World of Music* 32(2):81–97.

Bird, William H. 1789. *The Oriental Miscellany.* Calcutta: Joseph Cooper.

Bor, Joep. 1988. "The Rise of Ethnomusicology: Sources on Indian Music c. 1780–c. 1890." *Yearbook of Traditional Music* 1988 (20):51–73.

Bor, Joep, and Philippe Bruguiere. 1992. *Masters of Raga: Meister des Raga.* Berlin: Haus der Kulturen der Welt.

Capwell, Charles. 1986. "Musical Life in Nineteenth-Century Calcutta as a Component in the History of a Secondary Urban Center." *Asian Music* 18(1):139–163.

———. 1991. "Marginality and Musicology in Nineteenth-Century Calcutta: The Case of Sourindro Mohun Tagore." In *Comparative Musicology and Anthropology of Music,* ed. Bruno Nettl and Philip Bohlman, 228–243. Chicago: Chicago University Press.

Clements, Ernest. 1913. *Introduction to the Study of Indian Music.* London: Longmans.

———. 1920. *The Ragas of Tanjore.* London: Dharwar Gayan Samaj.

———. 1923. *Ragas of Hindustan.* 3 vols. Poona: Philharmonic Society.

Day, Charles R. 1974 [1891]. *The Music and Musical Instruments of Southern India and the Deccan.* London and New York: Novello; Delhi: Low Cost Publications.

Farrell, Gerry. 1988. "Reflecting Surfaces: The Use of Elements from Indian Music in Popular Music and Jazz." *Popular Music* 7(2):189–206.

———. 1997. *Indian Music and the West.* Oxford: Clarendon.

Jones, William. 1965 [1792]. "On the Musical Modes of the Hindoos." In *Hindu Music From Various Authors,* 3rd ed., ed. Sourindro M. Tagore,

125–160. Varanasi: Chowkhamba Sanskrit Series Office.

Khan, Inayat. 1979. *The Biography of Pir-o-Murshid Inayat Khan*. London: East-West Publications.

Manuel, Peter. 1994. *Cassette Culture: Popular Music and Technology in North India*. Chicago: Chicago University Press.

Massey, Reginald, and Jamila Massey. 1993. *The Music of India*. London: Kahn & Averill.

Mayer, John. 1978. "Indo-Jazz Fusions." *Composer* 34:5–11.

Mudaliyar, A. M. Chinnaswami. 1893. *Oriental Music in European Notation*. Madras: Ave Maria Press.

Neuman, Daniel. 1990. *The Life of Music in North India*. Detroit: Wayne State University Press.

Salter, Joseph. 1895. *The East in the West: Work among the Asiatics and Africans in London*. London: Partridge & Sons.

Shankar. Ravi. 1968. *My Music, My Life*. New York: Simon and Schuster.

Slawek, Stephen. 1993. "Ravi Shankar as Mediator between a Traditional Music and Modernity." In *Ethnomusicology and Modern Music History*, ed. Steven Blum, Philip Bohlman, and Daniel Neuman, 161–180. Urbana and Chicago: University of Illinois Press.

Tagore, Sourindro M., ed. 1965 [1882]. *Hindu Music from Various Authors*. Calcutta: I. C. Bose & Co.; Varanasi: Chowkhamba Sanskrit Series Office.

———. 1884. *The Musical Scales of the Hindus (with Remarks on the Applicability of Harmony to Indian Music)*. Calcutta: I. C. Bose & Co.

Willard, N. Augustus. 1965 [1834]. "A Treatise on the Music of Hindustan: Comprising a Detail of the Ancient Theory and Modern Practice." In *Hindu Music from Various Authors*, ed. Sourindro M. Tagore, 3rd ed., 1–122. Varanasi: Chowkhamba Sanskrit Series Office.

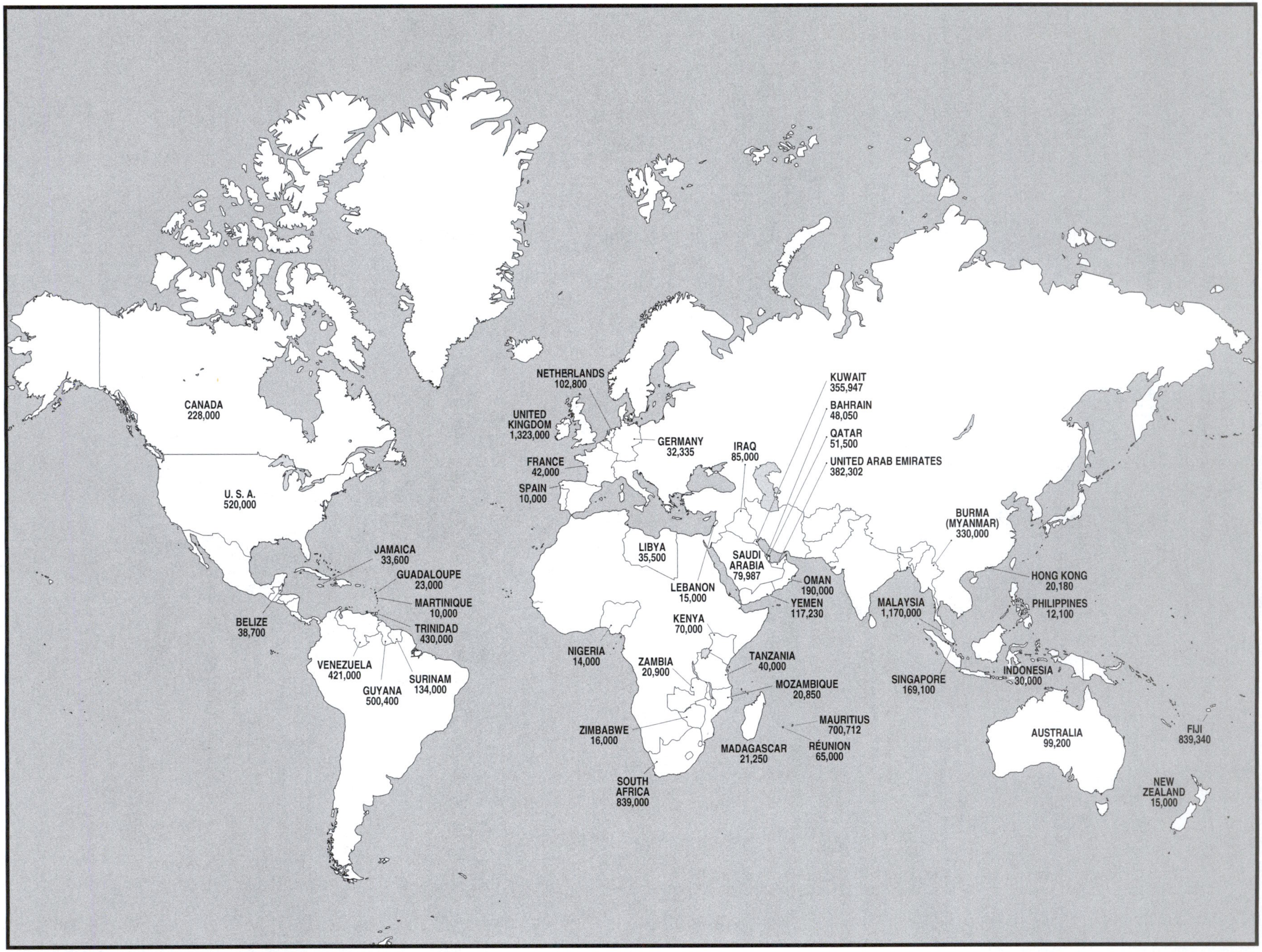
CANADA 228,000
U. S. A. 520,000
BELIZE 38,700
JAMAICA 33,600
GUADALOUPE 23,000
MARTINIQUE 10,000
TRINIDAD 430,000
SURINAM 134,000
GUYANA 500,400
VENEZUELA 421,000
UNITED KINGDOM 1,323,000
NETHERLANDS 102,800
FRANCE 42,000
SPAIN 10,000
GERMANY 32,335
NIGERIA 14,000
LIBYA 35,500
LEBANON 15,000
IRAQ 85,000
KUWAIT 355,947
BAHRAIN 48,050
QATAR 51,500
UNITED ARAB EMIRATES 382,302
SAUDI ARABIA 79,987
OMAN 190,000
YEMEN 117,230
KENYA 70,000
TANZANIA 40,000
MOZAMBIQUE 20,850
ZAMBIA 20,900
ZIMBABWE 16,000
SOUTH AFRICA 839,000
MADAGASCAR 21,250
MAURITIUS 700,712
RÉUNION 65,000
BURMA (MYANMAR) 330,000
MALAYSIA 1,170,000
SINGAPORE 169,100
HONG KONG 20,180
PHILIPPINES 12,100
INDONESIA 30,000
AUSTRALIA 99,200
FIJI 839,340
NEW ZEALAND 15,000

Music and the South Asian Diaspora

The first major exodus from South Asia occurred in the mid-1800s, when European imperialist nations recruited large numbers of unskilled Indian laborers to work as indentured servants in Guyana, Trinidad, Jamaica, South Africa, Madagascar, Fiji, Sri Lanka (then called Ceylon), Malaysia (Malaya), and Burma (Myanmar). Many remained in these countries, forming South Asian diasporic communities. Since that time, economic opportunities have attracted South Asians to various other parts of the world, particularly to the Middle East and North America.

For Indians, Pakistanis, Bangladeshis, and other South Asians far from their homelands, native languages, cultures, and religions form an essential part of their identity in the new environment. Among first-generation immigrants, South Asian music is an important aspect of cultural retention, while second and later generations often create new musical expressions reflecting their identity as descendants of immigrants. Such expressions combine popular styles of their own homeland with musical elements characteristic of their parents' or grandparents' South Asian birthplace.

MAP 3 The South Asian diaspora: major populations (over ten thousand) in the late 1980s. Sources: Arthur W. Helweg and Usha M. Helweg, *An Immigrant Success Story: East Indians in America* (Philadelphia: University of Pennsylvania Press, 1990), 22; Ceri Peach, "Three Phases of South Asian Emigration," in *Migration: The Asian Experience*, ed. Judith M. Brown and Rosemary Foot (Oxford: St. Martin's Press, 1994), 39.

The United Kingdom

Gerry Farrell

HISTORICAL BACKGROUND

South Asian populations have existed in the United Kingdom since the sixteenth century, although initially they were relatively small (Visram 1986; Mann 1992; Coleman and Salt 1996:7–8). By the nineteenth century, Indians resident in the United Kingdom—England, Scotland, Wales, and Northern Ireland—represented a wide spectrum of Indian society, from the nobility to domestic servants. There were princes and nawabs, many of whom came to the United Kingdom following sporadic upheavals in the Indian courts. Some became personalities in London's high society; figures such as Maharaja Dalip Singh (1838–1883) were favorites at the court of Queen Victoria (Bayly 1990:181–182). Other communities centered around large ports such as Liverpool, Bristol, and London, where Indian sailors or "lascars" jumped ship to live in the surrounding areas, often in poverty and slum housing. Christian missionaries recorded the musical life of these immigrants, particularly in the East End of London (Salter 1872, 1895). In the late nineteenth century, Indian vocalists and sitar and tabla players could be heard performing in the local public houses and streets of Shadwell and Bluegate Fields (Salter 1872:199). This part of London, the borough of Tower Hamlets, now has the largest Bangladeshi community in the United Kingdom.

After World War II, the South Asian population of the United Kingdom began to increase dramatically. This immigration was partly the legacy of the British Empire, and of India's central position in it. Former colonies became part of the British Commonwealth, and until the 1961 Immigration Act all citizens from these countries had British citizenship and were entitled to travel to the United Kingdom without restriction. At this time, other Western countries, notably the United States, were restricting immigration (Marshall 1996:332). At the same time, severe labor shortages in Europe followed the war, and migrant and immigrant labor met this economic need (Commission for Racial Equality 1986:1).

Initially the largest group of postwar immigrants to the United Kingdom came from the West Indies. Thereafter, immigration from South Asia increased, often for economic reasons or sometimes to escape persecution and discrimination, as was the case with the East African Asians who emigrated to the United Kingdom in the late

1960s and early 1970s. By 1991, the Office of Population Censuses reported that 1,479,645 persons of South Asian origin lived in the United Kingdom. This represented 2.7 percent of the total population of the United Kingdom (Owen 1996:88).

COMPOSITION OF THE SOUTH ASIAN COMMUNITY

The settlement pattern of South Asian immigrants initially centered on a number of specific locations in the United Kingdom. These were London and urban areas in the West Midlands, Yorkshire, Humberside, and the northwest. This settlement pattern further exhibited a South Asian regional division. Immigrants from Pakistan lived mainly in Greater Manchester and West Yorkshire, whereas London and the West Midlands had a larger population of immigrants from India and Bangladesh (Owen 1996:94–95). Further regional diversity existed within these broad national groupings, with the formation of specific communities from Kashmir, Punjab, Gujarat, and Sylhet (northeast Bangladesh), to name but a few. The heterogeneity of South Asian culture is also reflected in the languages spoken and the religions practiced. In India alone there are 325 languages and dialects employing twenty-five different scripts (Singh and Manoharan 1993:vii). South Asian languages spoken in the United Kingdom include Hindi, Gujarati, Urdu, Bengali, and Tamil, as well as many regional dialects. Among the religions practiced are Hinduism, Islam, Sikhism, Jainism, and Christianity. Such regional and cultural complexity within the South Asian community suggests the breadth and scope of musical life that exists within it.

SOUTH ASIAN MUSIC GENRES

The term "South Asian music" refers to musical genres with cultural roots in India, Sri Lanka, Pakistan, Afghanistan, Bangladesh, and Nepal. Although the term embraces a wide range of popular, classical, religious, and regional genres, unifying musical traits such as melodic and rhythmic organization, systems of notation, performance practices, and methods of learning have deep cultural roots and are common to various musical genres over this wide geographical area (Wade 1979).

Music performed by South Asians in the United Kingdom is not wholly representative of the diversity of South Asian music traditions, encompassing North and South Indian classical music, film and regional pop music, folk music, and religious and devotional music. However, there is a remarkable amount of music making that both replicates genres from the Indian subcontinent and adapts and fuses elements of South Asian and Western musical cultures.

The preponderance of immigrants from the northern part of the Indian subcontinent—Pakistan, North India, and Bangladesh—has resulted in the prevalence of North Indian music genres within the British South Asian community. A wide range of traditional musics are performed and taught, including North Indian classical music, various religious, light classical, and folk genres such as bhajan, qawwali, and *kīrtan*, and genres that are region- or language-specific such as the Bengali *Rabindra saṅgīt* 'songs of Rabindranath Tagore', Punjabi bhangra, and Urdu ghazal. Musical performance is also part of worship gatherings in Sikh gurdwaras and Hindu temples. South Indian classical musicians also perform in the United Kingdom, but Karnatak music has a relatively narrower distribution and community of interest.

The presence of a growing South Asian community in the United Kingdom and elsewhere has resulted in a wider audience in the West for classical musicians from India. This situation has led to the rise of impresarios within South Asian communities who regularly organize tours for visiting musicians. Several retailers of Indian instruments operate in the major cities, and there is at least one instrument maker now producing Indian instruments in England. South Asian immigrant musicians and dancers have started national organizations to promote their interests, with assistance from major funding sources such as the regional Arts Councils (Turner 1991). In addition, a growing number of musicians without South Asian cultural roots have taken up the study of Indian music and instrumental performance.

BHANGRA AND DEVELOPMENTS IN SOUTH ASIAN POPULAR MUSIC

Until recent years the main popular music of the South Asian community has been Indian film songs (*filmī gīt*). However, in the mid-1980s a new sound began to dominate British South Asian popular music. The music was bhangra, based on a folk music genre from the Punjab traditionally performed at the harvest festival of Baisākhī (Banerji 1988:208). The character of traditional bhangra is joyful, unrestrained, and highly rhythmic. According to Baumann, amateur bhangra bands performed at weddings and other social occasions among the London Punjabi community from the 1960s onward, but not until the late 1970s and early 1980s did a distinctive, commercial form of bhangra start to emerge (Baumann 1990:84).

The new incarnation of bhangra retained traditional elements of its folk forerunner, such as the use of the *ḍholak* 'double-headed barrel drum' and the characteristic syncopated eight-beat tala cycle *kaharvā*. Musicians added elements from Western pop such as electric keyboards, drum set, bass, guitars, and saxophone (figure 1); they also drew on the sounds and arrangements of Indian film music. However, the sound of bhangra is not as varied as that of movie songs. Bhangra is essentially dance music in which the driving beat is the central focus. The new sound quickly became popular among youth within the South Asian community in the United Kingdom, and bands such as Alaap (often cited as the founders of modern bhangra) and Heera have earned great success. The popularity of this dance music has led to the phenomenon of daytime discos filled with Asian kids playing truant from school (Banerji 1988:212; Baumann 1990:87).

The bhangra sound has not crossed over into mainstream Western pop music, despite its well-produced and highly professional presentation. No doubt there is a language barrier, as most bhangra are sung in Punjabi. Another contributing factor is the nature of recording distribution networks in the South Asian community, which are not connected to the wider popular music industry. Furthermore, the music's origins and the kinds of social experiences related in the songs are unique in British popular music.

Bhangra quickly became a cultural expression of South Asian youths, particularly in London, and was known as the "Southall beat" after the West London district where a large Punjabi community resides. The lyrics of "Munda Southall Da" 'The Boy from Southall', by the band Sitara, communicate the flavor of bhangra songs.

FIGURE 1 The British bhangra band Pardesi performing at a concert in Norway, 1997. Photo courtesy M. S. Jheeta.

They relate a love affair between a boy from Southall and a girl from the Midlands who is dressed up and "wears tight jeans like an English woman." The boy asks her to keep on coming to Southall and walk hand in hand with him on the Broadway (Farrell 1992:19; Sitara 1988; translated by Jaspal Bhogal).

> Hey girl, hey girl,
> You have fallen in love with a boy from Southall,
> And yet you come from the Midlands.
>
> You have come from the Midlands all tarted up
> Wearing tight jeans looking like an English woman.
> I feel like holding hands with you like the English do.
>
> Looking at your face, I feel like looking at you all the time,
> Let's go some place we have not been, and never look back again.
>
> Keep on coming to Southall, and walk on the Broadway and sing my song.
> Now let's get married and go on a honeymoon in Paris.

The emergence of a home-grown South Asian popular music in the United Kingdom has also functioned as a symbol of unity and identity for a community whose composition is, in reality, very disparate (Baumann 1990:83).

The South Asian music scene in the United Kingdom has continued to diversify. The work of artists such as Sheila Chandra and Najma Akhtar has brought together elements from Indian music, jazz, and a variety of world musics; artists like Apache Indian and Fun-da-mental fuse African American (particularly rap) and South Asian styles to produce commercial and often highly politicized music. The voice of Asian youth, no longer content to be contained within a minority community or within any particular aesthetic of South Asian music, comments on contemporary British society and the ills of racism, discrimination, and social deprivation. It is increasingly heard through the channels of popular music (Farrell 1997). To the youth of the South Asian community, music functions as a symbol of cultural identity, cultural pluralism, and social change.

MUSICAL TRANSMISSION WITHIN THE SOUTH ASIAN COMMUNITY

Much of the teaching of South Asian music takes place both formally and informally within the community. However, music teaching within the formal education system, particularly in elementary and secondary schools, now plays an important role in the transmission of South Asian musics in Britain.

In 1985 the Swann report, *Education for All*, proposed a model for multicultural education in United Kingdom schools that included a role for arts education (Swann 1985:333). By 1991, 18 percent of the local education authorities in England and Wales provided instruction on tabla, 17 percent on the Indian harmonium, and 15 percent on the sitar. For all three instruments this represented a doubling of the provision from 1986 (Sharp 1991:41). Farrell found that in Greater London twelve out of thirty-three boroughs provided instruction on South Asian instruments as well as instruction in a wide variety of musical styles, including North and South Indian classical, devotional genres such as bhajan and kirtan, and bhangra (Farrell 1990, 1994). These figures suggest the important role formal music education is playing in sustaining South Asian music teaching in the United Kingdom. Similar research findings exist on instruction in South Asian dance within the formal education sector (Turner 1991).

In higher education, South Asian music instruction is less widespread. Leeds College of Music in West Yorkshire provides such instruction, as do various private

Music teaching within the formal education system, particularly in elementary and secondary schools, now plays an important role in the transmission of South Asian musics in Britain.

institutions including the Bharatiya Vidya Bhavan in London, which was established in the early 1970s. However, there are signs that college-level teaching of South Asian music will increase; for example, at least one mainstream conservatory of music, the Birmingham Conservatoire, is planning to introduce degrees in Indian classical music.

SOURCES AND FURTHER READING

Despite the richness of South Asian musical life in the United Kingdom and its increasing prominence in popular music and music education, it has received relatively little attention in ethnomusicological literature. The place of South Asian music in the United Kingdom is nevertheless clearly important in relation to current ethnomusicological interest in the "micromusics" of the West (Slobin 1992), in the rise of "world music" within the popular music industry (Manuel 1988), and in the processes by which syncretic musical forms develop, in South Asia (Manuel 1994) and elsewhere.

Recent work on South Asian music in the United Kingdom has tended to focus on specific genres within specific sections of the community. Studies include Banerji and Baumann on bhangra (1988, 1990), and Baily on qawwali in Bradford and on music in three British Muslim communities (1990, 1995). One other area of focus is the relationship between South Asian music and formal music and dance education (Turner 1991; Farrell 1994). Such work has provided valuable "snapshots" of South Asian music in the United Kingdom, but there exists as yet no single study attempting to draw a broader picture of the South Asian community, exploring the complex connections between language, religion, regional background, demography, and musical genres. General studies of South Asians in the United Kingdom contain little discussion of music, despite its importance as a part of cultural identity and a symbol of both continuity and change.

REFERENCES

Baily, John. 1990. "Qawwali in Bradford: Traditional Music in a Muslim Community." In *Black Music in Britain*, ed. Paul Oliver, 153–165. Milton Keynes: Open University Press.

———. 1995. "The Role of Music in Three British Muslim Communities." *Diaspora* 4(1):77–88.

Banerji, Sabita. 1988. "Ghazals to Bhangra in Great Britain." *Popular Music* 7(2):203–213.

Banerji, Sabita, and Gerd Baumann. 1990. "Bhangra 1984–88: Fusion and Professionalization in a Genre of South Asian Dance Music." In *Black Music in Britain*, ed. Paul Oliver, 137–152. Milton Keynes: Open University Press.

Baumann, Gerd. 1990. "The Re-Invention of *Bhangra*. Social Change and Aesthetic Shifts in a Punjabi Music in Britain." *The World of Music* 32(2):81–97.

Bayly, Christopher Alan, ed. 1990. *The Raj: India and the British 1600–1947*. London: National Portrait Gallery.

Coleman, David, and John Salt. 1996. "The Ethnic Group Question in the 1991 Census: A

New Landmark in British Statistics." In *Ethnicity in the 1991 Census*, vol. 1, ed. David Coleman and John Salt, 1–32. London: HMSO.

Commission for Racial Equality (CRE). 1986. *Ethnic Minorities in Britain: Statistical Information on the Pattern of Settlement*. London: CRE.

Farrell, Gerry. 1990. "Survey of the Provision for Teaching Music Styles from the Indian Sub-Continent in the Greater London Area." Greater London Arts (GLA).

———. 1992. "The Music of India." *U208 Open University*. Milton Keynes: Open University Press.

———. 1994. *South Asian Music Teaching in Change*. London: David Fulton Publishers.

———. 1997. *Indian Music and the West*. Oxford: Clarendon.

Mann, Bashir. 1992. *The New Scots: Asians in Scotland*. Edinburgh: John Donald.

Manuel, Peter. 1988. *Popular Musics of the Non-Western World*. Oxford: Oxford University Press.

———. 1994. *Cassette Culture: Popular Music and Technology in North India*. Chicago: Chicago University Press.

Marshall, Peter James, ed. 1996. *The Cambridge Illustrated History of the British Empire*. Cambridge: Cambridge University Press.

Office of Population Censuses and Surveys (OPCS). 1992. *County Monitors 17/1 and 17/2: Inner and Outer London*. London: HMSO.

Owen, David. 1996. "Size, Structure and Growth of the Ethnic Minority Populations." In *Ethnicity in the 1991 Census*, vol. 1, ed. David Coleman and John Salt, 80–123. London: HMSO.

Salter, Joseph. 1872. *The Asiatic in England*. London: Seeley, Jackson and Halliday.

———. 1895. *The East in the West: Work among the Asiatics and Africans in London*. London: Partridge and Sons.

Sharp, Caroline. 1991. *When Every Note Counts: The Schools' Instrumental Music Service in the 1990s*. Slough: National Foundation for Educational Research.

Singh, K. S., and S. Manoharan. 1993. *People of India, Volume IX: Languages and Scripts*. Oxford: Oxford University Press.

Sitara. 1988. *Love Affair with Sitara*. The Gramophone Company, EMI. Audio cassette.

Slobin, Mark. 1992. "Micromusics of the West: A Comparative Approach." *Ethnomusicology* 36(1):1–89.

Swann, Lord M. 1985. *Education for All*. London: HMSO.

Turner, Alison. 1991. *Aditi South Asian Dance in Education Audit*. Bradford: Aditi.

Visram, R. 1986. *Ayahs, Lascars and Princes*. London: Pluto Press.

Wade, Bonnie. 1979. *Music in India: The Classical Traditions*. Englewood Cliffs, N.J.: Prentice-Hall.; rev. ed. New Delhi: Manohar Publications, 1987.

North America

Alison Arnold

Performance Contexts
Musical Meaning and Function
Genres and Instruments
Musical Education and Transmission
Music and Creativity
Music and Identity
Sources and Further Reading

Asian Indians constitute one of the fastest-growing North American immigrant populations as well as one of the more affluent and well-educated sectors of American society (Daniels 1989, 1994; Helweg and Helweg 1990; Saran 1985). The 1997 United States Current Population Survey lists 748,000 foreign-born Indians (U.S. Census Bureau 1997), up from 450,000 in 1990 and 203,000 in 1980, and the 1996 Canadian census reports 590,150 people of South Asian origin, also with recent large increases (from 450,000 in 1991 and 350,000 in 1981).

Among Indian- and Pakistani-American populations, musical performance reflects the cultural and social organization of the immigrant groups themselves. Indians have settled in many metropolitan centers of North America, particularly in the states of California, Illinois, New Jersey, New York, and Texas. Unlike earlier European immigrants, who formed urban ethnic enclaves, Indians and Pakistanis now live dispersed throughout middle-class suburban residential areas and tend to socialize within native regional communities (for example, Bengalis, Gujaratis, Tamils, and so on). Since the mid-1960s, when urban residential clustering did begin to some extent, Indian and Pakistani cultural and religious associations have sprung up in Atlanta, Chicago, Cleveland, Houston, New York, and other major cities, each group organizing its own social and religious functions promoting distinct native cultural traditions, languages, dress, food, and music (figure 1).

PERFORMANCE CONTEXTS

Many Indian- and Pakistani-American community events include musical performance, the contexts ranging from formal stage presentations to informal gatherings in private homes. Among immigrant communities, professional classical musicians and dancers are relatively few; Indian classical music and dance performance is consequently more often the preserve of visiting artists who perform for mixed Indian and American audiences. Notably, Indian audiences for North Indian (Hindustani) and South Indian (Karnatak) classical music concerts in North America tend to differ, in keeping with the two musical traditions and the two broad communities from North and South India, with their dissimilar cultures and languages. For example, an important venue for purely South Indian classical performances is the annual

FIGURE 1 Punjabi boys and girls perform bhangra at a celebration of the Baisākhī harvest festival hosted by the Punjab Cultural Society in Skokie, Illinois. Photo courtesy the Asia Society, New York.

Tyagaraja festival honoring the revered eighteenth- to nineteenth-century South Indian composer; the event, which is held in cities throughout the United States and often features major performers from India, attracts predominantly South Indian community members. In comparison with classical concerts, community performances by semiprofessional and amateur artists are more numerous, for the most part consisting of light classical, folk, and popular vocal music for local business, community, and family groups.

Two common occasions for local musical performance are evening music parties and wedding celebrations. An informal atmosphere generally characterizes such events, with audience movement and chatter during performances and audience participation through singing and clapping. At a Pakistani-American Muslim wedding anniversary in Chicago, for example, local musicians sit on the floor in traditional fashion, surrounded by family and friends, and sing Pakistani folk songs in the Pashto language, ghazals (Urdu couplets), qawwalis (mystical group songs), and Pakistani popular songs, with harmonium, tabla (drum), violin, and tambourine accompaniment (Arnold 1985); at a Sikh-Canadian wedding celebration, guests participate in dancing the traditional Punjabi bhangra folk dance (Qureshi 1972). Social and cultural events organized by community-wide associations incorporate broader-based South Asian musical and dance entertainment (figure 2), often with semiprofessional musicians performing film songs, ghazals, qawwalis, bhajans (devotional songs), or popular regional songs, depending on the cultural and religious makeup of the audience.

Indian- and Pakistani-Americans also perpetuate native musical traditions and practices within religious contexts. Members of institutionalized religious traditions (specifically Islam, Vedanta, and Christianity) follow worship rituals that include unaccompanied solo chanting of religious texts: Qur'ānic chanting in Muslim prayer sessions, prayer chanting in Vedanta temple services, and liturgical chanting within Christian congregations. Although Indian Christian worship also incorporates communal hymn singing, religious assemblies without a formal prayer leader or priest (Hinduism, Jainism, and the Sathya Sai Baba movement, for example) favor greater communal participation in musical devotion. Participatory singing of bhajans, eulogies (*stavan*), and Sanskrit couplets (*śloka*) forms a major part of religious worship among these assemblies.

FIGURE 2 A regional dance performance at the Bronx Zoo, New York City, for the Cultural Festival of India, sponsored by the India Tourist Office. Photo courtesy the Asia Society, New York.

Indian temples play an important role as cultural and musical centers, sponsoring festival celebrations and processions, religious programs and events, and music concerts on a regular basis. Over the past two decades, sizeable South Asian communities have funded and supported temple building in many North American cities, especially Hindu temples generally either for North Indians or South Indians (Bhardwaj and Rao 1990:215). In 1998, for example, a fund-raising dinner for the almost completed Murugan (Shiva) Temple in Lanham, Michigan, included the presentation of Tamil devotional songs by a vocal group that was invited to come from Houston, Texas, for the occasion; and the Sri Guruvaayoorappan (Krishna) Temple in Marlboro, New Jersey, celebrated its "grand opening" with ten days of religious, cultural, and musical activities.

MUSICAL MEANING AND FUNCTION

In its new cultural environment, native music takes on different meanings and aesthetic appeal for first-generation Indian and Pakistani immigrants, many of whom maintain close ties with family and friends back home. Familiar songs and musical styles create feelings of nostalgia and provide an emotional link with the past. Amateur Indian musicians in Chicago frequently perform Indian film and popular songs of past decades because of the native-born community's familiarity with and sentimental attachment to these old favorites.

As musical performance often takes place in the context of the larger Indian and/or Pakistani ethnic community, rather than of the nuclear family, native music and language simultaneously function to preserve the community's cultural heritage and identity in the New World. Audio- and video-cassette recordings, especially those available for rent in Indian grocery stores, as well as the constant traffic that flows between India and America, ensure that Indian-American music cannot become a fossilized tradition of musical memories from India and Pakistan. This is especially true in the realm of popular music, as Indian- and Pakistani-American musicians in North America frequently learn the latest Indian and Pakistani songs and styles to update their repertoire. Some are also interested in creating their own new immigrant musical traditions, and compose music and lyrics either in popular Indian musical styles or in new fusions of Indian and Western traditions. These hold special appeal for second- and third-generation immigrants, whose musical tastes tend to be greatly influenced by American pop culture.

GENRES AND INSTRUMENTS

First-generation immigrants tend to listen to and perform music native to India, Pakistan, and their other countries of origin (such as the Caribbean). As on the Indian subcontinent, a minority of the diasporic population in North America supports the classical traditions. Local artists generally practice and perform classical Hindustani and Karnatak music only as an avocation, not a profession, often also performing in lighter musical styles for the larger Indo-Pakistani community. Hindustani vocalists perform classical *khyāl* and light classical genres such as ghazal and *ṭhumrī*; instrumentalists present traditional raga performances that follow the *ālāp-joṛ-jhālā-gat* sequence. In view of the relatively low demand for classical concerts by local musicians as opposed to visiting Indian artists, together with the necessity of *riyāz* 'practice' to keep up this improvisatory art, it is not surprising that today few Indians continue to practice these traditions after settling in North America.

In contrast, the "light music" genres of ghazal, qawwali, *gīt* 'song', and film song—forms widespread in India and Pakistan and universally popular among South Asian communities in North America—require less musical knowledge and technique than classical forms for their comprehension, enjoyment, and performance, and are generally shorter in length. The incidence of semiprofessional and amateur singers and accompanists (tabla and harmonium) of these genres is consequently high. Folk music in the immigrant environment is less common, due to its localized and functional nature in South Asia; in the absence of folk musicians within these immigrant communities, cultural and religious organizations occasionally organize group performances of folk songs and dances, both as social entertainment and on occasion as part of larger community-wide events such as Indian Independence Day celebrations (August 16). The performance of traditional life-cycle or work songs in the new cultural environment is far less common and is limited mostly to intimate family or group gatherings.

Hindus, Muslims, Christians, and other religious groups within the Indo-Pakistani population strive to maintain musical traditions as practiced in their homelands, in some cases with increased enthusiasm and orthodoxy. Among Hindus, Sathya Sai Baba followers, and Hare Krishna members, solo and group devotional singing in Hindi and other Indian languages is indispensable to communal worship. The bhajan repertoire is in part dependent on the musical knowledge and memory of participants, although transmission of new material occurs through contact among North American communities and with devotees abroad. Participants at the Radha Krishna Temple in Evanston, Illinois, for example, sing devotional songs whose texts are published by the International Society for Krishna Consciousness, but no songbooks are used at religious gatherings—members learn the songs through repetition during leader-chorus singing, accompanied by harmonium, cymbals, and fiberglass barrel drums (*mridangam*).

For most Muslim communities, the traditional muezzin's call-to-prayer broadcast from the mosque five times a day is impractical in North American cities. Qu'rān chanting or recitation, in contrast, is a regular part of Muslim prayer sessions. Qu'rān chanters may not be traditionally trained in this art or even native Arabic speakers, but Islamic groups encourage this highly formalized and stylized manner of religious chanting as a fundamental component of their worship rituals.

The experience of Indian Christians in North America has differed from that of both Hindus and Muslims, since theirs is the majority religion in their new homeland. Early immigrants were immediately able to attend American Roman Catholic

A relatively new source for Indian cassette and CD recordings is the Internet, where large Indian record retail outlets can reach a national and even an international market with their mail-order service.

or Protestant church services and participate in familiar hymn-singing traditions. Nowadays many Indian Christian groups have taken over or arranged to use existing American church buildings, and hold services in their own languages. In Chicago, for example, the Indian Telugu United Methodist congregation, originally from Andhra Pradesh, sings hymns in Telugu and English as well as bhajans set to Western harmonies, accompanied by harmonium, cymbals, *kañjīrā* 'frame drum', Hawaiian guitar, and mridangam (or tabla if no South Indian drum is available). The Malayalam Eastern Orthodox congregation from Kerala sings unaccompanied and in unison. The liturgical singing employs scale pitches reminiscent of the ancient melodic modes of the Syrian Christians in Kerala, specifically two of which approximate the Greek Phrygian and Lydian modes. The use of traditional music and language among Indian and Pakistani religious communities suggests a low degree of acculturation and assimilation in American religious life; it further provides one explanation for the popularity and cultural significance of religious gatherings among the predominantly first- and second-generation immigrant population.

Most musical instruments traditionally employed in Indian classical and light classical performance can be found in South Asian communities in North America, generally purchased in India or Pakistan and imported. The North Indian sitar and *bāṅsurī* 'bamboo flute', and the South Indian vina are among the most common classical instruments. Yet the numbers of these are few in comparison with the profusion of popular and light classical accompanying instruments: harmonium, tabla, and *śruti* box 'small reed organ drone'. Occasionally South Asian groups blend tabla drums and harmonium with a Western drum set, electric and acoustic guitars, Afro-Cuban conga drums, and other non-Indian instruments. In virtually all musical contexts, vocalists and instrumentalists use electronic amplification. Folk instruments are less common, and are played largely among immigrants closely related by family or place of origin. At a typical gathering of Gujaratis from the Ahmedabad region, the *nāl* 'barrel drum', *ḍholak* 'cylindrical barrel drum', *mañjīrā* 'small hand cymbals', frame drum, and rattles accompany musical performance; the large *ḍhol* 'stick-beaten barrel drum' or the *ḍholak* is ever present for Punjabi bhangra dance performances.

MUSICAL EDUCATION AND TRANSMISSION

Many musical performers among the Indian- and Pakistani-American populations learned to sing and play instruments before emigrating to North America. A large percentage were introduced to music through family members at an early age and continued with musical education (often including some classical training) in school or private music lessons in India or Pakistan. Rarely did these musicians experience the traditional master-disciple (*guru-śiṣya*) relationship in which the student devotes his life to the practice and study of classical music [see THE CLASSICAL MASTER-

DISCIPLE TRADITION]. With the high demand for popular music entertainers in South Asian immigrant communities, average performers with relatively little musical training can achieve ministardom. For self-taught singers and instrumentalists, similarly numerous among the South Asian population, the acquisition of skills and repertoire involves listening to and imitating other musicians and memorizing popular songs and folk songs heard in live performances and on recordings.

Musical transmission among Pakistani- and Indian-Americans is primarily oral, following traditional practice in India. The strong desire among first-generation immigrants to pass on their native cultural traditions to the second and third generations has resulted in the establishment of some local Indian classical music and dance schools, where structured classes, often held in private homes, offer regular group and solo training for South Asian immigrants as well as the general American population. Part-time classical music teachers similarly serve the larger community, charge fees, transmit musical knowledge through performance demonstration and student imitation, and frequently include background study of Indian history, culture, and religion for non-Indian natives. The foundation of the Ali Akbar College of Music and Ravi Shankar's Kinnara School—both in California in 1967—brought Indian classical music and dance teaching to prominence on a national level. For light classical, popular, folk, and religious musics of South Asia, however, no systematic methods of transmission exist, although folk dances are taught in some Indian schools of dance. Local community musicians learn new repertoire, techniques, and styles largely from Indian and Pakistani cassette and CD recordings available in North America, from visiting friends and relatives, and on return trips to their native land. There is little direct transmission of these musical genres to second- or third-generation immigrants through teaching, largely due to a preference among younger Indian- and Pakistani-Americans for mainstream American culture and music, or for only the latest "desi" music (see below).

The transmission of recorded Indian music through cassette and CD players, radio, and television forms a significant part of the Indian- and Pakistani-American musical culture. Prerecorded music from India and Pakistan substitutes for live performance where none is available, in such contexts as small religious gatherings, classical-dance classes, and dance performances. In private homes, musical recordings provide performances by renowned and well-loved artists who tour North America infrequently. Owners of Indian restaurants and retail stores play popular and light classical recordings as background music, to create an Indian atmosphere for their clients. Indian cassette and CD recordings are generally available in Indian grocery stores, and Indian classical-music recordings can often be found on the shelves of larger American and Canadian record stores. A relatively new source for these is the Internet, where large Indian record retail outlets such as Shrimati's in Berkeley, California, can reach a national and even an international market with their mail-order service.

In metropolitan areas, South Asian communities have shown particular interest in broadcasting their popular music via radio, and more recently television. As in India, radio is a popular medium of communication, and in North America it plays an important role in advertising immigrant musicians to their local communities and even to the general population. The commercial broadcasting system in North America, unlike the Indian government-run All India Radio, allows Indian program hosts to air the most popular Indian film and light music exclusively. Television broadcasting by Indian- and Pakistani-Americans is less common, partly due to lack of financial support. One thriving venture is TV Asia, an Indian-American television network available nationwide via digital satellite, which was inaugurated in 1993 by the Hindi film star Amitabh Bachchan. In addition to its original news, talk show, and sitcom productions, TV Asia offers Doordarshan programs (the state-run Indian television network) and direct links with other South Asian networks.

MUSIC AND CREATIVITY

In the 1980s and 1990s, professional and semiprofessional Indian and Pakistani musicians in North America released audio-cassette and compact disc recordings blending Indian with American and Western musical traditions, following the pioneering efforts in such musical collaborations by Ravi Shankar, Yehudi Menuhin, and Jean-Pierre Rampal in the 1970s. Several renowned classical artists now residing in North America, including the violinists L. Shankar and L. Subramaniam and the tabla player Zakir Hussain, have produced such musical fusions with electronic synthesizers for American and international audiences (Shankar 1985, 1987, 1991; Subramaniam 1985). On a local level, some Indian- and Pakistani-American amateur music bands mix Indian and Western instruments and styles from both popular cultures, and a few produce commercial recordings. Other musicians compose new melodies and song lyrics within existing Indian musical styles, thereby creating music relevant to the immigrant experience in North America. The dissemination of this distinctly immigrant music remains limited to urban Indian- and Pakistani-American communities, but its growth and popularity among them indicates that these immigrants no longer wish to be dependent on their homeland for their musical culture, and that they are actively fostering the creation of their own music based on Indian, Pakistani, and American musical traditions.

Among American-born teens and young adults of Indian immigrants, a new desi (pronounced "day-shi") party scene emerged in the 1990s as a reaction to the South Asian traditions and community gatherings promoted by their parents. DJs play popular bhangra dance music in nightclubs and other locations, and create remixes combining Indian film songs with American dance music (such as hip-hop and techno) (Kvetko 1998). This desi music and dance provide young South Asians with a form of cultural expression that serves to identify their place between the world of their parents and that of mainstream American culture.

MUSIC AND IDENTITY

As a rapidly growing but minority Asian immigrant population, Indian- and Pakistani-Americans maintain transnational identity in North America. Before 1965, a pan–South Asian unity characterized the relatively small Indo-Pakistani immigrant population and was reflected in the community-wide organization of social events with varied music and dance performances. With the massive post-1965 influx of South Asians to the United States following the lifting of discriminatory immigration laws, regionalism emerged, and immigrants identified not only with India and Pakistan but with state and religious markers such as "Bengali" and "Sikh." Religious and cultural groups promoted separate regional identities within the larger ethnic population, and music performances often included devotional and regional traditions that served to define and segregate individual communities. Established Pakistani and Indian communities are now consumers of both South Asian and Western music, they are creating their own hybrid musical styles, and the young American-born generation is seeking its own musical identity, apart from that of its parents.

Social organization today reflects the larger South Asian community as well as the diverse communities it represents. National umbrella groups such as the Association of Indians in America, the India and Pakistan Leagues of America, and (among young adults) the Indian Students Association seek to promote common social identity among South Asian immigrants in North America by fostering coop-

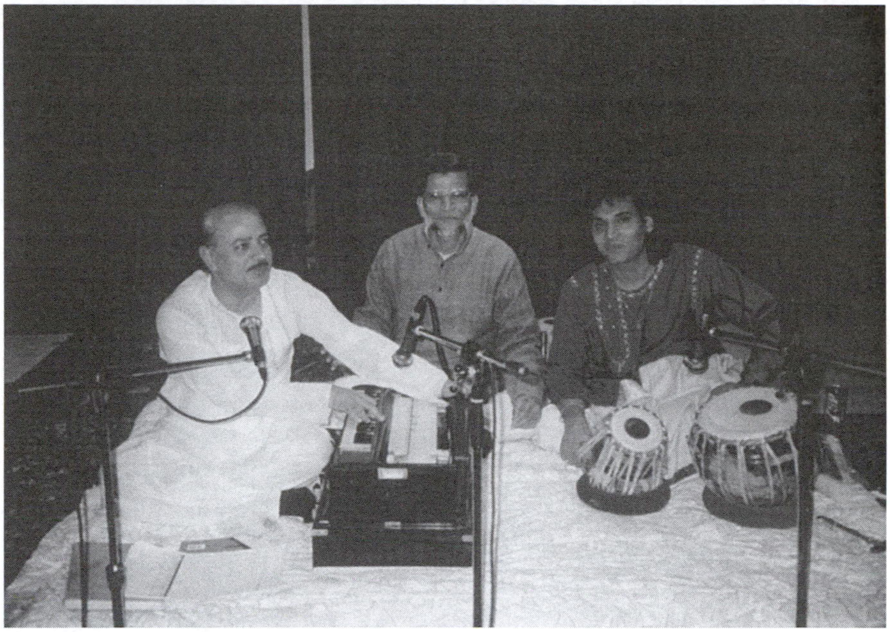

FIGURE 3 A vocal performance with harmonium and tabla accompaniment at a poetry and music event sponsored by the Gujarati Samaj of Montréal. Photo courtesy the Asia Society, New York.

eration and solidarity; urban organizations such as the Kannada Kuta and Gujarati Samaj celebrate regional heritage (figure 3). Similarly, the musical culture of Indian- and Pakistani-Americans encompasses broad traditions of classical and popular music and also varied light classical, religious, and other folk musics common to specific communities. Together with musical fusions and desi music of the second and third generations, this variety of musical expression clearly indicates the complexity of musical and cultural identity among Indian- and Pakistani-Americans.

SOURCES AND FURTHER READING

In contrast to other Asian immigrant populations, Indians and Pakistanis received relatively little scholarly attention prior to the 1980s: writers tended to focus either on the history of Indian immigration (Hess 1969; Jain 1971; Melendy 1977; Mishrow 1971) or on acculturation and adjustment to the new cultural environment (Bradfield 1970; Chandras 1974). In the past two decades scholarly interest has increased, with works ranging from broad social and cultural histories (Buchignani and Indra 1985; Johnston 1984) and studies of religious traditions (Fenton 1988; Williams 1988) to ethnographic research on individual communities (Fisher 1980; La Brack 1988). These authors penetrate various facets of the immigrant experience in North America—from the earliest arrivals in the 1890s to the post-1965 influx into the United States after the lifting of immigration quotas—but none addresses the areas of Indian- and Pakistani-American musical cultures.

The first publication devoted to the music of this immigrant group was Regula Qureshi's ethnomusicological study of East Indian (and Arab) communities in Canada (1972). This work laid the foundation for further research among Indian and Pakistani communities in North America. In 1980, Alison Geldard (now Arnold) carried out ethnographic research among the East Indian community in the Chicago metropolitan area (Geldard 1981), and in 1985 Gordon Thompson and Medha Yodh published their research on the music and dance of the Gujarati community in southern California (Thompson and Yodh 1985). Other scholars have looked at musical performance by visiting Indian artists and its impact on Indian music in North America (Erdman 1985; Neuman 1984), and have surveyed South Asian–American music (Jairazbhoy 1986). Interest in diasporic and transnational

Established Pakistani and Indian communities are now consumers of both South Asian and Western music, they are creating their own hybrid musical styles, and the young American-born generation is seeking its own musical identity, apart from that of its parents.

communities and musics in the 1990s (Farrell 1997; Gopinath 1995; Slobin 1994) has led to recent research on the music of children born in the United States in the 1970s to Indian-born parents, the "boom" generation nicknamed "ABCDs" (American-Born confused desis—*deśī* meaning "native, indigenous") (Kvetko 1998; McGee 1998).

REFERENCES

Arnold, Alison. 1985. "Aspects of Asian Indian Musical Life in North America." *Selected Reports in Ethnomusicology* 6:25–38.

Bhardwaj, Surinder M., and N. Madhusudana Rao. 1990. "Asian Indians in the United States." In *South Asians Overseas: Migration and Ethnicity*, ed. Colin Clarke, Ceri Peach, and Steven Vertovec, 197–217. Cambridge: Cambridge University Press.

Bradfield, Helen H. 1970. "The East Indians of Yuba City: A Study in Acculturation." M.A. thesis, Sacramento State College.

Buchignani, Norman, and Doreen M. Indra. 1985. *Continuous Journey: A Social History of South Asians in Canada*. Toronto: McClelland and Stewart.

Chandras, Kananur V. 1974. *The Adjustment and Attitudes of East Indian Students in Canada*. San Francisco: R. and E. Research Associates, Inc.

Daniels, Roger. 1989. *History of Indian Immigration to the United States: An Interpretive Essay*. New York: Asia Society.

———. 1994. "The Indian Diaspora in the United States." In *Migration: The Asian Experience*, ed. Judith Brown and Rosemary Foot, 83–103. Oxford: St. Martin's Press.

Erdman, Joan. 1985. "Today and the Good Old Days: South Asian Music and Dance Performances in Chicago." *Selected Reports in Ethnomusicology* 6:39–58.

Farrell, Gerry. 1997. *Indian Music and the West*. Oxford: Clarendon.

Fenton, John. 1988. *Transplanting Religious Traditions: Asian Indians in America*. New York: Praeger.

Fisher, Maxine. 1980. *The Indians of New York City: A Study of Immigrants from India*. Columbia, Mo.: South Asia Books.

Geldard [Arnold], Alison. 1981. "Music and Musical Performance among the East Indians in Chicago." M.M. thesis, University of Illinois at Urbana-Champaign.

Gopinath, Gayatri. 1995. "'Bombay, U.K., Yuba City': Bhangra Music and the Engendering of Diaspora." *Diaspora* 4(3):303–311.

Helweg, Arthur W., and Usha M. Helweg. 1990. *An Immigrant Success Story: East Indians in America*. Philadelphia: University of Pennsylvania Press.

Hess, Gary. 1969. "The 'Hindu' in America: Immigration and Naturalization Policies and India, 1917–1946." *Pacific Historical Review* 38:59–79.

Jain, Sushil K. 1971. *East Indians in Canada*. REMP Bulletin, suppl. 9. The Hague: Research Group for European Migration Problems.

Jairazbhoy, Nazir. 1986. "Asian-American Music, 1: Introduction; 5: South Asian." In *The New Grove Dictionary of American Music*, ed. H. Wiley Hitchcock. London: Macmillan.

Jensen, Joan. 1988. *Passage from India: Asian Indian Immigrants in North America*. New Haven, Conn.: Yale University Press.

Johnston, Hugh. 1984. *The East Indians in Canada*. Ottawa: Canadian Historical Association.

Kvetko, Peter. 1998. "The New Asian Kool: Music and Identity among Young Americans of South Asian Descent." Unpublished paper.

La Brack, Bruce. 1988. *The Sikhs of Northern California, 1904–1975*. New York: AMS Press.

Mayer, Adrian. 1959. "A Report on the East Indian Community in Vancouver." Working paper, Institute of Social and Economic Research, University of British Columbia.

McGee, Kristin. 1998. "From Bhangra to the New Desi Music: In Search of the International Groove." Unpublished paper.

Melendy, Howard B. 1977. *Asians in America: Filipinos, Koreans, and East Indians*. Boston: Twayne.

Mishrow, Jogesh C. 1971 [1919]. *East Indian Immigration on the Pacific Coast.* Stanford: R. and E. Research Associates,. Inc.

Muthanna, I. M. 1982. *People of India in North America (United States, Canada, W. Indies, & Fiji): Immigration History of East-Indians up to 1960,* 2nd ed. Bangalore: Lotus Printers.

Neuman, Daniel. 1984. "The Ecology of Indian Music in North America." *Bansuri* 1:9–15.

Qureshi, Regula. 1972. "Ethnomusicological Research among Canadian Communities of Arab and East Indian Origin." *Ethnomusicology* 16:381–396.

Saran, Parmatma. 1985. *The Asian Indian Experience in the United States.* New Delhi: Vikas.

Saran, Parmatma, and Edwin Eames, eds. 1980. *The New Ethnics: Asian Indians in the United States.* New York: Praeger.

Siddique, Muhammad. 1983. "Changing Family Patterns: A Comparative Analysis of Immigrant Indian and Pakistani Families of Saskatoon, Canada." In *Overseas Indians: A Study in Adaptation,* ed. George Kurian and Ram Srivastava, 100–127. New Delhi: Vikas.

Shankar, L. 1985. *Song for Everyone.* Compositions by L. Shankar (double violin) with Jon Garbarek (soprano and tenor saxophones), Trilok Gurtu (percussion), Zakir Hussain (tabla). ECM Records 823795 2. Compact disc.

———. 1987. *The Epidemic.* Compositions by L. Shankar (double violin) with Caroline Shankar (percussion and vocal), Steve Vai (guitar), Gilbert Kaufman (synthesizer), Percy Jones (bass). ECM Records 827522-2. Compact disc.

———. 1991. *M.R.C.S.* L. Shankar (double violin), Zakir Hussain (tabla), Vikku Vinayakram (ghatam), Jan Christianson (drums). ECM Records 841642–3. Compact disc.

Slobin, Mark. 1994. "Music in Diaspora: The View from Euro-America." *Diaspora* 3(3):243–251.

Statistics Canada. 1999. *Immigrant Population by Place of Birth, Showing Periods of Immigration 1981–1990 and 1991–1996, Canada, 1996 Census (20% Sample Data).* Available at http://www.statcan.ca/english/census96/nov4/imm2c.htm.

———. 1999. *Total Population by Ethnic Origin (1), for Canada, 1996 Census (20% Sample Data).* Available at http://www.statcan.ca/english/census96/feb17/eo2can.htm.

Subramaniam, L. 1985. *Expressions of Impressions.* Sonic Atmospheres SAS 206 (cassette), SAS 306 (compact disc).

Thompson, Gordon. 1985. "Songs in Circles: Gujaratis in America." *1985 Festival of American Folklife Program Book.* Washington, D.C.: Smithsonian Institution.

Thompson, Gordon, and Medha Yodh. 1985. "Garba and the Gujaratis of Southern California." *Selected Reports in Ethnomusicology* VI:59–79.

U.S. Census Bureau. *March 1997 Current Population Survey.* Available at http://www.bls.census.gov/cps/pub/1997/for_born.htm

Wade, Bonnie. 1978. "Indian Classical Music in North America: Cultural Give and Take." *Contributions to Asian Studies* 12:40–53.

Williams, Raymond B. 1988. *Religions of Immigrants from India and Pakistan: New Threads in the American Tapestry.* Cambridge: Cambridge University Press.

Trinidad

Helen Myers

The Bhojpuri Repertoire
The Devotional Repertoire
Local Classical Music
Film and Popular Music

Trinidad, the most southerly island of the West Indian archipelago, is situated off the northeastern coast of Venezuela. Valued in the seventeenth and eighteenth centuries for its rich sugarcane plantations, worked by African slaves, the island came under British rule in 1797. Not long after, a sudden labor shortage was brought about by the abolition of slavery throughout the British Empire and in 1838 brought the economy close to ruin. The subsequent introduction of indentured laborers from India into the British Caribbean colonies between 1845 and 1917 averted such a crisis. Some 144,000 Indians were brought to Trinidad; they were mostly from Uttar Pradesh, plus some five thousand from Madras. By the 1860s, East Indians represented the backbone of the island's single-crop plantation economy. Many of these "coolies," as they were known, remained on the island; at the turn of the millennium, their descendants still occupy the swampy land along the western coast and the central interior county of Caroni.

The earliest mention of the music of these impoverished immigrants is found in the logs of the ships that transported them from India to Port of Spain, Trinidad. These nautical records contain such expressions as "the Madrassee is a lively singing fellow" or "the Coolies are very musical" and "should be permitted to play their drums till 8 bells." Over the 150 years since this community became established in the New World, these Indians have abandoned certain aspects of their culture such as caste but have maintained others such as music, an important component of their cultural identity.

Trinidad's one million inhabitants include, besides those of African ancestry (45 percent) and East Indians (40 percent), notable groups of Europeans, Lebanese, Syrians, and some Venezuelans. Amid this racial diversity, ethnic groups often retain their own modes of dress, types of food, and artistic and musical forms. Most of the four hundred thousand Trinidadian Indians, for example, speak English as their first language, yet they sing songs in Indian languages—Hindi, Sanskrit, and Bhojpuri, the lingua franca of the old plantation system.

THE BHOJPURI REPERTOIRE

The Indian community in Trinidad still sang North Indian village songs in Bhojpuri as recently as the 1960s and 1970s, including those for weddings (*byāh ke gīt* and *lachārī*), for the ritual tattooing of the bride (*godna*), after childbirth (*sohar*), for the rainy season (*kajarī*), and for the springtime festival known as Phāguā or Holī (*cautāl*).

A three-day Hindu marriage ceremony would most likely include thirty to forty unaccompanied songs (*byāh ke gīt*) describing the marriage of Rama and Sita as told in the Hindu epic the *Rāmcaritmānas* 'The Lake of the Acts of Rama' by the illustrious Gosvami Tulsi Das (1552–1623). Groups of older women sang the strophic texts in leader-chorus style, using an old but somewhat creolized Bhojpuri of nineteenth-century India. The songs, surviving in recordings, typically have undulating melodies in a limited vocal range, with rhythmic groupings of eight or fourteen beats (as in *kaharvā* or *dīpchandī* talas). The women use a full-throated, sing-shout style with a low tessitura, similar to village singing in India. On the wedding night, they sing, "In the evening the clouds come in the sky and at midnight it starts to rain. Mother, open the sandalwood door and let Rama enter the *kohabar* [ritual bedroom]. Mother, open the sandalwood door and let Sita enter the *kohabar*" (figure 1).

Lachārī are amusing, gently teasing songs. A group of six to twelve women sing them as they cook for wedding celebrations, during wedding feasts, and for long periods while the marriage rites are performed. The women accompany themselves on the *ḍholak* 'double-headed barrel drum', *mañjīrā* 'finger cymbals', tambourines, *shak shak* 'rattles', and *ḍhantāl* 'iron rod struck with a curved metal beater' (the latter is no longer played in eastern Uttar Pradesh). The playful *lachārī* songs, which derive from a nineteenth-century Indian genre, recall India's past, a time when women entertained themselves in private and sang about the frustrations of male dominance with affectionate good humor. *Lachārī* are slowly being forgotten in Trinidad, as are some of the ceremonies they accompanied. In the Indian state of Uttar Pradesh, *lachārī* songs have now been largely replaced by rough, comic songs of sexual abuse called *gālī*.

Wedding processions and dancing are accompanied by a *tāssā* ensemble, which consists of two *tāssā* 'clay kettledrums' of Islamic derivation and a heavy cylindrical, double-headed bass drum. The *tāssā* drum repertoire consists of a series of "hands" (rhythmic patterns) comparable to certain duple-meter rhythmic cycles of North India; they are named after song genres, Indian festivals, or West Indian matters:

sāṅ– jha– i ba– ḍha– rā u– ma– ri ai– le ā– dhī rā– ti ba– ra– sa– i ho
mai– yā kho– le de– u cha– na–
na ke wa– ri– yā ra– mai– yā
jai– hāi ko– ha– ba– ra ho

FIGURE 1 Wedding song (*byāh ke gīt*), as sung by Trinidadian East Indian women in Bhojpuri. Transcribed by Helen Myers. The "key signature" indicates pitches that recur throughout the song, not a tonality. A straight line between notes indicates a pitch glide. The ♯ without bottom horizontal indicates a half sharp (approximately a quarter tone sharp).

tillānā, cautāl, kabīr, ulārā, "wedding," "one-way drum," "calypso-steel band," and "olé!"

Drummers also play *tāssā* during the Muslim festival of Hosay (known in the Middle East as Taziya), on the tenth day of the Islamic month of Muharram. This is a time of mourning, and is celebrated with high spirits in Trinidad. Neighborhood and family groups erect elaborate paper floats mounted on huge bamboo frames, decorated with giant birds, turrets, cornices, and a large onion dome. The festival concludes with a procession to the river that includes *gatak* 'stick fighting', "jumping up," and rum drinking, and is accompanied by special Hosay *tāssā* rhythms with such names as "preparation for battle," "full rage of battle," and "burial procession for Imam Hussein."

Around Carnival time, East Indian Hindus celebrate their springtime festival of Holī with lively men's songs (*cautāl*) accompanied by vigorous *ḍholak* drumming and the loud clang of cymbals (*jhāl*). In rice planting time and in the rainy season, village women sing songs of love and longing (*kajarī*), much as they do during the monsoon months in India.

THE DEVOTIONAL REPERTOIRE

During the so-called Hindu Revival of the late nineteenth and early twentieth centuries, reformist organizations in India sent Hindu missions overseas to outposts of the diaspora. In 1917, for example, missionaries from the Bombay-based Arya Samaj (Society of Aryans) visited Trinidad with the intent of reconverting Presbyterian East Indians to Hinduism. They taught the ancient Vedic rituals of *havan* (performed around a sacrificial fire) and *sanḍhyā* (performed at dawn, noon, and dusk), Vedic chants in Sanskrit (accompanied by drone instruments such as the harmonium or the *tambūrā* 'long-necked plucked lute'), and a new repertoire of Hindu bhajans (devotional songs). In 1951, Swami Purnananda from Calcutta arrived in Trinidad, and his teachings reinforced those of the earlier missionaries. The renowned Trinidadian writer V. S. Naipaul remembers the Aryan *havan* sacrifices from his childhood: "a pundit chanting in Sanskrit (or what in this far-off part of the world passed for Sanskrit), sitting in front of a low, decorated earthen altar, stuck with a young banana tree, and with sugar and clarified butter burning on an aromatic pitch-pine fire: old emblems of fertility and sacrifice" (Naipaul 1994: 241).

Since the 1960s, children have learned Hindi bhajans and Vedic mantras in Hindu elementary schools. These Trinidadian bhajans have unconventional leader-chorus forms in which the leader sings "cue lines" to signal the refrain or a new verse to the chorus. Bhajan singers use light, nasal head tones typical of Indian popular and classical singing. Many of the texts are in praise of Rama.

The texts of *nām-kīrtan*, another devotional song form, repeat the various names and epithets of a deity, as for example: "Rama Krishna Hare, Mukunda Murare, Sita Vallabha, Sita Rama, Vrindravana Govinda, Nanda Nandana," 'Hail Rama Krishna, enemy of Mura, lover of Sita, Sita Rama, cowherd of Vrindavan, son of Nanda'.

Ten percent of Trinidad's Indian population is Muslim, and Islamic devotional forms, including the call to prayer and Qu'rānic chant, are performed in city and village mosques. In Muslim elementary schools, children sing *qaṣīda* 'devotional songs'.

The Sai Baba movement from India reached Trinidad in 1974, bringing with it another style of worship and a repertoire of short catchy *kīrtan* songs. Devotees sing energetic, highly repetitive Sai songs; the performances emphasize accelerando and crescendo as the excitement builds, along with enthusiastic hand clapping and the loud accompaniment of *ḍholak,* harmonium, and small percussion instruments, all amplified by an in-house public address system. The melodious tunes and short texts serve the Hindu population well, as their knowledge of Hindi has deteriorated to such an extent that most East Indians now speak only English.

LOCAL CLASSICAL MUSIC

During the early years of the twentieth century, a distinctive local form of classical singing developed in Trinidad; its genres were known as *sargam*, *ghazal*, *ṭhumrī*, *dhrupad*, *tillāna*, and *dohā*. Early indentured laborers played tabla-like drum pairs and handmade *sāraṅgī* 'bowed fiddles' as accompaniment. In the nineteenth and early twentieth centuries, most formal singing took place at night, and all-night contests reminiscent of the song duels that are still popular in Uttar Pradesh villages took place between rival singers (Bhojpuri *gāyak*). Every hour of the night had its own prescribed song form, in the same way that classical Indian music assigns ragas to particular times of day and night. Performers also used raga names to identify melodic or compositional forms, referring to a song as "a *bhairavī*" or "a *kāfī*." (This does not mean that they followed the melodic modes referred to by these names in India.) An interesting "Quawali Song" recorded in the 1930s by the local star Jugrue Quawal praises both the Rajasthani Hindu poet-queen Mirabai and the Muslim Prophet Muhammad: "Among all poets the great Mirabai is the greatest, you drank poison from the blessed bowl. Oh, Mohammed you are the greatest of God's prophets, the beloved of everyone." Although some Western scholars have characterized this local classical music of Trinidad as a corrupted or distorted version of Indian classical music, such a characterization misses the charm of New World transformation. The classical Hindustani tradition was introduced to the island only in 1966 by the artist H. S. Adesh, and since this time tens of students have studied sitar and tabla playing as well as Hindustani vocal music.

FILM AND POPULAR MUSIC

An Indian sound film was shown for the first time in Trinidad in 1935. The showing of this film, *Bala Joban*, inaugurated a wave of local composition and led to the development of an island music industry. From the 1940s onward, Trinidadian singers were able to avail themselves of a vast source of popular music in the form of the glitzy products of the Bollywood studios in Bombay, which were themselves influenced by the Latin American and U.S. pop scenes.

In 1936, the first shipment of Indian film-song recordings reached Trinidad, together with new recordings of light classical music (ghazal and *ṭhumrī*), all providing fuel for the West Indian musical scene. Radio Trinidad, the island's first station, opened in 1947; by September of that year it had begun broadcasting a regular program of local Indian music, *Indian Talent on Parade*. By the 1960s, dozens of Indian orchestras were playing arrangements of film music at weddings, parties, bazaars, on the radio, and on the weekly television program *Mastana Bahaar*. These combos included electric guitars and keyboards, drum set, conga drums, bongos, trumpet, saxophone, violin, sometimes mandolin, and occasionally also traditional Indian instruments such as the *bāṅsurī* 'flute', *ḍholak*, or tabla.

Chutney

In the 1990s, pop songs of the youth culture are known as "chutney" or "Indian soca" (a word that combines the first letters of soul and calypso), and set the scene for drinking and dancing in nightclub settings. Songwriters mix the old local classical repertoire and traditional Indian instruments with a disco beat. Sharlene Boodram's 1994 competition-winning hit "Chutney Time" is typical, with its driving intensity, rap style, and English text with occasional Hindi vocabulary:

Chutney rap, chutney *jhūmar*, chutney lambada—the scene is alive with innovation as Caribbean styles are mixed with Bombay film music and American pop.

Tie your *dhotī* [loincloth worn by Hindus] man,
tie it up cause chutney down it extremely hot,
we say come down!
Form a little ring man,
and I do a little thing man,
and a wiggle of your body,
and I make your waist thin!

Chutney rap, chutney *jhūmar*, chutney lambada—the scene is alive with innovation as Caribbean styles are mixed with Bombay film music and American pop. Disco artists from India, notably the singer Kanchan and her husband Babla, have made hit arrangements of Trinidad soca and chutney songs such as Sundar Popo's "Chādar Bīchawo Bālma" 'Spread the Little Sheet Sweetheart', adding studio techniques used in Hindi film songs. Today the local recording industry in Trinidad is thriving, with many small private labels and one larger enterprise, Windsor Records in Port of Spain, which is run by the Mohammed brothers. East Indian recordings from Trinidad are readily available in the United States through various New York distributors, who provide prompt mail-order service for Indian-Trinidadian immigrants in North America.

REFERENCES

Arya, Usharbudh. 1968. *Ritual Songs and Folksongs of the Hindus of Surinam*. Leiden: E. J. Brill.

Bissoondialsingh, Tara. 1973. "Dhrupad Singing in Trinidad." B.I. Mus. thesis, Bharatiya Vidya Sansthhaan, Aranguez, Trinidad.

Carlile, James, ed. 1859. *Journal of a Voyage with Coolie Emigrants from Calcutta to Trinidad. By Captain and Mrs. Suntan, Late of the Ship 'Salsette.'* London: Alfred W. Bennett.

Chaudhuri, Shubha. 1989. "Sohar, Kajri, and Steel Bands: Helen Myers' Collection of Bhojpuri Songs from Felicity, Trinidad." *Samvadi, Newsletter of the Archive and Research Center for Ethnomusicology, New Delhi,* Summer/Fall.

Comitas, Lambros. 1968. *Caribbeana 1900–1965: A Topical Bibliography.* Seattle: University of Washington Press, for the Research Institute for the Study of Man.

Crowley, Daniel J. 1960. "Social and Cultural Pluralism in the Caribbean." *Annals of the New York Academy of Sciences* 83(20 Jan.):850–854.

———. 1954. "East Indian Festivals in Trinidad Life." *Caribbean Commission Monthly Bulletin* 7(9):202–204, 208.

———. 1957. "Plural and Differential Acculturation in Trinidad." *American Anthropologist* 59(5):817–24.

Cumpston, I.M. 1953. *Indians Overseas in British Territories, 1834–1854*. London: Oxford University Press.

Erickson, Edgar L. 1934. "The Introduction of East Indian Coolies into the British West Indies." *The Journal of Modern History,* 6(2): 127–146.

Freilich, Morris. 1960. "Cultural Diversity among Trinidadian Peasants." Ph.D. dissertation, Columbia University.

Gangulee, Nagendranath. 1947. *Indians in the Empire Overseas.* London: The New India Publishing House.

Grierson, George A. 1884. "Some Biharī Folksongs." *Journal of the Royal Asian Society* 18: 196.

———. 1886. "Some Bhoj'pūrī Folksongs." *Journal of the Royal Asian Society* 18: 207.

Hart, Daniel. 1866. *Trinidad and the Other West Indian Islands and Colonies*, 2nd ed. Port of Spain: The Chronicle Publishing Office.

Jayawardena, Chandra. 1968. "Migration and Social Change: A Survey of Indian Communities Overseas." *The Geographical Review* 58(3): 437–449.

Klass, Morton. 1961. *East Indians in Trinidad: A Study of Cultural Persistence.* New York: Columbia University Press.

———. 1991. *Singing with Sai Baba: The Politics of Revitalization in Trinidad.* Boulder, Colo.: Westview Press.

La Guerre, John, ed. 1974. *Calcutta to Caroni: The East Indians of Trinidad.* Port of Spain: Longman Caribbean.

Myers, Helen. 1980. "Trinidad and Tobago." *The New Grove Dictionary of Music and Musicians*, ed. Stanley Sadie. London: Macmillan.

———. 1983 (1978). "The Process of Change in Trinidad East Indian Music." In *Essays in Musicology*, ed. R. C. Mehta. Bombay and Baroda: Indian Musicological Society.

———. 1997. *Music of Hindu Trinidad: Songs from the India Diaspora.* Chicago: University of Chicago Press.

Naipaul, V. S. 1994. *A Way in the World.* New York: Alfred A. Knopf.

Schwartz, Barton M., ed. 1967. *Caste in Overseas Indian Communities.* San Francisco: Chandler Publishing Co.

Tewari, Laxmi G. 1974. "Folk Music of India: Uttar Pradesh." Ph.D. dissertation, Wesleyan University.

Tinker, Hugh. 1974. *A New System of Slavery: The Export of Indian Labour Overseas 1830–1920.* London: Oxford University Press.

Upadhyaya, Hari S. 1967. "The Joint Family Structure and Familial Relationship Patterns in the Bhojpuri Folksongs." Ph.D. dissertation, Indiana University.

———. 1988. *Bhojpuri Folksongs from Ballia.* Atlanta: Indian Enterprises Inc.

Upadhyaya, Krishna D. 1954–1966. *Bhojpuri Lokgit.* Parts 1 and 2. Allahabad: Hindi Sahitya Sammelan.

Martinique

Monique Desroches

The Caribbean island of Martinique has been a separate French overseas department since 1946. Its principal ethnic groups include Caribs, Africans, Europeans, and Asians; the latter are mostly Indians. The presence of this Indian population dates back to the manpower shortage faced by the sugar plantations of Martinique. Once slavery was abolished in 1848, the emancipated Black Creoles shunned this labor; it was for this reason that between 1854 and 1883 up to 25,000 Indians were brought over to Martinique to work on the numerous plantations. Most of these immigrants were recruited from Madras in southeastern India, were of low caste, and spoke Tamil.

Through emigration and due to assimilation with the Creoles, this population has diminished to its present size of approximately five thousand, and is largely concentrated in the northern part of Martinique, where the main plantations are located. Although the population now speaks Creole, the relative homogeneity of its ethnic origin has contributed to the survival of certain Tamil cultural features (Desroches and Benoist 1982; Desroches 1996). The ritual ceremonies Bon Dyé Coolies, or Sèvis Zendyen, as they are called in Creole, provide a good example.

TAMIL CEREMONIES

These ceremonies may take place in front of any one of the seven Tamil chapels on Martinique (figure 1), and are generally requested by a family either to obtain a favor from or to offer thanks to the family's deities. Three deities in particular are prominent: Maliemen, Maldevilin, and Nagoulou Mila. Maliemen, the goddess of fertility, is very popular in southern India, where she is known as Mariamma. (All the deities' original Indian names have been modified through oral transmission and syncretism with the Catholic religion.) The male deity Maldevilin is the most powerful of the three, and corresponds to the deity Madurai Viren in India. The third deity, Nagoulou Mila, the equivalent of the Muslim saint Nagour Mira in India, is worshiped to protect the Tamil population against storms and shipwrecks. Tamils dedicate to this latter deity the raising of the Indian flag that ends ceremonies symbolizing the arduous crossing of the Atlantic their ancestors made.

The main participants in any of these ceremonies are the priest, who enters a

FIGURE 1 Moulin l'Étang, one of the seven Indian chapels on Martinique. Photo by Monique Desroches, 1981.

trance state to speak Tamil with the deities; the interpreter, who translates into Creole the conversation between the priest and the deities (and also acts as a go-between for priest and family); and finally the drummers, who number between three and nine (figure 2). The drummers play a kind of tambourine (*tapou*) tied to the shoulder by a thin strap. Each drummer holds a cylindrical stick in the right hand, and in the left hand he holds a kind of small broom made from dried strips of coconut-palm leaves bound together with a thin rope. He plays with either hand. (For further information on this drum, see Desroches 1989.)

A ceremony comprises many stages, but the climax occurs when the priest falls into a trance through the influence of Maldevilin. Barefoot, the priest then stands on the sharp edge of a cutlass and converses with the deity in Tamil. The most spectacular moment, however, which all spectators await with impatience, is the animal sacrifice. The heads of an odd number of sheep and cocks must be severed with a single blow; otherwise, the sacrifice is a bad omen for the participants.

FIGURE 2 *Tapou* drummers on Martinique, 1979. Two (*from left*) play with coconut-palm strips in the left hand and three (*from right*) play with drumsticks in the right hand. Photo by Monique Desroches.

The importance and duration of each stage of the ceremony can vary depending on the priest or on the nature of the request being made to the deities. However, one element remains constant throughout the ritual: the drumming, whose rhythm or way of beating varies according to the section of the ceremony it accompanies. The drummers stop beating only to heat up their drums over an open fire. They claim that drying and tightening the skin improves the sonority of the drum and thereby increases the likelihood of pleasing the deities. The drums are also silent as the priest, balanced on the sharp edge of the cutlass, converses in Tamil with the interpreter.

These religious ceremonies, beyond their immediate sacred character, have helped improve the social status of the Tamil community within Creole society as a whole. The Indian priest's powers—his standing on the sharp edge of the cutlass, his curing of diseased persons while he is in a trance—all impress and somewhat frighten the black Creoles. This situation has helped the Tamils maintain their distinctive character in Martinique.

Furthermore, the Black Creoles not only attend Indian ceremonies, they occasionally also become supplicants, requesting and paying for a ceremony for themselves. When they do so they are acting on their view that the Tamil priest is a complementary, or opposite, sorcerer to the black sorcerer (called *quimboiseur* in the French West Indies): they believe that he will be able to obtain a favor the black sorcerer has been unable to get or provide an antidote for a bad omen already cast on someone by a black sorcerer.

Musical analysis

Nine rhythmic drumming patterns are used at the various Tamil ceremonies. Figure 3, which is based on the author's observations and analysis, presents these patterns—played by the cylindrical stick held in the right hand—and the various stages of the ceremony during which they are performed. The direction of the note stems indicates whether the drum is struck on its upper or lower part.

The first two rhythmic patterns, B-1 and B-1′, are played during the preparation for the ceremony, a phase that can last up to two hours. Participants bring food for the various deities, decorate the chapel with flowers, and sprinkle a holy mixture of mandja (an edible root), lemon, and sheep urine at the sacred place to purify the food offerings.

Inside the chapel with the interpreter and some of the supplicants, the priest deposits a tray filled with food on the floor and boils a mixture of rice and milk. The drummers play a new rhythm (B-2), which also precedes the animal sacrifices and is performed as the Indian flag is raised.

The priest then starts singing an invocation to Maliemen, at which time the drummers stop beating. They resume playing with the third rhythm, B-3, only when the priest shouts to them, "Let the drums beat," as the rice milk starts to boil. According to some ethnologists, the intensity and the speed of the drumming are linked to the boiling of the milk (Farrugia 1975). Just as it is very important that the animal sacrifice be carried out with a single blow, so also is it very important that the milk not boil over; otherwise, the result would again be a bad omen for the participants.

One rhythmic pattern, B-4, is not associated with any specific ritual or stage of one, and can be performed at any time. However, drummers tend to play it close to important events such as the boiling of the rice milk or the priest's falling into a trance. This pattern is more complex than the others and ends with a return to the first pattern, B-1.

After invoking the deities, the priest suddenly jumps from one foot to the other and sways and shouts: he is possessed by Maldevilin. The drummers switch to a new

FIGURE 3 Rhythmic drum patterns and the stage of a Tamil ceremony during which each is played.

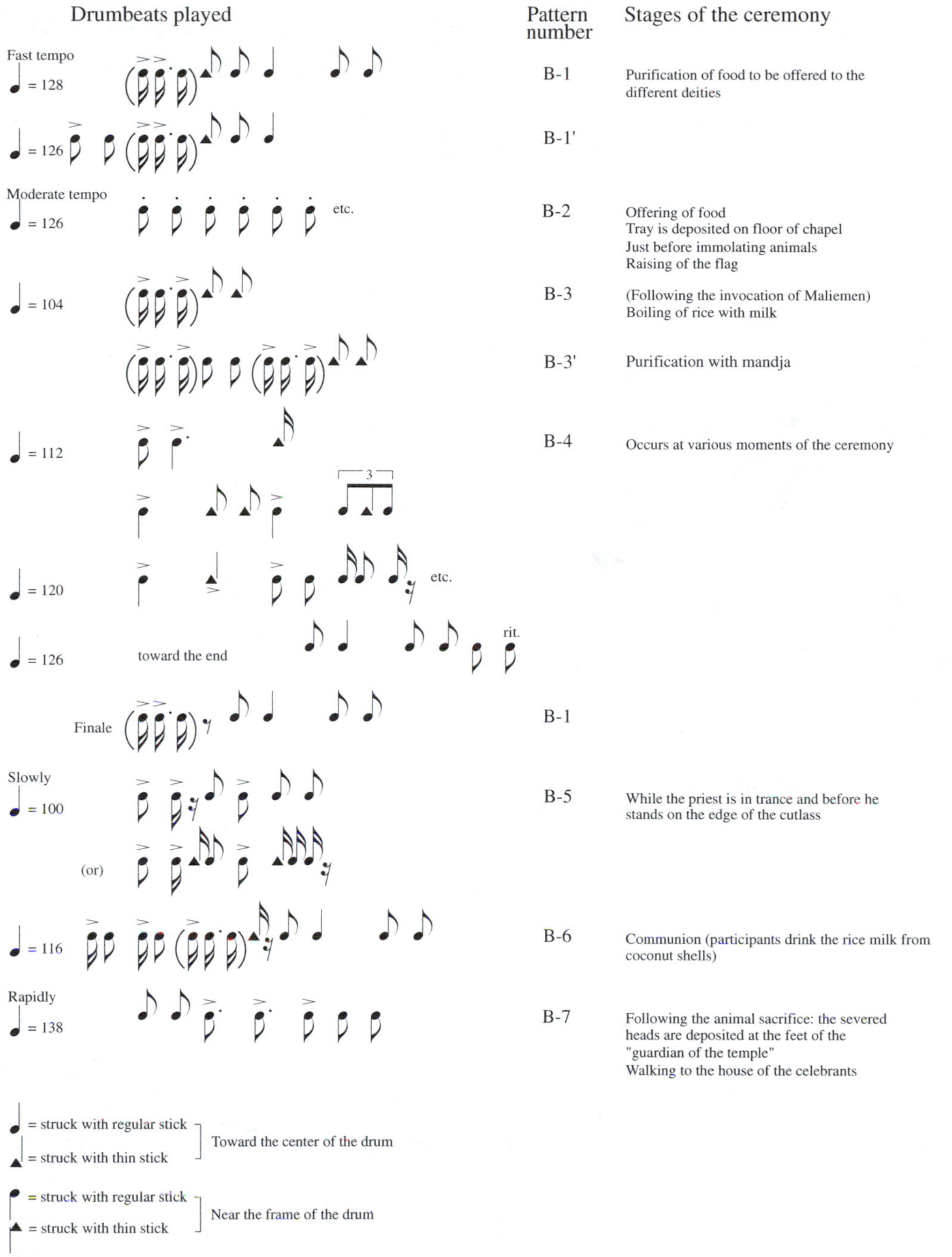
Drumbeats played
Pattern number
Stages of the ceremony
Fast tempo
= 128
B-1
Purification of food to be offered to the different deities
= 126
B-1'
Moderate tempo
= 126
etc.
B-2
Offering of food
Tray is deposited on floor of chapel
Just before immolating animals
Raising of the flag
= 104
B-3
(Following the invocation of Maliemen)
Boiling of rice with milk
B-3'
Purification with mandja
= 112
B-4
Occurs at various moments of the ceremony
3
= 120
etc.
= 126
toward the end
rit.
Finale
B-1
Slowly
= 100
B-5
While the priest is in trance and before he stands on the edge of the cutlass
(or)
= 116
B-6
Communion (participants drink the rice milk from coconut shells)
Rapidly
= 138
B-7
Following the animal sacrifice: the severed heads are deposited at the feet of the "guardian of the temple"
Walking to the house of the celebrants
= struck with regular stick
= struck with thin stick
Toward the center of the drum
= struck with regular stick
= struck with thin stick
Near the frame of the drum

rhythm, B-5; this rhythm precedes every occasion when the priest stands on the cutlass—and such occasions can number up to ten within a single ceremony (figure 4).

A communion follows these spectacular and impressive moments. Someone walks through the crowd and offers to each spectator food that has been prepared previously. During the communion, the drummers play pattern B-6. Finally the animals are sacrificed (figure 5), and then participants and spectators move to the house of the supplicants to take part in a feast, to the accompaniment of the drummers playing pattern B-7.

To the outsider, the drumming within the ceremonies poses several questions: What is the reason for associating a specific rhythmic pattern with one or more stages of a ceremony? What do these rhythmic patterns mean to the celebrants? Do these patterns have any function beyond mere musical accompaniment of the ceremony?

The carnivorous pantheon, which receives the sacrificial offering and is present during the dance, serves as a counterpoint to Maliemen, the vegetarian goddess who opens and closes the ceremony.

FIGURE 4 The priest, in a trance, standing on the cutlass. Photo by Monique Desroches, 1979.

According to several Martinicans connected with the ceremonies (drummers, an interpreter, an Indian family, and some Creoles), certain patterns—namely B-1, B-1′, B-3, B-3′, and B-6—are related to the deity Maliemen; pattern B-5 is related to Maldevilin. The insiders' view reveals that all the drumming patterns do indeed relate somehow to specific stages of the ceremony: some have an extramusical association with a deity. Interestingly, the rhythmic patterns related to the goddess Maliemen include a common rhythmic cell (♪♪.♪) not found in the other rhythmic patterns (indicated by parentheses in figure 3). Similarly, the B-5 pattern associated with Maldevilin is less syncopated than other rhythmic patterns and shows no obvious relationship with them. The identification of the rhythmic patterns with specific deities would thus appear to have a musical basis.

The ceremony outlined in figure 3 includes three events during which Maliemen is invoked: the initial period of the ceremony, when flowers and vegetarian foods are offered to the deity (with rhythmic patterns B-1 and B-1′); the preparation of the rice milk (patterns B-3 and B-3′); and the communal consumption of the vegetarian food (pattern B-6). (Although rice milk is offered to divinities all over India, it is particularly associated with Maliemen in cultures in which she is dominant.) These events represent the vegetarian phases of the ceremony, and the three rhythms associated with Maliemen separate these phases from the other parts of the service.

FIGURE 5 The animal sacrifice, which must be accomplished with a single stroke of the cutlass, is a highlight of the Tamil ceremony. Photo by Monique Desroches, 1979.

As a counterbalance to this vegetarian assembly around Maliemen, the rhythm sounded before each of the priest's steps on the edge of the cutlass, and which continues during his trance dance, is associated with Maldevilin. There is silence during the decapitation of the animal, but celebrants explicitly state that the sacrifice is carried out either for Maldevilin or for Cataveryen, not for Maliemen. The carnivorous pantheon, which receives the sacrificial offering and is present during the dance in which the priest responds to the main participants' wishes, serves as a counterpoint to Maliemen, the vegetarian goddess who opens and closes the ceremony. The music framing the portion of the ceremony devoted to Maliemen separates her from the bloodletting and simultaneously allows her presence. While Maldevilin is invoked during this animal sacrifice, the goddess Maliemen is seen as the divine sanctioner of the ceremony.

THE ROLE OF TAMIL DRUMMERS

The fact that these drummers are considered untouchables in India is not altogether unknown on Martinique. However, their presence and the indispensable role they assume in present-day Tamil ceremonies through their drums gives them a certain leverage against those who consider themselves superior. Their status on the island has been affected by their ceremonial role as well as by the social position of their ancestors, who arrived from South India as indentured laborers and took the place of the emancipated Black Creoles. The Creoles of African origin may dominate them, but would nevertheless be left powerless without them.

REFERENCES

Benoist, Jean. 1979. "L'organisation sociale des Antilles." *Études créoles*, 11–34.

Desroches, Monique. 1989. *Les instruments de musique traditionnels de la Martinique*. Fort-de-France: Ed. Bureau du Patrimoine, Conseil régional de la Martinique,

———. 1996. *Tambours des dieux*. Paris and Montréal: Harmattan.

Desroches, Monique, and Jean Benoist. 1982. "Tambours de l'Inde à la Martinique: Structure sonore d'un espace sacré." *Études créoles* 5(1/2): 39–59.

———. 1991. *Musiques de l'Inde en pays créoles*. University of Montreal UMM 201. Compact disc.

Farrugia, L. 1975. *Les Indiens de la Guadeloupe et de la Martinique*. Basse-Terre, Guadeloupe: Desormeaux.

L'Étang, Gerry, et al. 1994. *Présences de l'Inde dans le monde*. Paris: L'Harmattan.

Nattiez, Jean-Jacques. 1987. *Sémiologie générale et musicologie*. Paris: Christian Bourgeois.

Singaravelou. 1975. *Les Indiens de la Guadeloupe*. Bordeaux: Deniaud.

Guyana

Gora Singh (abridged by Karna Singh)

Guyanese Music with North Indian Roots
South Indian–Derived Ritual Music
Classical Music Traditions
Indo-Guyanese Popular Music

The many Indian musical traditions and influences found today in Guyana, and in Indo-Guyanese communities in the United States, are the legacy of Asian Indian immigrants who came to work on Guyanese sugar plantations in the nineteenth and early twentieth centuries, when the country was the British colony of British Guiana. These immigrants were indentured laborers brought in to replace African slaves on the colony's plantations following the abolition of slavery in 1834; the system of Asian Indian indentured labor began in 1838 and ended in 1917, half a century before Guyana gained its independence in 1966. People of Asian Indian ancestry in Guyana, and their culture, are commonly described as Indo-Guyanese, or simply East Indian (figure 1).

The overwhelming majority of indentured immigrants were Hindus, from villages in the Hindi-Bhojpuri linguistic region of North India (modern Bihar and Uttar Pradesh), and belonged to agricultural and artisan castes occupying the broad middle strata of the orthodox social hierarchy. Much smaller groups of Muslim and Christian immigrants, who had long been fully integrated into village and urban cultures and had centuries of religious and artistic syncretism behind them in Bihar and Uttar Pradesh, continued to participate actively in the predominantly Hindu-oriented, but equally syncretist, Indo-Guyanese culture on plantations and in village settlements.

GUYANESE MUSIC WITH NORTH INDIAN ROOTS

Hindi and Bhojpuri folk songs associated with the seasonal, agricultural, and life-cycle rituals and festivals of the traditional Hindu ritual calendar have flourished in these settings fairly vigorously, and remain very similar to their ancestral originals.

Chowtal (Hindi *cautāl*) is the communal music of Holī, the spring festival; songs with catchy verse rhymes are sung in a *gol*, a circle of singers made up of two sections, in a call-and-response style between the two parts, as each tries to outdo the other in diversity of verses, duration, and energy of singing. Singing begins slowly, in a kind of recitative, and rises to a crescendo with a joyful, boisterous energy and punctuated with ecstatic shouts. Each singer plays *jhāl* 'pair of hand cymbals', and a drummer

FIGURE 1 Choir of rural East Indian girls at the centennial celebrations commemorating the start of Asian Indian immigration to Guyana. Georgetown, 1938. Photographer unknown. Photograph from the Jung Bahadur Singh Photographic Collection. Courtesy Rajkumari Cultural Center, New York.

plays a *ḍholak* 'small double-headed drum', using both hands. Traditionally, *chowtal* was performed only by men; nowadays women also participate.

In contrast, traditional songs of birth and marriage have remained the exclusive territory of women, who often accompany themselves on the *ḍholak* drum. Usually, respected elderly grandmothers lead the singing with the chorus repeating the verses. *Sohar*, nativity songs offered at the birth of Hindu babies, are often sung unaccompanied in a steady, slow rhythm and with a tender treatment appropriate to cradle songs or lullabies. *Mouran* are songs performed just after birth, when an infant is taken to the waterside for the *mouran* ceremony, in which the baby's head is shaved in purification. This is followed by the *nahān*, a sacred healing bath in the water.

The *vivāh*, or Hindu wedding, includes a variety of women's songs. For example, two nights before the wedding, the bridegroom's mother goes in procession to the waterside, accompanied by female relatives and friends and male drummers. There the *matkor* ceremony takes place, in which earth is collected to form an altar to Mother Earth in the nuptial home. Women sing Bhojpuri songs in a light, fast tempo with bawdy, humorous texts on themes of fertility and procreation.

Another musical form from nineteenth-century North India that continues to flourish in Guyana is the ceremonial and processional *tāssā*-drum music played at seasonal and life-cycle ceremonies, as well as other outdoor events like *mela* 'fairs'. The traditional *tāssā* ensemble comprises a bass or "boom" drum (known as *bedam* or *dhāp*), at least two high-pitched, bowl-shaped earthenware kettledrums (*tāssā*, from which the ensemble gets its name), and a pair of large metal hand cymbals (*jhāñjh*). Continuous and repeated ostinato patterns are played on these instruments, with the exception of one *tāssā* drum, which is used for flashy, virtuoso improvisational passages.

Chutney or *chatni* (literally 'hot and spicy') is the most popular contemporary genre of Indo-Guyanese music. It derives from the kinds of songs with ribald texts that women sing at the *matkor* ceremony. Chutney has a spicy, playful musical style, and is used for relaxed social entertainment. Some of its characteristics reflect ancestral prototypes. Puns and other wordplay draw on the culinary arts to create sexual innuendo, such as the theme of flirtatious play within the joint family system involving the older sister-in-law and the brothers-in-law. The genre continues to serve as a frank expression of uninhibited sensuality and a benign tolerance of sexual indiscretion. New compositions, not only in Hindi but also in English creole (or a mix of the two), often comment on the Indo-Guyanese social scene, with satiric and comic treatment of the foibles and frailties of authority figures such as the sly, lascivious *paṇḍit* 'priest', the fun-loving *nānī* 'grandmother', and the domineering mother-in-law.

Some Indo-Guyanese art forms did not fare well with the passage of time. The pattern of agrarian settlement by indentured laborers who stayed on in Guyana and did not return to India was hospitable to ancestral village traditions, but in time the Guyanese English creole dialect, which included a strong mixture of Indic vocabulary, replaced the ancestral languages as the mother tongue of the Guyanese-born descendants. By the time Guyana became an independent nation in 1966, Guyanese of Asian Indian ancestry constituted the ethnic majority of the population, and almost all spoke only English creole. At the same time, there was a more widespread recognition of the decline of several heritage art forms, which are now kept alive by a few elder custodians and younger disciples, but in general are sadly neglected and without much fashionable contemporary appeal.

Two of these declining and increasingly obscure art forms are nevertheless the most distinctive Indo-Guyanese variations on ancestral originals. Formed during the first half of this century, they have a unique, local, diasporic flavor. In nineteenth-century North India, *birahā* singing and *nagārā* drumming and dancing existed as separate and distinct folk forms of the Ahīr caste, people who raised cattle especially for milk and butter (from which they made *ghī* 'clarified butter'). *Birahā* are Bhojpuri songs consisting of short rhymed couplets sung in a loud voice to a repeated melody by a solo male performer. The *nagārā* is a large, stately drum, 180 to 245 centimeters tall; drumming on the *nagārā* is accompanied by a vigorous male solo dance. In Guyana, these two performance expressions became fused; performers would sing a *birahā* couplet and then dance to the low, quick *nagārā* rhythm. The entire outdoor performance was also transferred from the open pastures to *mela* 'fairs', as popular entertainment with attractive prizes offered to competing artists.

SOUTH INDIAN–DERIVED RITUAL MUSIC

Although the Hindi-Bhojpuri legacy may be regarded as the "great tradition" of Indo-Guyanese culture, the heritage of the much smaller minority of Asian Indian immigrants from the Tamil language region of South India constitutes the "little tradition." People of Tamil ancestry—and their regional culture—are referred to as
TRACK –18 Madrasi. Madrasi culture centered on ritual worship (*pūjā*) of the South Indian folk mother goddess, Mariamma. Characterized by ecstatic dancing and continuous drumming on the *tappū*, a circular frame drum played with a thin wooden drumstick and a thin sliver of bamboo, these expressions developed in relative isolation during the first half of this century. Since the 1960s, however, a significant influx of Indo-Guyanese of North Indian ancestry into Madrasi temple communities has resulted in an integration of North Indian musical instruments and Hindi songs into Madrasi culture, while at the same time popularizing the "little tradition" beyond its regional and linguistic confines.

CLASSICAL MUSIC TRADITIONS

Tān saṅgīt is a distinct classical style of Indo-Guyanese vocal and instrumental music that flourished until the late 1960s and has since suffered a marked decline. It is practiced today by a small elite of elder custodians, younger masters, and cultivated patrons. The 1990s have seen a revival of interest among diaspora Guyanese in New York City. This style, according to oral history, dates from the late nineteenth century when a young woman immigrant, Subhagia Devi Prasad, performed and taught various vocal genres: a Banaras style of North Indian classical vocal music, including *dhrupad*, an austere temple style without much ornamentation, normally sung by men, and always dedicated to a Hindu deity; *tarānā*, syllabic patterns sung with playful improvisations; *ṭhumrī*, songs of love and separation encompassing phrases of lyrical poetry repeated several times with subtle musical nuances and variations; and ghazal, songs of Persian origin with Urdu texts. The first revered teacher was Guru Dihal, a leading disciple of Subhagia, who played the sitar, tabla, *sāraṅgī* 'bowed fiddle', and *esrāj* 'bowed lute' (figure 2). As musicians and musician-priests from Banaras and the Bhojpuri-speaking region of North India migrated to Guyana, the Guyanese classical style acquired regional musical elements, including the introduction of *jhāl* 'cymbals', *kartāl* 'clappers with metal jingles', and *ḍholak*. From the 1920s to the 1940s, Indian musicians from Lucknow, Calcutta, and Banaras performed concerts of classical music in Guyana, sponsored by wealthy Guyanese East Indians, but by this time *tān saṅgīt* had become a distinctive classical style (figure 3). Guyanese musicians blended elements of the traditional Indian genres with new Indo-Guyanese variations and fusions.

Indo-Guyanese music always recognized the distinction between *mārga* (classical music) and *deśī* (folk), but there was always a fluid symbiosis between the two, with a stronger *deśī* element. For example, bhajan, a popular genre with a rich corpus of

FIGURE 2 Performers from the theatrical production *Savitri*, Georgetown, 1929. *Tān saṅgīt* musicians (front row) include Prahalad Maselall, sitar (fifth from right); Dihal, *ḍholak* (fourth from right); Mrs. Mohammed Omar, singer (third from right); Mohammed Omar, *sāraṅgī* (second from right, partly hidden); and Tilack, *esrāj* (far right). Photographer unknown. Photograph from the Jung Bahadur Singh Photographic Collection. Courtesy Rajkumari Cultural Center, New York.

devotional Hindu songs, blends both *tān saṅgīt* and *deśī* styles. Both *mārga* (*tān saṅgīt*) and regional *deśī* singing styles in Guyana use the same accompanying instruments: *ḍholak*, a cylindrical double-headed drum with goatskin heads that is played with both hands; harmonium, a portable reed organ with bellows; and *ḍhantāl*, a rod struck with a palm-sized, U-shaped pin (both made of brass, iron, or steel). In both forms the human voice is the dominant melodic element. In *deśī* music—*chowtal*, *mouran*, and *matkor*—hand clapping is prominent in keeping the tala rhythm. Similarly robust bhajan and *tān* singing in temples often inspires devotional fervor among devotees, who join in with vigorous hand clapping.

INDO-GUYANESE POPULAR MUSIC

In the 1930s, the arrival of Bombay movies in Guyana gave birth to a new "filmi" musical culture, which became increasingly popular and glamorous, inspiring a new younger generation of "filmi" musicians and singers. This music continues to be a popular and integral expression of the Indo-Guyanese music scene. At about the same time, several musical instruments such as guitar, bongos, mandolin, clarinet,

FIGURE 3 Performers in the theatrical production *Footlights of Hindustan*, Georgetown, 1938. *Tān saṅgīt* musicians, seated on the floor (*left to right*): Mohammed Omar, *esrāj*; Latiff, tabla drum; Nalini Singh, a young dancer; Mrs. Mohammed Omar, harmonium, Maseelall Pollard, sitar. Photographer unknown. Photograph from the Jung Bahadur Singh Photographic Collection. Courtesy Rajkumari Cultural Center, New York.

The first popular East Indian orchestra in Guyana was the Uitvlagt Band, formed in the late 1940s. The group played locally made instruments as well as the tabla and harmonium imported from India, but soon incorporated the violin, guitar, and maracas.

FIGURE 4 The Leonora-Uitvlagt Indian Orchestra combined guitar and mandolin with traditional Indian instruments to play a repertoire that included folk, devotional, semiclassical, and film music. Photographer unknown, 1940s. Photograph from the Jung Bahadur Singh Photographic Collection. Courtesy Rajkumari Cultural Center, New York.

and saxophone began to make their appearance in both popular filmi orchestras and *tān saṅgīt* ensembles, influenced by Western popular music. Programs of *tān saṅgīt* and filmi music broadcast on the radio in Guyana popularized local performance talent among a much wider national audience.

The first popular East Indian orchestra in Guyana was the Uitvlagt Band, formed in the late 1940s (figure 4). The group played locally made instruments (*jhāl* 'cymbals' and *ḍhantāl* 'struck iron rod') as well as the tabla and harmonium imported from India, but soon incorporated the violin, guitar, and maracas, influenced by the use of these instruments in Bombay film music. Following Uitvlagt's lead, numerous popular groups formed all over Guyana, and by the mid-1960s many bands introduced the electric guitar, electric organ, and drum set then dominating Bombay film orchestras (figure 5). By the 1950s, Indo-Guyanese musical taste and performance were also becoming increasingly influenced by popular Afro-Guyanese creole folk songs and vibrant Afro-Caribbean musical expressions such as Trinidadian steel pan and calypso, Jamaican ska and reggae, and more recently, Afro-Indian Caribbean fusions like Trinidadian soca chutney.

Substantial Indo-Guyanese immigration to the United States since the 1960s has created vibrant communities (most of them in the New York metropolitan area) where both traditional and newer trends in music are integral to culture and the performance arts. More musicians and singers have found access to recording facilities, and the production of cassettes and CDs has added a more modern, mass-media dimension to Indo-Guyanese music. This in turn has stimulated a popular Indo-

FIGURE 5 The Swarangeet Orchestra, New York, performs popular filmi and chutney music styles with electric guitars, keyboard, saxophone, and drum set. These musicians reflect the glamorous influence of Western pop and Bombay film cultures. Mid-1990s. Photo courtesy Isardat Ramdehal.

Guyanese nightclub culture, where young people dance to styles such as chutney and soca chutney that have high-tech disco enhancements.

Dancing has been an integral aspect of several heritage music styles. In the past, men and women traditionally danced separately, but there has been an erosion of these restrictions, and nowadays male and female dancers perform together. At a Hindu wedding, women dance with the sensuous and graceful movements of the *matkor* ceremony and other events, but still often unseen by men; men dance in both male and female roles on the night before the wedding. Chutney is also a popular dance style; *nagārā* dancing features a male performer dressed in white knee-length trousers with appliqués of bright colored cloth, mica mirrors, silver beads, and dozens of copper bells. The bells make the costume a musical instrument in itself. *Rajdhar* dancing, with its rich display of intricate footwork, turns, and spins, and its lyrical, expressive face and hand gestures is accompanied by *tān* singing, usually of bhajan, *ṭhumrī*, and *tarānā*. Today, popular dancing by Indo-Guyanese youth—complete with coquettish facial expressions, sinuous arm movements, narrative hand gestures, fancy hip and waist movements, erotic pelvic thrusts and circles, and intricate footwork—echo the heritage of Asian Indian culture.

REFERENCES

British Broadcasting Corporation. 1992. *Worlds Apart; Following Fidel; Shades of Freedom.* New York: Ambrose Video Publishing. Videocassette.

Gosine, Mahin. 1988. *The East Indian Odyssey: Dilemmas of a Migrant People.* New York: Windsor Press.

Rauf, Mohammad A. 1974. *Indian Village in Guyana: A Study of Cultural and Ethnic Identity.* Leiden: Brill.

UNESCO. n.d. *Community Celebrations.* Port of Spain, Trinidad and Tobago: Banyan Studio. Videocassette.

Réunion Island

Monique Desroches
Brigitte DesRosiers

Plantation Temple Music
Urban Temple Music
Sega
Maloya

Réunion Island, an overseas French department situated in the Indian Ocean east of Madagascar, was first discovered by Europeans in the eighteenth century. Initially uninhabited, the island now has a population of approximately 520,000. During the eighteenth and nineteenth centuries, many West Africans (whose descendants are known in Creole as the Kaf), Indians (Tamil and Telugu speakers), and people from the coast of Zenguebar (Quiloa and Zanzibar) were brought to Réunion Island as slaves. The island's name aptly describes this assemblage of diverse peoples, none of whom is native to the island.

The end of slavery in 1848 followed by the immigration of more Indians, both Muslims (called Zarabs) and Hindus (called Malbars), as well as some Chinese and Comorians (from the Comoros Islands northwest of Madagascar) brought about major social changes. Among these changes was a division within the French population between the previous rich plantation owners (the Grands Blancs) and the poorer farmers (the Petits Blancs).

Music in this complex cultural mosaic plays the role of social identifier, although boundaries are fluid, determined not only by ethnic origins but also by values. Some Réunion musical styles remain within the confines of a particular ethnic group. Others transcend cultural boundaries, resulting in a form of musical expression that bonds the island to other creole islands (Desroches and Benoist 1991, 1997). Given the dynamics of social fragmentation, cultural identities tend to become somewhat blurred. People of Chinese descent, for example, can conceivably define themselves first and foremost as Réunion Islanders, then as Chinese, and then again as French. Some specialists in creole societies refer to this phenomenon as "cumulative identity" (Fuma and Poirier 1994) or "situational belonging" (Benoist 1994).

This article concentrates on two types of music in particular—ritual music of Indian origin among Indian descendants, and popular music of European, African, and Malagasy origin common to all Réunion Islanders. These two cases serve to identify the role music plays in building cultural identity among diasporic communities.

PLANTATION TEMPLE MUSIC

Musical practice among Réunion Islanders of Indian descent is an extension of the values, beliefs, and customs of their Indian ancestors. Contemporary Indian society on the island comprises two main religious as well as musical traditions: those of the Hindu temples on the plantations and those of the urban areas. (Muslims represent less than 5 percent of the total population.) Tamil Hindu music on the island invokes three deities: Mariemen (in India, Mariamman), Kali, and Pandyale (a heroine of the Mahabharata epic).

The coastal sugarcane plantations on Réunion Island shaped the island's economic and social life in the time of slavery. Musical performance in Hindu temples on the plantations stemmed from a deep-rooted village tradition in India. The style persists today, and is recognizable first and foremost by its instrumentation, composed almost exclusively of membranophones as well as certain percussion instruments such as *tāḷam* 'small cymbals' and bells.

The music of the plantation temples is essentially that of the drums. The *śakti* 'single-headed drum' and the *tapou* 'frame drum', also referred to by the islanders as Malbar drums, accompany the annual Marche dans le Feu 'firewalk' (Barat 1989; Desroches and Benoist 1997) (figure 1). Sometimes the *ulké* 'hourglass drum' (also called a *bobine*) joins the ensemble. The priest plays the hourglass drum, which permits him direct contact with the gods. This ceremony usually occurs in January or June and celebrates the virginity of the goddess Pandyale. The *tapou* drums also accompany the annual festival celebrating Kali, which is usually held sometime between June and October. Imported from southeastern India during the slave period, the *tapou* is struck by two sticks of different sizes, one of which sounds the fortissimo strokes, the other the pianissimo. Through a complex and delicate display of drum beating, the musicians produce a call to specific gods they wish to implore, a code that ensures the smooth running of the ritual.

TRACK 17

The music of the plantation temples is distinguished by the circularity of the musical message. Each ceremony has a structure based on a limited number of rhythmic patterns (between seven and eleven), and each pattern is associated either with a specific step of the ritual or with a call to a specific god. The drummers repeat the rhythmic pattern for the entire duration of the ceremonial phase or call, since it is important that the message be clearly heard by the gods. The drummers believe the

FIGURE 1 Two *tapou* 'frame drums' and a *śakti* 'single-headed drum' are played to accompany the Marche dans le Feu 'firewalk'. St. Gilles les Hauts, Réunion Island, 1988. Photo by Monique Desroches.

emphasis on repetition increases the chances of communicating successfully with the gods. The plantation temples use music to create gateways that match the profiles and specificities of the gods. The drums, for example, define whether the call is to a vegetarian or to a carnivorous god. In this way the drums assure the efficacy of the ritual (Desroches 1996; Desroches and Benoist 1983, 1997).

The musicians must all play the same rhythm at the same time, resulting in a strictly coordinated, vertical conception of music. The interpretation and improvisation that characterize other Indian musical spheres are here completely absent from musical practice.

URBAN TEMPLE MUSIC

This form of temple music follows a totally different religious and musical logic. Since the end of the nineteenth century, merchant associations have managed Hindu temples built in urban areas. Rich urban temple associations organize the teaching and performance of Indian classical music, which adds to the "Indianization" of the island culture. They have tended to transform and diversify the musical practices of the plantation temples, including instrumentation, musical styles, and melodies, as urban templegoers wish to distance themselves from the Indian village heritage. If ever an urban temple hires a plantation musician to play at a service, he must not bring his Malbar *tapou* drums since these serve to invoke the gods: in an urban temple, templegoers honor them. Urban temple music embellishes ritual rather than structuring it; the use of the drum for direct communication with the gods, as in the plantation firewalk, would be completely inappropriate.

Various instrumental ensembles perform during the Fête de Dix Jours 'Ten-Day Festival' dedicated to the god Muruga (Murugan in South India). The ensemble accompanying the festival procession comprises the *narslon* 'Indian oboe' of the *nāgasvaram* family, the *molon* 'double-headed cylindrical drum', with one head struck by a stick and the other by the hand, and the *tāḷam* 'small cymbals' (figure 2). This ensemble plays outside the temple; once the believers enter the temple, another ensemble joins the gathering. A portable harmonium, tablas, and cymbals accompany Tamil devotional bhajans inside the temple. The tablas introduce yet another conceptual and stylistic world. Improvisation and a more linear approach contrast with the circularity and repetition of the plantation firewalk.

FIGURE 2 Instruments played in the Fête de Dix Jours 'Ten-Day Festival' dedicated to the god Muruga: *molon* 'double-headed cylindrical drum' and *narslon* 'Indian oboe'. Saint-Paul, Réunion Island, 1988. Photo by Monique Desroches.

The ritual music of urban temples, like that of plantation temples, serves to promote the cultural identity of the templegoing community. Urban temple music reflects affiliation with contemporary India rather than any link with plantation values that are deemed inferior. Urban devotees, being strictly vegetarian, exclude animal sacrifices from their worship ceremonies, and consequently also exclude the *tapou* drums associated with such sacrifices in plantation temples. Use of the newly introduced portable reed organ (harmonium) symbolizes this "Indianity" trend. In contrast, rituals performed by devotees in rural plantation areas are rooted in insular traditions of the eighteenth- and nineteenth-century plantations that emphasize cyclical drumming patterns, trance possession, and animal sacrifice. The *tapou* drum is symbolically at the heart of this trend, known as "Malbarity" from the term *Malbars*, referring to Hindus living in rural plantation areas.

SEGA

If there is one musical style that links all Réunion Islanders, it is the popular genre *sega*, with the *maloya* a close second.

According to the linguist Robert Chaudenson (1981), the etymology of *sega* (originally pronounced "tsiega" or "tchega," and most likely from Swahili) seems to confirm the African origins of the word. It is a music characterized by a vivid and syncopated rhythm, the result of a fusion of African rhythms and European dance music.

Sega has undergone many transformations. The original accompaniment was the violin, but other instruments were gradually added—first the mandolin and then the banjo, which became so popular that the violin simply disappeared. The diatonic accordion joined the instrumentation, but was soon replaced by the chromatic accordion. Finally guitars and brass instruments appeared, with a full drum set providing the rhythmic support. The traditional *sega* may employ the *oulé* (*rouleur, ouleur*) 'large cylindrical drum' with a cowskin head; the *kayamb* (*kayamn, caimbe*), a raft-shaped rattle made from a double row of sugarcane sticks placed in a frame, between which vegetable seeds are inserted; a triangle; and sometimes a guitar or accordion.

Sega music today has simple tonic-dominant harmonies played on the guitar, a syncopated rhythm featuring the juxtaposition of binary and ternary rhythms, and lyrics of a light nature. Nowadays. the young tend to consider *sega* outmoded; it is largely confined to tourist productions in hotels or folkloric music festivals outside the island, but elements of *sega*, such as the guitar style as well as the harmony, have nevertheless penetrated the recent musical practices of young people.

MALOYA

The term *maloya* can refer not only to music but to certain dances and the songs that accompany them, to all appearances inherited exclusively from the Malagasy and African slave populations. The repertoire is wide ranging, including styles or creations along traditional lines as well as those of a modern character featuring elements usually associated with Western music. The *maloya* generally follows one of three main trends in performance practice.

The first style recalls the *maloya* tradition as preserved in rural areas and performed by older musicians such as Granmoun Lélé, Le Rwa Kaf, and Firmin Viry. This has a single vocal line with choral response, always sustained by a group of percussionists who sometimes act as chorus members. A dance traditionally accompanies the singing. As in the *sega,* the stressed rhythm has a characteristic juxtaposition of binary and ternary meters. LaSelve describes the music (LaSelve 1984:26, translated by Monique Desroches and Brigitte DesRosiers):

The political use of the *maloya* had a considerable influence on the development of popular music on Réunion Island, and resulted in a polarization between *maloya* and *sega* music. Proponents of each genre claimed that theirs was the authentic music of the island.

> The singer starts the first line of his recitative, provoking a response from the audience, or at least the rest of the band. This unaccompanied call is repeated with progressive support of all instruments, which, unlike the singers, will tirelessly provide a stressed rhythm. Quickly the music provokes a general corporal response from participants, who begin to dance in addition to answering the soloist.

The basic instrumentation consists of the *houlé* (*roulé, oulé*) 'cylindrical drum', which the player strikes with the hand while sitting on the front of the drum, the *kayamb* 'rattle', the *piké,* an idiophone made of bamboo mounted on an iron frame and played with sticks, the *sonbrer* 'a combination of two *piké*', and a triangle. A musical bow with affixed resonator (*bobre*) often augments this instrumental ensemble. The player strikes the bow with a thin stick, and embellishes the resultant sound with a small rattle of braided straw held in the same hand as the stick.

Autret divides this type of *maloya* into two subcategories: the *maloya* of the "cult of the dead," whose binary rhythms musicians call "warlike," and the "profane" *maloya*, played in "the cult honoring the ancestors" (*kabares*) and characterized by ternary rhythms (Autret 1993:38). The traditional *maloya* repertoire has now changed, and is performed in theaters, community halls, and nightclubs.

The second type of *maloya* relates closely to the first, retaining the traditional instrumentation and stylistic aspects of the accompaniment, but modifying the vocal themes with more politically engaging and socially relevant topics. This type appeared at the end of the 1960s, in conjunction with the social awareness of a specific Réunion identity. The most prominent practitioner of this category is undoubtedly the poet and singer Danyel Waro. Purist to some, integrationist to others, he is considered by the islanders to be the most accomplished artist of his generation. They refer to this particular style as *maloya sèk* 'dry', referring to the lack of electric amplification characteristic of this category.

The third stylistic current has appeared in recent years, marked by the inclusion of Western popular-music elements. Part of the emerging "world music" category, it is referred to as "electric *maloya*," "*maloya* moden" (meaning "modern"), or "*maloya* fusion." Groups such as Ziskakan, Basker, Ti Fock, and Na Essayé are representative of this style. Their foundations rest on a fusion of traditional *maloya* and *sega* with jazz and rock music that also incorporates African and Antillean rhythms such as reggae.

***Maloya* as a collective genre**

Until the end of the 1960s, *maloya* was exclusively rural in character. A convergence of events interrupted the peaceful existence of the *maloya,* hurtling it from relative obscurity into the public eye. Rural inhabitants were becoming increasingly aware of their cultural specificity and of longstanding social inequities. The Communist Party of Réunion Island (PCR) launched the *maloya* on a grand scale, using music to underline social and political claims.

The PCR promoted *maloya* as the music of the common people, whether Petit Blanc, Kaf (people of African descent), Chinese, or Malbar, since they shared the same social and economic problems. Composers combined lyrics expressing political ideas with traditional melodies and instruments. The *maloya* became the privileged vehicle of expression of the *fè nwar* (French: *fait noir* 'black deed'—clandestine or illicit activities).

The *maloya* thus acquired a stigma through its identity with the counterculture; this led to the government's banning existing *maloya* groups as well as any music expressing antiestablishment sentiment. The performance ban on militant musical groups such as Ziskakan (until the early 1980s) reflected a rejection of their autonomist stance as well as their association with the PCR.

The *sega-maloya* relationship

The political use of the *maloya* had a considerable influence on the development of popular music on Réunion Island, and resulted in a polarization between *maloya* and *sega* music. Proponents of each genre claimed that theirs was the authentic music of the island. A *sega* or *maloya* performance became an affirmation of allegiance, be it social, political, or cultural, and still is today. Those advocating *maloya* consider the *sega* a throwback to the time of slave-masters, colonialists, and capitalists that plays into the hands of those who would seek to dominate or exploit the island. Thus the terms *sega* and *maloya* refer not only to actual musical entities but to more abstract phenomena of mentality or spirit.

Sega and *maloya* crystallize the many dualities typical of Réunion society—purity/interbreeding, black/white, slave/colonialist, Native/European, old/young, and authentic/commercial—and symbolize the search for an identity by Réunion Islanders. This search could result in the synthesis of yet another new style that would serve as a sort of identifying flag for the whole of Réunion society, and might bring legitimacy through musical expression.

REFERENCES

Autret, Frédérique. 1993. "Introduction au maloya traditionnel de la Réunion, un genre musical en mutation." Master's thesis, University of Paris-Sorbonne.

Barat, Christian. 1989. *Nargoulan*. Saint-Denis, La Réunion: Du Tramail.

Benoist, Jean. 1994. "Le métissage: biologie d'un fait social, sociologie d'un fait biologique." In *Métissages*, ed. Bernard Cherubini, 13–22. Paris: L'Harmattan.

Chaudenson, Robert, et al. 1981. "Musiques, chansons et danses." In *Encyclopédie de la Réunion*, vol. 5, 75–107. Saint-Denis, La Réunion: Livres Réunion.

Desroches, Monique. 1996. *Tambours des dieux*. Montréal: Harmattan.

Desroches, Monique, and Jean Benoist. 1983. "Structure sonore d'un espace sacré." *Études créoles* 5(1–2):39–58.

———. 1991. *Musiques de l'Inde en pays creoles*. University of Montreal, UMM 201. Compact disc.

———. 1997. "Musiques, cultes et société indienne à la Réunion." *Anthropologie et Sociétés* 21(1):39–52.

DesRosiers, Brigitte. 1992. "Ile de la Réunion: musiques et identité." *Canadian Folk Music Journal* 20:47–54.

———. 1993. "Analyse de la relation entre les discours sur la musique et les stratégies identitaires à l'île de la Réunion." Master's thesis, University of Montreal.

Fuma, Sudel, and Jean Poirier. 1994. "Métissages, hétéroculture et identité culturelle." In *Métissages*, ed. Bernard Cherubini, 49–65. Paris: L'Harmattan.

LaSelve, Jean-Pierre. 1984. *Musiques traditionnelles de la Réunion*. Saint-Denis, France: Fondation pour la Recherche et le Développement dans l'Océan Indien.

Fiji

Donald Brenneis

The Republic of Fiji in the western South Pacific consists of approximately 320 islands, one-third of which are inhabited. About 350,000 descendants of indentured immigrants who arrived from India mostly between 1879 and 1919 now make up 46 percent of the population. About two-thirds of the immigrants arrived through Calcutta, coming primarily from the Gangetic plain; others, mostly Tamil- and Telugu-speakers, departed from Madras; a few were Gujarati merchants and Sikhs. About 11 percent of the present-day community are Muslims, and some are Christians, but most are Hindus. Fiji Hindi, a cluster of linguistic varieties most closely related to Bhojpuri (of eastern Uttar Pradesh), is the most widely spoken and sung language in the community.

The Fiji Indian musical world, though based on genres and instruments brought from India, includes new styles and genres from South Asia, introduced by visiting pandits and Muslim teachers through printed songbooks, Hindi films, and recordings; Western popular musics; and distinctively Fiji Indian kinds of performance, representing local transformations of these sources.

Some old genres, especially those associated with local subcastes (*jāti*), have disappeared or are known by only a few singers. Live musical performances and, since the rise of a national cassette industry and increased local programming on Radio Fiji, music recordings have consistently been a focus of entertainment, devotion, social life, and identity among Fiji Indians. Fiji Indian musical styles have distinctive forms and flavors, influenced by their South Asian antecedents but shaped by local interests, resources, and aesthetics (Brenneis 1983, 1985, 1987, 1991; Brenneis and Padarath 1975).

MUSICAL CONTEXTS AND GENRES

The most common ensemble is a trio: harmonium; *ḍhol,* a mid-size double-headed drum; and *bottil,* a pair of upright, empty, one-liter Fiji Bitter bottles, struck rhythmically on the neck with a pair of heavy nails, or *mañjīrā,* finger-held cymbals. Singers usually play harmonium. Performing secular music and devotional pieces, these ensembles figure centrally at Hindu and Muslim gatherings, weddings, and informal social evenings at home.

Most rural Fiji Indian music is song (*gīt*). The most commonly performed genre is *bhajan kavvali,* a style of Hindu devotional singing associated with *kavvali* (qawwali), a Muslim style. *Bhajan kavvali* consists of couplets, repeated whole or in part, with alternating slow and fast passages. Slow passages are usually sung solo and unaccompanied; faster passages, often multiple repetitions of the same couplet, add drum and bottles, and often a harmonium, doubling the melody.

The melodic form of slow passages is usually a descending terrace, the lowest pitches being sung in the middle of the line. The slower lines often invert the terrace: the singer's voice rises to the highest tone, and then descends. Since melodies stay toward the top of singers' ranges, this pattern combines a slow tempo with considerable vocal tension, giving such passages what villagers interpret as a sense of stress and intensity. In contrast to the usually antiphonal and choral form of South Asian qawwali, and of antecedent Hindu forms (like *harikīrtan*), *bhajan kavvali* is a solo style, as are related secular genres, including *Fiji kavvali,* narrative songs about historic or current events.

A second common genre, in this instance linked with the ritual calendar, is *cautāl* or *fāg,* named for the Hindu month when it is performed. A critical part of the Hindu festival of Holī, pieces in this genre stimulate in Fiji a sense of fun and hilarity. The songs are performed by a group of ten to twelve musicians, usually village men and boys, who go from household to household singing and being fed tea and sweets. Villagers call *cautāl* an archaic form. Two lines of four to six men, each line facing the other, sing responsorially. Several men on either side play *jhāñjh,* 10-centimeter-diameter brass cymbals. A *ḍhol* player sits at one end of the lines; at the other end, one person shakes a sistrum (*jhika*).

One singer begins a couplet, joined briefly by a drummed flourish at the end of the first line, and by the drum and the other singers on his own side at the couplet's end. The initial side may repeat the same couplet several times, at increasing speed. The opposing side then joins in, overlapping with the end of the first singers' couplets. Instrumentalists play throughout, initially striking the same duple pulses as the singers, but shifting to a triple rhythm against the singers' continuing duple as the repetition of each particular couplet comes to an end. A new couplet is then declaimed, and the pattern repeats.

Cautāl heard between 1970 and 1984 ranged from four to sixteen couplets in length. The melodic range is restricted when compared to that of *bhajan kavvali*; it usually stays within a fifth. The melody for each line of a couplet descends, though with frequent short midline rises. In contrast to *bhajan kavvali, cautal* are loud, multivoiced, and heard by their audiences as exceptionally exciting and festive. The moral didacticism of texts central to *bhajan kavvali* is unimportant for these songs, even when the texts are borrowed from the *bhajan kavvali* genre.

The basic harmonium ensemble is often supplemented by Western instruments (especially a clarinet), and by other Indian percussive instruments, especially the *daṅḍa tāl,* an iron bar struck rhythmically with an iron rod. Other instruments are used with particular genres of devotional singing. Tambourines (*kajalī*) are played with *ḍhol* (figure 1) in an antiphonal style associated with readings of the Ramayana, a sacred text.

For one variety of song, a soloist sings a *tambūrā bhajan* while accompanying himself on a two-stringed drone (*tambūrā*), plucked with one hand, and small paired wooden clappers with metal disks attached (*kartāl*), shaken with the other (figure 2). The *hudka,* an hourglass drum whose pitch is controlled by pulling or releasing the lacings around the head, is now primarily a curiosity, but was historically associated with specific lower castes in India. Similarly, the *mridang,* a large, double-headed drum brought to Fiji by members of the low-status Chamar subcaste, was initially

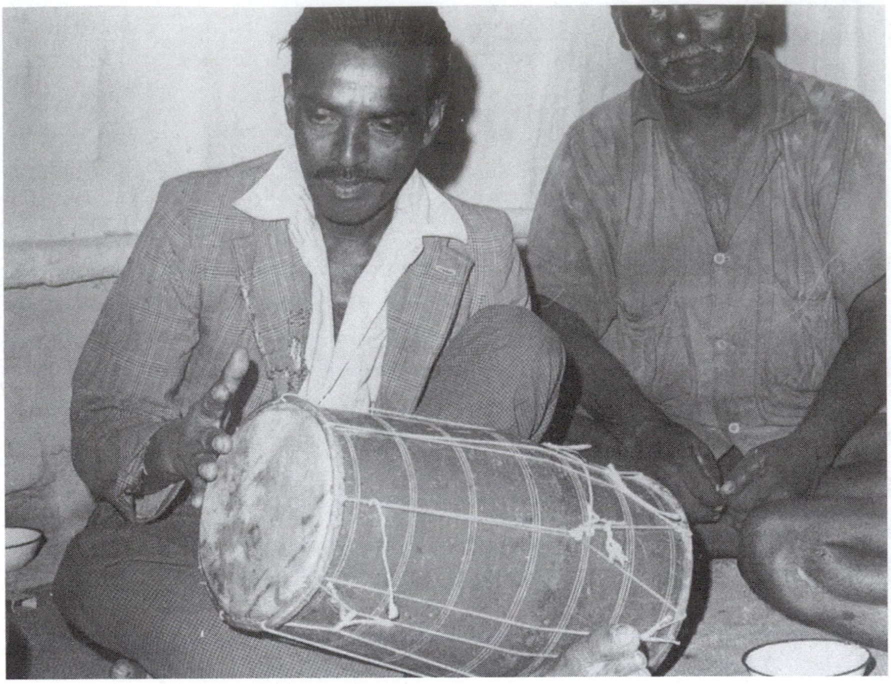

FIGURE 1 *Ḍhol* player at a *tambūrā bhajan* session, Bhatgaon, Fiji, early 1970s. Photo by Andrew Arno.

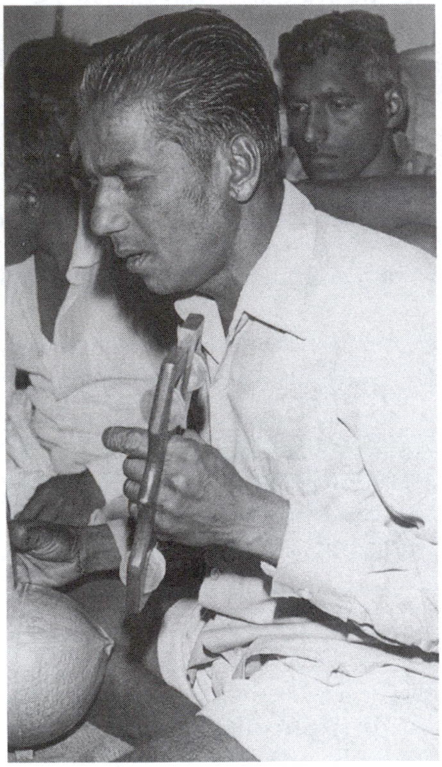

FIGURE 2 *Tambūrā bhajan* singer playing *kartāl* and *tambūrā*, Bhatgaon, Fiji, early 1970s. Photo by Andrew Arno.

used in caste-specific devotional and ritual settings, and now is occasionally played for secular performances, but not for religious music.

Some women have become known for singing *bhajan kavvali,* but women's most frequent public performances occur at Hindu weddings, whose events last several days. Songs for nuptial stages—anointing with oil (*telwan*), insulting the groom's party on its arrival at the bride's homestead (*gālī*) and on the day of the wedding—are still common, though women known to be specialists are often invited to help out. *Gālī* songs also figure in male singing at weddings and challenge-song sessions, in which two solo singers, each accompanied by harmonium, *ḍhol,* and bottles, question, challenge, and abuse each other. Such insults should be borne with good grace, though fights occasionally break out. In addition to older genres, film songs (*filmī gīt*) are exceptionally popular. As with earlier imports, they have provided a range of stylistic resources and inspiration for Fiji Indian singers.

REFERENCES

Brenneis, Donald. 1983. "The Emerging Soloist: *Kavvali* in Bhatgaon." *Asian Folklore Studies* 42:67–80.

———. 1985. "Passion and Performances in Fiji Indian Vernacular Song." *Ethnomusicology* 29:397–408.

———. 1987. "Performing Passions: Aesthetics and Politics in an Occasionally Egalitarian Community." *American Ethnologist* 14:236–250.

———. 1991. "Aesthetics, Performance and the Enactment of Tradition in a Fiji Indian Community." In *Gender, Genre, and Power in South Asian Expressive Traditions,* ed. Arjun Appadurai, Margaret Mills, and Frank Korom, 362–378. Philadelphia: University of Pennsylvania Press.

Brenneis, Donald, and Ram Padarath. 1975. "'About Those Scoundrels I'll Let Everyone Know': Challenge Singing in a Fiji Indian Community." *Journal of American Folklore* 88:283–291.

South Africa

Jayendran Pillay

Historical Context
The Musical Scene Today
Traditional Music Contexts

HISTORICAL CONTEXT

When South Africans speak of "Asians" they mean Indians, though the "Colored" category also includes other Asian strains and the handful of Chinese who live in South Africa. The first group of Indians to arrive were shipped by the British from India to South Africa in the 1860s as indentured laborers, to work in the sugarcane fields of Natal, one of South Africa's four provinces (Meer 1980). The Indians' arrival in South Africa was the result of a triangular pact among the governments of Natal (South Africa), India, and Great Britain, the British government being in control of the other two at that time (Pachai 1971). The shipments went on until 1911.

Indian South Africans had come from various parts of the Indian subcontinent, and they practiced different religions, belonged to different castes, and spoke different languages. The most common language among the immigrants was Tamil, followed by Hindi, Telugu, and Gujarati. All the Indians brought with them their (mainly Hindu) cultural and religious heritages. Today, Christianity and Islam are significant religious denominations among Indians, but the Indian Christian population consists largely of converts from the still-dominant Hindu culture. The Indian population as a whole is today divided as follows: 70 percent are Hindu, 20 percent Muslim, and 10 percent Christian; the caste system is now mostly extinct (Arkin et al. 1989:95). South Africa boasts the world's second largest Indian population outside India, after the United Kingdom.

South Africa's Indians are perceived as a "closed" group—as they have been since 1911, when the Indian government banned further recruiting of indentured laborers for service in Natal. Two years later, the South African government prohibited voluntary Indian immigration. Thus, nearly all Indians in South Africa today were born there (Pillay 1994b). And the cultural and racial diversity of South African society affords them a wide range of musical choices.

THE MUSICAL SCENE TODAY

The role of music in the Indian community is as profound as it is diverse. Indian music has limited exposure on television, although state-run and partially privatized

Adults and children affiliated with community-run Indian schools and local temples participate in annual local and national music competitions, which are an important means of maintaining Indian culture in South Africa.

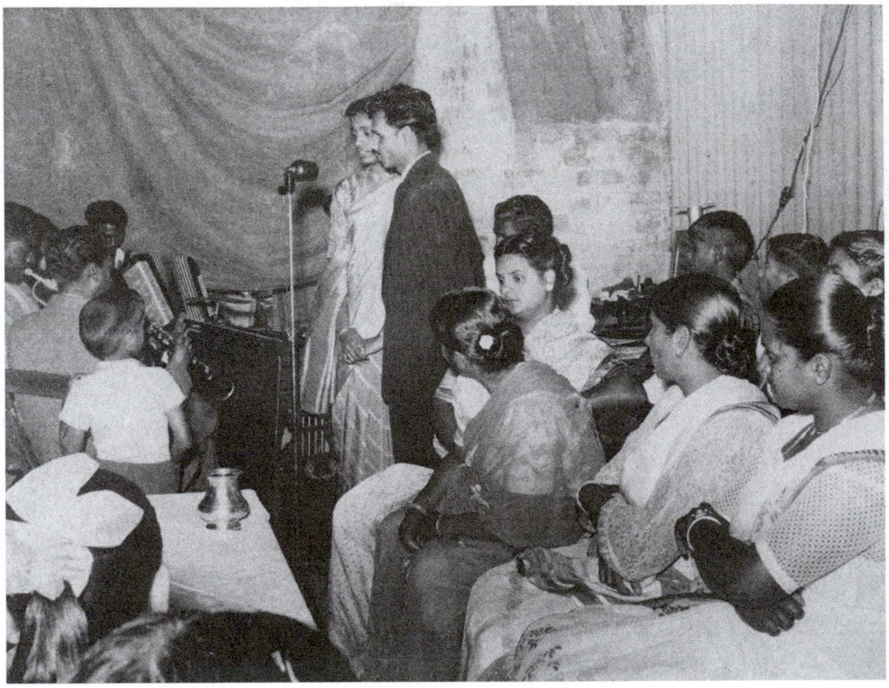

FIGURE 1 Savatri Pillay (*left*) sings a duet with Dorrie Francis (*right*) in a house concert in Durban, South Africa, early 1950s. Courtesy J. Pillay, personal collection.

radio stations targeting the Indian population of Natal and the Transvaal air primarily Indian film music. Many Indian homes receive these broadcasts, but it is hard to ascertain whether Indians regularly support them. Radio stations playing Western pop seem to be by far the more common choice of the Indian people, especially of teenagers and young adults. It is probably this influence that has produced many good jazz and pop artists among Indians, some of whom have made successful careers, although many aspiring artists were also discouraged through the apartheid system.

This is not to say that Indian music is ignored. On the contrary, many fine Indian music performers and dancers of varying ages also excel, with vibrant community support (figure 1). They might learn informally through a relative or friend, but the more accessible means is to attend a nearby Tamil, Telugu, Gujarati, or Hindi school, where a local resident teaches music, in addition to reading and writing in one of those languages. Adults and children affiliated with community-run Indian schools and local temples participate in annual local and national music competitions, which are an important means of maintaining Indian culture in South Africa.

Western classical music also has a presence disseminated through state-run television and radio networks and British-based public-school music programs. African music—whether work songs, or township music—finds its way through the airwaves, the streets, and marketplaces. It is not uncommon for an Indian to enjoy these musical genres and even for some to be fairly adept in performing them.

TRADITIONAL MUSIC CONTEXTS

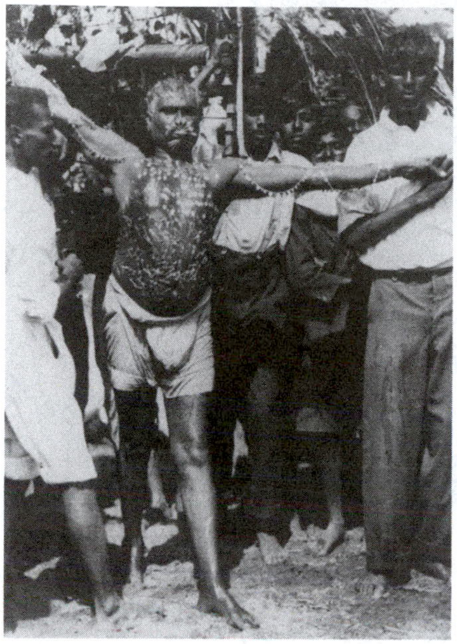

FIGURE 2 A Shaivite devotee, entranced with the spirit of Shiva, participates in the Kavadi Festival. He bears 108 pins on his body, signifying the 108 *mudrā* 'dance gestures' of Shiva. 1930s? Courtesy Local History Museum, Durban, South Africa.

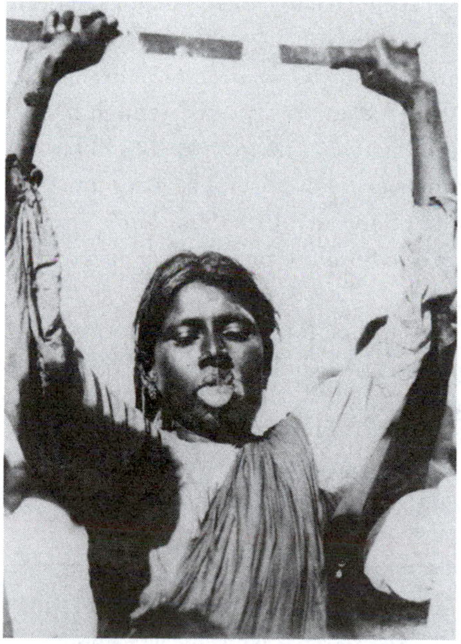

FIGURE 3 A woman entranced with the spirit of Shakti participates in a firewalking ritual honoring Draupati. Her tongue is pierced with the Shakti tridents, while she holds aloft a scythe. 1930s? Courtesy Local History Museum, Durban, South Africa.

Hinduism, Islam, and Christianity are the three principal religions of Indian South Africans (figure 2). Music is always performed in temples and churches; Muslims prefer the simple reading and chanting of scriptures from the Qur'ān in mosques. A fair number of Christians still have traditional Indian names and observe some Hindu customs, such as the lighting of lamps in their homes (but with portraits or statuettes of Christ instead of a Hindu deity, sometimes in combination with Hindu deities). Some of the hymns sung in churches have Tamil or Telugu texts.

Hindu South African temple music is related to the Tamil, Telugu, Gujarati, and Hindi calendar years as they are observed in India. For example, Tamils, who form the largest group within the Hindus of South Africa, celebrate aspects of transplanted "village India" culture, including the Tamil months of Chitrai, Vaikāci, Āni, Ādi, Āvani, Purattāci, Aipaci, Kārtikai, Mārkari, Tai, Māci, and Pankuni. Not only do Tamilians adhere to the rhythmic worship cycles for these months, but they also observe many rituals located within those time cycles. Many Tamils consider the month of Ādi, for example, to be important for invoking the deity Mariamman, the goddess who protects people against smallpox, cholera, and other contagious diseases. Mariamman is a local deity in India but enjoys pan-Hindu devotion in South Africa. Many temples in Natal and a few in Gauteng (the Transvaal) bear her name. The ceremony most identified with her in South Africa is the firewalking ritual. Devotees under trance summon her spirit (in the form of Mariamman, Kali, Durga, Shakti, or Draupati) into their bodies and walk across searing hot coals, showing no signs of pain or discomfort (figure 3). Devotees not under a trance also perform the same ritual, and are equally untouched by discomfort. Ritually, the participants are reenacting the epic moment from the Mahabharata when Draupati walks over fire to prove her faithfulness to the Pandava brothers, or—in a variant from a similar epic, the Ramayana—when Sita walks over fire to prove her chastity to Rama.

Other Indian rituals transplanted on South African soil, each containing a specific repertoire praising the special aspects and powers of particular gods and goddesses, include the Varalakshmi Vrata, Krishna Jayanthi, Vināyakar Chatūrti, Navrātrī, Dīpāvalī, Kārtikai Tīpam, Vaikunta Ekadāsi, Ārudra Darsanam, Ponkal, Tai-Pūsam, Shivarātrī, and the Pankuni Utiram. The *tēvāram* and *tiruvācakam* repertoires in praise of Lord Shiva and the *divyapprabandam* repertoire in praise of Lord Vishnu and his incarnations of Rama and Krishna are particularly popular. Bhajans (temple hymns) are performed generally by South Africans with both North and South Indian roots.

The specifically folk transplantations from South India to South Africa include *terukkūttu*, a ritual theater that reenacts an aspect of the Mahabharata or the Ramayana (figure 4); *nayyandi mēlam*, a processional music group of Indian drums supplemented today by percussion of African and Latin American origin; *kummi*, a dance with hand clapping and possibly lighted lamps; *kōlāttam*, a dance with struck sticks; *kāvaṭi*, a trance dance in honor of Lord Murugan; and *karakam*, a trance dance in honor of Shakti in the form of Draupati or Mariamman. *Kummi* and *kōlāttam* are widely performed in local Tamil schools and often at the temple or the public school in the late afternoons. *Kāvaṭi* and *karakam* dances are not associated with any school, since these are trance-inspired art forms connected with temple rituals. *Terukkūttu*, at one time confined to the rural areas of sugar estates in Natal, has found a new home in Indian townships such as Chatsworth and Phoenix.

FIGURE 4 A group of *terukkūttu* 'street drama' performers ready to participate in the folk version of the Ramayana on the Natal estates, Mt. Edgecombe, South Africa. 1930? Courtesy Local History Museum, Durban, South Africa.

Threatened with extinction, this art form has found new life in academic settings, such as the Speech and Drama Department of the University of Durban-Westville in Natal.

Temple music associated with the Hindi-speaking population is often in praise of Krishna and Vishnu, unlike that of the large Shaivite following among the Tamils. Bhajans (hymns), accompanied by tabla and harmonium, are common song forms at the temples. It is not unusual, however, for songs to be sung in praise of both Shiva and Vishnu at the same South African temple. Nor is it unusual for Hindu South Africans to use both North and South Indian instruments together in temples and in concert performances.

Since the turn of the century, both South and North Indian classical music has grown in popularity in the Indian South African community, even though many young people have turned to pop genres both in the West and in India. A number of local Indians have traveled to India to study music and dance and have returned to teach in South Africa. Also, since the demise of apartheid in 1994, a number of Indians from the motherland have immigrated to South Africa to teach music and dance.

Indian church music in South Africa draws its repertoire from a number of different affiliations, among them the Pentecostal, Catholic, Anglican, German Lutheran, and Seventh-Day Adventist churches, and a number of other Protestant denominations. In a few of these churches, songs are sung in Indian languages as well as in English.

REFERENCES

Arkin, A. J., K. P. Magyar, and G. J. Pillay, eds. 1989. *The Indian South Africans: A Contemporary Profile*. Pinetown: Owen Burgess.

Jackson, Melveen B. 1988. "An Introduction to the History of Music amongst Indian South Africans in Natal, 1860–1948: Towards a Politico-Cultural Understanding." M. Mus. thesis, Natal University.

Meer, Y. S. 1980. *Documents of Indentured Labour Natal 1851–1917*. Durban: Institute of Black Research.

Pachai, Bridglal. 1971. *The International Aspects of the South African Indian Question, 1860–1971*. Cape Town: Struik.

Pillay, Jayendran. 1988. "Teaching South Indian Music Abroad: Case Studies from South Africa and North America." M.A. thesis, Wesleyan University.

———. 1994a. "Music, Ritual, and Identity among Hindu South Africans." Ph.D dissertation, Wesleyan University.

———. 1994b. "Indian Music in the Indian School in South Africa: The Use of Cultural Forms as a Political Tool." *Ethnomusicology* 38(2):281–301.

Part 3
Music Regions

South Asia today comprises a handful of countries—India, Pakistan, Afghanistan, Bangladesh, Nepal, Bhutan, and Sri Lanka—but many diverse cultures. Its musical traditions reflect social and linguistic groupings, not political and geographical divisions. However, as India's state boundaries were drawn along linguistic lines in 1947 and soon after, in this volume its music regions are grouped by geographical area. Pakistan, Afghanistan, Sri Lanka, the Himalayas, and the former province of Bengal (now divided into Bangladesh and the Indian state of West Bengal) are treated as separate music regions.

Each music region thus represents a variety of musical cultures, linked by geographical proximity but mutually distinct in terms of socioeconomic status, religion, and other factors. In contrast to the classical and religious music traditions discussed in Part 2, which are common to broad geographical areas, the peoples and cultures treated in Part 3 represent the enormous diversity of local music and musicians in South Asia. Peoples and places not covered in this volume await the attention of future researchers.

Village women from a bridegroom's family celebrate in marriage rituals, dancing to the rhythms of the *dāireh* 'frame drum' and hand clapping. Herat, Afghanistan, 1977. Photo by Veronica Doubleday.

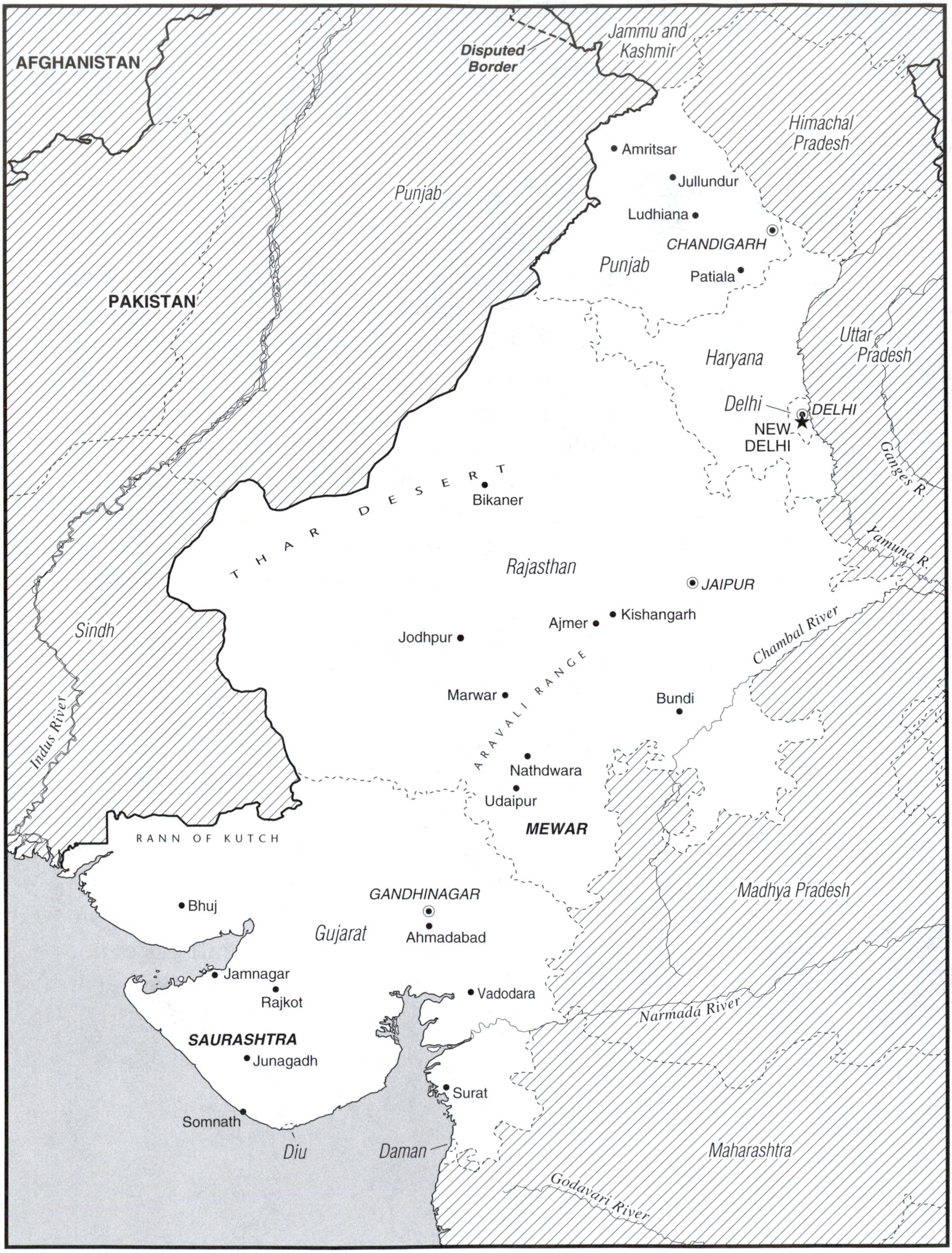
AFGHANISTAN
Disputed Border
Jammu and Kashmir
Himachal Pradesh
Amritsar
Jullundur
Punjab
Ludhiana
CHANDIGARH
Punjab
Patiala
PAKISTAN
Uttar Pradesh
Haryana
Delhi
DELHI
NEW DELHI
Ganges R.
THAR DESERT
Bikaner
Yamuna R.
Rajasthan
JAIPUR
Kishangarh
Ajmer
Jodhpur
Sindh
Chambal River
ARAVALI RANGE
Marwar
Bundi
Indus River
Nathdwara
Udaipur
MEWAR
RANN OF KUTCH
Madhya Pradesh
GANDHINAGAR
Bhuj
Gujarat
Ahmadabad
Jamnagar
Rajkot
Vadodara
Narmada River
SAURASHTRA
Junagadh
Surat
Somnath
Diu
Daman
Maharashtra
Godavari River

Northwest India

In the northwestern region of India, where ruling Rajput warrior clans were patrons of music as early as the sixth century, music and dance are now integral to people's daily lives. Among the majority Hindu population, as well as in the Muslim, Jain, Sikh, and tribal communities, secular and devotional traditions are still passed on from one generation to the next. *Garbā* and *rās* circle dances, devotional bhajans, *kīrtan* performances, Sufi qawwalis, ritual dance dramas, epic songs, and popular bhangra dances are just some of the many forms of musical expression that enrich people's lives in the northwestern states of Gujarat, Rajasthan, and Punjab.

Professional musicians belong to various hereditary musician castes and communities, both Hindu and Muslim. In times past they performed in the royal courts, in processions, and in temples; nowadays they entertain at weddings and festivals. Other professionals, including actors, jesters, genealogists, snake charmers, and epic storytellers, also include songs or instrumental performance in their presentations.

MAP 4 Northwest India

Gujarat

Gordon R. Thompson

The state of Gujarat, situated along India's northwest coast, consists of five major geographical areas: north Gujarat (deserts and mountains along the border with the state of Rajasthan), Kutch (adjacent to Pakistan), the Saurashtra Peninsula, Gujarat (centered around Ahmedabad and Vadodara), and south Gujarat (bordering the state of Maharashtra). Gujarati and Hindi are the primary languages spoken, with Marathi, Urdu, English, and tribal languages important in some areas.

In ancient times, the residents of this region traded with Egypt to the west and through the Indonesian Straits of Malacca, to the east. The physical location of Gujarat made it a convenient point of contact between sea routes and overland roads to the agricultural and military power bases of the Indo-Gangetic valley. Wealth generated by this trade made possible the building of palaces (notably at Junagadh and Vadodara), temples (the most famous of which was at Somnath), and merchants' mansions. In the twentieth century, Gujarat's merchants have not only maintained their economic influence but have gained national political power. Mohandas "Mahatma" Gandhi (who led India to independence) and at least one prime minister (Morarji Desai) were members of this middle class. Furthermore, Gujarati businesspeople and bankers have been in the forefront of building India's industries in the postcolonial era.

The growing affluence of the Gujarati middle class is transforming indigenous music and dance through its support of musical technology (for performance and recording) and the associated media (cassettes, radio, and television). This rise in power of the historically religious middle class is linked to the emergence of Hindu fundamentalism as a potent political and cultural force. Traditional art forms are now being given a nationalistic stamp of approval as defined by their association with identifiably Hindu forms of worship. Nevertheless, the musics of Gujarat reflect the input of peoples from elsewhere in India as well as from western central Asia, at the same time exhibiting a characteristic Gujarati flavor (Thompson 1987, 1997).

GARBĀ

The musical form most broadly associated with Gujaratis, both by outsiders and by themselves, is the *garbo*. Gujaratis generally use the plural form of the word, *garbā*,

FIGURE 1 On the evening before her wedding, the bride-to-be (*right*) dances *garbā* with her friends. Baroda (Vadodara), 1982. Photo by Gordon Thompson.

even when speaking in the singular, perhaps because they seldom perform a single *garbo*. The performance includes three different art forms—music, dance, and poetry—dedicated to Mataji, the collective representation of Gujarat's many mother goddesses. Today, a *garbo* might also be about Krishna, reflecting the incursion of this god's popularity into traditional feminine territory.

The term *garbo* probably derives from the perforated earthen lantern (*garbo*) of the kind around which devotees perform this ritual. However, other possible etymologies seem plausible. The root *garb* 'to go or move' perhaps describes the movement of the dance. The word *garbha* 'womb' (derived from *garbh* 'to conceive') also refers to the inner recess of a Hindu temple where the deity resides and may relate to the dance, which re-creates the shape of a temple around the deity's image.

The cultural origin of *garbā* lies in the celebration of female fertility. Family members and friends traditionally gather to sing and dance *garbā* at a girl's first menses and on the evening before her marriage (figure 1). Gujarati Hindu women (and some men) most typically and widely perform *garbā* during Navrātrī. This nine-night Hindu autumnal festival celebrates the fecundity of the harvest and the myriad mother goddesses worshiped in Gujarat. During this festival, every Gujarati neighborhood festoons an open space with colored lights, and in the evenings dancers and groups of musicians gather. The most important instruments have historically been the *ḍhol* 'large cylindrical, double-headed drum' and the *ḍholak* 'barrel-shaped double-headed drum'. Also common are various types of metallic idiophones such as the *jhāñjh* 'pair of flat cymbals' approximately 20 centimeters in diameter; the *mañjīrā* 'pair of small thick, cup-shaped cymbals'; and rhythmic instruments such as the tambourine. In past times, the *śahnāī* 'oboe' would have led the singing. Nowadays singers in more affluent contexts might accompany themselves on the harmonium or a synthesizer. Furthermore, amplified tapes provide an increasingly common replacement for live musicians.

Dance performance

Many modern urban and suburban Gujaratis value an idealized rustic agricultural past for which *garbā*, with their obvious agrarian associations, are an important metaphor. Modern *garbo* performances have nevertheless become highly stylized.

Women dancers dress in long, colorfully embroidered skirts inset with small mirrors and often decorated with gold or silver thread.

Women perform a *garbo* circle dance by rotating counterclockwise; bending and clapping accompany the responsorial singing. If the number of dancers is large or the dance space small, the women form concentric and oppositely moving circles. In the past, dancers in some locations balanced pots on their heads while dancing; in other locations, men danced holding structures festooned with lamps (*garbī*). In modern performances—in which the dancers' costumes have become effective displays of the wealth and position of their wearers—the dance steps have become increasingly complicated, with spins, twists, and gentle gestures added to the underlying form.

The center of the dance circle and the focus of the dancer's attention is either a pictorial representation of a mother goddess, such as Durga, or a symbolic representation of the goddess's creative aspect. This symbol might take the form of a perforated clay pot (*garbo*) with a lantern inside, or a brass vessel with water inside and a coconut in its mouth. The lantern light as well as the brass container and coconut represent life in the womb; the water represents the role of fluid in fertility. Some traditions employ a basket with sprouting seedlings as a symbol of the life springing from mother earth.

The *garbo,* in its most rustic and fundamental contexts, is a powerful representation of the circle of life and of human reliance on the fertility and productivity of the earth. Women dance and sing for hours (often after fasting) so that the spinning, bending, and repeated refrains provide a psychological release. The goddess rewards the devotees for their sacrifice and devotion. During their dancing and singing, the women see her amid the twinkling of their mirrored skirts.

Musical performance

The musical structure of a *garbo* is circuitous, like the dance. One or two singers begin by singing and repeating the fixed refrain. The leaders then sing a musical verse that is often, but not necessarily, set in a higher or contrasting tessitura. Each musical line connects directly or overlaps with the previous or following lines, the chorus alternating with the soloist(s). After the initial *garbo,* successive songs usually continue without a break.

Garbo texts extol Hindu goddesses both specific to the region, such as Becaraji, and of national recognition, such as Durga, all of whom may be referred to as Mataji or Ambama. In the famous *garbo* "Raṅgatāḷī" 'Painted Hands', the text describes the goddess and her devotees (Thompson and Yodh 1985). The refrain recurs after each verse line (figure 2).

FIGURE 2 The *garbo* "Raṅgatāḷī." Transcription by Gordon Thompson (Thompson and Yodh 1985).

Refrain
Raṅgatāḷī, raṅgatāḷī, raṅgatāḷī re, raṅgamā̃ raṅgatāḷī!
Verses
Mānhe atrīsa, batrīsa jāḷi re, raṅgamā̃, raṅgatāḷī!
Māthe kanakano garabo līdho re, raṅgamā̃, raṅgatāḷī!
Mānhe ratanano dīvaḍo kidho re, raṅgamā̃, raṅgatāḷī!
Mānī oḍhaṇī kasumbā coḷe re, raṅgamā̃, raṅgatāḷī!
Mā kare kankuḍā ghole re, raṅgamā̃, raṅgatāḷī!
Mānhī nānā te vidhanī bhāta re, raṅgamā̃ raṅgatāḷī!
Bhaṭṭa Vallabhane joyānī khānta re, raṅgamā̃, raṅgatāḷī!

Refrain
Painted hands . . . intoxicated with joy, painted hands!
Verses
Within the thirty-two lights/hands, intoxicated with joy, painted hands!
On her head a pot of gold is taken . . .
Inside, a lamp made of jewels . . .
Mother's scarf, saffron colored . . .
Mother's hands, turmeric rubbed . . .
Within these things, infinite designs . . .
Vallabh [the composer] yearns to see this . . .

A song text sometimes contains a devotee's request. In the following *garbo*, "Beṭānī Yācanā," the female devotee asks for a son and for items indicative of prosperity (Meghani 1973; Satyarthi 1951). The text also describes the traditional setting in which a woman lives in the home of her husband's family.

Refrain
Ambājī, āī Mā Becarājī Bāī Mā.
Uñcā, Uñcā oradā canāvo morī, Mā! Ambājī āī Mā!
Verses
Kayā bhāine beṭaḍo dho morī, Mā? Ambājī āī Mā!
Nānubhāine beṭaḍo dho morī, Mā. Ambājī āī Mā!
Nānī bahunī honś pūrī karo morī, Mā. Ambājī āī Mā!
Sonānā̃ pāranā̃ bandhāvo morī, Mā. Ambājī āī Mā!
Kinakhābanā khoyā̃ bandhāvo morī, Ma. Ambajī aī Ma!
Hīranī dorī bandhāvo morī, Mā. Ambājī āī Mā!
Faibā . . . , Bā hiñcoḷe morī, Mā. Ambājī āī Mā!
Dābā̃ te hāthamā̃ dorī morī, Mā. Ambājī āī Mā!
Janana te hāthmā̃ lāḍu morī, Mā. Ambājī āī Mā!

Refrain
Ambaji, O Mother Becaraji Bai.
Have high rooms built, Mother! O Mother Ambaji!
Verses
When will you give me a son, Mother? O Mother Ambaji!
Give a son to younger brother, Mother . . .
Fulfill the young daughter-in-law's desire, Mother. . .
Get a golden cradle made, Mother. . .
Have a cushion made, Mother. . .
Have silken thread used, Mother. . .
Auntie [husband's sister] . . . , will rock the cradle, Mother. . .
In her left hand is the string [used to rock the cradle], Mother. . .
In her right hand is a *lāḍu* [a sweet cake], Mother. . .

Early theologians saw in the *rās* circle dance a powerful symbol of the cosmic relationship between God and humankind.

FIGURE 3 A troupe of young women and girls performs *garbā* at a competition. Baroda (Vadodara), 1982. Photo by Gordon Thompson.

The *garbo* melody for "Raṅgatāḷī" serves both the verse and the refrain (see figure 2). The drum accompaniment at its most basic level is organized around a repeating duple-against-triple figure (*hiñc,* sometimes called *ek tāḷī* 'one clap'), which gives the music a continuous, driving rhythm. The first beat of the time cycle coincides with a clap by the dancers. In performance, the drum strokes are often made to stagger—sometimes ahead of the beat and sometimes behind—but always land squarely on beat 1.

A further propelling factor is the increase in speed and rhythmic density during *garbā* performances. The dancers and music move slowly and gracefully at the beginning of a series of *garbā,* with a single clap (*ek tāḷī*) in each cycle. As the music progresses, subsequent *garbā* are faster paced and the dancers insert two, three, and four claps into each rhythmic cycle.

In the late twentieth century, *garbā* are performed during Navrātrī not only for Mataji worship but also in competitions that attract hundreds of dance troupes (figure 3). Judges throughout the state and in most major Indian cities, as well as some international cities, evaluate the choreography and the costumes of young dancers. Local *garbo* performances are becoming more elaborate, as musicians playing synthesizers and traditional drums accompany the luxuriously garbed dancers of Gujarat's increasingly affluent cities. Even the most traditional of devotees can now learn new *garbo* songs from audiotapes and practice dances recorded on videotape.

RĀS

Rās, like *garbo,* is nowadays performed, both by sexually mixed and by segregated groups, on important occasions such as weddings and at Hindu festivals such as Navrātrī and Holī, which celebrates the arrival of spring. *Rās* performance, dedicated to the worship of Krishna, almost always occurs on the same evening as *garbo,* following the *garbā* performances. When the dancers finish *garbo,* they sing an invocation (*āratī*) to Mataji and retire Her image. They pick up brightly painted and lacquered wooden rods known as *ḍāṇḍiā* 'sticks' and reform a circle for the performance of *rās* (also known as *ḍāṇḍiā rās*). *Rās* is second in popularity only to *garbo,* and is related to a number of other musical, choreographic, poetic, and dramatic forms.

Early theologians saw in this circle dance a powerful symbol of the cosmic relationship between God and humankind. The dance represents the milkmaids of Vrindavan (*gopī*), dancing in a circle around Krishna; the early scholars interpreted this as a symbol of spiritual life revolving around God. With the popularity of Vaishnavism and the tenets of bhakti, the dance took on new meaning in the seventeenth and eighteenth centuries. Krishna simultaneously danced with each and every *gopī*, symbolically representing the individual's personal access to God. Gujarati temple artists have repeatedly employed this theme in their paintings and sculptures.

The tradition of dancing with sticks probably has numerous origins, of which two are most plausible. The first, originally suggested by Arnold Bake (1970), is that the *ḍāṇḍiā* refers to a stick (dibble) used by farmers to make a hole in the ground for planting seeds. Certain *rās* dance movements support this theory: the dancers kneel on one knee and alternately strike their sticks together and against the ground; and in some traditions dancers drop their sticks and act out events in the agricultural cycle related to the harvesting of wheat (*juwār*). Since only one stick is necessary for dibbling, however, agricultural practice does not explain why the dancers each hold two sticks.

The second possible origin for *rās* lies in the martial history of Gujarat and the local Rajput, Kathi, and Koli rulers. The medieval *rāso* epic poem recounts the battles and exploits of the region's kings and generals, and may have been performed with dance in some locales. The *ḍāṇḍiā* may suggest the actions of battle, with each dancer crossing weapons with another, then spinning and facing the next.

In staged performances, an offstage group of male musicians provides the music. Typically, the ensemble includes a singer playing a harmonium, one or more membranophones (*ḍhol, ḍholak,* and/or tabla) and one or more pairs of metallic concussion idiophones (*mañjīrā, kāsījoḍa,* and/or *jhāñjh*) played by the members of the chorus. Historical depictions of the dance show the dancers themselves singing and playing drums, cymbals, and what appear to be plucked drone instruments.

Dance performance

The dance configuration for *rās* consists of two integral and concentric circles moving in opposite directions. The two circles face each other, with the inner circle facing outward and the outer circle facing inward. Each dancer usually holds two *ḍāṇḍiā,* one in each hand. In the basic sequence of dance movements, the dancers (1) strike the outstretched right-hand stick of their current partner in the complementary circle, (2) strike their own two sticks together, (3) strike the left-hand stick of their partner, (4) strike their own two sticks together, (5) strike their partner's right stick again, (6) strike their partner's left stick again, (7) strike their sticks together, and (8) strike their sticks together again as they rotate to their right and to their next partner. The stick strokes occur on each beat of the eight-beat time cycle. Figure 4 shows this pattern, with "\" or "/"representing the right or left stick, respectively, reaching out to

FIGURE 4 *Rās* stick pattern.

beat	1	2	3	4	5	6	7	8
sticking	\	X	/	X	\	/	X	X

strike the partner's corresponding stick and "X" representing the dancer striking together his or her own sticks.

In some choreographies, the circles are interwoven in a "vine" pattern such that dancers alternately face the inside or the outside of the circle with each incremental rotation of their circle. A number of variations also exist on the above stick pattern, and twirls and partner variations may be added, increasing the complexity of the dance.

Musical performance

Men and women often perform *rās* together, and occasionally men perform it alone, but texts (sometimes described as *rāsaḍo*) are frequently feminine in perspective. Family politics and the worship of Krishna (and mother goddesses) are common topics and are usually stated from the viewpoint of the junior wife (as indicated by the kinds of kinship terms employed). Riddles and bittersweet observations may also be the subjects of *rās*, as well as descriptions of the dance and the dancers.

Rās singing is of two main types: responsorial and solo. The responsorial songs are often indistinguishable musically from *garbā*, and some tunes might even serve both. Solo singing is similar to the musical presentation of *chand*, the most rhythmic style of bardic verse (see below). The two types often occur as two parts of the same performance, the responsorial style coming first and providing much of the music, and the fast-tempo solo style (in which the singer recites the *rās* texts as in *chand*) closing the dance. The performers gradually increase the tempo, perhaps stringing several songs together.

BHAJAN

Perhaps the most popular form of devotional music in Gujarat—indeed in most of India—is the bhajan (sometimes also known as *pada*). Its most common structure is the rhymed couplet (*pada*): the first line, known as the *dhruvapada* 'fixed couplet', is sung at the close of each of the other couplets. Although generally devotional in content, bhajan texts are either didactic or biographical. Many verses by the Gujarati Narsinh Mehta (c. 1414–1481) and by Mirabai (c. 1500–1550), a Rajput from the contiguous Mewar region, are instructive, describing ideal behavior for worshipers to follow. A famous bhajan by Narsinh Mehta repeats as its *dhruvapada* how a religious person, particularly a devotee of the god Vishnu, should act:

Vaiśṇava jana to tene kahīe, je pīḍa parāī jāṇe re,
Paraduḥkhe upakār kare toye, mān abhimāna na āṇe re.

He who is a Vaishnav knows the pains of others,
Soothes others' sadness, is not conceited.

Other verses relate events in the lives of these two devotees, often concerning the clash between personal devotion and social obligations. For example, a bhajan ascribed to Mirabai has the refrain, "*Govindo prāṇ amāro re, māne jaga lāgyo khāro re*" (Govinda is my soul, the world repels me; I love only my Ramaji, I know no other). The bhajan recounts an oft-told story, in which the husband demands that she give up her life with religious mendicants and return to him; she refuses, and he then attempts to have her murdered.

Performers and performances

Devotees sing bhajans with a psychogenic intensity matched by few other cultural behaviors; for many Gujaratis, this is an ideal way to worship. At home, during quiet afternoons before dinner preparations begin, women may sit and sing softly from a collection of bhajan texts (*bhajanāvaḷī*). These might either be in the form of a hand-printed notebook or a published collection (for example, Hazrat 1981). Devotees might also join male or female bhajan groups (*bhajan maṇḍaḷ*) that commonly meet once a week on Thursdays, and on other occasions for festival celebrations (figure 5). Highly trained musicians perform bhajans in their concerts. In particular, classical musicians (especially Hindus) in the North Indian tradition often choose to sing a bhajan at the end of a concert. Skilled singers often render bhajans in tightly rehearsed and florid choral renditions called *sugam saṅgīt* 'sweet music'. Classical and *sugam saṅgīt* performances of bhajans are an important component of the growing cassette market. However, the most substantial representation in this market is by singers who straddle the folk-classical continuum.

A *bhajanik* is an individual with a special aptitude for or dedication to singing bhajans and whom a patron might hire to lead a *bhajan maṇḍaḷ* in an evening of bhajan singing. A *bhajanik* might join with others to form a bhajan group, traveling from village to town, singing in homes, in town squares, and in temple courtyards. Today, such groups reside in cities, where they can find a variety of patrons and their members can find other kinds of work during the day.

A bhajan devotional session commonly begins with the lighting of a small flame on a metal plate with raised sides. A devotee waves the flame in front of a representation of a deity while the bhajan group sings the *āratī*, commonly beginning with the words "*Jaya jagadīśa hare.*" Individual singers then commence bhajans by singing the refrain (*dhruvapada*), the others repeating the music and text couplet responsorially. In most responsorial bhajans, verses alternate with the refrain. The chorus joins in the refrain, although solo singers may present successive verses without refrains, with the chorus repeating each new utterance and the refrain recurring only at the end. Solo performances without chorus are often a combination of these two approaches. The soloist sings the refrain, then several verses followed by the refrain, and after that several more verses, ending with the refrain.

FIGURE 5 Women playing the roles of Radha and Krishna at a neighborhood *bhajan maṇḍaḷ* on the afternoon before the spring Holī festival. The seated women sing while the dancers act out the words. Baroda (Vadodara), 1982. Photo by Gordon Thompson.

The storyteller has been an important fixture in the religious lives of middle-class Gujaratis for several hundred years. His tales contain stories from the Hindu epics and from everyday life in Gujarat.

Musical performance

Singers refer to a bhajan melody as a *ḍhāḷ*, sometimes as a *dhun*. When devotees compose a number of texts to the same melody, they usually reference that tune with one particular text, usually the original text of the composition. Kalelakar's *Āśrama-Bhajanāvaḷī* (1975) provides an example of a bhajan melody identified by its association with a particular text: the bhajan "*Re śira sāṭe naṭavarane varīe*" 'Sacrifice your ego [to be] wed with Lord Krishna' has the instruction "*garabī-ḍhāḷ: Sagapan harivaranu sācū*" 'The [only] true relationship is with God'. This indicates that the singer of the bhajan is to sing the provided text "*Re śira sāṭe naṭavarane varīe*" to the *ḍhāḷ* (melody) of a *garabī* (a kind of *garbo* text), the refrain of which begins with the words, "*Sagapan harivaranu sācū*." Individuals thus compose new bhajans by applying a new text to an existing melody.

Many, if not most, bhajans have a more or less fixed melody. Variation in performance usually takes the form of ornamentation added to the melody or subtle rhythmic changes due to the text. A particular class of *ḍhāḷ*, however, approaches the abstract identity of a classical raga and is characteristically open to particular kinds of improvisation. These bhajan tunes often have names that parallel Hindustani ragas, although most are melodically distinct; they often have a time association as well. Singers associate the melodies *rāmagri* 'worship of Rama' and *prabhātī* 'sunrise' with the predawn and dawn, respectively, and *saṅdhyā* 'sunset' with the evening. Another kind of *ḍhāḷ* is related to different types of bhajan texts, and often has a relatively fixed melody. Such texts might "cut" like a "knife" (*kaṭārī*), contain ideas that should be "drunk" (*pyālo* 'drinking cup'), or contain prophecies (*agām*) (Thompson 1995).

KĪRTAN

Unlike bhajan, which anyone may perform, *kīrtan* is an expression of devotion to God by a religious instructor, often through a combination of music and spoken exegesis. Furthermore, whereas bhajan is a genre, *kīrtan* is more a kind of activity that includes a wide variety of musical forms. The word *kīrtan* derives from the root *kīrt*, meaning "to celebrate, praise, and glorify."

Two important contexts for Gujarati *kīrtan* are the *havelī saṅgīt* 'religious music' of the Vallabhacharya Vaishnav religious sect, and the *ākhyān* 'religious tales' of a storyteller such as the *māṇ bhaṭṭ* tradition. The title *kīrtankār* 'one who does *kīrtan*' describes the best-known musicians involved in these activities. The *kīrtankār* is generally a highly literate man (almost always Brahmin) who leads responsorial singing in a manner similar to that of a *bhajanik*. The *kīrtankār*, however, possesses more sophisticated musical knowledge and skills than the *bhajanik*. He draws on an eclectic musical repertoire that includes devotional songs, classical genres such as *dhrupad*, popular life-cycle songs such as wedding songs (*lagna gīt*) and lullabies (*hāḷaḍū*), and seasonal songs (*ritugīt*) (Meghani 1941). He may be a fine storyteller who, though without an affiliation with any particular temple or religious tradition, will praise

God by recounting stories from the Hindu epics such as the Mahabharata and the Ramayana, supplemented by texts such as the *Bhāgavata Purāṇa*. *Bhajanik* is an achieved status, and individuals who use this title often consciously attempt to obscure their caste affiliations (with notable exceptions). *Kīrtankār*, however, is partially an ascribed status, that is, a hereditary occupation characterized by rights and obligations to patrons' temples and families.

Havelī saṅgīt

For the Vallabhacharya Vaishnavs, a sect established by the Telugu religious scholar Vallabh (c. 1479–1531), *kīrtan* primarily takes the form of *havelī saṅgīt* [see RELIGIOUS AND DEVOTIONAL MUSIC: NORTHERN AREA]. Sect members worship Krishna in his *havelī* (mansion or temple) as a living deity to whom they offer food, clothes, and praises. The Brahmin celebrant is either a *pujārī* 'priest' who comes into direct contact with the image of Krishna in a separated area of the temple or a *kīrtankār* who leads worship through *kīrtan* performance.

When the image of Krishna grants an audience, the priests draw back the partitioning curtains and a male singer-drummer and one or more other musicians lead the devotees in *kīrtan* singing. The traditional drum is the *pakhāvaj*, a hand-played, double-headed barrel drum, but in some present-day performances the tabla drum pair is used. The accompanying instruments may include a *tambūrā* 'long-necked lute providing a drone', *surpeṭī* 'hand-pumped drone aerophone', harmonium, *jhāñjh* 'flat cymbal pair', *mañjīrā* 'small cup-shaped cymbal pair', or (less commonly) a *sāraṅgī* 'bowed, short-necked lute' and *bāṅsurī* 'bamboo flute'.

Worshipers gather in same-sex groups either facing each other (men to the right of the deity, women to the left) or in concentric circles (men closer to Krishna than women). All worshipers sing verses from bound books (often the *Gīta Govinda* of Jayadeva), which contain song lyrics and the name of an appropriate raga for each. The performance is responsorial; the singer-drummer sings a line that the other musicians and the audience then repeat.

The musical structure, according to performers, is *dhrupad*, an ancient form already mentioned in the *Nāṭyaśāstra*, a text written approximately two millennia ago. It consists of a repeating refrain (*dhruvapada*) set in the lower tetrachord of the octave (*sthāī*), and an evolving verse (*pada*) in the upper tetrachord (*aṅtarā*). The ragas employed include those familiar to Hindustani listeners such as *sāraṅg*, *kedār*, and *mālkauṅs*, and some that are more rare like *devgandhār*. *Dhrupad* are set in a variety of talas including *ektāl* (twelve beats), *dhrupad tāl* (fourteen beats), and *trītāl/tīntāl* (sixteen beats). On rare occasions, the *havelī* in some locations present dance dramas involving praise of Krishna (*ḍhāḍhilīlā, jogīlīlā,* and *maiyārilīlā,* for example) performed by hereditary professionals.

Māṇ bhaṭṭ ākhyān

Another type of *kīrtan* practiced in Gujarat is *ākhyān* 'legend, tale'. Its best-known form, *māṇ bhaṭṭ ākhyān*, involves a single male storyteller accompanying himself on a large globular metal pot (*māṇ*). *Bhaṭṭ* is a common surname among Brahmins in Gujarat and means "learned person," although it may have had other meanings in the past. The storyteller (*māṇ bhaṭṭ*) has been an important fixture in the religious lives of middle-class Gujaratis for several hundred years. His tales contain stories from the Mahabharata, the Ramayana, the Puranas, and from everyday life in Gujarat. Traditionally, he would deliver his stories to his merchant and middle-class patrons in a temple or household courtyard, or in a public area such as the town square.

According to the *kīrtankār* Sri Dharmiklal Pandya, the best-known living *māṇ bhaṭṭ* (figure 6), the poet Premanand (c. 1636–1734) translated portions of the epic

FIGURE 6 The best-known living *māṇ bhaṭṭ*, the *kīrtankār* Sri Dharmiklal Pandya performs, accompanied on tabla and harmonium by his sons. He creates rhythmic accompaniment to his religious storytelling by striking the rings on his fingers against the globular pot. Baroda (Vadodara), 1982. Photo by Gordon Thompson.

stories into Gujarati (Premanand 1979). Premanand placed his legendary characters in settings familiar to Gujaratis of his time. Pandya continues this tradition, inserting explanations that help modern listeners understand the ancient texts. *Māṇ bhaṭṭ* storytellers trace their literary and musical heritage to Premanand, a Brahmin from Vadodara whose many original stories and translations Gujaratis credit with the transformation of Gujarati into a recognized national language.

The *māṇ bhaṭṭ* accompanies the stories he sings by slapping rhythmically on the shoulders of the *māṇ*. This globular pot is about 60 centimeters in diameter and has a small neck with a narrow mouth. The performer adorns his fingers with metal rings so that his strokes emit sharp pings. The previous generation accompanied themselves on the *māṇ* while other family members played the cymbals (*jhāñjh*) and barrel drum (*pakhāvaj*). Today, Dharmiklal Pandya's sons accompany his singing and *māṇ* playing with tabla and harmonium.

The principal structural unit of *māṇ bhaṭṭ ākhyān* is the *kaḍavu* 'poetic verse'. The *māṇ bhaṭṭ* sets each *kaḍavu* to well-known tunes, poetic versifications, and repeating musical and poetic motifs. The form concludes with a couplet (*valaṇ*) that sums up the story just presented and often sets the tone for the next *kaḍavu*. The *māṇ bhaṭṭ* commonly pauses between verses to explain the text, sometimes drawing parallels between actions and events in the epics and in contemporary life. Besides the *kaḍavu*, the storyteller may incorporate into his story wedding, devotional, and seasonal songs, and any other musical form familiar to his audience, to make the drama more real.

DRAMATIC FORMS

Temple devotees enact relatively amateur presentations of religious stories (*ākhyān*) with songs and dances. The purpose of such dramatic performances is to present a story in which the temple deity figures prominently, thus honoring the deity. The retelling is itself an act of praise and often occurs on religious festivals.

Perhaps the best-known Gujarati musical drama form is the *bhavāī*. Performances may be professional or amateur, but virtually all honor a deity, usually a mother goddess and frequently the Mother Goddess Bahucharajimata. A professional *bhavāī* performer (*bhavāyā*) is male and traditionally belongs to a caste specializing in *bhavāī* performance.

The most distinctive accompanying instrument is the *bhungal*, a long, thin trumpet. Performers play rhythmic musical figures rather than melodies to create a sonic landscape against which the action takes place. Other accompanying instruments are the tabla, *ḍholak, mañjīrā, jhāñjh,* and nowadays the harmonium.

A *bhavāī* performance commonly begins with a *garabī* (alternative form of *garbo*) extolling the mother goddess and establishing the right emotional atmosphere. The discrete performance unit of *bhavāī* is a short playlet (*veśa*) that refers to the costume and makeup associated with the story. The subject matter either personifies a deity or presents pre-twentieth-century topical themes, particularly stories set in the period of the Gujarat sultans (c. 1600–1800). Troupes may update stories to reflect contemporary tastes (Desai 1972).

THE BARDIC TRADITION

In the early centuries of this millennium, two castes of bards began composing and reciting epic verses celebrating the exploits of their patrons, members of the warrior tribes of western India. By the twentieth century, these Cāraṇs and Bhāṭs (also known as Bāroṭs) played slightly different roles in the region's royal courts—historiographers and genealogists, respectively—but both castes were dedicated to maintaining their patrons' family histories (Thompson 1991, 1992–1993).

Cāraṇs and Bhāṭs developed their own poetic tradition, distinct from the epic stories in rhymed verse such as the Ramayana and the Mahabharata, that have long been a forte of South Asian bards. They employed the *rāso* (also called *rāsa* and *rāsaka*), a poetic structure consisting of several discrete poems that each tell a portion of the story, depict a scene, or serve as a vehicle for a character's speech. The most common *rāso* verse forms are the *duho* 'couplet' and *chand* 'extended verse'. The poetry relates stories of the patrons' heroes, battles fought to preserve family honor, and regional features such as animals (horses and lions, for example), religious shrines, and rivers. Verses can also be the vehicle for social commentary. Rulers in the past have given the bards relative freedom to speak their minds, no matter how distasteful to the patrons. A message conveyed in verse was apparently received and interpreted as self-evident truth rather than personal opinion.

The *rāj darbār* 'royal audience hall' or, in more humble estates, the men's quarters of the chief's compound was the traditional context for the presentation of this poetry. (Women are rare in this bardic tradition.) Today, the descendants of western India's royalty are either financially unable to sponsor Cāraṇs and Bhāṭs and their esoteric entertainment, or are uninterested in doing so. Some bards have turned to public performances of *duho* and *chand*, often mixed with regional religious and topical songs. Many have abandoned the family tradition in search of other occupations.

The Cāraṇ and Bhāṭ manner of presenting poetry in Gujarat, Saurashtra, and Kutch differs from bardic recitation in the adjacent states of Rajasthan and Madhya Pradesh. It is frequently described as "singing"; however, some poets declare they are "presenting" the words in a "high voice" (using the English phrase), in a *moṭī vāṇī* 'big voice' or a *nādavaibhava* 'magnificent voice'. In this style, bards intone their verses to standardized melodies that augment the structure of the verse, emphasize the rhythmic points, and serve as a medium through which the poet can project his voice.

Duho

The word *duho* (also known as *dohāro*) is usually translated as "couplet" and is derived from the Sanskrit-Hindi root *du* or *do* 'two'. In the days of Gujarat's royal courts, *duho* served as a medium for salutations, greetings, congratulations, rebukes, and praise, as well as part of larger epic poems. The following *duho* is from a *rāso*

> Some *chand* texts are simply lists of rivers, mountains, animals, people, or some other subject that can be catalogued. The most famous verses recount stories of kings and generals and their battles to protect their kingdoms and reputations.

about Siddhraj Jaisingh of Pattan and his confrontation with Chudasuma Ra Khengar of Sorath. The verse describes how forbidding Khengar and his fort of Girnar would have been to Siddhraj (Forbes 1922, I:210; 1924, I:157).

Bāwana hajāra bāndhiyā, ghoḍā gaḍha Giranāra;
Kayama haṭhe Soraṭhadhaṇī, khehaṇa daḷa Khengāra

Fifty-two thousand stallions hath he stabled in the fort of Girnar;
How obstinate the lord of Sorath, how complete the army of Khengar.

The primary melodic "sentence" is a series of three phrases, the second and third beginning one step higher than the last and reaching a slightly higher pitch, but all ending on the same pitch. The shape of the phrases is fundamentally descending. The actual pitch on which the presentation begins depends in large part upon the reciter's voice, since bardic performance almost always takes place without instrumental accompaniment. Bards most often present *duho* in free time, avoiding a sense of rhythmical pulse and meter.

Soraṭho

A very similar and almost as common versification form in the bardic repertoire is the *soraṭho,* named after the region around the city of Junagadh. The number of syllables per line is the same in both forms; however, in *duho* the first half of the line is longer and the rhyme occurs at the end of the line, whereas in *soraṭho* the second half is longer and the rhyme occurs in the middle. The following *soraṭho,* from the same *rāso* as above, describes a central point of conflict between the two kings (Forbes 1922, I:216; 1924, I:161). Khengar had abducted and married Siddhraj's fiancée, and now the lord of Pattan has defeated the interloper. However, as the widow of a Rajput king, she is now duty bound to commit *sati* 'ritual widow suicide'.

Uñco gaḍha Giranāra, vādaḷīthī vātũ kare;
Maratā̃ Rā Khengāra, raṇḍāpo rāṇaka devaḍī.

Lofty fortress of Girnar, speaking with the clouds;
[With] the death of Ra Khengar, a widow's royal tomb.

Chand

Although *duho* and *soraṭho* are the preferred mediums for the delivery of concise expressions, *chand* is the traditional vehicle for long narrative. Bards use the word *chand* interchangeably with *gīt* 'song'. They also distinguish different kinds of *chand* by poetic meter and rhyme scheme.

Some *chand* texts are simply lists of rivers, mountains, animals, people, or some other subject that can be catalogued. Others describe sounds that might be heard in a battle, during a storm, or from a dancer's ankle bells. The most famous verses recount stories of kings and generals and their battles to protect their kingdoms and reputations. *Chand* has been the most important vehicle for *lāmbā vīrkāvyo* 'long poetry about bravery', examples of which include the *Bharataśvarabāhubali* (composed by Salibhadra c. 1185), the *Raṇamalla Chand* (composed c. 1398), and the *Rājā Jaitsīno Chand* (composed c. 1595).

Each *chand* type has a particular organizational template. The pattern dictates where rhymes occur, the number of long and short syllables per line, how the line is divided, and in some cases, which words are repeated. In the following example of a *sinhacālūgīt*, the poetic structure imitates a "lion's walk" (*sinha cālū*). The lion is metaphorically represented as taking four steps forward and then retracting one step to be sure he is avoiding danger. Poetically, the last word or word cluster of each line is repeated at the beginning of the next. Sometimes a double meaning is emphasized. Poets describe this form as an example of how a king must conduct himself, always aware of potential treachery; the actual words of the verse describe how a lion conducts himself to be secure.

Kamare kasa, kativye kahe samare
Samare Śiva śakti dame, damo re,
Damore madanādi rave amo re,
Amore tujadebī male namo re.
Namore, buśī ho, gunake bhamare,
Bhamare, nakupanth sule, gamare,
Gamare, jaganām kare amare,
Amare mahā tu narahe kamare.

Brave one with absolute resolve in battle
Blessed with Shiva's strength,
Of whom creatures of vulgar taste are in fear,
To you we make obeisance.
Like the honeybee, you extract only good from others,
You defend the downtrodden, are brave,
and are kind to the world,
May you live forever in the world, brave one.

As with *duho* and *soraṭho*, opinions vary about whether *chand* presentation is singing or recitation. The musical line is similar to that of *duho*, starting from various pitches and descending a ninth, octave, sixth, or fifth to a tonic. However, bards recite *chand* in highly rhythmic and sometimes rapid-fire manner.

REFERENCES

Bake, Arnold A. 1970. "Stick Dances." *Yearbook of the International Folk Music Council* 2:56–62.

Desai, Sudha. 1972. *Bhavai: A Medieval Form of Ancient Indian Dramatic Art (Natya) as Prevalent in Gujarat*. Ahmedabad: Gujarat University.

Forbes, Alexander K. 1922. *Rās Mala Athwa, Gujarat Prantno Itihas*, ed. and trans. Ranchhordabhai Udayaram, 2 vols. Ahmedabad: Forbes Gujarati Sabha. In Gujarati.

———. 1924. *Rās Mala: Hindoo Annals of the Province of Goozerat in Western India*, ed. H. G. Rawlinson, 2 vols. London: Oxford University Press.

Hazrat, Kallolini. 1981. *Maro Garbo Ghumyo*. Bombay: Shrimati Nathibhai Damodar Takarsi Mahila Vidhyapit and Dr. Madhuri Shah Educational Foundation. In Gujarati.

Kalelakar, Dattatreya B. 1975. *Āśrama-Bhajanāvaḷī*. Ahmedabad: Navjivan Prakashan Mandir. In Gujarati.

Meghani, Zaverchand. 1941. *Cundadi: Gurjara Lagna-Gito*. Ahmedabad: Sambhulal Jagashibhao Gurjara Grantharatna Karyalay. In Gujarati.

———. 1973. *Radhiyali Rat*. Ahmedabad: Gurjara Grantharatna Karyalay. In Gujarati.

Premanand. 1979. *Premanandni Kavyakritio*, ed. Keshavram Shastri and Shivalal Tulsidas. Ahmedabad: Sahitya-Sanshodhan Prakashan. In Gujarati.

Satyarthi, Devendra. 1951. "Rajput War Poetry." In *Meet My People: Indian Folk Poetry*, 230–251. Hyderabad: Chetana Prakashan.

Thompson, Gordon. 1987. "Music and Values in Gujarati-Speaking Western India." Ph.D. dissertation, University of California at Los Angeles.

———. 1991. "The Carans of Gujarat: Caste Identity, Music, and Cultural Change." *Ethnomusicology* 35 (3):381–391.

———. 1992–1993. "The Barots of Gujarati-Speaking Western India: Musicianship and Caste Identity." *Asian Music* 24 (1):1–18.

———. 1995a. "Music and Values in Gujarati Western India." *Pacific Review of Ethnomusicology* 7:57–58.

———. 1995b. "What's In a *Ḍhāḷ*? Evidence of *Raga*-like Approaches in a Gujarati Musical Tradition." *Ethnomusicology* 39(3):417–432.

Thompson, Gordon, and Medha Yodh. 1985. "*Garbā* and the Gujaratis of Southern California." *Selected Reports in Ethnomusicology* 6:59–79.

Rajasthan

Mekhala Devi Natavar

Professional Musicians
Processional and Festival Music
Devotional Music
Women's Songs
Songs of Informal Men's Groups
Musical Epics
Folk Dance and Dance Drama
Musicians in the Late Twentieth Century

The Indian state of Rajasthan, whose name means "land of kings," lies on the Pakistani border in northwestern India. It is divided diagonally by the Aravali hills and comprises two distinct geographic regions: the vast Thar Desert in the west and north, which covers 212,000 square kilometers and is characterized by frequent famines, scanty rainfall, and sparse population; and the hilly, forested, fertile land to the south and east. These two regions exhibit different linguistic and artistic features; yet common to both are the traditions of martial honor and an exuberant joy of life that characterize the Rajasthani people. Ever since the sixth and seventh centuries, the conservative Rajput warrior clans ruling the various princely states patronized traditional music and dance in the feudal system known as *jajmānī*, in which services were exchanged for portions of the harvest. Rajasthan even attracted artists from other states, who came and received this generous patronage. Many Rajasthani dancer and musician castes have now migrated to other parts of North India to perform on Indian radio, television, stage, and in films.

The population consists of members of the Rajput warrior caste, Brahmin priests and scholars, Muslims (including Manganihārs, Laṅgās, Ḍāḍhīs), scheduled
TRACK 13 tribes (Bhīls, Mīnas, Garasias, Sahriyas, Dāngis, Gadūliya Lohārs), scheduled castes (formerly untouchables) (Chamārs, Bhangīs, Madaris, Naṭs, Jogīs, Bāzigārs, Bhāṇḍs), farmers (Jaṭs, Jāghidārs), and the Marwari mercantile community. Aside from the majority Hindus, other prominent religious groups include Jains, animists, and Muslims. Hindi, Urdu, and many dialects of Rajasthani are spoken throughout the state.

Music and dance are integral to daily life in Rajasthan. One significant reason for this may be the extended months of leisure time that farmers enjoy when sheep and cattle raising and agricultural work dwindle in the dry seasons (Kothari 1972:2). Rajasthanis sing and dance for mundane entertainment, for sacred devotional offerings to the gods and ancestors, for welcoming seasonal changes. They use singing and dancing as popular teaching tools by which villagers learn about their history, both worldly and otherworldly. Music is essential in celebrations of rites of passage and life-cycle rituals, such as the birth of a child, a boy's first haircut, puberty, marriage, and death.

Rajasthan has an elaborate system of professional musician groups that pass down their traditions orally to younger generations within their own caste.

PROFESSIONAL MUSICIANS

Musicians generally belong to one of two categories of performer: nonprofessional musicians, generally considered amateurs, who perform within their own communities, and professional musicians who perform for others in exchange for monetary remuneration. More often than not, men and women have different repertoires and perform separately, with performance contexts varying from formal to informal.

Many of the twenty-six districts making up modern-day Rajasthan were once princely states that provided the main source of patronage for the arts. The courts of the rajas of Bikaner, Jodhpur, and Udaipur were homes for many performers, but the most impressive and serious patrons were the rajas of Jaipur. For the several hundred years preceding India's independence in 1947, these kings employed professional musicians of both sexes and from both Muslim and Hindu backgrounds in the famed *Gunījankhānā* 'Department of Virtuosos' (Erdman 1985:82). Thus they supported generations of hereditary musicians, vocal artists, and dancers who were expected to perform in the court and in the adjoining temples as well as in royal processions. Due to such consistent patronage, the Dagar family was able to cultivate the vocal style of music called *dhrupad*, and the Jaipur *gharānā* 'stylistic school' developed within the prestigious classical dance style of North India, *kathak* [see HINDUSTANI VOCAL MUSIC; MUSIC AND DANCE: NORTHERN AREA].

Rajasthan has an elaborate system of professional musician groups that pass down their traditions orally to younger generations within their own caste. Some of these communities are sedentary, receiving regular patronage for their services and performances from local nobility. The Manganihārs, Laṅgās, Ḍāḍhīs, and Ḍholīs are four such performance communities in the western desert regions; in accordance with the *jajmānī* system, they provide musical services to the feudal lords, usually Rajput families. Other entertainers are migratory, traveling from Marwar to the more affluent eastern regions in search of new patrons and performance opportunities. These include the Bhāṇḍs, actors, mimes, and jesters who often parody the music of other groups; the Bhāṭs, genealogists (figure 1) who are also known for their *kathputlī* marionette shows, each troupe having male puppeteers, a female singer, and a *ḍholak* 'double-headed drum' player; the Jogīs (also called Saperās), snake charmers who play double clarinets with two tubes and a gourd wind chamber (*murlī* or *puṅgī*); the Naṭs, a community of actors, jugglers, and acrobats who accompany themselves on the *ḍhol* 'large double-headed drum', the *thālī* 'metal dish' played with sticks, and the *bāṅkiā* 'brass trumpets'; and the Bhopās, shamans and epic storytellers (although "Bhopā" refers to an occupation rather than to a specific caste).

FIGURE 1 A Turi Bhāṭ epic singer plays a *ḍholak* in a village near Sirohi, 1997. Photo by Nancy Martin.

Sedentary hereditary musician communities

The Laṅgā, a musician community and militant tribe of Rajput descent, are believed to have converted to Islam at the end of the seventeenth century when their patrons, the Sindhi and the Sipahi, became Muslims. Groups of male Laṅgā sing romantic

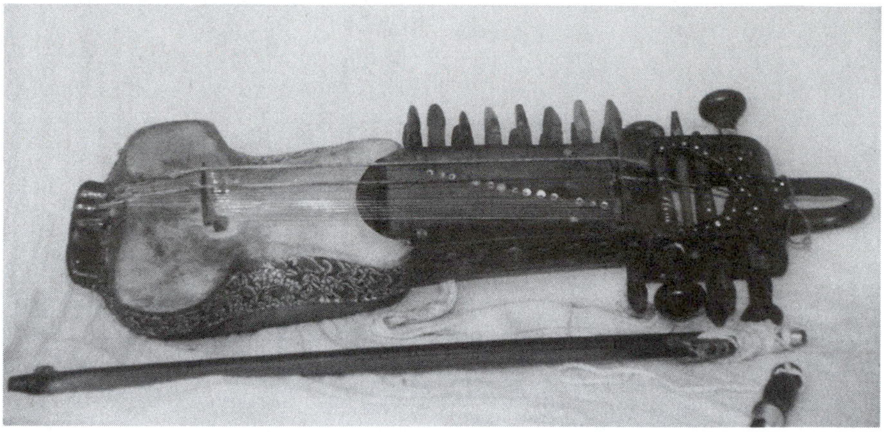

FIGURE 2 Bowed, unfretted lutes played by the Manganihārs: *above right, sindhī sāraṅgī; above, kamāychā.* Photos by Nancy Martin.

ballads accompanied by the *gujarātan* and *sindhī sāraṅgī,* bowed unfretted lutes with four playing strings and many sympathetic strings (figure 2), the *surindā,* a deep-waisted, bowed lute; the *satāra,* a flute comprising two six-holed wooden pipes, one played as a drone; the *murlī,* a single-reed instrument with gourd air chamber and twin finger-hole pipes for melody and drone; and the *morchaṅg* 'mouth harp'.

The Manganihār are also Muslim musicians, but they serve primarily Hindu patrons and perform devotional music in Hindu temples. They quite likely converted from Hinduism, for not only do they observe many Hindu customs, but their genealogies include Hindu names. Some prefer to be called Mīrāsī, referring to a category of hereditary musicians, rather than Manganihār, a term derived from the verb "to beg," which indicates low social status. Mīrāsī men and women perform professionally, though only the women and children dance. Male Manganihārs play the *kamāychā,* a bowed, round-bellied unfretted lute (figure 2). Nowadays the younger musicians play the harmonium (figure 3)—which is easier to learn than the *kamāychā*—as well as the *ḍhol* or *ḍholak* drum and *kartāl,* clappers consisting of four thin wooden slabs struck together, two in each hand. Two Manganihār communities specialize in playing the *surnāī* 'double-reed oboe' and *murlī* 'snake charmer's pipe' (Catlin 1977:167–168). Since the 1970s, some Laṅgās and Manganihārs have earned reputations from recordings and concert tours that have taken them around the world. Other musician groups include the Ḍāḍhīs (also Muslims who serve Hindu communities), Ḍoms, Rānās, Kalāvants, Damāmīs, Rāwals, and Nagārcīs.

FIGURE 3 A Manganihār singer accompanies himself on the harmonium at a performance in Shilpagram near Udaipur, 1993. Photo by Nancy Martin.

Ḍholīs are Hindu devotees of the goddess Chamunda Devi and of Bhaironji, a ferocious incarnation of Shiva. Ḍholīs serve only upper-caste Hindu patrons, mostly Rajputs and Cāraṇs. Ḍholī women, known as Ḍholans, are usually attached to a Rajput family, and sing for occasions like births, marriages, and deaths. The caste name derives from the huge *ḍhol* drum they play during celebrations and processions. However, they prefer to be called Kathaks, since their hereditary community takes credit for developing the North Indian classical dance style of that name. "Kathak" affords them a higher status in urban centers, where most prefer not to reveal their rural lower-caste Ḍholī identity. This community has not only enjoyed the patronage of the Rajasthani rajas, but has found employment in other courts from Hyderabad to Nepal. Since independence, Dholīs have become dance and music teachers and performers in major North Indian urban centers; a few have been influential film music and film dance directors. Yet they have not developed as successful a reputation as *kathak* dancers of higher, nontraditional castes and more prosperous backgrounds because of their illiteracy and childhood poverty. Furthermore, the younger generation is not learning to play the *ḍhol* and not carrying on the tradition.

Repertoire

The musical repertoire of professional Laṅgā and Manganihār performers consists of *moṭā gīt* 'big songs' and *choṭā gīt* 'small songs'. The *moṭā gīt* style is the more sophisticated and refined, exhibiting features related to Hindustani classical music. *Moṭā gīt* includes Hindu devotional compositions by poet-saints (*sūrpad*); songs in praise of kings, patrons, and deities (*hajra*); long and/or difficult songs; songs using the old poetic language of Rajasthan (*dingal*); raga-based songs often with rapid, improvised passages (*tān*) between lines; popular romantic ballads such as "Dhola-Maru" and "Moomal"; songs preceded by unmetered poetic couplets (*duhā*); characteristic vocal flourishes; and formal compositions with refrains (Jairazbhoy 1980:102). Most such songs derive from the men's repertoire, but occasionally women will perform a wedding song (*banrā*) in a more stylized, *moṭā gīt* manner. Musicians also employ this style in improvising instrumental compositions.

Choṭā gīt are men's songs derived from the women's repertoire. The lyrics often pertain to annual festivals, seasons, and celebratory occasions such as weddings and childbirth. They may also explore intimate feelings, such as the pain of separation from a loved one.

Both male and female professional vocalists perform *māṅd* songs to the accompaniment of a harmonium, *sāraṅgī*, tabla drums, and sometimes even a violin or sitar. The *māṅd* style, which may be undergoing classicization, is claimed as the origin of the North Indian *māṅḍ* raga (Neuman 1980:228); however, such use of a raga name in Rajasthan does not necessarily imply the melodic content of the classical raga bearing that name.

PROCESSIONAL AND FESTIVAL MUSIC

Up until India's independence in 1947, a *jajmānī* musician would lead royal processions playing a set of kettledrums (*nagāṛā*) with two curved beaters. Behind him a group of musicians would follow, playing instruments such as the bowed lute (*kamāychā*), double-reed oboe (*surnāī*), clappers (*kartāl*), harmonium, drums, and cymbals. These royal processions took place at coronations, festivals, on return from battle, to greet dignitaries, to accompany a bridegroom's party (*barāt*) to the bride's house, and on the birth of a male child (Jairazbhoy 1984:10). Nowadays, such bands play primarily at weddings. In the absence of feudal patronage, many rural musicians have switched from light classical and folk-music performance to employment in these more popular and lucrative bands.

Music is essential at all Rajasthani festivals, secular and religious, whether celebrated in the streets, in temples, or in private homes (figure 4). Parades and processions feature bands in regal costumes and male dancers. Prior to the twentieth century, courtesans (*tawāif*) employed by local rulers danced women's roles, but now cross-dressed males perform such parts. During the Holī festival, men's groups meet at night at certain crossroads to dance—often with obscene gestures—and to sing erotic or insulting songs (*gālī*) accompanied by a large frame drum (*daph* or *chāṅg*).

DEVOTIONAL MUSIC

Hindu temple celebrations are important performance contexts for singing and dancing by professionals and nonprofessionals of both sexes. Common throughout Rajasthan are all-night vigils (*jāgaran*) organized by temples and private patrons to commemorate and glorify specific deities through vocal and instrumental music. Performers offer prayers in the form of devotional songs (bhajan, *kīrtan*) and dance. Here also, on special occasions men may dress as women and dance in all-male nighttime gatherings.

TRACK 19

Hindus in Rajasthan worship the sacred in many forms, including plants such as

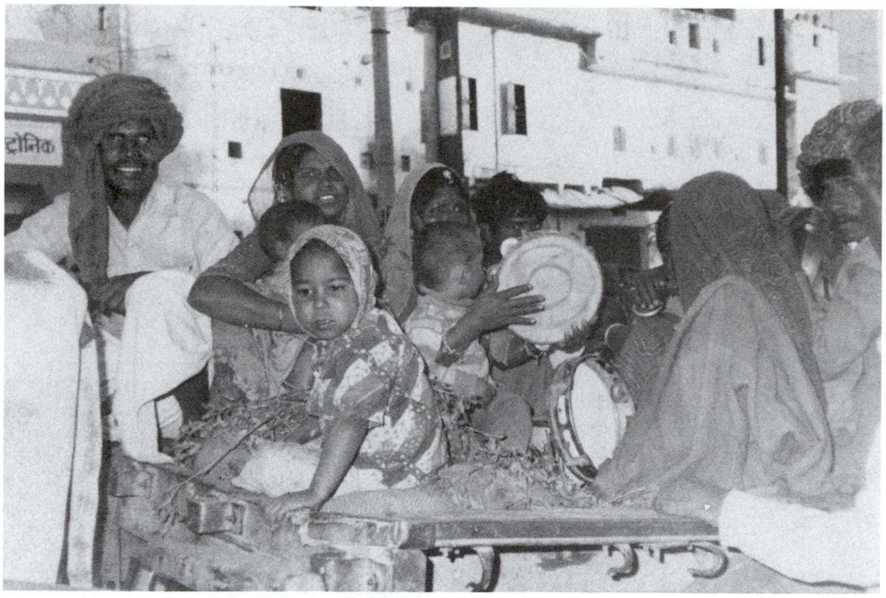

FIGURE 4 Lower-caste women play *kañjīrā* and sing during a Shivarātrī parade, Jaipur, 1984. Photo by Mekhala Devi Natavar.

the tulsi plant and the pipal tree and animals such as the cow and the monkey. They pay homage through song to major and minor Hindu divinities, as well as to many local deities. Of these, the five major folk gods—Pabuji, Gogaji, Mehaji, Harbhuji, and Ramdevji—are most important, as are the deified spirits (Bhomiya) of men who died heroic deaths while protecting the village community and the spirits of male and female kin who died young (Pitṛ/Pitṛānī) and have returned to bless and benefit the family. On many major occasions Rajasthanis also sing songs of worship to the spirits of women (Sati Mata) who followed their deceased husbands onto the funeral pyre by committing *sati* (the practice of self-immolation, which is now outlawed). Members of the dominant Rajput caste of Rajasthan and all those associated with them also worship Mataji or Devi, the Mother Goddess who bestows wisdom, wealth, victory, and peace. In performing for their Rajput patrons, professional musicians have gradually developed a large repertoire of songs in praise of her.

Certain centers in Rajasthan exist solely for Krishna worship. At the temple of Sri Nathji in Nathdwara, devotees offer Krishna poetic praise through *havelī saṅgīt* 'music of the Lord's home', a sophisticated light-classical vocal form. Full-time professional musicians of the Vallabhacharya sect of Vaishnavism sing at the eight daily services offered to the deity of Sri Nathji, to the accompaniment of *pakhāvaj* 'double-headed drum', harmonium and/or *sāraṅgī* 'bowed fiddle', and *jhāñjh* 'large brass cymbals'. Their devotional songs (*pad* and *kīrtan*), written by Surdas and the Aṣṭachāp saint-poets, describe Krishna's divine pastimes. Another center is Jaipur, a city of temples, the most famous of which was built by the rajas of Jaipur inside the City Palace gardens. At this temple, dedicated to Sri Radha–Govinda Devji, thousands of devotees gather daily to dance, play drums and cymbals, and engage in leader-chorus devotional songs written by poet-saints including Mirabai, the fifteenth-century Rajput princess who is the most important poet-saint of Rajasthan (figure 5).

Jogīs or Nāths are followers of Guru Gorakhnath; they often wander from village to village singing devotional songs and romantic ballads, accompanying themselves on a *sāraṅgī* 'bowed fiddle' or a *tambūrā* 'drone lute' (figure 6). Their repertoire reflects a branch of Hindu *nirguṇ bhaktī* 'devotion to God without attributes'. Their deep, meaningful songs expound a philosophy of detachment from the temporal world.

On dark new-moon nights, women sing songs dedicated to the ancestors, reassuring the spirits that they are loved and cared for by the living.

FIGURE 5 A devotee of Lord Krishna plays *kartāl* at the Sri Radha–Govinda Devi Temple, Jaipur, during the Holī festival, 1983. Photo by Mekhala Devi Natavar.

FIGURE 6 A Kalbeliā Jogī plays *tambūrā* and *kartāl* to accompany his bhajan singing, Jodhpur, 1996. Photo by Nancy Martin.

The two main types of Muslim music in Rajasthan are ghazal and qawwali. The ghazal is a form of Urdu love poetry, reflecting the Persian heritage that the Muslim invaders entering India from the west brought with them. Ghazal lyrics describe mundane erotic and romantic love; however, the poetry is heavily influenced by Sufi mysticism and is full of symbolic references to the divine. The poet's pain of separation from and joy at reunion with the beloved symbolizes the yearning and love for the divine. Male Sufis sing ghazals at all-night religious gatherings. The main vocal and dance music of courtesans and prostitutes is also the ghazal, and the form is very popular among light classical vocalists throughout North India and Pakistan.

Specialist musicians called Qawwāl perform lively qawwali, leader-chorus songs with stylized hand clapping, harmonium, and *ḍholak* or tabla drum accompaniment. Qawwali poetic verses are composed in Urdu or Persian, and express ideas of mystical love and praise for God, the Prophet Muhammad, and various saints. Qawwāli singing takes place year-round at the shrines of Sufi saints (*pīr*), and attracts crowds of both Muslims and Hindus at the saints' death anniversary celebrations (*ʿurs*). The most famous Sufi shrine (*dargāh*) in the world is that dedicated to Khwaja Moinuddin Chishti (1142–1236) in Ajmer. It holds an annual six-day *ʿurs* feast attended by people of all religions.

WOMEN'S SONGS

As with male musical performance, professional female musicians from communities such as the Mīrāsī, Dholī, and *tawāif* 'courtesans' may perform women's songs for their patrons. More commonly, women of all castes perform them informally within their own communities, and in mixed-caste gatherings during festivals, weddings, births, and other occasions.

A huge repertoire of women's group songs focuses on such themes as love, the changing of seasons, religious festivals, household activities, and life-cycle rituals such as marriage and childbirth. Women often sing devotional prayers (five in a row) at the beginning of a gathering. Following an invocation to Ganesh, the elephant-headed god of wisdom and remover of obstacles, they sing praise songs to the Mother Goddess in her forms as Durga and Gauri. Women also worship Bhaironji and Hanuman through hymns, as well as local deities and Sati Mata, who is identified variously as a clan deity or a queen deified for committing *sati*. Sitala Mata, the goddess of smallpox (and now, chickenpox), who both inflicts the disease on small children and protects them from it, must be appeased in order to ensure the well-being and good health of all young children and the community at large. Women direct songs to her during certain seasons, as well as whenever a child is stricken with either disease.

Groups of women gathering to sing devotional prayers (*bhajan maṇḍaḷi*) are a common feature of temple life, especially in urban areas. Leaving men to their own *bhajan maṇḍaḷi* groups, throngs of dedicated and pious women—mostly older housewives—come together to sing, either with *ḍholak* and harmonium or without accompaniment. They also dance in front of Hindu deities, twirling and acting out the meanings of the songs for hours at a time. Such activities take place at specific times of day all year long; in certain months, such as Phālgun (February–March) in the spring and Kārtik (October–November) in the fall, they are more popular for religious reasons, and attract many new or occasional worshipers.

On dark new-moon nights (*amavasya*), women, sometimes joined by their male relatives, sing songs dedicated to the ancestors. Through these prayers they seek to appease and please the spirits of dead children, ghost deities, and ancestors, reassuring the spirits that they are loved and cared for by the living. Contented spirits, such as Bhomiyaji and Piṭraji, are thought to be very beneficent to an individual or a family.

Secular song genres

Rajasthanis throughout the state celebrate the springtime Holī festival with uninhibited song and dance. Often the festivities last from the month of Phālgun to the following hot month of Chaitra (April), when the festival of Gangaur takes place. Two women's genres popular during this season are *keśyā* and *gālī*. Both are unabashedly bawdy, explicitly sexual, and express promiscuous desires for husbands and lovers (Gold 1994:39–45). *Keśyā* songs, sung by mixed-caste groups (not including Rajputs), deal with a range of women's feelings about love, often alluding to relational conflicts and misunderstandings as well as internal dilemmas. The *gālī* is a verbally abusive insult song female kin usually sing within the confines of their village home. Women may sing *gālī* at certain stages during marriage celebrations or at ceremonies associated with birth and child rearing. The explicit lyrics, about body parts, sexual intercourse, and infidelity, seem to express a sense of pride in the women's own sexuality and fertility. Men have separate venues for *gālī* songs but are sometimes exposed to these women's insult songs, since the women may not only sing in their presence but may specifically address certain male relatives, as at a wedding.

In contrast to the North Indian classical vocal genre *khyāl*, women's folk songs of the same name are sung just for pleasure, by and for women. These may include anything from plaintive songs of sorrow to playful songs expressing sexuality.

Women sing a variety of swing songs in the month of Sāvan (August) and the monsoon season, when young girls and women enjoy swinging on swings. Another seasonal genre is husband-wife dialogue songs in which the wife expresses her desire for love in terms of intimacy and gifts such as bangles and nice clothes. A pregnant wife may sing songs craving desired foods (*hūn*). Other popular women's songs include those admiring the bridegroom-prince (*banā*), songs describing the bride's loveliness (*banī*), lullabies praising a newborn male child (*hālariyo*), and birth songs (*jacchā kī gīt*). Still other songs reveal the frustrations of joint family life, the drudgery of domestic chores, problems with the mother-in-law, the new bride's fears, and the pain of a daughter's separation from her parents and family as she joins her new in-laws.

Women also sing songs at auspicious events celebrating puberty and fertility, such as the festival honoring the marriage between Tulsi, the holy basil plant, and Saligram, a form of Lord Krishna, during the month of Kārtik (October–November).

TRACK 19 Gangaur is perhaps the most popular and important festival for women, particularly unmarried girls who desire good husbands. Worship of the goddess Gauri, the spouse of Shiva, consists of elaborate rituals accompanied by song and dance.

SONGS OF INFORMAL MEN'S GROUPS

Men's songs are limited to work songs, reverential songs praising deities and legendary heroes, and those related to one or two festivals such as Holī, when song themes range from devotional to erotic. Men sing religious bhajans (figure 7) as well as ribald *gālī* songs, whose texts abuse and poke fun at people. Seasonal songs commemorating the arrival of spring or the monsoons describe the beauty of nature and the atmosphere of joy and love that prevails throughout the countryside.

MUSICAL EPICS

Rajasthan is famous for its romantic ballads and its heroic epics, narrated with the visual aid of painted scrolls. These epics describe the adventures and valiant deeds of Rajput kings. Two of the most popular traditional scroll epics are at least six hundred years old, and consist of sung prose and poetry passed down orally. One of these, *Pābujī kī par*, is a ballad performed by and for worshipers of Pabuji, a fourteenth-century hero. Believers in Pabuji's mystic powers invite epic singers (Bhopā), usually from the Thorī caste, into their homes in times of sickness and misfortune to sing the ballad at all-night vigils. The recitation takes place before an open painted scroll depicting Pabuji's life. Beginning at dusk and ending at dawn, the Bhopā sings and plays the *rāvanhatta* fiddle using a bow with attached *ghuṅghrū* bells (figure 8). He adds excitement to his recitation with occasional footwork enhanced by the sound of *ghuṅghrū* bells tied to his ankles. His wife (Bhopī) sings and sometimes dances, holding an oil lamp to illuminate Pabuji's images on the scroll at appropriate points in the narrative. The second epic describes the deeds of Devnarayan and the twenty-four Bagravat brothers, in nearly fifteen thousand verse lines and 335 songs. Epic singers commit the entire work to memory, and singers from different castes may collaborate in a performance taking thirty hours (Jairazbhoy 1984:15).

FOLK DANCE AND DANCE DRAMA

The four hundred-year-old *khyāl* dance-drama tradition differs from both the *khyāl* women's song genre described earlier and the North Indian classical vocal music of the same name. This folk-theatrical form draws from local legends, and consists of men's solo and duet dances interspersed with some stylized acting and touches of rustic vulgarity.

The Bhīl tribal people perform a ritual dance drama called *gauri* during the daytime in the rainy season, to ensure the well-being of the community and the village.

FIGURE 7 Mahesharam, a nonprofessional singer of the Meghwal caste of weavers and leatherworkers, accompanies himself on the *tambūrā*. Together with his group, he performs at all-night devotional singing sessions (*jāgaran*). Jodhpur, 1996. Photo by Nancy Martin.

FIGURE 8 A Bhopā musician plays the *gujarī* or *narelī* 'bowed fiddle', very similar to the *rāvanhatta*. Jodhpur, 1993. Photo by Nancy Martin.

The drama reenacts the fight between Shiva as Bhairav and the demon Bhasamasura. It encompasses mime as well as short skits on social or mythological themes. Some characters wear masks and dance in a circle around a *trishūl* 'trident' as the chief priest goes into a trance while dancing. The Bhīls of Rajasthan and the border areas of Gujarat reflect their fighting spirit by using bows and arrows in their dances. Their most popular dance is the *ghumer* (unrelated to the Rajput *ghūmar*). Men and women perform the dance year-round, accompanied by songs of heroism and romance.

In the feudal society of medieval Rajasthan, dancing was not considered a respectable profession, and those who engaged in it lost their social standing. Many dancers left their castes and formed a new community called the Bhavāī, believed to have been founded four hundred years ago by Nagoji Jat. Originally, males of this professional community performed *bhavāī* plays, which depicted scenes of daily life or local heroic or romantic tales. *Bhavāī* is now better known as a solo dance; male or female performers of various castes balance on their heads a series of pots or a column of alternating glasses and saucers, sometimes filled with colored water. There is often a spectacular element as the dancers step on the edges of sharp knives, on crushed glass pieces, or on the rim of a brass tray, rendering this a favorite dance with tourists, villagers, and the temple-going public.

Dance is an important part of every festive occasion, and each community enjoys its own regional dances. The *ghūmar* circle dance, however, is common throughout Rajasthan and has become a state symbol. Though *ghūmar* is associated primarily with the springtime festival of Gangaur, upper-caste Rajput women also dance *ghūmar* at marriages, festivals, and ceremonial occasions, either alone or in pairs or groups (figure 9). Fully veiled women wearing wide skirts twirl around and around, then stop abruptly and turn in the opposite direction. They wear *ghuṅghrū* 'ankle bells', and dance songs about women's lives, accompanied by the *ḍhol* 'double-headed drum'. The *panīhārī* dance is related to the *ghūmar* but differs in the elegant movements of the women, who carry earthen pots on their heads. During this group dance, individual performers show their skill by dancing independently.

Charī, also called *charwā*, is a circular dance performed by Mālī women. On their heads the veiled women balance pots topped with lighted lamps, as they dance with graceful hand movements close to the body, usually to welcome an honored guest such as a bridegroom on his arrival at the bride's home. The *ḍhol, thālī* 'metal dish' struck with a stick, and *bāṅkiā* 'brass trumpets' accompany the dance.

Women of the Kāmar caste perform a dance called *terā tālī* 'thirteen cymbals', usually in honor of Ramdevji, believed by locals to be an incarnation of Vishnu. Two or more seated and veiled dancers each have ten metal cymbals (*mañjīrā*) tied to their right leg and foot, one cymbal on each arm, another held in the left hand, and a fourteenth held in the right hand as a striker. The movements, as in other folk dances, derive from daily household chores such as winnowing rice, pounding grain, churning butter, kneading and rolling bread, spinning thread, and weaving cloth. Sometimes the dancers clench a small sword between their teeth and balance an ornamental pot on their heads. Male vocalists and musicians accompany the dancers on the harmonium, *ḍholak, mañjīrā*, and *tandūro* 'string drone'.

Kalbeliā snake charmers have a unique style of dance and music. The male members of this nomadic tribe entertain the public by playing the *bīn* and the *bhapang* to lure snakes. The *bīn* or *puṅgī* is a single-reed wind pipe inserted into the top of a gourd air chamber, from the bottom of which two parallel pipes extend for melody and drone; the *bhapang* is a plucked chordophone with a single metal string and a hollow, cylindrical base (figure 10). Sometimes the women join in to sing and perform *indoni, panīhārī*, and *shankariā* dances. Some women play the small *khanjarī*

Since many traditional professional-musician communities are of lower-caste status, members of the younger generation are pursuing more lucrative, higher-status professions, thus breaking with the traditional hereditary musical profession of their ancestors.

FIGURE 9 Wives, daughters, and sisters of Kathak-caste musicians dance the *ghūmar* in front of the Pitṛ (family ancestor) Temple during the Gangaur festival. Family members accompany them with hand clapping, harmonium, tabla, and *ḍholak* drum (instruments not shown). Lodhsar village, 1993. Photo by Mekhala Natavar.

FIGURE 10 Kalbeliā snake charmers play the *bhapang* (*left*) and the *bīn* (*right*). Jaipur, 1982. Photo by Mekhala Navatar.

'tambourine'. Veiled women in long, wide black skirts adorned with white cowrie shells simulate the serpentine movements of snakes, spiraling and spinning with deep back bends. The *shankariā* is a circle dance in which men and women enact a traditional story of unrequited love.

Certain dances are the exclusive domain of men. *Kacchī ghorī* is a colorful male dance rooted in the martial traditions of Rajasthan, and is performed mainly by the Bavaria, Kumhār, and Sargara communities in wedding processions. As many as four pairs of elaborately dressed dancers represent warrior bridegrooms, "wearing" colorful dummy-horses and brandishing swords. A *ḍhol* drum and *bāṅkiā* trumpets accompany the dancers, as do sometimes the songs of women. The Mīna of Mewar perform the *ger* dance during the festival of Holī. Men dance in a circle, while singers strike large *daph* 'frame drums'. Men perform many regional versions of circular stick dances during the month or more of the Holī festival, such as the *dandia ger* of Mewar and the *gīder* in the eastern region of Shekhavat. A combination of the *ger* and *ghūmar*, the springtime *ger-ghūmar* of the Bhīl tribe, is a complex circle dance with men in the outer ring and women in the inner ring. The dancers switch places with the changes in rhythm, while striking long decorated sticks with *ghuṅghrū* bells on the ends, which they hold in both hands. Also at the Holī festival, men dance the raucous *dhamāl*, often to the accompaniment of insult songs (*gālī*) and the large frame drum (*chāṅg* or *daph*).

A fire dance called *jasnāthi agni*, in honor of the saint Jasnath of the mystic Sidh Nāths of Bikaner, is a display of extreme devotion. To the gradually increasing tempo of horns and large drums, men and boys dance vigorously for up to an hour on a large pit of layers of burning charcoal and wood.

MUSICIANS IN THE LATE TWENTIETH CENTURY

Due to the breakdown of the old feudal *jajmānī* system of patronage at the village level, many Rajasthani musicians now depend on the Indian government and the state tourism department for funding. Some are lucky to receive employment as teachers in government institutions for the promotion of the arts or as musicians on All India Radio. Others find jobs in regional Rajasthani films. However, the situation is bleak for the majority of performers, who no longer receive the kind of economic sustenance necessary to flourish as a musical community. In addition, since many traditional professional-musician communities are of lower-caste status, members of the younger generation are pursuing more lucrative, higher-status professions, thus breaking with the traditional hereditary musical profession of their ancestors.

A few schools and colleges teach a variety of folk and some classical music and dance, but oral transmission is still the preferred method of musical training, especially in traditional families. Professional hereditary musicians still monopolize and keep alive most of the traditional arts. These musicians continue to play a vital role in the lives of the Rajasthani people.

REFERENCES

Catlin, Amy R. 1977. "Whither the Manganihars? An Investigation into Change among Professional Musicians in Western Rajasthan." *Bulletin of the Institute of Traditional Cultures*, Madras, Jan.–June, 165–178.

Erdman, Joan. 1985. *Patrons and Performers in Rajasthan*. Delhi: Chanakya Publications.

Gold, Ann G. 1994. "Sexuality, Fertility, and Erotic Imagination in Rajasthani Women's Songs." In *Listen to the Heron's Words: Reimagining Gender and Kinship in North India*, ed. Gloria G. Raheja and Ann G. Gold, 30–72. Berkeley: University of California Press.

Jairazbhoy, Nazir. 1980. "Embryo of a Classical Music Tradition in Western Rajasthan." In *The Communication of Ideas*, ed. J. S. Yadava and V. Gautam, 99–109. Tenth ICAES Series, no. 3. New Delhi: Concept Publishing Company.

———. 1984. *Folk Musicians of Rajasthan*. UCLA Video Series in Ethnomusicology. UCLA Music Dept., Los Angeles. Recorded August 1980. Videocassette and booklet.

Kothari, Komal. 1972. *Monograph on Langas: A Folk Musician Caste of Rajasthan*. Borunda, Jodhpur: Rajasthan Institute of Folklore.

Mathur, U. B. 1986. *Folkways in Rajasthan*. Jaipur: The Folklorists.

Neuman, Daniel M. 1980. *The Life of Music in North India*. Detroit: Wayne State University Press.

Vatsyayan, Kapila. 1976. *Traditions of Indian Folk Dance*. New Delhi: Indian Book Company.

Verma, Vijay. 1987. *The Living Music of Rajasthan*. New Delhi: Office of the Registrar General.

Punjab

Joyce Middlebrook

Bhangra
Giddhā
Other Punjabi Songs
Sikh Devotional Music
Entertainment Music

The word *Punjab* combines two Persian words, *panj* 'five' and *āb* 'water', to mean 'a land where five rivers flow'. Because India is surrounded by water to the south, east, and west and mountains to the north, its northwestern region—the Punjab—has historically presented the major overland access to the subcontinent. Over time, the many incursions by Persians, Greeks, Scythians, Kushans, Huns, Turks, and other peoples have resulted in a diverse group of permanent settlers in this region. From the 1100s to the 1800s, Turko-Afghan, Mughal, and Marāṭhā rulers dominated, followed by the British. At partition in 1947, the Punjab was divided into Indian and Pakistani territories. In 1966, further political reconfiguration of the Indian state of Punjab resulted in the creation of two new Indian states, Himachal Pradesh and Haryana. The present Indian state of Punjab has rich agricultural lands, with many songs and dances related to farming, harvesting, and village life.

BHANGRA

In the villages and cities of Punjab and in South Asian communities worldwide, Punjabi men perform bhangra, a lively, joyful dance. Five to eleven men, either in a circle or in one or more straight lines, execute vigorous movements. Usually an audience watches, and sometimes people in the audience also dance.

Many gatherings of villagers and urbanites, including annual festivals (such as Baisākhī, a harvest festival), fairs, weddings, birthdays, and other parties, feature bhangra as the main entertainment. Anticipation builds as the organizers erect a tent under which the dancers perform, in a park or schoolyard, on the flatbed of a truck, or in a parking lot or some other public place. In villages, invitations to friends and relatives circulate by word of mouth; in cities, announcements broadcast from loudspeakers placed on a car may advertise an upcoming bhangra event. Admission is always free, for sponsors or party hosts cover the costs of production. To find out where a dance group is appearing on any day, a newcomer need only inquire in a store or a restaurant, or from a passerby. An urban bhangra performance may attract thousands of people.

In Jullunder District in Punjab, four annual fairs (*mela*) host the largest bhangra competitions. The Nakodar and Madhlai Melas, established in the mid-1970s, attract as many as one million people. The Nakodar Mela formerly featured only performances of Muslim devotional songs (qawwali), but around 1990, after the success of the Madhlai Mela, it also began holding bhangra competitions. The Professor Mohan Singh Mela, also dating from 1990, draws between fifty and sixty thousand people, and in 1994 the foundation of the Shounky Mela provided a fourth location for bhangra competitions. Any bhangra group may participate by submitting a tape-recorded performance to the event's review committee. The committee selects entrants for the competition by listening to the tapes and assessing the popularity of groups. It then assigns performance lengths based upon popularity: perhaps three minutes for a relatively unknown group and fifteen minutes for a well-known one. Competing groups from Punjab, Canada, and England perform before an official committee that chooses the winners, who receive money, prizes, and instant fame. Even groups that fail to win the competition may gain such popularity with audiences that they, too, become well known.

Scholars have traditionally classified the songs accompanying bhangra as folk songs (*boliyāṅ*), but the word "bhangra" is now commonly used to refer to both the song style and the dances it accompanies. Song texts usually consist of one stanza of one to five lines repeated over and over for up to fifteen minutes. In addition to themes of farming and village life, texts may concern a particular celebration or deal with love, family, patriotism, or current social issues. Tempos tend to be fast.

Bhangra instruments and costumes

The traditional accompaniment for bhangra dancing is furnished by a drummer who plays and sings while standing, his music occasionally supplemented by the dancers' shouts ("hoi!" "shawa!" "bullay!"), roughly equivalent to the English exclamation *hey.* He plays the *ḍhol,* a barrel drum about 90 centimeters long and 60 to 75 centimeters in diameter, with goatskin heads 30 to 35 centimeters wide. Ropes laced through the drumheads and crisscrossed down the body serve to attach the skins and tune the drum. The drum hangs from the player's neck by a strap connected to the two ends of the drum. The upper head, played with a long, thin, bamboo stick, keeps a constant beat; the lower, tuned at a lower pitch, is struck with a thick wooden stick, and sounds most of the accents (figure 1).

FIGURE 1 The Punjabi drummer Malkiat Singh with the double-headed *ḍhol,* which commonly provides accompaniment for bhangra dancing. 1994. Photo by Ranjila Sandhu.

Other bhangra instruments include a smaller version of the *ḍhol,* called the *ḍholkī.* This drum is approximately 50 centimeters in diameter, with the upper head 15 to 22 centimeters wide and the lower, 17 to 25 centimeters wide. Its player sits cross-legged on the floor, holds the drum lengthwise across his lap, and with his hands strikes the heads, making various sounds. Both drums are tuned to either the tonic or the fifth, depending on the song. Ensembles may include tabla, metal tongs with jingles (*cimṭā*), and a single-stringed, short-necked, plucked lute (*tūmbī*).

The dancers wear brightly colored, often matching, costumes. Over long pants, the men wear a knee-length shirt (*kurtā*) and a vest, with a long cloth (*caddar*) tied around the waist. The latter three garments may be simple, or they may be lavishly embellished with gold or silver edgings or designs. The dancers' turbans have a fold of cloth standing up in the front like a peacock's tail.

Movements and props

The movements of the dance include bending, jumping, kicking, knee-bending, and complicated gymnastic formations in which the men lift one another to create a human pyramid, wheel, or other pattern. The steps have descriptive names, such as *phumhaṇiāṅ* 'jumping for joy', *jhummar* 'movements in an ancient game', and *cal* 'to walk'. The dancers often use props, such as the kind of long stick (*lāṭhī* or *ḍāṅg*) that farmers use for protection. In some farming songs, the dancers wield a *kāṭo*, literally 'squirrel', a stick about two feet long with a smaller stick attached to the top and a square of cloth tied to the opposite end; each dancer pulls a string connected to the small stick, and the cloth bobs up and down. For songs about snakes, dancers act out the stories with a *sāp* 'snake', a small, expandable, handheld trellis that the performers open and close while dancing.

Fusion of bhangra and Western music

Since the 1980s the blending of bhangra and Western music has become popular in England, Canada, and the United States. Song texts may be in English or Punjabi, or a combination of both. To the traditional instruments, new dance groups, often wearing Western clothing, have added electric guitars, synthesizers, saxophone, bongos, congas, and other percussion. Musicians combine old Punjabi melodies with newer styles, such as disco, hip-hop, house, jungle, ragga, rap, rave, reggae, techno, and trance, much to the joy of youthful listeners and the consternation of many of their elders. Some of these hybrid styles are being exported to Punjab through cassettes and videos; however, the new bhangra music heard and performed in Punjab is not so westernized as that produced in the United Kingdom or the United States.

Performing groups from Punjab attract as many as ten thousand people at overseas venues such as New York's Madison Square Garden. These variety shows for families include comedians, traditional dancers, and musicians playing newer bhangra styles. Groups in the United States and the United Kingdom give concerts or club performances with one hundred to three thousand young people in attendance, depending on the popularity of the band. In nightclubs, men and women dance together, in Western style.

GIDDHĀ

When Punjabi women gather to celebrate joyous occasions, they dance *giddhā* and sing folk songs. In village *giddhā*, a group of seven to fifteen women form a circle and begin clapping. One or two women step inside the circle and start singing a song of their choice. If others know the song, two to six will step into the circle and begin to dance and sing. As the women in the outer circle join in the singing, those inside the circle make gestures relating to the song. The basic step consists of putting weight on the back foot, slightly lifting the front foot, and alternating the feet with the same movement (figure 2). After each song (which lasts two to three minutes), the dancers inside the circle join the outer circle, and one or two other women step inside and choose a different song.

Songs and *giddhā* dancing are always a prominent part of wedding celebrations. Songs bless the bride with hope for a long and happy married life. The *ghoṛī* song blesses the bridegroom; it refers to the horse he rides into the bride's village. Women also sing songs as a paste of oil and turmeric is rubbed onto the bride's and bridegroom's hands and faces in separate ceremonies before the wedding. Also before the wedding, the bridegroom's family brings gifts for the bride, and close family members gather to sing. During the wedding, which takes place in the temple, friends and relatives, accompanied by devotional singing, come to bless the nuptial couple and present garlands and gifts of money. After the wedding, *giddhā* may take place in the home of the groom, where songs welcome the new bride and celebrate the marriage.

FIGURE 2 Punjabi *giddhā* dancers perform at a Baisākhī festival in the United States, c. 1996. Photo by Harry Singh.

A *giddhā* event can take place at the bride's or the bridegroom's house or at both houses. The gatherings are separate: if the bride's family hosts the event, the female relatives and close friends of the bride are invited; if the groom's family is the host, the groom's female relatives and close friends attend. On arrival at the house, the guests—women of all ages, and young male and female children—remove their shoes and begin to sit in a circle on the floor around the edge of a room or outdoors in the courtyard. As soon as several guests are present, the singing begins, during which there is often much talking, laughing, and moving about. Additional guests enter, greet others in the room, and seat themselves. Many women wear their best attire, including brilliantly colored pants and long shirts (*salwār kamīz*), sometimes decorated with intricate gold or silver embroidery, and beautiful gold jewelry. Widows tend to dress in white or light colors and do not wear jewelry. Formerly, widows were not allowed to attend these festivities because of a belief that they might bring bad luck.

Before the dancing begins, there is usually some singing of *siṭṭhṇī*, songs through which the female relatives on one side of the family formally insult the relatives on the other side. *Siṭṭhṇī* assert immoral sexual behavior in the other family and degrade that family's character, finances, and status. Some songs insult mothers-in-law, either directly or indirectly. The two families take turns singing *siṭṭhṇī* at one another. They do this with laughter, blushing, and sometimes covering their faces in embarrassment, either mock or real. Each group tries to outdo the other in the outrageousness of the insults. The participants consider this a joyous activity and do not actually feel insulted.

One explanation for the performance of *siṭṭhṇī* is that it relaxes the guests and promotes harmony at a time of tension, preventing serious hostility by its playful teasing. Unstated conflict and competition often exist between the bride's and groom's families, especially since all wedding arrangements and events are public knowledge, and families hold certain expectations regarding all the events associated with the wedding.

After about an hour, ten to twenty women may stand, form a circle, and begin dancing *giddhā*. Songs follow, in no prearranged order. The choice belongs to the singer who steps inside the circle; often, the women sing a set of five or six songs on a similar theme.

Indian films and videos have transformed the traditional *giddhā* into a much more complex, choreographed, often flashy routine performed by professional dancers frequently wearing matching costumes.

Giddhā songs

The vocal music accompanying the dancing of *giddhā* is monophonic and seldom accompanied. Occasionally, during special celebrations women play a *ḍholkī* (see above). Melodies are based on three- to six-note scales and usually move in stepwise motion or in major or minor thirds. Duple meters, eight-beat phrasing, and the use of spoken words to emphasize texts are common elements.

The lyrics concern daily work, such as spinning, weaving, churning butter, and making bread. They may relate to specific villages or exclaim on the joys of singing and dancing. They describe relationships with in-laws, husbands, brothers, sisters, and other relatives. They contain references to purdah (the covering of a woman's head and face), the application of henna (an herb that dyes and decorates the bride's hands), the status of women in the home, and family conflicts, especially problems with mothers-in-law. Many songs reveal an unmarried woman's concerns about her parent's choice of husband or her fears about living far away from her family after marriage. Through these songs women can express the hopes, joys, sadness, anger, and other feelings that they cannot reveal directly. Some songs have double meanings referring to sexual subjects.

Learning bhangra and *giddhā*

Mothers carry their babies to the celebrations where folk songs and dances take place. Children initially learn by watching the women dance, and are allowed to join in the dancing and singing as early as they wish. Girls start dancing as young as age three; boys usually begin between the ages of ten and eleven. Children may learn a variety of dances at school, and schools occasionally organize dances, either for the children or by outside groups. Those with the strongest interest become more proficient through practice rather than through formal training.

Indian films and videos have transformed the traditional *giddhā* into a much more complex, choreographed, often flashy routine performed by professional dancers frequently wearing matching costumes. In such staged performances, the dancers generally use prerecorded music, either recorded by the women themselves or on a commercial cassette. Young Punjabi women tend to imitate the latest steps and movements from film versions. Thus, during *giddhā* celebrations in the 1990s, many young women unfamiliar with old songs wait patiently (and sometimes not so patiently) until the older women are finished, so they can dance to a modern musical arrangement on cassette.

OTHER PUNJABI SONGS

Mahiāṅ songs originally became popular in western Pakistan and are now prevalent throughout Punjab; their texts refer to the legendary lover Ranjha and his amorous relationship with Heer. The *ḍholā* is a sentimental, lyrical song about love and beauty. *Ahaniāṅ* are songs sung at a man's death. The *lorī* is a lullaby mothers sing to rock their babies to sleep. *Birahā* is a song of separation, as in the separation of a bride and bridegroom because of work or war; women or professional female singers often sing separation songs at gatherings during the rainy season (in the summer months of July and August), when married women commonly return to the home of their birth to visit their families. The celebrations include swinging on swings, dancing *giddhā*, and singing songs of longing. Unmarried women sing songs longing for husbands they have not yet found.

SIKH DEVOTIONAL MUSIC

The principal religions practiced in present-day Punjab are Hinduism, comprising about 50 percent of the population, and Sikhism, comprising about 49 percent. Music in Sikh temples (*gurdwārā*) is related to Hindustani classical music, with the addition of elements from Muslim devotional and Punjabi folk music.

The Sikh religion was founded in Punjab by Guru Nanak, the son of a Hindu, in 1469, when the state of Punjab was under Muslim rule. Nanak was a holy man and a composer of devotional songs (*nirguṇ bhajan*). He rejected idolatry and caste, and this monotheistic religion attracted both Hindu and Muslim followers. The Sikh holy book, *Guru Granth Saheb*, has 1,343 of its 1,430 pages set to various kinds of music: long-established Hindustani ragas; *kīrtan* songs with poetry created by Sikh gurus and set to these established ragas; *gurbāṇī* songs composed by Sikh gurus; and *shabad* religious songs by Sikh gurus and other composers, including Muslims and Hindus. Unlike other religions that require practices such as celibacy, self-mortification, austerities, penance, and pilgrimage, Sikhism teaches that *kīrtan* singing is the sole requirement for communication with God and the most effective path toward spiritual fulfillment. Sikhs believe that singing *kīrtan* with true longing and love of God leads to a state of bliss.

The author G. S. Mansukhani identified five types of Sikh *kīrtan*, four involving solo vocal performance and the fifth being group singing (Mansukhani 1982). The first, the most purely musical, gives prominence to raga and tala and the technical perfection of the music, and subordinates the words and meanings of the texts. In the second, more hymnlike type, the performer emphasizes the words and intonation more than the raga and the tala. In the third type, the discourse-like *kīrtan*, musicians lecture about or comment on the hymns, giving more time to talking than singing. The fourth type is audience oriented; in it, musicians sing popular or audience-requested songs. Congregation members may place money in front of the musicians to show their appreciation. The last type is congregational singing.

The first Sikh musicians were Muslim professional singers (*rabābī*) who played the plucked lute (*rabāb*) and were attracted to the musical aspect of Sikhism. In the late 1500s, during a strike for higher pay by local professional lute players, amateur singers (*raggī*) performed hymns in their place. *Raggī* have continued to perform Sikh devotional music. The Ḍhāḍī musician caste represents a third type of Sikh musician, brought into a guru's service to sing about the heroic deeds of old warriors and to inspire the guru's soldiers. (Following the death of Guru Nanak, Sikhs had become a militant religious body under successive leaders.) Such musicians became popular because they used folk tunes and sang in a zealous and emotional style.

Sikh musicians use stringed, leather, metal, and clay instruments to provide rhythm, sound the tonic as a drone, or accompany vocal music. The harmonium, the double-headed *ḍholak* drum, the tabla, and metal tongs with jingles (*cimṭā*) are common Sikh instruments. Some purists consider the harmonium inappropriate for *kīr-*

FIGURE 3 Sikh musicians (*raggī*) perform devotional music on harmonium and tabla, 1996. Photo by Joyce Middlebrook.

tan performance, since its tempered tuning tends to impede a singer's use of microtonal intervals; however, most contemporary ensembles include it (figure 3).

In the 1990s, formally trained, professional Sikh musicians travel throughout the world to sing and play devotional music in gurdwaras, temples, and homes, for regular worship services, special festivals, or celebrations such as the birth of a son. They receive payment, accommodation, and hospitality either from a gurdwara or from private individuals.

ENTERTAINMENT MUSIC

Punjab's radio stations, operated by the Indian government, play both old and new Hindi songs. Privately owned TV channels broadcast new Hindi songs, modern versions of well-known folk tunes by popular Punjabi stars, MTV from Europe, and some Western pop songs by famous performers such as Michael Jackson. Popular Punjabi song subjects include love—especially unrequited love—and longing. Male bhangra groups and soloists have performed publicly for years; now, solo concerts by female singers are beginning to attract audiences (the first female solo concerts took place in the late 1970s).

Performances of Muslim devotional music take place several times a year. Musicians playing *ḍholkī*, harmonium, and tabla accompany a group of five to eleven male singers seated together on a stage. Most qawwali musicians are professionally trained singers who perform mystical poetry in leader-chorus format. Exuberant performance of such Muslim devotional music may last hours into the night.

In the 1990s, annual cassette production is increasing, with only a small percentage exported to other countries. This recorded music consists largely of older Punjabi folk songs performed in new musical styles, often with electronic instruments, by individuals or groups. Other recordings include devotional music and folk songs for *giddhā* dances.

REFERENCES

Bedi, Sohinder Singh. 1971. *Folklore of Punjab.* New Delhi: India National Book Trust.

Hershman, P. 1981. *Punjabi Kinship and Marriage.* New Delhi: Hindustan Publishing Corporation.

Henry, Edward O. 1975. "North Indian Wedding Songs." *Journal of South Asian Literature* 11(1, 2):61–93.

Mansukhani, G. S. 1982. *Indian Classical Music and Sikh Kirtan.* London: Oxford University Press.

Middlebrook, Joyce. 1991. "Customs and Women's Wedding Songs in Two Northern California Sikh Communities." Master's thesis, California State University, Sacramento.

Singh, Khushwant. 1978. *Hymns of Guru Nanak.* Bombay: Sangam Books.

Wade, Bonnie. 1972. "Songs of Traditional Wedding Ceremonies in North India." *Yearbook of the International Folk Music Council* 4:57–65.

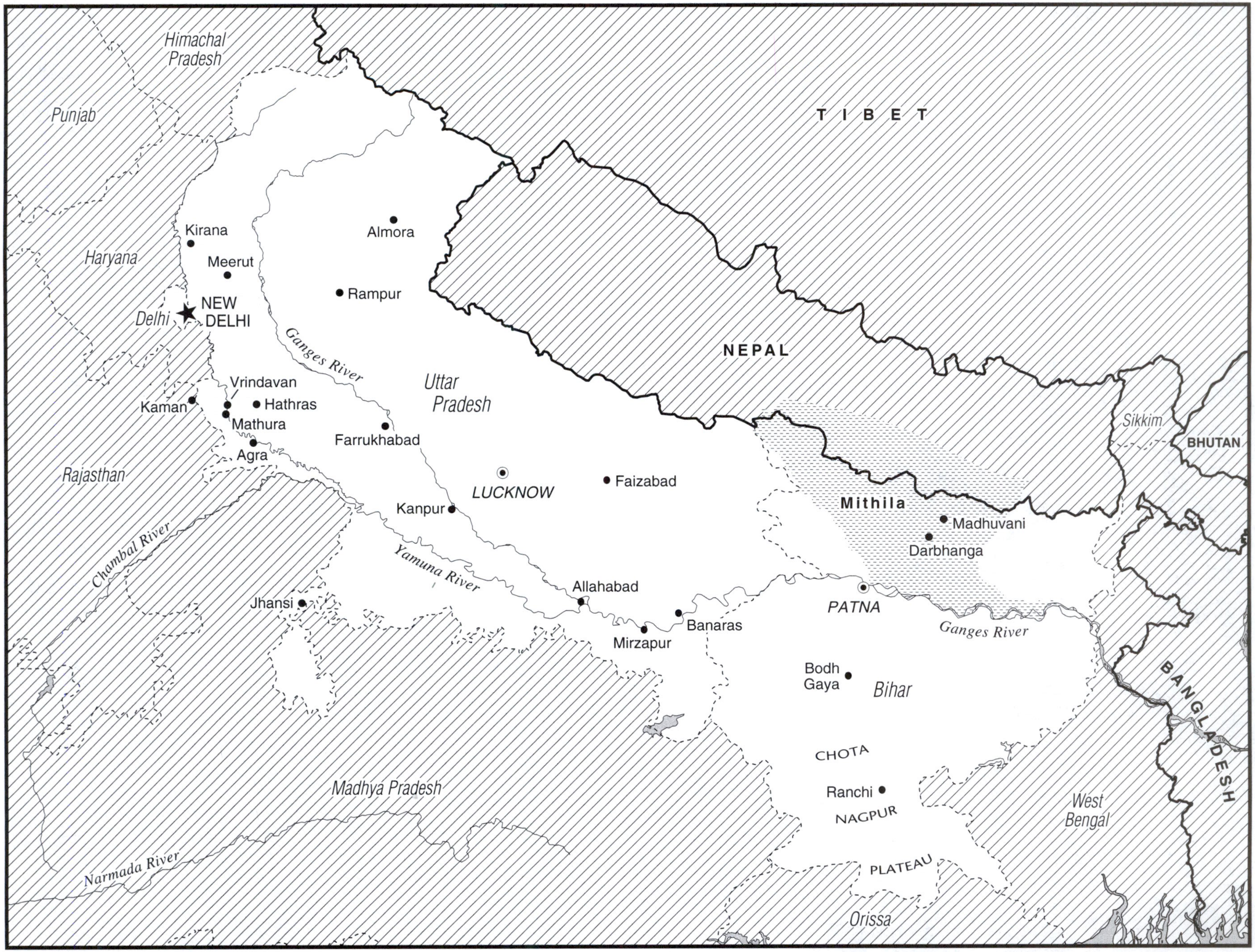
TIBET
NEPAL
BHUTAN
Sikkim
BANGLADESH
Himachal Pradesh
Punjab
Haryana
Delhi
NEW DELHI
Kirana
Meerut
Almora
Rampur
Ganges River
Uttar Pradesh
Vrindavan
Hathras
Kaman
Mathura
Farrukhabad
Agra
Rajasthan
LUCKNOW
Faizabad
Kanpur
Mithila
Madhuvani
Darbhanga
Chambal River
Yamuna River
Allahabad
Jhansi
PATNA
Banaras
Mirzapur
Ganges River
Bodh Gaya
Bihar
CHOTA
Ranchi
NAGPUR
PLATEAU
Madhya Pradesh
West Bengal
Narmada River
Orissa

North India

This densely populated region, through which the sacred Ganges River flows, is alive with music and dance, from the ubiquitous pop and film music that blares from loudspeakers, cassette players, radios, and televisions to the folk traditions and devotional songs of the many cultural and religious communities. Surrounding the urban centers—Delhi, Lucknow, Kanpur, Banaras (Varanasi), and Allahabad—where classical music has been nurtured and developed (see Part 2), the rural areas support the majority of the population that continues to maintain its own diverse music and dance forms.

Songs sung separately by women, by men, and by children reflect the region's geography and its linguistic and religious makeup, inherited partly from the region's former Hindu and Muslim kingdoms. Tribal and folk musics of the most northern areas, which extend into the massive Himalayan mountains, then give way to the regional and local musical traditions of the broad Gangetic plain—from the songs of North India's medieval Hindu poet-saints to qawwalis in praise of Sufi saints, from rural wedding songs to urban brass band tunes, and from epic singing to dance dramas.

MAP 4 North India

Uttar Pradesh

Edward O. Henry
Scott L. Marcus

Uttar Pradesh is the most populous state in India: the 1991 census showed 139 million inhabitants, a majority living rurally. Geographically and culturally, the state is not uniform. The northern part extends into the Himalayan Mountains; the southeastern part lies in the Vindhya Mountains of the Chota Nagpur Plateau. Between these extremes, the bulk of the land, and that with the highest fertility and human population density, is the flat, 160- to 320-kilometer-wide Gangetic Plain. Wheat is the primary food crop of the state, and sugarcane is the main cash crop, but more rainfall at the eastern end of the state also allows the cultivation of rice there.

Many important developments in Indian culture occurred in what is today Uttar Pradesh, including the great Hindu kingdoms at Ayodhya and Banaras (Varanasi), the numerous Muslim kingdoms culminating with the Mughal Dynasty, and the sacred Hindu complexes at Banaras and Mathura. Most important for the study of music, Uttar Pradesh was home to three of the greatest North Indian medieval poet-saints who wrote devotional hymns: Tulsi Das, Surdas, and Kabir. Their lyrics are still sung.

The state has three major language groups. The languages of the north, Garhwal and Kumaon, belong to the Himalayan family of Indo-Aryan languages. In the east, people speak Bhojpuri, which Indian linguists have classified as a member of the Magadhan family of Indo-Aryan; that this family includes Bengali, Oriya, and Assamese indicates how distant Bhojpuri is from the other Uttar Pradesh languages. The languages between the Himalayan and Magadhan families are interrelated members of the Western Hindi family. Most prominent are Khari Boli 'standing or standard speech', Hindi (the language of New Delhi and Meerut), and Urdu (the language spoken by Muslims, incorporating Persian and Arabic words). Though Hindi is not the language of a majority of Indians, it is the language with the largest number of speakers in India and the lingua franca of North India. Other Western Hindi languages—Avadhi, spoken around Lucknow, and Braj Bhasha, spoken in Mathura—are also important languages in Uttar Pradesh.

The music of Uttar Pradesh typifies the music of all North Indian regions in many respects, including the prevalence of monody, the distinctness of men's and women's music, the use of the barrel drum (*ḍholak*) and harmonium, and in large measure, the topics of song texts and the importance of devotion among them. Uttar Pradesh folk music divides into music performed by women and music performed by men, and people think of it as being divided into instrumental music (*bājā*) and vocal music (*gānā*), which they value more. Some women accompany their songs with the barrel drum, but only men perform purely instrumental folk music.

WOMEN'S SONGS

The largest body of folk music in Uttar Pradesh, or in India for that matter, is the songs that women sing: "In its effect on people's lives, there is no more important music in North India: these songs convey religious knowledge and social sentiments at the heart of everyday life, and the people who sing and hear them number in the hundreds of millions" (Henry 1988:25). Women's songs can be divided into *sanskār kī gīt*, which are part of life-cycle rituals (such as weddings and rites for births); songs sung at calendric rites or as part of such rites; and songs sung for recreation.

Women's recreational songs include those used specifically to accompany dance and those sung when women's work (such as grinding grain on hand-turned mills) or leisure allows them to sing. Both kinds of performance appear in the video *Dadi's Family* (1981) in the Odyssey series. Women also perform ritual laments and sing lullabies.

Musical style

Women's melodies usually have two phrases or strains, as in Irish jigs and reels, which can be called parts A and B. These parts combine in different ways to form structures, as in ABABA, and AABBAA, and so on. The songs never span more than one octave, but the B-part range is usually higher than the A-part range, and the scales of the parts sometimes differ (figure 1). The common melodic contour is a gentle arc: the melody rises from a starting tone, moving stepwise with occasional leaps of a third or fourth, and finally ends on the starting tone.

All women's songs are strophic, with more than one stanza sung to the same melody. Because the melody repeats many times in performance, and text lines tend to be formulaic (with a line or small cluster of lines repeating with only minor changes of wording), the songs are quite repetitious. (The song text in figure 1 has the typical structure, though it is unusually brief.) This trait, as in chanting, may have an important psychological benefit for the singers. Many women's songs have a regular beat, but probably a majority do not. Irregular meters and differences in topics, musical occasions, and purposes distinguish them from men's informal songs.

Song topics

Women's lyrics constitute a body of oral literature, and like any body of literature, their topics, functions, and significances are too diverse to admit easy generalization. Some patterns may be noted, however. One of their most important qualities is that they provide views of women far beyond the conventional images conspicuous in Hindu religious literature.

One type of women's lyric is that designated for a particular ritual or stage in a ritual process. Examples include the songs neighbors and resident women sing on the birth of a son, and in a preliminary wedding rite when turmeric is rubbed on the bride's skin. Turmeric (*haldī*) renders the skin a lustrous and auspicious hue. The lyrics of such songs often refer to the type of event at hand. Birth songs frequently concern the birth of the deity Ram, and wedding songs refer to ritual acts and actors in the wedding. In figure 1 (after Henry 1988:40), recorded during a turmeric-rubbing ritual before a wedding, the text refers to personnel involved in the rite: the *koirin* is the wife of a *koirī*, a man of the vegetable-growing caste; the *telin* is the wife of a *telī*, a man of the caste whose traditional job was to extract vegetable oils from

FIGURE 1 A typical women's melody from eastern Uttar Pradesh, with the B-strain having a slightly higher range and different scale (the sixth tone is a half step higher) from the A-strain. The structure of this performance is AABAA. Transcribed by Edward O. Henry.

seeds. The song expresses sympathy for the bride, who will soon leave her natal home and village to live with her husband in his natal family, all of whom are strangers to her.

> koirin koirin tū baṛī rānī re;
> kahāvāṅ ke haradī upar kāilū āj are
> hamarī rādhikā deī asa sukuvār re sahahi na jānelī
> haradiyā kā jhāṅkare
> telin telin tū baṛī rānī re;
> kahāvāṅ kā telavā upar kāilū āj are
> hamarī rādhikā deī as sukuvār re sahahi na jānelī
> kaṛūvā kā jhāṅkare

> *Koirin, koirin,* you are a great queen;
> From where have you brought the turmeric today?
> My Radhika Devi so tender cannot bear
> the harsh turmeric.
> *Telin, telin,* you are a great queen;
> From where have you brought the oil today?
> My Radhika Devi so tender cannot bear
> the harsh mustard-seed oil.

Some of these songs, with their lists of ritual objects, acts, or persons, serve as mnemonic devices, insuring proper performance of the ritual.

Another type of women's ritual lyric is the insult song (*gālī*), usually graphically obscene. Women frequently aim such songs at visiting male in-laws and other male outsiders (even Brahmin priests), especially at weddings but also on other occasions. In the following example (after Henry 1988:47), women at the wedding of a female relative insult their new female in-laws, accusing their new male in-laws of presenting jewelry to the bride in the wedding only to confiscate it afterward.

Māurū dekh jin bhulī hā e bābā māurū hav māṅgan kā
dulahā hav chinār kā; dulahin hav phacibaratā
kaṅganā dekh jin bhulī hā e bābā kaṅganā hav maṅganī kā

Look at the crown! Don't forget, mister, that the crown is borrowed!
The groom is of a whore; the bride is of a faithful woman!
Look at the bracelet! Don't forget, mister, that the bracelet is borrowed!

Women sing devotional songs both in the context of worship (figure 2) and in recreational sessions. The following text (after Henry 1988:90), recorded in a rite of worship of the Mother Goddess, shows that deity's power to award sons to the pious and disease to the unfaithful. In Bhojpuri, mother goddess songs are called *pacaṛā* and *mātā māī kī gīt.*

Maiyā morī pātarī pātarī kamaṛuā deśavā ārujhe ho
kekarā ke dehale śītalā (repeated)
kekarā ke dehale kālī
das pāṅc putavā ho (repeated)
kekarā ke kāinū nirasaṅtaniyā ho
dharamī ke dehalu sev kā
das pāṅc putavā ho.
garabhī ke kāila nirasaṅtaniyā
kekarā ke dehale maiyā
maiyā morī pātarī pātarī kamaṛuā deśavā ārujhe ho
das pāṅc gotiyā
kekarā ke pīṭhiyā aṅgaravā ḍaro ho nā
dharamī kā dehalo sev kā, das pāṅc gotiyā
garabhī kā pīṭhiyā ḍaro aṅgaravā ho
maiyā morī pātarī pātarī kamaṛuā deśavā ārujhe ho

Mother so thin, Omnipresence of Bengal,
To whom do you give, Sitala [the name of the smallpox goddess],
To whom do you give, Kali [another name of the Mother Goddess],
Five or ten sons?
Whom do you make childless?
I give to the pious, the devotees,
Five or ten sons.
I make the proud childless.
To whom do you give, Mother,
Mother so thin, Omnipresence of Bengal,
Five or ten pox?
On whose back do you rub hot coals?
To the religious devotees, five or ten pox.
I rub hot coals on the backs of the proud.
Mother so thin, Omnipresence of Bengal.

Hindus believe that hymn singing, like other kinds of worship, brings religious merit and, like all kinds of music performed in Hindu ritual contexts, is auspicious.

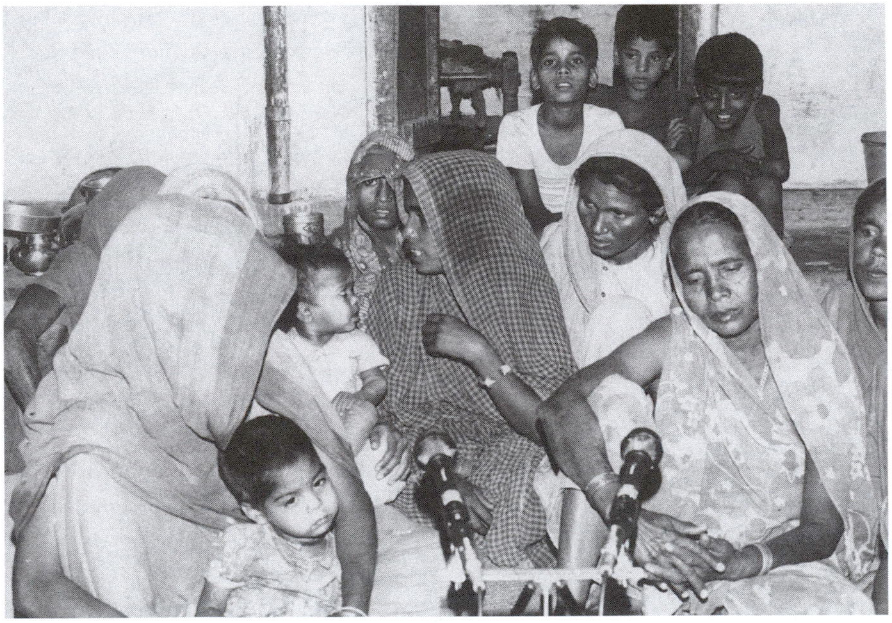

FIGURE 2 A women's informal song session on the outskirts of Banaras, 1978. Photo by Edward O. Henry.

In addition to the songs of life-cycle and worship rites, women sing many songs essentially for recreation. The songs cover a variety of topics; some of these are shared with men's music, like the songs of the spring rite called Holī, but many express primarily feminine concerns. Valued qualities are a good strong, uncracking voice and the ability of a woman to sing, but the outstanding aesthetic of women's song is the appropriateness of the song to the occasion.

SONGS OF INFORMAL MEN'S GROUPS

Village men also get together in informal groups to sing. Most common is the devotional group. Men gather at a shrine, temple, or home to sing devotional songs (bhajans) or the more repetitious hymns (*harikīrtan*) that feature repeated climaxes. Men of all castes may participate, just as women of all castes may participate in women's informal singing sessions, because recruitment is from the neighborhood group that includes castes of all levels above the so-called scheduled castes, or untouchables (*ādivāsī*). Scheduled castes live in separate, outlying hamlets.

The *ḍholak* 'double-headed drum' is the most important instrument used to accompany men's singing. As with many South Asian double-headed drums (*pakhāvaj* and *mridangam*), one of its heads has a higher pitch than the other, and produces busier patterns; the lower one provides complementary patterns of less frequent thumps and gulps. The drummer has primary control over the tempo and provides much of the rhythmic drive. Some drummers, including preadolescents, play

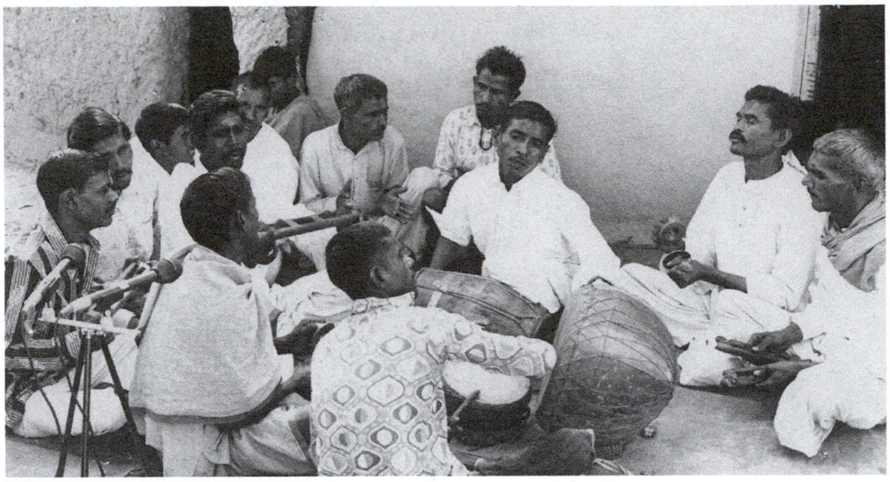

FIGURE 3 Men sing spring-season songs (*phaguā*) on the outskirts of Banaras, 1978. Instruments visible from left to right are: wooden clappers (*kartāl*, just behind microphone, and *jhāñjh*), hand cymbals (*jārī*, below *jhāñjh*), barrel drum (*ḍholak*), kettledrums (*nagāṛā*, front center, not typically part of *phāguā* sessions), hand cymbals (*jārī*), and wooden clappers (*kartāl*). Photo by Edward O. Henry.

with dazzling skill. Clapping provides other rhythmic support, as do two kinds of percussion instruments. Those struck together are the small hand cymbals (*mañjīrā*, *jārī*, or *jhāl*) and wooden clappers with metal disks that slide back and forth on pins (*kartāl*). A similar wooden frame instrument with sliding metal disks (*jhāñjh*) is oscillated like a tambourine (figure 3).

Performance of a *harikīrtan* begins at a moderate tempo and volume and increases in speed and intensity to an ecstatic climax, after which singing resumes at moderate levels to build to another peak, and so on. Traditional and popular songs (mostly film songs) provide the tunes. A performance may last for twenty minutes or more. Singers have said that while singing such songs they feel great devotion to God, their minds become entirely occupied with God, and a feeling of peace prevails. Hindus believe that hymn singing, like other kinds of worship, brings religious merit and like all kinds of music performed in Hindu ritual contexts, is auspicious (*maṇgal*). Devotional-singing groups provide sociability, intimacy, and affiliation, especially meaningful in impersonal urban contexts (Singer 1972).

Informal male groups also convene to sing seasonal songs. Outstanding among these are the songs associated with the rite of spring called Holī. Around Mathura (in western Uttar Pradesh) these songs are called *rasiyā*, and though they can address almost any topic and be sung at any time of year, they stereotypically concern the exploits of the deity Krishna, especially his playful exploits with Radha and the other milkmaids (*gopī*), and are sung most often around Holī (Manuel 1994). Singers choose from about twenty stock tunes, and the *ḍholak* and a harmonium (portable hand-pumped organ) provide the accompaniment.

In eastern Uttar Pradesh, the songs of the Holī season are called *phaguā*, and their style is similar to that of the *harikīrtan*. Women in eastern Uttar Pradesh also sing *phaguā*, but their performances lack the driving rhythm of the men's. The following excerpt (after Henry 1988:126) is a *phaguā* from eastern Uttar Pradesh, a dialogue between Krishna and Radha, his favorite milkmaid. Nanda Lal here means 'dear son of Nanda', Krishna's adoptive father, and Gval is the name of Krishna's caste.

Le lo dahī Nanda Lāl, Lāl dahiyā morī le lo
kahavā kā tū gop gvālī
kā tumāro nām. Lāl...
māthura kī ham gop gvāle
rādhā hamārā nām. Lāl...
ī dahiyā morī sāsu jamolī

becan calī ham āj. Lāl...
kab kar dūhal, kab kar jamāval
kab kar jaranav dāl. Lāl...
bhoravā kā dūhal, sānjh hī kā jamāval
sānjhavā joran dia dāl. Lāl...
i ha cahakavā kalp nāth pāṇde gāve
henarī baithale āj. Lāl...
āj kā dinavā hāue mehamanavā
holī kā hāue tyohār. Lāl...

Buy yogurt, Nanda Lal; dear boy, buy my yogurt.
Where are you from, milkmaid?
What is your name? Dear boy...
I am a Gval milkmaid of Mathura;
Radha is my name. Dear boy...
My mother-in-law made this yogurt
I came to sell today. Dear boy...
When was the milk taken from the cow? When did it thicken?
When did you add it to the lentils? Dear boy...
The morning's milking, it was thickened that very evening.
It was added to the lentils in the evening. Dear boy, buy my yogurt.
Kalp Nath Pande sings this song of Holī.
Henry sits today. Dear boy...
Today he is a guest,
The festival is Holī. Dear boy...

Many of the images of these songs pertaining to Krishna come from the poetry of Surdas and other medieval poet-saints.

During the monsoon season (July to September), both men and women sing songs thought especially appropriate for the rainy months, called *sāvan* (the name of a Hindu month in the monsoon season), *kajalī,* or *kajarī* (see below). These songs focus on lovers, in particular lovers who are separated.

BIRAHĀ AND *KAJALĪ*

Birahā

Birahā is a folk-music genre of the Bhojpuri region of northern India, which straddles the two Indian states of Uttar Pradesh and Bihar. Over the last one hundred years, the genre has developed from a song form performed only by the cowherd caste (Ahīr) and a few other closely related castes. Especially since the 1940s, the genre has developed to the point where it has become the region's most popular folk music, avidly sung by a broad section of both regions' lower castes. Present-day performances occur most commonly at either rural weddings or urban temple festivals; other occasions include housewarmings, yearly festivals, and births and deaths in musicians' families. Audiences are mostly male, and range from one hundred to over one thousand; women watch and listen from their houses and occasionally from the audience's periphery.

Performance ensemble

The *birahā* ensemble usually consists of five men; the group's leader and solo singer stands while his ensemble or "party" members sit in a semicircle around him. At one end of the semicircle sits a *ḍholak* 'double-headed barrel drum' player, at the other end a harmonium player. Two others sit behind the singer, providing vocal accompaniment and playing one of two hand-held idiophones. The most common idiophone is the *kartāl,* which comprises two pairs of narrow iron bars approximately 23 centimeters in length. The musician holds a pair in each hand and plays each pair independently, striking one bar of each pair against the other, thereby creating a high-pitched rhythmic accompaniment to the music. While this first type of idiophone is unique to *birahā,* a second type of idiophone, called *jhāñjh,* is widely used in other types of music. The *jhāñjh* consists of two pairs of wooden clackers, each mounted with multiple sets of tiny cymbals.

Ensembles take the name of the lead singer, as in "Hira Lal and Party." Many lead singers achieve substantial fame, and a handful of elite singers achieve superstar status throughout much of the Bhojpuri region. Performances commonly feature two "opposing" parties, with each group taking turns singing two songs at a time. The ensembles usually perform on a raised platform, and audience members sit between the two groups, turning to face each group as it sings. An explicit aspect of competition exists between the two groups, and audience members are quick to compare the two groups at the conclusion of the event.

Song genre

In the 1880s, the *birahā* genre consisted of two-line songs sung most notably by individual cowherders within the Ahīr community (Grierson 1884, 1886). According to popular belief, the Ahīr poet and singer Bihari Lal Yadav (1857–1926) of Banaras made several changes in this form, including the expansion of the poetic text to an unlimited number of lines, the insertion of a recurring refrain line, and the addition of two chorus singers and the iron-rod idiophones (Marcus 1995b). Present-day singers, especially older retired singers, claim that in Bihari's time *birahā* songs employed only one specific melody with variations.

Bihari's immediate disciples began occasionally to insert other melodies borrowed either from Bombay film songs or from other folk-music genres (Marcus 1993). Singers enlarged the accompanying ensemble, first adding the *ḍholak* and later the harmonium. With these melodic and instrumental changes, *birahā* performance spread beyond village settings to regional towns and cities, especially to Banaras.

Since the 1960s and 1970s, the prominent addition of film-song tunes and non-*birahā* folk melodies redefined the genre, and it developed into a suite form. A single song incorporated fifteen or more melodies, with the first four to eight text lines set to one melody, the next four to eight lines set to a new melody, and so on. In this suite form, the traditional *birahā* melody occurs only two or three times per song, usually for refrain lines that poetically encapsulate the song's main mood or message. Most songs are in eight-beat *kaharvā* rhythm, although performers also use six- and seven-beat rhythms. Over the last decades, *birahā* has appeared in the mass media, first on LP records from Calcutta-based companies and then on All India Radio broadcasts, LP and cassette recordings by local companies based largely in Banaras (Marcus 1995a), and most recently on television.

The first song performed at a typical event is a relatively short religious song of entreaty (*bandanā*) in which the singer asks for a specific deity's blessings to ensure a successful performance. All the subsequent performance items are usually narrative songs, each lasting up to 45 minutes. Singers nowadays include impromptu spoken prose passages in their sung texts to further the specific song's storyline, in contrast to past generations, when *birahā* songs contained only sung poetry. Songs might relate religious stories such as the birth of Lord Krishna (Marcus 1995b) or episodes from the Ramayana epic, nationalistic events such as the heroic deeds of those who died in the independence struggle against the British, or regional epic tales (*Canainī* and

In both city and village wedding performances, an important aspect of performer-audience interaction is the offering of tips or gifts (*inām*) by audience members during a song performance.

Ālhā). They may also offer social commentary (on dowry or alcohol abuse), news on topical themes such as a theft at an important temple (Marcus 1989), or recent changes in the national government.

Performance contexts

Temple performances usually take place as part of annual festivals of renewal and rededication (*shriṅgār* 'decoration'). The temple festival season generally runs from September to early December. Festival organizers raise money for these events by requesting donations from neighborhood stores and homes. Musical performances, commonly staged in the city street adjacent to the temple, start around 9:00 P.M. and continue through the night. The audience sits on tarpaulins spread on the ground, and generous displays of mini-bulbs (Christmas lights) create the effect of walls and (occasionally) the ceiling of an otherwise nonexistent pavilion. Loudspeakers strung above nearby streets invariably amplify the music throughout the neighborhood.

Other festival activities may include reading from religious books such as the Ramayana, creating wall paintings, repainting the temple itself, and in the case of two- or three-day festivals, showing a film or including a performance of other music genres such as qawwali or "covers" of Bombay film songs.

Village weddings with *birahā* performances usually occur from March to June, after the harvest, when the empty fields provide ample space for guests, who often number in the hundreds. For larger weddings a single large tent is erected, providing shade for one and all; smaller weddings often take place in village orchards.

In both city and village wedding performances, an important aspect of performer-audience interaction is the offering of tips or gifts (*inām*) by audience members during a song performance. The singer momentarily stops his song to acknowledge the giver and the specific gift, with words such as "My dear friend, Ram Narayan, has graciously presented 5 rupees and a garland of flowers." Members of both the *shriṅgār* organizing committee and the bride's and groom's immediate families are especially expected to participate in this gift giving.

Social organization

The *birahā* community of singers has explicit levels of social organization. On the broadest level, all singers must belong to a specific lineage or *akhāṛā,* with membership by either blood relation or ritual initiation. The five main lineages trace their origins back to Bihari Lal Yadav (see above), considered to be the founder of the modern *birahā* form (Marcus 1989). Among Bihari's many students, five established their own lineages, which eventually incorporated all their own sons and students. Other lineages beyond these initial five started when singers of another musical genre, *kajalī,* switched to singing *birahā.* (Interestingly, some former *kajalī* artists refer to their lineages as *gharānā,* the term for musical lineage in the North Indian classical music tradition.)

When two *birahā* groups are invited to perform at a single event, they are always from different lineages. The competitive element is thus not just a matter of two performing groups but of two lineages. Audience members are aware of lineage affiliations, as the last line of every song provides this information.

Birahā singers are affiliated not only with a lineage; each singer also associates with a poet, who creates most if not all of the songs that he performs. The poetic portions of *birahā* songs are fixed compositions that the singer obtains and memorizes prior to a given performance. (As with most North Indian folk music, *birahā* poets create new songs by setting new text to preexisting melodies.) The relationship between singer and poet is a formal one; the poet is recognized as the master or teacher (guru) and the singer as the student *(celā)*. A formal ritual establishes the relationship, after which the singer may perform the poet's compositions (as well as those of other poets of the same lineage). Poets incorporate into their songs' final lines both their own names and that of the singer's and poet's shared lineage affiliation.

Kajalī

Kajalī (also spelled *kajarī* or *kajrī*) is a folk-song genre of the Bhojpuri region performed during the rainy season—usually late June to September—when lush greenery reappears and agricultural labor begins again. Unlike *birahā, kajalī* performance is not confined to a specific caste or group of castes. It appears in various performance contexts: (1) as a women's genre sung to accompany a line dance, (2) as a women's or men's genre sung while swinging on swings during the rainy season, (3) as a men's genre sung as dance accompaniment (often a circle dance using pairs of sticks), (4) as a men's entertainment genre in which professional or semiprofessional groups perform on stage for formal occasions, and (5) as a vocal form in the repertoires of North Indian classical singers and instrumentalists.

Kajalī texts refer to the rains (often a drizzling rain), to black clouds and lightning, to various bird sounds, and to the swings that are set up in this season. The names of the months (Asāṛh, Sāvan, and Bhādoṅ) are an important part of the text symbolism. Because the rainy season is recognized as a time for love, song texts often describe the woman's longing while her beloved is away. "The black clouds have gathered; without my husband my heart is not happy" is a characteristic song line. Another image commonly evoked is the empty bed. *Kajalī* is thus considered a *virah gīt* 'song of separation', expressing the pains of being apart from one's beloved (Henry 1988). Song texts further exalt a particular association between *kajalī* and the city of Mirzapur in southeastern Uttar Pradesh. Many believe that the genre actually originated in this city. An annual festival there celebrates the city's main goddess, Vindhyachal Devi, with various *kajalī* performances, and takes place on a day called Kajalī.

Women's kajalī

The strength of the women's genre that accompanies the line dance rests, in part, on the association between *kajalī* and another festival called Tīj. That festival includes a fast that women undertake to ensure their husbands' good health, followed by feasting, the wearing of new clothes, and the singing of *kajalī* with its swaying dance.

Women's *kajalī* is not restricted to these two festivals, for village women sing whenever they get a chance during the rainy season. Many believe that *kajalī* is first and foremost a women's genre. There is no audience, and all women present participate by singing and dancing at the same time, generally without musical instruments, although a single seated woman may play the *ḍholak*. In the presence of a seated drummer, women sometimes sit around her and sing without the dance movements. Even when an occasion does not specifically call for *kajalī* songs, women during the rainy season may still sing *kajalī*. These songs are passed down from one generation to the next, and are thus popular during seasonal celebrations and activities, such as Lord Krishna's birthday, at rituals following childbirth, and as work songs while women transplant rice seedlings in the fields.

Men's kajalī

According to popular belief, men made several changes in the women's genre. In so doing they created two manifestations of *kajalī*—one that retained the dance movements (*dhunmuniyā kajalī*) and another that developed into a professional or semi-professional stage genre (*shāyarī kajalī*). In both formats, men instituted the position of the poet. A singer becomes the disciple (*celā*) of a specific poet (guru), after which he can receive and perform the poet's compositions. As in *birahā,* poets and their disciples belong to lineages (*akhāṛā* or *gharānā*) that are indicated in the last lines of songs, along with the poet's name, and performances often include competition between two groups from different lineages.

The men's texts include the standard *kajalī* themes, but new topics also abound, especially in the male dance-song form. Poets find topics in books and newspapers, and thus there are songs about the first people to climb Mount Everest, Mahatma Gandhi's confrontations with the British, and Indira Gandhi's death.

The professional stage genre (*shāyarī kajalī*) includes a formal performance ensemble consisting of a lead singer, instrumentalists, and chorus singers. Instruments include the *ḍholak* and/or tabla drums, the harmonium (commonly played by the lead singer), and often one other melody instrument (the double-reed *śahnāī,* the *bāṅsurī* 'bamboo flute', or the clarinet). The ensemble performs outdoors on a raised platform, with the audience commonly seated on chairs; the music is broadcast over loudspeakers to the surrounding neighborhood. In the early twentieth century, annual temple festivals often featured this type of *kajalī*. However, *birahā* singers have largely taken over these performances, leaving the professional *kajalī* in a state of decline. In response to this shift, some *kajalī* singers have changed over to singing *birahā*. Interestingly, *birahā* singers often sing short *kajalī* songs in their rainy-season performances.

Outside the Bhojpuri region, *kajalī* is known only as a genre performed by North Indian classical musicians whose roots are in eastern Uttar Pradesh and western Bihar. The most famous of these are the singers Girija Devi and Siddeshwari Devi and the *śahnāī* master Bismillah Khan. These musicians commonly end their rainy-season performances with one or more *kajalī* songs. When asked if classical musicians consider *kajalī* a light classical genre in such performances, Girija Devi replied that it is still folk music, to which they add their artistry; "we build it up and decorate it" (personal interview, Banaras, 1987). But to most people of the Bhojpuri region, *kajalī* remains a folk-music genre with no relation to classical music.

MENDICANT MUSICIANS' MUSIC

Mendicant is a polite word for beggar (*bhīk māṅgnewālā*). Most sensational are the snake charmers. They play a special instrument called *bīn* or *puṅgī* made from a gourd into which are inserted a windpipe and two bamboo tubes, and also sometimes a longer metal tube. The bamboo tubes contain single reeds, so the instrument—incorrectly called a flute in English—is really a clarinet. One tube has five to seven holes, which the player may stop with his fingers to produce different tones; the other tube or tubes produce the drone. The technique of circular breathing enables players to sound the melody and drone continuously without pausing for breath. The mouth and cheeks act as a chamber that is constantly refilled with air, in the manner of a bagpipe sack. These performers carry snakes (including harmless ones) that they allow to slither almost free during the show, and sometimes enormous pythons, but they "charm" only the cobras. Snakes have no ears; they respond more to the swaying of the player and his instrument than to the music. Though the cobras still have fangs, their charmers sever the ducts that supply them with venom (Skafte 1979).

A second kind of mendicant is the blind man. Singing devotional songs and playing the tambourine or a jingle-less version called *kanjīrā, daph,* or *caṅg,* they beg in trains and train stations and on the streets. In eastern Uttar Pradesh, people address them by the name of the blind poet-saint Surdas.

A third type of mendicant, called *jogī,* seems to be disappearing, though recordings of *jogī* music were made as recently as 1990. The mendicant in figure 4 plays a bowed stringed instrument called a *sāraṅgī* and sings hymns and epics. The prevailing type of hymn sung by the *jogī* and blind mendicants is the hymn of the formless
TRACK 20 Divine (*nirguṇ bhajan*). Such hymns convey beliefs in a deity without attributes, yet their texts focus not on the deity, but on the transitory nature of life, the inevitability of death, the temptations of maya—this world of illusion—and the importance of devotion for the rebirth of the soul. Most of these hymns contain the signature of the poet-saint Kabir.

PROCESSIONAL MUSIC

The most important and frequent processions are those of the bridegroom's party to the home of the bride or to another location where the wedding will take place. The poorest families can afford only a small drum ensemble. Informal in structure, such a group may use a frame drum (*daphalā*) about 60 centimeters in diameter, struck with a stick in one hand while the other hand holds a bamboo splint against the drumhead to add a buzzing sound; a pair of clay-bowl kettledrums beaten with sticks (*nagāṛā*); and other percussion instruments.

Slightly more expensive to hire is the *śahnāī* ensemble. The *śahnāī* is a double-reed instrument similar to the oboe, but with finger holes in a tapered cylindrical body. In this ensemble, one or more *śahnāī* players sound a drone, one plays the lead, and others play unison and supporting roles. A pair of kettledrums (*ḍuggī* and *khurḍak*) provide the percussive rhythm, played with fingers and hands like the tabla of classical Hindustani music.

FIGURE 4 A mendicant (*jogī*) accompanies himself on *sāraṅgī* in Ghazipur District, Uttar Pradesh, 1978. Photo by Edward O. Henry.

Still more expensive is the brass band, called English band (*aṅgrezī baiṅḍ*). The musicians usually wear uniforms, and the more expensive the group, the gaudier the uniform. Trumpets, cornets, and clarinets play the lead roles, and trombones, French horns, and euphoniums are supporting instruments. The percussion section may include maracas, cymbals, snare drum, bass drum, and the smaller Scottish bass drum. The bands play five kinds of music: Western folk and popular tunes; popular Indian music, mostly film songs; marches; Indian folk tunes such as *kajalī* and *purvī*; and Indian ragas.

The most expensive modern band has a distinctive flatbed wagon adorned with a large swan or other silhouette on each side. The vehicle carries or tows a loud, music-obscuring diesel engine that drives a generator to power the amplification and illumination systems. A singer or trumpeter rides on the wagon and uses the microphone, generating a sound that is heavily reverberated and always ear-splitting. The rest of the band trails behind, garishly illuminated even during the day by men carrying generator-powered fluorescent lights. In addition to leading the bridegroom's procession, the band provides musical entertainment when his party arrives at the wedding. Daring young men, and nowadays in the cities sometimes women, dance to this music, in a style influenced by music videos seen on television.

The most important venue for live musical entertainment is the wedding, at which the bridegroom's party and other guests enjoy chewing betel leaf and other delectables while they listen to the musical performance.

MUSIC FOR ENTERTAINMENT

The most important venue for live musical entertainment is the wedding, at which the bridegroom's party and other guests enjoy chewing betel leaf and other delectables while they listen to the musical performance. Informal bands are less expensive and more variable in composition than formal bands. Manuel reports that formal bands in western Uttar Pradesh specialize in performing the highly ornamented Hathrasi style of *rasiyā* songs (Manuel 1994). Formal bands in eastern Uttar Pradesh tend to specialize in either the Bhojpuri folk song genre *birahā* or "Hindi" qawwali, but also perform a kind of love song (*purvī*) as in the example below. The anguish of a woman separated from her lover or husband, a common theme, is thought to be intensified by certain natural phenomena like the call of the cuckoo and the scent of the *mahūā*-tree blossom, as in this text (after Henry 1988:210–211).

adhī adhī ratiyā ke bole koelariyā
cihuṅkī uṭhī goriyā sejariyā se ṭhāṛh
amavā mojarī gailaṅya mahuvā kocāī gailaṅya
mor birahiniyāṅ ke niniyā bhorāī gailaṅya
rahī rahī dehiyāṅ se bahailī bayariyā
khulan lāge sudhiyā ke dehalo kevāṛ
phulavā phulāī gailaiṅ bhaṅvarā lobhāī gailaiṅ
kavane kasuravā se piyā ghar nāhīṅ ailaiṅ?
likh likh patiyā paṭhavalī vipatiyā bahan lāge ratiyā
nayan jaladhār
paṅchi uṛan lāge gagan magan lāge
manavā ke pijaṛā se suganā bolan lāge
hamāro sanehiyā na gune niramohiyā
daiv ho jāne kahiyā le kaṭihani gāṛh
adhī adhī ratiyā ke bole koelariyā

At midnight, the cuckoo calls.
The pretty woman starts and stands near the bed.
The mango has blossomed; the *mahūā* has flowered.
The sleep of the lady separated from her lover has been broken.
The breeze blows over her body.
The door to memory begins to open.
The flowers have blossomed, the bee hovers near.
Why has my husband not come home?
She wrote her sorrows in a letter, posted it, and darkness began to descend.
Tears flow in her eyes.
Birds began to fly, and the sky began to lighten.
The parrot began to call from the cage of her heart.

The hardhearted one does not remember the love he gave to me.
God knows when he will remove this sorrow.
At midnight, the cuckoo calls.

"Hindi" (or popular) qawwalis derive from Sufi songs of the same name. Devotees within this tradition sing mostly Urdu qawwalis, principally on the anniversaries of Sufi saints at their shrines but also at other places and times. Unlike the Sufi songs, which express mystical experience, the Hindi qawwalis treat both love and Hindu mythological topics. The lyrics on the subject of love derive in part from another Indo-Muslim genre, the ghazal, usually about unrequited love—which may be interpreted as a woman's love for a man or God's love for humankind.

Qawwali bands employ a lead singer, often a harmonium player, a *ḍholak* player (who may also sing), and supporting vocalists who clap during the rhythmic portions. A qawwali performance alternates sections in free rhythm with sections in hard-driving, percussive rhythm that accompanies loud, florid, and sometimes high-pitched vocal passages. Hindi qawwalis evoke a surge of feeling, the primary aesthetic of entertainment music.

Epics

Another kind of entertainment music, no doubt less commonly heard nowadays, is the epic. The seminal study of South Asian oral epics edited by Blackburn and others (1989) shows the epic to be a diverse and widespread type of musical performance in India. Scholars have reported epics in Uttar Pradesh, including the *Ālhā*, the *Ḍholā*, and the *Lorik*—long, complex stories of scheming, magic, and battle, named after their protagonists.

Nonprofessionals perform the *Lorik* for the enjoyment of their companions and themselves, but paid specialists, both full-time and part-time, perform the *Ālhā* and the *Ḍholā* for weddings and other special occasions. Only in certain cases is there a connection between epic performance and caste. *Ālhā* performers witnessed in eastern Uttar Pradesh and Bihar were of the Naṭ caste, whose traditional occupations included that of acrobat (Henry 1988); however, near Allahabad, Uttar Pradesh, the ethnomusicologist Nazir Jairazbhoy recorded a Brahmin's performance of the *Ālhā* epic (1988). A *Ḍholā* singer near Agra, Uttar Pradesh, was of the water carrier caste (Kahār) but there is nothing to indicate this is a regular association, and his sidemen (instrumental accompanists) were of the tailor and Brahmin castes. In eastern Uttar Pradesh, members of the Ahīr caste (traditionally cowherds) consider themselves owners of the *Lorik* epic, but in Chattisgarh in southeastern Madhya Pradesh, people associate *Lorik* with the place rather than a caste.

All three epics may be performed as dance dramas, but are more commonly performed as vocal genres in which the lead vocalist alternates spoken, chanted, and sung portions to maintain interest and highlight events in the story. The vocalist's associate or assistant sings in unison or response. Solo *Lorik* singers observed by Henry in eastern Uttar Pradesh used no instrumental accompaniment; the *Ālhā* singers sang to the accompaniment of the *ḍholak*; and the *Ḍholā* performers near Agra played a small bowed lute, a metal percussion instrument, and the *ḍholak*.

MUSIC IN FOLK DRAMA

Three kinds of "folk" drama in Uttar Pradesh rely on music to communicate part of the story and enhance the presentation. The *rāmlīlā* depicts events in the *Rāmcaritmānas* (on the life of the Hindu deity Rama), the popular sixteenth-century vernacular version of the Ramayana story by the poet-saint Tulsi Das. *Rāslīlā*, like *rāmlīlā*, dates from the late medieval devotional religious movements in northern

India, but conveys events in the life of Krishna, especially his childhood in Vrindavan as a naughty but cute little boy, his youth as a lustful young man with the milkmaids, the circular dance (*rās*) of Krishna and the milkmaids, and the coming of Uddhav to try to bring Krishna back to Vrindavan.

The third kind of folk drama, *nauṭaṅkī*, is not really folk theater [see MUSIC AND DANCE: NORTHERN AREA]. It is staged in villages, but its actors are traveling professionals, not local people. The stories come from epics such as *Gopīcand* and *Puran Mal*, formerly circulated by bards of medieval religious cults. Among musics performed in this drama, one is special to it—the four-line stanzaic form called *caubolā*. Kettledrums (*nagāṛā*) and the harmonium are standard accompanying instruments.

CHANGING MUSIC AND CULTURE

The first mass medium to exploit folk music was the booklet containing lyrics, some already existing and some newly composed. Vendors still sell booklets here and there in the towns and cities of Uttar Pradesh. The booklets designate which traditional or popular tune can serve as the vehicle for the text. The 78-rpm records (and later, 45-rpm and 33-rpm) that followed became obsolete in the 1970s, when cassettes were introduced (Manuel 1993). Because cassettes are cheaper to manufacture, they are more widely produced than were records.

Cassettes are a mixed blessing. Clearly the great disadvantage is that they result in less live music. I observed weddings in which the bridal family played a *śahnāī* cassette of music in place of hiring a band, and where cassette jockeys played film music at blaring intensity, discouraging and replacing women's wedding songs. Manuel reports that some Hindus will just play a bhajan tape instead of going to a temple to sing bhajans. The significant results are less live performance, less communal music making (in keeping with the dwindling communal spirit of the village, noted by myself and others), the confinement of music to fewer specialists, and the loss of jobs for musicians and priests.

Much of the "folk" music heard on cassette is not in the rural style but has been "improved" by rearrangement (including the more frequent use of chords, played on keyboard or guitar) and the addition of nontraditional instruments including the keyed zither *benjo* or *bulbul taraṅg*, which Jairazbhoy has identified as the Japanese *taisho koto* (Jairazbhoy and Catlin 1993:176); mandolin; and the synthesizer or Casio keyboard. A substantial segment of newly composed "folk songs" features licentious lyrics. Cassette technology makes many different kinds of music more accessible and widely known, raises performance standards, generates income, and supports regional types of music by reproducing them and facilitating their broadcast.

SOURCES AND FURTHER READING

Though only one book (Henry 1988) has focused exclusively on Uttar Pradesh folk music and its cultural contexts, many scholars in anthropology, folklore, and musicology have written about it. Important Ph.D. dissertations submitted in the United States include those of Hari S. Upadhyaya on Bhojpuri songs and family dynamics; Laxmi Tewari on the songs of Kanpur (supplemented with some from Banaras); and Stephen Slawek on devotional songs (*kīrtan).* Anthropologists who have included lyrics or musical occasions as part of their ethnographic studies of the rural culture include Ruth and Stanley Freed, Ann Gold, Edward Henry (1988), Doranne Jacobson, Nita Kumar, Oscar Lewis, Leigh Minturn, Jack Planalp, Gloria Raheja, S. L. Srivastava, and Susan Wadley (Wadley 1983, 1994). Women's song outweighs all other topics in these ethnographies. The above-mentioned works show the omnipresence of music in the life of rural Indians in the twentieth century, that it is important in conveying a multiplicity of meanings, and that it is valued both as a way of interacting and as an accompaniment to interacting.

Studies focused more directly on the music itself include those of Edward Henry (1988), Nazir Jairazbhoy (1988), Peter Manuel (1993, 1994), Scott Marcus (1989, 1993, 1995 a and b), Regula Qureshi, and Bonnie Wade (on women's songs recorded in Haryana State and New Delhi, both of which are contiguous with Uttar Pradesh). Kathryn Hansen's book on *nauṭaṅkī* theater includes a sensitive analysis of its music.

Studies concerned primarily with interpretations of song texts include those of Shyam Pandey on the epic *Lorik* (1979, 1982, 1987); Indra Deva, George Grierson (1884, 1886), Shridhar Mishra, Krishna D. Upadhyaya (1957, 1966), and Hari S. Upadhyaya on Bhojpuri folk song; L. Winifred Bryce on the women's songs of Rajasthan (also contiguous with Uttar Pradesh); and Nisha Sahai-Achuthan on the folk songs of western Uttar Pradesh. LP disks, cassettes, and compact discs containing music from Uttar Pradesh have been published by Henry, Jairazbhoy, Lomax, Qureshi, Schlenker, and Tewari.

REFERENCES

Arya, Satya P. 1965. "Jhoda and Jhanjhi." *Folklore* 6(2):86–94.

———. 1966. "The Ritual Folk Song of Meerut of the Western Uttar Pradesh." *Folklore* 7(3):108–115.

Blackburn, Stuart H., Peter J. Claus, Joyce B. Flueckiger, and Susan S. Wadley, eds. 1989. *Oral Epics in India.* Berkeley: University of California Press.

Bryce, L. Winifred. 1961. *Women's Folk Songs of Rajputana.* New Delhi: Ministry of Information and Broadcasting, Government of India.

Dadi's Family. 1981. Odyssey series. Produced by Joseph Elder. Washington, D.C.: Corporation for Public Broadcasting. Film and videocassette.

Deva, Indra. 1989. *Folk Culture and Peasant Society.* Jaipur: Rawat.

Flueckiger, Joyce. 1989. "Caste and Regional Variants in an Oral Epic Tradition." In *Oral Epics in India*, ed. Stuart H. Blackburn, Peter J. Claus, Joyce B. Flueckiger, and Susan S. Wadley, 33–54. Berkeley: University of California Press.

Freed, Ruth S., and Stanley Freed. 1980. *Rites of Passage in Shanti Nagar.* New York: American Museum of Natural History.

Grierson, George A. 1884. "Some Bihari Folksongs." *Journal of the Royal Asiatic Society* 16:196–246.

———. 1886. "Some Bhojpuri Folk Songs." *Journal of the Royal Asiatic Society* 18:207–267.

———. 1967 [1903]. *Linguistic Survey of India.* Delhi: Motilal Banarsidass.

Hansen, Kathryn. 1992. *Grounds for Play: The Nautanki Theatre of North India.* Berkeley: University of California Press.

Henry, Edward O. 1981. *Chant the Names of God: Village Music of the Bhojpuri-Speaking Area of India.* Rounder Records 5008. LP disk.

———. 1988. *Chant the Names of God: Music and Culture in Bhojpuri-Speaking India.* San Diego: San Diego State University Press.

———. 1991. "*Jogīs* and *Nirgun Bhajan*s in Bhojpuri-Speaking India: Intra-Genre Heterogeneity, Adaptation, and Functional Shift." *Ethnomusicology* 35(2):221–242.

———. 1995. "The Vitality of the *Nirgun Bhajan*: Sampling the Contemporary Tradition." In *Bhakti Religion in North India: Community Identity and Political Action,* ed. David N. Lorenzen, 231–250. Albany: State University of New York Press.

Jacobson, Doranne. 1975. "Songs of Social Distance." *Journal of South Asian Literature* 9:45–60.

Jairazbhoy, Nazir A. 1988. *A Musical Journey through India 1963–64.* Los Angeles: Department of Ethnomusicology, University of California. Booklet and audio cassettes.

Jairazbhoy, Nazir, and Amy Catlin. 1993. "Review Essay: The JVC Anthology (India, Pakistan, Bangladesh, Sri Lanka, Nepal, and Bhutan)." *Asian Music* 24(2):159–180.

Kumar, Nita. 1988. *The Artisans of Banaras: Popular Culture and Identity, 1880–1986.* Princeton: Princeton University Press.

Lewis, Oscar. 1958. *Village Life in Northern India.* New York: Random House.

Lomax, Alan. N.d. *Indian Folk Music.* Columbia Records 9102021. LP disk.

Manuel, Peter. 1993. *Cassette Culture: Popular Music and Technology in North India.* Chicago: University of Chicago Press.

———. 1994. "Syncretism and Adaptation in Rasiya, a Braj Folksong Genre." *Journal of Vaiṣṇava Studies* 3(1):33–60.

Marcus, Scott L. 1989. "The Rise of a Folk Music Genre: Biraha." In *Culture and Power in Banaras: Community, Performance, and Environment, 1800–1980,* ed. Sandria Freitag, 93–113. Berkeley: University of California Press.

———. 1993. "Recycling Indian Film-Songs:

Popular Music as a Source of Melodies for North Indian Folk Musicians." *Asian Music* 24(1):101–110.

———. 1995a. "On Cassette Rather Than Live: Religious Music in India Today." In *Media and the Transformation of Religion in South Asia,* ed. Lawrence A. Babb and Susan Wadley, 167–185. Philadelphia: University of Pennsylvania Press.

———. 1995b. "Parody Generated Texts: The Process of Composition in *Birahā,* a North Indian Folk Music Genre." *Asian Music* 26(1):95–147.

Minturn, Leigh. 1993. *Sita's Daughters.* New York: Oxford University Press.

Mishra, Shridhar. 1965. "Elements of Culture in Bhojpuri Folk Songs." *Folklore* 6(1):28–39.

Pandey, Shyam M. 1979. *Hindi Oral Epic Loriki.* Allahabad: Sahitya Bhawan Private Limited.

———. 1982. *Hindi Oral Epic Canaini.* Allahabad: Sahitya Bhawan Private Limited.

———. 1987. *Hindi Oral Epic Lorikayan.* Allahabad: Sahitya Bhawan Private Limited.

Planalp, Jack M. 1956. "Religious Life and Values in a North Indian Village." Ph.D. dissertation, Cornell University.

Qureshi, Regula. 1995. *Sufi Music of India and Pakistan: Sound, Context and Meaning in Qawwali.* Cambridge: Cambridge University Press. With accompanying cassette.

Raheja, Gloria G., and Ann G. Gold. 1994. *Listen to the Heron's Words: Reimagining Gender and Kinship in North India.* Berkeley: University of California Press.

Sahai-Achuthan, Nisha. 1987. "Folk Songs of Uttar Pradesh." *Ethnomusicology* 31(3):95–406.

Schlenker, Rosina. N.d. *Middle Caste Religious Music from India: Musicians, Dancers, Prostitutes, and Actors.* Lyrichord LLST7323. LP disk.

———. N.d. *Lower Caste Religious Music from India: Monks, Transvestites, Midwives, and Folksingers.* Lyrichord LLST 7344. LP disk.

Singer, Milton. 1972. *When a Great Tradition Modernizes: An Anthropological Approach to Indian Civilization.* New York: Praeger.

Skafte, Peter. 1979. "Smoking Out Secrets of the Mysterious 'Snakers' in India." *Smithsonian,* October:120–127.

Slawek, Stephen. 1986. "Kīrtan: A Study of the Sonic Manifestations of the Divine in Popular Hindu Culture of Banaras." Ph.D. dissertation, University of Illinois at Urbana-Champaign.

Srivastava, S. L. 1974. *Folk Culture and Oral Tradition.* New Delhi: Abhinav Publications.

Tewari, Laxmi G. 1974. "Folk Music of India: Uttar Pradesh." Ph.D. dissertation, Wesleyan University.

———. N.d. *Folk Music of India (Uttar Pradesh).* Lyrichord LLST 7271. LP disk.

———. 1977. "Ceremonial Songs of the Kanyakubja Brahmans." *Essays in Arts and Sciences* 6:30–52.

———. 1991. *Traditional Music of the World 2: Folk Music of Uttar Pradesh, India.* Musicaphon BM 55802 ADD. Compact disc.

Upadhyaya, Hari S. 1967. "The Joint Family Structure and Familial Relationship Patterns in the Bhojpuri Folksongs." Ph.D. dissertation, Indiana University.

Upadhyaya, Krishna D. 1957. "An Introduction to Bhojpuri Folk Songs and Ballads." *Midwest Folklore* 7:85–94.

———. 1966. "Some Aspects of Indian Culture as Depicted in Bhojpuri Folk Song and Folk-Tales." *Folklore* 7(9):330–349.

Wade, Bonnie. 1972. "Songs of Traditional Wedding Ceremonies in North India." *Yearbook of the International Folk Music Council* 4:57–66.

Wadley, Susan S. 1983. "Dhola: A North Indian Folk Genre." *Asian Folklore Studies* 42:3–26.

———. 1994. *Struggling with Destiny in Karimpur 1925–1984.* Berkeley: University of California Press.

Mithila

Edward O. Henry

Women's Song
Other Ritual Song Forms

The territory called Mithila does not appear on contemporary maps of India, as it is no longer a defined political entity. Today, "Mithila" refers to the area where Maithili is spoken. The linguist George A. Grierson, who popularized the term (though he did not originate it), described this territory as bounded by the Kosi River on the east, the Ganges on the south, the Gandak on the west, and the Himalayas on the north. It thus straddles the India-Nepal border (Grierson 1967).

Geographically, culturally—and in particular linguistically—Mithila has more in common with West Bengal (to the south) than with Uttar Pradesh (to the west). Fish and rice are primary staples in this land of rivers, tanks (human-made ponds), and lush foliage. The worship of Shakti (the "wives" of Hindu gods) and Shiva is stronger than in Uttar Pradesh; the Durgā Pūjā festival dedicated to the goddess Durga is the greatest festival here, as in Bengal, though Vaishnav devotionalism—primarily devotion to Krishna—occurs.

Maithili is the only language in Bihar with a literary history not limited to the twentieth century, a fact in which Maithils take pride. This history goes back at least to the mid-1300s; the most prominent early figure was Vidyapati Thakur, who served as court poet to Raja Shiva Simha (r.1410–1414). Grierson published a collection of eighty-two song texts thought to have been composed by Vidyapati. Grierson had obtained these texts from blind singers and from the maharaja of Darbhanga. Most of the texts concern the love affair of Krishna and Radha. Many songs still sung in Mithila, including men's devotional songs, entertainment music, and women's ritual songs, carry the Vidyapati musical signature (*bhanītā*), though this is not always an authentic indication of authorship.

WOMEN'S SONG

Women's song in Mithila differs from that in regions to the south and west in important respects. First, it is intertwined with a body of courtly, literary poetry. Unlettered women commonly sing *baṭgamanī*, *samdāūn*, and many other genres that are literary poetic forms. The literary tradition continues in some families, in which authors of some women's ritual songs are known ancestors. Second, though the topics and contexts are largely the same as those to the south and west, Mithila women's songs have

Mithila women do not accompany their singing with a drum as Indian women do elsewhere.

more (and different) names for them. Anima Singh's collection contains forty-seven types of wedding song—one type for each perceived ritual or significant stage of a ritual (Singh 1970). (My recent fieldwork suggests that few if any women's groups can nowadays perform this many.) Ritual music was probably the focus of profound development, influenced by persons with a tendency to classify and categorize, notably Brahmin scholars. The royal support of both Brahmin scholarship and music is a part of Mithila's cultural heritage.

Third, Mithila women do not accompany their singing with a drum as Indian women do elsewhere. Fourth, some higher-caste groups sing exceptionally ornamented and challenging melodies, prompting the speculation that in the past the musical standard was from a more classical tradition. According to Dr. Shruti Dhari Singh, the director of the Center for the Study of Indian Traditions in Ranti, Madhubani, some of the women's tunes have possibly descended from an old vocal style of classical music, *dhrupad*. Finally, whenever Mithila women sing, they ideally begin with a *gosāūnī gīt*—a song to a mother goddess. All these factors distinguish the Maithili women's musical tradition from those of regions to the west and south.

OTHER RITUAL SONG FORMS

Occasionally, early in the morning—even before dawn—a man will sing a stately devotional song (*prātī*). Such songs also begin hymn sessions devoted to a mother goddess. The following *prātī* text, sung in Ranti by Mahavir Paswan in 1995, addresses Shiva, here called Bhola Nath. It contains Vidyapati's signature in the last line.

he Bholā Nāth kakhan harab dukh mor
dukh hī janam bhel dukh hī gamāol
sukh sapanau nahī bhel
akṣat candan aur gangā jal belpatr tori caṛhāyab
manahī Vidyāpati, he Bholā Nāth kakhan harab dukh mor

Hey, Bhola Nath, when will you remove my sorrow?
I was born in sorrow; I grew up in sorrow.
Even in my dreams there was no happiness.
Rice and sandalwood on the wood-apple leaf and incense wood I offer.
So sings Vidyapati: hey, Bhola Nath, when will you remove my sorrow?

Men sing this song to various tunes. The one sung by this singer is a variant of the tune he uses for singing the *Epic of Salheś*, a poem first studied by Grierson. Salheś or Salhesh is the name of a deity of the singer's caste, the Dusādh community. Caste members worship Salhesh in a special building containing icons. Singing the epic is part of that worship (figure 1).

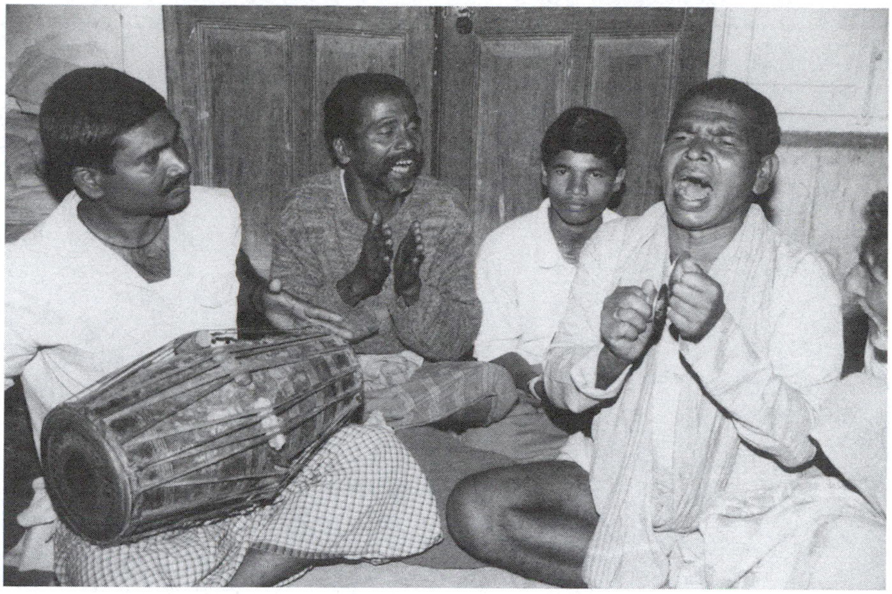

FIGURE 1 Mahavir Paswan (right, with cymbals) and his group sing the *Epic of Salhes*. Ranti, Madhubani District, Bihar, February 1995. Photo by Edward O. Henry.

The Musahar caste of this region also sings the *Dinā-Bhadrī*, an epic to the deities its members worship. The epic singers are men, like those of the Dusādh caste, and they also accompany themselves with drum and cymbals; the singing is in the strongly rhythmic and percussive mode typical of men's devotional music throughout North India. Other epics sung in Mithila include the *Ālhā*, *Gopīcand*, and *Behulā*.

The Maithili group that leads processions is called the *pipahī* ensemble. The *pipahī* resembles the double-reed *śahnāī* of regions further west but is shorter (22 centimeters long), with a cylindrical bore and seven finger holes. Several double reeds, accompanied by small kettledrums (*ḍigaṛī*, *khurḍak*) complete the ensemble, whose players are of the Camār caste.

Another musical tradition peculiar to Mithila is *jatā-jatin* 'boy-girl', a kind of folk operetta sung by women who divide into two sides. A member of one side plays the woman, and a member of the other side plays the man. The man asks the woman questions, to which the women on her side pronounce taunting responses, and vice versa. In 1995, women and girls of the Dhanuk caste performed *jatā-jatin* in Sarisab-Pahi, Bihar.

Changing musical culture

Perhaps at a slower rate than in other parts of India, performance of traditional music is declining in favor of popular cassette recordings, mostly of film music. Women sing less than before, and amplified cassette music is increasingly common. Now even the bullock carts that carry a groom to a bride's house for a wedding blare out wedding songs from commercial cassette recordings—which may not be in Maithili.

REFERENCES

Grierson, George A. 1967 [1903]. *Linguistic Survey of India*. Delhi: Motilal Banarsidass.

Mishra, Jayakanta. 1949. *A History of Maithili Literature*, vol. 1. Allahabad: Tirabhukti Publications.

———. 1950. *Introduction to the Folk Literature of Mithila*. Allahabad: Tirabhukti Publications.

Singh [Sinha], Anima. 1970. *Maithili Lok Git* [Maithili Folk Songs]. Calcutta: Lok Sahitya Parisad.

Northern Areas
North West Frontier Province
PAKISTAN
Disputed Border
Punjab
Punjab
LADAKH
SRINAGAR
Jammu and Kashmir
ZANGS-DKAR
Indus R.
Leh
Hemis
Disputed Border
LAHUL
Jammu
Basohli
Dharamsala
Himachal Pradesh
SPITI
SIMLA
Dehra Dun
Haryana
C H I N A
TIBET
Lhasa
Mustang
NEPAL
GANDAKHI ZONE
Pokhara
Gorkha
KATHMANDU
Bhaktapur
Sikkim
GANGTOK
Darjiling
Kalimpang
West Bengal
BHUTAN
THIMPHU
Arunachal Pradesh
Assam
Ganges River
Uttar Pradesh
Yamuna River
Chambal River
Bihar
BANGLADESH
I N D I A
Narmada River
West Bengal

Himalayan Region

The confluence of Indian, Tibetan, Nepalese, and Bhutanese cultures in the highest mountain chain in the world has resulted in musical traditions expressing varied ethnic and religious identities—Hindu songs in Nepal, Tibetan Buddhist chants in Ladakh and Himachal Pradesh, Muslim dance songs and Sufi ritual music in Kashmir, Gurung shaman recitation in Nepal, Manipa epic singing in Bhutan, and Beda and Mon instrumental performance in Ladakh, to name a few.

Political events of the twentieth century have dramatically affected people's lives and musical cultures in the Himalayan region. The massive influx of Tibetan peoples following China's occupation of Tibet reintroduced Buddhist music to parts of northern India. The ongoing civil war in Kashmir has caused an exodus of Hindus and Hindu musicians to more southern regions, and a corresponding decline in music making among Kashmiri Muslims. Yet where peace prevails, music and dance continue; performance traditions link the past and the present, and make possible the artistic expression of peoples' hopes for the future.

MAP 6 Himalayan region

Kashmir

Józef M. Pacholczyk
Gordon K. Arnold

Contemporary Musical Traditions ***Józef M. Pacholczyk***
Historical Sources ***Gordon K. Arnold***

Kashmir is today divided between India and Pakistan. The valley of Kashmir, the central and most densely populated region, is in Jammu and Kashmir, the northernmost Indian state. The mountainous northwestern parts of Kashmir—Gilgit, Hunza, and Baltistan—belong to Pakistan [see PAKISTAN: NORTHERN AREAS]. Through the 1980s, nearly 95 percent of the Kashmir Valley's population was Muslim, with the remaining 5 percent Hindu. But in the 1990s, political and social turmoil over the future of the valley led many Hindus to emigrate to other parts of India. Historically, Kashmir was strongly influenced by largely Hindu India as well as by Muslim Persia and Central Asia, and its culture can be considered a meeting point among them.

CONTEMPORARY MUSICAL TRADITIONS

Kashmiris perform a variety of musical genres in the villages and towns. Among the urban elite, musicians perform classical Sufi music (*ṣūfyāna mūsīqī*). In both urban and rural environments there are performers of many folk genres. Most of the music of Kashmir is in some way connected with religion, whether Islam or Hinduism; a variety of specifically religious ritual music is performed in mosques, in Sufi fraternity houses (*tekke* or *khanaqah*), and in Hindu temples. Many non-Kashmiri genres have also been imported, primarily from India, such as classical Hindustani music and Sufi devotional music (qawwali), not to mention Indian film and popular music. A few pandit artists are today creating a new hybrid music combining elements of Hindustani classical, Indian pop and film, Western, and Kashmiri traditions for a variety of shows and concerts. Western music is not popular in Kashmir; besides some local rock and pop bands performing in a few tourist hotels in Srinagar, the capital city of Kashmir, nationalized All India Radio broadcasts are the only source of Western classical, jazz, and pop material. This article covers the principal traditional genres of Kashmiri music, leaving out only those performed in the mosques.

Chakri

The most popular genre in Kashmir is *chakri*, a vocal genre sung in the villages and towns on various family and social occasions. *Chakri* is sung in responsorial style; vocal solo sections alternate with choral responses and instrumental interludes. The

FIGURE 1 Male dancer performing *bacha naghma*, with accompanying musicians seated in the background playing harmonium and two *sāraṅg*, 1979. Photo by Józef M. Pacholczyk.

music is lively and dynamic, with characteristic dotted rhythms and sharp changes in tempo and density. There are two kinds of *chakri*, Muslim and Hindu, but the Hindu variety is now rarely performed.

Muslim *chakri* functions as secular entertainment, by itself or in the context of folk-dance theatricals (*bacha naghma*); and also as ritual music for religious Sufi gatherings (*mehfil*). Within the Sufi ritual, only men perform *chakri*; women now also perform the secular form.

Secular contexts for *chakri* performance include weddings and circumcisions. The performance takes place under a large colorful tent, and often lasts into the early morning hours. The organizing family hires a musical ensemble, comprising a lead singer and other singer-instrumentalists. During such a night transvestite male dancers typically perform a short theatrical dance (*bacha naghma*) (figure 1). Elaborately dressed young boys depict the meaning of the text with feminine gestures, often incorporating comic sections. Occasionally a dancer invites a girl from the audience into the center of the circle and, holding her with crossed hands, whirls within the circle.

Dervishes from the Qādirī order (*silsila*) perform the ritual *chakri*. They are usually from the lower social strata and have limited education. The dervishes from the middle and upper strata usually prefer classical Sufi music. Ritual *chakri* texts are mystical poems in the Kashmiri language, and are often by the most renowned poets of Kashmir. They are similar to those used in Sufi music, and contain Sufi imagery common to both Persian and Kashmiri poetry. The most typical poetic themes are longing for a friend, who symbolizes God; a description of His beauty, sometimes presented in a sensuous way; and the intoxication that results from drinking wine, symbolizing spiritual ecstasy.

The chakri *ensemble*

The typical accompanying ensemble includes the bowed lute (*sāraṅg*), the plucked lute (*rebāb*), a goblet-shaped drum (*tumbaknarī*), and a struck clay pot (*nūt*). The *sāraṅg* is a variant of one of the most widely used string instruments in India, the *sāraṅgī*. In Kashmir, this lute has three gut melodic strings stretched over a skin head, and nine to thirteen sympathetic strings. The playing technique is similar to that of the Indian *sāraṅgī*. The player stops the strings by pressing from the side with the base of the fingernails, and bows the strings with a loose bow whose hairs are tightened with the fingers of the bowing hand. There is neither a standard size of *sāraṅg* nor a standard number of sympathetic strings. *Chakri* ensembles include one or two *sāraṅg* players.

The *rebāb* is a short-necked, plucked stringed instrument related to the Central Asian instrument of the same name and somewhat similar to the Indian *sarod*. It has a deep wooden belly, six gut playing strings, and sympathetic strings.

The *tumbaknarī* is a goblet-shaped, single-membrane clay drum similar to an instrument found all over the Near East and Central Asia called in Persian *dombak*, in Arabic *darabukka*.

The *nūt* is a large clay vessel somewhat similar to the South Indian *ghaṭam*. The right hand strikes against the opening of the vessel producing a deep sound similar to that of a drum. Players often strike the sides of the vessel with both hands, sometimes wearing rings on the middle finger that produce high-pitched sounds.

Three other instruments occasionally accompany *chakri*. The harmonium, a small hand-pumped organ, is an instrument of Indian manufacture that most likely became part of the *chakri* ensemble sometime in the nineteenth century. It is usually played by the lead vocalist. The *geger*, a brass vessel similar to the clay *nūt*, and the *chumta*, a forked rod with attached sets of cymbals, are also both part of the Hindu *chakri* ensemble.

Rūf

As with the *chakri* vocal genre, in Kashmir the name *rūf* refers to two distinct musical genres. The first is secular, associated with *chakri*; the second is a religious genre performed with dancing by women during Ramadan, the Muslim month of fasting.

The secular *rūf* is stylistically very similar to *chakri*—a vocal responsorial genre accompanied by the same kind of instrumental ensemble. In the past it was also associated with dance. Unlike *chakri*, the rhythm of the *rūf* is steady, and there are usually no instrumental interludes. Around 1948, Mohanlal Aima, a Kashmiri musician and musicologist, introduced the custom of coupling *chakri* with *rūf* in radio performances. Since then the practice has become common, both on the radio and at wedding celebrations.

During Ramadan, women in neighborhood compounds gather during the evening hours and perform religious *rūf*. They line up in two rows facing each other and sing antiphonally, with their arms draped on each other's shoulders, rhythmically moving in small steps forward and back. Their singing is loud, in full voice, most of the women straining their voices and after some time becoming unable to sing anymore. Several short melodies are used, and once they have settled on a particular melody, the women will repeat it for several minutes before moving to another melody. One group of women initiates a text line, and the other group answers with the refrain. The text is of a Muslim religious character, referring to fasting, holy shrines of Kashmir, or various Sufi saints, but can also refer to current events. Often the text has strong Sufi elements and uses typical Sufi imagery.

Nande baeth

Nande baeth are songs performed throughout the Valley of Kashmir during the planting, cleaning, and harvesting of rice. While a group of men or women moves in line through the rice field, a leader initiates the verse and the rest answer in responsorial style. The leader's singing style is often very elaborate and ornate, in contrast to the simpler style of the chorus response. *Nande baeth* songs have no instrumental accompaniment. The poetry is religious, some of it by well-respected Kashmiri Sufi poets.

Nande chakri

Nande chakri is similar to *nande baeth* in that a leader sings an elaborate opening of the poetic stanza, and the chorus answers in a simple style. Performances take place in the villages, but in homes rather than at work in the fields. One or more clay pots (*nūt*) and a goblet drum (*tumbaknarī*) accompany the songs.

Wanawun

Wanawun is a women's song genre performed at weddings, circumcisions, betrothals, and at the ceremony accompanying a boy's first haircut at age three (*zār*). Women perform *wanawun* with texts full of sorrow during funerals of young girls who have died unmarried, considering these songs as substitutes for the wedding *wanawun* that will never be sung for them. The singing style and accompanying movements are similar to those of a *rūf*. The women sing loudly and line up in two rows, again with arms on each others' shoulders, moving in small steps forward and back. The first group of women initiates the first line of text, and the second group responds with the second line, singing it twice. During a short rest, the groups quickly prepare the text of the next stanza. Whichever group happens to be ready first begins singing the next stanza at a given signal. The women improvise the text, usually on the topic of the particular occasion.

The *surnāy* ensemble

The *surnāy* ensemble consists of several double-reed instruments (*surnāy*), a single metal or ceramic kettledrum (*naqqārā*), and a double-headed barrel drum (*ḍhol*). The ensemble accompanies folk theatricals (*bānde pāther* 'musician's theater') that combine comedy, dance, and operetta and performs on a variety of village festive occasions, whenever the patron can afford to hire the group (figure 2).

In the theatricals, actors usually present a series of short stagings of folk stories, lasting from half an hour to an hour. The stories deal with a variety of subjects and often contain moral, social, and political commentary. Each troupe has a modest repertoire of stories, and the actors improvise much of the text. The *surnāy* musicians generally perform a prelude before the plays, and offer music again at the end, when they perform in alternation with the singing of transvestite dancers.

FIGURE 2 Performers of a folk theatrical ensemble (*bānde pāther*) from Drugmula. Musicians playing *surnāy* stand in the rear. Photo by Józef M. Pacholczyk, 1979.

Two kinds of ritual meetings employ Sufi music: weekly meetings lasting a few hours in the evening and all-night gatherings during major Islamic holidays.

At the beginning and end of theatrical performances, *surnāy* musicians also perform an instrumental repertoire of suites related to that of Sufi music (*ṣūfyāna mūsīqī*). Some *surnāy* musicians also play the long-necked lute (*setār*) and perform classical Sufi music for local Sufi gatherings.

Sufi music (*ṣūfyāna mūsīqī*)

Ṣūfyāna mūsīqī is the classical music of the urban elite in Kashmir, which consists of educated Sufis and Hindus who know Persian. The theoretical treatises associated with this music point to its origin at least as early as the first half of the eighteenth century. *Ṣūfyāna* performance takes place in both religious and secular contexts. Sufi meetings (*mehfil*), especially of the Qādirī order, constitute the former, with radio broadcasts providing the principal medium for the latter. Sufi music is neither broadcast on television nor available on commercial audio or video cassettes. Radio Kashmir, Srinagar, and the Sangeet Natak Akademi in New Delhi house archival recordings (Pacholczyk 1996:55).

Two kinds of ritual meetings employ Sufi music: weekly meetings lasting a few hours in the evening and all-night gatherings during major Islamic holidays such as *mi'rāj*, the commemoration of the Prophet Muhammad's mystical journey to heaven. All these meetings take place in the houses of well-to-do members of the fraternity. During the all-night sessions the dervishes (Sufi practitioners) sit or rather squat on mats around the perimeter of the room. In the center, a candle burns, symbolizing God. The sheikh, the leader of the order, sits on one side of the room surrounded by his closest male friends and disciples; the musicians sit in a corner and face the center.

The all-night performances are divided into two-hour periods. During each period, the musicians perform a particular *maqām* suite appropriate for that time of the night. The dervishes sit motionless in silence, listening to the music. When they feel the musicians are performing a favorite song particularly well, they join the musicians in singing. During the performance, some individual dervishes may go into ecstasy and exclaim the name of Allah, their arms outstretched.

Currently the most common secular performance situation is the radio broadcast. *Ṣūfyāna* music is aired several times a week on Radio Kashmir, Srinagar, the broadcasts usually lasting fifteen or thirty minutes. Once a month, All India Radio transmits a longer (one-hour) program of Sufi music. The A.I.R. musicians are experienced professionals who can adapt well to the different contexts of radio and ritual gatherings. Other secular contexts for Sufi music are the occasional concert before a ticket-buying audience or a performance by a regional folk music group representing Kashmir in other parts of India or abroad.

In the past, musicians also performed Sufi music in the context of a secular *mehfil*, but in the last few decades such secular meetings have become extremely rare. Although at the beginning of the twentieth century, during the reign of Maharaja

Pratap Singh of the Dogra dynasty in India, Sufi music was introduced at court, this practice ended with independence in 1947.

Sufi music in the eighteenth and nineteenth centuries was associated with professional female dancers (*ḥāfiẓa*). These professional dancers disappeared sometime early in this century, apparently because of their connection with prostitution. According to fragmentary musicians' accounts, solo dancers expressed the poetry with elaborate hand gestures, apparently in a style similar to the *kathak* dance of North India.

In previous centuries, all *ṣūfyāna* musicians belonged to a separate caste; in the twentieth century, many have come from outside the caste and become recognized masters of this still all-male musical tradition. A good Sufi musician has a very large repertoire of poems and melodies that have been passed on in the oral tradition. Proper voice quality is appreciated, although there is no particular training method used to develop it. Younger musicians apprentice themselves to sometimes aged masters and imitate their voice quality. These musicians are treated as servants; their patrons pay them their fee and dismiss them—with the exception of a small number of salaried staff musicians at Radio Kashmir, Srinagar.

Repertoire

TRACK 21 *Ṣūfyāna* is a composed choral music. Four to twelve musicians sing together and accompany themselves on instruments, each musician performing a slightly different version of the song. The result is a complex heterophony. In the 1980s regular *ṣūfyāna* ensembles developed their own styles and versions of the repertoire, and performed in Srinagar, Watora, Bij Bihara, the district of Kupwara, and other places.

Present-day Sufi repertoire consists of forty-seven suites (*maqām*), compound forms similar to those in classical, religious, and military repertoires throughout the Muslim Near East and Central Asia. The Kashmiri *maqām* is a collection of instrumental pieces and songs for performance in a specific melodic mode (melody type), also called *maqām*, and in a succession of specific rhythmic modes (talas) (Aziz 1963–1965). The term *maqām* also refers to a selection of items from this collection chosen for a specific performance. A performance of a *maqām* suite opens with a short, solo instrumental prelude (*shakl*) performed by the leader of the ensemble. Sometimes the leader follows this with a solo song, *nāther*. The main body of a *maqām* performance consists of several songs performed by the entire ensemble, with songs in longer talas preceding those in shorter talas. Sixteen talas are known today, ranging from four to thirty-two beats (*mātrā*).

All pieces within a single suite are in the same melodic mode. The melodic modes have proper names borrowed either from the terminology of Arabic and Persian modes or that of Indian ragas. Many Kashmiri modes have both Arabo-Persian and Indic names. In contrast to many classical traditions of the Near East, the Kashmiri modes do not always have different scales. All pieces in each mode, however, share the common set of short melodic phrases that are the musical determinants of that particular mode.

Sufi poetry

The number of poems associated with Sufi music exceeds 2,500; the number of tunes is considerably smaller. The *ṣūfyāna* song texts are mystical Sufi poems in Persian and Kashmiri by poets such as Hafiz, Sa'di, Omar Khayyam, and Jalalu'ddin Rumi of Persia, and Rasul Mir, Gami, Sarfi, and Iqbal of Kashmir. The texts are often in a ghazal, *dōbeitī,* or *rubā'ī* poetic form. A *ṣūfyāna* song in ghazal form usually employs only two or three lines of a ghazal text. Singers sing the first line in the first section of the song (*astāī*) and the second line in the following section (*aṅtarā*).

FIGURE 3 *Ṣūfyāna mūsīqī* ensemble from Srinagar. Instruments (*from left*) are two *setār*, *santūr*, *sāz-e-kashmīrī*, and *dokra*. Lying in the foreground is another *setār*. Photo by Józef M. Pacholczyk, 1977.

Sufi instruments

Four instruments are used in the performance of *ṣūfyāna mūsīqī*: the *santūr* 'trapezoidal zither', the *setār* 'long-necked lute', the now nearly extinct *sāz-e-kashmīrī* 'spike fiddle', and the *dokra* 'drum pair' (figure 3).

The *santūr*, a trapezoidal zither, has thirty courses of quadruple strings. A relative of the Persian *santūr*, it is played with two curved wooden mallets (*qalam*). The *setār* is a long-necked, fretted lute, and is related to the Persian instrument of the same name, but unlike its Persian counterpart, the Kashmiri instrument has a wide and slightly rounded bridge similar to that of the Hindustani sitar. The strings touch the surface of the bridge to produce a buzzing sound.

Few musicians now play the *sāz-e-kashmīrī*, and that only rarely. A relative of the Persian spike fiddle (*kamanche*), this bowed spike lute has three melodic strings and fourteen sympathetic strings on both the front and back of the round neck; it is no longer produced. The *dokra* is a set of Hindustani tabla, and is imported from India.

The future of Sufi music

Ṣūfyāna is now in a state of severe decline. The number of competent musicians is steadily diminishing and there are very few young students. *Ṣūfyāna* musicians still know and perform a large repertoire, with a majority of the texts in Kashmiri, but some melodic modes and talas are being forgotten. In the mid-1970s, the Jammu and Kashmir Academy of Arts, Culture, and Language introduced weekly class instruction in Sufi music to a group of young boys and girls. The principal purpose of this instruction was not to produce professional musicians but to generate an audience for the music. Presently, that instruction is no longer taking place, and it remains to be seen whether such efforts can prevent the disappearance of this tradition—even during the present generation.

HISTORICAL SOURCES

Though relatively remote, the Kashmir Valley has historically always been a crossroads for travel between Central Asia and the Indian subcontinent, serving as a place where cultural and religious traditions have mingled and been nurtured. Its geographic isolation helped to attract scholars and mystics when surrounding lands were being devastated by invading armies. According to early historical records, Buddhist schools flourished in Kashmir some two thousand years ago, and monks from Kashmir traveled throughout Asia preaching forms of Buddhism prevalent in their homeland. Artwork found in Central Asian excavations, such as those carried out by Sir Aurel Stein (Stein 1903, 1928), indicates that decorative arts traveled with the monks, and surviving pieces reveal that Kashmir enjoyed Persian, Central Asian, and Indian influences. From surviving pictures and sculptures of musical instruments, we can conclude that the music of Kashmir enjoyed the same cultural dispersion.

The first written history of the Kashmir Valley, Kalhana's twelfth-century *Rājataraṅgiṇī* 'River of Kings', is a chronicle in verse covering earliest mythology through A.D. 1152 (Stein 1961). Very little information on music exists from this period other than the mention of dancing and music taking place during times of peace and prosperity. In the medieval period, kings of Kashmir such as Sultan Zain-ul-Abdin (1420–1470) were well-known patrons of the arts, including music. Accounts of musicians arriving from distant places including Khurasan, of singing in the Melchas language, and of the use of *turushka* meters, all indicate the variety of musical influences in Kashmir resulting from royal patronage.

During the fourteenth century, one of the most famous Kashmiri mystics of the Triaka school of monastic Shaivism, Lal Ded, created song lyrics known as Lol-lyric, which are still sung today. A contemporary of hers, Sheikh Nur-ud-din (also known as Nund Rishi) of Char Sharif, was likewise a mystical poet who greatly influenced the blending of Hindu and Muslim mysticism. This blending of religious ideas served as a basis for the surviving ancient musical traditions of Kashmir. Indeed, the conversion of Kashmiri Hindus to Islam was gradual and by and large peaceful, and led to the fruitful mixing of mystical and musical traditions in the form of *ṣūfyāna kalām* (also called *ṣūfyāna mūsīqī*) 'Sufi music', the classical music of Kashmir.

Two treatises on music

Two treatises of the seventeenth and eighteenth centuries written in Persian—*Karāmat-e mujrā* 'The Flowing of Munificence' and *Tarāna-e sarūr* 'The Song of Joy'—are possibly the most detailed sources of Kashmiri musical theory and philosophy (Pushp 1962). These works serve as introductions to collections of poetry used as song lyrics during present-day performances of *ṣūfyāna kalām*. (All translations below are by Gordon K. Arnold.)

Karāmat-e mujrā

Karāmat-e mujrā would appear to be the older of the two treatises, since it is quoted in *Tarāna-e sarūr*. The work has no attributed author and begins with the following five sections:

1. Mythology on the origins of music, mostly from Arabic and Persian sources.
2. The organization of melodic modes (*maqām*) into a system of twelve, including their relationship with astrological signs and sounds of animals, and the effects of these modes on disease (a discussion based on the Aristotelian theory of humors).
3. Lists of melodic modes and their derivative *shabeh* 'divisions', all with Persian or Arabic names.
4. Some discussion of singing styles and performance practices.
5. Discussion of a list of seventeen meters with Persian or Arabic names.

The subsequent discussion of musical practice, of which a similar section appears in *Tarāna-e sarūr*, provides a relatively rare glimpse of performance practice

The beginning of the treatise *Tarāna-e sarūr* includes theory relating music to the act of creation and God's organization of the universe.

in this region prior to the twentieth century, particularly concerning the suite-like form that characterizes modern *ṣūfyāna kalām* performance (Pushp 1962:47–48):

> The incomparable master of the Pahlavi era, Abu Saayid, said that there were three ways of singing, i.e. *qullabī* [artful], *damāghī* [proud], and *ḥallaqī* [guttural]. The *qullabī* sound is the *saruchang* [cypress harp]. The *damāghī* sound is a neighbor to softness. The *ḥallaqī* sound is better whatever is sung. These three conditions have been taken from each *āvāz* [sound]. Some of the foundations of music, namely the meters, philosophers have taken from the motions of vibration. The origin of the foundation was named *ẕarb-al-qadīm* [the old beat]. After that, all who had ability contributed to this art. Five more meters were discovered, namely, *farakh, ufar, duyek, turkī ẕarb*, and *mukhammas*. There was an extension of meters from their *taṣnīf* [songs] in this way until Khwaja Safi al-Din, Abd-ul-Muman, and Ustad Ali nourished the spirit and Moulana Hasan Ghouri established seventeen [sic] meters: *ufar, duyek, chahār ẕarb, turkī ẕarb, mukhammas, durāfshān, dūrshāhī, chabar, fākhteh ẕarb, ifgāh turkī ẕarb, ṡaqīl, nīm ṡaqīl, khafīf, dūrkhejāz, ravānī,* and *ūsat*, which they say are blessed and a beneficent treasury of rhythm. But then several other meters, which were not included in the seventeen meters, had their duration of time increased. Also, *ẕarb al-malūk*, which is from modern *taṣnīf* [songs], and *ẕarb al-āsal,* which Nadir al-Aasri Ustad Sultan Muhammad Maauri established and fixed in several difficult *pishrav* [beginnings], were conforming to that [meter].

On the subject of song forms, the text continues (Pushp 1962:48–49):

> *Taṣnīf* [song] is in several parts in the science of music, that is, *naqsh* [picture], *ṣūrat* [face], *ʿamal kār* [doing work], *qūl* [speaking], *sarghazal* [the best ghazal], *tarāneh* [song], *rīkhteh* [mixed], *nīrū* [strength], *sarband* [wreath]. *Naqsh* is that which has two verses and has beats of each of the two *yallehlā*, and does not have *tan tan* [rhythm]. *Ṣūrat* is one high-pitched voice [section] and a repeated middle-pitched voice [section]. *ʿAmal* is two high-pitched voices [sections] in one manner and one middle-pitched voice [section], and is not repeated. Each two [high-pitched voice sections] begin low, and their rhythm is *tan tan* and does not have *yallehlā*. *ʿAmal kār* is not metric, is divine, and begins in rhythm, after which the verse is sung and again an excellent rhythm comes. It has two high-pitched voices [sections] in one manner. It does not have a middle-pitched voice [section] or repetition of a middle-pitched voice [section]. Its poetry is sometimes in Arabic, sometimes in Persian with its *darāmad* [beginning], sometimes from the verse, and sometimes from bringing in the rhythm. *Sarghazal* is low, not having high-pitched voice or middle-pitched voice [sections], and is repeated. Its *yalla* has three *gūsheh* [branches]. Whoever ornaments the verse does so with one and a half

praises and not also *yallehlā*, and it is mixed with words of rhythmical prose together with a verse sometimes of *tan tan* [rhythm] and sometimes of *yallehlā* before the music. *Sarband* is the best instrumental music. *Pishrav* [beginning] is one high-pitched voice [section] and a middle-pitched voice [section] and is not repeated; it is everywhere a necessity, heart-alluring, and an obligation of a kind. *Sarband* is in several meters. Its compositions were improvised each time the masters were together. From its extension a number of *sarband* were created, thus revealing from that [improvisation] their [the masters'] strength and ability.

Tarāna-e sarūr

Tarāna-e sarūr, written by Daya Ram Kachroo "Khushdil," presents a mixture of Persian, Arabic, and Indian theory and philosophy (Pushp 1962) (figure 4). The beginning of the treatise includes theory relating music to the act of creation and God's organization of the universe. For instance, the introduction of a soul into the body of earth is explained (Pushp 1962:1):

On the day when the Lord blew Adam's soul into the body,
The command was "Get in."
But from fear it did not enter the body.
The angels sang in the melody of David,
"Into the body, into the body, get into the body."

As in modern Sufi musical traditions in India and Pakistan, the eight musical notes are associated with mystical stages of enlightenment. Khushdil quotes from the *Mathnavī,* a 27,500-verse Persian poem on Muslim life and thought by Jalalu'ddin Rumi (1207–1273), and draws connections with Hindu mysticism (Nicholson

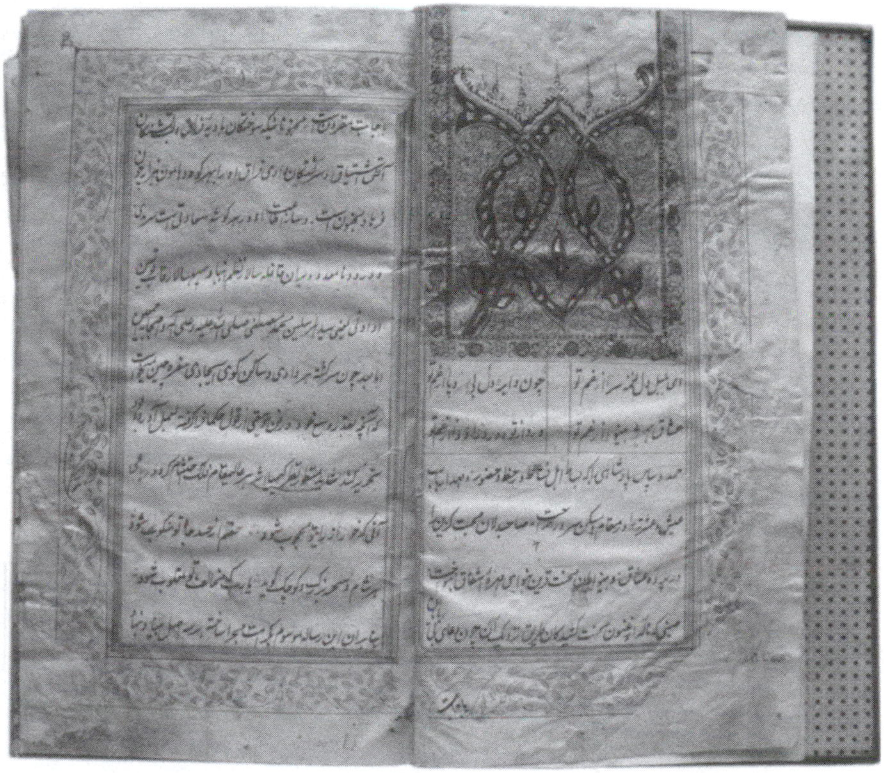

FIGURE 4 Pages from a copy of *Tarāna-e sarūr,* the Persian treatise by Khushdil on the musical theory and philosophy of Kashmir. Research Library, University of Kashmir, Srinagar. Photo by Gordon Arnold.

FIGURE 5 *Rāgmālā* picture from a manuscript copy of a *ṣūfyāna* poetry collection to which the Persian treatise *Tarāna-e sarūr* serves as its introduction. Research Library, University of Kashmir, Srinagar. Photo by Gordon K. Arnold.

1982). The author then relates a similar creation theme, linking it to music and sound as they are conceived in the Hindustani tradition. The melodic modes are divided into six raga families, and Khushdil describes their relationships with yogic traditions and their effects on nature. The treatise enumerates thirty-six ragas grouped into the six families, each of which in turn has one male (*rāg*) and five female (*rāgiṇī*) forms; it also details the appropriate times of day for each of the melodies to be sung (figure 5).

Rhythm and meter are the focus of the next section of the *Tarāna-e sarūr*. The author names and defines seventeen meters, including mnemonic syllables (*bol*) that approximate the sounds of the meters as played on a drum. For example, the syllables for *duyeka tāl* 'two one-beat meter' (which is different from the *duyek* cited in the *Karamāt-e mujrā*) are given in both Farsi (Persian) and Urdu: in Farsi, *dish dish tun tun, dish dish tun*; in Urdu, *da din nā, da din nā, da din nā, din nā* (Pushp 1962:16). Both Persian and Urdu names are similarly listed for each meter, indicating an attempt by the author to organize varied terms for the same meter. An appendix lists another set of mnemonic syllables, for a slightly different set of meters, which would imply some variance in the teaching and practice of drumming.

Tarāna-e sarūr continues with a discussion of the origin of various musical instruments. The following section is a good example of this discourse (Pushp 1962:19–20):

> The truth about instruments is as follows. When the titans, angels, rishis [saintly beings], nagas [snake gods], and genii assembled and by command of the power of God salinated the salty sea, Shri Vishnu was exhilarated by their sight and played upon them personally with his hands. From the primordial sound of *aumkār* that emerged from Shri Vishnu's playing, the entire creation became joyous and exultant and all of them started playing on bells as if their playing was the actual miracle of unity. Shrimati Saraswati Devi invented the vina and is still busy playing it. Indra and Chattarsen, the leaders of the *ghandarva* [heavenly musicians], cause kettledrums to appear, according to the entire range of rhythms. They invented the *surnāī* [double-reed instrument], *karnāī* [large brass trumpet], *būq* [trumpet], *qānūn* [zither], *zangūleh* [rattle], *daf* [large tambourine, with or without jingles], *dul* [large kettledrum], and the *damāmeh* [large double-headed drum]; the *dekhnabāj*, *ʿarab*, and *bajahteh* [wind instruments]; and the *qūs* [large military drum], the *kūrkeh* [large drum], and the *dādī*; and they are constantly engaged in playing these instruments. Shrimati Parvati Devi Bahavani invented the *tanbūr* [long-necked lute] without frets and gave it to Shri Birtibaljiv to play; and Shrimati Mata Parvati is the first *aum* [primordial sound] and the mother of all that is male and female; she is better, greater, and higher than all behavanis and gods. And Shri Narad Munisharjiv, namely Bashir, who in this world is unparalleled in this art, invented the flute, and in the service of Shri Vishnu plays the flute all day and night. Venus, who is the guardian of this science, plays the *rabāb* [lute], *kamāncheh* [spike fiddle], *chang* [harp], and *mūhchang* [mouth harp] with her hands and mouth.
>
> Kavir Novishrawan, the leader of all the yakshas and pishchas—that is, the filthy creation—invented and played the *ʾud* and *barbat* [lutes] until the beginning of the Kaliyuga [the last of four ages in Hindu cosmology]. Thereafter (in the Kaliyuga) Plato, the first teacher, invented the *arghūān* [organ] from his great intelligence. After him, Abu Ali Sina, while passing through a forest, suddenly arrived at a place where he saw a dead rooster caught in a branch whose body had rotted and whose dried veins had knotted on the bones. From the strings of these veins, a pleasant sound emanated. Having seen this, Abu Ali Sina made an imita-

tion of it, fashioning the *tanbūr,* with ninety-six frets so that ninety-six musical notes could be separately discernible. The Indians condensed this instrument and constructed one *sehtār* without frets and another with sixteen frets. Luqman made an imitation of this in the *santūr* [dulcimer], which has ninety-six strings. He also made the *chang* [harp] and the *mridang* [drum], an ancient instrument, along with the *dūkarah* and *māzīd.* An instrument was also made named the *mūsīqār,* which was similar to a *mūsīqār* bird with a thousand holes in its beak, each emitting a pleasant and happy note. The *ṭabl* and *tanbak* [drums] are from ancient times. This is the truth of the instruments, and all the learned men from the far reaches of this world are frustrated because none of them can claim proficiency in these instruments.

Khushdil's organization of music into *maqāmāt* 'melodic modes' reiterated details presented in the equivalent section of *Karamāt-e-mujrā,* possibly indicating his use of that text as a source. The author's discussion of *maqām* includes associations between the modes and astrological and medical theory, as in the following description (Pushp 1962:29–30):

> *Rāst* is associated with Aries, fire, heat, and dryness, and cures hemiplegia [a paralytic affliction of one side of the body] and the pains caused by cold and dry to the third degree.
>
> *Iṣfāhān*, from Taurus, is air, cold and dry to the second degree. Diseases caused by dryness and heat are cured by it.
>
> *'Irāq*, from Gemini, is earth, heat, and moisture and cures the afflictions of inflammation of the brain and contusions caused by excessive cold.
>
> *Kuchek*, from Cancer, is cold and moist, and cures pain in the ear and palpitations of the heart caused by fever.
>
> *Bazorg,* from Leo, is fire, hot, and dry, and cures intestinal diseases and contortions that have been caused by cold.
>
> *Ḥejāz,* from Virgo, is earth, cold, and dry, and cures colic, paralysis, and also pains caused by heat.
>
> *Busalīk*, from Libra, is wind, hot, and moist; it cures the pain of headaches caused by cold and helps sustain pregnancy.
>
> *'Ishāq*, from Scorpio, is water, cold, and moist, and cures afflictions of breathing caused by heat and dryness.
>
> *Ḥoseiny*, from Sagittarius, is fire, dry, and hot, and cures fever and feverish heat.
>
> *Zanguleh,* from Capricorn, is earth, and cures the diseases of colic and paralysis and pain caused by heat.
>
> *Navā,* from Aquarius, is earth, dry, and hot, and cures sciatica, hip gout, and chronic ulcers.
>
> *Rahāvy*, from Pisces, is water, cold, and dry; it cures diseases of the kidneys and bladder and thirst caused by heat.

The author reports from respected elders that the treatment of the sick, particularly of monarchs, was previously undertaken by singing songs and playing music. If this failed to cure the sick person, a remedy was sought through the control of food, including fine fruits and drink. Only as a final resort would medicines or seasonings be used.

The treatise lists some accomplishments of famous musicians, and ends with a discussion of musical performance practices similar to that cited above from *Karāmat-e mujrā.*

The atmosphere of modern gatherings for *ṣūfyāna kalām* performance is that of a supportive community striving to achieve a common mystical experience.

FIGURE 6 A gathering (*mehfil*) for *ṣūfyāna kalām* performance in Srinagar, 1982. The principal musician, Saz Nawaz, plays the *santūr* while seated between two Sufis attending the event. The other instruments are (*from left*) *dokra* (tabla), *setār*, and sitar. Photo by Gordon K. Arnold.

Glimpses of the past

Although it is risky to infer historical musical traditions from modern-day performance practices, I offer some observations on the *ṣūfyāna kalām* tradition, on the basis of *mehfil* (Sufi gatherings) I was privileged to attend in the early 1980s (figure 6). (My underlying assumption is that the theoretical treatises discussed above reflected, or at least had some connection with, historical practice.)

TRACK 21

The melodic and tonal content of present-day performance practice would seem diminished in variety and complexity as compared with that of the past. *Maqām* names in general, however, remain the same. The rhythms and meters discussed in the treatises are each presented in variant forms in terms of mnemonic syllable (*bol*) patterns, and these appear to have little relationship to the drumming observed in modern performances.

What has survived is the effectiveness of the practices in achieving mystical union. The atmosphere of modern gatherings is that of a supportive community striving to achieve a common mystical experience. The basic pulse of the music appears to be in harmony with the beating of the human heart, and it is possible that this music and its participatory singing may synchronize the heartbeats and breathing of those assembled. The mood of those gathered varies from a deep, meditative state during sections of halting rhythm, to more alert participation during sections in regular rhythm, when more men sing and more verses are introduced. At gatherings for *ṣūfyāna mūsīqī*, an atmosphere of calm and meditation contrasts with the energetic and at times agitated character of other Sufi gatherings in South Asia, such as qawwali performances. The spiritual and ecstatic nature of the lyrics tends to unite the gathering in common thought, and because of the participatory nature of the *mehfil*, many of the lyrics are well known to the Sufis who attend. The music, in general, serves to highlight the spiritual communion of the Sufis, and it is said that kindred spirits join in the chorus if one has ears to hear.

REFERENCES

Aima, Mohanlal. 1969. "Music of Kashmir." *Sangeet Natak* 11:67–73.

Aziz, Sheikh Abdul. 1963–1965. *Kōshur Sargam.* 3 vols. Srinagar: Jammu and Kashmir Academy of Arts, Culture, and Language.

Bamzai, Prithvi Nath Kaul. 1962. *A History of Kashmir.* New Delhi: Metropolitan Book Company.

Nicholson, Reynold A., ed. and trans. 1982 [1926]. *The Mathnawī of Jalālu'ddin Rūmī*, 3 vols. Cambridge: E. J. W. Gibb Memorial Trust.

Pacholczyk, Józef M. 1978. "Sufyana Kalam, the Classical Music of Kashmir." *Asian Music* 10(1):1–16.

———. 1979. "Traditional Music of Kashmir." *The World of Music* 21(3):50–59.

———. 1989. "Musical Determinants of the Maqam in Sufyana Kalam." In *Maqam, Raga Zeilenmelodik: Konzeptionen und Prinzipien der Musikproduktion*, ed. Jürgen Elsner, 248–258. Berlin: International Council for Traditional Music and Sekretariat Internationale Nichtstaatliche Musikorganisationen.

———. 1992. "Towards a Comparative Study of a Suite Tradition in the Islamic Near East and Central Asia: Kashmir and Morocco." In *Regionale Maqām–Traditionen in Geshichte und Gegenwart*, ed. Jürgen Elsner and Gisa Jähnichen, 429–463. Berlin: International Council for Traditional Music.

———. 1996. *Ṣūfyāna Mūsīqī: The Classical Music of Kashmir.* Intercultural Music Studies 9. Berlin: Verlag für Wissenschaft und Bildung. With accompanying CD.

Powers, Harold. 1980. "Kashmir." In *The New Grove Dictionary of Music and Musicians*, ed. Stanley Sadie. London: Macmillan.

Pushp, P. N., ed. 1962. *Taraana-e Saroor (On Music in Kashmir) by Daya Ram Kachroo "Khushdil."* Srinagar: Research and Publication Department, Government of Jammu and Kashmir.

Qalandar, Qaisar. 1976. "Music in Kashmir, an Introduction." *Journal of the Indian Musicological Society* 7(4):15–22.

Rafiqi, Abdul Qaiyum. n.d. *Sufism in Kashmir.* Varanasi-Delhi: Bharatiya Publishing House.

Stein, M. Aurel. 1903. *Sand Buried Ruins of Khotan.* London: F. Fisher Unwin.

———. 1928. *Innermost Asia: A Detailed Report of Explorations in Central Asia.* Oxford: Clarendon.

———, trans. 1961. *Kalhana's Rājataraṅgiṇī: A Chronicle of the Kings of Kashmir.* Delhi: Motilal Banarsidass.

Nepal

Pirkko Moisala

North Indian Classical Music in Nepal
Occupational Caste Musicians
Ethnic Musical Traditions
Nation-Building Politics and Modern Music
Current Trends

Nepal's music culture reflects interactions among native Nepalese, Tibetan, and Indian musical traditions, as well as the coexistence of Buddhist, Hindu, and animist traditions. Nepal's population consists of people of Tibeto-Burman and Indo-Aryan origin. Beginning with the migration of North Indian court musicians in the seventeenth century, Nepal has experienced a continuous influx of musical elements. Since the 1950s, this influx has included the adaptation of North Indian light classical music and Hindi film song characteristics into the modern Nepalese song repertoire. Influences from the North are evident in Buddhist music and in the music cultures of ethnic groups living in the northern parts of the country, such as the Sherpas [see TIBETAN CULTURE IN SOUTH ASIA].

The variety of music in Nepal arises from the country's many ethnic groups and castes (currently over thirty), each with its own music culture. Transportation difficulties in the mountainous land as well as caste hierarchy have favored the survival of separate musical traditions into the 1990s. The caste system—legalized in 1854 in the Muluki Ain civil code and officially abolished in 1951—is still often adhered to in practice. Within this system, castes (including those of musicians) and ethnic groups (also called *jāt* 'castes') rank within a complex ritual hierarchy that has deeply influenced musical practices. In rural areas, people belonging to lower castes may adopt music from an upper caste in an attempt to raise their status. In more liberal multicaste and multiethnic urban surroundings, musicians can adopt music from lower castes without harming their own status.

Nepal's music culture does not divide neatly into separate ethnic and sociomusical traditions, but rather includes the varied and overlapping repertoires and musical practices of different ethnic, social, caste, and age groups that share musical and cultural features while simultaneously supporting their own musical repertoires. Particularly during the *pancāyat* 'local council' era from the early 1950s to 1990, music-related institutions such as Radio Nepal, stage programs, and the recording and film industries promoted "modern music" (see below), which was to be shared by all ethnic groups as part of national unification. This music has spread throughout Nepal via mass media and has become popular nationwide (Anderson and Mitchell 1978).

A national cultural context for new Nepalese music has received much promotion. However, on the local level ethnic background still plays a more essential role in music making, along with the ritual hierarchical system and religion. The latter—whether Hinduism, Buddhism, or animism—is inseparably interwoven into musical thinking. Thus traditional characteristics coexist with the relatively rapid development of mass media and the general modernization of the country. Rural and urban surroundings today provide different opportunities for musical practices. Increasing hardships due to population growth and land erosion also affect musical behavior.

NORTH INDIAN CLASSICAL MUSIC IN NEPAL

North Indian classical music began to flourish in Nepal around 1800, when the ruling Rana family imported Indian musicians to perform in their courts and to teach the Hindustani tradition to Nepalese students. The students came from among the Ranas as well as from other upper-level social groups. Classical music in Nepal still remains an activity of high-ranking castes and groups. Although Nepal did not adopt the *gharānā* 'stylistic school' system of learning, a master-student relationship has been the basis of classical music teaching for a long time. Indian classical music flourished in Nepal until the 1950s, and Kathmandu was known as an important center for Hindustani music, cultivating frequent exchanges with similar centers in the Indian subcontinent.

Hindustani music in Nepal acquired high status due to the great proficiency it requires, but it has survived only among a small circle of performers and their audiences. Nowadays, classical music and its performers are said to be "on their last legs" (Sattaur and Wegner 1993:15). Indian masters who used to play and teach in Nepal have returned to their homes, and Nepalese musicians have difficulty surviving as classical musicians; they cannot find patrons, and the present-day music culture does not offer many work possibilities. A few play classical music in restaurants and some have employment with Radio Nepal, although the actual broadcast time of Hindustani music has been reduced to an hour a week. Classical music is possibly "too Indian" for present-day Nepal.

OCCUPATIONAL CASTE MUSICIANS

In Nepal, caste still determines to a great extent a person's social status and the power relationships that govern his or her life. The Nepalese caste hierarchy includes three occupational castes of musicians, the Damāis, Gāines, and Badis. These three castes are all scheduled castes (also known as untouchables) at the bottom of the social and economic scale. Before the Land Reform Act of 1964, they could not own land, and today many still do not have land of their own. As performing is not lucrative enough to make an adequate living, the Damāis also work as tailors, the Gāines do odd jobs for other castes, and the Badis fish and make handicrafts.

In the 1990s, members of scheduled castes still have few ways of improving their lives and social status. Many avoid revealing their caste name, and many have discontinued their traditional occupation to earn a living in other ways. Nevertheless, a few Damāis and Gāines have gained appreciation and status as professional musicians in cultural events, recording studios, and other mass media of urban Kathmandu.

The musical heritage of the occupational castes thus continues to be a part of their social role, but the future of this role is in question as Nepal modernizes and the importance of the caste hierarchy slowly diminishes. To continue their musical traditions, performers will have to adjust to new societal contexts and functions. Scholars have studied the music of Nepalese occupational castes with the exception of the Badis (Bech 1975; Helffer 1977; Helffer and Macdonald 1966; Macdonald 1975;

Tingey 1994; Weisethaunet 1992, 1997a, 1997b), but much scholarly work remains to be done.

Gāines and their music

The Gāines earn their living mostly by performing music, playing the four-stringed *sāraṅgī* 'bowed fiddle' and singing to any audience willing to pay. The first records of the Gāines date from the late seventeenth century; they may have arrived in Nepal from Rajasthan in the thirteenth and fourteenth centuries when escaping the Mughal conquerers. The Gāine population is concentrated in the Gandhaki zone of central Nepal, which supports Helffer's hypothesis (1977:50–54) that the ruler of Gandhaki played an important role in the establishment of the first Gāine settlements in Nepal.

The Gāines follow the Hindu order and accept their low-caste rank as part of their karma. They regard the talent for creating music as a gift from the gods that soothes the pain of poverty and low status (Bech 1975:32). Scheduled castes may not ask for services from higher Hindu castes, and the Gāines have developed their own Hindu rituals; one of the most important of these rites is *pūjā* 'worship' performed to music of the *sāraṅgī* and the *arbajo*, believed to be its predecessor. This takes place today at the Sri Panchami festival in honor of Sarasvati, the Hindu goddess of the arts. Gāines invoke Sarasvati to bless the family with the talents of *sāraṅgī* playing and singing.

Up to the mid-twentieth century, the Gāines functioned as "singing newspapers"; their songs passed on messages, stories, myths, and daily news to society at large. Even though their importance as transmitters of knowledge has decreased due to the development of electronic mass media, their role as messengers is still a part of their identification.

Most itinerant Gāine musicians are men; Gāine women generally stay home in their villages. Particularly after harvesttime (from mid-November to February), Gāine musicians walk from one village to another, from house to house, asking to play and sing for food: uncooked rice, chili, maize, or beans. For over thirty years performances for tourists have provided extra income to urban Gāines as well as to those living by the main roads. Many have also begun to sell decorative *sāraṅgī*—ornaments rather than true musical instruments. In the tourist quarters of Kathmandu, *sāraṅgī* players perform well-known Western tunes to attract tourists. These urban musicians, however, are only a modest reflection of the rich Gāine tradition of Nepal.

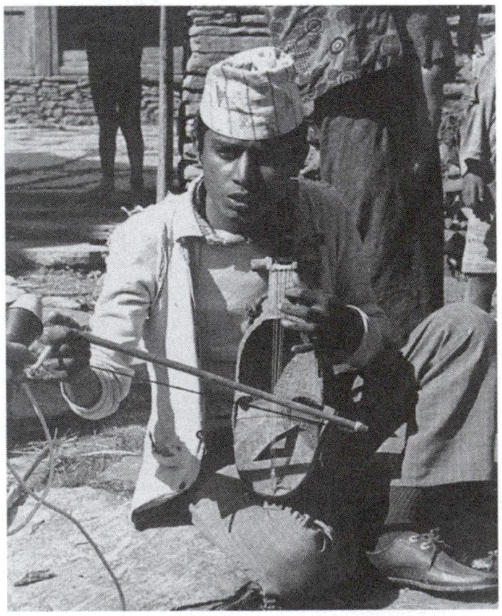

FIGURE 1 A Gāine musician plays the four-stringed *sāraṅgī* in Klinu village, 1976. Photo by Matti Lahtinen.

The four-stringed *sāraṅgī* fiddle is made out of a single block of wood; the lower part of the sound box has goatskin covering the front, while the upper part is left open (figure 1). The musician may put earned money into this upper part. Some musicians place a bell or bells at the end of the bow to provide rhythmic accompaniment. The strings are tuned to the scale degrees 5–1–1–5. The *sāraṅgī* player follows the melody of the song either in unison or heterophonically, and decorates the tune with occasional thirds and melismas. The interludes between verses are rather improvisational and sometimes even virtuosic.

The repertoire of Gāine songs is vast. It includes *jhyāure* popular dance songs, lyric songs, narrative songs (*karkhā*), religious songs (*astūti*), auspicious songs (*maṅgal*), love songs, laments, songs about life's hardships, and songs about particular events. For instance, the repertoire of the Gāines living in the Kathmandu Valley in 1961 included songs about the conquest of Everest by the Sherpa Tenzing Norgay and about the queen of England's visit to Nepal (Macdonald 1975). In many Gāine songs, criticism of society often blends with criticism of life.

The auspicious music of the Damāis

According to popular belief, the Damāi band (*damāi bājā*) originated in Middle

Eastern Islamic bands from the eleventh century onward, and traveled to Nepal, supposedly in the late fourteenth century, with court musicians of Rajput families fleeing from Muslim aggressors. In the process, peoples of the Himalayan foothills presumably adopted a court ensemble tradition. Historical records of Damāi instruments date from 1609. Today rural Damāis work as tailors, musicians, and occasional field workers within a traditional patronage system, receiving crops and grain after each harvest as payment for services. Damāis play music for their patrons and for other people.

Damāi music has both entertainment and auspicious functions. A Damāi band is an essential part of Nepalese weddings in rural and urban settings. The sound of the Damāi instruments echoes far distances to announce the celebrations; the band plays at the head of the wedding procession leading the bride to her new home. It also lends an auspicious aura to ritual functions: Damāi musicians perform for other life-cycle rites such as the first rice feeding of a baby, the birth of a son, funeral processions, and religious family services. Even though most of the Damāi repertoire is secular, band performance contexts are sacred or semisacred (having both sacred and secular functions) in nature.

Another name for the Damāi band, *pāncai bājā* 'five instruments', refers to the basic instruments of the band: the *śahnāī* 'shawm' played with circular breathing (figure 2), *damāhā* 'large kettledrum', *ṭyāmko* 'small kettledrum', *ḍholakī* 'double-headed drum', and *jhyāli* 'cymbals'. In practice, Damāi bands consist of varying groups and numbers of instruments. In central Nepal, the band has one or two curved natural horns (*narsiṅga*), while in the west a pair of natural trumpets (*karnāl*) with an occasional addition of a single *narsiṅga* is more usual. Sometimes the term *naumati bājā* 'nine instruments' is used to refer to a larger band.

The Damāi band repertoire consists of context-specific traditional items, such as seasonal rice-planting songs (*asāre*); music for the Hindu month of Phāgun (*phāgu*); the seasonal raga of the October Dasain festival (*mālaśrī rāg*); songs performed for the bride's departure at weddings (*beulī māgne*); music accompanying ceremonies and rites (*astūti*); popular folk dances; and modern folk songs and film tunes. But the younger generation of players no longer knows the older repertoire, which now exists principally in the memory of some older musicians.

Unlike seasonal ragas that have more complex melodic material, the popular repertoire consists mostly of pentatonic melodies. Damāi band performances used to

FIGURE 2 Damāi musicians play the *śahnāī* using circular breathing, 1985. Photo by Pirkko Moisala.

Popular Hindu legends have their Nepalese musical counterparts such as the Guruñg version of the story of Lord Krishna and the Magar performance of *Nachang*, the Hindu epic of Rama and Sita. Music creates a sacred space for ritual activities.

be largely tied to the devotional and agricultural year, with its repertoire reflecting the calendrical cycle, but nowadays popular and film music have largely replaced the "auspicious" ragas. Typical features of current Damāi band music are small intervals, stepwise melodic movement, short repetitive phrases frequently ending on the tonic—one of the *śahnāī* oboes often sounds the tonic pitch as a drone—and idiosyncratic fanfares played by the natural horn (*narsiṅga*) or natural trumpet (*karnāl*), not necessarily in tune with the oboes. Two meters predominate in the rhythmic accompaniment: *khyāli* (4/4 and 2/2) and *jhāure* (6/8 and 12/8) (Tingey 1994:114–115).

The Damāis also play ritual music at temples in central Nepal. A temple musician may receive a monthly salary in addition to ritual gifts (*bheti*). The temple bands differ from other Damāi ensembles in their composition: they include a *nagare* 'large kettledrum', *rāsa śahnāī* 'temple shawm', and *karnāl* 'natural trumpet', occasionally supplemented by other natural trumpets or by a complete *pāncai bājā* Damāi band. Temple bands play music for divine rather than human consumption, accompanying daily offerings, blood and other types of sacrifices to the presiding deities, and ritual processions. Their repertoires include some seasonal ragas of the popular bands in addition to their own musical material.

Nowadays, young Damāis may choose to leave the traditional patronage system and work for a regular salary in urban dressmakers' shops; education is beginning to open up other work possibilities. The ethnomusicologist Carol Tingey predicts that unless there is improvement in the economic condition or social status of the Damāi, the Damāi band tradition will steadily decline, and she doubts whether this "heartbeat of Nepal" will continue into the next century (1994:133).

ETHNIC MUSICAL TRADITIONS

The ethnic music of the Nepalese Himalayas represents a relatively uninvestigated field of ethnomusicological exploration. The rich musical heritage of the Newārs living in the Kathmandu Valley has been the subject of several studies (Bernède 1997; Grandin 1989, 1993a, 1994, 1995, 1997; Hoerburger 1970, 1975; Wegner 1986, 1987, 1988; Wiehler-Schneider and Wiehler 1980), and the songs of the Tamangs also living there have been surveyed (Hoerburger 1975). However, among the many ethnic music cultures outside of the Kathmandu Valley, only Guruñg music has been investigated (Gurung 1996; Moisala 1989a, 1989b, 1991, 1994, 1997).

The ethnic groups of Nepal fall into two broad categories: southern people of Indo-Aryan origin and northern people of Tibeto-Burman origin. The musical traditions of these people reflect this division, although many groups exhibit their own distinctive mixture of these backgrounds. In northern music, pentatonic scales without half tones dominate, whereas in the south melodies are more often based on heptatonic scales. Musical styles, musical terminology, and instrument names vary greatly from one area to another, a situation typical of oral traditions. Also, a wide variety of percussion instruments are used (Divas 1977; Helffer 1997a; Tingey 1992).

In addition to modern, mass-mediated music (see below), most if not all ethnic groups share popular *jhyāure* and *chuḍke* songs and dances as well as the song duels known as *dohori gīt*. Individuals or groups compete in the duels by inventing new verses, which they alternate with refrains sung jointly with others present.

Religious beliefs and music

Much ethnic music making is related either to the annual agricultural cycle—as in the *ya-rakma* dance of the Limbus, performed while threshing corn—or to the religious festival cycle. Ethnic groups honor gods and local deities with music in the hope of obtaining a good crop and to celebrate a new harvest. Various animist, Buddhist, and Hindu rites (for purifying the house, blessing the first-born son, and so on) include music, as do the annual religious festivals. Popular Hindu legends have their Nepalese musical counterparts such as the Guruñg version of the story of Lord Krishna and the Magar performance of *Nachang*, the Hindu epic of Rama and Sita. Music creates a sacred space for ritual activities.

The various religious authorities, shamans, lamas, and Hindu leaders all have distinct musical practices related to purification rites and rituals. Both shamans and laymen perform music as a medium for communicating with the gods, local deities, and ancestral spirits (Hitchcock and Jones 1976; Giannattasio 1988). Drum beating accompanies spiritual journeys made by shamans and spirit possessions of ordinary people.

Musical events, including religious rituals and festivals, serve to gather people together and create a special time and place for social interaction. Formal musical performances take place at religious festivals, in connection with rites of passage, and to honor important guests. Dance is an inseparable part of such musical performances. Both encapsulate the local cultural and ethnic identity: traditional musical genres carry a great deal of information about the history and traditions of an ethnic group as well as its current knowledge and beliefs.

The impoverishment of the rural areas has reduced the organization and frequency of lengthy, costly musical performances. In addition, the gradual modernization and development promoted by the state are decreasing the importance of musical genres related to animist belief systems and traditional ways of life.

Music making and music makers in the villages

Almost all ethnic Nepalese make music and dance at least at some point in their lives. People sing while working in the rice fields or carrying firewood. Spontaneous singing and dancing may occur during ordinary evening gatherings. Ethnic groups learn music through oral imitation, not necessarily through any specific form of teaching. From an early age, children imitate the music and dances of adults; there is no repertoire of children's songs. Nowadays, people listen to music on cassettes and radios more and more frequently to lighten work and long walks.

Popular, mass-mediated music also increasingly accompanies gatherings in local tea houses and shops. Most musical performances in the villages are spontaneous, but when work in the fields allows leisure time, villagers arrange performances either of traditional genres or of newly composed and adopted media music. Poor villagers must ration the use of radio and cassette players due to costly batteries, but they nevertheless adopt Nepalese and Hindi popular tunes into their local repertoires and compose songs in a similar style.

The sounds of musical instruments can carry long distances across mountainous terrain. Drumbeats or instrumental sounds signal that a wedding, funeral, or other event is taking place in another village—which may require many days of walking to reach.

Gender plays an essential role in the musical practice of Nepalese ethnic groups. In many communities, adult women are not allowed to perform, play, sing, or dance in public, particularly if they are married. Such groups may not actually articulate such prohibitions, but may enforce the restrictions by other means such as ridiculing women who participate in musical performances. However, some women's musical genres do exist, such as the *jhora gīt* sung by Magar women at the Hindu Tij festival celebrating Shiva and Parvati and the *maṅgalinī* 'auspicious songs' of the royal household (Tingey 1997). Among most ethnic groups married women may dance at their child's wedding. Furthermore, educated young women may break the restricting norms without losing respect.

The musical heritage of the Newārs

Newār culture has its roots in both northern lands—the Newār language belonging to the Tibeto-Burman family—and southern regions—through early and continuous cultural contacts with North India. Both Hinduism and Buddhism have coexisted in Newār culture since the early centuries of the common era. Songs and music form an important part of the Newār artistic heritage and have developed in contact with Indian music. The Newār concept of raga, however, as expressed in the hymns of two Newār traditions, *dāphā* and the Buddhist *cācā* (Widdess 1997), includes less improvisation than an Indian raga performance.

Most Newār music and dance groups have social functions that integrate religious practices and beliefs. Many neighborhoods contain a *nāsa dyā* 'shrine for the god of music' (Ellingson 1991). Particular occupational groups are assigned musical as well as other tasks and duties. These groups (castes) have social rank according to their religious duties. The task of gardeners (Gāthā), for example, is to organize and perform the *Nava Durgā* dance drama, which portrays the rice goddesses and which has existed since the sixteenth century. Mask makers (Chitrakār) prepare the secret masks worn by the dancers representing the rice goddesses. *Nava Durgā* performances take place during eight months of the year, mainly in the streets of Bhaktapur but also in other Newār towns and villages (Korvald 1994). Newār butchers (Nāy), at the bottom of the Newār ritual hierarchy, are occupational musicians.

Newār hymn-singing groups consisting usually of men from a particular neighborhood gather to sing *dāphā* hymns and bhajans; some groups are connected with a temple. They perform at shrines and take part in festival processions. Groups that sing *dāphā* are the earliest, estimated to date back at least three hundred fifty years. Members sing hymns in Newari and occasionally in Maithili to the accompaniment of the *khī* 'large barrel drum' and cymbals. A flute ensemble that plays the same hymn tunes may be connected with the group. In the more recent bhajan groups, members sing hymns in Sanskrit, Maithili, Newari, or Hindi accompanied by harmonium and tabla, as in Indian bhajan groups; these modern bhajans are delicate in their emotional expression. Many have appeared on cassettes (Henderson 1996).

A typical ensemble of Newār farmers is the *dhimaybājā*, whose roots may be in old Newār military music. The ensemble consists of *dhimay* 'cylindrical drums' and brass cymbals of varying sizes (*bhuchyāh* and *sichyāh*) (Wegner 1986). Musicians learn to play the *dhimay* drum orally, using drum syllables, under the guidance of a guru. The learning process involves many blood sacrifices to the associated gods of music. The *dhimaybājā* ensemble has regular performances in urban rituals as well as occasional performances in the group's neighborhood; the ensemble often plays while walking at the head of festival processions.

The *nāykhībājā* band of the Nāy 'butchers' consists of a *nāykhī* 'double-headed cylindrical or barrel drum' and two *sichyāh* cymbals. This ensemble also plays a dominant role in many town rituals and processions such as funeral processions (*sībājā*), in which musical sequences correspond with certain localities; it plays for pure enjoyment as well (Wegner 1988).

Up to the mid-twentieth century, the *guṭhī* system of land endowments and other local patronage provided essential support for musical performance. Nowadays for economic reasons music groups have increasing difficulty maintaining their musical traditions. According to the scholar Ingemar Grandin (1994), a little over 50 percent of Newār men are competent in one musical form or another, having taken music lessons from a guru. Almost all men over forty years of age have received musical training, whereas only half the younger ones have done so. Today, music in Newār culture is becoming the domain of specialists. At the same time, women, formerly not allowed to take part in music making, are now participating in modern stage programs as singers and dancers.

The Guruñgs as musical merrymakers

The Guruñgs are a Tibeto-Burman ethnic group of Mongoloid stock whose approximately 200,000 members live mainly in the hill area of central Nepal. Their traditional music is a significant repository of their ethnic identity. A most important Guruñg musical genre is the *ghā̃ṭu* dance drama, performed in its entirety at the full moon in mid-May. The performance takes three days and nights, and portrays the life story of King Pashram and Queen Yamavati (scholars have reached no consensus over whether the royal couple is legendary or historical). A group of male singers and some *mādal* 'double-headed cylindrical drum' players perform the *ghā̃ṭu* music. The dance visualizes the aesthetic aim of *ghā̃ṭu* performance, expressed in Nepali as *sallala pani page jastai* 'flowing like the water'.

TRACK 22

Ghā̃ṭu dancers must be young virgins who may continue as dancers until they marry (figure 3). At a specific point during the *ghā̃ṭu* performance, called *kusunda,* the dancers fall into spirit possession. Strict rules govern the *kusunda*; the Guruñg believe any mistake may result in blindness, madness, or even death. Due to these sanctions the *ghā̃ṭu* has maintained its unique *ghā̃ṭu* language, barely comprehensible to present-day singers or audiences, which may be an ancient Guruñg language.

Shamans of the two Guruñg shamanistic traditions, *poju* and *khlevri*, conduct death rites, which Guruñgs claim to be cultural items that separate them from other ethnic groups. The shaman recites oral narrations (*pé*) to the soul of the deceased.

FIGURE 3 Young Guruñg girls dance the *ghā̃ṭu* dance drama, accompanied by male singers and two *mādal* drummers, 1985. Photo by Pirkko Moisala.

According to traditional Guruñg musical thinking, one person alone cannot make *bājā* 'music'; *bājā* requires a group of people performing for an audience.

During the funeral procession and at the time of cremation, an ensemble consisting of *śaṅkha* 'conch shell trumpet', *sjō̃* 'bronze bell', *ngā̃* 'frame drum', and *jhyāli* 'cymbals' accompanies the recitation. Laymen perform a *serga* dance in honor of the deceased's soul as a part of the death rituals; the *serga* encourages the soul to find the path to heaven.

According to traditional Guruñg musical thinking, one person alone cannot make *bājā* 'music'; *bājā* requires a group of people performing for an audience. This comprehension corresponds with a cultural emphasis on collectivity. Both the *serga* and the *ghā̃ṭu*—as well as the *sorathī,* a third Guruñg musical dance-drama tradition—have pentatonic melodies sung in a continuous heterophonic style, reflecting the collective approach to music making (figure 4). *Mādal* drummers play the percussion accompaniment, based on slightly varied rhythmic patterns. In *sorathī,* as well as in the Krishna *caritra* (the story of Lord Krishna adapted to Guruñg usage in the 1930s), men dance female roles. In traditional Guruñg culture, music making by married women is not allowed; however, to the Guruñg, this does not contradict their cultural emphasis on collectivity.

From the 1930s on, the newer forms of Guruñg music, including the Krishna *caritra,* have been based on modal melodies and usually have *mādal* drum and harmonium accompaniment. Guruñg song compositions since the 1960s have been in popular radio and film styles. Love is the most common theme, but a song may also describe village life or the longing of a soldier (*gurkha*) serving in a foreign army. Guruñgs sing these songs in spontaneous gatherings, at the Rodi (a community-orga-

FIGURE 4 Pentatonic *ghā̃ṭu* dance drama melody, usually sung by male Guruñg singers in heterophonic style. In the *mādal* drum accompaniment, regular note heads indicate undamped strokes; note heads with a line through indicate damped strokes. Transcription by Pirkko Moisala, from 1985 field recording.

nized institution for youths) and in youth dance-theater performances. This new music does not relate to the animist worldview but connects Guruñg culture with the national culture of Nepal.

Even though Guruñgs regard performances of their traditional music as an important way of maintaining their culture, many villages lack the financial resources to arrange such occasions. They still perform parts of the *ghāṭu* and *sorathī* dance dramas at Guruñg-association festivals in Kathmandu, and many urban Guruñgs still prefer to have their funeral ceremonies carried out "with the drums," by traditional Guruñg shamans.

NATION-BUILDING POLITICS AND MODERN MUSIC

A Western visitor's first impression of the musical soundscape of Nepal's capital city, Kathmandu—is only a partial representation of Nepalese music. It is likely to be the music of urban orchestras that combine traditional Nepalese and foreign instruments and present a characteristic sonoric quality as they play tunes based on modal scales. Such orchestras consist of Western violins; solo melody instruments such as the *bāṅsurī* 'bamboo flute'; percussion instruments including the tabla, *ḍholak* 'barrel drum', *mādal* 'cylindrical drum', and possibly also a Western drum set; and a bass guitar, a harmonium (imitating the vocal melody), and a guitar, piano accordion, or mandolin to provide Western chordal harmony. The violins usually support the vocal sections heterophonically. Female vocalists sing with a tight voice quality and in a high register, while the male voices are soft and relaxed. The rhythmic accompaniment consists of short, repetitive rhythmic patterns (6/8 and 4/4 predominate).

This kind of Nepalese modern music (*ādhunik gīt*), which has spread throughout Nepal via radio broadcasting, closely resembles Hindi film tunes, borrowing elements from Western and other musical traditions. Even in remote mountain villages, Nepalese adopt and imitate this musical style. The most recent forms of *ādhunik gīt* incorporate Western rock and rap styles; original Western popular and disco music can also be heard in the tourist areas of Kathmandu, but only a small group of privileged urban youth listens to and performs this music.

New folk songs (*lok gīt*) combine tunes, rhythms, and instruments from various ethnic traditions with the modern *ādhunik gīt* orchestration. The song texts of both *lok gīt* and *ādhunik gīt* are most commonly on the subject of love. *Rāṣṭrīya gīt* celebrates patriotic and national themes with festive accompaniments, employing large orchestras with many violins and often brass instruments. However, *rāṣṭrīya gīt* forms only a minor part of mass-mediated music, and since 1990 (when Nepal changed to a democratic political system) it has lost its political importance. Yet another genre, a sophisticated variant of *ādhunik gīt*, is *gīṭi nāṭak*, which consists of sung narrative poems.

The popularity of mass-mediated music is a consequence not only of Nepal's modernization but also of the government's successful cultural politics between 1950 and 1990 during its promotion and formation of a unified nation-state. Radio Nepal was established in 1951; the Royal Nepal Academy in 1957; the Rastriya Nachghar (today the Sanskritik Sansthan), or national dance theater, in 1961; the Ratna Recording Trust (later the Ratna Recording Company) in 1962; and the Royal Nepal Film Corporation in 1971. The new musical genres—*ādhunik gīt, lok gīt,* and *rāṣṭrīya gīt*—developed in association with these state-owned institutions and followed the ideology of nation-building politics; the state restricted the broadcast of ethnic songs in languages other than Nepali. The institutions in turn provided a basis for the National Communication Service Plan, launched in 1971 to promote national unity, prestige, and dignity. But despite the one or two weekly programs produced by Radio Nepal introducing regional songs, and despite the national institutions becoming more commercially oriented in the 1980s, the enormously rich variety of indigenous ethnic musical traditions has clearly not enjoyed promotion equal to that given the modern genres. The full variety of ethnic traditions is featured only in state-arranged cultural tours to other countries and in cultural programs aimed at tourists. Unfortunately, these cultural performances usually consist of poor adaptations of indigenous genres far from their original cultural contexts.

CURRENT TRENDS

More recent liberal national policies have led to a revival of ethnic musical performance. Due to the political changes of 1990, ethnic groups are now allowed to promote their identities and establish their own associations. Musicians are working to strengthen their own traditions either by incorporating rural ethnic genres into the activities of urban associations and into stage programs, or by composing new songs in their mother tongues. One modern rock band now calls itself the Newārs.

Music with a political message may always have been a part of Nepalese music. Through their metaphorical songs of opposition, the Gāines have commented on and criticized state politics and the *pancāyat* 'local council' system for restricting ethnic politics. Political parties have used music as a propaganda tool, and the state of Nepal itself has understood the power of music as a political tool for unifying the country's diverse ethnicities.

After 1990, Radio Nepal stopped broadcasting many recordings of patriotic *rāṣṭrīya* and *lok gīt* songs from the *pancāyat* era. Nevertheless, the state-supported mass media continue to neglect ethnic musics. The author Kishor Gurung (1993:11) has noted the paradox in Nepal's official broadcasting policy, which seeks to establish cultural homogeneity—thus suppressing Nepal's cultural diversity—yet incorporates elements of Hindi film song, Indian and Pakistani ghazal, and Western music into its productions. Nepal TV, established in 1984, continues with the same politics, and "shows a lack of sensibility and even respect for cultural diversity" (Gurung 1993).

Modern urban society has found new uses for music, such as stage programs, and new support systems, such as professional music groups, restaurants, studios, educational institutions, and private tutoring. Professional music making is not restricted to lower-caste members of society but is the occupation of middle and high castes. In multiethnic, multicultural Kathmandu, musical specialization is respectable, and composers and performers may be Brahmins, Chetris, Newārs, or Guruṅgs. While music making moves from predefined assigned roles to achieved positions, music itself gains new status in modern society. Urban settings now allow women to perform as dancers and singers, although women instrumentalists are still extremely rare in public arenas.

The communal approach to music making has weakened among urban musicians as musical performance moves increasingly to the stage and the mass media. Similarly, as people replace the traditional agricultural way of life with modern occupations, they have fewer opportunities to participate in and thus maintain traditional musical genres tied to the agricultural cycle and an animist worldview. Studio musicians at Radio Nepal make new arrangements and provide new texts for songs collected in villages and brought to the capital. They broadcast the new songs back to their original location, and rural people who do not think of music as a source of copyright income are generally pleased and honored to hear "their songs" on radio and cassettes.

Kathmandu University has recently established a department of music that, in addition to granting B.A. and M.A. degrees, aims to preserve traditional music repertoires in sound archives. Also, since the second visit of Arnold A. Bake to Nepal in 1955, scholars have collected significant sound and film recordings (Bishop 1993;

Helffer and de Sales 1993). However, much scholarly work remains to be done to create a comprehensive picture of Nepal's rich musical traditions (Darnal 1997; Helffer 1997b; Tingey 1985a).

REFERENCES

Anderson, Robert, and Edna M. Mitchell. 1978. "The Politics of Music in Nepal." *Anthropology Quarterly* 51(4):247–259.

Bake, Arnold A. Collection of recordings from 1932 and 1956. British Sound Archives, London, and the School of Oriental and African Studies, University of London.

Bech, Terence. 1975. "Nepal, the Gaine Caste of Beggar-Musicians." *The World of Music* 17(1):28–35.

———. 1978. *Catalog of the Terence R. Bech Nepal Music Research Collection.* Bloomington: Indiana University Press.

Bernède, Franck, ed. 1977. *European Bulletin of Himalayan Research*, special double issue, *Himalayan Music: State of the Art* 12–13.

———. 1997. "Music and Identity among Maharjan Farmers: The Dhimay Senegu of Kathmandu." *European Bulletin of Himalayan Research*, special double issue, *Himalayan Music: State of the Art* (ed. Franck Bernède) 12–13:21–56.

Bishop, Naomi H. 1993. "Laura Boulton Audiotape and Film Collection from Nepal, 1950: A Report." *Himalayan Research Bulletin* 13(1-2):3–16.

Boulton, Laura. Collection of recordings from 1950, 1951, and 1956. Original audio tapes in the Office of Folklife Programs, Library of Congress; silent film footage on videotape in the Human Studies Film Archive, Museum of Natural History, Smithsonian Institution, Washington, D.C.; field notes at Columbia University, New York.

Darnal, R. S. 1997. "Bibliography of Nepali Music." *European Bulletin of Himalayan Research*, special double issue, *Himalayan Music: State of the Art* (ed. Franck Bernède) 12–13:240–251.

Divas, Tulsi. 1977. *Musical Instruments of Nepal.* Kathmandu: Royal Nepal Academy.

Grandin, Ingemar. 1989. *Music and Media in Local Life: Music Practice in a Newar Neighbourhood in Nepal.* Linköping: Tema.

———. 1993a. "Kathmandu, a Valley Fertile of Music." *Himal* 6(6):23–27.

———. 1993b. "Music as Message." *Himal* 6(6):24.

———. 1994. "Nepalese Urbanism: A Musical Exploration." In *Anthropology of Nepal: People, Problems and Processes,* ed. Michael Allen, 160–175. Kathmandu: Mandala Book Point.

———. 1995. "One Song, Five Continents, and a Thousand Years of Musical Migration." *Sargam* 1(1):56–65.

Ellingson, Ter. 1991. "Nasa:dya, Newar God of Music: A Photo Essay." *Selected Reports in Ethnomusicology* 8:221–272.

Giannattasio, F. 1988. "I rapporti tra musica e transe nello sciamanismo nepalese." In *La Terra Reale; Dèi, Spiriti, Uomini in Nepal*, ed. Romano Mastromattei, 183–226. Rome: Valerio Levi Editore.

Grandin, Ingemar. 1997. "Raga Basanta and the Spring Songs of the Kathmandu Valley: A Musical Great Tradition among Himalayan Farmers?" *European Bulletin of Himalayan Research*, special double issue, *Himalayan Music: State of the Art* (ed. Franck Bernède) 12–13:57–80.

Gurung, Kishor. 1993. "What Is Nepali Music?" *Himal* 6(6):8–11.

———. 1996. *Ghamtu: A Narrative Ritual Music Tradition as Observed by the Gurungs of Nepal.* Kathmandu: United States Information Service.

Helffer, Mireille. 1969. "Fanfares villageoises au Népal." *Objets et Mondes* 9(1):51–58.

———. 1977. "Une caste de chanteurs-musiciens: Les gaine du Népal." *L'Ethnographie* 73:45–75.

———. 1997a. "The Drums of Nepalese Mediums." *European Bulletin of Himalayan Research*, special double issue, *Himalayan Music: State of the Art* (ed. Franck Bernède) 12–13:176–196.

———. 1997b. "Bibliography of Himalayan Music." *European Bulletin of Himalayan Research*, special double issue, *Himalayan Music: State of the Art* (ed. Franck Bernède) 12–13:222–239.

Helffer, Mireille, and A. de Sales. 1993. "Nepalese Archives of the Department of Ethnomusicology in the Musée de l'Homme, Paris (1960–1975)." *European Bulletin of Himalayan Research* 5:24–25.

Helffer, Mireille, and Alexander W. Macdonald. 1966. "Sur un sārangi de gāine." *Objets et Mondes* 6(2):133–142.

———. 1975. "Remarks on Nepali Song Verse." In *Essays on the Ethnology of Nepal and South Asia*, ed. A. W. Macdonald, 175–265. Kathmandu: Ratna Pustak Bhandar.

Henderson, David. 1996. "Emotion and Devotion, Lingering and Longing in Some Nepali Songs." *Ethnomusicology* 40(3):440–468.

Hitchcock, John T. 1966. *The Magars of the Banyan Hill.* New York: Holt, Rinehart and Winston.

Hitchcock, John T., and Rex L. Jones, eds. 1976. *Spirit Possession in the Nepal Himalayas.* Warminster: Aris and Phillips.

Hoerburger, Felix. 1970. "Folk Music in the Caste System of Nepal." *Yearbook of the International Folk Music Council* 2:142–147.

———. 1975. *Studien zur Musik in Nepal.* Regensburg: Gustav Bosse Verlag.

Korvald, Tordis. 1994. "The Dancing Gods of Bhaktapur and Their Audience. Presentation of Navadurgaa Pyaakham: The Drama and the People Involved." In *The Anthropology of Nepal: People, Problems and Processes,* ed. Michael Allen, 405–415. Kathmandu: Mandala Book Point.

Lienhard, Siegfried. 1984. *Songs of Nepal: An Anthology of Newar Folksongs and Hymns.* Honolulu: Asian Studies, University of Hawaii.

Macdonald, Alexander W. 1975. "An Aspect of the Songs of the Gāine of Nepal." In *Essays on the Ethnology of Nepal and South Asia,* ed. H. K. Kuloy, 169–174. Kathmandu: Ratna Pustak Bhandar.

Moisala, Pirkko. 1989a. "An Ethnographic Description of the Madal-Drum and Its Making among the Gurungs." *Suomen Antropologi* 4:234–239.

———.1989b. "Gurung Music and Cultural Identity." *Kailash* 15(3-4):207–222.

———. 1991. *Cultural Cognition in Music: Continuity and Change in the Gurung Music of Nepal.* Jyväskylä: Gummerus.

———. 1994. "Gurung Music in Terms of Gender." *Etnomusikologian vuosikirja* 6: 135–147.

———. 1997. "Gurung Cultural Models in the Ghantu." *European Bulletin of Himalayan Research*, special double issue, *Himalayan Music: State of the Art* (ed. Franck Bernède) 12–13:152–175.

Mikame, Kiyotomo. 1979. "A Note on the Phaguwaa Festival of Chitwan Tharu." *Kailash* 7(3-4):227–246.

Rana, Jagadish. 1990. "Bhaktapur, Nepal's Capital of Music and Dance. A Study of Conservation & Promotion of Traditional Music and Dance." *Kailash* 16(1-2):5–12.

Sattaur, Omar, and Gert-Matthias Wegner. 1993. "Where Is Shastriya Sangeet?" *Himal* 6(6):15–17.

Tingey, Carol. 1985a. "An Annotated Bibliography and Discography of Nepalese Musics." *Journal of the International Council for Traditional Music (UK Chapter)* 11:4–20; 12:35–44.

———. 1985b. "The Nepalese Field Work of Dr. Arnold A. Bake." In *Ethnomusicology and the Historical Dimension,* ed. Margot Lieth-Philipp, 83–87. Ludwigsburg: Philipp Verlag.

———. 1991. "The Ethnomusicological Research of Dr. A. A. Bake." *The European Bulletin of Himalayan Research* 1:20–21.

———. 1992. "Sacred Kettledrums in the Temples of Central Nepal." *Asian Music* 23(2):97–104.

———. 1994. *Auspicious Music in a Changing Society: The Damāi Musicians of Nepal.* New Delhi: Heritage Publications; London: School of Oriental and African Studies, University of London.

———. 1997. "Music for the Royal Dasai." *European Bulletin of Himalayan Research*, special double issue, *Himalayan Music: State of the Art* (ed. Franck Bernède) 12–13:81–120.

Wegner, Gert-Matthias. 1986. *The Dhimaybājā of Bhaktapur: Studies in Newar Drumming I.* Stuttgart: Franz Steiner.

———. 1987. "Navadāphā of Bhaktapur. Repertoire and Performance of the Ten Drums." In *Nepalica 4/21,* ed. Bernard Kölver and Siegfried Lienhard, 469–488. Sankt Augustin: VGH Wissenschaftsverlag.

———. 1988. *The Nāykhibājā of the Newar Butchers: Studies in Newar Drumming II.* Stuttgart: Franz Steiner.

Weisethaunet, Hans. 1992. "Tradisjon og Destruksjon: Kastemusikere i Nepal." *Studia Musicologica Norvegica* 18:55–82.

———. 1997a. "The Performance of Everyday Life: The Gāine of Nepal." Ph.D. dissertation, University of Oslo.

———. 1997b. "My Music Is My Life." *European Bulletin of Himalayan Research*, special double issue, *Himalayan Music: State of the Art* (ed. Franck Bernède) 12–13:136–151.

Widdess, Richard. 1997. "Carya: The Revival of a Tradition?" *European Bulletin of Himalayan Research*, special double issue, *Himalayan Music: State of the Art* (ed. Franck Bernède) 12–13:12–20.

Wiehler-Schneider, Sigrun, and Hartmut Wiehler. 1980. "A Classification of the Traditional Musical Instruments of the Newars." *Journal of the Nepal Research Centre* 4:67–132.

Tibetan Culture in South Asia

Mireille Helffer

Music Outside the Monasteries
Musical Traditions of Tibetan Buddhism
Some Recent Changes
Research on Tibetan Musical Traditions in South Asia

Tibetan culture—whether speech, writing, a particular form of Buddhism, architecture, painting, sculpture, or music—extends far beyond the region often called the "roof of the world." For centuries, the peoples of this Himalayan region traveled up and down the Himalayan mountain chain. Today they live in India (Ladakh, Zangsdkar, Spiti, Lahul, Sikkim), Nepal (Humla, Dolpo, and Mustang districts, sherpa country), or Bhutan. Precise population statistics are lacking, but many Tibetan-speaking people live in these areas; they practice Tibetan Buddhism and the native Bon religion, and are ethnically and culturally Tibetan. When China occupied Tibet in 1959, waves of Tibetan refugees flooded out, about one hundred thousand according to standard estimates. Following the fourteenth Dalai Lama, they arrived in camps created specifically for them in India, and in Nepal to a lesser degree, and with the help of religious communities reestablished in exile they managed to find new ways to live. An especially large number of Tibetan refugees live in the northwest Indian state of Himachal Pradesh, where Dharamsala serves as the exiles' capital city and the home of the Dalai Lama. Refugees also live in Orissa and Karnataka in South India, on lands placed at their disposal by the Indian government. It is thus quite legitimate to speak of a Tibetan presence in South Asia today.

The musical culture among Tibetan refugees is subject to obvious regional variations, but it exhibits certain general musical characteristics. Vocal music is of primary importance to all who speak Tibetan or a Tibetan dialect. This is true of native Tibetans, peoples native to countries surrounding Tibet, those newly in the Himalayan region, and those in artificial situations in the camps. Furthermore, a sharp distinction exists between lay and monastic music. For this reason, songs sung by lay people and the rich musical tradition preserved in the monasteries are treated separately in this article.

MUSIC OUTSIDE THE MONASTERIES

In Tibetan culture, the practice of singing by individuals or groups is widespread. Song texts are almost exclusively in regular strophic form, and melodic improvisation is virtually absent. In each geographical area several tune types exist, each comprising one, two, three, or four melody lines, which singers repeat over and over again until

Epic storytellers wandered the roads of Tibet, telling of the many exploits of King Ge-sar. They sometimes crossed the Himalayan mountain passes, stopping in border villages where they entranced their audiences, eager for tales of marvels.

the end of the song. As a Tibetan scholar exiled in the West has observed, "In each region there exist a variety of melodies that may be applied to any of its *gzhas* [dance songs] (since all have the same metre); and similarly there are special tunes used for the drinking songs" (Namkhai Norbu Dewang 1967:209).

Lay women and men play very few musical instruments. These are primarily the *sgra-snyan*, a long-necked, plucked lute with four to seven strings; the *pi-wang*, a two- or four-stringed fiddle; and the *gling-bu*, a duct flute. To these instruments a drum, cymbals, or dulcimer is sometimes added. These instruments mainly accompany singing or dancing.

Common song repertoires

The genres discussed here have certain common stylistic elements, such as an abundance of repetition and onomatopoeia, but they differ in poetic structure according to the number of syllables per text line. Since the Tibetans have no single classification system for song types, common Tibetan terminology is applied here.

Glu is the most general term for a popular song. Such songs usually have seven or eight syllables per line. Within this category are marriage songs (*bag-ston gyi glu*), particularly extensive repertoires of which have been noted in Ladakh from the end of the nineteenth century (Francke 1941). These survive in manuscript collections that are carefully preserved by their owners, and even if they are seldom sung today, traces of them have been found in Ladakh (Tashi 1970), Spiti (Tucci 1966), and Humla (unpublished work of the ethnologists Nancy Levine and David Friedlander in 1991). In western Tibet, in neighboring regions, and even in other parts of Tibet, responsorial songs in which the groom had to answer traditional questions posed by members of the bride's family were evidently a major part of marriage ceremonies. Failure meant that the bride could not go to her future husband's village.

Other kinds of popular song common to the Tibetan community in exile are *chang-glu* 'drinking songs', sung when friends get together or at picnics; *gzhung-glu* 'songs of reunion', sung when groups gather; *chos-glu* 'religious songs' about monasteries or monks, and *gral-glu* 'line songs'. In the latter, two groups line up facing each other and compete in song. Particularly popular are songs of political criticism (*glu-shags* or *tshig-rgyag*).

In the epic of King Ge-sar (see "Specialist Song Repertoires" below), the term *glu* refers to all versified, sung passages that alternate with long prose sections. In Ladakh, these are known as *gling-glu* 'songs from Gling country'.

Gzhas generally refers to songs with six-syllable lines organized into quatrains (*tshig-rkang-bzhi*). This form includes songs attributed to the sixth Dalai Lama (Sorensen 1990), and also songs in the *nang-ma* and *stod-gzhas* repertoires popular with the Lhasa aristocracy in the 1930s and now widespread among Tibetans in exile in the border regions, including Bhutan. According to some scholars, *gzhas* differs from *glu* in its association with dancing. Round dances performed by both men and women with song accompaniment are called *skor-gzhas.*

Recent investigations in Mustang indicate that inhabitants of this distant northern Nepal region distinguish between *glu-gzhas, zhabs-bro glu* 'songs to accompany dancing', *gral-glu* 'line songs', *rta-gzhon glu* 'horseback riding songs', and *tshig-rgyag* 'songs of political criticism' (Friedlander 1991).

The term *mgur* applies to religiously inspired songs such as devotional songs to a religious master. These compositions generally have seven- or eight-syllable lines, similar to *glu* texts. Over the centuries singers have used *mgur*, like the Indian *doha*, to transmit the profound truths of Buddhism. A well-known example among Tibetans is Mi-la ras-pa's *Mgur-'bum* 'Hundred Thousand Songs', of which several English and French translations exist (Chang 1970).

Musical vocabulary

The minimal research carried out by scholars on the music of Tibetan songs has focused almost entirely on sound recordings of Tibetans in exile. Crossley-Holland (1961b, 1967) recorded about forty songs in Indian and Nepali refugee camps; Samuel (1976) worked with artists of the Tibetan Institute of the Performing Arts in Dharamsala; and Helffer (1977) analyzed Ge-sar epic songs. Until more systematic research takes place, scholars are limited to cautious generalities based on sound recordings that are very often published without contextual information. Such generalities have included the following observations:

- Contrast between songs with marked syllabic character and those with many melismas that incorporate nonsense syllables (*tshig-lhad*) between the text words;
- Often limited vocal range that can extend to a twelfth in the most elaborate songs (generally *glu*);
- The predominance of pentatonic melodies, with modal traces in the western Himalayan region (following contact with Kashmir and Central Asia);
- Generally regular rhythms, except in Ladakh (Trewin 1996);
- Alternating slow and fast tempos in the *nang-ma* and *stod-gzhas* repertoires popular in Lhasa during the first half of the twentieth century and since then throughout the culture.

Specialist song repertoires

Mendicant musicians who performed alone or in informally organized groups that sometimes traveled outside Tibet contributed to the spread of song repertoires to far corners of the region. Although many such mendicant traditions have now died out due to new socioeconomic conditions, a few of these musicians are discussed here.

The 'Dre-dkar wore masks and traditionally visited homes at the time of the Tibetan New Year declaiming songs of good fortune and hoping for alms. Still active during the 1960s, they seldom perform today. Folkloric demonstrations of their tradition sometimes take place in Dharamsala.

Epic storytellers (Sgrung-mkhan), often from Khams or the Byang-thang plateaus, wandered the roads of Tibet, telling of the many exploits of King Ge-sar. They sometimes crossed the Himalayan mountain passes, stopping in border villages like Dolpo or Kalimpong. Here in wintertime they entranced their audiences, eager for tales of marvels. The Sgrung-mkhan were soloists who sometimes wore the traditional hat of the bard and alternated prose recitation with sung verses, using different

FIGURE 1 A group of Beda musicians in Ladakh, playing *surnā* and *daman*. Photo copyright Helga Hirschberg, 1976.

tune types traditionally associated with the characters they were describing (Helffer 1977, 1978, tracks 2 and 3). In Ladakh, as Francke noted at the beginning of the twentieth century, a particular version of this epic tale has been preserved (Francke 1941). Some singers are still able to sing it today in a simplified form. In Bhutan, memory of the King Ge-sar epic is not completely lost, but only isolated songs are still known in oral tradition, separated from the story to which they once belonged. Such is the case of the tune "Ge-sar came from the North" (possibly translated "went to the North") (Levy 1971, vol. 4, tracks 7 and 9).

The now-frequent publication in China and Bhutan of most of the Ge-sar epic lyrics, edited in Western format, marks the transition of this repertoire from an oral tradition to a fixed written form. This has inevitably contributed to the disappearance of the Sgrung-mkhan.

The Manipa take their name from their primary role reciting or singing the six syllables of Avalokiteshvara's mantra *Om mani padme hum*. Their repertoire also consists of religious songs like the *Mgur-'bum* of Mi-la ras-pa or of such poet-saints as 'Brug-pa kun-legs. Formerly they traveled throughout Tibet, but today they survive only in Bhutan, where they perform outside the entrances to monasteries or the spectacular *dzong* fortresses so characteristic of Bhutanese architecture. In their songs they describe the little wooden structures known as *bkra-shis sgo-mang* that they carry with them. Recordings of Manipa singers were made by John Levy in the 1970s, without which the music of Bhutan would have remained unknown to the Western world (Levy 1971, vol. 3).

Organized troupes specializing in the repertoire of *a-lce lha-mo* musical theater, once performed in Tibet on various holidays, especially the yogurt festival (*zho ston*) at the end of the summer. The Tibetan government-in-exile has supported the re-formation of such troupes in Dharamsala, Orissa, and Nepal. Some tour India and Nepal and even Europe and the United States, performing abbreviated versions of or excerpts from the theater repertoire (Canzio 1985). This repertoire comprises about a dozen pieces of educational character, known generally by the name of their principal protagonists: Prince Nor-bzang, the virtuous Gzugs kyi Nyi-ma, the 'Don-grub and 'Don-yod brothers, and Padma 'od-'bar. Handwritten or printed booklets present the basic storyline, but this leaves ample scope for the actors' improvisation. Brilliantly costumed and accompanied by a large *rnga* 'frame drum' and a pair of cymbals, they recite, sing, and dance. As in the epic tales, lively declamation alternates with song. Performing these songs requires a particular vocal technique acquired only after long apprenticeship to highly qualified masters.

The Beda and Mon communities of musicians play a special role in the many festivals of the Ladakhi calendar, at which their presence is required. Their origin is uncertain, but they are without doubt not Tibetan, and in a mixed Buddhist-Islamic society their status is at the bottom of the social scale. Both are communities of
TRACK 23 instrumentalists who play the *surnā* 'oboe' and *daman* 'kettledrum' (figure 1). Sometimes the musicians' wives sing and dance while accompanying themselves on the *daph* 'frame drum'. The terms for the instruments are borrowed from the Indian world and recall the Mughal courts and the Indian *naubat* ensemble [see VISUAL SOURCES].

The Beda went from house to house receiving gifts in exchange for their performances. The Mon, in contrast, worked in a more formal manner, especially the Mkhar-mon who were once attached to the royal house of Ladakh. Today the Mkhar-mon retain some of these privileges, playing in honor of official persons or religious dignitaries, at archery and polo competitions, and during monastery and village festivals. Many demonstrate great virtuosity, especially in rhythmically complex pieces of the *lha-rnga* repertoire (Trewin 1990, 1993; Crossley-Holland 1961b, side B; Helffer 1978, tracks 4 and 5). Some today have employment as musicians on Leh radio.

It is quite possible that such musician groups provided a model for the *gar-pa*, troupes of young children attached to the Dalai Lama's house, first formed at the end of the seventeenth century (Trewin 1995). Like the Beda and Mon, they played oboes and kettledrums to accompany their dances and songs. The *gar-pa* tradition was recently revived in exile in Dharamsala, where children now play for certain festivals.

MUSICAL TRADITIONS OF TIBETAN BUDDHISM

Buddhism's spread to western Tibet, Ladakh, and the Indus valley dates back to the time of Rin-chen bzang-po (958–1055), to whom is attributed the construction of numerous monasteries in the region and the translation of many Sanskrit texts related to Buddhism. Throughout Tibetan history and the development of the various schools of Tibetan Buddhism, monasteries have been established in northwest Nepal (probably from the eleventh century in the Lo kingdom), in Bhutan (beginning in the fourteenth or fifteenth century), in Sikkim (at the end of the seventeenth century), and much later in the Shar-Khumbu region of Sherpa country (twentieth century).

Every school of Tibetan Buddhism (Bka'-brgyud-pa, Dge-lugs-pa, Rnying-ma-pa, Sa-skya-pa) now continues on the Indian subcontinent, but the Bka'-brgyud-pa tradition is predominant; the monasteries of Hemis, Lamayuru, and Phyang in Ladakh, and those in Bhutan enjoying the official support of the Bhutanese royal family, are all in this tradition. Since 1959, these monasteries have been cut off from Tibet, where formerly monks went to corresponding monasteries to complete their education before returning to their original monasteries.

Since the end of the 1960s, an extraordinary flourishing of exiled monastic communities has taken place. Dozens of monasteries have been built in India and Nepal (some with several hundreds of monks and novices), complete teaching cycles under the supervision of qualified masters have been developed, the observance of the principal rituals continues, and each monastery's musical tradition has been gradually reestablished.

The concern for faithful transmission has relied on religious texts and on the memory of precentors (*dbu-mdzad*) and the oldest monks who took the path of exile. Since 1985, some monks who avoided Chinese persecution have joined Indian monasteries and transmitted their expertise to younger generations. They have brought to India manuscripts with musical notation that preserve the traditions of the different monasteries. These writings concern the practice of singing (*dbyangs-*
TRACK 24 *yig*), the use of drums and cymbals (*rnga-tshig*), and the use of horns (*dung-tshig*).

FIGURE 2 Extract from a songbook of the Bka'-brgyud-pa tradition. Reprinted from Helffer 1978 with permission.

Whether ritual performances in exile retain all their former pomp is uncertain. Monks nevertheless perform the most important ones regularly.

FIGURE 3 Dge-lugs-pa monks perform a private ritual in Patan, Nepal, 1979. Instruments (*left to right*) are *dril-bu*, *ḍamaru*, *sbug-chal*, and *rnga*. Photo by Philippe Aubry.

Once reserved for use by precentors, these manuscripts now exist in facsimile reproductions (Helffer 1990) and are accessible to more users (figure 2). They constitute the best source of information on musical traditions connected with the practice of Buddhism in Tibet, but are largely unknown to Western musicologists.

Instruments were available in limited numbers during the early phase of exile, but specialist artisans, especially in Nepal, now produce instruments in quantity, though not always of good quality. These instruments are common to all Tibetan Buddhist traditions, and include:

- ritual instruments, such as the small hand bell (*dril-bu*) and small drum rattle (*ḍamaru*) (figure 3);
- timekeeping instruments, such as the large double-headed frame drum with handle, which is struck with a stick (*rnga*), and different kinds of cymbals (*sbug-chal* and *sil-snyan*);
- wind instruments, always played in identical pairs, such as the conch shells (*dung-dkar*), spectacular telescoping horns (*rag-dung* or *dung-chen*), short horns made of human bone or metal (*rkang-gling*); and oboes (*rgya-gling*) (Helffer 1994).

Whether ritual performances in exile retain all their former pomp is uncertain.

Monks nevertheless perform the most important ones regularly, including the *'cham* ritual ballets enacted in monastery courtyards during certain major festivals.

The abundance of published recordings (Helffer 1992) and tours of Western countries by groups of monks have enabled a wide audience to become familiar with this music, whose foreignness once so surprised both travelers and explorers.

SOME RECENT CHANGES

Small instrumental ensembles are playing an increasing role in musical life in Ladakh, in Bhutan at the Royal Academy of Performing Arts, and in Tibetan exile communities (such as at the Tibetan Institute of Performing Arts, Dharamsala). These most often consist of lute (*sgra-snyan*), fiddle (*pi-wang*), flute (*gling-bu*), and a kind of dulcimer (*yang-chin*). They accompany the *nang-ma* and *stod-gzhas* repertoires, and are slowly beginning to perform other song repertoires. Since these instrumental groups help preserve traditional repertoires, they frequently receive support from the authorities and from local radio stations. They are not necessarily limited to song accompaniment.

Just as Tibetans living under Chinese domination cannot escape the inevitable influence of the music they hear on local radio, television, and film, Tibetans in exile are exposed to Indian film music and Western pop. Young people have a hard time resisting the guitar (six-stringed, like the *sgra-snyan*); the accordion; the harmonium, a portable hand-pumped organ; and other nontraditional instruments. Many amateur groups compose new songs.

In Bhutan today, three kinds of music are prevalent: that of Tibetan origin (*Bod-sgra*), music of local origin (*gzhung-sgra*), and new music (*rigsar*). There is abundant audio-cassette production of the latter type, which is extremely popular among young people.

At the same time, Western musicians and composers of "world music" try to integrate elements of Tibetan music (or what they consider Tibetan music) into their own productions. Their zeal is reflected in errors such as their use of the term "Tibetan bowls" for ringing bowls, which were never used in Tibet.

RESEARCH ON TIBETAN MUSICAL TRADITIONS IN SOUTH ASIA

With notable exceptions, most published works to date have focused on the collection and translation of song lyrics, and reveal a wealth of repertoires. Worthy of special mention is the pioneering work of late-nineteenth-century Moravian missionaries in Ladakh, then better known as "Little Tibet." Although their interpretations reflect the prejudices of the era, modern scholarship is indebted to them for a multitude of songs associated with marriage rituals, calendric festivals, and the Ge-sar epic. The contribution of one particular missionary, A. H. Francke, to a French musical encyclopedia, complete with musical notation, long served as the sole reference for those wanting to know about Tibetan music (Francke 1922).

The turbulent 1960s saw a surge of interest in politically troubled regions; in the West, publications of song texts appeared with English translations from both the Spiti region (Tucci 1966) and various Tibetan provinces (Namkhai Norbu Dewang 1967). Locally, Ladakhi and Bhutanese scholars made fruitful attempts to collect songs, which were later published. Above all, thanks to progress in sound recording technology, this decade saw the first recordings of Tibetan musicians in South Asia through projects sponsored by UNESCO (Crossley-Holland 1961a and b).

Simultaneously, ethnographic works began to appear that dealt with Tibetan communities, and more systematic research was carried out on Tibetan refugees, including their music. Both were precious testimony to a threatened legacy (Crossley-Holland 1967, 1970).

Since 1959, the Tibetan government-in-exile, eager to preserve all aspects of Tibetan culture, has supported the development of the Tibetan Institute of Performing Arts, which has made many collections of music from elderly refugees and trained many young Tibetans. Through its publications, recordings, and performances, it has greatly contributed to the preservation and spread of the Tibetan musical legacy in India, Nepal, and the West (Jamyang Norbu 1986).

—TRANSLATED BY BETH G. RAPS

REFERENCES

Bourguignon, Serge. 1955. *Musique tibétaine du Sikkim.* Paris: Musée de l'Homme. Vogue LVLX 187. LP disk.

Canzio, Ricardo. 1985. *Ache Lhamo. Théâtre musical tibétain "Prince Norsang."* Paris: Disques Espérance. ESP-8433. LP disk and notes.

Chang, Garma C. C. 1970. *The Hundred Thousand Songs of Milarepa.* New York and London: Harper Colophon.

Crossley-Holland, Peter. 1961a. *Tibet.* Bärenreiter-Musicaphon BM 30 L20009-20011. 3 LP disks and notes.

———. 1961b. *Tibetan Folk and Minstrel Music.* Lyrichord LLST 7196 (reissued Albatross VPA 8449). LP disk.

———. 1967. "Form and Style in Tibetan Folk Song Melody." *Jahrbuch für Musikalische Volks und Völkerkunde* 3:9–69, 109–126.

———. 1970. "rGya-gling Hymns of the Karma-Kagyu: The Rhythmitonal Architecture of Some Instrumental Airs." *Selected Reports in Ethnomusicology* I(3):79–114.

Francke, Auguste H. 1922. "La Musique au Thibet." In *Encyclopédie de la Musique et Dictionnaire du Conservatoire,* ed. Lavignac, 3084–3093. Paris: Delagrave.

———. 1941. *A Lower Ladakhi Version of the Kesar Saga.* Calcutta: Bibliotheca Indica #1543. Compilation of author's major publications, 1905–1941.

Francke, Auguste H., and Anna Paalzow. 1931. "Tibetischer Lieder aus dem Gebiet des ehemaligen westtibetischen Königreiches." *Mitteilungen des Seminars für Orientalische Sprachen* 35:93–136.

Friedlander, David. 1991. "Rituels et Chants de Mariage Tibétain: Essai d'Exposition du Matériel Recueilli dans la Région Humla [Népal]." M.A. thesis, I.N.A.L.C.O., Paris.

Helffer, Mireille. 1977. *Les Chants dans l'Épopée Tibétaine de Ge-sar, d'après le Livre de la Course de Cheval.* Geneva and Paris: Librairie Droz.

———. 1978. *Ladakh. Musique de Monastère et de Village.* Le Chant du Monde LDX 74662. LP disk. Reissued as compact disc with 31-page booklet, LDX 274662/CM 251.

———. 1990. "Recherches récentes concernant l'emploi des notations musicales dans la tradition tibétaine." In *Tibet, Civilisation et société,* ed. Fernand Meyer, 59–84. Paris: La Fondation Singer-Polignac.

———. 1992. "An Overview of Western Work on Ritual Music of Tibetan Buddhism." In *European Studies in Ethnomusicology: Historical Developments and Recent Trends,* ed. Max P. Baumann, A. Simon, and U. Wegner, 87–101. Wilhelmshaven: Florian Noetzel.

———. 1994. *Mchod-rol, les Instruments de la Musique Tibétaine.* Paris: CNRS Éditions/Éditions de la Maison des Sciences de l'Homme.

Jamyang Norbu, ed. 1986. *Zlos-gar, Performing Traditions of Tibet.* Dharamsala (India): Tibetan Institute of Performing Arts.

Larson, Eric. 1982. *Tibetan Music from Ladakh and Zanskar.* Lyrichord LLST 7383. LP disk.

Lewiston, David. 1971. *Ladakh. Songs and Dances from the Highlands of Western Tibet.* Nonesuch Explorer H-72075. LP disk.

Levy, John. 1971. *Tibetan Buddhist Rites from the Monasteries of Bhutan.* 1: Rituals of the Drukpa Order; 2: Sacred Dances and Rituals of the Nyingmapa and Drukpa Orders; 3: Temple Rituals and Public Ceremonies; 4: Tibetan Bhutanese Instrumental and Folk Music. Lyrichord LLST 7255–58. Four LP disks and notes. Reissued as four compact disks, LYRCD 7255–58.

Liebermann, Fred, and Michael Moore. 1971a. *Music in Sikkim.* Command COMS 9002. LP disk.

———. 1971b. *Traditional Music and Dance of Sikkim.* Seattle: University of Washington Press. 16mm color film.

Namkhai Norbu Dewang. 1967. "Musical Tradition of the Tibetan People: Songs in Dance Measure." *Orientalia Romana: Essays and Lectures* 2:205–347 (Serie Orientale Roma XXXVI).

Samuel, Geoffrey. 1976. "Songs of Lhasa." *Ethnomusicology* 20(3):407–449.

Sorensen, Per K. 1990. *Divinity Secularized. An Inquiry into the Nature and Form of the Songs Ascribed to the Sixth Dalai Lama.* Vienna: Arbeitskreis für Tibetische und Buddhistische Studien, Universität Wien.

Tashi, Rabgyas. 1970. *Folk Songs of Ladakh.* Leh, Ladakh: Jammu and Kashmir Academy of Art, Culture and Language.

Trewin, Mark. 1990. "Rhythmic Style in Ladakhi Music and Dance." In *Wissenschaft und Gegenwärtige Forschungen in Nordwest-Indien,* ed. L. Icke-Schwalbe and G. Meier, 273–276.

Dresden: Staatliches Museum für Völkerkunde Dresden Forschungstelle.

———. 1993. "*Lha-rnga*: A Form of Ladakhi Folk Music and Its Relationship to the Great Tradition of Tibet." In *Anthropology of Tibet and the Himalaya,* ed. Ch. Ramble and M. Brauen, 377–385. Zurich: Ethnological Museum of the University of Zurich.

———. 1995. "On the History and Origin of '*Gar*', the Court Ceremonial Music of Tibet." *Chime Journal* 8:4–31.

———. 1996. "Rhythms of the Gods. The Musical Symbolics of Power and Authority in the Buddhist Kingdom of Ladakh." Ph.D. dissertation, City University, London.

Tucci, Giuseppe, coll. and trans. 1966. *Tibetan Folk Songs from Gyantse and Western Tibet,* 2nd rev. ed. Ascona, Switzerland: Artibus Asiae.

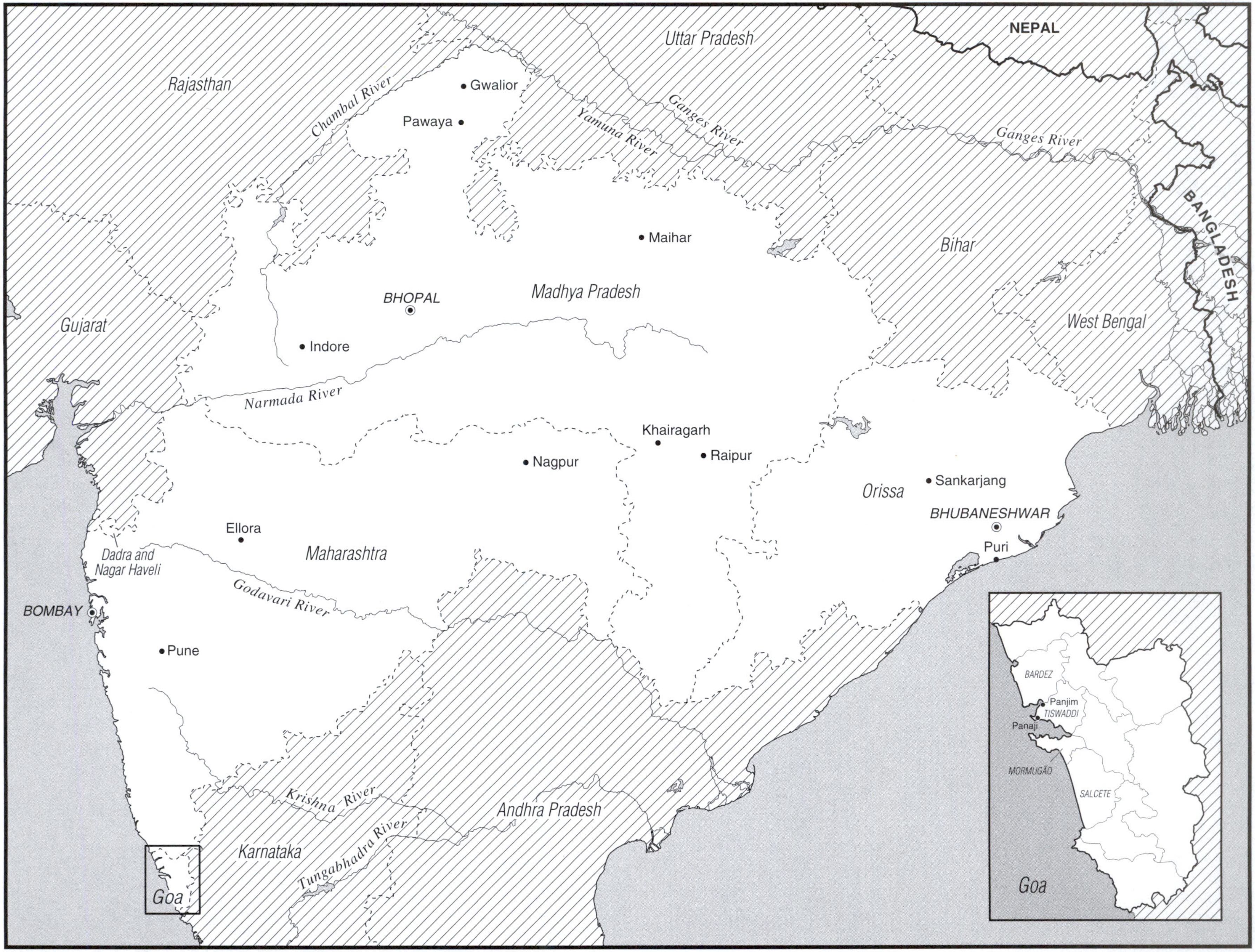
NEPAL
Uttar Pradesh
Rajasthan
Gwalior
Pawaya
Chambal River
Yamuna River
Ganges River
Ganges River
BANGLADESH
Maihar
Bihar
BHOPAL
Madhya Pradesh
West Bengal
Gujarat
Indore
Narmada River
Khairagarh
Raipur
Nagpur
Orissa
Sankarjang
BHUBANESHWAR
Puri
Ellora
Maharashtra
Dadra and Nagar Haveli
Godavari River
BOMBAY
Pune
Krishna River
Andhra Pradesh
Tungabhadra River
Karnataka
Goa
BARDEZ
Panjim
TISWADDI
Panaji
MORMUGÃO
SALCETE
Goa

Central India

The combination of dancing, singing, and instrumental music is essential to music making among the large tribal populations of central India. To the sounds of drums, flutes, and percussion, men and women of the Agaris, Bhīls, Gonds, Madias, and the many other *ādivāsī* groups of Madhya Pradesh, Maharashtra, and Orissa dance and sing to celebrate seasons, harvests, gods, and life-cycle events. And here as elsewhere in India, folk and devotional music traditions abound among the majority Hindu population.

Culturally distinct from these large central Indian states is the tiny state of Goa, strongly influenced for over four centuries by Portuguese colonization. Christians, Hindus, and Muslims cultivate their own music and dance traditions, which express not only their social identities, but also their own particular links with India and the West.

MAP 7 Central India

Madhya Pradesh

Ashok D. Ranade

Tribal Music
Folk Music
Devotional Music

This largest state in the Indian republic borders on seven other states: Uttar Pradesh, Bihar, Orissa, Andhra Pradesh, Maharashtra, Gujarat, and Rajasthan. Since the country was reorganized along linguistic lines in 1956, Madhya Pradesh has included seventeen Hindi-speaking areas as well as the former Rajasthani-speaking Sironj district. The state comprises twenty former princely states and 1,300 smaller estates (*jāgīr*). These had been seats of patronage for many diverse performing arts traditions, all of which over time contributed to the region's rich musical and theatrical culture. The seven river systems (Chambal, Betwa, Som, Narmada, Tapi, Mahanadi, and Indravati), together with the imposing Satpura and Vindhya mountain ranges and the tropical forests covering one third of the state, have also had a perennial influence on artistic expression.

The northern territory is populated largely by people of Aryan origin. In the southern and eastern parts live many tribal groups (*ādivāsī*) of Dravidian origin, including the Mudia, Madia, Paraja, Bhatra, Pando, Korwa, Oraon, Muṇḍa, Korku, Gond, Baiga, Zabua, Bhīl, and Bhilal. The state has the largest concentration of scheduled tribes in the country—and consequently a considerable range and variety of tribal music.

The Haihaya people of India's epic tales reportedly held sway here in ancient times; their centers were Avanti and Ujjain, both still culturally well known today. From the fourth to the second centuries B.C. the Mauryas resolutely ruled over the region. During his reign, the great Mauryan emperor Ashoka constructed the famous Buddhist stupa at Sanchi. Shungas, Satavahans, Kushans, Guptas, and Huns followed, all culturally different and all influential dynasties. In 1020, Mahmud of Ghazni invaded Gwalior; this began the phase of Muslim rule, although the land also remained under Rajput influence for another three hundred years. From the eighteenth to early nineteenth centuries, the Marāṭhās were in ascendancy, until they were overwhelmed by the British.

The four major religions of South Asia—Buddhism, Jainism, Hinduism, and Islam, each with its subsects and cults—have profoundly shaped life in Madhya Pradesh; this includes music as much as any other aspect of life. A major example from the Hindu pantheon is the way Lord Shankara (Shiva) and his derivative deities have influenced performing traditions.

The region's music history can be dated from 500 B.C., when King Udayan taught Princess Vasavadatta to play the vina. Milestones of the fourth and fifth centuries C.E. include the musical insights of the great Sanskrit poet Kalidasa as they appear in his dramatic works; Emperor Samudragupta's love of the vina, which he played himself; and the renowned arts patronage of his successor, Emperor Vikramaditya. From the Middle Ages up until modern times, more and less expansive dynasties ruled the region, including Gwalior, Chanderi, Kalinger, Malwa, Nimad, Gadha, Bundelkhand, Ratanpur, Raipur, Rayseen, and Asirgadh. Royal support from such families aided both the performing arts and scholastic traditions.

TRIBAL MUSIC

Diverse musical traditions exist among the state's large tribal population. Several features of this tribal music, however, are common not only in Madhya Pradesh but throughout the Indian subcontinent. First, musical performance generally combines dancing, singing, and instrumental playing: singing or dancing alone is rare. Second, general participation in music making is encouraged to such an extent that there is virtually no distinction between performers and audience. No one is entirely engaged in listening. The cultural group or community, not a solitary composer, is responsible for creating music.

Tribal music tends to respond to three great natural cycles, which in India largely determine the course of life: day and night, birth and death, and the seasons. Tribal populations make music not for its own sake, but for communion with some higher power. This evocative function of tribal music is used to the fullest in various tribal rituals. Tribal populations also use everyday objects and activities in symbolic ways, as well as tactile elements such as holding hands, stamping feet, and body thumping.

The following discussion serves to highlight the richness of tribal music in Madhya Pradesh.

Influence of agricultural and seasonal cycles

The *thandahar* dance of the Bastar tribe, in which both men and women take part, consists of body movements typical of agricultural work. The dance illustrates the constant collectivity of tribal music making not only by its non–gender-specific performance, but also in the tactile strategy of holding hands. The expression of collectivity, however, does not prevent individual initiative: in many of the less ritualistic performances, individuals modify and change musical features, without claiming individual credit. This kind of musical improvisation in tribal music, together with the absence of individualism, is sometimes described in India as the "copyright" element.

Tribal groups celebrate all the seasons with music and dance, but go to special lengths to mark those connected with fertility and productivity. Among the Gonds, one of the largest tribes in the state, the *bhīmul pandum* dance and music festival takes place prior to the monsoon, *harapu* and *bijja pandum* occur during the spring, *korta pandum* during the rains, and *jata pandum* and *kara pandum* in the postharvest autumn.

Sacred dance and music

For some tribal groups, including the Madias, music and dance are regarded not as recreation or a game but as a means of creating a bridge to an omnipotent god. Music and dance represent a form of prayer, and a duty. The *bhīmul pandum,* for example, is a premonsoon dance and festival of prayer for timely and adequate rain. Dance is thought to be a creation of Lingo (reminiscent of the Shaivite Linga), the Madia god who plays eighteen musical instruments. Madia dancers wear headdresses of decorated horns, believed to be gifts from the god Lingo. Great care is taken to ensure that the headgear does not fall off during the dance, for this would be considered extremely inauspicious. Other sacred seasonal dance events among the Madia are *irpu pandum,* which celebrates the harvest in February; *marka pandum*, held to solemnize the pounding of the first corn in April; *nukana-rendana pandum*, observed upon eating the new corn during the October autumn festivities; and *kara pandum*, preceding the cutting of bamboo.

The Gonds, who constitute almost one third of the tribal population in India, have dance and music associated with every occasion from birth to death. Their main music and dance forms include the collective dance known as *karam,* as well as the *dadariya*, *sajani*, *jharpat*, and *jhumar*. The Mudia Gonds celebrate young girls reaching puberty with a ceremony of body tattooing accompanied by singing and dancing. News of the event is announced with drumming on the *ḍhol* 'large double-headed cylindrical drum', and family members and friends travel long distances to witness a girl's entry into a new phase of life.

Among the Baiga, reportedly the oldest community of the Muṇḍa tribe (as Gonds are of the Dravidian tribes), everyone participates in the masked dance *karam*; dancing has so permeated their lives that the community even has a dance in which members partner ghosts. The dress of Baiga women facilitates dance and music, for they commonly wear ankle bells (*ghuṅghrū*). Other Baiga dances include the *saila*, a men's martial dance, and the *rīna*, a women's dance.

Improvisation

Among tribal populations, musical performances allow ample opportunity for improvisation. In bachelors' dormitories (*ghotul*), for example, Madia youths may begin to dance and sing at a moment's notice, and may continue their performance throughout the night into the early-morning hours. Such performances are generally unstructured: the performers often fit new words to known tunes. The music is common property, jointly held and changed by collective consent; individual efforts are not seen as such but are viewed as part of the common music-making process.

Instruments

Rhythm instruments are commonly used to accompany a wide variety of dances. They are also used in funeral rituals. Among the Madia Gonds, the priest in charge of funeral rites (*hangonda*) announces the death of a person by beating the *ḍhol*. The Korakus erect elaborate death stones, and the ceremony of laying the death stone is accompanied by an ensemble including three *ḍhol* players and one horn player, among others.

Buffalo horns are the most commonly used aerophones. Flutes are also played by all tribal populations, and are often made from bamboo tube, although gourds with large holes bored into them are also popular. The *kingiri* is a notable bowed chordophone with a coconut-shell resonator and wooden neck. Among membranophones, the *ḍhol* and its varieties are widely distributed, as is the *duff* 'frame drum'. The *ḍamaru*, an hourglass drum associated with Lord Shiva, enjoys a special distinction as well as dissemination. The Kahars play an hourglass drum called *dhudak* or *dahanki*. Tribal peoples also use ordinary objects or domestic utensils as instruments, such as winnowing baskets, water containers, metal dishes, and wooden strips and sticks.

FOLK MUSIC

The terms "tribal," "folk," "devotional," "art," and "popular" have frequently been used to categorize Indian music. However, they represent not exclusive but overlapping categories of a living tradition. Folk music is closer to tribal and devotional music than it is to art and popular music, yet folk music is distinguished from tribal music by characteristic stylistic features. Of particular importance is the great number of folk-music forms or genres, which can also be divided into categories such as riddles, proverbs and idioms, poetic couplets (*doha*), women's songs, men's songs, and children's songs.

Women's songs

Women's songs outnumber all other types of folk songs throughout India, and Madhya Pradesh is no exception. The major song types specific to women include those related to pregnancy, childbirth, puberty, marriage, and moving into the house of new in-laws, as well as festival and seasonal songs and songs of devotion.

Mixed orientations

Folk-music performance usually combines dance, drama, and music; rarely does one occur without the others. *Manch* and *kilagi-turra*, for example, are music- and drama-oriented performances, respectively; the latter also features more competitive
TRACK 25 poetry singing. Many dances have accompanying vocal and instrumental music; examples include *maṭkī kā nāc, adho nāc, ghumar, manch ke nāc,* and *garbā.*

Men's and children's songs

Songs specific to men encompass short story-songs; sung tales; *Ālhā* songs with the predominant sentiment of valor; seasonal songs such as *phāgu gīt, saire ke gīt,* and *divālī ke gīt*; amorous songs (*challa*); and devotional songs (*khayāl*). Songs accompanying agricultural work such as sowing the autumn crops (*bilwari*) are also notable for their question-and-answer structure. Children's songs are mainly nursery rhymes or game songs.

Song tales

Certain song tales warrant special mention since they blend prose, verse, and recitation. Notable examples are *sorath, nihal de, champa de,* and *sona rupa de.*

Oral epics

An important genre of folk music is the oral epic. Performances may feature recitation, singing, or a sung or danced reenactment of the Ramayana or the Mahabharata, the two enduring epic tales well known throughout all levels of Indian society. In oral epics of the Chattisgadh region, for example, the story of the Pandava brothers (in the Mahabharata) predominates. Lower castes have been the traditional performers and major repositories of the epics. Two main streams are known, *vedamati* and *kapalik*. The former features singing in a sitting posture, whereas the latter includes a standing posture as well as the use of more "acting." A third method, involving kneeling, is also in vogue. Sometimes the main singer is joined by a second performer or *ragi* 'one who brings color', who participates as a "character" reinforcing the epic performance. Accompanying instruments include the *tambūrā* 'string drone', *kañjarī* 'frame drum', *kartāl* 'clappers', harmonium, and *ḍholak* 'barrel drum' (figure 1); today even the banjo is gaining a foothold.

Rural communities often hold strong views for and against adhering to the

Devotees sing songs collectively at festivals and while on pilgrimages to temples or to the banks or confluences of sacred rivers.

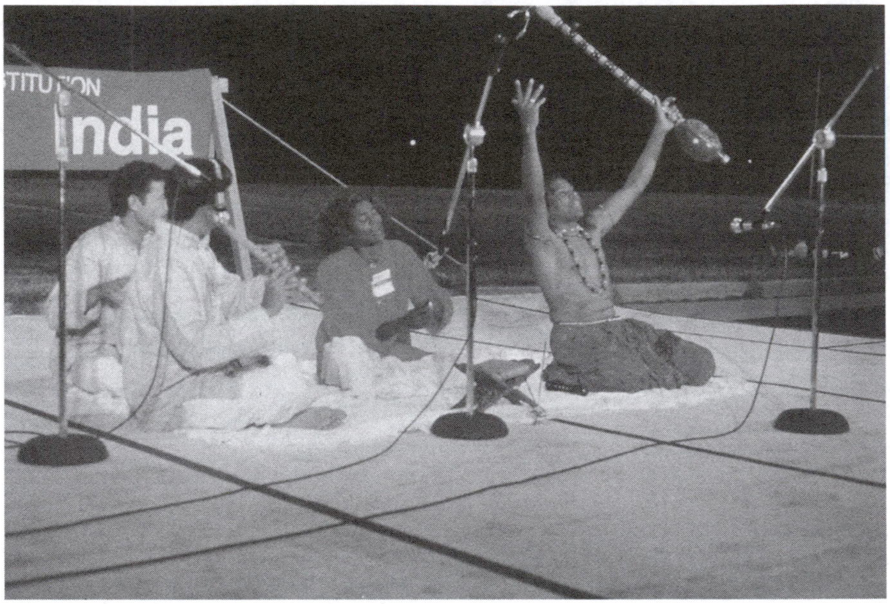

FIGURE 1 The Ramayana singer Purna of Madhya Pradesh (kneeling at right, holding his prop), accompanied by (*from left*) *ḍholak* (hidden behind flute player), *bāṅsurī*, and hand cymbals. Smithsonian Festival of American Folklife, Washington D. C., 1976. Photo courtesy Amy Catlin.

"original" epic narratives and modifying or distorting the "folk" versions of these tales. Equally varied opinions are expressed regarding the amount of singing or acting allowed during the narration. Such debates highlight the changing nature of the form as well as the expressive potential of oral epic singing.

DEVOTIONAL MUSIC

Devotional music consists mostly of songs of the celebrated poet-saints, such as Surdas, Kabir, and Tulsidas. Their poetic compositions (*pada*) are musically rendered as bhajans. Bhajans, however, are further classified according to various criteria: for example, *naradi bhajan* and *kañjarī ke bhajan* are mainly *nirguṇ* songs, that is, songs not in praise of any particular incarnation of a deity; *ramsatta* is a kind of *kīrtan* danced by youths; and *bhadaiya bhajan* is sung only on Janmashtami, the day celebrated as Lord Krishna's birthday.

Songs rendered collectively in acts of worship are numerous, such as *jas* compositions sung in praise of the Mother Goddess. Accompanied by *ḍholak, timki,* and *jhāñjh*, the renderings are expected to bring the priest (*ojha*) into a trance state. Similar compositions in the Bundeli dialect are known as *achari* or *devī ke gīt*. Devotees sing songs collectively at festivals and while on pilgrimages to temples or to the banks or confluences of sacred rivers (figure 2). *Bambulia* compositions belong to this class.

FIGURE 2 Mendicant devotional singers from Ujjain accompany themselves on frame drums (*daflī*) for the Mahāśivarātrī festival. Girnar, 1997. Photo by Amy Catlin.

REFERENCES

Hiralal, Shukla. 1986. *Ādivāsī Saṅgīt*. Bhopal: Madhya Pradesh Hindi Grantha Academy. In Hindi.

Kala, Shrikhande. 1995. *Madhya Pradesh meṅ Saṅgīt Ki Vikās Yātrā*. Delhi: Nirmal Publication. In Hindi.

Kothari, Komal S. 1968. *Indian Folk Musical Instruments*. New Delhi: Sangeet Natak Academi.

Parmar, Shyam. 1972. "Ballads and Narratives of Madhya Pradesh." *Sangeet Natak* 26.

———. 1978. "A Note on Folk Musical Instruments of Madhya Pradesh." *Folklore* (January).

Maharashtra

Ashok D. Ranade

Tribal Music
Folk Music
Devotional Music
Popular Music

The Indian state of Maharashtra is over 307,000 square kilometers in size and has natural borders on all four sides. To the north, the Narmada river flows west, marking the northern limit; the river Vainganga approximates the eastern border, along with the Deccan plateau, which levels off toward the east; the Sahyadri mountain ranges taper off in the south, forming the southern border; and to the west lies the coastline of the Arabian Sea. The Sahyadri ranges, running north-south for about 640 kilometers, also bifurcate Maharashtra into two distinct climatic regions: the lowland coastal strip known as Konkan, which enjoys a temperate climate, and the Deccan plateau known as Ghat or Desh, which extends to the east of the range and whose climate is more extreme.

Annual rainfall in Maharashtra markedly affects seasonal and agricultural cycles, and thus life-cycle celebrations and the associated musical events. The monsoon rains normally occur from June to September, with higher rainfall in the south. The copious water in one season and virtual absence of it in others directly affects agricultural work, which in turn affects the frequency and spacing of festivals. The number of festivals is in inverse proportion to the intensity of agricultural activities; of the thirty-odd festivals and ceremonial occasions that include musical performance, one third take place during the months-long rainy season.

Another geographical factor of cultural importance is the state's location within India, roughly midway on the country's north-south axis; repeated Puranic and epic references to Maharashtra as *dakshinapatha* 'the region in the southern path' show that this perception is an old one. People coming from the north and moving southward invariably lost momentum by this point, and tended to settle down in the region. Similarly, those arriving by sea frequently took up residence in Maharashtra. The state now borders two of the four South Indian states that are repositories of Dravidian culture, and has long been a meeting place for Aryans and Dravidians as well as for other indigenous and alien peoples in all historical periods. From ancient and Puranic times comes the story of Agasti, the first Aryan sage to secure a firm footing in non-Aryan territory south of the Narmada river and who accomplished this by establishing a settlement in Maharashtra. The later Islamic wave from the north stabilized in Maharashtra and ruled there from 1347 to 1630, unable to penetrate deep into the south for long. Then in the nineteenth century, British power could not subjugate the Marāṭhās until 1819, a fact indicative of the long duration of that confrontation.

Seven major world religions are practiced in the state; among the majority Hindu population, devotees worship not only the chief gods and goddesses of the Hindu pantheon, but also more than fifty village deities.

Three of India's twelve largest cities—Bombay, Pune, and Nagpur—are located in Maharashtra, with twenty-five other cities located in the state. This relatively high urban profile affects musical culture, which includes a greater variety of art and popular music than many other Indian states. With Bombay at its center, Maharashtra has become a unique melting pot of diverse cultural identities, and this is very much reflected in its music.

TRIBAL MUSIC

The prominent tribes in Maharashtra—the Agari, Bhīl, Mahadev Koli, Gond, Warli, Kokana, Thakur, Gavīt, Kolam, Korku, Andh, Malhar, and Pardhi—are concentrated mostly in the districts of Khandesh, Colaba, and Nasik and in parts of Pune and Ahmadnagar. Most music-making occasions among these groups involve dancing by both men and women. The *tarapi* and *ghor-nāc* of the Warli, and the Ganesh and Holī dances of the Agari are well known. All important life-cycle events such as childbirth, initiation, marriage, and death, as well as seasonal and agricultural cycles, have music associated with them.

The collective expression of music and dance among Maharashtran tribes, as among tribal groups in other Indian states, demands perfect synchronization of steps, movements, and vocalizations. It also features a hypnotic repetitiveness of patterns and timbres.

Tribal music employs instruments with loud, sharp tones and a clear sonority, such as small flutes, drums, and idiophones with sharp struck and scraped sounds. They are generally made from readily available inexpensive materials such as bamboo, hide, gourd, clay, and leaves. Instruments fashioned out of these materials in Maharashtra include the forked and jingling bamboo sticks, the *tarpe* 'aerophone with two gourd resonators', a rare scraped membranophone known as *dera* 'clay pot with covered mouth', *thāl* 'metal plate and scraping rod' that creates a hypnotic drone, and *ghuṅghrū* 'ankle bells'. For some tribes, musical instruments have a mythological significance: the Agari, for example, who are also known as the Ḍhol-Agari, claim that they were drummer-musicians to Ravana, the demon-king in the Ramayana.

FOLK MUSIC

Folk music refers not only to songs but also to the choreographic and histrionic elements that usually accompany them in performance. About sixty song types are current in the state, ranging in nature from sound effect to song, from movement to dance, and from routine action to dramatization. The following describes some of the folk-music genres of present-day Maharashtra.

Nandiwālā

A Nandiwālā is a specialist performer who gives animal-training shows in villages, using sound effects as music. Combining tricks with some soothsaying, the Nandiwālā employs a *gubgubī* 'double-headed, scraped membranophone', a *ghadyal-tipru* 'metal disc struck with a mallet', and tiny bells. Rhythmic playing, controlled verbalization, and loud thumping and scraping constitute the musical performance. After the show the performer asks for alms.

Bahurūpi

The performances of a Bahurūpi (literally 'one with many disguises')—a professional male entertainer who parades in different disguises and in return asks for alms—are examples of dramatized song. Bahurūpis are avowed devotees of the cult deities Bahiroba, Khandoba, Jakhai, and Janai and are widely known for composing humorous marriage proposal songs. Impersonations of females, pregnant women, young mothers, and so on form the dramatic repertoire. Song verses are full of rhymes and assonance; the Bahurūpi recites them in quick tempo without instrumental accompaniment.

Dhangari ovya

These movement-oriented songs are associated with goatherds, even though the word *dan* derives from the Kannada term for cattle. They center on Biruba, an incarnation of Lord Shiva. According to the associated myth, many flocks of sheep once emerged from an anthill and began destroying standing crops; Biruba was approached for redress, and created the Dhangars (herdsmen) to protect the crops. Dhangars worship the folk deity Biruba and sing *dhangari ovya* songs about his exploits.

In an open-air *dhangari ovya* performance, colorfully dressed Dhangars dance around players of a huge *ḍhol* 'cylindrical drum' and execute vigorous movements known as *gajanritya*. Broad, forceful rhythms, emphatic stanza endings, and powerful voice projections characterize the genre.

Vāsudev gīt

This genre exhibits elements of both dance and melodic solo singing. The performer represents Vasudev, an incarnation of Lord Krishna. He wears ankle bells and a distinctive peacock feather headdress, and plays the flute. He also sings, accompanying himself with a hand-held pair of cymbals (*mañjīrā*), and executes nimble, delicate dance steps and whirling dance movements. Such an itinerant singer performs in house courtyards in the mornings and asks for alms.

Vaghya-Muralī gīt

These songs form a subvariety of *gondhal*, a ritual theater form. The characters in the play, Vaghya and Muralī, are male and female devotees of the deity Khandoba, respectively. In the performance, known as *jāgaran* 'keeping awake', Murali is the chief dancer and Vaghya is her accompanist. The performance is distinguished by Murali's graceful and nimble dancing, her attractive and neat costume, and the pervasive, sensuous sophistication of her movements. The accompanying instruments are the *tuntune* 'one-stringed chordophone', which provides both rhythm and drone, *khanjiri* 'frame drum', *ghol* 'small bell', and ankle bells. Use of nonsense syllables and melodic phrases approximating ragas affirm the musical ambitiousness of this song type.

DEVOTIONAL MUSIC

The doctrine of bhakti (devotion) has been important in India since the fourth century, but specific musical styles inspired by devotional cults have existed only for about five hundred years. Poet-saints of each region have composed thousands of songs in regional languages and have passed them on orally.

Certain musical characteristics have allowed the continued performance of these songs by people at all levels of society. First, the performance of devotional music encompasses chanting, recitation, and singing, both solo and choral. Second, performers employ instrumental resources judiciously. The one-stringed drone vina provides melodic support, while the *mridang* 'double-headed barrel drum', *tāl* 'cymbals', and *ciplā* 'clappers' (wooden strips with inserted metal rings) provide rhythm. Rhythmic cycles of four and eight beats are common.

Devotional music genres such as bhajan, *kīrtan, sankīrtan* or *gāyan* use different musical resources in varied combinations. Among the variety of other devotional forms in Maharashtra are marriage songs sung by women (*dhavale*), poetic songs to the deity Vitthal (*abhaṅg*), devotional songs about Krishna and the milkmaids (*gaulan*), a semireligious dramatic musical performance (*bharud*), hymns of praise (*stotra*), collective singing in praise of a deity (*āratī*), devotional songs sung solo or in groups (*karunashtak*), Sanskrit couplets or hymns of praise (*śloka*), unaccompanied women's folk songs and devotional songs (*ovi*), a prosodic form set to a simple tune and quick rhythm (*katav*), and devotional songs about the separation of the beloved/ devotee from the lover/deity (*virani*).

POPULAR MUSIC

Maharashtra's importance in Indian popular music cannot be overestimated in both quantitative and qualitative terms. Metropolitan Bombay (now known as Mumbai) is a transcendent center of cosmopolitan activities in music, as it is in all cultural areas. Composers and producers of film music and other mass-mediated music, the two weighty components of the popular category, have found conditions in this city conducive to popular-music production. Of the four major Indian film-producing centers, two are in Maharashtra—Pune and Bombay. Bombay has also been significant in the history of Indian broadcasting and television. Though Maharashtra's heritage in popular music includes contributions in Hindi and other languages, the present discussion is restricted to Marathi works.

Beginning in 1843, a genre of Marathi theater developed that is usually described as music drama (*saṅgīt nāṭak*), although it was distinct from opera, musicals, and other existing forms combining music and theater. Its popularity led to the establishment of many theater companies. Authors wrote, adapted, and translated five-act plays; songwriters wrote between ten and two hundred songs for each music drama; producers invited composers—usually top-ranking vocalists from the Hindustani art music tradition—to select tunes; actor-singers received training from a young age; and touring drama companies gave hundreds of performances, traveling even into the interior of the state (figure 1). Stage music in the nineteenth century paralleled the earlier achievement of devotional music genres in spreading musical literacy among the populace (Ranade 1986).

FIGURE 1 Transportation vehicle for the touring music-drama company Anand Lok Natya Mandal, on the Pune-Aurangabad road, 1983. Photo by Gordon K. Arnold.

Stage music in the nineteenth century paralleled the earlier achievement of devotional music genres in spreading musical literacy among the populace.

The beginning of sound feature film production in India in 1931 led to the rise of Indian cinema and film music. Between 1931 and 1991, about 931 Marathi films were produced, most of them included several songs, which would become easily available through audio recordings, radio broadcasts, and (more recently) television and video cassettes. The introduction of the playback technique (dubbing studio-recorded singing into a film) in the mid-to-late 1930s brought about a revolution that remains in effect today; it became the norm for the actors' voices to be replaced during songs by those of new professionals from different cultural and performing backgrounds; this development added new singing-voice textures, intonation patterns, and dialects to the final product.

A concurrent development in popular music was the emergence of *bhāvgīt* 'songs of emotion'. These were topical in theme and combined many musical styles both Indian and foreign, employed fresh voices, introduced many instrumental colors, and were aimed at heterogeneous audiences with varied musical tastes. They generally depended on the new mass media for their presentation. The *bhāvgīt* genre reigned supreme from 1931 to about 1955, and continues to evolve today in a changing media and cultural environment.

REFERENCES

Ahmad, Nazir, ed. 1956. *Kitab-i-Nauras*. New Delhi: Bharatiya Kala Kendra.

Altekar, A. S. 1967. *Society, Religion and Culture: 200 B.C. to 500 A.D.* Bombay: Maharashtra State Gazetteer.

Ayyangar, R. Rangaramanuja. 1978. *Sangeet Ratnakara: A Study*. Bombay: Wilco Publishing House.

Bhatkhande, V. N. 1966. *Uttar Bharatiya Sangit Ka Itihas*. Hathras: Sangit.

Desai, Chaitanya. 1979. *Sangitvishayak Sanskrit Grantha*. Pune and Nagpur: Suvichar Prakashan Mandal.

Joglekar, S. A. 1956. *Halasatavahanachi Gathasaptashati*. Pune: Prasad Prakashan.

Karve, Iravati. 1968. *Maharashtra—Land and Its People*. Bombay: Maharashtra State Gazeteers.

Ketkar, S. V., and N. M. Kelkar. 1963. *Prachin Maharashtra: Political and Cultural History*. Pune: Venus Prakashan.

Paradkar, M. D. 1967. *Society, Religion and Culture: 500 A.D. to 1200 A.D.* Bombay: Maharashtra State Gazetteer.

Ranade, Ashok D. 1986. *Stage Music of Maharashtra*. New Delhi: Sangeet Natak Akademi.

Ranade, G. H. 1960. *Maharashtra Jeevan*, vol. II. Pune: Joshi-Lokhande.

———. 1967. *Music in Maharashtra*. New Delhi: Maharashtra Information Centre.

Shamashastry, R. 1926. *Abhilashitartha Chintamani*. Mysore: University of Mysore.

Velankar, D. K. 1958. *Sangit Chudamani: A Work on Indian Music by Kavichintamani Jagadekamalla*. Baroda: Oriental Institute.

Orissa

Ashok D. Ranade

The state of Orissa is located in eastern India, bordered by the Bay of Bengal to the east and by the states of Bihar, Madhya Pradesh, and Andhra Pradesh to the north, west, and south, respectively. Its physical features range from a plateau in the north and river valleys (the Mahanadi, Brahmani, and Vaitarini) in the central region to the mountainous area in the south. Forty-two percent of the land is jungle. In 300 B.C. the emperor Ashoka conquered Orissa, then known as Kalinga; the land was considered to be beyond the pale of Aryan civilization, which had been introduced by Indo-European-speaking peoples entering India in the second millennium B.C. It was here that Ashoka, realizing the futility of war and violence, embraced Buddhism and began a campaign propagating both the Buddhist religion and nonviolence. The later Jain, Satavahan, Gang, Bhaumakar, Soma/Kesari, and Surya dynasties ruled over the territory until 1568, when the Afghan sultan of Bengal took power and introduced Islam to the region. Thereafter the Mughals gained supremacy, although the Europeans began establishing trading centers in the early sixteenth century; British rule came in 1803. Until the recent past, the southern parts of Orissa were influenced by the Dravidian culture of the South Indian states.

Buddhism, Hinduism, and Islam have all played significant roles in Orissa's history. After Ashoka's conversion, Buddhism held sway until the seventh century. Even the Hindu lord Jagannath was considered to be a reincarnation of Buddha, until followers of Vishnu assimilated the deity. The Kesari kings, rulers from 940 to about 1100, were staunch followers of Shiva. From the fifeenth century, Vaishnavism became Orissa's main religion, influencing every aspect of life and culture. The coastal city of Puri is not only the center of Jagannath worship but a focal point for the cultural life of eastern India, encompassing the arts, philosophy, religion, and literature.

The language of Orissa, Oriya, dates back at least to the early centuries C.E. and is mentioned in Bharata's *Nāṭyaśāstra* as Odraja. Language scholars claim it evolved from a combination of Sanskrit, Bengali, and Mundari. From A.D. 1000 it was used as a literary language in the *boudha caryāgīt* 'Buddhist devotional songs' composed in ragas, and from the fourteenth century there survives Oriya poetry as well as translations of the Hindu Puranas (sacred writings of A.D. 300–750) and epics. The bhakti

Women of the nomadic Kela tribe are experts in tattooing. They sing songs describing female beauty and about how tattoos bring good luck.

cult, dating from the fourth and fifth centuries in South India and the fifteenth century in the North, produced an abundant literature of love and devotion. Theater and music also experienced parallel growth and development. The Hindustani or North Indian classical music system is predominant in Orissa, although vocal styles and vocalization patterns often remind listeners of Karnatak or South Indian classical music practice.

TRIBAL MUSIC

TRACK 26

Orissa's sizable tribal population has contributed much to the state's musical heritage. Of the many distinctive musical forms, two are mentioned here.

Members of the nomadic Kela tribe sing *keluni* songs. Kela men catch snakes and birds and earn their livelihood as snake charmers. Kela women are experts in tattooing. They sing songs describing female beauty and about how tattoos bring good luck. At one time the Kela used to play the *guduki*, a chordophone, to accompany their wives' singing and dancing.

Karam dance songs are performed by many tribes to propitiate either the male deity Karam Devta or the female deity Karamasani. Known especially among the Binjhal, Kisan Kol, Bhumij, and Santal tribes, *karam* songs vary from one group to another, with more or less scope for individual singers.

FOLK AND DEVOTIONAL MUSIC

The corpus of Orissan folk music consists of songs described broadly as devotional, mythological, festal, and community songs, dances, and ballads.

Among the common forms of devotional music, *janānā* (literally 'to inform') refers to solo songs sung by a Hindu devotee. The content of the songs is personal, informing God about the devotee's woes and miseries and seeking redress. Most *janānā* are addressed to Lord Jagannath, the ruling deity of Orissa.

The most popular devotional songs meant for group expression are *kāñjanī* bhajans. The *kāñjanī* is a frame drum held in the left hand and played with the right. Three other song forms also take their names from instruments associated with them: *kendra gīt*, *dundhukī gīt*, and *daskathi*. Most villages have small shrines dedicated to the *trimūrti* 'trinity'—the three major Hindu deities Brahma, Vishnu, and Shiva—and these are usually centers for bhajan singing groups. In addition to Hindu groups, Mahima Samaj, a Buddhist sect that worships *śūnya* 'the void', also sings its own bhajans.

Kīrtan is an important devotional song genre in Orissa connected with an ecstatic Vaishnav cult introduced from Bengal by Sri Chaitanya Deva. All villages have *kīrtan* groups that accompany the singing with a *khol* 'double-headed clay drum' and *kartāl* 'cymbals'. Special sessions of *kīrtan* singing known as *asht prahar* last twenty-four hours without interruption.

Professional balladeers sing *chanda,* a section of an epic tale in Oriya, along with some dance steps. *Chanda* songs are rhythmical, are set to a raga, and employ themes from the Ramayana, the Mahabharata, or the Puranas, and occasionally from love stories. The most popular of these ballads are *daskathia* and *pala*. Ballad singers perform *daskathia* (also called *rāmkathi*) in pairs, accompanying themselves with two wooden clappers fitted with a bunch of ankle bells. The witty main singer narrates different stories from the epics, which can last for hours. The assistant, known as the *palia*, repeats the refrain and participates in near-prose dialogue sections.

Another important variety of ballad is the *pala*, associated with the worship of Satyapir ("Satya" Hindu god, "Pir" Muslim saint), a synthesizing deity created during the seventeenth century to evoke Hindu-Muslim unity. A group of five to seven singers present the ballads. The main singer is known as the *gāyak*, the rhythm accompanist (*bāyak*) plays the *mridang* drum, and the remaining chorus (*palia*) provides vocal accompaniment and plays minor instruments such as the cymbals (*kartā l*).

A typical *chattīs* song consists of thirty-six stanzas, each beginning with a different consonant in the Oriya language. Folk singers and village elders sing these songs of mystical and didactic content.

Caupadi are four-stanza love songs describing feminine grace, charm, and the pangs of separation. They are commonly sung at village gatherings.

In the latter part of June, girls sing songs of fertility during the three-day Raja Sankranti festival. Swings are installed in every house and girls sing *ḍoli gīt* 'swing songs'. At the Kumārapūrṇimā festival on the full moon day in October, unmarried girls worship the sun god in the morning and the moon in the evening. Wearing new clothes, the girls sing *kumārapūrṇimā gīt* in chorus, adding and changing stanzas as they see fit.

Cowherds in Orissa perform songs and dances on various occasions, such as Giri Govardhan Pūjā (celebrating Krishna's lifting of Govardhan Mountain to save the people of Gokula, whom the god Indra tried to drown with torrential rains), Ḍola Yātrā (associated with Krishna and the festival of swings), and Gahama Purnima (a Krishna festival for young people). These dance-songs (*naudi gīt*) tell of Lord Krishna and his exploits and are accompanied with hand-held rhythm sticks.

Nirguṇ gīt are theological riddles in question-and-answer form, with more melodic variation in the answer section. The songs are not associated with any particular occasion or singers.

Followers of the Nāth cult sing *yogi gīt* to the accompaniment of a *kendara* 'bowed chordophone'. Itinerant musicians sing these mostly for audiences of women.

Various song and dance forms are associated with the Hindu Shakta cult. In the temples of the female deities Sarala Devi, Mangala Devi, and Karnika Devi, the *patna jātrā* festival dance is performed, while singers perform *danda jatra* songs in praise of Shiva. Instrumental accompaniment for these forms includes the *mahurī* 'double-reed aerophone', *gini* 'small cymbals', and *khol* 'double-headed clay drum'.

Chasa gīt 'cultivator's songs' are sung by laborers engaged in agricultural work; the lyrical content is often from the Ramayana or Mahabharata epics, or may be a narrative love song. Like *chasa gīt, halia gīt* are also songs concerned with agriculture, and are sung by bullockcart drivers and farmers.

Dandanata gīt are dance songs in question-and-answer form, sung by low-caste Hindus during the months of March and April. The singers perform intermittently during dancing accompanied by the *ḍhol* 'large cylindrical drum'. The song themes range from prayers to current affairs.

Dalkhai and *rasarkeli* are songs describing incidents from Lord Krishna's life or from the Ramayana, or humorous events from daily life. Sometimes competitions are held among youths who are encouraged to compose these polyphonic songs extempore. The large, sonorous *mādal* drum, often used by the Santals, accompanies these songs.

Other popular genres include the *chaiti ghoṛa nāc*, a ritual dummy-horse dance of the fishermen community performed beginning on the full moon day of Chaitra (March) to propitiate the horse-headed deity Basuli; and *desi karam*, a solo male dance performed in western Orissa to the accompaniment of the *mādal* earthen drum.

REFERENCES

Das, H. C. 1983. *Folk Culture*, vol. 4: *Folk Music and Dance.* Cuttack, Orissa: Institute of Oriental and Orissan Studies.

Dei, Santilata. 1988. *Vaisnavism in Orissa.* Calcutta: Punthi Pustak.

Mishra, Mahendra K. 1989. *The Folk Songs of Kalandi*. Bhubaneswar: Mayur Publications.

Patnaik, D. N. 1979. "Social Significance of the Folk Songs of Orissa." *Sangeet Natak* (July–Dec.). New Delhi: Sangeet Natak Akademi.

Prasad, Onkar. 1985. *Santal Music: A Study in Pattern and Process of Cultural Persistence.* New Delhi: Inter-India Publications.

Santhinathan, Santasheela. 1996. *Contributions of Saints and Seers to the Music of India*, Vol. II. New Delhi: Kanishka Publications.

Satpathy, Sunil Kumar. 1990. *Anthology of Santal Songs, Dance, and Music of Orissa*. Bhubaneswar: Indian Academy of Folk and Tribal Art.

Goa

Susana Sardo

Musical Contexts
Musical Instruments
Musical Genres
Musical Education and Transmission
Goan Music and the Social Order

Goa became the twenty-seventh—and most recent—state of the Indian Union on 30 May 1987. With a population of approximately 1,169,800 inhabitants (1991 census), Goa covers an area of 3,702 square kilometers on the west coast of India, bordered by Maharashtra to the north, Karnataka to the east and south, and the Arabian Sea to the west. The state is divided into eleven districts and has its political and administrative capital at Panjim. Prior to 1961, when Goa acquired the rank of Union Territory, agriculture always played an important role in the economy, especially the cultivation of rice, coconut, cashews, and flowers. Since that time, agricultural production has decreased, and today involves no more than 24 percent of the work force. Other sectors of the economy, particularly mining, education, and tourism, are now expanding.

Until the first half of the eighteenth century, Goa played a distinctive, almost emblematic role as the political capital of what was then called the "Portuguese Eastern Empire" and as the religious and educational center of Portuguese possessions in Asia and East Africa. Thus, two great cultural domains coexisted in Goa during the 451 years of Portuguese colonization (1510–1961), the European and the Indian. As a result of exchanges, rejections, and acceptances between these two cultures, Goa is today a land culturally distinct from other states in the Indian Union. Since 1961, Indians have migrated to Goa from other states; this has reversed the traditional pattern of emigration out of Goa, which in the past led to the settlement of Goan communities in Bombay, Toronto, London, Lisbon, and Dubai (Mascarenhas-Keyes 1987, 1993; Newman 1984).

Religious traditions, observed in rituals, food, and dress codes, directly affect daily life, and help maintain the boundaries between the two major religious groups, Hindus and Catholics (figure 1). Hinduism accounts for approximately 65 percent of the population, Catholicism for 31 percent, and Islam for 4 percent (1981 census).

Social organization among both Hindu and Catholic populations follows the caste system (*jāti*); four *varṇā* of Hindu society prevail here as in other territories of the Indian Union. Among the Catholics (converted Hindus), the caste system remains, but instead of four *varṇā* (Brahmin, Vaishya, Kshatriya, Shudra), there are only three: Brahmanes, Chardós, and Sudras (in Portuguese). The continuation of

The musical life of Goa is in large part a result of the activities of the Roman Catholic church during colonization.

FIGURE 1 Gavana, a professional group of Goan Christian musicians and dancers, in traditional Catholic dress: *fota-quimão* for women and *casaca* for men. Margão, 1988. Photo by Lorenz & Son.

the caste system as a principle of social organization among Catholics is probably the result of the mass conversion of Hindus to Christianity by the Portuguese rulers (Thomaz 1983). In Daman and Diu, Gujarat, where the Portuguese conversion to Christianity involved individual Hindus, Catholic society does not observe the caste system.

The official language of Goa is Konkani, although like the rest of India Goa is multilingual, and includes speakers of Hindi, Marathi, Urdu (spoken by Muslims), English, and Portuguese (spoken only by a small portion of the Christian community and a few Hindus). In 1987, when Konkani became the official language, the state adopted the Devanagari alphabet (Newmann 1988). Probably because of its predominantly oral history, Konkani pronunciation, intonation, and vocabulary differ among the social classes and districts where it is spoken. In the districts of greater Portuguese and Catholic influence (Salcete, Mormugão, Tiswaddi, and Bardez), oral Konkani contains more Portuguese words.

MUSICAL CONTEXTS

The musical life of Goa is in large part a result of the activities of the Roman Catholic church during colonization. The Portuguese colonizers transformed Hindu musical practices, substituting a European musical vocabulary and arriving at a distinctive musical idiom.

Music is primarily associated with three distinct activities: education (in schools or in the family), religion, and stage shows (for tourists or festivals). In stage shows, where musical performance is supported by the tourism industry, Hindu and

Christian musicians cohabit, whereas in education and religion the two remain apart. Christians have professional music associations whose members perform in hotels, bars, and festivals. Hindus are working toward the revival of their music; they perform mostly in festivals and sometimes for tourists, when hired for special events.

The practice of Indian (predominantly Hindustani) classical music in Goa continued during Portuguese rule; today, Hindus and Muslims teach this tradition in academies and perform in festivals and religious ceremonies. Catholics neither learn nor perform Indian classical music. Western art music, brought to Goa in the sixteenth century with the Catholic liturgy, is nowadays the exclusive domain of Christians. It is taught in academies (in most cases as supplementary education), is often associated with religious activities, and is performed in concert halls.

MUSICAL INSTRUMENTS

In contrast with Hindu and Western art music performed in Goa, Konkani music does not include purely instrumental genres, although instrumental accompaniment is essential to the performance of vocal pieces. The most common instruments used are the violin, the guitar, the mandolin, the piano, several types of metal or wood idiophones directly associated with dance, and the *gumatt,* a goblet-shaped clay drum with one end narrow and open, and the other end wide and covered with lizard skin (figure 2). Held at shoulder height or placed on the knees and played with the hands, the *gumatt* is a distinctive, essential element of Konkani music and is not used for any other type of Goan music.

MUSICAL GENRES

Goa's traditional music—transmitted orally—falls into two categories: (1) musical genres sung in Konkani that emphasize melody, are associated with harvest rituals (celebrating the harvest of coconut, flowers, and so on), and have strong Indian elements; (2) a heterogeneous repertoire consisting of musical genres sung in Portuguese, English, Hindi, or Konkani, linked to the Western harmonic tradition and usually performed as entertainment.

The first group comprises a monodic song repertoire of Hindu origin, always associated with dance and accompanied by idiophones and membranophones. It includes musical genres such as *dhalo*, *fugddi*, *talgaddi*, and *zagor*. Nowadays, Hindus—and occasionally Christians—usually perform these songs in tourist shows or festivals.

The second group, based on Western tonal harmony, consists, on the one hand, of "transplanted" song genres, including those in Portuguese (*corredinho*, *fado*, *marchas de Lisboa*), English (songs such as "My Bonnie Lies over the Ocean" popularized in Goa in the 1950s and 1960s), and Hindi (popularized by films and broadcast by All India Radio). Singers perform these songs in family circles and for tourists in hotels. On the other hand, this group includes a predominantly Catholic repertoire sung in Konkani. The choreography of accompanying dances, markedly distinct from that of Western dances, is very similar to some Indian dance forms, especially in their descriptive character. This repertoire includes genres such as *decknni*, *dulpod*, *mandó*, and *mussoll*.

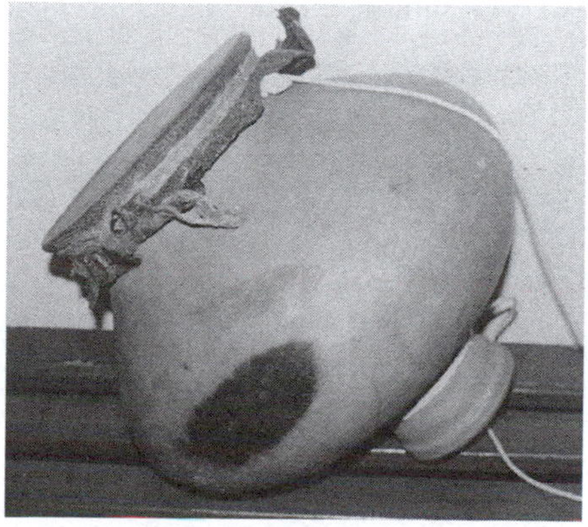

FIGURE 2 *Gumatt* used as accompaniment in all Goan musical genres. Photo by Susana Sardo.

The functions and performance practices of the traditional Konkani song repertoire are linked to Goa's social structure. The highest castes claim those musical genres directly associated with Western traditions, such as *dulpod* and *mandó*. Other genres are associated with the lower castes—mostly because they display a greater number of Hindu elements, but also because they are associated with agricultural work.

Several musical genres and dances have recently been revived in stage performances. A few go back to a remote past in rural Goa, such as the *kunnbi* dance, performed by the Kunnbi and Gauda castes and associated with the rice harvest, the sale of flowers, and other agricultural work. When professional musicians present these musical genres on stage, however, they modify them, as most performers have a purely commercial relationship with the music and choreography they perform. The following Konkani musical genres are the most common and representative.

Dhalo

Dhalo, a music and dance of Hindu origin, is performed exclusively by women. Up to the 1960s, women performed *dhalo* during the week of harvest celebrations in Paush, the tenth month of the Hindu calendar. The vocal melodies consist of short unison phrases; the texts draw on a wide variety of subjects ranging from religious to satirical. Metal idiophones and sometimes the *gumatt* 'clay goblet drum' accompany the dance. Today the *dhalo* is performed mostly in stage contexts; the choreography involves two rows of twelve women (each row with arms linked) moving forward and backward at different points.

Fugddi

Fugddi is a music and dance genre of Hindu origin and character performed exclusively by groups of women. Up to the 1960s, singers associated with the cult of the Hindu deity Ganesh performed it at harvesttime in praise and thanksgiving for the crops of the earth. More often than not, the choreography resembles movements of rice-plantation workers and mimics tasks associated with the cultivation of rice. The melody consists of short phrases repeated in unison. Today the text is no longer improvised or of religious character but focuses mostly on satires and humorous subjects; performances take place only on the stage danced in a circle to the accompaniment of metal idiophones and the *gumatt* goblet drum.

Decknni

TRACK 27 Christians compose and perform *decknni* music and dance, which is related to the Hindu female dance tradition of the *devadāsī* (whom the Christian Goans call *bailadeiras*). Only women perform the dance; men do not participate in the dance, but they do represent male characters in the story. Choreography focuses on corporal gestures, emphasizing the symbolic movement of arms and hands in a manner similar to the Indian classical dance genre *bharata nāṭyam*. Although *decknni* vocal and instrumental music incorporates Western tonal harmony, Christian Goans interpret *decknni* with many Indian musical characteristics such as repetitive rhythmic and melodic formulas, frequent use of half-tone melodic movement (as in raga melodies), recurring vocal ornaments and glissandi, recurring syncopated rhythms, and a nasal vocal tone. Gestures, costumes, and ornaments all imitate the stereotypical Indian *bharata nāṭyam* dance.

Dulpod

Dulpod, a musical genre of Christian origin, is associated with and performed after the *mandó* (see below)—especially the danced version of the latter—by women and men. It consists of two to four melodic phrases sung by one or two voices. After a *mandó* performance, the singers select several *dulpod* songs to perform at faster and faster tempos, successively increasing the pace of the dance. The number of *dulpod* to be performed after the *mandó* is not prescribed. Song texts usually refer to scenes of Goan daily life, such as the land itself, returning from work, or chatting between neighbors, or they relate satirical and humorous Goan popular tales. Text themes within a song may even be quite independent of each other, since the main objective is to test the ability of the dancers.

FIGURE 3 Stage performance of Goan singers accompanied by guitar and *gumatt*, at the Goan Mandó Festival, 1970s. Photo by Souza and Paul.

Fell

Christian men and women perform this musical genre during Carnival parade in the week before Lent. *Fell* consists of songs and theatrical numbers expressing the feeling of liberation from the daily routine, with emphasis on the main Carnival message of freedom in behavior and the promotion of happiness and joy. Two or more improvising voices can sing *fell*, depending on the versatility of the singers. *Fell* vocal performance uses Western tonal harmony and includes instrumental accompaniment, mostly by idiophones.

Mandó

The *mandó* genre, of Christian origin, consists of songs with instrumental accompaniment and sometimes also with dance. This is, for the Christian Goan, the musical genre perhaps most representative of Goa's cultural identity (figure 3).

The *mandó* is sung by two or three voices, in Western classical harmony. The arrangement is not fixed, but two voices moving in parallel thirds are common, as are three-voice textures employing contrary and oblique movement. Depending on their abilities, singers are free to introduce ornamental figures into their performances. Aside from this, there is one fixed, identifying *mandó* performance feature: a short vocal oscillation of indefinite pitch when two consecutive notes are linked. Performers call this oscillation *moll*.

The formal structure of the *mandó* is an ABA pattern. The A section consists of two phrases that repeat and are often in a minor key; the B section, or refrain, modulates to the relative major. Singers always perform the *mandó* in a slow tempo (*dolente*, as the performers call it); the expressive vocal performance and the corporal gestures dictated by the choreography constantly emphasize this slow tempo.

Mandó themes refer to stories that mark the daily life of Goans, both as individuals and as a people. Examples of the latter are political songs and texts that praise particular localities or natural phenomena such as the sun, the sea, or the monsoon. The majority of *mandó* songs nevertheless emphasize themes such as passion, lost love, false love, or flirtation.

Mussoll

Mussoll is a theatrical dance performed by Christian men of the Chardó social class in

Mussoll is a theatrical dance performed by the Christian men of the Chardó social class in the village of Chandor. The song texts associated with *mussoll* allude to Hindu gods, as in the evocation of Shiva, as well as to Catholic saints such as the Virgin Mary.

the village of Chandor, Salcete District. It is a martial dance intended to commemorate the victory of King Harihara II (son of King Bukka I of Vijayanagar) over the Cholas at the Chandrapur fortification in the fourteenth century. In Konkani, *mussoll* means "a stick to thresh grains." In the dance, a cane about 1.8 meters long, with two metallic discs the size of bottle caps attached to its upper end, represents the stick; the discs produce sounds when the lower end hits the floor. The stick serves to support the *mussoll* dancers in performance.

People begin organizing the *mussoll* on the Sunday before Carnival, but the dance itself takes place only during the actual three days of the festival. All men from Chandor participate in such activities as the procession, simulations of fights, and the *mussoll,* which a group of men sings and dances as it travels from house to house throughout the village. The songs associated with *mussoll* are slow, mostly pentatonic, sung in unison, and accompanied by several goblet drums, metal idiophones, and *mridangam* barrel drums. The song texts allude to Hindu gods, as in the evocation of Shiva, as well as to Catholic saints such as the Virgin Mary; substitution of Hindu devotions for Christian prayers is common. The choreography of the *mussoll* dance involves a group of men dressed in military garb, organized in a circle or in concentric circles, playing the sticks (*mussoll*) inside or around the circle.

MUSICAL EDUCATION AND TRANSMISSION

The profusion of musical genres in Goa and the important role of music in all activities of collective expression, whether family celebrations, rituals, parties, festivals, or tourist shows, signify a way of life in which informal musical education is crucial.

In the past, the formal teaching of music was very important, especially in the parochial schools first established in 1545 by the viceroy Dom João de Castro, and in the elementary schools first established in Goa in 1831 by decree of the Portuguese government. Access to these elementary schools was, however, very restricted, granted only to families of the Goan social elite. During these early years formal education was for boys exclusively, and wealthy families also maintained tutors (*mestri rebeko*) at home for complementary education. The first school for girls was established in 1845. Until then, education of girls in wealthy families took place at home. Even after the establishment of the *escola de meninas* 'school for girls', home tutors continued to educate females of the Christian elite. The practice of music was a necessity of family life until the mid-twentieth century, playing an important role in maintaining the family as an institution.

Today, Western art music remains essentially linked with conservatories: in addition to small private music schools, there are two art academies in Goa where European and Indian music and dance are taught: the Kala Academy in Panjim, founded in 1953, and the Escola de Música de Margão (Madgaon), established in 1955. These schools often submit their Western-music programs to English schools—Trinity College and the Royal College of Music, in London—for approval.

The Hindustani music tradition, widely performed in schools and broadcast on All India Radio, is part of Goan musical culture, cultivated by Hindu and Muslim Goans, but often rejected by the Catholics.

GOAN MUSIC AND THE SOCIAL ORDER

Goa's musical traditions reflect the state's hierarchical social system to a high degree. The various social groups can nevertheless rank particular musical traditions differently, depending on the group's perceived position in society. The music of Christians, for example, is defined by some as "folklore," by others as "art." Social groups identify with certain musical genres and practices, though there is some flexibility within this identification. The highest-caste Christians are an exception, as they do not recognize any validity or quality in performances of "their" music by other social groups.

A wide variety of musical genres exists in Goa, representing a continuum from classical Hindustani music to Western art music. Most music and dance performers identify more or less with one of these two paradigms, and thus through them with either India or the West. Hindu or Muslim Goans place fundamental value on Hindustani music and on the reproduction of musical genres that emphasize—through the use of Konkani—Goa's place within the multicultural Indian context. Christian Goans (especially those from the highest castes) attempt to insulate their music from all such indicators of "Indianness," emphasizing tonal harmony and the use of Western musical instruments. In the 1990s, Goans thus use individual musical expression to define their state within the larger context of India.

Although Goa has been the focus of some interest for ethnomusicologists (Sardo 1994, 1995; Pereira and Martins 1981), its various musical processes still await in-depth research. Among ethnographic works by native scholars, the extensive (though as yet unpublished) five-volume compilation of *mandó*, *dulpod,* and *decknni* songs organized and transcribed by Agapito de Miranda is significant.

—Translated by Cristina Magaldi

REFERENCES

Gune, V. T., ed. 1979. *Gazetteer of the Union Territory Goa, Daman and Diu.* Panaji: Gazetteer Department, Government of the Union Territory of Goa, Daman and Diu.

Mascarenhas-Keyes, Stella. 1987. "Death Notices and Dispersal: International Migration among Catholic Goans." In *Migrants, Workers and the Social Order,* ed. Jeremy Eodes, 82–97. London: Tavistock.

———. 1993. "International and Internal Migration: The Changing Identity of Catholic and Hindu Women in Goa." In *Migrant Women: Crossing Boundaries and Changing Identities,* ed. Gina Buijs, 119–143. Oxford: Berg Publishers Ltd.

Newman, Robert. 1984. "Goa: The Transformation of an Indian Region." *Pacific Affairs* 57(3):429–449.

———. 1988. "Konkani Mai Ascends the Throne: The Cultural Basis of Goan Statehood." *South Asia* 11(1):1–24.

Palackal, Joseph. In progress. "Mandó." In *The New Grove Dictionary of Music and Musicians,* 7th ed., ed. Stanley Sadie. London: Macmillan.

Pereira, José, and Micael Martins. 1981. "Song of Goa, an Anthology of Mandos." *Boletim do Instituto Menezes de Bragança* 128. Bastorá: Tipgrafia Rangel.

Sá, Mário Cabral e. 1997. *Wind of Fire: The Music and Musicians of Goa.* New Delhi: Promilla.

Sardo, Susana. 1994. "Goa—Sons e Silêncios." *Oceanos: Indo-Portuguesmente* 19/20:246–258.

———. 1995. "A Música e a Reconstrução da Identidade: Um Estudo sobre o Grupo de Danças e Cantares Goeses em Lisboa." Master's thesis, Universidade Nova de Lisboa.

———. In progress. "Singing Stories: Goan Catholic Music as a Strategy of Defining Identity." Ph.D. dissertation, Universidade Nova de Lisboa.

Sardo, Susana, and Rui Simões. 1989. "A Música e o seu papel no processo de cristianização em Goa." *Goa: Orgão de Divulgação Cultural da Casa de Goa* 1:13–18.

Thomaz, Luis Filipe. 1983. "Goa: Une Société Luso-indienne." *Boulletin des Études Portugaises et Brésiliennes* 42/43:15–44.

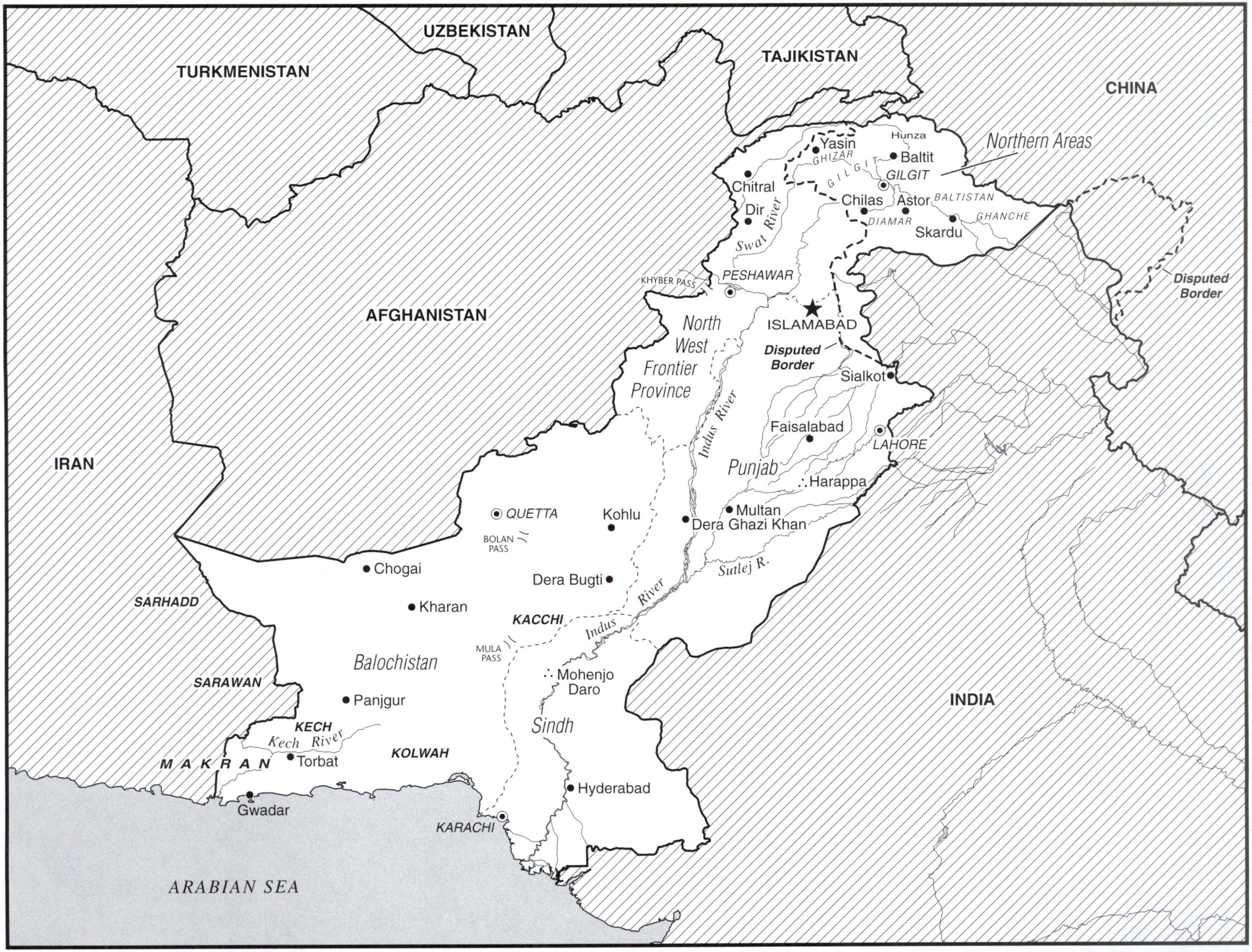
UZBEKISTAN
TURKMENISTAN
TAJIKISTAN
CHINA
Northern Areas
Hunza
Yasin
Baltit
GHIZAR
GILGIT
Chitral
Chilas
Astor
BALTISTAN
Dir
DIAMAR
GHANCHE
Skardu
Swat River
KHYBER PASS
PESHAWAR
Disputed Border
AFGHANISTAN
North West Frontier Province
ISLAMABAD
Disputed Border
Sialkot
Indus River
Faisalabad
LAHORE
IRAN
Punjab
Harappa
QUETTA
Kohlu
Multan
Dera Ghazi Khan
BOLAN PASS
Chogai
Dera Bugti
Sutlej R.
SARHADD
Kharan
KACCHI
River
Indus
MULA PASS
Balochistan
SARAWAN
Mohenjo Daro
Panjgur
INDIA
KECH
Kech River
Sindh
M A K R A N
Torbat
KOLWAH
Hyderabad
Gwadar
KARACHI
ARABIAN SEA

Pakistan

In the Islamic Republic of Pakistan, Muslim culture is expressed through various religious traditions: the call to prayer, Qur'ānic recitation, the chanting of religious poetry, and hymn recitation and chanting. Independent of Islamic orthodoxy, however, music and dance find expression in the varied regional traditions of Pakistan's cultural and linguistic groups, in the practice and performance (albeit declining) of Hindustani classical music, and in the thriving production of Westernized pop and rock music.

The songs and instruments of regional musics reflect the geographical and cultural proximity of neighboring Iran, Afghanistan, and India. In Balochistan, North West Frontier Province, and the Northern Areas, long-necked and short-necked lutes and drum-and-shawm ensembles are similar to those found in Islamic lands to the west; in the eastern province of Punjab, ballad and epic singing, musical folk theater, and accompanied puppet shows likewise have corresponding traditions in northeastern India.

MAP 8 Pakistan

Music, the State, and Islam

Regula Burckhardt Qureshi

Building a National Sound Culture: 1947–1960s
Cultivating Folk Music and Heritage
Musical Islamization
Musical Internationalization

The Islamic Republic of Pakistan is located in the northwestern part of the Indian subcontinent and includes the Indus river system as well as the surrounding mountains and desert. It consists of four linguistically and culturally distinct provinces—Punjab, Sindh, North West Frontier or Pathan Province, and Balochistan—three of which extend beyond Pakistan into India (Punjab), Afghanistan (NWFP), and Iran (Balochistan). It also encompasses the centrally administered Northern Area. Pakistan's national language is Urdu, the Muslim elite language and Muslim lingua franca of South Asia; the main regional languages are Punjabi, Sindhi, Balochi, and Pashto.

West and East Pakistan were established in 1947 when colonial India gained independence from British rule, created from areas with Muslim majorities in both the northwestern and eastern parts of what had been India up to then. In 1971, East Pakistan broke away and became the independent state of Bangladesh. Massive immigration of Muslims from India (and emigration of Hindus and Sikhs to India) decisively reinforced the Muslim character of the country, with Urdu espoused as the medium for developing a national culture largely in urban centers and by the mass media. Music reflects this constellation: art music and urban entertainment genres fall within the Indian musical style area, whereas each of the four major linguistic regions has a distinct musical identity.

As a new nation in search of cultural self-definition, Pakistan was guided by two paradigms: the negation of anything identified with India, and the affirmation of Muslim identity (figure 1). This identity is social and cultural as well as religious. Muslim culture, along with music, operated at two levels. At the elite or fine-art level, a single "Great Tradition" had flourished in the urban centers of Muslim domination in India, including Delhi, long the capital of Mughal India. The second level was local and mainly rural, rooted in the predominantly Muslim regions of Pakistan. For Pakistan to acquire a single cohesive cultural and musical base, these diverse "Little Traditions" would need to forge links with the Great Tradition.

Based on dynamics of class, ethnicity, and religion, an ongoing process of negotiation between these diverse identities has been taking place in the sonic arts, including music and the chanting of poetry and religious texts. Though "musical" in sound, chanted genres are considered not to be music but "recitation," characterized

FIGURE 1 King Faisal Mosque, an Islamic landmark in Pakistan's capital, Islamabad. Photo by Regula Burckhardt Qureshi, 1993.

FIGURE 2 A woman leads the women's hymn recitation at a Shia *majlis* (religious assembly) in PECHs *imāmbāṛā* (place of worship), Karachi, 1993. Photo by Regula Burckhardt Qureshi.

by the subordination of musical sound to religious and poetic texts. The sonic practice of Islam starts with the many forms of Qur'ānic recitation and of the call to prayer, and extends to the richly diverse vernacular hymns that mark major observances among all confessional groups including the Sunni majority, the Shia, and the Sufis (figure 2). [see PAKISTAN: DEVOTIONAL MUSIC].

The separation of religious recitation and music in the orthodox Islamic perspective implies a negative valuation of music. Indeed, Islamic orthodoxy disapproves of music altogether. At the same time, the historical record suggests that this unique categorical segregation of religious recitation left space for the development of a secular music as fine art, free from the constraints of religious ideology. And Pakistan inherited the tradition of private musical patronage at courts and feudal establishments, practiced during centuries of Muslim domination in South Asia. Part of this heritage is an eclectic spirit, an open attitude toward novelty, in terms of music and otherwise. Linked to the fundamentally transnational character of the Muslim polity, the Muslim courts through the centuries had experienced a fairly constant flow of musicians and poets who entered India generally from the Muslim regions to the northwest, mainly from Iran and Afghanistan.

The sonic arts have played an important part in the development of a cultural identity for Pakistan; this is also reflected in a continuous flow of writings in both English and Urdu (Ahmad 1964; Baloch 1965; Jalibi 1984; Malik 1982; Rauf 1965). This article outlines how the music of the newly created nation was the result of the meeting of opposites—tradition and innovation, secularism and orthodoxy, the center and the regions, immigrants and locals.

BUILDING A NATIONAL SOUND CULTURE: 1947–1960s

Pakistan's pursuit of the sonic arts as national culture was carried out pragmatically within a largely laissez-faire economy controlled by feudal-military elites. Initially, the only major cultural institution was Radio Pakistan. This was established by Director General Z. A. Bukhari on the model of All India Radio, a colonial version of the British Broadcasting Corporation (BBC), where Bukhari had apprenticed with the remarkably anticolonial, pro-Muslim founding director general, Lionel Fielden (Buchari 1966). Radio Pakistan and the ruling immigrant elite centered in Karachi, as well as the Punjabi elite in Lahore, at first served as a hub of patronage for classical

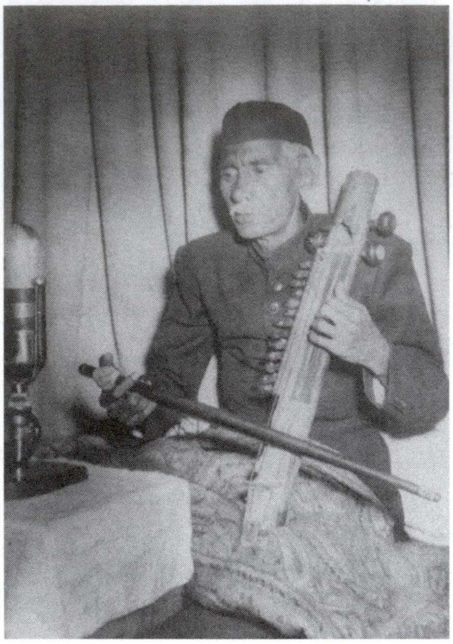

FIGURE 3 The legendary Bundu Khan with his original bamboo sāraṅgī, c. 1954. Photo courtesy Radio Pakistan.

musicians, mostly of Indian but also of Pakistani Punjabi origin. Each radio station also had a "rural" section that broadcast folk songs domesticated as studio music. Standard "light music" instruments were employed: tabla, *sāraṅgī*, and harmonium, as well as sitar, clarinet, and bowed strings as backups.

Radio Pakistan also created and widely disseminated a kind of national music, a choral song genre based on the Urdu verse of the national poet, Muhammad Iqbal. These creative compositions, labeled Iqbaliat, represented an attempt to combine a cheerfully martial style with the rhythm based on the verse meter. These performances were unique for a Muslim genre in that they included both men and women in the choral group.

More lasting was the use of the Sufi qawwali as a quasi-national music, whose strongly rhythmic, improvisational character, and flamboyant performance style were all retained and were showcased by many performers on state television from the 1960s onward. In fact, one of the first LP records of Pakistan, still famous today, was *Tajdar-e-Haram*, which launched the great Ghulam Farid Sabri and his qawwali group, later renamed the Sabri Brothers (Sabri Brothers 1996).

Hindustani music, unproblematically enriched by regional stylistic differences of *gharānā* 'musical lineage', was the classical music of Pakistan and served the elite across the country. The many outstanding classical musicians came from a traditionally mobile professional class of hereditary performers, the greatest of whom included Nazakat Ali, Salamat Ali, Sharif Khan Poonchwala, Bundu Khan (figure 3), Asad Ali Khan, Roshanara Begum, and Bade Ghulam Ali Khan. Their music was widely broadcast and recorded. Nevertheless, soon after Pakistan's capital was moved from Karachi to Islamabad—a newly constructed city too expensive and distant for musicians from the south—classical music went into a decline, especially in Karachi. Except for a few arts councils with sporadic classes, the lack of institutional support (music education and concert organizations) continued to leave art music largely dependent on dwindling feudal and personal patronage.

Pakistan's search for a national musical culture was based on a supralocal Islamic ideology, but it also faced the local reality of different musical cultures as in East versus West Pakistanis and immigrant versus indigenous communities. The main contest arose with the shift of elite power from immigrants to Punjabis that had already begun in the 1950s. Initially the cosmopolitan elites from all groups were satisfied with the representation of regional folk music in the form of homogenized studio versions of folk songs. These songs were commonly arranged into sets incorporating one song from each province and one or two from East Pakistan, and were disseminated on radio and through recordings. They were sonic representations of regional diversity contained and controlled within a centralized political as well as musical system.

Song composition was also seen as generating patriotism in this new country; poets such as Jamiluddin Aali and songwriters such as Sohail Rana created a folk-based popular song style that ranged from the sentimental to the martial. The popular songs "Jive Jive Pakistan" and "Sohni Dharti" are evergreen examples.

In the 1960s, the government-funded PIA Arts Academy sought to project a Pakistani identity abroad. An organ of Pakistan International Airlines, the academy employed a cross-section of classical and folk musicians and dancers to present eclectic mixtures of genres, including art music, within the general category of "folk heritage."

CULTIVATING FOLK MUSIC AND HERITAGE

In the seventies, the shift of power to indigenous elites, and a need to consolidate identity after the loss of East Pakistan, led to efforts to nationalize regional music and preserve the Pakistani heritage. These resulted in the founding of the National Institute for Folk Heritage, or Lok Virsa, in Islamabad, a model institution with a broad mandate that includes preservation as well as public display of the country's musical heritage. Lok Virsa has carried out research and documentation of the country's traditional music and is a regular sponsor of musical performances at folk arts festivals and in concerts and recordings. A complementary governmental initiative was the National Arts Council's sponsorship of the Urdu fine arts magazine *Saqafat* as well as books on music. The arts council also organizes music conferences and performances in Islamabad.

The greatest impact of the "folk music initiative" was felt, however, when folk artists were featured on television: every Pakistani old enough to have seen and heard them remembers the orange-robed mendicant singer Lallan Faqir and the intense vitality of Mai Bhagi's deep voice. Both were from Sindh, a region that was neglected until the ascent of a Sindhi prime minister, Zulfikar Ali Bhutto, and the international conference on "Sindh through the Centuries," sponsored by his government and held in 1975 (Qureshi 1981).

Prime Minister Bhutto's socialist agenda addressing and mobilizing the "people" placed a high priority on cultivating regional music and preserving the people's heritage. The Lok Virsa served both purposes. Regional music was showcased in its diversity, but also subsumed under a central authority. Interestingly, Lok Virsa has included classical as well as folk music in its mandate of recording Pakistan's heritage through the extensive and wide-ranging cassette collection on the Shalimar label. Lok Virsa also pioneered music videos presenting artists in the hosted format of a traditional performance (*mehfil*), a remarkable innovation that long preceded Western music videos.

An autonomous institution for studying regional culture, including music, was also founded in Sindh. Sindh University's Institute of Sindhology flourished under the outstandingly versatile scholar G. N. Baloch, who also authored important works on Sindhi music (1958, 1959, 1965, 1966, 1973). Interestingly, the same development did not extend to Punjab. Lahore was a center of classical music patronage and amateur learning since pre-independence days, supporting classical music classes run by the Al Hamra Arts Council as well as Pakistan's only annual music conference, up until the late 1990s. Thus, Lahore saw the establishment, by the great poet Faiz Ahmad Faiz, of a center specifically for classical music, named the Classical Music Research Cell. Today this remarkable archive is hidden in the basement of Radio Pakistan, but its staff of two continues to acquire and process valuable documents and recordings, and it remains a meeting place for musicians and music lovers alike.

MUSICAL ISLAMIZATION

Political Islamization during the 1980s meant musical Islamization of the public media, by extensive patronage of religious genres and by support for their musical "Arabization." An increasing cultural orientation toward the Middle East, beginning with the Islamic summit held in Islamabad in 1971 and reinforced by the growing Pakistani work force living in Arab environments, had already laid the foundation for this process.

This musical Islamization was strongly linked to the rapid spread of cassette recordings. The cassette medium introduced large numbers of privately and religiously produced recordings that reflected the interests of the market as well as the state. The low cost and accessibility of this technology effected an unprecedented spread of cassette production and dissemination. Of crucial importance during the 1980s was the influx of cassette recordings of standard Islamic recitation, especially the kind of highly elaborated Qur'ānic recitation (*qir'at*) cultivated in Egypt.

Rock bands create Pakistani forms of international pop music and are oriented to the West, international TV, and the Internet.

Reciting tours by outstanding Qur'ān reciters (*qāri*), and initiatives to introduce *qir'at* competitions as practiced in Egypt, had a palpable impact on vernacular religious chant. Qawwali singers beginning in the 1980s articulated and recorded texts with a strongly Arabic pronounciation, and some songs featured Arabic *darbukka* 'goblet drum' beats—Ghulam Farid Sabri's "Ya Mustafa," for example (Sabri Brothers 1996). Hymn texts focused more exclusively on the Prophet Muhammad rather than on local saints. Recordings of vernacular hymns, especially *na't*, in praise of the Prophet, became especially widespread.

The proliferation of cassette music has reduced the political importance of radio. In the 1980s, Radio Pakistan was transformed into a government tool and was starved of finances for cultural programming. The radio lost its pre-eminent role as patron of classical music, and its decision not to replace staff artists reduced this significant source of livelihood for classical musicians. The state media still remained a national touchstone for the sonic arts, only now in the form of television. With its extensive programming of religious recitation, PTV featured a musical Islamization that was also visibly performative, governed by strict rules of clothing (especially for women), and by restrictions on male-female performances.

Public patronage of religious recitation was strong, especially by mosques, but secular musical performance continued in private contexts, including small amateur groups in homes. The influx of video recorders in the 1980s helped perfect a public-private dichotomy of musical consumption, especially through the video boom of officially banned Indian films and their music. Public cinemas, however, were gradually closed down, crippling Pakistan's musically creative film and film-music industries.

MUSICAL INTERNATIONALIZATION

In the 1990s, the increasing use of Western popular and electronic instruments, especially among the westernized, English-educated elite, reflect both generational change and internationalization. Rock bands create Pakistani forms of international pop music and are oriented to the West, international TV, and the Internet. Aspects of westernization include television broadcasting of Western music dubs and the recasting of traditional music into various styles of fusion by artists such as Adnan Sami Khan and the late Nusrat Fateh Ali Khan.

At the same time traditional Pakistani genres, especially the ghazal and qawwali, enjoyed a revival and have now become an export specialty. Such reflected glory has in turn reinvigorated these musical forms at home, especially among the less westernized middle class. Of the two thriving export markets, India gives credible recognition to a broad range of artists, and expatriate Pakistani and Indian audiences in the West offer generous patronage.

Above all, the 1990s have seen the beginnings of substantial change in the social relations of music making, influenced by international exposure and patronage. Signs

FIGURE 4 Ataulla Khan Isa Khelvi performs for an elite audience at a five-star hotel in Karachi, 1992. Photo by Regula Burckhardt Qureshi.

of an incipient urban bourgeoisie appear in the permission for middle- and upper-class amateur music making, among proliferating amateur circles, and even more so among young professional rock musicians.

Throughout all these shifts, however, solo songs consisting of verses set to music remain the nationally preferred genre across musical styles, and elite patronage of ghazal artists remains the preferred display of status at fashion shows and weddings. An interesting aspect of the more liberal current musical scene is the lifting of a class taboo on listening to low-status music, so that a glamorous Punjabi elite gathering can enjoy listening to Punjabi village songs by an erstwhile truck driver, the famous Ataulla Khan Isa Khelvi (figure 4).

The bourgeoisification of exported sound recordings has also been driven by close contact between the artists and their personal hosts in the diaspora, for whom traditional performances invoke heritage and identification. Poetry recitals (*mushāira*) by teams of Urdu poets are favorites among expatriate Pakistanis.

Finally, the latter national/global developments are inevitably linked to the commodification of music and international capitalism. The country's continued openness toward the global market ultimately contributes to the present period of openness, eclecticism, and pluralism of musical styles, and represents a fruition of the laissez-faire attitude toward music and national culture that Pakistan initiated in its earliest years.

But there are social and artistic casualties. Hereditary professional musicians, especially classical musicians, bear the disadvantage of a low inherited status that few have had the means to enhance through education and linguistic skills (such as competence in English). For most, the rich oral heritage of the first Pakistani generation remains inadequately patronized and has therefore not been passed on to the second generation. The option to learn and perform the westernized music of the present is either financially impossible, given the cost of Western pop instruments in Pakistan, or artistically so, because of what today's foremost *sāraṅgī* player Nazim Ali Khan calls an inability to "dishonor" his classical art. Proactive means are required for the dissemination and patronage of the country's classical musical heritage to continue.

Another constituency that is as yet largely excluded from the pluralism and openness of the 1990s is women. Female singers are the most important bearers of the light classical tradition, especially the ghazal, an Urdu song tradition associated with courts, salons, and the dissemination of poetry across social classes. Pakistani ghazal singers include Iqbal Bano, Farida Khanam, Nur Jahan, Abida Parveen, Malka Pukhraj, and her daughter Tahira Syed. But for professional women musicians, social isolation remains a reality that places the continuing life of this quintessentially Pakistani music in double jeopardy. Middle-class respectability for women largely precludes even amateur music making in private, while the public domain is clearly a male preserve, even for westernized music. Recitation, however, is thriving among men and women. Many outstanding female reciters participate in the sanctioned "nonmusical" confines of religious assemblies (*milad, majlis*) and poetry sessions (*mushāira*), and these performances have been freely disseminated through recordings.

Pakistan's brief history as a nation is marked by diverse moves toward forging a South Asian Islamic identity through music. If there is one musical genre that has most consistently and eloquently articulated this identity, it is qawwali. Prominent in public musical life from the outset, qawwali embodies the qualities of verbal recitation as well as art music, in a unique and flexible constellation. Qawwali lives as Sufi religious practice and as a kind of national concert music; it has also become Pakistan's musical message to the world, thanks mainly to the great rhythmic and improvisational artistry of the late Nusrat Fateh Ali Khan, whose voice left Pakistan's indelible mark on world music (1997, 1999).

The last word goes to the media of music. Pakistan's eclectic openness to world markets has resulted in a strong and early presence for audio-visual media, and musical developments in Pakistan continue to be affected by them. It will be up to present and future governments and elites to ensure that Pakistan's musical artists can flourish and can continue to speak in and for their country.

REFERENCES

Ahmad, Aziz. 1969 [1964]. *Islamic Culture in the Indian Environment*, vol. 2. Oxford: Clarendon (esp. 108–166, 218–262).

Baloch, N. A. 1958. "Folk-Songs and Folk-Dances of West Pakistan." In *Traditional Culture in South-East Asia*, 253–265. Bombay: Unesco.

———. 1959. "Shah Abdul Latif (1690–1752), the Founder of a New Music Tradition." *Pakistan Quarterly* 9(3): 54–57, 68.

———. 1965. "The Traditional Cultures in West Pakistan." In *Perspectives on Pakistan*, ed. Anwar S. Dil, 167–203. Abbottabad, Pakistan: Bookservice.

———. 1966. *Musical Instruments of the Lower Indus Valley of Sind*. Hyderabad: Mehran Arts Council.

———. 1973. *Development of Music in Sindh*. Hyderabad: Sindh University Press.

Bukhari, Z. A. 1966. *Sarguzisht*. Karachi: Ma'arif Ltd. In Urdu.

Jalibi, Jameel. 1984. *Pakistan: The Identity of Culture*. Karachi: Royal Book Company.

Khan, Nusrat Fateh Ali. 1997. *Rapture*. Music Collection International 50019. Compact disc.

———. 1999. *Live at Islamabad, Volumes 1 and 2*. M. I. L. Multimedia MIL 2225. Compact disc.

Malik, M. Saeed. 1983. *The Musical Heritage of Pakistan*. Islamabad: Idara Saqafat-e-Pakistan.

Qureshi, Regula Burckhardt. 1981. "Music and Culture in Sind: An Ethnomusicological Perspective." In *Sind through the Centuries*, ed. Hamida Khuhro, 237–244. Karachi: Oxford University Press.

———. 1986. *Sufi Music of India and Pakistan: Sound, Context and Meaning in Qawwali*. Cambridge: Cambridge University Press.

Rauf, Abdur. 1965. *Renaissance of Islamic Culture and Civilization in Pakistan*. Lahore: Sh. Muhammed Ashraf Kashmiri Bazar.

Sabri Brothers. 1996. *Ya Mustapha*. Green Linnet Records, Xeno 4041. Compact disc.

———. 1997. *The Greatest Hits*. Shanachie 64090. Compact disc.

———. 1998. *Qawwali: Sufi Music from Pakistan*. Nonesuch Explorer 72080-2. Compact disc.

Devotional Music

Hiromi Lorraine Sakata

Musical Expressions
Movement and Dance Expressions
Music at Shrines

Devotional music forms part of the repertoire of almost every musical genre in Pakistan, and is performed and appreciated at every stratum of society. There is neither a special genre nor a special repertoire associated with the official state religion of Islam comparable to "church music" in the West. In fact, the concept of music *for* or *in* the mosque does not exist, for orthodox Islam does not sanction any form of musical performance in its services or prayers.

The most common and likely locus for the performance of devotional music is the shrines of Sufi saints, especially during annual pilgrimages and on saints' death anniversaries (*ʿurs*). Devotional songs and dances expressing the mystic spirit often play a central role in the commemoration and worship of these saints. The poet-saints themselves composed many such songs, which have great appeal for their followers and also for the masses. A large number refer to popular folk themes and stories, and use the heroes and heroines of regional romances to symbolize the mystic states of love, devotion, and separation. With these compositions the poet-saints also contributed to the development of regional languages to high literary levels, particularly Punjabi, Saraiki, and Sindhi.

MUSICAL EXPRESSIONS

Qawwali

Qawwali is the musical expression of Sufi poetry, and is central to the *samāʿ* 'listening; spiritual concert' of the Sufis of South Asia. The term *qawwālī* comes from the Arabic *qaul* 'to speak or say'. The etymology of the word thus carries an emphasis on the words or text of a song. The term *qawwāl* 'fluent, eloquent' came to be applied to singers, as in the celebrated eleventh-century Persian treatise on Sufism, *Kashf al-Mahjub*. Today, the term Qawwāl refers to singers of qawwali. The music is intended to make the listeners more receptive to the songs' messages.

The messages in qawwali texts identify love as the foundation of the relationship with God. The Sufi poetry often describes this spiritual love as if it were worldly love between a man and a woman. Sufi poets used worldly images to signify the mystic state and the Sufi mission. They use wine, the cupbearer, the tavern—all forbidden in

Sufi poetry may appear to be profane to the uninitiated, but it embodies sacred meaning to those who understand.

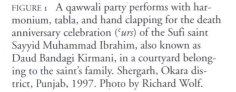

FIGURE 1 A qawwali party performs with harmonium, tabla, and hand clapping for the death anniversary celebration (*ʿurs*) of the Sufi saint Sayyid Muhammad Ibrahim, also known as Daud Bandagi Kirmani, in a courtyard belonging to the saint's family. Shergarh, Okara district, Punjab, 1997. Photo by Richard Wolf.

orthodox Islam in their outward form—as symbols of the mystic state. Wine is the catalyst that brings about the meeting of the mystic's soul and spiritual vision. Drunkenness is a metaphor for the ecstasy excited by divine love, and refers to a figurative drunkenness, a condition reached through ecstatic experience that enables the Sufi male, in the context of the *mehfil-e samāʿ* gathering, to discover a hidden dimension beyond his normal habits of thought. The cupbearer (*sāqī*) brings the wine of love and symbolizes the guide or teacher who leads the mystic to the drink of divine knowledge. The tavern refers to the heart of the mystic, or to the Sufi meeting place, a dwelling place of love. Intoxicated ones, those who are *mast* 'drunk', are lovers of God who have a vision of the Beloved, the Divine. Sufi poetry may appear to be profane to the uninitiated, but it embodies sacred meaning to those who understand.

The meaning of the song text is paramount, but it cannot be called qawwali until it is clothed in music performed by solo vocalists, a chorus of clapping singers, and harmonium (a small, portable hand-pumped organ) and drum accompaniment (figure 1). The traditional qawwali group is all male. The lead soloist selects the song verses, determines which lines the chorus should repeat or support, which themes or imagery to invoke, and most important, what textual or musical elements will communicate most effectively to the audience. According to popular belief, the qawwali style developed in the thirteenth century and is attributed to the great poet and musician Amir Khusrau (1244–1325), a disciple of the Sufi saint Nizamuddin Auliya, who was a luminary of the Chishti order of Sufis.

After a brief melodic introduction, the soloist intones the first lines of a poem in free rhythm. When the soloist arrives at a line of text to be emphasized, the chorus and rhythm instruments enter, adding strong rhythmic accents to the textual phrase, punctuating it with hand clapping and drumbeats. The elements of repetition, rhythmic beats, volume, and tempo build to a climax that totally envelops the listener and transports him to another plane. In this manner, qawwali generates spiritual arousal and conveys the message of the poetry. Qawwāl singers are responsible for setting the poems to music, establishing a mood appropriate for encouraging the intoxication of the listener, and ultimately leading the listener into an ecstatic trance. Then, having done so, they also have the responsibility of bringing the listener back gradually, by degrees, from the internal world to the external world.

The following text is a famous Sufi hymn (*qaul*) by Amir Khusrau. The first two lines constitute the Arabic *qaul*; the following lines, in Persian, are thought to symbolize the spiritual succession in Sufism as instituted by the Prophet Muhammad (Qureshi 1986:21):

Man kunto Maula	Whoever accepts me as master
Fā Alī-un-Maulā	Ali is his master too
Dar dil dar dil dar dānī	
Ham tum tānānā nānā tānānānā rī	
Yālalī yālalī yālā yālā rī	
Yālalalī yālalalī yālā yālā rī	

Among the best-known qawwali singers in Pakistan are the Sabri Brothers and the late Nusrat Fateh Ali Khan. The Sabri Brothers first introduced qawwali to American audiences in 1975. Until his untimely death in 1997, Nusrat Fateh Ali Khan was unquestionably the most famous Qawwāl in the world. He was instrumental in bringing this traditional, devotional genre to the attention of world popular-music audiences. As popular as they were, Nusrat's songs, including those in film sound tracks such as *The Last Temptation of Christ* and *Dead Man Walking*, nevertheless retained the element of spirituality.

Kāfī

Kāfī is a generic term for a mystic song, based on regional folk melodies, that contains references to heroes and heroines of regional romances. Typically, the heroine in these well-known and beloved tales becomes the symbol for the soul seeking union with the eternal Beloved. The songs symbolize the different facets of the mystical life and appeal to the general population. As a poetic form, *kāfī* is said to be inspired by the Arabic *qaṣīda*, an ode with a monorhyme at the end of each verse. The first and/or second text line serve as the refrain. The major Sufi poets of Punjab and Sindh used the *kāfī* form to relate to the common people. On a broader scale, the term *kāfī* became associated with a musical mode recognized in the Hindustani raga system. In Pakistan, however, singers perform *kāfī* songs in any musical mode. Some famous Sufi composers of *kāfī* are the poet-saints Sheikh Fariduddin Masud Ganj-i Shakar, Shah Husain, Bulleh Shah, Shah Abdul Latif, and Sachal Sarmast (see below).

True to its folk roots, *kāfī* is not associated with any particular musical style except in the sense that it is generally sung solo. Two contemporary solo *kāfī* singers are Pathana Khan and Abida Parveen. Pathana Khan uses harmonium, *sāraṅgī* 'bowed fiddle', and tabla accompaniment, a texture associated with the classical Hindustani tradition. Abida Parveen's ensemble includes a number of folk drums and percussion besides the harmonium and keyboard. Perhaps the best-known exponent of Shah Abdul Latif's *kāfī* songs was the late Ustad Manzoor Ali Khan, who sang them according to the *sur* (raga) specified by the saint himself.

Kāfī is generally recognized as the most popular form of music in Sindh. The Sindhi dervish (*faqīr*) sings *kāfī* while simultaneously dancing and accompanying himself on the *yaktāro* 'one- or two-stringed, plucked lute' and *chappar* 'wooden clappers'. A group of dervishes sing, dance, and play instruments in chorus, in what is called the *soung* (Sindhi, literally 'together') tradition. Such devotional song performances dedicated to the *murshid* 'Sufi guide or teacher' take place in his presence or at his *dargāh* 'court'.

A form related to the *kāfī* in Sindh is the *waī* of Shah Abdul Latif. A chorus of singers chants lyrical poems or couplets with a rhyming refrain, accompanied only by the *damboro* 'long-necked plucked lute' adopted by Shah Abdul Latif.

MOVEMENT AND DANCE EXPRESSIONS

Orthodox Islam frowns on dance and music in secular contexts, but the Sufis use such bodily response or expression as a mystical form of devotional experience. An eleventh-century Sufi, Ali ibn ʿUthman al-Jullabi al-Hujwiri, wrote (al-Hujwiri 1911:416):

> You must know that dancing (*raqṣ*) has no foundation either in the religious law (of Islam) or in the path (of Sufism), . . . but when the heart throbs with exhilaration and rapture becomes intense and the agitation of ecstasy is manifested and conventional forms are gone, that agitation is neither dancing nor foot-play nor bodily indulgence, but a dissolution of the soul. Those who call it "dancing" are utterly wrong. It is a state that cannot be explained in words: "without experience, no knowledge."

Dhamal

In Sindh, the folk dance called *dhamal* is associated with the mystic dance of the dervishes. One of the most popular Sufi saints of Pakistan, Lal Shahbaz Qalandar, is said to have practiced this mystic dance, a whirling, circling dance. Lal Shahbaz Qalandar was a thirteenth-century dervish referred to as *mast qalandar* 'the spiritually intoxicated *qalandar*'. A *qalandar* is one who is free from social and customary inhibitions and taboos, who lives a life of detachment from the world, entirely absorbed in the contemplation of the Divine. Today, thousands of pilgrims visit Lal Shahbaz's shrine in Sehwan Sharif, located in Sindh, to dance to the beat of the large ritual drums and reach the ecstatic state of their saint.

Zikr

Zikr 'remembrance of God' is formal mystical worship. Each Sufi order has an established pattern of meditation centering on this devotional practice. Some orders use it as a method of achieving ecstasy. Techniques for achieving an ecstatic state include prescribed breathing and postures as well as the repetition of formulaic phrases.

Chogān

Chogān is the spiritual music and dance of the Zikri sect of Islam, to which many Makrani Balochis of coastal Balochistan belong. The name of their ritual practice derives from the sacred space or open ground where they perform, known as *chogān* 'plain, field'.

MUSIC AT SHRINES

Musical life in Pakistan centers around the numerous shrines of Sufi saints. Musicians play on the grounds of local shrines on a daily basis, dependent on alms given to them by visitors to the shrines. The number of musicians increases on Thursday evenings and Fridays, as general attendance increases on the Muslim day of prayer. However, on the occasion of the saint's death anniversary, *ʿurs* (literally 'wedding', signifying a saint's union with God), the shrine turns into a busy fairground, bursting with pilgrims. There are stalls selling books, toys, bangles, and food; informal arenas (circles) of musical performance; and even areas for carnival rides and sideshows. These are occasions for the whole family, with important social as well as religious functions. And during these occasions, regional musicians have an opportunity to perform, listen to each other, exchange ideas, and earn some money.

Data Ganj Bakhsh

Data Ganj Bakhsh, the patron saint of Lahore, is the popular name of the eleventh-century Sufi Ali ibn ʿUthman al-Jullabi al-Hujwiri, who wrote the celebrated Persian treatise on Sufism, *Kashf al-Mahjub*. He spent the last years of his life in Lahore and is buried there. Its citizens revere him, and the city of Lahore has declared the anniversary of his death an official holiday. During this time, the shrine's kitchen is exceptionally busy feeding the thousands of pilgrims and dervishes who visit the shrine. Farmers from throughout the region bring great vats of milk; it is blessed and distributed to everyone. Groups of young men march in procession, carrying a large *chādar* 'cloth sheet' used to cover the saint's tomb as an offering. *Ḍholi* drummers playing large double-headed drums (*ḍhol*) accompany them, along with groups of men who dance all the way to the shrine.

The Data Ganj Bakhsh *ʿurs* consists of activities in and around the shrine as well as the *mehfil-e samāʿ* 'Sufi gathering for listening to qawwali', which has become the largest gathering of qawwal singers in Pakistan and possibly in the Indian subcontinent. Since 1965, a group of Lahore citizens has organized the gathering with the purpose of propagating spiritual music in their city. During the festival, hundreds of qawwali groups gather to participate. They come out of devotion for the saint, as well as for the money they often collect from the assembled Sufis, who shower them with such offerings when spiritually moved or inspired. This two-day, two-night gathering took place on grounds adjacent to the shrine until 1992, when the grounds were torn up to accommodate a large shopping mall. Since that time, the *mehfil-e samāʿ* has taken place on the grounds of a nearby boys' school. The organization of the gathering by a citizen's committee, rather than by the traditional descendants and keepers of the shrine, and the removal of this event from space adjacent to the shrine are just two of several factors that are contributing to a secularization of qawwali at the Data Ganj Bakhsh shrine.

Sheikh Fariduddin Masud Ganj-i Shakar

Sheikh Fariduddin Masud Ganj-i Shakar (1175–1265) is one of the most revered Sufi saints of South Asia. He established a principal seat of spiritual authority in Pakpattan (formerly Ajodhan), Punjab. Sheikh Farid was the spiritual guide of the renowned Sheikh Nizamuddin Auliya of Delhi, who became a leader within the Chishti order of Sufis and in turn the spiritual guide and teacher of Amir Khusrau. Like most South Asian mystics, Sheikh Farid was a scholar and a poet; he is credited with the early development of the Urdu language.

Sheikh Farid is said to have believed in the power of spiritual music (*samāʿ*) to move the hearts of listeners and stoke the fire of love in their hearts; he himself often danced in a state of ecstasy. His death anniversary is among the most important occasions for religious musical performance (figure 2), especially qawwali, because many qawwal singers attend as an act of devotion or as an offering. Qawwali performances take place on occasions such as *kacherī* 'court, assembly' in the presence of the official successor to the shrine (*dīvān*), *hāzerī* 'presence, attendance' at the shrine in front of the saint's tomb (*darbār*), and gatherings at other tombs of devotees buried in proximity to Sheikh Farid's tomb and shrine.

All Pakistanis embrace Bulleh Shah as a poet of the people who used images from Punjabi folklore and made symbolic references to local Punjabi customs and rituals.

FIGURE 2 Professional musicians play *ḍhol*, double-reed *śahnāī*, and *baghalbīn* bagpipe in a street beside the shrine of Sheikh Fariduddin Masud Ganj-i Shakar, Pakpattan, 1997. Photo by Richard Wolf.

Bulleh Shah

Bulleh Shah (1680–1758) is recognized as one of the greatest Sufi poets of Punjab. All Pakistanis embrace him as a poet of the people who used images from Punjabi folklore (particularly the Punjabi romance *Hīr Ranjha*) and made symbolic references to local Punjabi customs and rituals. He is known for his heterodox views, but his verses (*kāfī*) are nevertheless favorite inclusions in qawwali texts. The following lines appear in the qawwali "*Mā jogi de nal*," based on *Hīr Ranjha*. (Ranjha—a member of the Ranjha tribe—becomes a herdsman and the lover of Hir, daughter of the headman of the Sials.) Hir, who represents the devotee's love and devotion for the Beloved, expresses the poem's message. In his poem, Bulleh Shah uses both Hindu and Muslim imagery. (The qawwali text is from a performance by Nusrat Fateh Ali Khan and his party, Lahore, 1991; translation by Adam Nayyar.)

jadō di mā jogi di hoi,	Ever since I became the jogi's,
jadō di mā jogi di hoi	Ever since I became the jogi's,
mā vic mā mā rā gayi koi	no "I" has remained in me.
jogi mere nal nal, mā jogi de nal nal	The jogi is close to me, I am close to the jogi
ranjha jogi, mā jogyani	Ranjha is a jogi, I am a jogini,
ranjha jogi, mā jogyani,	Ranjha is a jogi, I am a jogini
is di khatir bhar sa pāni	for him I will fill water
jogi mere nal nal, mā jogi de nal nal	The jogi is close to me, I am close to the jogi

e ranjha ranjha kardi ni mā ape ranjha hoi ni sadio ni mānu tido	Oh, saying "Ranjha, Ranjha," I became Ranjha myself
ranjha, hir nā akho koi mā nahī o ap ha apni, ap kare diljoi jis de nal mā nyuṅ lagaya, jis de nal mā nyuṅ lagaya ohde vargi hoi	Call me Dhido Ranjha, no one should call me Hir It is not me, it is oneself that one tries to please
sayio, jogi mere nal nal, mā jogi de nal nal ahe, ni mā jana jogi de nal, kani mundrā pa ke e, kani mundrā pa ke mathe tilak laga ke ni mā jana jogi de nal, kani mundrā pa ke	Girlfriends, the jogi is close to me, I am close to the jogi Oh, I will go with the jogi, with earrings in my ears with earrings in my ears and a mark on my forehead Oh, I will go with the jogi, with earrings in my ears
ni, e jogi naī, koi rup ha rab da e jogi naī, koi rup ha rab da pes jogi da is nu bhabda is jogi mera man vic vasya sac akhā mā qasm quran e, jogi mera din iman e is jogi mānū kita rogi ni mā is jogi, ni mā is jogi, hun hor nā jogi	This is not a jogi, it is some manifestation of God The disguise of the jogi looks good on him This jogi tightened my hair This jogi settled in my heart I tell the truth, I swear by the Qur'ān The jogi is my religion, my faith This jogi has made me a sufferer I want this jogi, I want this jogi, now there is no other jogi
ni mā jana jogi de nal, kani mundrā pa ke kani mundrā pa ke, ni ma jana jogi de nal	Oh, I will go with the jogi, with earrings in my ears With earrings in my ears, oh, I will go with the jogi

Bulleh Shah was born in Uch, in Bahawalpur district, but moved to Kasur, Lahore District, where he lived until his death. Informal groups congregate to celebrate his death anniversary, both among the tombstones of the cemetery where he is buried as well as at Sufi gatherings, which include qawwali groups and soloists singing his verses.

Shah Abdul Latif

Undoubtedly the most famous and musically documented Sufi saint of Sindh is Shah Abdul Latif Bhitai (1690–1760). His poetry, known in the West through the works of scholars such as Herbert T. Sorley and Annemarie Schimmel, is based on the Qur'ān and the Prophetic traditions (*hadīth*) as well as the great mystical traditions of Persian poets. His rendering of these messages through the lips, emotions, and experiences of traditional Sindhi folk heroines made his poetry both accessible to and popular among the common people.

One of Shah Abdul Latif's favorite heroines was Sasui, of the romance *Sasui Punhun*. Punhun accompanies a camel caravan from Kech to Bhambhor, where he falls in love with Sasui. Punhun's father sends his other sons to bring Punhun back by force, and at night they kidnap him and return to Kech. In the morning Sasui finds her lover and his camels gone. In despair, she sets out on foot to track the camels. She endures great hardships and finally perishes while wandering the sandy deserts and barren mountains in search of her lover (Sorley 1940:366–367).

O mountain, you brought me grief.
I shall tell my friend when we greet.
There was terror at morning time
In your twists and turn deceit.
No boon did you work for me
Losing tracks of my loved one's feet.

O mountain, first to my friend
Shall I heap up your name with scorn:
How my feet were crushed by the stones,
How my soles to ribbons were torn.
Not a thought for me, not a jot
Of rue in your heart was borne.

"Tis the mountain that brings me woe,"
This my cry to heaven will soar.
O mountain, torture me not,
I have suffered much before.
No joy do I call to mind:
I remember of grief full store.

O mountain, on suffering ones
Should solace and help descend,
And largesse of sympathy come
To them who have lost their friend.
Then why, O stone, to their feet
Is it torture you extend?

O mountain, stricken forlorn
Folk come to tell you their woe.
To them who are broken and bruised
Should heartening solace flow.

They sit together, together they weep,
Afflicted woman and mountain steep,
To none telling aught of the flames
That within their hearts are aglow.

This poem comes from *Shah Jo Risalo*, a compendium of Shah's poetry, meant to be sung with musical accompaniment. Not all the poems included in the *Risalo* can be attributed to Shah Abdul Latif, nor are all his verses represented in the collection. The *Risalo* poems are arranged in twenty-nine chapters. Each chapter indicates a musical mode or raga (*sur*, literally 'tone, pitch') in which to sing the verses, and/or a mood or theme appropriate to the poem. Many musical modes are variants of Hindustani ragas, while others are based on local tunes. The verses from *Sasui*

Punhun quoted above come from the "kohiari" *sur*, a melody or melodic mode from the mountains.

The renowned Sindhi scholar Dr. N. A. Baloch has undertaken a ten-volume edition of *Shah Jo Risalo*. Volume 1, published by the Shah Abdul Latif Cultural Centre Committee in 1989, contains two chapters, *Sur Kalyān* and *Sur Yaman*. Volumes 2 through 7 include the other musical modes, making a total of twenty-nine. The remaining volumes include poetry by other poets, an epilogue, and indices.

Shah Abdul Latif adopted the *damboro* 'long-necked plucked lute' as an accompanying drone instrument for his sung poetry. A chorus of five or six followers devoted to the music of Shah Abdul Latif continue the tradition of singing songs from the *Risalo*. Every Thursday night and on other significant occasions such as the anniversary of Shah Abdul Latif's death, they sing in front of his shrine in unison or in octaves, each playing a *damboro*.

Shah Abdul Latif's death anniversary is celebrated with great fervor by the government and people of Sindh. The event includes speeches by Sindhi politicians, scholars, and representatives of the shrine at Bhitshah, literary conferences, wrestling tournaments (*malakhro*), carnival sideshows, and musical performances. The occasion attracts thousands of pilgrims who wish to remember this great Sufi saint and Sindhi poet and to celebrate their Sindhi culture.

Sachal Sarmast

Sachal Sarmast (1739–1826) is another beloved Sindhi poet-saint, one who followed in the footsteps of Shah Abdul Latif. His best-known poetry, created to be sung, consists of amatory/spiritual couplets (*kāfī*) in Arabic, Sindhi, Saraiki, Hindi, Punjabi, Urdu, and Persian; the following is a translation of a Sindhi text (Abbasi 1989:81):

> One wanton touch of the Beloved
> Has put me off my sense
> No longer care I for a fast
> Or for prayers have remembrance
> For wine I have ever fondness
> Whether it be night or day
> Be he a Mulla or a Kazi
> Cannot make me stay away

Sachal Sarmast's death anniversary celebration, like that of Shah Abdul Latif, takes place on the grounds of his shrine, in Daraza near the town of Ranipur in Khaipur District, Sindh. Each year followers reenact a turban-tying (crowning) ceremony of the official successor to the shrine (*sajjāda nashīn*). Throughout the ceremony, a group of Sindhi folk musicians called *faqīr* 'religious mendicants or dervishes' sing Sachal's verses and dance to the accompaniment of a *yaktāro* 'one- or two-stringed, plucked spiked lute' outside the shrine successor's home. After a private ceremony inside, during which the turban is tied around his head, his ardent followers lead him on a walk to the marble throne (*takht*), accompanied by musicians. The successor then visits the tombs of the saint and of his own family ancestors before returning home, again accompanied by the musicians and followers. Elsewhere on the shrine grounds, informal groups of musicians gather to play for each other and for the pilgrims, who have set up temporary camps.

Lal Shahbaz Qalandar

Uthman Marwandi (d. 1274), the thirteenth-century saint better known as Lal Shahbaz Qalandar, came from Marwand, Azerbaijan. He traveled widely with three

Lal Shahbaz Qalander is the most popular of all Sufi saints. Mystical songs heard throughout Pakistan invoke his name.

friends before finally settling in Sehwan, Sindh. He is the most popular of all Sufi saints, and his adopted name, Lal Shahbaz 'red royal falcon', derives from the color of the robe he always wore and from his soaring spiritual flights. Qalandar refers to a wandering mystic. Mystical songs heard throughout Pakistan invoke his name; the song "Mast qalandar," referring to him in his spiritually intoxicated state, was popularized on television and in film. He is also known as Jhule Lal 'red bridegroom', a reference to his failed attempt to marry a friend's daughter. This friend, Sheikh Bahauddin Zakariyya, promised Lal Shahbaz Qalandar his daughter's hand, but the sheikh died before the marriage could take place. According to popular belief, Lal Shahbaz Qalandar subsequently died of grief and disappointment when the sheikh's son refused to allow the marriage. The singers Nusrat Fateh Ali Khan and Michael Brook popularized this song among "world music" audiences during the 1990s (Sakata 1994:91; translation by Adam Nayyar):

dam mast qalandar mast mast	Breath enraptured *mast qalandar,* intoxicated, intoxicated,
mera vird hai dam dam ʿalī ʿalī	My refrain with every breath is Ali Ali
sakhi lāl qalandar mast mast	Generous red *qalandar,* intoxicated intoxicated
jhule lāl qalandar mast mast	Bridegroom red *qalandar,* intoxicated, intoxicated
ākhi jā malangā tū ʿalī ʿalī ʿalī ʿalī	O *malang,* keep on saying Ali Ali Ali Ali
ākhi jā malangā sach āpi man laiṇ ge	O *malang,* keep on saying the truth, they themselves will believe
āj naī te kal sāre ʿalī ʿalī kaiṇ ge	If not today, then tomorrow, all will say Ali Ali
mast, mast, mast, mast	Intoxicated, intoxicated, intoxicated, intoxicated

Lal Shahbaz Qalandar is said to have practiced *dhamal*, the mystical circling, twirling dance related to that of the Mevlevi Whirling Dervishes. To this day, musicians play large kettledrums (*bher*) in the courtyard of Lal Shahbaz Qalandar's tomb, and dervishes practice *dhamal* every evening after sunset prayers. Many visitors to the shrine, both men and women, dance to the drumbeats to the point of trance. The men, with arms raised, dance in place; the women toss their heads, letting their loose hair flow freely, while a few thrash about and roll on the floor in complete abandon.

Lal Shahbaz Qalandar's death-anniversary celebration comprises two main ceremonies commemorating the saint's life: the *dhamal* and the *mehṅdī* 'henna'. Each morning, assemblies of dervishes representing dervish hostels attached to the holy shrine gather at the shrine's main gate to dance the *dhamal* in turn. Each afternoon or evening, followers process to the shrine to the accompaniment of music, bringing *mehṅdī*, a symbol of Lal Shahbaz Qalandar as the bridegroom.

The Zikri pilgrimage to Torbat

A majority of the Makrani Balochis in Pakistan belong to the Zikri sect of Islam. The sect takes its name from the practice of *zikr*, or remembering God with short, repeated invocations. The Zikris make an annual pilgrimage to Koh-i Murad, their sacred mountain in Torbat, the administrative center of Makran District, where the sect's founder spent much of his time. Thousands of Zikris gather for this three-day event, during which they trek to the top of Koh-i Murad and offer short prayers. The actual *zikr* 'remembrance' ritual involves spiritual music and dance performance, which takes its name from the performance grounds (*chogān*) in front of the men's place of worship.

A singer leads the *chogān* singing words of praise. A group of men answer the leader with short, stock phrases while doing a dance of prescribed ritual movements. The tempo of the singing and dancing gradually builds up to a climax, leading some participants to a state of spiritual exaltation. Only men participate in the *chogān* dance, forming a large circle on the *chogān* grounds. The lead singer, standing in the center, has a good knowledge of the *chogān* repertoire and a strong voice. For as long as anyone can remember, the top lead singer has been a woman. The unquestioned leadership, authority, knowledge, and respect accorded to her during the pilgrimage stay with her and are carried into the community. For the Zikris, *chogān* is a symbol of their faith and a central communal ritual, performed at significant events in their lives [see BALOCHISTAN, figure 3].

The shrines discussed in this article are just a few of the well-known shrines of Pakistan. Literally scores of other shrines and sacred places play host to regional music, musicians, and dancers. It is here in the presence of the great spiritual leaders of Pakistan that all musical activities take on a devotional aspect that cannot easily be separated or distinguished from the secular cultural activities of people's daily lives.

REFERENCES

Abbasi, Muhammad Yusuf. 1992. *Pakistani Culture: A Profile*. Islamabad: National Institute of Historical and Cultural Research.

Abbasi, Tanveer, ed. 1989. *Sachal Sarmast*. Khairpur, Sindh: Sachal Chair, Shah Abdul Latif University.

al-Hujwiri, Ali ibn ʿUthman al-Jullabi. 1990 [1911]. *The Kashf al-Mahjub*, trans. Reynold A. Nicholson. Karachi: Darul Ishaat.

Baloch, Inayatullah. 1996. "Islam, the State, and Identity: The Zikris of Balochistan." In *Marginality and Modernity: Ethnicity and Change in Post-Colonial Balochistan*, ed. Paul Titus, 223–249. Karachi: Oxford University Press.

Baloch, N. A. 1973. *Development of Music in Sindh*. Hyderabad: Sindh University Press.

———. 1989–. *Shah Jo Risalo: A Critical Edition of the Text with a Comprehensive Introduction*. 10 vols. in Sindhi, with an introduction in English. Bhitshah, Sindh: Shah Abdul Latif Cultural Centre Committee.

Nizami, Khaliq Ahmad. 1973 [1955]. *The Life and Times of Shaikh Farid-u'd-din Ganj-i-Shakar*. Delhi: Idarah-i Adabiyat-i Delli.

Puri, J. R., and Tilaka R. Shangari. 1986. *Bulleh Shah: The Love-Intoxicated Iconoclast*. Amritsar: Radha Soami Satsang Beas.

Qazi, N. B. G. 1971. *Lal Shahbaz Qalandar*. Lahore: Ishfaq Ahmed.

Qureshi, Regula B. 1986. *Sufi Music of India and Pakistan: Sound, Context and Meaning in Qawwali*. Cambridge: Cambridge University Press.

Sakata, Hiromi Lorraine. 1994. "The Sacred and the Profane: Qawwali Represented in the Performances of Nusrat Fateh Ali Khan." *The World of Music* 36(3):86–99.

Schimmel, Annemarie. 1975. *Mystical Dimensions of Islam*. Chapel Hill: University of North Carolina Press.

Sorley, Herbert T. 1966 [1940]. *Shah Abdul Latif of Bhit: His Poetry, Life and Times*. Karachi: Oxford University Press.

Yusuf, Zohra, ed. 1988. *Rhythms of the Lower Indus: Perspectives on the Music of Sindh*. Karachi: Department of Culture and Tourism, Government of Sindh.

Punjab

Adam Nayyar

The Punjab is located at the crossroads of high cultures (Indian, Central Asian, and Iranian) and world religions (Hinduism and Islam). It is part of South Asia, yet its name, meaning "land of the five waters" (Farsi *panj* 'five', *āb* 'water'), is of Iranian origin. Its musical culture is the product of synthesis and assimilation in both repertoire and instrumentation.

The creation of the state of Pakistan in 1947 led to the traumatic division of the Punjab into Indian East Punjab and Pakistani West Punjab. In the massive exchange of population between the two halves, hundreds of Muslim musicians from East Punjab crossed over into the west. These musicians had traditionally been performers of Sikh religious music, and their departure was certainly a loss to the eastern section, but their arrival in the west resulted in the enrichment of the west's musical traditions. The family of Nusrat Fateh Ali Khan, for example, was among them; indeed, at that time, most of the classical musicians in the eastern half migrated to West Punjab.

The musical traditions of the Punjab in Pakistan today reflect the region's ethnic diversity. The majority of musicians belong to generally low-status occupational groups that pass on musical skills from one generation to the next. Apart from these, other individuals or groups who are willing to accept low social status voluntarily choose to learn and perform music. The occupational and regional variations in the status and role of musicians is wide: the spectrum traditionally ranges from the stigma and ambivalence associated with professional musicians to a positive role afforded amateur musicians.

INSTRUMENTS

Instrumentation in the Punjab generally follows the North Indian pattern and need not be described in detail here: preeminent are the tabla, sitar, sarod, and *sāraṅgī* 'bowed fiddle'. As elsewhere in South Asia, the ubiquitous harmonium is indigenized and manufactured in the Punjabi city of Gujranwala. The clarinet has also been integrated into the local musical context.

Certain instruments are common in rural Punjab: the *cimṭā*, a large pair of fire tongs played by slapping the tongs together with the right hand and striking the body of the instrument with a heavy iron ring attached at the end, held in the left

FIGURE 1 *Ḍhol* players and dancers at the death anniversary celebration (*ʿurs*) of the Sufi saint Sayyid Muhammad Ibrahim, also known as Daud Bandagi Kirmani, in Shergarh, Okara district, Punjab. 1997. Photo by Richard Wolf.

hand; the *king*, a two-stringed plucked lute; the *joṛi*, a pair of identical rosewood or cane duct flutes with five holes and no thumb hole, connected to one mouthpiece; and the *ḍhol*, a double-headed drum made from the trunk of a mango tree covered with goatskin stretched on mulberry switches, to which brass rings are attached for tension by a rope running through them (figure 1).

MUSICIANS

Professional musicians

Professional musicians belong to one of several endogamous groups that are ranked hierarchically according to their performance context and sophistication of repertoire. By far the largest and most important group is the Mīrāsī, hereditary musicians who refer to themselves as Kasbi, a Persian word meaning "one who works" (figure 2). The Mīrāsī refer to all nonhereditary musicians as Atai, an Arabic word meaning "to whom it is given."

Musicians, like other service-provider groups of the Punjab, are usually organized into endogamous patrilineal units within the traditional client-patron system. This *sēpi* system, by which clients provide goods and services to patrons, corresponds to the *jajmānī* system generally characteristic of South Asia. The status of all occupational groups not subsisting from agricultural activity is low. However, the role of the professional musician within the hierarchical South Asian caste system is unusual, for unlike other low-caste occupations, the musician does not deal directly with material culture. The shoemaker, the potter, the weaver, the carpenter, and the blacksmith all provide material services, whereas the professional musician provides services that take the less tangible form of music.

Mīrāsī: The core of Punjabi music

"You can recognize a true Mīrāsī by his black-bordered tongue." This saying from Mīrāsī lore means that the hereditary (male) musician's blessings and curses are equally effective.

The origins of the Mīrāsī are unknown. They claim to be an offshoot of the Quraysh, the tribe of the Prophet Muhammad, and to have come to the Punjab with the invading armies of Islam. As proof, they point out that their name is of Arabic origin: the term *mīrāsī* comes from the Arabic root for "inheritance," *miras*, and

FIGURE 2 Mīrāsī musicians from Multan play *śahnāī* and *naqqārā* at the Lok Virsa Festival, Islamabad, 1997. Photo by Richard Wolf.

relates to the professional male musician's traditional role of genealogist for the different kin groups living in the small universe of a village. It is the ancestral task of the Mīrāsī to commit to memory the names of previous generations, and the notable deeds of his patron's ancestors. The Mīrāsī enjoy the patronage of wealthy rural families, but also provide services to the common peasantry. As genealogists, they are summoned or appear by themselves at the birth of a son, to chant or sing about the infant's forefathers. They must enumerate the names of at least seven ancestors of the infant. If a shortage of noteworthy deeds exists, they often embellish mundane events to transform them into heroic deeds. In addition, in their capacity as musicians, they perform at fairs, rituals, and other festive occasions.

Despite their low status, the Mīrāsī have a ready wit. This ability, combined with their knowledge of the deeds of previous generations, arouses fear at the highest levels of the village hierarchy. Thus not only does the Mīrāsī know if the patron's ancestor was a train robber or a cattle thief, he also possesses a sense of humor that may render the patron open to ridicule. If a Mīrāsī makes a joke or remark that ridicules influential villagers, the entire concept of "face" or honor is endangered. Consequently, although the Mīrāsī is always obsequious to the point of servility in the presence of men of influence, the latter are very careful in dealing with him. The Mīrāsī on the one hand can risk punishment or even ejection from the village by making an influential farmer the target of his wit; on the other hand, taking offense at a person of such insignificant and obviously low status to the point of punishing him would make an honorable farmer look even more ridiculous. This forces the farmer to take a more tolerant approach and permit the Mīrāsī a degree of freedom not normally accorded other occupational groups of similar standing.

Among themselves, the Mīrāsī have evolved a private language of their own, rendering their conversation in public unintelligible to outsiders. They garble normal speech either by interspersing extra consonants or by attaching the last vowel of a word to its beginning. This ensures the transfer of secret or sensitive information publicly without danger of retribution. An atmosphere of external humor and internal fear and apprehension results, which is greatly conducive to a certain kind of high creativity. In this way, the safe expression of normally sensitive content is permitted in a ritualized setting.

Bhāṅḍ

Also known as Nakkāl (mimic), the Bhāṅḍ are Mīrāsī subgroups specializing in buffoonery and mimicry. They usually work in pairs and carry a large tanned leather clapper to accent their actions and jokes. Irreverent humor ranging from the political to the sexual marks the Bhāṅḍ, who strictly speaking are not performing musicians, even though they belong to the largest musician group of the Punjab.

Rās Dhāria

Another Mīrāsī group is the Rās Dhāria, which stages plays in villages after dark by the light of hurricane lamps (with glass chimneys) and torches. Their repertoire comprises mostly dramatic renderings of traditional folktales interspersed with songs, to the accompaniment of the shaken metal tongs (*cimṭā*).

Qawwāl

The Qawwāl are musicians of Mīrāsī background who sing only devotional songs at Sufi shrines throughout the Punjab (figure 3). The Qawwāl perform in groups of usually twelve male singers sitting six abreast in two rows, with the lead singers in the front row. The leader of the group (*mohri*) has a strong voice, supplemented by one or two chorus leaders (*āvāzia*) chosen for their sweet and melodious voices. Behind them in the second row is the tabla player, who plays the large qawwali tabla with wholemeal dough (*āṭā*) plastered on the left bass drum to make it louder and more resonant. The remaining performers comprise the chorus, and clap regularly in unison.

All Qawwāl emphasize that they harness the music in the service of the text, which renders their status higher than that of a Mīrāsī. Their lead singers are virtually always drawn from Mīrāsī groups, although they sometimes disavow linkage. The religious nature of their performance gives them slightly more prestige than Mīrāsī. Furthermore, the Qawwāl no longer work as genealogists, unlike the mainstream Mīrāsī musicians. The Qawwāl profess to emphasize not the music but the delivery of a Sufi message, based on the poetry of Muslim Sufi and Hindu bhakti masters in

FIGURE 3 The Muhammad Akram Arif qawwali party performing at the death anniversary celebration (*ʿurs*) of the Sufi saint Sayyid Muhammad Ibrahim, also known as Daud Bandagi Kirmani, in a courtyard belonging to the saint's family. Shergarh, Okara District, Punjab, 1997. Photo by Richard Wolf.

Between popular singers and high art-music vocalists are the singers of ghazal, a form of romantic love poetry introduced into the Punjab from Iran.

Arabic, Farsi, Punjabi, Purbi, and Urdu. The Qawwāl of the Punjab claim a musical tradition different from their counterparts further to the east, calling theirs the Punjabi *aṅg* 'style'. It is this particular style that put qawwali on the world music map through the performances of the late Nusrat Fateh Ali Khan.

Ghazalgoh

Between popular singers and high art-music vocalists are the singers of ghazal, a form of romantic love poetry introduced into the Punjab from Iran. Originally sung in Farsi, ghazal lyrics today are mainly in Urdu and Punjabi. Classified as semiclassical (*nīmklasīki*), this form of singing emphasizes the supremacy of the text. The music is considered to be subservient to the text, but must follow the rules of classical rendition. Ghazal singers (*ghazalgoh*) also sing other lighter forms of art music, such as the *ṭhumrī* and *dādrā*. Women are prominent among musicians of this art; two of the most highly regarded women ghazal singers of the Punjab today are Farida Khanum and Iqbal Bano. Together with the two leading male singers of ghazal, Mehdi Hasan and Ghulam Ali, they are the best-known living singers of this genre.

Gavayyā *and* sāzindā

Vocal art music follows the North Indian classical tradition. Both male and female singers (*gavayyā*) enjoy a high degree of respect among both musicians and their clientele, the urban and rural elite. Accompanying male instrumentalists (*sāzindā*) well versed in classical music are also respected, though they play a secondary role. The only instrumentalist considered on the same level as the singer is the sitar player (*sitār navāz*) or sarod player (*sarod navāz*). A master of either classical singing or sitar playing receives the Central Asian title of *khān* 'lord' or the Persian title of *ustād* 'teacher'. Even if such a person belongs to a Mīrāsī kin group (and most of them do), his virtuosity gives him respect and honor in society. Such masters usually belong to a hereditary school of classical music referred to as a *gharānā* 'house'. One universally accepted master leads each school, and the title of *khān* or *ustād* is hereditary if the master's offspring or close blood relatives achieve a high level of musical excellence. In former times such titles were reserved for singers, and sitar and sarod players (figure 4), but in recent times they have also been accorded to other instrumentalists who play classical music.

Non-Mīrāsī musicians

Bhirāīṅ

Close to the Mīrāsī yet different in status and role are the Bhirāīṅ, who are basically drummers. The Bhirāīṅ claim to be Mīrāsī, yet Mīrāsī groups reject the claim, considering themselves superior to the Bhirāīṅ. According to common belief, the Bhirāīṅ are also physically stronger and more robust than the delicately built Mīrāsī. The

FIGURE 4 Contemporary musicians within the traditional stylistic schools of classical music (*gharānā*) in the Punjab.

Name	Gharānā/Relationship	City
Vocalists (gavayyā)		
	SHAM CHAURASI *GHARĀNĀ*	
Salamat Ali Khan	Sham Chaurasi	Islamabad; U.S.A.
Sharafat Ali Khan	Elder son	
Shafqat Ali Khan	Younger son	
Zakir Ali Khan	Younger brother	Lahore
Badar uz Zaman, Qamar uz Zaman	Brothers, students of Niaz Hussain Shami	Lahore
Ghulam Shabbir Khan, Ghulam Jafar Khan	Brothers, students of Niaz Hussain Shami	
Riaz Ali, Imtiaz Ali	Brothers, students of Niaz Hussain Shami	
Rafaqat Ali Khan	Son of the late Nazakat Ali Khan	
	PATIALA *GHARĀNĀ*	
Fateh Ali Khan	Patiala	Lahore
Rustam Fateh Ali	Elder son	
Sultan Fateh Ali	Younger son	
Muhammad Ilyas Khan	Paternal first cousin	Karachi
Amir Ahmed Khan	Paternal first cousin	
Asad Amanat Ali Khan	Brother's son	Lahore
Hamid Ali Khan	Brother	
Rafaqat Ali Khan	Son of the late Nazakat Ali Khan	
	GWALIOR *GHARĀNĀ*	
Fateh Ali Khan	Gwalior	Hyderabad
Hameed Ali Khan	Elder brother	Hyderabad
Zafar Ali Khan	Paternal first cousin	Karachi
Ahmed Ali Khan, Rehmat Ali Khan	Brothers (not related to above family)	Karachi
	KAPURTHALA, TALVANDI, AND OTHER *GHARĀNĀ*	
Ghulam Hasan Shaggan, Qadir Ali Shaggan	Kapurthala/Gwalior	Lahore
Hafiz Khan, Afzal Khan	Talvandi Dhrupad	
Javad Ali, Fahim Ali	Students of Parvez Paras	
Munir Hussain Tawakkal	Son of Tawakkal Ali Khan	Bahawalpur
Ghulam Haider Khan	Son of Mando Khan	Lahore
Mahfuz Khokhar	Student of Sada Rang	Rawalpindi
Shahida Parvin	Daughter of Zahida Parvin	Lahore

(*continued*)

Bhirāīṅ play the large double-headed cylindrical drum (*ḍhol*) with great vitality at harvest, marriage, and other festivals, and also sing lullabies for infants to the deafening beat of the big drum. Apart from their musical activity, they are also agricultural workers, often helping with the harvest and functioning as sharecroppers. A Mīrāsī,

FIGURE 4 (*continued*) Contemporary musicians within the traditional stylistic schools of classical music (*gharānā*) in the Punjab.

Name	***Gharānā*/Relationship**	***City***
Instrumentalists (*sāzindā*)		
	Sitar	
Ashraf Sharif Khan	Son of Sharif Khan Punchvale	Lahore
Akhlaq Ahmed	Son of Imdad Hussain	Karachi
Nafis Ahmed	Son of Fateh Ali Khan	Rawalpindi
Ghulam Farid Nizami	Kirana *gharānā*	Islamabad
Rais Khan	Nephew of Vilayat Khan	Karachi
Muhammad Alam	None	Lahore
	Sāraṅgī 'bowed fiddle'	
Nazim Ali Khan		Lahore
Allah Rakha Khan		Rawalpindi
	Tabla	
Abdul Sattar Tari	Student of Shaukat Hussain Khan	U.S.A.; Lahore
Altaf Hussain "Tafu"		Lahore
Muhammad Ajmal	Student of Shaukat Hussain Khan	Islamabad
Muhammad Bashir		Karachi
Billah		Multan
	Bāṅsurī 'transverse flute'	
Salamat Hussain		Karachi
Babar Ali		Lahore
Arif Jafri		Islamabad
	Rubāb 'unfretted plucked lute'	
Bakhtiar Ahmed Khan		Peshawar
Mazhar Ali Khan	Rubabi	Lahore
	Sarod	
Asad Qizilbash		Islamabad
	Clarinet	
Sadiq Ali Khan Mando		Lahore
Sadiq Ali Khan		Faisalabad

in contrast, would not deign to do any professional work other than music. In the context of a commissioned performance, a Mīrāsī may play or sing with a Bhirāīṅ but would never marry one. Mīrāsī also spurn the Bhirāīṅ for using musical instruments for begging. The Bhirāīṅ directly and unashamedly solicit money for their performances, whereas the Mīrāsī are more subtle about it.

The Mīrāsī believe their repertoire is more sophisticated than that of the Bhirāīṅ, which gives them a feeling of superiority. The Bhirāīṅ, for example, play the *ḍhol*, which is relatively simple compared with the tabla played by the Mīrāsī, and the simple bowed fiddle (*choṭī sāraṅgī*), not the complex bowed *sāraṅgī* played by the Mīrāsī, which has both playing and sympathetic strings.

Perna

Among the diverse peripatetic groups of the Punjab are the Perna, who live in reed shelters at the periphery of villages and towns. Particularly well known are their itinerant female singers (*gaṛvivāliāṅ*) who use a small brass milk pot (*gaṛvi*) as an accompanying rhythm instrument. Perna women also allegedly work as casual prostitutes.

Qalandar

Another peripatetic group in the Punjab are the Qalandar, village entertainers who are accompanied by performing animals such as a bear, dog, goat, or monkey. They play popular tunes on a bagpipe (*baghalbīn*) and a small band drum (*ḍholak*).

Putlivālā

Puppeteers (*putlivālā*) are seminomadic groups that entertain villagers with string puppets (*putli*) on an impromptu stage assembled by borrowing village cots and bedsheets. The puppets portray characters from the Mughal emperor Akbar's court. A male puppeteer with a reed whistle in his mouth provides the dialogue for all characters. During the performance, a woman of the group sings popular songs backstage to the accompaniment of a small double-headed barrel drum (*ḍholak*) that she plays with her hands.

Chatu

Chatu are professional endogamous prostitute-and-pimp groups operating out of brothels. The professional female entertainers of this group, known primarily for their dancing, are called Kanjri. The men, known as the Sapardai, specialize in musical accompaniment on a large tabla and a loud harmonium, and also look after the needs of their performing women. They claim Mīrāsī origin—a contention disputed by the Mīrāsī.

Sāīṅ and faqīr

The graves and mausoleums of Muslim holy men and scholars are important centers for mystical religious music. The grave (*mazār, ziārat, dargāh*) becomes the focus of local religious activity, the high point of which is the celebration of the deceased's death anniversary. Punjabis consider the death of such a holy man to be his marriage with the eternal and celebrate it in much the same manner as a marriage. At almost every such celebration (*ʿurs*, Arabic 'marriage') in Pakistan, musicians perform devotional songs and music day and night. These musicians (the *faqīr* and the *sāīṅ*) are individuals who have broken away from traditional village life to wander from shrine to shrine. They have usually memorized the poetry of Sufi poets and recite and sing it at religious festivals. They are distinct from the Qawwāl, who also perform in religious rituals; for one thing, they often rely on cannabis for mystical inspiration.

The musical instruments used by the *faqīr* and the *sāīṅ* are simpler than those used by professional musicians; one instrument closely linked with these wandering religious mendicants is the *cimṭā* (see above), a pair of iron tongs struck together. The occupational group logically connected with the *cimṭā* is the blacksmiths (Lohār), but anyone may play it. Only the Mīrāsī reject it outright. Another instrument popular among the *faqīr* and the *sāīṅ* is the *king* or *iktār*, a hollow gourd with a stick through it, to which one or more strings are attached. To strike and pluck the strings, the player wears a metal thimble with a pick protruding from it on the right index

The central folk romance of the Punjab is the tale of Hir and Ranjha. Performers either recite the poem rhythmically or sing it with or without musical accompaniment.

finger. Both these instruments are linked to mystical religious traditions and are heard at shrines where *faqīr* or *sāīṅ* gather.

These mendicants come from all strata of village society and have no link to the Mīrāsī traditions regarding genealogy or patrons. Indeed, to the Mīrāsī, these mystical singers are stylistically naive upstarts who disturb the established pattern of life. The *faqīr* and the *sāīṅ* profess to spurn worldly activity (*dunyādāri*), confining themselves to the spiritual sphere. They form a central part of the subculture around shrines where great Sufi masters are buried and express the true religious sentiments of the peasantry of the Punjab. Depending on their expressive skills, these performers can gain fame and reputation far beyond their local area of activity, sometimes becoming nationally known. Those of widespread fame include the late *sāīṅ* Marna, with his simple *iktār* and delicate, haunting tunes, and the *sāīṅ* Akhtar Hussain, whose strong and powerful devotional songs still sway the people long after his death. A famous Sufi singer of today is Pathana Khan. Outside the mainstream music systems of Pakistan, these musicians belong to a tradition unique in its own right. Some specialize in rendering the work of one particular Sufi poet; for example, Pathana Khan's rendering of the poetry of Khwaja Ghulam Farid, the great poet of the desert, is an inimitable example of how mystical content can be expressed in musical form.

Naʿt Khwān

The Naʿt Khwān are singers of unaccompanied songs in praise of the Prophet Muhammad. They can be from any group, including the Mīrāsī.

Dāstāngoh

Another group of musicians are the storytellers (Ṭāḍi Dāstāngoh). Their repertoire consists of ballads, romances, and war tales; they usually perform in groups of three, and on occasion four. The lead ballad singer (*dāstāngoh*) plays a pressure drum (*ṭaḍ*), accompanied by a double flute (*joṛi*) and a plucked lute (*king*), which acts as a drone. The ensemble may also include a small bowed fiddle (*choṭī sāraṅgī*). The leader narrates a story in a loud voice, and the standing musicians break into song to illustrate particularly emotional parts. These ballad singers do not suffer the social stigma of the Mīrāsī and may belong to any ethnic group. They may also own land, which is unheard of for a Mīrāsī.

Khusrā

Eunuchs, hermaphrodites, and male transsexual entertainers dressing and living as women form an important group of non-Mīrāsī performers. They usually appear at the circumcision ceremony of a male child, where they sing and dance after the foreskin has been nailed to the upper right of the doorframe. The Khusrā take in any children of indeterminate gender as their own if a family parts with them. There is allegedly another manner of recruitment, in which a man renouncing the world voluntarily submits to the truncation of his genitalia and the subsequent cauterization of the wound by expert members of this group.

Nonprofessional musicians

Any person not belonging to a musician family who plays music for pleasure and not for profit is considered *shauqi*, from the term *shauq* 'hobby'. For example, a village farmer incurs no stigma or loss of status by playing the transverse flute (*vanjli*). However, in the vicinity of households with young unmarried women, family members may stop him from playing the flute, for its music is believed to affect women's hearts and render them romantic.

MUSICAL GENRES

Musical genres are inextricably linked to poetry in the Punjab, and often take their name from the type of poetry being rendered with music.

Secular genres

The most common musical genre is the *gīt* 'song', also called *lok gīt* 'folk song', sung to the accompaniment of *ḍholak* and harmonium by Mīrāsī and ballad singers (*dāstāngoh*). Ghazal singers perform a more sophisticated form of *gīt*. Women sing folk songs in chorus at marriages and festivals, accompanied by *ḍholak*. Specific types of *gīt* include: *māhiā*, a love song comprising stanzas of two rhyming lines, the first shorter than the second; *bolī*, a love song comprising stanzas of two nonrhyming lines, favored by competing women's groups at marriages and festivals; and *ṭappā*, usually an impromptu dialogue song in a three-line pattern, with the first line repeated after the second.

The ballad singer (*dāstāngoh*) sings ballads or stories (*dāstān*) at fairs and festivals, usually in a secular setting. Of the more than twenty existing *dāstān*, the lyrics are both secular and religious in content. Like the *dāstān*, the *vār* is a war tale extolling the great deeds of folk heroes. The same singers perform both *dāstān* and *vār*.

Shahānā are Punjabi songs sung at weddings. Women sing *mehṅdī* songs, with hand clapping and *ḍholak* drumming, while applying henna to the bride's hands. Nuptial songs for the groom are called *sĕhra.*

Mothers sing lullabies (*lori*) to their infants and children. Bhirāīṅ also sing these to the accompaniment of the *ḍhol* drum.

The ghazal is a romantic love song in Urdu or Farsi, at the interface between popular and classical music. The singer (*ghazalgoh*) renders the first line of text to the accompaniment of the tabla, *sāraṅgī*, and harmonium. Brisk, rhythmic tabla interludes (*ṭhāh dūṇī*) separate the first vocal line from the second, which together make up the couplet form of the ghazal.

Classical singing in the North Indian style belongs to the *rāgdāri* category. The singer concentrates on the music, employing only a few lines of text containing simple words. *Rāgdāri* also includes the rendition of raga on the sitar, and in recent years, accompanying instruments have started appearing as solo or lead instruments in this genre.

The central folk romance of the Punjab is the tale of Hir and Ranjha. Performers either recite the poem rhythmically or sing it in a specific style, with or without musical accompaniment. A performer may be any villager with a good voice, or a professional musician, and the performance of *Hīr*, named after the heroine, usually takes place at night.

Mirza is also a love story of the Punjab, in this case named after the hero. Singers (*dāstāngoh*) perform *Mirza* in a similar manner to *Hīr*, with double-flute (*joṛī*) and plucked-lute (*king*) accompaniment. According to tradition, the singer requires a great deal of strength in performance.

Religious and devotional genres

A sharp division exists among religious and devotional genres, separating orthodox religious genres from mainstream devotional Sufi music. As elsewhere in the Islamic world, orthodox Muslims do not consider an unaccompanied rendition (*qir'at*) of their sacred text, the Qur'ān, to be music. Neither do they consider unaccompanied songs in praise of God (*ḥamd*), the Prophet Muhammad (*naʿt*), Ali, the son-in-law of the Prophet, or Sufi saints (*manqabat*), or laments (*nohā, marsīya*) as music. Devotional singing with instrumentation is the domain of heterodox Sufi Islam, the folk religious sentiment of the Punjab.

Existing only in the Punjab and Sindh, *kāfī* is the rendering of mystical poetry with musical accompaniment [see PAKISTAN: DEVOTIONAL MUSIC]. Solo *faqīr* or *sāīṅ* singers perform *kāfī* at Sufi shrines. Singers specializing in *kāfī* follow a structural form similar to the ghazal, with *asthāī, aṅtarā*, and tabla or *ḍholak* rhythmic interludes. Qawwāl also sing *kāfī* in chorus as part of their repertoire.

Qawwali combines religious and devotional poetry and also draws from secular poetry in Arabic, Farsi, Urdu, and Punjabi. The usual performance context is a Sufi shrine on a Thursday evening, or the death anniversary celebration of a Sufi saint. Qawwali borrows from all musical genres, but maintains a leader-chorus structure with the chorus loudly singing the refrain along with hand clapping and drumming, following each solo verse rendition.

Singers perform laments and dirges (*nohā* and *marsīya*) bewailing the tragedy of Hussain's martyrdom at Karbala during the Islamic lunar month of Muharram. There is no instrumental accompaniment, although Muslims strike their chests with open or closed hands to provide rhythmic accompaniment.

Kīrtan songs in praise of the Sikh founder, Guru Nanak, and other luminaries of the faith are sung mostly by Muslim musicians and also by some Sikh musicians for Sikh pilgrims at Lahore, Sheikhupura, Hasan Abdal, and other Sikh shrines in the Punjab. Similarly, Punjabi Hindus sing devotional songs (bhajans)—mostly of the syncretic bhakti tradition—to the accompaniment of the one-stringed lute (*iktār*).

At esoteric meetings of the Sufi orders, professional musicians usually sing *hamāost* for the Sufi masters. This form of singing emphasizes the discovery of the secrets of the Self, and is usually unaccompanied.

REFERENCES

Bose, Fritz. 1967. "Pakistanische Musik." *Deutsche Gesellschaft für Musik des Orients* 6:18–23.

Catella, Martina. 1993. "Introduction au Qawwali: idiome musicale du soufisme en Inde et au Pakistan" (Introduction to Qawwali: The musical idiom of Sufism in India and Pakistan). Master's thesis, Université de Paris–IV Sorbonne.

Darshan, Abdul G. 1980. *Boliān*. Islamabad: Lok Virsa Publishing House. In Urdu/Punjabi.

Haidri, Iqbal. 1985. *Faisalabad, Vihari, and Bahawalpur*. Unpublished Field Report 200R-I. Lok Virsa Archives, Islamabad.

———. N.d. *Faisalabad Tour-Interviews, Lok Git*. Unpublished Field Report 243R-I. Lok Virsa Archives, Islamabad.

Hasan, Mumtaz, ed. 1973. *The Adventures of Hir and Ranjha*. London: Peter Owen.

Jadoon, Aslam. 1979. *Mahia*. Islamabad: Lok Virsa Publishing House. In Urdu/Punjabi.

Jairazbhoy, Nazir A. 1968. "L'Islam en Inde et au Pakistan." In *Encyclopédie des Musiques Sacrées*, 1, 454–463. Paris: Labergerie.

———. 1995. *The Rāgs of North Indian Music: Their Structure and Evolution*. Bombay: Popular Prakashan. With accompanying cassette.

Malik, Saeed. 1983. *The Musical Heritage of Pakistan*. Islamabad: Idara Saqafat-e-Pakistan.

Matringe, Denis. 1922. "Les particularités du soufisme au Punjab." *Revue de la Société Ernest Renan* 40:74.

Nayyar, Adam. 1988. *Qawwali*. Islamabad: Lok Virsa Research Centre.

Platts, John T. 1974. *Urdu Classical Hindi and English Dictionary*. Oxford: Oxford University Press.

Qureshi, Regula B. 1986. *Sufi Music of India and Pakistan: Sound, Context and Meaning in Qawwali*. Cambridge: Cambridge University Press.

Razia, Muhammad. *Survey of Lyallpur*. Unpublished Field Report 102 R-I. Lok Virsa Archives, Islamabad.

Sakata, H. Lorraine. 1993. *The Sacred and the Profane: The Dual Nature of Qawwali*. Berlin: International Institute of Traditional Music.

Sarmadee, Sarmad. 1975. *Musical Genius of Amir Khusrau*. New Delhi: Government of India, Ministry of Information and Broadcasting.

Balochistan

Sabir Badalkhan

Balochi Song Genres
Balochi Dances
Instrumental Musicians
Singers
Musical Instruments

The Baloch ethnic group inhabits Balochistan 'land of the Baloch', which comprises the Pakistani province of Balochistan, the Iranian province of Sistan-and-Balochistan, and the contiguous areas of southwestern Afghanistan. They also live in the Pakistani provinces of Sindh and the Punjab, in the Arabian peninsula, East Africa, and Turkmenistan. The Baloch are Muslims and speak Balochi, a language of northwest Iran. The number of Balochi-speakers is presently estimated at around 8 million, but the actual number of those belonging to original Balochi tribes and who no longer speak Balochi is estimated to be far higher.

Although Balochi music has remained more or less homogeneous throughout the Baloch region, the region can today be divided musically into three major areas: Makran, comprising the coastal area, Karachi, and the Arabian peninsula (hereafter called the "southern zone"); central and northern Balochistan, which runs from Quetta in northeastern Balochistan to the Sarhadd in Iranian Balochistan and includes Baloch areas of Afghanistan and Turkmenistan (the "northern zone"); and eastern Balochistan, extending from the eastern parts of the Bolan and Mula passes to the borders of the Punjab and Sindh and beyond (the "eastern zone"). These major zones can also be subdivided into several minor areas by dialect and regional style differences.

Among the Baloch, singing and instrumental music are related to festivities at birth, circumcision, and wedding ceremonies, harvests and religious festivals, and other private or collective celebrations. Music is played as an accompaniment to singing, to provide rhythm for dancing (including certain mystic dances performed as prayers and meditations), and for curing illnesses related to psychosomatic disorders.

BALOCHI SONG GENRES

The most common Balochi song genres are distinguished by their musical structure, manner of performance, the sex or social position of the performers, or the instrumental accompaniment. They include: *sipatt* 'prayer and praise songs on the birth of a child'; *nāzenk* 'praise songs for sons, brothers, and fathers'; *līlo* 'cradle songs'; *hālo* and *lāḍo* 'wedding and circumcision songs'; *sot* and *dastānag* 'short love songs'; *zahī-*

The *dastānag* used to be a short love song sung in one breath. The lyrics had two to seven lines, although the length depended "rather on the strength of the singer's lungs than any rule of composition."

rok, līko, and *ḍēhī* 'songs of separation and travel'; *shēr* 'verse narratives'; and *motk* 'elegies'. Certain song genres are accompanied by dances, including *chogān* 'religious songs'; *ambā* and *lēwā* 'fishermen's songs'; and *gwātī, shekī, shēparjā,* and *mālid* 'healing or spiritual songs'.

Sipatt

Sipatt (from Arabic *sifat* 'praise') are songs sung by women (occasionally joined by men) on the birth of a child, usually a son, from the first night to the sixth or for as many as fourteen, depending on the social status of the family. They are sung without instrumental accompaniment and are considered prayers. Women improvise on the song texts, except for the fixed refrains.

Nāzenk and *lolī*

Nāzenk and *lolī* (called *līlo* in the eastern zone) are both cradle songs, sung without musical accompaniment by women of all social backgrounds. *Nāzenk* (from *nāzenag* 'to praise') is mostly a praise song that is sometimes sung to honor elders (brothers, fathers, sons, daughters, and so on); *lolī* 'lullaby' is more soothing, though the aspect of praise is dominant here also.

Hālo and *lāḍo*

These chorus songs, sung by women on the occasions of betrothal, circumcision, and marriage, are subject to improvisation: the only fixed text is the refrain or hemistich. Their distinguishing feature is the inclusion of the words *hālo* or *lāḍo,* or variants such as *hālo, hāloē, lāḍoē,* or *lāḍūngē.* They are sung preferably to the accompaniment of a *ḍuhl* 'double-headed barrel drum', *ṭīmbuk* 'small double-headed barrel drum', and sometimes *surnā* 'oboe', which is played exclusively by Ludi men. The women clap their hands while singing and dancing.

Sot

TRACK-28, TRACK-29

Sot is a short song with a fixed refrain sung at circumcision and wedding ceremonies by a Sotī, generally a low-caste professional woman singer but occasionally a male singer from the same social level (figure 1). The Sotī may improvise on the song lyrics, and a chorus may join in singing the refrain. Song topics include love, separation, and the praise of a groom, son, or brother. *Sot* is the most popular song genre in the southern zone; it is also found in some parts of the northern zone, but is unknown in the east.

Sot are accompanied by any instrument current in Balochistan with the exception of the *suroz* 'bowed fiddle', *dambūrag* 'plucked lute', and *nal* 'flute'. The ideal instruments are the *bēnjo* 'keyed zither', *ḍukkur,* 'double-headed barrel drum', *kūnzag* 'earthen pot', *chinchir* 'cymbals', or *tāl* 'struck steel plate'.

FIGURE 1 Sharruk (also called Sharratunn), a Sotī, accompanied on the *bēnjo* by Usman Pullan, 1991. Photo by Sabir Badalkhan and A. Bakewell.

Dastānag

The *dastānag*, found exclusively in the eastern zone, used to be a short love song sung in one breath, accompanied by a long end-blown flute (*naḍ*) with eight to ten holes. The lyrics had two to seven lines, although the length depended "rather on the strength of the singer's lungs than any rule of composition" (Dames 1907, 1:184). The subject matter of some *dastānag* was tender love, others were comic; according to Dames (1907, 1:29), "nearly all [were] vivid and picturesque." Nowadays, *dastānag* lyrics can have over one hundred lines and their subject matter can include any topic of common interest.

The *dastānag* singer, called the *surrī* 'tune keeper', is accompanied by a *naḍī* 'flute player'. Both are upper-caste Baloch (men from inferior social backgrounds are not expected to perform *dastānag*). Since *dastānag* is believed to be the declaration of a love affair, it is sung only at male gatherings, where women are not supposed to be present.

A similar type of singing and *nal* playing exists in the rest of Balochistan, performed mostly by shepherds. One of them plays a pair of flutes, while the other keeps the rhythm with a dronelike voice. In the southern zone, the form is called *nal o guṭṭ kanag* (literally 'to accompany the flute with the voice of the throat').

Zahīrok, līko, and *ḍēhī*

Zahīrok (*zahīrīg, zahīronk*), from the term *zahīr* 'longing', is one of the most famous Balochi folk-song genres as well as the name of a famous tune (*sāz*) related to it (During 1997). It is current throughout southern Balochistan and parts of the central region.

Zahīrok, like *līko* and *ḍēhī*, consists of poetic couplets, sometimes with a third refrain line. It is sung by travelers, persons who are away from home, or relatives back home. Solitary workers in the fields or herding sheep and goats also sing *zahīrok*, as do women grinding grain, working on a loom, or doing other chores. As a work or travel song *zahīrok* is unaccompanied, but when sung for entertainment it is often accompanied by the *suroz* 'bowed fiddle'. *Zahīrok* tunes are named after periods of the night, regional or tribal names, famous *zahīrok* singers, composers of new *zahīrok* tunes, or the strings of a *suroz*.

In the southern zone, *zahīrok* is also employed in the singing of long narratives in verse (*shēr*). A good narrative singer (Pahlawān) is supposed to know all or most of the *zahīrok* tunes.

Līko and *ḍēhī* are work and travel songs found in the northern and eastern zones, respectively. *Līko* is most common in Sarhadd, Iran (Massoudieh 1989:644); Chagai and Kharan, Pakistan; Afghani Balochistan; and among the Baloch of Turkmenistan (Aksjonov 1990:3); *ḍēhī* is sung among the tribes inhabiting the eastern fringes of the Baloch region, as well as among the Baloch tribes of Dera Ghazi Khan in the Punjab. Both the *līko* and *ḍēhī* are accompanied by a *suroz* and a *dambūrag*, but the singer does not play a musical instrument while singing.

Shēr

Shēr is the most famous and refined genre of Balochi oral poetry. It is a descriptive narrative in verse form, with no refrain, sung by professional or amateur minstrels in formal settings. Some *shēr* can be categorized as epics. The singing is never accompanied by dancing. An alternate performance structure is *shērīdāstān* 'prosimetrics', in which the verse part is sung or recited and the prose section, containing the background of the episode and descriptive details of the actions, is chanted or narrated.

Shēr verses generally have a number of lines in a uniform meter and irregular rhymes: although different texts of a single *shēr* indicate some textual alterations, no intentional changes are either admitted by the performer or tolerated by his listeners.

The subject matter of a Balochi *shēr* can vary, but the Baloch generally distinguish three main types: *balochī*, which include war epics and historical and genealogical records; *ishkī*, love poems; and *pēgumbarī*, religious narratives dealing mostly with Islamic wars and the heroic exploits of Muslim heroes.

The *shēr* singer, known as Ḍomb in the east and Pahlawān in the rest of Balochistan, is always male and traditionally belonged to the Ludi caste. *Shēr* composers, however, are almost exclusively upper-caste Baloch.

Two types of stringed instrument always accompany the sung *shēr*: *suroz* and *dambūrag*. The two-stringed *dambūrag* is played by the singer himself, whereas the three-stringed version is played by his aide, called the *panjagī* 'helping hand'. When recited or chanted by men, regardless of social background or status, *shēr* is unaccompanied. Its recitation is considered a noble action (*xānwādahī kār*) and a prestigious pastime. Memorization, recitation, or chanting of a *shēr* without instrumental accompaniment is considered respectful, and almost every single Baloch knows some *shēr* or *shēr* fragments by heart.

Motk

Motk (called *modag* in the northern zone) is an elegy that was sung commonly until a few decades ago. Because of opposition from Muslim clergymen, it has now almost ceased to exist. A low-caste woman called *motk-kashsh* 'singer of elegies' usually led singing sessions, and other women joined in singing the refrain or last hemistich (Barker and Mengal 1969, 2:343–344; Massoudieh 1989:644). Such sessions continued up to six, fourteen, or even forty days, depending on the social status of the deceased. According to Barker and Mengal (1969, 2:344), a drum beaten by a Ludi or a Ḍomb accompanied a *motk* for a noble or chief in earlier times, but no further records indicate instrumental accompaniment to such singing.

BALOCHI DANCES

Dances of the Baloch can generally be classified into three main types on the basis of function as well as performance occasion: ceremonial dances, work dances, and ritual dances.

Chāp, suhbat, drīs

These three terms refer to similar dances in different parts of Balochistan: the famous Balochi *chāp* or *dochāpī* of the southern zone, the *suhbat* of the north, and the *drīs* in the eastern zone, which itself has almost become the "national dance" of the Baloch. They are all related to social and religious festivities, and are performed by men, although in the northern zone women also perform *suhbat* in close circles (Barker and Mengal 1969, 2:150).

Instrumental accompaniment for the three dance types is also similar. One or two *ḍuhl*, one or two *ṭīmbuk*, and one *surnā* accompany both the *dochāpī* and the *suhbat*. The musicians without exception are Ludi, craftsmen of the Baloch believed to be of Indian origin. The *drīs* is usually performed with a *suroz* and one or two *dambūrag*, although sometimes, in the absence of these instruments, the *ḍuhl* and *surnā* are also played.

A distinctive feature of the *drīs* dance is the performers' use of swords. Each dancer holds two swords (or even sticks nowadays) and crosses them with those of other dancers on the right and left in turns. *Drīs* was initially a war dance performed before or after wars to raise the morale of the tribe or to celebrate a victory, as well as on other occasions to keep the fighters fit. Since war was the business of the upper-caste Baloch, this dance is performed largely by them, with expert performers from a lower caste sometimes leading the dance. (The lower caste never fought in tribal wars, for it was deemed dishonorable for upper-caste Baloch to be engaged in war with persons of lower social rank.)

Occasionally low-caste singers perform chants, short songs, or couplets with refrains in accompaniment to the dance; some experts have a wide repertoire of such songs.

Lēwā

Lēwā is a festive dance of fishermen on the coast of Balochistan as well as of Baloch in Karachi who originally came from the coastal region. It is a group dance quite similar to *dochāpī, suhbat, drīs*, and *ambā*. Drums and percussion accompany the dance: two *ḍuhl* 'double-headed drums' (a large one called *rahmānī* and a slightly smaller one known as *kyāsa*), a *mugulmānī* 'large single-headed cylindrical drum carved with tripod legs', one or two *ṭīmbuk* 'small double-headed drums', and a *gurr* 'conch shell'. The drummers play either with sticks or with open hands. The performers wear loose shirts, put plumes around their heads and arms, and sometimes paint their faces. The effect gives the appearance of an African dance being performed on the Baloch coast.

Like other dances, *lēwā* is also accompanied by songs (*sot*) and chanted couplets with love themes, sometimes containing rude expressions about love affairs or in praise of women. The leader of the dancing group is called the *sarogān*.

Ambā

Ambā, or *ambao*, is a work song as well as a group dance performed by coastal fishermen on sea or land (figure 2). It was formerly sung when sailing ships were used for trade and transport. A crew of twelve to eighteen men, depending on the size of the vessel, needed to work together harmoniously to raise the sails and do the other work of the ship. A drummer would take his seat at the front of the vessel and lead the working crew in singing *ambā* songs. The lyrics are often very short, sometimes just single-word formulas repeated continuously. However, there are also long songs with refrains. Interestingly, the *ambā* repertoire contains a number of songs in Swahili that are presently sung by fishermen in Makran who do not understand their meanings. These have been transmitted orally from generation to generation, despite their lack of comprehension by the Baloch in modern times.

Mālid and *shēparjā* are rituals accompanied by music, singing, and dancing, presently performed for such purposes as self-purification of the performers and audience, protection of the surroundings from evil spirits and epidemics, or after the fulfillment of religious vows.

FIGURE 2 Musicians accompany an *ambā* song and dance at Ormara, Makran, playing (back row) *mugulmānī* drum and *gurr* conch shell, and (front row, *left to right*) *ṭīmbuk*, *ḍuhl*, and *ṭīmbuk* drums, 1991. Photo by Sabir Badalkhan and A. Bakewell.

The dance style and instrumental accompaniment of an *ambā* performance on shore are the same as for a *lēwā* performance, the only difference lying in the accompanying songs. In the case of an *ambā* dance, the songs have phrases that are designed to inspire collective effort; *lēwā* songs and couplets have purely love themes.

Chogān

Chogān (literally 'celebration') are religious songs, accompanied by a collective ritual, of the Zikri sect. The Zikri are a minority Muslim sect originating in the sixteenth century and found exclusively among the Baloch (Baloch 1996). These songs, also known as *sipatt* 'praise' (usually of God and the Prophet Muhammad) and less commonly *kishtī* (*Baluchistan District Gazetteers* 1906, 7:120), are unaccompanied by musical instruments and are performed on religious days as well as on other festive occasions such as circumcisions and wedding ceremonies, and after the summer and spring harvests.

Men form a large circle, with a female *shāir* 'singer' standing in the middle (figure 3). The *shāir* sings rhymed formulas, and the *jawābī* 'chorus' responds, moving their bodies, feet, and hands to the rhythm of the sung words. The lyrics are prayers and praises offered to God and the Prophet Muhammad, and are mostly in Balochi, with occasional words in Farsi (Persian). Three types of *chogān* can be distinguished according to body movement and syllabic length of the song lines. The *tarragī* involves the performers turning to the right side and then to the left, so as to face the performers on either side in turn, and then to the center (exactly as in the *chāp, suh-*

FIGURE 3 *Chogān* performance in Shapuk, 40 kilometers east of Turbat, with the female *shāir* singer surrounded by the men's chorus, 1991. Photo by Sabir Badalkhan.

bat, and *drīs* dances). In *raw-o-āī*, the performers step forward and backward, bending the body with each step. For the third *chogān* type, *jahl-o-burzī*, performers stand in one place and bend their bodies forward, then stand up straight, repeating this action with every half song line. In all three types of *chogān*, performers move extremely slowly to the right.

The *chogān* form comprises poetic couplets; the first line is sung, often improvised, by the female singer and the refrain line sung by the male chorus. The line lengths vary: *jahl-o-burzī* has two to four syllables, the *raw-o-āī* four to twelve syllables, and the *tarragī* five to twelve syllables. Each *chogān* begins with a line length of the maximum number of syllables. Every half hour or so, the *shāir* reduces the number of syllables per line; simultaneously, the movements of the chorus become progressively faster and their singing grows louder. This is the climax of a *chogān*, after which the *shāir* begins another song type. The entire session continues without a break until dawn.

Some female *shāir* singers inherit their positions; others are unrelated, talented women who accompany a famous *shāir* and learn the art. There are no social restrictions on becoming a *shāir*.

Mālid and *shēparjā*

Both *mālid* and *shēparjā* are rituals accompanied by music, singing, and dancing. *Mālid* was originally celebrated on the birth anniversary of the Prophet Muhammad or on the death anniversaries of Sufi saints. Nowadays, followers of a religious cult called Rifai (a subsect of the Sunni Muslims) perform *mālid*. Performance of the *shēparjā* was connected with Sheikh Fariduddin Masud Ganj-i Shakar (d. 1265), who is buried in the Punjab [see PAKISTAN: DEVOTIONAL MUSIC]. *Mālid* performers used to hold monthly meetings on the eleventh night of the lunar calendar; *shēparjā* meetings took place on Monday and Friday nights. Presently, both are performed on various occasions and for different purposes, such as self-purification of the performers and audience, protection of the surroundings from evil spirits (*jinn*) and epidemics, or after the fulfilment of religious vows (*kōl*).

Mālid and *shēparjā* groups both have leaders called *alīppa* (from the Arabic *k͟halifah* 'vicegerent of a saint'), who claim to have received their spiritual power in a dream from Ghos-i Azam or some other powerful *alīppa*. When an *alīppa* dies, his successor is selected by his disciples, or he may himself nominate one during his lifetime.

Some *mālid* performers I have observed during past years played seven *samā* 'tambourines' of different sizes. The *alīppa* sits in front of the group, facing the chorus and musicians and sings verses in praise of the Prophet Muhammad, Gaos-e Azam, Lal Shahbaz Qalandar, and other Islamic saints, to which the chorus responds by singing a refrain. The singing is known as *zigr* (Arabic *zikr*). In *shēparjā*, a *mugulmānī* 'large single-headed cylindrical drum' with red cloth covering the sides is placed in the center of a circle of dancers. Usually four drummers (two *ḍuhl* and two *ṭīmbuk* players) hang their double-headed drums from their shoulders and beat them with hands or sticks. The drummers take their place in the center near the *mugulmānī* player, facing and moving along with the circle of dancers. The *alīppa* leads the *zigr* singing, and the chorus responds, moving to the right around the drummers. In both *shēparjā* and *mālid* performances, the rhythmic intensity increases with each song, reaching a stage when most performers, sometimes joined by men and women in the audience, enter into trance. In a trance state the male dancers dagger themselves, lick red-hot-iron rods, rub burning chains with both hands, wash their hands in boiling oil, and perform other such actions. Each singing session lasts about half an hour, but the whole performance continues through the night with breaks for tea drinking and for warming the drum skins beside a burning fire. At the end of the performance, meat and rice or sweets are distributed.

Gwātī-ē lēb

Gwātī-ē lēb is a session in which instruments are played incessantly to accompany mystical songs and smooth dancing, and is meant to help a *gwātī* 'person possessed by an evil spirit (*gwāt*)' to enter into trance and be liberated from the evil spirit. (There are good *gwāt* as well as bad ones.)

Gwāt (literally 'wind, air') is a psychosomatic disorder common among the Baloch living in the southern zone, particularly on the Makran coast and in Karachi. The spirit-possession phenomenon and its treatment through music, singing, and trance, guided by a *shek* or *faqīr*, are also found with different names in other parts of Balochistan. *Gwāt* are considered to be spirits found everywhere in the universe, although their abodes are mostly in graveyards, isolated places, abandoned houses or villages, old trees, and places where a dead body has been washed before burial. A person who passes by any such place, especially at midday or during the night, risks being attacked and possessed by a *gwāt*. *Gwāt* also possess people who are not protected by a spiritual guide, who surpass their human limits, who hurt or disturb a spirit or a religious person, or, in the case of women, who are in a state of impurity (Sultana 1996:31). Possession by a *gwāt* is believed capable of being passed from one person to another; all spiritual healers are believed to have the power to cause people to be possessed by a *gwāt*.

When someone is suspected of being possessed by a *gwāt*, family members consult a spiritual healer, either a *gwātī-ē māt* 'mother of the *gwāt*-possessed person(s)' or a *shek* 'spiritual guide', to find out the causes of the illness and the methods for treating it. The spiritual healer reveals the type of *gwāt* involved and the appropriate *lēb* 'play' to be performed, which almost always includes music, singing, entering into trance, animal sacrifice, and food distribution. Different *gwāt* require different methods of treatment, taking from one to fifteen nights to be brought under control and forced to leave the patient. When the *gwāt* finally leaves the patient's body, the patient is given a *rahl* 'seal' in the shape of a ring or an incantation that is read and blown on a string, which the patient keeps with him at all times or stores safely at home in a box. As long as the person keeps the *rahl* and performs the *gwātī* or *shekī lēb* once or twice a year, she or he is protected and safe. If the person loses the *rahl* or a genie comes and steals it, then the *gwāt* returns infuriated and the person becomes very seriously ill, even risking death (Sultana 1996; During 1989:37–156).

Various musical instruments are used for different types of *gwāt* play (see Sultana 1996:39, table 1); however, the ideal instruments are the *suroz* and *dambūrag*. If these are not available, then the *lēb* is performed with other instruments chosen by the healer.

INSTRUMENTAL MUSICIANS

The Baloch term for both music and musical instruments is *sāz,* and instrumentalists are called *sāzī* 'musician' or *sāzinda* (literally 'expert in music'). Instrumental performance is a profession, and most instrumentalists are hereditary musicians, since musical skills have traditionally been passed down through the Ludi caste, the craftsmen of the Baloch. In the past, no upper-caste Baloch could keep or play any musical instrument other than the *nal* 'flute', or in rare cases, the *chang* 'mouth harp'. In recent years, socioeconomic developments have brought people of varied social backgrounds into the music profession, either as full-time or part-time musicians or singers. However, even in the present, the caste and social background of a musician or singer are recognizable from the musical instrument he plays, the type of songs he sings, or the occasions for which he performs. The flute, for example, is almost always played by high-caste Baloch, and in the eastern zone no person of low caste is supposed to play the flute or sing a *dastānag* 'short love song'. The *ḍuhl* 'double-headed drum' and *surnā* 'oboe', however, are traditional Ludi instruments, and are still played predominantly by them, although persons of other lower social levels sometimes play these instruments. The *dambūrag* 'long-necked lute' and the *suroz* 'bowed fiddle', although instruments of the lower castes, are nowadays played by a great number of upper-caste Baloch.

SINGERS

Baloch singers can generally be divided into three different categories on the basis of their social origin, the type of songs they sing, their instrumental accompaniment, and the occasions for their singing. The three groups are the *shēr* singers, the Sotī, and the Gwashinda.

Shēr singers

The singer of *shēr* 'long verse narratives', called Pahlawān 'the singer of heroic deeds' in the northern and southern zones, and Ḍomb in the eastern zone (Badalkhan 1994), is male and has traditionally come from the Ludi caste. Since the beginning of the twentieth century, men of other social backgrounds have also adopted this profession. *Shēr* singing is accompanied by one or two *dambūrag* lutes and one *suroz* fiddle (figure 4). A good Pahlawān never sings to the accompaniment of any other instrument. He sings sitting on a raised platform; at the height of his performance, he sits on bended knees.

In the past, each tribe had its own tribal Pahlawān or Ḍomb minstrel, who accompanied both the tribe in war and the tribal chief in his routine visits among his own tribe or when visiting others. The tribal minstrel sang the glory of the tribe and memorized poems composed by the tribal poet (*rezwār shāir),* whose job was to record events in verse. Tribal poets and minstrels received regular and established financial remuneration at harvesttime and/or on special occasions. Freelance minstrels also earned their living by singing *shēr,* wandering from tribe to tribe and village to village. Nowadays, the only source of income for a Pahlawān or Ḍomb is his earnings from performing at festivities or at gatherings of elders.

The *suroz*, a bowed fiddle with four playing strings and eight sympathetic strings, can surely be called the national instrument of the Baloch.

FIGURE 4 The Pahlawān Mahmad-i Haibitan (*center*) playing a *dambūrag* lute, accompanied by his *panjagī* or assistant *dambūrag* player (*left*), and his *suroz* player (*right*), c. 1989. Photo courtesy Mahmad-i Haibitan.

Sotī

TRACK 29

This term refers to singers of *sot*, short improvised songs with a fixed refrain, who belong exclusively to the Ludis or some other low social caste. Most are women, but some men sing *sot* as well. They earn their livelihood from donations and from compensation for their performances, usually at circumcision and wedding ceremonies. The Sotī sings to the accompaniment of any musical instrument current in Balochistan except the *suroz, dambūrag,* or *nal,* although the most commonly used are drums, *bēnjo* 'keyed zither', *tāl* 'steel plate', *zhāng* 'bells', and *kūnzag* 'earthen water pot'. Sotī themselves do not play musical instruments, with the exception of some female Sotī, who sing among women and accompany themselves with a medium-size *ḍuhl* or *ṭīmbuk* drum.

Gwashinda

Gwashinda (literally 'one who says') is a neologism for male singers who come from an upper-caste background. A Gwashinda sings short love songs composed by modern literate poets as well as special wedding songs. Almost all Gwashinda singers play the harmonium while singing. Unlike the Sotī singer, a Gwashinda never sings for dances, deeming it below his social status.

MUSICAL INSTRUMENTS

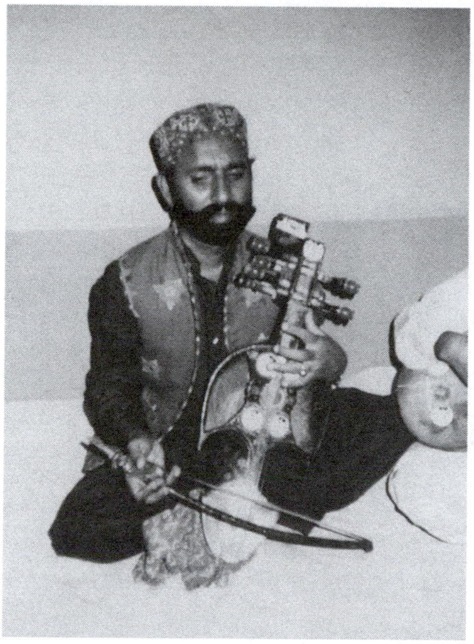

FIGURE 5 The *suroz* player Sachchu Khan Bugti of the Bugti tribe of eastern Balochistan, 1994. Photo by Sabir Badalkhan.

With no written historical sources on musical instruments, we learn through oral reports that most instruments currently played in Balochistan have been in use for virtually the same purposes since the fifteenth century. Stringed instruments include the *suroz*, a bowed fiddle with four playing strings and eight sympathetic strings that can surely be called the national instrument of the Baloch (figure 5), and the *dambūrag*, a long-necked, fretless lute with two to four strings that provides rhythm (figure 6). The *dambūrag* player strums the strings with his fingers; only in the eastern zone do musicians play melodies on a fretted *dambūrag*, accompanied by a small drum. Another chordophone is the *rabāb*, a plucked lute similar in shape to those found in Afghanistan and India. Until a few decades back, it was one of the popular instruments, used mostly to accompany *shēr* singing, but its use has greatly diminished.

Among keyed instruments is the *bēnjo* (CD track 28), a zither about 90 to 98 centimeters in length and 15 to 20 centimeters wide, with twenty-eight to thirty-two keys, two steel melody strings, and four sympathetic strings, two on either side of the bridge (see figure 1). The musician plays the two melody strings with a plastic plectrum. Another keyed instrument, the harmonium (used only by modern Gwashinda), was introduced by the Karachi Baloch only during the twentieth century.

Wind instruments include a variety of flutes, used in different contexts. The *naḍ*, a long, end-blown reed pipe, is one of the best-known instruments in the eastern zone. Other aerophones include the *bānsarī* 'small transverse steel pipe', a pair of double end-blown reed pipes (*donal* in the southern zone, *giraw* in the north, and *alghoza* in the east) (figure 7), *kānṭ* 'horn', and the *surnā* 'oboe'.

Various membranophones are played by the Baloch: the *ḍuhl* 'large double-headed drum,' *ṭīmbuk* 'small double-headed drum', *ḍukkur* 'medium-size cylindrical drum', *mugulmānī* 'large cylindrical drum' (resting on a tripod), tabla 'small cylindrical drum' (from India and Pakistan), and *samā* 'tambourine without jingles'. Idiophones include the *kūnzag* 'earthen water pot', *zhāng* 'bells tied in a string', *dapchang* 'mouth harp' (also called *chang*), *tāl* 'steel plate' fixed on a wooden platform and played with two sticks, and *chinchir* 'cymbals'.

FIGURE 6 The *dambūrag* player Samad (*left*) and the *suroz* player Gapur (*right*), musicians of the Pahlawān Mazar who belong to the famous Daudi family of instrumental musicians and singers. Gwadar, 1996. Photo by Sabir Badalkhan.

FIGURE 7 The *donal* double-flute player Peroz, accompanied on *dambūrag* by Allaidad, in Gwadar, 1991. Photo by Sabir Badalkhan and A. Bakewell.

REFERENCES

Aksjonov, Sergej. 1990. "Liko in the Poetical Folk Art of the Baluch of Turkmenistan." *Newsletter of Baluchistan Studies* 7:3–13.

Badalkhan, Sabir. 1994. "Poesia Epica e Tradizioni Orali Balochi: I Menestrelli Pahlawān del Makrān." Ph. D. dissertation, Istituto Universitario Orientale, Naples.

Baloch, Inayatullah. 1996. "Islam, the State, and Identity: The Zikris of Balochistan." In *Marginality and Modernity: Ethnicity and Change in Post-Colonial Balochistan*, ed. Paul Titus, 223–249. Karachi: Oxford University Press.

Baluch, Mohammad Sardar Khan. 1977–1984. *A Literary History of the Baluchis*. 2 vols. Quetta: Baluchi Academy.

Baluchistan District Gazetteers. 1986 [1906–1907]. 12 vols. vol. 3 (*Sibi*), vol. 7 (*Makran*). Quetta: Gosha-e Adab.

Barker, Muhammad Abd-al-Rahman, and Aqil Khan Mengal. 1969. *A Course in Baluchi*, 2 vols. Montreal: McGill University. (Vol. 2:263–349 contains samples of poetry and metrical analysis.)

Dames, Longworth M. 1907. *Popular Poetry of the Baloches*, 2 vols. London: The Folk-Lore Society; Quetta: Baluchi Academy, 1988.

During, Jean. 1989. *Musique et mystique dans les traditions de l'Iran*. Paris-Tehran: Institut Français de Recherche en Iran (pp. 33–233 on ritual music in Iranian Balochistan).

———. 1992. *Baloutchistan: Musique de l'extase et de guérison*. Ocora Radio France C 580017/18. 2 compact discs.

———. 1997. "The Baluchi Zahirig as a Modal Landscape and the Emergence of a Classical Music." In *The Structure of the ICTM Maqām Study Group Tampere-Virrat, Finland*, 2–5 October 1995, ed. Jürgen Elsner and Risto Pekka Pennanen, 39–64. Tampere: Department of Folk Tradition, University of Tampere.

Massoudieh, Mohammad Taqi. 1973. "Hochzeitslieder aus Balūčestān." *Jahrbuch für Musikalische Volks- und Völkerkunde*, 8:59–69.

———. 1985. *Mūsīqī-e Balochestān* (The music of Balochistan). Tehran: Entishārāt-i Sadāva Sīmāī, Jamhūrīya-e Islāmī-e Irān.

———. 1988. *Musik in Balūčestān*, 2 vols. Hamburg: Verlag der Musikalienhandlung Karl Dieter Wagner.

———. 1989. "Music of Baluchistan." In *Encyclopaedia Iranica*, ed. E. Yarshater, vol. 4: 644–645. London: Routledge and Kegan Paul.

Ryahi, Ali. 1977. *Zār va bād va Baloch* (*Zār*, wind, and the Baloch). Tehran: Tahuri.

Sultana, Farhat. 1996. "Gwat and Gwat-i-leb: Spirit Healing and Social Change in Makran." In *Marginality and Modernity: Ethnicity and Change in Post-Colonial Balochistan*, ed. Paul Titus, 28–50. Karachi: Oxford University Press.

North West Frontier Province

Mohammad Akbar

Vocal Genres
Performers and Audiences
Musical Instruments
Effects of Mass Media on Pakhtu Music

The North West Frontier Province (NWFP) is a mountainous region situated between Afghanistan and the Pakistani provinces of Balochistan, Punjab, and Gilgit (Northern Areas). Its population is over 15 million, including 3 million living in the tribal belt. Along with neighboring Afghanistan, the province is situated on the cultural crossroads between China, Iran, India, and Central Asia. For centuries, the Khyber Pass—with its formal entrance at the Jamrud Fort, located only 18 kilometers from the capital city of Peshawar—was to all actual and potential conquerors the most famous gateway to the fertile subcontinent.

The predominant sociocultural group is the Pakhtun people (Pashtun in Afghanistan), who also refer to themselves as Afghans [see SOUTHEASTERN AFGHANISTAN]. The Pakhtuns have a distinct culture and way of life known as Pakhtunwali; Pakhtu (Pashto), their language, is another name for their social order. The culture still has strong tribal bonds. Each tribe is confined to its own locality, and all the members of the tribe share the natural resources of that site.

Pakhtuns are great lovers of music and consider it an important aspect of their culture. Along with other craftsmen, however, musicians are not viewed as integral to the defense of this warrior nation, and so do not claim the same respect as do the religious or warrior core.

Historically, religion has always influenced Pakhtun views regarding music. Before the emergence of Islam, the Pakhtuns were followers of Hinduism and Buddhism and considered music sacred, employing it in many religious rituals. After the advent of Islam, music in Pakhtun society lost its sacred status but remained a great source of attraction. Pakhtuns use music not only for entertainment but also in war, in wedding and birth celebrations, and even during some religious events such as ʿĪdu'l-fiṭr (Taizai 1993). When tragic events take place, women sing melancholy songs (*sānde*) in the manner of an unaccompanied chant (Reshteen 1959). The media and the film industry have influenced music in NWFP, as has the large influx of Afghan refugees that arrived soon after the Soviet invasion of Afghanistan in the late 1970s. Although a source of financial hardship and political instability for NWFP, the Afghans are linguistically and ethnically the same people as the Pakhtuns; they have added to the musical riches of the province.

On social occasions men of all ages (including children) gather in a *hujra*, a guest house in a Pakhtun village or an open field. Women have their own soirées, playing and listening to music on occasions such as wedding parties.

VOCAL GENRES

Several vocal styles and genres can be identified in Pakhtu music. The *sandara* is either a solo song or a song accompanied by an instrumental ensemble. *Badalla, ghazal, loba,* and *bagathie* are Pakhtu song genres that differ only slightly in style, rhythm, and poetic structure. *Nīmakai* sounds similar to *loba* but starts with a more passionate and penetrating tone. The *landay* or *ṭappā*, said to be invented by women, is a single couplet; the first line has nine syllables, the second thirteen. This genre is associated with several styles of singing, all named after the regions in which they are popular, such as "Shulgarie," "Theerwala," and "Pekhawari."

Dīvāni ghazal is a poetic form that may be recited or sung. Texts may be selected from any popular poetry book, but the most common are those of Rehman Baba (for example, Baba 1984). After singing a *dīvāni ghazal*, a singer usually performs a *badalla*.

PERFORMERS AND AUDIENCES

Pakhtu singers entertain their audiences with different types of Pakhtu songs. On social occasions men of all ages (including children) gather in a *hujra*, a guest house in a Pakhtun village or an open field. Women have their own soirées, playing and listening to music on occasions such as wedding parties.

MUSICAL INSTRUMENTS

Rabāb

The *rabāb* is a short-necked lute with an elongated, oval belly usually made from red mulberry wood (figure 1). The *rabāb* typically has five playing strings and thirteen sympathetic strings, although special instruments may have fifteen. The strings are tied to small pegs made of cow or ox bone on the neck, and are stretched across a small bridge (*tātū*) of horny bone on the goatskin belly. The player strikes the strings with a plectrum also made of horny bone. There are sometimes three or five holes in the oval belly of the instrument.

Indian scholars have identified an instrument similar to the *rabāb*, the *waina*, which is mentioned in the ancient religious texts known as the Vedas (Reshteen 1959:68). The Indian author Naeem Kausar has written about yet another similar instrument called the *sarod* in a special musical issue of an Urdu-language magazine, *Aaj Kal* (August 1956). Kausar named Ustad Hafiz Ali Khan as one of the best *rabāb* players of his time, describing the artist as a Pakhtun from the Bangash tribe whose family settled in Afghanistan and whose grandfather, Ghulam Bandagi Khan, had traveled to India on business. The ustad took the *rabāb* from Kabul to India, made changes in it, and created the Indian instrument now referred to as the *sarod*. Some scholars argue that the *rabāb* originated in the Middle East, but Arabic and Persian dictionaries do not contain anything that could be considered the original form of

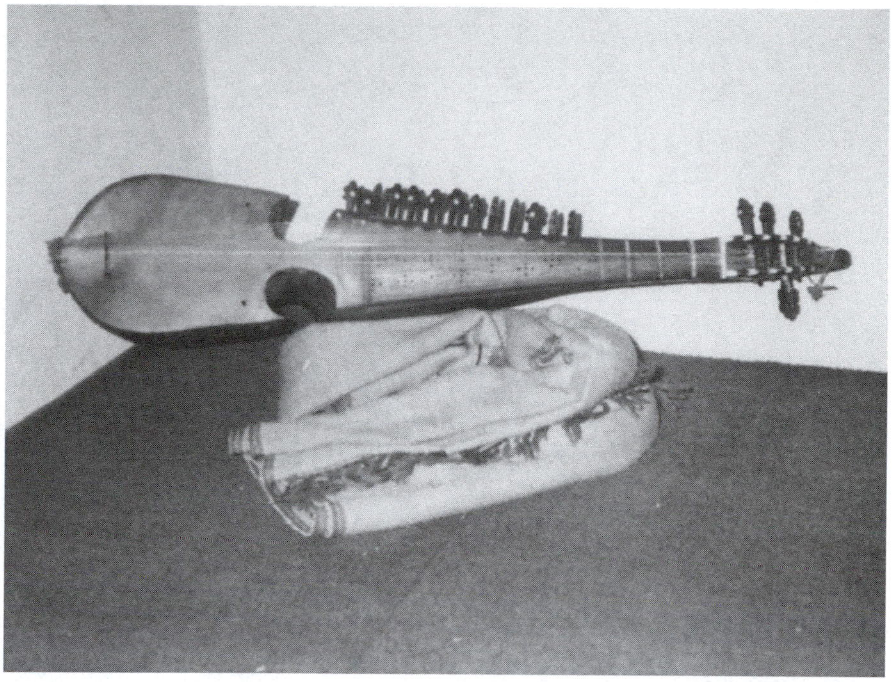

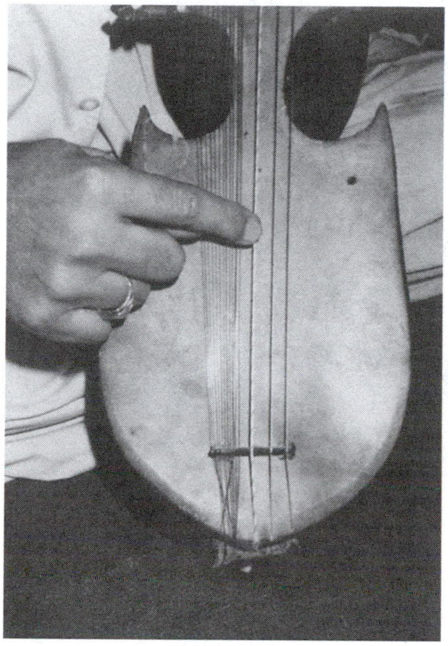

FIGURE 1 The *rabāb*: *right*, front view; *below*, lower part of the *rabāb's* oval belly showing the playing strings, sympathetic strings, and horn bridge (*tātū*). Photos by Mohammad Akbar, 1997.

this word. Sidiqullah Rekhteen, a Pashtun scholar and former head of the Pashtu Academy in Kabul, has traced the origin of the term to two Pakhtu words, *rap rap* or *rapup*, derived from *rap*, meaning "vibration." Currently, Ustad Bakhtiar is the best-known *rabāb* player in NWFP; from the previous generation, the late Ustads Mohammad Zamir and Din Mohammad Chacha stand out. Of the greatest *rabāb* makers, the late Ustad Samander Khan from Dabgari, Peshawar is most prominent.

Sitar

The word *sitār* is derived from the Hindi words for seven strings, *sāt tār*. The best-known type of sitar in NWFP is the *chitrāli sitār*, which is a long-necked lute made of mulberry wood devoid of oils (since wood containing oils disrupts the vibration process critical to the characteristic sound of a sitar). Mulberry wood also contains tiny pores that facilitate the vibrations of the strings by allowing air to pass through them (Booni 1993). The instrument is approximately 122 centimeters long and consists of a guitar-like neck and an oval-shaped, hollow base (figure 2).

The *chitrāli sitār* has six metal playing strings, including two main strings known as *joṛā* 'pair', and five sympathetic strings. Thirteen or fourteen frets (*parda*) made of plastic thread are each wrapped around the neck three or four times. All the strings cross a small, 5- to 8-centimeter bridge (*tātū*) of horny bone and are tied at the lower end to two metallic pegs.

The *chitrāli sitār* is a popular instrument throughout NWFP. It is played by amateur musicians not only in Chitral but also in areas such as Swat, Dir, and the central plains areas inhabited by the Yousafzai tribe. The sitar is usually accompanied by a *māngāi*, a clay pot used mainly for holding water, as well as a tabla drum pair, *rabāb* 'short-necked lute', *tamble* 'frame drum', and other locally made instruments. Among the outstanding sitar players of the past were Shad Mohammad, Gul Rooz, and Zainullah; of today's players, one of the most famous is Wahab Gul of Peshawar.

Sārīndā

Pakhtu musicians claim the *sārindā* was invented and used exclusively by Pakhtuns.

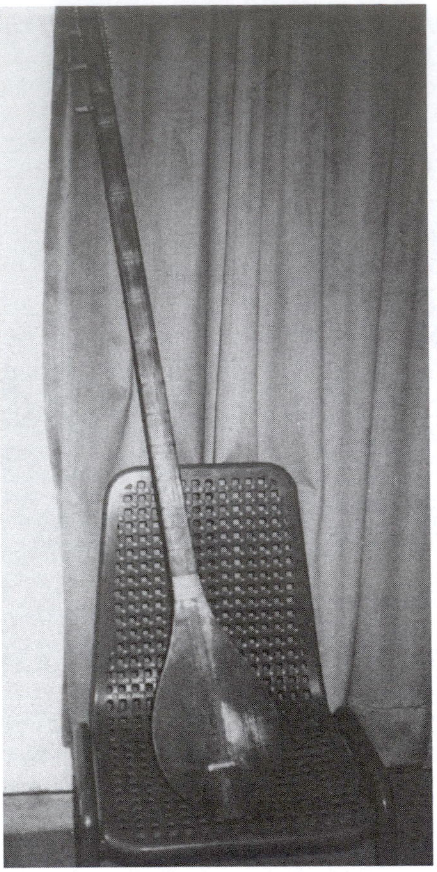

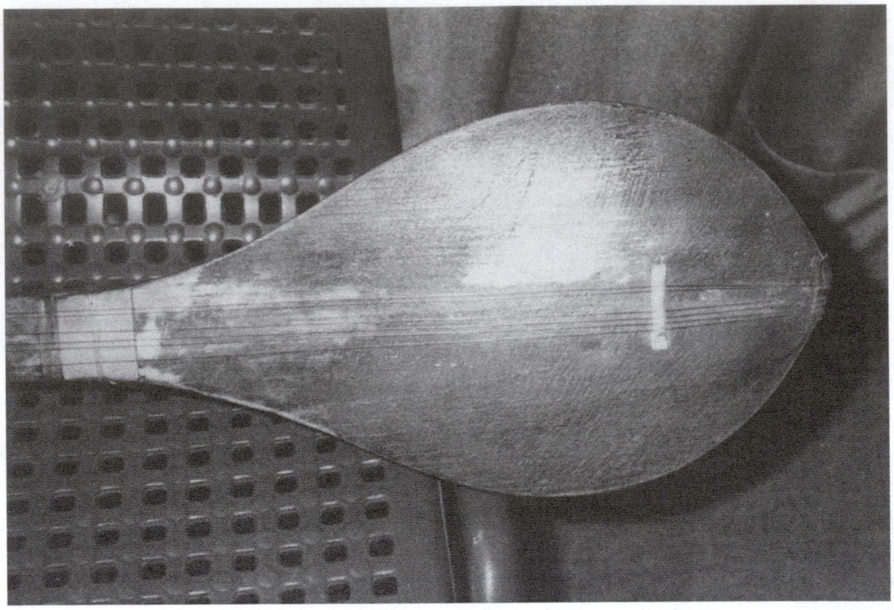

FIGURE 2 The *chitrāli sitār* 'long-necked lute': *above*, front view; *above right*, the six playing strings (sympathetic strings not visible) crossing the horn bridge (*tātū*). Photos by Mohammad Akbar, 1997.

According to the film, TV, and radio musician Ali Haider, the instrument originated in the Tera region of NWFP, which is inhabited mainly by the Pakhtun tribe known as the Afridi. In Tera, the instrument is called a *ghazhaka*, meaning an instrument with a fine soft sound. The name *ghazhaka* is similar to *ghījak*, referring to a spike fiddle of Northern Afghanistan, but the two instruments are different.

The *sārindā* is a short-necked bowed fiddle consisting of three parts: an oval belly, a short chest or neck section, and a curved upper end or head (figure 3). Like the *chitrāli sitār,* it is made of mulberry wood and has sympathetic strings in addition to the three main playing strings, known as *katai, bhum*, and *zhīl.* The belly is waisted with the upper half larger than the lower half and the upper half open whereas the lower half is covered with lamb's skin. The *sārindā* has eighteen pegs, four fixed on the short neck section and the remainder fixed at the upper end. The bow (*gaz*) has strings made of horse tail, and one end is covered with a piece of folded cloth.

Famous *sārindā* players include the late Ustad Pazeer Khan and his son, Munir Sarhadi. Currently Munir Sarhadi's son, Ijaz Sarhadi, is widely considered the foremost *sārindā* player (figure 4).

Shpelāi

The *shpelāi* is a duct flute usually made of bamboo or metal, sometimes of wood. In the high mountains of Swat district in northern NWFP, an eagle's wing bone is occasionally used to increase the penetration and effectiveness of the sound. The flute usually has six finger holes and occasionally a thumb hole in the back. The player holds the flute obliquely and blows through a hole in the upper end; some expert players use circular breathing. A second type of *shpelāi* is a side-blown flute with a closed upper end. The *shpelāi* is considered the musical instrument of lovers.

Da druzu shpelāi

The *da druzu shpelāi* is another kind of flute made from the pipelike stem of the wheat plant and found exclusively in Pakhtun areas. The inventor of this instrument is Zarnoosh Khan of the village of Jhagra near Peshawar. He is considered by many to be the only living expert on the instrument, and he speaks of inventing the instrument during his teenage years and gradually improving his skill.

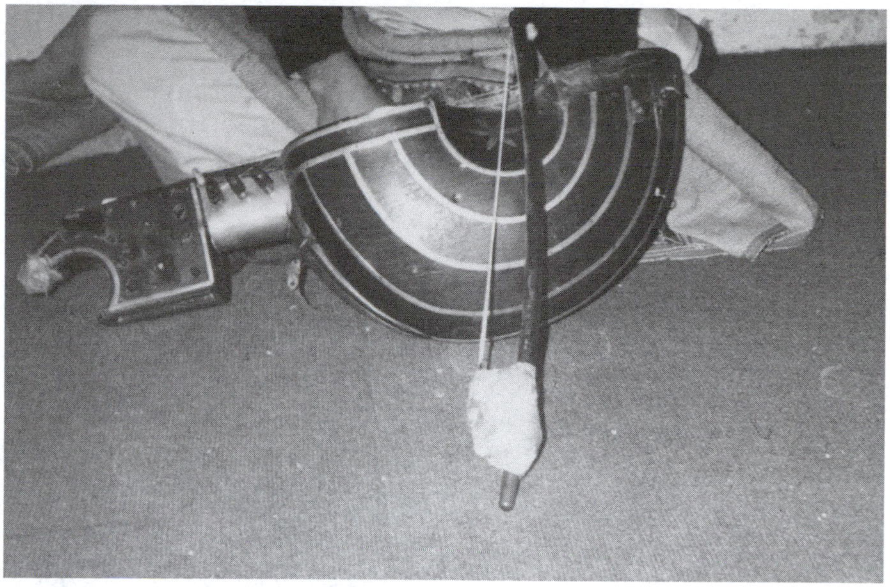

FIGURE 3 Side view of the *sārindā* with the *gaz* horsehair bow. Photo by Mohammad Akbar, 1997.

Sornāīe

The *sornāīe* is a double-reed aerophone frequently played with the *ḍhol* 'cylindrical drum' at weddings and other happy occasions, and to encourage soldiers in times of war. The term derives from two linguistic roots, *sorai* 'hole' and *nāī* 'pipe'.

Māngāi

The *māngāi* or *gaṛāi* is the clay vessel mentioned earlier that serves both as a water pot and as a musical instrument. It has a large round belly, an upper end or mouth, and a short cylindrical neck (figure 5). When played in ensemble with the *rabāb*, its mouth is covered with a circular piece of rubber. It is a popular instrument among Pakhtun youth and women.

The *māngāi* is played in one of two ways. Some players beat its upper end with one hand and the round belly with the other. In this case, they may wear a ring on one finger to produce a clicking sound. It is also played by beating on either side of the round belly with two hands at the same time.

FIGURE 4 Ijaz Sarhadi playing the *sārindā* in Ramdas, Peshawar, 1997. Photo by Mohammad Akbar.

Tamble

The *tamble* or *chamba* is a circular wooden frame drum covered on one side with goat, deer, or wolf skin (figure 6). It is sometimes referred to as *dar* or *daryal*; *dar* is a Sanskrit word for wood similar to the Pakhtu term *lar*, an abbreviation of *largai* 'wood' (Reshteen 1959). The *tamble* is particularly popular among Pakhtun women, who play it alone to accompany their soft, high-pitched singing voices.

Ḍhol

The *ḍhol* 'cylindrical drum' is an old Pakhtu instrument that has long been used on marches and in battles in times of war and at celebrations to accompany the Pakhtun *athuṇ*, the national dance. On such occasions the *ḍhol* player (*ḍholkaymor*) is able to raise the emotional intensity of an important public occasion. Sir Winston Churchill, in his renowned book *Malakand Field Force*, documented the role of such a drummer, a true hero who led the Pakhtun warriors and whom the English failed to capture alive (Churchill 1989). He provided the Pakhtuns with military messages coded into his drumbeats (Rokhan 1992). The importance of the drum in Pakhtu music can also be inferred from the eloquence of the Pakhtun term for the sound of a drum:

The national dance of the Pakhtuns is *athuṇ*, a group dance involving repetitive movements of the head, hands, legs, and feet that strictly follow the drum rhythm.

FIGURE 5 A pair of *māngāi* water pots, played by striking with the hands. Photo by Mohammad Akbar, 1997.

dum. With a slight change in pronunciation, the same word can also mean a singer or a musician.

Tabla

The tabla drum pair is also known in NWFP as *dupree* or *dolkay.* As elsewhere in Pakistan and in India, the smaller right-hand cylindrical drum produces a high-pitched sound (*zīr*), and the larger left-hand kettledrum sounds a deeper tone [see MUSICAL INSTRUMENTS: NORTHERN AREA]. The two drums usually stand on circular bases (*mangela*) made of intertwined ropes. The drumheads consist of a single layer of goatskin and a second layer of cowskin at the outer edge. Leather strips attach the drumheads to the body, passing through a leather hoop known as *gund* 'woven' at the rim. Famous tabla players of the older generation include the late Ustad Taj Mohammad and the late Ustad Gul Sanum. The present generation of players includes Fazal Rabbi and Wali Dad (figure 7).

FIGURE 6 Decorated wooden frame drum, *tamble* or *chamba.* Photo by Mohammad Akbar, 1997.

Harmonium

The harmonium is a free-reed keyboard instrument introduced to South Asia from Europe in the nineteenth century. It has been played more commonly in India than in Pakistan, but has recently emerged as an important component of the Pakhtu orchestra, enjoying prominence in Pakhtu music played on the radio and TV and in films. Renowned players include the late Dilber Raj and Rahdath Hussain and contemporary stars such as Musafer and Ali Haider. Other European instruments such as the guitar and the violin are also used in modern Pakhtu music.

EFFECTS OF MASS MEDIA ON PAKHTU MUSIC

FIGURE 7 The well-known tabla player Wali Dad performing in Ramdas, Peshawar, 1997. Photo by Mohammad Akbar.

Present-day mass media, particularly radio, TV, and film, have provided new avenues for the dissemination of Pakhtu music. In addition, recorded audio and videocassettes are sold by the thousands daily through music shops and street vendors. Interestingly, folk music remains the most popular musical category in NWFP, despite modern trends and foreign musical influences. However, in spite of a flourishing marketplace, singers and musicians often suffer financial hardships, due both to a lack of copyright protection and to the reluctance of music shop owners and videocassette producers to share their profits generously with the artists whose recordings they sell.

There is no formal school of Pakhtu music in NWFP, thus no music degree program or certificate is offered. The Abasin Arts Council in Peshawar is said to be accepting music students; in the Ramdas section of Peshawar, music teachers provide informal lessons to small numbers of students based on family or personal relations. This system keeps the transfer of musical knowledge at the one-on-one level.

Radio Pakistan Peshawar broadcasts more Pakhtu music than does Pakistan TV. Ironically, the total duration of Pakhtu programs from Peshawar TV does not reflect the demographic dominance of Pakhtuns in NWFP. Pakhtu film music has contributed significantly to Pakhtu music in recent decades, although the film industry gives the population quantity rather than quality. Pakhtu singers and musicians such as Gulzar Alam and Master Ali Haider regularly produce cassettes of Pakhtu pop music, despite limited financial resources.

Common contexts for music making are informal music concerts arranged for wedding parties and functions at educational institutions. Such events provide financial support for performing artists. Audiences participate in such concerts with vocal appreciation of the musicians and singers and with dancing. The national dance of the Pakhtuns is *athuṇ*, a group dance involving repetitive movements of the head, hands, legs, and feet that strictly follow the drum rhythm. *Athuṇ* may be danced by men, by women, or by both. Members of the Taliban or students of religious schools in Swat, Dir, and Bajur areas occasionally perform *athuṇ*. Their usual dance location is the lawn of the *madrassa* (religious school) or a room in the same building. Mixed gender *athuṇ* consists of an equal number of men and women and is still a common practice in the Kakaṛ tribe. Most tribes still dance *athuṇ*, although some including the Yousafzai have lost this lively custom. The Khattak tribe performs three common types of *athuṇ* dance: *bangra, shahdolla*, and *bulbula*. Young Khattak soldiers have gained international recognition through their *athuṇ* performances for foreign delegations to the NWFP.

Famous Pakhtu singers of past generations include Gulnar Begum, Ahmad Khan, Qamrojana, Sabz Ali Khan, and Fida Hussain. Among today's well-known singers are Ustad Khyal Mohammad, Hidayatullah, Kishwar Sultan, Khan Tehsil, Zarsanga, Gulzar Alam, and Sardar Ali Takkar. Significant music composers of the past include the late Rehdat Hussain, Farukh Sair Shama and Rafique Shinwari; those of the present day include Sunny, Fazle Rabbi Qais, and Ali Haider.

REFERENCES

Baba, Rehman. 1984. *Da Rehman Baba Kuleyat*, ed. Dost Mohammad Khan Kamil Momand and Qalandar Momand. Peshawar: Chapzai.

Booni, Shamsuddin. 1993. "Chitrali Sitar, a Musical Instrument of Central Asia." *The Frontier Post* 9 (119):12.

Churchill, Winston S. 1989 [1898]. *The Story of Malakand Field Force: An Episode of Frontier War.* London: Leo Cooper.

Reshteen, Sidiqullah. 1959. *Da Zhwund Sandara* (Song of Life). Kabul: Kabul State Press.

Rokhan, Fazal M. 1992. *Da Pukhtano Mosiqee* (On Pukhtun music). Mingora, Swat: Mingora Shoaib Sons, Publishers and Booksellers.

Taizai, Shirzaman. 1993. "Arts and Crafts in Puktoon Wali." *The Frontier Post* 8 (235):12.

Zarsanga. 1993. *Songs of the Pashtu.* Long Distance Music 662295. Compact disc.

Northern Areas of Pakistan

Anna Schmid

The Northern Areas are an administrative unit in northeastern Pakistan bordering Afghanistan to the north, China to the northeast, and India to the south. Lying in the Himalayan-Karakorum mountain ranges, the region has never had direct links with the lowlands, and relations with Central Asia and the Indian subcontinent have always been erratic. The population is characteristically segmented into valley societies, each encompassing one or part of one valley. Until recently, semiautonomous rulers reigned over some valleys, as in Astor, Baltistan, and the Gilgit District, while village councils organized other valley societies into so-called republics, as in the Diamar District. The urban centers are Gilgit and Skardu.

The main economic activity is irrigated agriculture, limited by the available land and water, with additional livestock keeping. The principal crops are wheat, barley, millet, buckwheat, legumes, maize, and potatoes, supplemented by fruits. Nowadays many families have one member employed in tourism or trade, but agriculture is still an important source of subsistence and income.

In contrast to this relative homogeneity in the economic and political domains, there is a rich diversity of language and religion (figure 1). In one valley several ethnolinguistic groups, with different religious affiliations, live together. In the whole area, more than ten different languages belonging to four language families are spoken, the most important being Shina, Balti, Burushaski, Wakhi, and Khowar. Muslims make up 99 percent of the population, belonging to four different Islamic groups, namely the Twelver Shia, Ismailiya, Sunna, and Nur Bakhshia.

The Northern Areas lie between Central Asia and India musically as well as geographically. Music there has incorporated influences from both regions—musicians were brought from Badakhshan (in northern Afghanistan) and were sent to the Mughal court of Akbar in Delhi—although it is not clear to what extent. Nonetheless, its diverse musical genres form a distinct musical area, with three major categories: amateur vocal music, amateur instrumental music, and professional performance by hereditary musicians.

FIGURE 1 Linguistic and religious diversity in the Northern Areas (excluding Diamar District), 1991. Based on Kreutzmann 1996:251 and personal communication.

District	Population	Distribution of Language Groups as a Percentage of the Population						Distribution of Religious Groups as a Percentage of the Population			
		Balti	Burushaski	Khowar	Shina	Wakhi	Others	Ismailiya	Twelver Shia	Sunna	Nur Bakhshia
Ghanche	135,400	96	—	—	3.4	—	0.6	—	43.2	7.9	48.9
Skardu	145,600	87	0.15	—	12.6	—	0.25	0.15	87.45	2.9	9.5
Ghizar	95,300	—	21	28.7	42	3.8	4.5	84.5	0.1	15.4	—
Gilgit	177,500	—	39.8	0.9	51.5	3.6	4.2	28.8	48.1	23.1	—
Northern Areas	553,800	46.5	16.4	5.2	27.9	1.8	2.2	23.8	49	12.4	14.5

AMATEUR MUSIC

Songs

Songs in the various languages, including Shina, Balti, Wakhi, and Khowar, represent the first musical category of amateur music. Those in Shina are most numerous; very few exist in the Burushaski language. Nowadays, amateur singing takes place mostly at private functions; singing on official occasions is rare, only occurring occasionally at weddings or festivals with the performance of one or two songs. Singers are primarily male. Since there is no formal teaching of singing, fathers pass on the vocal traditions to their sons, or send their sons to close relatives to learn songs. Those women who know songs usually learn them from hearing the men sing, and women are usually restricted to listening and watching men perform. Exceptions are some religious activities such as *zikr* 'remembrance', a kind of meditation in which Shia and Ismaili Muslims seek union with the Divine, when a man may accompany women's singing on a tambourine.

Official court occasions were formerly the scene of public vocal performance, both professional and amateur. Male singers were always selected according to their vocal ability, and often individual families encouraged such talent among sons. Frequently, two groups of up to twelve persons would chant alternately. Nowadays, an individual usually recites songs, although at some "women's evenings" during wedding celebrations the parties of the bride and bridegroom will sing alternately in the same way, to praise the outstanding personalities of the bride and bridegroom. The first party sings and the second interrupts with loud shouting, protesting and denying the praised qualities, and then begins to sing before the first group ends, the two groups overlapping. Most often, a drummer accompanies.

Personal relationships are a common topic of the texts; others include politics, history, sectarian clashes, joyful triumph, and praise of rulers, as well as love and other personal feelings.

In the Ismaili community, song performance occurs within religious contexts. To the sounds of the *rabāb* 'plucked lute' and sometimes a tambourine, male chanters (and occasionally female chanters) perform *ginān* (Nasiruddin n.d.), poetic religious compositions praising the imam (Muslim leader). *Ginān* chanting occurs mostly during *zikr* and thus follows the South Asian Sufic tradition. In Baltistan, men recite *marsīya* hymns during the first ten days of the month of Muharram that tell of the battle at Karbala, where Hussein, the grandson of Muhammad, died a martyr (Söhnen 1993).

Instrumental music

Playing an instrument as a leisure-time activity is the second category of amateur music in the Northern Areas. The *rabāb*, the sitar, and a simple fipple flute are the main instruments, and are played by men only. Performances are mostly indoors, in private places, except for flute playing by shepherds in the pastures. Men may play alone or in the company of friends, relatives, or members of age groups, with no specific occasion necessary. However, this kind of activity is not common, as very few people indulge in playing an instrument: the sitar and *rabāb* are considered refined instruments that can be mastered only by educated people who are knowledgeable about Indian classical music. Such amateur musical activities contrast sharply with the third category, professional performance by hereditary musicians.

PROFESSIONAL INSTRUMENTAL MUSIC

Hereditary musicians and their ensembles

Hereditary musicians called Ḍom in Shina and in other Indian languages, Mon in Balti, and Berico in Burushaski, perform the predominant instrumental music, *harīp* or *sāz*. These musicians migrated from North India, south of Kashmir, in several waves from an unknown time period up to about 1800 (Buddruss 1983; Fussmann 1972; Lorimer 1939). The name Ḍom often indicates a caste or ethnic group. Contrary to what is often repeated, this term does not denote a widespread single group, but is a generic term for several endogamous professional groups at the low end of the social hierarchy.

The phrase *ḍomogushpur rajogushpur* 'the dom prince the ruler prince' denotes that the hereditary musicians and the ruler descended from one ancestral source, the royal family, thus expressing the integration of music within society. Traditional narratives explain the original split into these two different groups. The former were sent away for education, but instead of learning to read and write they met the devil, Sheitan, who introduced them to music; the result was their acquisition of musical skills, but also their exclusion from royal succession. From then on, they had to accompany the ruler and play in front of him in processions, thus symbolizing royalty themselves. But it was the ruler who controlled the musicians, and thus also the musical events.

Ḍom ensembles embrace at least three musicians, each playing a different instrument: one aerophone—according to the occasion the player chooses either the double-reed *surnāī,* the fipple flute, or the transverse flute—and two membranophones, the *ḍaḍañ* 'double-headed drum' and *ḍāmal* 'pair of kettledrums', a combination common across Central Asia and throughout the Islamic world. Every musician specializes in one kind of instrument, and is named according to the one chosen: *surnāījī, ḍaḍañjī,* or *ḍāmaljī.*

The instrumental music performed by hereditary musicians is generally called *harīp.* The term also refers to music in general and to single tunes, which are further identified by adding the names of persons, places, regions, or events (as in *Qalandar-harīp*, Qalandar being a wandering mystic or entertainer). Another meaning of *harīp* is the instrumental musical style: the melody played on the wind instrument expresses the musical content, with the bass drum reinforcing and dramatizing the texture. The term *sāz* (of Persian origin) has a broader meaning, including all music of the Northern Areas, both professional and amateur. As used by the upper class, however, the term does not include the music of the hereditary musicians.

Until the early 1970s, music teaching for the most part took the form of copying the master and practicing in a *tamāshā* 'dance event'. The teacher, usually the father, gave his pupil some basic formal lessons, but students learned to play mostly by watching the teacher in performance and imitating him. The teacher would decide when his pupil was ready to join the ensemble and would announce the performance; the ruler or council would reward the pupil. After the local rulers were deposed in 1972–1974, this system of teaching was not replaced. Most professional musicians stopped teaching their children and sought formal schooling for them, hoping to guarantee them a far more promising future. However, some boys were fond of music and could not be discouraged from learning informally; they continued to practice the repertoire of *harīp* tunes on their own.

The Ḍom stress that being a musician is an entire lifestyle, and that for them no other activity is as important. Wherever they are, whatever they are doing, thinking about music and composing a tune must be possible—a way of life at odds with the necessities of an agricultural society and of a formal education. But for the Ḍom, becoming a renowned musician is possible only by concentrating totally on music.

Musical instruments

The *surnāī* is a double-reed wind instrument with a conical bore, seven finger holes and a thumb hole, similar to the Indian *śahnāī.* Sometimes silver or gold metalwork

The long transverse flute has mythological significance within Ḍom culture, for the sixth hole symbolizes the entrance for fairies during a seance.

decorates the ends of the wooden aerophone, thus signifying the honor and competence of the musician and often the gift of a local ruler. It is most often used for outdoor activities and to accompany dance. At indoor activities, or occasionally to intone sad, nondance melodies on outdoor occasions, musicians employ a fipple flute or small transverse flute. A long transverse flute exists but is played only at shamanic seances. Unlike the other aerophones, this has six front finger holes, of which only five are played. The instrument has mythological significance within the culture, for the sixth hole symbolizes the entrance for fairies during a seance. According to legend, the fairies prefer the sound of the long flute to that of the *surnāī* or the fipple flute, and consequently communicate their messages through the former. Seances are now largely tourist attractions and only rarely performed to cure illness, so the long flute is uncommon. Until the dismissal of the local rulers, seances were performed to predict political events and the future of the community, as well as to cure the sick and seek advice.

The *ḍaḍañ* 'double-headed drum' is also believed to be an instrument through which the fairies speak, but its employment is not restricted to seances. The player beats the left drumhead with the left hand and the right with a curved stick. In processions such as a bridal party, this bass drummer slings the instrument around his neck, but in all other musical activities the drummer—like the other musicians—sits cross-legged, with the drum on the floor in front of him. Either the musician himself or a local carpenter makes the drums, using specially selected apricot or willow wood and goatskin. For the copper-alloy *ḍāmal* 'kettledrums', drum makers import the metal bodies from Lahore but make the ox-leather membranes locally. Musicians play kettledrums with two straight sticks.

While performing, the musicians sit in fixed positions relative to each other, enabling them to hear the tuning of their instruments: the double-reed player sits on the right side, the bass-drum player on the left, and the kettledrum player in the middle (figure 2). This positioning also reflects a hierarchy of players' roles: the *surnāīj̄ī* (playing the only melody instrument) is the leader of the ensemble, the bass drummer follows the *surnāī* playing its keynote, and the kettledrum player is third in rank, playing the same pitch. Both drummers begin every tune playing the same rhythm; the kettledrum player continues with that rhythm throughout, while the bass drum varies its rhythms.

Performance contexts and dance ceremonies

Professional instrumentalists perform in a variety of contexts: shamanistic seances, seasonal festivals, religious events, polo matches, elections, inauguration ceremonies for newly constructed roads and buildings, and receptions for important guests. The musicians select melodies from the *dāni* or *harīp* categories, according to the occasion. For traditional events they perform prescribed tunes named after the occasion, though at contemporary gatherings the musicians have freedom to choose the music.

FIGURE 2 Hereditary musicians perform at a dancing ceremony in Baltit on the Muslim festival of ʿĪdu'l-fiṭr, July 1988. The money on the ground is from appreciative audience members. The instruments of the ensemble are, from left, two double-reed instruments (*surnāī*), kettledrums, and a double-headed bass drum. Photo by Anna Schmid.

FIGURE 3 A refined dancer performs after a polo match on the polo ground in Gilgit, June 1990. Two ensembles of musicians are sitting on the rear wall. At polo matches each team usually has its own band, and the two ensembles perform alternately, depending on whose team has the ball. Photo by Anna Schmid.

Any of these contexts may incorporate dancing (*tamāshā)* (figure 3). The location depends on the event—weddings take place in a certain house, celebrations for the beginning of the harvest occur along a specific canal. Close by the location or at the central village meeting place, organizers prepare a dancing area in the open; the place is purified, platforms are erected for distinguished guests, and the musicians take their places.

At the first drum sounds people start gathering either to dance or to watch, the spectators congregating around the dancing space in concentric circles. Formerly, the local ruler or village headman presided over a *tamāshā*, but since the early 1970s youth groups, political parties, or village organizations arrange them. The succession of tunes determines the order of events. The hereditary musicians claim that the opening tune was the first they composed when they arrived in the Northern Areas, and they always play this instrumental dance tune to begin a *tamāshā*. After this, groups of relatives, members of age groups, and renowned single dancers take their turn dancing, most often to specifically appropriate "ascribed" tunes (see below). In general there is no singing on such an occasion, although occasionally a respected singer may present one song between dances. These events may start in the late morning and last until dusk.

Similar entertainments in private houses, referred to as *bāzum* 'gathering', might celebrate the reunion of two friends after a long separation, or a successful business transaction; the only limiting factor generally is the cost of hiring musicians. Whereas in the nineteenth century, prior to British rule in this area, festivals and dancing were part of ritual celebrations, today people give priority to the dancing itself as an opportunity to interrupt the daily routine.

WOMEN AND MUSIC

Women participate in the *tamāshā* dancing as spectators standing in the background, and for many male dancers the women or one special woman are the most important audience. They appreciate a competent dancer and encourage him through hand clapping and exclamations. Until the mid-1930s, women danced in public, but they have not done so since that period, as conformity to Islamic dictates has become stronger. Occasionally women in the Ismaili areas (Hunza and parts of Gilgit and the

Yasin Valley) dance in private houses; in no sector of the Northern Areas do women play musical instruments.

THE POWER OF MUSIC

Public musical performance in the Northern Areas is synonymous with music performed by professional musicians, including *tamāshā* dance music. This identification means that professional musicians hold considerable power. They can greatly enhance or debase a dancer by their instrumental performance, influencing the dancer's status, as outstanding performances require a close relationship between musicians and dancer. If the musicians choose not to interact musically with the dancer, then the dancer cannot perform well and suffers humiliation and disgrace. Thus the dancers fear the professional musicians' power.

Society counteracts the musicians' power by according them low social status, in effect dictating that a group that monopolizes or controls certain powerful means like music may not assume power within the larger society. Professional musicians must live in separate quarters in villages, may not have representatives in political forums, and are generally considered inferior, unable to meet the standard requirements of social behavior and cultural values. Their participation in the power of music is thus contradictory: they produce the means (that is, music) to express central societal and cultural values, as in dancing ceremonies, and yet they are considered unable to fulfill these societal and cultural requirements.

MELODIC COMPOSITIONS

Musicians draw on a rich corpus of melodies composed over many generations. According to traditional narratives, musicians invented the first tune "when coming back from their educational journey." When both rulers and society had accepted this new musical style, the musicians proceeded to compose new tunes capturing specific atmospheres or moods, naming melodies after an occasion or a person. That first tune was assigned to the ruler, and was played to open all royal ceremonies. A whole category of tunes was in fact reserved for the ruler and his family, with special tunes for whenever the ruler moved, entered a village, or took his afternoon nap.

A second category comprises tunes for specific events such as seasonal festivals, weddings, and polo matches. The music for each event consists of a set of twelve melodies, denoting different phases in the event. In a third category are tunes composed for outstanding occasions such as triumphant battles, love affairs with political implications, or heroic deeds. This category contains the personally ascribed tunes which, when performed, give the celebrated man the privilege of dancing in the next *tamāshā.* The musicians in all three categories are concerned only with the composition of melodies, not with that of song lyrics.

Newly composed tunes further enlarge this rich melodic system. These are mostly songs that the Ḍom musicians adapt after hearing them on the radio. Shortly after the composition is completed, the "owner" of the tune invites his relatives, a singer, and some musicians to a first rehearsal. He will repeat the dance as the musicians play until the audience is satisfied with the performance.

The ownership of tunes, together with the composition process involving singer, musician, and owner, results in a multilayered interaction. Due to their competence, the musicians are the defining actors in this interplay: they decide when the composition is complete, they strongly influence the dance performance through their own performance, and they are in a position to allow the dancer to show off his skill, or to prevent him from doing so, turning the honorific action of dancing into a disgraceful humiliation. Dancers and audience alike recognize and fear this powerful position of the musicians, and this control by the musicians represents a significant force within the power of music as it is translated in dance ceremonies. Only recently have members of the Ḍom group been allowed to participate in the act of dancing itself, thereby loosening the restrictions traditionally placed on them.

HISTORICAL PERSPECTIVE

Long before the 1970s, when local rulers and political councils were still in command of musical performance and were simultaneously the patrons of the hereditary musicians, they rewarded extraordinary performances, paid the musicians in kind, encouraged new compositions, and sometimes were even responsible for the manufacture of new instruments, all the time considering political groupings and adjusting to their demands in order to maintain a fragile balance among various parties. The same was true of dancing ceremonies, through the assignment of dances and the ascription of tunes. But when the British gradually conquered the Northern Areas in the last quarter of the nineteenth century, this balance changed. The rulers no longer sought alliances with mighty clans but received support from the British, which resulted in an autocratic form of rulership. This slowly led to the decontextualization of musical activities, culminating in the final dismissal of local rulers in 1972–1974. The process received further support from a strengthened attitude toward Islam. Religious arguments were put forward against music in the Northern Areas; its value further declined, and the musicians were viewed as proponents of un-Islamic behavior. In some parts of the Northern Areas they were even expected to destroy their instruments to prove their religious ardor. The lowering of esteem for music in the local context, and the new reputation of music as un-Islamic drove many musicians to give up their profession.

Recent developments

To counter these developments, efforts are now being made to encourage music teaching. There are plans to establish a cultural center in Gilgit, representing the cultures of the neighboring valleys. Music and dance will be among the subjects taught; discussions about a formal curriculum have already taken place. However, the issue of how to constitute classes with hereditary musicians as teachers of pupils from other social groups remains problematic. Parents are concerned about the low social status of the teachers, and the hereditary musicians are concerned that their income will diminish if others become musical performers. Solutions to these problems have not been found.

Tourism is bringing an increased demand for local *tamāshā*. Not only is the remuneration for the musicians considerable, but the increasing interest stimulates them to continue professional music making. The local radio stations in Gilgit and Skardu broadcast local music and songs, mostly in Shina. Some musicians aim to be recorded for this programming, which they feel will augment the value of their work. Radio and cassette players provide a very strong incentive for musicians both to make music and to record it; they often transform songs from films into instrumental tunes. People play the cassette tapes in private and in public arenas such as transport vehicles or music shops in the bazaar.

REVIEW OF SCHOLARSHIP

The substantial literature on the Northern Areas ranges from reports of colonial officers and travel accounts to scientific research by scholars in various disciplines. Most publications mention musical activities, but only a few discuss them in any detail. Colonial officers often witnessed musical activities; they describe polo matches (Drew 1980; Haughton 1913), shamanic seances (Biddulph 1978; Lorimer 1931, 1935–1938, 1939), festivals such as weddings (Schomberg 1935) or seasonal celebra-

Radio and cassette players provide a very strong incentive for musicians both to make music and to record it; they often transform songs from films into instrumental tunes.

tions (Biddulph 1978; Leitner 1877, 1893a–c, 1894; Lorimer 1931, 1935–1938, 1939); some reports include songs (Biddulph 1978; Ghulam Muhammad 1905; Haughton 1913; Leitner 1877, 1893c, 1894).

In recent scientific publications, authors have included music and musical activities—specifically when they focus on religious topics and include shamanism (Dilthey 1971; Frembgen 1985, 1986, 1988; Friedl 1965; Jettmar 1961, 1975, 1979, 1983; Müller-Stellrecht 1973, 1979, 1980; Nayyar 1986). Only a few researchers have concentrated on music, musical activities, and musicians from either a linguistic, musicological, or anthropological perspective.

Linguists and amateur enthusiasts have recorded songs in different parts of the Northern Areas (Berger 1960, 1985; Biddulph 1978; Buddruss 1983; Jettmar 1983; Leitner 1877, 1893n, c, 1894; Lorimer 1935–1938; Söhnen 1983, 1993). In many instances, singers recited the songs especially for the fieldworker, so the description does not include the traditional context. Musicologists have also researched the musical culture; Farhana and others (1989) carried out a preliminary study of the musical culture of Baltistan, and Söhnen (1983) analyzed melodic structure on the basis of recorded songs. Huehns (1991) attempted an overview of the musical culture of the whole area, including the adjacent district of Chitral. Apart from their linguistic merits, the publications of Lorimer and Buddruss on Ḍomaakí, the language of the musicians and blacksmiths in Nager and Hunza, present the first insights into this group's worldview. In my own work, I have focused on social, cultural, and political aspects of the interethnic relationship between the hereditary musicians and blacksmiths and the wider society in Hunza and Nager (Schmid 1997). Two LP records preserve music of this area (Biltgen, Thomas, and Tissot 1962; Lewiston 1974). A thorough study of music in all cultures of the Northern Areas has not yet been undertaken.

REFERENCES

Berger, Hermann. 1960. "Bericht über sprachliche und volkskundliche Forschungen im Hunzatal" (Report on linguistic and folkloric research in the Hunza Valley). *Anthropos* 55:657–664.

———. 1985. "A Survey of Burushaski Studies." *Journal of Central Asia* 8(1):33–37.

Biddulph, John. 1978 [1880]. *Tribes of the Hindoo Koosh.* Lahore: Ali Kamran Publishers.

Biltgen, J., G. Thomas, and F. Tissot. 1962. *Cachemire vallées himalayennes* (The Himalayan valleys of Kashmir). BAM, LD 400 M. LP disk.

Buddruss, Georg. 1983. "Ḍomaakí *chot* 'Ton': Mit Beiträgen zur historischen Lautlehre" (Ḍomaakí *chot* 'tone': With contributions on historical phonetics). *Münchner Studien zur Sprachwissenschaft* 42:5–21.

———. 1984. "Ḍomaakí-Nachträge zum Atlas der Dardsprachen" (Ḍomaakí postscripts to the atlas of languages). *Münchner Studien zur Sprachwissenschaft* 43:9–24.

———. 1986. "Hindi *phūl,* Ḍomaakí *phulé.*" *Münchner Studien zur Sprachwissenschaft* 47:71–77.

Buddruss, Georg, and Sigrun Wiehler-Schneider. 1978. "Wakhi-Lieder aus Hunza" (Wakhi songs of the Hunza). *Jahrbuch für musikalische Volks- und Völkerkunde* 9:89–110.

Dilthey, Helmtraut. 1971. *Versammlungsplätze im Dardo-Kafirischen Raum* (Meeting places in the Dardic-Kafiri area). Wiesbaden: Otto Harrassowitz.

Drew, Frederic. 1976 [1875]. *The Jummoo and Kashmir Territories. A Geographical Account* (New Preface by C.-J. Charpentier). Karachi: Indus Publications.

Farhana Faruqi, Ashok Kumar, Anwar Mohyuddin, and Hiromi Lorraine Sakata. 1989. *Musical Survey of Pakistan: Three Pilot Studies.* Islamabad: Lok Virsa Research Center.

Frembgen, Jürgen. 1985. *Zentrale Gewalt in Nager (Karakorum): Politische Organisationsformen, ideologische Begründungen des Königtums und Veränderungen in der Moderne* (Central power in Nager [Karakorum]: Forms of political organization, ideological foundations of monarchy, and modern changes). Wiesbaden: Franz Steiner Verlag.

———. 1986. "Ethnographical Field-Research on the History and Culture of Nager: Some Preliminary Remarks on the Process of Settlement." *Central Asiatic Journal* 30(1–2):22–34.

———. 1988. "Polo in Nager. Zur Ethnographie eines orientalischen Reiterspiels" (Polo in Nager: On the ethnography of an eastern horseman's game). *Zentralasiatische Studien* 21:197–217.

Friedl, Erika. 1965. *Träger medialer Begabung im Hindukusch und Karakorum* (Median talent level in the Hindu Kush and Karakorum). Vienna: Österreichisch ethnologische Gesellschaft im Eigenverlag.

Fussman, Gérard. 1972. *Atlas linguistique des parlers Dardes et Kafirs* (Linguistic atlas of Dardic and Kafiri dialects), vol. I. Carte; Vol. II. Commentaire. Paris: École française d'extrème-Orient.

———. 1989. "Languages as a Source for History." In *History of the Northern Areas of Pakistan,* ed. Ahmad Hasan Dani, 43–58. Islamabad: National Institute of Historical and Cultural Research.

Ghulam Muhammad. 1905. "Festivals and Folklore in Gilgit." *Memoirs of the Asiatic Society of Bengal* NS 18(7):93–129.

Government of Pakistan. 1984. *1981 District Census Report of Gilgit.* Islamabad: Government of Pakistan.

Haughton, H. L. 1913. *Sport and Folklore in the Himalaya.* London: Edward Arnold.

Huehns, Colin. 1991. "Music of Northern Pakistan." Ph.D. dissertation, Cambridge University.

Jettmar, Karl. 1960. "The Cultural History of Northwest Pakistan." *Yearbook of the American Philosophical Society* 492–499.

———. 1961. "Ethnological Research in Dardistan 1958." *Proceedings of the American Philosophical Society* 105(1):79–97.

———. 1975. *Die Religionen des Hindukusch* (The religions of the Hindu Kush). Stuttgart: Kohlhammer.

———. 1977a. "Bolor—A Contribution to the Political and Ethnic Geography of North Pakistan." *Zentralasiatische Studien* 11:411–448.

———. 1977b. "Fragment einer Balti-Version der Kesar-Sage" (Fragment of a Balti version of the Kesar legend). *Zentralasiatische Studien* 11:277–286.

———. 1979. "Zur Kesar-Sage in Baltistan und Ladakh" (On the Kesar legend in Baltistan and Ladakh). *Zentralasiatische Studien* 13:325–338.

———. 1983. "Indus-Kohistan. Entwurf einer historischen Ethnographie" (Indus-Kohistan: Outline of an ethnographic history). *Anthropos* 78:501–518.

Kreutzmann, Hermann. 1995. "Sprachenvielfalt und regionale Differenzierung von Glaubensgemeinschaften im Hindukusch-Karakorum" (Language varieties and the differentiation of religious sects in Karakorum and the Hindu Kush). *Erdkunde* 49:106–121.

———. 1996. *Ethnizität im Entwicklungsprozeß: Die Wakhi in Hochasien* (Ethnicity in the course of development: The Wakhi of the Asian highlands). Berlin: Dietrich Reimer Verlag.

Leitner, Gottlieb W. 1877. *The Language and Races of Dardistan.* Lahore: Government Central Book Depot.

———. 1893a. "Dardistan. Legends, Routes and Wars in Chilas." *The Imperial and Asiatic Quarterly Review* 6(II):202–207.

———. 1893b. *The Hunza and Nagyr Handbook. Being an Introduction to a Knowledge of the Language, Race, and Countries of Hunza, Nagyr, and a Part of Yasin.* Woking: Oriental University Institute.

———. 1893c. "Legends, Songs, Customs and History of Dardistan." *The Imperial and Asiatic Quarterly Review* 5(I):143–182.

———. 1894. *Dardistan in 1866, 1886, 1893.* Woking: Oriental University Institute.

Lewiston, David. 1974. *Music in the Karakorums of Central Asia. Recorded in Hunza and Gilgit.* Nonesuch H-72061. LP disk.

Lorimer, David L. R. 1931. "An Oral Version of the Kesar Saga from Hunza." *Folk-Lore* 42:105–139.

———. 1935–1938. *The Burushaski Language.* 3 vols. Oslo: H. Aschehoug and Co.

———. 1939. *The Dumaki Language. Outlines of the Speech of the Doma, or Bericho, of Hunza.* Nijmegen: Dekker and van de Vegt N.V.

Müller-Stellrecht, Irmtraud. 1973. *Feste in Dardistan: Darstellung und kulturgeschichtliche Analyse* (Festive celebrations in Dardistan: Description and cultural-historical analysis). Wiesbaden: Franz Steiner Verlag.

———. 1979. *Materialien zur Ethnographie von Dardistan (Pakistan): Aus den nachgelassenen Aufzeichnungen von D. L. R. Lorimer* (Ethnographic material on Dardistan [Pakistan]: From the posthumous notes of D. L. R. Lorimer). Part I: Hunza. Graz: Akademische Druck- und Verlagsanstalt.

———. 1980. *Materialien zur Ethnographie von Dardistan (Pakistan). Aus den nachgelassenen Aufzeichnungen von D. L. R. Lorimer* (Ethnographic material on Dardistan [Pakistan]: From the posthumous notes of D. L. R. Lorimer). Part II: Gilgit; Part III: Chitral and Yasin. Graz: Akademische Druck- u. Verlagsanstalt.

Nasiruddin "Nasir" Hunzai. n.d. *English Version of Some Selected Gináns from DIWAN-I NASIRI.* Karachi: Kahnah-i Hikmat.

Nayyar, Adam. 1986. *Astor: Eine Ethnographie* (Astor: An ethnography). Wiesbaden: Steiner Verlag.

Schmid, Anna. 1993. *Die Dom zwischen sozialer Ohnmacht und kultureller Macht. Interethnischen Beziehungen in Nordpakistan* (The Ḍom between social stigma and cultural power: Interethnic relations in northern Pakistan). Wiesbaden: Franz Steiner Verlag.

Schomberg, Reginald C. F. 1935. *Between the Oxus and the Indus.* London: Martin Hopkins.

Söhnen, Renate. 1983. "On Reflections of Historical Events in Balti Folk Songs." In *Ethnologie und Geschichte. Festschrift für Karl Jettmar*, ed. Peter Snoy, 582–601. Wiesbaden: Franz Steiner Verlag.

———. 1984. "Treasures of Literary and Musical Traditions in Baltistan." *Journal of Central Asia* VII(2):39–48.

———. 1993. "Music from Baltistan." In *Contemporary German Contributions to the History and Culture of Pakistan*, ed. Stephanie Zingel-Avé Lallemant and Wolfgang-Peter Zingel, 109–126. Bonn: Deutsch-Pakistanisches Forum e.V.

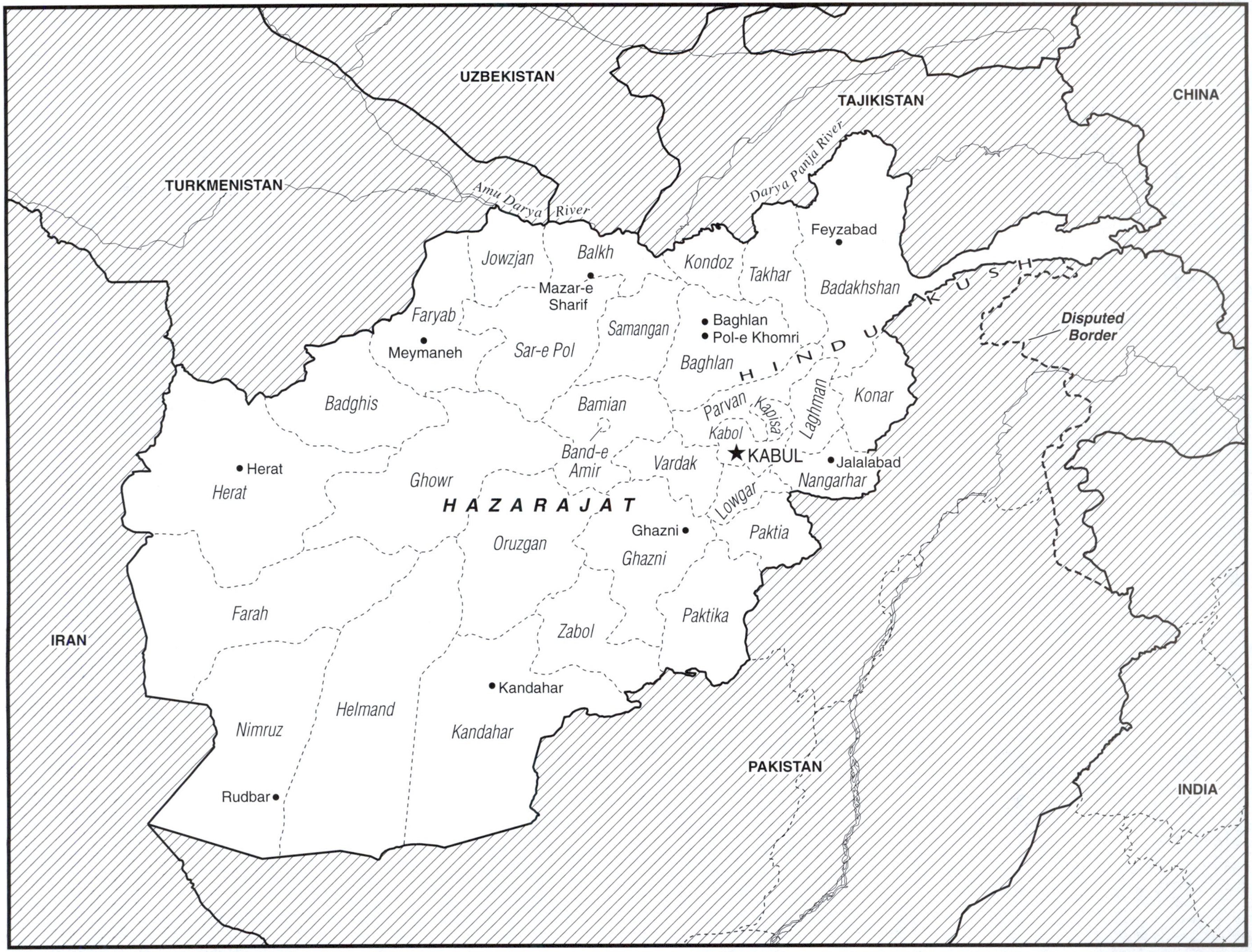

UZBEKISTAN
TAJIKISTAN
CHINA
TURKMENISTAN
Amu Darya River
Darya Panja River
Feyzabad
Jowzjan
Balkh
Kondoz
Takhar
Badakhshan
Mazar-e Sharif
Faryab
Samangan
Baghlan
Pol-e Khomri
Meymaneh
Sar-e Pol
Baghlan
HINDU KUSH
Disputed Border
Badghis
Bamian
Parvan
Kapisa
Laghman
Konar
Kabol
KABUL
Jalalabad
Band-e Amir
Vardak
Nangarhar
Herat
Herat
Ghowr
HAZARAJAT
Lowgar
Ghazni
Paktia
Oruzgan
Ghazni
Farah
Paktika
IRAN
Zabol
Kandahar
Helmand
Nimruz
Kandahar
PAKISTAN
INDIA
Rudbar

Afghanistan

Romantic ghazals, virtuosic lute playing, joyful wedding songs and dances, soothing lullabies, loud shawm-and-drum music, community recreational dances, epic songs—until recently all of these were part of the cultural landscape of Afghanistan. Women in groups sang to the accompaniment of frame drums, and men improvised poetic quatrains while accompanying themselves on long-necked lutes. However, increasingly severe restrictions on musical performance instituted by successive leaders, starting with the Communist government in the late 1970s, now leave in doubt the extent of current musical practice. The traditions described in the following articles represent the music of the Afghani people prior to and even in the midst of the present political situation.

MAP 9 Afghanistan

Music and the State

John Baily

The Afghan Court and Its Music
Radio Broadcasting and Afghan National Identity
Afghan Popular Music
The Marxist Regimes, 1978–1992
Music in the Post-Communist Era

In contrast to that of its neighboring countries Iran, Pakistan, and Uzbekistan, the history of music in Afghanistan remains largely undocumented. Alexander the Great conquered the region c. 330 B.C., and pockets of Greek culture survived for several centuries thereafter, but nothing is known of music in that epoch. Similarly, little is known about the music of the Ghaznavid (tenth to twelfth centuries) and Ghorid empires (twelfth and thirteenth centuries), which encompassed Afghanistan and parts of northern India and were largely responsible for the spread of Islamic culture over the Indian subcontinent. In the fifteenth century the city of Herat, in western Afghanistan, became the capital of the Timurid empire and was the cultural center of the Persian-speaking world. Some records exist of the court music of this era (Baily 1988:12–15). The musical instruments in use were those associated with the Middle East, such as the lute (*ūd*), end-blown flute (*ney*), spike fiddle (*ghīchak*), plucked zither (*qānūn*), and long-necked lute (*tambūrā*); the music was a sophisticated vocal and instrumental art based on Middle Eastern melodic modes (*maqām*). After the Timurids, there is another long gap in the musical record. With a dearth of written records, our understanding of the history of music in Afghanistan must draw largely on oral sources. These, together with extrapolation from contemporary performance practice, provide information dating back to the mid-nineteenth century.

The population of Afghanistan comprises a number of ethnic groups with distinct languages, identities, and cultures. In socioeconomic terms, they range from pastoral nomads to the mercantile classes of cities that have existed for many centuries. Few of these ethnic groups are confined to Afghanistan, as most belong to larger populations that inhabit adjacent countries as well—Iran, Pakistan, China, Tajikistan, Uzbekistan, and Turkmenistan—and share their Islamic faith, whether Sunni or Shia. Since the establishment of Afghanistan in 1747 as the distinct political entity known today, the Pashtuns have dominated the country. This most populous ethnic group, the "true Afghans," makes up about half the total estimated population of 15 million people. A second large group are the Tajiks, who number 3 or 4 million (according to pre-1978 estimates). Both groups extend over much of the territory of Afghanistan. The language of the Pashtuns is Pashto; that of the Tajiks is the form of Afghan Persian officially known as Dari and popularly referred to as Farsi. In addition, there are a number of other smaller localized groups: Aimaq, Baloch, Hazara, Kazakh, Kirghiz, Nuristani, Pashai, Turkmen, Uzbek, and others. Regional musics are associated with all of these groups, but there are also national types of music the whole country shares, most conspicuously in the cities of Herat, Jalalabad, Kabul, Mazar-e Sharif, and Kandahar.

THE AFGHAN COURT AND ITS MUSIC

The Pashtun Abdali tribesmen who established Afghanistan as a state in 1747 came from the southern part of the territory, and the southern city of Kandahar was the original capital of the new country. In 1776, Timur Shah moved the capital to Kabul, previously a mountain resort much favored by the Mughal emperors and burial place of Babur, the first Mughal ruler. In due course, the court of Kabul's amirs became an important center of musical patronage, especially of art-music genres adopted from North India. From the sixteenth to eighteenth centuries, when the eastern half of Afghanistan was part of the Mughal empire, Hindustani music was undoubtedly performed there. Evidence of Indian music in Kabul dates from the reign of the Afghan ruler Sher Ali Khan, who brought several Indian court musicians to the city in the 1860s. At least some came from Kasur, near Lahore. Ever since that time, the court music of Afghan's rulers has shown the strong influence of Hindustani music.

The male court musicians in Kabul cultivated vocal art music genres such as *dhrupad* and *khyāl*, and instrumental renditions of Hindustani modes, but they also developed two genres that constituted a distinctly Afghan art music: the *ghazal* song form and the extended instrumental form *naghma-ye kashāl.* Gradually, these court genres became more widely disseminated. From the 1860s to the 1970s, a succession of Afghan monarchs—Sher Ali, Abdur Rahman, Habibullah, Amanullah, and Zaher Shah—enthusiastically patronized music. The Indian court musicians and their descendants resided in a musicians' quarter in the old city, close to the royal palace (figure 1). They were known collectively by the name of *ustād* 'master, teacher', for their musical skills, their knowledge of Hindustani music theory, and their lineages.

FIGURE 1 The musicians' quarter in the old city, Kabul, 1974. Photo by Veronica Doubleday.

The Kabuli ghazal

The Kabuli ghazal is the main vocal art-music genre of Afghanistan. In Hindustani music, the ghazal is a well-established light-classical form, and the Kabuli version is based on the Indian model, with certain local characteristics. The ghazal is furthermore the principal form of Persian and Pashto poetry, consisting of series of couplets in a particular meter and rhyme scheme. The Kabuli ghazal generally consists of Persian texts, often from the great poets of the Persian language such as Sa'di (c. 1184–1292), Hafez (c. 1320–1390) and Bedil (d. 1872). Its music employs Hindustani ragas and talas.

The ghazal as a musical form has a cyclical organization, in which fast instrumental sections alternate with vocal text units. In performance, the text divides into refrain and verses; generally the first couplet functions as the refrain and the other couplets as verses, with the refrain repeated after each. The melodies for refrain and verse, termed *āstāī* and *antarā,* are distinct, the former having a lower tessitura than the latter. A third component of the ghazal form is the instrumental section (*duni*), an instrumental rendition of the *āstāī* melody. The song form is also cyclical with respect to tempo: the singer performs the verse in slow tempo, then accelerates for the refrain; the speed further increases in the instrumental section, which ends with a rhythmic cadence and a sudden drop back to the slow tempo for the next verse.

In the high art of ghazal singing, the vocalist skillfully quotes appropriate couplets from various poems, usually singing them in free rhythm. This manner of performance, reminiscent of Persian classical music, is a Tajik component of the Kabuli

FIGURE 2 Dad Mohammad (vocal and harmonium) and Fazl Ahmad (tabla), descendants of court musicians originally from the Lahore area, Pakistan, performing ghazals at home in the musicians' quarter, 1974. Photo by Veronica Doubleday.

ghazal form. The contrasts in tempo and the use of strong rhythmic cadences derive from Pashtun music [see SOUTHEASTERN AFGHANISTAN]. The Kabuli ghazal is thus a synthesis of Hindustani, Tajik, and Pashtun musical elements.

Since the 1920s, the ghazal singer has usually accompanied himself on the harmonium, backed by a small group including *rubāb* 'plucked lute', *sāraṅgī* and *delrubā* 'bowed lutes', *tānpūrā* 'drone lute', and tabla (figure 2). Apart from the *rubāb*, all these instruments came from India. The style spread beyond Kabul to other cities, such as Herat, Kandahar, and Mazar-e Sharif, where Kabuli musicians performed and acquired local pupils.

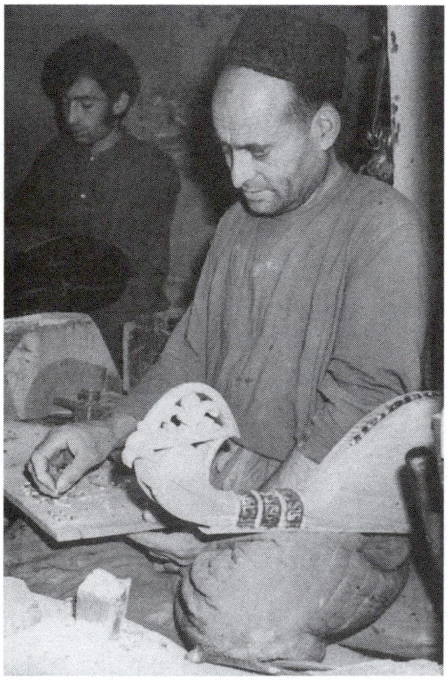

FIGURE 3 Joma Khan Qader in his *rubāb* workshop in the old city of Kabul, 1974. Photo by Veronica Doubleday.

The *naghma-ye kashāl*

The second genre of Afghan art music, also connected with Kabul, is the *naghma-ye kashāl* (literally 'the extended instrumental piece'). Instrumentalists favor this form as a vehicle for virtuoso solo performance on the *rubāb*, the short-necked plucked lute with sympathetic and drone strings that is the national instrument of Afghanistan (figure 3). The genre has obvious connections with Hindustani instrumental music, yet remains distinctly Afghan (Baily 1997).

The *naghma-ye kashāl* consists of three main parts. The first is an improvised prelude in free rhythm (*shakl* 'shape, features') in which the performer explores the melodic characteristics of the mode. The main composition (*āstāī*) follows, repeated many times with rhythmic variations produced by complicated right-hand stroke patterns. In the final section (*aṅtarā*), the musician plays a series of short compositions several times each, gradually accelerating toward the end of the piece. The tabla or *dohol* 'double-headed barrel drum' provides rhythmic accompaniment in the *āstāī* and *aṅtarā* but is silent during the improvised prelude. The drummer invariably plays the sixteen-beat metric cycle *tīntāl*.

Instrumental groups consisting of harmonium, *rubāb*, and tabla also play the *naghma-ye kashāl* to commence their performances at wedding parties or Ramadan concerts. The piece serves to establish the mode and warm up instruments, musicians, and audience. Figure 4 is a well-known *naghma-ye kashāl* composition obtained from the famous *rubāb* player Ustad Mohammad Omar in 1973.

FIGURE 4 A *naghma-ye kashāl* in *yemen* mode, taught to John Baily by the *rubāb* player Ustad Mohammad Omar in 1973. The *bhog* and *sanchāri* sections are part of the *aṅtarā*. Transcription by John Baily.

The flowering of court music in Kabul

The Afghan art-music genres, ghazal and *naghma-ye kashāl*, flourished especially at the court of King Amanullah in the 1920s, a progressive era inspired in part by the movement in Turkey to create a modern, westernized, and secular state. Many of today's Afghan art-music compositions are credited to the master musicians of that period. The principal vocalist was Ustad Qasem, a master ghazal singer, who combined a deep knowledge of Persian poetry with a broad training in Hindustani music. Other eminent Kabuli singers of that period include Ustad Ghulam Hassan, Ustad Nabi Gol, and Ustad Sheyda.

King Amanullah enjoyed a close friendship with Ustad Qasem. In a letter written to Qasem during the king's state tour of Europe in 1928, Amanullah addressed his friend in the warmest terms, saying how he missed him and had to console himself by listening to the 78-rpm records of Qasem he had brought with him. Soon after his return to Afghanistan in 1929, Amanullah was deposed by a popular uprising that rejected his modernist reforms.

In 1933, Zaher Shah came to power and was a considerable patron of music during his forty-year reign, inviting many musicians from India to perform at his court. In recent times, the most famous Afghan singer from this court tradition was Ustad Sarahang, who was also well known in India as a classical singer in the Patiala style. His grandfather had emigrated from Patiala to Kabul in the 1880s, and his father (Ustad Ghulam Hassan) was one of the great singers of the 1920s. An outstanding *rubāb* player of this time was Ustad Mohammad Omar. He belonged to the barber-musician caste, which is widespread in Afghanistan and remains distinct from the descendants of Indian court musicians.

RADIO BROADCASTING AND AFGHAN NATIONAL IDENTITY

The 1920s saw the beginnings of a deliberately national music. Ustad Qasem sang songs celebrating Afghanistan's independence from British hegemony at annual

Radio broadcasting in Afghanistan has been of crucial importance in the creation and development of Afghan popular music.

Independence Day festivities. Early radio broadcasting in Kabul in the 1920s probably helped consolidate such songs as an Afghan national music. The radio station opened in 1925, and for a few years radio achieved some headway, with an estimated one thousand radio receiver sets in Kabul by 1928. Ustad Qasem and other Kabuli singers recorded many 78-rpm records in India. Their market was primarily urban populations in Afghanistan and the sizable Afghan communities living in India.

After King Amanullah was deposed in 1929, the radio station—a symbol of modernity—was destroyed, and no serious attempt was made to resume radio transmissions until 1940. During the mid-1930s, a new nationalist movement emerged in Afghanistan: nationalist writers of the time viewed Afghanistan's ethnic diversity as one of the country's major problems, and they sought to establish a common history, religious background, and ethnic origin for all the peoples of Afghanistan, whom they claimed were descended from the same Aryan stock (Gregorian 1969). The nationalist ideology laid great stress on the Pashto language. The 1933 constitution specified Pashto and Dari for the first time as the official languages of the country. Nationalists also argued that Afghanistan needed to develop a modern national culture:

> Many urged that Afghanistan's folklore and traditional music be collected, and called for the development of a new literature reflecting both the nation's historical legacy and its present social realities, needs and aspirations. Poets and writers were exhorted to see themselves as vehicles of social change and their role as the awakening of the Afghan people (Gregorian 1969:349).

Radio Afghanistan officially resumed in 1940 with German technical assistance, although Afghanistan was neutral in World War II. During the war, difficulties in obtaining new equipment or spare parts seriously hampered broadcasting, and the government did not establish an effective service transmitting to most parts of the country until the mid-1940s. In order to ensure the dissemination of radio broadcasts, given the limited ownership of radio receivers, the government linked receiver appliances in several cities to loudspeaker systems in the main streets. The radio service broadcast news, music, and other programs to a predominantly male audience in public places. From the mid-1940s radio broadcasting started to replace the royal court as the principal patron of musicians and as the institutional sponsor of new developments in music. Radio Afghanistan employed most of the country's well-known musicians. Its stated aims were to spread the message of the holy Qur'ān, to reflect the national spirit, to perpetuate the treasures of Afghan folklore, and to contribute to public education. The government considered radio to be the quickest and most efficient means of communicating with and informing the public regarding its policies and development programs.

AFGHAN POPULAR MUSIC

Radio broadcasting in Afghanistan has been of crucial importance in the creation and development of Afghan popular music (*kiliwāli*). Regional music of Parwan and other mixed Pashtun-Tajik areas near Kabul provided models on which musicians based the new national popular music broadcast over the airwaves. Popular music from the 1950s to the 1970s brought together Dari or Pashto texts, Pashtun musical style, and Hindustani concepts and terminology. The descendants of Indian court musicians helped in its development, for their knowledge of Hindustani music theory and terminology and their high standards of performance were important in organizing small ensembles and large orchestras at the radio station. One such musician was Ustad Hashem, an excellent Punjabi-style tabla player, singer, multi-instrumentalist (sitar, sarod, harmonium, and *rubāb*), and composer and arranger in the manner of a Bombay film music director. The development of popular music also enabled a number of professional women singers to achieve fame as popular radio personalities. Mahwash was perhaps the best known of these within Afghanistan. In 1976, the Afghan government presented her with the honorific title Ustad Mahwash, a singular sign of official recognition.

Afghan popular music shows little in the way of Western influence, apart from the presence of a few Western instruments in ensembles. A major inspiration has been film songs from India and Pakistan that are heard in the cinemas of Kabul and the large provincial cities and are also available on cassettes. Indian film music is eclectic and in some ways quite Westernized, although Afghan popular music composers have not drawn specifically on its Western elements. One of Afghanistan's best loved popular singers, Nashenas, is also sometimes called "the Afghan Saigal" [see FILM MUSIC: NORTHERN AREA]. Nashenas, now more or less retired in London, performed songs sung by this legendary Indian film singer. The influence of Indian film songs extends much beyond their occasional adoption, either sung in Hindi/Urdu or with new lyrics composed in Dari or Pashto. Film music has inspired the composition of songs in the new popular style by educated singers like Khyal and Zaland, both from Kabul (figure 5). The period from the 1950s to the 1970s saw new opportunities emerge for amateur singers and instrumentalists alike to perform in public, and especially on the radio.

FIGURE 5 Khyal, a Radio Afghanistan singer and composer, performs at a Ramadan concert in Herat, with Western flute, *ḍholak*, and (hidden behind the singer) *delrubā*, 1976. Photo by Veronica Doubleday.

Other popular radio songs were local folk songs, either performed by provincial singers at the radio station or collected by station staff from different parts of the country. Radio broadcasting gave many Afghan folk songs a new lease on life in this manner. The radio service also transmitted the popular musics of Persian-speaking neighboring countries such as Iran and Tajikistan, and of the Pashto-speaking areas of Pakistan.

The 1950s to the late 1970s were the heyday of music in Afghanistan. The singer and songwriter Ahmad Zaher symbolized the extraordinary respect afforded music in this traditional Islamic society. (It should be remembered that many Muslims have questioned the lawfulness of music over the centuries.) Zaher came from an aristocratic family (Mohammadzai); his father, Dr. Abdul Zaher, was at one time prime minister of Afghanistan. He performed the most westernized form of Afghan music, playing the electric organ accompanied by trumpet, electric guitar, and trap drum set, and other much more traditional musicians readily adopted his songs at the local level.

THE MARXIST REGIMES, 1978–1992

Prince Mohammad Daud deposed his brother-in-law, King Zaher Shah, in 1973. Daud had socialist sympathies, and started to impose restraints on personal freedom. He closed down privately owned newspapers, magazines, nightclubs, and theaters. The media came under the firm control of the Ministry of Information and Culture, with local offices in every city. During the next five years, Daud imposed socialist ideas and policies adopted from the Soviet Union. His control became tighter, motivated not by religious puritanism but by a desire to limit free speech.

In 1978, a bloody coup by Nur Ahmad Taraki deposed Daud and inaugurated the dismal rule of the Communists. Two points of view were voiced at this time, from inside and outside the country. Singers who remained in Kabul felt compelled to praise the communist government, although they did this reluctantly, since they consequently feared assassination by the resistance. Those in exile extolled the bravery and fighting skills of the resistance. The communist government in Kabul, with its educated, secular, middle-class membership, supported music. Party members and their cohorts were enthusiastic patrons of live performance at small gatherings, and some musicians in Kabul prospered at this time.

In contrast, Afghan refugees in Pakistan and Iran were strongly discouraged from even listening to music on the radio. Musicians had to live and operate outside the refugee camps, which were run by the mullahs (religious leaders) in a state of perpetual mourning. The mullahs revived deep-seated reservations about the lawfulness of music from an Islamic point of view. The documentary film *Amir* recounts the experiences of one Afghan refugee musician as he plied a living on Dubgari Road, a musicians' business quarter in Peshawar, Pakistan (Baily 1985). Much of the oral history of the war survives in epic song texts recounting the exploits of various commanders and their *mujahedin* groups. In terms of stylistic parameters, music in the recent war years seems to have remained relatively static through the conflict, with little in the way of innovation. This is in marked contrast to the musical changes that took place between the 1860s and the 1970s.

MUSIC IN THE POST-COMMUNIST ERA

Since the fall of the communist regime in 1992, the Islamic government has more or less proscribed all music. The Kabul mullahs have cited the "soul-corrupting" aspect of music to justify this ban—as they did in 1929. Virtually all the remaining professional musicians left Kabul in 1992, after a number of rockets fell on the musicians' quarter. In 1997, little musical activity took place except in the north, in the city of

Mazar-e Sharif, which was controlled by the former Communist supporter General Dustam, an Uzbek. Until recently Radio Afghanistan broadcast a little music in some regions—unannounced and anonymous—and several cinemas were open to show Hindi movies. However, in 1996 Gulbuddin Hekmatyar, one of the most extreme *mujahedin* leaders, was appointed prime minister. He immediately closed all the cinemas in Kabul and banned music from Afghanistan's national radio and television stations. According to Pakistani press reports, he declared any sort of music played on the air to be illegal, because of its negative effect on peoples' psyches.

The Taliban movement, which had taken over 95 percent of the country by 1998, strongly reinforced this antimusical attitude on the part of the state and completely banned all musical instruments and associated music making in areas under its control. In the present political climate, music in Afghanistan is moribund. It is hoped that the musical traditions of Afghanistan will not be forgotten.

REFERENCES

Baily, John. 1981. "Cross-Cultural Perspectives in Popular Music: The Case of Afghanistan." *Popular Music* 1:105–122.

———. 1985. *Amir, an Afghan Refugee Musician's Life in Peshawar, Pakistan.* National Film and Television School, Beaconsfield, Bucks., England. 16mm film, videocassette.

———. 1988. *Music of Afghanistan: Professional Musicians in the City of Herat.* Cambridge: Cambridge University Press. With accompanying audio cassette.

———. 1997. "The *Naghma-ye kashāl* of Afghanistan." *British Journal of Ethnomusicology* 6:117–163.

Doubleday, Veronica. 1990. *Three Women of Herat.* Austin: University of Texas Press.

Gregorian, Vartan. 1969. *The Emergence of Modern Afghanistan.* Stanford: Stanford University Press.

Sakata, Hiromi Lorraine. 1983. *Music in the Mind: The Concepts of Music and Musician in Afghanistan.* Kent, Ohio: Kent State University Press. With 2 accompanying audio cassettes.

Slobin, Mark. 1974. "Music in Contemporary Afghan Society." In *Afghanistan in the 1970s*, ed. Louis Dupree and Linette Albert, 239–248. New York: Praeger.

———. 1976. *Music in the Culture of Northern Afghanistan.* Tucson: University of Arizona Press.

Music and Gender

Veronica Doubleday

Women's Domestic Music
Music at Weddings and Other Rites of Passage
Professional Entertainment
Women and Radio Afghanistan
Gender and Music in Civil-War Conditions

In Afghanistan, the physical segregation of women and men, the seclusion of women within the domestic space, and the veiling of women in public space are all consequences of a conservative interpretation of Muslim values. These conditions pervade village and city culture: only in the capital city of Kabul had large numbers of women become emancipated before communist rule began in 1978. Among nomad populations, women and men are not physically separated to the same degree, but tribal codes of honor secure men's interests at the expense of women's.

Gender ideology has had several important effects upon musical life. First, virtually all musical activity is segregated according to gender. Women perform in the privacy of domestic surroundings; men play in public, or in the separate guest rooms of private houses. Second, musical instruments have powerful gender associations. Third, religious and social ideals of modesty inhibit female musical expression. Fourth, a climate of covert prostitution surrounds some types of music and dance. Finally, men have tended to devalue women's music as unskilled and trivial, disregarding the fact that women are important transmitters of basic musical ability. Other articles in this volume relating to Afghan music deal with men's traditions; the emphasis here is on women's traditions.

WOMEN'S DOMESTIC MUSIC

Among women, the domestic space is virtually the only context for performance. The main types of women's informal music are songs—with or without accompaniment on the frame drum (*dāireh*)—and instrumental music, which is either drumming to accompany dancing or performance on the mouth harp (Persian: *chang*; Uzbek and Turkmen: *changko'uz*), a scantily researched tradition of northern Afghanistan.

Vocal music

There is considerable overlap in the vocal repertoires of women and men, who share the same musical culture and know the same local songs. In Herat in the west, Badakhshan in the north, and Hazarajat in the central part of the country, both women and men sing quatrains (*chahārbeiti*; *falak* in Badakhshan) in slow, unmetered regional styles (Sakata 1983:106–188). In the southeastern Pashtun areas, women and men sing a two-line verse form (*landay*) principally composed by women.

Women's and men's repertoires differ in matters relating to text and poetic form. Classical poetry such as the ghazal is composed by male poets and is a male preserve. Songs specific to women are distinguished by their female-oriented texts. The bride and the mother-daughter bond are central topics. A song from western Afghanistan entitled "ʿArus-e jān-e madār" 'Bride, dear to mother' refers to the sadness of a mother when her daughter leaves home to be married, as illustrated in the text refrain:

> ʿArus-e jān-e madār emshau mehmān-e madār
> Hāle ke tur miboram ātash be jān-e madār
>
> Bride, dear to mother, mother's guest tonight
> Now that they [the bridegroom's kinswomen] are taking you away, fire [of pain] on your mother's body.

Only women and girls sing lullabies, which are performed in the context of child care. They are improvised at the cradle, performed in a steady tempo, and normally have a rather narrow ambitus (within a tetrachord). In Hazarajat they consist of short stylized phrases in eight-syllable lines (Sakata 1989:91–93). In Herat they are based on traditional quatrains (*chahārbeiti)* (Baily 1996, track 11). A traditional Herati lullaby text contains spiritual and symbolic material, such as "Allāh hu" 'God is he', one of the main invocations in *zikr*, the Sufi ritual.

Allāh migum gol-e gorjeh Allāh hu	O God, I say, plum flower, "God is he"
Seta kaftar sar-e borjeh Allāh hu	Three pigeons on top of the tower, "God is he"
Yaki pokhteh yaki sukhteh khodā jan	One is cooked, one is burnt, dear God
Yaki zikr-e khodā gofte Allāh hu	One has said God's *zikr*, "God is he"

Performance styles also differ. The sounds of female voices, hand clapping, and frame drums are typical of women's music. Hand clapping is not a common rhythmic device among men, and men accompany their songs with a variety of instruments that women do not play. Women's performance is group oriented: several voices may support a lead singer, especially in refrains, whereas men's singing is soloistic or—especially in Pashtun areas—takes the form of a dialogue between two singers.

FIGURE 1 A young girl plays a frame drum (*dāireh*) in the playing position often used for dance rhythms. Herat city, 1974. Photo by Veronica Doubleday.

Instrumental music

Strict social and religious customs have deemed only two traditional instruments, the frame drum and mouth harp, suitable for women. The frame drum (*dāireh*) is generally considered a "women's instrument," although men play it in Badakhshan, where it is called *daf*. The instrument makers are people of lower-status groups derogatarily known as "Jat" (Rao 1982). The skin is usually goatskin, and the wooden frame often has iron rings and pellet bells or metal jingles set in it.

Throughout Afghanistan, drumming to accompany dancing is a popular form of entertainment for girls (figure 1). One drum may suffice, or two may be played together. If no drum is available, musicians substitute a metal tray. Specific rhythms accompany dances such as the *sehchakegi* 'three claps dance', *logari* 'dance in the style of the Logar valley', or *turisti* 'tourist dance'.

The mouth harp (*chang*) is a solo instrument locally manufactured by ironsmiths and played by women in northern Afghanistan and Kabul. Men also play the mouth harp but are ashamed, because they insist the instrument belongs to women and children. This nominal restriction of the mouth harp to women and youths is widespread in areas to the north of Afghanistan: Tajikistan, Kazakhstan, and Kirghizia (Slobin 1976:53). Significantly, although men may choose to override the shame of playing "women's instruments," women rarely claim the right to play "men's instruments."

MUSIC AT WEDDINGS AND OTHER RITES OF PASSAGE

Women play a significant musical role in marriage rituals (Doubleday 1990). Weddings (Persian: *ʿarusi,* Pashto: *tui*) are important in providing a legitimate outlet for formal female musical expression. Given the constraints placed on regular music making, women hold many all-female parties in connection with marriage that involve music, such as engagement parties and formal visits for exchanging gifts.

In cities, families may hire female professional musicians to entertain women's gatherings, but in rural areas the bridegroom's immediate kinswomen welcome the bride by playing music and dancing themselves. Notably, they escort the bride from her home to the wedding, which takes place at their house. Along the way they play ritual processional drumming, an exceptional instance of women's music being sanctioned in public space.

Ritual transitions also find expression in dance. In Hazarajat, women perform a group dance (*peshpu*) to welcome the bride. In Herat, women perform the national circle dance (*atan*) before the couple on their bridal throne. Pashtun women take turns to dance and sing the words "Harkahla ye rawaleh" 'May she [the bride] be welcome to come here anytime'. At weddings, continuous dancing is the definitive expression of celebration and joy.

Women sing wedding songs at particular ritual moments. "Heina ba kāra" 'Using henna' describes the dyeing of the bride's hands with henna on the eve of marriage (see Baily 1988:95–96 and Sakata 1983:140–144 for local Herati versions). "Asta bero" 'Go slowly' describes the slow procession of the bridal couple to their throne; the ethnomusicologist Mark Slobin recorded two female performances of this song in the north (1976:175–177). Local wedding songs also exist, as in the Herati "Olang olang" 'Oh, meadow' (Baily 1988:96–98). Wedding songs address the bride and bridegroom with conventional epithets and confer blessings on their union. They mourn the bride's departure, reinforce ideals of romantic love, and enjoin her to accept God's will.

Ceremonies relating to pregnancy and birth are the exclusive province of women, and are attended by family members and neighbors. A certain number of nights after a birth, or on several particular nights, women sit with the mother and her new baby expressly to ward off dangerous spirits (*jinn*) that may harm the baby. Singing, jokes, games, and sometimes dancing take place informally, with no ritual climax. The fortieth day after a birth is also a festive occasion.

Men celebrate the circumcision of boys. In the north, Uzbek circumcisions held during the long winter months include such pastimes as horsemanship matches (*buzkashi*) and feasts. Barber-musicians who perform the circumcisions play music on the shawm (*sornā*) and double-headed frame drum (*dohol*).

PROFESSIONAL ENTERTAINMENT

In some urban areas professional entertainers from particular low-status groups provide music at all-women festive gatherings, which include the bridegroom and his father in the crucial rituals. Gender ideology demands that these musicians be either female or young sexually immature boys. However, in Afghan society at large it is shameful for women to earn money through music, showing their physical talents and attractions to men outside their own family circle. (During "all-women" wedding rituals at least the bridegroom and his father are present and see the musicians.) The

FIGURE 2 Transvestite dancing boy at a clandestine party. Herat city, 1977. Photo by John Baily.

infringement of social boundaries that occurs with the presence of these professional musicians has led men to describe female professional musicians as prostitututes, which they are not.

A tradition of female professionalism has been well established in Herat since the late 1930s. Herati women's bands—which have been banned from working since 1993—employed instruments not traditionally assigned to women, such as the North Indian drum pair (tabla) and the Indian harmonium, as well as one or more frame drums. In the absence of an available woman tabla player, bands would recruit a young boy from the extended family [see WESTERN AFGHANISTAN]. In the north, female professional singers accompany themselves only on frame drums; in Pashtun regions, women do not undertake this work. In Kabul, Laghman, Jalalabad, and Logar, young boys from barber-musician families form bands led by a singer/harmonium player. For small sums of money, they entertain women's festive gatherings as a type of professional apprenticeship.

Connections between dancing, illicit sex, and prostitution have tended to sully the music profession's reputation. In western and northern Afghanistan, and across the border in Uzbekistan, there is an old tradition of training young boys as transvestite dancers (*bachehbāzigar*) to entertain men. Dancing-boy parties were held in cellar rooms and in secret (figure 2). A similar but more public and open tradition exists among the Pashtuns. These dancing boys are regarded as both highly erotic and sexually available (Slobin 1976:116–120).

Semi-itinerant groups loosely known as Jat or Ghorbat (Chelu in Herat) use music in the context of female prostitution. Clients come to their tented encampments on the cities' edges. Men play the bowed lute (*sārindā*), frame drum (*dāireh*) and small cymbals (*tāl*), and girls dance (Rao 1982). To the east, in Lahore (Pakistan) and in several large Indian cities, dancing girls perform in red-light districts, a tradition made familiar to Afghans through the Indian films that were extremely popular before the civil war but are now banned. Also before 1992, in the theaters then functioning in major Afghan cities, young women appeared on stage as singers and dancers; they were generally classed with prostitutes for seriously flouting social conventions of modesty.

The connection between music and prostitution has subjected professional female musicians to insults and disapproval. Conservative thinkers have labeled music "the work of the devil." This situation, compounded with the ideology of seclusion and economic dependency of women, has rendered music unacceptable as a profession for women, apart from the interesting exceptions described below.

WOMEN AND RADIO AFGHANISTAN

Those with conservative religious views consider it sinful for a woman's voice to be heard in public. The first woman to broadcast on Radio Afghanistan (then Radio Kabul), in 1947, was a news announcer, Latifa Kabir Seraj. She was from a prestigious Kabul family. In 1951, the station director persuaded a woman to sing on the radio for the first time. Parwin, the singer in question, was a member of a former princely family in Badakhshan and later became nationally famous. The high-status origins of these two female pioneers—and the backing of powerful men—gave them the confidence to overstep existing gender boundaries. The modernity and high status of radio broadcasting was also a factor in their popularity.

Parwin later recruited other female singers, from families with no professional musical connection, to receive training from male singers or music directors at the radio station. Thus female vocalists became a common feature of radio broadcasting, although conservative opinion still viewed such work as sinful. The hereditary musi-

Under communism, Kabul schoolgirls were recruited to perform group dances on television; then, with the fall of communism in 1992, the ruling party banned all music broadcasting.

cian families of Kabul still did not allow their daughters into the music profession, in order to protect their reputations as good Muslims.

In 1959, Queen Suraya made a public appearance unveiled. This caused a dramatic shift toward the emancipation of the women of Kabul, although it had virtually no impact outside the capital. Female singers soon appeared on stage singing for visiting dignitaries and traveling abroad to give concerts (Rahimi 1986:89). In 1977, the most prominent female singer, Mahwash, was given the honorific title of Ustad Mahwash (*ustād* 'master, teacher'), a move the government made not only to acknowledge her services to music but also to improve the status of women in the arts generally.

GENDER AND MUSIC IN CIVIL-WAR CONDITIONS

Since 1978, gender ideology has become highly politicized. The communist government sought to enroll women in the work force and promote the notion of equality for women. At the same time, conservative thinkers strove to enforce the strict seclusion of women and a culture of permanent mourning for the martyrs of war, with consequent avoidance of celebration and music.

Successive governments deliberately manipulated the position of women on radio and television. Under communism, Kabul schoolgirls were recruited to perform group dances on television; then, with the fall of communism in 1992, the ruling party banned all music broadcasting and dismissed all the women news announcers.

Under war conditions girls' domestic music making was discouraged. Full-scale weddings were often not practical, and this deprived girls of an important performance context. Boys' traditions also suffered. During the moonlit evenings of the holy month of Ramadan, boys in former times used to go begging for treats from door to door, singing particular Ramadan verses. Now, with nighttime dangers and curfews, the practice has ceased. Thus a whole generation has grown up with little musical performance. After a period of relaxation and liberalization that lasted from the 1950s to the 1970s, music and gender ideology have again become highly sensitive, contentious areas of life.

REFERENCES

Baily, John. 1988. *Music of Afghanistan: Professional Musicians in the City of Herat.* Cambridge: Cambridge University Press. Book and audio cassette.

———. 1996. *The Traditional Music of Herat.* UNESCO collection, Audivis D8266. Compact disc with accompanying notes.

Doubleday, Veronica. 1990. *Three Women of Herat.* Austin: Texas University Press.

———. 1999. "The Frame Drum in the Middle East: Women, Musical Instruments and Power." *Ethnomusicology* 43(1):101–134.

Rahimi, Fahima. 1986. *Women in Afghanistan.* Liestal: Stiffung Bibliotheca Afghanica.

Rao, Aparna. 1982. *Les Gorbat d'Afghanistan. Aspects Économiques d'un groupe itinérant "Jat."* Paris: Éditions Recherche sur les Civilisations.

Sakata, Hiromi Lorraine. 1983. *Music in the Mind: The Concepts of Music and Musician in Afghanistan.* Kent, Ohio: Kent State University Press. Book and two audio cassettes.

———. 1989. "Hazara Women in Afghanistan: Innovators and Preservers of a Musical Tradition." In *Women and Music in Cross-Cultural Perspective*, ed. Ellen Koskoff, 85–95. Urbana: University of Illinois Press.

Slobin, Mark. 1976. *Music in the Culture of Northern Afghanistan.* Tucson: University of Arizona Press.

Western Afghanistan

Veronica Doubleday
John Baily

Performance Contexts
Vocal Music
Instrumental Music
Professional Musicians in Herat City
Musical Characteristics
Religious Censure of Music in the 1990s

The vast expanse of mountains and desert that makes up western Afghanistan is dominated economically and culturally by the city of Herat. This ancient city, an important market center, is situated in a large riverine oasis nearly 130 kilometers in length that is dotted with cultivated fields and villages. Supposedly founded by Alexander the Great in the fourth century B.C., Herat later became part of the area then known as Khurasan, which reached its peak of civilization in the twelfth century.

The people of Herat consider the fifteenth century the time of their city's great flowering. As the capital of the Timurid empire, it boasted many fine religious buildings and was famous for its sumptuous court life with musical performance and its tradition of miniature paintings (Baily 1988:12–16) [see MUSIC AND THE STATE]. In 1976, UNESCO designated Herat a World Heritage Site and announced plans to restore its many important monuments. Within Afghanistan, Herat retains a reputation for excellence in the arts.

Persian is the language of western Afghanistan, which has strong historical links with Iran. Across the border—360 kilometers to the northwest—the Iranian city of Mashhad is a sister city to Herat, and the shrine of Imam Reza in Mashhad is an important Shia pilgrimage center for a significant proportion of Herat's urban population. (Although the inhabitants of Herat city are both Sunni and Shia Muslims, the people of western Afghanistan are predominantly Sunni.)

Herat Province has a long history as a center for Sufism, the mystical branch of Islam. The Herat valley is called "Dust of the Saints" (*khāk-e āuliyā*) on account of the many tombs of Sufi masters buried there. The shrine of Chisht-e Sharif, 160 kilometers along the Hari river to the east, is the place of origin of the Chishti Sufi order, which has been of great importance to religious music (qawwali) in India.

Ethnomusicologists have documented the musical culture of western Afghanistan (Baily 1988; Doubleday 1990; Sakata 1983) and sound recordings are available (Baily 1988, 1993, 1996; Sakata 1983). However, the recent civil war has had a marked impact on the musical life of the region. Between 1978 and 1992, communist forces in Herat city fought resistance forces holding the countryside. In 1995 the area came under the rule of Pashtuns of the Taliban movement.

Male professional musicians derive their chief source of income from playing at men's wedding gatherings, usually held in the courtyard of a neighboring house rented by the bridegroom's family for the gathering.

PERFORMANCE CONTEXTS

As in other parts of Afghanistan, music has two main uses: entertainment and ritual. The home is an important place for women's and men's informal music making, always physically separate. Women and girls sing, play frame drums (*dāireh*), and dance at home [see MUSIC AND GENDER]. Men hold parties for amateur music making, sitting apart in guest rooms reserved for male entertaining. Typically, they sing to the accompaniment of lutes (*dutār* or *rubāb*) or harmonium and the goblet-shaped drum (*zirbaghali*) or Indian tabla drum pair. Alternatively, music sessions may be purely instrumental.

In homes, musical performance also occurs in association with rites of passage, particularly the many women's parties for marriage celebrations. Weddings usually take place in the inner courtyard and several rooms of the bridegroom's house, where women gather and enact rituals. Women's singing and dancing continues thoughout the evening of the wedding and the following day until around dusk.

Male professional musicians derive their chief source of income from playing at men's wedding gatherings, usually held in the courtyard of a neighboring house rented by the bridegroom's family for the gathering. Bands comprise a singer with instrumental accompaniment. On the evening of the wedding, entertainment usually consists of classical poetry (ghazals), popular music (mainly songs learned from the radio), and instrumental music for solo or group dancing by the guests. The musicians often respond to requests from the guests to play particular items. Toward the end of the evening the musicians play specific wedding songs to honor the bridegroom before he leaves with his father to join the bride.

As elsewhere in the Islamic world, Qur'ān recitation and the call to prayer sung in mosques are part of daily life, although these are not considered music by Afghans. Western Afghanistan has a strong Sufi tradition. The Sufi ritual of the remembrance of God (*zikr*) took place until recently (and possibly still does) after the congregational prayers in Herat's "Friday Mosque," the principal mosque where devout Muslims pray together on Fridays. Muslims also perform it once a week in several Sufi lodges (*khāneqāh*) in the Herat valley. *Zikr* does not involve musical instruments. A circle of male devotees recite various religious formulas such as "*Allāh hu*" 'God is he' in a rhythmic manner, combining strong bowing movements of the body and circular movements of the head with forced breathing. One or more singers circumambulate the circle of devotees, singing Sufi poems in the ghazal form; some of the poems are composed by local poets such as Jami, who lived in the fifteenth century.

Spring country fairs (*meleh*) are a very popular form of seasonal entertainment (Baily 1988:136–139). The roots of this tradition are extremely old, connected with ritual new year observances at the spring equinox. These focus on an annual pilgrimage to Ali's shrine (cousin and son-in-law of Muhammad) at Mazar-e Sharif and the forty-day Tulip Festival there. In western Afghanistan, men and women hold separate mass gatherings at shrines and parks. Shawm and drum players (*sāzdohol*) stroll about the men's fairs, asking for money. Teahouse owners set up tents and hire musicians to entertain their male clients with regional songs or songs popularized on the radio. Male amateur musicians have picnics and play music for their own entertainment. Music making was formerly part of women's seasonal festivities, held separately in especially designated parks, but in the 1970s soldiers and policemen posted at park gates prevented women from playing to protect their privacy.

VOCAL MUSIC

The traditional sung poetry of this region falls into three main categories: quatrain singing (*chahārbeiti*), local folk songs (*mahali*), and ghazals.

The soloistic, improvisatory oral tradition of quatrain singing (*chahārbeiti*) is very old; it is assumed to be of rural peasant origin. *Chahārbeiti* is also the name of the quatrain form itself. Styles of singing these quatrains occur in all Persian-speaking areas of Afghanistan and across the border in Iran (Doubleday, forthcoming). In western Afghanistan the singing is unmetered, slow in tempo, and often has extended cadential phrases. Traditional melodies are in the Persian scales of *shur* and *homayun*. Musicians have named certain of these after specific localities, such as *chakhchurāni* and *koshki* that are named after small towns.

Male singers may perform *chahārbeiti* to their own accompaniment on the local *dutār* 'two-stringed lute'. This soloistic style is common in small towns and rural areas but less so in Herat city. *Chahārbeiti* melodies also form an important part of the *dutār* instrumental repertoire and may be played on other instruments. Sound recordings and analysis of *chahārbeiti* appear in Sakata 1983 (tracks 8–12 and pp. 129–137), and Baily 1996 (tracks 1 and 9).

The themes of unrequited love and separation from the loved one permeate this melancholy singing style. Romantic imagery derived from Sufism is prevalent: the nightingale serenading the rose and the moth burning itself in the candle flame both symbolize the consuming power of divine love. A body of these quatrains, attributed to Jalali, a twentieth-century folk poet from the mountainous region of Ghor, are famous throughout Afghanistan. Jalali's verses speak of his unresolved love for Siah Mu, whose father prohibited their marriage and caused Jalali to become deranged with passion.

Jalāli ʿasheq-e ru-ye Siāh Mu
Asir-e cheshm-e jādu-ye Siāh Mu
Konad sujd-e Jalāli az sar-e sedq
Be mehrāb-e du ābru-ye Siāh Mu

Alas, Jalali is in love with Siah Mu
Captivated by the bewitching eyes of Siah Mu
Jalali sincerely prostrates himself
Before the prayer niche of Siah Mu's eyebrows

Traditional local songs called *mahali* employ this quatrain form but have individual melodies and fixed chorus sections. The singer improvises verses based on locally known quatrains. The theme of love predominates, and many songs address loved ones, male or female, as for example "Mullāh Mohammad Jān" and "Hai Rebābeh." Recordings of such songs appear in Baily 1996, tracks 6, 12, and 13, with recordings of instrumental versions on tracks 7 and 8.

Normally only men sing the classical poetic form of ghazal. In urban areas, professional male bands perform ghazals in the Kabuli style (Baily 1988:60–67) [see

MUSIC AND THE STATE]. In rural areas, singers perform ghazals in a style closer to the regional *chahārbeiti* and *mahali* songs.

In Herat city, songs from outside sources whose popularity was transient and subject to changes in taste have always supplemented local genres. During the 1920s, Iranian classical music was in vogue and vocalists performed songs from the modal suites (*dastgāh*). In the 1930s, a fashion for the court vocal music of Kabul gradually replaced Iranian music. By the 1970s, Radio Afghanistan had become an important source of the popular music known among musicians as *kiliwāli*. Songs from Indian films (*filmī*) were also popular, gaining currency through the cinema in Herat, which has been closed during the civil war. Before the suppression of popular music in Iran under Ayatollah Ruhollah Khomeini's rule, Iranian songs had considerable popularity.

INSTRUMENTAL MUSIC

Musical instruments, particularly drums and lutes, are common in both solo performance and vocal accompaniment. As in other parts of Afghanistan, instrumental music is predominantly a male preserve.

The Herati long-necked lute (*dutār*)

The most characteristic indigenous instrument of western Afghanistan is the long-necked lute (*dutār*). Although fifteenth-century miniatures depict the lute as a court instrument, it is now associated with amateur rural traditions. Its original form has two gut strings and "simple fretting" (*pardeh rāsteh*) corresponding to the intervals of the Persian mode *shur*, with its characteristic neutral seconds. The player stops the first string only; the second sounds a continuous drone. The two-stringed *dutār* is played in rural areas from Herat Province into Ghor and Badghis, either solo or as accompaniment for the local style of quatrain singing (*chahārbeiti*).

Since the 1950s, the *dutār* has undergone notable transformations. At that time, a three-stringed form with a semichromatic fretting system enabled players to perform melodies in modes other than Persian *shur*, particularly the Afghani popular music that was being broadcast on the radio. Musicians refer to this fretting as *pardeh filmi* 'film fretting' or 'fretting for Indian film songs'. The three-stringed *dutār*, with steel strings and played with a small metal plectrum, has largely superseded the two-stringed *dutār*. It is widespread in the countryside, and players usually perform with the goblet-shaped clay drum (*zirbaghalī*) common throughout Afghanistan.

The most dramatic development occurred around 1965. A much larger fourteen-stringed lute (*dutār-e chārdeh jalau*) appeared, with a single main string and three drone strings complemented by ten or eleven sympathetic strings (figure 1). Players developed this form for use in urban bands, making it compatible with the short-necked lute (*rubāb*) and harmonium. Players of the fourteen-stringed *dutār* also perform the classical music (*klāsik*) of ghazals and ragas (Baily 1976, 1996) [see MUSIC AND THE STATE].

Music for shawm and drum

The shawm (*sornā*) and double-headed frame drum (*dohol*) form an instrumental pair always played together—never in combination with any other instruments. This pair is called the *sāzdohol* ensemble, and performs loud outdoor music throughout Afghanistan and across much of the Islamic world. In western Afghanistan, all its performers are members of a low-status group of barber-musicians called Jat or Gharibzadeh. The men who play this music work as barbers and perform circumcisions; they also manufacture their own instruments, frame drums (*dāireh*), kitchen sieves, and children's toys sold at spring fairs. In the past, these musicians also per-

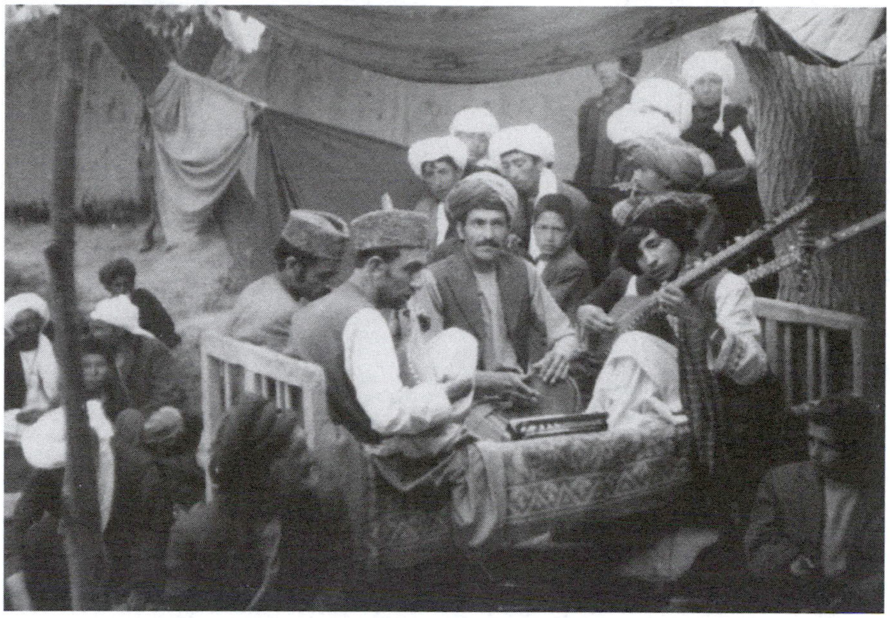

FIGURE 1 A *dutār* band consisting of three fourteen-stringed, long-necked lutes and a goblet drum (*zirbaghali*) plays at a spring fair (*meleh*) held at a shrine in Herat Province, 1977. Photo by John Baily.

formed a satirical folk drama (*seil*) as nighttime entertainment for wedding guests, but this tradition has virtually died out.

Contexts for shawm-and-drum music include weddings, circumcisions, religious festivals, and spring fairs. Occasionally, it is used to encourage group work activities such as harvesting wheat or cleaning irrigation canals (figure 2). An old style of *sāzdohol* music performed at weddings involved sung ritual verses, but this generally died out, possibly in the 1940s (Baily 1996, track 5). Shawm-and-drum players have a wide repertoire, encompassing traditional wedding songs, local songs, and new material gleaned from the radio or Indian films. The shawm playing is highly ornamented and continuous, employing circular breathing. The drum players use two sticks, one thinner and more flexible than the other.

Sāzdohol players perform mainly in villages and among nomad communities, but also appear in Herat at Muslim festivals such as ʿĪdu'l-fiṭr and the new year, when they go from house to house begging for payment. At urban weddings, they commonly arrive unannounced, asking for payment for a brief musical contribution to

FIGURE 2 Shawm-and-drum players (*sāzdohol*) provide music for men digging a ditch, Herat Province, 1974. Photo by Veronica Doubleday.

The characteristic themes and poetic imagery of the songs of western Afghanistan portray an idealized world of romantic love suffused with pain, longing, and religious devotion.

the ongoing rituals. These musicians are generally held in low regard and even feared. If they receive generous payment they shout praises and blessings on their patrons, but if dissatisfied they complain loudly with insults and ridicule.

Other traditional and imported instruments

Among other traditional instruments common in western Afghanistan, the frame drum (*dāireh*) is extremely popular. It is played mainly by women and is consequently regarded as a women's instrument [see MUSIC AND GENDER]. An urban classical-music instrument is the short-necked Afghan lute (*rubāb*) [see SOUTHEASTERN AFGHANISTAN]. The goblet-shaped clay drum (*zirbaghali*) is a common rhythmic accompanying instrument, played mainly by amateurs. Much less common is the long end-blown flute (*ney*), a solo instrument associated with shepherds and sometimes called the *ney chāpuni* 'shepherd's flute'.

Certain imported instruments have attained popularity. The North Indian tabla drum pair and the hand-pumped harmonium manufactured in India are both common in urban areas. In the 1920s, the double-chambered long-necked lute (*tār*), known locally as *chahārtār*, was imported from Iran and became popular in Herat city; it has since become obsolete in Afghanistan.

PROFESSIONAL MUSICIANS IN HERAT CITY

In the mid-1970s, there were many male professional musicians in Herat city, most of them members of hereditary musician families (*sāzandeh*) whose predominant profession was music. Others came from relatively modest, mainly artisan backgrounds. In recent years, with the prohibition of music, the profession has dwindled.

Male urban bands resemble those of other Afghan cities, having a lead singer accompanying himself on harmonium, rhythmic accompaniment on Indian tabla drums, and melodic support from plucked lutes. In Herat the lutes are either the short-necked Afghan *rubāb* or the large long-necked, fourteen-stringed *dutār*, or both.

Two hereditary musician families of Herat, the Khushnawaz and the Golpasand, form the basis of the city's professional community. The Khushnawaz are considered more senior. The singer and *rubāb* player Ustad Amir Jan, the founder of the Khushnawaz musical lineage, died in 1982. His eldest son, Ustad Mohammad Rahim, born in 1940, is a highly esteemed *rubāb* player. Ustad Amir Mohammad, a singer born in Kabul but semi-resident in Herat, led a highly prestigious band for many years in which Ustad Rahim played. Ali Ahmad, a singer, leads the Golpasand family. This hereditary lineage is also renowned for its women's bands.

Women from low-status barber-musician families used to work as entertainers for all-female gatherings in the city, singing and playing frame drums. From these *dāireh-dast* 'drum-in-the-hand' groups developed a tradition of women's professional bands unique in Afghanistan. Women from the Golpasand clan began operating in

FIGURE 3 A professional women's band of the Golpasand family plays at an engagement party in Herat city, 1974. *Left to right:* Gol Dasteh (vocal and harmonium), Urak (tabla), and Shahzadeh (*dāireh*). Photo by Veronica Doubleday.

urban-style bands in the late 1930s. Their patriarch, Golpasand, who died in the late 1960s, established three of his wives and a brother's wife in the first band. In the mid-1970s, a loose organization of five bands comprised about twenty-five women. In 1993, the Afghan authorities prohibited them from working, reflecting new strict religious principles concerning female modesty.

These women modeled their bands on the male urban-band sound. The lead singer played harmonium and was accompanied by tabla drums and one or two frame drums (*dāireh*) (figure 3). Having no formal training in music, the women made no attempt to tune the drums, and performed only a crude imitation of traditional Indian tabla strokes. They were also ignorant of technical terms for melodic modes and rhythms. However, their orally transmitted music was extremely popular at all-women festivities (Doubleday 1990:157–213).

MUSICAL CHARACTERISTICS

The music of western Afghanistan has close links with that of its neighbor, eastern Iran. The similarities include the refined and ornamented vocal style particularly characteristic of the indigenous *chahārbeiti* style. The use of neutral seconds in modal systems similar to those of Iran is most evident in local singing and in the fretting of the original two-stringed form of the long-necked lute (*dutār*). The songs of western Afghanistan employ mainly the Persian scale of *shur.*

Unlike eastern Afghanistan, with its emphasis on increases in tempo and dramatic climaxes, the music of western Afghanistan has a steady tempo. This applies equally to songs and dances. Dance rhythms are numerous and complex, whether performed on the frame drum, by the shawm-and-drum pair, or by other combinations of instruments. Girls and women perform these dances at home for entertainment and at weddings; likewise, men dance at weddings or at private outdoor recreational gatherings, particularly during springtime. The local men's circle dance *āushāri* is based on a fast six-beat rhythm (Sakata 1983:138–140). Another local tradition is men's stick dancing (*chubbāzi*), which employs a fast four-beat rhythm.

The characteristic themes and poetic imagery of the songs of western Afghanistan portray an idealized world of romantic love suffused with pain, longing, and religious devotion. Texts express an acceptance of difficulty and seek recourse through intercession with local saints. The songs emphasize human relationships, acknowledging the power of sexual attraction and the importance of emotional bonds within the family. After the civil war of 1978–1992, themes of war, chivalry, and epic feats were popular.

RELIGIOUS CENSURE OF MUSIC IN THE 1990s

Historically, music in this western region has often been condemned by religious and other leaders who regarded it as sinful due to its connection with dancing, illicit sex, and prostitution. This negative attitude toward music has come into play powerfully since 1992 with the end of the communist regime in Kabul.

The musical life of Herat city did not flourish under war conditions, with their attendant dangers and suffering. Then with the establishment of peace in 1992, the former resistance leaders governing western Afghanistan from Herat city endeavored to enforce strict controls on music. They ordered male musicians to carry license cards and to play only "religious and Sufi" music. They prohibited women musicians from performing at all, and jailed members of one band for disobedience.

For three years, the leaders allowed certain compromises. On local television musicians performed anonymously: viewers saw waterfalls or gardens instead of the musicians playing. In 1994, people celebrated the new year with public fairs including musical performance, although on one occasion authorities publicly confiscated musical instruments belonging to a band of licensed professional players. The principal musicians of the city were invited to compose and perform music for a large government political rally in the same year, but were not paid for their services. In 1995, Pashtun rulers from the Taliban movement came to power, with their even stricter views against music. They prohibited it completely—in theory if not in practice.

Since the civil war, the current wave of condemnation has ended music in many other Herat city contexts. Music formerly accompanied songs and dancing in the one theater in western Afghanistan, located in Herat city. The theater has now been closed. Musicians provided entertainment of a high standard during Ramadan, the month of fasting, when professional bands would come from Kabul to play evening concerts open to the public and villagers would travel to the city for this entertainment. New year and spring celebrations in parks and shrines formerly included music. Each year on Independence Day, in a park near the sports stadium, the city's shopkeepers' guilds would erect large booths, and visitors would be entertained with refreshments and music. Before the war there were also military parades, sports events, and other sorts of gala spectacles, all of which incorporated musical performance.

In addition to the loss of public music making, a generation of boys and girls has grown up with little opportunity to play, thus breaking the continuity of tradition. Nevertheless, in the past the people of western Afghanistan have recovered from similar disasters and social disruptions. The region's musical culture has deep historical roots: its survival would not appear to be under serious threat.

REFERENCES

Baily, John. 1976. "Recent Changes in the Dutar of Herat." *Asian Music* 8(1):29–64.

———. 1988. *Music of Afghanistan: Professional Musicians in the City of Herat.* Cambridge: Cambridge University Press. Book and audio cassette.

———. 1993. *Afghanistan. The Rubāb of Herat. Mohammad Rahim Khushnawaz.* VDE-Gallo AIMP XXV. Compact disc with accompanying notes.

———. 1996. *The Traditional Music of Herat.* UNESCO collection, Audivis D 8266. Compact disc with accompanying notes.

Doubleday, Veronica. 1990. *Three Women of Herat.* Austin: Texas University Press.

———. (forthcoming). "*Chahārbeiti.*" In *South Asian Folklore: An Encyclopedia,* ed. Peter Claus and Margaret Mills. New York: Garland.

Sakata, Hiromi Lorraine. 1983. *Music in the Mind. The Concepts of Music and Musician in Afghanistan.* Kent, Ohio: Kent State University Press. Book and two audio cassettes.

Northern Afghanistan

Jan Van Belle

Music in Social Life
Melodic Characteristics
Folk-Music Genres
Musical Instruments
Musicians, Music Learning, and Transmission
Mass Media

Northern Afghanistan, which includes the provinces of Badakhshan, Takhar, Baghlan, Kunduz, Samangan, Balkh, Jozjan, and Fariab, is separated from the nation's southern provinces by the Hindu Kush mountains and subsidiary ranges. About 1,290 kilometers of the rivers Amu Darya and Darya Panj form the northern border with Tajikistan, Uzbekistan, and Turkmenistan. Mazar-e Sharif is the principal city, with an estimated population of 150,000.

Reliable data on the various ethnic groups in northern Afghanistan is unavailable due to the lack of infrastructure and the ongoing civil war. According to existing sources (Slobin 1976; Sakata 1983; Jawad 1992), Tajiks, Uzbeks, Turkmen, Pashtuns, and Hazaras form the major ethnic groups. However, the numerical relationship and balance of power among these groups has changed dramatically in the last two decades with the flow of Pashtun refugees from the south. The major languages spoken in Afghanistan are Pashto and Dari, both of which belong to the West Iranian language family. All ethnic groups are Islamic and, regardless of their diverse religious tendencies within Islam, consider religion to be the dominant aspect of life and the founding principle of social cohesion. Most of the population is Sunni Muslim, with minority Shiite groups only in Baghlan and Badakhshan provinces that belong to the Nizari Ismailis and recognize the forty-ninth imam, the Aga Khan, as their spiritual leader.

Northern Afghanistan has a rich cultural history, but Western ethnomusicologists have paid little attention to its music. Only two major publications exist on music in northern Afghanistan (Slobin 1976; Sakata 1983). The inaccessibility of its mountains, the ethnic and linguistic diversity of its peoples and the resulting absence of a national identity, the bloody and violent nature of invasions in the past and of the present civil war, and the reputation of Afghans for austerity and aggression are among the major reasons for this lack of interest and field research. Afghanistan has no tradition of music research; music is not taught in schools or universities, and verbalized knowledge of music is limited to a few professional musicians. Bordering on Central Asia, the Indian subcontinent, and the Middle East, Afghanistan is related to each and yet distinct in many ways, as reflected in its musical culture. Local and regional musical styles still exist; but the spread of broadcasting and recordings and

Music in the Islamic culture of northern Afghanistan has always been an integral part of social life, despite the unfavorable attitude of Islam toward music.

the influx of refugees due to the ongoing civil war have brought changes in the musical landscape of northern Afghanistan.

The proclamation of the Islamic State of Afghanistan in 1992 marked a return of orthodox and fundamentalist forces. This regime has applied a strict and specific interpretation of Islamic law (*sharia*), according to which music is against public morals and must be banned from public life. In 1994 the fundamentalist Islamic militia known as Taliban began its march to power from southern Afghanistan, leading to the capture of the capital city, Kabul, in 1996. By 1998, the Taliban dominated 95 percent of the country. Archives, TV sets, and audio and video tapes have been destroyed, musicians beaten, and musical instruments broken during public and private performances. Prior to the takeover in the northern provinces, traditional Muslims saw themselves as the gatekeepers of public morals, but unlike the Taliban, they allowed music, and people were trying to keep up their rich musical tradition in spite of the difficult war situation. This article presents aspects of the musical culture in northern Afghanistan up to 1996.

MUSIC IN SOCIAL LIFE

Northern Afghans are related to the surrounding Islamic cultural area in their predilection for plucked lutes, bowed string instruments, specific rhythm instruments, solo voice within a small range, small ensembles, improvisation, and the use of specific scales. The human voice is predominant and plays a doubly important role, as the repertoire is preserved and disseminated mainly by oral transmission.

Music in the Islamic culture of northern Afghanistan has always been an integral part of social life, despite the unfavorable attitude of Islam toward music. Apart from religious and ritual functions, music serves as entertainment, pastime, and pleasure as in Western countries. Performers and listeners value music highly as a sensuous experience that involves a heightened state of consciousness. In live performances the atmosphere is informal, and listeners invariably offer sounds of appreciation and encouragement, clap rhythms, and dance, while the singers and instrumentalists often react with improvised songs extolling the virtues of audience members in a humorous way. Music and dancing in public, however, are exclusively male activities among the traditional nonfundamentalist Muslims of this area. Women are strictly separated from men, and sing, play, or dance only on specific domestic occasions like weddings or circumcisions, accompanying themselves on the frame drum (*dāireh*). Slobin (1976) has suggested that instrumental music and dance, which are offensive to Islamic morals, are associated with sexually loose behavior in Afghan society and are therefore either condemned or strictly segregated [see MUSIC AND GENDER]. One can, however, wonder why this is not universally the case in the Muslim world: Ismailis in neighboring Tajik Badakhshan do not segregate genders in a strict way, and men and women can dance together.

Music can be divided into four broad categories: religious music (*na*ʿ*t*), classical music (*musiqī-ye klāsik*), folk music (*musiqī-ye mahali*), and pop/film music. Northern Afghans will use these categories—inspired by Western musicology—if asked to describe their music culture, but they seldom volunteer such information. Also, in using these terms they may have in mind specifications and connotations different from those of such categories in Western music culture. As in many Islamic countries and other parts of Afghanistan, Qur'ānic recitation and the call to prayer are not considered music but rather forms of religious expression. In contrast, pieces of a religious nature (*naᶜt*) that musicians include in concerts are deemed music. Northern Afghans consider Hindustani music broadcast by Radio Kabul to be classical. They also put one type of local music—the Uzbek-Turkman *shashmaqām* style—in this category. Within the folk-music category, northern Afghanistan has a great variety of styles, which are discussed below. Youth culture greatly appreciates pop music, which arose in northern Afghanistan in the 1940s with the development of modern broadcasting and is inspired by imported Indian and Pakistani pop and film music. Apart from amplification and the introduction of some Western instruments, there is little direct influence from Western pop music.

MELODIC CHARACTERISTICS

The music of this region consists of melody and rhythm; the harmonic aspects of music familiar to Westerners are irrelevant here. Characteristic of most Afghan music is the use of specific scales called ragas (borrowing a term from North Indian Hindustani music). The most common is the *rāg bairami*, which corresponds to the Western Phrygian mode. Other ragas generally used are *beiru, pilu, pāri*, and *kesturi.* Although some musicians in northern Afghanistan use the Western sol-fa system, most indicate the relative pitch of the scale tones by the names *shadja* (*karj*), *rekap, gandār, madam, pancham, diwāt*, and *nikot*, which are derived from Hindustani music and abbreviated as Sa, Re, Ga, Ma, Pa, Da, and Ni. The term *karj* generally indicates the tonal center of a melody, often on Sa but in many cases transposed down a fourth to Pa for adult male voices (for more detailed information on Afghan scales, see Baily 1988).

FOLK-MUSIC GENRES

Musicians refer to folk-music genres according to geographical area (Kabuli, Herati, Shughnani), ethnic group (Pashtuni, Tajiki, Hazari, Uzbeki), song content (*'ishqi* 'love song', *lalai* 'lullaby', war songs), gender (*dāireh zanī* 'women's songs'), or poetical genre (*dubeiti, chahārbeiti, rubā'i, qaṣīda,* qawwali, and ghazal); they also refer to them as either dance songs (*raqs*) or pastoral songs (*chopāni*). Most professional performers and accomplished amateurs are all-round musicians, offering various Afghan styles and genres on request. Vocal music predominates over instrumental music, and there is no strict relationship between text and melody. Recordings of the well-known tune "Mullah Mohammad Jān," for example, have different texts, and the singer Hassan Besmil's recently composed texts on the war situation employ mostly existing melodies.

The relationship between poetic meter and melodic rhythm/meter tends to be loose or free in folk songs, and stricter in ghazals or other songs written by classical or modern poets. Duple and triple meters are quite common in Afghan music, as are combinations of duple and triple rhythms resulting in meters of five or seven beats. Specific to the eastern part of Badakhshan is a practice of singing a long series of poems, often with religious content, beginning in a slow, free rhythm, and continuing with a gradual increase of tempo and a steadier rhythm. Most folk songs are short, and sung in a steady slow or fast tempo, whereas the *qaṣīda*, ghazals, and epic songs like the *gorgholi* are longer.

Of the specific folk genres that still exist in northern Afghanistan, three are discussed here: the *falak*, the *kharābāt*, and the *gorgholi.* (Folk music of the Kazakh and Kirgiz minorities and Uzbek classical music in Bukhara style are not covered.)

TRACK 30 *Falak* 'fate, firmament', typical of Badakhshan, refers to a poetical form, its content and its melodic form. *Falak* verses are often in quatrain form, based on an AABA pattern, although there are many variations, which underscores the tendency to improvise. Texts are mostly melancholy, about unattainable love, longing for home, wandering, and so on. The melodic line is mostly descending, with the typical final interval an augmented or minor second. The narrow melodic range does not exceed a tetrachord or hexachord. Singers prefer the *ghijak* 'spike fiddle' as accompanying instrument, with the frame drum (*dāireh* or *daf*) or goblet-shaped drum (*zirbaghali*) joining later in the song to establish a steady rhythm. As accompaniment, the *ghijak* ornaments the melody with accented strokes, and plays the prelude, interludes, and postlude. The instrumental *falak,* played on *ghijak, dambura* 'long-necked lute', and *nay* or *tula* 'duct flutes', has an even narrower melodic range, and the *nay* and *tula* in particular play in a highly ornamental and melismatic style, with chromatic tones. These characteristics are also typical of Pamir Tajik musical style but are rare in other parts of Afghanistan.

Kharābāt 'ruins' is a poetical form in which the word *kharābāt* plays a leading role, often repeated in each text line. In Persian poetry the word *kharābāt* originally referred to taverns, where people gathered to enjoy drinking, eating, listening to music, and dancing. This meaning holds true in Kabul, where until recently Kharabat Street was a famous place where well-known musicians lived and private concerts took place [see MUSIC AND THE STATE, figure 1]. At a later stage, the term *kharābāt* took on a mystical meaning, in which sensual love and drunkenness are symbols of mystical love and spiritual elevation, respectively; the term is used to refer to a stage in the Sufi process of spiritual purification (De Bruijn 1992). *Kharābāt* singing is popular in Baghlan province among the Hazara Ismailis, who express a preference for mystical poets like Hafiz and Shams-e Tabrizi. The *kharābāt* singer accompanies himself mostly on harmonium or *dambura* 'long-necked lute' in a small ensemble of *rubāb* 'short-necked lute', *ghijak, zirbaghali* or tabla drums, and *tula.* The poetic form is often a ghazal, sung to a limited set of melodies and always preceded by an instrumental introduction. The *kharābāt* ghazal in figure 1 shows the instrumental introduction (played also as an interlude) and the text setting for the first two verses.

1a. Mardāna shitābēd ba maydān-i kharābāt
1b. Yārān maharāsēd zi 'unwān-i kharābāt

2a. In khāna-yi mihr ast na wayrāna-yi khaffāsh
2b. Bīnēd jamāl-i khur-i tābān-i kharābāt.

1a. Men, hasten to the square of the tavern
1b. Friends, don't be afraid of the inscription: tavern

2a. This is the house of love, not the ruins of the bar
2b. See the beauty of the brilliant sun of the tavern.

Gorgholi is an epic song related to a folk tale, popular in various Central Asian countries, that is loosely based on historical events. The tale is also still popular in Badakhshan; singers there render it in a special guttural vocal tone, mostly on winter evenings in performances lasting up to several hours. Like the *falak*, the melody has a

FIGURE 1 The instrumental introduction and first two verses of the *kharābāt* ghazal "Mardāna shitābēd." Transcribed by Jan Van Belle, 1996.

After this, 1a (once), 1b (2 times), instrumental interlude (2 times), verse 3a, 3b, etc.

limited range, typically with a minor second interval between the first and second scale degrees and a major or augmented interval between the second and third degrees. The singer accompanies himself mostly on the *dambura* lute, playing instrumental interludes (Sakata 1983).

Since the Soviet invasion of 1979, conceptions of genre have changed with migration movements and political shifts. The flow of predominantly Pashtun refugees, musicians, and instruments from the south has mixed with existing musical practices in the north, and contributed to the creation of broader and less characteristically local genres. In northeastern Afghanistan, particularly in Badakhshan province, inaccessible mountains have prevented any such flow; thus, traditional music still continues there. Furthermore, political division between east and west has contributed to a more liberal western and more rigorous eastern attitude toward music. In both areas, however, as elsewhere in Afghanistan, a new genre has appeared in which new lyrics sung to existing melodies deplore the war situation and express the desire for peace. The songwriter and singer Hassan Besmil, from Mazar-e Sharif, is a typical representative of this genre, and many others have performed his songs. Scenes witnessed in Jalalabad, where Taliban fundamentalists have taken music cassettes from cars and destroyed them in the streets, were still unheard of in northern Afghanistan in 1996, although the threat was painfully felt by the musicians and all inhabitants.

The political and economic situation has forced many professional musicians in northern Afghanistan to find other sources of income, and most well-known ensembles nowadays consist of both (former) professional and amateur players.

MUSICAL INSTRUMENTS

The most common instruments in the north are not exclusively "north Afghan," but exist in many neighboring regions and countries in varied forms. Morphological ties between certain types of instruments assume a pattern of cross-relationship between northern Afghanistan and neighboring countries, although the origin of instruments is not always clear. Instrument names are often borrowed from languages of other Islamic countries, like *tanbur* and *rubāb* from Arabic and sitar, *nay*, and *daf* from Persian. Among traditional instruments still played today in northern Afghanistan, the *dambura, tanbur,* and *dāireh* are the most widespread.

The *dambura* is a long-necked, fretless plucked lute, mostly of mulberry wood, with two nylon, gut, or (nowadays) metal strings and two frontal pegs. The pear-shaped body has small sound holes in various patterns on the wooden soundboard. The two strings are tuned to an interval of a fourth, and are plucked without a plectrum. Some *dambura* players intensify the rhythm by attaching a set of small metal bells (*zang-i kaftar*) to the right hand. The lute is a solo instrument, accompanied by *zirbaghali* or tabla drums, but is also played in small ensembles providing melodic and rhythmic support to the singer and/or instrumentalists. The *dambura* has always been a typical instrument for teahouse music. *Dambura* players, like all Afghan musicians, sit on the floor in a cross-legged position during concerts, holding the instrument across the lap. Listeners generally adopt the same cross-legged position.

The *tanbur* is a fretted, long-necked plucked lute with metal strings and an oval-shaped belly, made mostly of mulberry wood and having several decorative sound holes. It has six melody strings and a varying number of sympathetic strings. The number of nylon movable frets is variable, as is the tuning of the strings. The instrument of the well-known *tanbur* player Ustad Bahauddin is 130 centimeters in length, with ten sympathetic strings, diatonic tuning, and twenty-six frets. The *tanbur* is plucked with a twined thimble-like metal plectrum worn over the right forefinger. Slobin (1976) observed that the right thumb usually hangs free, but most players now use the thumb for special effects on the sympathetic strings. Like the *dambura*, the *tanbur* is both a solo and an accompanying instrument. In the Badakhshan province this instrument is called *setār* or *sitār* 'three strings', although it generally has more than three strings.

Another common plucked lute is the *dutār* 'two strings', which nowadays has more than two strings. Changes to the Herat *dutār* have possibly influenced developments in the north Afghan *dutār*. The instrument of renowned *dutār* player Shamsuddin Masrur, from Mazar-e Sharif, has fourteen strings and eighteen frets (Baily 1988) [see WESTERN AFGHANISTAN].

The *ghijak*, the only bowed instrument widely used in northern Afghanistan, is a spike fiddle generally with a tin-can resonator (figure 2) but sometimes with a round wooden belly covered with skin (figure 3); both are pierced with sound holes. A wooden or iron nail serves as a spike. Most *ghijak* have two gut or metallic strings

FIGURE 2 *Ghijak* with tin-can resonator. Photo by Jan Van Belle, 1996.

tuned to the interval of a fourth, although some Badakhshan variants have three or four strings, also tuned in fourths. The bow consists of horsehair tied to a curved stick. The *ghijak* produces a trembling, whining sound, and is played as a solo instrument, as vocal accompaniment, or in small ensembles.

The *zirbaghali* and *dāireh* drums are common in small ensembles in northern Afghanistan. The *zirbaghali* is a goblet-shaped drum made of pottery or wood, often richly decorated. The *dāireh*, also named *daf* in Badakhshan, is a single-skinned frame drum with metal rings sometimes fitted in the narrow frame. It is considered a woman's instrument and is used in domestic settings, although men play it in public concerts, especially in Badakhshan.

The most frequently used aerophones are the *tula* and the Badakhshan *nay* 'duct flutes'. The tula produces a rather mellow sound and is played solo on city streets or in ensembles. The Badakhshan *nay*, also frequently played by the Pamir Tajiks, is a regional instrument with a more penetrating sound, typically used for highly ornamental melodic patterns, especially in the *falak* genre.

Idiophones include the *chang* 'metal mouth harp', sometimes used in small ensembles to accompany the melody with repetitive patterns, and the *tāl* 'pair of finger cymbals', rarely played nowadays since the decline of teahouse concerts, the traditional environment for this instrument (Slobin 1976).

The influx of refugees into northern Afghanistan has resulted in new instrumental ensembles. Traditionally, plucked lutes—whether or not played by the singers—formed the main body, accompanied by *zirbaghali* or *dāireh* drums and/or flutes, mouth harp, and finger cymbals. Nowadays singers frequently accompany themselves on the Indian harmonium, first introduced into northern Afghanistan in the 1920s. Tabla drums are also widely used, often in combination with the Afghan *rubāb* and other more traditional instruments. The singer/harmonium player is usually the group's leader.

MUSICIANS, MUSIC LEARNING, AND TRANSMISSION

The traditional distinction between professional musicians (whether hereditary or nonhereditary) and amateur musicians (Sakata 1983) has become less relevant in the 1990s. The political and economic situation has forced many professional musicians to find other sources of income, and most well-known ensembles nowadays consist of both (former) professional and amateur players. All musicians are now *nawāzenda*, the term traditionally reserved for professional musicians.

FIGURE 3 *Ghijak* with skin-covered, round wooden belly. Photo by Jan Van Belle, 1996.

The ongoing war and lack of infrastructure and equipment has dramatically altered the position of musicians. Famous artists referred to as *ustād* 'master, teacher', such as Ustad Malang (*zirbaghali*), Ustad Bahauddin (*tanbur*), and Ustad Takhary (*ghijak* and *dambura*), who were once employed by Radio Kabul, have lost their jobs due to the prohibition of music and live in poor economic conditions in Mazar-e-Sharif. Local (northern) radio and TV stations, partly destroyed and badly in need of equipment and repair, cannot offer any employment on a regular basis. Many northern musicians have left Afghanistan altogether. Well-known professional musicians have fled to Western countries; a considerable number have settled in Peshawar, Pakistan, where in certain quarters Afghan music is very much alive (Baily 1985). Indeed, the whole northern Afghan population in these hard times has little money to spend on music, and the teahouses, formerly an important element of social life and a steady source of income for musicians, are no longer able to hire them.

Instrument builders too have had to stop their activities and seek other sources of income. Like many famous musicians, instrument makers have also emigrated to more comfortable and safer places where they continue building instruments in the traditional way. Unfortunately, they are often not in a position to transmit their knowledge in the traditional oral manner. Indeed, transmission of musical knowledge has generally become highly problematic. University music departments have conducted no music research during the last twenty years. In 1996, it was impossible to find a book on Afghan music in northern Afghanistan or for that matter in Kabul bookshops: the publishing industry had shut down.

The pedagogical tradition among instrument players in Afghanistan has always been the one-to-one relationship between master and pupil, taking place outside any formal schools. This oral tradition still survives in the north, although in a restricted form and mainly within the family, father to son.

MASS MEDIA

Local radio and TV stations in the north have always been strongly dependent on programs broadcast by Radio Kabul. Because of their limited means, homemade programs were few. Radio Kabul was thus the common musical denominator, setting norms and fashions. Since the war, transmission from Kabul has ended due to technical problems and prohibitive southern rules. The same technical problems also influenced the production of the few existing local programs. This situation has nevertheless created some unexpected positive aspects in the programming of local stations: once directed by the taste and wishes of Kabul programmers who traveled north to record northern music, local programmers are now responsible for the programming of their own music. Unfortunately, they badly lack the means to enjoy their new freedom. In 1996, according to Shamsuddin Masrur, a singer, *dutār* player, composer, and director of the music section of Balkh Radio and TV station in Mazar-e-Sharif, there were only three and a half hours of TV per day, of which only one hour was devoted to northern music genres, and the rest to sports, local news, and Qur'ānic reading. (The range of the TV station extends a maximum of 25 kilometers.) The radio station broadcast only two hours in the morning and two hours in the evening.

As regards the record industry, there is currently none in Afghanistan. Foreign records were available in the 1970s but are no longer so, partly pushed away by audio and video technology. In 1996, the Taliban took over northern Afghanistan. As elsewhere in the country, they prohibited all music and music making. Up to this time, all the main cities had local audio and video shops that sold cassettes and videotapes. Prices were reasonable, since only copies recorded on bad-quality tapes were for sale. The uncertain supply of electricity added to the poor quality. The bulk of sales consisted of Pakistani and Indian pop and film music, although people also asked for the local genres. The late Afghan pop singer Ahmad Zaher, called the Elvis Presley of Afghanistan, was still very popular, and his songs were widely available on audio tapes and in song-text booklets. Many people used to make their own recordings on cassette recorders, and some hired cameramen from local video shops to videotape domestic and public parties. This resulted from the lack of any copyright laws in Afghanistan, a fact that placed an additional financial burden on musicians.

REFERENCES

Baily, John. 1985. *Amir, an Afghan Refugee Musician's Life in Peshawar, Pakistan.* National Film and Television School, Beaconsfield, Bucks., England. 16mm film, videocassette.

———. 1988. *Music of Afghanistan: Professional Musicians in the City of Herat.* Cambridge: Cambridge University Press. Book and audio cassette.

De Bruijn, J. T. P. 1992. *The Legacy of Medieval Persian Sufism*, ed. Leonard Lewison. London: Khaniqahi Nimatullahi Publications.

Jawad, Nassim. 1992. *Afghanistan: A Nation of Minorities.* London: Minority Rights Group.

Sakata, Hiromi Lorraine. 1983. *Music in the Mind: The Concepts of Music and Musician in Afghanistan.* Kent, Ohio: Kent State University Press. Book and two audio cassettes.

Slobin, Mark. 1976. *Music in the Culture of Northern Afghanistan.* Tucson: University of Arizona Press.

Southeastern Afghanistan

Nabi Misdaq
John Baily

Pashtun Poets
Pashtun Musical Instruments
Pashtun Musical Style
Pashtun Music in the Postwar Situation

Stretching from Kandahar in the south to Jalalabad in the east, Southeastern Afghanistan is a region dominated by the Pashtuns, the ethnic group that has controlled Afghanistan since its establishment as a state in 1747 [see MUSIC AND THE STATE]. Central to Pashtun identity is the tribal law known as Pashtunwali, which stresses the virtues of honor (*izzat*), hospitality (*melmastia*), vengeance (*badāl*), surrendering oneself for acts of wrongdoing (*nanawatai*), and accompanying guests through dangerous territory (*badraga*). Pashtuns are everything from nomadic herdsmen to shopkeepers, merchants, and craftsmen in long-established cities such as Kandahar, Ghazni, and Jalalabad. Estimates of the population vary widely, from 7 to 14 million; an accurate census has never been carried out in Afghanistan. Another 7 to 14 million Pashtuns live in the North West Frontier Province of Pakistan, where they call themselves Pakhtuns, reflecting a slight difference in dialect. The Pashto language (Pakhtu in Pakistan) belongs to the Iranian family of Indo-European languages. Pashto has a long poetic tradition that has played a prominent role in the history of Pashtun music.

PASHTUN POETS

The first documented Pashtun poet was Amir Karor, born in 761 in Ghor, which Afghan scholars consider the original Pashtun homeland. The following lines are typical of his remarkable poetry:

> Za yam, zmaray puh dai narai la mā atal neshtah
> Puh Hendostan puh Takhar puh Kabul neshtah
> Bul puh Zabol neshtah la mā atal neshtah
>
> I am a lion, there is no equal of me in this world,
> Not in India, Takhar, or Kabul,
> Nor in Zabol. There is no one to equal me.

These lines show the principal characteristics of Pashto poetry: martial in spirit, dealing with topics such as struggle, conquest, and bravery—and hardly lacking in self-confidence. (The Pashto poetry cited here and elsewhere in this article has been pub-

Although Pashtuns enjoy listening to music, they do not generally consider it a respectable profession. A number of educated middle-class Pashtuns in Kabul have nevertheless become professional radio singers.

lished in rare and currently unavailable volumes in Kabul. All translations from the Pashto are by Nabi Misdaq.)

The warrior-chief Kushal Khan Khattak (1613–1689) is widely recognized as the greatest Pashtun poet. He was a leader in the fight against Mughal domination of the eastern part of Afghanistan and articulated the Pashtun desire for nationhood and self-determination.

The following well-known couplet brings out Khattak's zest for the struggle, in which he was engaged his entire life:

> Lā puh khob kai puh larzah praiwzi la kata
> Cha tre ghwago eh zema dai twuray shrang shi
>
> Even when asleep they will fall off their beds
> When the swishing of my sword reaches their ears

Some Pashtun poets, including the celebrated mystic Rahman Baba (c. 1671–1741), wrote in the Sufi tradition. Rahman Baba's poetry exemplifies a totally different approach to life:

> Le ka wanah mostaqim puh khpal makān yam
> Ka khazān rabandai rashi ka bahar
>
> Like a tree I am standing still in one place
> Whether it is autumn or spring

Hamid Mashughel (born 1722) is considered to be a link between the older Pashtun poets, before Afghanistan's statehood in 1747, and the modern ones after that time. His poetry employs language accessible to ordinary people and in particular lends itself to being sung with musical accompaniment. He is a favorite with Pashtun singers even today.

> Prot puh wino kai latpat sha yam puh pat kai
> Neh dai srozaro puh takht bandai bei pat
>
> I would rather swim in my own blood with honor
> Than sit on a golden throne without honor

Mashughel was skilled at weaving Pashto proverbs into his poetry, rendering it all the more attractive to his audience.

A more contemporary figure is Mohammad Amin, better known as Malang Jan (1917–1957). He showed great facility in the composition of stirring nationalistic poetry during the "Pashtunistan" movement, whose aim was the establishment of an autonomous state for the Pakhtuns of Pakistan. He also composed melodies for his poems, and through his exposure on Radio Afghanistan reached an audience of millions on both sides of the border. Some of his poetry is discussed below.

There are several genres of Pashto poetry, some of which are especially associated with music. Perhaps the most characteristic verse form is the *landay* (also known as *ṭappā*). These short poems are often composed by women wishing to encourage their men in times of struggle. The *landay* is a two-line verse; the second line is longer than the first, typically thirteen and nine syllables, respectively. The second line generally ends in the syllables *ma* or *na*. Another important and rather flexible verse form is the Pashto *chahārbeita* of two, three, or four lines. It is sung to a 6/8 meter called *dādrā*.

PASHTUN MUSICAL INSTRUMENTS

The musical instruments traditionally associated with the Pashtuns are the short-necked, waisted, plucked lute with sympathetic and drone strings (*rubāb*), the bowed lute (*sārindā*), and the double-headed barrel drum (*dohol*). The *rubāb* is regarded as the national instrument of Afghanistan. The harmonium and tabla, both introduced from India, became widely used in the early twentieth century, especially for urban music making. The *dohol* drum has an important symbolic role in Pashtun society, and the sound of a *dohol* being struck serves to announce important events, such as the birth of a boy; to accompany dancing; for weddings; and to signal an attack in wartime.

PASHTUN MUSICAL STYLE

Pashtun songs consist of a single melodic vocal line with instrumental accompaniment, with regular alternation between verses and short instrumental sections. Pashtun musical style bears a clear relationship to Pashto poetry: it tends to be forceful, loud, fast, and excited. The short instrumental sections are played at a fast tempo, with heavily emphasized rhythmic cadences followed by short breaks. In fact, these fast instrumental sections and rhythmic cadences are what most distinctly identify Pashtun music. In addition, they have influenced other genres of Afghan music, including the Kabuli ghazal and *naghma-ye kashāl*, such that the Pashtun musical style has now become the national style of Afghanistan. Radio broadcasting has strongly encouraged this development [see MUSIC AND THE STATE].

The tonal system is essentially diatonic, with little use of microtones. A division of the octave into twelve approximately equal half-tones is implicit in the fretting of the *rubāb* and the tuning of the harmonium. Pashtun music uses a simple system of melodic modes, corresponding approximately to the Ionian, Dorian, and Phrygian modes (*pāri*, *kesturi*, and *bairami*, respectively). The metrical modes such as *geda* (eight beats), *dādrā* (six beats) and *mogholi* (seven beats) are related to those of Hindustani music. (For a more detailed study of this music see Baily 1988:81–83.)

TRACK-31 The song "Yaqorbān" performed by Shah Wali, which appears on the CD accompanying this volume, exemplifies these musical characteristics. In 1985, Shah Wali was the leading Afghan refugee singer in Pakistan, and was frequently broadcast on Pakistani radio and television. He and the members of his band come from hereditary musician families occupying low positions in Pashtun society. For although Pashtuns enjoy listening to music, they do not generally consider it a respectable profession. Despite this prejudice, a number of educated middle-class Pashtuns in Kabul have nevertheless become professional radio singers.

Shah Wali and his band performed this song at a Pashtun wedding in the frontier region between Afghanistan and Pakistan in 1985. In this area, guns are readily available and, among other purposes, are used to enliven wedding celebrations. The wedding and the song performance are shown in the documentary film *Amir: An Afghan Refugee Musician's Life in Peshawar, Pakistan* (figures 1and 2). The song is in

FIGURE 1 Amir Mohammed Herawi playing the *rubāb* at a Pashtun wedding in Dean's Hotel, Peshawar, 1985. From the original footage of *Amir*, filmed by Wayne Derrick, produced by John Baily.

the Phrygian (E) mode (*bairami*) and composed by Malang Jan. It consists of four verses in the *landay* poetic form (figure 3).

Yaqorbān—Khodai ba mu bia Kabul ta buzi
Ma ta dai keli mashumān do'a kawina

Yaqorbān shema—watan zemā ze dai watan yam
Puh khplu srow wino ba'i tel āzādawameh

[instrumental section]

Yaqorbān shema—zeh dai watan dai bagh malyar yam
Mā Malang Jn puh kai khpuray kari dinah

Yaqorbān—'ashoqi nima padshahi dah
Cha ma'shuqa ya puh taraf walārwinah

I sacrifice myself—God take me back to Kabul,
The children of the village are praying for me.

I sacrifice myself for you—the homeland belongs to me and I belong to it;
With my red blood I will make it free forever.

[instrumental section]

I sacrifice myself for you—I am the gardener of my country
Because I, Malang Jan, learned to crawl in it.

I sacrifice myself—being in love is like having half a kingdom,
Particularly when the beloved is standing by one's side.

The song "Dalta rāndeh," performed on the same occasion, is in the *chahārbeita* form and uses a 6/8 rhythm much favored in Pashtun music. Malang Jan composed this song in the 1950s, when there were demands for an independent Pashtun state

FIGURE 2 Shah Wali (*right*) and his brother Wali (*left*) accompanying themselves on the harmonium, with other members of Shah Wali's band seated behind, performing for a Pashtun wedding, 1985. From the original footage of *Amir*, filmed by Wayne Derrick, produced by John Baily.

to be called Pashtunistan. Thirty years later, Shah Wali adapted the song to the circumstances of the war against the Russian occupation, changing the word "Pashtunistan" to "Afghanistan." The very enthusiastic response to this song from the frontier audience reveals that the listeners recognize its origins and applaud its implicit Pashtunistan sentiments. Shah Wali sings with his brother, and both play harmonium, accompanied by *rubāb*, clarinet, and tabla. The alternation of verses by two singers is typical of Pashtun music, and perhaps has its origin in the Pashtun practice of two poets sitting together trying to outdo one another with improvised verses.

Refrain:
Dalta rāndeh ousaydai neshi dai lido watan dai
Zemā watan dai shapiro watan dai

[instrumental section]

Verse 1:
Dalta kai her yaw Pashtun ous puh nāmo nang walār dai
Dai khplai khawri hefazat ta puh hemat walār dai
Sar cha puh khāwra warkawi dai jangyālu watan dai

Refrain:
Zemā watan dai shapiro watan dai
Dalta rāndeh ousaydai neshi
Zemā watan dai shapiro watan dai
Afghanistan dai shah zelmo watan dai

[instrumental section]

Verse 2:
Chai dai zelmo hara nārah chai dai izat daka dah
Dā sai ye pighlah dai hayā aw dai izat daka dah
Da namo nang izat Pashto aw dai Pashtun watan dai

The alternation of verses by two singers is typical of Pashtun music, and perhaps has its origin in the Pashtun practice of two poets sitting together trying to outdo one another with improvised verses.

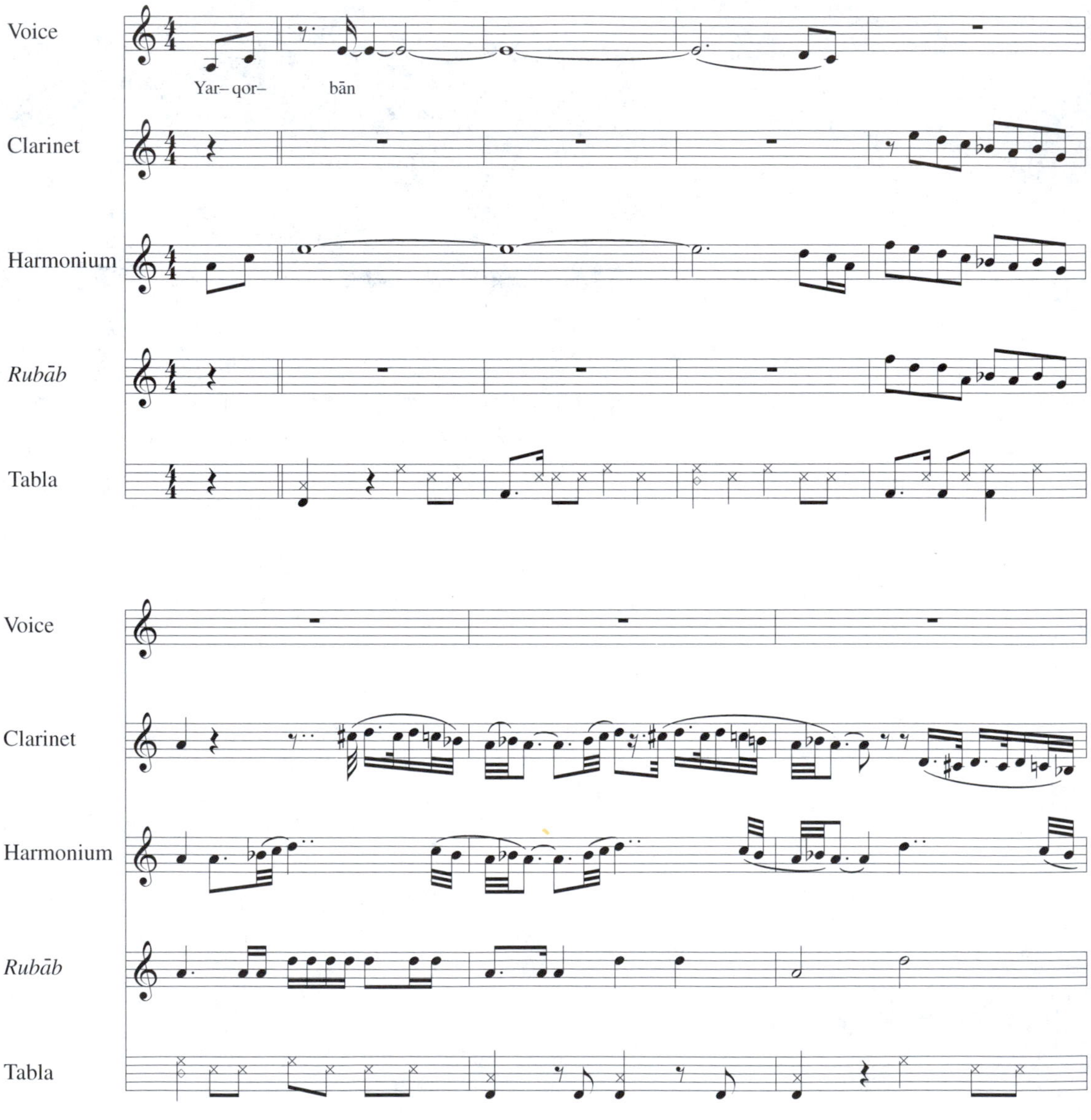

FIGURE 3
"Yaqorbān" 'I sacrifice myself', composed by Malang Jan and sung by Shah Wali at a Pashtun wedding in 1985. Transcription by Steve Hennings from a field recording by John Baily.

Refrain:
Zemā watan dai shapiro watan dai
Dalta rāndeh ousaydai neshi
Zemā watan dai shapiro watan dai

[instrumental section]

FIGURE 3 (*continued*) "Yaqorbān" 'I sacrifice myself', composed by Malang Jan and sung by Shah Wali at a Pashtun wedding in 1985. Transcription by Steve Hennings from a field recording by John Baily.

Verse 3:
Dā shari kandai kānai ghrounah bai dawā patai di
Cha dushmanan ye la ter ousa bai nawā pati di
Rashida haska ghāra gerza dai zemaro watan dai

Refrain:
Zemā watan dai shapiro watan dai
Dalta rāndeh ousaydai neshi
Zemā watan dai shapiro watan dai

Refrain:
The blind cannot remain here, this is the homeland of the sighted;
My homeland is the country of the angels.

[instrumental section]

Verse 1:
Here every Pashtun is standing up for his honor and grace;

He is standing up to protect his homeland with honor and courage.
Those who are prepared to die for their homeland are the defenders of their homeland.

Refrain:
My homeland is the country of the angels,
The blind cannot remain here.
My homeland is the country of the angels,
Afghanistan is the country of the heroic youths.

[instrumental section]

Verse 2:
As the cries of the warriors are full of zeal for freedom,
Similarly their maidens are modest and full of zeal.
The Pashtun way of life binds one to the Pashtun homeland.

Refrain:
My homeland is the country of the angels,
The blind cannot remain here.
My homeland is the country of the angels.

[instrumental section]

Verse 3:
As these rocks and mountains have not been exploited,
The enemies remain thwarted.
Rashid, move with your head held high because this is the country of the lions.

Refrain:
My country is the homeland of the angels,
The blind cannot remain here.
My homeland is the country of the angels.

PASHTUN MUSIC IN THE POSTWAR SITUATION

During the war waged by the *mujahedin* against the successive communist governments between 1978 and 1992, Pashtuns composed a great deal of Pashto poetry commenting on the conflict. Several million Pashtuns from Afghanistan found refuge across the border in Pakistan, mostly in refugee camps. Poetry was one of the few legitimate means of expression open to these people. Not surprisingly, given the political ethos of Pashto poetry, many political aspirations were expressed in this form. Despite the ban on music in the refugee camps by the fundamentalists, much of this poetry was set to music and recorded on cheap audio cassettes available in bazaars. Some of these recordings incorporated the sounds of authentic gunfire and the cry "God is great" (*Allah O Akbar*) to stir the passions of the listeners; others incorporated the sounds of gunfire imitated on the tabla. Apart from these small innovations, Pashtun musical style has not changed during this period of conflict.

Through the turbulent 1980s and 1990s in Afghanistan, the Pashtun people of the southeast have widely used Pashto song to articulate and disseminate every point of view, including criticisms of the various *mujahedin* leaders. A striking example are the songs of the Revolutionary Association of the Women of Afghanistan (RAWA), known in Farsi as Jamiat-e Enqalabi Zanan-e Afghanistan. These women refugees living in Quetta (Pakistan) have recorded a number of cassettes singing their own poetry (with instrumental accompaniment played by men) in the traditional style of praising the warriors and also condemning fundamentalists, communists, and those who stand in the way of the advancement of women. "Without women's participation no revolution will succeed!" is their slogan. Girls belonging to one of the two Afghan Refugee schools run by RAWA in Quetta composed, sang, and recorded the following poem:

Zerah dai Asia chai qahraman dai
Da watan mu gran Afghanistan dai

Soak chai puh yerghal der ta rāgheli dee
Goad aw puh ghāshuno mot wateli dee

So cha bāturan dai watan kai shori
Bia puh kazho strego soak nagori

Zerah dai Asia chai qahraman dai
Da watan mu gran Afghānistan dai

The heart of Asia [Afghanistan] is a hero,
This country dear to us is Afghanistan.

Those who have come to assault you
Have left limping with their teeth broken.

As long as your brave sons are in the country
No one will look at you [Afghanistan] with bad intentions.

The heart of Asia [Afghanistan] is a hero,
This country dear to us is Afghanistan.

REFERENCES

Baily, John. 1985. *Amir: An Afghan Refugee Musician's Life in Peshawar, Pakistan*. 52 mins. National Film and Television School, Beaconsfield, Bucks., England. 16 mm. Video cassette available from Documentary Educational Resources, Watertown, Mass.

———. 1988. *Music of Afghanistan: Professional Musicians in the City of Herat*. Cambridge: Cambridge University Press. With accompanying audio cassette.

———. 1990. *The Making of* "Amir: An Afghan Refugee Musician's Life in Peshawar, Pakistan." *A Study Guide to the Film*. Watertown, Mass.: sDocumentary Educational Resources.

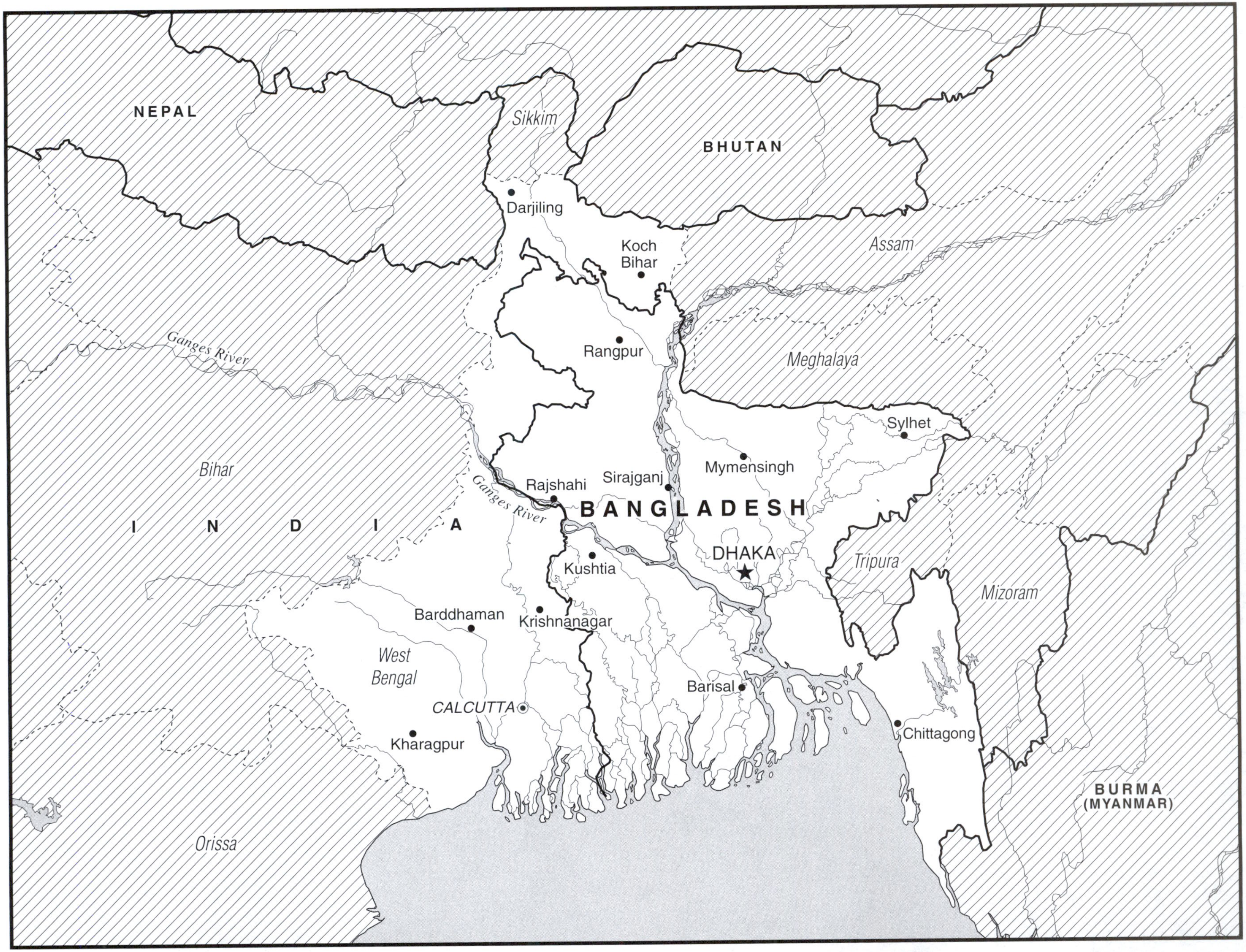
NEPAL
BHUTAN
Sikkim
Darjiling
Koch
Bihar
Assam
Rangpur
Meghalaya
Ganges River
Sylhet
Bihar
Mymensingh
Sirajganj
Rajshahi
BANGLADESH
Ganges River
I N D I A
DHAKA
Tripura
Kushtia
Mizoram
Barddhaman
Krishnanagar
West
Bengal
Barisal
CALCUTTA
Chittagong
Kharagpur
BURMA
(MYANMAR)
Orissa

West Bengal and Bangladesh

The eastern region of South Asia known as Bengal prior to India's independence has always been noted for its cultivation of literature and the performing arts. Bengali songs, in particular, have played a prominent role in the musical history of the region, ranging from the huge repertoire of devotional songs composed and sung by medieval Hindu poet-saints to the patriotic songs and Bengali ghazals of the twentieth century, and from the mystical songs of the Bāuls to the boatmen's songs of coastal areas.

Beyond classical music, instruments have played a subordinate role in both urban and rural music, largely that of accompaniment to the vocal line. Drums, plucked drums with single strings, percussion, and stringed instruments are most typical. Common among tribal groups of the region are bamboo and wooden flutes, and also drums.

MAP 10 West Bengal and Bangladesh

West Bengal and Bangladesh

Karunamaya Goswami

Devotional and Urban Music of Bengal before 1947
Post-1947 Musical Developments in West Bengal and Bangladesh
Bengali Folk Music

The music of West Bengal and Bangladesh is commonly known as Bengali music, after the Bengal region of northeast India that existed before the partition of 1947. In that year, Bengal was divided into East and West Bengal, and they became provinces of Pakistan and India respectively. In 1971, East Bengal fought a war with Pakistan to break away and become the independent nation of Bangladesh. West Bengal remained an Indian state. The two regions share a common musical tradition inherited from the pre-1947 period, as well as the Bengali language, in which song texts in that tradition were written.

DEVOTIONAL AND URBAN MUSIC OF BENGAL BEFORE 1947

Caryā gīti

The earliest extant writing in Bengali, from a time when the language was just evolving, is in the *caryā gīti* song genre. This song form was widely known and flourished over a long period, from the ninth to the twelfth centuries. Composers modeled the music after the stylized composition of a then-popular classical genre called *caryā,* and composed lyrics following a sonnet pattern. These poet-composers were part of a line of Buddhist mystic saints, who spoke symbolically about the secrets of spiritual success leading to nirvana. The singing pattern is believed to have been an alternation of solo and chorus. Individual *caryā* songs were governed by the rules of the raga in which the song was composed. Over a long period, *caryā* performers were able to develop and establish a popular musical model (Prajnanananda 1965).

Gīta Govinda

The *caryā* model dominated mainstream Bengali music until the second half of the twelfth century, when a great poet-composer of the Hindu Vaishnav sect (devotees of Vishnu), Jayadeva, appeared on the literary and musical scene of Bengal. He began creating a new form of music and poetry that centered on the great tradition of Radha-Krishna love lore. Born in a village in the district of Virbhum (now in West Bengal), Jayadeva was the court poet of Lakshmana Sena, a king of Bengal who ascended the throne in about 1178. A poet, musician, musicologist, and choreographer of a very high order, he composed a book of songs that not only shaped the later course of music and poetry in Bengal, but also influenced most profoundly the traditions of music, dance, and drama in other regions of India. Jayadeva called his song book *Gīta Govinda* 'Songs on Govinda'; Govinda is another name for Lord Krishna. *Gīta Govinda* is a collection of twenty-four songs on the love tales of Radha and Krishna, a theme endlessly represented in all Indian art forms. Jayadeva was a great performer of classical music and adopted an elaborate *dhruvapada* musical model for his songs, very close to the later *dhrupad* form [see HINDUSTANI VOCAL MUSIC]. The *Gīta Govinda* songs, written in sweet and simple Sanskrit, marked the beginning of a great Vaishnav musical era in Bengal that continued in full glory until the end of the eighteenth century.

Sri Krishna Kīrtan

Between 1450 and 1500, Baru Chandidas's songbook, *Sri Krishna Kīrtan,* enriched and diversified the musical and literary inheritance of the *caryā* poets and the *Gīta Govinda* poet Jayadeva. Whereas both *caryā* and *dhruvapada* musical forms were pan-Indian, Chandidas incorporated into his work purely Bengali musical and lyrical elements. Baru Chandidas made extensive use of the Radha-Krishna episode in his huge narrative work, which he arranged into hundreds of devotional songs (*kīrtan*). *Sri Krishna Kīrtan* was a grand song-drama that Baru Chandidas and his troupe performed on a simple stage. Critics regard it as a multidimensional work. Indeed, *Krishna Kīrtan* served as the basis for important musical and literary genres that developed and flourished in Bengal during the next one hundred years or more (Prajnanananda 1960).

Padāvalī kīrtan

The immediate impact of *Sri Krishna Kīrtan* was its influence on hundreds of Vaishnav poets who presented the lyrical songs of Sri Chaitanya's spiritual movement in Bengal. These poet-composers have been called *mahājana* 'saints', and their compositions *mahājana padāvalī* 'songs by saints'. The songs were popularly known as *kīrtan.* (Figures 1 and 2 show *kīrtan* performance in Uttar Pradesh.) Although Vaishnavites had composed and sung Vaishnav songs in the past, Sri Chaitanya gave them religious sanction by making singing in praise of Lord Krishna a compulsory part of the devotional practices he espoused (Prajnanananda 1970). Sri Chaitanya himself was an untiring singer of Vaishnav songs, and he also taught others how to sing. He is regarded as the father of *padāvalī* singing. His life and teachings became the subject of numerous songs. Many *padāvalī* composers possessed great poetic and musical talent, and succeeded in employing music to heighten the suggestivity of the lyrics. They brought this combination to such a high level of aesthetic accomplishment that it became an ideal for composers in Bengal, where the development of music took second place to that of poetry. This represents a vital distinction between Hindustani and Bengali composition (Ray 1973).

The musical ideas floated by Baru Chandidas developed into the great Vaishnav school of music in Bengal between 1550 and 1600. Narottama Thakur (1531–1587), a Vaishnav saint from Rajshahi (now in Bangladesh), took a leading role in founding the music school. Narottama was a renowned musicologist and a skilled performer who combined Hindustani classical genres like *dhrupad* with indigenous Bengali musical forms to promote the idea of the Vaishnav music school, which he presented at a grand Vaishnav convention held in his village, probably in 1584. The assemblage unanimously accepted the idea. Narottama's instance inspired others to evolve new schools of Vaishnav music, which in time reached five. Together they elaborately shaped the musical tradition typically known as Bengal's own contri-

FIGURE 1 *Kīrtan* singers, accompanied by a *ḍholak* drum and hand clapping, in Banaras, Uttar Pradesh, 1981. Photo by Stephen Slawek.

FIGURE 2 A *ḍholak* player accompanies *kīrtan* singing in Banaras, Uttar Pradesh, 1981. Photo by Stephen Slawek.

bution to Indian music. This Vaishnav music has an extremely intricate tala system (Sanyal 1989).

Śāktapada saṅgīt

The glorious age of *padāvalī* continued until the end of the eighteenth century, when song texts in Bengal invariably referred to Kanu, a popular name for Krishna. But in the second half of the eighteenth century, another musical tradition emerged, known as *śāktapada saṅgīt* 'songs on goddesses of power'. The poet-composers of these songs borrowed heavily from *maṅgala gān,* a renowned tradition of Bengali narrative composition on the power-cult gods and goddesses. Scholars believe that *maṅgala gān* was first composed in the fourteenth century (Bhattacharya 1958) and reached its climax in the compositions of Bharat Chandra Ray (1712–1760). *Śāktapada saṅgīt* were lyrical compositions in praise of the Hindu goddesses Kali and Durga that were sung as an essential part of their worship (*upāsanā*).

At the core of *śāktapada saṅgīt* texts is the eternal mother, symbol of infinite compassion and power; this contrasts with the Vaishnav *padāvalī* songs of perpetual love between the eternal feminine, symbolized by Radha, and the eternal masculine, symbolized by Krishna. For many years, songs on power-cult goddesses formed the principal trend of Bengali art music. One of the trendsetters was Ramprasad Sen (1720–1781), who created a new compositional form known as the melody of Ramprasad, combining elements of *bāul* (a Bengali folk form), classical melody, and *kīrtan*. This interaction between Bengali folk music and classical music represented a new compositional approach and gave rise to a new musical structure. Kamalakanta Bhattacarya (1772–1821), a talented poet and trained musician, composed similar *śāktapada saṅgīt*. Over the next one hundred fifty years or so, hundreds of poet-composers created a huge stock of songs glorifying the power-cult goddesses, particularly Kali. They accepted every prevailing school of music, classical or semiclassical, as the basis of their compositions. This stylistic approach of combining folk and raga-based melodies continued to dominate Bengali music during the nationalist movements of the early twentieth century, until the last of the great Bengali *śāktapada saṅgīt* composers, Kazi Nazrul Islam (1899–1976).

Ṭappā

At the beginning of the nineteenth century, a new musical genre emerged in Bengal called *ṭappā*. This was of historic significance, for the *ṭappā* poets sought a different, secular path for Bengali urban music. Bengali songs up to that time, whether *caryā, padāvalī kīrtan,* or *śāktapada saṅgīt,* had been religious songs, sung as part of religious obligations. *Padāvalī kīrtan* had embraced the subject of love, but love in a spiritual sense, between the two eternal entities: Radha, symbolizing the finite, and Krishna, symbolizing the infinite. The *ṭappā* poet-composers turned their backs on symbolism and spiritualism, and sought to portray love as a tender relation between man and woman. They emphasized mostly the aspect of separation (*viraha*).

Ramnidhi Gupta, popularly known as Nidhu Babu (1741–1839), was a gifted poet, musician, and performer who single-handedly took upon himself the responsibility of initiating a secular urban music tradition in Bengal. His center of activity was the city of Calcutta. Gupta learned *ṭappā* outside Bengal almost as soon as it was propagated by Golam Nabi (1742–1792), one of his contemporaries in Lucknow, a great center of Hindustani classical music. *Ṭappā* is one of the major styles of Hindustani music, the others being *dhrupad, khyāl,* and *ṭhumrī* [see HINDUSTANI VOCAL MUSIC]. It is widely believed that Golam Nabi combined the Lucknow *khyāl* with camel drivers' songs of the Punjab to arrive at the secular *ṭappā* style, which Ramnidhi Gupta learned. Acting as poet, composer, and performer, Gupta created hundreds of *ṭappā* songs, each with two stanzas of two lines each, expressing love as a human phenomenon in unambiguous terms. Ramnidhi significantly changed the jovial spirit of Hindustani *ṭappā*. He toned it down and made it perceptibly sad and slow, suiting the dejected mood of his lyrics, which portrayed the feelings of tearful heroines with little or no hope of union with the heroes.

Contemporary with Ramnidhi was Kalidas Chattopadhyay (1750–1820), a *ṭappā* poet, composer, and performer of a high order. He learned *ṭappā* in Banaras, home of the musical lineage of Golam Nabi. Kalidas did not favor Ramnidhi's secular approach to poetry and music, but rather chose to compose *ṭappā* songs about the power-cult goddesses, especially Kali. These two founding fathers thus began two distinct lines of Bengali *ṭappā*—a secular school of love songs and a religious line of *śāktapada saṅgīt.* Although at the beginning of the nineteenth century religious themes were the dominant content of Bengali music, many poet-composers of this period and after paid ample attention to Ramnidhi's secular trend, borrowing liberally from his *ṭappā* musical style (Goswami 1985).

Brahma saṅgīt

Nineteenth-century mainstream Bengali music included other important branches of development apart from *ṭappā,* two of which were *Brahma saṅgīt* and *swadeśī gān.*

Brahma saṅgīt 'Brahma songs' are inseparably linked to the new spiritual order founded by the Bengali thinker and religious reformer Raja Rammohan Ray (1774–1833). He preached *Brahma dharma* 'Brahma religion', and the Brahma songs were the new religion's prayer songs. In traditional Hinduism, God is one, but gods and goddesses symbolize His numerous attributes; traditional Hindu religious songs glorify these gods and goddesses. Rammohan Ray emphasized the oneness and indivisibility of God and introduced a new system of worship, which he explained in extensive inspirational writings. Ray strongly believed in the efficacy of music in purifying the human mind. He made prayer songs an inseparable part of his Brahma religious practice and composed new devotional songs for this purpose.

Rammohan Ray was a trained musician with a keen taste for classical music. For his own songs he followed the *ṭappā* model of his teacher, Kalidas Chattopadhyay. The *dhrupad* musical style soon came to be associated with Brahma songs, as

In 1872, the founding of the General Theater in Calcutta marked the beginning of professional theater in Bengal, and from the start the theater propagated patriotism through plays featuring songs.

Rammohan himself invited the noted *dhrupad* performer Vishnu Chakravarti to take charge of musical training in his Brahma religious organization. Rammohan died in England only five years after founding the Brahma religious society, in 1828. His *ṭappā* tradition did not last long, and instead composers of Brahma songs followed the *dhrupad* model. During his life, Rammohan Ray inspired some of his friends to compose Brahma songs, which they did with success. The Brahma religious movement with its prayer songs made a good start, and it continued to thrive in spite of the early death of its founder (Mukhopadhyay 1976).

Devendranath Tagore (1817–1905) became the next leader of the Brahma society. A philosopher, poet, and musician, Devendranath was passionately devoted to Rammohan's Brahma songs, and was also an admirer of Chakravarti and his *dhrupad* style. *Dhrupad* became the musical model for the Brahma sect under his leadership.

Members of the Brahma society did not always stand united. In 1866, Kesav Chandra Sen (1838–1884) founded a breakaway sect that he called the Indian Brahma Society, following a philosophical dispute with Devendranath. The musical model of this sect's prayer songs was *padāvalī kīrtan* instead of *dhrupad*. Shivnath Shastri (1847–1919) and Anandamohan Basu (1847–1906) then conflicted ideologically with Kesav Sen and founded a third stream of the Brahma sect called the General Brahma Society, but they retained Sen's style of prayer song.

A *dhrupad*-based musical style flourished in the prayer songs of Devendranath Tagore's sect, which became known as the Old Brahma Society. Devendranath turned his ancestral home at Jorasanko, in Calcutta, into a great center of musical activity, including performances of the sect's devotional songs. He himself composed some Brahma songs and inspired other family members to do so. His sons, who earned tremendous reputations as poets and musicians, composed hundreds of songs in the Old Brahma Society *dhrupad* style. Dwijendranath, Satyendranath, Jyotirindranath, and above all Rabindranath—all sons of Devendranath Tagore—composed brilliant Brahma songs and shaped the most remarkable chapter in the history of Bengali devotional music.

Patriotic songs

Bengali songs of patriotic spirit (*swadeśī gān*) arose in the mid-nineteenth century out of a sense of confrontation between the native Indian people and their British rulers. The patriotic call was first heard in the poems and songs of Ishwar Gupta (1812–1859). Poems by other nineteenth-century nationalist poets including Rangalal Bandyopadhyay, Hemchandra Bandyopadhyay, Madhusudan Datta, and Nabinchandra Sen heightened the spirit of Ishwar Gupta's patriotic call.

Exhibitions of native goods and talents known as *Hindu melā* gave great impetus to this new musical stream. Navagopal Mitra, a nationalist thinker, organized the first such exhibition of Indian-made goods in 1867 that lasted a week, to inspire Indians to look at the core of the problem of foreign rule. Devendranath Tagore and other members of the Jorasanko Tagore family assisted Mitra. It was a brilliant occasion, designed to display native goods and traditional acrobatic feats, to honor talented people, and, most important, to promote the singing of patriotic songs. A second *swadeśī*, or patriotic fair, in 1868 was inaugurated with a song composed by Vishnu Chakravarti with lyrics by Satyendranath Tagore. Satyendranath's song became widely popular, and is now regarded as the first great Bengali patriotic song of heroic sentiment. At subsequent sessions of the exhibition—which continued without break for fourteen years—performers sang patriotic songs in ever-increasing numbers.

Dwijendranath Tagore composed one song for the exhibition in *rāg nat bihāg* that described India under foreign rule as a weeping woman. The essential sadness of his patriotic feeling soon influenced many other poet-composers, and a stream of doleful Bengali patriotic songs appeared alongside the robust stream of heroic songs. Satyendranath and Dwijendranath, both sons of Devendranath Tagore, originated these two distinguished forms, but other eminent Bengali poet-composers like Manomohan Basu, Ganendranath Tagore, Hemchandra Bandyopadhyay, Govindachandra Ray, Vishnurama Chattopadhyay, and Rangalal Bandyopadhyay were soon also composing Bengali patriotic songs.

Rabindranath Tagore attended some of the later sessions of the exhibition and sang some of his own patriotic songs. His elder brother Jyotirindranath, a renowned poet and composer, formed the Rejuvenation Club, whose aim was to preach patriotism through writings and songs. Many patriotic songs were composed under the auspices of this club. In 1872, the founding of the General Theater in Calcutta marked the beginning of professional theater in Bengal, and from the start the theater propagated patriotism through plays featuring songs. Another event that proved inspiring for the growth of Bengali patriotic songs was the founding of the Indian National Congress in 1885. The singing of patriotic songs became customary at Congress sessions.

The movement opposing the partition of Bengal (1905–1911) provided a forum for the creation and performance of Bengali patriotic songs [see MUSIC AND NATIONALISM]. In 1905, Lord Curzon, then the governor general of India, declared the partition of Bengal in order to increase administrative efficiency. A movement—widely known as the *swadeśī* movement—was launched in opposition to British rule and the partition of Bengal. Patriotic songs played an important role in propagating the movement's message. Poets and composers such as Rabindranath Tagore, Dwijendralal Ray, Atulprasad Sen, Rajani Kanta Sen, Mukunda Das, and many others composed numerous songs in support of this movement. The movement soon spread throughout Bengal, and people composed and sang patriotic songs in huge numbers.

The enthusiasm for Bengali patriotic songs waned and the *swadeśī* movement declined when the partition was rescinded. By 1911, the chief musical exponents of the movement had either died or retired from composing patriotic songs. But this was only a temporary phase. The stream of patriotic songs in Bengal surged once again after a decade or so, when the Bengali people became locked into a tough confrontation with their foreign rulers. The movement for independence was gaining momentum, and Kazi Nazrul Islam (1899–1976), called the rebel poet of Bengal for his fiery anti-British outpourings, became its poetical and musical mouthpiece in this volatile time. He composed a fresh batch of explosive patriotic songs.

Jyotirindranath Tagore

Jyotirindranath (1849–1925) was a son of Devendranath Tagore and a great poet-composer, who infused a spirit of modernity into the Bengali urban music tradition and gave it a new aesthetic direction. He systematized nineteenth-century Bengali attitudes toward music by following the Western example of musical composition, instead of the Hindustani tradition of impromptu improvisation. Jyotirindranath is considered the forerunner of the five great Bengali poet-composers who created the "golden age" of modern urban music in Bengal: Rabindranath Tagore (1861–1941), Dwijendralal Ray (1863–1913), Rajani Kanta Sen (1865–1910), Atulprasad Sen (1871–1934), and Kazi Nazrul Islam (1899–1976).

Jyotirindranath was educated in Indian and Western music, and was known as a towering musicologist. He founded music schools, published music journals, and developed a notation system. His preference for composed music as opposed to improvised music inspired others to start composing. However, he had difficulty establishing the fixed nature of composed music and the authority of the composer; in the Hindustani tradition, song lyrics were unchangeable, but performers were at liberty, often extravagantly, to alter the musical composition. Jyotirindranath's works left no room for the performer to add or delete anything from the notation. This was a historic turning point for modern urban music in Bengal, and the impact of this new musical idea was immediately felt in the works of Jyotirindranath's disciple and younger brother, Rabindranath Tagore (Goswami 1993a).

Rabindranath Tagore

Rabindranath Tagore (1861–1941) is Bengal's greatest poet and composer. He is the only Indian poet ever to have won the Nobel Prize (1913), for his book of poems entitled *Gītāñjali* 'Song Offerings'. The collected poems represented some of the best of his compositional style. Rabindranath grew up in a home environment of classical music. He had little interest in rigorous training, but the diverse musical experiences in his home greatly enriched his sensibility. He did receive some musical instruction from his elder brother Jyotirindranath.

Rabindranath began to compose songs systematically from 1881. He completed about twenty-five thousand songs over his creative lifetime, which scholars have divided into three phases (Goswami 1993b; Majumdar 1990). During the first phase (1881–1900), Tagore prepared himself musically and poetically by composing songs modeled on existing Hindustani classical songs. In the second phase (1901–1920), Tagore made wide-ranging experiments, creating varied melodic patterns very different from those of Hindustani stock songs. He also paid keen attention to the folk music of Bengal, particularly songs of the Bāul religious sect (see below). Tagore composed most of his patriotic songs at this time, and many were profoundly influenced by Bāul music. The third phase (1921–1941) covers Tagore's compositions in what is now thought of as the "Tagore musical style." These compositions *par excellence*, created from a combination of folk forms (particularly those of the Bāul sect) and classical melodies and genres, represent the culmination of experiences gathered and of experiments made during the composer's previous forty years.

Rabindranath classified his songs into four major categories: *pūjā* 'worship', *swadeś* 'homeland', *prakṛti* 'nature', *prem* 'love', and two minor categories: *vicar* 'variety' and *ānushṭhanik* 'ceremonial'.

Rabindranath composed about six hundred fifty songs in the *pūjā* category, also known as *Brahma saṅgīt* 'Brahma songs'. They are mostly in *dhrupad* style, and their combined lyricism and music make the essence of allegiance to God universally inspiring. As a religious movement Brahmaism has declined, yet Tagore's Brahma songs have become increasingly popular with the music-loving population. His experimentation in these devotional songs gave new direction to Bengali urban music.

The category of *swadeś* songs comprises about seventy, including some of the best-known Bengali patriotic songs. Tagore began to compose patriotic songs as a young man, and continued this mission until 1911, when the *swadeśī* movement opposing the partition of Bengal declined. Thereafter he contributed little to this genre. Tagore composed his historic song "My golden Bengal, I love you," now the national anthem of Bangladesh, during the nationalistic *swadeśī* movement. In most of these songs, Tagore experimented with folk melodies, particularly Bāul tunes, which influenced his third and final phase of life as a composer.

Tagore composed nearly three hundred songs on the seasons of nature. His position in this respect is unique, in the sense that no other Bengali poet-composer worked so significantly and on such a huge scale in this song category. Tagore not only describes the visible changes in nature—in flowers, plants, creepers, wind, river, sky, and so on—but also communicates the corresponding states of the human mind. The relationship between music and nature has always been intimate, and assumed an organized form in Indian classical music with the composition of seasonal melodies and the linking of ragas with seasons. Nature has played an important role in shaping the aesthetics of people living in close harmony with it. However, as rural life declined, and cities grew and expanded into centers of modern industrial civilization, people were becoming increasingly cut off from nature. Rabindranath Tagore tried to revive the old, affectionate, and perhaps eternal relationship between man and nature in his seasonal songs. He himself lived much of his life in a pastoral environment, close to the Santiniketan University he founded in 1901. This closeness to nature inspired him keenly to describe in song the changing state of the Bengali mind during the yearly cycles of nature.

Rabindranath also composed love songs continually throughout his creative life, over four hundred in all. Inspired by the intrinsic charm and depth of human relationships, he presented the basic feelings of life in their endless shades and subtleties. The love songs of Tagore's first creative phase personalize relationships with robust feeling. Songs of the later phases show a gradual development from the level of personal feelings to a universal, philosophical expression. In the tradition of Bengali love songs, Tagore's never present a jovial mood. They are pensive songs that muse over a sense of separation between woman and man, both of them seeking a union that is frequently remote.

Tagore identified some of his songs as ceremonial. They are pertinent to particular ceremonies and festivals, and today Bengalis cannot think of holding many of their ceremonies without the performance of Tagore songs.

Rabindranath modeled his music on the four-movement structural design of *dhrupad*, and recognized this on many occasions. He once said: "We have got two things in *dhrupad*: one—vastness and depth; two—a sense of control and symmetry" (Tagore 1986:158). As a composer, he valued these qualities most. His prime objective was to heighten the lyrical suggestivity, which he pursued with a missionary zeal. Tagore never approved of the traditional extempore improvisation, which gave greater prominence to music than to poetry. Rather, he worked consistently and continuously to treat poetry and music equally. Rabindranath Tagore composed all the music for his songs, a concept unknown to Bengal before his elder brother, Jyotirindranath. He established fixed song composition by composing nearly twenty-five hundred songs in this manner, thus prescribing by example the absolute authority of a composer over his compositions. Tagore took careful steps in teaching his music, preparing his notations, and grooming a generation of performers so that his compositions would not be distorted through carelessness or wistful improvisations.

Modern developments of urban music in Bengal are indebted to Rabindranath Tagore. He provided a new aesthetic direction, and represents perhaps the highest model of composer-poet for future generations (Basu 1966).

Dwijendralal Ray was a major poet and composer of Bengal, and the first to create a musical style combining elements of Indian raga and Western music.

FIGURE 3 Dwijendralal Ray

Dwijendralal Ray

Dwijendralal Ray (1863–1913), popularly known as D. L. Ray, was a major poet and composer of Bengal, and the first to create a musical style combining elements of Indian raga and Western music (figure 3). He used *khyāl* and *ṭappā* genres creatively, in a personal way. The son of a renowned musician, Dewan Kartikayachandra Ray, D. L. Ray received his early music education from his father. After passing his M.A. in English in 1884, he went to England for higher education where he studied the history and theory of Western music. On his return to India, he joined government service as a deputy magistrate in Bihar, and began his illustrious career as a poet and composer. He acquired performing ability and a thorough musical knowledge of raga under S. N. Majumdar and others.

D. L. Ray's initial accomplishment as a poet-composer was with humorous songs. He excelled equally in witty satire and refreshing humor. He later earned phenomenal success as a composer of patriotic songs, which combined raga characteristics with Western musical traits such as the rise and fall of melodic phrases and the use of a vocal chorus. He was also a pioneer in Bengali marching music.

D. L. Ray's love songs exemplify his individual approach to raga, more particularly to *khyāl* and *ṭappā* and to a mixed form called *ṭap-khyāl*. He employed these stylistic forms, but within his own compositional structure. During his lifetime, his compositions were clearly overshadowed by the work of Rabindranath Tagore. However, present-day critics are publishing books and articles in recognition of his momentous contributions as a founder of modern Bengali urban music (Chaudhuri 1983).

Rajani Kanta Sen

Rajani Kanta Sen (1865–1910) is renowned for his accomplishments as a composer of devotional songs. Born in Sirajganj district (now in Bangladesh) to a poet-musician father, Guruprasad Sen, Rajani Kanta showed interest in singing and writing songs at an early age. He earned his reputation as a composer when he settled in Rajshahi as a lawyer. Rajani Kanta participated in the movement opposing the partition of Bengal (1905–1911), and composed patriotic songs on the movement's *swadeśī* ideas. During this time he lost his children tragically, then fell fatally ill, first with a kidney ailment and later with throat cancer. Even on his deathbed, Rajani Kanta Sen composed some sublime songs on the spirit of surrender to the will of God.

Although Rajani Kanta's favorite musical form was *khyāl*, his own musical style was unlike that of traditional *khyāl*; it fully communicated the depth of his feeling and the innocence of his urge for divine mercy and salvation. He also incorporated elements of Baul songs in some of his compositions.

Atulprasad Sen

The prime contribution of Atulprasad Sen (1871–1934) to Bengali music was the creation of a *ṭhumrī*-based foundation for Bengali art songs. Atulprasad was born in Dhaka. His grandfather, a poet, composer, and singer, took on the responsibility of raising him from a young age after his father died. Atulprasad spent his childhood in a literary and musical environment that nurtured his talents as a poet-composer and singer. On his return from London as a barrister, he joined the bar in Lucknow, where he lived and composed until the end of his life.

Sen divided his 210 song compositions into four broad groups: *devatā* 'god,' *prakṛti* 'nature,' *manava* 'man', and *swadeś* 'motherland.' His categories appear to be influenced by Rabindranath Tagore. Like D. L. Ray, Atulprasad was familiar with Western music from his stay in England, but he never borrowed a single Western melody or rhythm. Indian vocal music genres like *khyāl*, *ṭhumrī*, and ghazal were his principal musical sources, and he made occasional use of *ṭappā*.

Atulprasad Sen is regarded as the pioneer Bengali ghazal composer, although he composed only six or seven Bengali ghazals. Lucknow was renowned for its *ṭhumrī* and ghazal traditions, and Atulprasad's knowledge of Urdu gave him easy access to the ghazal poetry written in Urdu over the previous several hundred years. He began to compose Bengali ghazals but stopped after his first few creations, choosing to compose Bengali songs on the *ṭhumrī* model instead. During a lifetime lived far from Calcutta, the prime center for musical activities in Bengal, his contribution as a ghazal composer did not spread beyond a small, enlightened, intimate circle and was discovered only much later.

Bengali composers had employed *dhrupad*, *khyāl*, and *ṭappā* since the beginning of the nineteenth century, but not until Atulprasad Sen did Bengal hear compositions based on *ṭhumrī*. Bengali music lovers became enamored of the infinite tenderness and charm of his *ṭhumrī* style. Atulprasad established a trend of *ṭhumrī*-based songs by composing over a hundred such works. His *ṭhumrī*-based mode of composition became the most widely accepted musical style among post-Tagore Bengali composers writing popular and entertainment music.

Atulprasad Sen contributed significantly to the nationalist movement through his song compositions. In particular, his well-known song on the love of Bengali as the mother tongue drew upon Baul songs for its enchanting musical style. He borrowed largely from *khyāl*, Baul, and *kīrtan* for the musical style of his devotional songs and also from Hindustani forms like *khyāl* and *ṭhumrī* for his widely acclaimed love songs. A personal sense of failure in love shrouds all his compositions with a tremendous longing for union. Atulprasad Sen is the only major Bengali poet who wrote nothing of significance other than songs (Chakravarti 1990).

Kazi Nazrul Islam

The creative life of Kazi Nazrul Islam (1899–1976) as a Bengali poet-composer lasted for only twenty-two years. But within this short time period he composed over three thousand songs of remarkable variety. Nazrul came from a poor family in present-day West Bengal, India. He worked for folk-music troupes at an early age, and started his career as a writer, composer, and journalist after World War I. A strong opponent of British rule in India, he soon began writing poems expressing rebellious ideas and after 1922 was known as the "rebel poet of Bengal." In November of that year, he was arrested by the British Indian government on a charge of writing and publishing a seditious poem, and was sentenced to one year's rigorous imprisonment. He nevertheless continued composing patriotic songs.

From the end of 1926, Nazrul Islam began composing ghazals and concentrating more on music and literature than on politics. He joined the Gramophone Company of India in Calcutta in mid-1928 as a composer and trainer, marking the beginning of an exceptionally productive period as a songwriter and composer. He composed stage music and film music, and his contribution to the early talkies in Bengal is deemed historic. He also started broadcasting for All India Radio in Calcutta in 1938; the broadcasts, which aired at regular intervals, brought to light old obscure ragas and presented new ragas he composed himself. But at the height of his creative life—1942—Kazi Nazrul Islam fell seriously ill. He never recovered from this incapacitating illness, which caused him to lose his power of speech and mental faculties. Thirty years later, in May 1972, he was brought to Dhaka, after the emergence of Bangladesh as a sovereign state (1971). Nazrul lived with state honors until his death on August 29, 1976, when he was laid to rest in the compound of Dhaka University mosque. He is the national poet of Bangladesh.

Nazrul's life as a composer falls into four identifiable phases. The first phase of patriotic songs extends from 1920 to 1926; the second (ghazal) phase extends from the end of 1926 to mid-1928; the third phase, with the gramophone company, extends from 1928 to 1938; and the fourth (radio) phase from 1938 to mid-1942 (Goswami 1996a).

Kazi Nazrul Islam is considered the foremost composer of Bengali patriotic songs. He composed songs on a variety of *swadeśī* themes, including the freedom movement, communal harmony, and social awakening, such as *Bhāṅgārgān* 'Break down the iron gate':

Break down the iron gate of prison
And break down into pieces
The blood-bathed
Stone altar of the goddess of fetters.
O young god of destruction!
Play on your doomsday drum
Let the flag of destruction
Flutter on the wall of the East.

His compositions in such categories as "songs of socialist inspiration" and "songs of Muslim awakening" were new in the history of Bengali patriotic songs. Previous Bengali poet-composers had written about political freedom alone. Now Nazrul spoke of the economic emancipation of weaker sections of society, thereby laying the foundation of the progressive cultural movement in Bengal. His songs of Muslim awakening had also contributed to augmenting the Muslim renaissance in Bengal.

No Bengali poet-composer before Kazi Nazrul Islam had taken any effective interest in composing Bengali ghazals. Atulprasad Sen's work in this genre was little known in Bengal. Nazrul's ghazals awakened unprecedented interest among Bengali music lovers. No other musical genre had been received with so much immediate popularity in Bengal, or been paid so much immediate attention by all leading Bengali performers at one time. Nazrul created a new trend in modern Bengali music. His ghazals presented a different kind of poetic and musical expressiveness, sweet and melancholy with tender and subtle improvisations.

In the third phase of his life as a composer, working for the Gramophone Company of India in Calcutta as well as for stage and film, Nazrul composed songs on all possible themes, in many musical forms, and at incredible speed. Most of his three thousand songs were composed during this period. He was prominent in the first-ever large-scale commercial production of Bengali music by the recording and film industries. Notable at this time were his modern songs, devotional songs, songs based on folk-music traditions, and raga-based songs. A new musical genre, typically known as *ādhunik* 'modern', was a significant phenomenon in post-Tagore Bengali music. Produced as entertainment music, this new genre grew very fast with financial support from commercial music producers. Nazrul could spontaneously combine entertainment and art, and thus his compositions struck the hearts of the Bengali people. Hundreds of his modern songs built up a strong cultural basis for the emerging values in Bengali urban music. Many of Nazrul's immortal love songs belong to this trend.

Kazi Nazrul Islam occupies a singular position in Bengali music history for equally enriching the streams of Islamic and Hindu religious song. He was the first Bengali composer of Islamic devotional songs to lay a foundation for future composers by creating more than two hundred songs on various Islamic themes. He also wrote Hindu devotional songs in various musical styles. He fared equally well in the musical traditions of Vaishnav and Shaivite cults, composing almost six hundred songs chiefly glorifying the goddess Kali and the idols of eternal love, Radha and Krishna.

The record and film industries took keen interest in Nazrul's Bengali songs on folk-music models. Most of his compositions in this genre were for films. Of particular interest are his songs based on *jhumur,* an attractive genre of the Santal tribal people. None before Nazrul took any interest in creating an urban Bengali version of this ethnic music; its dancing movement and syncopated rhythmic pattern added new charm to Nazrul's songs.

Indian ragas formed the basis of most of Nazrul's compositions. He himself created seventeen new ragas and composed songs in all the major Hindustani forms, although he was particularly inspired by *khyāl*, *ṭhumrī*, and ghazal. Nazrul took part in two experimental program series for the Calcutta radio station, which he named *Hārāmaṅi* 'The Lost Gems' and *Navarāga Mālikā* 'The Garland of New Ragas'. In these broadcasts, Nazrul would sing his own compositions on unfamiliar ragas and on his personal raga creations. One of the outcomes of this experiment was a new genre, *rāg pradhān gān* 'classicomodern Bengali songs', which he pioneered.

Post-Tagore musical developments in Bengal follow by and large from the works of Kazi Nazrul Islam. The 1930s were a period of transition between the old and new Bengali urban music, and Nazrul stood as an important link. He was the last of the great Bengali poet-composers, and yet the originator of free musical tendencies representing the "modern" music (Goswami 1990). Important features of the emerging musical picture in Bengal include the division of labor between lyricist, composer, and singer in producing a song; improvements in recording technology; the introduction of "playback" (ghost) singing for movies; improvements in orchestration; and the expansion of radio musical programs.

Contemporaries of Nazrul

Many others contributed to the enrichment of urban music in Bengal during this period of transition. Lyricists include Hiren Basu, Hemendra Kumar Ray, Tulsi Lahiri, Anil Bhattacharya, Ajay Bhattacharya, Pranab Ray, Subodh Purakayastha, Sailen Ray, Vani Kumar, Saurindra Mohan Mukhopadhyay, Premendra Mitra, and Dhirendranath Mukhopadhyay. Significant among composers and music directors are Hiren Basu, Hemendra Kumar Ray, Tulsi Lahiri, Vinay Goswami, Himamsu Datta, Nitai Matilal, Kamal Dasgupta, Suval Dasgupta, Krishna Chandra De, Sailesh Dattagupta, Chitta Ray, Rai Chand Boral, Vishan Chand Varal, Pankaj Kumar Mullick, and Sachin Dev Burman. Singers include Angur Vala, Indu Vala, Harimati, Kamala Jharia, Radharani, Saila Devi, K. Mallik, Krishna Chandra De, Kanan Devi, Juthika Ray, Abbasuddin Ahmad, Satya Chaudhuri, Mrinal Kanti Ghosh, Jaganmay Mitra, Suprabha Sarkar, and Kundan Lal Saigal. The fast-developing recording and film industries came to dominate this new age of Bengali urban music.

From the 1930s on, film became the most influential branch of art in Bengal, even from a musical perspective.

Film music

Bengali film music is an extension of the music of Bengali professional drama. From the 1930s on, film became the most influential branch of art in Bengal, even from a musical perspective. When the age of talkies began in Calcutta in 1931, and the technique of playback singing was developed soon after, film music became very popular among cinema audiences. Drawing on the tradition of Bengali drama that depended on songs for commercial success, film producers did not fail to exploit this area of filmgoers' sentiment. Film music directors have been largely responsible for developments in urban Bengali music since 1931.

Hiren Basu, Pankaj Mullick, Rai Chand Boral, Krishna Chandra De, and Kamal Dasgupta were among the first composers and singers of Bengali film music. Their film songs derived mainly from light-classical Hindustani genres, but had a depth, weight, and expanse of their own. In successive decades, startling improvements were made in the technical aspects of film making. Film-song composition similarly changed in keeping with the changing patterns of entertainment, and traditional musical values no longer held sway in Bengali films.

Dilip Kumar Ray

The son of Dwijendralal Ray, Dilip Kumar (1897–1980) was a great composer-poet and musicologist who enriched the urban music of Bengal in many ways. He had extraordinary mastery in light-classical forms like *ṭhumrī*, *ṭappā*, and ghazal, and was also a master *kīrtan* singer. He developed a compositional style of his own that combined all these forms, and wrote lyrics on various themes, but his favorite genre was the devotional song. Dilip Ray was a close friend of Kazi Nazrul Islam, and fondly sang his ghazals and devotional songs. He was also an untiring commentator on musical aesthetics whose exchanges of opinion on music with Rabindranath Tagore have assumed historic importance.

Due to his retirement in 1928 to a saintly life at the Aurovinda yogic center in Pondicherry, he did not propagate his own compositional style. Dilip Ray nevertheless occupies an important place in the history of Bengali music for his tender lyrics, his distinguished compositional style, and his attractive vocal performances (Goswami 1985).

People's music

The Indian People's Theatre Association (IPTA) movement, founded in 1943 in the context of broad-based opposition to imperialism and fascism, influenced all creative pursuits in the South Asian subcontinent, including Bengal. Music was one of its dominant aspects. The Communist party of India was the driving force behind the movement, and a distinct genre of patriotic songs popularly known in Bengal as *gāna saṅgīt* 'people's songs' flourished under the auspices of the IPTA. The first bulletin of the IPTA, published in 1943, proclaimed:

> It is in this situation that the Indian People's Theatre Association has been formed to coordinate and strengthen all progressive tendencies that have so far manifested themselves in the nature of dramas, songs, and dances. It is a movement which seeks to make our arts the expression and the organizers of our people's struggle for freedom. It stands for the defense of culture against imperialism and fascism and for enlightening the masses about the causes and solutions of problems facing them. It tries to quicken their awareness of unity and their passion for a better and just world order.

Leaders of the movement considered songs an effective medium for organizing working people and realizing these newly formulated social ends. Activists of the People's Theatre movement composed most of the songs on themes like social change, forging a progressive society, and the unity and victory of the working people. Vinay Ray, Jyotirindra Maitra, Hemanga Biswas, and Salil Chaudhuri were the architects of this musical movement (Goswami 1986).

These were the major developments in mainstream Bengali music until 1947, when British rule in India came to an end and the subcontinent was divided into the two nation-states of India and Pakistan. Bengal was divided into two provinces: East Bengal, with its capital in Dhaka, became the eastern province of Pakistan, and West Bengal, with its capital in Calcutta, became an Indian province. East Bengal, or East Pakistan, emerged as the sovereign state of Bangladesh following the War of Liberation against Pakistani rule in 1971.

POST-1947 MUSICAL DEVELOPMENTS IN WEST BENGAL AND BANGLADESH

Musical developments in West Bengal following partition in 1947 concentrated chiefly on the diversified trends of modern music, patronized liberally by the film and record industries and by the government-run radio. A group of talented lyricists and composers joined those who had been working since the 1930s. The lyricists included Pulak Bandyopadhyay, Shivadas Bandyopadhyay, Mohini Chaudhuri, Shyamal Gupta, and Gauriprasanna Majumdar; among the successful composers were Abhijit Bandyopadhyay, Anal Chattopadhyay, Rabin Chattopadhyay, Salil Chaudhuri, Sudhin Dasgupta, Anupam Ghatak, Nachiketa Ghosh, Pravir Majumdar, Hemanta Mukhopadhyay, and Dilip Sarkar. A generation of talented singers performed in the modern musical styles: Pratima Bandyopadhyay, Dhananjay Bhattacharya, Pannalal Bhattacharya, Manna De, Syamal Mitra, Hemanta Mukhopadhyay, Manavendra Mukhopadhyay, Sandhya Mukhopadhyay, and Satinath Mukhopadhyay.

The songs of Rabindranath Tagore have gained strong popularity among the urbanized educated population. The Tagore birth centenary celebrations in 1961 provided great impetus to this trend, and performers from the Vishva Bharati University at Santiniketan, founded by Tagore, continue to support the growing interest in Tagore songs. Nazrul songs are once again popular in West Bengal, after falling out of fashion in the late 1940s and the 1950s.

In urban East Bengal (East Pakistan), which in 1971 became Bangladesh, the city of Dhaka faced a host of challenges in assuming the role of cultural capital of the newborn province. In old Bengal, Calcutta had assumed this role, and had indeed for many decades been a most illustrious spot on the cultural map of India. But the social and institutional supports for musical activities befitting a capital were yet to grow in Dhaka. Moreover, musical activities in the city had suffered an initial setback due to the large-scale migration of Hindus out of East Bengal into India, resulting in a lack of skilled performers, as the cultivation of music in Bengal had been limited mostly to the Hindus. Nevertheless, in the new East Bengal some stalwarts among the Muslims began to make their mark. Abdul Ahad, a great musical personality of Bangladesh, gave an authentic account of the musical situation in his autobiography (Ahad 1989). Ahad was one of the first Bengali Muslims to learn Tagore songs at Santiniketan during Rabindranath Tagore's lifetime and to become a Tagore-music celebrity. Like other Muslim musicians living in Calcutta, Abdul Ahad went to Dhaka in 1948 and joined the Dhaka radio station. He served the cause of music there for over four decades in various capacities, most notably as a composer of modern and patriotic songs. Abdul Ahad lovingly recalled the memory of those Muslim musicians who took a pioneering role, immediately following the partition of India, in filling the vacuum left by Hindu musicians in Dhaka and inspiring the next generation to learn and perform music.

A generation of music lovers and performers soon grew up in Dhaka. Abbasuddin Ahmad, already acknowledged as one of the great singers of undivided Bengal, came to Dhaka from Calcutta and rendered yeoman service while coping with the initial difficulties. Bimal Ray, Samar Das, Laila Arjumand Banu, Afsari Khanam, Anjali Ray, Sahjahan Hafiz, Sultan Alam, Abdul Halim Chaudhuri, Sheik Lutfar Rahman, Abdul Latif, and other singers and composers played important roles in building the tradition of modern music in Dhaka.

Initially, Dhaka lacked institutional support for the growth of modern music, in the absence of organizations producing records or films, and radio was the only institution able to extend tangible financial assistance. In the early 1960s, support began to come from cinema, and from television in the late 1960s. But still no significant record companies arose in East Bengal. Despite these limitations, however, lyricists such as Sikandar Abu Zafar, Mohammad Maniruzzaman, Abu Hena Mostafa Kamal, Azizur Rahman, and Syed Siddiqui and composers such as Abdul Ahad and Samar Das worked in close collaboration during the 1950s and 1960s to establish a solid foundation for modern music in the capital of present-day Bangladesh.

In addition to modern songs, post-partition musical developments in East Bengal included patriotic songs. These were characterized by a more lively and invigorating pulsation than the *ādhunik* 'modern' songs. East Bengal proved fertile ground for the growth of patriotic songs, especially as its people suspected a political plan hatched against them by the Pakistani ruling class soon after the foundation of Pakistan (1947). Speeches made by Mohammad Ali Jinnah, the founder of Pakistan, provided evidence that the West Pakistan minority had far-reaching plans to dominate and exploit the East Bengal majority. An incident on 21 February 1952, when police fired on and killed students and other activists demonstrating over the status of Bengali as a state language, became a great milestone in the cultural and political history of East Bengal, marking the beginning of a great struggle by East Bengal against West Pakistan's colonial tendencies. This struggle culminated in the War of Liberation in 1971 and the founding of the independent sovereign state of Bangladesh.

The long political struggle fostered many songs. The spirit of Bengali nationalism inspired some to take up songs composed years before by the great poet-composers Rabindranath Tagore, Dwijendralal Ray, Rajani Kanta Sen, Atulprasad Sen, and Kazi Nazrul Islam. Songs of the Indian People's Theatre Association were also sung. Meanwhile, poets and composers from all over East Bengal worked together to produce a huge repository of patriotic songs in a variety of musical styles. The great 1952 song of the Language Movement—"Can I forget 21 February which is tinged with the blood of my brother?" (lyricist, Abdul Gaffar Chaudhuri; composer, Altaf Mahmud)—remains one of the most prominent.

During the nine months of the War of Liberation—ending with the surrender of Pakistani forces in Dhaka on 16 December 1971—Independent Bangladesh Radio regularly broadcast a group of songs now known as the Liberation War songs. These included existing compositions, such as the great Bengali patriotic song "My golden Bengal, I love you" by Rabindranath Tagore, soon to become the national anthem of Bangladesh. They also comprised a host of new compositions communicating the spirit of the freedom struggle. Most renowned among these was the song "Victory to Bangladesh and victory to Bangladesh, Bangladesh will indeed be victorious," with lyrics composed by Gazi Mazharul Anwar and music by Anwar Parvez.

The emergence of Bangladesh as an independent state enabled the establishment of many cultural exchange programs with different countries, resulting in new modes of composition and performance among Bangladesh composers. A new generation is thus creating music befitting the spirit of hard-earned independence.

BENGALI FOLK MUSIC

The history of Bengali folk music dates back at least to the growth of *caryā* songs in the eighth century. Folk music and classical or semiclassical music in Bengal developed simultaneously, the former in villages, the latter flourishing in urban or semiurban hamlets. Generations of rural Bengali poet-composers created an enriched and varied tradition of folk music. The two musical traditions were not entirely distinct even during the golden days of classical music in nineteenth-century Bengal. Their occasional interaction resulted in mutual enrichment. For example, a popular folk-music form in Bengal, *bhātiāli* 'boatmen's song', is believed to have been based on a classical melody of the same name, and some distinguished urban compositional styles derive from *bāul,* another popular Bengali folk-music form (Bhattacharya 1969). Particularly notable in the history of Bengali music is a combination of classical and folk-music styles, even though a recognizable distance between these two musical traditions exists, reflecting the two distinct cultural worlds, rural and urban. With the growth of organized city life over hundreds of years, this sense of distance has actually widened, as rural traditions in Bengal decline and urbanization becomes increasingly synonymous with modernization and development. In this situation, a large number of minor Bengali folk-music forms have died out; fortunately, the major ones have survived the onslaught of time.

These major Bengali folk-music forms are *bāul, bhātiāli, bhāwāiyā, gambhīrā,* and *jhumur.* The general names cover many regional varieties of differing musical style and textual expression. Folk ballads popularly known as *pālāgān* constitute a distinct genre. Some simple forms like *jārigān* and *puthipāṭh* are also widely performed. Ceremonial songs, which once constituted the bulk of Bengali folk music, are largely on the wane, with only a few genres still performed (Dev 1996).

Bāul

TRACK 32 In textual and compositional variety, *bāul* songs form the richest stream of Bengali folk music. Bāul is a mystical cult, popularly described as a folk religion, that follows a distinct spiritual and philosophical discipline expressed through song (Bandyopadhyay 1976; Bhattacharya 1969). Towering poets like Lalan Shah (1792–1890) of Kushtia and Hasan Raja (1854–1922) of Sylhet—both in Bangladesh—have left behind *bāul* songs on their metaphysical thoughts, rich in lyricism and music. Countless other Bāul singers and composers from the different regions of Bengal have performed songs in their own regional musical style (figure 4). Bāuls accompany themselves on a one-stringed instrument known as *ektārā* or *gopīyantra* (figure 5) and a simple drum (*ḍugi*). In an exalted mood, Bāuls perform a dance popularly known as *bāul* dance. Like all the other folk dances of Bengal except *chau* and *nācni,* Bāul dance is nothing more than a simple body movement to the rhythm of the song (Capwell 1989). Bāul song, with its enriched lyricism and music, has greatly

At one time, Bengal was infested with poisonous snakes, and a nomadic tribe of snake charmers would move about, mostly in boats, catching snakes and treating snake-bitten people. They would sing songs in praise of Manasa, the goddess of snakes.

FIGURE 4 Bāul singers of Bangladesh performing at the American Institute of Indian Studies in Calcutta, 1983. The instruments (*left to right*) are *gopīyantra, dotārā, ḍugi, gopīyantra,* and *kartāl.* Photo by Charles Capwell.

influenced the development of Bengali urban music. Rabindranath Tagore himself improvised his own musical style from a combination of *bāul* and classical forms like *khyāl* and *ṭappā* (Ghose 1978; Goswami 1994).

Bhātiāli

Bhātiāli songs, popularly known as boatman's songs, are in vogue largely among the boatmen of Bangladesh and West Bengal. They sing *bhātiāli* songs in their leisure hours, while their boats sail downriver. The songs are believed to have originated in low-lying areas of Bengal where boats were once the only means of transport. *Bhātiāli* songs have long melodic phrases that begin in the middle of the scale and gradually move upward. Ample references exist in the medieval musical literature of India to a raga known as *bhātiāli* or *bhātiārī.* Musicologists presume that the present-day *bhātiāli* form of Bengali folk music derived initially from this classical raga.

Bhāwāiyā

Bhāwāiyā is a generic name referring to various song forms of the high, dry lands of Rangpur in Bangladesh and Koch Bihar in West Bengal. Each form has a distinct name and possesses its own characteristic "voice-breaking" features, whereby the voice momentarily stops the melody with a discordant sound. *Bhāwāiyā* covers a wide range of themes, from light to serious.

Gambhīrā

Singers perform this popular genre in the Rajshahi district of Bangladesh and the

FIGURE 5 A Bāul musician playing a *gopīyantra,* Calcutta, 1983. Photo by Charles Capwell.

Maldaha district of West Bengal. The word *gambhīra* refers to Lord Shiva, and in past centuries, *gambhīrā* was a kind of composition about Shiva or dedicated to Shiva. In more recent times, composers have created *gambhīrā* with either nominal reference to Shiva or none at all. Nowadays the term refers to a new type of narrative composition with texts about mundane affairs and that combines singing, dancing, and acting. In this form, *gambhīrā* is a Bengali folk-dramatic work, performed for entertainment. Nevertheless, the *gambhīrā* composition is often serious in tone, dwelling on all the social evils rural people constantly confront.

Jārigān

Jārigān '*jāri* song' is a popular Bengali folk narrative song that predominantly describes the tragic events related to the historic war of Karbala. In the story, one of the grandsons of the Prophet Muhammad, the founder of Islam, is killed. *Jārigān* follows the style of *pāṭha-saṅgīt* 'recitative music', but is a little more complex. The leading musician in a *jāri* performance is called *bayāti,* the narrator of the story who is, by tradition, supported by a *dohār* 'singing band'.

Jhāpān

Jhāpān is a kind of Bengali folk music that belongs to the community of snake charmers. At one time, Bengal was infested with poisonous snakes, and a nomadic tribe of snake charmers would move about, mostly in boats, catching snakes and treating snake-bitten people. They would also play and perform snake games. Whatever the occasion, they would sing songs in praise of Manasa, the goddess of snakes. These songs are *jhāpān*. Among various types of *jhāpān,* one known as *sākhī* has a question-and-answer structure performed by two singing troupes.

Jhumur

Jhumur refers to a type of song and dance of the Santals, who are among the earliest native peoples of the subcontinent, now living in various linguistic regions. *Jhumur* songs consequently vary in language, but have similar musical features. Bengali *jhumur* is largely prevalent among the Santals living in the Burdwan-Birbhum district of West Bengal and those in the northern districts of Bangladesh. It has a sharp rhythmic character, making frequent use of syncopation. A bamboo flute and cylindrical drum (*mādal*) usually accompany *jhumur* songs and dances.

Kavigān

Equally popular in cities and in the countryside, *kavigān* has an elaborate musical system of its own. It takes the form of a contest between two singing parties, each party being led by a *kaviẏāl* 'lead poet' who is given musical support by a singing troupe called the *dohār*. The musical performance revolves around a question, usually from Indian mythological literature, which the lead poet of the first party poses to the lead poet of the second. The argument between the two parties, and the question of which party wins victory, keeps the performance interesting and alive. The whole recital continues for several hours, divided into sessions with some breaks. The history of organized *kavi* performances dates back to the beginning of the eighteenth century.

Letogān

Leto is a popular folk musical genre of the Burdwan region in West Bengal. *Leto* combines the question-and-answer form of *kavigān* with the dancing and acting of folk drama. Two singing parties take part in a contest in which they fight each other on a certain question posed by the party that sings first. The question-and-answer process takes place through song. A lead poet (*godā kavi*) directs each party in composing impromptu songs to answer the question thrown by the lead poet of the other party. *Leto* is in effect a contest between the two poet-leaders of the two singing bands.

Pālāgān

Pālāgān is a kind of a musical performance narrating the stories of proverbial heroes and heroines of Bengali folk literature. The lead performer of this folk-ballad singing is called the *baẏāti* 'narrator'. His troupe, the *dohār*, provides musical support. Members collectively sing refrains as the musical narration unfolds, and sometimes members break into sequences of dialogue with the narrator. The lead performer and his troupe have an assigned place in the middle of the performance space (*āsar*), and the listeners sit around the *āsar*. *Pālāgān* combines music, poetry, recitation, and dialogue, as well as some simple dancing gestures by the lead performer.

Puthipāṭh

Puthipāṭh, a type of folk-ballad rendition traditionally known as "reading," is in fact a form of singing. Performers produce a kind of repetitive chanting of a simple melody that consists of only three or four notes and simple rhythms. It is a very popular musical exercise in rural Bengal.

Sārigān

Scholars and critics often broadly divide Bengali folk music into two groups: leisure music and work music. All music sung by rural Bengali people during working hours belongs to the *sārigān* genre. It encompasses a diverse group of songs that people sing in different work situations. The principal idea behind *sāri* group singing is to invigorate the singers to work hard in a rhythmical manner. *Sārigān* is a chorus-style performance with sharp, fast rhythms. With the mechanization of working processes, the tradition of Bengali *sārigān* is rapidly declining.

REFERENCES

Ahad, Abdul. 1989. *Āsā Yāoār Pather Dkāre* (Waiting by the way.) Dhaka: Banla Academy.

Bandyopadhyay, Sudhansu M. 1976. *Baul Songs of Bengal.* Calcutta: United Writers.

Bhattacharya, Deben. 1969. *The Mirror of the Sky: Songs of the Bāuls from Bengal.* London: Allen and Unwin; New York: Grove Press.

Basu, Arun Kumar. 1966. *Bāṅlā Kāvya Saṅgīt o Rabīndra Saṅgīt.* Calcutta: Rabindra Bharati.

Bhattacharya, Asutosh. 1958. *Bāṅlā Maṅgala Kavyer Itihās.* Calcutta: A. Mukherjee & Co. Pvt. Ltd.

Capwell, Charles. 1989. *The Music of the Bauls of Bengal.* Kent, Ohio: Kent State University Press.

Chakravarti, Sudhir. 1990. *Bāṅlā Gāner Sandhāne.* Calcutta: Aruna Prakasani.

Chaudhuri, Narayan. 1983. *Bāṅālīr Gitacarcā.* Calcutta: Jijnasa.

Dev, Chittaranjan. 1966. *Bāṅlār Palligīti.* Calcutta: National Book Agency.

Ghose, Santidev. 1978. *Music and Dance in Rabindranath Tagore's Education Philosophy.* New Delhi: Sahitya Akademi.

Goswami, Karunamaya. 1985. *Saṅgīt Kosh.* Dhaka: Banla Academy.

———. 1986. *Bāṅ lā Gān.* Dhaka: Banla Academy.

———. 1990. *Aspects of Nazrul Songs.* Dhaka: Nazrul Institute.

———. 1993a. *Bāṅlā Gāner Vivartan.* Dhaka: Banla Academy.

———. 1993b. *Rabīndra Saṅgīt Parikramā.* Dhaka: Banla Academy.

———. 1994. *History of Bengali Music in Sound.* Dhaka: Losauk.

———. 1996a. *Music and Dance of Bangladesh.* Khulna, Bangladesh: Silpakala Academy.

———. 1996b. *Nazrul Gīti Prasaṅga.* Dhaka: Banla Academy.

———. 1997. *The Splendours of Old Bengali Songs.* Dhaka: Ford Foundation. Six audio cassettes.

Goswami, Utpala. 1991. *Bhāratīya Uccaṅga Saṅgīt.* Calcutta: Dipayan.

Majumdar, Devajyoti Datta. 1990. *Rabīndra Saṅgīter Kramavikāś.* Calcutta: Sahityalok.

Mukhopadhyay, Dilip Kumar. 1976. *Bāṅālīr Raga Saṅgīt Carcār Itihās.* Calcutta: Firma KLM Private Ltd.

Prajnanananda, Swami. 1960. *Historical Development of Indian Music.* Calcutta: Firma KLM Private Ltd.

———. 1965. *Historical Study of Indian Music.* Calcutta: Anandadhara.

———. 1970. *Padāvalī Kīrtaner Itihās.* Calcutta: Sri Ram Krishna Vedanta Math.

Ray, Dilip Kumar. 1938. *Sāṅgītikī.* Calcutta: Calcutta University.

Ray, Sukumar. 1973. *Music of Eastern India.* Calcutta: Firma KLM Private Ltd.

Sanyal, Hitesranjan. 1989. *Bāṅlā Kīrtaner Itihās.* Calcutta: K. P. Bagci and Co.

Tagore, Rabindranath. 1986. *Saṅgīt Cintā.* Calcutta: Vishva Bharati.

Godavari River
Maharashtra
DECCAN
Godavari River
Madhya Pradesh
Orissa
Bobbili
Srikakulam
Vizianagaram
EASTERN GHATS
Bidar
HYDERABAD
Gulbarga
Rajahmundry
Bijapur
Vijayawada
Guntur
Machilipatnam
Krishna River
PLATEAU
WESTERN GHATS
Hubli
Vijayanagar
Andhra Pradesh
Tungabhadra River
Bay of Bengal
Karnataka
Tirupati
Tiruvarur
MADRAS
BANGALORE
Kolar
Kanchipuram
Kaveri River
Mysore
Kollegal
Dharmapuri
ARABIAN SEA
Pondicherry
Salem
Tamil Nadu
Chidambaram
Bokkapuram
Ooty
Kaveri River
Srirangam
Coimbatore
Kozhikode
LACCADIVE SEA
Palghat
Trichy
(Tiruchchirappalli)
Thanjavur
Trichur
Pudukkottai
Ernakulam
Cochin
Madurai
Kerala
Tirunelveli
Tuticorin
TRIVANDRUM
Kanyakumari
SRI LANKA

South India

The four states of South India—Karnataka, Andhra Pradesh, Tamil Nadu, and Kerala—are culturally and linguistically related due to their Dravidian roots. Although there is no single Dravidian music culture, the Karnatak classical music tradition is shared, while each geographical area has its own varieties of the common regional forms: life-cycle, work, and religious songs, sung narratives, community dances, and dance dramas. Also common to the entire region is the enormously popular Indian film and pop music.

Throughout this southern region, Hindus, Muslims, Christians, and Jews maintain their own religious and ritual music traditions, which in some cases include popular commercial song forms. Among tribal groups, generally living apart from the general population—often in remote mountainous regions—music making likewise underscores group identity: male Sidhis in Karnataka paint their bodies white and dance with flowered headgear and belts of bells; tribal women and men in Kerala dance together singing in vocables; and in Tamil Nadu, Mullu Kurumbas chant without instrumental accompaniment while performing circle dances, and Kotas play in ensembles made up of double reeds, frame drums, cymbals, and horns.

MAP 11 South India

Karnataka

Gayathri Rajapur Kassebaum
Peter J. Claus

Situated in southwestern India, the state of Karnataka lies on the ancient Deccan plateau and is surrounded by the states of Goa, Maharashtra, Andhra Pradesh, Tamil Nadu, and Kerala. The state has a long western coastline along the Arabian Sea that stretches from Goa in the north to Kerala in the south. With a land area of 192,204 square kilometers, Karnataka in 1991 had a total population of 44 million—roughly the same as Egypt, Poland, or South Korea.

Karnataka came into being as a collection of princely states during the seventh century. Following a long period under Hindu, Jain, and Muslim rulers, ending with the fall of Tippu Sultan in 1799, British rule was established in the nineteenth century. After India achieved independence in 1947, it was not until 1956 that the modern state of Karnataka was formed. Kannada was declared the state language, although Telugu, Tamil, and Urdu were spoken in the south and Marathi, Hindi, and Urdu—among others—in the north. (Tulu and Konkani are relatively more common in the southern coastal Dakshin Kannad district, coastal Konkani in the northern district of Uttar Kannad.)

Many religions and sects have influenced people's lives and musical traditions in Karnataka. It is the birthplace of Virashaivism, for example, a revolutionary form of Shiva worship combined with egalitarian principles that was popularized by the saint Basavanna and the poetess Mahadeviakka in the twelfth century.

In many regions, particularly in Gulburga, Bijapur, and Bidar, the influence of Islam is noticeable. Songs by Muslim composers such as Sharif Saheb and Nana Saheb are in the repertoires of regional musicians. Many of these performers belong to the scheduled castes, previously known as untouchables, at the lowest level of the Hindu caste hierarchy (also popularly called Harijans 'God's people', a name given them by Mahatma Gandhi, or Dalits). In recent years, some Harijans in Karnataka have been identified as Adi Dravidians 'first dwellers', others as Adi Karnataka 'ancient Karnataka settlers'. These communities can be credited with preserving the many regional music genres that they have been performing for centuries.

REGIONAL MUSIC TRADITIONS

Regional music in India is identified as *janapada* (*jana* 'people', *pada* 'song'). This label serves not only to differentiate folk-music traditions from classical traditions but also to emphasize that this is a music created and performed by local people, that is, mostly farmers, hired laborers, small service tradesmen, and artisans such as potters, iron smiths, and stonecutters. Regional music is an oral tradition, performed by nonliterate musical and cultural specialists, that emphasizes local versions of the Hindu epics and thus complements classical literary traditions. Many regional musicians are wanderers and itinerant song specialists popularly called *alamāri* 'mendicants', and are identified either by the costume they wear or the musical instrument they play. Their performances often take place in simple houses, huts, or in other ordinary settings.

The term *folk music*, sometimes in the Indian context used interchangeably with *regional music*, can refer to simple songs ordinary people sing to ease their work or to accompany home-related tasks. Clearly, this would not accurately describe all regional music performances. Many regional performers are initiated and apprenticed, learn long texts, and must coordinate several musical elements in their performances. Theirs is the work of a skilled musician who has been taught by people who derive their living from music. Regional music is nevertheless music of the people, for it expresses the oral tradition of a specific community that has limited means of propagating its culture, a tradition not viewed by society in general as high art. Regional musicians, even the many of low caste, nevertheless hold a position of respect because this music making is associated with the divine and is believed to lead both performer and listener to a higher plane of consciousness.

Indeed, the function of regional music is really to educate ethnic and caste groups through performances rich in local history, legend, and myth, lore that is always linked to worship and belief. Performers belonging to Muslim communities sing about the Prophet Muhammad and about local Sufi masters and their teachings. Hindu communities sing about local deities and venerate heroes and heroines possessing half-human, half-miraculous, godly powers. The stories they narrate are Dravidian in origin, although some involve the pan-Indian Hindu gods and goddesses (notably Shiva and Vishnu) as well as the Roman god Saturn. Mixed performances in which both Muslims and Hindus join in singing songs related to Shiva, the Prophet Muhammad, or Sufi masters are in fact not uncommon.

Regional music includes many types of songs, dances, story narratives, instrumental ensembles, costumed performances, and other elements. Songs are invariably accompanied by dance or body movement, often with instrumental accompaniment. Group dances are usually performed on festival days and also as a diversion after a day of long, hard labor in the fields. In some parts of northern Karnataka, Muslim groups perform ritual dances during the annual Muharram festival, in which Hindus sometimes participate. Dance, song, or instrumental music tied to the worship of local deities often includes "black magic," spirit worship that can induce a trance state in performance. Dances are also sometimes used in curing certain psychological illnesses. Song texts are created telling the fortune of a particular individual, family, or village. The performers suggest a particular gift; in return, they perform a ritual that may help solve or ease specific problems. Having such rituals performed with song and dance is believed to bring good luck to the families or communities involved.

Among the myriad forms of regional music are congregational singing, especially the popular bhajan form and the solo song genre called *tatva*, which is accompanied by a single-stringed lute (*ēktāri*) and wooden clappers (*ciṭike*). *Sampradāya* 'traditional song' is a genre performed mostly by women. Another tradition, often identified as *katha* and sometimes called *mēḷa* 'small ensemble', consists of the performance of story narratives combining song, dance, drama, and recitation. The performers often accompany themselves on a drum, cymbals, flute, or chordophone while enacting the drama. This genre is very popular in the rural areas of Karnataka. Many regional music genres are rendered in domestic settings (*akam*), which are thought to include both home and temple rituals; but they may also be performed in public (*pūram)* as entertainment, despite their religious basis.

Regional music traditions and performances may be classified into six categories: song forms (*pada*), sung narratives (*katha*), instrumental ensembles (*mēḷa*), costumed performances (*vēṣa*), dance performances (*kuṇita*), and miscellaneous traditions by itinerant performers, such as puppet theaters and the singing of praises in honor of the goddess Maramma.

SONG FORMS

Pada is a general term for "song" that encompasses a variety of forms. All *pada* forms feature short texts, consisting of stanzas with refrains, and strophic melodies that are usually recognizable popular tunes. These melodies need not always be in any recognized classical raga, but they must have a clear melodic contour. Many songs append characteristic phrases to each melodic line, such as "*tandana tāna*" or "*suvvi,*" which do not have linguistic meaning but generally connote good luck, in terms of a good harvest or timely rain, and good fortune in general. *Pada* are all metered, 4/4, 3/4, and 7/4 structures being the most common. Some are sung as solos (without dance or instrumental accompaniment), but a large number are sung with instrumental accompaniment or body movement. Singers also commonly ornament the melodies with slides and quick vocal turns.

Some *pada* are performed for recreational purposes, others for specific rituals; many are performed during ceremonies in the home and at annual festivals. These songs may be used for healing and tattooing, or may represent a community myth and be related to fortune telling. There are women's songs, men's songs, and songs sung by both men and women as well as solo and group songs. In general, *pada* can be grouped into types based on function. Four representative examples are discussed here: life-related songs; philosophical songs; political, moral, and ethical songs; and predicting songs.

Life-related songs

One of the important and popular types of *pada* found all over Karnataka is life-cycle songs, including those popularly called *sampradāya* songs, and wedding songs (*śobāna pada*). Generally, *sampradāya* and *śobāna* songs are not accompanied by instruments, and are sung predominantly by women (figure 1), although some men in northern Karnataka also sing them. The songs are often passed on from mother to daughter. However, the tradition is not necessarily hereditary, and older performers do some teaching of youth outside the family.

Sampradāya songs are sung by high-caste Brahmin women, by low-caste Harijans, and by many in between. The texts are devotional, praising a local deity or addressing a family issue such as a dowry, mother-in-law and daughter-in-law conflict, or the status of a childless woman, or life-cycle events such as childbirth, pregnancy, or marriage. Other *pada* topics include prayers to local village deities that refer to local legends and myths. These are sung at village social functions and in homes where the singers are invited for weddings or other festivities. Harijan women sing in village dialect and are considered song specialists, although they earn their living by working in the fields. Brahmin women, most of them householders, sing songs in a Sanskrit-based Kannada; some of them have studied Karnatak music.

FIGURE 1 Woman performing *sampradāya* songs at Gāḷēramma Temple in Hampi, 1996. To the right of the performer, a woman holds (but is not playing) a *caudike* string drone. Photo by Gene Kassebaum.

Philosophical songs

Philosophical songs (*tatva*) are known by various names in different parts of Karnataka: *ēktāri mēḷa*, for example, are songs sung by a one-stringed drone lute player; *tambūri mēḷa* are songs named for the classical four-stringed lute that provides the drone for a solo singer. *Tatva* performers often sing with rhythmic accompaniment such as *damḍi* 'tambourine' and *ciṭike* 'wooden clapper', which keeps the time cycle. In some parts of the state, *tatva* songs are also sung to the accompaniment of a harmonium 'small hand-pumped reed organ' instead of the *ēktāri* drone. *Tatva* songs are not gender-specific; both women and men perform, many of whom are mendicants, though some are householders.

The *tatva* genre can be divided into three schools. The first is the Kannada tradition, carried on by mendicants of a Shiva sect that traces its lineage back to the twelfth-century *śaranaru* 'servants of Shiva'. *Tatva* songs in Telugu represent the second school, performed mainly in southern Karnataka, especially in the southwest districts of Kolar and Bangalore city. The performers trace their origins to the seventeenth-century singer Kaivara Naranappa, a glass-bangle seller. Moreover, Naranappa's song tradition is alive today, not only in small villages but in the small temples and shrines of metropolitan Bangalore, among its Telugu-speaking population.

The third tradition of *tatva* is that of the Muslim composer Sharif Saheb and his Hindu contemporaries of the early nineteenth century, whose texts bear universal, nonsectarian messages.

Group singing of the bhajan genre is popular throughout the state; both men and women participate. Usually a solo singer initiates the songs, and the followers sing certain portions of it in a call-and-response manner. Bhajan groups are often made up of professionals and amateurs together. A main singer typically plays the harmonium as the melody instrument, and tabla drums and a tambourine (*damḍi*) provide further accompaniment. Both *tatva* philosophical song texts and congregational bhajan singing convey the message that the nature of the self is reformable and stress the importance of the guru (philosophical guide) and his blessings.

Political, moral, and ethical songs

Specialist male singers perform *lāvṇi* 'political, moral, or ethical songs' throughout Karnataka; they improvise both tune and lyrics, alternate chant with song, and

Katha is a musical performance that tells a story. *Katha* performers sing about their communities, about individual members, and about their beliefs, their gods and goddesses, and their heroes, to the accompaniment of instruments and often dance.

accompany themselves on a large tambourine. Many song texts are about contemporary events or characters—for example, an increase in the price of rice, wheat rationing, a fraudulent politician, a corrupt bank official, or an abusive or unfaithful husband. *Lāvṇi* performers also narrate historical stories using a song form that may have originally come from Maharashtra during the fifteenth century. The art of *lāvṇi* singing is hereditary, and has been passed on within families from one generation to another. Politicians and government officials have often hired *lāvṇi* and *gīgī* singers as "media brokers," traveling to many villages and disseminating socially relevant information such as techniques for controlling mice in the fields or family planning.

TRACK 33 *Gīgī pada* is a type of *lāvṇi* performed only in the northern district of Dharwar. It is distinguished by its refrain, "*gīya gā gāgīya gā gīya gīya gī*," from which its name derives. Both women and men perform *gīgī pada,* with two to four performers in a group taking turns singing. The principal performer usually plays a large tambourine called a *dappu,* and all the performers join in singing the end of the refrain, "*gīya gīya gī*" (figure 2).

Predicting songs

Among the various types of songs that predict the future is *kāla jñana,* a type sung by *sāruvayya,* male mendicants who have embraced the Lingāyat (Shaivite) sect. The *sāruvayya* priest is also called *jangama* 'the mover' as opposed to *sthāvara* 'settled in one location'. The *sāruvayya* walks from village to village comforting those who are in distress, singing songs predicting the future, and reading the fortunes of the individuals and families they help. *Koravanji* are women artists who sing fortunes and tattoo people of the village. They also serve as matchmakers. While tattooing, they sing songs and make jokes to ease the pain of the needle penetrating the skin.

SUNG NARRATIVES

Katha is a musical performance that tells a story. *Katha* performers sing about their communities, about individual members, and about their beliefs, their gods and goddesses, and their heroes, to the accompaniment of instruments and often dance. While enacting stories, the performers communicate using symbols of personal and communal significance, including items of dress, instruments, the community name, or the local deity's name. *Katha* narratives, unlike *pada* songs with their short texts and their emphasis on melody, are much longer—usually lasting all night—and have texts that are more complex.

Katha performers come from rural villages (even if many now live in urban areas), and belong to closed sects with hereditary and religious lineage connections to local folk deities. Religious practice dedicates infants at birth to the local deities; nonhereditary adults can become performers only after initiation into the religious sect. Descriptions of the local gods in *katha* texts combine spiritual and human qualities;

FIGURE 2 Strophic song with *gī gī* refrain. The melodies of stanzas 2 and 3 are similar to that of stanza 1. Transcription by Gayathri Rajapur Kassebaum, 1994.

Refrain

										Melodic Form
P:	**N N**	**N P**	**N N**	**S S**	**SNN**	**S S S SNN**	**S S**	**S S**	**S**	
T:	**Ha-ra**	**Ha-ra**	**Ha-ra**	**gī-ya**	**gā**	**gā-gī-ya gā**	**gī-ya**	**gī-ya**	**gī**	
Tr:	God	God	God							

Stanza 1

P:	G G G G	P P P	D S S D D	P P	**A**
T:	so-se-yar-na	ka-du-va	at-yam-ma-rel-la	ni-va	
Tr:	You the mothers-in-law who torment your daughters-in-law,			You	

P:	P D D P	GRS R	R G RS S	**A1**
T:	ch-ta-vit-tu	ke-li-ri	ku-ta-kon-da	
Tr:	sit down and listen carefully,			

P:	P P	P D D P	GRS R	R G RS S	
T:	ni-va	ch-ta-vit-tu	ke-li-ri	ku-ta-kon-da	**A1**
Tr:	You sit down and listen carefully.				

SPEECH MODE **B**

T:	ut-tu-ma so-se-id-re
Tr:	If you have a gentle-natured daughter-in-law,

P:	G G G	G R S	R S	G R R S	SR G MGRS	**B1**
T:	in-nis-tu	ka-dti-ri	ot-ti	at-tu-ti-ri	sam-sa-ra	
Tr:	you torment her and push her and her family			nearly to breaking.		

Refrain:

P:	S S SNN S S S SNN S S SNN S S S SNN S S S
T:	**gī-ya gā gā-gī-ya gā, gī-ya gā gā-gī-ya gā, gī-ya gā**

Text Translation

1. You the mothers-in-law who torment your daughters-in-law,
You sit down and listen carefully
You sit down and listen carefully
If you have a gentle-natured daughter-in-law,
you torment her and push her and her family nearly to breaking. **(gī-ya gā. . .)**

2. Being cruel and cruel, at once, you push her into a well
You better treat your daughter-in-law with care
You better treat your daughter-in-law with care
Grandmother!! You better treat your daughter-in-law with care
If you have a gentle daughter-in-law,
you torment her and push her and her family nearly to breaking. **(gī-ya gā. . .)**

3. Leaving their father, mother and relatives,
Leaving their natal home, they have come
If you have a gentle daughter-in-law,
you torment her and push her and her family nearly to breaking. **(gī-ya gā. . .)**

P: Pitch represented in Indian solfège notation (S, R, G, M, P, D, N, S)
T: Transliterated Kannada text
Tr: Free translation
Repeated texts are in **boldface**.

these gods may be endowed with "good" and/or "bad" magic power. Most *katha* performers are musical specialists and itinerant alms seekers. A performing group usually consists of a teacher and three to four disciples who sing stories accompanied by an instrument that serves as an icon of their particular sect. *Katha* audiences may be rural or urban, and typically include both sect members and nonmembers.

The narrative stories serve as religiously based guides to life issues and concerns for their listeners. Such concerns include status and caste, untouchability, good and bad luck, heaven and hell, love, lust, hate, and adventure. In particular, the stories emphasize women's issues such as a woman's vulnerability in marriage, the stigma of being childless (*banje*), widowhood, and complex family conflicts involving mothers-in-law, daughters-in-law, and sisters-in-law. Some genres of *katha* are sung genealogies of a family or a village, and a family or community will invite song specialists to its village to perform one.

Katha performers narrate their stories in leader-chorus fashion using song, chant, and speech. They use both Karnatak and Hindustani tune families and employ melodic formulas with repetition, imitation, and reduction techniques, as well as chant and dramatic speech. In figure 3, the leader and follower in turn sing progressively shorter segments of the first musical and text phrase. After the leader's second phrase, the follower repeats and reduces the first phrase before repeating the second. Of the many types of *katha* performed throughout Karnataka, two representative types—*kamsāḷe* and *caudike*—serve as examples.

Kamsāḷe

Kamsāḷe performers are males dedicated to and initiated into a sect that worships Madesa, originally a hill-tribe deity, now widely revered in the Virashaiva (Shaivite) tradition as a bachelor deity. Madesa is identified with the tiger on which he rides, and with the golden cobra, which is his personification; both are fertility symbols in many narrative stories. The performers sing stories about this hero/god figure and his miraculous powers, in which he responds to the call of needy and helpless women. They take their name from the *kamsāḷe,* a pair of large cymbals that are used to accompany the singing; the top part of one cymbal is struck against the hollowed lower half of the other, which is in the shape of a bowl (figure 4). The bowl symbolizes the alms-seeking practice of the performers, who travel only in the districts of Mysore, Nanjangud, and Kollegala in southern Karnataka. The Madesa temple is situated in the hills along the Tamil Nadu border.

Caudike

Caudike is the name given to both a genre of sung narrative and a symbolic instrument played by a performing sect devoted to the female deity Ellamma (and her personifications). This genre is also identified as *caudike padagāraru* '*caudike* songsters'. The instrument *caudike* (see below) is related to the sacred Hindu Puranic story of Parasurama and his mother Renuka. Renuka has appeared as the popular goddess Ellamma in the present age (the last of four epochs in Hindu chronology) in order to protect the lower castes and *dēvadāsi,* women dedicated to the goddess Ellamma. The story is linked to the ancient Hindu epic, the Mahabharata, but the *caudike* version centers on regional and local beliefs.

In southern Karnataka, the authorized priests of Ellamma shrines and temples and the performers of *caudike katha* are always male. In the north, women and transvestite men are the primary *caudike* performers (figure 5). Some performers belong to the Adi Karnataka and Adi Dravidian castes (subdivisions of the Harijans, traditionally called Holeya and Mādiga).

FIGURE 3 An excerpt of reduction and repetition technique employed in *katha*. Transcribed by Gayathri Kassebaum, 1994.

Reduction and repetition

[section repeated below]

P: S S D S S S S RG G G G G G G [R G G G R S S S S R R GRR]
L: Ai-yyamo-da-le ni-mma pa-da-va ne-ne-ve-nu **[ma-ti-ga-la ka-ru-ni-su ma-ha-de-va]**
Tr: Sir, first I think of your feet, grant me intelligence, Mahadeva

P: R G G G R S S S S R R GRR
F: ma-ti-ga-la ka-ru-ni-su ma-ha-de-va
Tr: grant me intelligence, Mahadeva

P: S R R R R R R P
L: ma-ti-ga-la ka-ru-ni-su
Tr: grant me intelligence

P: S R R GRR
F: ma-ha-de-va
Tr: Mahadeva

P: R G G G RG G R G G G RG G R G G G G G R G G **[MGRS] LF**
L: Ya-ti-ga-la pra-sam a-ri-ya-da na- vu dru-du mo-ksa-nja-na gu-ru-de-**va**
Tr: Not knowing the mysteries as the sages do, we believe in release from bondage, our guru and god.

P: R G G R G GRG G G G G G G R G G P P M M M M M M MG
F: mo-da-le ni-mmapa-da-va ne-ne-ve-nu **ma-ti-ga-la ka-ru-ni-su ma-ha-de-va**
Tr: First I think of your feet [grace], grant me intelligence, Mahadeva

P: R G G G R S S S S R R GRR
LF: ma-ti-ga-la ka-ru-ni-su ma-ha-de-va .....pitch drop....
Tr: Grant [us] intelligence, Mahadeva

P: P P P P P PM M M M M M MG R G G G G G R G G MGRS
F: Ya-ti-ga-la pra-sam a-ri-ya-da na-vu dru-du mo-ksa-nja-na gu-ru-de-va
Tr: Not knowing the mysteries as the sages do, we believe in release from bondage, our guru and god.

P: Pitch represented in Indian solfège notation (S, R, G, M, P, D, N, S).
L: Leader's part in transliterated colloquial Kannada text.
F: Follower's part in transliterated Kannada text.
LF: Leader and followers singing in unison, in transliterated Kannada text.
Tr: Free translation

Repeated texts are in **boldface**: **Ma-ti-ga-la ka-ru-ni-su ma-ha-de-va**

The main performer—a priest in southern Karnataka—sings the story and accompanies himself on the *sruti caudike,* while the disciple, also a singer, plays the *bārike caudike* imitating the end phrases of the main melody. The *sruti caudike* is a plucked chordophone with a membrane-covered cylindrical wooden body and a single steel wire string. The player plucks the string with a thin stick to produce rhythmic patterns. The *bārike caudike* is similar, a chordophone with one thin twisted gut string attached to the membrane inside the cylinder. Here the player pulls and releas-

The tiger costume dance is usually performed by a man whose body is painted like a tiger's, with yellow and white dots, and who wears a tiger's mask on his face and a tail made of dried grass.

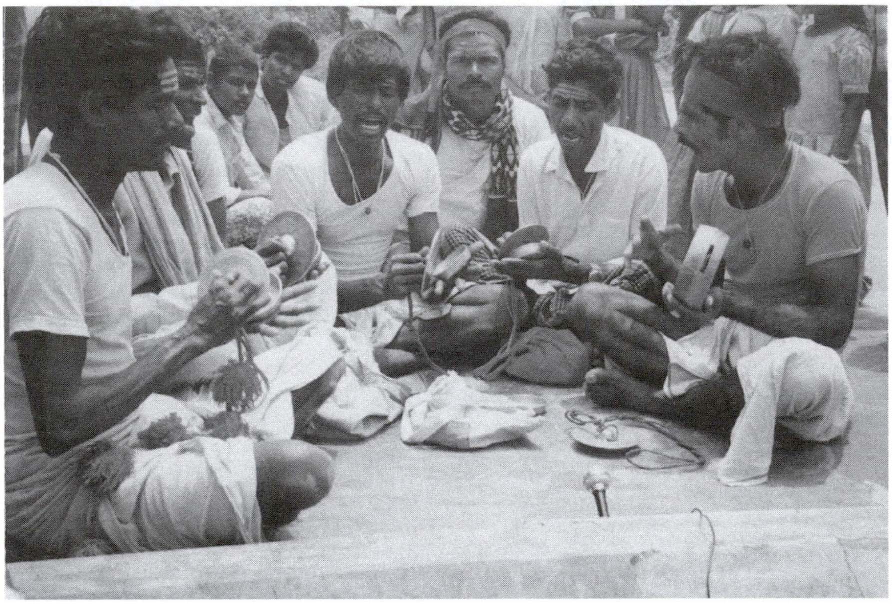

FIGURE 4 *Kamsāḷe* performers in Mahadevapura, Kollegal District, 1993. The performer seated far right is playing a *damḍi* tambourine. Photo by Gene Kassebaum.

es the gut string with a pick to produce a friction sound and to play syncopated rhythmic patterns.

INSTRUMENTAL ENSEMBLES

The word *mēḷa* refers to a "gathered group" such as the performers and audience at a village folk festival. *Mēḷa* also means a small ensemble performing a genre of local music, and in some contexts it refers to purely instrumental groups.

Many musical instruments are made in villages with locally available materials. Drums of the same type may have different names in different locations. Double-headed drums in Karnataka are often played with sticks and mallets. Many sizes of cymbal are used all over the state, and gongs shaped like brass plates struck with a mallet are also popular. Double-reed instruments, bugles of varying types, and animal horns are important in local and regional traditions.

Karḍi majalu, in northern Karnataka, is an ensemble consisting of a cymbal, drums, and double-reed instruments. Its music features different rhythmic sequences; the performances end with a climax featuring changing tempi. The ensemble performs at household rituals, village festivals, and on special ceremonial occasions such as an event welcoming a political guest.

The *kombu kahaḷe* ensemble consists of animal and brass horns. The *kahaḷe* is made of brass tubes in the shape of the letter S that are assembled before a performance. Although the sound quality of these two instruments differs considerably, they are played together. In many villages, horns and bugles are considered important

FIGURE 5 *Caudike* performer in Gāḷēramma Temple, Hampi, 1993. Photo by Gene Kassebaum.

instruments. They are played at village gatherings (*jātra*), especially during annual festivals when a village market is set up. In ancient India, the *kombu* and *kahaḷe* were used to announce the arrival of an enemy and to alert a king's soldiers. Today the ensemble is used for welcoming village dignitaries and politicians, to announce a bridegroom's arrival, and often to honor the arrival of a guru (religious teacher).

COSTUMED PERFORMANCES

Vēṣa literally means "costume" or "disguise," and a *vēṣa* performance includes the use of a mask or headdress to portray a character in a folk myth. A typical example is an animal costume, of which the most popular are the tiger (*huli*), monkey (*ānjanēya*), bear (*karaḍi*), and cow (*kōle*).

The tiger costume dance (*huli vēṣa*) is usually performed by a man whose body is painted like a tiger's, with yellow and white dots, and who wears a tiger's mask on his face and a tail made of dried grass. The performer imitates the movements of a tiger and shows his acrobatic skills in the dance. Two or three people generally assist him, particularly by moving the tiger's tail. The tiger costume dance is performed in village and city streets on Hindu and Muslim holidays.

For the monkey costume dance (*ānjanēya vēṣa*), the performer wears a crown on his head and heavy makeup. He holds a bell in his left hand and a club in his right. Another performer usually accompanies him with a large tambourine (*tamaṭe*) and stick, or a double-headed drum (*ḍōlu*). The monkey dance is performed in village festivals, especially during Rāmanavami, in April. The monkey represents Hanuman (Anjaneya in Kannada), king of the monkeys in the Ramayana epic.

During the Hindu festivals of Divālī 'festival of lights' and Gouri 'festival for women worshipping the goddess Parvati' and the Muslim festival of Muharram, performers in parts of Kodagu district wear a bear costume and dance in the streets to entertain village communities. Performers of the bear dance (*karaḍi vēṣa*) are members of the Muslim and Dalit communities. During harvest time, performers wear the bear costume and dance from house to house. Some itinerant performers even catch bears in the forest and train them to dance like humans. When training the animals, the performers dance wearing a bearskin costume and ankle bells. This street entertainment is popular among both young and old. The performer may play any instrument as background music, but the double-headed *ḍōlu* drum and *tamaṭe* 'tambourine' are most common. During the performance, enthusiasts without costumes may join in the dancing. On rare occasions the performers switch roles, and the trained bear imitates the human trainer while the trainer acts out physical movements of the bear.

Kōle basava (literally 'decorated cow'), also called *basavāṭa gangettinavaru* in some parts of southern Karnataka, is a street performance in which a trained cow or bull and a musician put on brief skits in front of houses. The musicians are hereditary wandering artists who perform in both urban and rural neighborhoods. In the skits, the cow listens to the performer and obeys his requests, usually circling or shaking her head at appropriate points. The performer also plays a double-reed aerophone (*nāgasvaram*) between the acts.

In some kinds of costume performance, the performers endure piercing triangular needles in their jaws as part of their costume. These performers may play an instrument or dance, but their act in itself is considered a ritual performance. Piercing the body with needles, especially part of the face or tongue, signifies power and is a kind of rite of passage in achieving spirituality. Among the folk community, inflicting pain is believed not only to increase awareness but also to endow the performer with special powers. The warrior costume dance (*poṭi vēṣa*) provides an example of such body piercing, performed by Harijans and Dalits to the sound of the *tamaṭe* frame drum. Although the sight of the performer induces fear, his dance is very attractive.

DANCE PERFORMANCES

Throughout Karnataka, many types of *kuṇita* (dance) are performed, having various functions among the local communities. For example, dance performances will often serve to commemorate a Muslim religious leader's memorials or to represent Hindu myths, most importantly regional variations of the classical epics, the Ramayana and Mahabharata. The names of the gods and goddesses for whom the dances are performed by Hindus are also local and change according to the location. Dances often celebrate Mariyamma, a South Indian personification of the Hindu deity Kali. (In regional dance performances, most dances are performed to honor a specific goddess.)

Dances may be performed by women, by men, or by both women and men. When men dance for female deities, women are often excluded from the performances. In some contexts, men are required to wear women's clothes when they dance.

In many dances, performers balance ritual objects on their heads and dance in a trance state. The headdress, often a symbolic representation of a local goddess, is an everyday object such as a vessel, a rice-pounding pestle, a basket, or a pole. It is decorated with vermilion, turmeric powder, flowers, betel leaves, and other good-luck items.

Dance in Karnataka cuts across religious and social lines. Hindus and Muslims join together to dance in some parts of the state, even though the dances may celebrate a Muslim saint. Tribal and nontribal people may dance together in villages. Dolls are used to represent local male gods, who are often related to the goddess either as a son or a lover.

Mask dances are an important type of dance in Karnataka. The mask dancers are considered the guardians of the local village goddess, whom their masks may represent. Also common are dances to worship cobras and other snakes, and even snake lairs (often old termite mounds). The dance movements in such performances imitate the snake.

Dance closely interweaves religion, ritual, entertainment, and recreation. A few representative Karnataka dance types are presented here.

Tribal dance

The Sidhi people who live in northern Karnataka and the border areas of Shimogga have their own social structure and musical genres that are distinct from those of the general population. Members of Sidhi communities are descendants of African slaves brought to western India by Arab or European traders (Palakshappa 1976). They have embraced Hindu, Muslim, and Christian religious practices, but their social customs and life-style closely resemble those of the Hindus. Among those Sidhis who embrace the Islamic faith, social dancing (*āligum kuṇita*) is accompanied by chanting "*Āli āli āli,*" for in their dancing the performers commemorate Ali, the cousin and son-in-law of the Prophet Muhammad.

Sidhi male dancers wear shorts and paint a white paste on their body before performing. They wear headgear prepared with flowers and a belt of bells at the waist and carry a leather belt in one hand. *Āligum kuṇita* is a group dance that any number of people can join, but there are usually two dancers who dress up in costume.

There is no accompaniment except for the *Āli* chant and the belt of bells worn by the dancers. Often they stop and hit themselves with the belt before starting to dance again. For them the self-inflicted pain heightens the religious experience.

Festival dance

The Holī festival, which celebrates the end of winter and the new beginnings of spring, is most important in Karnataka. In southern districts, the Holī festival celebrates the destruction of desire (*kāma*), and communities build wooden effigies of *kāma* in the shape of a man, which they then set on fire. Villagers throw grains of rice and wheat on the burning image, at which point dancing begins. The community known as Kuduba in southern Karnataka dances the *holī kuṇita* to the sound of the *gumaṭe* 'bottle-shaped drum' and *tāla* 'cymbals'. They sing songs in the Kuḍubi language, some with texts in a conversational mode, others in story form.

Male deity dances

Kāse kuṇita is a group dance performed by men in northern and central Karnataka in which the dancers wear a special costume and hold a knife in their hands. Accompanied by song, the dance depicts a war between two groups, with themes such as the beginning and end of the world, good and evil, gods and demons. A similar dance called *vīragāse* is performed in central Karnataka, where the costumes are different and the story is related to the male god Virabhadra.

Sindīrana kuṇita is a dance performed by Harijan fishermen and washermen in the districts of Bangalore and Kolar. The dance takes place at the village fair (*jātra*) in front of the goddess temple and also at other village rituals, and is named after Sindir, a son of the mother goddess in the form of Kali. Both deities are worshipped through the dance. A large doll of Sindir is made of wood and decorated with crooked teeth and a mustache. The doll carries a knife in one hand and a hammer in the other, and is smeared with vermilion and turmeric powder; the image produces fear in the audience. A main dancer carries the doll on his shoulder and dances to the *pare* and *tamaṭe* frame drums.

Sword dance

Caudammana kuṇita is a kind of sword dance performed at village gatherings and festivals, mostly in the north Karnataka district of Kalburgi. According to legend, Virabhadra was born from the forehead of Shiva to destroy the demon

Making *sōma* masks is a religious act; the hereditary mask makers who are also devotees of the goddess select a single type of tree dear to the goddess and carve it carefully with the right dimensions.

Dakshabrahma. Virabhadra kills the demon, but from the blood falling on the ground immediately sprout new demons. To overcome these, the female goddess Caudamma is created, a form of the mother goddess Kali. The communities that worship Virabhadra and those that worship Caudamma are both called *pancāla*; thus they belong to same lineage. Some weaving communities have embraced the Caudamma sect.

Once a year, the Caudamma festival is celebrated in a gathering called a *jātra*. Usually a male performer wears a mask of the goddess Caudamma. In his left hand he carries a lamp called *bāla belaku* 'life lamp' and in his right hand he carries a symbolic sword (*katti*). The performance consists of dances and narrative songs about a ten-day fight with the demons. On the last day of the celebrations, two male performers wear Caudamma masks and dance with inspiration. The accompanying instruments are the double-reed *śahnāī*, a large tambourine called *halage,* and other kinds of percussion instruments.

Drum dance

Halage is a generic word for membranophone in northern Karnataka. In *halage kuṇita,* a group of dancers perform to various drum timbres and asymmetric drum rhythms. Such a performance is very spectacular to watch and is very popular in the region. In *ḍōlu kuṇita*, men dance while playing a *ḍōlu* 'double-headed drum'. Varied forms of this dance include acrobatic jumping, touching the ground, or wearing stilts while playing the *ḍōlu*.

Mask dance

The ritual *sōma* dance is performed annually in villages to honor the local goddess. There are always two mask dancers, called "yellow *sōma*" and "red *sōma*," who are considered her representatives and guardians (figure 6). The names for the *sōma* performers and the colors they wear may vary from one part of the state to another. One dancer is considered mild and the other wild and fear-producing. In some areas one mask is considered male and the other female.

Making *sōma* masks is a religious act; the hereditary mask makers who are also devotees of the goddess select a single type of tree dear to the goddess and carve it carefully with the right dimensions. The mask is attached to a bamboo frame and colorful saris are densely hung on the side and back. Dancers wear the whole frame as they dance, often while in a trance state.

Only the priests of the family goddess have been initiated to perform this religious mask dance. The mask dancer generally wears a bell on his ankle and tight silver bracelets (*kaḍaga*). He wears a necklace with a brass or silver engraving of the goddess and holds long bamboo sticks in his hands. The dance is usually performed in front of the goddess temple, just before an icon of the main goddess is taken out in procession. The devotees carrying the icon walk on fire, and an animal is sacrificed to

FIGURE 6 *Sōma* masks and dancers, 1989. Photo by V. Srinivasamurthy.

the goddess. The *sōma* mask dance is performed at the time of the animal sacrifice. On occasions when a village goddess does not respond to the blood of the animals, the presence of the *sōma* mask dancers is essential. At such times the *sōma* dancers are possessed by the goddess and dance in a trance until the goddess relieves them.

OTHER ITINERANT PERFORMERS

Puppet traditions

Although wandering musicians flourish in Karnataka, the puppet performance traditions are disappearing due to a lack of patrons and because younger family males are moving to urban areas to make a living. This younger generation is not able to get training from the elders. Puppet traditions are now preserved only by folk music promoters—individual collectors, scholars, university teachers of Kannada culture, and folk institution heads—who seek to arrange performances and advertise or describe performers to potential sponsors or audiences.

Puppets with strings (*sūtra gombeyāṭa*) were once popular in Karnataka. Now only a few families are well-versed in this performance art. The puppet show plots are related to the Ramayana and Mahabharata Hindu epics; the puppets are decorated to resemble characters in those tales. A small double-reed instrument (*mukhavīṇa*) provides melodic accompaniment, and a double-headed drum (*tāla maddaḷe*) and cymbals provide the rhythm. Singers narrate the story while the puppets are manipulated.

Shadow puppets are made of animal hide (*togalu bombē*). A puppeteer manipulates them on a screen by the light of an oil lamp. Men and women both participate in the performance singing and the voicing of different characters while accompanying themselves on harmonium, tabla, and cymbals. This art is hereditary; some performers travel from village to village, giving all-night performances.

Uri Maramma performance

In the villages, the female goddess Maramma (or Mariyamma) is one of the most powerful female deities. She is feared for her curse of smallpox (figure 7), but also welcomed, for a visit from her is believed to ease life's problems for the inhabitants. In southern Karnataka, Maramma has several identities, including the village curing

FIGURE 7 Mariyamma at a crossroads in Ballary District, Hampi, 1993. Photo by Gene Kassebaum.

goddess (Uru Maramma), wind goddess (Gali Maramma), and basket visiting goddess (Hotado Maramma; see below). In the north Maramma is called by such names as Durugi, Murugi, and Murugavva.

A community of itinerant priests devoted to Maramma carry a decorated icon of the goddess in a basket and sing her praises in front of houses, to the accompaniment of a small double-headed drum (*urume*) played with a bent stick. In this way, these wandering performers make their living.

In this Uri Maramma performance, a priest's wife carries the box containing the icon and sings "Mariyamma has come to the town, Mariyamma has come to the village" while playing the *urume* drum. The priest usually circles his wife, cracking the whip as he dances in a trance state. Villagers believe that the welts he raises with the whip on his own body will bring peace to the goddess and also to the village. While the priest sings or talks, his wife accompanies him on the drum and sings a refrain, "*Tana tandana.*" She shakes the icon of Maramma to attract the attention of the villagers and let the audience know of the deity's presence. The priest blesses the villagers and their children, and in return for his religious service the villagers offer gifts of grain, coins, saris, or whatever they can afford.

URBANIZATION, MEDIA, AND INSTITUTIONS

Since the early 1960s, increased population, urbanization, and industrialization in Karnataka have affected even the smallest towns and villages. Television and radio have brought information everywhere, and employment—or the promise of it—and the expansion of public transportation have stimulated migration to urban areas. Urbanization and mass media have also directly affected the village way of life, introducing secular practices that are being assimilated.

Most performers of regional music belong to the scheduled castes. Those who move away from the countryside may absorb certain urban ways of life but they tend to keep their rural nature and continue practicing local traditions they bring with them such as ritual worship of local deities, *bhangi* 'cannabis, marijuana' consumption, *tāḍi* 'fermented palm wine' offerings to the goddess, and dedication of their children to the deity. These religious traditions sometimes link with and sometimes diverge from Hindu traditions. Their meanings appear in the texts and stories they perform.

In the past, the villages provided these performers with economic and spiritual support. Even for those who remain in the villages and small towns and continue their performing practices and alms seeking, their traditional occupations are changing along with their patrons. Both are in transition. Alms-seeking is now kept to a minimum as a religious act, and some performers have taken to farm labor or factory work, while others have formed performing groups that offer services to the public. Initiation into sects continues, but the youngsters attend village schools and divide their time between learning school subjects and practicing performance skills. Secular education and training has now replaced full-time apprenticeship. This may result in a different kind of performance in the near future.

Institutions such as the Janapada and Yakshagana Academies in Bangalore, as well as various folk music scholars and collectors, have produced cassette recordings and have also introduced these performers to television and radio broadcasting. Some folk artists have won prizes and certificates, and this recognition has helped them gain higher status as folk artists. Although the majority of folk performers in Karnataka are still isolated and have received no such acclaim, awareness among them is growing and they are altering their performances to suit more public situations. However, as Bruno Nettl has noted, change is almost inevitable: "[m]usic once ceremonial becomes entertainment [even if] its sound has been substantially maintained" (Nettl 1985:163).

The hill temples of the gods and goddesses previously had the limited function of recruiting members for the sect and offering initiation ceremonies with *lingāyat* priests. Recently, these centers have become popular pilgrimage destinations, offering tourist accommodations and hostels for people attending the annual fairs and festivals. Although such changes together with the availability of advanced technology will no doubt affect regional music performances in the future, at present many performers still uphold relatively traditional practices.

COASTAL KARNATAKA

Coastal Karnataka, formerly called the Canara Coast, is the part of India's southwestern coastline north of Kerala and south of Goa. Linguistically and culturally complex, the area is quite distinct from the regions of Karnataka east of the Western Ghat mountain range. The dominant language of the southern coastal area is Tulu, an autonomous Dravidian language probably spoken throughout the Canara coast in earlier times. In the north, a distinctive coastal dialect of Kannada has become the predominant language, and throughout coastal Karnataka, Konkani, spoken in Goa, is a significant minority language. Prior to India's independence in 1947, the British divided the region into two districts, South Canara and North Canara, each under separate presidencies. After independence, they were renamed Dakshina 'South' Kannada and Uttara 'North' Kannada, respectively.

The musical traditions of coastal Karnataka reflect the history of the region, with the music of the Tuluvas (Tulu-speaking people) in many cases forming a foundation that was then modified and supplemented over time by immigrant groups. Two major groups of Konkani immigrants, the Roman Catholic Christians and the Gauda Saraswat Brahmins, are exceptions to this generalization, as their musical traditions exhibit little or no Tuluva influence. At present, while the Tuluva musical traditions have been fairly well researched, those of the Kannada- and Konkani-speaking communities have received little specific attention. The following section concentrates on the distinctive music of theTuluvas.

Tuluva musical traditions developed within an agricultural economy based on a system of rice cultivation in which wealthy landlord families rented plots of land to sharecropping tenants. These wealthy and powerful landlords were major patrons of

Women sing *pāḍdana* songs while pulling the paddy seedlings from their seed beds; they sing *kabita* as they replant the seedlings in the growing fields.

the arts and of religion. Tuluva social structure is multicaste, with typical villages having fifteen to twenty castes. Unlike elsewhere in southern India, villages consist of houses scattered along the numerous waterways. Clusters of houses, with permanent shops and tea stalls, exist only around a few major temples and administrative centers. The predominant Tuluva religious celebration is the *bhūta kōla*, in which family deities and caste heroes are honored with songs extolling their deeds. Spirit possession also takes place, during which the deities manifest themselves in a spirit medium, bless the people, and promise continued protection and bounty.

Song traditions

Pāḍdana

In this sociocultural context song traditions developed far more extensively than did instrumental music. The most important musical tradition is *pāḍdana* (from the Dravidian root *pāḍ* 'to sing'), a genre of sung narratives associated with *bhūta* worship. The genre consists of several closely related singing traditions or subgenres. The over two hundred individual songs range in length from one to twenty hours; most take two to four hours to sing. These songs may be variously classified as epics, ritual songs, or ballads, depending on their purpose or the context in which they are sung. Most subject matter concerns the deeds of local deities, classed as *bhūta* and *daiva*.

Pāḍdana denotes at least two distinct traditions, sometimes identified by the terms *nāṭṭina pāḍdana* 'planting songs' and *sandi* 'ritual songs', although these terms tend to be used indiscriminately. *Nāṭṭina pāḍdana* are normally sung by women; *sandi* are sung in a ritual context by the men and women of the professional bardic castes—the Pambadas, Paravas, and Nalkes. The two traditions are historically related and share a common story repertoire, but they exhibit numerous stylistic and compositional differences. Women's field songs are comparatively longer, with strong narrative and lyrical qualities. While the ritual songs of the Paravas are also fairly long and strongly narrative (which suggests a close link to the women's songs), the Nalkes' and Pambadas' songs are normally much shorter and often have highly abbreviated texts. Men usually accompany their singing with a drum (*tembere*), and their *pāḍdana* have a distinctive rhythm that is coordinated with the drum's.

Women's field-song *pāḍdana* and men's ritual *pāḍdana* also differ markedly in melody. The women's repertoire of a region includes a half-dozen or so basic tunes; a singer will frequently use two or more tunes and rhythms in singing a single *pāḍdana*, shifting as the tragedy and tension mount and the song's central deity appears. The ritual songs sung by men of the bardic castes do not usually contain this melodic change. However, there are several distinctive singing styles, which vary from one caste and region to another. The Paravas, along the Western Ghat foothills, for example, sing the *Kōṭi-Chenayya pāḍdana* in a staccato style with short text lines called *naḍapu*. Both men (but not of the three bardic castes) and women sing the *Siri pāḍḍana*, a group of five songs associated with the class of supernatural beings called Siris, that are rapid, have a particularly long line, and end with a drawn-out tone. Early recordings by Arnold Bake, and even a few contemporary recordings from Dakshina Kannada, reveal that several other *pāḍḍana* are sung in this style, although this is now rare.

The earliest collection of *pāḍḍana* was made by members of the Basel Mission in the nineteenth century and published in Tulu in 1886, using a modified Kannada script, under the title *Pāḍḍanolu*. The *Indian Antiquary* published many of these texts in both transliteration and translation between 1894 and 1898, and more recent articles by Claus and Upadhyaya contain transcriptions and English translations or summaries of major *pāḍḍana* from both ritual and field-song traditions (Claus 1975, 1979, 1986, 1989, 1991; Upadhyaya and Upadhyaya 1984).

The traditional *pāḍḍana* has been a major inspiration for modern Tuluva writers. The first Tulu films were based on these epic-length stories (*Kōṭi-Chenayya*, *Siri*) and became highly successful. Collaborating songwriters and poets recomposed portions of the songs, which provided most of the music for these films and became enormously popular on cassette recordings throughout the district. These film-music versions were then introduced into the ritual context, piped over loudspeakers as dance songs for the costumed *bhūta* dance of the Nalkes and Paravas. Several of the same *pāḍḍana* had been earlier recomposed into *yakṣagāna*-style songs.

Hogalikke

In the Kannada-speaking areas of Dakshina Kannada there is another song tradition, similar to *pāḍḍana,* called *hogalikke*, a term meaning "to extol or praise"—in this case the names and deeds of deities. The Nalkes, a dancer caste (called Panars in this region), sing *hogalikke* in the context of several ritual forms closely related to the Tuluva *bhūta kōla*. These songs, like the *pāḍḍana* sung by the bardic castes, often tell of the places where a deity is worshiped and the names by which it is known there. They differ significantly from *pāḍḍana,* however, in singing style and in their much shorter length. There are no Kannada variants of this genre sung by women as field songs.

Kabita

Kabita is an extremely popular Tuluva field-song genre sung by women of all castes during the rice-planting season. Like *pāḍḍana, kabita* is sung in leader-chorus style, however, whereas *pāḍḍana* is usually sung by two women, one leading with a long poetic line and the other repeating it, *kabita* is sung by a group, with one woman singing a relatively short poetic line and the others joining in with a chorus that is repeated throughout the song. Women sing *pāḍḍana* while pulling the paddy seedlings from their seed beds; they sing *kabita* as they replant the seedlings in the growing fields. *Pāḍḍana* are overwhelmingly tragic in ethos; *kabita* are light and playful. The subject matter of *kabita* songs is varied, ranging from mnemonics (recalling the names of trees, types of ornaments, parts of a bull, and so on) to narratives (telling of a woman propitiating a deity in order to become pregnant, or a series of events in a landlord-tenant relationship, for example). Some *kabita* story episodes bear a strong resemblance to (and a historical connection with) certain *pāḍḍana* texts. But there is no tradition of either women or men singing *kabita* in a ritual context.

Analogous to the women's work songs are men's plowing songs, known as *ural,* which are not narrative and are very short, rarely more than a few poetic lines focusing on a single image.

Dakke bali

Dakke bali, also called *nāga mandala,* is a tradition of ritual worship of the cobra (*nāga*), which is possibly historically related to both *bhūta kōḷa* and *pāḍdana*. Men of the Vaidya caste perform the ritual, which combines song, pictorial art (drawing of a mandala), costumed dance, and spirit possession. The Vaidyas play the *dakke* hourglass-shaped drum, a variant of the *ḍamaru* that is distinctive in the Tuluva ritual context but associated elsewhere in South India with Shaivite traditions. The heads of the *dakke* are made of kidskin tightly stretched on hoops of brass and strung together with cotton twine around the outside. A cane hoop slung around the player's shoulder secures the drum at his left side such that by pressing down on the drum with the left hand, the player further stretches the string binding the two heads, raising the pitch. The drum can thereby provide rhythm on varying pitches. The songs of the Vaidyas are mostly semiclassical Kannada compositions in the Vaishnavite tradition; in the northern, Kannada-speaking areas, Panars perform in virtually the same tradition.

Koraga performance

As is true among many South Indian castes, several Tuluva musical traditions are named after the drums used, as in *dakke bali*. Most noteworthy is the drumming tradition of the Koragas, the "lowest" of the Tuluva castes, classified by the government as tribals. The Koragas are most closely associated with the *ḍōlu*, a cylindrical wooden drum almost a meter long and about 46 centimeters in diameter, with heads of cowhide. The drum hangs from the player's neck and is beaten with both hands in simple rhythms. Its sound is deep and travels far. Koragas can be heard at virtually all community celebrations, from *bhūta kōla* to weddings, drumming, singing, whistling, and dancing in the distance. (Although they remain unseen, their music is essential. According to ancient Tamil Cankam poetry, the sound of drumming has the capacity to protect people from evil influences that may lurk in the shadows of any celebration.) Among the most impressive contexts for Koraga performance is the royal buffalo race at Wandar: in a particular field adjacent to the one where the race will be held, the princely head of the manor formally receives the numerous vassal lords who have just led their tenants in grand processions to the site of the celebration; Koragas entirely encircle the 8-hectare field, enfolding the event with the sound of their drumming. The earth literally trembles.

Itinerant singers

Certain castes walk from house to house during particular seasons singing songs and performing brief dances. The most widespread song genre is the *madira*, in most areas performed only by members of the Nalke 'dancer' caste. The performing group usually consists of two people—either husband and wife or mother and daughter—with one (the husband or the mother) singing and the other dancing. Many *madira* songs are similar to *pāḍdana* in content, but the melody and rhythm are adapted to a simple dance step. Others, perhaps derived from the *kabita* tradition, consist of two-line stanzas (resembling proverbs) that satirize local castes with humorous comparisons and puns involving readily identifiable character traits. These stanzas are coupled with a repeated chorus line, "*Madira, madira...*" In the southeastern part of coastal Karnataka, the *karangolu* tradition is similar to *madira*. Manseru women travel from house to house in the rainy season singing *lēlē* songs (see below). These are reputed to ensure health and prosperity for the coming year. In return for their visit, villagers give the women small quantities of rice.

Life-cycle songs

Only a few Tuluva song genres are associated with life-cycle rituals, and these are connected with particular castes. Wedding songs, though common in many parts of India, are not prominent in the repertoire of most Tuluva castes. The *pāḍdana* of Kōṭi-Chenayya, the Billava caste heroes, is sometimes sung at Billava weddings, during the *madringi pāḍunu* ceremony when members of the bride's party make henna designs on their hands the day before the wedding. Brahmins and related temple castes sing wedding songs (*śobāna*), but these are mostly in Kannada and closely resemble the wedding song traditions of eastern Karnataka. Tulu wedding songs in this genre appear to be either translations of Kannada songs or inspired by them.

In many parts of Karnataka *śobāna* songs, normally thought of as wedding songs, are also sung at girls' puberty rituals (*doḍḍāki*). A similar singing tradition may have existed in the distant past among the Tuluva communities, but none do today. In fact, it is now rare to mark a girl's puberty with any ritual at all.

Ensemble music

The two most widespread kinds of ensemble music, *yakṣagāna* and *vādya,* are both context-specific, the former a part of a theater tradition of the same name, the latter associated with ritual.

Yakṣagāna

Yakṣagāna is a category of semiclassical theater found throughout southern India. In coastal Karnataka, it is more popularly known as *bailāṭa* (*bailu* 'field', *āṭa* 'drama'). Though the term *bailāṭa* refers more to the traditional performance context, the term *yakṣagāna* hints at its musical origins: *yakṣa* indicates a class of deities and *gāna* designates a specific form of vocal music.

Historically, this form reached an extremely high level of sophistication and gained widespread patronage in coastal Karnataka. Two distinct forms developed somewhat independently: *baḍaga* 'north' *tiṭṭu,* around Udupi; and *tenka* 'south' *tiṭṭu,* around Mangalore. Both forms require a similar ensemble of actors, musicians, and musical instruments, but they differ in costume, dance style, and musical delivery. The instruments are the *maddale* 'double-headed, hand-beaten drum'; *ceṇṭa* 'double-headed, stick-beaten drum'; *tāḷa* 'pair of cone-shaped, hand-held cymbals' in the south, 'hand-held bronze gong' in the north; and *śruti* 'small, portable reed-organ drone'. The southern form is particularly noted for its intense *ceṇṭa* drumming [see KERALA]; the northern form is noted for its complex *maddale* rhythms.

A singer (*bhāgavata*) directs the entire performance, initiating the musical interludes with his *tāla* and singing the story line (*prasanga*) while the actors dance. The story line ends with lines that the actors then proceed to elaborate on extemporaneously with spoken dialogue. Both story line and dialogue are in a literary type of Kannada, although certain "folk characters" sometimes speak in more colloquial Kannada or even Tulu.

Yakṣagāna drum rhythms, particularly those of the *maddale,* have developed in conjunction with the tradition's dance configurations and thus differ somewhat from other South Indian tala conventions in both the terminology used to identify particular rhythms (*bol* patterns) and in style of execution (Rao 1983).

In coastal Karnataka today, *yakṣagāna* is an enormously popular and vibrant tradition. Troupes have devoted followers, and every village has its aficionados. All the renowned *bhāgavata* and *maddale* artists have made cassette recordings that are generally commercially successful. People from many walks of life know the popular sto-

Many temples have special drums or other instruments that have been donated to the temple along with fields to support a family of musicians.

ries, and many have had some experience with acting. Expert singers and *maddale* players are held in high esteem.

Vādya

The most ubiquitous instrumental ensemble is simply called *vādya* 'musicians'. The players belong to the Śērigāra caste, and through family lineages they have inherited the right to play at particular village *bhūta kōla* (religious celebrations). The basic set of instruments consists of *tācśe* 'shallow drum', *sammēla* 'set of two drums bound together', *nāgasvaram* 'double-reed oboe', and *kombu* 'curved brass horn'. This ensemble may play along with other musicians at other kinds of events, but at *bhūta* ceremonies it functions to control the ritual: its various ragas demarcate the sequences of the ritual and establish a supportive environment. The intensity of the music at key points in the ceremony is said to stimulate possession, or, if need be, to lessen the intensity of possession by placating the *bhūta* 'family deity or caste hero'. The musicians set the rhythms for the possession dance of the *bhūta*. Their music is one of the gifts presented to the *bhūta,* and the musicians are honored during the ceremony.

Most temples also retain musicians of the Śērigāra caste on the basis of hereditary right. Their basic set of instruments is the same as that for a *bhūta koḷa* performance. Many temples have special drums or other instruments that have been donated to the temple along with fields to support a family of musicians. These rights are inherited—as is the obligation to play. At many temples, the Śērigāra musicians perform at each day's major worship ceremonies (*pūjā*).

Another instrumental group, known as a 'band', consists of several of the instruments mentioned above plus any of the following: trumpet, drum, saxophone, or clarinet. The musicians are also of the Śērigāra caste but are not directly associated with religious rituals; their main function is to provide a festive air to the activities and to escort dignitaries (including deities). Bands also play at a variety of secular events such as political rallies, and at other ceremonial functions such as weddings.

Musicians of the Śērigāra community are musical craftsmen: although they must be competent, they need not be virtuosos. Band musicians are paid in rupees for each performance and are usually able to support themselves solely on the basis of their music at village *bhūta* ceremonies, weddings, funerals, and other special occasions. Many have the right to play at particular ritual functions, in addition to occasional work at private celebrations. Some achieve high reputations as musicians, either through personal effort or having trained under a classical music master, and in doing so they join the ranks of talented artists of various castes. Śērigāra rarely join *yakṣagāna* troupes, generally only as *ceṇṭa* players.

Koḍagu musical traditions

Kodagu, formerly known as Coorg, is a district of southern Karnataka with a distinctive language (Koḍagu) and culture. Its core area is a high, fertile valley nestled between spurs of the Western Ghat mountains, which separate it from neighboring Kerala to the southwest, Karnataka to the east, and the Tulu-speaking area of coastal Karnataka to the northwest. Kodagu is famous throughout Southern India as the source of the Kaveri River. Considered a goddess, this sacred river runs through the center of the district, and is central to much of the religion and culture of the Koḍagus.

The Koḍagus (or Coorgis), who are regarded as the original inhabitants of Kodagu district, are primarily a farming community and own most of the cultivated rice fields. In recent times, Koḍagu music has shown influences from other southern Karnataka traditions, although many distinctive Koḍagu musical genres have basic formal affinities with those of coastal Karnataka and Kerala, particularly of the tribal and lowercaste communities (Iruva, Kurumba, Manseru, Muggeru [also called Mēra], Malekuḍiya, and others) along the western slopes of the Western Ghats. Most other communities in the district—primarily speakers of Kannada, Tulu, and Malayalam—consider themselves immigrants and retain the identity and traditions of their home culture.

The most distinctive musical tradition of the Koḍagus is a form of circle-dance singing, of which both male and female variants exist. Men perform songs (*pāṭü*) accompanied by a drum (*duḍi*) that often include dance: the basic form is the *boḷkoṭ* 'lamp dance'. Variant song traditions are known individually either by the occasion on which they are sung (such as the *pūttari pāṭü* 'new rice ceremony'), or by the implements used (stick dance, sword dance, whisk dance, deer-antler dance, and so on). Other songs praise local deities and are named after them, such as the *mandakkana pāṭü,* to the goddess Mandakkana.

The drum commonly played by Koḍagu men is the *duḍi*, a wooden hourglass-shaped membranophone. Drummers hold the *duḍi* horizontally. The head on the right side is made of cow skin, that on the left of goat skin; both heads are tied with leather thongs. In the center of the body is a wooden or bone peg to which bells are attached with a copper wire. A similar drum, also called *duḍi*, is characteristic of Muggeru, Manseru, and Malekuḍiya musical traditions in Dakshina Kannada.

Women also perform circular dances around a lamp, the most common being the *umattāṭa* dance. This perhaps has its origin in the form called *tummattāṭa*, which is performed at a girl's first menstruation (from which the name is derived). In this dance, after her final purificatory bath, the girl stands in the center of a circle of women, who dance around her singing songs to the goddess Kaveri. The women keep time using small bronze cymbals. Songs to other deities and legendary heroes are also included. The puberty song performance is similar to a more generalized form used for any festive occasion on which women dance around a special lamp (*dīpa*). This more expanded form is often linked, as is much Koḍagu worship, to the pan-Indian god Vishnu. The circle-dance performance enacts a variant of a classical Hindu myth: when the ocean was being churned, the gods and demons brought the mountain, Meeru, to serve as a churning post. Vishnu took on a female form, Mohini, and used Parvati's dances to enchant the demons while the gods distributed the nectar among themselves. *Ummattāṭa* is believed to be the expression of that dance. The sound of the bronze cymbals (*kanci*) is said to signify the seed-syllable *ōmkara,* specially used in worshiping the family deity. Variants of the women's dances parallel certain forms of the men's stick and sword dances in the manner in which the women strike not only their own cymbals, but, in complex alternating patterns, those of the dancers on either side of them.

Video and audio recordings of a number of Koḍagu musical and religious traditions can be found in archives of the Regional Resource Centre for Folk Performing Arts, Udupi.

REFERENCES

Ashton, Martha B., and Bruce Christie. 1977. *Yakshagana: A Dance Drama of India*. New Delhi: Abhinav Publications.

Ashton-Sikora, Martha. Forthcoming. "*Yaksāgāna*." In *South Asian Folklore: An Encyclopedia,* ed. Peter J. Claus and Margaret Mills. New York: Garland.

Bhatt, Haridas. 1983. "Transmission of Yakshagana Art through the Generations." In *Dance and Music in South Asian Drama*, ed. Richard Emmert et al., 180–187. Tokyo: The Japan Foundation.

Blackburn, Stuart H., and A. K. Ramanujan, eds. 1986. *Another Harmony: New Essays on the Folklore of India*. Berkeley: University of California Press.

Blackburn, Stuart H., and Joyce Flueckiger. 1989. "Introduction." In *Oral Epics in India*, ed. Stuart Blackburn, Peter Claus, Joyce Flueckiger, and Susan Wadley, 1–11. Berkeley: University of California Press.

Blackburn, Stuart H., Peter Claus, Joyce Flueckiger, and Susan Wadley, eds. 1989. *Oral Epics in India.* Berkeley: University of California Press.

Burnell, A. C. 1894–98. "The Devil Worship of the Tuluvas." *Indian Antiquary,* 23 seq.

Channabasappa, G. R., ed. 1977. *Karnataka Janapada Kalegalu* (A brief introduction to the folk arts of Karnataka). Bangalore: Kannada Sahitya Parishat. In Kannada.

Chidananda, Murthy. 1972. *Basavanna*. New Delhi: National Book Trust, India.

Chinmaya Dasa, Sivacandra, and Nanjundayya. 1957. *Yakshagana: Shani Devara Mahatme* (Yakshagana: the power of the planet, Saturn the great). Bangalore: T. Narayana Ayyangar. In Kannada.

Claus, Peter J. 1975. "Siri Myth and Ritual: Description of a Mass Possession Cult of South India." *Ethnology* 14(1): 47–58.

———. 1979. "Mayndala: A Myth and Cult of Tulunad." *Asian Folklore Studies* 38(2): 95–129.

———. 1986. "Playing Cenne: The Meanings of a Folk Game." In *Another Harmony: New Essays on the Folklore of India*, ed. Stuart Blackburn and A. K. Ramanujan, 265–293. Berkeley: University of California Press.

———. 1989. "Behind the Text: Performance and Ideology in a Tulu Oral Tradition." In *Indian Oral Epics in India,* ed. Stuart Blackburn et al., 55–74. Berkeley: University of California Press.

———. 1991. "Kinsongs." In *Gender, Genre, and Power in South Asian Expressive Traditions*, ed. Arjun Appadurai, Frank J. Korom, and Margaret Mills, 3–29. Philadelphia: University of Pennsylvania Press.

———. Forthcoming. "*Pāḍdana*." In *South Asian Folklore: An Encyclopedia*, ed. Peter J. Claus and Margaret Mills. New York: Garland.

Elmore, W.T. 1984 [1913]. *Dravidian Gods in Modern Hinduism*. New Delhi: Asian Educational Services.

Jogan, Shankar. 1990. *Devadasi Cult: A Sociological Analysis*. New Delhi: Ashish Publishing House.

Kambar, Chandrasekhar. 1972. "Ritual In Kannada Folk Theatre." *Journal of the Sangeet Natak Academy* 25:5–22.

Karanth, Shivarama K. 1975. *Yakshagana*. Mysore: University of Mysore.

Kassebaum, Gayathri R. 1994. "Katha: Six Performance Traditions and Preservations of Group Identity in Karnataka, South India." Ph.D. dissertation, University of Washington.

Kulakarni, Ya. Gu. 1987. *Renuka Mahatme: Yelu Kollada Sri Ellammana Caritre* (Renuka's power: seven sacred ponds, Ellamma's story). Dharwad: Pratibha Publishers (in Kannada).

Nagegouda, H. L. 1987. *Prasasti Padeda Mahaniyaru* (Folk Art Awardees 1980–1986). Bangalore: Karnataka Janapada Yakshagana Academy. In Kannada.

Nettl, Bruno. 1985. *The Western Impact on World Music: Change, Adaptation, and Survival.* New York: Schirmer Books.

Palakshappa, T. C. 1976. *The Siddhis of North Kanara.* Delhi: Sterling Publishers.

Parama Sivaiyya, Gi Sam. 1978. *Kamsaleyavaru* (Kamsale players). Bangalore: IBH Prakasana. In Kannada.

———. 1980. *Karnataka Janapada Vadyagalu* (Folk musical instruments of Karnataka). Bangalore: IBH Prakasana. In Kannada.

Ramanujan, A. K. 1986. "Two Realms of Kannada Folklore." In *Another Harmony: New Essays on the Folklore of India*, ed. Stuart H. Blackburn and A. K. Ramanujan, 131–164. Berkeley: University of California Press.

———. 1987. "Foreword." In *Folktales of India*, ed. Brenda E.F. Beck, Peter Claus, Praphulladatta Goswami, and Jawaharlal Handoo, xi–xxi. Chicago: University of Chicago Press.

———. 1991. "Toward a Counter-System: Women's Tales." In *Gender, Genre, and Power in South Asian Expressive Traditions*, ed. Arjun Appadurai and Frank Korom, 3–29. Philadelphia: University of Pennsylvania Press.

Rangathan, Ashok. 1990. "Karnataka." In *Insight Guide: South India,* ed. Manjulika Dubey and Bikram Grewal, 153–217. Singapore: APA Publications.

Rao, H. Gopala. 1983. "Rhythm and Drums in Badagatittu Yakshagana Dance-Drama." In *Dance and Music in South Asian Drama*, ed. Richard Emmert et al., 188–204. Tokyo: The Japan Foundation.

Sumitra, L. G. 1974. "The Folklore of Karnataka: Collection, Documentation, and Research Work Done So Far—A Critical Survey." *Journal of the Indian Musicological Society* 5: 8–18.

Thurston, E. 1975 [1909]. *Castes and Tribes of South India*, vol. IV-K-M, 99–106. Delhi: Cosmo Publications.

Upadhyaya, U. P., and Sushila Upadhyaya. 1984. "Jumadi Paddana." In *Bhuta Worship*, 27–50. Udupi: Regional Resource Centre for Folk Performing Arts.

Wadley, Susan. 1986. "The Katha of Sakat: Two Tellings." In *Another Harmony: New Essays on the Folklore of India*, ed. Stuart H. Blackburn and A. K. Ramanujan, 195–232. Berkeley: University of California Press.

Whitehead, Henry. 1976 [1921]. *The Village Gods of South India*. Delhi: Sumit Publications.

Andhra Pradesh

Gene H. Roghair

Cinema Music
The Integrative Role of Folk Music
Oral Narrative Song

When the boundaries of the modern Indian state of Andhra Pradesh were created in 1956, the attempt was made to include a majority of the Telugu-speaking people who inhabit the area. Significant minorities of Telugu speakers still live in the surrounding states, particularly in Tamil Nadu and Karnataka; within Andhra Pradesh itself, there are many linguistic minority groups as well. The largest of these linguistic minorities is the Urdu speakers, concentrated in and around Hyderabad, the current capital (as well as former capital of a large Muslim state of the same name that maintained a separate identity up until Indian independence). Andhra Pradesh has an area of over 275,000 square kilometers and a population of more than 60 million—both a little greater than those of the United Kingdom. Although Hyderabad is a major metropolis, the state is largely rural, ranging from rich rice-growing deltas to dry, rocky uplands.

The traditional music of Andhra Pradesh can be divided into two distinct streams, although such division oversimplifies a complex cultural evolution. One stream is the classical tradition, which adheres to standards laid out in authoritative texts and handed down by upper-caste elites. The development of this tradition was integrally connected with the court and temple history of South India. Even today, performers, audiences, and connoisseurs almost deify revered composers. Practitioners of this art typically start at a very young age and spend years learning from a musical guru.

Educated elites, both Indian and foreign, categorize the diverse traditions of the second stream as folk music. Folk music being less self-conscious than classical music, its standards are not delineated anywhere in Sanskrit or classical Telugu. Nevertheless, it has its own aesthetic as well as a complex interrelationship with everyday life, culture, and religion. Unlike the recognized composers of classical music, folk composers remain largely anonymous. This music is considered the common heritage of those who sing it and those who participate as audiences. However, it is erroneous to assume that it comes strictly from the villages; much of it also has historical connections with temples and courts. With the passage of time, some of its masters have gradually lost influence, due to the vagaries of their patrons' power and influence.

All native Telugu music, whether classical or folk, has emerged from the rhythms

Lullabies and cradle songs used to quiet a baby every day comprise some of the earliest religious and cultural instruction for the child. Some are about Lord Krishna, whom mothers often worship as a divine child; others are about Rama and Sita, the ideal royal couple.

of life as it is lived at various levels. Classical performances are now generally more secular and independent of time and place; folk music continues to blend with the sounds of life in its daily, yearly, age-old mytho-religious rhythms.

For example, the sounds and rhythms of daily activities provide an audible background to village life in Andhra Pradesh. Some sounds are common to all Telugu-speaking people, others are peculiar to particular regions or zones, but each village and neighborhood has its own peculiar pattern, its own variations on the constant themes: the early morning milking of buffalo, the churning of curds into butter, and the sweeping out of houses, as well as boys driving cattle to the village fields, men plowing fields with bullocks and wooden-shafted plows, and women filling brass water pots from the village well. Joining these work sounds are other sounds of daily life: adult conversation, children running and playing, a mendicant calling for a handout, a bus clattering down the street. Some sounds are seasonal: planting, transplanting, cultivating, harvesting, threshing, and transporting. Sounds of birth, marriage, and death signal the great cycles of life. Spiritual and religious events—festivals, pilgrimages, and parades—honor cosmic time; the changing patterns of all sounds together measure historical time. And the background music of life in Andhra Pradesh is always changing in tempo and pitch, as new sounds are added and old ones fall away.

Combining with this ambient symphony are the musical traditions of the Telugu people. Songs and instrumental music express the same rhythms of life as do the background noises. Some of these musics are old and familiar, tied to a caste, a temple, a way of life, or a region, and may die out with changing circumstances. Some are new, transmitted by cinema, radio, television, audio cassette, and compact disc. Driven by industry and by an emerging consumer consciousness, the new sounds are indeed rooted in tradition, but their appeal is associated with novelty and cinema stars. Just as the sounds of motor rickshaws, lorries, automobiles, trains, and factories have augmented Andhra's soundscape, so too has cinema music become ubiquitous in the lives of the Andhra people.

CINEMA MUSIC

It would be difficult to overestimate the importance in the urban environment of this popular form of musical entertainment. India in fact has the largest movie industry in the world, and Indians constantly listen to cinema music. It is always part of their lives [see FILM MUSIC: SOUTHERN AREA], its influence reaching even into the smallest villages, where working boys and girls, endeavoring to emulate the stars, learn all the lyrics of the latest songs. This music is also accessible outside India. Tapes and compact discs are available from Indian groceries in towns and cities all over the world, wherever Indians have made their homes. Indian students and recent immigrants in the United States discuss the latest developments on the Internet with fellow Telugu-speakers in India. As in much of the rest of the world, the sheer volume of popular music tends to obscure the old traditions and diminish their role. Nevertheless, the richness of the traditional music lies waiting to be tapped by those who take the time to appreciate it and its connection with life on its many levels.

THE INTEGRATIVE ROLE OF FOLK MUSIC

Folk music is not an indigenous term or concept; there is no analogous traditional term in Telugu. Each type of song, whether lullaby, work song, epic, or devotional hymn, has its own individual style of singing. Many, even most, have specific contexts in which they are sung or performed. One Telugu term that does encompass this diversity has come into common parlance in recent decades, primarily among educated elites: *janapada gēyālu* 'people's songs', alternatively *janapada sāhityam* 'people's literature'.

Valuable collections and surveys of the various song types have been published in Telugu. Notable among these is an extensive study by Biruduraju Ramaraju that includes descriptions of various traditions and summaries of some narrative works (Ramaraju 1958). A much smaller work by Nedunuri Gangadharam (1968) provides transcriptions of many short folk songs. These studies suggest the diversity of musical traditions, but in-depth examinations of individual traditions are few.

Scholars have classified Telugu folk music in various ways. Most traditional songs fit into several different classifications. A song can be defined by the context in which it is sung as, for example, spinning-wheel songs; the same song can be categorized by who sings it, perhaps according to gender or caste. Singing style is another means of classification. Certain field songs are called "ah" songs because, following each narrative passage sung by the lead singer, the other workers sing a long, drawn-out, responsive "ah." The same songs can also be classified as rice-transplanting songs, according to their context. Subject matter further results in a wide range of categories: devotional, cultural, love, Puranic, Vaishnavite, Shaivite. But people sing songs in all these categories informally, for their own enjoyment, rather than in a formal performance context.

The fluidity of the categories suggests an overall integrative function. Lullabies and cradle songs used to quiet a baby every day comprise some of the earliest religious and cultural instruction for the child. Some are about Lord Krishna, whom mothers often worship as a divine child; others are about Rama and Sita, the ideal royal couple (manifestations of Vishnu and Lakshmi, respectively). A historical French officer named Bussy, who led a destructive campaign in central and coastal Andhra Pradesh, emerges as a bogeyman in some lyrics. Others name foods, commonly used articles, and different family members. As children grow older, they learn other songs from parents and peers, many associated with games. At the same time, the songs instill cultural and religious values. Sprightly tempos and repetitive structures make the songs easy to sing and remember. The verbal content stays with the children throughout their lives.

Work songs

Hundreds of traditional songs accompany the various jobs that people do. Agriculture is particularly rich in songs that range from prayers for rain to ribald songs sung by crews of women as they weed or harvest. Every sort of traditional work has its own songs, whether it is road building, quarrying, or housework. The rhythm is often connected with the work at hand, but the content may deal with entirely unrelated subjects. Mortar-and-pestle songs (*rōkaṭi pāṭalu*) maintain a rhythm that allows three people to slam heavy pestles into the same mortar safely (figure 1). Such songs ease the drudgery of the work, and their content deals with other dimensions of life of particular interest to the people singing, voicing their concerns, dreams, and desires.

FIGURE 1 A mortar-and-pestle song (*rōkaṭi pāṭa*) helps three workers maintain a constant rhythm. Guntur District, Andhra Pradesh, 1969. Photo by Gene H. Roghair.

Life-cycle songs

Songs accompany the stages of life from birth to death, and their respective festivities. These songs transmit the values of the culture that gives rise to them. For example, all members of a wedding party have songs that define their roles and society's expectations of them [see SEASONAL AND LIFE-CYCLE RITUALS].

Religious songs

Hindu devotion is very important in Andhra Pradesh. Devotional songs to one deity or another exist in both the classical and folk traditions, often dedicated to one of the many goddesses: Sarasvati, goddess of learning and the arts; Lakshmi, goddess of good fortune; Gauri, consort of the great god Shiva; Annapurna, generous bestower of food; Durga, manifestation of the energy of all the gods and protector of the earth; and the village goddesses such as Ankamma, Ganga, and Nukalatalli. There are popular songs of devotion to Hanuman, the monkey god; to Vinayaka (Ganesh), the elephant-headed god who overcomes all obstacles; and to Krishna and Rama, popular incarnations of Vishnu. They are sung in a great variety of contexts; women, for example, will frequently make a vow to perform a religious task or observance in order to conceive, to protect a husband, or to attain some other desirable end. Songs will often accompany these vows, sometimes with the text focusing on a serpent or a sacred plant.

ORAL NARRATIVE SONG

Of particular interest in Andhra Pradesh is a type of oral narrative song that has never appeared in some parts of the world, and that has faded away in most others. Long and sophisticated, these songs have an ancient lineage; they are not sung for pleasure, but as a powerful instrument of cultural integration, enrichment, and transmission.

Telugu-speakers maintain a rich tradition of extended oral narrative literature drawn from a wide range of times, places, and cultural and religious traditions. Singers and storytellers present this literature, to the accompaniment of musical instruments, in a combination of song and prose narration, a form of singing distinct from the informal type of singing discussed thus far.

Although particular castes and vocal traditions perform these narratives, the traditions have a low profile and a tendency to blend into the environment that often characterizes folk music; but specific standards exist, because the music has been passed on orally from generation to generation.

Classical and folk literature

To understand these narrative songs, it is helpful to note that there exists a rich and diverse extant classical literature in Telugu, dating back to an eleventh-century Telugu rendition of the Mahabharata. This literature exhibits a strong Sanskrit influence, as its writers have been predominantly Brahmins, fluent in Sanskrit and participants in the pan-Indian cultural tradition transmitted via Sanskrit. Called *mārga* 'the path', this literature has shaped cultural and religious standards and values in the region.

An alternative body of oral literature, however, as old as or older than the standard literature, has shown itself more flexible and capable of changing with the times than the elitist classical literature. This rich tradition is the legacy of low-caste or even outcast individuals; its method of transmission remains fundamentally oral, but it is at least as important as the classical literature in transmitting cultural and religious values, although it receives little formal acknowledgment for this role. Telugu culture is bipolar in this respect, both poles influencing the majority of the population as well as each other, in an ongoing rich, historical interaction.

Divisions of Telugu narrative song

One indigenous way of classifying Telugu narrative song is by type of accompanying instrument. Subject matter is also used: mythological, religious, heroic, fairy-tale, historical. There are further subdivisions according to who sings: only certain castes and/or singing traditions concern themselves with some narratives; a variety of people sing others, and in different styles. Most of the stories are more or less well known by a broad spectrum of society. Some singers have regular patrons for whom they perform; others rely on a more diverse audience. (An audience is seldom restricted to the patron; others are generally allowed to enjoy the performances. Although there are some restrictions on who sings and who does not, few restrictions are of a proprietary nature.)

Instruments

A variety of instruments is employed, including string, wind, and many percussion instruments, all of which generally differ from those used for classical music.

Gummeṭa *and* tambūrā

One of the most popular drums employed by narrative singers is the *gummeṭa* (figure 2). Generally made of brass, but sometimes of clay, the *gummeṭa* has the shape of a small-necked jug. The jug's neck is open; the opening in the base is covered by a tightly stretched skin head tied with thongs. The player suspends the instrument with a strap around the neck, so that it lies horizontally at about waist level, and strikes the head with the fingers of one hand, usually the right, and cups the palm of the other hand over the open neck. While striking the drumhead, the drummer controls the opening at the other end by alternately cupping or removing his or her palm. The result is a unique and variable resonant sound, unlike any other drum.

The *tambūrā*, a long-necked lute, often accompanies the *gummeṭa* in narrative performances (see figure 2). The lead singer carries the lute over his or her shoulder while pacing back and forth, singing the story. The *gummeṭa* players may simply drum and sing on the refrains, or may also join in humorous repartee with the lead singer. One of them may even tell a humorous or bawdy *piṭṭa katha* 'little bird story'

One of the most popular drums employed by narrative singers is the *gummeṭa*, which has the shape of a small-necked jug and produces a unique and variable resonant sound.

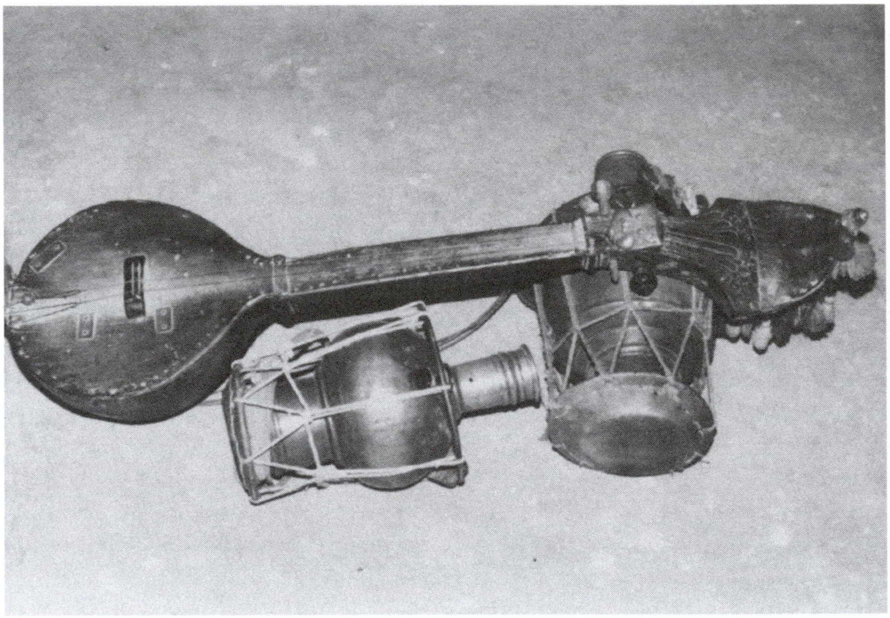

FIGURE 2 *Tambūrā* and two *gummeṭa* drums, used to accompany Telugu narrative song. Andhra Pradesh, 1974. Photo by Gene H. Roghair.

having no particular connection with the main narrative; sometimes they even draw audience members into the story as characters. In recent years, nontraditional singers have also adopted the instrumental combination of *gummeṭa* and *tambūrā* (see "*Burra katha* stories" below).

Jamikiḷi

Many narrative singers like to accompany themselves on the *jamiḍiki* or *jamikiḷi* (figure 3). This is a brass or wooden drum, tapering slightly from the skin head to the open end. A string is attached to the head and emerges from the open end of the drum with a short piece of wood attached to its loose end. The player cradles the drum in one arm, tightens the string by holding the piece of wood with the hand of the same arm, and plucks the string with the free hand. By changing the tension on the string while plucking, the player can vary the pitch. The instrument is particularly characteristic of Bavanīlu or Jamikiḷi singers, whose names come from the varieties of this instrument they use. Two distinct versions exist: a small type that emits a sharp twang, and a much larger instrument with a deeper sound.

Pambajōḍu, titti, *and* kommu

The *pambajōḍu* is a pair of double-headed drums, each about 45 centimeters long and 10 to 12 centimeters in diameter (figure 4). In some cases both drums are made of brass; in others, one is brass and the other wood. The player supports the drums at

FIGURE 3 *Jamikiḻi*, played by plucking the string inside the drum. Andhra Pradesh, 1974. Photo by Gene H. Roghair.

about waist height with a harness, striking one head with a small stick and the other with the fingers of the left hand. Sometimes players attach bronze bells to the front drum. *Pambajōḍu* drummers usually perform together with players of finger cymbals, jangling ankle bracelets, and *titti* 'bellows', a simple bagpipe-like instrument made from an entire goatskin. Two of the leg holes are sewn shut, as are the neck and rump. From one leg opening emerges a small bamboo tube through which the player blows to inflate the bag. When the bag is full, the musician folds the leg skin over the tube to prevent air from escaping. Another bamboo tube, fitted with a double reed, is inserted into the remaining leg opening. As the air escapes, it produces a buzzing hum. By alternately blowing in the tube and squeezing the bag, the musician is able

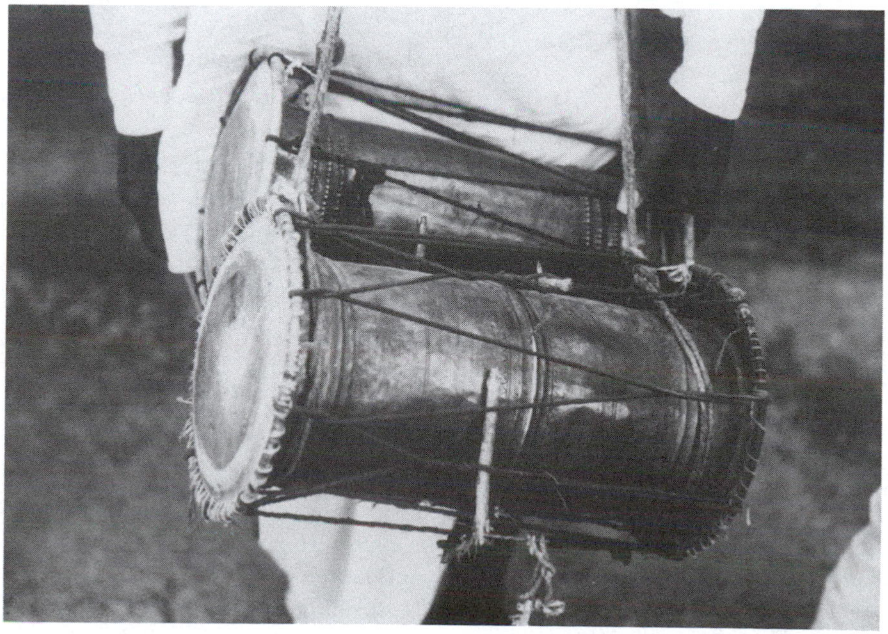

FIGURE 4 *Pambajōḍu*, used in performance of the *Epic of Palnāḍu* and *Kāṭamarāju Katha*. Andhra Pradesh, 1980. Photo by Gene H. Roghair.

FIGURE 5 Herding-caste epic singers (Golla Suddulu) perform *Kāṭamarāju Katha* accompanied by (*from left*) *pambajōḍu*, *titti*, and *kommu*. Guntur District, Andhra Pradesh, 1980. Photo by Gene H. Roghair.

to maintain a steady, uninterrupted tone throughout the entire performance. In some narrative traditions, a crescent-shaped brass horn called a *kommu* joins the drum and bagpipe (figure 5). The *kommu* also appears frequently in parades.

Other instruments

Folk instruments less commonly used in narrative performance include the hourglass Shiva drum (*oggu*), flat drum (*ḍappu*), large double-headed drum, castanet, sticks, finger rings, other lute-like instruments, conch, flute, and *nāgasvaramu* (known elsewhere as *mahuḍi* or *puṅgī*), a gourd wind instrument played by snake charmers (figure 6). In addition, various classical instruments have found a place in folk music, including the North Indian tabla drum pair and the double-reed *sannāyi*. The harmonium, a small hand-pumped organ, accompanies many village performances. Even brass bands have a folk music repertoire, performing for funeral processions in cities and towns.

Narrative song topics

Many of the narrative songs take their subject matter from the Sanskrit classics, the pan-Indian epics, and the Puranas (Hindu myths and legends). Many of these were derived from oral traditions current among the common people, as high-caste Sanskrit writers used popular songs and stories for their own purposes, modifying them as they saw fit. The narrative songs also draw on folk traditions, some of them inspired by the Sanskrit epics and their regional-language versions. Not surprisingly, the content and emphasis varies according to who uses them and for what purposes. Unlettered Telugu-speakers distinguish between these fabricated stories (*kaṭṭu kathālu*) and true stories (*jarigina kathālu*), which took place in what they perceive to be real time and space. In other words, there is an indigenous division of time into mythological and historical realms, as understood by the singers and their audiences. They consider the local epics and legends that feature places and social divisions with which they are intimately acquainted to be true and to have happened in real time, however tenuous the connection with events that actually happened. The pan-Indian myths, however, they regard as fabricated by poets, even when sung in their local variations.

FIGURE 6 A snake charmer plays the *nāgasvaramu* (known elsewhere as *mahuḍi* or *puṅgī*). Guntur District, Andhra Pradesh, 1968. Photo by Gene H. Roghair.

Folk versions of mythological stories

Telugu narrative songs from the Ramayana and the Mahabharata may differ substantially from both Sanskrit and classical Telugu versions. Actually, many popular stories related to the Ramayana and the Mahabharata are not in the classical texts. Others are expanded versions of minor stories in the classical tradition. Virtually all Indians know the main outline of the Ramayana, but certain episodes capture people's hearts, and they want to hear them again and again. People never tire of hearing the stories of the monkey king, Hanuman, and those of Lava and Kusha, the sons of Rama and Sita. Some of these are in the classics and some are not. Popular stories from the Mahabharata are often quite peripheral to the main action. Savitri, an ideal wife, follows Yama, the god of death, to the netherworld and returns to the land of the living with her husband, Satyavat, in one popular tale.

Another corpus of Puranic tales are those of Krishna, which also appear in the *Bhāgavata Purāṇa* and are part of both oral Telugu and pan-Indian tradition. These stories lead up to the birth of Krishna and tell of his boyhood and youth with the cowherd women, as well as of his various wives and heroic exploits. We do not know exactly how the oral and written versions have interacted over time; although these stories often fit into the Hindu religious tradition, in most cases their appeal is mythological and reaches beyond narrow religious boundaries. The oral renditions, a prime source of mythological information, form an important part of the region's cultural fabric.

Religious narrative songs

Another category of narrative song is religious, and closely connected with one or another of the great divisions of the Hindu religion: Shaivite, Vaishnavite, or Devi worship. Vaishnavite stories include those of the various incarnations of Vishnu, who appears from time to time to rescue the world and its inhabitants from one threat or another. Here, too, are stories of Lakshmi, goddess of fortune and consort of Vishnu. These are known all over India and are present in Sanskrit as well as many regional languages. Other Vaishnavite stories are of a more regional nature.

Most singers of tales in Andhra Pradesh are mendicant entertainers, at least part time.

Shiva stories include those about Devi in her various manifestations as Parvati, Ganga, Gauri, and other female deities. The marriage of Ganga and Shiva is a well-loved example. Regional traditions reflect the militant devotionalism of South Indian Shaivism. As a test, Siriyalu and his wife are asked to serve their only son as a meal to Shiva, who appears as a leprous mendicant devotee, and they do so. The story is found in medieval Tamil and Telugu sources, and exists in most South Indian languages.

Heroic narrative songs

Telugu heroes and heroines constitute one of the most highly developed categories of extended narrative songs. Although the oldest of these, the *Palnāṭi Vīrula Katha* (also called the *Epic of Palnāḍu*), has its historical roots in the twelfth century, and some elements of the tradition may be much older, newer heroic stories take the listener into the late twentieth century. The *Epic of Palnāḍu*—long, involved, and full of motifs common to epics throughout the world—can take up to a month to perform. It integrates diverse cultural and religious material into a comprehensive worldview from the perspective of the main battlefield and present hero temple (both in the town of Karempudi). One of the earliest recordings (and translations) of a Telugu oral epic, the *Epic of Palnāḍu*, as performed by the accomplished singer Alisetti Galeyya, was made by Gene Roghair in 1974 (Roghair 1982).

Stories in the epic cycle associated with the Golla herding caste of Andhra Pradesh, dating to the thirteenth century, are even longer than the *Epic of Palnāḍu*. The best known is *Kāṭamarāju Katha*, the story of the hero Katamaraju. Tangirala Venkata Subbaravu has published a monumental work in Telugu on this tradition, comprising both a study and an anthology (Subbaravu 1976–1977). These stories integrate the cultural and religious experience of the Golla into a coherent worldview.

TRACK 34 Many heroic narratives involve recognizable periods of Telugu history. *Bobbili Yuddha Katha* 'Story of the Battle of Bobbili' refers to a fort and a minor kingdom, and dates to the mid-eighteenth century, when the French were present in coastal Andhra. It recounts a military and tax-collecting expedition from Hyderabad along the coast that ends with the destruction of a small fort in Srikakulum district. A more recent account tells of Alluri Sitaramaraju, who was involved in a twentieth-century uprising in Telugu lands previously ruled by the nizam of Hyderabad. The people of Andhra Pradesh accept such stories as history—*jarigina kathālu* 'stories that happened'—as distinct from *kaṭṭu kathālu,* the fabricated stories of mythology.

Narratives of deified female martyrs

Although many stories have female characters, even heroines, there is a particular type of heroine story in a class by itself. Singers and audiences consider these stories to be about women who actually lived; thus they are of the historical type. And just as people have deified heroes of the Telugu epics, so too have they deified these heroines, although for different reasons. The story of Kanyaka is one example. A local king wants to marry Kanyaka, the daughter of a wealthy merchant and the most beautiful woman in the world. Instead, Kanyaka immolates herself along with other members of her caste, establishing a code of conduct for the caste, and becomes a goddess. Such stories of women who become martyrs for a principle abound in Andhra Pradesh. In all of them, a woman whose virtue is challenged responds heroically and consequently dies, following which she is deified, worshiped, and celebrated at local or regional festivals. In most cases, singers and audiences believe the events took place in the not-too-distant past; an existing temple marks the ground where the transformation is supposed to have taken place. The stories, told by a cross-section of narrative singers, sometimes exist in Sanskrit or literary Telugu versions.

Burra katha *stories*

In the 1950s the Communist party of Andhra Pradesh, seeking to attract the attention of the common folk, approached the singer Muhammad Nazir. He began writing simplified and shortened versions of traditional stories and presented them with the traditional *tambūrā* 'lute' and *gummeṭa* 'drum' accompaniment. He also utilized the *piṭṭa katha* technique of digressing from the main story to verbalize the political agenda. In this manner he successfully brought his message to large, often urban, audiences. He was in fact so successful in adapting the folk style for his own purposes that soon many were following in his footsteps, and today much of the urban and educated populace regards this style, which came to be known as *burra katha,* as a folk tradition and a prime example of oral narrative performance.

Burra katha remains popular to this day. But although it is a lively art, it is quite different from the original folk tradition. Written forms of the *burra katha* stories appear in cheaply printed editions, from which singers memorize and perform them for general audiences. In the process, longer and more involved versions of the stories that had been handed down by oral transmission have been pushed into the background, and those who still know them are largely ignored.

Narrative singers

As already mentioned, singers of the Telugu oral narratives are of different types. Some sing primarily Shiva songs, whereas others may sing stories from only one of the Telugu epics or even from a variety of stories, as secular entertainers. Others are characterized by their caste or social group, or by that of their audience, or by instruments or singing style. But what do all the different singers of tales have in common?

Mendicant singers of tales

Andhra society labels most present-day Telugu narrative singers as *biksha* 'beggars or mendicants'. This Telugu term encompasses a wide variety of individuals and lifestyles. Most of them are not narrative singers. An old village woman, for example, finds herself reduced to seeking daily handouts in order to eat. Religious mendicants roam over vast areas, spending their lives asking for alms. Snake charmers, scorpion handlers, and a variety of other small-time entertainers beg for a living while providing diversion. Most singers of tales in Andhra Pradesh are mendicant entertainers, at least part time. The singers, perhaps a father and son or a husband and wife, come walking into a town. One may shoulder a *tambūrā* that she strums as she walks along singing a few lines of a story. As the pair enters a residential street, the inhabitants become aware of their presence. By the song and instrument, residents know what kind of singers these are; they may stop and play for a while in front of a house before giving a call for alms. The woman of the house may emerge and give them a handful of rice or a small coin or two, or may send a child out with something for the singers. The singers then move on to the next house, singing and looking for another handout. They seldom play for long at any one place, although occasionally they may be approached by someone interested in feeding them for a few days or even providing them with additional payment of some kind, in which case they will stay longer.

Performances take place in a temple courtyard or in the street. Substantial crowds may stay up long past their usual bedtimes to hear the stories. Or perhaps the affair is more private, in the courtyard of some person of means. The singing continues for as long as the singers, patrons, and guests are all agreeable. At length, the patron may reach the end of his willingness to pay, the crowds may become restless, or the singers may have more pressing engagements elsewhere. When the performance is over the singers move on, and life in the village or neighborhood resumes its normal patterns.

But do these singers spend all of their lives roaming from place to place? There may be more logic to their movements than is initially obvious. It is unlikely that they move about randomly from village to town, up and down this street and that. Many establish connections with one caste or another, and with particular patrons in specific villages. In some villages, singers have permanent residences, and make up as much as half the population. During the agricultural season they work in the fields of landowners, receiving payment in kind for their services, then fan out over large portions of the state during the slack seasons. Far from their homes, they engage in their second livelihood as mendicant singers. There may be a clear understanding among the singers as to who will cover what territory, and even an understanding with other singers of the same type from elsewhere in the state. Sometimes patrons will send someone to a village to seek the singers out and engage their services for a wedding, festival, or funeral. In such cases, the arrangements have all been made before the singers journey to the patron's location.

Not all singers follow these patterns. The Vīravidyavantulu, singers of the *Epic of Palnāḍu*, usually have, or at one time have had, temple lands dedicated to their use, in payment for services rendered to the temple at certain times of year. (Control of temple lands has often been lost through family debts.) This does not mean that the Vīravidyavantulu are wealthy or even better off than mendicants; they also have to do farm labor and other low-paid work for their main incomes.

Jangam singers

Jangam singers are all Shaivites, although there are numerous subgroups; their primary patrons are of the various Shaivite castes. Both men and women perform on a regular basis, playing a small version of the jug-shaped *gummeṭa* drum made of brass or bronze. Their repertoire includes Shiva stories from the classical texts as well as from the South Indian Shaivite tradition. They also sing historical works like *Dēśingurāju Katha* 'The Story of Raja Desingu' and *Sarvāye Pāpaḍu*, the story of a Telugu Robin Hood character. Next to the Dāsari, the Jangam are perhaps the best-known narrative singers in Andhra Pradesh. As such, and because they sing for a broad spectrum of society, they often know large numbers of songs.

Dāsari singers

TRACK 34 Dāsari singers are all Vaishnavites; their name means "devotees of Vishnu." Men and women both sing a wide range of songs including heroic, Vaishnavite, and fairy tales. They have traditionally used many different instruments, such as the conch and bell, but now seem to use the *gummeṭa* and *tambūrā* most frequently. Their vocal performance style is very active, with rapid notes. The main singer, carrying the *tambūrā*, moves about throughout the performance; the drummers actively engage in exchanges with the lead singer. The Dāsari may be the most commonly known narrative singers throughout Andhra Pradesh. Muhammad Nazir, the originator of the *burra katha* style, credits them along with the Jangam singers for the style he further developed.

Jamikiḷi singers

The Jamikiḷi, also known as Bavanīlu, take their name from the string drum that they play. Widespread throughout Andhra Pradesh, they are devotees of various village goddesses such as Ankamma, Ellamma, and Renuka, about whom they sing many songs, men and women alike. With a diverse selection of songs, they are mendicant entertainers. They also officiate at feasts featuring goat sacrifices.

Piccukaguntḷu singers

The primary patrons of the Piccukaguntḷu are the Reḍḍi, a major agricultural caste in Andhra Pradesh, but they also sing for the Golla or herding caste. They know all the Reḍḍi and Golla lineages and family histories, and sing heroic songs about characters from these castes. Typically they play the bell and *titti* 'bagpipe drone', but they have also adopted the commonly used *gummeṭa* and *tambūrā.* These singers worship Shiva and various local goddesses, and sing tales about these divinities.

Vīravidyavantulu singers

The Vīravidyavantulu are exclusively male singers who perform only stories from the *Epic of Palnāḍu*. These performances are acts of devotion and worship, both of the epic's heroes and of Ankamma, a local goddess and patron of the heroes. The singers first make offerings to the goddess, offer obeisance to their sacred instruments, and worship the deified heroes in the form of weapons. After these preliminaries, the lead singer begins the chosen story for the night.

The singers present the *Epic of Palnāḍu* in a combination of song and heightened prose. They accompany their performance with the *titti* 'bagpipe drone', *pambajōḍu* 'drum pair', finger cymbals, and ankle bracelets. Although many oral-narrative performances are quick and lively, epic singing is slower and more methodical. It is not surprising that the lively Dāsari or Jangam performances have become popular entertainment, whereas epic singing remains of interest primarily to devotees of the goddess or the heroes. However, the epic style is very powerful, as it is an ancient art form capable of holding an audience for long periods of time. An accomplished singer knows over thirty nights' worth of stories, and can captivate an audience as he covers a vast range of diverse subjects and integrates them into a coherent local ideology.

When the bagpipe drone begins, the lead singer commences the narrative. Single drum beats, the clang of finger cymbals, and vocal interjections by the drummer punctuate each phrase. Again rapid drum beats, cymbals, and a drawn-out melodic line sung by the accompanists conclude each sentence. This line repeats a portion of the lead singer's preceding line, and ends with the extended name of a god or hero who is integral to the hero cult. The presentation is enhanced by the actions of the lead singer, who brandishes a sword in one hand and a brass shield in the other. Bells on the sword and jangling ankle bracelets complete the overall effect.

During performances of the *Epic of Palnāḍu,* people frequently interrupt to offer monetary gifts, large or small, to the singers. When a gift is proffered, the singer acknowledges the giver not with a simple thank-you or nod; he breaks off the narrative and launches into a formulaic response that includes blessings for the person offering the gift or in whose name it is offered. This acknowledgment can extend into a lengthy, often humorous, story about the giver. The audience thoroughly enjoys

An accomplished narrative singer knows over thirty nights' worth of stories, and can captivate an audience as he covers a vast range of diverse subjects and integrates them into a coherent local ideology.

FIGURE 7 A member of the Golla herding caste plays the crescent-shaped brass horn, *kommu*. Guntur District, Andhra Pradesh, 1980. Photo by Gene H. Roghair.

these interruptions, becoming more engaged with the performance and becoming more connected with the heroes of old.

Golla Suddulu singers

The *Kāṭamarāju Katha* epic of the Golla Suddulu singers (see figure 5) is very similar to the *Epic of Palnāḍu*. These singers are also all male, and employ the same basic instruments and singing style as the Vīravidyavantulu. Performances are very long and involved, and draw from an extensive range of stories. The singers select which portion of the epic to perform, depending on the occasion, the demands of the audience, and their own skill. The Golla Suddulu do not use the sword and shield. Their performances may also include the large, brass, crescent-shaped horn known as a *kommu* (figure 7). The herding castes have an affinity for this instrument, and use it also in parades and ritual situations.

REFERENCES

Gangadharam, Nedunuri. 1968. *Minnēru: Jānapada Gēya Ratnāvaḷi* (River of the sky: a necklace of folk songs). Rajamahendraramu, Andhra Pradesh: Pracina Grandhavali. In Telugu.

Ramaraju, Biruduraju. 1958. *Telugu Jānapadagēya Sāhityamu* (Telugu folk-song literature). Hyderabad: Andhra Racayitala Sangham. In Telugu.

Roghair, Gene H. 1982. *The Epic of Palnāḍu: A Study and Translation of Palnāṭi Vīrula Katha*. Oxford: Clarendon.

Subbaravu, Tangirala Venkata. 1976–1977. *Kāṭamarāju Kathālu* (The stories of Katamaraju), 2 vols. Hyderabad: Andhra Pradesh Sahitya Akadami. In Telugu.

Tamil Nadu

Richard K. Wolf
Zoe C. Sherinian

Masinagudi Mariyamman Festival *Richard K. Wolf*
Musical Regions *Richard K. Wolf*
Social Status, Identity, and Musical Style *Richard K. Wolf*
Ensembles *Richard K. Wolf*
Vocal Traditions *Richard K. Wolf*
Christian Music *Zoe C. Sherinian*

About 63 million Tamils live in India, most of them concentrated in Tamil Nadu 'Tamil Country', India's southeasternmost state. The Tamil language they speak is the oldest Dravidian language for which written evidence exists. In addition to its roughly 90 percent Hindu population, Tamil Nadu has a substantial number of Christians and Muslims, and some Jains. The hills host some of the state's tribal populations—Kurumbas, Iruḷas, Kotas, Todas, and Paṇiyas—all of whom speak Dravidian languages. These tribes do not consider themselves Tamils, although they do participate in Hindu worship and in some cases identify themselves as Hindus. Some have converted to Christianity.

MASINAGUDI MARIYAMMAN FESTIVAL

Before the onset of the rainy season each year, Tamils of many faiths and castes participate in colorful fairlike festivals devoted to the goddess Mariyamman. Like other large religious events in India, Mariyamman festivals are not only matters of ritual or solemn devotion but also complex social and economic encounters among often diverse populations. Mariyamman controls rain, healthy crops, and fertility; she protects her devotees from diseases, such as chicken pox, that are caused—according to indigenous belief systems—by excessive heat in the body. Music and dance are two important means of propitiating the goddess, making her happy and keeping her "cool"; when devotees become possessed, the music and dance performances also become vehicles for the goddess's presence.

Along the road between Ooty in the Nilgiri hills (westernmost Tamil Nadu) and Mysore (southern Karnataka) is the town of Masinagudi, home of the goddess Maciniyamman, one of Mariyamman's sisters, and the tribal village of Bokkapuram, home of another form of the goddess. In February, thousands gather for the Masinagudi festival: rural villagers, forest-dwelling tribal peoples, urbanites who wish to fulfill a vow or are simply curious, and a host of professionals with both commercial and spiritual interests. These professionals include musicians, vendors, priests, puppeteers, circus troupes, gamblers, forest guards, police, and welfare officials of one sort or another.

Such Tamil festivals coalesce around central events often connected with the

The pot carriers danced as they moved forward, bending each leg in time with every three-beat unit, each man keeping the pot on his head balanced with the right hand, sometimes also with the left.

reenactment of local mythologies; in the case of Mariyamman, the event usually involves a conflict between the goddess and a demon. Highly visible and palpable is a sprawling multitude of localized kin- or community-based activities, including bhajan singing or dancing by clusters of devotees and processions of colorfully outfitted people bouncing jauntily, water pots balanced on their heads. Near certain sites, such as temples or rivers, devotees must take turns filling brightly decorated pots with water, or receiving the goddess's blessings through divine vision (*darśan*, *taricanam* in Tamil).

A processional

The family of a young man named Subramaniam, who worked in a budget tourist hotel in Ooty, came every year to the Masinagudi festival. While conducting fieldwork in Tamil Nadu in 1991, I found his family in leisurely repose under a temporary canopy, elaborately decorating narrow-necked, round-bellied brass water pots with yellow and white flowers to form cone shapes (according to local tradition, the festooned flowers are shaped one way for gods and another for goddesses). On one side of each cone they affixed a metal image of the goddess. If the procession leader, in this case Subramaniam, has undergone several days of dietary restrictions and has carefully observed rules of ritual purity, he may carry a special pot (*śakti karakam*) containing the goddess's power or *śakti* (Tamil *satti*).

Subramaniam led the procession, consisting mostly of female relatives dressed in red saris. Members draped large garlands of the yellow and white flowers around their necks and carried the decorated water pots on their heads. Facing the pot carriers and walking backward was a father-and-son team of professional priest-singers. The musicians' function was to invite the goddess forward and make her happy with agreeable music and words. The goddess was seen to reside at various times and in various senses inside the pot, in the metal image affixed to the pot, in each of the individual processioners (if they were possessed), and especially in the leader of a group.

M. Virarakavan, the senior priest-singer, sang while squeezing the strings of an hourglass-shaped tension drum (*kōṭānki*) with his left hand and striking it with the fingers of his right hand. The drum, sometimes called *uḍukkai* (usually a smaller version of the same drum), had a fiber snare and projected a thick penetrating sound. Kopalan, the son, rapped two sticks, one thin and one thick, on the *tappaṭṭai*, a frame drum about 35 centimeters in diameter. These professional singers had learned the song texts from printed sources. They played the drums so close to their mouths that individual words were obscured, rendering the singing and drumming a continuous, efficacious entity.

The drummers played a particular 6/8 rhythmic pattern associated with the *karakam* procession and dance in Tamil Nadu: the hourglass drum player emphasized beats 1, 3, 4, and sometimes 6, occasionally introducing an additional duple subdivision in beats 1–3 and 4–6 (figure 1), creating a tension between duple and triple that

FIGURE 1 *a*, Typical 6/8 drumming pattern for *karakam* procession and dance; *b*, variation emphasizing duple meter.

is typical of many Tamil drumming styles. The pot carriers danced as they moved forward, bending each leg in time with every three-beat unit, each man keeping the pot balanced on his head with the right hand, sometimes also with the left. Other women clapped their hands and jumped up and down in time with the music, sometimes swooning in possession, sometimes putting vermillion on the heads of men to give them "power." These processions typically proceeded from a temple to a river and back to a temple. The final destination for this festival procession was the temple at Bokkapuram, whose guardians and priests were Iruḷas, a tribal community respected for their abilities as musicians and sorcerers.

Community and itinerant musicians

Along the road to Bokkapuram were many private groups of devotees (families, friends, or acquaintances from a particular town or village), and several kinds of musical ensembles. At one point I could see Kota tribal women dancing around a Tamil female medium of the goddess and singing songs to her in the Kota language (figure 2), as in the following excerpt of a song composed by Rajammal of Trichagadi village in the Nilgiris:

macanī amā macanī amā māyakārī macanī amā
bokkapūrē amanikē pavaḷa tērē kacuvēmē
cikkaminē vēcuvēmē cinadu keṛē vāmē amā
ukēramā ukēramā unacirēnē pācuvēmē

Macani mother! Magical one, Macani mother!
We build a red coral palanquin for Bokkapur mother!
We pray to Cikka mother, please come to us with a gold umbrella!
We sing to Uker mother with emotion.

Two ensembles of tribal instrumentalists, one Kota and one Iruḷa, were playing for circles of their respective community dancers just a few yards away from one another. A possessed man clad entirely in yellow was the center of attention for the

FIGURE 2 Kota tribal women singing in Trichagadi village near Ooty, 1984. Photo by Amy Catlin.

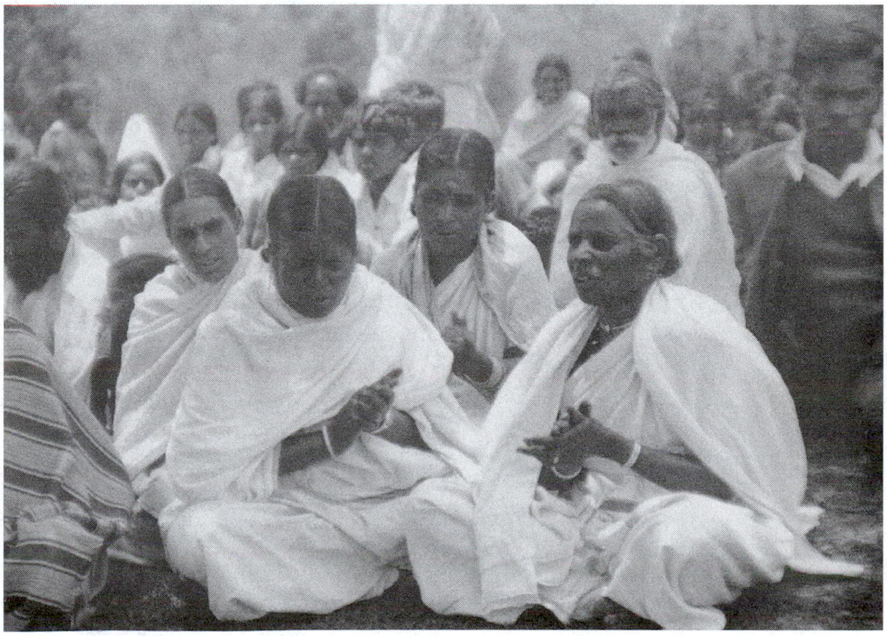

moment, as a venerable if somewhat-decrepit looking Iruḷa priest with long gray hair and a long, thick, curly gray beard whipped him. In this part of Tamil Nadu, according to Virarakavan, the goddess would order the priest to whip the devotee whom she had possessed until his or her trance state wore off when the goddess vacated the devotee's body.

Along the road I encountered Icvari and Matavan, itinerant musicians of the Vēṭar caste, who are traditionally hunters. Wearing a red-flowered cotton sari, Icvari sang Tamil and Kannada devotional and film songs while accompanying herself expertly on the *kañcirā* 'tambourine'. Matavan, a sinewy, strong-featured man wearing a color-coordinated pale-green bandana and safari shirt, played a harmonium suspended from his shoulder, and matched the pitch and rhythm of Icvari's melodies with uncanny precision. Their performance wove together variegated, now inseparable, strands of history and cultural tradition: favoring minor modal harmonies, Matavan elaborated on Icvari's folk rendition of movie songs. Icvari looked around while she sang; her voice was neither the mellifluous, high-pitched, thin voice of film songs nor the shouting, tonally imprecise voice of many professional Tamil stage actor-singers, but was deep and harmonically rich, loud, and penetrating. Her large lips, chapped and cracked from the dryness of the season, moved in almost exaggerated fashion around the "u" and "o" vowels of the song, plaintively heightening the shading of doubt these final sounds add to Dravidian interrogative phrases.

Scenes from Bokkapuram

At Bokkapuram, hundreds of tents were set up adjacent to the temple, some housing hastily erected shops, others sheltering whole families. Vendors hawked bright-hued flowers, fruits, bangles, and religious items as thousands of people walked by, turning the grassy areas into mud. Groups congregated around campfires or in tents to sing devotional songs, mostly in Tamil, Kannada, or Malayalam. I counted five different gambling games underway. Four ferris wheels were powered by men standing inside the wheel and nimbly stepping forward like hamsters on circular exercise equipment. Among the most popular entertainments was a finger-puppet show with dances choreographed to cinema songs, and a young girl's seductive dance, also to film songs. In another area, a member of a traditional barber caste shaved young children's heads, after which their parents offered the hair to the goddess. In a somewhat less-visited tent, family-planning movies ran almost continuously through the evening hours.

Buses, trucks, and cars came and went throughout the day and night, kicking up dust in dry areas, making deep ruts in wet places, and adding the diesel and petrol odors to the air without which an Indian *mēlā* 'festival' is never complete. Regiments of pot carriers arrived and departed, each exhibiting its own style of music, dress, and pot decoration.

MUSICAL REGIONS

Common throughout the state are certain traditional ritual, entertainment, and devotional musics that might be termed "classical" because they employ Karnatak tala and raga (or *paṇ*, the equivalent in ancient Tamil music), but styles and schools are regionally distributed. Traditions that do not employ tala and raga or that do so in ways that do not conform to scholarly treatment of these entities are somewhat more localized, defined sometimes according to their musical characteristics or style, frequently according to textual content, context, or instrumentation. The following overview of Tamil music divides the state geographically into three sectors: East and South; Central and North; and West.

FIGURE 3 The metrical pattern of a Tuticorin fishermen's song organized in groups of three (*top*), shown in relation to the rhythm of the oar strokes (*bottom*).

East and South

In cities of the eastern seaboard such as Tuticorin, fishermen sing distinctive songs while rowing or drawing in large nets. The "meters" of these songs, like those of most Tamil folk songs, are equivalent to duple, triple, and compound-duple time in Western terminology; songs sometimes begin with vocalizations in free rhythm. Most if not all of the fishermen's songs are antiphonal, pitting a single man or alternating individuals against a heterophonic chorus. The relationship between rowing and the sung meter is neither simple nor regular. A field recording illustrates the coordination between the creaking of the oars and the song's brisk triple meter (figure 3). The melodic phrases, particularly those in triple meter, do not resolve themselves into regular patterns of four, six, or eight; rather, the phrases overlap, as do the metric orientations of the sung phrases, providing an overall phrasing effect reminiscent of some Indian tribal musical traditions.

TRACK 15

In the southern districts of Tirunelveli and Kanyakumari, a ritual storytelling form called the bow song (*villuppāṭṭu*) is characteristic; it is named after the bow-shaped percussion instrument it features in performance (figure 4). This tradition places extraordinary emphasis on the sanctity of the written text, which is preserved on palm leaves (Blackburn 1988). These southern districts are also famous for the lament form called *oppāri* or *pilākkaṇam*. Tamil laments usually feature a nonmetrical, recitative-like descending melody interspersed with sobs. The texts are highly alliterative lists that enunciate what the deceased will no longer be able to do, what the mourner will be deprived of without the loved one (items and activities), and how wonderful the dead person was when alive (favorable comparisons).

Central and North

From the mid-seventeenth century, musical patronage during the reigns of the Telugu Nāyaks and Marāṭhās led to the flourishing of Karnatak music in the east-central district of Tanjavur. The northern kingdoms also brought with them their own regional musical forms that took hold and developed in the district. One such form of religious narrative was the *kālakṣēpam*, which included singing and instrumental music. In the late nineteenth century, Tanjore Krishna Bhagavatar is widely

FIGURE 4 The *villupāṭṭu* troupe Sivalingam Nadar plays (*left to right*) *tāḷam* cymbals, *villu* bow (using *vīsukkōl* rattle beaters), *kaṭṭai* (wooden clappers), and *kuḍam* brass pot on which the bow rests, struck with a *pālai* beater. Kanyakumari, 1984. Photo by Amy Catlin.

The Todas do not play instruments, with the tiny exception of the one aging performer who can still play the *puxury*, a bamboo trumpet.

FIGURE 5 Tep Venkatacalam Tevar Pillai sings the *kāman-pāndigai* debate form, also known as *lāvṇi*, and plays the *tēp*, also called *tappaṭṭai*, Madurai, 1984. Photo by Amy Catlin.

credited with combining Tamil folk styles, Karnatak music, and Marāṭhi *kīrtan* 'devotional song' to create the highly popular, modern *kālakṣēpam* form (Gurumurthi 1989; Nixon 1988; Premeela n.d.).

Bhāgavata mēḷā, a classical dance-drama enacted before temple idols by all-male troupes, also developed in Tanjavur district. According to popular belief, the form grew out of the Telugu dance form now called *kuchipuḍi*, which spread into Tamil Nadu after Muslim invaders drove the Nāyak rulers of the Vijayanagar empire south. The form has all but died out, although efforts to preserve and revive it in villages such as Melattur have been underway since the 1930s (Arudra 1986; Khokar n.d.).

Tradition also credits the Marāṭhās with introducing to Tanjavur the *lāvṇi* folksong genre, in which two parties engage in a musical debate on philosophical or mythological themes. The primary theme concerns whether or not the god of love, Kama, was consumed by the fire of Shiva's third eye. The *tappaṭṭai* 'frame drum' and the *tuntina*, a Marāṭhi plucked drum, accompany the *lāvṇi* (Lakshmanan Chettiar 1980) (figure 5).

Wet-paddy cultivation provides the context for an invocatory song form, *kuravai*, sung with melody only in Tanjavur district. In other parts of Tamil Nadu women perform a kind of ululation also called *kuravai* in conjunction with agriculture, on festive occasions, and at auspicious moments during rituals. The latter *kuravai* is an important marker of significant ritual moments but is not a form of singing.

A dramatic narrative form, *terukkūttu* (or simply *kūttu*) 'street drama/dance/music', is most popular in central and northern Tamil Nadu. Drawing on some of the same textual traditions as the southern bow song (*villuppāṭṭu*), such as the Mahabharata epic, it often recounts stories of local deified heroes and performers. Unlike the bow song, performers act out the stories instead of describing them, and both performers and audience members become possessed by the characters represented (Frasca 1990).

Another related form of sung narrative is the *uḍukkai pāṭṭu* of the Konku section in Coimbatore district in west-central Tamil Nadu. *Villuppāṭṭu*, *terukkūttu*, and *uḍukkai pāṭṭu* all describe or enact epic events of regional importance, and thus come under a more general label, *katai pāṭṭu* 'story-song'. *Uḍukkai pāṭṭu* derives its name from the *uḍukkai* 'small hourglass drum' with which the male singer accompanies himself (Beck 1982).

West

In westernmost Tamil Nadu, bordering the states of Kerala and Karnataka, lie the Nilgiri hills, home of South India's most celebrated tribal populations. The Todas have gained fame as objects of fascination to Westerners since the Italian missionary Jacome Finicio wrote the first authoritative account of them in 1603. Among Nilgiri tribes, they have a highly distinctive singing style characterized by deep, guttural, but tuneful undulation. They do not play instruments, with the tiny exception of the one aging performer who can still play the *puxury,* a bamboo trumpet.

The Nilgiri tribes can be divided into two major groups: those inhabiting the plateau and nearby slopes (Todas, Kotas, Alu Kurumbas, and Iruḷas), and those who live in the northwestern part of the district (Mullu Kurumbas, Beṭṭa Kurumbas, Kāṭṭu Nāyakkas, and Paṇiyas). The Todas, numbering some twelve hundred, live primarily on the Nilgiri plateau in many small isolated hamlets. Until the early twentieth century, they subsisted through the production of dairy products, but now practice agriculture and work in semiurban jobs. They used to fulfill a Brahmin-like role among the Nilgiris, serving as honored attendees at ceremonies of Baḍagas, Kurumbas, and Kotas. Until the onset of a modern cash economy in the past century, all Nilgiri tribes engaged in a system of reciprocal ritual and economic cooperation structurally resembling the *jajmānī* system elsewhere in India. The Hindu Baḍagas (some are now Christians), who considered themselves socially and politically superior to the Nilgiri tribals, were also singers, not instrumentalists. Now numbering nearly 150,000, the Baḍagas perform on pan-Indic instruments such as harmonium and tabla to accompany bhajan singing.

Until the late 1930s, Baḍagas and Todas used to hire Kotas (who number about fifteen hundred) to perform essential instrumental music for funerals. The Kotas, increasingly aware of the low status associated with performing music for other peo- TRACK 12 ples' funerals in Hindu society (although they still perform for their own), eventually discontinued this service (with rare exceptions), for they do not consider themselves inferior. The Kotas were not only musicians but also skilled wood and metal workers, basket makers, potters, hunters, and procurers of traditional medicines. They maintain these skills today, but on a diminished level, and no longer for other tribes.

The Iruḷas and Kurumbas provided services and forest produce to all three of these groups—Baḍagas, Todas, Kotas—and occasionally also performed music for them. Along with the Kotas, these two large groups (numbering perhaps ten thousand or more) play related musical styles in similar shawm and drum ensembles; their dance styles and rhythms also exhibit similarities. Now that Kotas no longer play funeral music for Todas and Baḍagas, Kurumbas and Iruḷas sometimes perform this function.

The Todas and Baḍagas also frequently hire small bands of Tamil or Kannada-speaking plains people to play at funerals. The bands consist of a clarinet, one or more tom-toms and/or snare drums, and metal maracas. Outfitted in brightly colored (though frequently tattered and stained) military band uniforms, the musicians provide essential instrumental music alongside the tuneful wailing of Todas. The kind of music Todas patronize has changed over the last half-century, but its importance and its ritual function (to honor the dead, among other things) have not.

Among the other major group of Nilgiri tribes in the extreme northwest, the most elite—the Wynad Ceṭṭis, a Malayalam-speaking Hindu caste, and the Mullu Kurumbas—have an elaborate verbal art but do not perform musical instruments. Instead they chant while performing circle dances around a sacred lamp, an art the Mullu Kurumbas call *vaṭṭakaḷi.* The two communities also perform several varieties of stick dances called *kōlāṭṭam,* also while circling a lamp. The middle-ranking communities, the Beṭṭa Kurumbas, Iruḷas, and Kāṭṭu Nāyakkas, utilize musical instruments and play musical styles almost identical to those of Kotas, Iruḷas, and Kurumbas elsewhere. At the low end of the hierarchy, Paṇiyas play double-reed instruments and drums of slightly different construction, and move differently while playing these instruments and while dancing. The Paṇiyas also perform an indigenous style of musical drama, which they are reviving from the state of decline it reached in recent decades.

SOCIAL STATUS, IDENTITY, AND MUSICAL STYLE

The division of musical labor in the Nilgiri hills in many ways parallels that found on the plains of Tamil Nadu. Three important similarities are (1) the association between ritual rank and the type of vocal or instrumental music performed: those of higher rank specialize in vocal forms, those of lower rank play drums and reed instruments; (2) the articulation of ritual rank through the differential status of patrons and hired musical performers: higher-status performers have higher-status patrons; patrons usually equal or outrank performers; and (3) the articulation of status by the auspiciousness of the event for which a musician performs, and the performer's proximity to the focus of an event.

Ritual rank and type of music

The musical culture of the highest castes in Hindu society, the Brahmins, like that of the high-ranking Nilgiri tribe, the Todas, focuses on vocal music and the power of correctly pronounced, intoned, or chanted words and sounds. The music of the lowest castes (Dalits or scheduled castes), in contrast, emphasizes percussion, rhythm, and the power or meaning of nonverbal sound. Scheduled castes (see below) have adopted the drum as a cultural emblem, although not all Tamil scheduled castes are in favor of this occupational link with drummers. One such caste, the Paṟaiyars, is named for the *paṟai* (another term for *tappaṭṭai*), the cowhide frame drum with which this caste is associated.

Brahmins do not perform ritual roles as instrumentalists because this would compromise their rank, making them musical 'servants' to their ritual patrons, but among themselves they do perform a wide variety of song types, some specific to particular occasions. Most varieties of Brahmin song, whether ritually specific, generically devotional, or domestic, tend to be based on Karnatak ragas (or at least compatible with South Indian raga classification). Lullabies are generally in *nīlāmbari rāga*; wedding songs sung when the bride and groom sit on a swing are often in *kuranji rāga*. Brahmins and other affluent communities generally have access to and resources for education in classical music, but there is nothing specifically Brahmin about classical music. Lower-caste performers of ballads, work songs, and folk-dance songs place less conscious emphasis on Karnatak raga melodies or talas, although they may incorporate classical pieces, or emulations of classical styles, into these genres. In many forms of Tamil folk music, vocal embellishments have classical counterparts; voice quality and intonation, however, tend toward norms different from those characteristic of Karnatak music.

Ritual rank and social status

Musicians belonging to the upper-middle-caste Iśai Veḷḷāḷars dominate in the most important and ubiquitous type of temple music in South India, that of the *periya mēḷam* 'big ensemble.' Until the 1930s, they were the traditional dance teachers, musicians, and dancers of *catir,* the temple dance now called *bharata nāṭyam*. The ensemble associated with the dance was called the *cinna mēḷam* 'small ensemble'. The musical styles of both are based on Karnatak ragas and talas; the repertoires and performance practices are somewhat different [see KARNATAK RAGA].

Iśai Veḷḷāḷars are not the only caste to perform in the *periya mēḷam*, but they have been the only ones to master both *periya mēḷam* and *cinna mēḷam* performance styles. This caste has historically been concentrated in the Tanjavur district, an important "seat" not only of Karnatak concert music but also *periya mēḷam* music. Iśai Veḷḷāḷar musicians in this district also perform for weddings and other auspicious occasions of Brahmins and high-ranking non-Brahmin castes.

The Naidus (*nāyuṭu*, a title associated with the Nāyaks), who migrated to Tamil

Nadu from Andhra Pradesh, are another set of castes associated with the *periya mēḷam*, and are especially known for their performance on the clarinet. They have helped popularize the practice of playing Karnatak music on Western band instruments (Terada 1992).

Scheduled castes

The scheduled castes, also referred to as untouchables, or Dalits, are the lowest-ranking members of the Hindu social order, outside the four classes of Brahmins, Kshatriyas, Vaishyas, and Shudras. The two best-known scheduled drummer castes are the above-mentioned Pa̱raiyars and the Telugu-speaking Cakkiliyars. The Pa̱raiyars are concentrated in east-central and northern Tamil Nadu, and the Cakkiliyars predominate in western Tamil Nadu. In areas where they overlap, both provide services as drummers. Neither drummer caste would participate in functions of the highest castes, but they do participate in various ensembles for village or district temple festivals attended by people of differing ranks and backgrounds. At these functions, the upper-caste *periya mēḷam* generally performs in close proximity to the temple or next to a temple cart (*tēr*) taken out on procession, whereas the scheduled-caste ensemble performs some distance away. In some locations, a nonscheduled caste drummer will perform on two cylindrical drums (*pampai*), one tied on top of the other, just a few feet away from the temple's central shrine, with a *periya mēḷam* just beyond this, and the scheduled caste further away. This arrangement represents both a caste and an organological hierarchy, for the *pampai* double drum and its player are credited with special supernatural powers.

Lower-caste musicians perform music at distances from the temple in inverse proportion to their ranks because higher castes believe them to be polluting to their temples, to their gods, and to their persons. Scheduled castes are not allowed inside higher-caste temples, despite laws to the contrary. The anthropologist Michael Moffatt found that the music of the *periya mēḷam* was considered auspicious or "good," and that of the Pa̱raiyars was believed to frighten away various classes of malevolent beings (Moffat 1979). Although this is certainly the function of some kinds of music in Tamil Nadu, it is not the only function of all music performed by untouchables, nor is it the function of music performed only by untouchables. Research remains to be conducted that explores scheduled-caste perspectives on their own roles as drummers.

Tamil language and Tamil music

The independence movement in India in the 1930s and 1940s not only fostered a sense of nation, of a primarily Hindu "unity" expressed in the arts through such reinvented traditions as *bharata nāṭyam* dance, it also stimulated an appreciation of "diversity" by fostering interest in regional art forms and languages. The poet Subramania Bharati, who died a quarter of a century before India gained freedom, revitalized the Tamil language, adapting it to suit the nationalist cause while also glorifying its own venerable past. Bharati composed songs and poems of social and political relevance, employing traditional forms derived from both ancient Tamil literature and contemporary folk songs, and instilled in his compatriots new pride in all things Tamil (Baskaran 1981; Roy 1974). Bharati was perhaps the most significant inspiration for the Tamil Iśai 'Tamil Music' movement of the 1940s.

In the decades leading up to the 1940s, Telugu and Sanskrit were the languages of classical music and dance and English was the colonial administration's language; in public life, Tamil was relegated to colloquial speech and scholarly and religious writings. Since most Tamils could not understand Telugu or Sanskrit, their understanding of music remained incomplete, especially since Tamil culture pays great lip

There is a substantial market for cassettes of folk music arrangements; the cassettes do not include descriptive notes, but some include song texts.

service to the importance of song texts (*sāhitya*). In the 1940s the proponents of Tamil music began to insist on the inclusion of Tamil-language Karnatak music compositions in every concert, and in some venues the performance of Tamil compositions exclusively (Ramachandran 1983). This led to a great controversy in the music world that continues to some extent today, a debate over whether the essence of music (*rasa* and *bhāva*) lies in pure sound (*nāda*) or in the language of song.

An organization called the Tamil Iśai Sangam was formed in 1943 to encourage the composition and performance of Tamil songs. To this day, the Sangam sponsors performances of Karnatak music compositions almost exclusively in the Tamil language, even if the performances are rendered instrumentally. The Sangam also sponsors research into Tamil music traditions of the past as well as those (such as *tēvāram*) not central to the concert tradition. The organization is particularly interested in demonstrating the link between the music described in ancient Tamil texts and modern-day classical music.

Indian musicologists have paid little serious attention to the many regional nonclassical traditions of Tamil Nadu, usually couching descriptions invidiously in terms of Indian classical music and omitting insiders' perspectives. Some writers with a performer's bent, such as Vijayalakshmi Navanitakrishnan, M. Navanitakrishnan, and K. Kuppuswami, have collected and learned Tamil folk songs and rearranged, orchestrated, and performed them in a light classical style. Proponents of Tamil folk music argue that although these performers change and decontextualize the songs, they also raise Tamil awareness of folk music and introduce it to a wider audience. There is a substantial market for cassettes of such folk music arrangements; the cassettes do not include descriptive notes, but some include song texts.

ENSEMBLES

The term for ensemble in Tamil is *mēḷam*, derived from the Sanskrit root *mil-* 'to gather, meet or join'. In North India, the Hindi word *mēlā* refers to a fair or festival. In Tamil, *mēḷam* refers either to a gathering of musical instruments or to the collection of frets on the vina. By extension, *mēḷam* has also come to refer to drums (especially the *tavil* 'barrel drum'), because drums are conspicuous at outdoor instrumental-music parties; *mēḷam,* however, does not mean "drum" in any literal or historical sense. Other terms for ensemble include *koḷvar*, an ensemble of double-reed instruments (*koḷ*) and drums (*par* 'cylindrical drum', *tabaṭk* 'frame drum') among the Kotas of the Nilgiris.

Periya mēḷam is composed of one or more *nāgasvaram* 'seven-holed shawm', one or more *tavil* 'barrel drum', *tāḷam* 'finger cymbals', and a drone, formerly an *ottu* 'shawm without finger holes' but now a *śruti peṭṭi* 'bellows-driven reed organ'. Performing for auspicious occasions such as weddings and temple festivals, these ensembles have historically been known for extensive unmetered improvisation (*ālāpana*) on the *nāgasvaram* and solo rhythmic improvisation on the *tavil.*

Classical and quasi-classical dance and drama ensembles

The *cinna mēḷam* of the 1930s and earlier, associated with temple dance, comprised a female dancer, a male dance master (*naṭṭuvanār*) who sang the rhythmic dance syllables (*jati*) while playing the finger cymbals (*tāḷam*), a junior dance master who also sang, possibly additional women singers, and instrumentalists playing flute or *mukhavīṇā* 'double-reed instrument', *mridangam* 'barrel drum', and bagpipe drone. Formerly the ensemble stood behind the dancer and moved forward and backward on stage according to her movements. The modern ensemble sits to one side of the stage. South Indian bamboo flute and clarinet came to replace the *mukavīṇai*; additional instruments include the vina. A bellows-driven reed organ, the *tamburā* string drone, or an electronic drone now replaces the bagpipes.

The *cinna mēḷam* instrumental grouping appears to persist in another transformation in the all-male Tamil drama form *terukkūttu*, which predominates in the central and northern parts of the state (Frasca 1990). As in *cadir* and *bharata nāṭyam*, the musical ensemble retains a close relationship with the drama company, remaining attached to it throughout the careers of the performers. On stage, the ensemble sits on an elevated platform in the rear, playing instruments from stage right to left generally as follows: pedal harmonium (*peṭṭi* 'box'), which replaces the drone-shawm (*ottu*), providing melodic support; an upright *mridangam* 'barrel drum' with left head facing down, shorter and squatter than its classical counterpart, thus providing a higher pitch; a horizontal *ḍholak* modified by the addition of a small bamboo stick for striking the right head; a 30-centimeter-long *mukhavīṇā* 'double reed'; and *tāḷam* 'finger cymbals'. The actors/dancers themselves sing, receiving vocal support (*pin pāṭṭu*) from the harmonium and from off-stage actors.

A related form of theater is *icai nāṭakam* 'music drama' or special *nāṭakam* 'special drama', with large actors' associations in Madurai, Pudukkottai, and fourteen other smaller towns. This form differs from *terukkūttu* in its inclusion of women as actresses and the practice of individually booking each actor and musician: there are no troupes or rehearsals, but rather a shared repertoire of dramas. *Icai nāṭakam* shares with *terukkūttu* a rather informal approach to classical forms (ragas and talas) and the linking of specific ragas with certain kinds of scenes; it also employs musical styles derived from folk genres and commercial film song. Two drummers provide the musical accompaniment: a *mridangam* player uses both vertical and horizontal drums similar to *terukkūttu,* and sometimes also the North Indian tabla; the other drummer, called the "all round," plays special effects on two bongos, tom toms (using face and rims), large cymbals, and other percussion instruments. The most prestigious musician in the ensemble plays the leg (*kāl*) harmonium, with bellows driven by a foot pedal, and provides vocal melodic support; following him in status are the *mridangam* player, the "all round," and finally the player of the finger cymbals.

Folk ensembles

Whereas the *periya mēḷam* and *cinna mēḷam* are classical-music ensembles associated with ritual and dance, respectively, the *naiyāṇṭi mēḷam* is a folk ensemble associated with both ritual and dance. The melodies are based not on ragas but on specific song tunes (*meṭṭu*), and the percussion patterns are organized into talas that are closer to the *ṭhēka* 'specific ostinato patterns' of Hindustani music than to classical Karnatak tala: folk talas tend to be specific percussion patterns on which the performer can elaborate in particular ways on individual instruments.

The distinction between "folk" and "classical" may be analytically difficult to draw in some musical traditions, but Tamils today do make the distinction linguistically. Tamil terms referring to "the folk" appear to describe indigenized versions of nineteenth-century European notions, and the twentieth-century Western disciplines

FIGURE 6 A *naiyāṇṭi mēḷam* ensemble of Kallar men playing (*left to right*) *pampai, tavil, śruti* box, two *nāyaṇam, jālra, tavil, tamukku, pampai,* and *uṟumi* (rubbed membranophone). Usilampatti, Madurai district, 1984. Photo by Amy Catlin.

of folklore and anthropology have also contributed to the development of this terminology. *Nāṭṭupuṟam* 'countryside' is used as an adjective with words such as song (*pāṭal*), art (*kalai*), and literature (*iyal*) to denote folk song, folk arts, and folk literature, respectively. Tamils similarly employ other adjectives, some specifying village rather than city.

Naiyāṇṭi mēḷam *folk ensemble*

The Tamil word *naiyāṇṭi* means "teasing" or "cajoling," and refers to the light-spirited, raucous, sometimes slightly obscene tenor, behavior, and performance of this kind of folk ensemble. The *naiyāṇṭi mēḷam* performs on festive occasions, for dance-dramas or for demonstrations, and consists of players from varying backgrounds. The ensemble usually accompanies professionalized versions of ritual dances such as *karakam* and *kāvaṭi* (a dance associated with the god Murugan, in which dancers perform with a bow-shaped burden on their shoulders), or other staged folk dances such as the hobby-horse (*poy kāl kutirai* 'false leg horse'), *kuṟavan-kuṟatti* (the playful, erotic banter of a romanticized tribal/gypsy couple), and buffoon dances (the standardized comic role in a drama).

The *naiyāṇṭi mēḷam* usually consists of two *nāyaṇam* 'shawm slightly shorter than the *nāgasvaram*', one *ottu* 'double-reed drone', one or two *tavil* 'barrel drums', a tension drum consisting of two cylindrical drums laced together (*pampai*), a pair of conical drums tied around the player's waist and played with curved sticks (*kirikaṭṭi* or *kuṇṭalam*), a small kettledrum played with thin leather straps (*tamukku*), and finger cymbals (*jālra*) (Deva 1987; Sambamurthy 1971) (figure 6). Unlike Karnatak music, where the tempo as articulated by the tala remains fixed, the music of the *naiyāṇṭi mēḷam* speeds up considerably at the conclusion of certain kinds of pieces.

Other ensembles

In some ensembles, the association of a particular piece with a particular dance or ritual is indicated both by the percussion pattern employed and by the melody. In moving down the hierarchy of ensembles, diagnostic musical features of a piece (and characteristics that identify pieces with particular rituals or dances) change, from ragas and melodies (in the *periya mēḷam*) to melodies (*meṭṭu*) and percussion patterns (in the *naiyāṇṭi mēḷam*), and finally to rhythm alone. In the latter ensembles, invariably composed of scheduled caste (Paṟaiyar and Cakkiliyar) drummers, the relationship among percussion instruments is foremost; the melody moves to the background, remaining inaudible or entirely absent, and when audible, does not exhibit significant variation from piece to piece. Performers often number the rhythmic patterns: one beat (*oraṭi*), two beats (*reṇḍaṭi*), and so on, each increasing in density and complexity. The numbers appear to refer to groups of drum strokes, not to *mātrā* counts characteristic of Karnatak tala [see KARNATAK TALA].

In these latter ensembles, which I have located in Dharmapuri and Salem districts, the leader is a *tappaṭṭai* 'frame drum' player, the figurative king (*rāja*) of the ensemble. Specially featured in some of these groups are one or more double-headed ceramic barrel drums (*mattaḷam*) and one or more shallow kettledrums (*tāca*), which are suspended from the player's waist and beaten with two sticks.

Some communities associate an ensemble composed of *nāgasvaram*, *pampai*, and *uṟumi*, sometimes called an *uṟumi mēḷam*, exclusively with inauspicious occasions such as funerals. The *uṟumi*, an hourglass-shaped rubbed membranophone, is widely believed to have positive supernatural powers, particularly among the Telugu-speaking Kampalattar Nāyakar caste. When the ensemble plays for Kampalattar Nāyakar all-male line dances (*tēvarāṭṭam*) followed by circle dances (*cēyvaiyāṭṭam*), the ensemble consists of two or three *uṟumi* players, one of whom serves as the leader. This form involves no singing. It is unusual in the Tamil context that the dancers play two instruments while they dance: the *cēkaṇṭi* 'bronze gong' affixed to the dancer's waist and played with a 30-centimeter-long stick attached to the left index finger, and the *cēvai palakai* 'lizard-skinned tambourine' (Vicayalatcumi 1983).

Tribal ensembles in the Nilgiris

TRACK 12 The Kotas, Iruḷa subgroups, and Kurumba subgroups (except for the Mullu Kurumbas) play a cognate set of musical instruments in ensembles consisting of at least two double reeds of up to 46 centimeters in length (Kota *koḷ*), a frame drum (Kota *tabaṭk*), usually two or more cylindrical drums (Kota *par* or *kinpar*), and occasionally cymbals and long S- or C-shaped brass horns (Kota *kob*) (figure 7). Kotas use a large conical drum (*ērtabaṭk*) in addition to the brass horn for making announcements or to mark important ritual moments (in Tamil society, the *paṟai* drum fulfills

FIGURE 7 Kota musicians playing (*left to right*) *kob*, two *koḷ*, *tabaṭk*, *kinpar*, *kob*, *kinpar*, and *dhopar* in Kolimalai village near Ooty, 1984. Photo by Amy Catlin.

Illiterate villagers have created many folk songs, which should be described as "intuitively" composed; however, there is a long tradition of highly literate Tamil poets composing folk songs.

FIGURE 8 Common Kota rhythmic patterns presented in skeletal form: *a*, ten-beat *cādā dāk*; *b*, six-beat *cādā dāk*; *c*, seven-beat *cādā dāk*; *d*, eight-beat *tiruganāṭ dāk*.

this function). Iruḷas of the eastern, south-central, and western Nilgiris employ clay barrel drums (*kaḍime*, *tavil*, and *poṟe*, respectively) in these areas.

For solo instruments, most of the tribes employ end-blown bamboo trumpets (Kota *bugīr*) with five or six holes, on which they play songs and some of the shawm repertoire. This trumpet, along with a simple idioglottal bamboo clarinet (Kota *pulaṇg*), serve as the principal practice instruments for the shawm as well as for informal music making in domestic contexts.

The shawms of all the tribes have six holes, except that of the Paṇiyas, which has seven. The melodies sometimes tend toward diatonicism, but often a single note will fall between two diatonic intervals (such as a major and minor third). The variance from diatonic intervals is notable because Indian classical and popular musics are usually built on a twelvefold division of the octave, and other Nilgiri tribal songs tend be diatonic or at least have discrete pitches that correspond with South Indian classical pitches.

Melodies define instrumental ensemble pieces and tend to be short, with two to four phrases. The emphasis on melody in distinguishing one piece (and thus one significant context) from another represents a distinct break from observed behavior among lower-caste Tamils, who value percussive rhythmic elaboration and differentiation. The Nilgiri tribes share a limited number of rhythmic patterns. The most common are in cycles of six beats (compound duple), seven, eight, ten, and twelve beats. Figure 8 shows Kota versions of these rhythmic patterns (*dāk*) (Wolf 1997).

VOCAL TRADITIONS

Vocal traditions in Tamil Nadu, like those of instrumental ensembles, are almost always associated with the performance of dance, drama, or ritual. Some have instrumental accompaniment, and most instrumental melodies (except those of Nilgiri tribes) are based on songs. Singing styles and melody types vary enormously according to location, community, education, modernization, and degree of westernization. As mentioned above, Brahmin and other higher-caste vocal styles tend to share significant features with Karnatak music. Not only are these styles based on ragas or raga-like melodic entities, they also share with classical music features of vocal production: clear lyrics, distinct pitch definition, comparatively relaxed throat muscles, and mild nasalization. In contrast, non-Brahmin folk music, particularly of the lowest castes, tends to contain highly colloquial lyrics that are often significantly distorted by their musical renditions. Professional singers, who are often dancers and/or actors as well, tend to sing with very tight throats and significant nasalization. They also tend to shout or to sing with extreme forcefulness (*kaṭṭu pāṭukiṟatu*) in order to be heard over long distances. Shouting styles and some of the unaccompanied narrative styles may involve melodies of indefinite pitch, due either to wide vibrato or an almost spoken style, but pitches generally tend toward diatonic intervals.

Classical and folk melodies further differ in their pitch sets. Nonclassical regional singing, whether chant or sung narrative texts, women's circle dance songs (*kummi*), or devotional songs, tends to remain within restricted vocal ranges, sometimes as small as a fourth or fifth and containing only four or five tones. Seldom do songs range the entire two octaves or more of classical music. Folk melodies are similar to light classical ragas in their inclusion of more than one variety of a pitch class (*svara*), as in the use of both pitches approximating the Western minor and major third. While classical ragas may include two varieties of certain pitches, their use is usually quite restricted—either to an ascent or descent, or to rare phrases in which their novelty is highlighted. Folk melodies and light ragas (*rāga behāg,* for example) tend to make greater use of alternative pitches; there are no general rules along the lines of classical ragas that govern such melodies as a collectivity. Most common is the alternation of phrases using two varieties of the third degree. Thus the alternation of "major" third and "minor" third—and the frequent appearance of pitches lying between the two—suggests that conceptions of pitch differ between folk and Karnatak music.

Illiterate villagers have created many folk songs, which should be described as "intuitively" composed; however, there is a long tradition of highly literate Tamil poets composing folk songs. These literary folk-song forms have become part of mainstream village repertoires; in some cases, poets and scholars invented the genres. The songs recall ancient Tamil rules of prosody, which need to be considered in the definition of some folk genres. In general, meter and prosody are central to folk-music forms, particularly those connected with communal dancing. Meters tend to be duple, compound duple, triple, and septuple. At the beginning of an *oyilāṭṭam* or *kummi* song, for example, singers establish the rhythmic/poetic meter and the melody by singing syllables such as *ta na na ne*. This vocalization is then repeated beween verses as a type of refrain. In the *oyilāṭṭam* transcription (figure 9), the vocalization is indicated by syllables appearing directly below the notation. In rendering verses or composing new ones, singers must preserve the sequence of long and short motives set up in the vocalization. One line of Tamil-language text, shown below the vocalization in figure 9, provides an example of how the lexical text is articulated in relation to the vocalized pattern. The fourth bar shows how alterations in the rhythmic pattern are introduced to accommodate vowel length in the text. The song text describes a pilgrimage to a hill temple, and the text line roughly translates as "I playfully came along the path to the Kunta Malai hills." The clay pot accompaniment illustrates a common ostinato pattern in which duple and triple subdivisions of the half-note beat are played.

Song genres and their contexts

Virtually any day of significance is an occasion for song in Tamil Nadu [see SEASONAL AND LIFE-CYCLE RITUALS]. The most prominent occasions are annual reli-

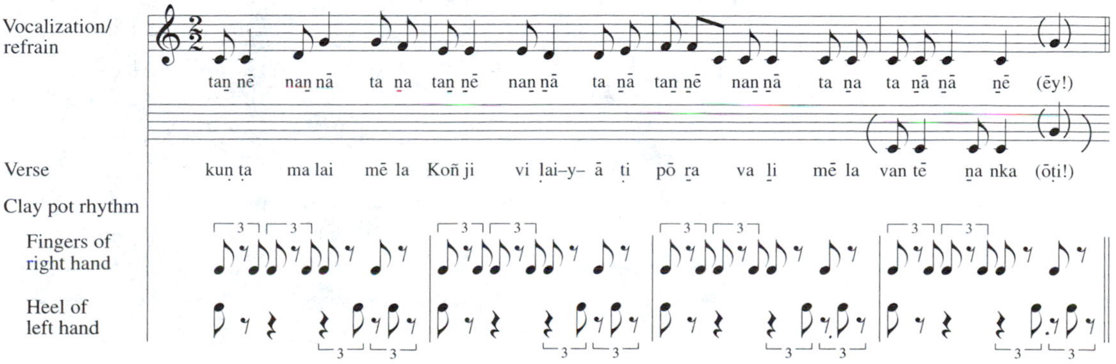

FIGURE 9 Tamil *oyilāṭṭam* song recorded by Richard K. Wolf in Madurai, 1982. The syllables directly below the notation are vocalizations on the song melody and rhythm; below the vocalizations is one line of Tamil song text indicating the relationship between the lexical text and the vocalized pattern. The clay-pot ostinato accompaniment sounds both duple and triple subdivisions of the half-note beat.

FIGURE 10 Bhajan procession with harmonium and *tambūrā* in Madras, 1977. Photo by Amy Catlin.

gious festivals, regular temple worship, and domestic events. In regularly scheduled singing sessions or in a temple during a festival, devotees, accompanied by an experienced leader, sing bhajans in a traditional order according to generally agreed-on rules (*padhati*). On other occasions, such as during a procession, devotees may sing whatever they wish (figure 10). In the morning during the month of Mārkaḻi, devotees sing *tiruppāvai* in Vaishnavite temples and *tiruvempāvai* in Shaivite temples; the verses are similar in form and content; both have intense, devotional (bhakti) texts in which the poet assumes the persona of a female devotee (Cutler 1979, 1987). Other parties of bhajan singers, called *kōṭṭi* (Sanskrit *gōṣṭhi*), may parade in the streets singing *nāmāvaḷi* 'string of names', antiphonal songs (usually in eight-count *ādi tāḷa*), *divyanāma sankīrtana* 'divine names and praises' (often sung while devotees circumambulate a sacred oil lamp), *tēvāram* (hymns composed by seventh-century Tamil Shaivite saints), *tiruppugaḻ* (complex metered devotional songs to Murugan composed by the fifteenth-century saint-poet Arunagirinadar), and other hymns.

Women and men sing and perform festival dance forms separately; the most important of these are *kummi*, *kōlāṭṭam*, and *oyilāṭṭam*. Song texts often recount mythological stories of general Hindu significance, which may or may not relate to the principal deity of a given festival. *Kummi* and *kōlāṭṭam* in particular are ubiquitous in Tamil Nadu, including most tribal communities, and in an extraordinary variety of styles.

Work songs and ritualized work songs

Folk songs accompany virtually every type of work, although they are on the decline in Tamil Nadu, due in large part to technological changes in the way work is accomplished in villages and in some measure to the proliferation of film songs. Just as ululation songs (*kuravai*) accompanied rice-seedling transplantion during wet-paddy cultivation, so also did special songs accompany sowing, plowing, and harvesting. Songs called *ēṟṟap pāṭṭu* once accompanied the hoisting of water buckets from an irrigation well by means of a bamboo pole. Sometimes these songs could serve several functions at one time: a mother could sing her child to sleep while performing the rhythmic irrigation work and singing. These songs were often of the counting variety, each stanza mentioning successive numbers. With the completion of each stanza, the singer would know how many buckets had been drawn.

Songs occasionally become part of a carefully circumscribed ritual performed before a potentially dangerous task. The Jēnu Kurumba tribe of the Nilgiris collects honey from nests lodged in rocky, often vertical slopes. Honey collectors sing to the bees (*jēn-paduna*) while hanging from ropes and smoking out the nests.

Until recently Toda culture was concerned almost exclusively with ritualized dairy farming, and Todas performed nearly every major kind of work—feeding salt to the buffaloes, rethatching a temple/dairy, preparing buttermilk coagulant—as a religious ritual accompanied by formulaic songs. Toda work songs, like Toda work and singing generally, are gender-segregated: women sing their own genre of work songs, called *tīm*.

Dance songs

Besides bhajans, the most important communally shared type of folk song in a Tamil village, particularly among women, is that associated with dance. Special ritual songs, such as those for weddings, are generally known only by a few women. Dance songs frequently involve a leader and chorus, thus enabling all to participate while at the same time learning the songs.

Kummi *and* oyilāṭṭam

Usually a circle dance, *kummi* invariably consists of a group of women singing while performing a variety of hand clapping patterns (*kummiyaṭi*) and dance steps (*aṭavu*) (figure 11). A leader and chorus perform some varieties of *kummi*, whereas in others all participants sing at once. In Dharmapuri district women perform a less common form of *kummi*: women sing antiphonally in two facing lines, clapping their hands while bending forward and not moving their feet. Men practice a similar form called *oyilāṭṭam* (also called *oyiṟkummi*), although the dances are different (figure 9 presents an *oyilāṭṭam* song). Men dress up in turbans, put on anklets, and dance in rows brandishing handkerchiefs in both hands. The song subjects are local historical tales or episodes from pan-Indic Hindu myths such as the Ramayana. Singers perform *kummi* either along with the dance or simply as songs: set pieces in a Tamil drama or illustrations of moral/religious points in a didactic context. Tamil Christians and

FIGURE 11 Girls and women demonstrating the *kummi* dance in Tuvariman village, Madurai District, 1996. Photo by Richard Wolf.

Noṇṭi cintu 'lame song' is the song form associated with Tamil Nadu's one-man music-drama genre. The play is a moral tale and a spectacle: the actor must perform for several hours with arm and leg bound up.

Muslims also use the *kummi* form to sing about their own religious traditions (Caktivel 1991; Perumal 1982).

The songs usually comprise pairs of short antecedent-consequent phrases of two or four counts. Each count is usually subdivided into three beats; if the tempo is slow, triple, duple, and compound-duple subdivisions may appear alternately as hemiola or simultaneously as polyrhythm. Performers clap out counts simply, one clap per count, or in a variety of patterns. Two pairs of phrases make up one line; lines are usually organized in couplets. Non-Brahmin women's *kummi* songs in Madurai and Dharmapuri district villages seldom exceed three tones. It appears from initial observation that men's *oyiṟkummi* may exhibit a wider ambitus than that of women's *kummi* in communities where both are performed. Also, in *oyiṟkummi* singers place more emphasis on rhythmic intricacy, the rhythm tends to be vocalized more frequently (using "tan nā nē" and so on), and the ends of songs usually speed up signficantly. Brahmin *kummi* tends to exhibit greater tonal range and, as with other genres, is sometimes set to classical ragas.

Kōlāṭṭam

Women perform *kōlāṭṭam* by knocking sticks held in each hand against one another and, often in complex patterns, with those of other dancers in a circle. Anklet-wearing dancers knock the sticks of their partners, skip one or more dancers in the circle, turn around and return to a new partner. In *pinnal kōlāṭṭam*, colorful ribbons join dancers' arms to a central pole—the dancer creates spiraling, lanyard-like knots of the colored ribbons, and unravels them by reversing the direction of the dance at the end. Although *kōlāṭṭam* still holds a place in ritual contexts (weddings, puberty ceremonies), it has been widely adopted for social occasions and public displays because Tamils find it interesting not only to participate in the dance but also to watch.

Cintu

Cintu was originally a song type with three divisions: *pallavi*, *anupallavi*, and *caraṇam*, as in the Karnatak *kīrtana* [see KARNATAK VOCAL AND INSTRUMENTAL MUSIC]. It is now usually a strophic song (the *caraṇam* section only) with a short melody and many verses. Often the *cintu* appears as a solo melody, such as when rendered on the double-reed *nāyaṇam* in a festival context. Musically, the *cintu* shares rhythmic features with *kummi* song—the prevalence of triple meter, sometimes in tension with duple meter, but also other meters. Unlike *kummi*, *cintu* is named for particular kinds of activity with which it is associated, and is thus similar to occasional songs, such as marriage songs or instrumental melodies of Nilgiri tribals, many of which are named for associated rituals or dances (Muttappan 1983).

Noṇṭi cintu

Noṇṭi cintu 'lame song' is the song form associated with Tamil Nadu's one-man music-drama genre, the *noṇṭi nāṭakam*, which flourished under the Tirunelveli petty chieftains or Poligars (*pāḷaiyakkārar*) of the eighteenth and nineteenth centuries. The drama depicted a parable of a debauched man's life. In punishment for a crime the man is subjected to the ancient Tamil punishment of *māṟu kāl māṟu kai*: amputation of an arm on one side of the body and a leg on the other. After his subsequent discovery of God, in recognition of supreme self-sacrifice and devotion, he regains his lost limbs. The play is a moral tale and a spectacle: the actor must perform for several hours with arm and leg bound up. Later versions of this dramatic form have diverged from the original plot, omitting the story of the cripple entirely, yet the actor still performed the drama, singing and dancing as if he were a cripple, with arm and leg bound.

The dialogue for this drama was composed in a special *noṇṭi cintu* meter. Like *kummi*, *noṇṭi cintu* is composed in two-line couplets, but unlike *kummi*, the first line is usually shorter than the second—the form thus iconically reproduces the physical condition of the protagonist. Typically the actor sings a passage and then dances while a *nāyaṇam* player repeats the melody in the background (Palacupiramaniyam 1991).

Kāvaṭi cintu

An ensemble sings or plays a *kāvaṭi cintu* while a Murugan devotee bears on his shoulders a large bow-shaped burden (*kāvaṭi*). The music induces possession and the devotee moves to the intoxicating meter of the *cintu* in a sort of dance (*kāvaṭiyāṭṭam*). According to popular belief, the Tamil poet Annamalai Reddiyar (1861–1891) created the musical-poetic genre when he was commissioned to compose devotional works on Murugan by a Tirunelveli Tēvar (a dominant landed caste) chieftain.

Verses have three, five, or seven lines rendered in alternate slow-fast-slow tempi. At the end of each verse the drummers perform a rapid interlude on the *nāyaṇam,* simultaneously sung by the devotees, to which the bow-shaped-burden carrier attempts to dance. The melodies are frequently raga-based, but in performance are not subject to the same grammatical strictures as classical music (Manikkam 1991; Subramaniam 1990).

Other cintu *varieties*

Many other *cintu* types exist, some quite obscure. It is unclear whether they all share musical or structural features with one another. *Vaḻinaṭai cintu* is a type of song that pilgrims or travelers sing to while away the time on a long journey. The song's metrical character tends to match the traveler's gait. *Vipattu cintu* recounts accidents; *nīti cintu* is a moral song; *kōlai cintu*, popular in the late nineteenth and early twentieth centuries in Tamil Nadu, recounts tales of famous murders; and *valaiyal cintu* is a song form sung by bangle sellers on special ritual occasions. Tamil converts to Islam, such as Acan Ali Pulavar, have composed *cintu* on the Prophet Muhammad, called *pūvaṭi cintu* (literally 'flower-feet song').

CHRISTIAN MUSIC

India's diverse spiritual and cultural landscape includes 20 million Christians. The state of Tamil Nadu is home to 3 million Christians, who make up 5.8 percent of its population—twice the national percentage. Portuguese Catholics were the first to convert Tamils to Christianity in the sixteenth century, followed by German Lutherans in the eighteenth century and British and American Protestants in the nineteenth century (Grafe 1990). More recently, Pentecostal and other independent denominations have started churches in South India (Caplan 1987). In 1947, a majority of the Christians associated with the disparate Protestant mission groups united to form the Church of South India (C.S.I.), creating a common liturgy and ecclesiastical system. Despite this merger, however, there is still great diversity of social identities and musical practices within the C.S.I. and throughout the Tamil Christian community.

Tamil Christians have a variety of social identities—including caste (Forrester 1980), class, denominational background, language, geographic location, and theological orientation—that correlate with their musical styles and forms. Tamil Christian music can be divided into three major groups: (1) English-language hymns and choruses using Western instrumentation; (2) *pāmalai* and *ñanapāṭṭu* (Western hymns translated into Tamil while retaining their English or German tunes and meters); and (3) indigenous Christian music sung in the vernacular and using musical styles, poetical forms, and instruments that express culturally contextualized Christian hermeneutics. These indigenous styles include Karnatak (classical or light classical), folk, and light music, the latter fusing elements of Western pop with Indian folk and light classical music (Innasi 1994).

Western Christian music

Tamil Christians use German hymn tunes as well as American popular choruses and pop or folk-style songs composed by Indian youth. English-speaking congregations, particularly in the larger cities, regularly sing choruses like "What a Friend We Have in Jesus" and pieces from standard collections such as *Hymns Ancient and Modern.* Many C.S.I. congregations have continued to practice the liturgical and musical traditions of the conservative Anglican missions in which they are rooted. They employ the organ instead of indigenous instruments and Western hymns more than Tamil *kīrtana*, a Hindu religious song form.

The use of European music reflects a larger movement that began in the early nineteenth century, promoting westernization and identification with Britain and America as well as with the values of capitalism, materialism, and, often, evangelical Christianity (Grafe 1990; Hardgrave 1969; Wilson 1982). The English-speaking urban congregations that employ European music consist of educated upper- and middle-caste/class Tamil Christians, although some are upwardly mobile middle-class Shudras and Dalits (formerly called untouchables). Due to the influence of missionaries, these lower-caste people have strongly identified with Western education and Victorian puritanism in order to raise themselves from their former status. Singing hymns in English symbolizes their new cultural identity.

Western hymns translated into Tamil

Western missionaries began translating the Bible and Western hymns into Tamil in the seventeenth century. They employed European hymn tunes, and attempted to adapt their Tamil translations to their musical meters. Unfortunately, they were unable to preserve the linguistic character and classic poetic structure of Tamil, rendering the lyrics almost meaningless. The result of this musical fusion was two genres: *pāmalai*, used by the C.S.I., and *ñanapāṭṭu*, used by Lutherans. Today, in the liturgy of most urban middle- and lower-class Protestant churches, three out of four musical pieces are *pāmalai*. In contrast, poor rural congregations never used hymns; from the eighteenth century onward, Protestant missionaries employed Karnatak *kīrtana* 'devotional songs', which were musically closer to village traditions than were Western hymns.

Indigenized Christian music

The contemporary movement toward indigenizing Christianity in India began in the

FIGURE 12 The Tamil Nadu Theological Seminary Community Carol Service Choir, directed by the Reverend James Theophilus Appavoo, 1993. Photo by K. Sam Ilango.

mid-twentieth century among both Catholics and Protestants who believed in contextualizing Christian hermeneutics in Indian culture and art (Amirtham and David 1990). The Catholics started ashrams (religious retreats), built churches in Hindu architectural style, and began Karnatak music and dance schools. The locus of the Protestant movement for indigenizing Christianity is the Tamil Nadu Theological Seminary in Madurai (figure 12). The seminary has created six Tamil music liturgies in Karnatak style as well as hundreds of classical, folk, and light songs.

Christian Karnatak music

The Italian Jesuit Robert de Nobili first composed Christian Karnatak music to attract potential Brahmin converts in the early seventeenth century. Upper-caste converts brought the classical poetic and musical traditions of Hinduism to Indian Christianity, along with caste divisions and the practice of ritual separation. Until recently, they controlled positions of influence in the church as priests, bishops, pastorate committee members, theologians, and choirmasters. Consequently, they have had a tremendous impact on indigenized music and theology, particularly in promoting Karnatak music as the ideal indigenized style.

Indigenous Christian music includes *kīrtana* 'three-part devotional song form' (also commonly called "lyrics" in Indian English), bhajan (devotional call-and-response form), and *Tamil iśai vaḻipāṭṭu* 'Tamil music liturgy'. *Tamil Church Hymnal and Christian Lyrics* contains more than four hundred Christian *kīrtana*, many of which were composed in the eighteenth and nineteenth centuries by famous upper-caste Christian poets such as Tanjore Vedanayakam Sastriar and H. A. Krishna Pillai (Francis 1988). The American Congregational missionary Edward Webb first published this Tamil hymnal in 1853 and disseminated it among Protestants of all class and caste levels as a more meaningful hymn collection for Tamil speakers than English hymns or *pāmalai* (Chandler 1913). Many Protestants still use *kīrtana*, although the songs are not accessible to the majority of Christians today because their lyrics use either sanskritized or literary Tamil and Brahminical theology.

Tamil iśai vaḻipāṭṭu are musical liturgies in Karnatak style that use both *kīrtana* and bhajan form. They appear in both the C.S.I. prayer book and the Tamil hymnal. Karnatak musicians teach these liturgies in seminaries, and the young pastors then transmit them to their congregations.

Tamil Christian light-music troupes often employ Western rock instrumentation or "orchestras" that include violins, flute, harmonium, and tabla along with drum set and electric guitars.

Christians view raga, tala, and the three-part *kīrtana* or call-and-response bhajan form as Karnatak characteristics of this indigenous Christian music. While most Christians sing *kīrtana* and bhajans in congregations, a few have had the opportunity to receive advanced training in Karnatak vocal music and sometimes perform solos in a service or wedding. The degree of "classicalness" in such a performance depends on the individual's ability to interpret the *rāga gamaka* 'microtonal pitch ornaments' or to improvise variations. Most Christian choirs sing a simplified, codified tune that represents only the skeleton of the raga, although they often perform rhythmically complex *svara* (solfège) passages with complex rhythms in unison.

Christian Karnatak accompanying instruments differ from Hindu Karnatak instrumentation. Christians employ either harmonium and tabla in a light classical style, or they fuse raga-based melodies with Western harmonic organ accompaniment. On special occasions a violin or flute accompanies the melody in unison. Since the 1940s, traditional *kīrtana* sung in urban Protestant churches have had organ accompaniment. However, pitches in the chords that are used tend to undermine the rules of raga, resulting in a Western hymn quality rather than a Karnatak sound.

Christian light music

Tamil people use the designation "light music" for film music and other orchestral or band music that imitates the film-song sound. The term "film music" is rare. Tamil Christians, especially middle- and lower-middle-class urbanites, have used this light style widely in the last twenty-five years, often referring to it by the common Tamil translation *mel iśai*, literally 'soft music'. Evangelical groups in particular have exploited the mass appeal of commercial film style to attract gospel-convention audiences and to communicate their messages of *āsirvādam* 'blessing' theology. But liberation theologians have also used its simpler language and musical forms, as these are more accessible to poor and less educated Christians.

Christian light music includes simple choruses in functional harmony as well as elaborate film-style orchestrated arrangements. Its transmission is primarily through cassette recordings and live performance at gospel meetings, festivals, weddings, and events sponsored by Christian educational institutions. Until the late 1980s, formal church services rarely included light music because of its association with Indian film song; with the 1988 edition of the Tamil hymnal, which incorporated a number of popular light-music songs, its use has increased. Light-music troupes often employ Western rock instrumentation or "orchestras" that include violins, flute, harmonium, and tabla along with drum set and electric guitars.

Among the most famous Indian gospel singers are the Reverend Dinakaran Sara Navaroji, Father S. J. Berkmans, and the Reverend Ezekiel George. One of India's most famous commercial film playback singers, Yesudas, has also recorded many cassettes of Christian devotional music. Recently, Protestant theologians such as M.

Thomas Thangaraj added their light-music compositions to the 1988 edition of the Tamil hymnal as a new section entitled "Songs of New Life" (Francis 1988).

Christian folk music

Christian villagers have used Tamil folk music (*girāmiya pāṭṭu,* literally 'village songs') since at least the mid-twentieth century for Christmas and other festivals (Grafe 1990; Innasi 1994). Some American missionaries encouraged the transmission of Bible stories through musical genres like *kālakṣēpam* 'sacred epic story narration' and *kummi* 'women's circle dance'. Yet because missionaries and high-caste Christians considered folk music culturally degraded, they allowed its performance only outside the sanctity of the village church; the congregations inside sang classical *kīrtana* during services. Urban congregations virtually never use folk music.

Since the 1980s, liberation theologians have begun questioning the accessibility and meaningfulness of classical *kīrtana* singing to the poor and lower-caste people who make up 75 percent of the Tamil Christian community. These theologians have proudly reclaimed folk music's positive value for use in the church, as it reflects the experience and values of the Tamil majority (Clarke 1994; Prabhakar 1989; Webster 1992; Wilfred 1992; Wilson 1982). As a result, clergy and musicians in both Protestant and Catholic churches have begun to incorporate Christian texts set to traditional folk songs into meetings, conferences, and services as a means of consciousness raising and unification against social and economic oppression in both the church and the greater society. Some Christian folk-song books have been published and distributed among congregations; much of this music is transmitted orally (Appavoo 1986).

In 1994 the Reverend James Theophilus Appavoo, a C.S.I. theologian, composed one of the first liturgies entirely in folk-music style. He conservatively followed the C.S.I. liturgical structure, since this innovation was very progressive, but he replaced the traditional high literary and sanskritized Tamil with spoken Tamil. He also used music, metaphorical language, and content integral to Tamil Nadu folk culture. Instead of employing the upper-caste metaphor of Jesus as a powerful king riding a horse, for example, Appavoo portrays Jesus as a farmer who "removes the weeds and *nerinji* thorns from the fields of his people's hearts" (Appavoo 1994). Appavoo's version of the Lord's Prayer is illustrative, as in the opening text (translated by Theophilus Appavoo and Zoe C. Sherinian) (figure 13):

> Vānattila vāḻukiṟa pettavarē sāmi [repeated]
> Āmā pettavarē sāmi, [repeated]
> on pērveḷaka vēṇum sāmi viḍatalai varavēṇum [repeated]
>
> The divine one, our parent living in heaven (repeated)
> our parent divine one, yes our parent divine one
> let the meaning of your name be "let there be freedom" (repeated)

The text continues: "We don't want the rule of the wicked but your just rule. Let the flag of your will be in this world as it flies in heaven, and give us daily the '*Oru olai*' [communally shared, literally 'one pot'] food."

The music in Appavoo's folk liturgy draws from the rhythm, melody, and moods of Tamil folk genres, for example, *kummi* 'women's circle dance', *oyilāṭṭam* 'men's line dance', *temmāngu pāṭṭu* 'duet with alternating vocal lines', and laments. In his 6/8 meter setting of the Lord's Prayer, Appavoo creates a rhythmic tension of three beats against two in the melodic rhythm and percussion pattern typical of lively Tamil folk dance. Men and women sing in octave unison (figure 13 shows the women's line

FIGURE 13 Opening text and verse setting of the Lord's Prayer by James Theophilus Appavoo (1994). The vocal line shows alternating leader and chorus melodies. The drum accompaniment includes *uḍukkai*, tabla (replacing the more common *tavil*), and *paṟai*. Transcription by Zoe Sherinian. Reprinted with permission.

only) in a leader-chorus format with a rotating leader. Village drums accompany the singing: an *uḍukkai* 'small hourglass drum'; *tavil* 'barrel drum', or a Western-style snare drum without snares played with a soft mallet and hand; and *paṟai* 'frame drum'. When available, instruments such as the bamboo flute, harmonium, *nāgasvaram* 'double-reed aerophone', and tabla also provide accompaniment.

Appavoo is actively reclaiming folk culture as a legitimate source of Christian liturgical expression in order to build a sense of self-esteem and cultural pride among poor and Dalit Christians. He encourages his students and their village congregations to indigenize or recompose his songs to fit their contexts and thus participate fully in the construction of a Christian theology that reflects their identities, values, and needs.

Besides this Christian folk music movement, the most recent Christian musical trends are light-music arrangements of classical *kīrtana* and folk songs for guitar or film-style orchestras. More individual Christians are studying Karnatak singing, instrumental performance, and dance. Although caste and class remain among Tamil Christians, these social differences do not prevent access to particular musical styles, as they did in past decades.

REFERENCES

Alavantar, R. 1981. *Tamiḻar Tōṟ Karuvikaḷ* (Leather instruments of the Tamils). Madras: International Institute of Tamil Studies.

Amirtham, Samuel, and C.R.W. David. 1990. *Venturing into Life.* Madurai: Tamil Nadu Theological Seminary.

Appavoo, James Theophilus. 1986. *Folk Lore for Change.* Madurai: Tamil Nadu Theological Seminary.

———. 1994. *Girāmiya Isai Vaḷipāṭṭu* (Worship in folk music). Unpublished liturgy from the Tamil Nadu Theological Seminary, Madurai. In Tamil.

Arudra. 1986. "Bhagavata Mela: The Telugu Heritage of Tamil Nadu." *Sruti* 22:18–24.

———. 1986. "The Resurrection of the Bhagavata Mela." *Sruti* 22:25–28.

Balakrishnan, Shyamala. N.d. "Folk Music of Cholamandalam." *Kalakshetra Quarterly* 9(4): 16–18.

Balakrishnan, Shyamala, Padma Subramanyam, K. S. Vasudevan, and N. Vasudevan. *Folk Music of Tamilnadu.* N.d. Gramophone Company of India, ECSD 3233. LP disk.

Baskaran, S. Theodore. 1981. *The Message Bearers: The Nationalist Politics and the Entertainment Media in South India 1880–1945.* Madras: Cre-A.

Beck, Brenda. 1982. *The Three Twins: The Telling of a South Indian Folk Epic.* Bloomington: Indiana University Press.

Blackburn, Stuart H. 1988. *Songs of Birth and Death: Texts in Performance.* Philadelphia: University of Pennsylvania Press.

Blackburn, Stuart H., and A. K. Ramanujan, eds. 1986. *Another Harmony: New Essays on the Folklore of India.* Berkeley: University of California Press.

Caktivel, S. 1991. "Kummi-Kōlāṭṭam." In *Vāḻviyaṟ Kaḷañcuciyam,* vol. 2, 643–645. Tanjavur: Tamil University. In Tamil.

Canmukacuntaram, C. 1980. *Tamiḻil Nāṭṭuppuṟap Pāṭalkaḷ* (Tamil folk songs). Chidambaram: Manivacakar Nulakam. In Tamil.

Caplan, Lionel. 1987. *Class and Culture in Urban India: Fundamentalism in a Christian Community.* Oxford: Clarendon.

Chandler, John S. 1913. *Seventy-Five Years in the Madura Mission.* Madurai: American Madurai Mission.

Chandrasekharan, K. n.d. "Kuravanji Dance of Kalakshetra." *Kalakshetra Quarterly* 3(4):7–14.

Clarke, Sathianathan. 1994. "Christ as Drum: A Constructive Proposal for Indian Christian Theology." Ph.D. dissertation, Harvard Divinity School, Harvard University.

Cutler, Norman. 1979. *Consider our Vow (Translation of Tiruppāvai and Tiruvempāvai into English).* Madurai: Muttu Patippakam.

———. 1987. *Songs of Experience: The Poetics of Tamil Devotion.* Bloomington: Indiana University Press.

Deva, B. Chaitanya. 1987. *Musical Instruments of India: Their History and Development.* 2nd rev. ed. Delhi: Munshiram Manoharlal.

Folk Songs of South India. N.d. Gramophone Company of India, MOCE 1004. LP disk.

Forrester, Duncan B.1980. *Caste and Christianity: Attitudes and Policies on Caste of Anglo-Saxon Protestant Missions in India.* London: Curzon.

Francis, Dyanandan, ed. 1988. *Christian Lyrics and Songs of New Life.* 15th ed., enlarged and revised. Madras: Christian Literature Society.

Frasca, Richard. 1990. *The Theatre of the Mahābhārata: Terukūttu Performances in South India.* Honolulu: University of Hawaii Press.

Grafe, Hugald. 1990. *History of Christianity in India,* vol. 4, part 2: "Tamilnadu in the Nineteenth and Twentieth Centuries." Bangalore: Church History Association of India.

Gurumurthi, Prameela. 1989. "The Evolution of Harikatha." *Sruti* 53:37–39.

Hardgrave, Robert L., Jr. 1969. *The Nadars of Tamilnad: The Political Culture of a Community in Change.* Berkeley: University of California Press.

Hart, George L. 1975. *The Poems of Ancient Tamil: Their Milieu and Their Ancient Counterparts.* Berkeley: University of California Press.

Innasi, S. 1994. *Dimensions of Tamil Christian Literature.* Madras: Mariyakam.

Jayalakshmi, Salem S. 1990. "Tamil Music: A Survey." In *Encyclopedia of Tamil Literature,* vol. 1, 175–186. Madras: Institute of Asian Studies.

Khokar, Mohan. N.d. "Bhagavata Mela Nataka." *Kalakshetra Quarterly* 9(3):23–25.

———. N.d. "Kuravanchi Natakam." *Kalakshetra Quarterly* 9(3):26–27.

———. N.d. "Bommalattam" (Puppetry). *Kalakshetra Quarterly* 9(4):23.

Kuckertz, Joseph. 1969. *Südindische Tempelinstrumente,* ed. Dieter Christensen. Klangdokumente zur Musikwissenschaft KM 0001. Berlin: Museum für Völkerkunde. LP disk.

Kunacekaran, K. A. 1988. *Nāṭṭuppuṟ Maṇṇum Makkaḷum* (Folk country and people). Madras: New Century Book House. In Tamil.

Lakshmanan Chettiar, S. M. L. 1980. *Folklore of Tamilnadu,* 2nd ed. New Delhi: National Book Trust.

Lourdu, D. 1990. "Folklore in Tamiḻnāṭu: A Survey. " In *Encyclopedia of Tamil Literature,* vol. 1, 451–68. Madras: Institute of Asian Studies.

Manikkam, M. 1991. "Kāvaṭi Cintu." In *Vāḻviyaṟ Kaḷañcuciyam,* vol. 2, 266–267. Tanjavur: Tamil University. In Tamil.

Moffatt, Michael. 1979. *An Untouchable Community in South India: Structure and Consensus.* Princeton: Princeton University Press.

Muttappan, Pala. 1983. *Cintu Ilakkiyam* (Cintu grammar). Madras: International Institute of Tamil Studies.

Nixon, Michael. 1988. "Nantaṉār Carattiram in Performance: An Item in the Tamil Musical-Dramatic Repertoire." M.A. thesis, Wesleyan University.

Palacupiramaniyam, R. 1991. "Noṇṭi Cintu." In *Vāḻviyaṟ Kaḷañcuciyam*, vol. 2, 858–860. Tanjavur: Tamil University.

Periyakkaruppan, Ram. 1991."Tālāṭṭu" (Lullaby). In *Vāḻviyaṟ Kaḷañcuciyam*. Tanjavur: Tamil University.

Perumal, A. N. 1981. *Tamil Drama: Origin and Development.* Madras: International Institute of Tamil Studies.

———. 1982. *Kummi Pāṭalkaḷ* (Kummi songs). Madras: International Institute of Tamil Studies. In Tamil and English.

———. 1984. *Tamḻar Icai* (Music of the Tamils). Madras: International Institute of Tamil Studies.

Prabhakar, M. E. ed. 1989. *Towards a Dalit Theology.* Delhi: ISPCK, published for the Christian Institute for the Study of Religion and Society.

Premeela, M. N.d. "Harikatha—A Composite Art Form." *Kalakshetra Quarterly* 9(4):24.

Radhakrishnan, N., ed. 1982. *The Beating Drum and the Dancing Feet: An Introduction to Indian Folk Performing Arts.* Kerala: National Centre for Development Education and Performing Arts.

Raghavan, A. Srinivasa. N.d. "Rama Nataka Kirtanas." *Kalakshetra Quarterly* 6(2):22–24.

Ramachandran, Anandhi. 1983. "The Tamil Isai Movement: A Battle of Words." *Sruti* 2:4–9.

———. 1983. "Oduvars: A Hoary Tradition of Hymn Singing." *Sruti* 2 (Nov):12–13.

Ramanathan, S. 1960. "A Survey of the Traditions of Music, Dance and Drama in the Madras State." *Bulletin of the Institute of Traditional Cultures, Madras* 2:214–221.

Ramasamy, Thulasi. 1987. *Tamil Yakṣaganas.* Madurai: Vizhikal.

Ramasubramaniam, V. N.d. "Kamban's Epic as Shadow Play." *Kalakshetra Quarterly* 3(4): 25–34.

Roy, Kuldip K. 1974. *Subramanya Bharati.* New York: Twayne Publishers.

Sambamurthy, P. 1971. *A Dictionary of South Indian Music and Musicians,* vol. 3. Madras: Indian Music Publishing House.

Singer, Milton. 1980 [1972]. "The Rādhā-Krishna *Bhajanas* of Madras City." In *When a Great Tradition Modernizes: An Anthropological Approach to Indian Civilization*, 199–249. Chicago: University of Chicago Press; Midway Reprint.

Siromoney, Gift. n.d. "Musical Instruments from Pallava Sculpture." *Kalakshetra Quarterly* 2(4):11–20.

Srinivas, M. N. 1944. "Some Tamil Folksongs," parts 1 and 2. *The Journal of the University of Bombay*, vol. 12, parts 1 & 4. July 1943: 48–80, and Jan. 1944: 6–86. Reprint.

Subramaniam, V. 1990. "Annamalai Reddiar's Kavadichindu: Beautiful Songs for Dance—But Neglected." *Sruti* 67:36–38.

Terada, Yoshitaka. 1992. "Multiple Interpretations of a Charismatic Individual: The Case of the Great Nagasvaram Musician, T. N. Rajarattinam Pillai." Ph.D. dissertation, University of Washington, Seattle.

Vallavan, C. 1985. *Nāṭṭuppuṟaviyal Kaṭṭuraikaḷ* (Tamil folk literature). Madras: Maitili Patippakam.

Vanamamalai, N. 1981. *Interpretation of Tamil Folk Creations.* Trivandrum: Dravidian Linguistics Association.

Vatsyayan, Kapila. 1987. "The Deccan, Eastern and Western Ghats." In *Traditions of Indian Folk Dance*, 2nd rev. enl. ed., 303–368. New Delhi: Clarion Books.

Vicayalatcumi, P. 1983. "Tēvarāṭṭam." Ph.D. dissertation, Madurai Kamaraj University, Madurai, Tamil Nadu.

Webster, John C. B. 1992. *A History of the Dalit Christians in India.* San Francisco: Mellen Research University Press.

Wilfred, Felix. 1992. *Leave the Temple: Indian Paths to Human Liberation.* Maryknoll: Orbis.

Wilson, Kottapalli. 1982. *The Twice Alienated Culture of Dalit Christians.* Hyderabad: Booklinks.

Wolf, Richard. 1997. "Of God and Death: Music in Ritual and Everyday Life. A Musical Ethnography of the Kotas of South India." Ph.D. dissertation, University of Illinois at Urbana-Champaign.

Kerala

Rolf Groesbeck
Joseph J. Palackal

Kerala became an Indian state shortly after Indian independence in 1947; its boundaries were drawn on linguistic lines. Kerala was specifically defined as the state whose native language is Malayalam, one of the seventeen official state languages of India. Although the two use different alphabets, Malayalam is closer to Tamil than to any other Indian language, for the original language of the Kerala region was an archaic form of Tamil. Malayalam only emerged as a distinct language around the tenth century (for more on Kerala's history, see Sreedhara Menon 1988).

Kerala is situated on the southwest coast of India, bordered by the Western Ghat Mountains on the east and the Arabian Sea on the west. The population of Kerala is now around 29 million, and largely rural. There are several major cities, but none has more than about half a million people. The population is about 58 percent Hindu, 19 percent Christian, and 23 percent Muslim, with a small number of Jews. Rice, tapioca, and spices are important crops.

The musics of Kerala exhibit a remarkable diversity, which scholars and laypersons have categorized into a threefold scheme. The first category is popular music, referring to music disseminated primarily through the mass media and the recording industry. Popular music includes a large amount of film music (the Malayalam film industry is one of the largest regional cinemas in India) comparable in style with that of the rest of India [see FILM MUSIC: SOUTHERN AREA]. It also incorporates an equally important amount of vocal sacred music (*bhaktigāṇa*) unconnected with film, though stylistically related to film music. Trivandrum and the central Kerala cities of Trichur and Palghat are centers of classical Karnatak music, the second category [see KARNATAK VOCAL AND INSTRUMENTAL MUSIC]. The third category comprises a vast range of predominantly vocal (though occasionally instrumental) folk musics—that is, anything that does not fit comfortably into either the popular or the classical category—some of which is associated with dance and drama. The temple music of high-ranking Hindu castes discussed in this article does not fit easily into any of these three categories; it is related to Karnatak music in some ways but not in others. The later sections of the article survey Christian, Muslim, and Jewish music as well as some of Kerala's popular music.

A common village scene in central or northern Kerala is a street procession of elephants followed by an ensemble composed mostly of drummers.

HINDU DRUMMING TRADITIONS

One of the first things you notice as a visitor to a village in central or northern Kerala is the drums. Especially if you come between mid-November and mid-May, roughly the dry, hot season, a common scene is a street procession of elephants followed by an ensemble composed mostly of drummers, with a crowd of enthusiastic townspeople in the rear. Near a temple you will quite likely hear drummers playing, particularly during the temple's annual festival. If you pass the house of a Mārār (drummer/singer temple caste), you may even hear the sounds of drumming very early in the morning. Drumming is indeed ubiquitous around temples and processions in Kerala. Since the heart of music in Indian Hindu worship is singing, why is drumming so crucial in this region of the country?

Part of the answer lies in the role of drums in South India's ancient history. In his study of ancient Tamil poetry of two millennia ago (1975), the writer George Hart notes that one type of drum typically followed Tamil kings into battle, and was beaten when they awoke in the morning. This drum was given daily baths and had a bed of its own. Taking an enemy king's drum after vanquishing him in battle gave the conqueror the rights to the enemy's kingdom. Before a battle, another drum was beaten to assemble soldiers, and yet another accompanied courtesan dance. The vast majority of musical instruments mentioned in these poems are drums, and they apparently played a wide variety of preeminent roles in ancient South Indian society. Much has changed in Kerala since that time—the introduction of temple worship, the dominance of the Brahmin community and of Sanskritic Hinduism, the institution of the modern caste system, the many recent political and economic changes—but the centrality of drums has remained constant.

HINDU MUSICIAN CASTES AND THEIR DUTIES

Approximately two-thirds of Kerala's Hindus are low-caste (*avarṇa*). Particularly large lower castes are the Iḻavas (producers of toddy, an alcoholic drink), the Āśāris (carpenters), and the Pulayas (agricultural workers), among others. Of the high-caste Hindus, most are Nāyars (formerly warriors), while about 3 percent of the population belongs to even higher castes: the most important, in descending rank, include the Nambudiri Brahmins (priests), Brahmins from other states (mostly Ayyars from Tamil Nadu), and a number of temple servant castes. The Mārār drummer/singer caste is one of the latter. Partly because many Ayyars live in Trivandrum, the capital city in the far south, the culture of southern Kerala (particularly as manifested in its architectural style and temple music) is in some ways more closely related to that of Tamil Nadu than to the rest of Kerala.

The drummers, other instrumentalists, and even singers who perform temple music in Kerala have particular responsibilities to their home temples. Families from several high castes are assigned to play specific instruments for daily rituals as well as for an annual festival (often as long as ten days) and several smaller festivals.

Instrumentalists also accompany dance and theatrical stage performances, in the temples and elsewhere. Mārārs, members of the principal high-ranking musician caste, often live in houses adjacent to their village temples and play for the temples' rituals between about 6:00 A.M. and 9:00 P.M. The vast majority of drummers (both Mārārs and others) are male, with just a few female *ceṇṭa* 'double-headed cylindrical drum' players, who are usually not Mārārs and do not play for rituals. Formerly, the temples compensated the Mārārs with shares of rice paddy every month, gardens in which to grow vegetables, and cows to provide milk for yogurt, so that ideally they would be able to devote themselves entirely to music. Within the last thirty years, as temples have replaced this arrangement with a monthly salary, few families are able to live on the income, and many Mārārs have become freelance performers who tour sporadically six months of the year. Others leave the family profession altogether and take white-collar jobs, such as official political positions.

Other high-ranking musician castes include the Cākyār Nambiyārs, who play a drum that accompanies the Sanskrit drama genre *kūṭiyāṭṭam*; the Kuṟuppās, who make drawings with colored powders and sing songs to propitiate a deity (Jones 1982); and the Nambiśśans, who are principally garland makers but a few of whom play barrel drums for temple rituals. Together with the Mārārs, these castes among others are "temple servants." The Nāyar caste, though not primarily a musician caste, includes a number of families of instrumentalists. In most Hindu musician castes, men from a given family inherit their temple musical rights and responsibilities from their mother's brothers, although less so today than in the past.

Additionally, a number of the lower castes perform music as part of their caste jobs. The Puḷḷuvas assist in the snake-god (Naga) propitiation ritual called *pāmpin tuḷḷal.* They make drawings similar to those created by the Kuṟuppās; they also sing, perform a dance in which they rub their bodies with a lighted torch, assist the Nāyar priest in his stewardship of the ritual, and play musical instruments (Neff 1995). Pāṇans go from house to house singing songs late at night at certain times of the year, and also take charge of the drumming performances at low-caste temple festivals (comparable to performances by Mārārs and Nāyars in the high-caste temples). Paṟayans are mostly agricultural workers, but sometimes drum for low-caste festivals as well. Lastly, Vaṇṇāns (generally herbal physicians and tailors), Malayans (umbrella makers), and Vēlans (basket weavers) often sing and play instruments for the low-caste *teyyam* ritual in northern Kerala, which propitiates a variety of local heroes, war gods, and incarnations of the Mother Goddess. A ritual specialist, possessed by a deity, performs the ritual acts (Freeman 1991; Ashley 1993).

Instruments

The principal instruments played by the Mārārs are the *ceṇṭa*, 'cylindrical drum' played with one or two sticks (figure 1); the *iṭaykka*, 'small tension drum' played with a stick (figure 2); the *timila*, 'hourglass hand drum'; the *maram*, 'cylindrical hand drum' used only in special rituals; a conch shell; and a flat gong used to keep time. Every Mārār drummer must master all of these. In addition, Mārārs must learn the principal Kerala style of temple singing, called *sōpānam saṅgītam (sōpānam* 'steps', referring to the steps that lead to the temple's inner sanctum; *saṅgītam* 'vocal or vocally based music'). There are three genres of *sōpānam saṅgītam*, including one based on the twelfth-century North Indian poem *Gīta Govinda*.

The other high castes of musicians specialize more. Some of the Cākyār Nambiyārs play only a huge pot drum (*miḻāvu*); the drummer Nambiśśans and a few members of other castes play the *maddaḷam* 'barrel drum' (figure 3); and those Nāyars who are instrumentalists for the most part play either the *maddaḷam*, *kompả* 'semicircular horn', *kurum kuḻal* 'small shawm', a pair of cymbals, or one of the

FIGURE 1 *Ceṇṭa* drummers and cymbal players in a *ceṇṭa mēḷam* ensemble. Irinjalakuda, Kerala, annual temple festival, May 1989. Photo by Rolf Groesbeck.

instruments in the *periya mēḷam* ensemble: the *nāgasvaram* 'large shawm', or the *tāvil* 'barrel-shaped drum' played with one hand and one stick. The latter ensemble provides the core of instrumental music in most South Indian temples; in the central and northern sections of Kerala, however, it is usually of secondary importance. Most musicians learn to play instruments at home from older male relatives, starting often around the age of seven and studying in the very early morning (some get up as early as 4:00 A.M. to start their technical exercises) and in the evening. When they have mastered the basic lessons on their instruments, they give a ceremonial first performance (*araṅṅēṟṟam*), after which they may perform either publicly or for rituals (for more on Kerala instruments, see Rajagopalan 1974).

Although some low musician castes play the same instruments as the high castes, others play less common instruments. The Puḷḷuvas play three instruments: a musical bow strummed with a polished piece of wood (*kuṭam*), a one-stringed bowed lute normally played as a drone (*vīṇā*), and cymbals roughly comparable to those used by the Nāyars (Neff 1995). The castes that perform for the *teyyam* ritual play a smaller version of the Nāyar *kurum kuḻal*, the same *ceṇṭa* drum played by Mārārs, sometimes the *nantuṇi* (a drone instrument also formerly played by Kuṟuppās), and a small pair of cymbals (Freeman 1991; Ashley 1993). The Pāṇans and Paṟayans today perform on the same instruments played by the Mārārs and Nāyars.

FIGURE 2 D. Parameswara Kurup (next to his house) with his *iṭaykka* tension drum. Alleppey District, Kerala, 1990. Photo by Rolf Groesbeck.

Genres

The musician castes learn a huge number of compositions and genres. For the most part these genres relate to specific ritual and stage contexts. One of the most important temple musical genres is *koṭṭippāṭissēva* 'drumming-and-singing offering' (Omchery 1969); Mārārs present this vocal performance with *iṭaykka* 'tension drum' accompaniment before the *pūjā*, the priest's adoration of the deity in his or her sanctum. Since these adorations usually take place five times daily throughout Kerala, Keralites associate the sound of the *iṭaykka* drum with temple worship. Two other ensembles that frequently accompany processions of the deity through the temple grounds or the streets are the *pañcavādyam* 'five instruments' and the *ceṇṭa mēḷam* 'drum ensemble', respectively. These terms refer both to the specific ensembles and to the genres they perform. The *pañcavādyam* ensemble includes roughly ten *maddaḷam*

FIGURE 3 Students at the Guruvayur Vadyavidyalayam (temple arts institution) play *maddaḷam* drums and dummy *nāgasvaram.* Guruvayur, Kerala, 1990. Photo by Rolf Groesbeck.

'barrel drums', ten to fifteen *timila* 'hourglass hand drums', one or two *iṭaykka* 'hourglass tension drums', ten *kompā* 'semicircular horns', and fifteen cymbals—thus "five [types of] instruments"—as well as a conch shell to start the performance. Solo passages alternate with unison playing. The *ceṇṭa mēḷam* (also referred to simply as *mēḷam*) includes roughly forty-five *ceṇṭa* 'cylindrical drums', fifteen *kompā* 'semicircular horns', fifteen *kurum kuḻal* 'small shawms', and thirty pairs of cymbals (see figure 1). In both ensembles the numbers are not fixed; usually the richer the temple and the more special the occasion, the larger the number of instruments.

When certain processions come to a halt inside the temple grounds, there is often a series of instrumental performances by smaller groups. Hindus believe that their deities, like cultured humans, are lovers of the arts and will be pleased if a particularly talented soloist shows his abilities. The four performances, always in the following order, are *tāyampaka,* usually a *ceṇṭa* drum solo with cymbals and other *ceṇṭa* drums as timekeepers (although occasionally two, three, or even five drums will share the solo role) (Rajagopalan 1967; Groesbeck 1995); *kēḷi,* a solo for *maddaḷam* drum (or duet for *maddaḷam* and *ceṇṭa,* or ensemble piece for several *maddaḷam* drums) with cymbals and flat gong as timekeepers (*kēḷi* is largely a transcription of *ceṇṭa tāyampaka* for *maddaḷam*); a solo or duet for the *kompā* horn, with cymbals as timekeeper; and a solo for *kurum kuḻal* shawm and *ceṇṭa* accompaniment, again with cymbals keeping time. Finally, immediately before certain processions, a few Mārārs play a piece for *maram* 'cylindrical hand drum' or *timila* 'hourglass hand drum' called *pāṇi* (literally 'palm of the hand'). Mārārs believe that *pāṇi* is particularly important, its purpose being to call the gods to attend a ritual; they believe that the drummer must play *pāṇi* perfectly in order to call the gods correctly, and that if he doesn't, he will die within a year.

A number of dance and theatrical genres also have drum accompaniment. The most famous of these is the dance-drama *kathakaḷi* 'story-play', a nine-hour series of scenes mainly from the Hindu epics Mahabharata and Ramayana, accompanied by *ceṇṭa, maddaḷam,* and singers, who keep time with the flat gong and cymbals (Jones 1983; Jones and Jones 1970; Zarrilli 1984) [see MUSIC AND DANCE: SOUTHERN AREA]. The *iṭaykka* plays a minor role. *Kūṭiyāṭṭam* 'acting together', a liturgical drama based on Sanskrit literature from over a millenium ago, has accompaniment by the *miḻāvu* and a pair of tiny cymbals (Richmond, Swann, and Zarrilli 1990). *Mōhini*

Every day, many Kerala Hindus go to the temple before work and are likely to hear the temple's drummer, who stands at the steps leading to the inner sanctum, playing the *iṭaykka* drum and singing.

āṭṭam 'dance of the enchantress' is a solo dance recital for a woman and is accompanied by *iṭaykka*, occasionally by *maddaḷam*, and usually also by a Karnatak music ensemble (Venu and Paniker 1983; Kalyanikutti Amma 1990). A dance-drama closely related to *kathakaḷi* is *kṛshṇāṭṭam* 'play of Krishna', which is accompanied by *maddaḷam* drums, *iṭaykka*, and singers. Nowadays, most performances of these genres are cultural programs not connected with temple ritual; they were once part of court entertainment. Many leading landowning and royal families in Kerala used to support *kathakaḷi* troupes, allowing the members to live and rehearse in their homes.

In general, temple drums do not participate in modern, film-influenced stage genres such as *nāṭakam* 'drama' and *bālē* (cognate of "ballet"); the music for such performances is closer to film music.

A variety of castes provide music for a number of nonspecialist vocal genres. These include the songs for *tiruvātira kaḷi*, a women's group activity that also features dancing and hand clapping, and is often performed as an offering for an auspicious marriage, usually in December; and occasional songs such as boat songs, songs celebrating the lives of heroes, and agricultural songs.

MUSICAL CONTEXTS

Music in daily temple rituals

How does temple music fit into the daily life of an ordinary Kerala Hîndu? Every day, many Hindus wake up close to daybreak and go to the temple before work. On arriving, they might hear the temple's Mārār drummer, who stands at the steps leading to the inner sanctum, playing the *iṭaykka* drum and singing music from the *sōpānam saṅgītam* tradition. The vocal tradition is dying out more quickly than the drumming traditions, for nowadays many Mārārs only play the *iṭaykka* and dispense with the singing. The priest then cues the drummer to stop playing by opening the doors of the sanctum (the priest is the only person allowed inside), revealing the deity and thus initiating the worship ritual; worshipers crowd around the sanctum (or the door to the temple's cloister), craning their necks to get a glimpse of the deity. Direct eye contact (*darśan*) with the deity is a very important part of Hindu devotion in Kerala as elsewhere in India. The worshipers pray and give money to the priest, who in turn gives them flowers, sandalwood paste, and/or sweets. After some time, the Mārār may resume playing. Later, the priest may remove a portable replica of the deity from the sanctum and carry it in procession around the sanctum, then around the temple's cloister, giving offerings to stones representing the temple's minor deities as he goes. This procession ritual, which typically occurs three times a day in the wealthier temples, is called *śīvēli*; it gives the devotees an opportunity to worship the deity in the open air. Before this procession, the Mārārs play *pāṇi* to invite the gods, and during this they and some Nāyars play a small version of the *ceṇṭa mēlam* ensemble. Other temple servants in the procession carry lamps, and the devotees follow the procession, all the while attempting to view the deity.

After one or two worship rituals in the sanctum and one *śīvēli*, Kerala Hindus look at their watches and leave for work. Temples often close down in the middle of the day, particularly during the afternoon, when most Keralites are taking naps after their lunch. However, devotees attempt to go back to the temple around sunset, during which time there is another *pūjā* adoration, another *śīvēli* procession, and a sunset adoration called *dīpārādhana* 'worship with lamps'. In this last devotion, hundreds of lighted wicks adorn the inner sanctum and the cloister as the drummers perform a composition similar to *kēḷi* (or else a segment of *tāyampaka*, if the temple has no resident *maddaḷam* player). After the last *pūjā* of the day the temple closes its doors and worshipers go home, perhaps to do further worship at their household shrines. The centrality of worship in the daily life of Kerala Hindus and the ubiquity of drumming (and to a lesser extent singing) in temple worship can hardly be overstated.

Music in festivals and non-Brahminical temple rituals

During the dry season, the nightlife in Kerala's villages, particularly its high-caste temples, perks up significantly. Keralites often celebrate during all-night festivals; the Kerala author K. R. Vaidyanathan once described the temple as a "house of prayer, a social club, and a cultural center," and this characterization is particularly apt during festivals (Vaidyanathan 1977). The people continue their normal working schedules during the day and get scarcely any sleep at night.

What happens at these nighttime temple festivals? The principal events are expansions of processions—of which large temples may hold twenty or more within a ten-day period—and cultural programs on stages located within the temple grounds. These cultural programs may include *kathakaḷi* dance-drama, *mōhini āṭṭam* and other South Indian solo female dance genres, Karnatak music concerts, *periya mēḷam* performances, and live concerts of Malayalam popular music and theater genres. In procession, the accompanying *ceṇṭa mēḷam* (or *pañcavādyam*) performance is typically expanded from a few minutes to one, two, or even four hours. The procession usually contains a pause during which the replica of the deity is removed from its perch atop an elephant (at temple festivals there are typically around fifteen elephants, all dressed up in bright ornamental coverings) and placed on a stool, from which it watches the series of instrumental solos (see "Genres" above). Of these, by far the most important is *tāyampaka*, with *ceṇṭa* cylindrical drums and cymbals; sometimes several *ceṇṭa* soloists will perform *tāyampaka* on a given day. All of the temple festivals are garish and ornate, a few remarkably so; the Puram festival in Trichur (a city in central Kerala), for example—*pūram* refers to both a constellation and the festival held under that constellation—features a display of brightly colored umbrellas under which the elephants stand, many *pañcavādyam* and *mēḷam* ensembles, and typically about a quarter of a million spectators.

Kerala temples are the sites of other activities besides festivals, including regular nonspecialist group devotional singing (bhajan). But the most popular temple events are the festivals at large Brahminical temples that include major performances of *pañcavādyam*, *mēḷam*, and the other drumming genres, in addition to *kathakaḷi* and solo dance. Indeed, these festivals are the primary arenas not only for religious activity but also for social life in general (outside the home) in most of Kerala. (Restaurants, cinemas, and tea shops are also important social centers, but the first two are attended primarily by men.)

Why are festivals so important? A young Mārār, an engineering student, once responded to my question of why he had forsaken his caste job to move into another profession by answering another question: why Mārārs in general continue doing their caste job. He said, "When Bhagavati [the wrathful Mother Goddess] is happy, she showers her blessings onto us, and we are happy. We want to keep her happy, so we play *mēḷam.*" Indeed, Kerala's folklore is full of stories about Bhagavati's rage when she has not been propitiated sufficiently, and Keralites clearly consider festivals necessary transactions; the greater the number of musicians, the greater the sound they make; the more impressive the procession, the greater the likelihood that Kerala's gods will be pleased and will spread good fortune among their devotees.

In addition to the high-caste temple festivals, a number of propitiation rituals, mostly by low castes, contribute to Kerala's dry-season religious and cultural life. These include the *pāmpin tuḷḷal* snake-god ritual lasting several days, and the *teyyam* propitiatory ritual lasting a full night and into the next morning. The *muṭiyeṯṯu* is a mother-goddess propitiation ritual performed only in south-central Kerala by about eight Mārār and Kuṟuppā families. It features singing, *ceṇṭa* drumming, and cymbal playing (Caldwell 1995). The *pāna* is another mother-goddess propitiation ritual in which the *ceṇṭa* players are Nāyars. Various regions of Kerala feature other all-night or longer rituals, often to the Mother Goddess, but many of these are becoming increasingly rare (Tarabout 1986).

MUSICAL STRUCTURES

The rhythmic and formal structures of temple drum compositions are very different from each other. In particular, *tāyampaka* and *kēḷi* are far more complex than *ceṇṭa mēḷam*. Yet virtually all drum genres exhibit the key concepts of repetition and reduction, of which the latter is particularly crucial. Early in my own *ceṇṭa* drum studies, my *āśān* 'preceptor' grabbed my field notebook and drew a series of rectangles: a long horizontal one at the bottom, a slightly shorter one above, and several more on top of this, each shorter and narrower than the last, with a very narrow one at the top, and finally a straight vertical line (figure 4). He explained to me that each rectangle was analogous to a section of *tāyampaka*. At the time he compared his own drawing to the Eiffel Tower, but a few years later he equated it with the pyramid-shaped tower adorning the entrances to many South Indian temples (*gōpuram*). Kerala intellectuals, and less frequently drummers, often argue that the rhythmic principle of reduction actually derives from the architectural feature. In any event, this visual image is pivotal to an understanding of drummers' conceptions of their musical forms.

Structure of *ceṇṭa mēḷam*

The processional compositions of the *ceṇṭa mēḷam* ensemble clearly exemplify the two concepts of repetition and reduction. One group of *ceṇṭa* drums repeats a specific pattern several times, then finishes with a cadence (*kalāśam*); in figure 5*a*, the

FIGURE 4 Picture drawn in Rolf Groesbeck's scratch notebook by V. V. Balaraman, *ceṇṭa* teacher, Kerala Kalamandalam, Cheruthuruthy, Kerala, 1988 (Groesbeck 1995:379).

FIGURE 5 Excerpts from *pañcāri mēḷam,* Kerala temple processional drumming composition for *ceṇṭa mēḷam* ensemble, performed at the Kottakkal annual temple festival, 1989: *a*, *ceṇṭa* pattern and cadence (*kalāśam*); *b*, cadence starting in half time that marks the end of a drum pattern repetition (*a*); *c*, new section in the original tempo. Tala keepers are other *ceṇṭa* drums and cymbals. (This represents a simplification of the cymbal part.) Transcription by Rolf Groesbeck.

a Twenty-four-beat *pañcāri tāḷa* (third *kālam*)

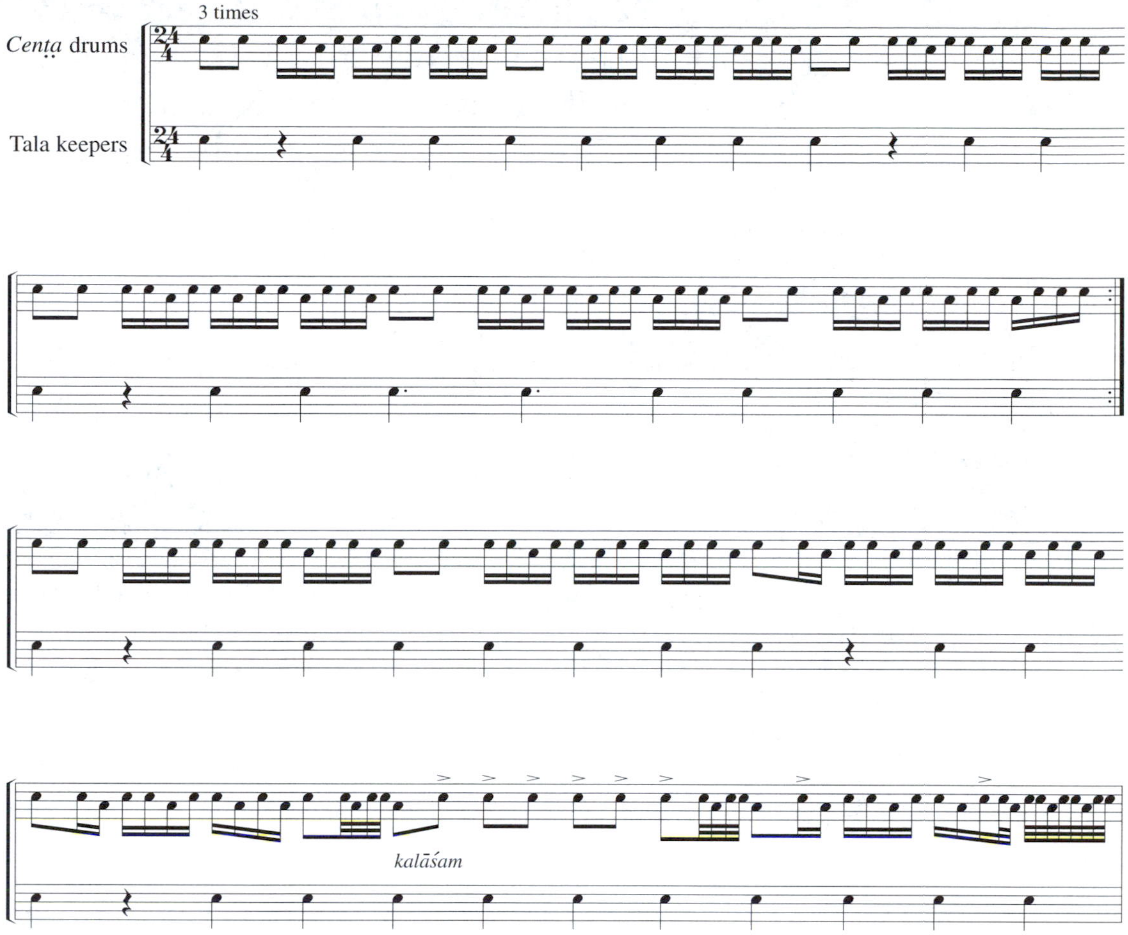

b

c Twelve-beat *pañcāri tāḷa* (fourth *kālam*)

twenty-four-beat tala pattern, played by *ceṇṭa* drums and cymbals, repeats three and a half times before the cadence (the *kompā* and *kurum kuḻal* parts are not shown). This pattern or a slight variant followed by the cadence repeats many times, each repeat slightly faster than the previous one. At one point in the composition another varia-

Toward the end of a four-hour-long performance, Keralites express the excitement caused by the increase in tempo, rhythmic density, and volume, and the decrease in tala cycle length by jumping ecstatically and waving their arms in the air.

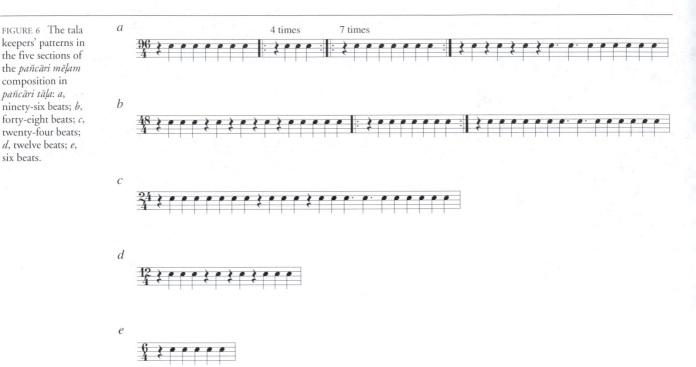

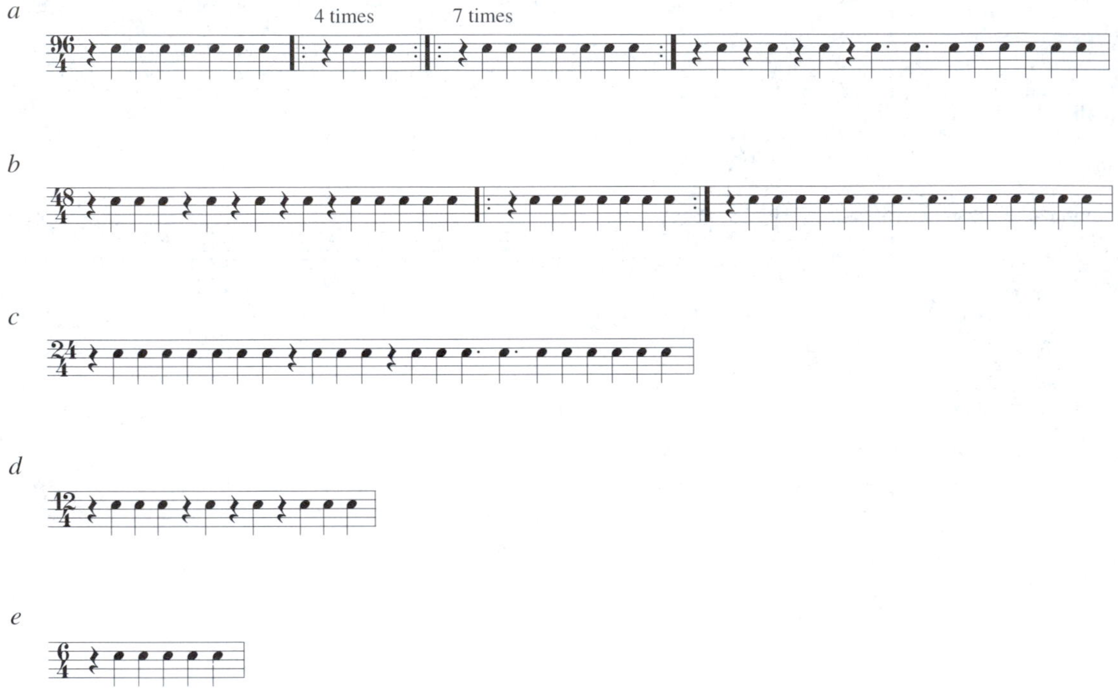

FIGURE 6 The tala keepers' patterns in the five sections of the *pañcāri mēḷam* composition in *pañcāri tāḷa*: *a*, ninety-six beats; *b*, forty-eight beats; *c*, twenty-four beats; *d*, twelve beats; *e*, six beats.

tion of the *ceṇṭa* pattern is used, but the overall shape of the sequence is retained. When the tempo becomes (in theory) exactly twice as fast as the initial speed, the *ceṇṭa* drums play a *kalāśam* 'cadence' starting in half time (figure 5*b*) and moving into a new section with a twelve-beat tala pattern in the original tempo (figure 5*c*).

The sections of a *ceṇṭa mēḷam* composition are distinguished from one another by the number of beats (*akṣara* or *mātrā*) per tala cycle (*kālam*). The most frequently played composition is in *pañcāri tāḷa* and has five main sections: in the first, each tala cycle (*tāḷavaṭṭam*) has ninety-six beats, which a group of *ceṇṭa* drums (the tala keepers) and cymbal players delineates throughout (figure 6*a*). The *kompā* horns and *kuḻal* shawms take turns playing, each repeating short unison patterns throughout the composition. In the second section, the tala cycle decreases to forty-eight beats, and the timekeeping drum pattern changes slightly as well (figure 6*b*). The tala cycle in the third section is only twenty-four beats (figure 6*c*), in the fourth twelve beats (figure 6*d*), and in the fifth six beats (figure 6*e*). In a coda called *nālām iraṭṭi* 'fourth doubling', the tala beaters play straight accented beats while the other drummers play a new series of patterns, the tala in this last section being in effect one beat per cycle. In a sense, all five sections of *pañcāri mēḷam* are in the same tala (*pañcāri*), which theoretically denotes a six-beat cycle; however, in practice a cycle of *pañcāri tāḷa* can contain six, twelve, twenty-four, forty-eight, or ninety-six beats.

Some talas used in other genres are even more flexible; for instance, *pañcavādyam* is theoretically in seven-beat *tripuṭa tāḷa*, but the various sections of *pañcavādyam* use tala cycles with seven, fourteen, twenty-eight, fifty-six, 112, 224, 448, 896, and even 1,792 beats! (In practice, musicians start from 112 or fifty-six beats per cycle.) The increases in tempo within a section, and the ever-decreasing number of beats per cycle, are audible as the initial two- to three-minute cycles are reduced to those lasting only a few seconds each. The effect is particularly powerful in four-hour-long *ceṇṭa mēḷam* compositions, such as occur in the most famous festivals. Here the ninety-six-beat tala section in theory lasts two hours, the forty-eight-beat segment one hour, the twenty-four-beat section thirty minutes, and so on until the coda, which finishes after a few minutes. Toward the end of such a performance Keralites express the excitement caused by the increase in tempo, rhythmic density, and volume, and the decrease in tala cycle length by jumping ecstatically and waving their arms in the air with index fingers pointed.

Relationship between the Kerala and Karnatak musical systems

The metric and percussive aspects of the Karnatak system differ in several ways from those of the Kerala temple musical system. The notion of constantly increasing tempo and decreasing tala cycle is largely foreign to Karnatak music; in most Karnatak genres, the tempo and the tala cycle ideally remain constant. The concept of more than two different numbers of beats for a given tala—for instance, *pañcāri* in six, twelve, twenty-four, forty-eight, or ninety-six beats—is uncommon in Karnatak music. In the Kerala system, each genre employs a particular tala or set of talas, and within the same tala, the number of beats per cycle often differs from one genre to another. For instance, most *tāyampaka* and *kēḷi* are in eight-beat *campaṭa*, but the *kathakaḷi* dance-drama uses the sixteen- and thirty-two-beat varieties of *campaṭa* as well, and *campaṭa mēḷam* (a *ceṇṭa mēḷam* composition in *campaṭa tāḷa*) uses all of these plus the sixty-four-beat variety. In performance, tala-keeping instruments beat the varieties of one tala differently, so that in a sense thirty-two-beat *campaṭa* is not merely quadruple eight-beat *campaṭa*, but sounds like a completely different tala. Also, instrumentalists often beat a given variety of tala in a slightly different way for different genres.

The structure of talas in the modern-day Kerala system is distinct from the Karnatak *sūlādi tāḷa* system; the latter consists of seven principal tala types, each with five varieties based on the differing lengths of the *laghu* (a component part of the tala), for a total of thirty-five talas [see KARNATAK TALA]. These five varieties do not exist in the Kerala system. Furthermore, the Kerala talas are not merely equivalents of the Karnatak tala types. For example, the tala *muri aṭanta* (very fast seven or six pulses per cycle) in *kathakaḷi* does not have a parallel in Karnatak music, and the common Kerala *eka tāḷa* (one or two beats per cycle) is not identical to *eka tāḷa* in Karnatak music (three, four, five, seven, or nine beats depending on the length of the *laghu*).

Other differences between the systems stand out. First, whereas Karnatak music devotees and performers keep tala (particularly in vocal concerts) through a system of claps, waves, and finger counts, in Kerala drumming genres percussionists keep the tala through their rhythmic performance; rarely do audience members or temple devotees clap the tala. Second, Kerala drummers tend to place the central beat (*samam*) of a tala cycle either at the end of the cycle or at the beginning and at the end; in Karnatak music, by contrast, *samam* is always the first beat of the cycle. Thus, a Kerala drummer plays eight-beat *campaṭa* either as . . . X . X . X (where X indicates a full drum stroke, and . indicates a rest or muted stroke), emphasizing the last beat, or X . . . X . X . X, where the final drum stroke is the first beat of the next cycle, always sounded for emphasis; by contrast, the Karnatak drummer claps eight-beat *ādi tāḷa* X . . . X . X . Finally, the genres of Kerala temple instrumental music are by and large quite distinct from those of Karnatak music. There is no Karnatak equivalent, for instance, of *pañcavādyam* or *tāyampaka*; nor is there a comparable Kerala temple counterpart to the drum solo (*tani āvartanam*) in a Karnatak concert.

There are, however, similarities between Kerala temple instrumental music and Karnatak music. Like Karnatak genres, sung compositions (*padam*) in *kathakaḷi* are for the most part in Karnatak ragas; Kerala temple music of course uses tala as an organizing metric principle; and Kerala talas bear some resemblance to certain Karnatak talas (Venkitsubramonia Iyer 1969). As an example of the latter, fourteen-beat *khaṇḍa jāti āṭa tāḷa* in Karnatak music is clapped X 1 2 3 4 X 1 2 3 4 X O X O (where X refers to a clap, O to a wave of the palm, and numbers to finger counts against the thigh or other palm); in Kerala, fourteen-beat *aṭanta tāḷa* is beaten . X X X X . X X X X . X . X. Finally, the performers in both cases are highly trained specialists once patronized by Brahmins, royalty, and large landowners.

Its similarities with Karnatak music provide evidence that Kerala temple music and drumming do not fit well into the category of folk music. Then again, the distinctions between Kerala temple music/drumming and Karnatak classical music underscore that these are largely separate systems, not to mention separate music cultures. Since both performers and audience members point out the distinctions between the two, the one (Kerala temple culture) cannot be regarded merely as a subset of the other.

PEDAGOGY AND THE LIVES OF PERFORMERS

Daily routine of the student

Male members of the musician castes tend to begin musical study at an early age with an *āśān* 'preceptor', usually an older male relative. Musicians from outside these castes frequently study in modern arts institutions that are open to all Hindus and even to non-Hindus as well, and are often patronized by large temples or the state. The Mārārs start by giving the *āśān* an offering of betel nut, betel leaf, a white cloth of the kind Kerala men normally wear wrapped around the waist *(muṇṭa)*, and some money. They then prostrate themselves on the ground in front of him to express their subservience. After learning an introductory drum pattern, which is an invocation to Ganesh, the god of auspicious beginnings, they learn a technical exercise for their particular drum, called *sādhakam* 'practice'. On the *ceṇṭa,* this practice consists of one of four short patterns, repeated around ten thousand times in four different tempi, each twice the speed of the previous one, usually for about two hours.

Once the young student has mastered these patterns, he begins a demanding regimen that he maintains throughout the monsoon season (roughly June to August): *sādhakam*, 4:00 A.M. to 6:00 or 7:00 A.M.; shower and breakfast, then off to school; after returning from school, lessons in an elementary form of a composition (*tāyampaka* on the *ceṇṭa* drum, the most rudimentary form of *pañcavādyam* on a *timila* hourglass hand drum, perhaps *koṭṭippāṭisseva* on an *iṭaykka* tension drum) until bedtime. Mārārs often start learning on *ceṇṭa*, first mastering the most elementary student *tāyampaka*—about thirty separate fixed compositions called *eṇṇam* 'numbers', lasting approximately half an hour in total—and thereafter go on to study *kēḷi* and *mēḷam*. After learning these basic lessons on *ceṇṭa*, the student might do the same on each of the other Mārār drums in turn, as well as in the Kerala style of temple singing (*sōpānam saṅgītam*). His regimen continues between September and November, but perhaps not so intensely. When his *āśān* starts to perform in the festival season, the student may accompany him from village to village, carrying the *ceṇṭa*, tightening the drumheads, and fetching him lunch or tea. At this point, the student's formal lessons will probably halt, to resume in June. After completing the beginning lessons and giving first performances (*araṅṅēṯṯam*) in all aspects of his caste job—a process that may take several years—the student can take advanced lessons from his first *āśān* or more likely from a well-known drummer in another village. Some students travel as much as 240 kilometers from their homes to take short advanced courses.

The drummers' daily lives

Young Mārārs nowadays apparently spend much less time with their drumming than their elders did in previous generations. Many older drummers left school at age seven, eight, or nine to devote all their time to their caste job. One older performer noted the following schedule for much of his youth: 4:00 to 6:30 A.M., *iṭaykka sādhakam*; 6:30 to mid-morning, accompanying his father to the temple to watch him perform for the daily ritual; late morning, *ceṇṭa* compositions; mid-afternoon, more *iṭaykka sādhakam*; late afternoon, *timila sādhakam*; and later, *ceṇṭa sādhakam* and more *ceṇṭa* lessons. Such older musicians often regret that today's drummers are unable to immerse themselves in drumming as much as they themselves did, and in particular remember a practice from their youth called "moonlight *sādhakam*," in which drummers would play from the rising to the setting of the moon, up to twelve hours at a time.

Since one or two Mārārs can perform most music for the daily temple rituals, and since Kerala families are typically large, not all Mārārs in a household are needed to play for these rituals. Because of this, there often exists a hierarchy among the males of a family; the oldest and most talented tend to spend the monsoon season teaching and the dry season as freelance performers, traveling (usually by bus) from village to village to perform at festivals at the request of local temple committees. Many make enough money from these performances to support their families and leave the task of the daily ritual, which as noted earlier is much less remunerative today, to younger or less talented family members. There is clearly a pecking order among drummers, with freelance festival performers (and *kathakaḷi* drummers) at the top and ritual specialists at the bottom.

Gender

Although some temple servants are women—certain actors and cymbal players in the Sanskrit drama *kūṭiyāṭṭam*, and occasionally flower gatherers—women almost never play any of the temple drums. Recently a few women have started playing *ceṇṭa* for *tāyampaka* or *kathakaḷi*, a few more have sung for *kathakaḷi*, and a great many women learn *kathakaḷi* acting as amateurs, but the musicians performing the Kerala musical forms discussed in this article are mostly men. One reason may lie in the centrality of goddess worship in Kerala; drumming often exists for the purpose of pleasing—and thus influencing the behavior of—these goddesses (as, for example, in *muṭiyeṯṯu* performances; Caldwell 1995), and also reflects the Sanskritic concept of a man's ability to accrue power by harnessing feminine energy. However, much research needs to be done to test this hypothesis, especially as it applies to high-caste worship. Nevertheless, temple music and drumming in Kerala are largely the province of men, much more so than with dance or drama.

High-caste professional women performers are found frequently in the solo dance *mōhini āṭṭam*, and often in a monodrama called *oṭṭan tuḷḷal*. *Mōhini āṭṭam*, like the Tamil dance style *bharata nāṭyam*, often consists of a series of items, several of which have the same names as *bharata nāṭyam* items (such as *jatisvaram*, *varṇam*, *padam*, and *tillāna*). The Kerala dance differs in its characteristic body position and in the dancer's typical costume and hairstyle. The relationship between contemporary

A drumming lesson in Kerala is quite a different experience from a typical music lesson in the West. First, lessons are almost always in groups. Second, there is little notation. Third, drumming is not so much studied theoretically as incorporated into the body through practice.

mōhini āṭṭam and female dancing that is referred to in tenth-century and later Kerala temple records and literature is unclear. However, references in Malayalam literature clearly indicate that a dance of this name existed as early as the sixteenth century. Like so many of India's solo female dances, *mōhini āṭṭam* underwent a decline in the late nineteenth century but was revived in the 1930s, when the newly founded Kerala Kalamandalam emphasized it in its curriculum (Venu and Paniker 1983; Kalyanikutti Amma 1990).

Teaching and learning

A drumming lesson in Kerala is quite a different experience from a typical music lesson in the West. First, lessons are almost always in groups. Since all drum compositions require ensemble members to beat the tala, there is no point in studying privately. (Many Westerners in Kerala and amateurs attempting to become more knowledgeable connoisseurs study *kathakaḷi* privately, but this practice is very unusual among those who wish to be professionals.) Second, there is little notation. The *āśān* teaches his students by rote, and rarely if ever explains the structures of the compositions he teaches. A single pattern may be played and repeated back for an hour or more until the student can play it perfectly. Students can thus take a long time to learn to play even a small musical segment. I [Rolf Groesbeck] recall the case of a drumming student in my own group (at the institution at which I studied) who took about three months to learn the first *eṇṇam* 'fixed composition' of *tāyampaka,* about two minutes in length. I thought he would be dismissed from the school for ineptitude, but he then learned the rest of *tāyampaka* in about a month. Once he had absorbed the basic structure, he could sense how the rest of the piece would proceed and could play it perfectly from memory.

A third important contrast with Western musical learning is that drumming in Kerala, like acting and dancing, is not so much studied theoretically as incorporated into the body through practice; a student can scarcely forget his drum patterns because he cannot remove himself from them. Whereas a Western musical score or recording is a tangible object that exists separately from the student, Kerala drumming is rarely written down and student versions of compositions are never recorded, so no separation is possible. The teacher corrects the student not only by saying something, but by grabbing the student's arm, shoulder, or wrist, implying that the body can remember more surely than the brain alone. The student is required to play his compositions exactly the way his *āśān* teaches him, for usually no improvisation is permitted in drumming pedagogy, or initially in singing or acting either, which gives the *āśān* extraordinary power.

This power was alluded to earlier in the description of the ritual offerings marking the beginning of pedagogy. The teacher's power is manifested in other aspects of pedagogy as well. The *āśān* hits the thigh or the arm of students who repeatedly fail to learn, and students (in my experience) never criticize their *āśān* for doing so, even long after their studies are over. Another display of recognition of the *āśān*'s power relates to his compensation; in general the teacher charges no fee but accepts grandiose gifts on an irregular basis. During my musical research in Kerala in 1988–1990, one of my informants reported having allowed his *āśān* to take his *ceṇṭa*; another reported having accepted special cloths worn around the waist (*muṇṭā*) from his students on holidays; another boasted that if he were to ask one of his former students for several thousand rupees (a vast sum), the student would surrender the money immediately. The likely reason is that if the student were to pay the *āśān* a fixed regular fee, the *āśān* would feel that his services were worth exactly that amount; by typically paying the *āśān* nothing (except on special occasions), the student is showing that no amount of money can measure the *āśān*'s value. In general, the student's attitude and behavior towards his *āśān* express extreme indebtedness, subservience, and devotion. This attitude, along with the drum patterns the *āśān* teaches, is in a sense embodied physically in the student by means of the daily experience of pedagogy, instead of existing merely as an abstract ideology.

Creativity and aesthetics

According to popular belief, as noted above, a single mistake—a deviation from the version a drummer learns from his *āśān*—in performing the composition *pāṇi* causes the drummer to die within a year. No individual variation is allowed in *mēḷam* either, for the first group of *ceṇṭa* drums (those not keeping the tala) play in unison throughout. (The only exception is the lead *ceṇṭa* and lead *kuḻal* players' decisions over the length of each section.) However, *pañcavādyam* does allow limited scope for individual improvisation—much of the piece consists of a series of improvised solos by all of the drummers in turn—and *tāyampaka* permits quite a lot. Moreover, at least in *tāyampaka*, performers tend to insist that they do not learn improvisation from their *āśān* but develop it on their own, generally after the conclusion of their studies (Groesbeck 1999). How can the emphasis on exact replication of patterns taught by a student's *āśān*, in the pedagogy of these drumming forms, be reconciled with the valorization of individual imagination in performance?

Drummers I interviewed contended that they could define their personal styles, prove their skills, and ultimately win the admiration of the audience more in festival performances of *tāyampaka* using *manōdharmam* ('improvisatory segments') than in such performances emphasizing student compositions (mostly *eṇṇam*), due to the advanced and idiosyncratic nature of *manōdharmam*. At the same time, many lauded the idea of a performance dominated by *eṇṇam* compositions, calling it "scientific" and looking back fondly on a barely remembered past in which performers putatively adhered to the patterns they had learned as students. In general, performers who improvise frequently are celebrated for their originality and paid very well, but are often criticized for being eccentric (in their personal habits as well as their playing) or "unscientific," whereas those who follow a consistent model are championed by older connoisseurs for being faithful to the ways of the past. These latter drummers, however, draw smaller crowds and often less enthusiasm. Clearly, the aesthetic of improvisation conflicts to some degree with the values associated with the patterns learned from an *āśān*.

This schism may in part derive from the social separation between student and teacher, and the different behaviors expected of each. Students must wake up daily at 4:00 A.M. for *sādhakam*, whereas teachers often sleep in; students do not wear facial hair (even by and large those in late adolescence), but teachers often do; students rarely get angry, although teachers are frequently so. This phenomenon may in turn derive in part from the Sanskritic emphasis on *āśrama dharma* 'life-stage duty', according to which each of four stages in the life of the ideal Hindu high-caste male (including the first "student" stage and the second "householder" stage) requires a separate set of goals and activities. This in turn explains the importance of the "first performance" as a rite of passage, in which the drummer theoretically leaves the student stage and enters that of the adult performer. Perhaps since student and performer are two such different roles, it makes sense that each has his own rhythmic pattern in *tāyampaka*.

This explanation does not account for the contention of most drummers that performances in *tāyampaka* with much improvisation are relatively new, or that in *pāṇi* and *mēḷam* improvisation is absent. More likely the tension between improvised *tāyampaka* and the student model derives to some degree from recent socioeconomic changes in Kerala, notably the land reforms enacted between 1956 and 1970 that endangered the well-being of Kerala's temples and landowning families, many of whom were important connoisseurs of the arts. Whereas prior to the land reforms, wealthy landlords patronized many temple festivals and daily rituals, the festivals now owe their existence by and large to temple committees whose members go door to door collecting money for the deity. The daily rituals have thus declined, and most of the festivals no longer have single patrons who are also connoisseurs. Mārārs, unable to support themselves by their daily ritual duties at their home temples, more frequently become itinerant festival performers who, because different temple committees pay them each night, are ultimately beholden to none of them. Additionally, with the decline in importance of the landowner/connoisseur, performers perceive themselves as increasingly independent and impervious to outside suggestions on how to practice their art. In short, the student is bound to his teacher, and must play what his teacher instructs; the teacher is less bound to anyone—his own (former) teacher, his temple, or his patron/connoisseur—and is freer to do as he wishes. Since the above economic situation dates to some degree only from the last quarter century or so, the debate over improvisation is, according to my informants, a relatively recent phenomenon.

Despite a host of trends—changes in festival patronage and programming, the decline of the daily ritual and other special rituals, complaints about the new styles in *tāyampaka* and about the lesser skills of the newest *kathakaḷi* performers, and the decline of other forms such as Kerala temple singing and *kūṭiyāṭṭam*—the temple is still the undisputed center of Kerala ritual and stage performance. Performances of *pañcavādyam*, *kathakaḷi*, and *tāyampaka* as well as grandiose temple festivals with elephant processions still abound in almost every village in central and northern Kerala. Much of the core of Kerala social life still revolves around mass worship of powerful deities, reminiscent of the heroic military kings of ancient South Indian lore, and the most important musical means of celebrating these deities' powers remains drumming compositions indigenous to Kerala, now as in the past.

CHRISTIAN MUSICAL TRADITIONS

According to traditional belief, Christianity came to Kerala in the first century through the preaching of Saint Thomas the Apostle. In the fourth century, the early Christian community gathered strength with the arrival of Christians from Persia (present-day Iran and Iraq); in the fifth century, the Church in Kerala was affiliated with the Church in Persia, adopting in the process the Chaldean (East Syrian) liturgy. Portuguese missionaries established the Latin rite in the early 1500s. Many divisions then took place among the Kerala Christians after the mid-1600s. In the early nineteenth century, the Protestant missions became active in the state, and these contacts led to a rich and varied repertoire of Christian music, combining indigenous and foreign traditions. Kerala's Christian churches in the late twentieth century include the

Syro-Malabar Church, the Nestorian Church, the Syrian Orthodox (Jacobite) Church, the Syro-Malankara Church, the Mar Thoma Church, the Latin Church, and the Protestant churches.

According to the 1991 census, there are 5.6 million Christians in Kerala, who constitute approximately 19 percent of the total population (29.1 million). Their religious music comprises four major categories distinguished by genre and location: liturgical music, dance and theater music, music in the home, and devotional music.

Liturgical music

The liturgical music of Kerala comprises music of the mass, communion service, Office of the Hours, and paraliturgical services. The Syro-Malabar and the Nestorian churches follow the Chaldean liturgy in East Syriac. Even after the vernacularization of this liturgy in 1962, some of the ancient Syriac melodies continue to be sung with Malayalam texts, along with new hymns. The Syrian Orthodox and Syro-Malankara churches adopted the Antiochean liturgy in West Syriac, which is now partly vernacularized. The music of these churches preserves the ancient *Ekkāra* (from Syriac *ekkōro* 'root') canon, which prescribes rules regarding the use of eight ecclesiastical modes (*niṟam* 'color') in the Office and the sacraments, conceptually similar to the eight modes of Gregorian chant. The liturgical music of the Mar Thoma Church is a compendium of West Syriac chants, Anglican hymns, and Malayalam compositions in Karnatak musical style. The Latin Church in Kerala vernacularized its liturgy in 1967. Unison singing of Malayalam hymns replaced Western chants in Latin and the polyphonic singing style. In the absence of any standardization, new hymns are being composed and sung independently in each church. Many of the Protestant churches in Kerala continue polyphonic singing. Congregations sing English hymns, German chorales with Malayalam translations, and Malayalam hymns composed by local musicians.

Dance and theater music

The early 1980s saw a revival of some traditional Christian theater and dance forms of Kerala, such as *mārgamkaḷi* 'dance of the Christian way', *paricamuṭṭukaḷi* 'dance with striking shields', and *caviṭṭunāṭakam* 'foot-stamping drama'. The first two are pre-sixteenth-century dance traditions of the Kerala Christians, both combining devotion with entertainment. *Mārgamkaḷi* is popular among the Syro-Malabar and the Syro-Malankara Christians. Men perform the dance in groups, and since the 1980s young women have also formed dance groups (figure 7). The dancers themselves sing the *mārgamkaḷi* songs in unison call-and-response form, the lyrics recounting the missionary activities and martyrdom of Saint Thomas the Apostle. *Paricamuṭṭukaḷi*, an artistic adaptation of the Kerala martial-arts tradition (*kaḷari*), is popular among Syro-Malabar, Syro-Malankara, Syrian Orthodox, and Latin Christians. Male groups perform the dance, in which the dancers each carry a sword and shield and strike them against each other's in time with the song's rhythm. The group leader or maestro (*āśān*) sings each line of the song for the group to repeat in unison. The leader controls the song's tempo and the speed of the dancers' movements.

Caviṭṭunāṭakam, a theatrical tradition of the Kerala Latin Christians, dates from the second half of the sixteenth century (Richmond et al. 1990). The name refers to the vigorous, high-arching steps of the male characters who pound the wooden platform, especially during rhythmic cadential formulas (*kalāśam*) at the ends of songs. Actors and, more recently, actresses sing (in Malayalam) and dance enactments of chivalrous stories from Western Christendom, supported by an orchestra placed at rear center-stage. The orchestra consists of Western (violin and harmonium) and

Among composers and performers of Christian music in the 1990s there is an increasing demand for Western musical instruments such as synthesizers, electric guitars, and electronic drum machines.

FIGURE 7 *Mārgamkaḷi* performed by the students of St. Mary's Girls High School, Fort Kochi. 1994. Photo courtesy the newspaper *Rashtra Deepika*.

Indian instruments. The music and dance styles in *caviṭṭunāṭakam* are adaptations of South Indian classical and folk traditions.

Music in the home

Among the songs generally sung in the home environment are wedding songs, *R̲abbān pāṭṭu* (a song about Saint Thomas the Apostle, written by Rabban Thomas Maliekkal), historical songs about individual churches and communities, songs for home liturgy (different from the hymns sung in the church), didactic songs, and narrative poems such as *Puttan pāna* (a composition that narrates biblical events, written in the eighteenth century by John Ernest Hanxleden). Christians sing these songs unaccompanied, either solo or in group unison. Some of the song melodies show the considerable influence of Syriac liturgical music (Palackal 1995).

Commercialized devotional music

A new genre of Christian devotional songs (*kr̲istīya bhaktigānaṅaḷ*) became popular in the 1970s with the introduction of cassette technology in Kerala. Both Christians and non-Christians compose such Christian songs for commercial recordings. The arrangements employ Western and Indian instruments. On average, about four hundred prerecorded cassettes of Christian devotional songs in Malayalam are released annually.

In the 1990s, two contrasting trends are noticeable in the Christian music of Kerala: westernization and Indianization. Among composers and performers of Christian music there is an increasing demand for Western musical instruments such as synthesizers, electric guitars, and electronic drum machines. Some composers use these instruments for chordal and rhythmic accompaniment, creating a homophonic texture, in live and recorded performances of liturgical and devotional songs. The wide popularity of westernized Christian song arrangements reflects recent changes in musical taste. Other composers attempt to Indianize Christian music by drawing inspiration from Indian classical, folk, and bhajan styles. Examples include Christian bhajans with Malayalam and Sanskrit lyrics (Palackal 1979) and the Christian *kīrtana* compositions of George Panjara, with Malayalam lyrics in Karnatak musical style (Panjara 1988).

MUSLIM MUSIC

The Muslims of Kerala, known as Mappilas, have an identity distinct from that of other Indian Muslim communities (Miller 1992). Mappilas are the descendants of Arab settlers and Hindu converts to Islam. They number 6.8 million, or 23 percent of Kerala's population. The nonliturgical musical tradition of the Mappilas (*māppiḷappaṭṭu* 'Mappila songs') is at least seven centuries old and blends Kerala and Arab musical styles. The Mappila spoken language, and also the language of their song texts, is Arabi-Malayalam, which follows Malayalam syntax but mixes Malayalam words with words from Arabic, Persian, Urdu, Hindi, Tamil, and Kannada. A single couplet of a song may contain words from four or five languages. The only exception to this is a genre called *arabi-baith* 'Arabic song' that is composed exclusively in Arabic. Singers of Mappila songs have a peculiar voice fluctuation that serves the vocalization of Arabic phonemes.

A wide variety of themes are found in Mappila songs. Most popular among them are praises of the Prophet Muhammad and Muslim saints, holy wars (Fawcett 1901), and the love and romance of legendary heroes as well as of common people. M. N. Karassery recently discovered some old Mappila songs that narrate stories from the Hindu epic Ramayana (Karassery 1992).

A distinctive mark of Mappila song texts is their metric structure (*isal,* from the Arabic word *aṣl* 'principle'). This is based on a combination of Arabic and Dravidian systems of prosody. The character of a meter depends upon the number of long and short syllables in a poetic line, and the order in which they occur. Over one hundred meters are currently popular. A composer may combine parts of two or more meters to create a new one. The composition of a song text is thus called *pāṭṭukeṭṭuka* 'to tie a song'. Some of the norms regarding rhyme and rhythm in tying a song are similar to those of Malayalam prosody. However, the norms regarding tempo are specific to Mappila songs. Slow tempo is called *cāyal* 'slanting'; fast tempo, *muṟukkam* 'tightening'.

Music and dance are integral to Mappila festive occasions. *Oppana* 'proximity, sitting together' is the most popular dance, performed separately by women's and men's groups, on occasions such as weddings and the celebration of a girl's first menstruation. In women's *oppana* during weddings, the performers dance around the seated, finely dressed bride (figure 8). Intricate dance steps and hand clapping accompany the singing. The lead singer sings each line of the song, which the group repeats. The performance begins in a slow tempo and progresses through a variety of meters (7/8, 4/4, 6/8, and so on) and tempi.

Kōlkkaḷi 'dance with sticks' is a dance for men that is performed during wedding celebrations. The dancers hold 30-centimeter-long sticks in each hand and move in circles, rhythmically striking the sticks. The group leader, called *gurukkaḷ* 'teacher', controls each stage of the dance, which starts in a slow tempo and gradually builds up speed. Like the women's *oppana,* the accompanying song is in leader-chorus response form.

Another men's dance in wedding celebrations is *paricamuṭṭukaḷi* 'dance with striking shields', performed by twelve dancers. The *paricamuṭṭukaḷi* of the Muslims

FIGURE 8 Women's *oppana* dance, performed by the students of Holy Cross High School, Thellakom. 1995. Photo courtesy the newspaper *Rashtra Deepika*.

and Christians share a similar vocabulary of body movements. The songs, however, are different. Those of the Muslims, known as shield songs (*paricappāṭṭu*), narrate events related to the holy wars.

A few musical genres do not have dance accompaniment. *Kattupāṭṭu* 'letter song' is the most popular; it takes the form of a letter sung by a young woman whose husband lives abroad. The themes of such songs include love, pain of separation, longing for reunion, and even detailed description of personal lives. Letter songs were once sung unaccompanied in the privacy of Muslim homes, but are now performed in public with instrumental accompaniment (such as harmonium, tabla, or guitar) and are published on commercial cassettes.

Daffmuṭṭu 'striking the *daff*' is popular among certain sectors of Mappila society. Men play the *daff*, an Arab frame drum, in accompaniment to songs praising the Prophet Muhammad and Muslim saints. The singing is in a loud voice. On the birth and death anniversaries of Muslim saints, groups of *daff* players may visit rich Muslim homes and perform for a remuneration.

The performance contexts of Mappila songs have expanded over the years from home and public places of worship to performance halls, political party conventions, and school and college youth festivals. Even non-Mappilas compose songs for such occasions, and performers also come from different religious backgrounds. Change in performance contexts has influenced the choice of musical instruments for accompaniment. Besides traditional instruments such as the frame drum (*daff*), a larger frame drum (*aravāna*), and a double-reed aerophone similar to the North Indian *śahnāī* (*māppiḷaṣehnāī*), synthesizers, electric guitars, and electronic drum machines have found a place in contemporary performances for chordal and rhythmic accompaniment.

JEWISH MUSIC

The first Jewish immigrants arrived in Kerala after the destruction of the second temple in Jerusalem, c. A.D. 70 (Koder 1968). There were several migrations of Jews from the Middle East and Europe in the fourth, fifth, and fifteenth centuries. After 1948, many Jews migrated from Kerala to Israel. According to Jacob Cohen, a senior member of the Jewish community in Kerala, there were only seventy-seven Jews in the state in 1996. They belong to two different endogamous communities, the Sephardim and the Ashkenazim. Both communities gather for prayer at the only functioning synagogue in Kochi (formerly Cochin). They share the same musical traditions, with minor variations.

The Jewish musical repertoire in Kerala may be divided into Hebrew songs and Malayalam songs. Hebrew songs, comprising cantillation of the Torah, prayer, and semireligious songs, are sung by both men and women in the synagogue and during ceremonies at home. Some songs are simple and strictly metrical, while others are governed by syllabic-poetic rhythm and meter. They exhibit intercultural influences: traces of Yemenite and Babylonian styles in the cantillation of the Torah, for example, are indications of early contacts between Kerala Jews and these cultures (Ross 1978). The Jews in Kerala do not play musical instruments either for accompaniment or entertainment. However, Sarah and Jacob Cohen, who live in "Jew Town" in Kochi, recall that until the early 1960s Hindu and Muslim instrumental ensembles used to be invited to perform during wedding celebrations in front of the bride's and groom's homes.

The Jewish songs in Malayalam are of three kinds: historical songs that narrate events related to Jewish settlements and the history of various synagogues in Kerala, biblical songs, and secular songs. Women sing these songs at home during festive gatherings and wedding celebrations. They are passed on orally from one generation to the next, and their authorship is unknown. Some are set to Hebrew song melodies, but the vocal quality and ornamentation in performance are typically Keralite. The songs range from isometric (such as 4/4, 6/4, and 3/4) with symmetrical rhythms, to nonmetrical with melismatic recitatives. Generally, women sing these songs in groups. A few songs are in call-and-response style, in which the lead singer sings the stanzas and the group repeats the chorus line (*kuṟukkan*, literally 'fox'). Kerala Jews seldom perform Malayalam songs now, and the tradition is going out of vogue.

TRIBAL MUSIC

The 1991 government census lists thirty-five tribes living in Kerala. Each has its own language and music; most tribes live in cluster houses called *ur*, in the mountainous regions of the Wynad, Palakkad, and Idukki districts. Music and dance are part of the daily lives of these women, men, and children, who sing and dance together. Only men play musical instruments. General characteristics of Kerala tribal music include a brisk rhythm, a predominance of drums, a call-and-response style of unison singing, and relatively few melodic patterns employed for almost all occasions.

Death and annual temple festivals are two important occasions on which singing and dancing take place. The tribes in Attappady, in Palakkad district, announce death by a special beating on two drums, *peṟa* 'kettledrum' and *davil* 'double-headed drum'. Men and women dance around the corpse, which is placed in the *ur* courtyard. The dance begins with a rhythmic production of sounds and vocables followed by songs with words. The music is strictly metrical and contains simple melodic phrases of four or eight beats. A wooden reed instrument called *kokal* doubles the melody at the upper octave. Singing and dancing continue until the corpse is buried. Death anniversaries are also occasions for musical celebrations, as are weddings and a girl's first menstruation.

FOLK MUSIC

Kerala has a rich repertoire of folk songs called *nāṭōṭippāṭṭu* 'songs that run through the region', sung mostly by the lower castes. These songs are associated with work, rituals, and entertainment. They record the history and social practices of the people who sing them.

Kerala folk songs fall into two categories: southern songs (*tekkan pāṭṭu*) and

As elsewhere in India, film songs receive the maximum television and radio broadcast time afforded any type of music in Kerala.

FIGURE 9 Section of a reaping song (*koyttupāṭṭu*) that employs the *vāyttāri* technique, as sung by Esthappan Ouseph, 1995. Transcribed by Joseph J. Palackal.

northern songs (*vaṭakkan pāṭṭu*). Boat songs are a specialty of the south, which has many rivers and backwaters, while the north is well known for heroic songs. Agricultural songs are common to both areas.

One of the popular techniques employed in the composition of folk songs is called *vāyttāri*, a combination of sounds and syllables that set the metric structure and, in some cases, the melodic phrase of a song. A *vāyttāri* may be formulated from simulations of sounds produced by percussion instruments, such as the *ceṇṭa* 'double-headed cylindrical drum', *maddaḷam* 'barrel drum', and *uḍukkai* 'small hand drum'. Figure 9 is an example of this technique in a reaping song (*koyttupāṭṭu*).

A composer-singer fits individual words or complete text lines into the *vāyttāri* structure, and in the process, he or she may borrow lines from popular songs or compose lines instantly. The act of composing a song is thus to tie a song (*pāṭṭukeṭṭuka*). When singers use a *vāyttāri* in performance, the leader first sings the *vāyttāri* once or twice for the group to repeat, after which they all sing the song in call-and-response style.

FILM MUSIC

Film is the most popular entertainment form in Kerala. Seventy-five to a hundred films in Malayalam are released every year. The financial success of a film depends on several factors, one of the most critical being the inclusion of songs and dances. Each film may include three to six songs. Approximately 135 music directors, all men, work in the Malayalam film industry, and most are from Kerala (Nair 1994). They draw on a huge variety of musical genres, from Indian classical and folk to Western pop and rap. Almost 95 percent of film songs have the same musical structure: three stanzas of four lines each, presented in an A B A C A form, with stanza A serving as a refrain. Music directors orchestrate their songs using both Western and Indian musical instruments; in addition to accompanying the singer(s), the studio orchestra plays instrumental interludes between the song stanzas. Film songs are generally up to five minutes in length [see FILM MUSIC: SOUTHERN AREA].

As elsewhere in India, film songs receive the maximum television and radio broadcast time afforded any type of music in Kerala. They are released on commercial cassettes, and more recently on compact discs. Film song artists, known as playback singers, are second only to movie actors/actresses and politicians in popularity.

REFERENCES

Ashley, Wayne. 1993. "Recodings: Ritual, Theatre, and Political Display in Kerala State, South India." Ph.D. dissertation, New York University.

Caldwell, Sarah. 1995. "Oh, Terrifying Mother: The Mudiyettu Ritual Drama of Kerala, South India." Ph.D. dissertation, University of California at Berkeley.

Choondal, Chummar. 1988. *Christian Folklore*, vol. I. Thrissur: Kerala Folklore Academy.

Embrantiri, Kalamandalam, et al. 1993a. *Le Mahabharata: musiques, chants, et rythmes du Kathakali.* Auvidis/Ethnic B 6778. Compact disc.

———. 1993b. *Le Ramayana: musiques, chants, et rythmes du Kathakali.* Auvidis/Ethnic B 6779. Compact disc.

Fawcett, F. 1901. "War Songs of the Mappilas of Malabar." *Indian Antiquary* 30:499–508, 528–537.

Freeman, John Richardson, Jr. 1991. "Purity and Violence: Sacred Power in the Teyyam Worship of Malabar." Ph.D. dissertation, University of Pennsylvania.

Groesbeck, Rolf. 1995. "Pedagogy and Performance in 'Tayampaka', a Genre of Temple Instrumental Music in Kerala, India." Ph.D. dissertation, New York University.

———. 1999. "Cultural Constructions of Improvisation in *Tāyampaka*, a Genre of Temple Instrumental Music in Kerala, India." *Ethnomusicology* 43(1):1–30.

Hart, George. 1975. *The Poems of Ancient Tamil.* Berkeley: University of California Press.

Jones, Betty True. 1983. "Kathakaḷi Dance-Drama: An Historical Perspective." In *The Performing Arts in India: Essays on Music, Dance, and Drama*, ed. Bonnie Wade, 14–44. Berkeley: University of California, Center for South and Southeast Asian Studies.

Jones, Betty True, and Clifford Jones. 1970. *Kathakaḷi: An Introduction to the Dance-Drama of Kerala.* New York and San Francisco: American Society for Eastern Arts.

Jones, Clifford. 1982. "Kalam Ezuttu: Art and Ritual in Kerala." In *Religious Festivals in South India and Sri Lanka*, ed. Guy Welbon and Glenn Yocum, 269–294. New Delhi: Manohar.

Kalyanikutti Amma, O. 1990. "Mohini attam." In *Studies in Indian Music and Allied Arts*, 4, ed. Leela Omchery and Deepti Omchery Bhalla, 121–129. Delhi: Sundeep Prakashan.

Karassery, M. N. 1992. *Māppiḷappāṭṭukaḷuṭe sāhitya sāmskārika mōlyam* (Literary and cultural significance of Mappila songs). Ph.D. dissertation, Calicut University. In Malayalam.

Koder, Sattu S., et al., eds. 1968. *Cochin Synagogue Quarter Centenary Souvenir.* Ernakulam: Thilakam Press.

Marar, Maniyan. 1989. *Festive Drums of Kerala.* Seven Seas (World Music Library) KICC 5120. Compact disc.

Miller, Roland E. 1992. *Mappila Muslims of Kerala*, 2nd ed. Madras: Orient Longman.

Nair, Madhusudanan B. 1994. *Malayāḷa calaccitṛa sangētam 50 varṣam: citṛagāna smaraṇika* (Fifty Years of Malayalam Film Music: A Souvenir of Film Songs). Kollam: Author. In Malayalam.

Nambiar, Unnikrishnan, et al. 1997. *The Kudiyattam Dance-Drama: An Ancient Sanskrit Performance from Kerala.* JVC VICG 5037-2. Compact disc.

Neff, Deborah. 1995. "Fertility and Power in Kerala Serpent Ritual (India)." Ph.D. dissertation, University of Wisconsin.

Omchery, Leela. 1969. "The Music of Kerala: A Study." *Sangeet Natak Academy Journal* 14:12–23.

Palackal, Joseph J. 1979. *Christian Bhajans.* Bangalore: Deccan Records. LDEC 102. LP disk.

———. Forthcoming. "Christian Music." In *The New Grove Dictionary of Music and Musicians*, ed. Stanley Sadie. London: Macmillan.

———. 1995. "Puttan pāna: A Musical Study." Master's thesis, Hunter College, City University of New York.

Panjara, George. 1988. *Christian Classical Music Concert.* Thodupuzha: Nadopasana NC 101. Audio cassette.

Pillai, Kadammanitta Vasudevan. 1993. *Paṭeni.* Thiruvananthapuram: Kerala Bhasha Institute.

Rajagopalan, L .S. 1967. "Thayambaka: Laya Vinyasa." *Journal of the Music Academy, Madras* 38:83–102.

———. 1974. "Folk Musical Instruments of Kerala." *Sangeet Natak Academy Journal* 33:40–55.

Richmond, Farley P., Darius L. Swann, and Phillip B. Zarilli, eds. 1990. *Indian Theatre: Traditions of Performance.* Honolulu: University of Hawaii Press.

Ross, Israel J. 1978. "Cross-Cultural Dynamics in Musical Traditions: The Music of the Jews of Cochin." *Musica Judaica* 2(1):51–72.

———. 1979. "Ritual and Music in South India: Syrian Christian Liturgical Music in Kerala." *Asian Music* 11(1):80–98.

Sankarankutty, Mattanur. 1997. *Kerala: Le Thayambaka.* Ocora (Harmonia Mundi) C 560047. Compact disc.

South India Ritual Music and Theater of Kerala. 1989. Notes by Pribislav Pitoeff. Le Chant du Monde (Harmonia Mundi) LDX 274910. Compact disc.

Spector, Johanna. 1972. "Shingli Tunes of the Cochin Jews." *Asian Music* 3(2):23–28.

Sreedhara Menon, A. 1988. *A Survey of Kerala History.* Madras: S. Viswanathan Pvt. Ltd.

Tarabout, Gilles. 1986. *Sacrifier et donner à voir en pays Malabar. Les fêtes de temple au Kerala: étude anthropologique.* Paris: École Française d'extrême Orient.

Usman, Muhammad M., ed. 1986. *Folk Arts Directory*, 2nd ed. Thrissur: Kerala Sangeetha Nataka Academy.

Vaidyanathan, K. R. 1977. *Sri Krishna, the Lord of Guruvayur.* Trivandrum: Bharatiya Vidya Bhavan.

Venkitsubramonia Iyer, S. 1969. "Some Rare Talas in Kerala Music." *Sangeet Natak Academy Journal* 14:5–11.

Venu, G., and Nirmala Paniker. 1983. *Mohiniyattam.* Trivandrum: G. Venu.

Zarrilli, Phillip. 1984. *The Kathakaḷi Complex: Actor, Performance, and Structure.* New Delhi: Abhinav Publications.

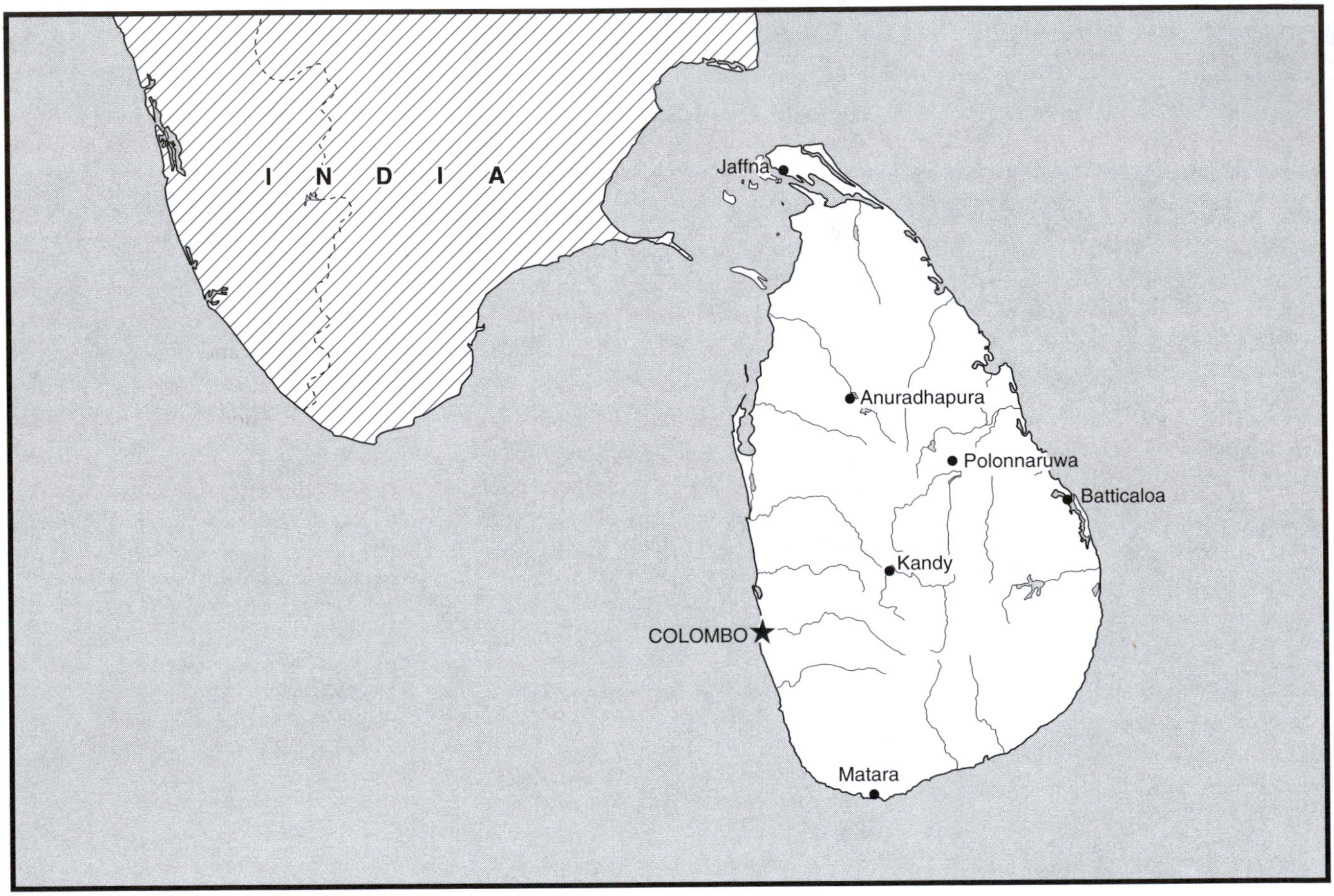
INDIA
Jaffna
Anuradhapura
Polonnaruwa
Batticaloa
Kandy
COLOMBO
Matara

Sri Lanka

Buddhist chants, kettledrum-and-oboe ensembles, verses sung to Hindu guardian spirits, Sinhala drum music, masked theater, temple processions, popular Afro-Portuguese-influenced dance music, and Sinhala pop all contribute to the musical soundscape of present-day Sri Lanka. The island's population is composed largely of the Sinhala people—descendants of Indo-Aryans who emigrated from India in the fifth century B.C.—and Tamils, whose ancestors emigrated from South India from the third century B.C. through the twelfth century C.E. In their daily lives, music enriches their rituals, expresses their social and cultural identities, and reveals influences from old indigenous religious practices as well as modern pop styles of North America, Africa, and elsewhere.

Contemporary pop musicians employ trumpets, saxophones, electric guitars, and synthesizers in their experiments with native pop music and dance genres. The results are heard in nightclubs, festivals, open-air stage shows, and television programs, and add to the rich musical diversity of this island nation.

MAP 12 Sri Lanka

Sri Lanka

Anne Sheeran

Sri Lanka, formerly Ceylon, is located in the Indian Ocean roughly 39 kilometers from the southern tip of India, 970 kilometers north of the equator. It is an island approximately 65,610 square kilometers in size, with a population of around 18.1 million in 1996.

Bordered on the west by the Arabian Sea and on the east by the Indian Ocean, Sri Lanka occupied a central point on the maritime trade routes that linked India, Africa, Europe, and Asia. Until the early 1800s, several competing regional power centers and kingdoms operated in Sri Lanka, sometimes as allies of Indian kingdoms while at other times under the occupation of one or another Indian power. Strategic matrimonial alliances between elite families in Sri Lanka and India appear to have been routine; immigrations from India under the auspices of such alliances were not uncommon. By the sixteenth century, natural resources—including salt, spices, plumbago, and gems—made Sri Lanka a target for European colonial expansionism: beginning in 1505, Sri Lanka was occupied successively by the Portuguese, the Dutch (1658), and the British (1796). The African diaspora had at least two components: the first Africans came as slaves of the Portuguese during the seventeenth century; during the early nineteenth century they served as soldiers for the British. Ceylon won independence in 1948 and became the Republic of Sri Lanka in 1972.

Music and performance practices in Sri Lanka bear the imprints of these extensive regional and international connections, from which several diasporic groups emerged. The Sinhala people constitute roughly 73 percent of the population; the Sri Lankan Tamils about 13 percent of the population. "Estate" or "Indian" Tamils, brought by the British to Sri Lanka during the nineteenth and early twentieth century to work in the plantations, make up about 6 percent of Sri Lanka's population. A heterogeneous Muslim community, which includes Moors, Malays, Bohras, Memons, Khojas, and Afghans constitutes about 7 percent of all Sri Lankans. Fewer than 1 percent are Burghers, a census category that refers to those Sri Lankans who intermarried with Portuguese and Dutch. Statistically smaller groups are Chetties, Parsis, and Eurasians, as well as a group of people known as "kaffirs"—descendants of African slaves and soldiers. Although they are few in number, their performance genres are a rich source of information about the African diaspora in South Asia as well as the forging of creole cultures—Iberian, African, Asian, European—in the shadow of colonial occupation.

Roughly 78 percent of the population lives in the rural areas. The Sinhala community is thought to have at least three regionally distinctive musical subcultures: low country, up country, and Sabaragamuwa. These subcultures differ according to musical instrumentation, genre, drum patterns, and vocal style. The south, or "low country," is also known by the name of a historically important kingdom and power center for the Sinhalese, Ruhunu. "Up-country" refers to the mountainous interior regions, the locus of several administrative power centers and kingdoms including Anhuradhapura (137–1000), Polonnaruwa (1055–1255) and Kandy (1469–1815). In practice, however, "up-country" conveys an almost exclusive focus on the Kandyan area. The central areas in between up-country and low-country are generally thought to constitute a third Sinhala musical cultural area, usually referred to by the name of an important province, Sabaragamuwa.

No similar regional profiles have yet been published (in the English literature) about music in the Muslim, Tamil, and Burgher communities. The Burgher community historically has been most numerous in the southern and southwestern coastal areas of the country. About two-thirds of the Muslim community are in the southern and central areas; the remaining third is in the east. Roughly three-quarters of the Sri Lankan Tamil community reside in the northern and eastern regions, while the remaining quarter lives in the central and southern regions.

Religion is intertwined with the political, economic, military, and artistic histories of Sri Lanka's diasporic groups. In the 1990s, roughly 18 percent of the population (mostly Tamil) practices Hinduism; almost 67 percent (mainly Sinhala) practices Theravada Buddhism. Around 7 percent of the population practices some form of Christianity; a roughly similar percentage practices Islam. Sinhala people also recognize another network of religious practices and ideologies. Characterized simply as the "older religion," this network includes elements found throughout South Asia, such as worship of localized spirit entities, popular Hinduism, and astrology. It has been referred to variously as the "Little Tradition" (Obeyesekere 1963), the "pre-Buddhist indigenous religion," the "sub-religion" (Kulatillake 1991:47), the "spirit religion" (Gombrich and Obeyesekere 1988), and "animism" (Gunawardana 1976). Formally, it recognizes four major guardian deities whose influence is such that each Buddhist temple contains a *dēvālē* 'shrine' for them. There are also secondary spirit beings whose spheres of influence tend to be rooted in specific locales, as well as planetary entities, malevolent and beneficent. A Buddhist religious specialist, the *kapurala*, presides over the worship of the guardian deities, and lay Buddhists (*âdurā*, also *yakâdurā*, and *kaṭṭāḍiya*) are the chant and drumming specialists who control the communication with the secondary spirit beings and the planetary forces. The repertoires of verse and drumming performed by these ritual specialists, though not systematically studied so far, contain rich information about older, heterogeneous music cultures that underlie contemporary South Asian musical cultures.

This article does not claim to be a complete survey of Sri Lanka's multiethnic, multireligious society. For reasons to be explained below, music research in Sri Lanka is sporadic and uneven. Scholars writing in English have begun to take note of music and performance in Sri Lanka, but only rarely refer to the scholarship written in the Tamil and Sinhala languages. Further, the Sinhala musical arts have been almost the exclusive focus of attention. It should be emphasized, therefore, that this is not a survey of music in Sri Lanka, but rather, of necessity, a survey of music in only one of its diasporic groups, the Sinhala. Given the rich artistic interchanges among all of Sri Lanka's diasporic groups over the centuries, a discussion of Sinhala music, including the social history of each genre, will undoubtedly be one of the many benefits of a more broadly inclusive approach to music and performance arts in Sri Lanka.

SRI LANKA AND THE MUSICOLOGY OF SOUTH ASIA: ISSUES AND PERSPECTIVES

Sri Lanka belongs to the broad South Asian musical-culture area. Its chanted prose and sung verse styles are evocative of the practice of intoned recitation of the oldest religious system in India, the Vedic religion, which took root in India around 1500 B.C. As in Vedic recitation, a narrow, three-tone scale is typically found in chanted prose and sung verse in Sinhala Sri Lanka. The poetic meters of Sanskrit, the classical literary language of the Hindus, and the meters of Pali, a language with mixed Vedic and Sanskrit heritage, provide the framework for vocal and instrumental rhythms. With the influence of a number of regional languages still to be thoroughly explored, however, prosody and its social history remain a rich topic for future research. Drum music is highly valued and operates within the cyclic and additive principles found elsewhere in South Asian drum music. Drums, along with sung, intoned, or recited vocalization, provide the basic ensemble structure, with the not infrequent addition of aerophones and *tāḷam* (hand cymbals). Chordophones of diverse kinds appear to have been common in earlier times. Nowadays, chordophones that are most typically "South Asian"—sarods, sitars, and so forth—tend to be used in the orchestrations of Tamil and Sinhala light classical music (see below). The S-shaped *kombu* is sometimes incorporated into low-country ceremonies, not as a musical instrument but as a ceremonial prop.

Music in Sri Lanka can easily be understood as distinctively South Asian, but many of Sri Lanka's performance genres and musical practices—including its most beloved popular music, an Afro-Iberian genre called *bailā*—do not seem South Asian at all. In anthropology and ethnomusicology alike, studies on South Asian music have been greatly influenced by the "Great Tradition" model of culture and society (Singer 1972:xi), in which India's intellectual, ethical, and aesthetic achievements were thought to be contained in its sacred texts, written in Sanskrit and preserved and interpreted by educated, urban literati. "Sanskritization," the assumption that social processes in India ultimately were brought under the sway of the Sanskrit texts, is an example of the Great Tradition perspective as it operates in the subcontinent. As an artifact of colonialist scholarship, this model authorized the "invention" of an Indian tradition (Dirks 1987), which takes as its point of reference a standardized Hindu ideology, the Sanskrit texts, and a Brahmin-centered social hierarchy.

In South Asian musicology one of the important consequences of this incomplete and misleadingly homogeneous notion of "India" has been the concentration on classical, urban-centered models and a relative deemphasis on other streams of musical and cultural influence. Among these, at least three can be mentioned in the Sri Lankan context: the practice of intoned recitation, Indian Buddhist music, and the music of Islam. As noted above, much of the vocal music in Sri Lanka's older performance traditions retains an overall orientation toward a narrow, three-tone scale. This scale is at least evocative of Vedic chant and, as such, its popularity in Sri Lanka may richly illustrate the dissemination and retention of some of the region's oldest musical forms. Yet it is classical music, not Vedic music, that bears the designation of "normal music" for India, where "normal" is strictly limited to music discussed in early Sanskrit music theory texts (*saṅgīta śastra*) (Powers 1980:73–74). Similarly deemphasized is the music of early Indian Buddhism, which appears to have been the basis of some of the musical principles and practices that are now understood to be "Indian" (Ellingson 1979, 1980). Buddhism largely disappeared from the Indian scene, but its oldest extant branch, Theravada, has survived in Sri Lanka since around the third century B.C. In Sri Lanka, Theravada musical forms coexisted and competed with music of the older religion and with a vibrant spectrum of music and performance arts of heterodox Buddhist branches, including the South Indian Dhammaruci sect of the Tantric school. To complete the overview of the multiple streams of commonly accepted "non-Indian" musical influence in Sri Lanka, it may be observed that music emerging from broadly Islamic contexts appears to have been absorbed into Buddhist musical offerings.

Sorting out the relative importance of these varying streams of influence presents an array of thorny historical and interpretive issues. More broadly inclusive scholarship—on music in early India as well as on the musics of Sri Lanka's diasporic groups—can most certainly lay the groundwork for that task. In the meantime, it is important to keep in mind that to approach Sri Lanka's musical cultures one needs in a sense to push aside the notion or expectation of a Hindu-centered "Indian" music and rethink any underlying assumptions.

Music in Sri Lanka's communities requires two further refinements of the conventions of South Asian musicology in addition to the consideration of Vedic music, Indian Buddhist music, the music of Buddhism's various branches as they operated in Sri Lanka over time, and the regional music and performance arts among the diasporic groups in Sri Lanka, including the music of Islam. First, in contrast to the Brahmin-centered ritual hierarchies of the Hindu-centered "India," Sinhala religious specialists are not always, or even most of the time, members of high-caste groups. In the old religion, drummer-performers are members of the Beruva (and sometimes the Oli) castes, considered extremely low in the Sinhala caste hierarchy. Ritual specialists, *kapuralas*, who control communications with the guardian deities, are usually from the Govigama (farmer) caste, considered to be the highest caste in the Sinhala caste hierarchy. At times the two groups, usually consisting entirely of lay Buddhists, work together. Although their caste position may dictate who can and cannot make contact with the highest-level deities, a ceremony's dependence on the knowledge of both groups appears to complicate conventional expectations of caste hierarchies governed by rigid rules of purity and pollution.

The second point to remember in exploring music in Sri Lanka is that, unlike the two canonical musical traditions of India, musical knowledge in Sri Lanka has not been consolidated into any single theoretical system. Among Sinhala musicians, for example, *guru paramparā* 'teacher lineages' compete with one another to assert proprietorship over varied dance, vocal, and drumming systems and techniques. The systems in use among drummer families are so diverse, according to the Sinhala musicologist Cyril de Silva Kulatillake, that each could probably constitute its own theory (Kulatillake 1980:35). This degree of nonstandardization varies substantially from the Great Tradition model of Indian music, which assumes a fundamental degree of standardization over time. The absence of any overarching model has had several consequences, one of which is that musical studies in Sri Lanka raise the issue of diversity in a way that the Hindu-centered model of Indian music does not.

A final point may be made concerning musicology in Sri Lanka. Colonial scholars and travelers, not finding equivalents to the Sanskrit *saṅgīta śāstra* in Sri Lanka, concluded that the Sinhala had no music to speak of, dismissing it as nothing more than noise, "the bellowings of an enraged buffalo, alternated with the howling of a hungry dog" (Sirr 1850:260). Music in the Tamil and Muslim communities was largely ignored or considered to be in a "fallen" state. It was assumed that the music of these diasporic communities could not have retained the riches, or the purity, of the homeland. Even today it is common to hear someone declare "we Sri Lankans have no music." At the turn of the century Sinhala nationalists attempted to counter these derogatory notions by asserting the presence of an ancient, Kandyan musical

In the older religious networks, the practices that involve the expulsion of any of eighteen different malignancies are associated with particular melodies and drum repertoires.

tradition (Sheeran 1997). However, on the whole the impact of colonial-era biases has been both to stereotype Sri Lanka as a region of derivative, uninteresting music and to create an incomplete body of scholarly research in all languages about its performance traditions.

THE MUSIC OF MUSLIM AND TAMIL COMMUNITIES

One of the consequences of the negative stereotyping of music in Sri Lanka is that scholars have not pursued research into music in the Muslim and Tamil communities. It is not possible, therefore, to report on the music and performance arts in these communities except in a cursory way. The Muslim musical milieu includes, for example, varying styles of Qur'ānic recitation, for which students are sent for training to Western Asia. It also appears to include a broadly Western Asia–influenced devotional music, which is performed within the grounds of the mosque at the great southern pilgrimage center, Kataragama. This music is associated with trance and is organized around singing, dancing, and the percussive rhythms of the *daff* 'hand-held frame drum' and the tambourine.

Given the extensive trading networks that linked Western Asia and Sri Lanka over the centuries, as well as the Islamic conquest and rule in India, it is not surprising that Islamic musical ideas and influences traveled to Sri Lanka. One of the most provocative indications of this influence has been observed in the kettledrum and oboe ensemble for Buddhist musical offerings, *hēvisi* (see below). Oboe-type instruments in India are generally understood to have emerged from West Asian contexts. The Sri Lankan oboe is distinctive because, unlike the double-reed oboes of West Asia, it is a quadruple-reed instrument. Whatever its historical provenance, both its incorporation into the Buddhist musical ensemble and its use in that ensemble of characteristically West Asian instruments are fertile topics for further study.

The lack of available scholarship also makes it difficult to report on music and performance traditions in the Tamil communities. The Hindu temple ensemble, consisting of the *tavil* and the double-reed *nāgasvaram*, is ubiquitous in Sri Lanka. It appears that the great cultural capital of northern Sri Lanka, Jaffna, occupies a position of some prominence in South India for its *nāgasvaram* players. It would also appear that the Sinhala folk-opera genre, *nādagama*, was greatly influenced by the Tamil folk opera *Natukūttu*. (Whether the *Natukūttu* may still be found in Sri Lanka's northern and eastern regions is unclear.) Tamil prosody, a topic of considerable interest for the social history of music and performance arts among Sri Lanka's diasporic communities, is probably one of the richest troves for future study. One important Tamil compositional form, *cintu*, seems to have been transformed into the Sinhala *sindu*, a lyrical form that flourished in a variety of contexts in Sinhala Sri Lanka, including Buddhist and secular praise singing and in *nādagama* (Ariyaratne 1989).

SINHALA MUSICAL FORMS AND RHYTHMS

Most of the available information about music in Sri Lanka covers what is now understood to be music of the Sinhala people. Cyril de Silva Kulatillake is one of the few Sinhala scholars to publish in English on Sinhala meter, melody, and rhythm (1974–1975, 1980, 1991). A considerable portion of the following discussion is drawn from Kulatillake's analyses. Understandings of a variety of Sinhala musical forms and their multicultural histories, particularly the popular musical forms of the late nineteenth and twentieth centuries, are indebted to Sunil Ariyaratne, a Sinhala musicologist who has published extensively in the Sinhala language (1985, 1986, 1987, 1988, 1989).

One of the first seemingly atypical aspects of Sinhala music is that there is no centralized, text-based music theory to use as a point of departure. In the Sinhala language, for example, there appears to be no real analog to the Sanskrit *saṅgīta śāstra*. Certain musical idioms, genres, and metrical frameworks are thought to have developed under the auspices of one dynastic era or another. However, much of what constitutes the "traditional" music in Sri Lanka appears to have developed outside homogenizing influences of centralized state or court networks, and in fairly regionally specific contexts. Certain teacher lineages retain proprietary rights to repertoires and styles that, in turn, are related not to any particular "school" or "system" of music but to particular kinds of practices. In the older religious networks, for example, the practices that involve the expulsion of any of eighteen different malignancies (*sanni yakka*) are associated with particular melodies and drum repertoires; the *gam maduwa* 'village ceremony', which seeks blessings from various important deities, has its own, generally distinctive, repertoire.

In Sinhala chanted prose and sung verse (*kavi*), prescribed sequences of long and short syllables (*mātra*) usually shape the melodic rhythm. As a matter of convention, the term *meter* is used to refer to a combination of stanza form and syllable count, with the duration of the *mātra* giving each *kavi* its particular character. Four categories of meter may be mentioned. The *gi* meters are characterized by the quatrain form (the first and third lines are equal in length, the second and fourth lines are unequal). The *sivpada* meters contain lines of equal length. *Akasara-vrutta* meters are defined by the number of syllables in each line rather than by their duration. A fourth category, *sindhu* meters, appear to be flexibly structured, with any number of lines and what Kulatillake has characterized as "a mixture of metres and also metro-rhythms" (1980:12).

Kulatillake has examined the workings of poetic meters in Sinhala prosody in relation to three languages: Pali, Sanskrit, and an older language of Sri Lanka, Athuva. The phonometrical (*phono-*, referring to phonology, the science of speech sound, phonetics, and phonemics; *metrical*, meaning composed in meter) principles of these languages, he believes, shaped "melody regions"—relations of tones to one another—rather than discrete scales or ragas. An analysis of melody," he writes, "has to be done in terms of the styles present in songs rather than on the basis of a system" (Kulatillake 1980:16). Among these melody regions six can be mentioned. *Tovil* songs are typified by a narrow melodic range in which the *gi* meter predominates. The *sivpada* meter has generated several melody regions, including the *seepada* and *samudraghōsha* types. The *samudraghōsha* melody region, apparently used only rarely for religious prose or song, emerged from compositional styles made popular during the Kotte period. (Kotte refers to a southwesterly kingdom, 1371–1597.) Kulatillake calculates that as many as 80 percent of Sinhala folk melodies—occupational songs such as boatmen's songs, carters' songs, miners' songs, and so forth—are composed in *sivpada* meters. They, too, tend to have narrow melodic ranges. *Pasam* 'passion hymns', a corpus of music developed in the seventeenth century and influenced by

Portuguese Catholicism, involve what Kulatillake characterizes as "full-scale" singing (1980:20–21) and thus constitute their own melody region. The up-country *vannam*, consisting of apparently unique "phonometrical" arrangements, constitutes another melody region. It has been suggested that the up-country *vannam* is related to the Tamil genre *varṇam*. Interestingly, the up-country *vannam* appears to be distinct from the thirty-two *vannam* associated with the Dondra Temple in the south, near Matara. Finally, the *praśasti* 'praise songs' (also known as *virudu*) form a melody region that probably bears the imprint of southern Indian compositional forms. This melody region emerged from the court of the up-country Sinhala king Narendrasinghe (reigned 1707–1739) and appears to have flourished during the reign of his brother-in-law and successor, Rajasimha (reigned 1739–1747), who belonged to the Telugu-speaking Nāyakkars of Madurai.

Little is known of the musical legacies of the southern kingdom, Ruhunu. It is home to the great Kataragama Temple, one of the seven holiest pilgrimage destinations in South Asia and also, historically, the power base of important rulers as well as pretenders to political power elsewhere in Sri Lanka. A study of its musical forms (as in the case of those discussed above) may serve to shed light on the waxing and waning of the political, religious, and social influence of various diasporic groups over time.

A theory of Sinhala drum music is mentioned in a Sinhala chronicle, *Wādankusa-ratnamāla* 'Science of Music', a manuscript that is presumed to be from the eighteenth century and in which several South Indian terms are used. In 1908, a Sinhala scholar, Mahawalatenne Bandar, presented the *wādankusa-ratnamāla* system to the Royal Asiatic Society as proof that the Sinhala possessed an ancient system of music theory. It is Kulatillake's conclusion, however, that attempting to understand drumming systems in Sri Lanka within the framework of an overarching theory, including South Indian drum theory, "will lead us nowhere" (Kulatillake 1980:35). Although as many as 90 percent of Sinhala drum repertoires are named for specific dance sequences in the practices of the older religion, drummer families that specialize in various repertoires claim their own unique approaches. (An attempt to reconcile these differences may be found in a 1962 publication, *Hela-gee Maga*, by the Sinhala musicologist W. B. Makulloluwa.)

A fruitful direction for research is the social history of Sinhala compositional styles, which bear the imprints of complex interactions among religious, military, and political forces through the centuries. Pali and Sanskrit meters, for example, are both found in prosody of the older religion. The more common compositional framework is the Pali-based *gi* meter, characterized as "the oldest form of song in Sri Lanka" (Kulatillake 1991:60) and which is thought to have predated the arrival of Buddhism to Sri Lanka in the third century B.C. The Sanskrit *akasara-vruttu* meter's integration into the music of the older religion may be the result of slightly later Mahayana Buddhist influence. However, a full social history of meters in the practices of the old religion would probably also reveal the operation of Tamil and Telugu prosody since heterodox Buddhist branches in Sri Lanka used regional languages in addition to Sanskrit.

MUSIC IN THE OLDER RELIGIOUS NETWORKS

The performance genres practiced in the context of the older religion contain an important corpus of Sinhala vocal and instrumental repertoires. In the shrines for Hindu guardian deities (*dēvālē*) the Buddhist specialist (*kapurala*) communicates through chanted prose and sung verse; drum music may figure importantly in the efficacy of the rituals. The communications of the *kapurala* as well as those of the lay

Buddhist performers (*âdurā*, also *yakâdurā*, or *kaṭṭāḍiya*) occur within the context of clusters of rituals known as *bali* (offerings to the planetary deities) or *tovil* (expulsion of malignant influence).

A significant aspect of the performers' and teachers' lives and their interactions with their "clients" is their caste status. The religious specialists in the old religion, as mentioned above, come from two castes, the Beruva caste and, less commonly, the Oli caste. Prejudice against drummers as low-caste people is so intense that they may go to great lengths to conceal their profession. Sons are routinely encouraged to seek other occupations rather than face the prejudices associated with their caste. Drummer-performers' "clients" in many cases are members of higher castes, who may look down on them in other contexts. According to one recent study, members of the higher caste, Govigama, are seeking training from Beruva performers of the old religion while still expressing disdain for them (Simpson 1997).

What follows is an overview of the major contexts for Sinhala vocal and drumming music associated with the older religion. Most of Sri Lanka's performances, whether associated with the old religion or with the promotion of the latest pop music band, occur during what Ellingson has described as Sri Lanka's "cultural prime time"—from around 10:00 P.M. until dawn (Ter Ellingson, personal communication). They are usually open to anyone who wants to come. A recent study has noted that well-known episodes from *tovil* ceremonies have begun to form the basis of all-night stage shows (*sandarśanaya*). The appearance of one or another of the less frightening demons is not unusual in another performance context—the nightlong stage shows of popular music (*saṅgīta sandarśanaya*) that feature the latest in Sinhala, Western, and occasionally Tamil pop bands, solo singers, and dance troupes.

Tovil

In both the up-country and the low-country, drummers and religious specialists engage in a nexus of practices that involve control and expulsion of a variety of malignant influences. These practices became a focus for colonial administrators and missionaries, who characterized them as "devil worship" and as "devil dancing"—blatant evidence of heathenism that would inspire citizens back home to sustain funding for Christian missionaries and the colonial occupation. The consequent notoriety of the *tovil* has given rise to numerous studies on dance, exorcism, religion, and healing (Ames 1977; de Zoete 1957; Kapferer 1983; Obeyesekere 1969; Pertold 1973; Raghavan 1967; Wirz 1954). The drum and vocal repertoires, as well as their conceptual significance, have not received wide attention, however. This is probably due in part to the disciplinary specializations of the researchers or to an assumption that music is somehow autonomous, or extra.

Tovil practices are diverse and may focus on such powerful entities as Mahasona, Suniyam, and Iramudun Samayama, and the eighteen malignancies (*sanni yakka*). The cluster of practices that constitute a *tovil* usually involves a possession as well as appearances of the various malignancies and negative influences in masked form. Each malignancy, referred to colloquially as a "demon," has its own drum pattern (Becker n.d.:8). The principles of vocal production in these performances appear to have some basic connection to styles of Vedic chant and Buddhist *pirit* 'protective recitation'. Pitch ranges are generally narrow: three to four half tones common in the low-country, a slightly broader range in the up-country. As discussed above, *gi* meters account for an array of chanted prose and sung verse styles found throughout the network of *tovil* music.

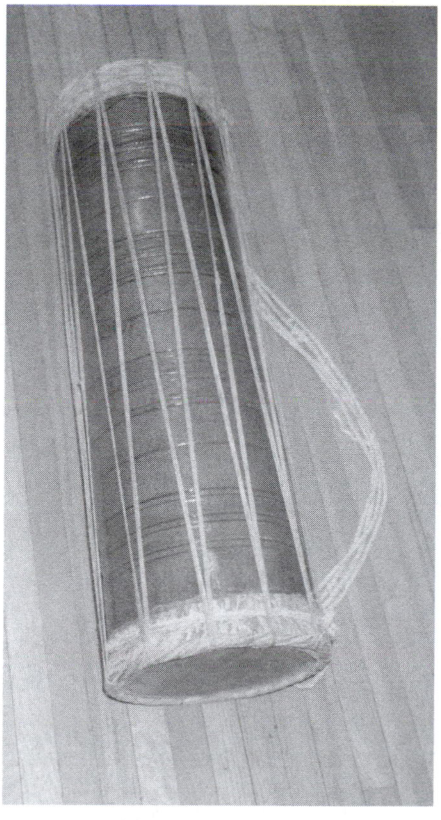

FIGURE 1 *Yak bera* drum of southern Sinhala Sri Lanka; also called *devol* or *ruhunu bere*. Photo by Anne Sheeran, 1998.

In the southern regions, the drum used in *tovil* ceremonies is the *yak bera* (figure 1), a double-headed cylindrical drum, roughly 67 centimeters long, that is suspended from the player's waist with a rope and played with two hands. The term *yak* carries

When it is understood what planetary influences are causing the patient's upset, clay effigies of the relevant planetary beings are constructed, and narratives and musical offerings are directed to these planetary beings.

the connotation of evil or malevolence, taking its name from a cluster of practices known as *yaktovil*. Depending on the context, the drum may also be referred to as the *devol bera* (Devol being the name of an important deity), or the *ruhunu bera* 'southern or low-country drum'. Among the distinctive sonic qualities of the drum are its ringing harmonies and sharp, almost barking tones. Nowadays, because of restrictions on the felling of woods like *jak*, or *kos*, the low-country drum is usually made from coconut wood. Cow intestines are a common material for the drumhead.

Bali

An important cluster of practices in Sinhala Sri Lanka is the *bali śanti karma* (*śanti* 'peace', *karma* 'action'). During the 1990s, the Ministry of Ayurvedic Medicine sponsored several *bali* ceremonies, which are thought to bring peace and good health, and to restore equanimity. Astrologers cast and explore the astrological chart of a "patient." When it is understood what planetary influences are causing the patient's upset, clay effigies of the relevant planetary beings are constructed. It is to these planetary beings that narratives and musical offerings are directed. The low-country *bali* places less overall emphasis on painting the effigies, whereas in the up-country, one may find effigies painted in a variety of colors, including vibrant reds, blues, and yellows.

Although an extensive body of scholarship on *bali* is available in Sinhala (Dissanayake 1990; Kariyawassam 1976; Piyasena 1988; Sederaman 1964, 1967), little has been drawn into the English-language treatments of the genre so far. Kulatillake suggests that *bali* meters range closer to Sanskrit theories of metrics than to Pali theories (1980:3–5), implying, he suggests, influences of the heterodox Mahayana and Tantric Buddhisms that began to flourish in Sri Lanka beginning around the second century C.E. Wijesekera (1987:131) mentions that the specialists (*santikāraya*) for *bali* are not of the Beruva caste but rather of the Oli. Other than these notes, a few general points on the ceremonies, drawn from personal observation, may be noted. The ethos of up-country and low-country *bali* appear to be somewhat different. In the low country, for example, *bali* performers play complex microrhythms with immense gentleness rather than the competitive bravado common in *tovil*, so as to help foster feelings of peacefulness and serenity in the patient and audience. Drummer-dancers use hand-held bells to create an encompassing sonic envelope; they move gently and quietly, with their feet supposedly never lifted from the floor. Even the singing in parallel fourths, perhaps somewhat jarring to the unaccustomed ear, helps to delineate an arena of peace and tranquillity.

Both low-country and up-country *bali* feature hand-held bells and ankle bells to create a constant, unbroken sound that provides a sonic parallel to the sacred thread (*nula*) that extends from the altar to the patient and through the crowd of spectators for the duration of the performance. In the low-country, the singing is antiphonal, at times in parallel fourths. Up-country *bali* troupes appear to prefer to integrate more acrobatic kinds of dance, as well as episodes of competitive drumming. "We have to keep the audience awake!" was the explanation given by one drummer.

Music of the *dēvālē*

One component of the older religious nexus is the worship of major and minor deities. For example, a *gam maduwa* (literally 'village shelter or hall') may be held to worship the goddess Pattini. A lay Buddhist religious specialist who is responsible for the particular *dēvālē* 'shrine' impersonates the goddess and recites verses that describe her life and accomplishments. Kulatillake identifies some of the meters used in such a ritual as Sanskrit (1980:4). The *kapurala* works in coordination with the Beruva drummers, whose drum rhythms appear to invoke the presence of the particular deity as well as control the pacing of the worship.

The social history and present practice of the *dēvālē* ceremonies constitute a rich topic for further research. Scholars have long recognized the complexity of the interaction between Buddhism and the old religion, including the eventual consolidation of the old religion within the overall Buddhist framework (Gombrich and Obeyesekere 1988; Obeyesekere 1963). A history of the musical styles in *dēvālē* ceremonies would probably help to illuminate the multiple forces that flowed through this interaction, and that continue to make them vibrant forums of social, political, and religious commentary.

Kohomba kankāriya

A now rarely performed set of practices of considerable musicological significance is the *kohomba kankāriya*. This is a series of ceremonies of supplication and healing offered to a special group of spirit beings thought to be powerful in the up-country regions. Among them is the god Kohomba. The purpose of the *kohomba kankāriya* is to bring about general auspiciousness such as a good harvest, the end of a drought, or peace in the community. The stories of the gods are presented in chanted-prose and sung-verse styles; these alternate with comic episodes in which, for example, specialists explore the intricacies of caste hierarchies by arguing back and forth about the proper way to address one another (Walcott 1978). The spirit of argumentation and competition often extends to displays of virtuosity among the drummers, as (in teams or individually) they try to outdo one another and the dancers in demonstrations of their art. The *kohomba kankāriya* is expensive to coordinate and requires weeks of preparation, specialists in a variety of arts including as many as sixteen drummers, and eighty-four different episodes, which may take days to perform; as a result, full-scale performances have become infrequent. During the late nineteenth and early twentieth centuries, elements of the ceremony came to signify a generalized Sinhala identity; what is known as "Kandyan dance" takes its basic forms from the *kohomba kankāriya* (Reed 1991).

The *kohomba kankāriya* is a wellspring of information about Sinhala music in Sri Lanka. Kulatillake has indicated that the practices contain the entire repertoire of drum music for the main up-country drum, the *gâṭa bera* (Kulatillake 1980:28). Walcott has explored its many styles of vocal music, and suggests that the presentation of the gods' stories through song is at the heart of the offering's efficacy (1978:19). He has identified singing styles within the syllabic *akasara-vrutta* meter, which appears to be a common framework for introductory, unaccompanied offerings to spirit beings and for praise to Buddha. These introductory *kavi* 'songs', known as *anistippuva*, generally use four tones of a pentatonic scale and involve "lines sung in a 'parlando' (spoken), syllabic style with the last syllable of the first and fourth lines prolonged in a florid melisma" (Walcott 1978:20). Walcott has also noted the use of a diatonic scale in connection with one of the singing styles, *ura yakkama*. As noted earlier,

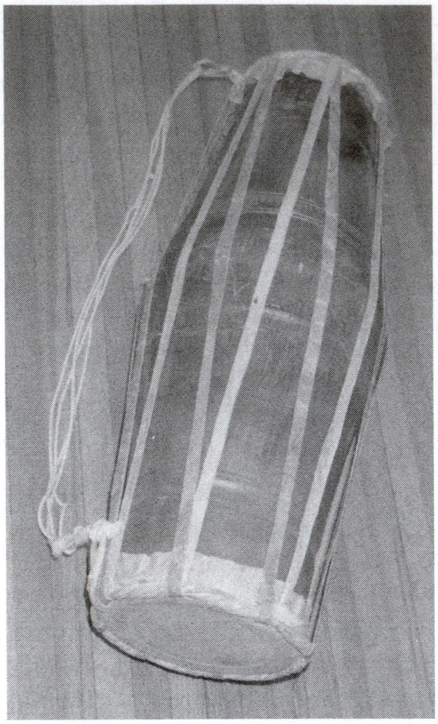

FIGURE 2 *Gâṭa bera* drum of the Sinhala up-country, with tapered ends and waisted middle; also called Kandyan drum. Photo by Anne Sheeran, 1998.

Kulatillake traces the Sanskrit *akasara-vrutta* meter to the era of Mahayana Buddhist activity in Sri Lanka; he notes, further, that the ability to sing the eulogies (*Deva Stortra*) in Sanskrit was considered by some to be "a mark of competency" (1980:5).

The *gâṭa bera* (figure 2) is a double-headed barrel drum. Like the *yak bera*, it is played with both hands and is suspended from the player's waist with a rope. It measures roughly 68 centimeters in length and roughly 86 centimeters in diameter at the widest part. The drumheads measure about 20 centimeters in diameter. The *gâṭa bera* has a higher-pitched tone produced with the right hand and a duller tone produced with the left hand. It shares with the *yak bera* the capacity for a sharp, almost barking timbre that carries over considerable distances. It too tends to be constructed from coconut wood; some drum makers say that using goat rather than cow intestine for the drumheads produces a louder sound.

Raghavan refers to the *gâṭa bera* as "undoubtedly the most important" of all Sinhala drums (1967:175), but there is no reason to suppose that this is true. During the independence struggle at the turn of the century, when cultural activists attempted to consolidate a "Kandyan" musical tradition, many of the region's characteristics were labeled as the oldest and purest examples of Sinhala Sri Lankan culture (Reed 1991; Sheeran 1997). It is in that context, which lacks an appreciation of the rich regional diversity operating within the overarching Sinhala identity, that we may understand Raghavan's assertion. Raghavan also refers to the *gâṭa bera* as the *magul* 'auspicious' *bera* (1967:175). However, the term *magul bera* refers to a particular drum pattern that may be played on the *daule* (see below), the *yak bera* or the *gâṭa bera*, and also to the context of the performance—either inaugural or festive occasions.

Popular genres and instruments

Kolam is a Sinhala masked theater associated with the southwestern areas of Sri Lanka. Scholars have suggested that its genesis may be examined in reference to the eighteen diseases that form the basis of a cluster of *tovil* practices (see above). *Kolam* music requires two instruments, the *horanâva* 'quadruple-reed aerophone' and the *yak bera* drum, as well as a "master of ceremonies" and a chorus of young female singers. As in most Sinhala melody, the melodic range is narrow (about three tones); melodic rhythm is structured by the combination of long and short syllables of the verse (Sarachchandra 1966:82). Kulatillake suggests that *kolam* music absorbed and transformed elements of *nādagama* melody, a Sri Lankan version of the southern Indian *natukūttu* drama (Kulatillake 1980:32). Another popular form of musical theater in southwestern Sri Lanka that may be related musically to the *nādagama* is *rukkada*, or puppet theater.

Sokari is a Sinhala dramatic genre of the central and up-country regions that incorporates mime, impersonation, masks, and a great deal of slapstick comedy. *Sokari* usually centers on the adventures of a cast of characters attempting to immigrate from India to Sri Lanka, where they hope to find work. The play is accompanied by the up-country drum, the *gâṭa bera*. Dialogue alternates with sung verses in unison and at times in parallel approximate seconds. The drama unfolds with characters moving clockwise in a circular motion on the "stage"—usually a clearing of some kind. Buddhist temples sometimes sponsor *sokari* performances, which take place usually between April and June each year.

A number of Sinhala dance and performance genres use the *rabāna*, a popular hand-held frame drum. The *rabāna* generally comes in two sizes: the *at* 'hand-held' *raban* is generally about 25 to 30 centimeters in diameter, and the *banku raban* is roughly 60 to 75 centimeters in diameter. At holidays like the Sinhala New Year groups of women are thought to have gathered around the *banku-raban*, which is placed on the ground, to play it simultaneously. Little appears to be known about this tradition. Kulatillake mentions it in connection with announcements of a girl's first menstruation or the consummation of her marriage (1984–1985:32); nowadays, young school-age girls, at least in the Colombo metropolitan schools, may study the *banku raban* as a "traditional" cultural activity.

At raban troupes often participate in public festivals, such as the processions (*perahera*) of Buddhist temples, where they alternate spinning the drum with playing it while dancing. The *at raban* is also used widely as an accompaniment to the vocal genre *virudu* (also *praśasti* 'praise songs'), one of the melody regions thought to have been strongly influenced by South Indian melodies (see "Sinhala Musical Forms and Rhythms" above). Nowadays, *virudu* is a popular framework for sung storytelling.

BUDDHIST MUSIC

Theravada Buddhism survived longest in southeastern India and Sri Lanka, moving from Sri Lanka to southeast Asia around the eleventh century. Wherever Theravada exists one finds music associated with it that can be distinguished from the music of Mahayana Buddhist traditions by its more restrictive character. Although many scholars have interpreted certain restrictions as evidence that music was negatively valued in the Theravada tradition, in fact the reverse is true: music was understood to be so powerful a means of affecting perception and cognition that forms were developed to harness and control that power (Ellingson 1979:151). Nevertheless, scholars have tended to characterize Theravada as essentially antimusic, the locus of no significant music theory or styles. Kulatillake, for example, notes that without Mahayana Buddhism and its "licence for lavish festivities and ceremonies" the more orthodox Theravada Buddhism would never have been able to survive. "Had it not been for [the] accommodation of Mahayanic elements, Buddhism in its pure Theravada ideals could not have stood the intrigues of Hinduism in particular" (1991: 39).

Although by far the most widely accepted assessment of music in Sinhala Theravada Buddhism, Kulatillake's understanding of Theravada music may be complicated in several respects. First, it too coincidentally echoes the preferences of European colonial scholars who, during the eighteenth and nineteenth centuries, promoted the notion of Buddhism as an essentially austere, wholly "rational" religion. Second, making the case for any one "essentially" Theravada characteristic implies a degree of certainty that may be unwarranted: the Theravada canon was not committed to writing until the first century B.C., thus postdating the rise of the Mahayanic branches and suggesting at least the possibilities of Mahayana-Theravada interactions. Third, even the canon offers a somewhat different perspective on the place of music in Theravada Buddhist worship, as well as on its forms. In the *Maha-Parinibbana-Sutta*, for example, Buddha talks of the grand vitality of the city of his own demise, Kusinara, with reference to the sensuous mingling of musical sounds of drums, vina, singing, and cymbals. He also suggests that instrumental musical offerings by lay people constitute important forms of worship. He discusses styles of chanting in detail in the *Cullavagga*, advocating chant ("intoned recitation") as a form of musical worship.

Music and performance at the Daladā Maligawā Temple

One of the most interesting examples of diverse musical strands operating within a Theravada Buddhist framework is the music and performance associated with the Daladā Maligawā in Kandy. This temple is known as the Tooth Relic Temple, or the Temple of the Tooth, because it holds one of the Buddha's teeth in safekeeping. During the reign of King Narendrasinghe (1707–1739), the Tooth Temple underwent a considerable increase in status and importance. The relic began to be included

A temple band of musicians called *hēvisi* makes an offering of sounds at Buddhist temples, usually three times each day.

in the annual *asala perahera*, which had hitherto been connected to worship of the major Hindu deities; it also shed its identity as an object of Mahayana worship and began to acquire a Theravada identification. At the same time, the *kavikāra maḍuva* was developed, involving high-caste lay Buddhists performing eulogies to the Buddha within the temple chambers more or less in secret.

The early rulers in the Nāyakkar dynasty in Sri Lanka (1739–1815), to which Narendrasinghe's court was connected, are thought to have sought out the support of the Sinhala Theravada monastic community (*sangha*), and it was to bolster their claim to authority in Sri Lanka that they became patrons of Buddhist worship. Under their patronage, several important musical forms flourished, including *praśasti*, 'praise songs'. Ariyaratne has suggested that they are closely related, if not directly analogous, to the Tamil *cintu* (Sinhala, *sindu*), a five-line composition with a shortened first line (*pallavi*) and a long second line (*anupallavi*) (Ariyaratne 1989:179–181). Other elements of *kavikāra maḍuva* musical performance, such as the incorporation of the *udakki* 'hourglass drum' and the *panteru* 'tambourine', reflect the broad religious and musical influences operating within Theravada Buddhist contexts. The *udakki*, also known as the *ḍamaru*, is an hourglass drum identified with both the cosmic dance of Shiva and Buddhist tantric practice. The *panteru*, an idiophone, is a metal-frame instrument with jingles that are thought to signify the circle of planets. The *panteru*, like other elements of the *kavikāra maḍuva* musical performance, is of great antiquity and exemplifies the diverse social histories that are inscribed in the music of Theravada Buddhist worship.

Buddhist musical offerings now found in Sinhala Sri Lanka, including chanted recitation of religious texts by monks (Bhikkus) and instrumental musical offerings by lay people, appear to be broadly consistent with the portrayal of music in the Theravada texts. Three examples will be discussed: the music of the lay Buddhist instrumental ensemble (*hēvisi*); Buddhist chanting (*pirit*); and the system of instrument classification (*pañcatūrya nāda*) [See CLASSIFICATION OF MUSICAL INSTRUMENTS]. Yet even in these cases, the interplay of historical processes calls for a broadening rather than a narrowing of what is conceived as "Buddhist" music. Certainly, Sinhala Buddhist chanting would appear to qualify as Buddhist music, but ease of identification generally breaks down on consideration of specific elements of performance. Temple processions (*perahera*), for example, involve professional and amateur dance, music, and theater troupes that draw from diverse musical sources and temporal strata. Such processions are often contexts for political commentary and fun, as when the colonial overseer in his pith helmet appears, harassing groups of dancing tea pluckers. The *pappara*, a snare drum and trumpet ensemble, is a regular feature; its jazzy melodies and rhythmic drive are also popularly associated with the high-energy cheering sections at cricket matches. West Asian musical instruments have been incorporated into the primary lay Buddhist instrumental ensemble, *hēvisi*. Both the Theravada and the Mahayana branches of Buddhism in Sri Lanka have nourished

FIGURE 3 *Tewa pada*, a sixteen-beat drum tala with three levels of accents—heavy, light, and silent—played as a musical offering by the *hēvisi* ensemble while circumambulating the Buddhist temple in Sinhala Sri Lanka.

--		.	--		.	--		--							
1	2	3	4	5	6	7	8	9	10	11	12	13	14	15	16
--		.	--		.	--		--							

-- first level of accentuation (clap)
. second level (wave)
third level (no mark)

or provided a framework for the flowering of diverse performance genres, styles, and contexts. As a result, forms authorized in the canon as well as the heterogeneous music and performance arts that flourish in everyday contexts of Buddhist worship are included under the heading of Buddhist music.

Hēvisi

A temple band of musicians called *hēvisi* makes an offering of sounds (*śabda pūjā*) at Buddhist temples, usually three times each day. Their musical offering is also known as *hēvisi pūjā*, sometimes translated as "homage of the drums" (Seneviratna 1979:52). The basic *hēvisi* ensemble consists of two drums (*daule* and *tammâṭṭa*) and the oboe (*horanâva*). On important occasions or in more affluent temples the *tāḷam* 'hand cymbals' and the conch shell are commonly added to this basic ensemble.

Specific drum rhythms accompany each significant moment of the *hēvisi pūjā*. The rhythm for circumambulating the temple is the *tewa pada* (figure 3), a sixteen-beat cycle with three levels of accentuation: heavy emphasis on beats 1, 4, 7, and 9; lighter on beats 3 and 6; and none on beats 10 through 16. As they arrive at each of the four gates, representing the four cardinal directions, the musicians shift to the *buddha pada* (figure 4), a sixteen-beat cycle with two levels of accentuation: strong accents on beats 1 and 2, 5 and 6, 9 and 10; and no accents on the rest. Specific rhythms also delineate moments in the lunar cycle and accompany homages to the major and minor deities of the Sinhala pantheon (Seneviratna 1979: 53–55). In an unpublished series of lectures, Ter Ellingson has explored the movement of these specific rhythms through time and their structured elaboration of underlying Buddhist cosmological principles (Ellingson, personal communication).

The *daule* 'double-headed barrel drum' is 41 centimeters long and has large drumheads 34 centimeters in diameter (figure 5). It hangs suspended from the drummer's waist and is played with a stick in the right hand and the bare left hand. Historically, the *daule* is associated with rituals of state, including the announcement of royal edicts and the funeral processions of important state and court personages. Also known as the Sabaragamuwa (central-region) drum, the *daule* is commonly used for funerals and temple processions, and in the *bali* rituals of the central region.

The *tammâṭṭa* (*pokuru*) *bera* is a pair of kettledrums tied together (figure 6). It is played suspended from a player's waist and beaten with two supple, spring-loaded sticks (*kaduppu*) that are partially covered in cloth. The *tammâṭṭa* elaborates on the rhythmic cycle given by the *daule*. Colonial observers referred to it inaccurately as the "tom-tom." Both kettles are roughly 18 centimeters high. The diameter of one head

FIGURE 4 *Buddha pada*, sixteen-beat drum tala with two levels of accents—heavy and silent. Played as a musical offering by the *hēvisi* ensemble at each of the four gates of a Buddhist temple, in Sinhala Sri Lanka.

--	--			--	--			--	--						
1	2	3	4	5	6	7	8	9	10	11	12	13	14	15	16
--	--			--	--			--	--						

-- first level of accentuation (clap)
second level (no mark)

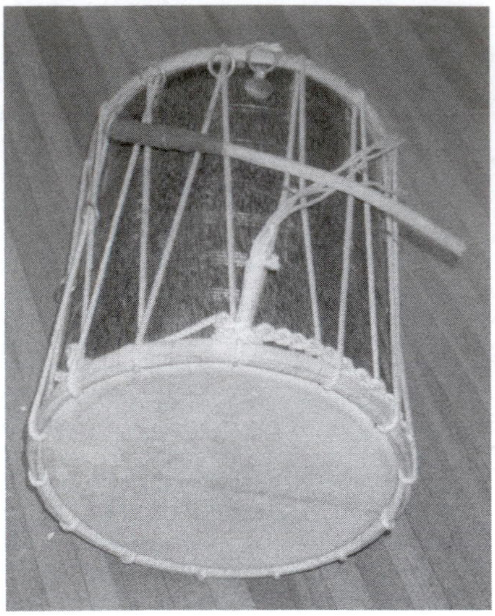

FIGURE 5 *Daule* drum used in the *hēvisi* ensemble; sometimes referred to as the Sabaragamuwa drum. Photo by Anne Sheeran, 1998.

is about 18 centimeters, the other roughly 22 centimeters. The right-hand drum is higher pitched than the left-hand drum.

The *horanâva* is a conical-bore, quadruple-reed oboe. It can vary in size, anywhere from 20 to 36 centimeters in length, and can have six to eight finger holes. It is an instrument with an extremely piercing, "high energy" sound (Ellingson 1987: 188). In the *hēvisi* ensemble the *horanâva* player embellishes a series of set, skeletal melody patterns. In *kolam* music, the *horanâva* alternates with the singers. The *horanâva* player may use melodies drawn from a variety of sources, and the relationship between a melody pattern and its embellishment appears to be intricate. This intricacy, it may be observed, was completely lost on many colonial observers, to whom the "shrill" sounds of the instrument were a glaring example of what they found intolerable about Sinhala music (Sheeran 1997).

Pañcatūrya nāda

Another window into Buddhist musical principles is a system of instrument classification called the *pañcatūrya nāda*. According to Seneviratna the *pañcatūrya nāda* is "the nucleus of the Buddhist Music of the Theravada tradition in Sri Lanka" (1980:12). It is a fivefold system of instrument classification that is the "Buddhist counterpart of the classical-Hindu four instrument classes" (Ellingson 1980:433). References to the *pañcatūrya nāda* are found in the sixth-century Pali commentary the *Vamsatthappakasini* (Seneviratna 1979:50). The five categories are *ātata*, *vitata*, *ātatavitata*, *ghana*, and *suṣira*. The first three categories are types of drums: *ātata* refers to a single-headed drum; *vitata* refers to a double-headed drum; and *ātatavitata* refers to stringed drums. *Ghana* refers to idiophones, *suṣira* to aerophones [see CLASSIFICATION OF MUSICAL INSTRUMENTS].

According to Kulatillake, in the nineteenth century the three drum classifications began to refer to the manner in which the drums were played—with sticks, or hands, or with combinations of sticks and hands (Kulatillake 1991:70–71). *Ātata* then came to refer to drums played with the hands, *vitata* to drums played with sticks, and *ātatavitata* to drums played with both hands and sticks.

Kulatillake has also surveyed interpretations of another fivefold classification system, *panca tāḷa*. Some dancer families link the term to five basic dance positions. However, the term has also been interpreted to refer to five sources of musical sound, sometimes to five purportedly basic drum sounds. Typically, *panca tāḷa* references five basic rhythmic patterns, although there is little consensus among drummer families about which five patterns should be included (Kulatillake 1980:37-39).

Pirit

Pirit (from *paritta* 'protection' in Pali) refers to Buddhist chant. It is a style of intoned recitation (*sarabhanna*) based on phonological properties of the Pali language, but restricted melodically to the Vedic three-tone scale. As the oldest among all the Theravada traditions outside India, the Sinhala Theravada chant traditions may afford rich insights into Indian Buddhist musical principles. The exploration of this point, however, would have to include weighing the relevance of several subsequent influences. Among these influences are two important reformist movements, in the twelfth and eighteenth centuries, during which the Sinhala Theravada monastic community sought to revitalize Theravada Buddhism in Sri Lanka through contacts with Burmese and Thai Theravada traditions. Ellingson has observed that there are obvious differences among Sinhala, Burmese, and Thai chants and speculates that in the Sinhala case, traditions older than chant have probably been retained (personal communication). Thai and Burmese influences may also constitute an ideological overlay whose influence cannot be ruled out without further scholarship.

This engagement with Thai Theravada Buddhism is collectively remembered in

FIGURE 6 *Tammâṭṭa* (*pokuru*) *bere*, used in the *hēvisi* ensemble. Photo by Anne Sheeran, 1998.

the annual *dorakadarśane* ceremony. A small boy is dressed in what may be the robes of Thai royalty to reenact the arrival of the predominant Thai Theravada Buddhist ordination lineage, the Siam Nikaya, in Sri Lanka in 1753. An energetic temple procession delivers the boy to the temple. This procession has a *hēvisi* at one end, a *pappara* brass band at the other, and traditional Kandyan dancers in the middle, along with troupes of students demonstrating their skills in the winnowing dance, *rabāna* twirling, and the *lī-keḷi* stick dance (from the Tamil *kōlāṭṭam* dance). At the temple, the entire neighborhood is engulfed in the sounds of amplified *pirit* chanting.

Kulatillake asserts that *pirit* chanting was introduced through Mahayana Buddhism, and suggests that it may be "one of the oldest institutions of singing in Sri Lanka" (1982:20). This differs somewhat from accounts in the Theravada texts, in which Buddha makes statements authorizing monks to chant. Furthermore, the practice of chanting protective formulas has been known in South Asia since pre-Buddhist times (de Silva 1981:3–27). An integral part of Sri Lanka's political, religious, and musical history, *pirit* chanting gradually became a focus for state patronage. As a result, full-fledged ceremonies developed that elaborate in symbolic form the interdependence among the state, the Buddhist monastic community, and the laity.

Nowadays, *pirit* ceremonies mark any occasion when protection or blessings are sought, from the opening of a new factory to the commemoration of a family or neighborhood anniversary. The ceremonies, which can last anywhere from one hour to seven days, are usually conducted by Buddhist monks (and, in some cases, Buddhist nuns), and, if the sponsors can afford it, may include a *hēvisi* band. Abbreviated *pirit* recitations are heard daily on the state-controlled radio, while neighborhood temples broadcast cassette-recorded chanting over loudspeakers each evening.

SINHALA STAGE AND POPULAR MUSIC

A broad spectrum of contemporary popular music opens the window onto Sinhala Sri Lanka's more recent musical history and illustrates the genesis of Sinhala musical forms in a multiethnic, transnational context. Of these, four popular forms—*nṛtya*, *bailā-kaffriñgā*, Sinhala pop, and *sarala gī*—will be considered.

Disco *bailā* constitutes the climax of an evening's nightclubbing, bringing almost everyone out onto the dance floor for one last high-energy fling.

Nṛtya

In the 1870s Parsi and Marathi theater troupes from North India began touring in Sri Lanka. Their music incorporated a range of genres from the ghazal to harmonium accompaniment. In 1877, Sri Lanka's leading playwright, C. Don Bastian, popularized this music by translating its songs directly into Sinhala. By the following year the public's "madness for Hindi songs" had laid the foundations for the transformation of this music into a popular genre, *nṛtya* (Ariyaratne 1986). By the turn of the century, *nṛtya* and the vibrant Sinhala musical theater, Tower Hall, became inseparable; its chief playwright, John de Silva, began inviting North Indian musicians (Vidhan Ameer Khan, Mahadeva Jothinatha, and Janji Maharaj) to Colombo to compose for his theater. By 1906, the genre had become an obvious choice for the first series of gramophone recordings of "Sinhala" music. *Nṛtya* music dominated the urban popular scene in Sri Lanka until the emergence of Indian film music in the 1930s. Contemporary Sinhala pop musicians, such as the band Shakti, occasionally incorporate elements of *nṛtya*—the harmonium, or a well-known *nṛtya* tune—into their compositions.

Bailā-kaffriñgnā

Bailā is a popular music and dance genre with probable roots in Afro-Portuguese performance traditions in Sri Lanka (Sheeran 1997). It is understood to have a core set of seventeen or eighteen melodies (thought to be of Portuguese origin), and a 6/8 meter. Its identity, however, is strongly tied to its instrumentation: whether synthesized or acoustic, the *bailā* features combinations that include the banjo or mandolin, violin, guitar, *rabāna*, and a pair of conga drums. Its styles are varied. Some bands orient the *bailā* toward the Iberian side of its lineage by adding instruments typical of mariachi bands (mariachi being a product of Spanish colonialism and thus conflated with perceived "Iberian-ness"). This style of *baila* is generally considered to be graceful and moderate and is associated with a type of dance known as the *kaffriñgnā*. Since the songs usually consist of verses sung by a soloist with refrains sung by a chorus, they are known as "chorus *bailā*." Another style of chorus *bailā* is probably more common. Sometimes referred to as "disco" *bailā*, this style is more aggressive, fun, and free wheeling than its Iberian-oriented counterpart. Whereas the latter emphasizes gentility and romance, the disco *bailā* stresses raucousness and sarcastic, assiduously unromantic attitudes. It is generally the kind of *bailā* that one hears at the all-night popular musical shows (*saṅgīta sandarśanaya*) and, if the nightclub has not banned it altogether for being too low class, it also constitutes the climax of an evening's nightclubbing, bringing almost everyone out onto the dance floor for one last high-energy fling. With the rise of regional broadcasting beginning in the 1930s and 1940s, the *bailā* drew from a variety of popular musical influences from Africa, the Carribbean, and the United States. The 1970s version of *bailā*, "disco" *bailā*, was greatly influenced by the 1970s "made-in-the-U.S.A." version of Trinidadian calypso.

Some performers use the music of *bailā* as a framework for storytelling or for commentaries on popular events, moral issues, tributes to teachers, good citizenship, patriotism, and so on. Others use the music as a framework for a tradition of competitive, theatricalized word dueling and verbal competition. This is known as *wāde* 'debate' *bailā*, in which performers extemporize on a melody and a topic of the judges' choosing. The performers' skill in working within the metrical basis of the melody is one of the challenges of the genre. *Wāde bailā* competitions are not uncommon and, like most of Sri Lanka's entertainment genres, can begin around 10:00 P.M. and go on until dawn. The "All Ceylon *Bailā* Champions" tour as a group and are especially busy during the two festival seasons in Sri Lanka, the Christmas holidays and the Hindu and Sinhala New Year (April–June).

Debate and chorus *bailā* probably emerged from a network of African-Iberian performance traditions that flourished in Sri Lanka between the late sixteenth and early twentieth centuries. The term *bailā* is used to denote many genres, ranging from dancing, debating, or brawling to weighing or measuring (Sheeran 1997). *Che koetie* (*chichothi*) is a term sometimes associated with eighteenth- and nineteenth-century references to *bailā* and appears to have had a figurative relationship with verbal competition: something hard edged, meant to ridicule or confront (Jackson 1990). During the eighteenth and nineteenth centuries, the performance milieu came under the influence of European and North American racial politics. By the 1850s, writings of the Sri Lankan middle- and upper-class intelligentsia and of English residents clearly indicate that blackface minstrelsy had become especially influential as a template for thinking about people of the lowest racial strata—Africans and those of mixed African-Portuguese ancestry (Sheeran 1997). As their music became more popular, these groups came to be represented as innately musical, fond of dancing, carefree, and impecunious—all stereotypes taken directly from minstrelsy. These stereotypes probably explain to some extent the genre's eventual elaboration into its two dominant forms—the gentle, fit-for-the-drawing-room *kaffriñgnā*, and the purportedly low-caste, raucous *bailā*. Likewise, during the twentieth century, the genre's wide popularity and its notoriety as an African-Portuguese music made it a target of criticism among some Sinhala nationalists. The *kaffriñgnā-chicothi-bailā* nexus is thus a rich source of information not only about the African diaspora in South Asia, but also about the forging of creole cultures and the growing emphasis in Sri Lanka on music as a politics of nationalism.

Sinhala pop

Given its rich history in Sri Lanka, *bailā* music seems somehow excessive or untamed to many people. This point comes out in diverse contexts, but perhaps most intriguingly in relation to another popular commercial genre, Sinhala pop. "Sinhala pop" is a cover term for music that is usually organized around a solo singer and an instrumental ensemble comprising three primary instruments: electronic drum sets, synthesizers, and electric guitars. Its diverse influences include Indian film songs, Western pop music, and reggae, though during the 1960s Latin sounds (such as those of the group Los Paraguayos) were in the forefront of the genre. Like *bailā*, Sinhala pop can be heard in a variety of contexts: on long-distance buses and television musical shows, blaring out of kiosks at the market, and at open-air stage shows. Further research will deepen our understanding of Sinhala pop music, but it may be noted that Sinhala pop is often counterposed to *bailā*, as in "I like *bailā* music, but I like normal music, too" (Sheeran 1997). The genre seldom outsells *bailā* music, but from time to time in the mid-1990s, it seemed poised to gain the commercial edge.

Sarala gī

Sarala gī is a subset of a larger category of music that the British Broadcasting Corporation (BBC) characterized as "oriental," that is, music from India and Sri Lanka rather than from the West. Known as *visarada* 'music experts', its proponents in the past usually earned an advanced degree in music from Bhatkhande University in Lucknow, or from Santiniketan in Bengal (now West Bengal). *Sarala gī* is considered to be the music of educated Sinhalese. Most often translated as "light classical" music, *sarala gī* is contemplative and introspective music, intended to settle the mind. It is usually performed by a single vocalist accompanied by an "Oriental orchestra" that includes sitars, violins, tablas, flutes, and sarods. Song topics may range from religious devotion to folk themes involving life in the village, love, romance, and longing. The music is far less commercially successful in Sri Lanka than the other two dominant Sinhala popular genres, *bailā* and Sinhala pop. During the late 1980s one hundred thousand or more copies of a popular *bailā* cassette would sell within one or two years. With few exceptions, sales of the best *sarala gī* cassette would number only between fifteen and twenty thousand over several years.

Sarala gī has had an important bearing on the development of Sinhala musical politics during the twentieth century. It came of age during an era of backlash against Indian film music, which to cultural nationalists in both India and Sri Lanka seemed to symbolize the general deterioration of musical, and hence cultural, sensibilities of the Sri Lankan people. Sinhala nationalists felt that film music was particularly menacing in light of the belief, widespread in India and Sri Lanka by the 1940s, that if there had been a genuinely "ancient" system of Sinhala music, four hundred years of colonial domination had all but buried it. Just as the All India Radio programmers had encouraged such artists as Rabindranath Tagore to develop innovations based on Bengali folk melodies, authorities in the Sinhala section at Radio Ceylon (later, the Sri Lankan Broadcasting Corporation) likewise encouraged Sinhala musicians to use the framework of Sinhala folk tunes as a basis for experimentation. Ceylon Radio artists were auditioned by musical experts from the Marris College of Music in Lucknow; Sinhala musicians were encouraged to study at Santiniketan, Tagore's musical institute in Bengal. The great exponents of Sinhala folk music, Devar Surya Sena and Neelum Devi, were part of the musical activism associated with Santiniketan. Ananda Samarakoon (1911–1962) also studied there and is considered by some to be the father of the *sarala gī* genre. Sunil Shanta (1915–1981) studied at Santiniketan and at Bhatkhande University. Shanta, however, appears to have been interested in breaking away from what he considered the dominance of North Indian music. His music contains a rich variety of influences, including American country music, Hawaiian guitar, and in particular the swing music of 1940s southern California dance halls (Richard Jones, personal communication).

REFERENCES

Ames, Michael M. 1964. "Magical-Animism and Buddhism: A Structural Analysis of the Sinhalese Religious System." In *Religion in South Asia*, ed. Edward B. Harper, 21–52. Seattle: University of Washington Press.

———. 1977. *Tovil, the Ritual Chanting, Dance, and Drumming of Exorcism in Sri Lanka*. New York: Performing Arts Program of the Asia Society.

Amunugama, Sarath. 1978. "John de Silva and the Nationalist Theatre." *The Ceylon Historical Journal* 25(1–4):285–304.

Ariyaratne, Sunil. 1985. *Baila Kapirinna*. Maradana: S. Hewkapuge. In Sinhala.

———. 1986. *Gramafpon gi yugaya*. Kolamba: Dayavamsa Jaykodi. In Sinhala.

———. 1987. *Karol, Pasam, Kantaru: A Survey of Sinhala Christian Hymns in Sri Lanka*. Colombo: Supersun Educational Services Ltd.

———. 1988. *Ananda Samarakoon Adhayanaya*. Colombo: S. Godage and Brothers. In Sinhala.

———. 1989. *Sindu Vistaraya: An Investigation into the Word "Sindu" in Sinhala Literature and Music*. Colombo: Dayawansa Jayakody & Co.

Bandar, Mahawalatenne. 1908. "Kandyan music." *Journal of the Royal Asiatic Society (Ceylon Branch)*. 21:129–164.

Becker, Judith. N.d. "A Preliminary Investigation of Drumming, Dancing and Singing in the Sri Lankan Yak Tovil." Manuscript.

Berberich, Frank J., III. 1974. "The Tavil: Construction, Technique, and Context in Present-Day Jaffna." Master's thesis, University of Hawaii.

Callaway, John. 1829. *Yakkun Natannawa und Kolma Nattanawa, A Cingalese Poem, trans. by John Callaway*. London: J. Murray.

Carter, John Ross. 1983. "Music in the Theravada Buddhist Heritage: In Chant, in Song, in Sri Lanka." In *Sacred Sound: Music in Religious Thought and Practice*, ed. Joyce Irwin, 127–147. Chico, Calif.: Scholars Press.

Casinader, Rex A. 1981. *Miners' Folk Songs of Sri Lanka*. Göteborg: Göteborgs Ethnografiska Museum.

Daluwatte, Chandrasena. 1992?. *Pahatarata Natum*. Colombo: Daluwatte Printers.

de Silva, Lily. 1981. "*Paritta*: A Historical and Religious Study of the Buddhist Ceremony for Peace and Prosperity in Sri Lanka." *Spolia Zeylanica* 36/1. Colombo: National Museums of Sri Lanka.

de Zoete, Beryl. 1957. *Dance and Magic Drama in Ceylon*. London: Faber and Faber.

Dirks, Nicholas B. 1987. *The Hollow Crown: Ethnohistory of an Indian Kingdom*. Cambridge: Cambridge University Press.

Dissanayake, Mudiyanselage. 1990. *Uderate Santi Karma Saha Gami Natya Sampradaya*. Colombo: S. Godage and Brothers.

Egan, Michael J. 1969. "A Structural Analysis of a Sinhalese Healing Ritual." Ph.D. dissertation, Cambridge University.

Ellingson, Ter. 1979. "The Mandala of Sound: Concepts and Sound Structures in Tibetan Ritual Music," 112–204. Ph.D. dissertation, University of Wisconsin–Madison.

———. 1980. "Ancient Indian Drum Syllables and Bu Ston's *Sham Pa Ta* Ritual." *Ethnomusicology* 24(3):431–452.

———. 1987. "Review of *Śri Lānka: Kōlam—The Masked Play*." *Ethnomusicology* 31(1):187–189.

Gombrich, Richard, and Gananath Obeyesekere. 1988. *Buddhism Transformed: Religious Change in Sri Lanka*. Princeton, N.J.: Princeton University Press.

Gooneratne, D. de Silva. 1954 [1865]. "On Demonology and Witchcraft in Ceylon." *Journal of the Royal Asiatic Society (Ceylon Branch)*. 4(13):1–117.

Goonatilleka, M.H. 1976. *Sokari of Sri Lanka*. Colombo: Department of Cultural Affairs.

———. 1978. *Masks and Mask Systems of Sri Lanka*. Colombo: Tamarind Books.

———. 1982. "Drum Dictates the Tune in Kolam of Sri Lanka." *Sangeet Natak* 63:6–14.

———. 1984. *Nadagama, the First Sri Lankan Theatre*. Delhi: Sri Satguru Publications.

Gunawardana, A.J. 1976. *Theatre in Sri Lanka*. Colombo: Department of Cultural Affairs.

Halverson, John. 1971. "Dynamics of Exorcism: The Sinhalese Sanniyakuma." *History of Religions* 1(4):332–359.

Jackson, K. David. 1990. *Sing without Shame: Oral Traditions in Indo-Portuguese Creole Verse*. Amsterdam and Philadelphia: John Benjamins Publishing Company and Instituto Cultural de Macau.

Kapferer, Bruce. 1983. *A Celebration of Demons*. Bloomington: Indiana University Press. In Sinhala.

Kariyawassam, Tissa. 1975. *Rata wakuma hewat riddi yagaya*. Colombo: Prakasayo Press. In Sihala.

———. 1976. *Santi karma ha Sinhala Samajaya*. Colombo: Indika Mudunalaya. In Sinhala.

———. 1986. *Bali yaga Piliwela*. Colombo: S. Godage and Brothers. In Sinhala.

———. 1990. *Gam Madu Puranaya*. Colombo: Samaywardena Printers. In Sinhala.

Karunatileke, Narada. *Sokari Natkaya*. Colombo: S. Godage and Brothers.

Keuneman, Herbert. 1973. "Traditional Drums of Ceylon." *Arts of Asia*, 3(2):28–33.

Kulatillake, Cyril de Silva. 1974–1975. "'Samudraghosha' Metre and the 'Seepada Styles' of Singing in Sri Lanka." *Mitteilungen der Deutschen Gesellschaft für Musik des Orients* (Berlin) 13:39–55.

———. 1976. *A Background to Sinhala Traditional Music of Sri Lanka*. Colombo: Department of Cultural Affairs.

———. 1977. "The 'Gi' Metre in Sinhala Music." *Proceedings of the National Symposium on Traditional Rural Culture of Sri Lanka*, 123–133.

———. 1980. *Metre, Melody, and Rhythm in Sinhala Music*. Sinhala Music Research Bulletin no. 2. Colombo: Sinhala Music Research Unit, Sri Lanka Broadcasting Corporation.

———. 1982a. "Buddhist Chant in Sri Lanka, Its Structure and Musical Elements," *Jahrbuch für musikalisches Volks- und Völkerkunde* 10:20–32.

———. 1982b. *The Vannams in Sinhala Traditional Music*. Colombo: Sangita Paryesana Amsaya, Sri Lanka Buvan Viduli Samsthava.

———. 1984–1985. "Raban-Sellama and Its Music." *Journal of the Royal Asiatic Society (Sri Lanka)* 29:19–32.

———. 1991. *Ethnomusicology, Its Content and Growth; and, Ethnomusicological Aspects of Sri Lanka*. Colombo: S. Godage and Brothers.

Laade, Wolfgang. 1993–1994. "The Influence of Buddhism on the Singhalese Music of Sri Lanka." *Journal of Asian Music* 25(1-2):51–68

Makulloluwa, W. B. 1962. *Hela-gee Maga*. Nugegoda, Sri Lanka: Saman Press.

———. 1976. *Dances of Sri Lanka*. Colombo: Department of Cultural Affairs.

Malagamma, J. C. 1972. *Udarata Tala Sastraya*. Giragama: Aesthetic Education Souvenir. In Sinhala.

McGilvray, Dennis B. 1983. "Paraiyar Drummers of Sri Lanka: Consensus and Constraint in an Untouchable Caste." *American Ethnological Society* 10:97–115.

Mudiyanse, Nandasena. 1967. *Mahayana Monuments in Ceylon*. Colombo: M.D. Gunasena.

Nell, Louis. 1856–1858. "An Introductory Paper on the Investigation of Sinhalese Music." *Journal of the Royal Asiatic Society (Ceylon Branch)* 3:181–186.

Obeyesekere, Gananath. 1958. "Organization of a Sinhalese Ritual." Master's thesis, University of Washington.

———. 1963. "The Great Tradition and the Little in the Perspective of Sinhalese Buddhism." *Journal of Asian Studies* 22(2):139–153.

———. 1966. "The Buddhist Pantheon in Ceylon and Its Extensions." In *Anthropological Studies of Theravada Buddhism*, ed. Manning Nash, 1–26. Cultural Report Series, no. 13. New Haven: Yale University Press.

———. 1969: "The Ritual Drama of the *Sanni* Demons: Collective Representations of Diseases in Ceylon." *Comparative Studies in Society and History* 11(2):174–216.

Peiris, Edmund. 1974. "The Origin and Development of Simhala Nadagam." *Journal of the Royal Asiatic Society (Sri Lanka)* 18(N.S.):27–40.

Pertold, Otakar. 1973. *The Ceremonial Dances of the Sinhalese: An Inquiry into Sinhalese Folk Religion*. Dehiwala: Tisara Prakasakayo.

Piyasena, Dharmasiri. 1988. *Uva Bali Yaga Santiya*. Colombo: S. Godage and Brothers.

Powers, Harold S. 1980. "India, subcontinent of, I," *The New Grove Dictionary of Music and Musicians*, ed. Stanley Sadie. London: Macmillan.

Raghavan, M. D. 1967. *Sinhala Natum: Dances of the Sinhalese*. Colombo: M. D. Gunasena.

———. 1971. *Tamil Culture in Ceylon: A General Introduction*. Colombo: Kalai Nilayam.

Reed, Susan. 1991. "The Transformation of Ritual and Dance in Sri Lanka: *Kohomba Kankariya* and the Kandyan Dance." Ph.D. dissertation, Brown University.

Roberts, Michael. 1990. "Noise as a Cultural Struggle: Tom-Tom Beating, the British, and Communal Disturbances in Sri Lanka, 1880s–1930s." In *Mirrors of Violence: Communities, Riots and Survivors in South Asia*, ed. Veena Das, 240–285. Delhi and New York: Oxford University Press.

Sarachchandra, E. R. 1966. *The Folk Drama of Ceylon*, 2nd ed. Colombo: Department of Cultural Affairs.

Sathasivam, W. 1910. "The Music of the Sinhalese and Tamils." *The Ceylon National Review* 3(9):126–129.

Scott, David. 1994. *Formations of Ritual: Colonial and Anthropological Discourses on the Sinhala Yaktovil*. Minneapolis: University of Minnesota Press.

Sederaman, J. E. 1959. *Nrytaratnakaraya*. Colombo: M. D. Gunasena. In Sinhala.

———. 1962. *Udarata Natum Kalava*. Colombo: M. D. Gunasena. In Sinhala.

———. 1964. *Lankawe Bali Upata*. Colombo: M. D. Gunasena. In Sinhala.

———. 1967. *Bali Yaga Vicharaya*. Colombo: M. D. Gunasena. In Sinhala.

Seneviratna, Anuradha. 1975. "Musical Rituals of the Dalada Maligawa Pertaining to the Temple of the Sacred Tooth." *Sangeet Natak* 36:21–42.

———. 1979. "*Pañcatūrya Nāda* and the *Hēwisi Pūjā*." *Ethnomusicology* 23(1):49–56.

———. 1980. "Music and the Theravada Tradition in Sri Lanka." Paper presented at the Third Conference of the International Association of Buddhist Studies, Winnipeg, Manitoba, Canada.

———. 1981. "Some Notes on 'Gaman Hewisi' (March beats): An Aspect of Sinhala Drum Music of Sri Lanka." *Sangeet Natak* 61–62:5–13.

———. 1984. *Traditional Dance of Sri Lanka*. Colombo: Central Cultural Fund, Ministry of Cultural Affairs, Sri Lanka.

Sheeran, Anne. 1997. "White Noise: European Modernity, Sinhala Musical Nationalism, and the Practice of a Creole Popular Music in Modern Sri Lanka." Ph.D. dissertation, University of Washington.

Simpson, Bob. 1985. "Ritual Tradition and Performance: The Berava Caste of Southern Sri Lanka." Thesis, University of Durham.

———. 1997. "Possession, Dispossession and the Social Distribution of Knowledge among Sri Lankan Ritual Specialists." *Journal of the Royal Anthropological Institute* (N.S.) 3:43–59.

Singer, Milton B. 1972. *When a Great Tradition Modernizes.* New York: Praeger.

Sirr, Henry Charles. 1991 [1850]. *Ceylon and the Cingalese : Their history, government and religion, the antiquities, institutions, produce, revenue and capabilities of the island, with anecdotes illustrating the manners and customs of the people*. London: W. Shoberl. Reprint, New Delhi: Asian Educational Services.

Surya Sena, Devar. 1962. "Folk-songs of Ceylon." *Ceylon Today* 11(7):18–21.

Tilakasiri, J. 1976 [1961]. *Puppetry in Sri Lanka*, rev. ed. Colombo: Department of Cultural Affairs.

Vasantha, Kumara. 1993. *Symphony of the Temple Drums: Buddhist Symbolism through Ritual Art.* Kandy: Vanantha Kumara.

Walcott, Ronald. 1978. "*Kohomba Kankariya*: An Ethnomusicological Study." Ph.D. dissertation, University of Sri Lanka, Vidyodaya Campus.

Wijesekera, Nandadeva. 1987–1989. *Deities and Demons, Magic and Masks.* 2 vols. Colombo: M. D. Gunasena.

Winslow, Deborah. 1984. "A Political Geography of the Deities: Space and the Pantheon in Sinhalese Buddhism." *Journal of Asian Studies* 43(2):273–291.

Wirz, Paul. 1954. *Exorcism and the Art of Healing in Ceylon*. Leiden: E. J. Brill.

Yalman, Nur. 1964. "The Structure of Sinhalese Healing Rituals." *Religion in South Asia*, ed. Edward B. Harper, 115–150. Seattle: University of Washington Press.

Glossary

All terms in **bold** are defined elsewhere in the glossary. Page numbers in *italic* indicate pages on which illustrations appear.

abhang (also *abhaṅg, abhanga*) Devotional songs of Maharashtra and Gujarat (250, 253, 549, 729)

abhaṅga Posture used in ***oḍissi*** dance (520)

abhinaya Portrayal of emotions or expression through gestures, postures, and facial expression (21, 104, 267, 411, 492, 513, 520–22)

abhishēka Ritual bathing of deity's statue in various sacred substances (211)

ābhog Fourth section of ***dhrupad*** composition (169, 198–99, 250)

ācārya (also ***paṇḍit***) Learned individual qualified to serve as a **guru** (460)

achari (also *devi ke gīt*) Songs in the Bundeli dialect in praise of the Mother Goddess (724)

aḍavu Dance steps used in ***mōhini āṭṭam*** dance (149, 512)

adbhuta 'Wondrous', one of the eight emotional states (***rasa***) codified in the ***Nāṭyaśāstra*** (69, 313)

adho nāc Malwa dance with vocal and instrumental accompaniment (723)

ādhunik gān 'Modern song', popular urban entertainment music produced largely by Bengali recording and film companies in Calcutta, early 1930s (854, 858)

ādhunik gīt Modern song (550, 705)

ādī tāḷa (also *ādi tāḷam*) Eight-beat metrical cycle in Karnatak music (219, 223, 227, 323–24)

ādivāsī 'Original inhabitants'; replaced the British colonial term "scheduled tribe," referring to tribal peoples (288, 292, 501, 502, 664, 720)

âdurā (also ***kaṭṭādiya, yakâdurā***) Term for drummer-priest of the **old religion** in Sri Lanka (955, 961)

aerophone Musical instrument whose sound is produced by air vibrating inside or immediately around it (20, 322, 324, 326, 327, 339–41, 831, 876, 968)

Afghani *rabāb* Short-necked, unfretted, plucked lute in Afghanistan, northwestern Pakistan, and Kashmir (193, 336, 337, 344, 786, *787*)

agnicayana Vedic ritual involving construction of a large fire altar (238–39)

Agra *gharānā* Stylistic school of singing whose exponents originally came from the city of Agra (172, 177, 378, 443, 465)

ākam (also *akam*) Domestic or home performance (509, 868)

akhāṛā Social and artistic lineages found in some Bhojpuri folk music communities (668, 670); (2) Centers for training and rehearsal of folk performing genres (474)

ākhyān Legend or tale in Gujarat (632, 634)

akṣara Beat, in a Karnatak **tala** cycle (142, 938)

ākṣiptikā (1) Metrical song demonstrating the properties of a raga (35); (2) 'Tossing outward', the first statement of the Karnatak ***ālāpana*** (214)

alamāri Wandering performing group in Karnataka (867)

alaṅkāra (1) Embellishment, beauty (82); (2) Exercises; pieces for students by Purandara Dasa (141, 216)

ālāp Nonmetric exposition of a **raga**; introductory section of a raga performance; improvisation within a Hindustani composition (39–40, 48, 69, 82, 84–85, 119, 164, 165–68, 172, 174, 177, 195–96, 198–99, 202, 203, 206, 336, 337, 581)

ālāpana Nonmetric improvisation on a **raga** (89, 90, 94, 99, 100–103, 104, 106, 214–15, 218, 384, 389, 451, 452, 453, 912)

alārippu Invocatory dance that begins a ***bharata nāṭyam*** performance by a solo dancer (522)

a-lce lha-mo Traditional Tibetan musical theater (712)

alghoza (also *algojā, alghozā , alghozah , donal, giraw*) Double duct flute in northwestern India and Pakistan (*7*, 286, 345, 783)

Ālhā Sung epic poem in North and Central India (401, 668, 673, 679, 723)

āligum Sidhi tribal dance in Karnataka (877)

alpa Relatively weak tone in a raga (68)

alpatva 'Weakness'; weak pitches in a Hindustani raga (64, 68)

alta Red liquid applied to the palms, fingertips, and soles of the feet by female ***oḍissi*** dancers (521)

ambā Fishermen's work songs (774, 777, *778*)

ambalavāsi Female temple dancers in Kerala (521)

ānandalaharī Plucked string instrument in which the string is attached on one end to a membrane-covered resonator and on the other to a small membrane-covered pot (328, 329, 365)

aṅg (also *aṅga*) (1) Style of music (188–89, 193, 195–98, 203, 206–207, 766); (2) Complex hand gestures combined to form **tala** structures (139)

aṅgrezī baiṅḍ 'English band', brass band that plays processional music in North India (671)

anibaddh 'Unbound', Hindustani ragas rendered without meter (**tala**) (82)

ānjanēya vēṣa Monkey-costume dance in Karnataka (875)

aṅtarā Second section of a Hindustani composition emphasizing the upper octave tonic (164, 169, 172–73, 180, 185, 191, 192, 195, 198–99, 250, 532–34, 633, 687, 772, 805–806)

anubandham Coda (216)

anudātta Accent in Vedic recitation that normally precedes the ***udātta*** accent (240, 242)

anulōma Diminution in Karnatak music, by which a theme is repeated twice at double speed and four times at quadruple speed (217)

anulōma-pratilōma Diminution and augmentation in Karnatak music (217)

anupallavi Second section of a Karnatak composition, following the ***pallavi*** (145, 216–17, 219, 221–22, 225–26, 228–29, 230, 269, 544, 920, 966)

anuvādi (also *anuvādī*) Subordinate tone in raga (68, 95)

ārādhana Celebration of the anniversary of a saint's death (210, 383, 385, 390, 393–94)

arangēṟṟam (also *arrangētram*) Debut performance (157, 392)

āratī (1) Devotional form of collective singing (255, 631, 729); (2) Clockwise, vertical circling of a flame before an image of a deity (275, 629)

arched harp Harp of Indian antiquity with a boat-shaped resonator and curved neck (323, 326)

ariccantiran nāṭakam Tamil folk drama about the mythological figure Harishcandra (277)

āroh (also *arōhaṇa*) Ascent of scale pitches in a raga (67, 75, 84, 90, 93)

ārudi (also *aṟuti*) Arrival point in a Karnatak composition (146, 217)

Arya Samaj Hindu social-reform organization founded by Swami Dayananda in the early twentieth century; now powerful among the Indian diasporic populations of Trinidad and Mauritius (590)

āśān 'Preceptor' in Kerala (936, 940–43, 945)

asāre Music for rice-transplanting season in Nepal (699)

asht prahar Special sessions of ***kīrtan*** singing in Orissa, sometimes lasting twenty-four hours (732)

āsirvādam (also *asi*) Literally 'blessings', 'good wishes', or 'prosperity' in Tamil; also contemporary term for Pentecostal or evangelical theology promising rewards in heaven for those who are saved (924)

astāī (also ***sthāī***) 'Stable', the first line or section of a composition (687, 772, 805–806)

aṣṭapadī (also *aṣṭapadi*) Eight-stanza song form used by Jayadeva in the ***Gīta Govinda*** (105, 231, 262, 520, 522)

astūti Music played at shrines in Nepal (698, 699)

ātata Category of single-headed drums, as well as drums played with the hand, in the Buddhist ***pañcatūrya nāda*** system (327–29, 968)

ātatavitata Category of stringed drums, also drums played with both hands and sticks, in the ***pañcatūrya nāda*** system (327–29, 968)

aṭavu Dance steps in Tamil Nadu (919)

Atharvaveda Collection of magical formulas and spells; one of the four religious and cultural texts (**Vedas**) of the Vedic Aryans (238, 507)

athuṇ (also ***attan***) National Pakhtun dance (789, 791)

Atman World Soul (37)

at-raban Hand-held frame drum in Sri Lanka (964)

attan Pashtun dance considered a national expression of Afghanistan (506, 814)

avanaddha vādya Musical-instrument category in the ***Nāṭyaśāstra*** referring to **membranophones** (322, 351)

avanaddha varga Drum ensemble associated with performances of Sanskrit drama (323)

avaroh (also *avarōhaṇa*) Descent of scale pitches in a raga (67, 75, 84, 90, 93)

āvartan (also *āvarta*) One complete cycle of a **tala** (112, 141)

bacha naghma Muslim folk-dance theatricals of Kashmir (683)

bād Notebooks in which Vaishnav singers keep their songs (470)

bag͟halbīn Bagpipe played by the **Qalandar** in Punjab, Pakistan (*756*, 769)

Bahurūpi 'One with many disguises', professional male entertainer of Maharashtra (728)

bahutva 'Strength'; strong tones in a Hindustani raga (64, 68)

bāī Professional female singer (373, 374, 375, 376, 378, 380, 381)

bailā (also *bayala*) Popular Sinhalese music and dance genre in Sri Lanka incorporating Portuguese rhythms (427, 556, 956, 970–71)

bailadeira Portuguese Goan term for ***devadāsī*** (738)

Baisākhī Punjabi harvest festival featuring the **bhangra** dance (500, 574, *579*, 650, *653*)

bāj Playing style or lineage in Hindustani instrumental music and drumming (133, 190, 192, 206, 342, 378)

bājā (1) Instrumental music in Uttar Pradesh (661); (2) Musical instrument, ensemble, or music in Nepal (698, 704)

bali Name of an important cluster of rituals associated with Sri Lanka's **old religion** (961–62, 967)

bambulia Songs sung collectively by devotees in Madhya Pradesh (724)

bānam Bowed string instrument of Orissa with a coconut resonator and a bamboo neck (345)

bandanā Song of entreaty addressed to a specific deity in Uttar Pradesh (667)

bānde pāther 'Musician's theater', folk theatricals of Kashmir (498, *685*)

bandiś 'Composition' in Hindustani music (172, 179, 180, 195, 196)

bāni Stylistic performance traits unique to an individual artist (231, 378)

bāṅkiā Brass trumpet played in Rajasthan (640, 647–48)

banku-raban Large frame drum of Sri Lanka (964–65)

bāṅsurī (also *bāṅsī*) North Indian bamboo flute (188, 339, *340*, 350, 424, 497, 535, *536*, 582, 591, 633, 670, 705, *724*)

bapla 'Marriage', Santal marriage songs (474)

bārahamāsā Twelvemonth song of Uttar Pradesh; the primary theme is a husband's separation from his wife (277)

baṛā khyāl Hindustani ***khyāl*** performance in slow or medium speed (172–73, 175, 183, 190, 195–96,)

bārike Barrel-shaped, skin-covered instrument in the ***caudike*** tradition of Karnataka (873)

barmasa (also *choumasa*) Songs describing the rainy season in Madhya Pradesh (475)

Basant Spring festival in North India and Pakistan (276)

basavāṭa gangettinavaru (also ***kolē basava***) Street performance involving a cow and a musician, in Karnataka (876)

basavi (also ***dēvadāsi***) Female temple dancer in Karnataka and Tamil Nadu (521)

bass Large double-headed cylindrical drum played in Trinidad with ***tāssā*** drums (589)

batu Second dance number in an ***oḍissi*** performance (520)

Bāul Mystical sect of Bengal, noted for its unique religious and musical practices (343, 344, 405, 411, 436, 503, 846, 850, 853, 859–60)

Bavanīlu Telugu narrative singers; in performance, they usually play the ***jamikiḷi*** (894, 901)

bāyak Musician who plays the ***mridang*** and cymbal and accompanies the presentation of ***pala***, in Orissa (733)

bāyāṅ (also ***ḍagga***) Larger, lower-pitched left drum of the tabla pair (*122*, *339*, *341*, 342, 346)

bāzum Social gathering in the home for dancing, in the Northern Areas of Pakistan (797)

Beda Ladakhi folk musician, player of oboe or kettledrum (*712*)

begum Respectable lady (373, 374, 381)

Behulā Sung epic poem in Mithila (678)

bēnjo Keyed zither common among the Baloch in Karachi and southern Balochistan (774, *775*, 782–83)

Beruva Sinhala caste of drummers in Sri Lanka (957, 961–63)

bhadaiya bhajan **Bhajan** sung only on the day celebrated as Krishna's birthday (724)

bhāgavata mēḷā (also *bhāgavata mēlam*) Form of classical dance drama in South India; enacted before temple idols by all-male troupes (270, 516–18, 908)

Bhāgavata Purāṇa Sanskrit text containing stories of Krishna (249, 263, 515, 633, 897)

Bhāgavatar (1) Tamil Vaishnava devotional music leader (106, 270, 390); (2) ***Harikathā*** performer (270, 390); (3) Director and conductor of a ***yakṣagāna*** drama (515–16)

bhajan (also *bhajana, bhajane*) Devotional hymn; Hindu devotional song (89, 105, 106, 211, 229, 246, 249, 253, 254–56, 262, 267–68, 273, 345, 347, 358, 364, 376, 390, 391, 401, 410, 413–14, 415–16, 419, 425–26, 452, 533–34, 539, *549*, 573, 575, 579, 581, 590, 602, 605, 608, 617–18, 623, 630–32, 642, 646, 664, 674, 702, 724, 729, 732, 772, 869, 909, *918*–19, 923–24, 935, 947)

bhajanik Bhajan singer (401, 631, 632)

bhajan kavvali Hindu devotional song genre of the Fiji Indian community (613–14)

bhajan maṇḍaḷ Male or female devotee singing groups in Gujarat (*631*, 645)

bhakti Hindu tradition of devotion and love directed toward a personal god, encompassing religious practices, literature, and philosophy (11, 15, 69, 72, 96, 105, 106, 163, 209, 220, 248, 254–55, 256, 260, 262, 263–65, 306, 308, 313, 416, 493, 503, 518, 555, 629, 643, 728, 732, 765, 918)

bhakti *gīt* (also *bhaktigāna*) Devotional songs, mostly in vernacular languages (248, 929)

bhakti yoga Path of devotion (220)

bhamakalapam Female temple dance of Andhra Pradesh (516)

bhānd (also *bhagat*) Male professionals who perform ***bānde pāther*** in Kashmir (498, *499*, 640)

bhand-jashna Folk drama of Kashmir (485)

bhangra Lively folk music and dance style of the Punjab; adapted as a popular, syncretic style (426–27, 500, 506, 540, 550, 568, 573, *574*–76, *579*, 582, 584, 623, 650–52, 654, 656)

bhangi Cannabis, often smoked by performers of regional music, in Karnataka (880)

bhapang Plucked **chordophone** with a single metal string and a hollow, cylindrical base, in Rajasthan (647, *648*)

bharata nat Theater of the ***ādivāsī*** tribal populations in the Mastar region of Madhya Pradesh (471)

bharata nāṭyam South Indian classical dance form (104, 108, 149, 262, 358, 360, 366, 383, 388, 390, 400, 410, 512, 517, 520, *521*–23, 738, 910–11, 913, 941)

bharud Hymn of praise in Maharashtra (729)

bharyā 'Daughter-in-law', a category of the ***parivār*** classification system dividing ragas into family groups consisting of one male **raga**, five or six wives (***rāgiṇī***), sons (***putra***), and daughters-in-law (314)

bhātiāli Bengali boatmen's songs (859–60)

bhāva Emotion; passion (69, 91, 93, 107, 269, 298, 512, 513, 521, 912)

bhavāī Dramatic performance involving music and dance in Gujarat and Rajasthan (419, 485, 501, 634–35, 647)

bhavana Religious drama of Assam (486)

bhavāyā Performer of ***bhavāī*** (634)

bhāvgīt 'Songs of the emotions', popular, topical songs of Maharashtra (730)

bhayānaka 'Terrible', one of the eight emotional states (***rasa***) codified in the ***Nāṭyaśāstra*** (69, 313)

bheṇṭ Hindi devotional songs to the Mother Goddess (247)

bher Large, stick-played folk kettledrum (346, 760)

bherī Double-headed drum of medieval India played with one hand and a stick (328)

bhīmul pandum Dance and music festival of Madhya Pradesh; takes place prior to the monsoon (721–22)

bhogum (also ***kalavantulu, sani***) Female temple dancers in Andhra Pradesh (521)

bhopā (1) Folk priest or medium in Rajasthan who provides curing and other ritual services (288, *292*, 640); (2) Professional ballad singers in Rajasthan (345, 640, 646, *647*)

bhuchyāh Cymbals in Nepal (702)

bhūta kōla Traditional worship in Tulunad in which family deities and local caste heroes, both called *bhūta*, are honored with songs and through spirit possession (882–84, 886)

bhūtam (also ***teyyam***) 'Spirits' in Kerala (511)

bidāī gīt 'Departure song' sung in North India when a woman leaves her natal home after marriage (275)

bidesia Folk drama of Bihar (485)

Bijja Pandum Gond festival, which takes place in the spring (721)

biksha Mendicant or beggar (899)

bilwari Men's songs accompanying agricultural work (723)

bīn (1) (also ***rudra vīṇā***) Plucked stick zither with gourds attached to each end (119, 164, 170, 188, 190, 308, 332, *333*, 334, 335, 336, 337, 343, 563); (2) (also *murlī*, ***puṅgī***) Single-reed horn pipe popularly associated with snake charmers in South Asia (345, *469*, 506, 647, *648*, 670)

bīṇ bājā Arched harp of present-day central India (329)

biṅdī (also ***tilak***) Red dot worn on the forehead of a ***bharata nāṭyam*** dancer; also worn as a sign that one is a Hindu (522)

birahā (1) Bhojpuri men's folk song genre (550, 666–69, 672); (2) Songs of separation in Punjab (655); (3) Rhyming poem sung by Guyanese Indian livestock herders (602)

Bobbili Yuddha Katha Telugu epic dating from the mid-eighteenth century (898)

bobine (also ***ulké***) Hourglass drum played on Réunion Island (607)

bobre Musical bow played on Réunion Island (610)

bol Word or syllable representing a drum stroke; the drum stroke itself (111, 132, 175, 201–*202*, 494, 692, 694, 885)

bolālāp In Hindustani vocal music, melodic improvisation on a text (173, 174–75)

bol banāo In Hindustani vocal music, variation and elaboration of a text (180, 197, 198)

bol bāṅṭ In Hindustani vocal music, rhythm-oriented improvisation on a text (169, 175, 176)

bolī (pl. *boliyāṅ*) Punjabi folk songs (500, 651, 771)

boḷkoṭ Koḍagu circle dance around a lamp, accompanied by song and sometimes drumming (887)

boltān In Hindustani vocal music, fast melodic figure sung to a text (173, 175, 201)

boudha caryagīt (see also ***caryā gīt***) Buddhist devotional songs of the tenth to twelfth centuries in Orissa (731)

Brahmasaṅgīt Songs in praise of Brahma; prayer songs of the Brahma Samāj religious sect, founded in Calcutta in 1828 (847–48, 850)

Brahmin (*Brāhmaṇ*) Traditionally, the highest group or class (***varṇa***) of Hindu society, many of whom served as priests (9, 45, 227, 239, 240, 243, 262, 263, 274–75, 385, 386–95, 398, 400–401, 544, 557, 632, 639, 678, 706, 735, 868, 881, 893, 910–11, 916, 956)

Braj Bhasha Western Hindi language used in devotional poetry and song texts (5, 183, 247, 252, 256, 495, 660)

bugīr (also *buguri*) Kota end-blown bamboo trumpet; same as Toda ***puxury*** (366–67, 916)

bummâḍiya Sri Lankan pot drum with clay body, short flaring neck, and iguana-skin drumhead (367)

burra katha Popular style of Telugu narrative singing derived from a folk model (899, 901)

byāh ke gīt Bhojpuri wedding song (*589*)

cācā Newār Buddhist hymn repertoire in Nepal (702)

cadir Ritual dance form of Tamil Nadu that evolved into modern-day ***bharata nāṭyam*** (910, 913)

caitī Love song genre of Uttar Pradesh (277)

caiti ghoṛa nāc Dance form associated with the Hindu Shakta cult in Orissa; ritual dummy-horse dance of the fishing community of Orissa (733, 734)

cakkardār Type of ***paran*** (***pakhāvaj*** composition) played three times (118–19, 121, 201)

cākyār Temple performance genre for solo actor-storyteller in Kerala (510)

cākyār kūttu Dramatic performance by the Cākyār community of Kerala (511)

calan (also ***gat-qā'ida***) Tabla composition (130)

campanti Tamil marriage songs in which the groom's and bride's families make fun of each other (275)

candrasārang North Indian bowed, fretless lute invented by Alauddin Khan (337)

***Cankam* literature** Anthologies of Tamil poetry dating from about the first to fourth centuries C.E. (319, 326, 884)

caraṇam The "foot" or verse of a song in Karnatak music (145, 146, 216–17, 219, 221–22, 225–26, 228–29, 230, 262, 265, 266, 269, 920)

caryā gīt (see also ***boudha caryāgīt***) Principal song genre in Bengal from the ninth through twelfth centuries, with Buddhist texts (844–45, 847, 859)

caudike Single-stringed, barrel-shaped drone instrument in Karnataka; also a type of ***katha*** (869, 872, *875*)

caupadi Love songs sung at village gatherings in Orissa (733)

cautāl (also *chowtal, fāg*) Men's festive songs of the springtime **Holī** season in Trinidad, Guyana, and Fiji (589–90, 600–601, 603, 613)

cautārā Drone lute played by devotional singers in Rajasthan (343)

caviṭṭunāṭakam Foot-stamping drama performed by the Latin Christians of Kerala (*485*, 945–46)

cēkaṇṭi Bronze gong tied to the waist and played with a stick in Tamil Nadu (915)

ceṇṭa Double-headed cylindrical drum of Kerala, played with two curved sticks (350, 351, *362*, 363, 511, 513, 515, 885–86, 931, *932*, 935, 936–38, 940–41, 943, 950)

ceṇṭa mēḷam Ritual music ensemble of Kerala (361, 362, 932–35, *936*, *937*–39)

ceṅṅala Small hand-held gong of Kerala (360, 362)

cēvai palakai Tambourine with a lizard-skin head in Tamil Nadu (915)

cēyvaiyāṭṭam Dance performed by Kampalattar Nāyakars in Tamil Nadu (915)

chahārbeiti Persian-language folk song form of four-line verses, western Afghanistan (812–13, 819–20, 823, 827, 835–36)

chakri Vocal genre of Kashmir (475, 682–84)

chālīsā Common Hindu prayer form (549)

challa Men's amorous songs of Madhya Pradesh (723)

'cham Tibetan ritual ballet, performed in monastery courtyards (502, 505, 715)

champa de Song tale of Madhya Pradesh, blending prose, verse, and recitation (723)

chand (also ***gīt***) Extended poetic verse, in Gujarat (630, 635–37)

chanda Section of Oriya oral epic tale sung by professional balladeers in Orissa (732–33)

chang Mouth harp played in Afghanistan (781, 783, 812–13, 831)

chāṅg Large shallow-rimmed frame drum of Rajasthan (642, 648)

chappar Wooden clappers (753)

chaprī Rectangular wooden clappers (506)

chasa gīt 'Cultivator's songs' sung by agricultural laborers in Orissa (733)

chatni (also **chutney**) 'hot and spicy', popular-music genre of the Indo-Guyanese (601)

chattīs Mystical and didactic songs sung by folk singers and village elders in Orissa (733)

chāu Dance form of eastern India, performed by men during spring festivals (496, *497*, *498*, 859)

che koetie (also *chichothi*) Old Sri Lankan term probably referring to a performance tradition involving word dueling and verbal competition (971)

chelā Pupil, student (461)

chili-gari-ai 'Juniper and goat', purifying ritual theater of the Northern Areas of Pakistan (488)

chimta (also ***cimṭā***) Metal tongs with brass discs attached (651, 655, 769)

chinchir Cymbals played in Balochistan (774, 783)

chitrāli sitār Long-necked lute popular throughout the North West Frontier Province (787, *788*)

chogān Ritual spiritual music and dance of the Zikris of Pakistan (754, 761, 774, 778, *779*)

chopāni Pastoral shepherd song of northern Afghanistan (827)

chordophone Musical instruments whose sound is produced by one or more vibrating strings (20, 322, 323, 326, 327, 332–339, 873)

choṭā gīt 'Small songs', men's songs derived from women's repertoire, sung by the **Laṅgās** and **Manganihārs** in Rajasthan (642)

choṭā khyāl Hindustani vocal music genre in medium or fast tempo (172, 173–74, 179, 183, 195, 206)

choṭī sāraṅgī Small bowed lute of Punjab, Pakistan (769–70)

chuḍke Popular dance and instrumental piece in Nepal (701)

chutney (also Indian soca, soca chutney) Hot, spicy songs in traditional Bhojpuri culture; lively, sexy dance songs in Trinidad (591–92, 601, 604–605)

chutti Curved white frame used in ***kathakaḷi*** face makeup (*513*)

cikāra (also *cakārā*) Short-necked and spike fiddles played in Madhya Pradesh, Rajasthan, and Kashmir (345)

cikārī Drone strings on many North Indian plucked string instruments (199)

Cilappatikāram 'The Tale of the Anklet', first great Tamil epic (24, 260, 319, 327, 518)

cimṭā (also ***chimta***) Two flat iron bars joined at one end with metal platelets attached, used in folk and devotional music of northern regions (347, 762, 765)

cine pāṭṭu South Indian film songs (368)

cinna kaṭci 'Small faction' of devotees at a Tyagaraja festival (389, *391*, 393, 394)

cinna mēḷam 'Small ensemble' of musicians with a dancer (104, 360, 383, 387, 389–390, 509, 910, 913)

cintu Strophic song with a short melody and many verses, in Tamil Nadu (920–21, 958, 966)

ciplā Pair of wooden clappers with metal jingles, in South India (267, 364)

ciplyā Clappers, wooden strips with inserted metal rings, used for rhythm in the devotional music of Maharashtra (728)

ciṭike Wooden clapper used in Karnataka to keep time in ***tatva*** singing (867, 869)

citrāvīṇā 'Artful *vīṇā*' stopped with a sliding stick (*233*)

citrā vīṇā Arched harp of Indian antiquity with seven strings (*299*, 326)

citta svara Composed ***svara*** passages occasionally included in Karnatak ***kriti*** and ***varṇam*** (216–17, 230)

cīz Vocal composition, in Hindustani music (172)

conga drum Afro-Cuban barrel-shaped or tapering drum (347, 368, 544, 582, 591, 970)

conkā Folk rhythm instrument of Maharashtra; produces variable-pitch sounds, similar to the ***khamak*** (343)

corredinho Portuguese song genre of Goa based on Western tonal harmony (737)

ḍaḍañ Double-headed drum of the Northern Areas of Pakistan (796)

dadariya Important Gond music and dance form of Madhya Pradesh (722)

dādrā Light classical vocal form, in Hindustani music (162, 179, 183, 373, 412, 424, 766)

ḍaf (also *daf, daff, daph,* ***duff****, duph*) Frame drum with wood or metal frame (346, 642, 648, 671, 692, 712, 813, 828, 830–31, 948, 958)

ḍagga (also ***bāyāṅ***) Left-hand kettledrum of the **tabla** pair (*122, 339, 341*)

dāhinā (also ***dāya,*** **tabla**) Smaller, higher-pitched right-hand drum of the **tabla** pair (*122, 339, 341*)

dā'irā (also *dāireh,* ***daf***) Frame drum with jingles (305, 310, 812, *813*, 815, 818, 820, 822, *823*, 826, 828, 830–31)

dāk Kota percussion rhythm pattern (*916*)

dakke Hourglass-shaped pressure drum used to accompany ***dakke bali*** (884)

dakke bali (also *nāga mandala*) Form of cobra (*nāga*) worship with circular dancing, singing, and drumming (883–84)

ḍakkinī Trumpet of Indian antiquity (326)

dakṣiṇā Gift given to a **guru** by his student in place of payment for lessons (459)

Dalit Literally 'broken' or 'oppressed', communities formerly called untouchables or Harijans (875, 876, 910–11, 922)

dalkhai (also *rasarkeli*) Songs of Orissa describing incidents in Krishna's life (733)

damāhā Large kettledrum played in Nepal (699)

ḍāmal Kettledrum pair of the Northern Areas of Pakistan (795–96)

daman Tibetan kettledrum pair (*712*)

ḍamaru (also ***ḍamrū***) Small hourglass-shaped drum with knotted strings that strike the heads when the drum is rotated (110, 325, 346, 365, *367*, *485*, *714*, 722, 966)

damburā (also *damburo, dambura, danburo, dhambura*) Long-necked, unfretted, plucked lutes of Pakistan and Afghanistan (344, 506, 754, 759, 828–29, 830–31)

dambūrag Long-necked unfretted lute of Balochistan, used as a rhythm-keeping instrument, mostly with the ***suroz*** and ***nal*** (774, 776–77, 781, *782, 783, 784*)

damḍi Small tambourine of Karnataka, with iguana-skin head (869, *874*)

danda jatra Songs sung to accompany the ***patna jatra*** dance in Orissa (733)

dandanata gīt Dance songs of Orissa in question-and-answer form (733)

daṅḍa tāl (see also ***ḍhantāl***) Iron bar struck rhythmically with an iron rod in Fiji (613)

ḍāṇḍiā rās (also ***rās***) Stick dance of Gujarat (347, 405, 427, 501, 629)

dāni Category of tunes accompanied by ***surnāī*** or transverse flute, in the Northern Areas of Pakistan (796)

dapchang (also ***chang***) Mouth harp, one of the most common musical instruments of the Baloch (783)

dāphā Hymn-singing tradition of the Newārs in Nepal (702)

daphalā Frame drum of Uttar Pradesh (671)

ḍappu (also *dappu*) Frame drum of Andhra Pradesh and Karnataka (870, 896)

darbār (also ***rāj darbār***) Royal court (375)

darbukka Arabic goblet drum (748)

dargāh Muslim mausoleum housing a saint or other important personage (401, 644, 754, 769)

darśan Visual contact with a god, the embodiment of a god, or a highly respected personage (279, 393, 904, 934)

Dāsari Oral narrative singers in Andhra Pradesh, devotees of Vishnu (900–901)

dasi āṭṭam (also ***sadir kacheri***) Obsolete term referring to the ***bharata nāṭyam*** dance (521)

daskathia (also *ramkathi*) Popular type of ***chanda*** song sung by balladeers in Orissa (732–33)

dāstān Ballads or stories sung by a ballad singer (Dāstāngoh) in Punjab, Pakistan (771)

dastānag Short love songs of eastern Balochistan, accompanied by a single-reed pipe (773, 775, 781)

daule (also *daula, sabaragamuwa* drum) Double-headed barrel drum in the ***hēvisi*** Buddhist ensemble of Sri Lanka (329, 363–64, 964, 967)

dāya (also ***dāhinā,*** **tabla**) Right-hand conical wooden drum of the **tabla** pair (*122, 339, 341*)

dbyangs Type of solemn chanting in Tibetan Buddhist rituals (13, 713)

dbu-mdzad Tibetan precentor (713)

debate *bailā* Word dueling and verbal repartee in Sri Lanka (971)

decknni Goan music and dance genre, performed by Christians (737–38, 741)

ḍēhī (also ***līko, zahīrok***) Songs of separation, travel, and work popular in eastern Balochistan (774, 775–76)

delrubā Bowed lute of western Afghanistan (806, *809*)

dera 'Clay pot with covered mouth', a scraped **membranophone** of Maharashtra (727)

dervish Religious mendicant (683, 686, 753–54, 760)

deśī (1) Regional musics of the medieval period (20, 24, 33, 34, 75, 76, 299); (2) Relatively unrefined, regional traditions and practices (326, 372, 398, 400, 492, 583–84, 586, 602–603)

desi karam Solo male dance of western Orissa (734)

deśī sitār Folk **sitar** of Gujarat (*344*)

***deśī* tala** Regional rhythmic pattern in cyclic form (110)

Dēśingurāju Katha Popular Telugu oral narrative song (900)

devadāsī (also *dēvadāsi*) Hereditary female temple and court dancers (211, *263*; 386–87, 392–93, *400*, 407, 409, *518*, 521, 738, 872)

dēvālē Shrine for Hindu guardian deities in Sri Lanka (955, 960, 963)

devatā Minor divinity; term used to refer to **ragas** (313, 853)

devī (1) Local or regional goddess (291); (2) Respectable lady (373, 374)

Devr 'God', annual festival of the Kotas (278, 281, 285)

devr koḷ Special "god melodies" played at the annual **Devr** festival of Kota worship (278, 281)

ḍhāk Mina hourglass pressure drum of Rajasthan (292)

ḍhāḷ Melody in Gujarat; particularly, one adaptable to several different texts (632)

dhalo Goan music and dance of Hindu origin performed by women (475, 737–38)

dhamal Mystic **dervish** dance of Sindh (754, 760)

dhamāl (1) Drum rhythm often associated with **Sufi** shrines (281); (2) Dance associated with Holī, in Rajasthan (648)

dhamār Hindustani vocal genre similar to ***dhrupad*** (170, 250, 373)

dhāmi Nepali term for shaman (289)

dhamsa Large kettledrum (497)

dhangari ovya Song and dance genre of the Dhangars of Maharashtra (728)

ḍhantāl (see also ***ḍaṅḍa tāl***) Meter-long iron rod struck rhythmically to accompany Indian songs in Trinidad and Guyana (589, 603–604)

dhāp Locally made bass "boom" drum of the Indo-Guyanese (601)

Ḍhaṛhī Lower-class Muslim minstrel in North India (122–23)

dharma Predestined spiritual duty (9, 20, 375, 943)

dhavale Marriage songs sung by women in Maharashtra (729)

dhimay Cylindrical drum of Nepal (702)

dhimaybājā Music and musical ensemble of Nepal (702)

ḍhol Large double-headed cylindrical drum played by hand or stick, widespread in northern regions of South Asia (*8, 273*, 275, 279, *280*, 281, *282*, 283, 328, 346, 347, 360, *415*, 426, 489, 497, 500, 501, 506, 582, 612–13, *614*, 625, 629, 640–41, 647–48, *651*, 685, 722, 728, 733, 755, *756, 763*, 767–68, 771, 774, 789)

ḍholā Sung epic poem in North India (655, 673)

ḍholak (also *ḍholakī*) Double-headed barrel drum played with sticks or hands, widespread throughout the northern regions of South Asia (*123*, 131, 133, 248, 342, 346, 347, 368, *403*, 472, *475, 495, 499*, 500, 502, 505, 506, 534, 535, *549*, 550, 574, 582, 589–91, 600, 602–603, 625, 629, 635, *640*–41, 644–45, 647, 655, 660, 664, *665*, 666–67, 669–70, 673, 699, 705, 723–24, 769, 771–72, *808, 846*, 913)

ḍholī Ḍhol player; a class of ritual musicians including drummers (7, 280, 403, *415*, 476, 640–41, 644, 755)

ḍholkī Smaller version of the ***ḍhol*** (651, 654, 656)

dhrupad Preeminent Hindustani court vocal and instrumental music genre of the premodern era (15, 42, 69, 83, 84, 116, 119, 120, 125, 132, 136, 162, 163–70, 171, 172, 174, 175, 177, 179, 184, 188, 190, 196, 198, 199, 202, 207, 224, 229, 246, 250, 251, 252, 253, 254, 333, 335, 336, 342, 373, 378, 379, 410–11, 435, 591, 602, 632–33, 640, 678, 805, 845, 847–48, 850–51, 853)

dhruvapada (1) Repeated refrain in a **bhajan** or ***dhrupad*** (630–31, 633); (2) Literally 'song on God'; ancient musical style believed to be the precursor of Hindustani ***dhrupad*** (845)

dhudak (also *dahanki*) Hourglass drum of the Kahars in Madhya Pradesh (722)

dhūmsa Double-headed drum of Rajasthan (280)

dhun Light classical genre in Hindustani music (194, 198, 203, 632)

dhunmuniyā kajalī Form of Bhojpuri ***kajalī*** in which performers dance while they sing (670)

ḍhyāngro Double-headed frame drum used by Nepali shamans (290)

ḍigaṛī Small kettledrum of Mithila (679)

dilrubā North Indian bowed, unfretted, long-necked lute similar to the ***isrāj*** (234, 336)

Dīpāvalī (also Dīvālī) Hindu "festival of lights," celebrated October–November (252, 277–78, 617, 875)

divālī ke gīt Men's seasonal songs of Madhya Pradesh (723)

dīvāni ghazal (also *ragām, rubāyi*) Poetic form, either recited or sung in the North West Frontier Province (786)

divyanāma sankīrtana Divine names and praises in Tamil Nadu, often sung while devotees circumambulate a sacred oil lamp (105, 918)

Divya Prabandham 'The Sacred Collection', four thousand Tamil verses by the Vaishnava Āḻvārs (260–61, 617)

dōbeitī Poetic form of Kashmir (687)

dodāta Theater tradition of north Karnataka (104)

dohol Double-headed drum of Afghanistan (806, 814, 820, 835)

dohori gīt Song duel; competition song in Nepal (701)

dokra Drum pair; Hindustani **tabla** imported into Kashmir from India (*688*)

doli gīt 'Swing songs' sung by girls in Orissa (733)

ḍōlu Popular double-headed folk drum of Karnataka (875–76, 878, 884)

Ḍom Various professional musician groups in the northern region (641, 794–95, 798–99)

Ḍomb Musicians and singers of the Ludi caste in eastern Balochistan (776, 781)

donal (also ***alghoza, giraw***) Double flute of southern Balochistan (783, *784*)

dorakadarśane Annual Buddhist ceremony in Sri Lanka celebrating the arrival of the Siam ordination lineage from Thailand in 1753 (969)

dotārā Unfretted lute of Bengal played by the Bāuls (344, *860*)

dotāro String drone instrument of western India resembling the ***ektār*** (344)

'Dre-dkar Tibetan itinerant musician who recites auspicious songs at the Tibetan new year (711)

dril-bu Tibetan handbell used in Buddhist rituals (*714*)

drut Fast tempo in Hindustani music (111, 192, 193)

drutam Hand gesture comprising a clap and a wave (two beats) in Karnatak music (139, 141, 144)

duḍi Hourglass-shaped drum of the Koḍagu and Tulu in Karnataka (887)

duff (also *ḍaf, duph*) Shallow-rimmed, large frame drum (506, 722)

ḍuggī (also *ḍugi, ḍukkaṛ,* ***khurḍak***) One or a pair of small hand-played kettledrums in North India (328, 340, 503, 671, *860*)

ḍuhl Any of various double-headed barrel drums, played mostly for festive occasions in Balochistan by a Ludi drummer (*ḍuhlī*) (774, 777, *778*, 780, 781–82, 783)

duho (also *dohāro*) Poetic couplet in Gujarat (635–37)

ḍukkur Double-headed barrel drum of Balochistan (774, 783)

dulpod Goan music and dance genre performed by Christians (737–38, 741)

dundhukī Folk rhythm instrument of Orissa with variable-pitch sounds; similar to the ***khamak*** (343, 732)

dung-dkar End-blown conch-shell trumpet of Tibet, known elsewhere in South Asia as ***śaṅkh*** (713, 714)

dupree (also *dolkay,* **tabla**) Drum pair (790)

dutār Long-necked, fretted plucked lute of Afghanistan (344, 818–19, 820, *821*, 822–23, 830, 832)

eḍuppu Point in a Karnatak **tala** cycle where the song text begins (146, 156)

ektār (also *ekanādā, ēktāri, iktār*) Single-stringed, plucked drone lute (344, 365, 366, *400*, 428, 769–70, 772, 859, 867, 869)

ektārā (also ***gopīyantra***) Single-stringed, plucked drum (343, 347, 859)

Epic of Palnāḍu (also ***Palnāṭi Vīrula Katha***) Extended Telugu oral epic with roots in the twelfth century (898, 900–902)

ēṟṟap pāṭṭu Now rarely performed, a Tamil work song for accompanying the hoisting of water buckets from a well (918)

ērtabaṭk Kota kettle drum, Tamil Nadu (278, 915)

ettugaḍa svara 'Deceiving' melodic passages in Karnatak genres such as ***varṇam***; a type of ***citta svara*** (216–17)

fāg (also ***cautāl***) Song genre of Fiji Indians performed during the **Holī** festival (613)

falak Folk genre of melancholic nature from Badakhshan (812, 828, 831)

faqir (*faqīr*) Religious mendicant, **dervish**, devotee (753, 759, 769–70, 772, 780)

farmaiśī Complex form of ***cakkardār*** composition for North Indian ***pakhāvaj*** (118–19)

fell Musical genre performed by Christians in Goa (739)

Fiji kavvali Secular narrative songs of Fiji Indians (613)

filmī gīt 'Film song', composed and recorded for commercial Indian films (127, 407, 412, 420, 531, 560, 574, 614, 820)

firozkhānī gat Fast-tempo Hindustani instrumental composition (126, 189, 193–94)

fugddi Goan women's music and dance genre of Hindu origin (737–38)

gaekwad (also **maharaja**) "Great ruler" (443)

gālī Insult song sung during weddings and on other occasions in North India (275, 415, 589, 614, 642, 645–46, 648, 663)

gamaka Musical ornament (31, 33, 36, 39, 91, 93–94, 197, 199, 200, 232, 352)

gāna (1) Incidental music, in the early Indian theater (20, 25); (2) Popular music genre in Tamil Nadu (557)

gānā Singing or song, vocal music in Uttar Pradesh (661)

ganasaṅgīt 'People's songs' with heroic sentiments upholding the socialist cause, composed and sung by Indian Communist party activists (856)

gandā bandhan (also *gaṇḍā bandhan*) Initiation ceremony by which a ***śiṣya*** becomes a disciple (377, 459)

gāndharva Ritual music for the early Indian theater (20, 25)

gangettinavaru See ***basavāṭa gangettinavaru***

ganika Dancing girl or courtesan (408)

gar Tibetan dance form (713)

garabī Type of ***garbo*** text, and alternative type of ***garbo***, in Gujarat (632, 635)

garba Malwa dance form with vocal and instrumental accompaniment (723)

garbī Alternative form of ***garbo*** dedicated to Krishna or sung from a male point of view (626)

garbo (pl. *garbā,* also *garbī*) Gujarati devotional song and dance, usually dedicated to mother goddesses (277, 474, 501, 550, 623, 624, *625*, *626*, 627–28, 629–30)

gat (1) Hindustani instrumental composition (188–208, 335, 581); (2) Compositional genre in the **tabla** repertoire (130–31, 133–34, 135)

gâṭa bera (also up-country drum, Kandyan drum) Double-headed barrel drum used in the Buddhist ***hēvisi*** *pūjā* ensemble in Sri Lanka (329, 364, 963, *964*)

gaṭibhēda Subdivision of the basic pulse into 3, 5, 7, or 9 in Karnatak music (218)

gat-qā'ida **Tabla** composition (130)

gātra vīṇā Literally 'body instrument'; singer, in the ***Nāṭyaśāstra*** (321, 327)

gaulan Devotional song genre of Maharashtra with texts on Krishna's pranks and his teasing of the milkmaids in Gokul (729)

gauri kalyāṇam 'Marriage of the goddess Gauri', an auspicious song (274)

gavayyā Male and female singers in the North Indian classical tradition (766)

gāyak Main singer who presents ***pala*** ballads and leads a chorus (***palia***) (591, 733)

gāyakī aṅg 'Singing style', the imitation of vocal styles in Hindustani instrumental music (195, 196, 232)

gāyan (see also ***samāj-gāyan***) 'Singing'; in Maharashtra, a wide spectrum of vocal expression; a devotional song form (729)

gāyanśālā North Indian vocal music school (563)

gaz Horsehair bow used for playing the ***sārindā***, in North West Frontier Province (788, *789*)

Ge-sar King and hero of Tibetan epic (711–12, 715)

ghada Clay 'pitcher drum' of Kashmir (476)

ghadyal-tipru Metal disc struck with a mallet, in performances by a **Nandiwāla** (727)

ghana Category of **idiophones** in the ***Nāṭyaśāstra*** and the Buddhist ***pañcatūrya nāda*** systems (327, 968)

***ghana* ragas** 'Weighty' ragas; set of five specific **ragas** in Karnatak music (100, 218)

ghana rāga pañcaratna (see ***pañcaratna***) Five songs in medium tempo composed by Tyagaraja in the five ***ghana* ragas** (451)

ghana vādya Musical instrument category in the ***Nāṭyaśāstra*** designating **idiophones** (322, 327, 351)

gharānā Musical lineage; stylistic school of musical practice in Hindustani music (8, 15, 57, 67, 83–84, 134, 136, 137, 176–78, 189, 194, 195, 196, 204–208, 342, 373, 375, 376, 377–78, 379, 380, 409–10, 413, 443, 460, 465–67, 494, 526, 640, 668, 670, 697, 746, 766, *767–68*,)

ghaṭam Clay pot percussion instrument, in Karnatak music (149, *150*, 235, 357–58, 368, 452, 684)

ghāṭu Guruṅg dance drama in Nepal (*703*–705)

ghazal Urdu poetic genre; light classical vocal genre with Urdu text (107, 127, 162, 179, 183–86, 192, 255, 256, 373, 376, 381, 410–11, 412–13, 424, 425–26, 435, 494, 532, 534, 539, 548–49, 573, 579, 581, 591, 644, 673, 687, 706, 749–50, 766, 771–72, 786, 805–807, 818, 819–20, 827–28, *829*, 853–56, 970)

ghichak West Asian bowed lute (305)

ghīchak (also ***ghijak, kemanche***) Persian spike fiddle used in medieval Indo-Persian courts and still found in Afghanistan (305, 345, 788, 804, 828, 830, *831*)

ghol 'Small bell' of Maharashtra (728)

ghora nāc gīt Song form associated with the Hindu Shakta cult in Orissa (733)

ghūmar Popular circle dance that has become the state symbol of Rajasthan (647, 648, 723)

ghuṅghrū Small metal bells played or worn as ankle bells by dancers (476, 494, 497–98, 506, 646, 648, 722, 727)

giddhā Punjabi women's folk dance (500, 506, 652, *653*, 654–56)

gīgī Song form with "*gī ya gī ya*" refrain text in Karnataka (870, *871*)

ginān Chanted religious compositions in the Northern Areas of Pakistan (794)

gini Small cymbals of Orissa (733)

giraw (also ***alghoza, donal***) Double flute in northern Balochistan (783)

gīt (also *gīta*) (1) Song; a nonclassical song in a regional language (19, 20, 21, 104, 127, 266, 347, 581, 613, 661, 678, 771); (2) Poetic versification in the context of bardic poetry (636)

Gīta Govinda Twelfth-century love poems by Jayadeva (105, 452, 510, 519, 521–22, 633, 844–45, 931)

gītam Song passed down in the ***prabandha*** tradition; some are simple songs created for teaching purposes (452)

gīti Song text, or song text and music (844)

gīti nāṭak Modern, sophisticated genre of sung narrative poems in Nepal (705)

gling-bu Bamboo duct flute of Tibet (710, 715)

glu Tibetan folk-song genre (710–11)

Golla Suddulu Narrative singers of the Telugu herding caste (902)

gondhal Ritual theater form of Maharashtra (728)

gopī Milkmaid (493, 495, 501, 503, 629, 665)

Gopīcand Sung epic poem of North India used in ***nauṭaṅkī*** folk drama (674, 679)

gopīyantra (also ***ektārā***, *gopīyantro*) Plucked string drone; the string is attached at one end to a membrane-covered resonator, at the other to the instrument's forked bamboo frame (*328*, 343, 859, 860, *861*)

gorgholi Epic songs in Badakhshan and other Central Asian regions (827–28)

gotipua Young male temple dancers in Orissa (519)

goṭṭuvādyam (also ***citravīṇā***) Unfretted vina played as a slide lute (100, 104, 233, 334, 352, 354, 365, 424)

grāma (also *grama*) Scale (45, 51, 73–74, 106)

gubgubī Double-headed, scraped **membranophone** played by a **Nandiwālā** in performance (727)

guduki **Chordophone** of the nomadic Kela tribe (732)

gujarātan sāraṅgī Small bowed unfretted lute played by the Laṅgā musicians of Rajasthan (345, 641)

gumaṭe Double-headed pot or brass drum with variable pitch, in Karnataka (877)

gumatt Goan clay pot drum (*737*–38, *739*)

gummeṭa Jug-shaped drum played by Telugu oral narrative singers (893, *894*, 899–901)

gurbāṇī Sikh devotional songs (426, 655)

gurdwara Sikh place of worship (256, 573, 655–56)

gurr Conch shell played during festive dances in Balochistan (777, *778*)

guru Music teacher and master; spiritual guide (150, 232, 376, 391, 457–67, 470–73, 482, 520, 582, 669–70, 703, 869)

guru dakṣiṇā Student-teacher relationship in which the student does not live in the teacher's home (***gurukul***) but pays a form of tuition (***dakṣiṇā***) (459)

gurudeva Honorific, a respectful term of address to one's guru (457)

gurudvāra Guru's residence (457)

gurukul Household of the guru; student-teacher relationship in which the student lives with the teacher (457, 459)

Gurupañcāśikā 'Fifty Verses of Guru Devotion', a poem from the first century B.C. describing the guru-student relationship (457–58)

gurupūrṇimā Day on which pupils honor their gurus, celebrated on the day of the full moon in the Hindu month of Asāṛh (457)

guru-śiṣya (see also ***ustād-śagird***) (1) Master-disciple; relationship with a Hindu teacher (213, 376, 455, 457, 465, 582); (2) ***guru-śiṣya paramparā***, Master-disciple tradition (66, 86, 220, 457, 459–61, 464, 465, 467, 957)

Gwalior *gharānā* Hindustani vocal style and lineage whose exponents were originally from the city of Gwalior (206, 378, 443–44, 465–66)

Gwashinda Upper-caste male singers in Balochistan (781–82)

gwātī Person possessed by an evil spirit known as *gwāt* 'wind', who is treated with music, singing, and animal sacrifices and liberated from the *gwāt* by a healer (*gwātī-ē māt*) when both enter a state of trance (*774*, 780–81)

gzhas Tibetan folk-song genre usually accompanied by dance (710–11, 715)

hadīth Traditional sayings of the Prophet Muhammad (282, 757)

ḥāfiẓa Professional female dancers of the eighteenth and nineteenth centuries in Kashmir (687)

hāḷaḍū Lullabies, in Gujarat (632)

halage Generic term for **membranophones** in Karnataka (878)

halia gīt Songs sung by bullock-cart drivers and farmers in Orissa (733)

hālo (also *lāḍo*) Wedding and circumcision songs of Balochistan (773–74)

hand Drum pattern in Trinidad (589)

hangonda Gond priest in charge of funeral rites (722)

Harapu Gond festival that takes place in the spring (721)

harikathā 'The story of the Lord'; narrated and sung stories of Lord Vishnu, which may include drama and dance (89, 105, 106, 270, 390, 453)

harikīrtan Repetitious devotional hymn (613, 664–65)

harīp (1) Music; instrumental music; tune, in the Northern Areas of Pakistan (794–96); (2) Music of the Burusho double-reed and drum ensemble, in the Northern Areas of Pakistan (283)

harmonium Portable hand-pumped organ widely used for devotional and light classical music (171, 180, 186, 188, 235, 248, 251, 257, 338, 340, 352, 364, 426, 494, 495, *496*, 497, 515, 520, 534, 535, 543, *549*, 550, 555, 563, 575, 579, 581–82, *585*, 590, 603–604, 608–609, 612, 614, 618, 633, *634*, 635, 641–45, 655, *656*, 660, 665, 667, 670, 673–74, 715, 723, 746, 752–53, 762, 771, 790, *806*, 808, 818, 822, *823*, 828, *837*, 869, 896, 909, 913, *918*, 924, 948, 970)

hāsya 'Comic', one of the eight emotional states (***rasa***) codified in the ***Nāṭyaśāstra*** (69, 313)

havan Vedic ceremony performed at dawn, noon, and dusk; still performed in Trinidad (590)

havelī Literally 'mansion'; house of worship (251, 280, 401, 633)

havelī saṅgīt Music performed as part of the worship in a Vallabhacharya ***havelī*** (250–51, 252, 401, 632, 633, 643)

havelī saṅgītkār Musician of the Vallabhacharya religious tradition (401)

Hawaiian guitar Electric guitar played with a slide (339, 347, 582, 972)

hēvisi (also *hēvisi pūjā*) Buddhist kettledrum-and-oboe ceremonial ensemble in Sri Lanka (13, 329, 351, 361, 363–64, 958, 966, 967–69)

Hindustani music Classical music of North India

hogalikke 'To praise the name and deeds of deities'; a Kannada variant of the Tulu ***pāḍdana*** (883)

Holī North Indian Hindu festival celebrating the defeat of the mythical ruler Hiranyakasipu by the man-lion incarnation of Vishnu (170, 276, 471, 473, 490, 501, 504, 589, 629, 642, 645, 648, 664–65, 727, 877)

horanâva Quadruple-reed, conical bore **aerophone** of Sri Lanka, used in the lay-Buddhist musical ***hēvisi*** ensemble and in diverse secular contexts (329, 363, 366, 964, 967–68)

Hotado Maramma In Karnataka, icon of the popular goddess Maramma in a basket (880)

hotṛ Chief **Ṛgveda** priest in Vedic rituals (241)

hudka Hourglass pressure drum played by Fiji Indians (613)

huḍki (also *huṛuk, huḍukka*) Hourglass pressure drum of the western Himalayas (291, *304*, 305, 346)

huli vēṣa Tiger-costume dance in Karnataka (875)

icai nāṭakam (also special *nāṭakam*) Music drama; a form of Tamil drama employing performers who do not rehearse together (913)

iḍakku (also *iṭaykka*) Variable pitch hourglass drum of Kerala (363)

ʿĪd-ĕ-aẓḥā Muslim holiday commemorating Abraham's sacrifice of Isaac (277)

idiophone Musical instrument whose sound is produced by the vibrations of the instrument itself (20, 322, 324, 327, 342–43, 358, 470, 737, 966, 968)

ʿĪdu'l-fiṭr Muslim holiday celebrating the end of **Ramadan** (277)

imām Title for Shia religious leader (280)

imāmbāṛā Building in which Shia services are held to commemorate the martydom of Husain and his family (279)

inām Gift or reward given to a musician during a performance (668)

Indian *rabāb* (also *dhrupad rabāb*) Long-necked plucked unfretted lute with skin-covered body and gut strings (obsolete) (188, 190, 337, 345)

irpu pandum Madia sacred harvest celebration in Madhya Pradesh (722)

Iśai Vēḷḷāḷar South Indian upper-middle caste of musicians, dancers, and dance teachers (387, 910)

isal Metric structure of Mappila (Muslim) songs of Kerala (947)

'ishqi Love song of Northern Afghanistan (827)

isrāj (also *esraj*) Bowed long-necked fretted lute combining features of the **sitar** and the ***sārangī*** (248, 251, *336*, 494, 602)

iṭaykka (also ***iḍakka***) Small hourglass drum of Kerala (360, 361, 513, 931–34, 940–41)

iyal Literature of Tamil Nadu (914)

jāgaran (1) All-night event of singing and dancing, usually devoted to a deity or ancestor (642); (2) ***Gondhal*** ritual theater in Maharashtra (728)

Jaiminīya School of Sāmavedic chanting (242–43)

jajmān (also ***jajmānī, yajmān***) Patron, one who conducts or sponsors a ritual (400–401)

jajmānī (also ***jajmān***) Hereditary patron-client relationship (476, 639–40, 642, 649, 909)

jālra Small, flat cymbals of Tamil Nadu and Kerala (*914*)

jaltarangam (also *jaltarang*) Set of porcelain bowls filled with different levels of water, played by striking the edges with bamboo sticks (342–43, 352, 354–55)

jamikiḷi (also *jamiḍiki*) Drum played by plucking a string attached to the head (894, *895*, 901)

jan Santal charm song with curative powers (476)

janaka (also ***mēḷa***) Seven-tone scale capable of generating ragas (77, 97)

janānā 'To inform', solo devotional songs sung by Hindu devotees in Orissa (732)

janapada gēyālu People's songs; folk songs in Andhra Pradesh (891)

janapada sāhityam People's literature; folk literature in Andhra Pradesh (891)

jangam Devotee of Shiva and singer of Shaivite narrative songs (900–901)

jangama 'One who moves', mendicant (870)

jantar Stick zither of northwest India related to the North Indian ***bīn*** (343–44)

janya Karnatak **raga** derived from ***janaka*** scale (97)

jārī (also *jhāl*) Hand cymbals (*665*)

jas Compositions sung in praise of the Mother Goddess in Madhya Pradesh (724)

jatā-jatin 'Boy-girl', folk operetta sung by women in Mithila (679)

jata pandum Gond festival that takes place in autumn (721)

jati South Indian dance master's spoken syllables (214, 913)

jāti (1) Ancient mode class (27, 33, 34, 74, 75, 45, 96); (2) Class of rhythms in Karnatak music (140); (3) (also *jāt*) Caste or species (9, 398, 612, 696, 735)

jatisvaram Second part of the ***mōhini āṭṭam*** dance (512, 522, 941)

jātra Village fair in Karnataka (877–78)

jātrā (1) Bengali folk theater (419, 486, 488–89, 503, 505, 550); (2) Fairs and festivals connected with deities in Nepal (490)

javā Triangular coconut-shell plectrum used with the **sarod** and other instruments (336)

jāvaḷi Light vocal genre used to accompany South Indian dance performances; sung Karnatak performances (103, 104, 107, 219–20, 389, 411, 414, 452, 517)

jawābī 'Respondents', chorus of a singing group in Balochistan (778)

jayamangaḷa gâṭa Sinhala blessing songs (557)

jēn-paduna Songs sung by Jēnu Kurumba tribal people while gathering honey (919)

jhāl (1) Brass cymbals played in Trinidad with ***tāssā*** and bass drums (590); (2) Locally made variant of traditional Indian cymbals played by Hindu musicians and singers in Guyana (600, 602, 604)

jhālā Fast, virtuosic improvisatory section with rhythmic pulse following ***joṛ*** in Hindustani instrumental music (194, 198–199, 202, 203, 206, 581)

jhāñjh (1) Pair of cymbals (248, 251, 279, *280*, 347, 505, 601, 613, 625, 629, 633–35, 643, 724); (2) **Idiophone** consisting of four wooden frames with small cymbals, two held in each hand (*665*, 667)

jharpat Gond music and dance form of Madhya Pradesh (722)

jhelā Responsorial singers in ***samāj-gāyan*** devotional singing (251)

jhika Sistrum played by Fiji Indians (613)

jhora gīt Magar women's songs sung at the Tij festival in Nepal (702)

jhūmar Gond music and dance form of Madhya Pradesh (592, 722)

jhyāli Cymbals in Nepal (699, 704)

jhyāure (1) Popular dance piece in Nepal (698, 701); (2) 6/8 and 12/8 meters in Nepal (700)

jindua Song genre of the Punjab in solo-chorus style (475)

jōḍippaṭṭu Vocal duet in Karnatak music (227, 232)

Jogī Caste of hereditary mendicant musicians in Uttar Pradesh (345, 488, 639–40, 643, *671*)

jogīā sārangī Bowed, unfretted, two-string lute played by **Jogīs** to accompany their ballad singing (345)

joṛ Solo instrumental section with recurring pulse in the introductory ***ālāp*** of a Hindustani **raga** performance (198–99, 202, 203, 206, 581)

joṛā 'Pair', the two main playing strings on a ***chitrāli sitār*** of the North West Frontier Province (787)

joṛi Pair of cane duct flutes connected to one mouthpiece (763, 770–71)

jugalbandī (1) Pair of Hindustani soloists who play instruments of contrasting timbre (205, 380); (2) South Indian concert combining Hindustani and Karnatak instruments (351)

kabita Popular Tuluva women's field-song genre; sung during rice-planting season (883–84)

kaccēri Concert of Karnatak music (212, 384)

kaḍaga Silver bracelets worn by ***sōma*** dancer in Karnataka (878)

kadambaka 'Series, collection'; early name for ***rāgamālikā*** (218)

kaḍavu Poetic verse; text providing the principal structure for ***māṇ bhaṭṭ ākhyān*** (634)

kaḍime Iruḷa clay barrel drum (916)

kaffriñgnā Dance and music genre associated with African-Portuguese performance traditions in Sri Lanka (970–71)

kāfī Mystical poetry of the Punjab and Sindh (12, 753–54, 756, 759, 772)

kahaḷe Indigenous brass instruments of Karnataka (874)

kaikkottikkali Clap dance; village dance form in Tamil Nadu (518)

kājal Charcoal used by women as eye makeup (274)

kajalī (also *kajarī*) (1) 'Dark eyes', romantic songs for the rainy season in North India; also sung in Trinidad (589–90, 666, 668, 669–70, 671); (2) Tambourine played by Fiji Indians (613)

kalai Art (914)

kālakṣēpam Musical epic storytelling and preaching genre, performed by a lead singer or preacher playing wooden clappers and accompanied by a small orchestra (262, 270, 907–908, 925)

Kalāvant Professional, highly skilled singer or instrumentalist in the Hindustani tradition (379, 409, 476, 641)

kalavantulu (also ***bhogum, sani***) Female temple dancers in Andhra Pradesh (521)

kālgūc āṭ Kota dance performed at the beginning of any set of dances (278)

kalpanā sangīta Improvised music (89, 99)

kalpana svara (also ***svara kalpana***) Improvised solfège passages in Karnatak music that return to a main theme (217–18)

kalpita (also *kalpita saṅgīta*) Literally 'already conceived'; composed music (89, 99)

kalyāṇam Marriage (274, 275)

Kāmasūtra Medieval Indian manual of love and courtesan life (407–408, 551)

kamaicā (also *kamāychā*) Bowed unfretted lute played by the Manganihārs of Rajasthan (345, *641*, 642)

kamanche (also ***kemanche***) Persian spike fiddle (345, 688, 692)

kampita Ornamental shake (36, 94)

kamsāḷe A ***katha*** tradition in Karnataka; medium-size cymbal (872, *874*)

kancha karuvi Tamil musical instrument category referring to **idiophones** (327)

kanci Hand cymbals in Karnataka (887)

kāñjanī (1) Frame drum of Orissa (732); (2) ***kañjanī*** **bhajan**, popular devotional song form for group expression in Orissa (732)

kañjanī ke bhajan (also ***naradi bhajan***) *Nirguṇ* songs; those not in praise of a particular incarnation of a deity (724)

kañjarī (also *kañcira, kañjīrā*, ***khanjarī***, *khanjira, khanjiri*) Frame drum, often with small cymbals attached (149, 235, 346, 357, 364, 452, 582, *643*, 671, 723, 728, 906)

kānṭ Balochi horn, usually an oxen horn (783)

kapalik Oral epic performance genre of Madhya Pradesh (723)

kapurala Lay Buddhist ritual specialist in the **old religion** of Sri Lanka (955, 957, 960, 963)

kara pandum Gond festival that takes place in autumn (721–22)

karaḍi vēṣa Bear-costume dance in Karnataka (875)

karakam Clay vessel; South Indian ritual folk dance with clay vessels balanced on the dancers' heads (277, 518, 617, 904, 914)

karam Tribal dance/song form of central and eastern India (501, 722, 732)

karḍi majalu Ensemble of northern Karnataka (874)

karkhā Narrative songs of the Gāines (698)

karnāl Natural trumpet in Nepal (699–700)

Karnatak music Classical music of South India

kartāl (1) (also *kartāḷa*) Pair of wooden or iron clappers, sometimes with metal discs attached, played with one hand in folk and devotional musics (248, 251, 347, 364, *403*, 497, 602, 613, *614*, 641–42, *644*, *665*, 723); (2) Clappers consisting of four iron rods, two held in each hand, used in the ***birahā*** genre of Uttar Pradesh (667); (3) (also ***khartāl***) Cymbals (504, 732–33)

karuṇa 'Compassionate', one of the eight emotional states (***rasa***) codified in the ***Nāṭyaśāstra*** (69, 313)

karunashtak Devotional songs consisting of eight stanzas, sung by a soloist or in a group in Maharashtra (729)

karuvi General term for musical instrument in Tamil (327)

kārvai Any group of unarticulated pulses; gaps between three statements of a Karnatak ***mōrā*** cadence (155)

kāse Dance performed for the male deity Virabhadra in Karnataka (877)

Kashmiri *setār* A small **sitar** closely resembling the Iranian ***setār*** (344)

kāsījoḍa Pair of hand-held cymbals slightly heavier than the ***mañjīrā*** (629)

katai pāṭṭu Tamil story-song (908)

Katamaraju Hero of *Kāṭamarāju Katha*, an extended Telugu oral epic with roots in the thirteenth century, (898)

katav Prosodic form used for descriptive and didactic songs with quick tempos and simple tunes, in Maharashtra (729)

kathā (also *katha, kathālu*) Story; sung narrative (493, 549–50, 867–68, 870, 872, *873*, 896, 898)

kathak Classical dance of North India (119, 131, 132, 179, 180, 325, 342, 410, 487, 493–94, 495, 564, 640, 687)

kathakaḷi Dance drama of Kerala (90, 104, 324, 351, 361, 362–63, 490, 511, 513–14, 516, 542, 564, 933–35, 939–42, 944)

kaṭṭādiya (see also ***âdurā***, ***yakâdurā***) Drummer who controls communication with spirits of the **old religion** in Sri Lanka (955, 961)

kaṭṭaikkūttu Tamil dance drama based on stories from Hindu epics (*515*–16)

kaṭṭ pāṭukiṟatu Manner of shouting or singing with great forcefulness in Tamil folk music (916)

Kauthuma School of Sāmavedic chanting (242, 243–44)

kāvaṭi (1) Bow-shaped burden carried on the shoulders in honor of the Tamil deity Murugan, especially during the ***kāvaṭiyāṭṭam*** dance (518, 914, 921); (2) Tamil dance associated with the god Murugan (617, 914)

kāvaṭi cintu Tamil musical poetic genre sung or played to accompany the ***kāvaṭiyāṭṭam*** dance (921)

kāvaṭiyāṭṭam Tamil dance associated with the god Murugan in which a possessed dancer carries a ***kāvaṭi*** on the shoulders (921)

kavikāra maḍuva Group of lay Buddhist singers who perform in secret at the Daladā Māligawa, the Buddhism Temple of the Tooth in Sri Lanka (966)

kayamb (also *kayamn, caimbe*) Raft-shaped cane rattle played by Indians on Réunion Island (609–10)

keluni Songs of the Kela tribe of Orissa (732)

kemanche (also ***ghīchak***, ***kamanche***) Persian spike fiddle of the medieval Indo-Persian courts; still found in Afghanistan (345)

kendara Bowed **chordophone** of Orissa (733)

kenrā Bowed instrument of Bihar, with a coconut resonator and bamboo neck (345)

keśyā Bawdy songs sung on a variety of occasions in Rajasthan (277, 645)

kēṭṭi mēḷam 'Loud, robust ensemble'; rapid, loud playing of all instruments in a South Indian ensemble (usually ***tavil*** and ***nāgasvaram***) used to draw attention to an important moment and drown out inauspicious sounds (275, 279, 286)

kẖālī Hand gesture (wave) signifying an unstressed, "empty" subdivision of a Hindustani **tala** (112)

khamak Folk rhythm instrument of Bengal consisting of a small drum with a string attached that produces variable-pitch sounds when plucked (343)

khanaqah (also *khāneqāh*, ***tekke***) **Sufi** fraternity house (682, 818)

khānḍana Rice-pounding or swing songs sung during more general rites by girls of south Gujarat, to secure favorable husbands (274)

khanjani Small cymbals (505)

khanjarī (also ***kañjarī***, *kañjīrā, khanjiri*) Small frame drum with jingles (452, 647, 723, 728)

kharābāt Folk genre of Baghlan derived from Persian mystical poetry (828, *829*)

khartāl (also ***kartāl***) Cymbals (495, 503)

khayāl Devotional songs of Madhya Pradesh (723)

khī̄ Newār drum in Nepal (702)

khol Double-headed clay barrel drum of northeastern India (346, 356, 503, 732–33)

khurḍak (also *ḍuggī, ḍukkaṛ*) Small hand-played kettledrum pair of North India (340, 671, 679)

khyāl Since the late eighteenth century, the preeminent Hindustani vocal genre (15, 69, 83, 84, 119, 123, 125, 126, 127, 132, 134, 162, 163, 164, 169, 170–79, 180, 184, 195, 196, 197, 200, 202, 206, 207, 229, 256, 333, 335, 336, 338, 373, 378, 379, 381, 410–11, 413, 533, 581, 645, 646, 805, 847, 852–53, 855, 860)

khyāli 4/4 and 2/2 meters in Nepal (700)

kilagi-turra Folk drama form of Madhya Pradesh featuring competitive poetry singing (723)

kiliwāli Popular music in Afghanistan (809, 820)

king (1) Stick zither of Jammu and Kashmir, related to the North Indian ***bīn*** and the medieval *vīṇā* (343); (2) Plucked lute of Punjab, Pakistan (763, 769–70, 772)

kingiri Bowed **chordophone** with a coconut shell resonator, in Madhya Pradesh (722)

kinnarī vīṇā Stick zither described in medieval musicological texts (343)

kirikaṭṭi (also *kuṇṭalam*) Pair of conical drums tied around the player's waist and played with curved sticks, in Tamil Nadu (914)

kīrtan (1) (also *kīrtana*) Devotional praise song (42, 106, 211, 216, 219, 221, 250–51, 253–54, 262, 265–67, 268, 347, 411, 416, 503, 517, 522, 549, 573, 575, 590, 623, 632–34, 642–43, 655–56, 674, 724, 729, 732, 772, 845, *846*, 856, 908, 920, 922–25, 927, 947); (2) (also ***sankīrtan***) Congregational dancing and chanting of a holy name, often that of Krishna (503, 643, 729)

kīrtankār Performer of ***kīrtan*** (632–33, *634*)

klāsik (also *musiqī-ye klāsik*) Classical music in Afghanistan (820, 827)

kob Kota curved brass horn (278, *915*)

kohomba kankāriya Important ritual to bring about peace, a bountiful harvest, and the general welfare, in Sinhala Sri Lanka's up-country (364, 963)

kokkara Metal scraper of Kerala, used in sorcery (367)

koḷ Kota double-reed **aerophone** with conical bore (912, *915*)

kōlai cintu Songs popular in the late nineteenth and early twentieth centuries in Tamil Nadu, recounting tales of famous murders (921)

kolam Sinhala masked theater of southern and southwestern Sri Lanka (491, 964)

kōlāṭṭam South Indian stick dance, accompanied by song (518, 617, 909, 918, 920, 969)

kōle basava Performing cow, in the Karnataka ***basavāṭa gangettinavaru*** street performance (875–76)

kōlkkaḷi Stick dance in Kerala (947)

koḷvar Instruments central to a Kota ensemble: ***koḷ, par,*** and ***tabaṭk*** (278, 912)

komal 'Flatted', as a flatted note (67, 79, 445)

kombu (also ***kompà***) Animal horn; curved brass horn (874, 886, 956)

kombu kahaḷe Bugles; ensemble of animal and brass horns (874, 886)

kommu Crescent-shaped brass horn used particularly by singers of the Telugu herding caste (*896, 902*)

kompà (also ***kombu,*** *śṛṅga*) Semicircular trumpet of South India (360, *361*, 362, 363, 366, 931, 933, 937, 938)

konakkoḷ Gurgling syllables recited to rhythmic patterns in Karnatak music (214)

koraippu Section of a Karnatak drum solo involving more than one drummer (159, *160*)

koravanji (see also ***kuravanji***) Women tattoo artists and singers in Karnataka villages (870)

korta pandum Gond festival that occurs during the rainy season (721)

kōrvai Intricate rhythmic composition in a Karnatak drum solo (154, 155–56, *158*, 159)

kōṭānki Small, hourglass-shaped pressure drum in Tamil Nadu (904)

kōṭṭi Tamil party of **bhajan** singers (Sanskrit *gōṣṭhi*) (918)

koṭṭippāṭisēva 'Drumming-and-singing offering', temple music genre of Kerala (932, 940)

kovur pancaratnam (also ***pañcaratna***) Five songs composed by Tyagaraja on the deity Sundaresvara, who presides at the main temple at Kovur, near Madras (451)

kriti Karnatak classical vocal genre derived from the ***kīrtan*** devotional tradition (36, 94, 97, 99, 100, 145, 149, 209, 211, 216, 217, 218, 219, 220, 221–23, 224–26, 228, 229–30, 231, 267, 268–69, 385, 388, 389, 390, 393, 394, 410–11, 414, 451, 452)

kriyā Hand movements that mark subdivisions of Karnatak **talas** (139)

Kṛshṇa Janmāṣṭāmī North Indian festival celebrating the birthday of Krishna (276)

kṛshṇa līlā Theatrical performance of Krishna's pastimes with the milkmaids, performed by boys in Bangladesh (505)

Kṛshṇalīlātaraṅginī Seventeenth-century Sanskrit musical poem by Narayanatirtha on the Krishna theme (452)

kṛshṇāṭṭam Ritual temple dance drama of Kerala (351, 362, 363, 510–11, *512*, 514, 934)

Kshatriya (*Kṣatriya*) Traditionally the second-highest group or class (***varṇā***) in Hindu society, whose members served as rulers and fighters (9, 386, 398, 735, 911)

kuchipuḍi Classical dance form originating in Andhra Pradesh (104, 270, 358, 515–18, 521, 908)

kuḍam Struck brass pot on which *villu* bow rests (365, *907*)

kuḻal Small South Indian double-reed pipe or bamboo flute (234, 350, 352, 354, 360, 361–62, 389, 931–33, 937–38, 943)

kumārapūrṇimā gīt Songs sung by girls in Orissa at the Kumārapūrṇimā festival (733)

kummi Tamil women's circle dance (277, 278, 283, 617, 917–18, *919*–21, 925)

kummiyaṭi Hand clapping in ***kummi*** songs of Tamil Nadu (919)

kuṇita Generic term for dance in Karnataka (868, 876)

kunnbi Dance associated with agricultural work performed by Goan Christians (737)

kuṇṭalam (also ***kirikaṭṭi***) Pair of conical drums tied around the player's waist and played with curved sticks in Tamil Nadu (914)

kūnzag Earthen water pot used as a rhythm-producing instrument; played by a *kūnzagī* (774, 782, 783)

kuranji South Indian **raga** name; often used in Tamil swinging songs (275)

kuravai Tamil song form associated with agriculture; also, a type of ululation performed by women at important ritual moments (908, 918)

kuravanji (see also ***koravanji***) Dramatic form about gypsies, in Tanjavur (518, 519)

kuṟavan-kuṟatti Dance and song in the form of playful, erotic banter between a gypsy man and woman, in Tamil Nadu (914)

kutam Musical bow of Kerala (932)

kutapa Melodic ensemble associated with Sanskrit drama, consisting of a singer, players of hand cymbals marking the meter and tempo, and string and flute players (322, 323)

kutirai 'Horse dance', processional dance performed in village festivals in Tamil Nadu (518)

kūṭiyāṭṭam Sanskrit dance drama of Kerala (361, 363, 399, 484, 486, 509, *510*, 511, 515, 931, 933, 941, 944)

kūttambalam 'Drama hall', a room in a temple in which dance dramas are staged (509, 515)

kūttu (also ***terukkūttu***) Popular street dance and drama in Tamil Nadu (908)

lachārī Saucy women's songs for weddings and childbirth celebrations, sung in Trinidad and Bhojpur (589)

laggī Short, fast-tempo Hindustani **tabla** composition (128, 132, 181–83, 186, 198)

lakṣaṇa Characteristic feature (22, 28)

lakṣmi kalyāṇam 'The Wedding of Lakshmi'; song played during Tamil weddings (275)

lalai Lullaby of northern Afghanistan (827)

lāli Lilting tune in ***kuranji*** **raga**, sung during the swinging ceremony at Tamil weddings (275)

lāmbā vīrkāvyo Long poems about bravery, in Gujarat (637)

landay (also *tappa*) Two-line verse form in the southeastern Pashtun areas of Afghanistan and Pakistan (506, 786, 813, 835–36, *838–39*)

Laṅgā Caste of hereditary musicians in Rajasthan (345, 398, 402–*403*, *476*, 639-42)

lāsya (see also ***taṇḍava***) Feminine aspects of dance; one of the main principles of dance in the twelfth-century treatise *Abhinaya Chandrika* (494)

lāvṇi (1) Song form with improvised text, in Karnataka (869–70); (2) Tamil form, of Marathi origin, in which two parties engage in a musical debate on philosophical or mythological themes (908)

laya (also *lay*) Tempo or rhythm (101, 111, 148, 149, 200, 452)

laykārī Complex rhythmic play in Hindustani music (111, 136, 169, 175, 178, 200)

lehrā Sindhi folk composition believed to drive evil spirits from the body of a possessed woman (286)

lēwā Festive dance common among fishermen along the Baloch coast; also performed by coastal Baloch living in Karachi (774, 777–78)

light music (also ***mel iśai***) Popular style of Tamil music, often combining Western harmony on guitar or keyboard with Indian melody, Indian folk or dance rhythms, and film-style vocals (924–25)

lī-keḷi Sinhala stick dance now performed in Buddhist temple processions (***perahēra***) (969)

līko (also ***ḍēhī, zahīrok***) Songs of separation, travel, and work, popular in northern Balochistan (774, 775–76)

līlā (see also ***kṛshṇa līlā, rās līlā***) Religious drama of North India (419, 495)

līlo Cradle songs and lullabies in Balochistan (773–74)

linga (also *lingam*) Phallic symbol of Shiva's creative power (224)

lithophone Musical instrument comprising

separate pieces of stone that sound successive scale pitches when struck (*320*–21)

lok gīt 'Folk song', in Nepal (705–706, 771)

lorik Sung epic poem in North India (673, 675)

macakkaippāṭṭu Morning-sickness song sung for newly pregnant Tamil women (275)

mādal Large double-headed cylindrical drum of Nepal (*703*–704, 705, 734, 862)

maddaḷam South Indian double-headed barrel drum (360, 361, 362, 513–15, 931–32, *933*, 934–35, 950)

maddaḷe Double-headed drum (885–86)

madhya (also *madhyama*) (1) Medium or middle, as in medium tempo or middle register (96, 111, 153, 167, 192); (2) (also *madhyam*) Intermediate level of college education in North India (447)

Māgha Hindu month (January–February) (277)

Mahabharata One of the great ancient Hindu epics, consisting of a hundred thousand verses (11, 361, 399, 408, 482, 492, 509, 513, 516, 607, 617, 633, 635, 723, 733, 876, 879, 893, 897, 908, 932)

mahali (also *musiqī-ye mahali*) Folk music; also, local or regional styles in Afghanistan (818, 819–20, 827)

Mahā-Parinibbāna-Sutta Pali Buddhist text describing lay-Buddhist instrumental musical offerings (965)

maharaja (also **gaekwad**) "Great ruler" (229, 443)

mahāri Female temple dancers in Orissa (519)

mahurī (also ***mohurī***) Double-reed **aerophone** of Orissa (733)

majlis (also *majilis*) Shiite mourning session, usually during **Muharram** (256, 284, 286, *745*, 750)

makuṭam 'Crown'; concluding melodic or rhythmic passages involving repetitions (228)

mālai mārrira pāṭṭu Garland-exchange song of Tamil Nadu (275)

Malbar drum (also ***tapou***) Frame drum of Réunion Island (607)

mālid Ritual dance of Balochistan performed on various occasions, accompanied by tambourines (***samā***) (774, 779–80)

mallāri Repertoire of compositions without texts, played by ***nāgasvaram*** or ***tavil*** players (234)

maloya Popular musical genre on Réunion Island encompassing several styles (609–11)

māṇ (also *gāgar*) Large globular metal pot of Gujarat (633, *634*)

māṇ bhaṭṭ Kīrtan singer who accompanies himself on the ***mān***, in Gujarat (7, 632–33, *634*)

māṇ bhaṭṭ ākhyān Religious stories told by a ***māṇ bhaṭṭ*** (401, 633–34)

Mān Kutūhal Early sixteenth-century music treatise (45, 314, *315*)

manch Musical-theater form in Madhya Pradesh (471–72, 723)

manch ke nāc Malwa dance form with vocal and instrumental accompaniment (723)

māṅd Rajasthani folk-song type (642)

maṇḍala sthāna Dance position in ***kathakaḷi*** (514)

mandó Goan Christian song and dance genre (737–39, 741)

māngāi (also *gaṛāi*) Clay water pot **idiophone** (787, 789, *790*)

maṅgal (also *maṅgaḷa*) Auspicious song (556, 698, 702)

maṅgala gān Medieval Bengali narrative songs in praise of power-cult goddesses such as Manasa and Candi and gods such as Dharma (846)

mangaḷa vādyam 'Auspicious musical instruments', ensemble including ***nāgasvaram*** and ***tavil*** common in South Indian temples, rituals, and processions (210)

maṅgalācaraṇ Slow invocatory dance including ***pushpāñjali*** and ***raṅgbhūmi pranām***; the first dance in an ***oḍissi*** performance (520)

mangaḷam Short ending piece of a Karnatak concert; auspicious concluding song (220, 275)

Manganihār Professional musician caste in Rajasthan (7, 273, 345, 476, 639–40, *641*, 642)

Manipa Tibetan itinerant musician whose repertoire includes the **mantra** *Om mani padme hum* and religious songs (712)

mani-rimdu Sherpa Buddhist folk dance drama of Nepal (490)

mañjīrā Small cup-shaped hand-held cymbals used in North Indian and diaspora dance and devotional music accompaniment (342, 347, *400*, 505, 582, 589, 612, 625, 629, 633, 635, 647, 665, 728)

manodharma Improvised material in a Karnatak **raga** (99, 451, 455, 943)

mantra Sacred word or phrase with magical powers (225, 261, 469, 590, 712)

maqām Melodic mode or melody type; also, a collection of instrumental pieces and songs for performance in a specific melodic mode in Kashmir (686, 687, 693, 694, 804)

maram Cylindrical hand drum of Kerala (931, 933)

Marche dans le Feu 'Firewalk'; annual ceremony celebrating the virginity of the goddess Pandyale on Réunion Island (*607*)

mardala Drum (Sanskrit); cognates throughout India refer to a variety of different drums (520)

mārga (1) Ancient classical music (20, 33, 34, 300, 400, 492); (2) Culture of a high or refined "way" or "path" usually associated with social elites at important cultural centers (602–603); (3) Governed by rules of **raga** and **tala** (372); (4) Telugu classical literature (893)

mārgam 'Path'; an ideal suite for dance concerts as codified c. 1800 (508)

margamkali *The Play of the Way*, performed by the Christians of Kerala (945, *946*)

marka pandum Sacred Madia festival held to solemnize the pounding of the first corn in April (722)

Mārkaḻi Tamil month (mid-December to mid-January) (918)

maro dandorā Telugu folk drum-music genre (556)

marṣīyā (also *marṣiya, marsīya, marṣiyah*) Elegy chanted or sung by Shiite Muslims (277, 772, 794)

maśak Bagpipe played by the *bhopā* community of Rajasthan (345)

masītkhānī gat Slow-tempo Hindustani instrumental composition allegedly created by Masit Khan in the eighteenth century (125, 126, 189–191, 192, 195, 197, 198, 202, 206)

mast Intoxicated, drunk; mad; excited (752, 754)

mat 'Opinion'; attribution of raga family groupings to a particular author or theoretician (77, 314)

mātam Self-flagellation, usually beating oneself on the breast with the hands, practiced by Shias in Pakistan (*280*)

maṭkī kā nāc Malwa dance with vocal and instrumental accompaniment (723)

mātrā (1) Beat; the duration of two beats (112, 241, 687, 915, 938, 959); (2) Pulse groups in Karnatak **tala** beats (142)

mattaḷam Tamil double-headed ceramic barrel drum (915)

maulūd Sindhi men's song genre honoring the Prophet Muhammad, especially on his birthday (278)

mehfil Assembly, congregation (203, 413, 493, 527, 686, *694*–95, 747, 752, 755)

mel iśai 'Soft music'; ***light music*** (Tamil) (924)

mēḷa (1) (also ***janaka***) seven-tone scale capable of generating Karnatak **ragas** (97); (2) (also ***mēḷam***) Ensemble (387, 867–68, 874, 933, 935–36, 940, 943–44)

mēlā Festival (Tamil) (602, 650, 906, 912)

mēḷam Ensemble of instruments; or frets on a vina (912)

melody regions Scales, ragas (term proposed by the Sinhala musicologist C. de S. Kulatillake) (959)

membranophone Musical instrument whose sound is produced by the vibrations of a stretched membrane (20, 322, 324, 326, 327, 341–42, 737)

meṅhdī Muslim and Hindu wedding ritual in northern regions, in which henna is applied to the hands of the bride (275, 771)

meṭṭu Melody; fingerboard of the vina (Tamil) (913–14)

mgur Tibetan song form on a religious theme (712)

milād (also *milad, milād*) 'Birth'; especially, the birthday of the Prophet Muhammad (256, 278, 411, 750)

miḻāvu Oversize pot drum of Kerala (*363*, 510, 511, 931, 933)

mīṇḍ Glide between two or more tones, in

Hindustani instrumental music (191, 197, 199, 202)

Mīrāsī Caste of hereditary musicians in North India and Pakistan (7, 123, 273, 283, 345, 379, 409–10, 476, 506, 641, 644, 763–71)

mitatru karuvi 'Throat instrument', referring to a vocalist (Tamil) (327)

mizrāb Wire plectrum worn on the forefinger, used to play the **sitar** and other stringed instruments (201, 334)

mohan vīṇā Modified slide guitar developed by Vishwa Mohan Bhatt (467)

mōhini āṭṭam 'Solo dance of the divine temptress'; semiclassical dance of Kerala dedicated to the goddess Mohini (358, 511–14, 521, 933–35, 941–42)

mohṛā Brief melodic fragment ending an improvisation, in Hindustani music (117–18, 166, 198–99)

mohurī (also ***mahurī***, *mohorī*) Double-reed folk **aerophone** (346)

mokṣa Spiritual liberation from the Hindu cycle of reincarnation (20, 70, 375)

mokṣa nata Fast-tempo dance, the concluding item in ***oḍissi*** dance performance (520)

moll Short vocal oscillation, in Goa (739)

molon Double-headed cylindrical drum on Réunion Island (*608*)

Mon Ladakhi folk musician, player of oboe and kettledrum (712, 794)

mōrā Karnatak rhythmic cadential structure (154–55, 156, *157*, 158, 159)

morchaṅg Wrought-iron mouth harp played by **Laṅgās** in Rajasthan (641)

morsing (also *murcing*) South Indian mouth harp played as a percussion instrument (222, 235, 358)

moṭā gīt 'Big songs', sophisticated and refined songs sung by the **Laṅgās** and **Manganihārs** in Rajasthan (642)

motk Elegies of Balochistan (774, 776)

mouran Guyanese Indian women's songs performed after birth; infant head-shaving ceremony (601, 603)

mṛdang (also ***pakhāvaj***) North Indian barrel drum (*299*, 342)

mridang Barrel-shaped double-headed classical and folk drum of South Asia (114, 342, 503, 613, 693, 728, 733)

mridangam 'Clay unit'; double-headed barrel drum, nowadays of wood, played in Karnatak music (104, 107, 114, 147, 149, 150, 151, *152*, 153, 159, 161, 222, *233*, 235, 267, 307, 324, 325, 326, 350, 356, *357*, 358, 360, 361, 364, 365, 366, 384, 389, 452, 513, 517, 522, 543, 555, 560, 581–82, 664, 740, 913)

muḍivu In a Karnatak **tala**, the starting point of the first half of a ***pallavi*** theme (217)

mudra 'Stamp', 'insignia', or signature of the composer, integrated in the text of a song; also, the name of the song's **raga**, **tala**, other musical features, or deity integrated in the song text (224, 452)

mudrā Hand gesture used by Vedic reciters and chanters (*242*, 243, 520)

muezzin Religious caller to Islamic prayer (581)

mugulmānī Large single-headed, cylindrical tripod drum played on festive occasions and for ritual dances in coastal Balochistan and among the Baloch in Karachi (777, *778*, 780, 783)

Muharram Muslim month; also, a holiday of special importance to Shiites memorializing members of the Prophet Muhammad's family who died defending Islam on the battlefields of Karbala, Iraq, in A.D. 680 (277, 285, 590, 794, 875)

muhurtam Auspicious hour-and-a-half period during which the central ritual of a Hindu wedding must be performed (275)

mukhavīṇā Small South Indian double-reed instrument (366, 387, 879, 913)

mukhiyā Lead devotional singer in North Indian ***samāj-gāyan*** (*248*, 251)

mukhṛā Opening section of Hindustani instrumental composition, serving to emphasize the first beat of a **tala** cycle (117–18, 128, 172, 174–75, 181, 191, 193, 197, 200)

mukhtai svara Solfège passage sometimes performed following the ***anupallavi*** in some Karnatak ***varṇam***; a type of ***citta svara*** (216–17)

mūrccanā Process of creating new Karnatak ragas by shifting the tonic to a different scale tone (97)

murlī (also ***bīn***, ***puṅgī***) Double clarinet with a gourd wind chamber (345, 640–41)

mushāira Urdu poetry reading (284, 749–50)

mūsīqī Music (Urdu) (285)

mussoll Musical genre associated with a Christian martial dance, in Goa (737–39)

naḍ (also ***nal***) Flute, in Balochistan; usually a shepherd's instrument (775, 783)

nāda Primordial sound; musical sound (34, 70, 91, 221, 313, 327, 452, 912)

Nāda-Brahman Cosmic primordial sound, in yoga and music (70, 247)

nādagama (also *nadagam, nadhagam*) Nineteenth-century Sinhala theatrical genre (422, 491, 958, 964)

nāda yoga Spiritual path of devotion to musical sound (220)

nagārā Double-headed cylindrical folk drum of Guyana, two meters or more in height and played by one or two men with thick rounded sticks; also, performing drummer group and Ahīr singer-dancers of Guyana (602, 605)

nagāṛā (also *nagare*, ***naqqārā***) Pair of clay or metal kettledrums played with two curved beaters; used in folk, popular, and temple contexts (342, 346, *496*, 497, 502, 642, *665*, 671, 674, 700)

nāgasankīrtan Processional singing of devotional songs (267)

nāgasvaram Large South Indian double-reed **aerophone** with a conical bore, played in temples, rituals, and processions (90, 103, 108, 161, 210, 212, 230, 232, 234, 270, 275, 286, 323–24, 350, 352, 354, 355, *359*, 360, 387, 389, 390, 392, 393, 394–95, 452, 544, 556–57, 608, 876, 886, 912, 915, 925, 931, *933*, 958)

nāgasvaramu Gourd wind instrument played by snake charmers in Andhra Pradesh (896)

naghma-ye kashāl Afghan instrumental form (805, 806–*807*, 835)

nā'ī West Asian horizontal flute (305, 306)

naiyadi Kandyan dance form of Sri Lanka (490)

naiyāṇṭi mēḷam Tamil folk instrumental ensemble consisting of drums and double reeds (913, *914*)

nal Flute, in Balochistan (774–75, 781–82)

nāl Folk barrel drum played by Gujaratis in the United States (582)

nalunku Tamil wedding ritual in which the bride and groom apply paint to one another's feet, joke with one another, and sing (275)

nāmasiddhanta Recitation of holy names as a path to enlightenment in South India (221)

namaskāram (also *namaste*) Putting the hands together as in prayer or prostrating the body, as greeting or obeisance; also traditional verbal greeting (275, 472)

Nambudiri Brahmin caste in Kerala that practices ancient forms of Vedic recitation and chant (241–42)

nām-kīrtan Singing the names of God, in North India (248, 250, 253, 590)

ñanappāṭṭu European (particularly German) hymns translated into Tamil and sung primarily by Lutherans in Tamil Nadu (922)

nande baeth Unaccompanied songs performed throughout the Valley of Kashmir during the planting, cleaning, and harvesting of rice (684–85)

nande chakri Song genre similar in style to ***nande baeth***, but performed in homes with instrumental accompaniment (685)

Nandiwālā Specialist performer who gives animal-training shows in the villages of Maharashtra (727)

naqqārā (also ***nagāṛā***, *nagare*) Stick-played kettledrum pair (122, 123, 131, 133, 279, 280, *304*, 305, 346, 347, 401, 402, 506, 685)

nāṛ Obliquely held, end-blown folk flute of Sindh and Rajasthan (345)

naradi bhajan (also ***kañjanī ke bhajan***) ***Nirguṇ*** songs: those not in praise of a particular incarnation of a deity (724)

Nāradīyaśikṣā Treatise providing practical instruction for the chanting of Sāmavedic hymns, compiled in the fifth or sixth century (18, 24, 30–33)

narampu karuvi Tamil musical category referring to **chordophones** (327)

narsiṅga Long curved natural horn of Nepal (699–700)

narslon Oboe of the ***nāgasvaram*** family on Réunion Island (*608*)

naʿt Religious music honoring the Prophet

Muhammad and his offspring (278, 748, 772, 826–27)

nāther Optional solo song following the ***shakl*** in a Kashmiri ***maqām*** performance (687)

nāṭṭupuṟam 'Countryside', 'folk' (Tamil) (914)

naṭṭuvanār Dance master, especially of ***bharata nāṭyam*** (104, 149, 521–22, 913)

nāṭya Drama, acting and a combination of dance and drama, from which come both pure dance (***nṛtta***) and that which displays sentiment (***nṛtya***) through expression (***abhinaya***) (21, 44, 492, 507–509, 511, 513–14, 516, 518–19, 521)

nāṭya kaccēri Dance concert honoring a deity as part of a village festival in Tamil Nadu (518)

nāṭya saṅgīt Marathi musical drama (423)

Nāṭyaśāstra Celebrated Sanskrit treatise on drama, music, and dance by Bharata, dated c. 200 B.C.–A.D. 200 (18, 22, 23–24, 25–30, 32, 43, 51, 52, 73, 104, 110, 139, 140, 228, 262, 298, *299*, 313, 317, 319–29, 350, 351, 356, 363, 372, 399, 408, 470, 480, 482, 492, 507, 515, 519, 521, 523, 633, 731)

naubat Outdoor court ensemble of trumpets, drums, cymbals, and double-reed instruments, in medieval North India (301, *303*, 305, 340, 342, 712)

naubat khānā Ensemble of kettledrums, sometimes including double-reed instruments with conical bores; also, building where such an ensemble plays (*279*, *280*)

naudi gīt Dance songs of Orissa telling of Krishna and his exploits (733)

nauḥah Lament sung by Shiites during **Muharram**, often accompanied by self-flagellation (***mātam***) (277)

Naukācaritram Telugu musical story by Tyagaraja, consisting of verses and announcements woven around Krishna songs (452)

naumati bājā Damāi ensemble of nine instruments, in Nepal (699)

nauṭaṅkī North Indian folk musical drama (346, *410*, 419, 485, *496*, *549*, 674, 675)

navagraha kriti Songs on the nine houses, or planets, in their deified form; the best-known set of such Karnatak compositions is by Muttusvami Dikshitar (1775–1835) (224, 451)

Navrātrī 'Nine nights', Hindu festival of North and South India (230, 277, 501, 550, 617, 625, 628, 629)

nawāzenda Musician or instrumentalist; formerly professional performers only (831)

nay (also *ney*) Flutes of the recorder family; in Badakhshan, a conical end-blown fipple flute (804, 822, 828, 830–31)

nāyaka nāyikā 'Hero-heroine' theme of women in love, found in South Asian literature (313)

nāyaṇam South Indian double-reed instrument, slightly shorter than the ***nāgasvaram*** (*914*, 920–21)

nāykhī Barrel drum of Nepal (702)

nāzenk Praise songs sung for male relatives in Balochistan (773–74)

ngā Frame drum of the Guruṅg shaman (704)

nibaddh 'Bound'; Hindustani **ragas** rendered with meter (**tala**) (82)

nibal de Song tale of Madhya Pradesh, blending prose, verse, and recitation (723)

nīmakai Passionate song of North West Frontier Province (786)

nipuṇ Supplementary or final level of college education in North India (447)

niraval (also *neraval*, ***sāhitya prastāra***) Improvisation in Karnatak music that retains the text of the original composition but changes the melody (99, 147–48, 217, 451)

nirguṇ (see ***kañjanī ke bhajan***) Bhakti tradition describing God in ineffable form (249, 253, 256, 345, 643, 655, 671, 724)

nirguṇ gīt Songs of Orissa that present theological riddles in question-and-answer format (733)

nirvāhaṇa Entrance of the first character in ***kūṭiyāṭṭam*** dance drama (510)

nīti cintu Tamil morality songs (921)

nizam Formerly, Muslim ruler of Hyderabad State (now Andhra Pradesh) (898)

nom-tom ālāp Improvised ***ālāp*** section with rhythmic pulse in Hindustani vocal music (168, 173, 175, 198–99, 215)

noṇṭi cintu Song form associated with ***noṇṭi nāṭakam***, the one-man musical-dramatic genre of Tamil Nadu (920–21)

noṇṭi nāṭakam One-man musical-dramatic genre in Tamil Nadu (921)

nṛtta (1) (also *nritta*) Nonrepresentational or "pure" dance (20–21, 149, 180, 492, 494, 513, 519, 521–22); (2) (also *nritya*, *nṛtta*) Representational dance (21, 44, 104, 149, 180, 492, 519, 521)

nṛtya (also *nurti*) Sinhala popular music based on Marathi and Parsi theater music of the late nineteenth and early twentieth centuries (491, 970)

nṛtya-nāṭya Dance drama in Bangladesh (505)

nukana-rendana pandum Madia sacred autumn festivities (722)

nūt Struck clay pot **idiophone** of Kashmir, similar to South Indian ***ghaṭam*** (683–85)

oḍissi Major classical dance form of India, with roots in temple dance of Orissa (519–21)

Oduvar Hereditary temple singers of the ***tiruppugaḻ*** hymns in South India (216)

oggu Small hourglass-shaped drum of Shiva in Andhra Pradesh (896)

ojapali Religious drama form of Assam (486)

old religion One of the two primary religions of the Sinhala in Sri Lanka; includes worship of localized spirit entities, popular Hinduism, and astrology (955, 960–65)

ōmayṇ Sound of all instruments playing simultaneously in a Kota ensemble (278)

oppana Popular dance of the Mappilas (Muslims) of Kerala (947, *948*)

oppāri Tamil lament (907)

oraṭi 'One beat' (Tamil) (915)

oru olai Literally 'one cooking pot'; as used by the liberation theologian Theophilus Appavoo, the pooling together by poor people of Tamil Nadu of their financial and labor resources to fight social oppression and perform daily worship (925)

ōṭam Boat songs in Tamil Nadu (518)

oṭṭan (also ***paṛayan, sīthangan***) One of three kinds of popular dance drama (***tuḷḷal***) in Kerala (514, 516, 941)

ottu South Indian double-reed drone pipe (103, *359*, 360, 912–14)

oulé (also *houlé, ouleur, roulé, rouleur*) Large cylindrical drum on Réunion Island (609–10)

ovi Women's songs of Maharashtra; also, an unaccompanied devotional song genre of central India with a loosely structured form allowing singers freedom for extempore composition (729)

oyilāṭṭam (also *oyiṟkummi*) Tamil men's line dance with athletic movements and call-and-response vocals (*917*–20, 925)

pachvāṅ 'Western'; a style of **tabla** playing, in North India (134)

pacaṛā (also *mātā māī kī gīt*) Mother goddess songs, sung by women in Uttar Pradesh (663)

pad Maharashtran song (162, 643)

pada (1) In the early period, a word or line of a poem referring to the verbal element of music or song (current term in South India is *matu*) (20, 724); (2) Song text (630, 633); (3) Various song types, in Karnataka (868, 870)

padam South Indian dance and song form; a song to the Divine Lover (103, 104, 107, 219–20, 229, 266–67, 389, 410–11, 452, 512, 517, 940–41)

padāvali kīrtan Refined Bengali devotional music (250, 253, 505, 845–48)

pada varṇam Major South Indian dance genre (217, 517)

pāḍdana Tulu genre of sung narratives associated with an indigenous Tuluva category of deities called *bhūta* (415, 882–85)

padhati Received tradition or rules for performing a particular piece or genre (918)

padyam (also ***viruttam***) Style of singing poetry without a pulse (215, 218)

Pahlawān Male singer of ***shēr*** in Balochistan, accompanied by stringed instruments (776, 781, *782*)

pakaṛ Identifying or catch phrase of a Hindustani **raga** (446)

pakhāvaj (also ***mṛdang***) North Indian double-headed barrel drum (111, 114–*121*, 122–25, 127, 130–31, 133–36, 164, 168, 169, 197, 248, 251, 341–42, 346, *378*, 402, 448, 494, 520, 633–34, 643, 664)

pala Popular type of ballad in Orissa, associated with the worship of Satyapir (486, 733)

palia Group of five to seven singers led by a main singer (***gāyak***), presenting ***pala*** ballads (733)

pallavi First section of a Karnatak composition; improvisational section, with text and **tala** (100, 141, 145, 213, 215, 216–218, 219, 221–222, 225–226, 228–229, 230, 262, 265, 266, 269, 410, 455, 544, 920, 966)

Palnāṭi Vīrula Katha (also ***Epic of Palnāḍu***) Extended Telugu oral epic with roots in the twelfth century (898)

pāmalai American and British hymns translated into Tamil, sung primarily in the Church of South India and former British and American missions in Tamil Nadu (922–23)

pambajōḍu Pair of double-headed drums used in Telugu epic performances (894, *895*, *896*, 901)

pampai South Indian double cylindrical drum (286, 911, *914*–15)

paṇ Ancient melody of Tamil Nadu described in early texts on Tamil music and believed to be the precursor of all South Indian **ragas** (96, 216, 260, 906)

pāncai bājā (also *pañcai bājā*) 'Five instruments', Damāi ensemble of Nepal equivalent to the ***naubat khānā*** (280, 286, 699–700)

pancāla Worshipers of the male deity Virabhadra (878)

pañcaratna 'Five jewels', a set of compositions by Tyagaraja (211, 217, 393, 394, 395)

pañcatūrya nāda Buddhist fivefold system of instrument classification, in Sri Lanka (327–29, 966, 968)

pañcavādyam South Indian ritual percussion and wind ensemble (351, 360, 361, 365, 932, 935, 939–40, 943–44)

paṇḍit Hindu teacher's honorific title (380, 444, 460, 462, 464, 465, 601)

pāṇi 'Palm of the hand', drum patterns played on the ***timila*** to summon the gods to a ritual (933–34, 943–44)

pantheru Kandyan dance form of Sri Lanka (490)

par Kota cylindrical drum in Tamil Nadu (912, *915*)

paṟai (also *pirai*) Tamil frame drum played by hand or with two thin sticks; the traditional occupation of the Paṟaiyar caste (367, 910, 915, 926)

paramparā Tradition, as in ***guru-śiṣya paramparā*** (389, 457, 957)

paran Hindustani ***pakhāvaj*** drum composition (117–18, 119, 120–21, 130, 131, 132, 158, 494)

parani gi Sinhalese classical music style (557)

paṛayan (also ***oṭṭan, sīthangan***) One of three kinds of popular dance drama (***tuḷḷal***) in Kerala (514)

parda Frets consisting of plastic thread wrapped around the neck of a ***chitrāli sitār*** (787)

pardeh Frets on the Afghani ***dutār*** (820)

paricamuṭṭukaḷi Dance with swords and shields performed by the Christians and Muslims of Kerala (945, 947–48)

parivār 'Family' system of **raga** classification that grouped each of the six primary ragas with five or six wives (***rāgiṇī***), and could be extended to include sons (***putra***) and daughters-in-law (***bharyā***) (73, 76–77, 314, *315*, *316*)

pasam Passion hymns; corpus of Sinhala Christian religious songs ascribed to Jacome Gonsalvez, a Goan priest (1767–1842) (959)

pasu In Sri Lanka, masked folk drama that is a Roman Catholic passion play (491)

pāṭal Song (Tamil) (914)

pāṭhya Recitation (21)

patna jatra Festival dance performed at temples in Orissa (733)

paṭṭāpiṣēkam 'Coronation', of Rama as king in the ***rāma nāṭakam*** drama (279)

pattiyam Wedding ritual in Tamil Nadu, in which the bride sings of all her wishes and desires (275)

pāṭü 'Song' (Kodagu), in Karnataka (887)

pāwā (also ***satāra***) Paired flute of Rajasthan with one pipe used as a drone, played by the **Laṅgās** (345)

pellet drum Hourglass drum struck by two pellets attached to the ends of strings tied to the drum's narrow middle section. Twirling the drum back and forth activates the striking action (325)

pellet rattle Small, generally spherical clay rattle, with a hollow center containing a few pellets that cause the instrument to sound when shaken (319, 321)

pena Bowed string instrument of Manipur with a coconut resonator and bamboo neck (329, 345)

perahēra Buddhist temple processions in Sri Lanka (491, 965, 966)

periya kaṭci 'Large faction', referring to a devotee group at a Tyagaraja festival (391–92, 393, 394)

periya mēḷam (also ***mangaḷa vādyam***) Large ensemble of ***nāgasvaram*** and ***tavil*** players who perform for auspicious occasions in South India (103, 234, 323–24, 351, 358, *359*, 360, 383, 387, 388, 389, 390, 393, 394, 509, 910–11, 912–14, 931, 935)

Persian *rabāb* Persian unfretted plucked lute; used at medieval Indian courts (337, 692)

peṭṭi (also ***śruti* box**, *śruti peṭṭi*) 'Box'; bellows-driven reed organ in South India (913)

Phāguā Holī springtime festival in Trinidad (589)

phaguā Songs of the **Holī** season, in Uttar Pradesh (665–66)

phāgu gīt Men's seasonal songs of Madhya Pradesh (723)

Piccukaguntlu Telugu narrative singers who sing primarily for certain agricultural and herding castes (901)

piké **Idiophone** of bamboo mounted in an iron frame, on Réunion Island (610)

pilākkaṇam Tamil lament (907)

piḷḷari gīta 'Ganapati songs'; Karnatak beginners' pieces honoring Ganesha, the Lord of Beginnings (216)

pinnal kōlāṭṭam Stick dance in which dancers hold colorful ribbons tied to a central pole in Tamil Nadu (920)

pin pāṭṭu Vocal support parts in Tamil drama (913)

pipahī Double-reed **aerophone**; ensemble accompanied by kettledrums (679)

pīr Muslim holy man or saint; **Sufi** saint (644)

pirit Buddhist chant in Sri Lanka (961, 966, 968–69)

piṭṭa katha Digression from the main story, in a Telugu oral narrative performance (894, 899)

pi-wang Small Tibetan spike fiddle, used to accompany songs in most Himalayan areas (710, 715)

playback singer Vocalist who records songs for Indian commercial film productions (420–21, 531, 538–39, 855, 924)

polli gīt Bengali folk songs (550)

pop bhajan Popular devotional songs (**bhajans**) influenced by the Urdu pop **ghazal** (11, 255)

poṟe Iruḷa clay barrel drum in Tamil Nadu (916)

poṭi vēśa Warrior-costume dance in Karnataka (876)

powada Heroic ballad genre of Maharashtra (474)

poy kāl kutirai Tamil dummy-horse dance (914)

prabandha (also *prabandham*) Medieval song form (33, 36, 163, 164, 250, 517)

pracaya Accentless syllables in Vedic chant that often follow the sounded accent (***svarita***) (240, 242)

praśasti Songs of praise; Sinhala vocal genre sometimes characterized as Kandyan court music (960, 965–66)

pratham Initial or primary level of college education in North India (447)

prātī Mithila devotional songs (678)

prayōga Melodic phrase of a Karnatak **raga** (91)

premtāl Folk rhythm instrument of northern India consisting of a small drum with a string attached that produces variable-pitch sounds when plucked; similar to ***khamak*** (343)

pūjā Worship ritual; any of many different ritual ceremonies honoring deities (211, 254, 255, 323, 391, 549, 556, 602, 698, 850, 886, 932, 935)

pujārī Priest who has direct contact with both an image of a deity and the offerings to the deity (633)

pulang Kota simple idioglottal clarinet with down-cut reed, made of bamboo (916)

pullavān kuḍam Plucked **chordophone** with a pot resonator, in Kerala (365, *366*)

pullavān vīṇā Small folk fiddle of Kerala (350, 365, *366*)

pung Hand-played barrel drum of Manipur (346, 494, 504)

puṅgī (also ***bīn, murlī***) Snake charmer's instrument consisting of a wind pipe inserted into the top of a gourd air chamber, and two single-reed pipes extending from the bottom, which sound the melody and a drone (345, 350, 405, *469*, 640, 647, 670, 896)

purab 'Eastern'; a style of **tabla** playing in North India (134, 192)

pūram (also *puṛam*) Public performances, as opposed to performances in a domestic context (509, 868, 935)

Purana (see ***Bhāgavata Purāṇa***) Hindu sacred texts containing ancient historical and cosmic stories (11, 497, 633, 731, 733, 896)

puṛappāṭu First part of a ***kūṭiyāṭṭam*** dance drama, during which the dancer performs movements behind a curtain (510)

purusha Male ragas, in the classification of **raga** families (313)

purvaṅga First part of a ***pallavi*** theme, in Karnatak music; precedes the ***uttaraṅga*** (217)

pūrvaraṅga Ritual prelude to a play (25)

pushpāñjali (see also ***mangalācaraṇ, raṅgbhūmi pranām***) 'Offering of flowers', part of the ***mangalācaraṇ*** in ***oḍissi*** dance (520, 522)

putra 'Sons'; a category of the ***parivār*** classification system dividing ragas into family groups of one male **raga**, five or six wives (***rāgiṇī***), sons, and daughters-in-law (***bharyā***) (314)

pūttari pāṭu Koḍagu "new rice ceremony," in Karnataka (887)

pūvaṭi cintu 'Flower-feet' song, about the Prophet Muhammad; sung by Tamil converts to Islam (921)

puxury Toda end-blown bamboo trumpet; same as Kota ***būgir*** (909)

qā'ida Hindustani theme-and-variations composition for **tabla** (128–29, 130, 131)

qalam Curved wooden mallets used to strike the ***santūr*** while playing (688)

qalandar Wandering mystic; one who has abandoned family, friends, and possessions (754, 760, 769, 780, 795)

qānūn Persian box zither, played at the medieval Indo-Persian courts of North India (332, 339, 692, 804)

qāri Qur'ān reciters (748)

qaṣīda Long ode with rhyming couplets related to the **ghazal**, often in praise of the Prophet Muhammad's family (278, 284, 590, 753, 827)

qaul Speech, word, or saying (751, 753)

Qawwāl A singer of **qawwali** (426, 644, 751, 765–66, 769, 772)

qawwali (also *kavvali*) Solo-chorus **Sufi** devotional song form (12, 125, 179, 256, 347, 403, 416, 419, 426, 532, 534, 535, 540, 549, 568, 573, 576, 579, 581, 613, 623, 644, 651, 656, 672–73, 682, 746, 750, 751–53, 755–57, 772, 817, 827)

qir'at Highly elaborated style of Qur'ānic recitation cultivated in Egypt (747–48, 772)

rabab (see also ***rabāb, rebāb, rubāb***) Six-stringed unfretted plucked lute, from which the Indian **sarod** developed (190, 196, 308, 329, 337, 344, 506, 655)

rabāb Short-necked lute with five playing strings and thirteen to fifteen sympathetic strings (783, 786, *787*, 789, 794)

rabābī Muslim professional singer of Indian Punjab (655)

rabāna Frame drum of Sri Lanka (964, 969, 970)

rabga Double-headed conical drum played with sticks, in Bihar (502)

Rabindra saṅgīt Songs of the Bengali poet and musician Rabindranath Tagore (162, 254, 336, 550, 562, 573)

raga (also *rāg, rāga*) System governing melody; melodic mode; melodic resource for composition and improvisation (20, 46–47, 50–51, 52, 64–87, 89–108, 115, 138, 163, 164–65, 168, 171, 172, 173, 174, 180–81, 184, 192, 193, 194, 195, 196, 197, 198–99, 200, 203, 209, 214, 215, 216, 217, 218, 219, 220, 221, 225, 228, 234, 250, 251, 252, 253, 256, 262, 266, 269, 301, 305, 312–18, 337, 359, 372, 373, 377, 383, 384, 389, 400, 433, 445–48, 452, 456, 463–64, 466, 521–22, 529, 532, 534, 543–44, 557, 565, 567, 581, 591, 632–33, 642, 655, 671, 687, 692, 699–700, 702, 731, 733, 738, 753, 758, 805, 820, 827, 851–52, 855, 860, 886, 906, 910, 913, 917, 920–21, 924)

rāga gamaka (see also ***gamaka***) Microtonal ornamentation of **raga** pitches (924)

rāgamālikā (also ***rāgmālā***) Karnatak nonmetered improvisation on different **ragas**; presentation of several ragas in sequence, employed in various Karnatak genres (97, 99, 107, 215, 217, 218–19, 225)

rāgam-tānam-pallavi Karnatak genre consisting of improvisation on a **raga** followed by variations on a texted theme (***pallavi***); requires the highest level of musicianship from a Karnatak performer (94, 100, 159, 213, 217–18, 225, 388, 389, 455)

rāga tāḷa mālikā Karnatak melody in a series of **ragas** and **talas** (219)

rāgdāri Classical singing in North Indian style in Punjab, Pakistan (771)

rāgdhyāna (also *dhyāna*) Written **raga** visualizations (73, 313, 314)

rag-dung (also *dung-chen*) Long metal trumpet, used in Tibetan Buddhist rituals in South Asia (714)

raggī Musician who performs devotional music in Indian Punjab (655, *656*)

ragi 'One who brings color', a second "character" who joins the main singer in oral epic performances in Madhya Pradesh (723)

rāgiṇī Female **ragas**; the "wives" of the main (male) ragas in the ***parivār*** classification system of **raga** families (47, 51, 73, 313, 314, 318, 692)

rāgmālā (1) 'Garland of ragas', iconographic and poetic personification of **ragas** (44, 46, *47*, 48, 73, 301–302, 307, 309, 312–18, *692*); (2) (also ***rāgamālikā***) In Hindustani music, improvisation on different **ragas** in sequence (97, 99, 107, 197, 203, 215, 217, 218–19, 220)

rāg pradhān gān Bengali songs in Hindustani classical style, particularly ***khyāl***, by composers working for gramophone companies in Calcutta during the 1930s (855)

rājā Ruler (443, 915)

rājadāsi (see also ***dēvadāsi***) Performers for kings at the royal courts of Tamil Nadu (518)

rājasik Passionate, greedy, vain; antiheroic character type in ***kathakaḷi*** dance drama (*513*)

rāj darbār (also ***darbār***) Royal audience hall, court (635)

Ramadan Islamic month of fasting (277, 816, 824)

rāma nāṭakam Tamil dance drama based on stories of the god Rama (275, 277, 279)

rāmanāṭṭam Dance drama on the life of Rama; a temple dance of Kerala (510, 511)

Rāmaṇṇa Style of Sāmavedic chanting (243–45)

Ramayana Epic tale of Lord Rama, his wife Sita, and the demon king Ravana (11, 220, 261, 353, 361, 408, 482, 490, 509, 513, 516, 613, 617, 633, 635, 667, 673, 723, 727, 733, 876, 879, 897, 933)

rāmlīlā Devotional dance drama of Uttar Pradesh depicting events from Rama's life (673)

ramsatta Kīrtan danced by youths in Madhya Pradesh (724)

Rāṇāyanīya School of Sāmavedic chanting (242, 243)

raṅgbhūmi pranām 'Obeisance to the earth'; part of the ***maṅgalācaraṇ*** in ***oḍissi*** dance (520)

raqs Dance or dance music, in Northern Afghanistan (827)

raqṣ Dance or dancing, in Pakistan (754)

rās (also ***dāṇḍiā rās***) Stick dance and its music in northwest India (405, 495, 501, 503, 504, 550, 623, 629–30)

rās garbā Folk dance music of northwest India that has evolved into a popular style (427)

rasa 'Essence', emotion (21, 26, 29–30, 33, 67, 69, 71–72, 101, 247, 263, 299, 313, 317, 484, 508, 514, 912)

rāsa (1) Temple music played by Damāis in Nepal (700); (2) (also ***rāso***, *rāsaka*) Epic poem recounting the battles and exploits of Gujarat's kings and generals (629, 635)

rasika Connoisseur of aesthetic bliss (69, 262, 384)

rasiyā Vulgar folk song of the Braj region of North India (550, 551, 665, 672)

rās līlā Devotional dance drama portraying Krishna and the milkmaids, performed by boys in Uttar Pradesh (*440*, 441, 494, *495*, 673)

rāso (also ***rāsa*** and *rāsaka*) Epic poem recounting the battles and exploits of Gujarat's kings and generals (629, 635)

rāṣṭrīya gīt National song (705–706)

raṭa yakuma Sri Lankan ceremony performed to ensure the safety of a child or fetus (274)

raudra 'Furious', one of the eight emotional states (***rasa***) codified in the ***Nāṭyaśāstra*** (69, 313)

rāvanhatta (also *rāvaṇahatthā*) Long-necked, two-stringed bowed lute made from a long bamboo stick inserted in a half coconut shell covered with membrane; played by the Bhopā singers of Rajasthan (345, 646, *647*)

razākhānī gat Fast-tempo Hindustani instrumental composition allegedly composed by Ghulam Raza Khan in the nineteenth century (126, 191–93, 194, 197, 198, 206)

rebāb Short-necked plucked stringed instrument of Kashmir (683–84)

relā Hindustani theme-and-variations composition for **tabla**; similar composition for ***pakhāvaj*** barrel drum (119)

reṇḍaṭi 'Two beats' (Tamil) (915)

rezwār-shāir Official poet of a tribe in Balochistan, who would record all important events in verse, and teach each of these to the tribal minstrel; the minstrel then sang them at public gatherings and tribal assemblies (781)

Ṛgveda Oldest religious and cultural text (**Veda**) of the Vedic Aryans, consisting of hymns addressed to the Vedic gods (238, 239, 240–42, 243, 469, 507)

rgya-gling Tibetan oboe used in Buddhist rituals, played with circular breathing technique (714)

rīna Baiga women's dance of Madhya Pradesh (722)

riyaz (also *riāz, riyāz*) Dedicated and regular music practice (373, 581)

rkang-gling Tibetan trumpet, originally made from a human femur (714)

rnga Large double-headed frame drum of Tibet (712–13, *714*)

rōkaṭi pāṭalu Songs sung while working with a mortar and pestle in Andhra Pradesh (891, *892*)

rol-mo (also *sbug-chal*) Brass cymbals of Tibet (*714*)

rubāb Short-necked plucked lute of western Afghanistan (*806*–807, 808, 818, 822, 828, 830–31, 835, *836*–37)

rubā'i Poetic genre, often in quatrain form (687, 827)

rudra vīṇā (also ***bīn***) North Indian plucked stick zither (164, 196, 197, 199, *303*, 308, 332)

rūf Secular vocal genre in Kashmir related to ***chakri***; religious song and dance genre in Kashmir performed by women during **Ramadan** (475, 498, 684–85)

rukhsat In Pakistan, departure of the bride from her parents' home (276)

śabda pūja Offerings of sound in Buddhist temple worship, in Sri Lanka (967)

śabdam Dance item in a ***bharata nāṭyam*** performance (502)

sabhā (also ***sangīt sabhā***) Music society; organization that arranges music, dance, and drama performances for public entertainment (106, 270, 454, 557)

sāddhanā Self-realization; in religious disciplines such as fasting and worship, music is a path to achieving this goal (313)

sādhakan 'Practice', technical exercise for drum students in Kerala (940–41, 943)

sadir kacheri (also ***dasi āṭṭam***) Obsolete term referring to the ***bharata nāṭyam*** dance (521)

sāhitya (also *sāhityam*) Song text (138, 145, 385, 513, 912)

sāhitya prastāra (also ***niraval***) In Karnatak music, improvisation that retains the text of the original composition but changes the melody (99)

śahnāī (also *ṣanai,* ***sannāyi, surnāī,*** *surnāīe*) North Indian double-reed **aerophone** used in concert, popular, and folk musics (188, 195, 207, 273, 280, 283, 285, *304*, 305, 336, 340, *341*, 346, 347, 351, 359, 360, 361, 363, 401, 402, 424, *475*, *495*, 497, 506, 625, 670, 671, 674, 678, *699*–700, *756*, *764*, 795, 878, 948)

saila Baiga men's martial dance of Madhya Pradesh (722)

saire ke gīt Men's seasonal songs of Madhya Pradesh (723)

sajani Gond music and dance form of Madhya Pradesh (722)

śāktapadasaṅgīt Literary song genre of West Bengal and Bangladesh devoted to power-cult gods and goddesses and employing music of various styles including ***dhrupad***, ***khyāl***, ***ṭappā***, and even ***kīrtan*** (846–47)

sakti Single-headed drum on Réunion Island (607)

śakti (also *satti*) Power (Sanskrit), especially that of a goddess (904)

sam (also *sama*) First beat of a **tala** cycle (112, 146, 170, 198, 201)

samā Tambourine without jingles, played for ritual dances by a *samāī* (780, 783)

samā' 'Listening to, hearing'; a spiritual concert (294, 751–52, 755)

samabhaṅga Posture in ***oḍissi*** dance (520)

samādhi Holy person's death that occurs during meditation; the place where it occurs (210, 211, 259, 391)

samāj-gāyan Vaishnav devotional singing of Braj, northern India (250, 251–52)

sāman Hymn of the **Sāmaveda** (38–39)

Sāmaveda The musical **Veda**, a religious and cultural text of the Vedic Aryans composed of notated melodies set mostly to **Ṛgveda** texts (96, 222, 238–39, 240, 242–45, 261, 492, 507)

sampradāya (1) Tradition passed on through a teacher-student lineage of Karnatak music, similar to the Hindustani ***guru-śiṣya paramparā*** (14, 42, 97, 231, 247, 259, 390, 465); (2) Genre of women's life-cycle songs in Karnataka (867–68)

samskara (also *saṅskār*) 'Mental impression'; an imprint left on the subconscious that shapes and colors life; therefore, a ritual that seeks to make a beneficial impression on the life of an individual or community (472)

samudraghōsha Popular meter of most Sinhala thematic songs such as carter's songs and boatmen's songs, in Sri Lanka (959)

samvādi (also *samvādī*) Second most important tone in a **raga** (64, 68, 74, 84, 95, 445)

sañcārī Third section of a Hindustani ***dhrupad*** composition (169, 198–99, 250)

sañcāri gita Teaching song illustrating a raga's characteristics (216)

sandara Solo song; also, song accompanied by music in North West Frontier Province (786)

sānde Melancholy song recited by women during tragic events in North West Frontier Province (785)

sanḍhyā Ancient Vedic ceremony centered around a sacrificial fire, still practiced in Trinidad (590)

sangam Meeting, conference, congress, organization (912)

saṅgati Melodic variation, often in a progressive series (145, 217, 221–22, 226)

saṅgīt nāṭak Marathi music drama genre (729)

saṅgīta (also *sangīt*) 'Music' (Sanskrit); includes vocal and instrumental music as well as dance (19, 25, 33, 99, 246, 372, 513, 931, 956–57, 959)

saṅgītācārya One who has vast knowledge of music (460, 465)

Saṅgītaratnākara Thirteenth-century music treatise by Sarngadeva (18, 21, 24, 25, 33–37, 43, 44, 45, 52, 69, 70, 75, 96, 111, 198, 215, 262, 324–25, 356)

sangīta sabhā (also *sabhā*) A music society (212)

sangīta sandarśanaya All-night popular music shows in Sri Lanka (961, 970)

sani (also ***bhogum, kalavantulu***) Female temple dancers in Andhra Pradesh (521)

śaṅkh (also *śaṅkha, śaṅku*) Conch shell trumpet played mostly in rituals (326, 345, 360, 361, 363, 704)

sankīrtan Devotional music genre emphasizing collectivity, iteration of God's name, and dancing (250, 504, 729)

sannāyi (also ***śahnāī***) Double-reed instrument used in classical and folk music in Andhra Pradesh (896)

sanni yakku Curative dance form in Sri Lanka (490, 959, 961)

śānti muhurtam Tamil ritual associated with a married couple's first night together (275)

santūr Box zither played with two light wooden hammers; used as a Hindustani concert instrument as well as in regional music of Kashmir (82, 207, 332, 338, *339*, *688*, 693, *694*)

sanyāsin One who has renounced the world (210, 228)

sarala gī 'Straight' or 'simple' song; twentieth-century genre of Sinhala light classical music (970, 972)

śaranaru Devotees of Shiva in Karnataka (869)

sarāng (also *sarān*, ***sārindā***, ***surindā***) Any of various bowed **chordophones** of southern Afghanistan, Pakistan, and North India (683–84)

sāraṅgī (also *sāraṅg*) Bowed **chordophone** with a short neck, a waisted, skin-covered body, and metal strings; used as both a solo and an accompanying instrument in Hindustani classical and folk music (*55*, 171, 175, 177, 179, 180, 181, 182, 186, 194, 195, 207, 234, 248, 251, 256, 307, *335*, 336, *338*, 341, 344–45, 347, 378, 380, 402–*403*, *477*, 494, 535, 560, 591, 602, 633, 642–43, *671*, 683–84, *698*, *746*, 749, 753, 762, 769, 771, 806)

sarasvatī pūjā Worship of Sarasvati, the goddess of learning and music, on the ninth day of **Navrātrī** (9, 211, 277)

sarasvatī vīṇā Plucked stringed instrument associated with Sarasvati, in Karnatak music (*211*, 232, 324, 325, 350, 352, *353*, 355, 365)

sargam (also ***svara* syllables**) Indian sol-fa syllables (52, 173, 176, 252, 591)

śāgird Student (376, 377, 460–61)

sārindā (also *sarān*, ***sarāng***, ***surindā***) Bowed folk **chordophone** with a distinctive deeply waisted double body and a deep, arched back (337, 344–45, 506, 787–88, *789*, 815, 835)

sarod Short unfretted plucked lute with a deep-waisted, skin-covered body that narrows into a metal-plated neck; one of the premier concert instruments of Hindustani music (*4*, *133*, 188, 189, 194, 204, 205, *206*, 207, 307, 336, *337*, 338, 339, 344, 378, 411, 462, 536, 560, 565, 684, 762, 766, 786, 808, 972)

sarogān Leader of a singing group in Balochistan (777)

sāruvayya Mendicant fortune teller (870)

śāstra Treatise, field of study (21, 22, 42, 86)

śāstriya Based on a rule or treatise (75, 372)

satāra (also ***pāwā***) Paired flute of Rajasthan with one pipe used as a drone, played by **Laṅgās** (345, 641)

satti (also ***śakti***) 'Power' (Tamil), especially of a goddess (904)

satvik Divine, noble, heroic, generous, refined; character type in ***kathakaḷi*** dance (*513*)

saùñ Arched harp of Burma, with a tradition that continues today (329)

savāl javāb Question-and-answer rhythmic exchange between instrumental soloist and accompanist in a Hindustani performance (132, 204)

sāz (1) Classical music or melody, in northern Pakistan (795); (2) Music or musical instrument (775, 781)

sāz-e-kashmīrī Spike fiddle, a relative of the Persian ***kamanche*** (*688*)

sāzdohol Shawm and drum pair, in western Afghanistan (818, 820, *821*)

sāzī Musicians; instrumentalists, in Balochistan (781)

sāzinda Musicians; instrumentalists or instrument makers in Punjab, Pakistan (766, 781)

sega Popular musical genre of Réunion Island (609–11)

sēpi Patron-client relationship in Punjab, Pakistan, that corresponds to the ***jajmānī*** system (763)

serga Guruñg funeral dance of Nepal (704)

setār (also *sehtar*) Long-necked fretted lute of the Persian music tradition (335, 344, *688*, 693, 830)

sgra-snyan Long-necked lute of Tibet and the entire Himalayan region (710, 715)

sgrung-mkhan Tibetan bard whose repertoire is centered around the hero Ge-sar (711–12)

shabd kīrtan (also *shabad*) Sikh song form (250, 257, 655)

shahānā Punjabi songs sung at weddings (771)

shāir Poet in Balochistan (778–79)

shakl Solo instrumental prelude to a ***maqām*** performance in Kashmir (687, 806)

sharia 'The path to follow'; Islamic law (826)

shāyarī kajalī Professional or semiprofessional form of the Bhojpuri folk music genre ***kajalī*** (670)

shekī Performance (*lēb*) including music, singing, sacrifice, and trance, performed by a *shek* (spiritual guide) or *gwātī-ē māt* (spiritual healer) (774, 780)

shēparjā In Balochistan, ritual dance performed with drum accompaniment (774, 779–80)

shēr In Balochistan, long verse narrative without refrain, sung by minstrels with string accompaniment or recited by common people without musical accompaniment (774, 776, 781, 783)

shpelāi Duct flute of the North West Frontier Province (788)

Shudra (*Śūdra*) Group or class (***varṇa***) in Hindu society, traditionally the artisans and laborers (9, 228, 386, 398, 735, 911, 922)

sichyāh Cymbals, in Nepal (702)

śikṣā Phonetic manual (30)

silsila **Dervishes** from the Qādiri order in Kashmir (683)

sindhī sāraṅgī Small bowed unfretted lute played by **Laṅgā** musicians of Rajasthan (345, *641*)

sindīrana Mythic male doll representing a son of Kali; the dance in which the doll is carried by dancers (877)

sipatt Prayer and praise songs sung on the birth of a child, in Balochistan (773–74, 778)

śiṣya Disciple; music student (97, 101, 150, 376, 377, 384, 389, 390, 461, 464–65, 582)

sitar Hindustani long-necked, fretted, plucked lute; one of the premier concert instruments of Hindustani music (107, 188–89, 191, 193–94, 196, 198, 205, 206, 307, 325, 333, *334*, *335*, 336–39, 351, 368, 378, 411, 414, 424, 465, 494, 520, 529, 535, 543, 560–61, 562, 566, 572, 575, 582, 591, 602, 642, 746, 762, 766, 771, 787, 808, 830, 972)

sīthangan (also ***oṭṭan***, ***paṛayan***) One of three kinds of popular dance drama (***tuḷḷal***) in Kerala (514)

siṭṭhnī Songs of insult in Indian Punjab (653)

śīvēli Temple procession ritual in Kerala (934–35)

sivpada Quatrain with lines of equal length; popular framework for prosody in the Kotte period (1371–1597) (959)

siyāhī Circle of black paste placed on the heads of Hindustani drums to aid tuning and resonance (115, 122, 341)

sjõ Bronze bell of the Guruñg shaman in Nepal (704)

śloka (1) Metrical couplet; verse (21, 99, 104, 107, 215, 218, 261–62, 579); (2) Ancient prosodic meter used for devotional and didactic texts, usually recited in a highly stylized manner (729)

smṛti Tradition (21, 43)

śobāna Wedding songs performed by women in Karnataka (868, 885)

sohar Songs sung at the birth of an Indian baby, in Trinidad and Guyana (589, 601)

śolkaṭṭu Spoken rhythms derived from drum sounds in Karnatak music (104, 150, *152*, 230)

sokari Folk play of the up-country Sinhala people of Sri Lanka (491, 964)

sōma Mask dance of Karnataka (878, *879*)

sona rupa de Song tale of Madhya Pradesh blending prose, verse, and recitation (723)

sonbrer 'Combination of two ***piké***', played on Réunion Island (610)

sōpāna 'Stone steps'; praise songs of Kerala, sung on the steps leading to the image of a deity (230, 231, 363, 931, 934, 940)

sorath Song tale of Madhya Pradesh blending prose, verse, and recitation (723)

sorathī Guruñg dance drama in Nepal (704–705)

sornā Shawm; double-reed wind instrument of Afghanistan, played in the open air (814, 820)

sornāi Double-reed **aerophone** in the North West Frontier Province (789)

sot Short love songs sung on Balochi festive occasions by **Sotī** singers (774, 777, 782)

Sotī Lower-caste male or female singer of ***sot*** and wedding songs (774, *775*, 781–82)

soz Shia lament (282, 284)

special *nāṭakam* (also ***icai nāṭakam***) 'Special drama', in Tamil Nadu (913)

Śrī Jayantī South Indian celebration of the birth of Krishna (276)

śṛngāra (also *śṛṅgāra*) 'Erotic', one of the eight emotional states (***rasa***) codified in the ***Nāṭyaśāstra*** (69, 72, 313)

śruti (also *sruti*) (1) Microtone; drone; intonation (31–32, 39, 67, 74, 81, 91, *93*, 101, 351, 355, 384, 445, 715, 872, 885); (2) 'That which has been heard,' knowledge received orally, referring to the learning of the sages transmitted through the **Vedas** (21, 43, 70)

śruti* box** (also ***peṭṭi, *śruti peṭṭi*; see also ***surpetī***) Small bellows-driven reed organ that provides the drone pitch (103, 249, 355–56, 360, 364, 582, 912, *914*)

stavan Eulogy (579)

sthāī (also *sthāya*) First melodic phrase or section of a Hindustani composition; first section of a Hindustani composition emphasizing the lower tetrachord of the octave (36, 164, 169, 172–73, 174, 180, 181, 185, 191, 195, 198, 200, 250, 532–34, 633)

sthāvara 'Settled in one location', as opposed to wandering (870)

stotra Large combinations of chants (239, 261–62, 268, 729)

strī Female ragas (313)

Sufi Islamic mystic; mystic cult of Islam (256, 265, 293–94, 313, 339, 376, 460, 503, 534, 540, 568, 623, 644, 659, 673, 682–84, 686–89, 691, 694–95, 745–46, 750, 751–57, 759, 765, 769–70, 772, 794, 813, 817, 818, 824)

ṣūfyāna (also *ṣūfyāna kālam*, *ṣūfyāna mūsīqī*) 'Sufi music', classical music of the urban elite in Kashmir, with roots in Persian music (339, 682, 686–90, 694)

sugam saṅgīt Carefully rehearsed unison choral presentations of religious song (631)

suḥbat 'Company'; spiritual conversation in Sufism (460)

sūlādi Karnatak compositional form (139, 266, 939)

sur Pitch, tone; melody or melodic modes (753, 758–59)

surbahār Large **sitar** invented to emulate the sound and repertoire of the Hindustani ***bīn*** (196, 197, 204, 205, 335–36, 414)

surindā (also *sarān*, ***sarāng***, *sārindā*) Any of various bowed **chordophones** of southern Afghanistan, Pakistan, and North India (345, 641)

surnā Double-reed oboe played to the accompaniment of drums by lower-caste musicians (340, *712*, 774, 777, 781, 783)

surnāī (also *śahnāī*) Double-reed **aerophone** (346, *499*, 506, 641–42, 692, 795–96, *797*)

surnāy Double-reed **aerophone** of Kashmir; instrumental ensemble accompanying folk theatricals (***bānde pāther***) in Kashmir (685–86)

suroz Spike fiddle, the only bowed stringed instrument in Balochistan used for multiple purposes; the national instrument of the Baloch, similar to the Iranian ***ghīchak*** (774, 775–77, 781, *782*, *783*)

surpetī (see also ***śruti peṭṭi***) Hand-pumped drone **aerophone** of Gujurat (633)

sursiṅgār Modification of the *dhrupad rabāb*, with a wooden face and metal strings (obsolete) (196, 337)

suṣira Category of **aerophone**s in the Buddhist ***pañcatūrya nāda*** system (327, 968)

suṣira vādya **Aerophone** (instrument category), in the ***Nāṭyaśāstra*** (322, 326, 351)

sūtra Saying, maxim, aphoristic verse (21, 471–72, 557)

sūtradhāra 'Chief musician, narrator' of a dance drama, who keeps the beat with a pair of cymbals, recites dance syllables, and may join in the dancing (517)

sūtra gomeyāṭa String-puppet play, in Karnataka (879)

suvvi Refrain used in songs in Karnataka (868)

svara (1) Scale degree; pitch in general (20, 24, 31–32, 33, 67, 90–91, *93*, 218, 224, 228, 230, 243, 451, 917, 924); (2) (also *dhatu*) The melodic aspect of music (452)

***svara* exercises** Musical passages of increasing complexity based on ***svara* syllables**, as exercises for beginning music students (451)

svara kalpana Karnatak melodic improvisation (***manodharma***) using sol-fa syllables (98–99, 148, 218, 384, 451)

svara pallavi Section following the ***batu*** in an ***oḍissi*** dance performance (520)

svara sthānam (also *svara-sthān*) Pitch location, within the system of twelve ***svara*** to the octave (67)

svara* syllables** (also ***sargam) Indian sol-fa syllables Sa, Ri, Ga, Ma, Pa, Dha, Ni, used as text material in musical composition and improvisation (100, 451)

svarajāti (1) Didactic form, in Karnatak music (228); (2) Composition based on a ***svara* syllable** form and given a meaningful text (451)

svarākṣara Punning use of ***svara*** names in a Karnatak song text (224, 230)

svaraprastāra Raga development in Karnatak music (215)

svarāvali Melodic exercise pieces for students of Karnatak music (216)

svarita Transitional sounded accent, in Vedic recitation; often follows the ***udātta*** accent (240, 242)

svarlipi Indian music notation (446)

svarmaṇḍal Box zither, strummed and plucked as background filler for a Hindustani vocal performance (332, 520)

swadeśī gān Patriotic songs (848–54)

tabaṭk Kota frame drum of Tamil Nadu (912, *915*)

ṭabl Drum (Arabic) (341, 693)

tabla Pair of hand-played tuned drums used for Hindustani classical, semiclassical, and film musics; also, the right-hand drum of the tabla pair, also known as the ***dāhinā*** or ***dāya*** (*4*, *62*, 111, 121–34, 136–37, 171, 172, 179, 180, 181–83, 186, 188, 195, 197, 251, 257, 307, 325, 326, *335*, *339*, 341, 342, 346, 351, 356, 364, 368, 378–79, 380, 402, 424, 448, 494, 529, 534, 535, 536, 543, 549, 555–57, 560, 566, 572, 575, 579, 581–82, *585*, 591, 602, 604, 608, 618, 629, 633, *634*, 635, 642, 644, 651, 655, *656*, 670, 671, 746, 753, 762, 765, 768, 771–72, 783, 787, 790, *791*, *806*, 808, 814, 818, 822, *823*, 828, 838, 909, 913, 924–25, 948, 972)

tablātarang Pitched row of tuned ***dāhinā*** (right-hand tabla drums) (136)

tāca Tamil version of ***tāshā*** drum (915)

tahareta Meaningless syllables used by Santals to teach melodies that can accompany different texts (474)

tāl (1) Large cymbal pair of Rajasthan and Uttar Pradesh (347); (2) Steel plate with a wooden handle, played with two sticks in Balochistan (774, 782, 783)

tala (also *tāl*, *tāḷa*) The organization of time, rhythm and meter in Indian music; a metric cycle (20, 24, 26–27, 29, 33, 39, 44, 99–100, 110–37, 138–61, 162, 168–69, 172, 173, 174–75, 181, 182, 183, 184–85, 193, 194, 196, 198, 201, 212, 216, 219, 228–29, 250, 253, 255, *299*, 342, 372, 373, 377, 383, 389, 447–48, 452, 494–95, 510, 514, 521–22, 543, 565, 574, 589, 603, 633, 655, 687, 805, 906, 910, 913, 924, 938–40, 943)

tāla (also *tāl*, *tāḷam*) Pair of small metal hand cymbals used to mark metrical patterns and indicate tempo (103, 104, 149, 270, 305, 322, 323–24, 342, 358, 359, 360, 364, 365, *366*, 368, 557, 607, 608, 728, 815, 831, 877, 885, 907, 912–13, 956, 967)

tāḷamālikā 'Garland of talas'; rhythmic or melodic piece performed in a series of **talas** (218)

tālampoṭa Pair of large cymbals used in the Buddhist ***hēvisi*** *pūjā* ensemble of Sri Lanka (329)

tālāṭṭu Tamil lullaby (556)

tālī Clapping gesture signifying a stressed subdivision of a Hindustani **tala** (112)

tālīm Training; musical training or lessons (465)

tāl-maddale (also *tāla maddaḷe*) 'Cymbal and double-headed barrel drum'; narrative drama of Karnataka believed to be the precursor of ***yakṣagāna*** (515–16, 879)

tamāśā Folk drama of Maharashtra (419, 423–24, 485)

tamāshā Dance ceremony; public entertainment in the Northern Areas of Pakistan (795, *797*, 798, 799)

tāmasik 'Evil', 'cruel'; vicious character type in ***kathakaḷi*** dance (513)

tamaṭe Large tambourine played with sticks, in Karnataka (875–77)

tamble (also *chamba, dar, darjal*) Frame drum popular among Pakhtun women of the North West Frontier Province (787, 789, *790*)

tambūr (also ***tanbur***) Long-necked fretted lute of Iran and elsewhere in the Middle East, popular at medieval Indo-Persian courts of India (164, *309*, 310, 332, 344, 692–93)

tambūrā (see also ***tambūri***, ***tānpūrā***) Long-necked, unfretted, plucked drone lute (*4*, 74, 104, 165, *171*, 222, 232, *233*, 307, 308, 332, 334, 343, 355, *356*, 360, 364, 368, *378*, 384, 392, 494, 522, 556–57, 590, 613, *614*, 633, 643, *644*, *647*, 723, 804, 893, *894*, 899–901, 913, *918*)

tambūrā bhajan Solo song genre of the Fiji Indians (613, *614*)

tambūrī Small ***tambūrā*** carried by devotees of the poet-saint Tukaram, in Maharashtra (343)

Tamil Iśai 'Tamil Music' movement of the 1940s (105, 231, 390, 911)

tamil isai vaḷipāṭṭu 'Tamil music liturgy', seven Tamil musical liturgies, including one in folk style, in use at the Tamil Nadu Theological Seminary (923)

tammâṭṭa (also *tamukku*) Kettledrum pair used in the Buddhist ***hēvisi*** ensemble of Sri Lanka (329, 363, 364, 367, *914*, 967, *969*)

tān Improvisatory melodic phrase, often in fast tempo, in Hindustani vocal and instrumental music; sometimes used synonymously with ***vistār*** (83, 170, 173, 175–80, 181, 191, 197, 198, 199, 200, 202, 642)

tān saṅgīt Form of Indo-Guyanese classical music (602–*603*, 604)

tānam Unmetered, pulsed improvisation on a Karnatak raga (100, 215, 218, 451)

tanbur (also *tanbūr*) Long-necked, fretted, plucked lute with oval body, in northern regions (692, 693, 830–31)

tandana tāna (also *tana tandana*) Refrain of a song in Karnataka (868, 880)

tāṇḍava (see also ***lāsya***) Masculine aspects of dance; one of the main principles of dance in the twelfth-century *Abhinaya Chandrika* (494, 519)

tanduro Unfretted plucked lute used to provide a drone in Rajasthan (647)

tani āvartanam Extended percussion solo in a Karnatak concert (148, 158–59, 219, 223, 235, 356, 384, 940)

tānpūrā (also ***tambūrā***) Long-necked, unfretted, plucked drone lute (188, 249, 251, 465, 806)

Tantric Referring to an esoteric cult within Hinduism and Buddhism (503, 520, 957)

ṭap-khyāl Mixed form of ***ṭappā*** and ***khyāl*** popular among Bengali urban composers, in the nineteenth and first half of the twentieth centuries (852)

tapou (also **Malbar drum**) Frame drum of Martinique and Réunion Island (595, *607*, 608–609)

tappaṭṭai Frame drum of Tamil Nadu (904, *908*, 910, 915)

ṭappā Vocal form based on Punjabi song (162, 229, 413, 771, 786, 847–48, 852–53, 856, 860)

tappū Locally made frame drum played with a bamboo stick, in Guyanese Tamil music (602)

tār śahnāī North Indian bowed, long-necked, fretted lute related to the ***isrāj*** (336)

tarānā Rhythm-oriented Hindustani vocal genre using vocables (162, 164, 178–79, 220, 229, 602, 605)

tarpe **Aerophone** with two gourd resonators, in Maharashtra (727)

tāś Stick-played folk kettledrum of North India (346)

tāshā Shallow bowl-shaped drum in Pakistan (279, *280*, *283*)

tāssā Earthenware kettledrum with laced goatskin head, in Trinidad and Guyana (589–90, 601)

tata vādya **Chordophone** (instrument category), in the ***Nāṭyaśāstra*** (322, 323, 327, 351)

tātū Small bridge of horny bone on the **Afghani *rabāb*** (786, *787*, *788*)

tatva Abstract philosophical song genre in Karnataka (867, 869)

tāus Bowed, long-necked, fretted lute shaped like a peacock (obsolete) (336)

tavil Double-headed drum played in South Indian temples, rituals, and processions (103, 161, 210, 212, 234, 270, 275, 286, 323–24, *359*, 360, 361, 363, 390, 393, 394–95, 452, 912, *914*, 916, 926, 931, 958)

tawāif Courtesan singer and dancer (373, *374*, 409, 424, 642, 644)

tāyampaka Temple performance in Kerala (933, 935, 939–44)

tekke (also ***khanaqah***) **Sufi** fraternity house in Kashmir (682)

telwan Nuptial songs sung by the Fiji Indians (614)

temmāngu pāṭṭu Tamil song form in which two singers (sometimes representing lovers) sing alternate lines (556, 925)

terukkūttu (also *terrukkūttu pāṭṭu*) 'Street drama/dance/music' (Tamil); popular dramatic narrative form in Tamil Nadu (90, 516, 542, 556, 617, *618*, 908, 913)

tēvāram (also *tevāram*) 'Garland of the Divine'; a collection of Tamil hymns to Shiva, composed by Tamil Shaivite saints from the seventh to ninth centuries (105, 107, 216, 231, 260–61, 617, 912, 918)

tēvarāṭṭam Dance genre performed by Kampalattar Nāyakars in Tamil Nadu (915)

teyyam Gods, in Kerala; ritual form of worship of folk and tribal gods, goddesses, and benevolent or malevolent spirits (***bhūtam***) (287, 511, 514, 931–32, 936)

thālī (also *thāl*) Metal plate struck with a stick (291, 292, 640, 647, 727)

thandahar Dance of the Bastar tribe of Madhya Pradesh (721)

ṭhāṭ Parent scale in Hindustani music theory (46, 51, 52, 67, 77, *79*, 445)

ṭhekā Drum pattern representing a Hindustani **tala** (44, 112, 124, 153, 169, 172, 174, 913)

Theravada Buddhism Doctrine of the Elders; considered the most orthodox form of Buddhism, thought to have begun in Sri Lanka c. 250 B.C. and spread to Southeast Asia around the eleventh century (12, 955, 965–69)

ṭhumrī Light classical Hindustani vocal form and style; associated with dance and dramatic gesture (15, 69, 107, 123, 126, 127, 128, 132, 162, 179–83, 184, 186, 192, 194, 197–98, 202, 203, 219, 373, 376, 379, 381, 410–11, 412–14, 424, 435, 494, 533, 581, 591, 602, 605, 766, 847, 852–53, 855–56)

tihāī Hindustani cadential pattern consisting of a musical phrase repeated three times, ending at the ***mukhṛā*** or ***sam*** (129, 155, 183, 198, 200, 201, 202)

tilak (also ***biṅdī***) Red dot worn on the forehead of a ***yakṣagāna*** dancer or a ***bharata nāṭyam dancer***; also worn as a sign that one is a Hindu (515, 522)

tillāna Lively, fast-paced song form that is the last piece of a ***bharata nāṭyam*** dance concert (104, 107, 178, 219–20, 229, 414, 452, 512, 522, 590, 591, 941)

tīm Toda women's work-song genre in Tamil Nadu (919)

ṭīmbuk Small barrel drum (***ḍuhl***) played as rhythmic accompaniment (774, 777, *778*, 780, 782, 783)

timila Elongated double-headed hourglass drum of Kerala (*360*, 931, 933, 940)

ṭīpaṇī Gujarati song and dance form associated with the work of compacting earthen floors (474, *475*, 501)

tiruppāvai Vashnavite devotional genre of Tamil Nadu (274, 918)

tiruppugaḻ Tamil devotional songs to the deity Murugan, from the fifteenth and sixteenth centuries (105, 106, 145, 216, 918)

tiruvarutpā Nineteenth-century hymns to the deity Murugan (216)

tiruvempāvai Shaivite devotional genre in Tamil Nadu (274, 918)

titti Goatskin bagpipe drone used in Telugu epic performance (895, *896*, 901)

tīvra 'Sharped', as a sharped note (67, 79, 91, 126, 445)

togalu bombē Puppets made from hide in Karnataka (879)

toghorā Funeral piece played by the Burusho people, Northern Areas of Pakistan (283)

tokara Folk rhythm instrument of Assam, consisting of a small drum with a string attached that produces variable-pitch sounds when plucked; similar to the ***khamak*** (343)

tole karuvi **Membranophones** (Tamil instrument category) (327)

toppi madaḷam 'Barrel drum and vina'; obsolete ensemble once used to accompany ***mōhini āṭṭam*** (513)

tovil Nexus of rituals in Sinhala Sri Lanka performed for the control or expulsion of a variety of malignant influences (959, 961–62, 964)

tribhanga 'Three bends'; posture in the ***oḍissi*** dance (*520*)

ṭukṛā Tabla composition based on a ***pakhāvaj*** barrel drum ***paran*** (131, 132, 494)

tuḷai karuvi **Aerophones** (Tamil instrument category) (327)

tuḻḻal 'Jumping'; dance drama of Kerala based on Hindu epics (514, 516)

tumbaknari Open-ended goblet drum similar to the West Asian *dombek* (476, 683–85)

tūmbī Single-stringed, short-necked, plucked lute, in Indian Punjab (651)

tuntina (also *tuntune*) Marathi plucked drum (343, 544, 728)

tūrya 'Musical instrument' (327)

tūryaugha Ensemble of musical instruments (327)

tutari High-pitched horn of Bhutan (489)

tūtī Double-reed folk **aerophone** of North India (346)

ṭyāmko Small kettledrum of Nepal (699)

uḍakkai (also *udakki, uḍukkai, uḍḍukā*) South Indian hourglass pressure drum with a snare (293, 368, 544, 904, 908, 925, 926, 950, 966)

udātta Principal, raised accent in Vedic recitation (240–42)

udekki Kandyan dance form of Sri Lanka (490)

uḍukkai pāṭṭu Sung narrative, in the Konku region of Tamil Nadu (908)

ulké (also ***bobine***) Hourglass drum played on Réunion Island (607)

umattāṭa Dance performed by Koḍagu women in Karnataka (887)

ūñcal Tamil swing song in a slow tempo; sung at weddings (275)

uncavritti (also *uñcavritti bhajana*) Procession with singing at a Tyagaraja festival (211, 391, 393, 394, 395)

uñjal 'Swing songs' of Tamil Nadu (518)

upanayana Elaborate initiation ceremony that students undergo before they can begin study with a **guru** (459)

uṟaccal tōṟṟam Songs to urge the onset of possession in ***teyyam*** in Kerala (287)

ural Tuluva plowing songs of Karnataka (883)

'urs (also *urs*) Death anniversary of a **Sufi** saint (276, 284, 498, 644, 751, *752*, 754–55, *763, 765*, 769)

urume Double-headed drum played with sticks in Karnataka (880)

uṟumi Hourglass-shaped rubbed **membranophone** of Tamil Nadu (544, *914*–15)

ustad (also *ustād*) Master musician; honorific title for a Muslim teacher (376, 443, 459–62, 465–66, 766, 786, 805, 816, 831)

ustād-śagird (also ***guru-śiṣya***) Master-student; relationship with a Muslim teacher (376, 459–60)

utsava-sampradāya-kīrtana 'Song form used in the tradition of festivity'; songs that accompany the various daily rituals in the worship of a deity (452)

uttaraṅga Second part of a ***pallavi*** theme, in Karnataka music; follows the ***purvaṅga*** (217)

uṭukkai pāṭṭu Tamil folk drum music (556, 908)

vādi (also *vādī*) Most important tone of a raga in Hindustani and Karnatak systems (64, 68, 84, 95, 445)

vādya Musical instrument (Sanskrit); instrumental music (20–21, 33, 104, 232, 322, 351, 885–86)

vāggeyakāra 'Word-song-maker'; composer (209)

vaidika Vedic (209)

Vaishya (*Vaiśya*) Traditionally the third-highest group or class (***varṇa***) in Hindu society consisting of merchants and traders (9, 386, 398, 735, 911)

valaiyal cintu Tamil song form sung by bangle sellers in Tamil Nadu on special ritual occasions (921)

valaṇ Verse summarizing the preceding story section, in ***māṇ bhaṭṭ ākhyān*** (634)

vaḻinaṭai cintu Tamil song sung by pilgrims or travelers to pass the time on a long journey (921)

vaṁsī (also *baṁsī, vaṃśa*) Transverse bamboo folk flute in northern regions (326, 345)

varṇa Group or class; one of the four major divisions of Hindu society: **Brahmin, Kshatriya, Vaishya,** and **Shudra** (9, 386, 398, 735)

varṇam Karnatak composition, performed at the beginning of Karnatak concerts (104, 149, 216–17, 218, 228, 229, 451, 452, 512, 522, 941, 960)

vāsudev gīt Melodic solo songs of Maharashtra performed by an itinerant male singer-dancer (728)

vaṭṭakaḻi Mullu Kurumba chant/song and circle dance around a sacred lamp in Tamil Nadu (909)

Veda Any one of four compilations that comprise the religious and cultural texts of the Vedic Aryans; the earliest Hindu sacred writings (10–11, 238–45, 247, 261, 507)

vedamati Oral epic performance genre of Madhya Pradesh, performed in a sitting posture (723)

vēṇu Karnatak bamboo flute (234, 350, 354)

ves Kandyan dance form of Sri Lanka (490)

veśa Short play, part of a ***bhavāī*** performance, in Gujarat (635)

vēṣa Costumed performance in Karnataka (868, 875)

vessel flute Instrument in the form of a vessel with one or more finger holes on the circumference (320)

vībhatsa 'Disgusting'; one of the eight emotional states (***rasa***) codified in the ***Nāṭyaśāstra*** (69, 313)

vicitra vīṇā Hindustani stick zither constructed like an unfretted ***bīn***, played by sliding a glass ball over the strings and stroking them with wire plectra (207, 333–34, 354)

vidhināṭak Religious drama of Andhra Pradesh (486)

vidūṣaka Buffoon character common in South Indian regional dance forms (516)

vidvān Mature, accomplished Karnatak performer (385, 388, 393)

vikram samvat Hindu calendar (276)

vilambit (also *vilamba*) Slow tempo (111, 153, 191, 192)

villādi vādyam Eight-foot-long musical bow of Tamil Nadu (*367*, 368)

villuppāṭṭu 'Bow song'; Tamil ritual storytelling form named for the musical bow featured in its performance (368, 401, 556, *907*–908)

vilōma anulōma/pratilōma Augmentation, a variation technique in Karnatak music in which the theme or the meter is made twice and then four times as slow (218)

vina (also *vīṇai*) South Indian fretted plucked lute (21, 25, 48, 49, 73, 100, 104, 106, 164, 170, 207, *211*, 215, 217, 218, 221, 232, *233*; 247, 261, 301, 305, 307, 308, 315, 325, 351, 352–53, 355, 368, *378*, 389, 411, 414, 452, 513, 522, 543, 555, 557, 582)

violin Western stringed instrument adopted as a solo and accompanying instrument in South Asia, with some alteration as to playing position, tuning, and playing technique (100, 106, 171, 194–95, 204, 207, 217, 232–33, 338, 347, 351–52, 355, 360, 364, 368, 384–85, 389, 391, 411, 452, 520, 522, 543, 563, 579, 609, 642, 705, 735, 790, 924, 945, 972)

vipañcī vīṇā Arched harp of Indian antiquity, played with a plectrum (299, 326)

vipattu cintu Tamil song form recounting accidents (921)

vīra 'Heroic'; one of the eight emotional states (***rasa***) codified in the ***Nāṭyaśāstra*** (69, 313)

vīragāse Dance of Karnataka venerating the male deity Virabhadra (877)

virah gīt Songs of separation of Uttar Pradesh (669)

virani Devotional songs of Maharashtra on the separation of the beloved (devotee) from the lover (deity) (729)

Vīraviyavantulu Traditional singers of the ***Epic of Palnāḍu***, in Andhra Pradesh (900–902)

viruttam (also ***padyam***) Karnatak style of singing poetry without a pulse (99, 107, 215)

viśārad Advanced level of college education in North India (447)

vishṇupad Vaishnav songs in ***dhrupad*** style (250)

vistār 'Expansion'; variations or improvisations following the composition in Hindustani instrumental music; in melodic improvisation, sometimes used synonymously with ***tān*** (83, 129, 191, 198)

vitata Category of double-headed drums played with sticks, in the Buddhist ***pañcatūrya nāda*** system (327–29, 968)

vīthināṭaka Street-theater form of Andhra Pradesh (516)

Wādankusa-ratnamāla 'Science of Music'; eighteenth-century Sinhala chronicle containing theory of drum music (960)

waī Sindhi lyrical poems sung by a chorus (754)

wanawun Women's song genre in Kashmir (685)

yajmān (also ***jajmān, jajmānī***) One who conducts or sponsors a ritual (400, 401)

yajmānī Patronage (400, 401–403)

Yajurveda Collection of sacrificial verses and prose formulas used in Vedic sacrifices; one of the four religious and cultural texts (**Vedas**) of the Vedic Aryans (238, 243, 261, 507)

yakâdurā (see also ***âdurā, kaṭṭādiya***) Drummer of the **old religion** in Sri Lanka who controls communication with spirits (955, 961)

yak bera (also *devol bera*, low-country drum) Double-headed cylindrical drum of Sri Lanka (*961*, 964)

yakṣagāna (also *yakṣagāna bayalata*) Elaborate masked and costumed temple dance drama of Karnataka (90, 104, 270, 361, *362*, 401, 476, *486*, 514, *515*–17, 883, 885–86)

yaktāro One- or two-stringed plucked lute, used by Sindhi ***faqir*** to provide a rhythmic drone (753, 759)

ya-rakma Limbu dance performed at corn threshing in Nepal (701)

yati Rhythmic shape of text phrases in Karnatak music (147, 224)

yogi gīt Songs sung by itinerant followers of the Nāth cult in Orissa (733)

zahīrok (also ***ḍēhī, līko***) Songs of separation, travel, and work; most popular in southern Balochistan (773–74, 775–76)

zār Ceremony in Kashmir that accompanies a boy's first haircut (685)

zhāng Bells tied in a string, in Balochistan (782, 783)

zikr 'Remembrance of God'; ritual formula for Shia worship (754, 761, 780, 794, 813, 818)

zirbaghali Goblet-shaped single-headed pottery drum of Northern Afghanistan played with two hands (818, 820, *821*, 822, 828, 830–31)

A Guide to Publications

REFERENCE WORKS

Barnett, Elise B. 1970. "Special Bibliography: Art Music of India." *Ethnomusicology* 14:278–312.

———. 1975. *A Discography of the Art Music of India*. Ann Arbor, Mich.: Society for Ethnomusicology.

Bech, Terence R. 1978. *Catalog of the Terence R. Bech Nepal Music Research Collection*. Indiana: Indiana University Press.

Bhowmik, Swarnakamal, and Mudrika Jani. 1990. *The Heritage of Musical Instruments (A Catalogue of Musical Instruments in the Museums of Gujarat)*. Vadodara: Department of Museums.

Bor, Joep. 1988. "The Rise of Ethnomusicology: Sources on Indian Music c. 1780–c. 1890." *Yearbook for Traditional Music* 20:51–73.

Darnal, R.S. 1997. "Bibliography of Nepali Music." *European Bulletin of Himalayan Research* 12–13:240–251.

Dasgupta, Kalpana, and Bhagwan K. Prasad, comp. 1982. *Mass Communication in India: An Annotated Bibliography*. New Delhi: Indian Institute of Mass Communications.

Helffer, Mireille. 1997. "Bibliography of Himalayan Music." *European Bulletin of Himalayan Research* 12–13:222–239.

Hornbostel, Erich M. von, and Curt Sachs. 1961 [1914]. "Classification of Musical Instruments: Translated from the Original German by Anthony Baines and Klaus P. Wachsmann." In *The Garland Library of Readings in Ethnomusicology*, ed. Kay K. Shelemay, vol. 6, 119–145. New York: Garland.

Katz, Jonathan. 1983. "Indian Musicological Literature and Its Context." *Puruṣārtha* 7:57–75.

Kendadamath, G. C. 1986. *Indian Music and Dance: A Select Bibliography*. Varanasi: Indian Bibliographic Centre.

Kinnear, Michael. 1985. *A Discography of Hindustani and Karnatic Music*. Westport, Conn.: Greenwood Press.

———. 1994. *The Gramophone Company's First Indian Recordings 1899–1908*. Bombay: Popular Prakashan.

Kuppuswamy, Gowri, and M. Hariharan. 1981. *Index of Songs in South Indian Music*. Delhi: B. R. Publishing Corporation.

———. 1981. *Indian Dance and Music Literature: A Select Bibliography*. New Delhi: Biblia Impex.

Mehta, R. C., ed. 1993. "Directory of Doctoral Studies in Indian Music." *Journal of the Indian Musicological Society* 24:1–74.

Menon, Raghava R. 1995. *The Penguin Dictionary of Indian Classical Music*. New Delhi and New York: Penguin Books.

Nijenhuis. Emmie te. 1977. *Musicological Literature*. Wiesbaden: Otto Harrassowitz.

Rajagopalan, N. 1990. *A Garland: A Biographical Dictionary of Carnatic Composers and Musicians*. Bombay: Bharatiya Vidya Bhavan.

Sambamurthy, Pichu. 1952–71. *A Dictionary of South Indian Music and Musicians*. 3 vols. Madras: Indian Music Publishing House.

———. 1962. *Catalogue of Musical Instruments Exhibited in the Government Museum, Madras*. 3rd ed. Madras: Government of Madras, Controller of Stationery and Printing.

Subbha Rao, B. 1993 [1956–1966]. *Raga Nidhi: A Comparative Study of Hindustani and Carnatic Ragas*. Madras: The Music Academy.

Sundaram, B. M., comp. 1987. *Tala Sangraha: Compendium of Talas in Karnatak Music*. Bangalore: Percussive Arts Centre.

Tingey, Carol. 1985. "An Annotated Bibliography and Discography of Nepalese Musics." *Journal of the International Council for Traditional Music (U.K. Chapter)* 11:4–20; 12:35–44.

Who's Who of Indian Musicians. 1968. New Delhi: Sangeet Natak Akademi.

GENERAL

Allen, Matthew. 1998. "Tales Tunes Tell: Deepening the Dialogue between 'Classical' and 'Non-Classical' in the Music of India." *Yearbook for Traditional Music* 30:22–52.

Appadurai, Arjun, Frank J. Korom, and Margaret Mills, eds. 1991. *Gender, Genre, and Power in South Asian Expressive Traditions*. Philadelphia: University of Pennsylvania Press.

Archer, William G. 1974. *The Hill of Flutes*. Pittsburgh: University of Pittsburgh Press.

Arnold, Alison. "Popular Film Song in India: A Case of Mass-Market Musical Eclecticism." *Popular Music* 7(2):177–188.

———. 1991. "Hindi Filmī Gīt: On the History of Commercial Indian Popular Music." Ph.D. dissertation, University of Illinois at Urbana-Champaign.

———. In press. "India, Film Music." In *The New Grove Dictionary of Music and Musicians*, 7th ed., ed. Stanley Sadie. London: Macmillan.

Ashton, Roger, ed. 1966. *Music East and West.* Bombay: Indian Council for Cultural Relations.

Baily, John, and Paul Oliver. 1988. "South Asia and the West." *Popular Music* 7(2) (entire issue). Published separately as *Popular Music in India.* New Delhi: Manohar, 1988.

Bake, Arnold A. 1970. "Stick Dances." *Yearbook of the International Folk Music Council* 2:56–62.

Banarjee, Jayasri. 1986. "The Methodology of Teaching Indian Classical Music: A Statement on the Problem." *Sangeet Natak* 79:11–48.

Banerji, S. C. 1976. *Fundamentals of Ancient Indian Music and Dance.* Ahmedabad: L. D. Institute of Indology.

Bandyopadhyaya, Shripada. 1980. *Musical Instruments of India (with Forty-Six Rare Illustrations).* Varanasi and Delhi: Chaukhambha Orientalia.

———. 1985. *Indian Music through the Ages: 2400 B.C. to the Present Era.* Delhi: B. R. Publishing Corp.

Barreto, Lourdino. 1968. "Aesthetic Indian Music as a Bridge between Christian and Indian Religious Music." Ph.D. dissertation, Pontifical Institute of Sacred Music.

Beck, Guy L. 1993. *Sonic Theology: Hinduism and Sacred Sound.* Columbia: University of South Carolina Press.

Bharata. 1926–1964 [second century]. *Nāṭyaśāstra of Bharatamuni, with the Commentary Abhinavabhāratī by Abhinavaguptācārya*, ed. M. Ramakrishna Kavi and J. S. Pade. 4 vols. Gaekwad's Oriental Series 36, 68, 124, and 145. Baroda: Oriental Institute.

———. 1951–1961 [second century]. *The Nāṭyaśāstra*, trans. Manomohan Ghosh. 2 vols. Calcutta: Asiatic Society.

Bhattacharya, Sudhibhushan. 1968. *Ethnomusicology in India.* Calcutta: Indian Publications.

Bhimani, Harish. 1995. *In Search of Lata Mangeshkar.* New Delhi: HarperCollins India.

Blackburn, Stuart. 1988. *Singing of Birth and Death: Texts in Performance.* Philadelphia: University of Pennsylvania Press.

Blackburn, Stuart, Peter Claus, Joyce Flueckiger, and Susan Wadley, eds. 1989. *Oral Epics in India.* Berkeley: University of California Press.

Booth, Gregory D. 1990. "Brass Bands: Tradition, Change, and the Mass Media in Indian Wedding Music." *Ethnomusicology* 34(2):245–62.

———. 1997. "Socio-Musical Mobility among South Asian Clarinet Players." *Ethnomusicology* 41(3):489–516.

Bor, Joep, and Philippe Bruguière. 1992. *Masters of Raga.* Berlin: Haus der Kulturen der Welt.

Bose, Sunil Kumar. c. 1990. *Indian Classical Music: Essence and Emotions.* New Delhi: Vikas Publishing House.

Daniélou, Alain. 1959. *Textes des Purāṇa sur la Théorie Musicale.* Pondicherry: Institut français d'indologie.

Dattila. 1988 [second century]. *Dattilam,* rev. ed., trans. and ed. Mukund Lath. New Delhi: Indira Gandhi National Centre for the Arts.

de Tassy, Garcin. 1995. *Music Festivals in India and Other Essays*, trans. and ed. M. Waseem. Delhi: Oxford University Press.

Deva, B. Chaitanya. 1981. *The Music of India: A Scientific Study.* Delhi: Munshiram Manoharlal.

———. 1986. *Indian Music.* New Delhi: Indian Council for Cultural Relations.

———. 1993 [1978]. *Musical Instruments of India: Their History and Development*, rev. ed. Delhi: National Book Trust.

Ebeling, Klaus. 1973. *Ragamala Painting.* Basel: Ravi Kumar.

Erdman, Joan, ed. 1992. *Arts Patronage in India: Methods, Motives and Markets.* New Delhi: Manohar Publications.

Farrell, Gerry. 1997. *Indian Music and the West.* Oxford: Clarendon.

Flora, Reis. 1987. "Miniature Paintings: Important Sources for Music History." *Asian Music* 18(2):196–230.

Gangoly, Ordhendra C. 1989 [1934]. *Ragas and Raginis.* New Delhi: Munishiram Manoharlal.

Gautam, M. R. 1980. *The Musical Heritage of India.* New Delhi: Abhinav Publications.

———. 1989. *Evolution of Raga and Tala in Indian Music.* New Delhi: Munshiram Manoharlal.

Goswami, O. 1957. *The Story of Indian Music: Its Growth and Synthesis.* Bombay: Asia Publications.

Hardgrave, Robert L., Jr., and Stephen M. Slawek. 1997. "Instruments and Music Culture in Eighteenth-Century India: The Solvyns Portraits." *Asian Music* 20(1) (1988–1989):1–92. Reprinted in *Musical Instruments of North India: Eighteenth-Century Portraits by Baltazard Solvyns.* New Delhi: Manohar.

Holoien, Renee A. 1984. "Ancient Indian Dramatic Music and Aspects of Melodic Theory in Bharata's Natyasastra." Ph.D. dissertation, University of Minnesota.

Howard, Wayne. 1977. *Sāmavedic Chant.* New Haven and London: Yale University Press.

———. 1982. "Music and Accentuation in Vedic Literature." *The World of Music* 24(3):23–34.

———. 1987. "The Body of the Bodiless *Gāyatra*." *Indo-Iranian Journal* 30:161–173.

Jairazbhoy, Nazir A. 1980. "The South Asian Oboe Reconsidered." *Ethnomusicology* 24(1):147–156.

———. 1988. *A Musical Journey through India 1963–1964*. Los Angeles: UCLA Ethnomusicology Publications. With three accompanying cassettes.

Jackson, K. David. 1990. *Sing without Shame: Oral Traditions in Indo-Portuguese Creole Verse*. Amsterdam and Philadelphia: John Benjamins Publishing Company and Instituto Cultural de Macau.

Joshi, G. N. 1988. "A Concise History of the Phonograph Industry in India." *Popular Music* 7(2):147–156.

Kabir, Nasreen, and Rupert Snell. 1994. "Bollywood Nights: The Voices behind the Stars." *World Music: The Rough Guide*, ed. Simon Broughton et al., 219–222. London: The Rough Guides (Penguin).

Kakar, Sudhir. 1982. *Shamans, Mystics and Doctors: A Psychological Inquiry into India and its Healing Traditions*. New York: Alfred A. Knopf.

Katz, Jonathan, ed. 1992. *The Traditional Indian Theory and Practice of Music and Dance*. Proceedings of the 7th World Sanskrit Conference, Kern Institute, 1987. Leiden and New York: E. J. Brill.

Kaufmann, Walter. 1968. "Some Reflections on the Notations of Vedic Chant." In *Essays in Musicology: A Birthday Offering for Willi Appel*, ed. Hans Tischler, 1–18. Bloomington: Indiana University School of Music.

Knight, Roderic. 1985. "The Harp in India Today." *Ethnomusicology* 29(1):9–28.

Kothari, Komal S. 1968. *Indian Folk Musical Instruments*. New Delhi: Sangeet Natak Akademi.

Kramrisch, Stella. 1965. *The Art of India: Traditions of Indian Sculpture, Painting, and Architecture*, 3rd ed. London: Phaidon Press.

Krishna Murthy, K. 1985. *Archaeology of Indian Musical Instruments*. Delhi: Sundeep Prakashan.

Krishnaswamy, S. 1971. *Musical Instruments of India*. Boston: Crescendo.

Kuckertz, Jozef. 1976. "Reception of Classical Indian Music in Western Countries during the 20th Century." *Journal of the Indian Musicological Society* 7(4):5–14.

Kuppuswamy, Gowri. 1984. *Royal Patronage of Indian Music*. Delhi: Sundeep Prakashan.

Kuppuswamy, Gowri, and M. Hariharan, eds. 1980. *Indian Music: A Perspective*. Delhi: Sundeep Prakashan.

———, eds. 1982. *Glimpses of Indian Music*. Delhi: Sundeep Prakashan.

———, eds. 1989. *An Anthology of Indian Music*. Delhi: Sundeep Prakashan.

Lath, Mukund. 1978. *A Study of Dattilam: A Treatise on the Sacred Music of Ancient India*. New Delhi: Impex India.

Lutgendorf, Philip. 1991. *The Life of a Text: Performing the Rāmcaritmānas of Tulsidas*. Berkeley: University of California Press.

Manuel, Peter. 1988a. "Popular Music in India: 1901–86." *Popular Music* 7(2):157–176.

———. 1988b. *Popular Musics of the Non-Western World*. New York: Oxford University Press.

Marre, Jeremy, and Hannah Charlton. 1985. "There'll Always Be Stars in the Sky: The Indian Film Music Phenomenon." In *Beats of the Heart: Popular Music of the World*, 137–154. New York: Pantheon.

Massey, Reginald. 1992. "From Bharata to the Cinema: A Study in Unity and Continuity." *Ariel: A Journal of International English Literature* 23(1):59–71.

Massey, Reginald, and Jamila Massey. 1993. *The Music of India*. London: Kahn and Averill.

Matanga. 1928. [ninth century]. *The Bṛhaddeśī of Mataṅgamuni*, ed. K. Sambasiva Sastri. Trivandrum: Sanskrit Series.

———. 1992–1994 [ninth century]. *Bṛhaddeśī of Śrī Mataṅga Muni*, trans. and ed. Prem Lata Sharma. 2 vols. New Delhi: Indira Gandhi National Centre for the Arts.

Nanyadeva. 1869–1870 [twelfth century]. *Sarasvatīhṛdayālaṁkāra, or Bharatabhāṣya*. Govt. MS no. 111. Poona: Bhandarkar Oriental Research Institute Library.

Narada. 1986 [n.d]. *Nāradīya Śikṣā, with the Commentary of Bhaṭṭa Śobhākara*, trans. and ed. Usha R. Bhise. Poona: Bhandarkar Oriental Research Institute, 1986.

Nijenhuis, Emmie te. 1974. *Indian Music: History and Structure*. Leiden: E. J. Brill.

———. 1977. *The Ragas of Somnatha*. Leiden: E. J. Brill.

———. 1992. *Saṅgītaśiromaṇi: A Medieval Handbook of Indian Music*. Leiden and New York: E. J. Brill.

Neuman, Daniel. 1978. "Journey to the West." *Contributions to Asian Studies* 12:40–53.

Pal, Pratapaditya. 1967. *Rāgmālā Paintings in the Museum of Fine Arts, Boston*. Boston: Museum of Fine Arts.

Pandey, Kanti Chandra. 1963. *Abhinavagupta: An Historical and Philosophical Study*, 2nd rev. ed. Varanasi: Chowkhamba Sanskrit Series.

Parmar, Shyam. 1977. *Folk Music and Mass Media*. New Delhi: Communication Publications.

Parsvadeva. 1925. [thirteenth century]. *The Saṅgītasamayasāra of Saṅgītākara Śrī Pārśvadeva*, ed. T. Ganapati Sastri. Trivandrum: Sanskrit Series.

Popley, Herbert. 1950. *The Music of India*. Calcutta: YMCA Publishers.

Post, Jennifer. 1989. "Professional Women in Indian Music: The Death of the Courtesan Tradition." In *Women and Music in Cross-Cultural Perspective*, ed. Ellen Koskoff, 97–109. Urbana: University of Illinois Press.

Powers, Harold. 1965. "Indian Music and the English Language: A Review Essay." *Ethnomusicology* 9:1–12.

———. 1980a. "Illustrated Inventories of Indian Rāgamālā Painting." *Journal of the American Oriental Society* 100(4):473–493.

———. 1980b. "India, Subcontinent of, I, II." In *The New Grove Dictionary of Music and Musicians*, ed. Stanley Sadie. London: Macmillan.

Prajnanananda, Swami. 1973 [1960]. *Historical Development of Indian Music.* Calcutta: Mukhopadhyay.

———. 1979. *Music: Its Form, Function and Value.* New Delhi: Munshiram Manoharlal.

———. 1981 [1965]. *Historical Study of Indian Music.* New Delhi: Munshiram Manoharlal.

Pringle, B. A. 1962 [1894]. *The History of Indian Music.* Delhi: Susil Gupta.

Qureshi, Regula. 1991. "Whose Music? Sources and Contexts in Indic Musicology." In *Comparative Musicology and Anthropology of Music: Essays on the History of Ethnomusicology*, ed. Bruno Nettl and Philip Bohlman, 152–168. Chicago: University of Chicago Press.

Raghavan, V. 1967. *The Number of Rasa-s.* Madras: Adyar Library.

———. 1979 [1966]. *The Great Integrators: The Saint-Singers of India.* New Delhi: Ministry of Information and Broadcasting.

Ramanathan, S. 1979. *Music in Cilappatikaaram.* Madurai: Madurai Kamaraj University.

Ranade, Ashok D. 1992. *Indology and Ethnomusicology: Contours of the Indo-British Relationship.* Springfield, Va.: Nataraj Books.

Randhawa, M. S. 1971. *Kangra Rāgmālā Paintings.* New Delhi: National Museum.

Rangacharya, Adya. 1986. *Natyasastra.* Bangalore: IBH Prakashana.

Rowell, Lewis. 1977. "Abhinavagupta, Augustine, Time and Music." *Journal of the Indian Musicological Society* 13(2):18–36.

———. 1992. *Music and Musical Thought in Early India.* Chicago: University of Chicago Press.

Sarngadeva. 1943–1953. [thirteenth century]. *Saṅgītaratnākara of Śārṅgadeva, with Kalānidhi of Kallinātha and Sudhākara of Siṃhabhūpāla,* ed. S. Subrahmanya Sastri. 4 vols. Madras: Adyar Library.

———. 1945 [thirteenth century]. *Saṅgītaratnākara of Śarnadeva* (vol. 1, ch. 1), trans. C. Kuhnan Raja. Madras: Adyar Library.

———. 1976 [thirteenth century]. *The Saṃgītaratnākara of Śārṅgadeva,* trans. K. Kunjunni Raja and Radha Burnier. Vol. 4. Madras: Adyar Library.

———. 1978–1989. [thirteenth century]. *Saṅgītaratnākara of Śārṅgadeva. Sanskrit Text and English Translation with Comments and Notes,* trans. R. K. Shringy and Prem Lata Sharma. Vol. 1, Delhi: Motilal Banarsidass; vol. 2, New Delhi: Munshiram Manoharlal.

Santhianathan, Shantsheela. 1996. *Contributions of Saints and Seers to the Music of India*, vol. 2. New Delhi: Kanishka Publishers.

Schubel, James. 1993. *Religious Performance in Contemporary Islam: Shi'ia Devotional Rituals in South Asia.* Columbia: University of South Carolina Press.

Sharma, Amal Das. 1993. *Musicians of India.* Calcutta: Naya Prokash.

Shirali, Vishnudass. 1970. *Sargam: An Introduction to Indian Music.* New Delhi: Abhinav Publishers.

Silver, Brian Q. 1996. "Another Musical Universe: The American Recording Industry and Indian Music, 1955–1965." In *Seminar on Indian Music and the West*, ed. Arvind Parekh, 225–236. Bombay: Sangeet Research Academy.

Simon, Robert L. 1984. *Spiritual Aspects of Indian Music.* Delhi: Sundeep Prakashan.

Somesvara. 1925–1961 [1131]. *The Mānasollāsa of King Someśvara,* ed. G. K. Srigondekar. 3 vols. Gaekwad's Oriental Series nos. 28, 84, and 138. Baroda: Oriental Institute.

Staal, J. Fritz. 1961. *Nambudiri Veda Recitation.* The Hague: Mouton.

Stooke, Herbert J., and Karl Khandalavala. 1953. *The Laud Rāgamālā Miniatures: A Study of Indian Painting and Music.* Oxford: Bruno Cassirer.

Sudhakalasa. 1961. *Saṅgītopanishat Sāroddhāra,* Edited by U.P. Shah. Gaekwad's Oriental Series. Baroda: Oriental Institute.

Tagore, Sourindro M. 1976 [1875]. *Yantra Kosha or A Treasury of the Musical Instruments of Ancient and of Modern India, and of Various Other Countries.* New York: American Musicological Society.

Tarlekar, G.H., and Nalini Tarlekar. 1972. *Musical Instruments in Indian Sculpture.* Pune: Vidyarthi Griha Prakashan

Thielemann, Selina.1996. "Offering, Blessing, Expression of Divine Love: The Role of Music in Several Religious Contexts in India." *Journal of the Indian Musicological Society* 27:1–16.

Vidyarthi, Govind, trans. 1959a. "Melody through the Centuries." *Sangeet Natak Akademi Bulletin* 11/12:13–26 [trans. of portion of *Ma'dan-ul-Mūsīqī* ('Mine of Music'), c. 1860].

———. 1959b. "Effects of Raga and Mannerism in Singing." *Sangeet Natak Akademi Bulletin* 13/14:6–14 [trans. of portion of *Ma'dan-ul-Mūsīqī* ('Mine of Music'), c. 1860].

Wade, Bonnie. 1979. *Music in India: The Classical Traditions.* Englewood Cliffs, N. J.: Prentice-Hall; rev. ed. New Delhi: Manohar Publications, 1987.

Wade, Bonnie C., ed. 1983. *Performing Arts in India: Essays on Music, Dance, and Drama.* Berkeley: University of California Press; Lanham, Md: University Press of America.

———. 1984. "Performance Practice in Indian Classical Music." In *Performance Practice: Ethnomusicological Perspectives*, ed. Gerard

Béhague, 13–52. Westport, Conn. and London: Greenwood.

Wade, Bonnie C., and Ann M. Pescatello. 1979. "The Status of Women in the Performing Arts of India and Iberia: Cross-Cultural Perspectives from Historical Accounts and Field Reports." In *The Performing Arts: Music and Dance*, ed. John Blacking and Joanne W. Kealiinohomoku, 119–137. The Hague: Mouton.

Widdess. D. R. 1980. "The Kuḍumiyāmalai Inscription: A Source of Early Indian Music in Notation." *Musica Asiatica* 2:115–150.

———. 1995. *The Ragas of Early Indian Music: Modes, Melodies, and Musical Notations from the Gupta Period to c. 1250.* Oxford: Clarendon.

———. 1996. "The Oral in Writing: Early Indian Music Notations." *Early Music* 24(3):391–405.

Yule, Paul, and Martin Bemmann. 1988. "Lithophones from Orissa—The Earliest Musical Instruments from India?" *Archaeologia Musicalis* 1/88:46–50. In German, *ibid.*:41–46.

MUSIC IN NORTHERN AREAS

Ahmad, Najma Perveen. 1984. *Hindustani Music: A Study of Its Development in the Seventeenth and Eighteenth Centuries.* New Delhi: Manohar.

Alter, Andrew B. 1994. "*Gurus, Shishyas* and Educators: Adaptive Strategies in Post-Colonial North Indian Music Institutions." In *Music-Cultures in Contact: Convergences and Collisions*, ed. Stephen Blum and Margaret J. Kartomi, 158–168. Sydney: Gordon and Breach.

———. 1997a. "Garhwali Bagpipes: Syncretic Processes in a North Indian Regional Musical Tradition." *Asian Music* 29(1):1–16.

———. 1997b. "Key Processes in the Oral Transmission of Hindustani Vocal Music." *Journal of the Musicological Society of Australia* 20:61–83.

Anderson, Robert, and Edna M. Mitchell. 1978. "The Politics of Music in Nepal." *Anthropology Quarterly* 51(4):247–259.

Arnold, Alison. 1991. "Hindi Filmī Gīt: On the History of Commercial Indian Popular Music." Ph.D. dissertation, University of Illinois at Urbana-Champaign.

———. 1992–1993. "Aspects of Production and Consumption in the Popular Hindi Film Song Industry." *Asian Music* 24(1): 122–136.

Babiracki, Carol. 1991. "Musical and Cultural Interaction in Tribal India: The *Karam* Repertory of the Mundas of Chotanagpur." Ph.D. dissertation, University of Illinois at Urbana-Champaign.

Baily, John. 1976. "Recent Changes in the Dutar of Herat." *Asian Music* 8(1):29–64.

———. 1981. "Cross-Cultural Perspectives in Popular Music: The Case of Afghanistan." *Popular Music* 1:105–122.

———. 1988. *Music of Afghanistan: Professional Musicians in the City of Herat.* Cambridge: Cambridge University Press. With accompanying audio cassette.

Baloch, N. A. 1973. *Development of Music in Sindh.* Hyderabad: Sindh University Press.

Baloch, Nabi B.K.B. 1975. *Musical Instruments of the Lower Indus Valley of Sindh,* 2nd ed. Hyderabad, Sindh: Zeb Adabi Markaz.

Bandyopadhyay, Sudhansu M. 1976. *Baul Songs of Bengal.* Calcutta: United Writers.

Bech, Terence. 1975. "Nepal: the Gaine Caste of Beggar-Musicians." *The World of Music* 17(1):28–35.

Beck, Guy L. 1996. "Vaiṣṇava Music in the Braj Region of North India." *Journal of Vaiṣṇava Studies 4*(2):115–147.

Bernède, Franck. 1997. "Music and Identity among Maharjan Farmers. The Dhimay Senegu of Kathmandu." *European Bulletin of Himalayan Research* 12–13:21–56. (Special double issue, *Himalayan Music: State of the Art*, ed. Franck Bernède).

Bhatkhande, Vishnu Narayan. 1971. "A Short Historical Survey of the Music of Upper India." *Journal of the Indian Musicological Society* 2:1–43.

———. 1972 [1941]. "A Comparative Study of Some of the Leading Musical Systems of the 15th, 16th, 17th, and 18th Centuries." *Journal of the Indian Musicological Society* 3:1–61. Also published separately, Baroda: Indian Musicological Society, 1972.

———. 1981. *Bhātkhaṅde Saṅgīt-Śāstra: Hiṅdustānī Saṅgīt-Paddhati.* 4 vols. Trans. into Hindi by Sudama Prasad Dube et al. Hathras: Sangeet Karyalaya.

———. 1985. *Hiṅdustānī Saṅgīt-Paddhati: Kramik Pustak-Mālikā.* 6 vols. Trans. into Hindi by Vaman N. Bhatt et al. Hathras: Sangeet Karyalaya.

Bhattacharya, Deben. 1969. *The Mirror of the Sky: Songs of the Bāuls from Bengal.* London: Allen and Unwin; New York: Grove Press.

Bhattacharya, Jotin. 1979. *Ustad Allauddin Khan and His Music.* Ahmedabad: B. S. Shah Prakashan.

Bhimani, Harish. 1995. *In Search of Lata Mangeshkar.* New Delhi: HarperCollins Publishers India.

Bor, Joep. 1986–1987. "The Voice of the Sarangi: An Illustrated History of Bowing in India." *National Centre for the Performing Arts Quarterly Journal* 15 (3-4)/16(1):1–183.

Bryce, L. Winifred. 1961. *Women's Folk Songs of Rajputana.* New Delhi: Ministry of Information and Broadcasting, Government of India.

Capwell. Charles. 1986a. "Musical Life in Nineteenth Century Calcutta as a Component in the History of a Secondary Urban Center." *Asian Music* 18(1):139–63.

———. 1986b. *Music of the Bauls of Bengal.* Kent, Ohio: Kent State University Press.

———. 1991. "Marginality and Musicology in Nineteenth-Century Calcutta: The Case of Sourindro Mohun Tagore." In *Comparative Musicology and Anthropology of Music,* ed. Bruno Nettl and Philip Bohlman, 228–243. Chicago: University of Chicago Press.

Catlin, Amy R. 1977. "Whither the Manganihars? An Investigation into Change among Professional Musicians in Western Rajasthan." *Bulletin of the Institute of Traditional Cultures, Madras* Jan.–June:165–178.

Chakrabarty, Ramakanta. 1988. "Vaiṣṇava Kīrtan in Bengal." In *The Music of Bengal: Essays in Contemporary Perspective*, ed. Jayasri Banerjee, 12–30. Bombay and Baroda: Indian Musicological Society. Repr. in *Journal of Vaiṣṇava Studies* 4(2) (1996):179–199.

Chandola, Anoop. 1977. *Folk Drumming in the Himalayas: A Linguistic Approach to Music.* New York: AMS Press.

Chang, Garma C. C. 1967. "Form and Style in Tibetan Folk Song Melody." *Jahrbuch für Musikalische Volks- und Völkerkunde* 3:9–69, 109–126.

———. 1970a. *The Hundred Thousand Songs of Milarepa.* New York and London: Harper & Row.

———. 1970b. "rGya-gling Hymns of the Karma-Kagyu: The Rhythmitonal Architecture of Some Instrumental Airs." *Selected Reports in Ethnomusicology* I(3):79–114.

Chaudhuri, Debu, ed. 1993. *Indian Music and Ustad Mushtaq Ali Khan.* New Delhi: Har-Anand Publications.

Dahmen-Dallapiccola, A. L. 1975. *Ragamala-Miniaturen von 1475 bis 1700.* Wiesbaden: Otto Harrassowitz.

Daniélou, Alain. 1980. *The Ragas of North Indian Music.* New Delhi: Munshiram Manoharlal.

Dasasarma, Amala. 1993. *Musicians of India: Past and Present Gharanas of Hindustani Music and Genealogies.* Calcutta: Naya Prokash.

Deodhar, B. R. 1973. "Pandit Vishnu Digambar in His Younger Days." *Journal of the Indian Musicological Society* 4(2):21–51.

———. 1993. *Pillars of Hindustani Music*, trans. Ram Deshmukh. Bombay: Popular Prakashan.

Deshpande, Vamanrao Hari. 1972. *Maharashtra's Contribution to Music.* New Delhi: Maharashtra Information Service.

———. 1987 [1973]. *Indian Musical Traditions: An Aesthetic Study of the Gharanas in Hindustani Music.* Bombay: Popular Prakashan.

Dhar, Sheila. 1995. *Here's Someone I'd Like You to Meet: Tales of Innocents, Musicians and Bureaucrats.* Delhi: Oxford University Press.

Dhar, Sunita. 1989. *Senia Gharana—Its Contribution to Indian Classical Music.* New Delhi: Reliance Publishing House.

Dhar Chowdhury, Sisirkona. 1982. "Acharya Allauddin Khansahib." *Journal of the Department of Instrumental Music,* Calcutta: Rabindra Bharati University.

Dick, Alastair. 1984. "Sarod." In *The New Grove Dictionary of Musical Instruments*, ed. Stanley Sadie. London: Macmillan.

———. 1984. "Sitar." In *The New Grove Dictionary of Musical Instruments*, ed. Stanley Sadie. London: Macmillan.

Divas, Tulsi. 1977. *Musical Instruments of Nepal.* Kathmandu: Royal Nepal Academy.

Doubleday, Veronica. 1990. *Three Women of Herat.* Austin: University of Texas Press.

Dvivedi, H. 1954. *Mānsimha aur Mānkutūhal.* Gwalior: Vidya Mandir Prakasan. In Hindi.

Ellingson, Terry J. 1979. "The Mandala of Sound: Concepts and Sound Structures in Tibetan Ritual Music." 2 vols. Ph.D. dissertation, University of Wisconsin–Madison.

———. 1980. "Ancient Indian Drum Syllables and Bu Ston's *Sham Pa Ta* Ritual." *Ethnomusicology* 24(3):431–452.

———. 1991. "Nasa:dya, Newar God of Music: A Photo Essay." *Selected Reports in Ethnomusicology* 8:221–272.

Erdman, Joan L. 1978. "The Maharaja's Musicians: The Organization of Cultural Performance at Jaipur in the Nineteenth Century." In *American Studies in the Anthropology of India*, ed. Sylvia Vatuk, 342–367. New Delhi: Manohar.

———. 1985. *Patrons and Performers in Rajasthan.* Delhi: Chanakya Publications.

Farhana, Faruqi, Ashok Kumar, Anwar Mohyuddin, and Hiromi Lorraine Sakata. 1989. *Musical Survey of Pakistan: Three Pilot Studies.* Islamabad: Lok Virsa Research Centre.

Flora, Reis. 1988. "Music Archaeological Data from the Indus Valley Civilization, c. 2400–1700 B.C." In *The Archaeology of Early Music Cultures, Third International Meeting of the ICTM Study Group on Music Archaeology,* ed. Ellen Hickmann and David Hughes, 207–221. Bonn: Verlag für Systematische Musikwissenschaft.

———. In press. "Music Archaeological Data for Culture Contact between Sumer and the Greater Indus Area, c. 2500–2000 B.C.: An Introductory Study." In *Hearing the Past: Essays in Historical Ethnomusicology and the Archaeology of Sound,* ed. Ann Buckley. Liège: Université de Liège Presse.

Fox-Strangways, Arthur. 1965 [1914]. *The Music of Hindoostan.* Oxford: Clarendon.

Gaston, Anne-Marie. 1994. "Continuity and Tradition in the Music of Nāthdvāra: A Participant Observer's View." In *The Idea of Rajasthan: Explorations in Regional Identity,* ed. Karine Schomer et al., vol. 1, 238–277. Columbia, Mo.: South Asia Publications.

———. 1997. *Krishna's Musicians: Musicians and Music Making in the Temples of Nathdvara, Rajasthan.* New Delhi: Manohar.

Gautam, M. R. 1980. *The Musical Heritage of India*. New Delhi: Abhinav Publications.

Ghose, Santidev. 1978. *Music and Dance in Rabindranath Tagore's Education Philosophy*. New Delhi: Sahitya Akademi.

Gold, Ann G. 1994. "Sexuality, Fertility, and Erotic Imagination in Rajasthani Women's Songs." In *Listen to the Heron's Words: Reimagining Gender and Kinship in North India*, ed. Gloria G. Raheja and Ann G. Gold, 30–72. Berkeley: University of California Press.

Goswami, Karunamaya. 1990. *Aspects of Nazrul Songs*. Dhaka: Nazrul Institute.

———. 1994. *History of Bengali Music in Sound*. Khulna, Bangladesh: Losauk.

———. 1996. *Music and Dance of Bangladesh*. Dhaka: Silpakala Academy.

Gottlieb, Robert S. 1977. *The Major Traditions of North Indian Tabla Drumming*. 2 vols. Munich: Musikverlag Emil Katzbichler.

———. 1993. *Solo Tabla Drumming of North India: Its Repertoire, Styles and Performance Practices*. 2 vols. Delhi: Motilal Banarsidass. With two audio cassettes.

Grandin, Ingemar. 1989. *Music and Media in Local Life: Music Practice in a Newar Neighbourhood in Nepal*. Linköping: Tema.

———. 1994. "Nepalese Urbanism: A Musical Exploration." In *Anthropology of Nepal: People, Problems and Processes*, ed. Michael Allen, 160–175. Kathmandu: Mandala Book Point.

———. 1997. "Raga Basanta and the Spring Songs of the Kathmandu Valley: A Musical Great Tradition among Himalayan Farmers?" *European Bulletin of Himalayan Research* 12–13:57–80.

Greig, J. Andrew. 1987. "*Tārīkh-i Sangīta*: The Foundations of North Indian Music in the Sixteenth Century." Ph.D. dissertation, University of California, Los Angeles.

Gupt, Bharat. 1982. "Origin of Dhruvapada and Krishna Bhakti in Brijabhasha." *Sangeet Natak Akademi Bulletin* 64/65:55–63.

Gurung, Kishor. 1993. "What Is Nepali Music?" *Himal* 6(6):8–11.

———. 1996. *Ghamtu: A Narrative Ritual Music Tradition as Observed by the Gurungs of Nepal*. Kathmandu: United States Information Service.

Hamilton, James Sadler. 1988. *The Sitar Music of Calcutta*. Calgary: University of Calgary Press.

Hardgrave, Robert L., and Stephen M. Slawek. 1988–1989. "Instruments and Music Culture in Eighteenth-Century India: The Solvyns Portraits." *Asian Music* 20(1):1–92. Enlarged and revised as *Musical Instruments of North India: Eighteenth-Century Portraits by Baltazard Solvyns*. Delhi: Manohar, 1997.

Hawley, John S. 1984. *Sūr Dās: Poet, Singer, Saint*. Seattle: University of Washington Press.

Helffer, Mireille. 1977. "Une caste des chanteurs-musiciens: les gaine du Népal." *L'Ethnographie* 73:45–75.

———. 1990. "Recherches récentes concernant l'emploi des notations musicales dans la tradition tibetaine." In *Tibet, Civilisation et Société*, ed. Fernand Meyer, 59–84. Paris: La Fondation Singer–Polignac.

———. 1992. "An Overview of Western Work on Ritual Music of Tibetan Buddhism." In *European Studies in Ethnomusicology: Historical Developments and Recent Trends*, ed. Max P. Baumann, A. Simon, and U. Wegner, 87–101. Wilhelmshaven: Florian Noetzel.

———. 1994. *Mchod-rol, les Instruments de la Musique Tibetaine*. Paris: CNRS Editions/ Editions de la Maison des Sciences de l'Homme.

———. 1997. "The Drums of Nepalese Mediums." *European Bulletin of Himalayan Research* 12–13:176–196.

Helffer, Mireille, and Alexander W. Macdonald. 1966. "Sur un sarangi de gaine." *Objets et Mondes* 6(2):133–142.

———. 1975. "Remarks on Nepali Song Verse." In *Essays on the Ethnology of Nepal and South Asia*, ed. H. K. Kuloy, 175–265. Kathmandu: Ratna Pustak.

Henderson, David. 1996. "Emotion and Devotion, Lingering and Longing in Some Nepali Songs." *Ethnomusicology* 40(3):440–468.

Henry, Edward O. 1975. "North Indian Wedding Songs." *Journal of South Asian Literature* 11(1,2):61–93.

———. 1988. *Chant the Names of God: Music and Culture in Bhojpuri-Speaking India*. San Diego: San Diego State University Press.

———. 1991. "*Jogis* and *Nirgun Bhajans* in Bhojpuri-Speaking India: Intra-Genre Heterogeneity, Adaptation, and Functional Shift." *Ethnomusicology* 35(2):221–242.

———. 1995. "The Vitality of the *Nirgun Bhajan*: Sampling the Contemporary Tradition." In *Bhakti Religion in North India: Community Identity and Political Action*, ed. David N. Lorenzen, 231–250. Albany: State University of New York Press.

———. 1998. "Maithil Women's Song: Distinctive and Endangered Species." *Ethnomusicology* 42(3):415–440.

Hoerburger, Felix. 1970. "Folk Music in the Caste System of Nepal." *Yearbook of the International Folk Music Council* 2:142–147.

Howard, Wayne. 1986. *Veda Recitation in Vārāṇasī*. Delhi: Motilal Banarsidass.

Huehns, Colin. 1991. "Music of Northern Pakistan." Ph.D. dissertation, Cambridge University.

Hurie, Harriotte Cook. 1980. "A Comparative Study of Khyal Style: Pandit Omkarnath Thakur and His Student Pandit B. R. Bhatt." M.A. thesis, Wesleyan University.

Imam, Mohammad Karam. 1959. "'Melody through the Centuries': A Chapter from *Ma'danul Musiqi* (1857)." Trans. Govind Vidyarti. *Sangeet Natak Bulletin* 11:13–26, 33.

Jairazbhoy, Nazir A. 1977. "Music in Western

Rajasthan: Continuity and Change." *Yearbook of the International Folk Music Council* 9: 50–60.

———. 1980. "Embryo of a Classical Music Tradition in Western Rajasthan." In *The Communication of Ideas*, ed. J. S. Yadava and V. Gautam, 99–109. 10th ICAES series, no. 3. New Delhi: Concept Publishing Company.

———. 1995. *The Rāgs of North Indian Music: Their Structure and Evolution*, 2nd ed. Bombay: Popular Prakashan. With accompanying audio cassette of Ustad Vilayat Khan, sitar, and Ustad Umrao Bundu Khan, *sāraṅgī* and voice.

Jairazbhoy, Nazir, and A. W. Stone. 1963. "Intonation in Present-Day North Indian Classical Music." *Bulletin of the School of Oriental and African Studies* 26 (1):119–132.

Jamyang Norbu, ed. 1986. *Zlos-gar, Performing Traditions of Tibet.* Dharamsala: Tibetan Institute of Performing Arts.

Karnani, Chetan. 1976. *Listening to Hindustani Music.* Bombay: Orient Longman.

Kaufmann, Walter. 1965. "Rasa, Rāgamālā and Performance Times in North Indian Rāgas." *Ethnomusicology* 9(3):272–291.

———. 1968. *The Ragas of North India.* Bloomington: Indiana University Press.

Khan, Ali Akbar, ed. 1996. *The Classical Music of North India.* Book.2: *Evening Rags of Asawari That,* vol. 1: *Rag Darbari Kanra*; vol. 2: *Rag Chandranandan*; vol. 3: *Rag Kirwani.* Notation by George Ruckert. [Staunton, Va.]: East Bay Books.

———, ed. 1998 [1991]. *The Classical Music of North India.* Book 1: *Introduction to the Classical Music of North India*, vol. 1: *The First Year's Study.* [Staunton, Va.]: East Bay Books.

———, ed. In press. *The Classical Music of North India.* Book 1: *Introduction to the Classical Music of North India*, vol. 2: *Instrumental Compositions in Morning Ragas.* Notation by George Rucket. [Staunton, Va.]: East Bay Books.

Kippen, James. 1988. *The Tabla of Lucknow: A Cultural Analysis of a Musical Tradition.* Cambridge: Cambridge University Press..

———. 1989. "Changes in the Social Status of Tabla Players." *Journal of the Indian Musicological Society* 20(1, 2):37–46.

Korvald, Tordis. 1994. "The Dancing Gods of Bhaktapur and Their Audience. Presentation of Navadurgaa Pyaakham: The Drama and the People Involved." In *The Anthropology of Nepal: People, Problems, and Processes,* ed. Michael Allen, 405–415. Kathmandu: Mandala Book Point.

Kothari, Komal. 1972. *Monograph on Langas: A Folk Musician Caste of Rajasthan.* Borunda, Jodhpur: Rajasthan Institute of Folklore.

———. 1977. *Folk Musical Instruments of Rajasthan: A Folio.* Borunda: Rajasthan Institute of Folklore.

Kumar, Nita. 1988. *The Artisans of Banaras: Popular Culture and Identity, 1880–1986.* Princeton, N.J.: Princeton University Press.

Levy, Mark. 1982. *Intonation in North Indian Music: A Select Comparison of Theories with Contemporary Practice.* New Delhi: Biblia Impex.

Lienhard, Siegfried. 1984. *Songs of Nepal. An Anthology of Newar Folksongs and Hymns.* Honolulu: University of Hawaii Press.

Malik, M. Saeed. 1983. *The Musical Heritage of Pakistan.* Islamabad: Idara Saqafat-e-Pakistan.

Mansukhani, Gobind Singh. c. 1982. *Indian Classical Music and Sikh Kirtan.* London: Oxford University Press.

Manuel, Peter L. 1979. "The Light-Classical Urdu Ghazal-Song." M.A. thesis, University of California, Los Angeles.

———. 1988/1989. "A Historical Survey of the Urdu Gazal-Song in India." *Asian Music* 20(1): 93–113.

———. 1989 *Ṭhumrī in Historical and Stylistic Perspectives.* Delhi: Motilal Banarsidass.

———. 1993. *Cassette Culture: Popular Music and Technology in North India.* Chicago: University of Chicago Press.

———. 1994. "Syncretism and Adaptation in Rasiya, a Braj Folksong Genre." *Journal of Vaiṣṇava Studies* 3(1):33–60.

Marcus, Scott L. 1989. "The Rise of a Folk Music Genre: Biraha." In *Culture and Power in Banaras: Community, Performance, and Environment, 1800–1980,* ed. Sandra Freitag, 93–113. Berkeley: University of California Press.

———. 1993. "Recycling Indian Film-Songs: Popular Music as a Source of Melodies for North Indian Folk Musicians." *Asian Music* 24(1):101–110.

———1995a. "On Cassette Rather than Live: Religious Music in India Today." In *Media and the Transformation of Religion in South Asia,* ed. Lawrence A. Babb and Susan Wadley, 167–185. Philadelphia: University of Pennsylvania Press.

———. 1995b. "Parody-Generated Texts: The Process of Composition in *Birahā*, a North Indian Folk Music Genre." *Asian Music* 26(1):95-147.

McDaniel, June. 1989. *The Madness of Saints: Ecstatic Religion in Bengal.* Chicago: University of Chicago Press.

McNeil, Adrian. 1992. "The Dynamics of Social and Musical Status in Hindustānī Music: *Sarodiyās, Seniyās*, and the *Mārgī-Deśī* Paradigm." Ph.D. dissertation, Monash University.

Meer, Wim Van Der. 1980. *Hindustani Music in the 20th Century.* The Hague: Martinus Nijhoff.

Middlebrook, Joyce. 1991. "Customs and Women's Wedding Songs in Two Northern California Sikh Communities." M.A. thesis, California State University.

Miner, Allyn. 1993. *Sitar and Sarod in the 18th and 19th Centuries.* Wilhelmshaven: Florian Noetzel Verlag. First Indian ed., Delhi: Motilal Banarsidass, 1997.

Misra, Susheela. 1985. *Music Makers of the Bhatkhande College of Hindustani Music.* Calcutta: Sangeet Research Academy.

———. 1990. *Some Immortals of Hindustani Music.* New Delhi: Harman.

———. 1991. *Musical Heritage of Lucknow*. New Delhi: Harman.

Moisala, Pirkko. 1989a. "An Ethnographic Description of the Madal-Drum and Its Making among the Gurungs." *Suomen Antropologi* 4:234–239.

———.1989b. "Gurung Music and Cultural Identity." *Kailash* 15(3-4):207–222.

———. 1991. *Cultural Cognition in Music: Continuity and Change in the Gurung Music of Nepal.* Jyväskylä: Gummerus.

———. 1994. "Gurung Music in Terms of Gender." *Etnomusikologian vuosikirja* 6:135–147.

———. 1997. "Gurung Cultural Models in the Ghantu." *European Bulletin of Himalayan Research* 12–13:152-175.

Moutal, Patrick. 1991. *Hindustānī Rāgas Index*. New Delhi: Munshiram Manoharlal.

———. 1991. *A Comparative Survey of Selected Hindustānī Rāgas Based on Contemporary Practice.* New Delhi: Munshiram Manoharlal.

Nag, Deepali. 1985. *Ustad Faiyaaz Khan*. New Delhi: Sangeet Natak Akademi.

Narayan, Kirin. 1986. "Birds on a Branch: Girlfriends and Wedding Songs in Kangra." *Ethos* 14(1):47–75.

Nayyar, Adam. 1988. *Qawwali*. Islamabad: Lok Virsa Research Centre.

Neuman, Daniel. 1978. "*Gharanas*: The Rise of Musical 'Houses' in Delhi and Neighboring Cities." In *Eight Urban Musical Cultures: Tradition and Change*, ed. Bruno Nettl, 186–222. Urbana: University of Illinois Press.

———. 1980. *The Life of Music in North India: The Organization of an Artistic Tradition.* Detroit: Wayne State University Press. Reprint, Chicago: University of Chicago Press, 1990.

Oldenburg, Veena Talwar. 1990. "Lifestyle as Resistance: The Case of the Courtesans of Lucknow, India." *Feminist Studies* 16(2):259–288.

Ollikkala, Robert. 1997. "Concerning Begum Akhtar, 'Queen of Ghazal.'" Ph.D. dissertation, University of Illinois at Urbana-Champaign.

Owens, Naomi. 1983. "The Dagar Gharānā: A Case Study of Performing Artists." In *Performing Arts in India. Essays on Music, Dance, and Drama*, ed. Bonnie C. Wade. Lanham, Md.: University Press of America. Reprint, *Asian Music* 18(2) (1987):158–195.

Pacholczyk, Józef M. 1978. "Sufyana Kalam, the Classical Music of Kashmir." *Asian Music* 10(1):1–16.

———. 1979. "Traditional Music of Kashmir." *The World of Music* 21(3):50–59.

———. 1989. "Musical Determinants of the Maqam in Sufyana Kalam." In *Maqam, Raga Zeilenmelodik: Konzeptionen und Prinzipien der Musikproduktion*, ed. Jürgen Elsner, 248–258. Berlin: International Council for Traditional Music and Sekretariat Internationale Nichtstaatliche Musikorganisationen.

———. 1992. "Towards a Comparative Study of a Suite Tradition in the Islamic Near East and Central Asia: Kashmir and Morocco." In *Regionale Maqām—Traditionen in Geshichte und Gegenwart*, ed. Jürgen Elsner and Gisa Jähnichen, 429–463. Berlin: International Council for Traditional Music.

———. 1996. *Ṣūfyāna Mūsiqī, the Classical Tradition of Kashmir*. Berlin: International Institute for Traditional Music.

Paintal, Ajit Singh. 1971. "The Nature and Place of Music in Sikh Devotional Music and Its Affinity with Hindustani Classical Music." Ph.D. dissertation, University of Delhi.

Pandey, Shyam M. 1979. *Hindi Oral Epic Loriki*. Allahabad: Sahitya Bhawan Private Limited.

———. 1982. *Hindi Oral Epic Canaini.* Allahabad: Sahitya Bhawan Private Limited.

———. 1987. *Hindi Oral Epic Lorikayan.* Allahabad: Sahitya Bhawan Private Limited.

Parmar, Shyam. 1977. *Folk Music and Mass Media.* New Delhi: Communication Publications.

Patel, Madhubhai. 1974. *Folksongs of Southern Gujarat.* Baroda: Indian Musicological Society.

Pereira, José, and Micael Martins. 1981. "Song of Goa, an Anthology of Mandos." *Boletim do Instituto Menezes de Bragança* 128. Bastorá: Tipgrafi Rangel.

Post, Jennifer C. 1982. "Marathi and Konkani Women in Hindustani Music, 1880–1940." Ph.D. dissertation, University of Minnesota.

———. 1992. "Professional Women in Indian Music: The Death of the Courtesan Tradition." In *Women and Music in Cross-Cultural Perspective*, ed. Ellen Koskoff, 97–109. New York: Greenwood Press.

Powers, Harold. l980a. "Classical Music, Cultural Roots, and Colonial Rule: An Indic Musicologist Looks at the Muslim World." *Asian Music* 12(1):5–13.

———. 1980b. "Illustrated Inventories of Indian Rāgamālā Painting." *Journal of the American Oriental Society* 100(4):473-493.

———. 1980c. "Kashmir." *The New Grove Dictionary of Music and Musicians*, ed. Stanley Sadie. London: Macmillan.

Prasad, Onkar. 1985. *Santal Music: A Study in Pattern and Process of Cultural Persistence.* New Delhi: Inter-India Publications.

Qalandar, Qaisar. 1976. "Music in Kashmir, an Introduction." *Journal of the Indian Musicological Society* 7(4):15–22.

Qureshi, Regula B. 1972. "Indo-Muslim Religious Music: An Overview." *Asian Music* 3:15-22.

———. 1981a. "Islamic Music in an Indian Environment: The Shi'a Majlis." *Ethnomusicology* 25:41–71.

———. 1981b. "Music and Culture in Sind: An Ethnomusicological Perspective." In *Sind through the Centuries*, ed. Hamida Khuhro, 237–244. Karachi: Oxford University Press.

———. 1986. *Sufi Music of India and Pakistan: Sound, Context and Meaning in Qawwali.* Cambridge: Cambridge University Press.

———. 1990. "Musical Gesture and Extra-Musical Meaning: Words and Music in the Urdu Ghazal." *Journal of the American Musicological Society* 43(3):457–97.

———. 1993 "Text, Tune, and Context: Analyzing the Urdu *Ghazal*." In *Text, Tone and Tune: Parameters of Music in Multicultural Perspective,* ed. Bonnie C. Wade, 133–158. New Delhi: Oxford and IBH Publishing. With audio cassette.

———. 1997. "The Indian Sarangi: Sound of Affect, Site of Contest." *Yearbook for Traditional Music* 29:1–38.

Rana, Jagadish. 1990. "Bhaktapur, Nepal's Capital of Music and Dance: A Study of Conservation and Promotion of Traditional Music and Dance." *Kailash* 16(1-2):5–12.

Ranade, Ashok D. 1984. *On Music and Musicians of Hindoostan.* New Delhi: Promilla.

———. 1986. *Stage Music of Maharashtra.* New Delhi: Sangeet Natak Akademi.

———. 1989. *Maharashtra: Art Music.* New Delhi: Maharashtra Information Centre.

———. 1990. *Hindustani Classical Music: Keywords and Concepts.* New Delhi: Promilla.

Ranade, Garesh H. 1960. *Music in Maharashtra.* New Delhi: Maharashtra Information Centre.

———. 1971. *Hindusthani Music: Its Physics and Aesthetics,* 3rd ed. Bombay: Popular Prakashan.

Ray, Sukumar. 1985. *Music of Eastern India.* Calcutta: Firma KLM.

———. 1988. *Folk-Music of Eastern India: With Special Reference to Bengal.* Shimla: Indian Institute of Advanced Study.

Roach, David. 1971. "The Sitar: Its Tradition, Technique and Compositions." M.A. thesis, Wesleyan University.

———. 1972. "The Benares Bāj–The *Tablā* Tradition of a North Indian City." *Asian Music* 3(2):29–41.

Roche, David. 1996. "Devi Amba's Drum: Mina Miracle Chant and the Ritual Ostinato of Spirit-Possession Ritual Performance in Southern Rajasthan." Ph.D. dissertation, University of California, Berkeley.

Row, Peter. 1977. "The Device of Modulation in Hindustani Art Music." *Essays in Arts and Sciences* 6(1):104–20.

Ruckert, George. 1991. *Introduction to the Classical Music of North India.* St. Louis: East Bay Books—MMB Music Inc.

Sá, Mário Cabral e. 1997. *Wind of Fire: The Music and Musicians of Goa.* New Delhi: Promilla.

Sahai-Achuthan, Nisha. 1987. "Folk Songs of Uttar Pradesh." *Ethnomusicology* 31(3):395–406.

Sakata, Hiromi Lorraine. 1983. *Music in the Mind: The Concepts of Music and Musician in Afghanistan.* Kent, Ohio: Kent State University Press. With two accompanying audio cassettes.

———. 1989. "Hazara Women in Afghanistan: Innovators and Preservers of a Musical Tradition." In *Women and Music in Cross-Cultural Perspective,* ed. Ellen Koskoff, 85–95. Urbana: University of Illinois Press.

———. 1993. *The Sacred and the Profane: The Dual Nature of Qawwali.* Berlin: International Institute of Traditional Music.

———. 1994. "The Sacred and the Profane: Qawwali Represented in Performances of Nusrat Fateh Ali Khan." *The World of Music* 36(3):86–99.

Samuel, Geoffrey. 1976. "Songs of Lhasa." *Ethnomusicology* 20(3):407–449.

Sardo, Susana. In progress. "Singing Stories: Goan Catholic Music as a Strategy of Defining Identity." Ph.D. dissertation, Universidade Nova de Lisboa.

Sarmadee, Shahab. 1975. *Musical Genius of Amir Khusrau.* New Delhi: Ministry of Information and Broadcasting, Government of India.

———. 1976. "About Music and Amir Khusrau's Own Writings on Music." In *Life, Times, and Works of Amir Khusrau Dehlavi,* 241–269. 7th centenary commemoration volume. New Delhi: Shri Hasnuddin Ahmad for the National Amir Khusrau Society.

———. 1984–1985. "*Mankutuhal* and *Rag Darpan*—Reflections of a Great Seventeenth-Century Scholar-Musician." *ISTAR Newsletter* 3–4:15–28.

———, ed. 1978. *Ghunyat-ul-Munya: The Earliest Known Persian Work on Indian Music.* Bombay: Asia Publishing House.

Satpathy, Sunil Kumar. 1990. *Anthology of Santal Songs, Dance, and Music of Orissa.* Bhubaneswar: Indian Academy of Folk and Tribal Art.

Shankar, Ravi. 1968. *My Music, My Life.* New York: Simon & Schuster.

Shepherd, Frances. 1976. "Tabla and the Benares Gharana." Ph.D. dissertation, Wesleyan University.

Silver, Brian. 1976. "On Becoming an Ustad: Six Life Sketches in the Evolution of a Gharana." *Asian Music* 7(2):27–58.

Singh, Khushwant. 1978. *Hymns of Guru Nanak.* Bombay: Sangam Books.

Slawek, Stephen M. 1986. "Kirtan: A Study of the Sonic Manifestations of the Divine in the Popular Hindu Culture of Banāras." Ph.D. dissertation, University of Illinois at Urbana-Champaign.

———. 1987. *Sitār Technique in Nibaddh Forms.* Delhi. Motilal Banarsidass.

———. 1988. "Popular *Kīrtan* in Benares: Some 'Great' Aspects of a Little Tradition." *Ethnomusicology* 32(2):77–92.

———. 1991. "Ravi Shankar as Mediator between a Traditional Music and Modernity." In *Ethnomusicology and Modern Music History,* ed. Stephen Blum, Philip V. Bohlman, and Daniel M. Neuman, 161–180. Urbana: University of Illinois Press.

———. 1996. "The Definition of Kirtan: An Historical and Geographical Perspective." *Journal of Vaiṣṇava Studies* 4(2):57–113.

Slobin, Mark. 1974. "Music in Contemporary Afghan Society." In *Afghanistan in the 1970s*, ed. Louis Dupree and Linette Albert, 239–248. New York: Praeger.

———. 1976. *Music in the Culture of Northern Afghanistan*. Tucson: University of Arizona Press.

Söhnen, Renate. 1993. "Music from Baltistan." In *Contemporary German Contributions to the History and Culture of Pakistan*, ed. Stephanie Zingel-Avé Lallemant and Wolfgang-Peter Zingel, 109–126. Bonn: Deutsch-Pakistanisches Forum e.V.

Solis, Theodore. 1976. "The Sarod." M.A. thesis, University of Hawaii at Manoa.

Sorensen, Per K. 1990. *Divinity Secularized. An Inquiry into the Nature and Form of the Songs Ascribed to the Sixth Dalai Lama.* Vienna: Arbeitskreis für Tibetische und Buddhistische Studien, Universität Wien.

Sorrell, Neil, and Ram Narayan. 1980. *Indian Music in Performance: A Practical Introduction.* Manchester: University of Manchester Press.

Srivastava, Indurama. 1980 [1977]. *Dhrupada: A Study of Its Origin, Historical Development, Structure and Present State.* Delhi: Motilal Banarsidass.

Stewart, Rebecca M. 1974. "The Tablā in Perspective." Ph.D. dissertation, University of California, Los Angeles.

Tagore, Sourindro Mohun. 1965 [1875]. *Hindu Music from Various Authors.* Varanasi: Chowkhamba Sanskrit Series Office.

Tewari, Laxmi. 1974. "Folk Music of India: Uttar Pradesh." Ph.D. dissertation, Wesleyan University.

———. 1977. "Ceremonial Songs of the Kanyakubja Brahmans." *Essays in Arts and Sciences* 6:30–52.

Thielemann, Selina. 1997. *The Darbhangā Tradition: Dhrupada in the School of Pandit Vidur Mallik.* Varanasi: Indica Books.

Thompson, Gordon R. 1987. "Music and Values in Gujarati-Speaking Western India." Ph.D. dissertation, University of California, Los Angeles.

———. 1991. "The Cāraṇs of Gujarat: Caste Identity, Music, and Cultural Change." *Ethnomusicology* 35:381–391.

———. 1992–1993. "The Bāroṭs of Gujarati-Speaking Western India: Musicianship and Caste Identity." *Asian Music* 24(1):1–17.

———. 1995a. "Music and Values in Gujarati Western India." *Pacific Review of Ethnomusicology* 7:57–78.

———. 1995b. "What's in a *Ḍhāḷ*? Evidence of *Raga*-Like Approaches in a Gujarati Musical Tradition." *Ethnomusicology* 39(3):417–432.

Tingey, Carol. 1992. "Sacred Kettledrums in the Temples of Central Nepal."*Asian Music* 23(2):97–104.

———. 1994. *Auspicious Music in a Changing Society: the Damāi Musicians of Nepal.* New Delhi: Heritage Publications; London: School of Oriental and African Studies, University of London.

———. 1997. "Music for the Royal Dasai." *European Bulletin of Himalayan Research* 12–13:81–120.

Trewin, Mark. 1990. "Rhythmic Style in Ladakhi Music and Dance." In *Wissenschaft und Gegenwärtige Forschungen in Nordwest-Indien,* ed. L. Icke-Schwalbe and G. Meier, 273–276. Dresden: Staatliches Museum für Völkerkunde Dresden Forschungstelle.

———. 1993. "*Lha-rnga*: A Form of Ladakhi Folk Music and Its Relationship to the Great Tradition of Tibet." In *Anthropology of Tibet and the Himalaya,* ed. Ch. Ramble and M. Brauen, 377–385. Zurich: Ethnological Museum of the University of Zurich.

———. 1995. "On the History and Origin of '*Gar,*' the Court Ceremonial Music of Tibet." *Chime Journal* 8:4–31.

———. 1996. "Rhythms of the Gods. The Musical Symbolics of Power and Authority in the Buddhist Kingdom of Ladakh." Ph.D. dissertation, City University, London.

Verma, Vijay. 1987. *The Living Music of Rajasthan.* New Delhi: Office of the Registrar General.

Wade, Bonnie C. 1972. "Songs of Traditional Wedding Ceremonies in North India." *Yearbook of the International Folk Music Council* 4:57–65.

———. 1984a. *Khyal: Creativity within North India's Classical Music Tradition.* Cambridge: Cambridge University Press. Reprint, Delhi: Motilal Banarsidass, 1997.

———. 1984b. "Performance Practice in Indian Classical Music." In *Performance Practice: Ethnomusicological Perspectives*, ed. Gerard Béhague, 13–52. Contributions in Intercultural and Comparative Studies no. 12. Westport, Conn. and London: Greenwood Press.

———. 1990. "The Meeting of Musical Cultures in the 16th-Century Court of the Mughal Akbar." *The World of Music* 32(2):3–25.

———. 1996. "Performing the Drone in Hindustani Classical Music: What Mughal Paintings Show Us to Hear." *The World of Music* 38(2):41–67.

———. 1998. *Imaging Sound: An Ethnomusicological Study of Music, Art and Culture in Mughal India.* Chicago: University of Chicago Press.

Wadley, Susan S. 1983. "Dhola: A North Indian Folk Genre." In *Asian Folklore Studies* 42:3-26.

Waldschmidt, Ernst, and Rose L. Waldschmidt 1967. *Miniatures of Musical Inspiration in the Collection of the Berlin Museum of Indian Art. Part 1: Rāgamālā-Pictures from the Western Himālaya Promontory.* Bombay: Popular Prakashan.

Wegner, Gert-Matthias. 1986. *The Dhimaybaja of Bhaktapur—Studies in Newar Drumming I.* Stuttgart: Franz Steiner.

———. 1988. *The Naykhibaja of the Newar*

Butchers—Studies in Newar Drumming II. Stuttgart: Franz Steiner.

Widdess, Richard. 1981. "Aspects of Form in North Indian *ālāp* and *dhrupad*." In *Music and Tradition: Essays on Asian and Other Musics Presented to Lawrence Picken*, ed. D. R. Widdess and R. F. Wolpert, 148–181. Cambridge: Cambridge University Press.

———. 1994. "Festivals of *Dhrupad* in Northern India: New Contexts for an Ancient Art." *British Journal of Ethnomusicology* 3:89–109.

———. 1997. "Carya: The Revival of a Tradition?" *European Bulletin of Himalayan Research* 12–13:12–20.

Wiehler-Schneider, Sigrun, and Hartmut Wiehler. 1980. "A Classification of the Traditional Musical Instruments of the Newars." *Journal of the Nepal Research Centre* 4:67–132.

Yusuf, Zohra, ed. 1988. *Rhythms of the Lower Indus: Perspectives on the Music of Sindh.* Karachi: Department of Culture and Tourism, Government of Sindh.

MUSIC IN SOUTHERN AREAS

Ames, Michael M. 1977. *Tovil, the Ritual Chanting, Dance, and Drumming of Exorcism in Sri Lanka.* New York: Performing Arts Program of the Asia Society.

Ariyaratne, Sunil. 1987. *Karol, Pasam, Kantaru: A Survey of Sinhala Christian Hymns in Sri Lanka.* Colombo: Supersun Educational Services Ltd.

———. 1989. *Sindu Vistaraya: An Investigation into the Word 'Sindu' in Sinhala Literature and Music.* Colombo: Dayawansa Jayakody & Co.

Atikal, Ilanko. 1993 [fifth century]. *The Cilappatikāram of Ilanko Atikal: An Epic of South India,* trans. R. Parthasarathy. New York: Columbia University Press.

Ayyar, S. Venkita Subramonia. 1975. *Swati Tirunal and His Music.* Trivandrum: College Book House.

Balakrishnan, Shyamala. N.d. "Folk Music of Cholamandalam." *Kalakshetra Quarterly* 9(4): 16–18.

Baskaran, S[undararaj] Theodore. 1981. *The Message Bearers: The Nationalist Politics and the Entertainment Media in South India 1880–1945.* Madras: Cre-A.

Beck, Brenda. 1982. *The Three Twins: The Telling of a South Indian Folk Epic.* Bloomington: Indiana University Press.

Berberich, Frank J., III. 1974. "The Tavil: Construction, Technique, and Context in Present-Day Jaffna." M.A. thesis, University of Hawaii.

Blackburn, Stuart H. 1988. *Songs of Birth and Death: Texts in Performance.* Philadelphia: University of Pennsylvania Press.

Blackburn, Stuart H., and A. K. Ramanujan, eds. 1986. *Another Harmony: New Essays on the Folklore of India.* Berkeley: University of California Press.

Booth, Gregory D. 1996. "The Madras Corporation Band: A Story of Social Change and Indigenization." *Asian Music* 28(1):61–86.

Brown, Robert. 1965. "The Mṛdaṅga: A Study of Drumming in South India." 2 vols. Ph.D. dissertation, University of California, Los Angeles.

Carter, John R. 1983. "Music in the Theravada Buddhist Heritage: In Chant, in Song, in Sri Lanka." In *Sacred Sound: Music in Religious Thought and Practice*, ed. Joyce Irwin, 127–147. Chico, Calif.: Scholars Press.

Casinader, Rex A. 1981. *Miner's Folk Songs of Sri Lanka.* Göteborg: Göteborgs Ethnografiska Museum.

Catlin, Amy. 1980. "Variability and Change in Three Karṇāṭak Kritis: A Study of South Indian Classical Music." Ph.D. dissertation, Brown University.

———. 1985. "Pallavi and Kriti of Karnatak Music: Evolutionary Processes and Survival Strategies." *National Centre for the Performing Arts Quarterly Journal* 14(1):26–44.

———. 1991. "'Vatapi Ganapatim': Sculptural, Poetic, and Musical Texts in a Hymn to Ganesa." In *Ganesh: Studies of an Asian God*, ed. Robert L. Brown, 141–169. Albany: State University of New York Press.

Cutler, Norman. 1987. *Songs of Experience: The Poetics of Tamil Devotion.* Bloomington: Indiana University Press.

Day, Charles. 1974 [1891]. *The Music and Musical Instruments of Southern India and the Deccan.* Delhi: B. R. Publishing.

Deva, B. Chaitanya. 1989. *Musical Instruments in Sculpture in Karnataka.* Delhi: Motilal Banarsidass.

Dickey, Sara. 1993. *Cinema and the Urban Poor in South India.* New Delhi: Foundation Books.

Diksitar, Subbarama. 1963–1983 [1904]. *Saṅgīta Sampradāya Pradarşiṇi.* Madras: The Music Academy.

Francis, Dyanandan, ed. 1988. *Christian Lyrics and Songs of New Life,* rev. ed. Madras: Christian Literature Society.

Gowrie, Kuppuswamy, and M. Hariharan, eds.. 1989. *An Anthology of Indian Music.* Delhi: Sundeep Prakashan (articles mostly on Karnatak music).

Greene, Paul D. 1995. "Cassettes in Culture: Emotion, Politics, and Performance in Rural Tamil Nadu." Ph.D. dissertation, University of Pennsylvania.

———. In press. "Sound Engineering in a Tamil Village: Playing Audio Cassettes as Devotional Performance." *Ethnomusicology* 44.

Groesbeck, Rolf. 1995. "Pedagogy and Performance in 'Tayampaka,' a Genre of Temple Instrumental Music in Kerala, India." Ph.D. dissertation, New York University.

———. 1999a. "'Classical Music,' 'Folk Music,' and the Brahmanical Temple in Kerala, India." *Asian Music* 30(20):87–112.

———. 1999b. "Cultural Constructions of Improvisation in *Tāyampaka*, a Genre of Temple Instrumental Music in Kerala, India." *Ethnomusicology* 43(1):1–30.

Gurumurthi, Prameela. 1989. "The Evolution of Harikatha." *Sruti* 53:37–39.

Hart, George L. 1975. *The Poems of Ancient Tamil: Their Milieu and Their Ancient Counterparts.* Berkeley: University of California Press.

Higgins, Jon. 1976. "From Prince to Populace: Patronage as a Determinant of Change in South Indian (Karnatak) Music." *Asian Music* 7(2):20–26.

Howard, Wayne, ed. 1988. *Mātrālakṣaṇam: Text, Translation, Extracts from the Commentary, and Notes, Including References to Two Oral Traditions of South India.* New Delhi: Indira Gandhi National Centre for the Arts; Delhi: Motilal Banarsidass.

Jackson, William J. 1991. *Tyagaraja: Life and Lyrics.* Madras: Oxford University Press.

———. 1994. *Tyagaraja and the Renewal of Tradition: Translations and Reflections.* Delhi: Motilal Banarsidass.

———, ed. 1994. *The Power of the Sacred Name: V. Raghavan's Studies on Namasiddhanta and Indian Culture.* New Delhi: India Book Centre.

Janaki, S. S., ed. 1989. *Bibliography of* [V. Raghavan's] *Writings on Music, Dance.* Madras: Kuppuswami Sastri Institute.

Jayalakshmi, Salem S. 1990. "Tamil Music: A Survey." In *Encyclopedia of Tamil Literature,* vol. 1, 175–186. Madras: Institute of Asian Studies.

Jayaraman, Lalgudi G. 1986. "The Violin in Carnatic Music." *Kalakshetra Quarterly* 8(1/2):28–34.

Kaufmann, Walter. c. 1976. *The Ragas of South India.* Bloomington: Indiana University Press.

Kassebaum, Gayathri R. 1975. "Gamaka in Alapana Performance in Karnatic Music." M.A. thesis, University of Hawaii.

———. 1987. "Improvisation in Alapana Performance: A Comparative View of Raga Shankarabharana." *Yearbook for Traditional Music* 19:45–64.

———. 1994. "Katha: Six Performance Traditions and Preservations of Group Identity in Karnataka, South India." Ph.D. dissertation, University of Washington, Seattle.

Keuneman, Herbert. 1973. "Traditional Drums of Ceylon." *Arts of Asia* 3(2):28–33.

Khokar, Mohan. N.d. "Bommalattam" (Puppetry). *Kalakshetra Quarterly* 9(4):23.

———. N.d. "Bhagavata Mela Nataka." *Kalakshetra Quarterly* 9(3):23–25.

———. N.d. "Kuravanchi Natakam." *Kalakshetra Quarterly* 9(3): 26–27.

Kulatillake, Cyril de Silva. 1974–1975. "'Samudraghosha' Metre and the 'Seepada Styles' of Singing in Sri Lanka." *Mitteilungen der Deutschen Gesellschaft für Musik des Orients* 13:39–55.

———. 1976. *A Background to Sinhala Traditional Music of Sri Lanka.* Colombo: Department of Cultural Affairs.

———. 1977. "The 'Gi' Metre in Sinhala Music." *Proceedings of the National Symposium on Traditional Rural Culture of Sri Lanka,* 123–133.

———. 1980. *Metre, Melody, and Rhythm in Sinhala Music.* Sinhala Music Research Bulletin no. 2. Colombo: Sinhala Music Research Unit, Sri Lanka Broadcasting Corporation.

———. 1982a. "Buddhist Chant in Sri Lanka, Its Structure and Musical Elements." *Jahrbuch für musikalische Volks- und Völkerkunde* 10:20–32.

———. 1982b. *The Vannams in Sinhala Traditional Music.* Colombo: Sangita Paryesana Amsaya, Sri Lanka Buvan Viduli Samsthava.

———. 1984–1985. "Raban-Sellama and its Music." *Journal of the Royal Asiatic Society (Sri Lanka)* 29:19–32.

———. 1991. *Ethnomusicology, Its Content and Growth; and Ethnomusicological Aspects of Sri Lanka.* Colombo: S. Godage and Brothers.

Kuppuswamy, Gowri, and M. Hariharan, comps. 1981. *Index of Songs in South Indian Music.* Delhi: B. R. Publishing Corporation.

Laade, Wolfgang. 1993–1994. "The Influence of Buddhism on the Singhalese Music of Sri Lanka." *Asian Music* 25(1-2):51–68.

L'Armand, Kathleen, and Adrian L'Armand. 1978. "Music in Madras: The Urbanization of a Cultural Tradition." In *Eight Urban Musical Cultures,* ed. Bruno Nettl, 115–145. Urbana: University of Illinois Press.

McGilvray, Dennis B. 1983. "Paraiyar Drummers of Sri Lanka: Consensus and Constraint in an Untouchable Caste." *American Ethnological Society* 10:97–115.

Mohan, Anuradha. 1994. "Ilaiyaraja: Composer as Phenomenon in Tamil Film Culture." M.A. thesis, Wesleyan University.

Nelson, David P. 1991. "*Mṛdaṅgam* Mind: The *Tani Āvartanam* in *Karṇāṭak* Music." Ph.D. dissertation, Wesleyan University.

Nijenhuis, Emmie te. 1987. *Sacred Songs of India: Dikshitar's Cycle of Hymns to the Goddess Kamala.* Winterthur, Switzerland: Amadeus.

Palackal, Joseph J. 1995. "Puttan pāna: A Musical Study." M.A. thesis, Hunter College, City University of New York.

———. In press. "Christian Music." In *The New Grove Dictionary of Music and Musicians,* 7th ed., ed. Stanley Sadie. London: Macmillan.

Parthasarathy, T. S. 1975. "Contemporaries and Disciples of Sri Muthuswami Dikshitar." *Birth Bi-Centenary of Sri Muthuswami Dikshitar.* Special issue of *Journal of the Indian Musicological Society* 6(3):28–32. Baroda: Indian Musicological Society.

———. 1982. *Music Composers of India*. Madras: C. P. Ramaswami Aiyar Foundation.

Pattabhi Raman, N. 1994. "Carnatic Music during the Decade: How It Was Ten Years Ago." *Sruti* 125 (July), 21–37. Excerpt from a six-part series from *Sruti* 3 (December 1983).

Pesch, Ludwig. 1999. *The Illustrated Companion to South Indian Classical Music*. Delhi: Oxford University Press.

Peterson, Indira V. 1989. *Poems to Siva: The Hymns of the Tamil Saints*. Princeton, N.J.: Princeton University Press.

Premeela, M. N.d. "Harikatha—A Composite Art Form." *Kalakshetra Quarterly* 9(4):24.

Raghavan, A. Srinivasa. N.d. "Rama Nataka Kirtanas." *Kalakshetra Quarterly* 6(2):22–24.

Raghavan, V. 1979. *The Great Integrators: The Singer-Saints of India*. New Delhi: Ministry of Information, Government of India.

———, ed. 1975. *Muttuswami Dikshitar.* Special issue (September) of *National Center for the Performing Arts Quarterly Journal.* Bombay: National Centre for the Performing Arts.

Raghavan, V., and C. Ramanujacari. 1981. *The Spiritual Heritage of Tyāgarāja*. Madras: Sri Ramakrishna Math.

Rajagopalan, L. S. 1967. "Thayambaka: Laya Vinyasa." *Journal of the Madras Music Academy* 38:83–102.

———. 1974. "Folk Musical Instruments of Kerala." *Sangeet Natak Academy Journal* 33:40–55.

Rajagopalan, L. S., and Wayne Howard. 1989. "A Report on the Prācheena Kauthuma Sāmaveda of Palghat." *Journal of the Indian Musicological Society* 20(1–2):5–16.

Rajagopalan, N. 1990. *A Garland (Biographical Dictionary of Carnatic Composers and Musicians).* Bombay: Bharatiya Vidya Bhavan.

Ramachandran, Anandhi. 1983. "Oduvars: A Hoary Tradition of Hymn Singing." *Sruti* 2 (Nov):12–13.

Raman, V. P. 1966. "The Music of the Ancient Tamils." *Tamil Culture* 12:203–21. Reprinted in *Readings on Indian Music*, ed. Gowrie Kuppuswamy and M. Hariharan, 80–99. Trivandrum: College Book House, 1979.

Ramanathan, S. 1960. "A Survey of the Traditions of Music, Dance and Drama in the Madras State." *Bulletin of the Institute of Traditional Cultures, Madras* 2:214–221.

Ramanathan, Subrahmanya. 1974. "Music in Cilappatikaaram." Ph.D. dissertation, Wesleyan University.

Ramanujachari, C., and V. Raghavan. 1981. *The Spiritual Heritage of Tyagaraja*, 3rd ed. Madras: Ramakrishna Matha.

Ramanujan, A. K. 1981. *Hymns for the Drowning*. Princeton, N.J.: Princeton University Press.

Rangaramanuja Ayyangar, R. 1972. *History of South Indian (Carnatic) Music: From Vedic Times to the Present.* Madras: Author.

Ravikiran, Chitravina N. 1997. *Appreciating Carnatic Music*. Madras: Ganesh and Co.

Roberts, Michael. 1990. "Noise as a Cultural Struggle: Tom-Tom Beating, the British, and Communal Disturbances in Sri Lanka, 1880s–1930s." In *Mirrors of Violence: Communities, Riots and Survivors in South Asia*, ed. Veena Das, 240–285. Delhi and New York: Oxford University Press.

Roghair, Gene H. 1982. *The Epic of Palnāḍu: A Study and Translation of Palnāṭi Vīrula Katha*. Oxford: Clarendon Press.

Ross, Israel J. 1978. "Cross-Cultural Dynamics in Musical Traditions: The Music of the Jews of Cochin." *Musica Judaica* 2(1):51–72.

———. 1979. "Ritual and Music in South India: Syrian Christian Liturgical Music in Kerala." *Asian Music* 11(1):80–98.

Rothenberg, Jerome, ed. 1968. *Technicians of the Sacred*. New York: Doubleday.

Sambamurthy, Pichu. 1952–1971. *A Dictionary of South Indian Music and Musicians*. 3 vols. Madras: Indian Music Publishing House.

———. 1962–1970. *Great Composers.* 2 vols. Madras: Indian Music Publishing House.

———. 1963-1973. *South Indian Music.* 6 vols. Madras: Indian Music Publishing House.

———. 1967. *The Flute*. Madras: Indian Music Publishing House.

Sankaran, Trichy. 1975. "The Nagaswaram Tradition Systematised by Ramaswami Dikshitar." In *Birth Bi-Centenary of Sri Muthuswami Dikshitar*. Special issue of *Journal of the Indian Musicological Society* 6(3):16–21. Baroda: Indian Musicological Society.

———. 1984. "Bangalore Nagaratnammal: A Devadasi True." *Sruti* 4:14–16.

———. 1989. "Fiddle Govindaswamy Pillai (1879-1931): A Prince Among Musicians." *Sruti* 55:19–25.

———. 1994. *The Rhythmic Principles and Practice of South Indian Drumming.* Toronto: Lalith Publishers.

Sarma, Harihara. 1969. *The Art of Mridhangam*. Madras: Sri Jaya Ganesh Talavadya Vidyalaya.

Sastri, S. Subrahmanya, ed. 1937. *The Mela-Raga-Malika of Maha Vaidyanatha Sivan* (Iyer). Adyar: The Adyar Library.

Seetha, S. 1981. *Tanjore as a Seat of Music during the 17th, 18th, and 19th Centuries*. Madras: University of Madras.

Seneviratna, Anuradha. 1975. "Musical Rituals of the *Dalada Maligawa* Pertaining to the Temple of the Sacred Tooth." *Sangeet Natak* 36:21–42.

———. 1979. "*Pañcatūrya Nāda* and the *Hēwisi Pūjā*." *Ethnomusicology* 23(1):49–56.

———. 1981. "Some Notes on 'Gaman Hewisi' (March Beats): An Aspect of Sinhala Drum Music of Sri Lanka." *Sangeet Natak* 61-62:5–13.

Shankar, L. 1974. "The Art of Violin Accompaniment in South Indian Classical Music." Ph.D. dissertation, Wesleyan University.

Sheeran, Anne. 1997. "White Noise: European Modernity, Sinhala Musical Nationalism, and the Practice of a Creole Popular Music in Modern Sri Lanka." Ph.D. dissertation, University of Washington, Seattle.

Simpson, Bob. 1985. "Ritual Tradition and Performance: The Berava Caste of Southern Sri Lanka." Ph.D. dissertation, University of Durham.

———. 1997. "Possession, Dispossession, and the Social Distribution of Knowledge among Sri Lankan Ritual Specialists." *Journal of the Royal Anthropological Institute* (N.S.) 3:43–59.

Singer, Milton. 1980 [1972]. "The Rādhā-Krishna *Bhajanas* of Madras City." In *When a Great Tradition Modernizes: An Anthropological Approach to Indian Civilization*, 199–249. Chicago: University of Chicago Press; Midway Reprint.

Siromoney, Gift. N.d. "Musical Instruments from Pallava Sculpture." *Kalakshetra Quarterly* 2(4):11–20.

Spector, Johanna. 1972. "Shingli Tunes of the Cochin Jews." *Asian Music* 3(2):23–28.

Srinivas, M. N. 1943–1944. "Some Tamil Folksongs." Parts 1 and 2. *The Journal of the University of Bombay* 12(1, 4), July 1943: 48–80 and Jan. 1944: 6–86. Reprint.

Srinivasa Iyer, P. S. 1937. *Articles on Indian Music.* Tirupapuliyur: Kamala Press.

Sruti: South Indian Classical Music and Dance Monthly. Madras: P N. Sundaresan.

Staal, J. Fritz. 1961. *Nambudiri Veda Recitation.* The Hague: Mouton.

Subramaniam, Karaikudi S. 1985. "An Introduction to the Vina." *Asian Music* 16(2):7–82.

Subramaniam, V. 1990. "Annamalai Reddiar's Kavadichindu: Beautiful Songs for Dance–but Neglected." *Sruti* 67:36–38.

Terada, Yoshitaka. 1992. "Mutiple Interpretations of a Charismatic Individual: The Case of the Great *Nagasvaram* Musician, T. N. Rajarattinam Pillai." Ph.D. dissertation, Wesleyan University.

Vasantha, Kumara. 1993. *Symphony of the Temple Drums: Buddhist Symbolism through Ritual Art.* Kandy: Vanantha Kumara.

Vedavalli, M. B. 1995. *Ragam Tanam Pallavi: Their Evolution, Structure, and Exposition.* Bangalore: M. R. J. Publications.

Venkitasubramonia Iyer, S. 1969. "Some Rare Talas in Kerala Music." *Sangeet Natak* 14:5–11.

———. 1975. *Swati Tirunal and His Music.* Trivandrum: College Book House.

Vidya, S. 1948. *Kritis of Syama Sastri*, vol. 3. Madras: C. S. Iyer.

Viswanathan, Tanjore. 1975. "Rāga Ālāpana in South Indian Music." Ph.D. dissertation, Wesleyan University.

———. 1977. "The Analysis of Rāga Ālāpana in South Indian Music." *Asian Music* 9(1):13–71.

Wadley, Susan. 1986. "The Katha of Sakat: Two Tellings." In *Another Harmony: New Essays on the Folklore of India*, ed. Stuart H. Blackburn and A. K. Ramanujan, 195–232. Berkeley: University of California Press.

Walcott, Ronald. 1978. "*Kohomba Kankariya*: An Ethnomusicological Study." Ph.D. dissertation, University of Sri Lanka.

Wolf, Richard. 1997. "Of God and Death: Music in Ritual and Everyday Life. A Musical Ethnography of the Kotas of South India." Ph.D. dissertation, University of Illinois at Urbana-Champaign.

DANCE AND DRAMA

Allen, Matthew. 1997. "Rewriting the Script for South Indian Dance." *TDR (The Drama Review)* 41(13):63–100.

Amunugama, Sarath. 1978. "John de Silva and the Nationalist Theatre." *The Ceylon Historical Journal* 25(1–4):285–304.

Arnold, Alison. 1998. "Film Musicals: Bollywood Film Musicals." *The International Encyclopedia of Dance*. Oxford: Oxford University Press.

Arudra. 1986a. "Bhagavata Mela: The Telugu Heritage of Tamil Nadu." *Sruti* 22:18–24.

———. 1986b. "The Resurrection of the Bhagavata Mela." *Sruti* 22:25–28.

———. 1986-1987. "The Transformation of a Traditional Dance." *Sruti* 27/28:17–36.

Ashley, Wayne. 1993. "Recodings: Ritual, Theatre, and Political Display in Kerala State, South India." Ph.D. dissertation, New York University.

Ashton, Martha B., and Bruce Christie. 1977. *Yakshagana: A Dance Drama of India*. New Delhi: Abhinav Publications.

Ashton-Sikora, Martha. Forthcoming. "*Yaksāgāna.*" In *South Asian Folklore: An Encyclopedia,* ed. Peter J. Claus and Margaret Mills. New York: Garland.

Bhatt, Haridas. 1983. "Transmission of Yakshagana Art through the Generations." In *Dance and Music in South Asian Drama*, ed. Richard Emmert et al., 180–187. Tokyo: The Japan Foundation.

Bruin, Hanne de. 1994. "*Kaṭṭaikkūttu*: The Flexibility of a South Indian Theatre Tradition." Ph.D. dissertation, University of Leiden.

Caldwell, Sarah. 1995. "Oh Terrifying Mother: The Mudiyettu Ritual Drama of Kerala, South India." Ph.D. dissertation, University of California, Berkeley.

Chandrasekharan, K. N.d. "Kuravanji Dance of Kalakshetra." *Kalakshetra Quarterly* 3(4):7–14.

Dance and Music in South Asian Drama: Chhau, Mahakali Pyakhan and Yakshagana. 1983. Report of Asian Traditional Performing Arts (ATPA) [III], 1981. Tokyo: The Japan Foundation.

Desai, Sudha. 1972. *Bhavai: A Medieval Form of Ancient Indian Dramatic Art (Natya) as Prevalent in Gujarat.* Ahmedabad: Gujarat University Press.

De Zoete, Beryl. 1957. *Dance and Magic Drama in Ceylon.* London: Faber & Faber.

Folk Dances of India. 1956. Publications Division, Ministry of Information and Broadcasting, Government of India.

Frasca, Richard A. 1990. *The Theatre of the Mahābhārata: Terukkūttu Performances in South India.* Honolulu: University of Hawaii Press.

Freeman, John Richardson, Jr. 1991. "Purity and Violence: Sacred Power in the Teyyam Worship of Malabar." Ph.D. dissertation, University of Pennsylvania.

Gaston, Anne-Marie. 1991. "Dance and the Hindu Woman: Bharata Natyam Re-ritualized." In *Roles and Rituals for Hindu Women*, ed. Julia Leslie, 149–173. London: Pinter Publishers.

———. 1996. *Bharata Nāṭam: From Temple to Theatre.* Delhi: Motilal Banarsidass.

Goonatilleka, M. H. 1982. "Drum Dictates the Tune in Kolam of Sri Lanka." *Sangeet Natak* 63:6–14.

———. 1984. *Nadagama, the First Sri Lankan Theatre.* Delhi: Sri Satguru Publications.

Gunawardana, A. J. 1976. *Theatre in Sri Lanka.* Colombo: Department of Cultural Affairs, Government of Sri Lanka.

Hansen, Kathryn. 1992. *Grounds for Play: The Nautanki Theatre of North India.* Berkeley: University of California Press.

Higgins, Jon B. 1993. *The Music of Bharata Nāṭyam.* New Delhi: Oxford and IBH Publishing.

Jogan, Shankar. 1990. *Devadasi Cult: A Sociological Analysis.* New Delhi: Ashish Publishing House.

Jones, Betty True. 1983. "Kathakaḷi Dance-Drama: An Historical Perspective." In *The Performing Arts in India: Essays on Music, Dance, and Drama*, ed. Bonnie Wade, 14–44. Berkeley: University of California Center for South and Southeast Asian Studies.

Jones, Betty True, and Clifford Jones. 1970. *Kathakaḷi: An Introduction to the Dance-Drama of Kerala.* New York and San Francisco: American Society for Eastern Arts.

Jones, Clifford. 1982. "Kālam Ezuttu: Art and Ritual in Kerala." In *Religious Festivals in South India and Sri Lanka*, ed. Guy Welbon and Glenn Yocum, 269–294. New Delhi: Manohar.

Kambar, Chandrasekhar. 1972. "Ritual in Kannada Folk Theatre." *Sangeet Natak* 25:5–22.

Karanth, Shivarama K. 1975. *Yakshagana.* Mysore: University of Mysore Press.

Kersenboom, Saskia. 1995. *Word, Sound, Image: The Life of the Tamil Text.* Oxford: Washington, Berg Publishers.

———. 1996 [1987]. *Nityasumangali, Devadasī Tradition in South India*, 2nd ed. Delhi: Motilal Banarsidass.

Khokar, Mohan. 1987. *Dancing for Themselves: Folk, Tribal, and Ritual Dance of India.* New Delhi: Himalayan Books.

Kliger, George, ed. 1993. *Bharata Natyam in Cultural Perspective.* New Delhi: Manohar/American Institute of Indian Studies.

Kuppuswamy, Gowri, and M. Hariharan. 1982. *Bharatanatya in Indian Music.* New Delhi: Cosmo Publications.

Makulloluwa, W. B. 1976. *Dances of Sri Lanka.* Colombo: Department of Cultural Affairs, Government of Sri Lanka.

Marglin, Frédérique. 1985. *Wives of the God-King: The Rituals of the Devadasis of Puri.* Oxford: Oxford University Press.

Massey, Reginald, and Jamila Massey. 1989. *The Dances of India: A General Survey and Dancers' Guide.* London: Tricolour Books.

Misra, Susheela. 1989. *Invitation to Indian Dances.* New Delhi: Gulab Vazirani for Arnold Publishers (India).

Mukhopadhyay, Durgadas, ed. 1978. *Lesser Known Forms of Performing Arts in India.* New Delhi: Sterling Publishers.

Nambiar, Balan. ?1981. "Gods and Ghosts, *Teyyam* and *Bhūtam* Rituals." *Marg* 34(3): 63–75.

Nanda, Serena. 1990. *Neither Man nor Woman: The Hijras of India.* Belmont, Calif.: Wadsworth.

Neff, Deborah. 1995. "Fertility and Power in Kerala Serpent Ritual (India)." Ph.D. dissertation, University of Wisconsin.

Nixon, Michael. 1988. "Nantaṉār Carattiram in Performance: An Item in the Tamil Musical-Dramatic Repertoire." M.A. thesis, Wesleyan University.

Omchery, Leela. 1969. "The Music of Kerala: A Study." *Sangeet Natak* 14:12–23.

Ostor, Akos. 1980. *The Play of the Gods: Locality, Ideology, Structure, and Time in the Festivals of a Bengali Town.* Chicago: University of Chicago Press.

Pani, Jiwan. 1992. *Sonal Mansingh: Contribution to Odissi Dance.* Delhi: Motilal Banarsidass.

Patnaik, D. N. 1971. *Odissi Dance.* Bhubaneswar: Orissa Sangeet Natak Akademi.

Peiris, Edmund. 1974. "The Origin and Development of Simhala Nadagam." *Journal of the Royal Asiatic Society (Sri Lanka)* 18 (N.S.):27–40.

Pertold, Otakar. 1973. *The Ceremonial Dances of the Sinhalese: An Inquiry into Sinhalese Folk Religion.* Dehiwala: Tisara Prakasakayo.

Perumal, A. N. 1981. *Tamil Drama: Origin and Development.* Madras: International Institute of Tamil Studies.

Radhakrishnan, N., ed. 1982. *The Beating Drum and the Dancing Feet: An Introduction to Indian Folk Performing Arts.* Kerala: National Centre for Development Education and Performing Arts.

Raghavan, M. D. 1967. *Sinhala Natum: Dances of the Sinhalese.* Colombo: M. D. Gunasena.

Raha, Kironmoy. 1980 (reprint). *Bengali Theatre.* New Delhi: National Book Trust.

Raman, Indu. 1995. "Vanishing Traditions: Bhagavatha Mela Natakams of Melattur." *Journal of the Indian Musicological Society* 26:52–64.

Ramasamy, Thulasi. 1987. *Tamil Yakṣagaanas*. Madurai: Vizhikal.

Ramasubramaniam, V. N.d. "Kamban's Epic as Shadow Play." *Kalakshetra Quarterly* 3(4): 25–34.

Ranade, Ashok D. 1986. *Stage Music of Maharashtra*. New Delhi: Sangeet Natak Akademi.

Rangacharya, Adya. 1971. *The Indian Theatre*. New Delhi: National Book Trust.

Rao, H. Gopala. 1983. "Rhythm and Drums in Badagatittu Yakshagana Dance-Drama." In *Dance and Music in South Asian Drama*, ed. Richard Emmert et al., 188–204. Tokyo: The Japan Foundation.

Reed, Susan. 1991. "The Transformation of Ritual and Dance in Sri Lanka: *Kohomba Kankariya* and the Kandyan Dance." Ph.D. dissertation, Brown University.

Richmond, Farley P., Darius L. Swann, and Phillip B. Zarrilli, eds. 1990. *Indian Theatre: Traditions of Performance*. Honolulu: University of Hawaii Press.

Samson, Leela. 1987. *Rhythm in Joy: Classical Indian Dance Traditions*. New Delhi: Lustre Press Private Ltd.

Sarachchandra, E. R. 1966. *The Folk Drama of Ceylon*, 2nd ed. Sri Lanka: Department of Cultural Affairs.

Seneviratna, Anuradha. 1984. *Traditional Dance of Sri Lanka*. Colombo: Central Cultural Fund, Ministry of Cultural Affairs.

Srampickal, Jacob. 1994. *Voice to the Voiceless: The Power of People's Theatre in India*. Delhi: Motilal Banarsidass.

Tarlekar, T. G. 1991. *Studies in the Natyasastra*, 2nd ed. Delhi: Motilal Banarsidass.

Varadpande, M. L. 1983. *Religion and Theatre*. New Delhi: Abhinav Publications.

Vatsyayan, Kapila. 1974. *Indian Classical Dance*. New Delhi: Ministry of Information and Broadcasting.

———. 1980a. "India, VII: Dance." *The New Grove Dictionary of Music and Musicians*, ed. Stanley Sadie. London: Macmillan.

———. 1980b. *Traditional Indian Theatre: Multiple Streams*. New Delhi: National Book Trust.

———. 1982. *Dance in Indian Painting*. Atlantic Highlands, N.J.: Humanities Press.

———. 1987 [1976]. "The Deccan, Eastern and Western Ghats." In *Traditions of Indian Folk Dance*, 2nd ed., 303–368. New Delhi: Clarion Books.

———. 1996. *Bharata, The Nāṭyaśāstra*. New Delhi: Sahitya Akademi.

Venu, G., and Nirmala Paniker. 1983. *Mohiniyattam*. Trivandrum: G. Venu.

Zarrilli, Phillip. 1984. *The Kathakaḷi Complex: Actor, Performance, and Structure*. New Delhi: Abhinav Publications.

Zarrilli, Phillip, Farley Richmond, and Darius Swann, eds. 1990. *Indian Theater: Traditions of Performance*. Honolulu: University of Hawaii Press.

SOUTH ASIAN DIASPORA

Arnold, Alison. 1985. "Aspects of Asian Indian Musical Life in North America." *Selected Reports in Ethnomusicology* 6:25–38.

Arya, Usharbudh. 1968. *Ritual Songs and Folksongs of the Hindus of Surinam*. Leiden: E. J. Brill.

Baily, John. 1990. "Qawwali in Bradford: Traditional Music in a Muslim Community." In *Black Music in Britain*, ed. Paul Oliver, 153–165. Milton Keynes: Open University Press.

———. 1995. "The Role of Music in Three British Muslim Communities." *Diaspora* 4(1):77–88.

Baily, John, and Paul Oliver, eds. 1988. *Popular Music* 7(2). "South Asia and the West" issue.

Bake, Arnold. 1953. "The Impact of Western Music on the Indian Musical System." *Journal of the International Folk Music Council* 5:57–60.

Banerji, Sabita. 1988. "Ghazals to Bhangra in Great Britain." In *Popular Music* 7(2):207–13.

Banerji, Sabita, and Gerd Baumann. 1990. "Bhangra 1984-1988: Fusion and Professionalization in a Genre of South Asian Dance Music." In *Black Music in Britain*, ed. Paul Oliver, 137–152. Milton Keynes: Open University Press.

Baumann, Gerd. 1990. "The Re-Invention of *Bhangra*: Social Change and Aesthetic Shifts in a Punjabi Music in Britain." *The World of Music* 32(2):81–97.

Brenneis, Donald. 1983. "The Emerging Soloist: Kavvali in Bhatgaon." *Asian Folklore Studies* 42:67–80.

———. 1985. "Passion and Performance in Fiji Indian Vernacular Song." *Ethnomusicology* 29:397–408.

———. 1987. "Performing Passions: Aesthetics and Politics in an Occasionally Egalitarian Community." *American Ethnologist* 14:236–250.

———. 1991. "Aesthetics, Performance and the Enactment of Tradition in a Fiji Indian Community." In *Gender, Genre, and Power in South Asian Expressive Traditions*, ed. Arjun Appadurai, Margaret Mills, and Frank Korom, 362–378. Philadelphia: University of Pennsylvania Press.

Brenneis, Donald, and Ram Padarath. 1975. "'About Those Scoundrels I'll Let Everyone Know': Challenge Singing in a Fiji Indian

Community." *Journal of American Folklore* 88:283–291.

Chaudenson, Robert, et al. 1981. "Musiques, chansons et danses." In *Encyclopédie de la Réunion*, vol. 5, 75–107. St. Denis, La Réunion: Livres Réunion.

Desroches, Monique. 1996. *Tambours des Dieux*. Montreal: Harmattan.

Desroches, Monique, and Jean Benoist. 1997. "Musiques, cultes et société indienne à la Réunion." *Anthropologie et Sociétés* 21(1):39–52.

DesRosiers, Brigitte. 1993. "Analyse de la relation entre les discours sur la musique et les stratégies identitaires à l'île de la Réunion." M.A. thesis, University of Montreal.

———. 1992. "Île de la Réunion: musiques et identité." *Canadian Folk Music Journal* 20:47–54.

Erdman, Joan. 1985. "Today and the Good Old Days: South Asian Music and Dance Performances in Chicago." *Selected Reports in Ethnomusicology* 6:39–58.

Farrell, Gerry. 1994. *South Asian Music Teaching in Change*. London: David Fulton Publishers.

Geldard [Arnold], Alison. 1981. "Music and Musical Performance among the East Indians in Chicago." M.M. thesis, University of Illinois at Urbana-Champaign.

Jackson, Melveen B. 1988. "An Introduction to the History of Music amongst Indian South Africans in Natal, 1860-1948: Towards a Politico-Cultural Understanding." M. Mus. thesis, Natal University, South Africa.

Jairazbhoy, Nazir. 1986. "Asian-American Music, 1: Introduction; 5: South Asian." *The New Grove Dictionary of American Music*, ed. H. Wiley Hitchcock and Stanley Sadie. London: Macmillan.

Klass, Morton. 1991. *Singing with Sai Baba: The Politics of Revitalization in Trinidad*. Boulder, Colo.: Westview Press.

Manuel, Peter. 1997. "Music, Identity, and Images of India in the Indo-Caribbean Diaspora." *Asian Music* 29(1):17–35.

Middlebrook, Joyce. 1991. "Customs and Women's Wedding Songs in Two Northern California Sikh Communities." M.A. thesis, California State University, Sacramento.

Myers, Helen. 1980. "Trinidad and Tobago." *The New Grove Dictionary of Music and Musicians*, ed. Stanley Sadie. London: Macmillan.

———. 1983 [1978]. "The Process of Change in Trinidad East Indian Music." In *Essays in Musicology*, ed. R. C. Mehta. Bombay and Baroda: Indian Musicological Society.

———. 1997. *Music of Hindu Trinidad: Songs from the India Diaspora*. Chicago: University of Chicago Press.

Neuman, Daniel. 1984. "The Ecology of Indian Music in North America." *Bansuri* 1:9–15.

Pillay, Jayendran. 1988. "Teaching South Indian Music Abroad: Case Studies from South Africa and North America." M.A. thesis, Wesleyan University.

———. 1994a. "Music, Ritual, and Identity among Hindu South Africans." Ph.D. dissertation, Wesleyan University.

———. 1994b. "Indian Music in the Indian School in South Africa: The Use of Cultural Forms as a Political Tool," *Ethnomusicology* 38(2):281–301.

Qureshi, Regula. 1972. "Ethnomusicological Research among Canadian Communities of Arab and East Indian Origin." *Ethnomusicology* 16:381–396.

Thompson, Gordon. 1985. "Songs in Circles: Gujaratis in America." *1985 Festival of American Folklife Program Book*. Washington, D.C.: Smithsonian Institution.

Thompson, Gordon, and Medha Yodh. 1985. "*Garbā* and the Gujaratis of Southern California." *Selected Reports in Ethnomusicology* 6:59–79.

Upadhyaya, Hari S. 1988. *Bhojpuri Folksongs from Ballia*. Atlanta: Indian Enterprises Inc.

Wade, Bonnie C. 1978. "Indian Classical Music in North America: Cultural Give and Take." *Contributions to Asian Studies* 12:29–39.

A Guide to Recordings

GENERAL

Encyclopedia of Musical Instruments. N.d. Covers Western and world instruments; over 120 minutes of audio and video performances. QCD 7037W-E. Distributed by Multicultural Media:http://www.worldmusicstore.com. CD-ROM for Windows only.

The Four Vedas. 1969. Recorded by Fritz Staal. Asch Mankind Series AHM 4126. LP disk.

The Language of Rhythm: Drumming from North and South India. N.d. Produced by Bob Haddad, notes by David Nelson. Features Bikram Ghosh, tabla, and Trichy Sankaran, mridangam. Music of the World MOW 150. 2 compact discs.

L. Subramaniam and Bismillah Khan—Live in Geneva. 1991. Instrumental duet with L. Subramaniam, Karnatak violin, and Bismillah Khan, Hindustani shahnai. Audiorec ACCD 1020. Compact disc.

A Musical Anthology of the Orient: India I. 1965. Recorded by Alain Daniélou. Barenreiter Musicaphon BM 30 L 2006. LP disk.

A Musical Journey through India 1963–1964. 1988. Recordings by Nazir A. Jairazbhoy. Los Angeles: UCLA Ethnnomusicology Publications. 3 audio cassettes and booklet.

Pandit Bhimsen Joshi and Balamurali Krishna—Live. 1991. Duet with the Hindustani vocalist Bhimsen Joshi and the Karnatak vocalist Balamurali Krishna, and Shashikant Muley, tabla. Ragas Darbari Kanada, Malkauns/Hindolam, and Bhairavi. Navras Records NRCD 0022. Compact disc.

Rough Guide to the Music of India and Pakistan. N.d. Artists include Ali Akbar Khan, Bismillah Khan, Amjad Ali Khan, Shiv Kumar Sharma, Hariprasad Chaurasia, the Sabri Brothers, Nusrat Fateh Ali Khan, and Purna Das Baul. Distributed by Multicultural Media WMNW-1008. Compact disc.

Vintage Music from India: Early Twentieth Century Classical and Light-Classical Music. 1993. Produced by Richard Spottswood, with notes by Peter Manuel. Rounder Records CD 1083. Compact disc.

MUSIC IN NORTHERN AREAS

Afghanistan: On Marco Polo's Road. The Musicians of Kunduz and Faizabad. 1997. Produced by Stephen McArthur. Music of the Earth series. Multicultural Media MCM 3003. Compact disc.

Afghānistān: Musique Instrumentale et Chant. 1990. Recorded by Hubert de Fraysseix, notes by George Wen. Sunset-France, Playa Sound PS 65058. Compact disc.

Afghanistan: Ritchak, Zer-Barhali, Toolah, Rabab, Tumbur, Tabla. 1990. Playa Sound PS 65058. Compact disc.

Afghanistan: Rubab et Dutâr. 1995. Performed by Ustad Rahim Khushnawaz, rubab; Gada Mohammad, dutar; and Azim Hassanpur, tabla. Notes by John Baily. Ocora C 560080. Compact disc.

Afghanistan. The Rubāb of Herat. Mohammad Rahim Khushnawaz. 1993. Recorded by John Baily. VDE-Gallo AIMP XXV. Compact disc with accompanying notes.

Alisha: Madonna—Jadoo. 1989. "Indipop" artist. The Gramophone Company of India Ltd. PSLP 5111. Compact disc.

Amdo: Tibetan Monastery of Labrang. N.d. Distributed by Multicultural Media C-56101. Compact disc.

Amjad Ali Khan—Touch of Class. 1990. Hindustani sarod performance, ragas Desh and Hemavati, and two bhajans, with Sukhvinder Singh, tabla. Audiorec ACCD 1009. Compact disc.

Ananya: Ustad Amir Khan—Navras Nav-Ratna, The Great Masters. N.d. Khyal vocal performance of ragas Yaman, Hansadhwani, Puriya, and Abhogi. Live performance recorded c. 1965. Navras 0091/92. 2 compact discs.

Anindo and His Tabla: Anindo Chatterjee. 1992. Tabla solos in tintal, dhamar, pancham sawari, and ektal, with Ramesh Mishra, sarangi. Audiorec ACCD 1016–1017. Compact disc.

Anthology of World Music: North Indian Classical Music. N.d. Original UNESCO LP recordings digitally transferred to CD. Multicultural Media 5101–5104. 4 compact discs with a 40-page booklet.

Anup Jalota—In Classical Mood. 1995. The ghazal singer Anup Jalota performs three bhajans in ragas Yaman, Malkauns, and Gurjari Todi, with tabla, guitar, and santur accompaniment. Navras Records NRCD 0055. Compact disc.

Artistic Sound of Sarod: Ali Akbar Khan. N.d. Hindustani sarod performance of raga Basant Mukhari with Jogia. Chhanda Dhara 3386. Compact disc.

Ashit Desai—Songs of Narsinh Mehta, Vols.1–3. 1996. Gujarati devotional songs. Song texts and descriptions in Gujarati only. Navras Records NRCD 0062–0064. 3 compact discs.

Ashit Desai—Jai Jai Srinathji. 1995. Gujarati devotional songs sung by Lata Mangeshkar, Jagjit Singh, Anup Jalota, and others. Navras Records NRCD 0069. Compact disc.

Baloutchistan: Musiques d'extase et de guérison/Baloutchistan: Ecstasy and Healing Musics. 1992. Recorded and with notes by Jean During. Ocora Radio France C 580017/18. 2 compact discs.

Bardes de l'Himalaya: Népal [et] Inde: Épopées et musiques de transe/Bards of the Himalayas: Nepal [and] India: Epics and Trance Music. 1997. Recorded and with notes by Frank Bernède. Le Chant du Monde CNR 274 1080. Compact disc.

The Best of Shakti. N.d. Compilation of pieces from three albums, 1975–1977, by the fusion group Shakti: John McLauglin, Shankar, Zakir Hussain, and T. H. Vinayakram. Moment Records MRCD 1011. Compact disc.

Bhajan Lal Sopori—A World of String and Sound. 1993. Santur performance of ragas Ahir Lalit, Marwa, and Mishra Kafi, with Mohammad Akram Khan, tabla. Academy of Indian Music AIMCD 003. Compact disc.

Brilliancy and Oldest Tradition: Tabla Solo and Duet (with Kumar Bose). 1993. Kishan Maharaj. Chhanda Dhara SNCD 70493. Compact disc.

Buddhadev Das Gupta, Sarod: Morning Concert. 1989. Hindustani sarod performance of raga Ahir Bhairav, with Anand Gopal Bandopdhyay, tabla. Raga Records 206. Compact disc.

Captivating Melodies of Sitar: Ustad Vilayat Khan. N.d. Raga Mian Ki Todi. Produced by Rangasami Parthasarathy. Oriental Records CD 120. Compact disc.

Chants in Praise of Krishna. 1990. Recorded in Dwarikadhish Temple, Mathura, India. JVC World Sounds JVC VICG 5034. Compact disc.

Chant the Names of God: Village Music of the Bhojpuri-Speaking Area of India. 1981. Recorded by Edward O. Henry. Rounder Records 5008. LP disk.

Classical Music of North India: Sitar and Tabla I. N.d. Manilal Nag, sitar, performs raga Suha Kanada. King World Music Library 5111. Compact disc.

The Dagar Brothers: Rag Kambhoji. 1989. Vocal dhrupad performance. Produced by Bob Haddad. Music of the World CDT-114. Compact disc.

Dagar Brothers: Raga Miyan ki Todi. 1988. Hindustani vocal dhrupad performance. Jecklin Disco JD628-2. Compact disc.

The Day, the Night, the Dawn, the Dusk: Nusrat Fateh Ali Khan. N.d. Qawwali performance. Shanachie 64032. Compact disc.

Dhrupad: Vocal Art of Hindustan. 1990. The Dagar Brothers. JVC World Sounds VICG 5032-2. Compact disc.

The Emperor of Sarod: Live, Vol.1, Ali Akbar Khan. N.d. Performance of raga Bageswari Kanada. Chhanda Dhara 71090. Compact disc.

Evergreen Hits from Old Films. 1994. Songs from Hindi films, 1936–1949. The Gramophone Company of India Ltd. PMLP 5831. Compact disc.

Festival of India: A Hindustani Sampler. N.d. Artists include Sultan Khan, *sāraṅgī*; V. G. Jog, violin; G. S. Sachdev, South Indian flute; Purna Das Baul, Bengali folk ensemble; and the Dagar Brothers, dhrupad vocal music. Produced by Bob Haddad. Music of the World MOW 121. Compact disc.

Folk Music of Nepal. 1994. Includes Gaine musicians, *mādal* drumming, and popular music. World Music Library 74. Seven Seas/King Records KICC-5174. Compact disc.

Folk Music of Uttar Pradesh, India. 1991. Recorded by Laxmi Tewari. International Institute for Comparative Music Studies/Musicaphon BM 55802 ADD Compact disc.

Flutes of Rajasthan. 1989. Recorded and with notes by Geneviève Dournon, produced by CNRS/Musée de l'Homme. Le Chant du Monde LDX 274645. Compact disc.

Gangubai Hangal; The Voice of Tradition. N.d. Hindustani khyal performance of ragas Shuddha Kalyan, Abhogi, and Basanta. Wergo (Welt Musik) SM 1501. Compact disc.

Gavana—Goa: A viagem dos sons/The Journey of Sounds. 1998. Music of the Goan Catholic community; accompanying booklet by Susana Sardo. Tradisom VS01. Compact disc.

Gauhar Jan—Malka Jan. 1994. Historical recordings of Hindustani vocal music by Gauhar Jan and Malka Jan from 1902 to 1907. Gramophone Company of India Ltd. CMC 882517/18. 2 compact discs.

Ghalib—Portrait of a Genius: A Ghalib Centenary Presentation. Ghazal. Begum Akhtar and Mohammed Rafi. 1968. Gramophone Company of India Ltd. ECSD 2404. LP disk.

Ghazals. 1991. Begum Akhtar sings ghazals. Music India CDNF 154. Compact disc.

Girija Devi. 1989. Live performance of Hindustani vocalist Girija Devi, with Zakir Hussain, tabla. Khyal in raga Puriya Kalyan, tappa, and thumri. Moment Records MRCD 1004. Compact disc.

Gopal Krishan: Dhrupad and Khyal. N.d. Three ragas performed on *vicitra vīṇā*. Multicultural Media C-560078. Compact disc.

The Greatest Hits. 1997. The Sabri Brothers. Shanachie 64090. Compact disc.

Greatest Hits of the 50s, Vol.3. 1997. Hindi film songs by the music directors C. Ramchandra,

Naushad, O. P. Nayyar, Shankar-Jaikishen, and others. The Gramophone Company of India Ltd. CDF 130121. Compact disc.

Greatest Hits of the 60s, Vol.3. 1997. Hindi film songs by the music directors Naushad, Shankar-Jaikishen, S. D. Burman, Lakshmikant-Pyarelal, and others. The Gramophone Company of India Ltd. CDF 130126. Compact disc.

Greatest Hits of the 70s, Vol.3. 1997. Hindi film songs by the music directors R. D. Burman, Shankar-Jaikishen, Lakshmikant-Pyarelal, Kalyanji-Anandji, and others. The Gramophone Company of India Ltd. CDF 130136. Compact disc.

Greatest Hits of the 80s, Vol.1. 1997. Hindi film songs by the music directors Shiv Hari, Lakshmikant-Pyarelal, R. D. Burman, Khayyam, and others. The Gramophone Company of India Ltd. CDF 130118. Compact disc.

Great Master, Great Music: Ustad Abdul Wahid Khan. 1976. Hindustani khyal performance. Gramophone Company of India Ltd. ECLP 2541. LP disk.

Great Masters of the Rudra-Veena: Ustad Zia Mohiuddin Dagar. 1988. Raga Pancham Kosh. Auvidis A 6131. Compact disc.

G. S. Sachdev—Spirit. 1995. Hindustani flute performance in ragas Bihag, Kalavati, and Chandrakauns, with Zakir Hussain, tabla. Audiorec ACCD 1029. Compact disc.

Gundecha Brothers—Raga Darbari. 1997. Hindustani vocal dhrupad performance, with Shrikant Mishra, pakhavaj. Audiorec ACCD 1036. Compact disc.

Hirabai Barodekar and Saraswati Rane—Classical Vocal. 1992. Gramophone Company of India Ltd. HMV 04B 7434/35. 2 compact discs.

Hypnotic Santur: Shivkumar Sharma. 1988. Shafaat Ahmed Khan, tabla; Shefali Nag, tambura. Raga Gorack Kalyan and Dogri Folklore. Produced by Shefali Nag. Chhanda Dhara SP 83088. Compact disc.

Immortal R.D. Burman—His Own Voice. 1997. Hindi film songs composed and sung by R.D. Burman. Polygram India Ltd. CDF 201. Compact disc.

Inde Centrale/Central India: Traditions musicales des Gond/Musical Traditions of the Gond. 1990. Recorded by Jan Van Alphen 1978–1981. AIMP XX, Archives Internationales de Musique Populaire. VDE/Gallo CD 618. Compact disc.

Inde du Nord: L'art de la vichitra vina. N.d. Performance of ragas Bairagi and Jog by Gopal Krishan. Ocora/Radio France C 560048/49. 2 compact discs.

Inde du Nord/North India: Mithila: Chants d'amour de Vidyapati/Love Songs of Vidyapati. 1995. Notes by Georges Luneau. Ocora C 580063. Compact disc.

India Festival. N.d. A multimedia celebration of India's fairs and festivals. Magic Software Pvt. Ltd., F-6 Kailash Colony, New Delhi 110048. Available from www.magicsw.com/cd-rom/index.htm. CD-ROM.

India Musica. N.d. An interactive guide to Hindustani music. Magic Software Pvt. Ltd., F-6 Kailash Colony, New Delhi 110048. Available from www.magicsw.com/cd-rom/index.htm. CD-ROM.

India Mystica. N.d. An interactive multimedia encyclopedia of Indian culture, traditions, and beliefs. Magic Software Pvt. Ltd., F-6 Kailash Colony, New Delhi 110048. Available from www.magicsw.com/cd-rom/index.htm. CD-ROM.

Indian Folk Music. N.d. Recorded by Alan Lomax. Columbia Records 9102021. LP disk.

Indian Night Live Stuttgart '88: Memorable Tabla Duet. 1991. Zakir Hussain and Sultan Khan. Chhanda Dhara SNCD 70891. Compact disc.

India: Traveling Artists of the Desert—The Vernacular Musical Culture of Rajasthan. 1997. Recorded by Keiji Azami. Multicultural Media MCM 3002. Compact disc.

Inédit—Shâhjahân Miah—Chants mystiques bâuls du Bangladesh (Mystical Baul songs of Bangladesh). 1992. Notes by Pierre Bois. Maison des Cultures du Monde W 260039. Compact disc.

Instrumental Music of Rajasthan: Langas and Manganiyars. N.d. World Music Library KICC-5118. Compact disc.

Jaffar Hussain Khan—The Voice of the Mystics. 1992. Qawwali ensemble. Academy of Indian Music AIMCD 001. Compact disc.

Jagdeep Singh Bedi—Sitar and Surbahar: Soft and True. N.d. Produced by Martha Lorantos and Bob Haddad. Performed with Kailash Chandra Sharma, flute; and Ravi Kumar, tabla. Music of the World MOW 108. Compact disc.

The King of Dhrupad: Ram Chatur Mallik in Concert. 1988. Ragas Vinod, Sindura, Paraj. Recorded in Vrindavan in 1982, by Gottfried Düren. Produced by Peter Pannke. Wergo Spectrum SM 1076-50. Compact disc.

Kirvani: Tarun Bhattacharya, Santur, and Bikram Ghosh, Tabla. N.d. Produced by Bob Haddad. Music of the World MOW 139. Compact disc.

Kishori Amonkar. 1991. Hindustani khyal performance. Music Today CD A-91006. Compact disc.

Kishori Amonkar—Sadhana. 1997. Vocal performance of religious bhajans. Audiorec ACCD 1035. Compact disc.

Kohinoor Langa Group: Music from the Desert Nomads. N.d. Vocal and instrumental music. Multicultural Media WDR-34. Compact disc.

Ladakh: Musique de Monastère et de Village; Ladakh: Monastic and Village Music. 1989. Recorded by Mireille Helffer. Le Chant du Monde LDX 274662/CM 251. Compact disc with 32 page booklet.

Ladakh: Songs and Dances from the Highlands of Western Tibet. 1971. Recorded by David Lewiston. Nonesuch Explorer H-72075. LP disk.

Lakshmi Shankar—Bhakti Ras. N.d. Lakshmi Shankar sings bhajans. Navras Records NRCD 0056. Compact disc.

Lakshmi Shankar—Live in London. 1992. The Hindustani vocalist performs khyal in raga Madhukauns, thumri in raga Mishra Kafi, and bhajan, with Shiv Shankar Ray, tabla. Navras Records NRCD 0006. Compact disc.

The Legendary Lineage: Ustad Hafiz Ali Khan, Ustad Amjad Khan, Amaan and Ayaan Ali Bangash. 1996. Three generations of this musical family are presented: Hafiz Ali Khan (c. 1968) performs ragas Bilaskhani Todi, Yaman Kalyan, Desh, and Pilu Jungala; Amjad Ali Khan (1966) performs raga Darbari Kanada; Amaan and Ayaan Ali Bangash (1966) perform raga Bhairav. Navras Records NRCD 0084/85. 2 compact discs.

Legends: Lata Mangeshkar "The Nightingale." 1997. Digitally remastered Hindi film songs sung by Lata Mangeshkar between 1949 and 1997. The Gramophone Company of India Ltd. CDF 130111/15. 5 compact discs with accompanying 32-page booklet.

Lower Caste Religious Music from India: Monks, Transvestites, Midwives, and Folksingers. N.d. Recorded by Rosina Schlenker. Lyrichord LLST 7344. LP disk.

The Lyrical Tradition of Dhrupad—6: Uday Bhawalkar. N.d. Hindustani vocal dhrupad performance in raga Gurjari Todi. Makar Records 031. Compact disc.

The Lyrical Tradition of Khyal—1: Ustad Iqbal Ahmad Khan—Delhi Gharana. N.d. Hindustani khyal performance in ragas Komal Rishab Asavari and Mian ki Todi. Makar Records 003. Compact disc.

Maestro's Choice: Alla Rakha and Zakir Hussain. 1991. Hindustani tabla. Music Today A19013. Compact disc.

The Majestic Tabla of Swapan Chaudhuri. 1993. Chhanda Dhara SNCD 71093. Compact disc.

Mallikarjun Mansur in Concert. Vol.1: Morning Ragas. N.d. Hindustani khyal performance of ragas Bibhas, Yamani Bilawal, and Bhairavi. Pyramid Classical 7008. Compact disc.

Mallikarjun Mansur: The Legend Lives On. N.d. Hindustani khyal performance of ragas Savani and Shivmat Bhairav. OMI Magnasound D4HV 0589. Compact disc.

Manilal Nag, Sitar—Dawn Raga Lalit. 1989. Hindustani sitar performance with Anand Gopal Bandopadhyay, tabla. Raga Records 213. Compact disc.

Masters of Raga: Sarangi Solo. Ram Narayan in Concert. 1994. Performance of ragas Marwa and Misra Pilu recorded in 1976. Suresh Talwalkar, tabla. Wergo (Welt Musik) SM 1601. Compact disc.

Masters of Tala: Pakhawaj Solo. N.d. Raja Chatrapati Singh. 1989. Wergo SM1075–50. Compact disc.

Mehdi Hassan—Classical Ghazals. 1990. Pakistani ghazal singer presents ghazals and thumris, with Sultan Khan, sarangi; and Shaukat Hussain, tabla. Navras Records NRCD 0001–0003. 3 compact discs.

Memories of Herat: Music of Afghanistan. N.d. Performed by Aziz Herawi, *dutār* and *rubāb* lutes; Siar Ahmad Hazeq, tabla; and Omar Herawi, *zirbaghali* drum. Produced by Bob Haddad. Music of the World LAT50602. Compact disc.

Middle Caste Religious Music from India: Musicians, Dancers, Prostitutes, and Actors. N.d. Recorded by Rosina Schlenker. Lyrichord LLST7323. LP disk.

Music from the Shrines of Ajmer and Mundra. N.d. Reissue of 1970s recordings by John Levy. Multicultural Media TSCD-911. Compact disc.

Music in Sikkim. 1971. Recorded by Fred Liebermann and Michael Moore. Command COMS 9002. LP disk.

Musiques du Pendjab pakistanais/Music from the Punjab Province of Pakistan: Vol.2: Le Ghazal. 1995. Performed by Farida Khanum, vocal. Arion ARN 64301. Compact disc.

Musiques du Toit du Monde: Ladakh et Nepal/Roof of the World Musics. 1988. Recorded at the monastery of Hemis by Gérard Kremer. Sunset-France, Playa Sound PS 65021. Compact disc.

The Mystic Fiddle of the Proto-Gypsies: Masters of Trance Music. 1997. Recordings and notes by Jean During, produced by Theodore Levin. Shanachie SH 65013. Compact disc.

Najma—Qareeb. 1989. Pop ghazals. Shanachie SH 64009. Compact disc.

Nepal: Musique de fête chez les Newar. 1989. Recorded by Marguerite Lobsiger-Dellenbach (1952) and Laurent Aubert (1973). AIMP XIII, Archives Internationales de Musique Populaire. VDE/Gallo VDE CD 553. Compact disc.

Nikhil Bannerjee: Raga Misra Kafi. 1990. Sitar performance with Swapan Chaudhuri, tabla. Raga Records 204. Compact disc.

North India: Instrumental Music of Medieval India. N.d. Ustad Asad Ali Khan, rudra vina, performs ragas Darbari Kanada and Gunakali. Anthology of Traditional Musics series. Auvidis Unesco D 8205. Compact disc.

Nusrat Fateh Ali Khan: Intoxicated Spirit. 1996. Qawwali music of Pakistan. Shanachie SH 64066. Compact disc.

Nusrat Fateh Ali Khan—Qawwali: The Vocal Art of the Sufis I–II. 1996–1997. JVC Music VICG 5029-2/5030-2. 2 compact discs.

The Other Side of Naushad—Aathwan Sur. 1997. Ghazals composed by the Hindi film music director Naushad Ali, sung by Hariharan and Preeti Uttam. Navras Records NRCD 0102. Compact disc.

Padmashree M. S. Gopalakrishnan: Raga Bhimpalasi/Raga Puriya. N.d. Hindustani violin performance. OMI Magnasound C5CI 5013. Compact disc.

Pakistan: The Music of the Qawal. 1990. Recorded and with notes by Alain Daniélou. Anthology of

Traditional Musics. Auvidis Unesco D 8028. Compact disc.

Pakistani Music: The Rubab of Kashmir. N.d.. Subhan Rathore, rubab and vocal, with Abdul Ghani, tumbaknari. World Music Library KICC-5109. Compact disc.

Pandit Bhimsen Joshi—Bhakti. 1992. Four devotional bhajans. Audiorec ACCD 1024. Compact disc.

Pandit Jasraj—Tapasya. 1995. Hindustani vocal performance with Anindo Chatterjee, tabla. Ragas Marubihag, Des Ang Jaijaivanti, and Bhairavi. Audiorec ACCD 1031. Compact disc.

Pandit Kartick Kumar—Atma. 1990. Hindustani sarod performance in ragas Bihag and Jhinghoti, with Sukhvinder Singh, tabla. Audiorec ACCD 1004. Compact disc.

Pandit Kumar Gandharva—Raga Bhairav ke Prakar. 1978. House concert with Vasant Achrekar, tabla. Navras Records NRCD 0042. Compact disc.

Pandit Ravi Shankar, Sitar/Ustad Ali Akbar Khan, Sarod, in Concert, 1972, with Alla Rakha, Tabla. 1996. Apple/EMI 7243 8 53817 2. 2 compact discs.

Pandit V. G. Jog. 1991. Live recording of Hindustani violin performance in Berkeley, May 1991, with Zakir Hussain, tabla. Ragas Jog and Rageshri. Moment Records MRCD 1003. Compact disc.

Playback—The 50 Melodious Years: The Fabulous Years 1946–1956. 1991. Contains 23 Hindi film songs. The Gramophone Company of India Ltd. CDF 1.30024. Compact disc.

Playback—The 50 Melodious Years: The Melodious Decade 1956–1966. 1991. Contains 18 Hindi film songs. The Gramophone Company of India Ltd. CDF 1.30025. Compact disc.

Playback—The 50 Melodious Years: The Exciting Era 1976–1986. 1991. The Gramophone Company of India Ltd. CDF PMLP 5407. Compact disc.

Prayer Music of Sikh: In Bangra Sahib Temple, Delhi. 1988. JVC Ethnic Sound series 21, VID 25035. Compact disc.

Purushotamdas Jalota—Praising Krishna. 1993. Songs of the eight Astachap poet-musicians of the fifteenth and sixteenth centuries. Audiorec ACCD 1013. Compact disc.

Purushotamdas Jalota—Songs of Kabir. 1992. Songs of the Indian mystic and poet Kabir. Audiorec ACCD 1012. Compact disc.

Purushotamdas Jalota—Songs of Surdas. 1991. Krishna bhajans of the sixteenth-century Hindu poet-saint Surdas. Audiorec ACCD 1011. Compact disc.

Qawwali: Sufi Music from Pakistan. 1998. Sabri Brothers. Nonesuch Explorer 72080-2. Compact disc.

The Raga Guide: A Survey of 74 Hindustani Ragas. 1999. By Joep Bor. Nimbus Records NI 5536/9. 4 compact discs with book.

Raga Lalitadhvani: Sarod Maestro Amjad Ali Khan. N.d. JVC Music VICG-5451-2. Compact disc.

Ram Narayan: Raga Lalit. N.d. Hindustani sarangi performance. Indian Classical Masters series. Nimbus 5183. Compact disc.

Ras Rang—Evolution of Thumri, Vol.1. 1997. Collection of thumris sung by Parween Sultana Birju Maharaj, Sipra Bose, Shobha Gurtu, Ghulam Mustafa Khan, and others. Navras Records NRCD 0081. Compact disc.

Ras Rang—Evolution of Thumri, Vol.2. 1997. Collection of thumris sung by Girija Devi, Birju Maharaj, Sipra Bose, Shobha Gurtu, Ghulam Mustafa Khan, and others. Navras Records NRCD 0082. Compact disc.

Ravi Shankar—Concert for Peace at the Royal Albert Hall. 1993. Live performance in London, 9 November 1993. Ravi Shankar, sitar; Partho Sarathy, sarod; and Zakir Hussain, tabla, perform ragas Jait, Kirwani, and Misra Khammaj. Moment Records MRCD 1013. 2 compact discs.

Ravi Shankar: Concerto for Sitar and Orchestra. 1990. Angel Classics 69121. Compact disc.

The Sabri Brothers: Greatest Hits. 1997. Qawwali performance. Shanachie SH 64090. Compact disc.

The Sabri Brothers: Ya Mustapha. 1996. Produced by Richard Blair. Green Linnet Records, Xeno 4041. Compact disc.

Sacred Ceremonies: Ritual Music of Tibetan Budhism: Monks of the Dip Tse Chok Ling Monastery, Dharamsala. 1990. Fortuna Records 17074-2. Distributed by Celestial Harmonies, P.O. Box 30122, Tucson, Ariz. 85751. Compact disc.

Sargam: Santur, Shenai and Tabla—Tarun Bhattacharya. N.d. Produced by Bob Haddad. Music of the World MOW 132. Compact disc.

Satya Sai Baba Chants the Bhajans. N.d. Recorded at Prasanthi Nilayam and Vrindavan. Distributed by Sathya Sai Book Center of America, 305 First Street, Tustin, Calif. 92680. Stereo SC-002. Audio cassette.

Sharda Sahai—The Art of the Benares Baj. 1993. Tabla solo in the Banaras style. Audiorec ACCD 1034. Compact disc.

Shiela Chandra—Silk. 1991. "Indipop" fusion album of Chandra's songs recorded 1983–1990. Shanachie SH 64035. Compact disc.

Shiva Mahadeva: Dagar Brothers: Dhrupad, Classical Vocal Music of North India. 1996. Nasir Zahiruddin Dagar and Nasir Faiyazuddin Dagar, vocal; ragas Malkauns, Darbari Kanada, Adana, and Bhatiyar. Pan Records 4001/02. 2 compact discs.

Shujaat Khan, Sitar; Shyam Kane, Tabla. 1992. Ragas Shahana Kanada and Pahari. India Archive Music IAM CD 1009. Compact disc.

Songs of the Bauls II: Purna Chandra Das. 1993. JVC World Sounds JVC VICG5267. Compact disc.

The Songs of Distant Sands. 1995. Music of the Langas and Manganihars of Rajasthan. Navras Records NRCD 0059. Compact disc.

The Soul of Tabla. 1993. Swapan Chaudhuri. Interworld Music CD 809092. Compact disc.

Sri Lanka: Musiques rituelles et religieuses. 1992. Reissue of Ocora 558 552. Ocora C580 037. Compact disc.

String Craft: Nishat Khan. N.d. Hindustani sitar performance. JVC Music VICG 5452-2. Compact disc.

Tabla Lahara. Pandit Shamta Prasad. 1988. Concord Records 05015. Audio cassette.

Tabla Lahara. Ustad Afaq Husain Khan. 1991. Concord Records 05023. Audio cassette.

Tabla Tarang: Melody on Drums. 1996. Performed by Pandit Kamalesh Maitra, tabla tarang (set of tabla tuned to pitches of a musical scale), and Trilok Gurtu, tabla. Recorded by Walter Quintus, with notes by Laura Patchen. The World's Musical Traditions 10. Smithsonian/Folkways CD SF 40436. Compact disc.

Talking Tabla—Bikram Ghosh. N.d. Music of the World MOW 143. Compact disc.

Thumri and Dadra: Vocal Art of Hindustan [II]. 1994. Rita Ganguly, vocal; Sabri Khan, sarangi; Rashid Mustafa, tabla; and Sajjad Ahmed, harmonium. JVC World Sounds JVC VICG 5347. Compact disc.

Thumri: Vocal and Instrumental Light Classical Music of North India. 1994. Produced by Lyle Wachovsky, with notes by Peter Manuel. India Archive Music IAM CD 1012. Compact disc.

Tibet—Monks of the Sera Jé Monastery: Ritual Music and Chants of the Gelug Tradition. N.d. Recorded by Angelo Ricciardi (January 1997) at a monastery-in-exile in South India. With 96-page color booklet. Distributed by Amiata Media, P.O. Box 405, Chappaqua, N.Y. 10514, http://www.amiatamedia.it. Compact disc.

Tibetan Buddhist Rites from the Monasteries of Bhutan. N.d. 1. Rituals of the Drukpa Order; 2. sacred dances and Rituals of the Nyingmapa and Drukpa Orders; 3. Temple rituals and public ceremonies; 4. Tibetan Bhutanese instrumental and folk music. Recorded by John Levy. Lyrichord LYRCD 7255–58. Four compact discs.

Tibetan Music from Ladakh and Zanskar. 1982. Recorded by Eric Larson. Lyrichord LLST 7383. LP disk.

The Traditional Music of Herat. 1996. Recorded by John Baily. UNESCO collection, Audivis D8266. Compact disc with accompanying notes.

The Tradition of Dhrupad on Rudravina 1. N.d. Bahauddin Dagar performs ragas Bhairav and Komal Re Durga. Makar Records 006. Compact disc.

The Tradition of Dhrupad on Rudravina 2. N.d. Bahauddin Dagar performs ragas Kanakangi and Ragvardhani. Makar Records 033. Compact disc.

Trésors du Pakistan/Pakistan Treasures. 1991. Includes performances on rabab, sarinda, sarangi, Baluchi sarinda, and tabla. Playa Sound PS 65082. Compact disc.

The "Ultimate" in Taal-Vidya: Solo Masterpieces in Teentaal and Jhaptaal. Alla Rakha. 1989.OMI Magnasound D4H10079. Compact disc.

Ustad Ali Akbar Khan—Passing on the Tradition. 1995. Hindustani sarod performance of ragas Marwa and Puriya Kalyan, with Swapan Chaudhuri, tabla. Alam Madina Music Production AMMP 9608. Compact disc.

Ustad Ali Akbar Khan Plays Alap. 1992. Hindustani sarod performance of ragas Shri, Pilu Baroowa, and Iman Kalyan. Alam Madina Music Production AMMP 9303. Compact disc.

Ustad Ali Akbar Khan—Signature Series. N.d. Vol.1: Three ragas–Chandranandan, Gauri Manjari, Jogiya Kalingra (original recordings 1966–1969). Vol.2: Medhavi, Khammaj, Bhairavi Bhatiyar with ragmala (original recordings 1969–1970). Alam Madina Music Productions AMMP CD 9001–9002. 2 compact discs.

Ustad Alla Rakha and Zakir Hussain, Tabla Duet. 1991. Live performance at the Ramkrishna Mission Auditorium, Calcutta, January 1991. Duet in tintal. Moment Records MRCD 1001. Compact disc.

Ustad Amir Khan: The Legend Lives On. N.d. Khyal vocal performance of ragas Nand, Bahar, and Darbari Kanada. OMI Magnasound D3HV 0636. Compact disc.

Ustad Imrat Khan: Rag Madhur Ranjani. N.d. Sitar performance. Produced by Bob Haddad. Music of the World MOW 123. Compact disc.

Ustad Latif Ahmed Khan—The Great Tabla Wizard. c. 1983. Tabla solo in tintal, Delhi Gharana style. Academy of Indian Music AIMCD 003a. Compact disc.

Ustad Muhammad Umar—Robab-Music from Afghanistan. N.d. Classical and folk music. Academy of Indian Music AIMCD 004. Compact disc.

Ustad Munawar Ali Khan and Raza Ali Khan. 1990. Homage to Ustad Bade Ghulam Ali Khan, sung by his son and his uncle, with Tanmoy Bose, tabla. Ragas include Komal Rishabh Asavari, Gaud Sarang, Bhimpalasi, Megh, and Rageshwari. Audiorec ACCD 1003-S. 3 compact discs.

Ustad Nizamuddin Khan. 1994. India Music Archive IAM CD 1014. Compact disc.

Ustad R. Fahimuddin Dagar: Raga Kedar. N.d. Hindustani vocal dhrupad performance. Jecklin Disco JD635. Compact disc.

Ustad Sabri Khan: Raga Darbari/Raga Multani. N.d. Hindustani sarangi performance. Auvidis Ethnic B 6754. Compact disc.

Ustad Sabri Khan—The Family Tradition. 1991. Hindustani sarangi performance by Sabri Khan with his sons Kamal Sabri, sarangi; and Sarvar Sabri, tabla. Ragas Nat Bhairav, Shri, Shyam Kalyan, and a dhun in raga mand. Audiorec ACCD 1018. Compact disc.

Ustad Vilayat Khan: Raga Darbari Kanada. N.d.

Hindustani sitar performance. EMI India CDNF 150186. Compact disc.

Ustad Vilayat Khan: Raga Jaijaivanti. N.d. Hindustani sitar performance. India Archive of Music 1010. Compact disc.

Ustad Zia Mohiuddin Dagar: Raga Yaman. N.d. Hindustani rudra vina performance. Nimbus/ Indian Classical Masters 5276. Compact disc.

Veena Sahasrabuddhe—Live in Concert. 1994. The khyal singer from Maharashtra performs the morning raga Bhupal Todi in the Gwalior Gharana style, with Sanjay Deshpande, tabla. Navras Records NRCD 0031. Compact disc.

Venu: Hariprasad—Zakir Hussain. 1989. Hindustani flute performance of raga Ahir Bhairav, with Zakir Hussain, tabla. Produced by Zakir Hussain and Mickey Hart. Rykodisc RCD 20128. Compact disc.

Vicitra Vina: The Music of Pandit Lalmani Misra. N.d. Performance of the evening raga Kausi Kanhada. Distributed by Multicultural Media D-8267. Compact disc.

Vishwa Mohan Bhatt, Guitar: Ragas Bihag and Desh. 1996. Hindustani performance on guitar with Sukhvindar Singh, tabla, recorded live in Pittsburgh in 1989. Raga Records 208. Compact disc.

Vocal Music of Rajasthan: Langas and Manganiyars. N.d. World Music Library KICC-5117. Compact disc.

Vocal Phenomenon: Sri Bhimsen Joshi Live. 1992. Ragas Lalit and Jogia, and bhajans. Produced by Shefali Nag. Chhanda Dhara SNCD 70392. Compact disc.

Zakir Hussain and Sultan Khan. 1987. Chhanda Dhara SNCD 4487. Compact disc.

Zarsanga: Songs of the Pashtu. 1993. Songs of Pakistan, accompanied by *rabāb, ḍholak,* and tabla. Produced by Alain Weber and Armand Amar. Long-Distance Music 662295. Compact disc.

Zia Mohiuddin Dagar: Live in Seattle 1981. 1999. Hindustani rudra vina performance in ragas Todi, Ahir Lalit, and Pancham Kauns recorded live at the University of Washington, 27 February 1998. Raga Records 219. Compact disc.

MUSIC IN SOUTHERN AREAS

An Anthology of South Indian Classical Music. 1990. A broad selection of vocal and instrumental performances by various artists including Semmangudi Srinivasa Iyer (vocal), M. S. Subbulakshmi (vocal), L. Subramaniam (violin), T. R. Mahalingam (flute), and Palghat T. S. Mani Iyer (mridangam). Ocora/Radio France C590001-04. 4 compact discs.

Ariyakudi Ramanuja Iyengar. N.d. Karnatak vocal performance with M. N. Krishnan, T. N. Krishnan, P. Subramania Pillai, and Bangalore Manjunath; an All India Radio release. EMI India CDNF 147750. Compact disc.

Aruna Sayeeram: Chant Karnatique/Karnatic Song. N.d. Karnatak vocal performance, with Sundar Rajan and Bombay S. Shankaranarayanan, recorded in France. Auvidis Ethnic B6747. Compact disc.

Bombay Sisters: Mutthuswamy Dikshitar's Navagraha Kritis. N.d. Karnatak vocal performance of Diksitar's Navagraha kriti cycle on the planets, with Usha Rajagopalan, Kamala Vishwanathan, K. V. Prasad, and N. Govindarajan. EMI India CDNF 170503. Compact disc.

Cascades of Carnatic Music: M. L. Vasanthakumari. 1990. The Karnatak vocalist and distinguished disciple of G. N. Balasubramaniam performs with T. Rukmani, Palghat T. S. Mani Iyer, S. D. Sridhar, S. V. Raja Rao, and Hari Shankar. Oriental 158–159. 2 compact discs.

Christian Bhajans. 1979. Sung by Joseph Palackal. Bangalore: Deccan Records LDEC 102. LP disk.

Christian Classical Music Concert. 1988. Performed by George Panjara. Nadopasana/ Thodupuzha NC 101. Audio cassette.

Connoisseurs Delight: V. Ramachandran. N.d. Karnatak vocal performance with Nagai R. Muralidharan, Guruvayur Dorai, and T. H. Subashchandran. OMI Magnasound D5CV 5043. Compact disc.

Divine Sounds of the Bamboo Flute, "Mali." N.d. Karnatak flute performance by T. R. Mahalingam, with Dwaram Mangathayaru, Karaikkudi R. Mani, and Gurumurthy. Oriental 183/184. 2 compact discs.

D. K. Jayaraman. N.d. Karnatak vocal performance, with T. Rukmini, Srimushnam V. Raja Rao, and T. H. Subhashchandran. EMI India CDNF 168307. Compact disc.

D. K. Pattammal. N.d. Karnatak vocal performance, with T. Veeraraghavan, Sivakumar, and K. M. Vaidyanathan. EMI India CDNF 147729. Compact disc.

The Doyen of Carnatic Music: Dr. Semmangudi Srinivasa Iyer. N.d. Karnatak violin performance with V. V. Subramaniam, Guruvayoor Dorai, and V. K. Krishnan. Oriental 163–164. 2 compact discs.

Dr. L. Subramaniam: Raga Hemavati. N.d. Karnatak violin performance. Nimbus NI 5227. Compact disc.

Dr. M. L. Vasanthakumari—Carnatic Concert. N.d. Karnatak vocal performance, with Sudha Raghunathan, A. Kanyakumari, and R. Ramesh. Super Audio (Geethanjali) 020. Compact disc.

Dr. N. Ramani: Classical Carnatic Flute. N.d. Karnatak compositions and a ragam Tanam pallavi ragamalika. Nimbus 5257. Compact disc.

Dr. S. Ramanathan. N.d. Karnatak vocal performance, with Karaikudi R. Mani and M. S. Gopalakrishnan. OMI Magnasound C5CV 5017. Compact disc.

Folk Music of Tamilnadu. N.d. Recorded by Shyamala Balakrishnan, Padma Subramanyam, K. S. Vasudevan, and N. Vasudevan. The Gramophone Company of India ECSD 3233. LP disk.

Folk Songs of South India. N.d. The Gramophone Company of India MOCE 1004. LP disk.

Guru Padam: K. V. Narayanaswamy. N.d. Karnatak vocal performance, with Padma Narayanaswamy, G. Chandramouli, J. Vaidhyanatha, H. Siwaramakrishnan. Koel 063. Compact disc.

The Immortal Sounds of the Veena: Dr. S. Balachander. N.d. Karnatak vina performance, with S. V. Raja Rao, R. Harishankar, Karaikudi R. Mani, and T. H. Vinayagaram. Oriental 119. Compact disc.

Inde du Sud: Kerala—Le Thayambaka/South India: Kerala—The Thayambaka. 1997. Performed by Mattanur Shankarankutty; recording and notes by Jean-Paul Auboux. Ocora C560 047. Compact disc.

Jon Higgins. c. 1970. The Gramophone Company of India CDNF 147728. Compact disc.

Karaikudi R. Mani—Layapriya. 1995. Karnatak drumming by the mridangam player Karaikudi R. Mani, with violin, ghatam, kanjira, and morsing. Audiorec ACCD 1028. Compact disc.

Karnatak Music of Andhra. 1997. Voleti Venkateswarlu, voice; R. Subba Rao, vina; K. Kannan, flute; Anawarupu Gopalam, mridangam, morsing; Yella Venkateswara Rao, mridangam; N. C. H. Krishnamacharyulu, violin; D. Pandurangaraju, violin; and A. Gopalan, ghatam. Recorded by Nazir Jairazbhoy. Apsara Media for Intercultural Education. Audio cassette.

K. S. Narayanaswami—Veena. N.d. Karnatak vina performance, with Trichur Narendran. Oriental AAMSCD 202. Compact disc.

Lalgudi G. Jayaraman: Live Concert at Sri Krishna Gana Sabha, Vol. II. N.d. Karnatak violin performance, with G. J. R. Krishnan, Trichy Sankaran, and G. Harishankar. OMI Magnasound C5CI 5031. Compact disc.

Laya Vinyās: The South Indian Drumming of Trichy Sankaran. 1990. Music of the World CDT120. Compact disc.

L. Subramaniam—Distant Visions. 1991. Karnatak violin performance, including ragamalika, with K. Gopinath, mridangam, and K. M. Rajah, kanjira. Audiorec ACCD 1021. Compact disc.

L. Subramaniam—In Praise of Ganesh. 1992. Live Karnatak violin performance with Karaikudi Krishnamurti, mridangam, Anindo Chatterjee, tabla, and T. H. Subashchandran, ghatam. Ragas Abhogi and Kapi. Audiorec ACCD 1027. Compact disc.

The Lyrical Tradition of Carnatic Music—1: Aruna Sayeeram. N.d. Karnatak vocal performance, with B. Anantharaman and S. Shankaranarayam. Makar Records 013. Compact disc.

Maharajapuram V. Santhanam. N.d. Vocal performance by the late Karnatak vocalist. Music Today/Maestro's Choice C 91016. Compact disc.

M. S. Gopalakrishnan. N.d. Karnatak violin performance, with Srimushnam V. Raja Rao and E.M. Subrahmanyam. EMI India CDNF 168311. Compact disc.

M. S. Subbulakshmi. 1991. Live Karnatak vocal performance at the United Nations Building, Washington D.C., on 23 October 1966, with Radha Viswanathan, V. V. Subramanian, T. K. Moorthy, and T.H. Vinayakram. EMI India CD PMLP 5306/07. 2 compact discs.

M. S. Subbulakshmi—Live at Carnegie Hall. N.d. Karnatak vocal performance, with Radha Viswanathan, A. K. S. Alagiriswami, and Guruvayur Dorai. EMI India CDNF 147808/09. 2 compact discs.

Music of South India—Karaikudi Veena Tradition: Surabi—Rajeswari Padmanabhan. N.d. Karnatak vina performance, with Mannargudi Easwaran. SonicSoul Acoustics 60. Compact disc.

Music of the Veena I: S. Balachander. 1990. Recorded in 1974. JVC World Sounds VICG-5036-2. Compact disc.

Music of the Veena II: Raajeswari Padmanabhan. 1990. Karnatak performance by Raajeswari Padmanabhan and Sreevidhya Chandramouli, vina, and Tanjore Upendran, mridangam. JVC World Sounds VICG-5038. Compact disc.

Naadha Manjari—Lalgudi G. Jayaraman. N.d. Karnatak violin performance, with G. J. R. Krishnan, Karakudi R. Mani, and T. H. Vinayakram. AVM Audio CD 1066. Compact disc.

Nadanubhava—Horizons of Carnatic Music. 1998. K. N. Shashikiran and Sowmya. Produced by Carnatica, Chennai (India). Distributed in the U.S. by KalaiOli Musicals, 16806 Soaring Forest Dr., Houston, Tex. 77059-4006, phone (888) 376-3758, e-mail shrie@msn.com. CD-ROM.

Nadhaswaram: Sheik Chinna Moulana. Musical Herolds [sic] from South India. N.d. Karnatak performance on the double-reed nagasvaram, with Sheik Kasim, Sheik Babu, and Sheik Subramaaniam. Wergo/Haus der Kulturen der Welt SM 1507. Compact disc.

Nadopasana—My Own Carnatic Tutor. 1998. By K.N. Shashikiran and Sowmya. Produced by Carnatica, Chennai (India). Distributed in the U.S. by KalaiOli Musicals, 16806 Soaring Forest Dr., Houston, TX 77059-4006, phone (888) 376-3758, e-mail shrie@msn.com. CD-ROM.

Pallavi South India Flute Music. 1973. Tanjore Viswanathan. Nonesuch Explorer Series H-72052. LP disk.

Ramnad Krishnan: Vidwan, Music of South India. N.d. Vocal performance of three kritis and a ragam tanam pallavi. Elektra/Nonesuch: Explorer Series 9 72023-2. Compact disc. Originally released as LP disk, 1967.

Sangeeta Kalanidhi V. Doreswamy Iyengar: Live at Music Academy Hall, Madras (1984). N.d. Karnatak vina performance with D. Balakrishna,

K. Viswanatha Iyer, and K. S. Manjunathan. EMI India CDNF 147774. Compact disc.

Sangita Kalanidhi M. S. Subbulakshmi. N.d. Karnatak vocal performance, with Radha Viswanathan, V. V. Subramanian, T. K. Moorthy, V. Nagarajan, and T. H. Vinayakram. EMI India CDNF 147701. Compact disc.

Sangita Kalanidhi Semmangudi Srinivasa Iyer. N.d. Karnatak vocal performance, with Palghat T. S. Mani Iyer, mridangam; and L. Shankar, violin. Oriental AAMS 186. Compact disc.

Semmangudi R. Srinivasa Iyer. N.d. Karnatak vocal performance, with P. S. Narayanaswami, T. N. Krishnan, and S. V. S. Narayanan. An All India Radio release. EMI India CDNF 147752. Compact disc.

South Indian Classical Flute: Tanjore Viswanathan. N.d. Karnatak flute performance, with V. Thyagarajan and Ramnad V. Raghavan. JVC Music VICG 5453-2. Compact disc.

Sri Muthuswami Dikshitar's Sri Kamalamba Navavaranam: S. Rajeswari. N.d. Karnatak vocal performance of Muttusvami Diksitar's Sri Kamalamba Navavaranam song cycle. EMI India CDNF 147782/83. 2 compact discs.

Sri Lanka—Buddhist Chant: Mahâ Pirit—the Great Chant. 1990. Recorded by Wolfgang Laade in 1979. Jecklin-Disco JD 651-2. Compact disc and booklet in English.

Südindische Tempelinstrumente. 1969. Recorded by Joseph Kuckertz, ed. Dieter Christensen, Museum für Völkerkunde, Berlin. Klangdokumente zur Musikwissenschaft KM 0001. LP disk.

Sunada: Karaikudi S. Subramaniam and Trichy Sankaran. 1992. Vina and mridangam; music from the classical tradition of South India. 1992. Produced by Bob Haddad. Music of the World CDT 127. Compact disc.

Swara Bushani. N.d. Compilation by Balamurali Krishna of vocal performances by various artists. Oriental AAMS 166/167. 2 compact discs.

The Tradition of Carnatic Music on Veena 1: Shri R. Pichumani—Tanjore Vani. N.d. Karnatak vina performance, with S. Karthick. Makar Records 024. Compact disc.

The Tradition of Carnatic Music on Veena 2: Ranganayaki Rajagopalam—Karaikudi Vani. N.d. Karnatak vina performance, with S. Karthick. Makar Records 029. Compact disc.

A Tribute to Adolphe Sax: Kadri Gopalnath. N.d. Karnatak performance on saxophone, with A. Kanyakumari, T. Bhakthavatsalam, S. Kartik, and B. Rajasekar. Oriental 228/229. 2 compact discs.

Tribute to the Great Masters: Ravikiran. N.d. Karnatak performance on the citravina (gottuvadyam), with Vellore Ramabhadran. Chhanda Dhara 71194. Compact disc.

Vadya Lahari: South Indian Instrumental Ensemble. 1992. Features A. Kanyakumari, violin. Produced by Bob Haddad. Music of the World MOW 125. Compact disc.

V. Doreswamy Iyengar. N.d. Karnatak vina performance recorded in 1991, with Vellore Ramabhadran. Music Today/Maestro's Choice C 91014. Compact disc.

Veena Virtuoso / Balachander. N.d. Karnatak vina performance recorded in 1982, with R. Ramesh. King World Music Library 5110. Compact disc.

Violin Virtuoso: Lalgudi G. Jayaraman. N.d. Karnatak violin performance, with G. J. R. Krishnan, Karaikudi R. Mani, and T. H. Vinayakram. Includes an extended ragam tanam pallavi in raga Simhendramadhyamam. Oriental AAMS 125. Compact disc.

The Vocal Artistry of Trichur V. Ramachandran. N.d. Karnatak vocal performance, with Delhi P. Sunder Rajan, Srimushnam V. Raja Rao, and Vaikom Gopalakrishnan. Oriental 230–231. 2 compact discs.

DANCE AND DRAMA

Ache Lhamo. Théâtre Musical Tibétain "Prince Norsang." 1985. Recorded by Ricardo Canzio. Disques Espérance (Paris) ESP-8433. LP disk.

Devadasi Murai: Remembering Devadasis. 1998. Coproduced by Saskia Kersenboom. A coproduction of Cultural Informatics Group, Indira Gandhi National Centre for the Performing Arts, Delhi, and Parampara Foundation for Traditional Arts of South India, Utrecht. Distributed by Parampara, Postbus 417, 3500 AK Utrecht, Netherlands, e-mail parampara@worldonline.nl. CD-ROM.

Inde du Sud: Musiques Rituelles et Théâtre du Kerala/South India: Ritual Music and Theatre of Kerala. 1990. Recorded and with notes by Pribislav Pitoëf 1981–1983. Le Chant du Monde LDX 274 910. Compact disc.

Indian Classical Dance. Includes 60 minutes of video performances and over 400 color photos on *bharata nāṭyam, kathakaḷi, mōhini āṭṭam, kuchipuḍi, oḍissi, kathak,* and *manipuri.* ICD-01. Distributed by Multicultural Media at http://www.worldmusicstore.com. CD-ROM for Windows only.

Indian Dance: Bharata Natyam. 1996. Info-drive Sofware, Madras. CD-ROM for PC.

Orissi Dance Music: An Ancient Performance from Orissa. 1993. JVC World Sounds JVC VICG 5268. Compact disc.

Pandit Birju Maharaj—A Kathak Performance. 1991. Live Hindustani kathak performance, with Zakir Hussain, tabla. Navras Records NRCD 0044. Compact disc.

Le Râmâyana: Musiques, chants et rythmes du Kathakali. 1993. Recorded in 1978, with notes in English and French. Ethnic/Auvidis B 6779. Compact disc.

Raslila (The Dance of Krishna): Folkloric Dance Play of India. 1988. CD Ethnic Sound Series 19. JVC VID-25033. Compact disc.

Sri Lanka: Comédies et opéras populaires. 1995. Performed by the Dhamma Jagoda ensemble and the T. W. Gunadasa ensemble. Recorded and with notes by Henri Lecomte. Le Chant du Monde CMT 274 1006. Compact disc.

SOUTH ASIAN DIASPORA

Jaya, Jaya Devi: Traditional Tamil Songs from the Madrasis of Guyana. 1996. Recorded in New York City. Produced and distributed by Errol G. Virasawmi.

Musiques de l'Inde en pays creoles. 1991. Recorded by Monique Desroches and Jean Benoist. University of Montreal UMM 201. Compact disc.

A Guide to Films and Videos

GENERAL

Discovering the Music of India. 1994. Distributed by Multicultural Media. AIMS 8705. Video cassette.

Folk Performers of India. 1984. Produced by Nazir Ali Jairazbhoy. UCLA Ethnomusicology Publications. Video cassette.

There'll Always Be Stars in the Sky: The Indian Film Music Phenomenon. 1992. Jeremy Marre. Harcourt Films. Video cassette.

MUSIC IN NORTHERN AREAS

The Adaptable Kingdom: Music and Dance in Nepal. N.d. Produced by Deben Bhattacharya. Distributed by Multicultural Media AFV-72534. Video cassette.

Ali Akbar Khan Allauddin Festival 1990. 1990. Sound Photosynthesis. Video cassette.

Amir, an Afghan Refugee Musician's Life in Peshawar, Pakistan. 1985. Produced by John Baily. National Film and Television School, Beaconsfield, Buckinghamshire, England. Video cassette, 16mm film.

Between Time: A Tibetan Village in Nepal. 1984. Produced by Ken and Ivory Levine, on the Bhotia culture. Iris Film and Video, 720 Blane St., Seattle, Wash. 98109. 16mm film.

The Bhands of Kashmir. c. 1980. Produced by Siddharth Kak. A Cinema Vision India film. 16 mm film.

Bhimsen Joshi; Girija Devi. 1994. Hindustani vocal music. Alurkar Music House. AV 132. Video cassette.

Bhimsen Joshi; Gangubai Hangal. 1992. Produced by Suresh Alurkar. Hindustani vocal performance at the Savai Gandharva Music Festival, Pune. Alurkar Music House AV 108. Video cassette.

The Dragon Bride. 1993. Directed by Joanna Head. The wedding of a teenage girl to four brothers of the Nyimba people of the Nepalese Himalayas. Distributed by BBC Enterprises, London. Video cassette.

Echoes from Tibet. N.d. A Tibetan refugee settlement in the western Himalayas; includes an excerpt of a ritual dance drama staged for the Dalai Lama's visit. Distributed by Multicultural Media. AFV-72336. Video cassette.

Faces of the Forest: The Santals of West Bengal. N.d. Music and dance in the daily life and religious ceremonies of this *ādivāsī* 'tribal' community. Distributed by Multicultural Media AFV-72533. http://www.worldmusicstore.com. Video cassette.

The Fair at Dharamtalla. 1984. Acrobats, healers, and snake charmers at a market in India. Sharpe Film Collective, 172-3 Rash Behari Ave., Calcutta. 16mm.

Folk Musicians of Rajasthan. 1984. Recorded by Nazir Jairazbhoy, August 1980. UCLA Video Series in Ethnomusicology. UCLA Music Department, Los Angeles. Video cassette and booklet.

Hariprasad Chaurasia; Zakir Hussain. 1993. Hindustani performance by Hariprasad Chaurasia, flute; and Zakir Hussain,tabla at theSavai Gandharva Music Festival, Pune, 1992. Alurkar Music House AV 111. Video cassette.

Himalayan Herders. 1997. Directed by John and Naomi Bishop. Ethnographic video showing rituals in Buddhist temples, villages, and mountains of central Nepal. Distributed by Documentary Educational Resources, Watertown, Mass. Video cassette.

Hindustani Slide: Indian Classical Guitar by Debashish Bhattacharya. 1995. Mark Humphrey, project coordinator. Vestapol (division of Stefan Grossmann's Guitar Workshop, Inc.). Distributed by Rounder Records, Cambridge, Mass. Video cassette.

India Cabaret. 1986. Film on a Bombay nightclub, by Mira Nair. Filmmakers Library, New York. 16mm film, video cassette.

Indian Classical Music. 1994. Includes performances by Ali Akbar Khan, sarod; Alla Rakha, tabla; Amjad Ali Khan, sarod; Hariprasad Chaurasia, flute; and Ravi Shankar, sitar. Distributed by Films for the Humanities and Sciences, P.O. Box 2053, Princeton, N.J. 08543, http://www.films.com. AYP5066. Video cassette.

The Instrumental Artistry of Vishwa Mohan Bhatt. Mohan vina player, modified slide guitar. 1997. Vestapol (division of Stefan Grossmann's Guitar Workshop, Inc.) V-13068. Distributed by

Multicultural Media and Rounder Records. Video cassette.

Khandan: The Musical Heritage of Shujaat Khan. 1998. Produced by Arundhati Neuman. India Performing Arts. Video cassette.

Krishna in Spring. 1992 [1988]. Directed by Deben Bhattacharya. Temple ceremonies in India celebrating spring. Distributed by Audio-Forum V72182, Guilford, Conn. Video cassette.

Lord of the Dance: Destroyer of Illusion. 1994 [1985]. Directed by Richard Kohn and Franz-Christophe Giercke. Documentary on Mani Rimdu, an ancient Tibetan Tantric ritual, as practiced in a Buddhist monastery in Nepal. Distributed by Mystic Fire Video, P.O. Box 1092, Cooper Station, New York, New York 10003. Video cassette.

Menri Monastery. 1993. Produced by Roslyn Dauber. Film on the relocated religious center of the Bonpo, pre-Buddhist Tibetans, at Menri Monastery, Himachal Pradesh, India. Includes rarely performed ceremonies. Distributed by the Center for Media and Independent Learning, University of California Extension, Berkeley. Video cassette.

Musical Instruments of Kacch and Its Neighbors. 1999. Nazir Jairazbhoy and Amy Catlin. Van Nuys, Calif.: Apsara Media for Intercultural Education. Video cassette.

Painted Ballad of India. 1992 [1988]. Directed by Deben Bhattacharya. Sussex Tapes V72183. Distributed by Audio-Forum, Guilford, Conn. Video cassette.

Pandit Jasraj. 1992. Hindustani vocal performance at the Savai Gandharva Music Festival, Pune, 1992. Alurkar Music House AV 109. Video cassette.

Raga. 1992. Directed by Deben Bhattacharya. Includes performance of raga Sindh Bhairavi by Halim Jaffar Khan. Distributed by Audio-Forum, Guilford, Conn. Video cassette.

Raj Gonds. 1982. Produced by Melissa Llewelyn-Davies. The Dandari Festival of central India. Films Inc., 5547 Ravenswood Ave., Chicago, Ill. 60640. 16mm film, video cassette.

Ravi Shankar in Concert. 1994. Sitar performance with Alla Rakha, tabla. Distributed by Films for the Humanities and Sciences, P.O. Box 2053, Princeton, N.J. 08543, http://www.films. com. BVL5070. Video cassette.

Ravi Shankar: The Man and His Music. 1994. Produced by Anne Schelcher and Pascal Bensoussan. Distributed by Films for the Humanities and Sciences, P. O. Box 2053, Princeton, N.J. 08543. BVL4345. Video cassette.

Ravi Shankar: Raga. 1991. Produced by Howard Worth. Mystic Fire Video, P.O. Box 1092, Cooper Station, New York 10003. MYS 76239. Distributed by Multicultural Media. Video cassette.

Retooling a Tradition: A Rajasthani Puppet Takes Umbrage at His Stringholders. 1994. Produced by Nazir Jairazbhoy and Amy Catlin. "Fictive Documentary." Van Nuys, Calif.: Apsara Media for Intercultural Education. Video cassette.

Shivkumar Sharma and Gangubhai Hangal. 1994. Hindustani performance at the Savai Gandharva Music Festival, Pune. Alurkar Music House AV 126. Video cassette.

South Asia 2. 1988. Hindu devotional songs, git, and bhajans; Sikh bhajan. JVC Video Anthology of World Music and Dance, vol. 12. C3525. Video cassette.

South Asia 3. 1988. Rudra vina; sitar; Pabuji-ki-phad of Rajasthan; kathputli puppets of Rajasthan; bhatiyali, sari-gan, and Baul folk songs of Bengal. JVC Video Anthology of World Music and Dance, vol. 13. C3526. Video cassette.

South Asia 4: Pakistan, Bangladesh. 1988. Qawwali, hamd, manqabat, trance ritual. JVC Video Anthology of World Music and Dance, vol. 14. C3527. Video cassette.

South Asia 5: Sri Lanka, Nepal, Bhutan. 1988. Tovil, kohomba kankariya ceremonial dance, Devol ritual dance, Vedda hunting song. JVC Video Anthology of World Music and Dance, vol. 15. C3528. Video cassette.

The Story of a Musician: Ustad Yunus Husain Khan. 1994. Produced by Arundhati and Daniel Neuman. Van Nuys, Calif.: Apsara Media for Intercultural Education. Video cassette.

Tales of Pabuji: A Rajasthani Tradition. 1996. Directed by Axel Horn, produced by Joseph C. Miller et al. Distributed by Filmakers Library, New York. Video cassette.

There'll Always Be Stars in the Sky: The Indian Film Music Phenomenon. 1992 [1983]. Produced by Jeremy Marre. Beats of the Heart series. Distributed by Shanachie Records, 37 E. Clinton St., Newton, N.J. 07860, http://www.shanachie.com. Video cassette.

Traditional Music and Dance of Sikkim. 1971. Produced by Fred Liebermann and Michael Moore. Seattle: University of Washington Press. 16mm color film.

Waves of Joy: Anandalahari. N.d. The Bauls, religious poet-singers, at the annual celebration of the twelfth-century poet-composer Jayadeva in West Bengal. Distributed by Multicultural Media. AFV-72431. Video cassette.

MUSIC IN SOUTHERN AREAS

Bake Restudy 1984. 1991. Produced by Nazir Jairazbhoy and Amy Catlin. Van Nuys, Calif.: Apsara Media for Intercultural Education. Video cassette with accompanying monograph.

Buddha and the Rice Planters. 1992. Directed by Deben Bhattacharya. The importance of Buddhism in Sinhalese life, religion, art, and music in Sri Lanka. Distributed by Audio-Form, Guilford, Conn. Video cassette.

The Flying Bird: A Portrait of Savitri Rajan, Vina Artist. 1989. Produced by Vishnu Mathur and C. S. Lakshmi. Montreal: Les Productions la Fête.

Video cassette, 16mm film.

Shiva's Disciples. 1985. Produced by Simon Kurrian, on South Indian music and dance. Centre Productions, 1800 30th St., #208, Boulder, Colo. 80301. 16mm film.

South Indian Classical Music House Concert with M. D. Ramanathan, vocalist; T. N. Krishnan, violin; and Umayalpuram Sivaraman, mridangam. 1994. Produced by Fredric Lieberman and Amy Catlin. Van Nuys, Calif.: Apsara Media for Intercultural Education. Video cassette.

DANCE AND DRAMA

Balasaraswati: A Vintage Video of Balasaraswati Dancing "Krishna ni Begane Baro." 1998. Directed by John Frazer. Originally filmed at Wesleyan University in 1968. Bharata natyam classical dance. Available from World Music Archives, Olin Library, Wesleyan University, Middletown, Conn. Video cassette.

Circles and Cycles of Kathak Dance: The Lucknow Tradition. 1989. Produced by Robert Gottlieb. On kathak classical dance of North India. R. & L. Gottlieb Productions; also University of California, Extension Media Center, 2176 Shattuck Ave., Berkeley, Calif. 94720. 16mm film, video cassette.

The Cosmic Dance of Shiva. 1992. Produced and directed by Deben Bhattacharya, Jose Montes-Baquer, and Mario Dublanka. Documentary interpretation of Shiva's cosmic dance in Indian classical dance style by the dancers Raja and Radha Reddy. Audio-Forum V72409. Distributed by Sussex Video/Multicultural Media, R.R. 3, Box 6655, Granger Road, Barre, Vt. 05641, http://www.worldmusicstore.com. Video cassette.

A Dance the Gods Yearn to Witness. 1997. Documentary on the classical bharata natyam dance. Distributed by Filmakers Library, New York. Video cassette.

Dancing Girls of Lahore. 1993. Produced by Ahmad Jamal. Portrait of two courtesans of Lahore, Pakistan, contrasting their lives with courtesan life under the Mughals. Distributed by Filmakers Library, New York. Video cassette.

Given to Dance: India's Odissi. 1985. Produced by Ron Hess, South Asian Studies, 1216 Van Hise Hall, University of Wisconsin, Madison, Wisc. 53706. On Oriyan music and dance. 16mm film.

India—The Cosmic Dance of Shiva. N.d. Distributed by Multicultural Media AIMS 8705. Video cassette.

Kalakshetra: Devotion to Dance. 1985. Produced by Anthony Mayer, Centre Productions, 1800 30th St., #208, Boulder, Colo. 80301. Documentary on the Kalakshetra academy of music and dance in South India. 16mm.

Music and Dance of the Baiga People of Madhya Pradesh, India. 1993. Produced by Roderic Knight. Original Music. Video cassette.

Radha & Raja Reddy: Kuchipudi Nritya. 1993. Kuchipudi classical dance performance at the Savai Gandharva Music Festival, Pune, 1992. Alurkar Music House AV 117. Video cassette.

South Asia 1. 1988. Covers bharat natyam, kathakali, manipuri, kathak, Manipuri folk dance, and dhol cholam (drum dance). JVC Video Anthology of World Music and Dance, vol. 11. C3524. Video cassette.

South Asia 2. 1988. Includes the chhau (of Purulia), the chhau (of Seraikela), and yakshagana. JVC Video Anthology of World Music and Dance, vol. 12. C3525. Video cassette.

SOUTH ASIAN DIASPORA

Two Homes, One Heart: Sacramento Sikh Women and Their Songs and Dances. Joyce Middlebrook. P.O. Box 120, Brownsville, Calif. 95919. Video cassette.

Notes on the Audio Examples

Except for tracks 7 and 11, all CD selections are excerpts from longer recordings.

1. Hindustani *baṛā khyāl,* in *rāg kāmod, ektāl* (2:00)
   A slow-tempo vocal performance by Balvant Rae Bhat, with Ishvar Lal Misra playing tabla, and *tambūrā* drone accompaniment. The soloist begins the performance with a brief unmetered introduction of the raga pitches using vocables and accompanied only by the *tambūrā.* The vocalist then sings the first phrase of the song, after which the tabla joins in, presenting in this excerpt two cycles of the twelve-beat tala.
   Recorded by Stephen Slawek in Banaras, North India, 1975.

2. Hindustani *joṛ* improvisation on *vicitra vīṇā* in *rāg bairāgī* (2:19)
   An instrumental improvisation played on the *vicitra vīṇā* 'concert stick zither' by Lalmani Misra, accompanied by *tambūrā* drone lute. In a *joṛ* (which follows the unmetered *ālāp* in a Hindustani instrumental raga performance), the soloist introduces a pulse by sounding the drone strings and the melody strings alternately, with some degree of regularity.
   Recorded by Stephen Slawek in Banaras, North India, 1974.

3. Hindustani *khyāl aṅg gat,* moderately fast tempo, in *rāg miyāṅ malhār, tīntāl* (3:12)
   An instrumental performance by Lalmani Misra playing *vicitra vīṇā* 'plucked stick zither', with Ishvar Lal Misra on tabla, and *tambūrā* drone accompaniment. The soloist first presents the composition within one tala cycle of sixteen beats, and repeats this before beginning his improvisation. The composition can be heard again midway through the excerpt and at the end, following a rapid improvisational passage (*tān*).
   Recorded by Stephen Slawek in Banaras, North India, 1975.

4. Karnatak vocal *ālāpana* in *rāga śankarābharaṇa* (1:58)
   A vocal improvisation by Srimati Brindamma, with *tambūrā* drone accompaniment. The soloist begins her *ālāpana* performance on the fifth scale degree (Pa) of the raga, from which she descends to explore the raga's lower notes. By the end of this excerpt, her unmetered improvisation has returned once again to Pa.
   Recorded by Gayathri Rajapur Kassebaum at the University of Hawaii, Honolulu, on 24 June 1977.

5. Karnatak instrumental *tānam* in *rāga hamsānandi* (1:45)
   An instrumental improvisation performed by R. Subba Rao on the *sarasvatī vīṇā* 'plucked lute', accompanied by *tambūrā* drone lute. In this *tānam* excerpt, the soloist creates a pulsating style of improvisation on the raga by repeating single notes and brief melodic patterns. *Tānam* is nowadays performed only within the *rāgam-tānam-pallavi* genre.
   Recorded by Nazir Jairazbhoy in Vijayawada, Andhra Pradesh, on 12 December 1963. From *Karnatak Music from Vijayawada,* Apsara Media compact disc, 1999. Used with permission.

6. Karnatak vocal *kriti*, "Budham āśrayāmi" 'Taking refuge in Budha (Mercury)' in *rāga nāṭakurañji, jhampā tāḷa* (2:11)
   A vocal performance by the late M. D. Ramanathan, with T. N. Krishnan, violin, and Umayalpuram Sivaraman, *mridangam*. This excerpt of a *kriti* from the Nine-Planet Cycle of Muttusvami Diksitar presents the first line of the *pallavi* section, followed by several *saṅgati* variations and the beginning of the *anupallavi*, in a ten-beat tala cycle [see KARNATAK VOCAL AND INSTRUMENTAL MUSIC, figure 7].
   Recorded by Fredric Lieberman and Amy Catlin in Adaiyar, Madras, 27 December 1977. From *South Indian Classical Music House Concert*, Apsara Media videocassette, 1994. Used with permission.

7. Hindustani tabla *peshkār* in *tīntāl* (3:26)
   A solo drum composition in a sixteen-beat tala cycle and in theme-and-variations form performed by Ahmad Jan Thirakva, c. 1930s–1940s, with *sāraṅgī* accompaniment. This performance, taken from a 78-rpm recording, exhibits a style of playing free from the complex rhythmic divisions characteristic of present-day tabla playing.
   Gramophone Company of India 78-r.p.m. disk HMV N.5996 (OML.4774). From the collection of Mr. and Mrs. Dinkar Manjeshwar, Bombay.

8. Karnatak *tani āvartanam* on *mridangam* barrel drum, in *ādi tāḷa* (3:50)
   The beginning of an extended drum solo in eight-beat *ādi tāḷa* performed by Karaikudi R. Mani, employing slow-tempo rhythmic figures and patterns. The excerpt ends with a more elaborate cadential design (*kōrvai*).
   Recorded by David Nelson in Srinivasa Sastri Hall, Madras, on 28 February 1988

9. Ṛgvedic recitation by Nambudiri Brahmins (1:34)
   Two Brahmins, T. N. Paramesvaran Nambudiri and his brother T. N. Sankaranarayanan Nambudiri, recite the Ṛgveda text (1.20.1), beginning with the words "janmane stomaḥ," according to the Nambudiri *jaṭāmātrā*. This recitation form has the temporal values of the mnemonic braid pattern (*jaṭā*).
   Recorded by Wayne Howard in Trichur, Kerala, on 4 July 1971.

10. North Indian devotional song, "Subhaga varaṇa tana" 'Your beautiful color', of the Haridāsī sect (1:58)
    Responsorial devotional singing (*samāj-gāyan*) by the monks of the Haridāsī Vaishnav sect, with harmonium, *jhāñjh* 'metal clappers', and *pakhāvaj* 'barrel drum' accompaniment. The song describes the beautiful face of Krishna [see RELIGIOUS AND DEVOTIONAL MUSIC: NORTHERN AREA, figure 4].
    Recorded by Guy Beck in Haridas Nagar, Vrindavan, in July 1992.

11. South Indian devotional *kriti*, "Girirājasutā" 'Son of the mountain king's daughter', in *rāga bangāla, deśādi tāḷa* (3:14)
    A devotional *kriti* composition in four-beat *deśādi tāḷa* by Tyagaraja honoring the deity Ganesha, sung by members of the Indian Classical Music Association of Purdue University at a Saint Tyagaraja conference. The vocalists Padma Subramaniam, Sreedevi Kanth, and Vyjayanthi Manian are accompanied by Chakri Amburi (vina), Nandkumar (flute), Seshatare Natarajan (violin), Chandramouli Prasanna (*mridangam*), and Prashant Srikhande (*tambūrā*).
    Recorded by the Indian Classical Music Association of Purdue University, West Lafayette, Indiana on 5 December 1998. From *Saint Thyāgarāja Sammelan*, ICMAP cassette. Used with permission.

12. Dry funeral song of the South Indian Kota tribe (1.00)
    Kotas perform this song at their annual "dry funeral," held in December in memory of all who have died during the preceding year. The instrumental ensemble comprises three trumpets *(kompu)*, two

high-pitched hand drums (*kinpar*), a frame drum played with a stick *(tabaṭk)*, and two double-reed instruments *(koḷ)*.
Recorded by Amy Catlin and Nazir Jairazbhoy near Ootacamund, Tamil Nadu, on 13 April 1984. From *Bake Restudy 1984*, Apsara Media videocassette, 1990. Used with permission.

13. Spirit possession chant, "Devī Ambāv ro ḍhāk," of the *bhopā* priest mediums of the Mīna *ādivāsī* 'tribe' of southern Rajasthan (2:13)
Performed by Puna Pargi Mina, lead vocal and *ḍhāk* drum, Amar Pargi Mina, vocal and *ḍhāk* drum, and Vesa Pargi Mina, vocal and *thālī* percussion plate. The narrative lyric describes an unprecedented gathering that is to take place at Devi Amba's mountain palace. Note the lead singer's high-pitched ecstatic vocal style, indicating the onset of spirit-possession when other nonmusician *bhopā* priest mediums will be possessed by the goddess and her assisting divinity, Bheruji.
Recorded by David Roche in Chota Undri village, Udaipur District, Rajasthan, on 18 February 1983. Copyright © 1984 by David Roche. Used with permission.

14. Double fipple flute (*joḍiyā pāwā*) piece, "Sārang kā Sorath" 'Springtime in Surat', Gujarat (2:02)
Yakub Hasam Jat plays both melody and drone through the two pipes of the *joḍiyā pāwā* flute, using circular breathing to maintain a constant sound.
Recorded by Amy Catlin and Nazir Jairazbhoy in Jatwand village, Kutch, Gujarat, on 5 February 1998. From *Musical Instruments of Kacch and Its Neighbors*, Apsara Media videocassette, 1999. Used with permission.

15. Tamil *villuppāṭṭu* bow song (1:42)
A sung prayer to the elephant-headed god Ganapati (Ganesh), performed in a goddess temple in Kottara by a *villu* ensemble: Agasta Lingam Pillai, vocal and *villu* 'musical bow'; Ganapati Chettiar, *jālā* 'bottlecap rattle'; Ayappan Chettiar, *kuḍam* 'struck brass pot on which the bow rests'; Ramayya Chettiar, vocal and *jālrā* 'small cymbals'; Ramasami Chettiar, *kaṭṭai* 'wooden clappers'; Tangam Nadar, *uḍukkai* 'hourglass tension drum'; and Minatci Nathan Pillai, harmonium. As he sings, the main performer strikes the bow with two *vīsukkōl* beaters, each of which has a donut-shaped metal rattle near the handle. The beaters sound together with the struck bowstring and the bells hanging from the bow. The brass pot is struck on the mouth with a palm-sheaf paddle and on the sides with a coin.
Recorded by Amy Catlin and Nazir Jairazbhoy in Kottara, near Nagercoil, Tamil Nadu, on 18 March 1984. From *Bake Restudy 1984*, Apsara Media videocassette, 1990. Used with permission.

16. North Indian kathak dance syllables (1:28)
The dancer Archana Joglekar recites mnemonic syllables (*bol*) for the first two rhythmic compositions presented in a *kathak* dance recital: *āmad* 'to arrive' and *uthān* 'to take off'. A tabla accompanist performs a slow *tritāl* of sixteen beats. A gap of one tala cycle separates the two rhythmic compositions; in the second half of this cycle a brief introductory syllable pattern leads into the faster and sharper *uthān* composition.
Recorded by Baba Santoshi at Radio Wani Studio, Bombay, 1995. Copyright 1995 by Archana Joglekar. Used with permission.

17. Firewalk (Marche dans le Feu) drum and percussion music, Réunion Island (1:24)
Frame drums (*tapou*), kettledrums (*sakti*), and small bells (*tālam*) are played by Réunion Islanders of Indian descent for the annual firewalk that takes place in connection with coastal plantation temples. Drumming patterns include calls to specific deities.
Recorded by Monique Desroches in St. Gilles les Hauts, in June 1988. From *Musiques de l'Inde en Pays Créoles*, University of Montreal compact disc UMMUS 201, 1991, track 20. Used with permission.

18. Guyanese Madrasi devotional song, "Aeyoh veedeoh anda maganay" 'O Lord give me that blessing' (1:29)
Mukain Nagapoollay, singer and drummer (playing *matalam* 'double-headed drum'), and Chinapa Virasawmi, harmonium player, perform a traditional Tamil song from the Mahabharata *nargam* 'popular dance drama'.
Recorded in New York by Errol G. Virasawmi. From *Jaya, Jaya Devi: Traditional Tamil Songs from the Madrasis of Guyana*, compact disc Copyright © 1996 by Jaya, Jaya Devi. Used with permission.

19. Kathak women's devotional song of Rajasthan (1:13)
Women of the Kathak caste sing at an all-night vigil (*jagarān*) to honor and call on an ancestor (Pitṛ), a boy who died at a young age. This Kathak family celebration marks both the boy's birthday and the annual springtime festival of Gangaur, when women worship Gauri (the wife of Shiva) to ask for blessings on their menfolk, husbands, and husbands-to-be. The women accompany their singing with *ḍholak* drum and *mañjīrā* finger cymbals; a male relative plays the harmonium.
Recording by Mekhala Devi Natavar in Lodhsar, Churu District, Rajasthan on 21–22 March 1996.

20. *Nirguṇ bhajan*, hymn of the formless divine, "Re man musāphir" 'Hey, mind-traveler', Uttar Pradesh (1:52)
The mendicant musician Kalamu Jogi sings and accompanies himself on the *sāraṅgī* 'bowed fiddle'.
Recorded by Edward O. Henry in Khalsa village, Azamgarh District, Uttar Pradesh, on 4 January 1990.

21. *Ṣūfyāna mūsīqī*, Sufi music of Kashmir (1:49)
In a ritual gathering (*mehfil*) for the performance of Sufi music, lead musician Ghulam Muhammad Qalinbaf sings mystical poetry in *maqām ḥusaynī* and plays a *setār* 'long-necked lute', joined in chorus by other musicians also playing *santūr* 'box zither', *setār*, and *dokra* (Indian tabla drums).
Recorded by Sheikh Abdul Aziz in Srinagar, Kashmir, 1984.

22. *Ghāṭu* dance drama song of the Guruṅgs of Nepal (2:10)
A group of male singers, together with drummers playing *mādal* 'double-headed drums', perform music for the *pha laba ghāṭu* dance drama of the Guruṅgs near Pokhara, central Nepal.
Recorded by Pirkko Moisala and Matti Lahtinen in Klinu, Lamjung District, Nepal, on 16 February 1976.

23. Oboe and kettledrum music for archery in Ladakh (1:41)
Two Beda musicians play *surnā* 'oboe' and *daman* 'kettledrum' to accompany village archery games. A melodic and rhythmic pattern is repeated with variations; the change in tempo indicates that a marksman has hit the target.
Recorded by Mireille Helffer in Ladakh, August 1976. From *Ladakh: Musique de Monastère et de Village/Ladakh Monastic and Village Music*, Le Chant du Monde compact disc LDX 274662, 1989, track 4. Used with permission.

24. Buddhist ritual music and chant in honor of A-phyi, Ladakh (1:57)
Buddhist monks of the Sgang-sngon Bkra-shis Chos-rdzong monastery of Phyang offer ritual music and a prayer of invitation in vocalized chant (*dbyangs*) to the tutelary goddess of the monastery, A-phyi. The instruments are two long trumpets (*dung-chen*), two oboes (*rgya-gling*), cymbals (*sbug-chal* and *sil-snyan*), and a double-headed frame drum (*rnga*).
Recorded by Mireille Helffer in Ladakh, August 1976. From *Ladakh: Musique de Monastère et de Village/Ladakh Monastic and Village Music*, Le Chant du Monde compact disc LDX 274662, 1989, track 1. Used with permission.

25. Bhaṅgī drumming in Madhya Pradesh (1:28)
Six male Metars, a lower-caste Hindu community of Bhaṅgīs (sweepers), play eight-sided frame

drums (*ḍaplā*) to accompany a female Berni dancer on the morning after a Rajput wedding.
Recorded by Nazir Jairazbhoy in Penchi, Chanchora Taluk, Madhya Pradesh, on 16 February 1964.

26. Paraja antiphonal courtship song, Orissa (2:01)
Five young men and nine young women of the Paraja tribe sing during the harvest festival, Push. To the men's phrases, "You should not go now while I am singing / Please girl, don't go now and leave me," the women respond, "We are already so much in love that even if we don't meet here we will meet in the other world." The men then reply, "No, no, we will be reborn in this world and meet here." Each man plays a single-stringed spike lute with gourd resonator (*ṭoilā* or *ḍuḍuṅgā*) as the women dance.
Recorded by Nazir Jairazbhoy in Sano Chindri village near Koraput, Orissa, on 31 December 1963.

27. *Decknni* dance song "Borieche tari" 'Borim boatman', Goa (1:45)
The professional group Gavana [see GOA, figure 1] performs a traditional Goan song about the *devadāsī* temple dancers of South India, arranged by T. A. Sequeira. The soloists are Margarida Távora e Costa and Silvano Fernandes; in the women's dance, each dancer holds two burning candles as she imitates gestures of *bharata nāṭyam* classical dance.
Recorded by Susana Sardo. From *Gavana Goa: A Viagem des Sons/The Journey of Sounds*, Tradisom compact disc VS01, 1998, track 11. Used with permission.

28. *Bēnjo* 'keyed zither' performance in Balochistan (2:40)
The legendary *bēnjo* player Bilawal Biljiam (d. 1980) of Karachi plays a popular Balochi tune on the *bēnjo*, a keyed zither with between twenty-eight and thirty-two keys and two steel melody strings that are struck with a plastic plectrum. He is accompanied by a *ḍukkur* 'double-headed barrel drum', a tabla drum pair, and *chinchir* 'cymbals'.
Recorded in Karachi in the 1970s.

29. *Sot* wedding song of Balochistan (3:06)
Sharruk, a professional female Sōtī [see BALOCHISTAN, figure 1], sings a short song (*sot*) for a wedding on the Makran coast, Balochistan, accompanied by *ḍukkur* 'double-headed barrel drum', *chinchir* 'cymbals', and a *bēnjo* 'keyed zither' played by Usman Pullan.
Recorded by Sabir Badalkhan and Anderson Bakewell in Jiwani, Makran coast, Balochistan, in November 1991. Copyright © Anderson Bakewell. Used with permission.

30. *Falak* folk song "Ey shox sar-i" 'Hey, you impudent giggler', northern Afghanistan (1:44)
Ustad Rahim Takhary, vocal and spike fiddle (*ghījak*), and Ustad Malang Najrabi, goblet-shaped drum (*zirbaghali*), perform a *falak* folk song; the metered section in this excerpt is generally preceded by an unmetered prelude.
Recorded by Jan Van Belle in Mazar-e Sharif, Northern Afghanistan, on 24 July 1996.

31. Pashtun wedding song, "Yaqorbān" 'I sacrifice myself for you', of southeastern Afghanistan (2:23)
Shah Wali Khan and his band [see SOUTHEASTERN AFGHANISTAN, figures 2 and 3] perform for a wedding in the frontier region between Pakistan and Afghanistan; Shah Wali Khan and his brother Wali sing and play harmonium, with Amir Jan on plucked lute (*rubāb*), Mustafa on clarinet, and Mena Gol playing tabla drums.
Recorded by John Baily in a village near Mardan, North West Frontier Province, Pakistan, on 9 May 1985. From *Amir: An Afghan Refugee Musician's Life in Peshawar, Pakistan*, 16mm and videocassette, 1985. Used with permission.

32. Bāul song of Bangladesh, "Khanchar bhitar achin pakhi" 'Human soul—a mysterious bird' (1:56)
This representative *bāul* song of Lalan Shah is performed by Chandana Majumdar, granddaughter of a well-known Baul from Bengal, accompanied by a two-stringed lute (*dotārā*), single-stringed lute

(*ektārā*), plucked string drone (*gopīyantra*), bamboo flute, violin, double-headed drum (*khol*), and tabla.
Recorded by Karunamaya Goswami in Dhaka, 1997. From *The Splendours of Old Bengali Songs*, cassette 6 (Dhaka: Ford Foundation, 1997).

33. *Gīgī pada* song of northern Karnataka (1:58)
Hanumanthappa Hadukosa sings this *gīgī pada* and plays a large tambourine (*dappu*); his assistants, Govindappa Krishnappa Dosasa and Sanappa Krishnappa Biolkarri, join in singing the characteristic refrain, "*gīya gīya gī.*"
Recorded by Gayathri Rajapur Kassebaum in Dharwar town, northern Karnataka, on 6 June 1988.

34. Telugu epic narrative song, *Bobbili Yuddha Katha* 'Story of the Battle of Bobbili', Andhra Pradesh (1:53)
The Dāsari singers Bavurubilli Suryanarayana, lead singer and *tambūrā* 'drone lute' player, and Bavurubilli Apparavu, playing *gummeṭa* 'jug-shaped drum' and *tāḷālu* 'finger cymbals', perform this excerpt from the Telugu epic narrative in alternation.
Recorded by Gene Roghair in Vishakhapatnam, Andhra Pradesh, on 23 July 1974.

Index

Page numbers in *italic* indicate pages on which illustrations appear.